CONTEMPORARY CHINESE LAW AND LEGAL SYSTEM

Contemporary Chinese Law and Legal System is a rich source for teaching, study, and research in Chinese law and the legal system and a useful guide for legal practitioners who are engaged in international practices involving China. The book provides an in-depth overview of modern Chinese law and legal systems, with a thorough analysis of the basic legal infrastructure, civil code, and legal mechanisms of international civil litigation in Chinese courts and foreign arbitration in China. It includes the most recent judicial opinions and practices pertaining to implementing the civil code and enforcing foreign arbitral awards and judgments. Detailed and comprehensive, *Contemporary Chinese Law and Legal System* provides profound knowledge about the law and legal infrastructure in modern China.

Mo Zhang is a professor of law at Temple University Beasley School of Law, USA, teaching conflict of laws, contract, international commercial transactions, international commercial arbitration, and Chinese law. Legally trained both in China and in the United States, Zhang has published numerous law journal articles and is the author of *Chinese Contract Law, Theory and Practice*, 2nd ed. (Brill, 2020), and *Introduction to Chinese Torts Law* (Tsinghua University Press, 2014).

Contemporary Chinese Law and Legal System

FUNDAMENTALS, CIVIL JUSTICE AND PROCESS

MO ZHANG
Temple University

CAMBRIDGE
UNIVERSITY PRESS

CAMBRIDGE
UNIVERSITY PRESS

Shaftesbury Road, Cambridge CB2 8EA, United Kingdom

One Liberty Plaza, 20th Floor, New York, NY 10006, USA

477 Williamstown Road, Port Melbourne, VIC 3207, Australia

314–321, 3rd Floor, Plot 3, Splendor Forum, Jasola District Centre, New Delhi – 110025, India

103 Penang Road, #05-06/07, Visioncrest Commercial, Singapore 238467

Cambridge University Press is part of Cambridge University Press & Assessment, a department of the University of Cambridge.

We share the University's mission to contribute to society through the pursuit of education, learning and research at the highest international levels of excellence.

www.cambridge.org
Information on this title: www.cambridge.org/9781009690423

DOI: 10.1017/9781009690478

First published 2026

A catalogue record for this publication is available from the British Library

Library of Congress Cataloging-in-Publication Data
NAMES: Zhang, Mo (Law teacher) author
TITLE: Contemporary Chinese law and legal system : fundamentals, civil justice, and process / Mo Zhang.
DESCRIPTION: Cambridge, United Kingdom ; New York, NY : Cambridge University Press, 2026. | Includes index.
IDENTIFIERS: LCCN 2025040973 (print) | LCCN 2025040974 (ebook) | ISBN 9781009690423 hardback | ISBN 9781009690447 paperback | ISBN 9781009690478 epub
SUBJECTS: LCSH: Justice, Administration of–China | Law–Study and teaching–China | Civil law–China | Civil procedure–China | Dispute resolution (Law)–China
CLASSIFICATION: LCC KNQ1572 .Z4345 2025 (print) | LCC KNQ1572 (ebook) | DDC 347.51–dc23/eng/20250904
LC record available at https://lccn.loc.gov/2025040973
LC ebook record available at https://lccn.loc.gov/2025040974

ISBN 978-1-009-69042-3 Hardback
ISBN 978-1-009-69044-7 Paperback

To Frances, Elizabeth and Henry

Contents

Preface

Chinese law and the Chinese legal system are both old and young. They are old because China is a country that has a several-thousand-year history in which the law and legal system evolved. They are young for the reason that the law and legal system in the country have experienced fundamental changes during the modern era, especially after 1949, when the People's Republic of China was founded. The civil law tradition in the Chinese law and legal system is a major part of the changes that occurred after the Opium Wars in the nineteenth century. The socialism that China has been pursuing since 1949 has dramatically reshaped the law and legal system of the country. The Open Door policy and other reforms undertaken in China for nearly half a century further exposed the country to the outside world, so that its law and system became connected with the international community more closely than ever before.

The vast amount of legislation in the past few decades and the establishment of a socialist legal system with Chinese characteristics witness the further development of the legal infrastructure in China. The promulgation of the Civil Code in 2020 constitutes a milestone in the country's legal landscape that marks a new era of comprehensive codification of the laws governing civil relations and affairs. Both the 2023 Amendments to the 1991 Civil Procedure Law and the 2025 revision to the 1995 Arbitration Law signify the country's effort to move toward international standards and common practices in resolving civil disputes through both litigation and non-litigation means.

China now is at a crossroads: steadily moving forward to a rule-based civil society with a democratic system through extensive and in-depth reforms, or going backward to an authoritarian regime that left the country with the Cultural Revolution nightmare. Although a general belief in China is that the trend of reform and opening up in the country is irreversible, the resistance to further reform in the political arena remains strong, especially when the leadership of the Communist

Party of China is at stake. Externally, the US–China relationship has become a driving force that affects in many ways the direction China is heading.

The half-century-long reform and legislation in China have resulted in a rapid development of law and the legal system in the country. It is fair to say that laws in China now are very well in place, and many of them are surprisingly well written. But law on paper is one thing, and law actually in action is another. One of the greatest challenges facing China is how to turn law on paper into law really in action. At the heart of the matter is the enforcement of law. Given the deep-rooted officialdom culture in the country, the bureaucrat-centered mentality continues to generate strong resistance to the effective implementation of law.

China does seem to have ambition to further improve its legal system under the rule of law. There are, however, many minefields lying on the road ahead. Questions that inevitably arise include, among others:

a. Which is supreme under the rule of law in the country: the Constitution or a political party?
b. To whom should the government be accountable, to the people or to superior leaders?
c. What is the primary purpose of law: to restrain government power or to impose obligations on the people?
d. How can government corruption be prevented and public power be free from abuse absent an effective mechanism of checks and balances?
e. How can the law be enforced impartially without independence of the judiciary?

This book is not intended to provide answers to these questions but rather examines what the current law and legal system are, and how they operate in the country. Given the very broad coverage of Chinese law and the legal system, both in subject and in content, the book is limited to an analytical review of them from a civil law perspective, with a focus on (1) fundamentals of the current legal infrastructure bearing Chinese characteristics; (2) basic rules of the newly adopted Civil Code; and (3) foreign-related civil dispute settlement mechanisms. The book offers in-depth analysis and discussion of theoretical and practical issues confronting the Chinese legal system in general, and civil law in particular. It also takes a deep dive into the legal matters involved in civil disputes with foreign elements, including litigation and arbitration.

The book consists of three parts. Part I provides an overview of Chinese law and the legal system. It begins with a review of Chinese legal history and culture, followed by an issue-specific discussion of classic Chinese legal philosophies, distinctions of the Chinese legal tradition, and civil law influence. The focal point then turns to the theoretical foundation and sources of modern Chinese law under the brand of a socialist legal system with Chinese characteristics. Also covered in

Part I are the structure of the Chinese government, the role and powers of the Chinese judiciary, the Chinese Bar, and legal education in the country.

Part II is comprised of Chinese civil law under the newly adopted Civil Code. In addition to the general provisions of the Civil Code, the discussion extends to each of the subjects contained in the Civil Code. Due to the limited coverage of the book, Part II tends to cover civil and commercial matters only within the realm of the Civil Code. On those grounds, the substance of Part II includes such subject matters as Property (Right to Things), Contract, Rights of Personality, Marriage and Family Relations, Succession, and Torts.

Part III concentrates on the mechanism of civil dispute settlement. It mainly deals with procedural matters in resolving civil disputes through litigation and non-litigation means. It discusses the major issues encountered in foreign civil litigation in Chinese courts and international commercial arbitration in the country. In litigation, the jurisdiction of Chinese courts in foreign cases, choice of law, and recognition and enforcement of foreign judgments are the center of discussion, while in arbitration, the focus is on the legal framework of foreign arbitration in China, arbitration agreements, and enforcement of foreign arbitral awards.

The book is designed as a reading book for teaching Chinese law and a reference book for those who practice law related to China. It tends to serve multifaceted goals: (a) to facilitate teaching the Chinese legal system and the Civil Code in a systematic way; (b) to provide a useful guide for legal practitioners to engage in legal practice in China; and (c) to provide researchers with a source pertaining to their research and study in modern Chinese law and the legal system.

Acknowledgments

I am greatly indebted to my colleagues and students at Temple and scholars around the world who provided invaluable comments, suggestions, and input toward the production of this book. Special thanks are owed to Temple University Beasley School of Law and Dean Rachel Rebouché for their generous support. I am especially grateful to the late Professor Jiang Ping, Professor Robert Reinstein, and Professor Jacques deLisle for their mentorship and guidance.

My acknowledgments also go to the journals that published my articles from which several chapters of the book are developed. Included in the list are (in alphabetical order): *Berkeley Business Law Journal* (2008), *Boston College International and Comparative Law Journal* (2008), *Cardozo International & Comparative Law Review* (2021), *Emory International Law Review* (2006), *North Carolina Journal of International Law and Commercial Regulation* (2011), *Northwestern Journal of International Law and Business* (2006), *Richmond Journal of Global Law and Business* (2011), *San Diego International Law Journal* (2018), *Temple International & Comparative Law Journal* (2000, 2010), and *Washington International Law Journal* (2017).

A particular debt of gratitude is due to Laura M. Stanton, Temple JD '25, for her assistance with edits and proofreading. All errors and mistakes are mine.

Introduction

The modern history of China consists of two periods, with 1949 as the dividing year. However, there exist different views about the first period. Some Western historians took the year 1911 as the beginning of the first period,[1] but the general consensus in Chinese history books is that the first period started in 1840.[2] In Chinese history, both 1840 and 1911 were historically significant because they were associated with events that instrumentally and dramatically changed the country.

The year 1840 was an important turning point in Chinese history. The Opium Wars, in which joint foreign forces defeated China, turned China from a self-sufficient feudal empire into a semi-colonial and semi-feudal state. In 1911, the republican revolution broke out, which led to the fall of the Qing Dynasty, the last feudal dynasty in the country. The birth of the Nationalist government – the fruit of the revolution – brought to an end the imperial history that had lasted over 2,000 years in China, from 221 BC to AD 1911.

The second period of modern Chinese history is from 1949 onward. In 1949, the Communist Party of China (CPC) won the civil war against the Nationalist government. As a result, the CPC took control of the country and the People's Republic of China (PRC) was founded. The most notable change in China after 1949 was the establishment of a socialist system under the leadership of the CPC. The change was significant because it was not simply a transition of government but a transformation of the nature of the country. Because of this change, the second period in China is marked as a new era, referring to the contemporary history of the country.[3]

1 See Chicago Public Library, *Timeline of China's Modern History*, available at www.chipublib.org/timeline-of-chinas-modern-history/ (2025). See also HarvardX History of China, *The Modern Era*, available at www.edx.org/course/creating-modern-china-the-republican-period-to-the (2025).

2 See the Overseas Chinese Affairs Office of the State Council, Common Knowledge about Chinese History, 148 (China Travel Press, 2013).

3 See *id.*

Ever since 1949, China has struggled with the development of its law and legal system under a socialist brand. The past seventy-plus years have witnessed how the building of legal infrastructure took place in the country. At the very beginning, the CPC government abolished all the laws that existed during the Nationalist period, leaving the country an empty "plain paper" in the areas of law and the legal system. However, in order to quickly put in place a new legal system, the country in almost every aspect followed the model of the former Soviet Union. In 1954, the first Constitution of the PRC was adopted.

But the effort to build a socialist legal system was soon interrupted by mass movement maneuvered by Chairman Mao in pursuit of his philosophy of class struggle. With the notorious Anti-Rightist Campaign in the country in 1957, followed by the Great Leap Forward in 1958, China rapidly descended into political fanaticism and legal nihilism. The chaos of lawlessness reached its peak in the country during the ten-year Cultural Revolution from 1966 to 1976. Not until 1978 was the gear of China reversed, moving away from Mao's class struggle and turning onto the economic development. Along with vast economic reforms came the effort to rebuild the nation's legal system.

The economic reforms, which began in 1978, were aimed at modernizing China through an opening-up policy. It was these reforms that produced significant changes in the country from both economic and legal perspectives. Economically, China shifted from a planned economy to a market-oriented economy,[4] which helped the nation step into the mainstream of the world economy and become one of the fastest-growing countries globally in terms of economic development.[5] More significantly, the economic reforms paved the way for China to become a member of the World Trade Organization (WTO) in 2001. In addition, with a large absorbance of foreign capital in order to boost economic development, foreign direct investment (FDI) became a major component of the country's economy. In 2022, China's FDI inflows reached $189 billion, making the nation the world's second-largest FDI recipient after the United States.[6]

Legally, China has had massive legislation in the past decades in which many laws were adopted to regulate the politically and economically changing society. During the thirty years from 1949 to 1979, there were about 134 laws that were

[4] In 1992, the 14th National Conference of the CCP set as the goal of China's economic reform the establishment of a socialist market economy in China. One year later, in 1993, the 1982 Constitution was amended to provide that the state was to pursue developing a socialist market economy. The amendment also provided that the state shall enhance economic legislation and improve macro-control of the economy.

[5] According to former Chinese President Hu Jintao, China's GDP grew at an average rate of 9.4 percent annually for the twenty-six years from 1978 to 2004. See Hu Jintao, Keynote Speech at 2005 Fortune Global Forum. A full text of the speech is available at http://politics.people.com.cn/GB/1024/3392948.html. For detailed statistics, see www.stats.gov.cn.

[6] See the UNCTAD, The 2023 World Investment Report. A full text of the report is available online at https://unctad.org/system/files/official-document/wir2023-annex_tables-1_en.pdf.

adopted at the national level. By 1979, only about twenty-three were still in effect. After 1979, legislation in China entered a high-speed process. In the year of 1979, for example, the National People's Congress (NPC), the top legislative body of the state, passed seven laws in a single session,[7] making it a "magnificent feat" in modern Chinese legislative history. It has also become a common scenario that foreign laws and legal systems are referred to in the law-making process of the country in order to help the country better connect to the world.

As of December 2024, over 305 laws were adopted by the NPC and its Standing Committee,[8] including, among others, 51 Constitution and related laws, 24 civil and commercial laws, 96 administrative laws, 83 economic laws, 28 social laws, 4 criminal laws, and 11 litigation and non-litigation procedural laws.[9] In addition, there were about 597 administrative regulations, more than 200 departmental regulations, over 16,000 local regulations, and 800 local government regulations.[10] Moreover, the Supreme People's Court (SPC) has issued numerous judicial interpretations for the implementation of laws. More importantly, as part of judicial reform, the SPC since 2011 has established a "guiding case" system in people's courts to help promote the uniform application of law.

In 1997, the CPC set a goal for the nation to establish a "socialist legal system with Chinese characteristics" by 2010. Interestingly, in 2008, the CPC government proclaimed that such a legal system had been preliminarily established, meaning that the 2010 goal would be reached as planned. In its "White Paper on China's Rule of Law," published on February 28, 2008, the Press Office of the State Council of China described the development of such a legal system as the greatest achievement in the advancement of the rule of law in the country.[11] In March 2011, the NPC proclaimed that a legal system of socialist nature with Chinese characteristics had been established in the country by the end of 2010.[12]

It is important to note that China is a highly centralized unitary country, but the unitary system applies only to the mainland. In the late 1990s, China established

7 The seven laws included the Criminal Law, Criminal Procedural Law, Election Law, Local Government Organization Law, Organization Law of People's Courts, Organization Law of People's Procuratorates, and Sino-Foreign Joint Venture Law.

8 See Huang Haihua, *The Legislative System of China*, 2 J. People's Cong. (2025), available at www.npc.gov.cn/npc/c2/c30834/202502/t20250218_442863.html.

9 See China Legislation Data 2023, available at www.163.com/dy/article/IE7MNTNM05149C2O.html.

10 See Haihua, *supra* note 8.

11 See the Information Office of the State Council of China, *White Paper on the Rule of Law in China*, available at www.china.org.cn/government/news/2008-02/28/content_11025486.htm.

12 See the Information Office of the State Council of China, *White Paper on the Socialist Legal System with Chinese Characteristics*, available at www.china.org.cn/government/whitepaper/node_7137666.htm (hereinafter *Legal System White Paper*); see also Wu Bangguo, *Work Report of the Standing Committee of the National People's Congress of the First Session of the 12th National People's Congress of the People's Republic of China*, March 8, 2013, available at http://theory.people.com.cn/n/2013/0308/c49150-20726969.html.

special administrative regions (SARs) based on the concept of "one country with two systems" to deal with Hong Kong and Macao, former British and Portuguese dependencies, after their handover. Under the "one country with two systems" scheme, the SARs are granted autonomous power in executive, legislative, and judicial aspects, and are allowed to keep intact their social and legal systems inherited from the colonial period.[13] Although there has been growing concern about Hong Kong's autonomous status in recent years, the common law tradition inherited from the British legal system in the region remains intact. In this regard, the contemporary law and legal system of China do not include the laws and legal systems of the SARs.

1. SOCIALIST LEGAL SYSTEM WITH CHINESE CHARACTERISTICS

In the contemporary world, in addition to civil and common law traditions, the socialist legal tradition is also considered highly influential.[14] One possible reason is that the socialist legal system used to be employed in all countries of the former Soviet bloc and is still practiced in China, the country with the largest population and fastest-growing economy in the world. Another reason is that countries with the socialist system differ sharply from many other countries of either common or civil law systems in their governing ideologies and political structures. The socialist legal system with Chinese characteristics particularly signifies these differences.

According to the Information Office of the State Council, the socialist legal system with Chinese characteristics is a legal system that "is based on the conditions and reality of China, meets the needs of reform, opening up and the socialist modernization drive, and reflects the will of the CPC and the Chinese people."[15] In its substance, the legal system is "headed by the Constitution, with laws related to the Constitution, civil and commercial laws and several other branches as the mainstay, and consisting of laws, administrative regulations, local regulations and other tiers of legal provisions," and "ensures that there are laws to abide by in economic, political, cultural and social development, as well as in ecological civilization building."[16]

In describing the nature of the socialist legal system with Chinese characteristics, much of the Chinese legal literature follows the wording verbatim as set by the CPC, although the term itself is quite vague and subject to different interpretations.

[13] For example, under the Basic Law of Hong Kong, the socialist system and policies of the mainland shall not be practiced in Hong Kong, and the common law system in Hong Kong shall be maintained for fifty years. See the Basic Law of Hong Kong, Preamble, and arts. 5 and 8. A full text of the Basic Law of Hong Kong is available at www.basiclaw.gov.hk/en/basiclaw text/images/basiclaw_full_text_en.pdf.

[14] See John Henry Merryman, The Civil Law Tradition: An Introduction to the Legal System of Western Europe and Latin America, 1 (2nd ed., Stanford University Press, 1985).

[15] See the Information Office of the State Council, *Legal System White Paper*, *supra* note 12.

[16] See *id.*

Some in the country have endeavored to further articulate the features of Chinese characteristics,[17] but their articulation has mostly offered nothing more than certain political slogans. A true reality in China is that government opinion always speaks too loudly and powerfully to leave any room for individuals' views to be heard.

A. *Socialism*

Theoretically, the concept of socialism has its intellectual roots back in ancient Greek times. The term was originally used to describe a type of collective society. During the Industrial Revolution in the late eighteenth century, the socialist system emerged as an alternative to the expanding capitalist system, with an emphasis on public ownership of the means of production. Karl Marx, known as the founding father of communism, infused socialist ideology with the theory of classes.[18]

According to Marx, society was made up of classes, and when certain classes controlled the means of production, they used it to exploit the vast working class. It was Marx's belief that socialism could only be established through a revolution of class struggle so as to make public the ownership of the means of production. Marxist socialism was introduced to, and practiced in, the former Soviet Union and the socialist bloc through the work of Vladimir Lenin.[19]

In China, ever since 1954, when the first socialist constitution was adopted, Marxism-Leninism has been the ruling orthodoxy that governs the country. Mao himself was very keen on Marx's thoughts of the revolutionary clash between capital and labor and made it his top priority to carry on the torch of class struggle. After Mao's death, China abandoned the notion of class struggle and refined the socialist course for the nation.

In the late 1950s, facing serious backlash to the "Great Leap Forward" campaign, Mao realized that the development of a socialist system in China would need to take place in two stages: a preliminary stage and a developed stage.[20] In the preliminary stage, the primary goal of the state had to deal with poverty and economic development. This idea, however, was soon superseded by Mao's zeal for continuing revolution. Not until the economic reforms that took place in the late 1970s did the country's focus begin to turn from the continuing revolution to the development of the economy.

17 These features include: (a) under the guidance of the theory of socialism with Chinese characteristics and the ideology of socialist legality, (b) reflection of the common will of the vast majority of people led by the working class, (c) pursuit of internal harmony and unification of the system, (d) in light of the material living condition of modern China, and (e) an open, involving, and continuously improving system. See *id.* at 24–29.

18 For general discussion on socialism, see Stanford Encyclopedia of Philosophy, Archive, Fall 2019 Edition, available at https://plato.stanford.edu/archives/fall2019/entries/socialism/.

19 See *id.*

20 See The Collected Works of Mao Zedong, Vol. 8, 116 (People's Press, 1999).

In 1981, the Chinese government restated the concept of a preliminary stage of socialism and for the first time explicitly set it as the basic tone for the country.[21] Six years later, in 1987, the theory of the primary stage of socialism was further elaborated to include "one center and two adherences."[22] As the nation's development strategy, one center means a focus on economic construction, while the two adherences refers to adherence to the opening-up policy and adherence to the so-called four basic principles.[23]

Thus, the basic notion underlying Chinese characteristics is that China is a socialist country and the Chinese socialist system is at the preliminary stage. The preliminary stage of socialism approach not only prompts the need for an opening-door policy but also justifies the adoption of a market economy – a core element of capitalism – and incorporates it into the socialist system. Under this approach, the principal contradiction in Chinese society was described for years as the contradiction between the people's growing material and cultural needs and backward social production.

In 2017, in his report to the 19th National Congress of the CPC, Xi Jinping redefined the principal contradiction as the contradiction between unbalanced and inadequate development and the people's ever-growing needs for a better life.[24] According to Xi, the evolution of the principal contradiction represents a historic shift that affects the whole landscape and creates many new demands.[25] On that basis, the reform and economic development lying ahead in the country were tailored to suit the need for establishing and improving a mature and vibrant market economy under a socialist system.

In comparison with legal systems elsewhere, the socialist legal system with Chinese characteristics has several distinctive features. First, despite its socialist nature, the contemporary legal system of China remains within the family of civil law both in its roots of development and in its legislative and juristic pattern.[26] Thus, the socialist legal system with Chinese characteristics can be described as a civil law system governed by socialist ideology, along with Chinese tradition and reality. Second, as far as the legal system is concerned, Chinese characteristics contain the nation's ancient heritage, represented mainly by *Confucian* ethos. Third, the

[21] See the CPC, *Resolutions on Several Historical Issues of the Party since the Founding of the People's Republic of China*, passed in 1981, available at www.china.com.cn/chinese/archive/131144.htm.

[22] See Zhao Ziyang, *Report at the 13th National Congress of the Communist Party of China*, October 25, 1987, available at http://news.cntv.cn/china/20120902/102051.shtml.

[23] The four basic principles are the ruling principles of the country set forth by the CPC, which include: (a) the socialist road, (b) the proletarian dictatorship, (c) the leadership of the Communist Party, and (d) Marxism-Leninism and Mao Zedong Thought.

[24] See Xinhua News, *Principal Contradiction Facing Chinese Society Has Evolved in New Era: Xi*, October 18, 2017, available at www.xinhuanet.com/english/2017-10/18/c_136688132.htm.

[25] See *id.*

[26] See Information Office of the State Council, *Legal System White Paper*, *supra* note 12, at 24.

development of law and legal system in China has been, and remains to be influenced by the country's reception of foreign law as a reference in both legislation and the application of law.[27]

B. *Leadership of the CPC*

But the most striking aspect of Chinese characteristics is the supremacy of the CPC's leadership. Under the Chinese 1982 Constitution,

> both the victory in the New-Democratic Revolution of China and the success in its socialist cause have been achieved . . . under the leadership of the Communist Party of China ... the Chinese people of all nationalities will continue under the leadership of the Communist Party of China . . . to make China a socialist country that is prosperous, powerful, democratic and culturally advanced.[28]

Unlike any political party elsewhere, the Communist Party is the single and only ruling party in China that actually possesses all powers of the nation, including the military.[29]

Under article 1 of the 1982 Constitution, the socialist system is the basic system of China. Article 1 also makes it imperative that disruption of the socialist system by any organization or individual is prohibited.[30] In 2018, the 1982 Constitution was amended for the fifth time. The 2018 amendment modified article 1 of the 1982 Constitution by adding a new provision that the defining feature of socialism with Chinese characteristics is the leadership of the CPC.[31] The 2018 amendment further underscores the constitutional basis for the CPC's leadership.

Also in the 2018 amendment was the abrogation of term limits for the presidency of the country, a position now held by the chairperson of the CPC. The repeal of presidential term limits is widely considered a huge setback from the political reform that has been sought in the country for decades.[32] In the eyes of foreign observers,

27 See Perry Keller, *Sources of Order in Chinese Law*, 42 Am. J. Comp. L. 711, 712 (1994) (Chinese possesses ... a highly sophisticated Confucian based legal history which once formed the philosophic backbone of imperial law and continues to resonate in contemporary legal culture. The country has also undergone a series of experiments in the reception of foreign law.).

28 See 1982 Constitution of the People's Republic of China (as amended), Preamble. An English version is available at http://english.peopledaily.com.cn/constitution/constitution.html.

29 Some similarities might be seen in a few socialist countries like North Korea, Cuba, and perhaps Vietnam.

30 See *id.*, art. 1.

31 The 1982 Constitution was amended in 1988, 1993, 1998, 2004, and 2018, respectively. An English version of the 2018 Amendments is available at www.loc.gov/item/global-legal-monitor/2018-05-18/china-2018-constitutional-amendment-adopted/.

32 It was previously provided in article 79 of the 1982 Constitution that the term of office of the President and Vice-President of the People's Republic of China is the same as that of the National People's Congress, and they shall serve no more than two consecutive terms. The amended provision in 2018 eliminates the second clause. The term limits on key leadership in

this change heralds an end to the era of collective leadership and sets the stage for a return to individual autocracy.[33]

In the process of legislation, the CPC's leadership is dominant. First, it is an unpublished but unyielding principle that all draft major laws of national importance must be examined and approved by the Central Committee of the CPC before they may be reviewed by the NPC.[34] This principle was explicitly stated in a 1991 internally circulated official document of the Central Committee of the CPC.[35] Although the document limited the application of this principle to important laws primarily in political, economic, and administrative areas, virtually all laws passed by the NPC were pre-reviewed and approved by the Central Committee of the CPC.

The adoption of amendments to the 1982 Constitution is typical to help better explain the role of the CPC in the nation's legislation. Take the 2004 amendment, for example. On December 12, 2003, the Central Committee of the CPC made a proposal to the Standing Committee of the NPC to amend the 1982 Constitution. An important amendment in the proposal, among others, was to add former President Jiang Zemin's idea of "Three Represents" to the Constitution in line with

the 1982 Constitution were the centerpiece of a systemic reform to help prevent the recurrence of personality cult and dictatorship in the country.

33 See Suzuki Ken, *China's New "Xi Jinping Constitution": The Road to Totalitarianism*, Nippoon Communications Foundation, November 27, 2018, available at www.nippon.com/en/in-depth/a05803/?cx_recs_click = true.

34 See Qin Qianhong, *The Impacts of the Communist Party of China on Legislation*, Beijing University China Law Info., available at http://article1.chinalawinfo.com/Article_Detail.asp?ArticleID = 23338.

35 The document was named "Several Opinions of the Central Committee of the Communist Party of China on the Strengthening of the Leadership over the State Legislative Work" (Zhongfa, 1991 No. 8). Under the Opinions, the Central Committee of the CPC shall retain control of the legislative process in the following four ways: (a) any amendment to the constitution and certain draft laws of political importance or of vital economic or administrative importance, before being submitted to the National People's Congress for review, must be examined by the Politburo of the Central Committee of the CPC, and all other proposals for constitutional amendments must also be submitted through the party organization of the NPC to the Central Committee of the CPC for review; (b) for any law in a political area, before it is drafted, the Standing Committee of the NPC must have the legislative thought and principles of the law reported to the Central Committee of the CPC for approval; (c) any draft law in a political area or of important economic and administrative areas must be reported to the Politburo or Standing Committee of the Central Committee of the CPC for approval before it is submitted to the NPC for review; and (d) the Central Committee of the CPC shall exercise its leadership uniformly over all law drafting work. All laws drafted by the NPC and its Standing Committee must be reported by the party organization at the NPC to the Central Committee of the CPC for approval, and all laws drafted by other competent government departments, if review by the NPC is required, must also be reported to the Central Committee of the CPC for approval. See *id.* In order to implement the Opinion, the Provincial Committee of the Communist Party of Zhejiang issued "matching opinions" entitled "Opinions of the Committee of the CPC of Zhejiang Province on Further Advancement of Local Legislation" in order to assure the party's leadership over local legislation. A full text is available at http://china.findlaw.cn/fagui/gj/22/16011.html.

Marxism-Leninism, *Mao Zedong* Thought, and *Deng Xiaoping* Theory as the governing ideology of the country.[36]

This proposal met widespread criticism, especially from legal scholars, because they believed that the "Three Represents" was no more than a norm guiding the Communist Party itself as well as its members, and therefore should not be provided in the Constitution that governs the country as a whole. Some also pointed out that the use of abbreviations in the Constitution would cause confusion and also set a bad precedent of legal vagueness.

But all the criticisms were ignored. The NPC at its national session in March 2004 adopted the CPC's proposal without changing a single word. Among the 2,903 delegates present, 2,863 voted for, 10 voted against, and 17 abstained. Interestingly, the vote as to the several amended articles was taken on an "all or nothing" basis. This voting pattern in fact left many delegates with no choice but to take the whole package because they disagreed with the provision of "Three Represents" but did not want to lose other provisions in the amendment (e.g., protection of private property and safeguarding of human rights).

The 2018 amendment is another example. As noted, the 2018 amendment was very controversial for its removal of the presidential term limits from the Constitution. When the amendment proposal was introduced by the CPC, it met criticism from the public, the legal community, in particular because of the concern that the scrapping of the term limits would reverse the gear of reforms in the country. But in order to justify the CPC's claim that they were making the move in response to popular demand, all criticisms of the move were filtered out via state censorship, mostly on the Internet. As a result, the only information available to the public was the official statement that the amendment had won support from both inside and outside the CPC and its historic significance was to ensure the prosperity and lasting security of the country.

Second, it has become a political norm that in addition to the constitutional mandate, leadership of the CPC must also be provided in particular laws. The requirement of a "party leadership clause" in legislation came after the 18th National Congress of the CPC, which called for the political construction of the CPC in 2012.[37] During recent years, the Standing Committee of the NPC in its annual legislative work plans explicitly held that the leadership of the CPC clause is an indispensable part of laws and regulations. In its 2022 Legislative Work Plan, for example, the Standing Committee of the NPC stated it as the "highest political principle" to "unswervingly uphold the CPC's overall leadership in legislative

36 The "Three Represents" states that the CPC represents the development trends of advanced productive forces, represents the orientation of an advanced culture, and represents the fundamental interests of the overwhelming majority of the people of China. The idea was put forward by Jiang Zemin in 2000.

37 See Liu Yida, *The Specific Forms and Evolution of the "Party Leadership" Clause in the Law*, 1 J. Rsch. in the CPC Rules (2022), available at www.cicjc.com.cn/info/1040/14387.htm.

work," "resolutely implement the Party Central Committee's major decisions and arrangements," and "make the CPC's ideas become the will of the country through legislation."[38]

The CPC's leadership clause is provided in laws and regulations in three different formats: (a) a general expression of the CPC's leadership to the effect that the party leads certain specific work; (b) a stipulation that the party instrumentality, alone or jointly with administrative agencies, takes charge of certain legal responsibilities; and (c) a provision that makes support for the CPC's leadership a legal obligation and criterion for working in public offices.[39] For any major national legislative matters determined by the CPC Central Committee, the Standing Committee of the NPC is required to promptly seek instructions from and report to the CPC Central Committee during the entire legislative process.[40]

C. *Public Ownership*

In China, public ownership is considered the core of socialism and viewed as the crown jewel of the country's economic system. The nation's economy is currently structured with public ownership as the main body, with a common development of multiple ownerships. Under this economic structure, there is an established distribution system in which distribution is mainly made according to work, while multiple distribution methods coexist.

In the Chinese economy, there are two basic forms of public ownership: whole people ownership and collective ownership. Article 6 of the 1982 Constitution (as amended) explicitly provides that the basis of the socialist economic system of the PRC is socialist public ownership of the means of production, namely, ownership by the whole people and collective ownership by working people.[41] Article 7 further defines the whole people ownership economy as the state-owned economy and categorizes it as a leading force in the economy of the nation.[42]

Collective ownership refers to public ownership in rural areas. Under article 8 of the 1982 Constitution (as amended), collective ownership by working people includes all forms of cooperative economy in rural areas, such as producers' supply and marketing, credit, and consumers' cooperatives.[43] Pursuant to article 8, rural collective economic organizations shall run under a dual operation system that combines centralized operation with decentralized operation by households under a contract.[44]

[38] See the 2022 Legislative Work Plan of the Standing Committee of the NPC, published on May 6, 2022, available at www.npc.gov.cn/npc/c2/c30834/202205/t20220506_317718.html.

[39] See Yida, *supra* note 37.

[40] See the 2022 Legislative Work Plan of the Standing Committee of the NPC, *supra* note 38.

[41] See 1982 Chinese Constitution (as amended 2018), *supra* note 28, art. 6.

[42] See *id.*, art. 7.

[43] See *id.*, art. 8.

[44] See *id.*

For many decades until 1988, public ownership was the only legally recognized and protected ownership in China. Conceptually, for quite a long period of time, especially in Mao's era, socialism was interpreted and understood in China as a system that should not tolerate private ownership. It was in part affected by Lenin's proposition, translated from Russian into Chinese, which was taken as a biblical tenet: that "we do not recognize private law,"[45] meaning that everything in the economy must be in the public's hands. The non-recognition of private ownership also came from Mao's revolutionary doctrine that private ownership was the source of all evils and that the ultimate goal of the Communist Party was to eliminate it.[46]

The attitude toward private ownership in China changed after the economic reform that started in 1978. But the official recognition of private ownership in the nation was ten years later in 1988, when the 1982 Constitution was amended.[47] The 1988 Amendment, however, did not use the term private ownership but rather the term "private sector of the economy." And further, according to article 11 of the 1982 Constitution as amended in 1988, the private sector of the economy was only deemed "a complement to the socialist public economy."[48] In the 1999

45 This proposition was stated in the instructive opinions of Lenin to the draft civil code of the Soviet Union in 1922. Many in China now believe that there was a mistranslation of Lenin's words. According to them, what Lenin meant was that "we do not recognize anything 'private,'" and its purpose was to enhance government control over private matters. See Jiang Ping, *Roman Law Spirit and Modern Chinese Legislation*, in Jiang Ping, ed., Commentary on Civil and Commercial Law, 69 (China University of Politics and Law Press, 2018). See also Shen Weixing, *Construction of Property Law of China under the Balance of Public and Private Rights*, 4 Contemp. L. Rev. 46 (2008).

46 See Hu Fuchen, *Is the Private Ownership the Source of All Evils?* A full text of the article in Chinese is available at http://wuliucun.ycool.com/post.3036184.html. In the mid 1950s, believing in the communist principles stated in Karl Marx's Manifesto of the Communist Party (one of such principles was to get rid of private ownership), Mao declared that China must root out capitalism and say no to private ownership. Based on that belief, Mao launched a nationwide campaign of socialist transformation from 1953–1956. One primary purpose of the campaign was to nationalize, in whole or in part, all privately owned enterprises and to make public ownership the sole ownership of the country.

47 Before the 1988 amendments, the Constitution allowed the existence of an "individual economy of urban and rural people." But as many believed in China, in a legal sense, the "individual economy" and "private economy" were two different concepts. For example, one typical feature of individual economy is that the individual is the owner of the means of production but at the same time is the worker himself. The private economy involves employment of others. Thus, in the 1988 Amendments, the private economy was added in line with the individual economy.

48 The new paragraph added in the 1988 Amendment to article 11 of the 1982 Constitution reads:

> The State permits the private sector of the economy to exist and develop within the limit prescribed by law. The private sector of the economy is a complement to the socialist public economy. The State protects the lawful rights and the interests of the private sector of the economy, and exercises guidance, supervision and control over the private sector of the economy.

Amendment, the private sector of the economy was escalated to "an important part of the socialist market economy."

As noted, the current economy in China is labeled as a socialist market economy – an economy that is purposed to follow market rules but maintain its socialist nature. The concept of a socialist market economy was formally adopted in China in the 1993 amendments to the 1982 Constitution. It marked the country's official departure from a planned economy. Although the term socialist market economy was never clearly defined, a general understanding in China is that the adoption of a socialist market economy in China will by no means affect the leading status of public ownership in the nation's economy. It is an economy in which diverse forms of ownership coexist and develop while public ownership remains the mainstay.

Therefore, it is impossible to describe the socialist legal system with Chinese characteristics in China without addressing the role of the CPC and public ownership.

Both the leadership of the CPC and the dominance of public ownership constitute the main themes of present Chinese society and the legal system, and also determine the trend of future development. On the other hand, the formation of a socialist legal system with Chinese characteristics provides legal assurance of the legitimacy of the CPC's sole leadership and the controlling status of public ownership.

China's vast economic reform in past decades has changed the country dramatically. As noted, with its fast economic growth, China has now become the second-largest economy in the world. Along with economic development, however, there is a growing demand in the country for political reform, reform in response to public outcry for social equity and justice, and for legal safeguards against government corruption and abuse of power.

In pursuing political reform, the state seems to have taken a stance of strong commitment on the surface. At the top level of the CPC, political reform has become a frequent topic of the working agenda. But as far as the substance of political reform, words seem to be much more powerful than actions. It has been highly questionable where political reform should lead. A question frequently asked is how far political reform may go. Realistically, there are so many minefields in making reform politically, and the mobility to step forward is extremely limited in almost all politically sensitive areas, particularly when the issue comes directly to the controlling power of the CPC.

The development of the rule of law in the country is a good example. The issue was actually raised as early as the beginning of the economic reform in 1978,[49] but

[49] In December 1978, Deng Xiaoping announced in a working meeting of the Central Committee of the CPC a new legal policy aimed at establishing a rule-based legal system. The policy is abbreviated in sixteen Chinese characters: "There must be law to rely upon; law must be followed; enforcement of law must be strict; and violation of law must be corrected." See The Selected Works of Deng Xiaoping, Vol. 2, 147 (People's Publishing House, 1993).

not until 1999 did China formally make it a constitutional mandate that China governs the country according to, and builds a socialist country ruled, by law.[50] Although it is now acclaimed that the rule of law in China has been established, such establishment is by and large still at the stage of enactment of laws, and the trends set in motion in terms of exercising the rule of law in both legislation and enforcement remain quite winding. In addition, there are certain areas, categorized as politically sensitive, that stay untouchable.

Nevertheless, in the course of development of the socialist legal system with Chinese characteristics, there has been judicial reform undertaken by the SPC, the highest judicial body of the nation. Unlike the general political reform that requires extensive institutional and structural changes in the government, and even in the ruling party, judicial reform is narrowly circumscribed to the judicial system. It might be true that political reform and judicial reform can hardly be separated, especially when judicial independence is at issue. But judicial reform, as many expect in the country, could take place on a manageable scale and scope.

2. JUDICIAL REFORMS

Judicial reform in China began in the late 1990s as a response to public outcry for justice and fairness in judicial proceedings and as an effort to restore public confidence in the judicial system. At the early stage of the judicial reforms, the focus was on three aspects: the trial function of the courts, openness of trials, and judicial professionalism.[51] A part of the reform was the publication of cases, which was aimed at providing guidance for the lower courts in order to help promote judicial efficiency and transparency. Years later, the reform was extended to cover such areas as the organization of courts, the judge system, litigation procedures, methods of trial, an enforcement mechanism, and management of judicial work.[52]

A. *Reform Plans*

In 1999, the SPC issued the first "five-year" outline for judicial reform. Since then, the SPC has updated its reform plan every five years. The latest one was the sixth "five-year" reform outline, which was adopted in February 2024 to cover the period from 2024 to 2029. But again, the reforms may only be made without diminishing the leadership of the CPC. In 2014, the CPC issued the Decision on Several

[50] See the 1982 Constitution (as amended), *supra* note 28, art. 13.

[51] See the SPC Report, *Judicial Reforms of Chinese Courts 2013–2018*. A full text of the report is available at www.chinadaily.com.cn/specials/ChineseCourtJudicialReform2013-2018.pdf (hereinafter referred to as *Judicial Reform 2013–2018*).

[52] See *id.*

Important Issues Concerning the Comprehensive Promotion of Governing the Country by Law, making it imperative to persist in the leadership of the CPC.[53]

According to the 2014 Decision, the leadership of the CPC "is the most essential trait of Socialism with Chinese characteristics and is the most fundamental guarantee for Socialist rule of law."[54] The 2014 Decision further stresses that letting the CPC leadership "penetrate into the entire process and all aspects of ruling the country to the law is a basic experience of the construction of our country's Socialist rule of law."[55]

Under this condition, the 2014 Decision calls for continuing judicial reform to improve the judicial system.[56]

B. *Changes*

The past two decades of judicial reform have brought notable changes to the Chinese judiciary, and most of the changes have resulted from efforts made by the courts to pursue juridical justice and transparency. One major change resulting from the judicial reform is a shift of trial method from the traditional approach of the court *ex officio* to the mechanism of enhancing the role of the parties, particularly in civil cases. As early as 1998, the SPC issued the *Several Rules on the Matters Concerning Reform of Civil and Economic Trial Methods*, where the SPC specifically addressed such issues as (a) burden of proof of the parties, (b) fair trials, (c) improvement of court proceedings, and (d) evidence examination and determination. Those issues then became the major contents of the judicial reform contained in the 1999 "five-year" reform guidelines.[57]

The outcomes of the reform on trial methods are twofold. On the one hand, it introduced into the Chinese trial system a principle of "whoever makes a claim bears the burden of proof." The principle is purposed to impose the burden on the parties instead of the courts to produce evidence. Under this principle, a party who fails or is unable to present evidence will lose on the claim. The court is charged with a minimum burden of collecting evidence and will only do so on an as-needed basis.

On the other hand, the reform places the focus of the trial on the process of the court hearing. In the past, the court would need to make a pre-trial investigation for the purpose of gathering information on the case and collecting evidence. Under

[53] See the CPC Central Committee, *Decision on Several Important Issues Concerning the Comprehensive Promotion of Governing the Country by Law*, issued on October 23, 2014. An English version of the Decision is available at www.chinalawtranslate.com/en/fourth-plenum-decision/.

[54] See *id.*

[55] See *id.*

[56] See *id.*

[57] See Mo Zhang & Paul Zwier, *Burden of Proof: Developments in Modern Chinese Evidence Rules*, 10 Tulsa J. Compar. & Int'l L. 419, 433 (2002).

the reformed trial methods, the investigation will mainly be conducted during the trial and the determination of the facts will be made on the evidence provided by the parties through a "cross-examination" in the hearing. An advantage of this method is to avoid possible bias the judge may have before the trial.

Another change relates to the establishment of the so-called judicial accountability system. At the core of such a system is the notion that the judge adjudicating a case shall have the power to decide it and shall also be responsible for the decision made. Its intended purpose is to help ensure the power and authority of the judge in judicial proceedings and, in the meantime, to reduce the role of the judicial committee, a special decision-making body in the court system, in the determination of cases.[58] There has always been criticism that the judicial committee acts as a backseat driver in the trial and interferes with the independence of the judges in their rulings.

The notable components of the judicial accountability system include the presiding judges' conference and the case allocation mechanism. The presiding judges' conference is a newly established channel by which the presiding judges in various cases discuss and exchange views on the pending cases. According to the SPC, the presiding judges' conference is purposed to provide guidance and reference for judges to accurately apply the law, promote the unification of adjudication rules and standards, summarize trial experience, and improve trial management.[59]

Depending on the topics and nature of cases to be discussed, the presiding judges' conference may invite experts, scholars, other relevant professionals, as well as NPC delegates or members of the Chinese People's Political Consultative Conference (CPPCC), to attend. The cases submitted to the presiding judges' conference for discussion at the request of a presiding judge or collegiate panel include (a) those that are new, difficult, complicated, and have great social impact; (b) those involving rules and standards of judgment that need to be unified or have general guiding significance in the application of laws; (c) those in which the judgment to be made will be inconsistent with the rules and standards in the judgment of similar cases decided by the court or higher people's courts; (d) those for which the opinions of the members of the collegial panel are quite different; (e) those in which the presiding judge who holds a minority opinion thinks that it is necessary to invite

[58] In China, the trial committee is a body of collective leadership within the people's courts of all levels for trial work. Consisting of a president, vice presidents, and division heads of a court, the trial committee functions under the rule of democratic centralism to discuss major or difficult cases and other issues related to trial work, and in many cases has the final say as to the final decision. In the SPC, for example, the trial committee is the leading group of the SPC dealing with major or difficult cases and other issues related to trial work. The SPC trial committee members include the President, Executive Vice President, Vice Presidents, Directors and Deputy Directors of Chambers, and certain senior judges.

[59] See the SPC, *Guiding Opinions on the Improvement of the Working Mechanism of the Presiding Judges Conference of the People's Courts (Provincial)*, issued on December 24, 2018. A full text of the Opinion is available at www.chinacourt.org/law/detail/2018/12/id/149823.shtml.

discussion; (f) those in which a reversal, a change of the judgment, a remand for a new trial, an appellate review, or an order for a retrial is to be made; and (g) others that need to be submitted for discussion.[60]

Case allocation refers to the method of distributing cases among the judges. The reform has put in place a system under which random allocation is the mainstay, supplemented by assignment in limited cases. The allocation of cases is made randomly among the judges on the basis of subjects of law and the complexity of the cases. After allocation, for such reasons as recusal, job transfer, health condition, or risk of corruption, the judge handling the case may be replaced. The replacement, however, is subject to the review and approval of the division head or president of the court under their respective authority. If a replacement is made, a timely notice shall be given to the litigants and shall also be made public on the case's platform online.[61]

The judicial accountability system includes lifetime responsibility for the quality of the case adjudicated and disciplinary action against the judge for misconduct committed during the process of adjudication. The lifetime responsibility is aimed at ensuring the quality of cases adjudicated. According to the SPC, a judge shall be responsible for the quality of case adjudication for life and shall be held liable for illegal adjudication if the judge intentionally violates the law or commits gross negligence when adjudicating the case that results in a wrong judgment causing serious consequences.[62]

Disciplinary action takes place when a judge is found to have violated the duty of adjudication. The violation is assessed and determined by the provincial disciplinary committee consisting of representatives from the high, intermediate, and trial people's courts, as well as civilians. The type of discipline taken against a particular judge is dependent on whether an illegal adjudication has been committed and whether the judge acted intentionally or through gross negligence.[63]

The third major change concerns openness and transparency of judicial proceedings. As noted, the judicial reform began with the promotion of judicial transparency by the publication of cases. Since 2013, judicial transparency has been more closely linked to an extensive scale of openness in judicial proceedings. Under a concept called judicial democracy, the SPC has established nationwide channels for the public to access trial proceedings, court hearings, judgment documents, and enforcement procedures.[64] According to the SPC, the establishment of these channels is to help advance in the Chinese judiciary a principle of full and substantive disclosure according to the law.[65]

[60] See *id.*, art. 4.
[61] See the SPC, *Judicial Reform 2013–2018*, *supra* note 51.
[62] See *id.*
[63] See *id.*
[64] See *id.*
[65] See *id.*

Take court hearings, for example. In order to make the court trial open and transparent, the China Court Live Broadcasting Website was established in December 2013 under the auspices of the SPC. The website was then upgraded in 2016 to provide nationwide live online broadcasting of court trials of all cases that can be made public under the law. Through this website, the public can watch a trial live online or obtain a video of the trial via the Internet. In addition, all trial information online can be shared through Weibo (a microblogging website) or WeChat.[66] Now all 3,525 courts across the country are connected to the court's digital network. In recent years, however, the openness and publication of cases seem to have suffered a serious setback due to the tightened control of information dissemination in the nation.

The fourth major change is the structural or organizational change of the courts. This change has occurred in several aspects. The first aspect is the creation of circuit courts. Chinese courts comprise four tiers in terms of jurisdiction: at the top is the SPC, and under the SPC are the basic people's courts, intermediate people's courts, and high people's courts. In 2015 and 2016, six circuit courts were created to handle multi-provincial cases.[67] The circuit courts are purposed to handle inter-regional and serious administrative, civil, and commercial disputes, and in the meantime minimize or avoid the influence of local interests.[68]

Note, however, that the creation of circuit courts does not add an extra tier into the current court system in China. The circuit courts are merely dispatched branches of the SPC and are charged with the power to adjudicate cases as assigned by the SPC. The judgments and rulings by the circuit courts have the same effect as those made by the SPC. In addition, the presidents of all six circuits are the senior justices of the SPC. The work of the circuit courts is considered important to improve judicial efficiency and help effectively maintain social harmony and stability.[69]

The second aspect of the structural change involves the expansion of specialized courts. Before the reform, in addition to the regular people's courts, there were several specialized courts, including military courts, maritime courts, railway transportation courts, forest courts, land reclamation courts, and oil courts. In 2014, three Intellectual Property (IP) Right Courts were established in Beijing, Guangzhou, and Shanghai to adjudicate IP-rights-related cases. In addition, as of 2019, nineteen IP

[66] See *id.*

[67] The six circuit courts are located in Shenzhen, Shenyang, Nanjing, Zhengzhou, Chongqing, and Xian, respectively.

[68] See the SPC, *Rules on Several Issues Concerning Adjudication of Cases by Circuit Courts*, issued on January 5, 2015, available at www.court.gov.cn/zixun-xiangqing-13148.html. According to the SPC Rules, the Circuit Courts hear eleven types of cases, including administrative, civil, and commercial cases of first instance which are of significance or have major impacts on the country, appeals from the High People's Courts, procedural matters involving judicial supervision or the decisions of the High People's Court, and civil and commercial cases involving judicial assistance or parties from Hong Kong, Macau, or Taiwan.

[69] See the SPC, *Judicial Reform 2013–2018*, *supra* note 51.

Chambers were formed in sixteen provinces. The latest one was the IP Chamber of the SPC, which was established in January 2019 to deal with appeals of highly specialized and technical cases, such as patent infringement.[70]

In addition, on August 20, 2018, the Shanghai Financial Court was formed with special jurisdiction over finance-related civil, commercial, as well as administrative cases that used to be adjudicated in intermediate people's courts. The cases adjudicated by the financial court mainly involve disputes concerning liabilities for misrepresentation in securities, financial loan contracts, corporate bond trading, repurchase of pledged securities, financial leasing contracts, and business trusts.[71] Under the SPC rules, the financial court also has jurisdiction over (a) bankruptcy cases in which financial institutions are the debtors; (b) judicial review requested for the arbitration of finance-related civil and commercial disputes; and (c) applications for recognition and enforcement of foreign judgments and rulings on finance-related civil and commercial disputes.[72]

Moreover, in 2017 and 2018, three Internet courts were established in Hangzhou, Beijing, and Guangzhou. These courts are missioned to experiment and implement the SPC's initiative of "online resolution of online disputes." The Internet courts are aimed at promoting judicial efficiency by using the Internet to facilitate online verification of a litigant's identity, collection of evidentiary materials, and service of process.[73] The SPC anticipates that the Internet courts will be able to draw and refine from their practices rules for adjudicating Internet-related cases so as to help effectively and fairly adjudicate newly emerged difficult and complicated online cases, including, for example, ownership of big data, liability for contracting fault in online shopping, and ownership of copyrights on IP works.[74]

A highly notable development in this regard is the establishment of the China International Commercial Court (CICC) under the SPC. In response to the rapid expansion of international commercial transactions between China and other countries, and as an effort to help implement the country's "Belt and Road" initiative,[75]

[70] See *id.*

[71] See *id.*

[72] See the SPC, *Rules on Jurisdiction of the Shanghai Financial Court*, adopted on August 7, 2018, available at www.chinacourt.org/law/detail/2018/08/id/149788.shtml.

[73] See the SPC, *Judicial Reform 2013–2018*, *supra* note 51.

[74] See *id.*

[75] The Belt and Road Initiative (also known as the One Belt, One Road) refers to the massive infrastructure development launched by China in 2013 that involves vast investment in numerous countries and regions. From China's viewpoint, the initiative is to help promote the economic prosperity of the countries along the Belt and Road and regional economic cooperation. See China State Council, *Action Plan on the Belt and Road Initiative*, March 30, 2015, available at https://english.www.gov.cn/archive/publications/2015/03/30/content_281475080249035.htm. In the West, however, it is viewed as an ambitious and multifaceted foreign economic policy initiative to expand China's global economic reach and influence. See Congressional Research Services, *China's "One Belt, One Road" Initiative: Economic Issues*, March 16, 2024, available at https://crsreports.congress.gov/product/pdf/IF/IF11735.

the SPC in 2018 created a special court named the "International Commercial Court" to adjudicate international commercial cases in a fair and timely manner in accordance with the law, equally protect the legitimate rights and interests of Chinese and foreign parties, and create a stable, fair, transparent, and convenient international business environment ruled by law.[76] There are two CICCs established by the SPC. The First CICC is located in Shenzhen, and the Second CICC is in Xi'an. The CICC is defined as the SPC's "permanent judicial body" specializing in handling international commercial disputes. But since the creation of the CICC is purposed to serve the "Belt and Road" initiative and guarantee its implementation, its international function and effectiveness remain to be seen.

The third aspect is the formation of pilot courts for transregional trials. In December 2014, in order to maintain and enhance judicial credibility with the public, the Fourth Intermediate People's Court in Beijing and the Third Intermediate Court in Shanghai were established as pilot courts to conduct trials across administrative regions. The two courts are designated to be responsible for adjudicating major civil, commercial, administrative, environmental resource protection, food and drug safety cases, and some major criminal cases that involve different administrative regions. The very purpose of the transregional trials is to ensure that cases involving local interests are fairly adjudicated.[77]

What is worth noting here is the effort to establish a centralized budget system at a provincial level for all intermediate and trial courts. As part of the reform on judicial finance management dictated in the 2014 Decision, the centralized budget intends to have the expenditures of the intermediate and trial courts in the province covered by the provincial rather than the local government. The purpose is to sever local courts from possible influence and interference by the local government. But absent financial assistance from the central government, the judicial budget centralization has met more resistance than expected in many provinces due to the lack of sufficient and sustainable fiscal capacity to implement it.

Another major change resulting from judicial reform concerns the qualifications and roles of people's assessors. China does not have a jury system, but instead has people's assessors in judicial proceedings. As a normal practice, people's assessors form a collegial panel with a judge in the trial. Since 2015, the SPC has been carrying out a reform of the people's assessor scheme with a focus on such matters as criteria and methods for the selection of people's assessors, expansion of the scope of people's assessors' participation and power in the trial, and advancement of the job security of people's assessors.[78]

[76] See the SPC, *Provisions on Several Issues Concerning the Establishment of International Commercial Tribunals*, issued on June 25, 2018, amended December 5, 2023. A full text of the amended provisions (effective January 1, 2024) is available at http://gongbao.court.gov.cn/Details/26f41d00009ec973d5c70c2c82ca86.html.

[77] See the SPC, *Judicial Reform 2013–2018*, *supra* note 51.

[78] See *id.*

The purpose of the reform concerning people's assessors is to put in place a new mechanism that will help better employ the advantages of people's assessors in their familiarity with social reality and public opinion, and turn their role mainly to the finding of facts of the case rather than the issue of application of law. In other words, under the new mechanism, the people's assessors, when participating in the trial, will only have the power to vote on factual issues.[79]

The new mechanism is intended to bring about four conversions: (a) selection of people's assessors is transformed from reliance mainly on recommendations by certain organizations to random selection from a people's assessor pool; (b) the power of the people's assessors is changed from full participation in the trial to the finding of facts; (c) the collegial panel turns from a three-member panel to a seven-member panel so as to increase the number of people's assessors participating in the trial; and (d) the evaluation of cases attended by the people's assessors shifts from quantitive evaluation to qualitive evaluation.[80]

In 2018, the first People's Assessors Law of China (PAL) was adopted.[81] Many provisions in the PAL actually derive from outcomes of the reforms. For example, article 14 of the PAL provides that when the people's assessors and judge form a collegial panel to adjudicate a case, the judge should serve as the presiding person, and the collegial panel can be a three-member or seven-member panel.[82] Also, under article 19 of the PAL, if people's assessors are required for the formation of a collegial panel, they shall be selected randomly from a list of the people's assessors, depending on the nature of the particular case.[83]

C. *Unfinished Business*

To the extent that judicial efficiency is to be maintained and the law is to be observed, the decades-long judicial reform has dramatically improved the Chinese judiciary. The public confidence and trust in the judiciary, however, do not seem to have reached the levels desired. Judicial independence remains in limbo. The problem is that the courts are still deemed a tool to serve the interests of the CPC. The tone set clearly by the CPC for the country is that

[79] See *id.*

[80] See *id.*

[81] The People's Assessors Law (PAL) was adopted by the Standing Committee of the NPC on April 27, 2018, available at www.npc.gov.cn/zgrdw/npc/lfzt/rlyw/2018-04/27/content_2054207.htm. On April 25, 2019, the SPC issued the Interpretation on Several Issues Concerning Application of the People's Assessors Law to implement the PAL. According to the SPC, the people's court shall randomly select people's assessors from the list of people's assessors seven days before the hearing (art. 3). A text of the PAL is available at www.court.gov.cn/fabu-xiangqing-154792.html.

[82] See *id.*, PAL, art. 14.

[83] See *id.*, art. 19.

China must never follow the path of Western constitutionalism, separation of powers, or judicial independence.[84]

On February 27, 2019, the SPC issued its Fifth Five-Year Reform Outline of the People's Court (2019–2023), entitled the Opinions on Deepening the Comprehensive Supporting Reform of the Judicial System of the People's Courts.[85] According to the SPC, a fundamental principle that governs the continuing reforms in the people's courts is the absolute leadership of the CPC over the work of the people's courts. Thus, it is imperative that judicial reform must always be under the leadership of the party, and the CPC's core role in holding the reins of all government branches, including the judiciary, must be maintained. But a question inevitably raised is how to restore and maintain the public trust and confidence in the judiciary without judicial independence.

3. ISSUES FACING THE CHINESE LEGAL SYSTEM

The notion of a socialist legal system with Chinese characteristics seems quite abstract. It in essence implicates that the development of a legal system in the country shall be premised on the nation's political, social, and cultural reality.[86] Ever since the inception of the rebuilding of the legal system after ten years of chaos due to the Cultural Revolution, there has been a general holding that China must walk its own path to develop a legal system that is fit for the country. As noted, a centerpiece of Chinese characteristics is the CPC's leadership. An iron rule is that the development of a legal system must not entrench upon the absolute leadership of the CPC.[87]

However, a legal system consists of a set of laws and the process of their interpretation and enforcement. It functions to prescribe the rights and responsibilities of all members of society in various ways. Although the law may be defined differently, it serves as a social instrument to set the rules of conduct, to punish violations, and to maintain good order. In one respect, law is considered to represent, and also ensure adherence to, the will of the state. In the other respect, however, law is deemed the

[84] See Charlotte Gao, *Xi: China Must Never Adopt Constitutionalism, Separation of Powers, or Judicial Independence* – The Chinese president calls for strengthening the Communist Party's leadership over law in China, The Diplomat, February 19, 2019, available at https://thediplomat.com/2019/02/xi-china-must-never-adopt-constitutionalism-separation-of-powers-or-judicial-independence/.

[85] See the SPC, *Opinions on Deepening the Comprehensive Supporting Reform of the Judicial System of the People's Courts: The Fifth Five-Year Reform Outline of the People's Court (2019–2023)*, available at www.court.gov.cn/fabu-xiangqing-144202.html.

[86] See People's Daily Editorial Article, *Perfection of Socialist Legal System with Chinese Characteristics*, People's Daily, March 15, 2009, at p. 1. The article is a restatement of the official opinion of the nation set in the Second National Session of the 11th National People's Congress held in Beijing from March 5 to March 13, 2009. A full text of the article is available at http://opinion.people.com.cn/GB/8962404.html.

[87] See *id.*

science of justice and the art of justice,[88] meaning that the very purpose of law is to achieve, preserve, and sustain justice.

Thus, a well-functioning legal system does require a certain level of judicial independence or neutrality, especially in situations where justice is at stake. It is then vitally important that a country run under the rule of law rather than the will of a man, a particular party, or a political organization. On the other hand, in a legally sound society it is held self-evident that nobody is above the law. In this context, there are several issues that are indeed critical to the development of the legal system of socialist nature bearing Chinese reality on the basis of the rule of law.

A. *Theme of the Legal System: Obligation-Based v. Right-Based*

Rights and obligations are the two fundamental values contained in any legal system. A right in general is a legal or moral entitlement, while an obligation is regarded as a course of action imposed by law, society, or conscience by which one is bound or restricted.[89] Both the notion of rights and the interaction between rights and obligations determine the character and nature of a society, which in turn affects the legal structure of that society.[90] In a society that is legally ordered and administered, rights are necessarily the center of attention because they are directly related to the dignity of human beings as well as the basic order of human society.[91] In addition, rights are deemed vitally important in the theory of justice.[92]

The concept and contents of rights may vary from country to country, but they are commonly classified into two major categories. One category is called "universalist and egalitarian" and the other is referred to as "authoritarian and hierarchical." The former is the modern conception of rights, which holds that equal rights are granted to whole people. The latter represents the historical notion that different rights ought to be granted to different people depending on status, and as a result some should have more rights than others.[93]

In addition, there are two main conceptions of rights in the modern world: natural rights and legal rights. The idea of natural rights holds that there is a certain list of rights enshrined in nature that cannot be legitimately modified by any human

[88] For general discussion, see Lysander Spooner, Natural Law; or the Science of Justice (Part One) (A. Williams & Co., 1882); see also Morris Cohen, Law, the Art of Justice (Hugh Lauter Levin Associates, 1992).

[89] See H. L. A. Hart, The Concept of Law, 170–171 (2nd ed., Oxford University Press, 1994); see also Daniel Elazar, *Changing Conceptions of Rights in the United States and the West*, 22 J. Federalism 14 (Spring 1992).

[90] For scholarly discussion, see H. L. A. Hart, Essays on Bentham: Jurisprudence and Political Philosophy (Oxford University Press, 1982).

[91] See Hart, *supra* note 89, at 269.

[92] See *id.* at 162–183; see also Jeanne Duly & Judith Lumley, *Individual Rights and Social Justice*, 28 Austl. & N.Z. J. Pub. Health 507 (2004).

[93] See Stanford Encyclopedia of Philosophy, available at https://plato.stanford.edu/entries/egalitarianism/.

power. The theory of natural rights is closely related to natural law. Legal rights, however, are considered human constructs, created by society, enforced by governments, and subject to change.[94] Natural rights are commonly defined as the rights "not contingent upon the laws, customs, or beliefs of any particular culture or government," while legal rights are considered as the rights "bestowed onto a person by a given legal system."[95]

China is a country in which obligations are weighed significantly over rights, and hardly any right may be deemed natural. Historically, the country was deeply immersed in and bound by *Confucian* norms of morality that placed great emphasis on the hierarchy and order of social status. The *Confucian* creed that "the ruler must be like a ruler, the subject like a subject, the father like a father and the son like a son" set an insurmountable boundary that defined the propriety of the behavior of a person in reference to the person's social status.[96]

The very focus of the creed was the obligations of loyalty and filial piety, upholding a fundamental principle that one must commit his life to serve in order to be loyal, and one must devote all he could in order to show filial piety. Of all Confucian virtues, filial piety stood at the top. Thus, with regard to the law, the theme was mainly to impose duties and obligations through punishment rather than to recognize rights and protect entitlements.

Again, the legacy of *Confucianism* not only forged Chinese legal culture but also had a long-lasting influence on the development of the Chinese legal system. In Mao's era, for example, the obligations-based theme became such a strong political force that no one dared to mention individual rights. At that time, everything was centered on serving the public interest for society as a whole. Pursuant to Mao's proletarian class theory, people in the working class should claim nothing as their own. As a result, for many decades, all in the country were subject to social and public interest, and every individual must subordinate his/her rights to the great cause of socialism.

The development of a market economy in China, however, has generated a drive to reverse course to place more attention on rights. Since the 1990s, there has been a growing demand in the country for the respect and protection of individual rights or human rights. In the late 1990s, a national debate emerged among scholars on whether the socialist legal system in China should be premised on rights rather than

94 See Randy Barnett, *A Law Professor's Guide to Natural Law and Natural Rights*, 20 Harv. J.L. & Pub. Pol'y 655–681 (1997); see also Online Library of Liberty, Natural Law and Natural Rights, available at https://oll.libertyfund.org/groups/102.

95 See History of Western Civilization II, ch. 20, The Age of Enlightenment, § 19.1.3: Natural Rights, available at https://courses.lumenlearning.com/suny-hccc-worldhistory2/chapter/natural-rights.

96 See "*The Analects of Confucius*" (*Lunyu*) (Raymond Dawson trans., Oxford University Press, 1993). See also Cai Dingjian & Wang Chenguang, China's Journey toward the Rule of Law: Legal Reform, 1978–2008, 22 (China Social Science Academic Press, 2008).

on obligations.[97] Those who opposed the obligation-based legal scheme argued that the pursuit of a market economy in China raised a great necessity to place civic rights ahead of obligations. They believed that socialist law in modern China should rest on a basic assumption that rights should take priority over obligations.[98]

Although the debate did not produce an immediate change institutionally in favor of a rights-based legal system and no consensus was reached, it undoubtedly helped increase public awareness as well as consciousness of civic and civil rights. Partly for those reasons, the debate was deemed a major breakthrough against the conventional ideology in the country that overly stressed obligations and belittled rights.[99] In addition, many saw the legislation trending in recent years toward the protection of the rights of the consumer as well as weak groups as a sign of change in social values appreciating, and a legal framework shedding light upon, the importance of rights.[100]

In addition, the commitment made by the CPC to "putting people first"[101] and the "building of a harmonious society,"[102] though quite policy-driven, also implicates a policy change in the government's attitude toward concern for the people. This commitment, initiated in 2003 and reinforced in 2006, was a direct response to the growing anger of the public over spreading corruption in the government, including the judiciary. Its purpose was to alleviate public concern over the degeneration inside the Communist Party, to improve and enhance the governing ability of the CPC, and to help maintain the stability of society. Nevertheless, it demonstrates that more importance is being attached to people's rights.

Another indication of recognition of rights was the 2004 Amendments to the 1982 Constitution. In the 2004 Amendments, it became a constitutional principle in China that lawful private property is inviolable. The 2004 Amendments also mandate that the state protect the rights to private property and its inheritance, and to

97 See Dingjian & Chenguang, *supra* note 96, at 22.

98 See *id.*

99 See *id.*

100 See *id.*

101 In its 3rd Annual Meeting of the 16th Central Committee, which was held in Beijing on October 11, 2003, the CPC called for an effort to "stick with putting people first, establish an outlook of comprehensive, coordinated, and sustainable development, and promote overall development in economy, society and people." See the *Bulletin of the 3rd Annual Meeting of the 16th Central Committee of the CPC*, published on October 14, 2003. A full text of the Bulletin is available at http://news.sina.com.cn/2003-10-14/21231921305.shtml.

102 In 2006, the Central Committee of the CPC set forth a national goal to establish a harmonious society in China. It is a policy-driven concept because such a society must be established on the condition of adherence to the principles of (a) putting people first, (b) scientific development outlook, (c) reform and opening-door policy, (d) socialist democracy and legality, (e) properly handling the relationship among reform, development, and social stability, and (f) the Communist Party's leadership. See the *CPC's Resolution on Several Major Issues Concerning Establishment of a Socialist Harmonious Society*, adopted on October 18, 2006. A full text of the Resolution is available at http://news.xinghuanet.com/politics/2006-10/18/content_5218639.htm.

make compensation for private property expropriated or requisitioned for the public interest in accordance with the law.[103] Those constitutional provisions strengthened the legal protection of private property rights and expressed to respect and safeguard human rights.

Despite the progress, however, the theme of the legal system in China has not yet shifted to a rights-based system. Among others, the institutional hurdles of the CPC and the traditional "power-driven" political culture have made it extremely difficult, if not impossible, to routinely put people first or duly respect the rights of people. It remains typical that government officials at all levels are appointed, and in many cases are handpicked, by the Communist Party committee at the corresponding level. An unwritten but quite settled protocol is that the officials, once appointed, tend to be responsible only to their superiors and are most concerned with satisfying them.

Thus, for Chinese officials, there is no such concept as constituency or constituent. As discussed *infra* in the book, in China's long history, the tradition has always been that politics are bureaucrat-oriented rather than people-oriented. Given that power is unchecked and directly linked to all privileges and benefits, legal or illegal alike, the official rank or status matters and carries significantly more meaning than anything else. More importantly, as a general pattern, an officer may hold a certain position for a certain period of time, but the privileges and benefits associated with his or her rank or status would stay with him or her for a lifetime.

Therefore, despite the commitment repeatedly made by the CPC and the central government to respect the rights of people, the general public at large somehow remains skeptical. In this regard, it remains to be seen in China whether and how the theme of the socialist legal system will turn to be rights-based rather than obligation-based. There are two fundamental questions that are still unsolved. What are the basic rights that are unalienable to people? And how will these rights be adequately and effectively protected?

B. *Role of the CPC: Supremacy of Party v. Supremacy of Law*

The toughest issue facing the Chinese socialist legal system is the position and the role of the CPC vis-à-vis that of the law. On their face, the provisions of law appear to be clear. Under the 1982 Constitution (as amended in 2004), people of all nationalities, all state organs, the armed forces, all political parties and public organizations, and all enterprises and institutions in the country must take the Constitution as the basic standard of conduct, and must uphold the dignity of the Constitution and

[103] *The 2004 Amendments to the 1982 Constitution* were adopted by the NPC on March 14, 2004. An English text is available at www.cecc.gov/resources/legal-provisions/2004-amendment-to-the-constitution-of-the-peoples-republic-of-china.

ensure its implementation.[104] Also, there is a constitutional requirement that no organization or individual be privileged to be beyond the Constitution or law.[105]

It is logical to infer from the Constitution that all parties in China, including the CPC, shall act under and in compliance with the Constitution. And in this context, it appears that the Constitution is the supreme law of the country. But in fact, the power of the Constitution is always challenged by the power of the CPC, and in many cases, the CPC is actually placed above the Constitution. This often casts serious doubt in the public as to whether the Constitution or the CPC has superiority in the country. A seemingly unsolved puzzle is whether the CPC must also be subject to the law. There are several attributes to this confusing but real phenomenon embedded in the political structure of the nation.

The first attribute is the Constitution itself. Although the 1982 Constitution (as amended in 2018) provides that the country is to be governed by the law, it explicitly emphasizes the leadership of the Communist Party[106] and upholds the single-party ruling system. The amended Constitution firmly states that the CPC-led system of multi-party cooperation and political consultation shall exist and develop for a long time to come.[107] The 2018 Amendments further prescribe the leadership of the CPC as "the defining feature of socialism with Chinese characteristics."[108] The CPC leadership is also positioned as the most fundamental basis of the rule of law in the country.

There are, however, at least two major loopholes. One loophole is that the Constitution places the CPC above all others and provides the CPC with absolute power. The danger is that once a power becomes absolute, abuse of such power may become inevitable. The other loophole is the lack of a proper check on the CPC. Without a constitutional check, it would be impossible to prevent the CPC from abusing power. Consequently, the CPC becomes the most binding force, leading the general public to believe that the CPC is much more powerful than the Constitution. Even worse, the unchecked power of the CPC unavoidably becomes the breeding ground for corruption. Although the CPC has been trying to employ a so-called self-correction mechanism against corruption, such self-vigilance never seems to have worked effectively.

The second attribute is the official conception of law adopted in China. Deeply rooted in Marxist theory, law in China is commonly viewed as a manifestation of the will of the ruling class, and legislation is the process of turning the will of the ruling class into the will of the state.[109] Further, since the CPC is characterized as the only

[104] See the 1982 Constitution, *supra* note 28, Preamble.
[105] See *id.*, art. 5.
[106] See *id.*, Preamble.
[107] See *id.*, art. 4.
[108] See the 2018 Amendments, *supra* note 31.
[109] See Shen Zongling, Jurisprudence, 32 (2nd ed., Higher Education Press, 2004). See also Zuo Zeyuan, An Introduction to Law, 19 (Law Press, 2007).

representative of the ruling class (namely the working class) in China, the will of the ruling class ultimately becomes the will of the CPC. Thus, no law, including the Constitution, may be enacted without the consent of, or approval by, the CPC.

Because the "will" theory underlies all legislation in China, the CPC holds the real legislative power, although under the 1982 Constitution (as amended in 2018), the NPC is the highest legislative body of the state,[110] and the NPC and its Standing Committee exercise the nation's legislative power.[111] Thus, despite its constitutional standing as the country's top legislature, the NPC in reality must follow the leadership of the CPC. As noted, the legislative work of the NPC is to make the CPC's opinion become the law or will of the state through the NPC's legislation. In addition, the NPC must make all efforts to ensure that all candidates recommended by the CPC for various government posts are elected or appointed.[112] For those reasons, the NPC is often nicknamed the "rubber stamp."

The third attribute is that the CPC controls the election of delegates to the NPC. Pursuant to the 1982 Constitution (as amended in 2018), the NPC is composed of delegates elected from the provinces, autonomous regions, municipalities directly under the central government, SARs, and the armed forces. The facts, however, tell a different story. The direct election of delegates only takes place at the county level, and all other delegates are elected from the candidates recommended by the CPC. In addition, the election of delegates to the NPC is made on the basis of a quota, and the allocation of the quota is determined by the Standing Committee of the NPC under a framework authorized by the CPC.

Among the total number of delegates to be allocated, about 10 percent are directly controlled by the NPC, following the opinion of the CPC. Direct control means that the NPC earmarks a certain number of delegates to certain provinces, and such provinces ensure that these earmarked delegates are duly elected, even though the delegates have little or nothing to do with the people of a particular province. Another notable point is that among the delegates of the NPC, a vast majority are members of the CPC.[113] As a general principle, all delegates who are CPC members must vote for whatever proposals the CPC has made for the NPC.

Moreover, during NPC meetings, delegates indulge in conversations among themselves, or express their views, about how wonderful the CPC leadership is and how significant the achievements made at all levels of government have been.

[110] See the 1982 Constitution, *supra* note 28, art. 57.

[111] See *id.*, art. 58.

[112] See Wu Bangguo, Chairman of the CPC, The Working Report of the Standing Committee of the NPC to the Second Annual Assembly Meeting of the 11th NPC, March 9, 2009. A full text of the Working Report is available at www.npc.gov.cn/huiyi/dbdh/11_2/2009_03/16/content_1493472.htm.

[113] For example, in the first NPC, 54.49% of delegates were members of the CPC, the second NPC 57.75%, the third NPC 54.83%, the fourth NPC 76.8%, the fifth NPC 72.78%, the sixth NPC 62.5%, the seventh NPC 66.9%, the eighth NPC 68.4%, the ninth NPC 71.5%, and the tenth NPC 72.99%.

Delegates rarely criticize the work of the CPC or the government. In the 2009 NPC annual assembly meeting, as one delegate from Guangdong sharply noted, for every ten-minute speech allowed per delegate during the group discussion at the NPC meeting, some eight minutes were used to offer flattery or praise the work of the government and their own self-achievement, leaving little or even no time to address any serious and legitimate business or social concerns.[114]

The fourth attribute relates to the CPC's control of the judiciary. Prescribed in the 1982 Constitution (as amended in 2018), the people's courts of China have the independent power of adjudicating cases in accordance with the law and are not subject to interference by any administrative agencies, public organizations, or individuals. However, it is unclear whether the constitutional power of independence reserved for the Chinese courts is subject to challenge by the CPC. Although the Constitution is vague in this regard, it appears that no judicial power may trump the authority of the CPC.

The CPC's control of the judiciary is easily discernible from many aspects. First, all courts in China are bound by a stated principle that judicial work must adhere to the leadership of the CPC. The foremost responsibility of the judiciary is to provide legal safeguards so that the leadership of the CPC is not tarnished. Second, the appointment of judges is generally made with the purpose of best serving the interests of the CPC. Particularly, most presidents of the courts, if not all of them, are political appointees, many of whom do not even have a legal background.[115] Third, all people's courts at different levels are directly under the supervision of the political and legal affairs committees of the CPC at their corresponding levels, and all major cases must be reported to such committees before a court judgment is made.

A descriptive catchphrase that exemplifies the relationship between the CPC and the people's courts was the doctrine of the "Three Supremes." Introduced by the CPC in 2007, the "Three Supremes" included "supremacy of the cause of the CPC, supremacy of the interests of the people, and the supremacy of the Constitution and law."[116] Since the "three supremacies" should be observed in that particular order, the top priority must be given to the cause of the CPC. In 2008, the doctrine of the "Three Supremes" was adopted by the SPC as the guiding principle of the courts. Under that doctrine, all judicial work must serve to uphold the interests of the CPC and to maintain social stability.

[114] See Zhong Nanshan, We Shall Not Use 8 Minutes to Sing Praises during Our 10-Minute Talk in the Congress. Zhong is a delegate from Guangdong province and is well known as a bold speaker making comments on politics. The context of the above comments is available at http://cpc.people.cpm.cn/GB/64093/64387/8942249.html.

[115] For example, the President of the Supreme People's Court, appointed in March 2008, was not a trained lawyer.

[116] See David Bandurski, *"Three Supremes,"* available at http://chinamediaproject.org/2010/11/12/three-supremes.

However, many in China have criticized the doctrine of the "Three Supremes" as fatally flawed. On its face, the doctrine creates a serious logical problem because supremacy should not have three juxtapositions. It seems evident that there would be no supremacy if all were deemed supreme. In addition, the content of the doctrine is quite subversive of the general notion that the Constitution is the fundamental law and has the highest legal status. Thus, in a society ruled by law, nothing may surpass or be side by side with the Constitution. Encountering furious criticisms, the CPC quietly phased out the doctrine of the "Three Supremes" years later.

In October 2019, the CPC Central Committee issued the Decision on Several Major Issues of Upholding and Improving the Socialist System with Chinese Characteristics to Promote the Modernization of the National Governance Mechanism and Capacity.[117] In the Decision, the "Three Supremes" was replaced with the "Supremacy of Constitution and Law" alone.[118] The Decision set it as a goal to form and improve an institutional mechanism that guarantees the full implementation of the Constitution. But still, the prerequisite is that the leadership of the CPC must be maintained in all aspects of national governance.[119] Then the question that remains is whether the CPC should also be subject to the Constitution and law, and how.

C. *Limits on Government Authority: Public Power v. Private Rights*

China is widely referred to as an authoritarian country with a powerful and highly centralized bureaucratic system.[120] The government power at both central and local levels is so extensive and far-reaching that its tentacles not only reach every aspect of the country's political and economic fields but also extend to the realm of private rights.[121] In *Mao*'s era, as noted, nothing was deemed private and all could be penetrated for the cause of the party.[122] Since the gear of the country was reversed from class struggle to economic development after Mao's death, private rights have emerged to become the center of attention.[123] The boundary between public power

[117] See the CPC Central Committee, *Decision on Several Major Issues of Upholding and Improving the Socialist System with Chinese Characteristics to Promote the Modernization of the National Governance Mechanism and Capacity*, issued on October 31, 2019, available at www.xinhuanet.com//mrdx/2019-11/06/c_138532143.htm (hereinafter referred to as the 2019 CPC Decision).

[118] See *id*., art. 4(1).

[119] See *id*.

[120] See Carl Minzner, *Countries at the Crossroads 2011: China*. A full text of the article is available at https://freedomhouse.org/sites/default/files/inline_images/ChinaFINAL.pdf.

[121] See Jiang Ping, Essentials of Civil and Commercial Law, 68 (Chinese University of Political Science and Law Press, 2019).

[122] See Jiang Ping, Ups and Downs, Withering and Flourishing: Autobiography at the Age of Eighty, 276–288 (Law Press, 2010).

[123] See Wang Limin, *Toward a New Era of Protection of Private Rights*, in Studies in the Law of Torts, I–VII (Renmin University Press, 2010).

and private rights has ever since been a hot topic that prompts nationwide discussions and debates.

In Chinese legal literature, public power is described as referring to the authorities held by state agencies and government officials to manage state affairs, maintain social order, and protect the welfare of the public, including, among others, the legislative, administrative, and judicial authorities.[124] Private rights, on the other hand, mean individual rights (natural person or entity) of a private nature, which consist of both personal and property rights.[125] In addition, public power has two basic functions: to maintain order, including economic order, political order, social order, cultural order, etc., and to provide necessary public services, while private rights are the rights comprising private interests and personal will on an individual basis.[126] Furthermore, public power in general possesses coercive force, but private rights are basically premised on the principles of party autonomy and voluntariness.[127]

In a society, public power and private rights are always interconnected. When public power is exercised, private rights are often at stake because all power is susceptible to abuse.[128] Thus, the possible conflict between public power and private rights is an issue that constantly arises.[129] A major problem China is encountering in its course of building the country under the rule of law is how to prevent public power from being abused so that private rights are not harmed.[130] Since China does not have a tradition to place constraints on government, it has become a spiraling social outcry against unlimited public power.[131] As early as 2013, the Third Plenary Session of the 18th CPC Central Committee, in response to the call for a battle against corruption, set as a requirement that "power must be locked in the cage of regulation."[132]

But since there is no effective system to place the government on a leash, the abuse of public power and infringement of private rights and interests persist and

[124] See Jiang Ping, *The Track and Curve of the Development of the Rule of Law over the Past Thirty Years*, The Beijing News, April 27, 2009, available at www.sinoss.net/c/2009-04-27/532775.shtml.

[125] See *id.*

[126] See Liu Yingying, *On the Conflict of Private Rights with Public Power and Restrictions*, 10 Contemp. Educ. Theory Practices J. 163 (2011).

[127] See *id.*

[128] See, in general, Richard H. Fallon, Jr., *Individual Rights and the Power of Governments*, 27 Georgia L. Rev. 343 (1993).

[129] See Limin, *supra* note 123, at I–II.

[130] See Chen Min, *Properly Handle the Conflict between Public Power and Private Rights*, 1 The Mag. Leadership Dig. 53 (2006); Ruan Chuansheng, *The Boundary of Public Power and Private Rights*, Study Times, November 12, 2012; Liu Haibing, *Limits on Public Power and Protection of Private Rights*, 10 Legal Sys. Soc'y 12 (2011).

[131] See Yang Xiejun, *Reconstruction of the National Public Power Supervision System in the Process of Comprehensive Reform*, 70 Wuhan U. J. Phil. Soc. Sci. 10 (2017).

[132] See Communiqué of the Third Plenary Session of the 18th Central Committee of the Communist Party of China, available at www.gov.cn/ducha/2015-06/09/content_2877546.htm.

remain in an endless stream in the country.[133] There are two fundamental issues with which China is still struggling. The first issue involves the intended purpose of law, that is, whether the law is purposed to limit government power or to prescribe the scope of private rights.[134] As discussed, in Chinese history, all individual rights were considered to be granted rather than inherent in individuals. Under that notion, the law was primarily not to deal with how public power or government authority should be limited but to provide what rights may be granted to private individuals. Although efforts have been made to alter this notion in order to shut power in the cage of regulation, nothing seems substantial in action.[135]

The second issue concerns the exercise of public power and the entitlement of private rights. It is believed that a country governed by the rule of law shall adhere to the principle that no public power can be exercised without explicit authorization by law and all private rights can be freely enjoyed unless otherwise provided by law.[136] Put differently, in the public field, the government can only do what is allowed under the law, and in civil areas, private individuals may do whatever is not prohibited by law. The rudimental concept is that the power of the government is not obtained naturally but endowed by law, while private rights inherently exist and may not be taken away without due process of law.[137]

In China, it has also become a common belief that to better protect private rights, government power should be limited.[138] But the path to turn the common belief into reality is both rocky and stormy.[139] Bureaucratic resistance is strong, and hurdles are high. First, the lack of an effective mechanism to oversee public power makes it hard, if not impossible, to confine the government to act within the statutory boundary.[140] Second, the absence (even denial) of a check and balance scheme inevitably leads to the overexpansion and excessive use of public power.[141] Third, the vague and unclear provisions of law and regulations in prescribing public power often result in the abuse of public power to infringe private rights.[142]

133 See Wang Shoulin, *Why Is Corruption So Common Among Top Leaders? How to Solve the Supervision Problem?*, Procuratorate Daily, June 9, 2020, available at www.spp.gov.cn/dj/llyj/202006/t20200609_464878.shtml?eqid= c98c7e78003e8894000000066473613b.

134 See, in general, Jiang Ping, Still Cautiously Optimistic: The History and Future of the Rule of Law in China (Zhejiang People's Press, 2016).

135 Caitlin E. Schultz, *Placing Power in the Cage of Law: Judicial Independence in China*, 44 Cap. U. L. Rev. 393 (2016).

136 See Ping, *supra* note 122, at 466–467.

137 See Ping, *supra* note 121, at 132–138.

138 See Limin, *supra* note 123, at I–II.

139 See *id.* at II.

140 See Shoulin, *supra* note 133.

141 See Mingwen, *supra* note 130.

142 See Xiejun, *supra* note 131.

D. *Dominance of Public Ownership: Public Domain v. Private Interests*

The past decades have witnessed sweeping changes in China as a result of vast economic reform. One significant change was the change in the ownership structure of the country from single public ownership to a coexistence of multi-ownerships. Since 1988, when a private economy was formally legalized in the nation,[143] the protection of private ownership has become an issue generating a great deal of debate and controversy. Among the highly debated issues is whether private ownership shall enjoy the same rights and protection as public ownership does.

Despite the reform and changes, what remains intact is the dominant position of public ownership. In 1992, the ultimate goal of economic reform was rephrased to establish a "socialist market economy" system.[144] The term "socialist" clearly refers to the guarantee of public ownership, and state ownership in particular, which is characterized as the "leading force" of the nation's economy. Private ownership, as defined in the 1999 Amendments to the 1982 Constitution, is at most "an important component of the socialist economy."[145]

In its 2019 Decision, the CPC Central Committee reiterated that the basic economic system of China contains (a) public ownership as the mainstay with common development of multi-ownership economies, (b) the scheme of "to each according to his work" as the main body of the distribution coexisting with multi-distribution methods, and (c) the socialist market economy.[146] Under this economic system, the state is said to unswervingly consolidate and develop the public ownership economy, and in the meantime encourage, support, and guide the development of the non-public ownership economy.[147]

It should be noted that since 2004 there have been two important pieces of legislation aimed at protecting private ownership, or the interests of private property. The first piece was the 2004 Amendments to the 1982 Constitution. The 2004

[143] The 1988 Amendments to the 1982 Constitution added to article 11 the following paragraph:

> The State permits the private sector of the economy to exist and develop within the limits prescribed by the law. The private sector of the economy is the complement to the socialist public economy. The State protects the lawful rights and interests of the private sector of the economy, and exercises guidance, supervision and control over the private sector of the economy.

See the 1982 Constitution, *supra* note 28.

[144] At the 14th National Conference of the Communist Party, held October 1–18, 1992, establishing the socialist market economy system was officially prescribed as the ultimate goal of economic reform. See Xinhua News Agency Report on the Conference, available at http://news.xinhuanet.com/ziliao/2003-01/20/content697129.htm.

[145] See the 1982 Constitution, *supra* note 28.

[146] See the 2019 CPC Decision, *supra* note 117, art. 6. The socialist distribution system under Marxism is known as "from each according to his ability to each according to his work."

[147] See *id.*

Amendments legally recognized the inviolable nature of private property, alleviating the previously entrenched hostility to private property in the country. The second piece of legislation was the Property Law. Passed on March 16, 2007, and effective October 1 in the same year, the Property Law for the first time in Chinese history granted equal protection to all property rights, public and private alike, and altered the orthodox notion of the nation against private ownership.

However, the protection of private property rights and private interests does not seem to rest with ease. On the contrary, the public demand for equal protection of private property still meets strong resistance from the traditional holding of the superiority of socialist public ownership over all other forms of ownership. One legitimate concern, for example, is how the Property Law is to be implemented. A thorny problem is how to change the ideology of the predominance of public property so that a legal framework can provide equal protection to private property, especially where the public domain and private interests conflict.

It is even more difficult in the country to limit the government's power to interfere with individual liberty and private property rights. The interference in most cases originates from the government's strong appetite for control, in conjunction with its desire to maintain social stability. Surely, there is nothing wrong with the government maintaining social stability, but the issue is whether stability should be achieved at the cost of loss of property or violation of the rights of particular individuals, or if it should be maintained by preventing the misconduct of government.

Unfortunately, the focus of social stability in China has been largely on how to constrain the conduct of people rather than the actions of government.[148] As noted, it is a common phenomenon that lower-level Chinese government officials often care more about their job performance and their superiors' satisfaction than about the interests of the general public.[149] For example, during the 2020–2023 pandemic period, China forcefully put into place a notorious "Zero Covid" policy with massive compulsory tests and abrupt lockdowns in buildings, neighborhoods, and even whole cities. Despite the huge negative impacts on people's lives, food shortages, loss of jobs, etc., and mounting public anger, governments at all levels in the country

[148] For example, in a "nail house" situation, the owner of the household is normally blamed for not respecting the government, and rarely are people led to think that there was something wrong with the government. See Su Sengxiang, *How Should We Treat "Nail House"?* March 22, 2007. A full text of the article is available at http://news.xinhuanet.com/legal/2007-03/22/content_5879558.htm.

[149] See Cai Huihong, *Cultural Shackles – On the Slow Pace of the State Owned Enterprises Reform of China*, available at www.myshow.com.cn/class/0Barticle1.htm. In China, local, county, and provincial government overlords all have an interest in power, and were they to coincide, the power is going to come down very hard on the neck of the average citizen. See Patrick Randolph, Speech at the 2003 Congressional-Executive Commission on China Roundtable, Ownership with Chinese Characteristics: Private Property Rights and Land Reform in the People's Republic of China, available at www.cecc.gov.

raced to strictly enforce the policy in order to maintain a high degree of consistency with the top leader of the CPC.[150]

E. *Government Power Structure: Allocation of Powers v. Separation of Powers*

In the development of the socialist legal system with Chinese characteristics, one fundamental issue is how state power should be exercised under the leadership of the CPC so that the tragedy of the Cultural Revolution will not be repeated. An important lesson the country learned from the Cultural Revolution was that state power should not be excessively concentrated on any individual, the party chief or the state head alike. For many years, there have been efforts to establish a mechanism for the separation of the party and the government, but no promising result has ever been produced.

In many countries in modern times, government responsibilities are divided among different branches, and each branch is constrained to its own authority. The very notion of such division is the doctrine of separation of powers. In a constitutional government, the system of separation of powers is purposed to prevent the concentration of power in the hands of individuals or groups and to provide for a mechanism of checks and balances. In the U.S., for example, three government branches, the Executive, Legislative, and Judiciary, are structured separately and independently to ensure that each can limit the powers of the others and no one branch may become too powerful. With checks and balances, the usurpation of power would be prevented.

In China, the concept of separation of powers was accepted as early as the early 1910s when Dr. Sun Yat-sen, the founding father of the Nationalist government, proposed the five-power constitution. According to Dr. Sun, to form a democratic government after the fall of the imperial regime in the country, there must be a five-power constitution without which a government would not be complete and could not do its best work for the people.[151] The five powers referred to five branches of government, including executive, legislative, judicial, examination, and censorate branches.[152] The last two branches were deemed as China's imperial

[150] For comments on the Zero Covid policy and its impacts, see Michaeleen Doucleff, *Why China's "Zero COVID" Policy Is Finally Faltering*, available at www.opb.org/article/2023/08/15/why-china-s-zero-covid-policy-is-finally-faltering; and VOA China News, *What Is China's "Zero-Covid" Policy?*, November 8, 2022, available at www.voanews.com/a/what-is-china-s-zero-covid-policy-/6854291.html.

[151] See Sun Yat-sen, *The Principle of Democracy (1924)*, from Sources of Chinese Tradition: From 1600 through the Twentieth Century, compiled by Wm. Theodore de Bary and Richard Lufrano, Vol. 2 (2nd ed., Columbia University Press, 2000), 323–324, available at http://afe.easia.columbia.edu/ps/cup/sun_yatsen_democracy.pdf.

[152] The examination branch was designed to be responsible for the selection of candidates for bureaucracy through centralized examinations, while the censorate served as a high-level supervisory agency to check up on the behavior of the government.

heritage of political structure because they were traditional Chinese administrative components.[153]

In March 1921, the Nationalist government began to draft the Constitution structured on the five powers. However, not until 1946 was the Nationalist Constitution formally adopted. Provided in the Nationalist Constitution was a central government with five branches in order to ensure a balanced division of powers. But because of the civil war and the communist boycott, the Nationalist Constitution was not effectively implemented in the country. In 1949, when the Communist Party took control, the Nationalist Constitution, along with other laws adopted by the Nationalist government, was entirely abolished.

Since 1949, the notion of separation of powers has never been recognized in China because the leadership of the CPC is considered the core of the political structure of the nation. An unshakable mindset created in the general public is that the CPC should and must have control of everything in the country. It is a firmly upheld governing principle that government, military, society, and schools; north, south, east, west, and central, the CPC leads them all.[154] In recent years, as a response to the call for the establishment of a constitutional government under the rule of law,[155] the CPC once again took a clear stance against the adoption of constitutionalism, separation of powers, or judicial independence in the country.[156] As a result, the CPC's power over all aspects of Chinese society continues to expand.[157]

Thus, government powers in China are not separated but allocated among different government branches under the umbrella of the people's congress system. All government branches, central or local, are required to be responsible to the people's congress at the corresponding level. The congress, as noted, is under the direct control of the CPC. But due to the lack of checks and balances, corruption and abuse of power have long become a chronic disease of the government, and even within the CPC. As noted, the CPC took a great deal of pride in a self-correction mechanism, but the effectiveness of the self-correction is always in serious doubt.

[153] See Ernest Caldwell, *Chinese Constitutionalism: Five-Power Constitution*, in Rainer Grote, Franke Lachenmann & Rüdiger Wolfrum, eds., Max Planck Encyclopedia of Comparative Constitutional Law (Oxford University Press, 2017).

[154] See Nectar Gan, Xi Jinping Thought – *The Communist Party's Tighter Grip on China in 16 Characters*, South China Morning Post, October 25, 2017, available at www.scmp.com/news/china/policies-politics/article/2116836/xi-jinping-thought-communist-partys-tighter-grip-china.

[155] For general discussion, see Thomas Kellogg, *Arguing Chinese Constitutionalism: The 2013 Constitutional Debate and the "Urgency" of Political Reform*, 11 U. Pa. Asian L. Rev. 337 (2016); see also Samson Yuen, *Debating Constitutionalism in China: Dreaming of a Liberal Turn?*, Open Edition Journal – China Perspectives, April 2013.

[156] See Gao, *supra* note 84.

[157] See Jack Kamensky & Erin Slawson, *Five Takeaways from China's Fourth Plenum*, China Business Review, November 7, 2019, available at www.chinabusinessreview.com/five-take aways-from-chinas-fourth-plenum/.

It should also be noted that in recent years there has been a new reporting system developing in the country under which all CPC Politburo members must make a personal working report annually to Xi Jinping. A similar report shall also come from the NPC, State Council, SPC, and the Supreme People's Procuratorate (SPP). A clear signal from the reporting system is that Xi is the supreme leader of the country. But a question in many people's minds both at home and abroad is how the power of the top leader of the country is to be checked and limited under the rule of law China is pursuing.

PART I

Chinese Law and Legal System in General

Law and legal systems vary in different countries, and they are deeply rooted in the historical background and traditions of each country. In the context of the meanings and functions of the law and legal system, social and political dynamics often interact with the legal philosophies that shape the approaches taken by different legal schools of thought. Justice and law are always issues that have to be viewed and addressed in light of social changes and developments. Therefore, the discussion of law and legal systems would be meaningless without taking into consideration the social and political distinctions of a particular country.

Law and the legal system in China possess Chinese distinctions. Part I of this book offers a general view of these distinctions. It begins with Chinese legal history, followed by a discussion on of the theoretical foundation of modern Chinese law. The focus then turns to the Chinese Constitution and political infrastructure. Thereafter, a review is made of both the Chinese judiciary and sources of law. In the end, the discussion is centered on Chinese legal education and the function of the Chinese bar. The very purpose of this part is to help understand the evolution and current state of law and the legal system in China.

1

Chinese Legal History and Culture

INTRODUCTION

China is considered one of the oldest countries in the world, with a history spanning some five thousand years. It would be impossible to comprehend Chinese law and the legal system without first looking into its history and the aspects of legal culture and tradition. There are at least two reasons to do so: First, any legal system, however old or young, is always in a process of change, and history offers a great prospect for understanding such changes.[1] Second, legal tradition itself plays an important role in shaping legal changes,[2] and it also determines the pattern as well as the direction of the changes.[3] In addition, the development of law and legal systems is largely influenced by the legal tradition that operates and ultimately becomes a part of legal culture.

Although there is a lack of agreement among legal scholars on what "legal culture" is exactly and what it should contain,[4] it is generally regarded as the notion concerning the features or the role of law and the patterns of legally oriented social behavior and attitudes.[5] It is further understood that legal culture involves capturing the distinctive quality of social discourse through which issues are conceived and which responses are formulated.[6] Therefore, in order to address legal culture and describe the legal tradition of a certain society, it is necessary to examine such elements as the legal mechanism, forms of legal behavior, legal values and mentalities, the role of lawyers, as well as the function of courts.

1 See Alan Watson, *Legal Changes: Sources of Law and Legal Culture*, 131 U. Pa. L. Rev. 1121, 1122 (1983).
2 See *id.* at 1152.
3 See *id.* at 1134.
4 See David Nelken, *Using the Concept of Legal Culture*, 29 Austl. J. Leg. Phil. 1, 2 (2004).
5 See *id.* at 1.
6 See Jeremy Webber, *Culture, Legal Culture, and Legal Reasoning: A Comment on Nelken*, 29 Austl. J. Leg. Phil. 27, 36 (2004).

However, among all relevant elements of legal culture, the role and rule of law are deemed most significant. They not only are the indicator of social order that implicates a particular legal culture but also serve as the basis on which a specific legal tradition is formed. But to the extent that the legal culture and tradition of a country are meaningfully described, the role and rule of law should be viewed within the course of development of the legal system and be judged from the evolving characteristics of the law in the entire history of the country. With that in mind, the discussion of Chinese legal culture and tradition will focus on historical development and changes.

1. CHINESE LEGAL HISTORY IN BRIEF

To speak broadly, Chinese legal history can be divided into four different periods. The first period began with the formation of *Huaxia* tribes (2850 BC to 2205 BC) and ended during the time of Spring and Autumn and Warring States (770 BC to 221 BC). This period was also called in short the period of "Three Sovereigns and Five Emperors" (*San Huang Wu Di*)[7] and the *Xia* (2070 BC to 1600 BC), *Shang* (1600 BC to 1046 BC), and *Zhou* Dynasties (1046 BC to 221 BC).[8] Generally, any time before the *Xia* Dynasty in China was classified as the "prehistoric age." In addition, the *Zhou* Dynasty was divided into the *Western Zhou* (1046 BC to 770 BC) and the *Eastern Zhou* (770 BC to 221 BC), and the *Eastern Zhou* was further divided into "Spring and Autumn" (770 BC to 476 BC) and "Warring States" (476 BC to 221 BC).

Xia was the first dynasty of China, and it also symbolized the early *Huaxia* civilization (Chinese civilization). The founder of *Xia* was named "*Yu*." The *Xia* Dynasty was considered historically significant because it made China a formal "state" and marked the beginning of a slavery society in the country. In addition, *Xia* was also regarded as the embryonic stage of the Chinese legal system, developed from the custom-based religious rites formed in the period of *Shan Huang* and *Wu Di*.

More significantly, on the basis of religious rites evolving from *Xia* to *Zhou*, a number of etiquettes were established in this first period as social norms and eventually became behavioral rules governing the country. All such etiquettes, taken together, were collectively called "*Li*." Commonly translated as "the rules of

[7] Since the "Three Sovereigns and Five Emperors" were mythological rulers of China during the period of pre-history, Chinese historians have offered various interpretations about who they were. One well-accepted interpretation is that the "Three Sovereigns" were referred to as "*Nüwa*," "*Fuxi*," and "*Shennong*" (also called "*Yan Di*"), and the "Five Emperors" were the "Yellow Emperor" (or "*Huang Di*"), "*Zhuanxu*," "*Ku*," "*Yao*," and "*Shun*."

[8] This dynastic history and time periods were based on the "*Table of Dynastic Periods of Xia, Shang and Zhou*" published in 2000 by the Research Group organized through the State Commission of Science and Technology under a State grant.

propriety" or simply "rites," "*Li*" was further developed into the "standardized and systemized" social norms in the West *Zhou* Dynasty called "*Zhou Li*."[9]

In the *Zhou* Dynasty, there developed four major systems in the country, including enfeoffment, square-fields, patriarchal clan, and ritual systems. These four systems constituted the foundations of the country's political, economic, social, and cultural structures. Enfeoffment was a mechanism of land granting as rewards to the descendants of heroes or nobles and clan members, upon which vassal states were formed. Square-fields referred to state ownership of land held by nobles. As a land management scheme, each piece of land was divided into nine squares, within which the eight outer squares were allocated to serfs who had to cultivate the central one for the serf owner. Since the divided nine squares looked like the Chinese character "井" (well), the scheme was also called the well-field system.[10] The patriarchal clan represented the kindred relationship established between the ruler and the ruled.

In contrast to the other three systems, the ritual system played a more specific role in maintaining social stability and political order of the country. The ritual system in the *Zhou* Dynasty contained two major parts: "*Li*" (rites) and "*Yue*" (music). "*Li*" consisted of the norms that governed human behavior. The system established a pattern that determined human identities and formed a hierarchy based on social status. It was believed that the joint work of "*Li*" and "*Yue*" would produce social harmony and social happiness – which is the ultimate aim of the state.[11]

"*Yue*" was the established protocols and ceremonial procedures reflecting human identities and social status. The type of music was strictly limited to the level of status, and any disorder would violate the corresponding rites. Put differently, "*Li*" was the basic rules under which the country would function as desired, while "*Yue*" was the formality to ensure the enforcement of the rules. In other words, if the people follow the rules of "*Li*," they must meet the requirements of "*Yue*."

The detailed etiquettes of the *Zhou*'s ritual system were recorded in the book "*Zhou Li*." Although there has always been debate among historians about the actual author of the *Zhou Li*, it is commonly believed that the book was written by *Zhou Gongdan*, a politician and military strategist of the Western *Zhou* Dynasty.[12] The contents of "*Zhou Li*" were quite extensive, from topics as large as politics and the military to as small as food and clothing. There were six parts in the *Zhou Li*,

[9] See Zhang Jinfan, The Tradition and Modern Transition of Chinese Law, 4 (2nd ed., Law Press, 2005).

[10] Under this system, the lands were all owned by the king and were allocated to the officials as their salaries, and the officers could then let their serfs cultivate the land for crops. The amount of allocated land was dependent on rank, and all land so allocated could not be transferred but could be inherited.

[11] Jinfan, *supra* note 9, at 20–21.

[12] See generally Peng Lin, History of Zhou Li (National Library Publishing House, 2019).

including Heaven, Earth, Spring, Summer, Autumn, and Winter. Each part addressed different functions of government offices. For example, government in general was under the "Offices of Heaven," education under "Offices of Earth," social and religious institutions under "Offices of Spring," the military under "Offices of Summer," justice under "Offices of Autumn," and population, territory, and agriculture under "Offices of Winter."[13]

As a comprehensive code of conduct, the *Zhou Li* served a dual function: a political means of maintaining social stability and an ideological strategy for governing the *Zhou* Dynasty under clan relationships and hierarchy. More importantly, the rites in the *Zhou Li* not only represented the customized rules in the *Zhou* Dynasty but also shaped the *Confucian* classic theory developed by *Confucius*. It was later acclaimed that an exercise of "*Li*" could help "govern the country, stabilize the society, appease the people, and benefit future generations."[14]

Closely related to "*Li*" was the concept of "*Xing*," which emerged in the *Xia* Dynasty. "*Xing*," meaning punishment, was used to implement "*Li*." In the *Xia* Dynasty, a violation of "*Li*" would constitute a criminal offense upon which a penalty would be imposed. In Chinese legal history, "*Xing*" is considered the initial form of criminal law because it is mainly comprised of penalties for criminal offenses. By the time of the *Zhou* Dynasty, there had developed the so-called *Wu Xing* (Five Punishments) to help maintain "*Li*" and social order. The "*Wu Xing*" included "*Mo*" (tattooing the face), "*Yi*" (chopping off the nose), "*Yue*" (cutting off the feet), "*Gong*" (castration), and "*Dapi*" (the death penalty or decapitation).[15]

The most distinctive feature of the legal system in the *Xia*, *Shang*, and *Zhou* Dynasties was the intimate entanglement of "*Li*" with "*Xing*," under which the country was basically "ruled by *Li* and run by *Xing*."[16] Specifically, whatever was not allowed by "*Li*" would be prohibited by "*Xing*," and anything that was in compliance with "*Li*" would necessarily be permissible by "*Xing*." In other words, "*Li*" was not only the basis of "*Xing*" but also enforced by "*Xing*." Thus, while the rule of "*Li*" played a dominant role at that time, the law was essentially a combination of "*Li*" and "*Xing*."

The second period of Chinese legal history is referred to as the "imperial period," stretching over two thousand years from the founding of the *Qin* Dynasty (221 BC) to the fall of the Qing Dynasty (1911). During this period, China witnessed more than a dozen dynasties that encompassed feudal as well as semi-colonial societies.[17] With

[13] See *id.*

[14] See Zuo Commentaries, available at https://so.gushiwen.org/guwen/bookv_46653FD803893E4FACE837B4EA6F8571.aspx (accessed August 25, 2025).

[15] See Zhang Zhongqiu, Legal Culture in Comparative Vision (sic), 52 (Law Press, 2003).

[16] See Gao Minxuan & Zhao Bingzhi, Evolution of Chinese Criminal Legislation, 1 (Law Press, 2007).

[17] Those dynasties were *Qin* (221–206 BC), *Han* (206–220), *Three Kingdoms and Wei* (226–280), *Jin* (265–420), *Southern and Northern Empires* (420–589), *Sui* (581–618), *Tang* (618–907), *5 Imperia and 10 Kingdoms* (907–960), *Song* (960–1279), *Yuan* (1206–1368), *Ming* (1368–1644),

regard to the legal system, the country carried the tradition of a combination of "*Li*" and "*Xing*" as formed in the *Xia*, *Shang*, and *Zhou* Dynasties, and developed it into a synergy of "*Li*" and "*Fa*" (law). Moreover, codified law became the primary legal source. Out of all of the legal codes enacted in this period, the *Tang* Code was regarded as the most influential in the entire history of imperial China.

The major development of the legal system in the second period of Chinese legal history was that "*Li*" became the mainstay of the legal system, while law was simply the secondary means to supplement "*Li*." During the imperial times, the heart of "*Li*" was to uphold the power and protect the authority of the emperor. In addition, the patriarchal and kinship-premised social system and tradition made the emperor both the ruler of the country and the ultimate source of law. Because of this distinction, imperial China was commonly classified as being ruled by men rather than by law. Another distinction of the imperial legal system was that the majority of laws were criminal-oriented and there was no distinction between criminal law and civil law.

The third period of the Chinese legal system spanned from 1911 to 1949. A fundamental change in this period was that the imperial system ended and was replaced with a republic system. For that reason, the third period was also called the "republic period." The most significant characteristic of the republic period was that the traditional chain between "*Li*" and "*Fa*" *was* broken, and a new legal system formed. On this ground, the third period is deemed a transitional period in modern Chinese legal history.

The dramatic changes in the "republic period" were driven by two significant and unprecedented forces: one external and one internal. Externally, the Opium Wars in the 1840 signaled the death of China's long-held policy of self-seclusion and forced China to open its doors to the Western world. As a result of foreign occupation, Western ideologies were ushered into the country and clashed with "*Li*" as well as with the patriarchal Chinese tradition. Hence, China entered into an era of social change that eventually led the country away from both feudalism and the imperial system.

Internally, realizing that the glory of imperial power had faded as a result of the unexpected defeat by foreign forces during the Opium Wars and other subsequent losses, a group of political elites within the central government tried to revive China by calling for "learning from the West." They opined that in order to make China strong again, it was necessary to imitate the Western countries both politically and economically. To that end, they launched a campaign historically called the "Westernization Movement" (*Yangwu Yundong*, 1863–1879) in the nation, aimed at developing national industries and the army.

and *Qing* (1644–1911). Note that among these dynasties, some coexisted in different areas, and some overlapped because when the new one was founded, the existing one had not yet been completely overthrown.

In the late nineteenth century, another group of reformists emerged, leading the "1898 Legal Reforms" (*Wuxu Bianfa*). They believed that in order to remove China from its state of backwardness, it must undergo political and legal reforms. With that in mind, they studied Western political systems and attempted to introduce some aspects into China as a means of revitalizing the nation. Their hope was that the reforms would help establish a constitutional monarchy in the country.

But in the face of strong resistance from the ruling conservative power in the Forbidden City, neither the "Westernization Movement" nor the "1898 Legal Reforms" succeeded. Nevertheless, the two historical events inevitably brought Western political concepts and democratic ideologies to China, which in part planted seeds for the "1911 Revolution" (*Xinhai* Revolution). It was this Revolution that relegated China's more than two-thousand-year-old imperial system into the annals of history.

A significant achievement of the "1911 Revolution" was the establishment of a republic government formed under the "Three Principles of the People"[18] and the theory of a "Constitution of Five Powers"[19] advocated by Dr. *Sun Yat-sen*, the founding father of the Republic of China. In the meantime, the "1911 Revolution" brought to an end the "*Li*"-based and imperial-power-centered classic Chinese law and legal tradition.

Unfortunately, however, due to constant internal conflicts, the war against Japanese occupation, and the civil war, the newly born republic was never actually stabilized. Consequently, the concept of the "Three Principles of the People" and the "Constitution of Five Powers" were barely implemented. Although under the Nationalist government led by *Chiang Kai-shek*, a set of laws known as the *Six Codes*, reflecting Dr. *Sun Yat-sen*'s ideology, were compiled and promulgated, they were not applied effectively as intended and were eventually abolished by the Communist government in 1949.

But it is important to note that the civil law impact on the Chinese legal system after the Opium Wars was significant in that Chinese laws began to bear a strong civil law tradition. From the "Westernization Movement" and the "1898 Legal Reform," the traditional Chinese legal system evolved into a mixture of Chinese legal classics and civil law substantive contents as well as procedural formalities. A highly notable feature, for example, was the application of written law and legal principles, and legal codification.

The fourth period of Chinese legal history started with the founding of the People's Republic of China in 1949. This period, commonly called the "socialist period," can be further classified into *Mao*'s era (*Mao Zedong*) and the post-*Mao*

[18] The three principles were "nationalism," "people's democratic rights," and "people's well-being."

[19] Under Dr. *Sun Yat-sen*'s doctrine, a constitution in China should set forth five independent powers, namely legislative power, executive power, judicial power, examination power, and supervisory power.

era. As noted, during *Mao's* era from 1949 to 1976, China followed former Soviet-style socialism and was then maneuvered by *Mao* to be fully engaged in the "revolutionary movements" that were sought to keep the color of China "red," meaning to resist capitalism. During the period from 1949 to 1976, there were at least fifty-five "revolution movements" launched in the country, including the 1957 "Anti-Rightists" campaign, the 1958 "Big Leap Forward" movement, and the 1966 "Cultural Revolution" (more than twice a year on average, and many of them lasted for several years). In the legal area, *Mao* annulled all laws enacted by the Nationalist government before 1949 and attempted to replace them with socialist laws or "the people's laws."[20]

Unfortunately, due to *Mao*'s zealotry in the "class struggle,"[21] the country's endeavor to establish legality was entirely shelved in 1957 when the nationwide "Anti-Rightists" campaign was launched to suppress intellectuals. After that, legal work in China stalled. During the ten years of the Cultural Revolution (1966 to 1976), the whole country became a place that had no law at all, and every effort was made to build up the personality cult of *Mao*. For that reason, many regarded *Mao*'s era as a dark period of "lawlessness,"[22] or legal nihilism in the country. According to a foreign observer, under *Mao*'s reign, the vast land of China lived in a legal vacuum for thirty years.[23]

Mao's death in 1976 made it possible for China to move in a different direction. The most striking changes were the abandonment of *Mao*'s "class struggle" theory and the shifting of the country's focus to "economic development" rather than "political movements." In 1978, a nationwide economic reform was initiated to modernize the country. Along with the economic reform was an explosion of legislation, resulting in a significant number of laws and regulations. In 1982, China rewrote its Constitution, attempting to bring the country back to a society of legality. As noted, the 1982 Constitution was amended in 1988, 1993, 1999, 2004, and 2018, respectively.[24]

Since 1978, China has been on a course of fast development both in restructuring the economy and in rebuilding the legal system. The economic reform has not only helped China become an emerging power of the world economy, but has also

[20] According to *Mao*, the laws in Communist China "are made by the working people themselves." See Selected Works of Mao Zedong, Vol. V, 359 (People's Press, 1977).

[21] In his famous article "On the People's Democratic Dictatorship" published on June 30, 1949, *Mao* made it clear that the State apparatus, including the army, the police and the courts, is the instrument by which one class oppresses another, and to the antagonistic class, it is violence and not benevolence." See Selected Works of Mao Zedong, Vol. IV, 418 (People's Press, 1961–1976).

[22] See Laszlo Ladany, Law and Legality in China: The Testament of a China-watcher, 52 (University of Hawaii Press, 1992).

[23] See *id.* at 55.

[24] Under article 5 of the 1982 Constitution (as amended in 1999), the People's Republic of China governs the country according to law and makes it a socialist country ruled by law.

introduced two Western concepts that drastically changed the country. The first concept is the "market economy," which set a goal for economic reform in the country. Although the term "market economy," as used in China, is squared with the word "socialist," the country is determined to reshape its economic system under the rules of the market.

The second concept is the rule of law. China had a reputation for having a rule of men in its history, and even in *Mao*'s era. In order to restructure its legal system, the country made a move to incorporate the concept of rule of law into it so that the country is to be governed under the law. In 1999, when the 1982 Constitution was amended for the third time, the provision "to rule the country by law" became a constitutional mandate for the nation, though the notion of rule by law is not necessarily the same as the concept of the rule of law.[25]

Another change worth noting is the absorption of common law ideologies and principles into the current Chinese legal system. In the process of legal drafting, common law rules are often taken as reference and, in certain cases, are adapted into laws. In legal proceedings, judges are given more discretionary power to rule on cases, and precedent has a role to play in the form of guiding cases. Thus, in terms of legal distinctions, the current Chinese legal system contains features that combine Chinese heritage, civil law tradition, and common law practice. But still, titled with "socialist" and "Chinese characteristics," the legal system in China is replete with Chinese realities and stands out as one of the major legal systems in today's world.[26]

Whatever the present state of the Chinese legal system may appear to be, it still embodies a distinctive tradition evolved from its history. Many aspects of this tradition have had, and will continue to have, powerful and unique effects on the current development of the legal system and legal theories. The philosophic tenets inherent in the traditional legal system are clearly discernible in the course of such development. Therefore, a closer look at Chinese legal philosophy and tradition will certainly help better understand modern developments.[27]

2. CLASSIC CHINESE LEGAL PHILOSOPHIES

The traditional Chinese legal philosophies can be traced back as early as the period of Spring-Autumn (770 BC to 475 BC) and Warring States (476 BC to 221 BC).[28] In Chinese history, the Spring-Autumn and Warring States periods were so

[25] See Ralph H. Folsom, John H. Minan, & Lee Ann Otto, Law and Politics in the People's Republic of China in a Nutshell, 1 (West, 1992).

[26] Civil law, common law, and socialist law are regarded as the three highly influential legal traditions in the contemporary world. See John H. Merryman, The Civil Law Tradition, 1 (2nd ed., Stanford University Press, 1985).

[27] See Folsom et al., *supra* note 25, at 1.

[28] In the *Xia*, *Shang*, and Western *Zhou* Dynasties, there had already developed certain legal thoughts such as the patriarchal-clan-based "*Li*," but the more systematical legal thoughts were developed in the periods of Spring-Autumn and Warring States.

significant that they command lengthy discussion in all history books in China. During these periods, China transitioned from a slave society to a feudal society. There were three major changes in this transition.

The first major change was the collapse of the square-fields land system. As noted, under the square-fields system, the king owned all of the land. In *The Book of Songs*, a collection of Chinese folk songs describing part of China's history during the Western *Zhou* Dynasty, there is a very famous verse: "all land under the heaven belongs to the King and all people on the earth are the subjects of the King," which typically reflects land ownership in the *Zhou* Dynasty.

The most significant social change during the Spring-Autumn period was the emergence of independent "little kingdoms" (dukedoms), comprised of former territories enfeoffed by the king to nobles, including relatives and family members of the king. As a result of this change, the land that used to be owned by the king or the state was transferred into the hands of landlords. Consequently, all land in the little kingdoms was privatized, and the square-fields land system was replaced with individual private ownership.

The second major change was the disruption of "*Zhou Li*."[29] The change in land ownership led to the erosion of the king's power and then all etiquettes that were aimed at maintaining the authority of the king were broken down. As the little kingdoms each arose as a sovereign state independent from the king, and the nobles struggled with each other for power, the king's power was seriously weakened. Consequently, royal authority was diminished and then gradually sank out of sight. Because of the decline of "*Li*," Spring-Autumn was deemed as the period of "collapse of ritual propriety and fall of literal culture," meaning that both "*Li*" and "*Yue*" established in the *Zhou* Dynasty were broken down.[30]

The third major change was the abolishment of enfeoffment, replaced by an administrative system consisting of prefectures and counties. Enfeoffment was an entitlement to land and other properties granted on the basis of a patriarchal clan. The prefecture-county system, however, was a top-down government structure with two local administrative levels under the central government. It was this system that laid the foundation of the totalitarian government – or government with highly centralized power – which has existed in China ever since.

As a response to these changes, legal reform took place in the states that had evolved from the previous little kingdoms. The centerpiece of the reform was active legislation, putting in place new laws to regulate society. This legal reform led to two developments that had great impacts on Chinese legal history: the promulgation of separate or individual written law and the codification of laws and customary rules.

29 See Wu Shuchen, History of China Legal Thoughts, 79 (Law Press, 2004).

30 See Yang Duorong, The Mutual Cultivation of Self and Things: A Contemporary Chinese Philosophy of the Meaning of Being (Chad A. Meyers trans.), 156 (Indiana University Press, 2016).

The adoption of specific law on an individual basis was viewed as historic progress in legislation.

Corresponding with the dramatic political and social transition in the Spring-Autumn period was the flourishing of new theories and thought. Many intellectuals affiliated with different "little kingdoms" competed to find "good theory and philosophy" to govern their state and make it stronger than others. As a result, there grew a diverse intellectual force called "hundred intellectuals" (*zhu zi bai jia*). Each of the intellectuals not only developed his/her own thoughts and ideas but also openly debated with others. These intellectual debates on politics and social order gave rise to a historical social environment in which the "hundred intellectuals" contended.

The debates mainly involved four major relationships: *Tian* and *Ren* (nature and human beings), *Li* and *Fa* (rites and law), *Jia* and *Guo* (family and state), and *Jun* and *Chen* (ruler and ruled). It was believed that if these relationships were dealt with properly, the stability and prosperity of society would be achieved. If, however, any of these relationships were disordered, social chaos would follow. But opinions differed sharply on how these relationships should be addressed and structured.

The intellectual debates produced many schools of thought, which eventually yielded four major ones (the "big four") that had tremendous impact on Chinese legal philosophy and jurisprudence. The big four included the *Confucianists* (*Ru Jia*), *Taoists* (*Dao Jia*), Legalists (*Fa Jia*), and *Mohists* (*Mo Jia*). Much of the significance of these four schools of thought is due to the fact that each of the schools was directly associated with one of China's most famous ancient philosophers. Among the big four, *Confucianists* and Legalists were the most influential in the development of the traditional Chinese legal system.

A. Confucian *School of Thought*

The *Confucian* school was founded by *Confucius* (551 BC to 479 BC) and then was further developed by *Mencius* (372 BC to 289 BC). Both *Confucius* and *Mencius* were regarded as great thinkers and philosophers in the history of China, and they were commonly referred to as "the Sages" in the nation. In addition, *Confucius* was also hailed as a great educator because he devoted much of his life to education and legendarily had seventy-two bright disciples (*Xianren*) and three thousand followers (*Dizi*).[31] The philosophy and ideology held by *Confucius* and *Mencius* as well as their followers were together called "the Doctrine of *Confucius – Mencius*" (*Kong-Meng Zhidao*), which was branded as "*Ru*," or collectively as *Confucianism*.[32]

[31] Many stories about Confucius's life and teaching were described by *Sima Qian* (145–87 BC), the Prefect of the Grand Scribes of the *Han* Dynasty, who wrote a series of history books known as "Records of the Grand Historian" (*Shiji*).

[32] The literal meaning of "*Ru*" is "learned man," and it also implicates benevolence and morals.

Confucius, named *Qiu* and styled *Zhongni* (commonly called), was born in the state of *Lu* (today's Shandong Province). A poor descendant of a deposed noble family, he had a rough childhood – his father died when he was three years old, and his mother passed away when he was seventeen. Upon reaching adulthood, he had to support himself by undertaking petty jobs such as managing a warehouse and caring for livestock. In the meantime, *Confucius* was quite interested in politics, but not until the age of fifty was he made a city magistrate of *Lu*. *Confucius* then was appointed the Secretary of Justice of *Lu*, and finally Chief Minister of *Lu*.[33]

Although *Confucius* had great ambition to serve the state of *Lu*, his political career was not promising. He resigned from the post of Chief Minister at age fifty-five because his political views were at odds with the Duke of *Lu*. He left *Lu* thereafter to begin traveling in different states. He returned to *Lu* in 484 BC and spent the rest of his life teaching and writing. *Confucius* died in 479 BC at 72 (or 73 according to the traditional Chinese method of calculation).[34]

Confucius' early life was strongly influenced by his mother, who taught him how to appreciate and practice rites during his childhood. From a young age, he extensively studied the rites of the *Zhou* Dynasty and was reputed to be a man of fairness, politeness, and a love of learning. He was also an avid music lover because he believed that music could help mold kindness and uprightness of character. As noted, the most important part of *Confucius*' life was teaching. He taught not only rites and philosophy but also poetry and music.

Many of *Confucius*' philosophic thoughts and apothegms were based on conversations with his students. The collection of these conversations was later compiled by his disciples into a famous book named "*The Analects of Confucius*" (*Lunyu*). While being engaged in education, *Confucius* also put tremendous effort into editing "*The Book of Songs*" (*Shijing*), "*The Book of Documents*" (*Shanghsu*), and "*I Ching*" *(the Book of Changes* or *Yijing* or *Zhou Yi)*, revising "*The Records of Rites*" (*Liji*), and writing "*The Spring and Autumn Annals*" (*Chunqiu*).[35] These books constituted the theoretical basis for the *Confucian* school of thought.

Confucius devoted all of his work to the restoration of "*Li*" formed in the *Zhou* Dynasty. He regarded "*Li*" as the very basic rule of conduct. When asked by one of

33 For more general information about *Confucius*, see Jeffery Riegel, *Confucius*, Stanford Encyclopedia of Philosophy, available at https://plato.stanford.edu/entries/confucius/.

34 Under Chinese tradition (the lunar year system), people normally use "nominal age," which means that one more year is added to the real age. For example, you would be one year old already in the year you were born.

35 In Chinese history, there was a well-known collection of classics called the "*Four Books and Five Classics*" (*Si Shu Wu Jing*). The "*Four Books*" were "*The Great Learning*" (*Da Xue*), "*The Doctrine of the Mean*" (Zhong Yong), "*The Analects of Confucius*" (*Lunyu*), and "*The Mencius*" (*Mengzi*). The Five Classics were "*The Book of Songs*" (*Shijing*), "*The Book of Documents*" (*Shujing*), "*The Book of Changes*" (*Yijing*), "*The Book of Rites*" (*Liji*), and "*The Spring and Autumn Annals*" (*Chunqiu*). Among the "*Four Books and Five Classics*," five were related to *Confucius* and *Confucian* doctrines.

his students about studying "*Li*," Confucius replied that one would find oneself at a loss as to where to stand without studying "Li,"[36] meaning that the rites or etiquettes are what helps prevent one from descending into savagery, or in today's words, "manners maketh man" (referring to the belief that politeness, good manners and civility are essential to humanity).[37] Thus, in *Confucius'* mind, "*Li*" ought to be the code of conduct for everyone.

In his effort to uphold "*Li*," *Confucius* focused on the establishment of an aristocratic system premised on "*Li*" ideology. He believed that a country must have a social order under which all people behaved within the boundaries of "*Li*." He tried to promote a rigidly stratified hierarchy in which no one could ever step beyond the limits. In his words, a good country would embody the order of "*Jun Jun, Chen Chen, Fu Fu, Zi Zi*," meaning that the ruler must be like a ruler, the subject like a subject, the father like a father and the son like a son.[38]

On the basis of "*Li*," *Confucius* made morality a norm of politics and behavior and refined the Spring-Autumn moral thought by developing the standards of benevolence and faithfulness. More specifically, Confucius considered family the cornerstone of society. He promoted a notion that harmony premised on "*Li*" in the family, particularly between husband and wife, is critical to social stability.

Mencius, named *Meng Ke*, was a well-known philosopher in the period of the Warring States, and a loyal advocate and defender of the *Confucian* school against rival philosophic doctrines. *Mencius* was said to study with *Confucius'* grandson *Zisi*. Like *Confucius*, *Mencius* tried to use his thoughts to influence politics throughout his life by traveling from state to state, but was unfortunately not successful. Nevertheless, he was regarded to have made great contributions to the *Confucian* school of thought by explicitly interpreting *Confucianism* and developing the *Confucian* theory into a system of philosophic thinking.

The most representative collection of *Mencius'* philosophic views was his book "*Mengzi*," where he elaborated on *Confucianism* as well as his own political approaches. Because of his strong advocacy for *Confucian* doctrines as well as his creative work in expounding *Confucianism*, *Mencius* became the "master" after *Confucius* and was lauded as the "Second Sage" (*Ya Shen*). One of the great contributions *Mencius* made to *Confucianism* was his theory that all people are naturally good. He further developed the idea of benevolence and believed that people have the inherent ability to become benevolent but require cultivation to exercise benevolence well.[39]

36 See "*The Analects of Confucius*" (*Lunyu*), *Ji Shi* Sixteen. An English translation of "*The Analects of Confucius*" is available at www.hm.tyg.jp/~acmuller/contao/anatects.html.

37 See James Hastings, *The Expository Times*, Vol. 31, at p. 332 (T. & T. Clark, 1920).

38 See *id.*, *Yan Yun*, Twelve.

39 According to *Mencius*, an infant has no lack of knowledge of how to love his parents, and when he grows up, he knows naturally how to respect his older brothers. Loving one's parents is benevolence and respecting one's older brothers is rightness – these principles penetrate all

An important addition the *Mengzi* made to *Confucianism* was the concept of benevolent policy (*Ren Zheng*). According to the *Mengzi*, a benevolent ruler would be the one who made the interest of the people his top priority. In the words of the *Mengzi*, people should come first, and then the state; the last in line should be the ruler.[40] Thus, a ruler must first try to gain the confidence and support of his people. It was *Mencius*' belief that a non-benevolent ruler may hold the reins of a state but would never gain the trust of the people.[41]

In addition to *Confucius and Mencius*, another *Confucian* master worthy of mention is *Xunzi* (313 BC to 238 BC). Named *Kuang* and styled *Qing*, *Xunzi* was a very sophisticated and also influential philosopher in the Warring States period. Reputed to be the epitome of the *Confucian* school of thought, *Xunzi* consolidated Confucian tradition with Legalist ideas. He viewed "*Li*" and "*Fa*" (legal standards or law) as deriving from the same source, interpreting "Li" in light of "*Fa*." He believed that the integration of "*Fa*" into "*Li*" would best serve both the legal tradition and reality.[42] The major book containing the writings of *Xunzi* was "The *Xunzi*."[43]

The most notable aspect of *Xunzi*'s philosophy was his doctrine of "bad human nature." In opposition to *Mencius*, *Xunzi* believed that all people were born with "bad" nature, but this "bad" nature could be fundamentally transformed through education as well as social discipline.[44] From *Xunzi*'s viewpoint, there is nothing higher than the transformation of man in harmony with natural order. According to *Xunzi*, human nature provides a significant barrier to moral improvement, but the barrier can be overcome. The disposition of people ultimately depends on what they acquire as a result of education and socialization.[45]

More importantly, in addition to his advancement of "*Li*," *Xunzi* put great emphasis on "*Fa*." He strongly believed that "*Li*" and "*Fa*" complement each other to maintain social order together: "*Li*" encourages positive behaviors of people while "*Fa*" deals with negative selfish behaviors by punishing them. *Xunzi* also actively

people. See "*Mencius*," *Jin Xin* (Part One). It is also *Mencius*'s belief that the goodness of human nature is just like the downward tendency of water, and just as all water has a down-running tendency, all people have a tendency toward goodness. See "*Mencius*," *Gao Zhi* (Part One).

40 See the *Mengzi*, *Jing Xin* (B), ch. 38.

41 See *id.*

42 See Zhao Min, An Introduction to Pre-Qin Confucian Political Philosophies, 36–41 (Beijing University Press, 2004).

43 "The *Xunzi*" consists of thirty-two chapters and most of them are believed to be *Xunzi*'s own work.

44 The term "bad" used by Xunzi was to implicate the self-regarding desire or instinct by birth – each person has his or her own desire, and without proper guidance through being educated or disciplined, the unregulated pursuit of or struggle for the personal desire could cause social turmoil and ultimately lead to strife and disorder. See Min, *supra* note 42, at 38–39. See also Patricia Ebrey, Chinese Civilization: A Sourcebook, 24–26 (2nd ed., Free Press, 1993).

45 See Cui Yongdong, "Doctrines of State Administration" of Political Thinkers, 48–49 (China University of Political Science & Law Press, 2007).

advocated that "*Fa*" be equally applied to everyone regardless of his or her social status.[46] *Xunzi*'s idea of the application of law is believed to have had a strong influence on the development of legalism.

Historically, *Xunzi* was regarded as having developed the "Doctrine of *Confucius – Mencius*" in a reformative way. According to *Xunzi*, "*Li*" has three roots: "Heaven and Earth are the root of life, Forebears are the root of kinship, and Lords and teachers are the root of order."[47] He divided "*Li*" into two different functions: to serve as the ideological foundation of the country and to serve as a basic value of the family.[48] In *Xunzi*'s view, the stability of both a country and a family would depend on a good practice of "*Li*."[49]

But *Xunzi* associated "*Li*" more with the political structure than with the clan system. Unlike *Confucius* and *Mencius*, *Xunzi* opposed the aristocratic hereditary system and favored a bureaucrat-based centralization of state power.[50] For example, *Xunzi*'s political views included a desire "to esteem those who are knowledgeable and to employ those who are capable."[51] Thus, in *Xunzi*'s opinion, an appointment of any public officer should be made on the basis of merit rather than family status.

As a very influential classic philosophy in China, *Confucianism* established a system comprising social-political values and transcendent ideals of traditional Chinese society. A core tenet of the system was the concept of the Three Cardinal Guides and Five Constant Virtues. These guides and virtues formed a significant part of the Chinese social fabric and way of life and became Chinese traditional ethics and moral standards that lasted for thousands of years.

The Three Cardinal Guides were stated as "ruler guides subject, father guides son, and husband guides wife," which reflects a special moral relationship between ruler and subjects, father and son, and husband and wife under the *Confucian* standard. The core of the Three Cardinal Guides is that subjects, son, and wife must absolutely obey and be loyal to the ruler, father, and husband. It was also required under the Three Cardinal Guides that the ruler, father, and husband set an example for the subjects, son, and wife. The whole idea is that if the Three Cardinal Guides are followed, society would be in good order.

The Five Constant Virtues include benevolence (*Ren*), righteousness (*Yi*), propriety or ritual (*Li*), wisdom (*Zhi*), and faithfulness (*Xin*).[52] Benevolence refers to love or kindness, and in particular infers that a good ruler or government must

46 See Shuchen, *supra* note 29, at 151.

47 See John Knoblock, Xunzi: A Translation and Study of the Complete Works, Vol. 3, 58 (Stanford University Press, 1994).

48 See *id.*

49 See *id.*

50 See Shuchen, *supra* note 29, at 150.

51 See "*Xunzi*," *supra* note 43, at ch. 9 *Wang Zhi* (System of King).

52 The "Five Constant Virtues" of *Confucianism* originated from *Confucius*'s three virtues "benevolence, righteousness, rituals." Mencius then added "wisdom." Dong Zhongsu in the Han Dynasty expanded them into five by including "faithfulness."

be people-oriented. Righteousness means fitfulness or integrity, requiring the way of thinking or acting to be in accord with defined norms. Propriety implicates courtesy or modesty, which requires certain rites to be followed. Wisdom represents knowledge, talent, or intelligence. Faithfulness refers to honesty, credibility, and accountability.

The very focus of the Three Cardinal Guides and Five Constant Virtues is on two principles: loyalty and filial piety. Loyalty refers to the duty owed to the ruler, while filial piety is an obligation of obedience and care for one's parents and elderly family members. Both loyalty and filial piety originated from two major canons in *Zhou Li*, namely "Zun Zun" (respect those who should be respected) and "Qin Qin" (stay close to family members). In substance, "Zun Zun" implies loyalty," and "Qin Qin" suggests "filial piety."[53] Developed from *Zhou Li*, *Confucianism* made it a fundamental ruling strategy that one should be loyal to the ruler and show filial piety to parents,[54] which was reflected particularly in the Three Cardinal Guides. Notably, a society that has established loyalty and filial piety prioritizes no rights, only obligations.

B. *Legalist School of Thought*

The antithesis of *Confucianism* is legalism, a pragmatic political philosophy propagated by legalists such as *Shang Yang*, *Han Fei*, and *Li Si*.[55] *Shang Yang* (390 BC–338 BC), also called *Wei Yang* or *Gongsun Yang*, nicknamed "Lord of *Shang*," came from the state of *Wei* to the state of *Qin* in 361 BC to serve Duke *Xiao* of *Qin*. He took with him to *Qin* a copy of the Canons of Law (*Fa Jing*), the classic law book of *Li Kui*.[56] Supported by Duke *Xiao*, *Shang Yang* launched two reforms (in 359 BC and 350 BC) in *Qin* (known as the Reform of *Shang Yang* or "*Shang Yang Bian Fa*") and enacted sweeping changes. The reform helped transform *Qin* from a weak to a strong state. Ultimately, *Qin* unified the country by conquering the other six rival states and established the first imperial dynasty of China, the *Qin* Dynasty, in 221 BC.

A significant part of *Shang Yang's* reform was the abolishment of the "Square-fields" land system. As noted, the "Square-fields" system was a product of enfeoffment. In his reform, *Shang Yang* privatized land by stripping nobles of their rank

53 See Zhang Zhongqiu, Comparative Studies of Chinese and Western Legal Culture, 134–135 (Chinese University of Political Science & Law Press, 2006).

54 See Kwang-Kuo Hwang, *Filial Piety and Loyalty: Two Types of Social Identification in Confucianism*, 2 Asian J. Soc. Psych. 163, 170 (April 1999) (*Confucians* recognized a simple fact on the basis of Chinese cosmology: individuals' lives are the continuation of their parents' physical lives).

55 Among the major legalists also were *Li Kui* (455–395 BC) of the state of *Wei*, *Shen Dao* (395–315 BC) of the state of *Zhao*, and *Shen Buhai* (?–338 BC) of the state of *Chu*.

56 *Li Kui* served as Prime Minister of the state of *Wei* from 445 BC to 396 BC. The most influential piece of his writing was *Fa Jing* (the Canons of Law).

and privileges obtained under enfeoffment. He assigned land to soldiers based on their military successes and rewarded farmers who exceeded harvest quotas. *Shang Yang* replaced the "Square-fields" system with individual ownership of property and allowed land to be transferred through purchase.[57]

Shang Yang's political views and philosophical thoughts were stated in the Book of *Lord Shang* (*Shang Jun Shu*), a book compiled by scholars.[58] The *Lord Shang* recorded *Shang Yang*'s reform initiatives and addressed his view of the origin and role of law. *Shang Yang* emphasized the importance of law in governing a country and promoted the idea of equal punishment (*Yi Xing*). According to *Shang Yang*, the imposition of punishment should not take into account the social status of the person being punished.[59]

Politically, *Shang Yang* was keen on centralized control of the state. He divided the territory of *Qin* into prefectures and counties administered by the central government. He opposed the criterion of heredity in government office in favor of bureaucratic term appointments. By building the prefecture-county-based administrative structure, *Shang Yang* created the statewide bureaucracy in China, in which the political loyalty of appointed officers was to the person who appointed them, and ultimately to the head of the state.[60]

Note, however, that the changes *Shang Yang* effected in *Qin* included severe punishments and a tyrannical government. *Shang Yang* regarded people as being inherently selfish and unable to know how to attain prosperity. He believed that only a uniform legal system of rewards and punishments would bring order to society. He held the notion that the imposition of a harsh penalty for a minor violation of law could prevent a felony or serious offense, and ultimately that moral goals may only be attained through overtly immoral means.[61] Ironically, *Shang Yang* made Qin a powerful state but died from a torture tactic he invented: his body was pulled apart by chariots and his whole family was executed.

Han Fei (280 BC–233 BC), a descendant of a noble family of the state of *Han*, was a disciple of *Xunzi* and a great philosopher of his time. *Han Fei* studied all the legalist ideas and developed a comprehensive theory of legalism in his book "The

[57] For a general discussion of Shang Yang and his reforms, see Li Yu-Ning, Shang Yang's Reforms and State Control in China (The China Book Project) (Routledge, 1977).

[58] There has been a long debate on who wrote the Book of Lord *Shang*, and *Shang Yang* was the putative author. But at present, a majority of Chinese scholars believe that the Book of Lord *Shang* was a compilation of *Shang Yang*'s views and thoughts by scholars at a later time. See Zhang Weiren & Chen Jingquan, Early Chinese Political and Legal Thought, 234 (People Press, 2006).

[59] See Rosemary Roberts, *Shang Yang and the Performance of Historical Drama in Reform-Era China*, in L. Ruru, ed., Staging China, Chinese Literature and Culture in the World (Palgrave Macmillan, 2016).

[60] See History of China, Vol. 1 (Haiyan Press, 2001).

[61] See Y. Pines, *Legalism in Chinese Philosophy*, Stanford Encyclopedia of Philosophy, available at https://plato.stanford.edu/entries/chinese-legalism/.

Han Feizi," consisting of fifty-five chapters.[62] Because of his contributions, *Han Fei* was acclaimed as the person who epitomized legalist thoughts and systemized the theory of legalism. *Han Fei* tried many times to promote reform in the state of *Han* but was unsuccessful because his political ideas were not accepted by the king of *Han*. After being disappointed at home, he went to *Qin* in 234 BC and found favor with the king of *Qin*, who was later crowned as the first Emperor of China, *Qin Shi Huang*. Unfortunately, *Han Fei* was jailed a year later due to a false charge and committed suicide while in jail.

Li Si (284 BC–208 BC) was a powerful and highly controversial political figure. Like *Han Fei*, *Li Si* was also a student of *Xunzi*. He helped the state of *Qin* win the war against all its neighboring states and unify the country with the founding of the *Qin* Dynasty. While serving as prime minister for both *Qin Shi Huang* and his son, *Qin Er Shi* (229 BC–207 BC), *Li Si* managed to put legalist theory into practice and enacted harsh laws to implement it. For example, in order to stabilize *Qin*'s power, *Li Si* persuaded *Qin Shi Huang* to suppress intellectual dissent by burning all books and records containing key *Confucian* texts and burying some 460 *Confucian* scholars – the incident historically known as "Burning Books and Burying Intellectuals" (*Fen Shu Keng Ru*). In addition, according to *The Records of the Grand Historian* written by *Sima Qian* of the *Han* Dynasty, *Li Si* also caused the death of *Han Fei* out of his envy for *Han Fei*'s intellect.

The Book of Lord *Shang* and the *Han Feizi* were the principal sources of Legalist doctrine. The *Han Feizi* essentially restated the previous legalist ideologies and advocated a system of laws that enabled the ruler to govern efficiently, and even ruthlessly.[63] Unlike *Confucianism*, which upheld "rule by *Li*," Legalism strove for "rule by law." As described in the *Han Feizi*, a ruler did not devote himself to virtue but to law, and made no arbitrary judgments himself but used law as a measurement of merit.[64]

The most significant and influential part of the *Han Feizi* was the description of political strategies of governance. It synthesized the "*Fa*" approach of *Shang Yang*, the "*Shu*" method of *Shen Buhai*,[65] and the "*Shi*" notion of *Shen Dao*[66] into a general scheme for the ruling of the country. "*Fa*" encompasses the laws, rules, or

62 The current version of the *Han Feizi* was the one compiled by *Liu Xiang* (77–6 BC) in the *Han* Dynasty, but most of the chapters in the book were written by *Han Feizi*.

63 See *Han Feizi* (Burton Watson trans.), The Way of the Ruler (Columbia University Press, 2003).

64 See *id*.

65 *Shen Buhai* (385–337 BC), legalist, native of the state of *Zheng* that was later taken by the state of *Han*. As a reformer, *Shen*, in addition to stressing the law like other legalists, introduced the concept of "*Shu*" – ruling strategies, emphasizing on methods of appointment, supervision, and evaluation of the ruler's subordinates.

66 *Shen Dao* (390–315 BC), legalist from the state of *Zhao*. He held that the people should be ruled by the monarch, and all matters should be determined by law. He advocated "*Shi*," namely power, and advocated "governing without doing anything," believing that only when the monarch has power, can the law be enforced.

legal norms that helped establish desired social standards and regulate human behavior, and ultimately maintain the power of the ruler and state. "*Shu*" denoted the strategies or measures by which the power of the ruler was exercised and decisions were carried out. "*Shi*" represented the authority and power that rested with the ruler and commanded full respect and obedience from the ruled.[67]

According to *Han Fei*, the "*Fa*" "*Shu*," and *Shi*" were three indispensable components of being a ruler. Without "*Fa*," the country would become uncontrollable since "Fa" lays a foundation and makes governance possible; short of "*Shu*," the "*Fa*" would not be effectively implemented and as a result the country would be mismanaged; absent "*Shi*," the "*Fa*" would not be respected and the role of the ruler would be diminished. Thus, it was *Han Fei*'s belief that a country would be well under control if the ruler could rely on "*Fa*" and live with "*Shi*."[68] He also emphasized that a ruler could not afford to lose either "*Fa*" or "*Shu*" because "*Fa*" served as the premise of "*Shi*," and "*Shu*" functioned as the means to realize and maintain "*Shi*."[69]

In short, Legalism advances the idea that the law was designed to support the ruler and the state. The legalists advocated that law should be given absolute authoritativeness so that it would become the sole criterion by which to judge right from wrong.[70] On the other hand, the legalists favored heavy punishments because they considered it vitally important to equip the law with great "deterrent force."[71] In the meantime, the legalists promoted equal application of the law with the notion that if the punishments were harsh and the law equally applied, neither the powerful nor the weak would be able to escape state control and the authority of the ruler.[72]

Many in China now view the legalists as having essentially created a concept of "rule of law" that placed the law above all others in terms of state power and administration.[73] However, it is important to note that the rule of law advanced by the legalists had a clear focus on punishment and the maintenance of power by the ruler. Conceptually, it differed sharply from the meaning of the rule of law commonly held in Western countries, in that the rule of law under the legalists' concept had nothing to do with the separation of powers, impartial justice, accountability of government, or judicial independence. Rather, the rule of law theory, if there was any, as employed in ancient China was intimately related to maintaining the supremacy of imperial power.

[67] See Shuchen, *supra* note 29, at 142.
[68] See *id.*
[69] See Yongdong, *supra* note 45, at 176–200.
[70] See Shuchen, *supra* note 29, at 140–141.
[71] See *id.* at 139.
[72] See *id.* at 140.
[73] See Yongdong, *supra* note 45, at 145–150. See also Shuchen, *supra* note 29, at 135–136.

C. Taoist *School of Thought*

Taoism was one of the major philosophies in Chinese history that had a great impact on the development of Chinese law and legal culture. The origin of *Taoism* can be found in the period of Spring-Autumn and Warring States, and the founder of *Taoism* was *Laozi*, an ancient philosopher of China. The life of Laozi was legendary, and some questioned whether there was really a historical *Laozi*. Although there was debate on where *Laozi* was born, it was commonly believed that *Laozi* was a native of *Chu* (part of today's Henan Province). The family name of *Laozi* was "*Li*" and given name "*Er*," styled "*Dan*" (also as "*Boyang*").

Laozi was believed to be an acquaintance of *Confucius* and was also consulted by *Confucius* about "*Li*." *Laozi* committed his whole life to self-cultivation and the practice of virtue. Not until late in his life did *Laozi* start writing to express the meaning and his understanding of virtue. *Laozi* was credited to be the author of the book "*The Laozi*," also called "*Dao De Jing*," commonly translated as the "*Classic of the Way and Virtue*." However mythical the author of the book may be, "*Laozi*" was considered the authoritative source of *Taoism*.[74]

It should be noted that, at the beginning, *Taoism* was a philosophical doctrine, but it later became not only an independent school of thought but also a major religion in the Eastern *Han* Dynasty (AD 25–220). Therefore, in modern Chinese history, the term *Taoism* may refer to either a philosophical tradition or an organized religion, because in the Chinese language the former is identified as *Daojia* (the *Taoist* school) while the latter as "*Daojiao*" (the *Taoist* religion or simply *Taoism*). Of course, these two are very closely related in both their origin and foundations.[75] For the purposes of this book, the term *Taoism* is used to designate this particular school of thought or philosophy.

The "*Laozi*" was a short book containing 81 chapters with only some 5,000 characters. The book mainly addressed "*Dao*" (translated as "the Way") and "*De*" (Virtue), but the core of the book was "*Dao*." The word "*Dao*," as used in the "*Laozi*," contained a truly complicated philosophical meaning, and as such "the Way" was only a literal translation which did not (and could not) implicate the actual intention or connotation of the word "*Dao*." What *Taoism* intended to promote were three "treasures," namely compassion (love), moderation (appropriateness), and humility (humbleness).

According to the "*Laozi*," "*Dao*" was a mysterious and superior noumenon from which all things in the universe originated. The basic notion of *Taoism* was that

74 In 1993, a set of bamboo slips (used as the medium for writing in ancient times in China) were unearthed from a Warring States Period tomb located in Guodian, Jingmen of Hubei Province, and the slips recorded a handwritten copy of a simplified version of the *Laozi*. Many then believed that the slips proved that *Laozi* was the author of the "*Laozi*."

75 Some in China were of the opinion that *Daojiao* originated in the "*Laozi*." But some disagreed and thought that it came from the pre-history belief in God or Divinity.

"*Dao*" itself, born before heaven and earth, was a spiritual object beyond the perception and reach of human beings. But it was such a spiritual object that created all beings on earth. To be more specific, from the *Dao* there developed "*Qi*," meaning vitality or energy, and with the "*Qi*," "*Yin*" (negative force) and "*Yang*" (positive force) came into play. Because of the function of *Yin-Yang*, all things on the earth were formed and nourished. Given the abstrusity of "*Dao*," the school of *Taoist* learning, known as the "Doctrine of Mystery," was developed thereof.

Thus, the cornerstone of *Taoism* was the "*Dao*," meaning "thing-in-itself." It was believed that from *Dao*, various tenets or principles that govern human beings and human life were derived. Under those tenets or principles, there developed strategies and rules through which all political matters and problems of the state were solved. An important political theory of *Taoism* was that oneself and the state were ruled the same way by "*Dao*," and therefore the understanding of "*Dao*" for oneself was the understanding of "*Dao*" for everything, including political matters. What was essential under the doctrine of *Daoism* was to let nature take its own course.

On the basis of "*Dao*," two functional canons were promoted: "self-cultivation" and "non-action." According to the *Laozi*, everything has its own way or path to grow and develop, so any effort contrary to "naturalness" would be counterproductive and doomed to failure. "Self-cultivation" focused on the value of one's spirit and virtue as well as moral discipline, while "non-action" was primarily meant to govern the state by doing nothing that was against nature (*Wu Wei Er Zhi*). In short, as long as "*Dao*" was followed, everything would be well organized and in order.

With regard to law, the *Laozi* divided it into two categories: norms of *Dao* and enacted statutes. According to the *Laozi*, human beings were ruled by earth, earth by heaven, heaven by *Dao*, and *Dao* by nature.[76] Therefore, the norms of *Dao* were the ultimate authority or the highest standards. The statutes enacted by human beings were often affected by man-made factors and had the tendency to contradict the norms of *Dao*.[77] Hence, it was vital that statutes strictly followed the norms of *Dao*.[78]

D. Mohist *School of Thought*

Mohism was a school of thought that flourished during the Warring States and was as equally influential as *Confucianism* at that time. The master of *Mohism* was *Mo*

[76] See Yongdong, *supra* note 45, at 93.

[77] In China, scholars have disputed whether the *Laozi* attached any importance to man-made laws. Some argued that since the *Laozi* enshrined *Dao* by diminishing the role of law, it virtually promoted legal nihilism. Others disagreed and pointed out that the *Laozi* addressed both *Dao* and law, and its emphasis on *Dao* over law was consistent with its philosophical belief that law should derive from *Dao*.

[78] See *id.*

Di (490 BC–403 BC), another legendary philosopher in ancient China. *Mo Di* was legendary not only because where he was from was little-known (scholars debate whether *Mo Di* was from the state of *Lu* or the state of *Song*) but also because knowledge of his original family name was speculative, due to the fact that "*Mo*," meaning "ink" in Chinese, is an unusual family name in China.[79] The major work of *Mo Di* was the book "*Mozi*," which was actually a compilation of *Mo Di*'s dialogues, comments, and anecdotes. Although its author was unknown, the compilation was made by *Mo Di's* followers.

The central tenet of *Mohism* was the doctrine of inclusive care that focused on benefiting others. According to *Mo Di*, there were two interests in society: personal interest and others' interest. Ignorance of others' interest in favor of personal ones was considered the direct cause of evil or social turmoil. Therefore, it was important that people cared about each other and mutually benefited in their dealings. In order to achieve inclusive care, any aggression must not be sought, because like theft, robbery, or murder, aggression brought harm to others and ultimately hurt society as a whole. Inclusive care, in *Mo Di*'s words, was purposed to help build a society where people treat others' country, others' family, and others' body like their own.[80] More simply put, inclusive care and non-aggression constituted the very foundation of *Mohist* philosophy.

The social standard *Mohism* tried to promote was "*Ren*." Similar to *Confucianism*, *Mohism* interpreted "*Ren*" as benevolence and humanity. A notable feature of *Mohism* was its pursuance of a lifestyle of austerity and self-sacrifice for impartial care or universal love. The *Mohists* regarded self-sacrifice as an important ethical principle to fulfill the duty of universal care and to act out of concern for the well-being of all others. In this context, *Mohism* shares the same value as altruism.

Thus, from the *Mohist* viewpoint, unnecessary luxuries and excessive expenditures must be eliminated, and as such a "*Ren*" person must avoid wasting resources on extravagant things as well as funerals. As some have observed, the *Mohists* saw themselves primarily as a moral, political, and religious advocacy group devoted to realizing what they saw as a morally right society and way of life, and the *Mohists*' ethical theory was an interesting, complex form of consequentialism that posits a plurality of intrinsic goods, which were to be promoted through a variety of strategies.[81]

Mo Di's political view was utilitarianism. He believed that social stability was dependent on the wealth of the general public, and that meeting the wants of the

[79] Since the word "*Mo*" is an unusual family name, many suspected that it was an epithet given to him because he was once a slave or convict, whose faces were often branded or tattooed with dark ink.

[80] See Yongdong, *supra* note 45, at 127.

[81] See Stanford Encyclopedia of Philosophy, *Mohism*, available at http://plato.stanford.edu/entries/mohism.

ruler must be within the boundary of necessity for the ruled and their basic living. Hence, the very purpose of the *Mohists*' advocacy for thrift in utilization was to help accumulate the wealth of the nation for the benefit of the general public. In accordance with *Mo Di*, if the country had a "*Ren*" ruler, the country's wealth could be multiplied because the "*Ren*" ruler would not tolerate any waste of resources.[82]

Related to *Mohism's concept of* inclusive care was the theory of promoting uniformity and elevating the worthy. The purpose of uniformity was to establish a unified conception of morality, and such morality was to be achieved by encouraging people to conform upward to the good moral standard set for society under the will of the Heaven. Pursuant to *Mohism*, the most important thing was to make the greatest worthy person the Son of Heaven to rule the country, followed by creation of a centralized government with a hierarchical bureaucracy. "Elevating the worthy" was to help ensure that appointments to the bureaucracy were made on the basis of ethical merit and professional ability.

In essence, the *Mohists* advocated a unified ethical and political structure premised on the concept of impartial care for all, to maintain a stable social and economic order. The *Mohist* ideology was to establish an authoritarian country ruled by a virtuous and benevolent sovereign, and to run the country hierarchically by a government formed by all merit-based bureaucrats. An ultimate goal of the *Mohists* was to build objective standards that would guide judgment and action reliably and impartially so as to produce beneficial, morally right consequences,[83] because they believed that conformity to traditional rites itself, as promoted by *Confucians*, did not ensure that actions were morally right.

In Chinese legal history, *Mohism* was characterized as the philosophy of petty handicraftsmen. There were a number of reasons for this. First, *Mohism* emerged from a rising class of craftsmen and merchants that grew in size and influence during the Warring States period, and many of them lived a hard and thrifty life. Second, *Mohists* opposed exploitation and had a strong hostility toward the aristocratic system. They believed a good society should be one where equality was applied and benefits were promoted for all under heaven. Third, as noted, *Mohists* favored self-sacrifice and valued thrift over luxury. In this context, the *Mohist* doctrine was also labeled as a civilian doctrine, a doctrine that advocated civilian interests and upheld an idea of universal brotherhood.

Unfortunately, the *Mohist* school of thought never became the ideologically dominant force. As a matter of fact, it was pushed out as an outsider and gradually faded away as an "obsolete approach" after *Confucianism* became the orthodox doctrine of the country. This was in part because *Mohism* was regarded as contradictory to the basic concept of "*Li*" that was central to *Confucian* thought. But *Mo*

[82] See Yongdong, *supra* note 45, at 138.
[83] See Stanford Encyclopedia of Philosophy, *Mohism*, *supra* note 81, at 1.

Di and his *Mohism* remained influential due to their doctrine of inclusive care for the welfare of "all under heaven" and their idea of promoting a harmonious and peaceful social order.

3. TRADITIONAL CHINESE LEGAL SYSTEM

As discussed, China's legal system has its roots in the *Xia*, *Shang*, and *Zhou* Dynasties. But it did not become a real "system" until after the *Qin* Dynasty. First, the unification of China into a single state in the *Qin* Dynasty made it possible to have a statewide legal system, applying uniformly across the country. Second, in the *Han* Dynasty, when *Confucianism* became the state orthodox ideology, the Chinese legal system embarked on the development of the "Li"-premised tradition that dominated China for nearly two thousand years and remains highly discernible today. Finally, in the *Tang* Dynasty (AD 618–AD 907), the Chinese legal system fully developed as a "system," represented by the "*Tang* Code." The *Tang* Code laid a foundation for the traditional Chinese legal system, which included several historical features.

A. *Dominance of the* Confucian *School and Integration of* Li *and* Fa *with* Li *as the Core*

The most striking characteristic of the ancient Chinese legal system was its concomitance with *Confucian* philosophy. As noted, in the *Qin* Dynasty, *Confucians* had once sunk into diminishing status because *Legalism* was in the first emperor's graces, particularly during the dark period of "Burning Books and Burying Intellectuals" (212 BC). But since the *Qin* Dynasty had a very short lifespan, this period soon ended. A dramatic change after the quick fall of the *Qin* Dynasty was the revival of *Confucianism*.

In the *Han* Dynasty, at the suggestion of *Dong Zhongshu*, Emperor *Wu Di* adopted a state policy of "proscribing hundred[s] of other schools of thought and espousing *Confucian* ideology only."[84] As a result, *Confucianism* emerged again. At that time, however, *Confucianism* had developed from its original appearance during the Spring-Autumn and Warring States periods to incorporate elements of other schools of thought such as Legalism and Taoism, to keep pace with the times. Due to its patriarchal ideas and clan-based ruling strategies, *Confucianism* was enthroned as the orthodox ideology and mainstream thought of the country, which lasted for almost the entire period of Chinese imperial history.

[84] Dong Zhongsu (179–104 BC) was a famous scholar in the *Han* Dynasty who served both Emperor *Jing* Di and *Wu Di* of *Han*. He was often quoted as the man who helped make *Confucianism* the official ideology of ancient China, mainly because he suggested eliminating all other schools of thought and replacing them with *Confucianism*.

Out of all of the factors credited for the dominance of *Confucianism* in Chinese legal history, three are most notable. The first factor was the *Confucian* system of social estate that aimed at maintaining imperial power and deifying the autocratic kingship. Under the *Confucian* Three Cardinal Guides, the social estate system established was an imperial-power-centered social and political order under which the country was structured and governed.

The second factor was the clan-based ethic standard established by *Confucianists*. The ethic standard served as an ideological device to unify the country around the emperor. Based on traditional etiquette, *Confucianism* believed that the essence of state power was in the country, and the essence of the country was at home.[85] *Confucianists* regarded the whole country as a family in which the emperor was the head. Thus it was important and necessary to establish a patriarchal and ethical relationship so as to ensure that the head of a family possessed absolute power to control.

The third factor was the totalitarian structure of bureaucrats created under imperial power to govern the country. *Confucianism* advocated a benevolent government. Although *Confucian* benevolent ideology attached great importance to public opinions and people's livelihood, it mainly revolved around creation of a harmonious relationship between the ruler and the ruled. In particular, the *Confucian* conception of superiority of imperial power in fact helped form a theoretical basis to justify the totalitarian nature of the government.

As noted, when *Confucianism* was upheld as the state orthodox ideology in the *Han* Dynasty, it began to mix with the methodologies of other schools of thought. Since the *Han* Dynasty, the *Confucian* "*Li*" and Legalist "*Fa*" had become the major driving forces in the development of the Chinese legal system. Thus, Chinese legal history was virtually a history of the interplay and integration of "*Li*" and "*Fa*." The ideological core of the traditional Chinese legal system was "*Li*," supplemented by "*Fa*."[86]

Again, as originated in the *Zhou* Dynasty and refined by *Confucianism*, "*Li*" is a classic Chinese social construct used extensively to refer to the norms of social behavior and moral standards.[87] From the Western viewpoint, "*Li*" is a very complicated concept because it is a Chinese ideograph that embodies the entire spectrum of interaction with humans, nature, and even material objects.[88] In Chinese history, "*Li*" played a significant role in both regulating human activities and defining the relationship between humans and nature. The conception of "*Li*" and all theories developed under this sacred rubric constituted the main theme of traditional Chinese social and legal culture.

[85] See Zhai Tongzu, Chinese Law and Chinese Society, 5–6 (Zhonghua Book Company, 1981).

[86] See Shi Guangquan, The Compromise of Li and Law and Historical Changes of Chinese Traditional Legal Culture (*sic*), 31–47 (Law Press, 2006).

[87] See Jinfan, *supra* note 9, at 3.

[88] See Wikipedia, "*Li*," available at http://en.wikipedia.org/wiki/li_(confucian).

From its inception, "*Li*" was rooted in the religious rites used to worship heaven and ancestors. Not until the West *Zhou* Dynasty did "*Li*" begin transitioning to systemized norms of conduct. When the Lord of *Zhou* stipulated a set of "*Li*," known as "*Zhou Li*," "*Li*" was infused with political functions to serve as a primary means to govern the state. At that time, as noted, the very purpose of "*Li*" was to help build a political and social system under which a hierarchical order was established and maintained. Pursuant to the order, people were each ranked on the basis of their social status and were classified as noble, respected, inferior, or lowly. Thus, upon the enactment of "*Zhou Li*," "*Li*" evolved from religious rites to social norms.

According to "*Zhou Li*," the order of the hierarchy must be strictly followed and cannot be violated by anyone. Therefore, in a state, everyone was subservient to the king. Additionally, the inferior should not offend the noble, and the poor may not be treated the same as the wealthy. Similarly, in a family, the younger members must be obedient to their elders, sons must be servile to their fathers, and the lowly must listen to the respected. In the view of the Lord of *Zhou*, when "*Li*" was observed, everything in the state would be well ordered and the country would be strong; otherwise the whole society would descend into chaos.

As discussed, during the period of Spring-Autumn and Warring States, China experienced a dramatic change, transforming from a slavery society to a feudalistic society. This change, along with social upheavals, led to a moment to abandon "*Zhou Li*." Believing that "*Li*" was essential to stability and development of the state, *Confucius* focused much of his effort on restoring "*Zhou Li*." On the one hand, *Confucius* stressed the importance of maintaining "*Zhou Li*" for an orderly society. On the other hand, as noted, he introduced into "*Li*" his idea of *Ren* (benevolence), making "*Li*" and "*Ren*" the two key components of *Confucianism*.

According to *Confucius*, if a person lacked "*Ren*," he could fail to observe "*Li*." Thus, in order to comply with "*Li*," it was essential to behave with such morals as filial submission, brotherliness, righteousness, good faith and loyalty, the basic norms of virtue. To that end, *Confucius* strongly advocated the rule of virtue by emphasizing a political approach of "guiding with virtue and regulating with '*Li*'." When speaking of "*Li*," *Confucius* and his followers believed that adherence to "*Li*" would lead people to abide by virtues and follow the rites appropriate to their social, political and personal status.

In *Confucian* texts, "*Li*" comprised various rites. The most influential work that contained texts of "*Li*" was the book of *Li Ji* (Records of *Li*). In the *Li Ji*, *Confucius* addressed "*Li*" as extensively as to include some "300 major and 3000 minor rules of ritual."[89] When discussing "*Li*" in the *Li Ji*, *Confucius* addressed *Li* in a very diverse range of topics, from eating and drinking, women's walking, clothing, and mourning

89 See *Li Ji*, *Li Qi*, 10, para. 11.

to learning, attitude to elders, loyalty to superiors and ultimately loyalty to the ruler of the state.[90]

But no matter how extensive and dynamic it may be, "*Li*" basically served two major functions: being a moral standard and acting as the norms of conduct. Again, the central idea of "*Li*" was to promote a social scheme under the Three Cardinal Guides and Five Constant Virtues, and to help establish an emperor-centered aristocratic political system. It was *Confucius*' strong belief that if the ruler acted like a ruler, the subject like a subject, the father like a father, and the son like a son, the order of society and the stability of the state were readily attainable.

However, at the beginning of the feudal period of Chinese history, especially during the *Qin* Dynasty, *Confucianism* was merely a scholarly doctrine and did not play much of a role in the social and political arena. For a long period of time, legalists were vehemently opposed to the *Confucian* ideology. As noted, it was in the *Han* Dynasty that *Confucianism* became more and more influential and ultimately was made the state orthodoxy.

When *Confucianism* was upheld as the governing ideology of the country, it began to combine with the methodology of "*Fa*" promoted by legalism. It was a legalist belief that "*Fa*" was indispensable in the ruling of a country. Therefore, during the *Han* Dynasty, China entered into a period in which the development of law and the legal system consisted of integration between *Confucian* "*Li*" and legalist "*Fa*," making "*Li*" the mainstay while "*Fa*" was the means to supplement and implement "*Li*."

A historical reason for *Confucianism*'s acceptance in the *Han* Dynasty was the swift fall of the *Qin* Dynasty (221 BC–206 BC). Notorious features of the *Qin* Dynasty were tyranny and excruciations. A lesson the *Han* learned from the *Qin* was that in order to rule the country properly, all policies must be tempered with benevolence and mercy. For that reason, Emperor *Wudi* took *Dong Zhongshu*'s advice and adopted *Confucianism* as the government ideology of the country. The Confucian "*Li*" then became a basic means to help create a benevolent government. Ever since, "*Li*" had become an important part of the Chinese legal system.

The integration of "*Li*" and "*Fa*" in the *Han* Dynasty began with the use of *Confucian* classics to interpret law and even to determine legal cases. The most notable phenomenon at that time was that all cases were adjudicated in line with the ideology and spirit of classic *Confucian* work, namely the "*Spring & Autumn Annals*."[91] As part of the integration effort, *Dong Zhongsu* compiled all relevant cases together into his famous book named "Adjudication of Cases under the '*Spring*

[90] See *id.*

[91] The classic Confucian works consist of four books and five classics known as "*Si Su Wu Jing*." The Five Classics refer to the *Book of Songs* (*Shi Jing*), the *Book of History* (*Shu Jing*), the *Book of Changes* (*Yi Jing*), the *Book of Rites* (*Li Jing*), and the *Spring & Autumn Annals* (*Chun Qiu*). The Four Books are the *Great Learning* (*Da Xue*), the *Doctrine of the Mean* (*Zhong Yong*), the *Analects of Confucius* (*Lun Yu*), and the *Mencius* (*Meng Zi*).

& Autumn Annals' (Chun Qiu Jue Yu)." *Dong*'s book is deemed the first casebook in Chinese legal history. In this context, a result of the integration was the *Confucianization* of law.

The practice of adjudication under the "*Spring & Autumn Annals*" was in place until the *Tang* Dynasty (618–907) when the *Tang* Code was promulgated (653). As the first comprehensive codification of law in China, the *Tang* Code was very influential in many ways. Most significantly, the *Tang* Code became the legislative blueprint for all dynasties thereafter. In the *Tang* Code, the integration of "*Li*" and "*Fa*" was more systemized and formal. In fact, many in China regarded the whole *Tang* Code as an outward legal expression of "*Li*," not only because the *Tang* Code was deeply rooted in "*Li*" but also because it legalized "*Li*" as the basic social norm of conduct.

Under the *Tang* Code, "*Li*" served as the foundational influence on Chinese legal policies, using punishment as the means to implement policies.[92] On that basis, the *Tang* Code heavily relied on the conception of "*Li*" and used "*Li*" as the principal guideline of the code. Under the provisions of the *Tang* Code, violations of the Three Cardinal Guides would face serious punishment, including the death penalty. In addition, several provisions in the *Tang* Code were simply the parallel of rites in the "*Zhou Li*." Moreover, "*Li*" was also employed in the process of adjudication to determine such matters as the severity of punishment and sentencing.[93]

In sum, through embedding the *Confucian* Three Cardinal Guides in statutes, the *Tang* Code formally codified "*Li*" and made "*Li*" the foundation of law. In light of "*Li*," the very focus of the *Tang* Code was essentially on maintaining the ultimate authority of imperial power. The reason behind this is simple and obvious. As noted, of the Three Cardinal Guides, the outmost guide was "ruler over subject," which emphasized "loyalty," and the remaining guides of "father over son" and "husband over wife" were concerned with "filial piety." Both "loyalty" and "filial piety" were fundamental values of "*Li*."

Because of its explicit implication of "*Li*," the *Tang* Code was historically viewed in China as an agglomeration of the legislation of "*Li*" and "*Fa*." In particular, the *Tang* Code was hailed as a typical representation of the legal system in which the "*Li*" and "Fa" were well synthesized.[94] As discussed, the significance of the *Tang* Code was that it was followed as a model by almost all dynasties thereafter. Thus, the promulgation of the *Tang* Code marked the beginning of the era in Chinese legal history in which the combination of "*Li*" and "*Fa*" was codified as the legal

[92] See *Tang* Code – *Table of Rules* (*Ming Li*).

[93] A typical example in this regard was the provision about an assault upon a family member. If one assaults his brother, he will be sentenced to jail for two-and-a-half years; if one assaults his uncle, aunt, or maternal grandparent, the sentence will be doubled; if one assaults his parents or paternal grandparent, the death penalty will be imposed.

[94] See Jinfan, *supra* note 9, at 23.

substance of the law and the legal system. This era lasted until the end of the *Qing* Dynasty in 1911.

B. *Patriarchal Clan-Based Social Order and Imperial-Power-Centered Bureaucrats*

The development of law and the legal system in Chinese history was closely intertwined with the evolution of the patriarchal clan system. Clan, as an anthropological term, is "a non-corporate descent group in which genealogical links to a common ancestor are assumed but are not actually known."[95] The term is often used to describe "an expanded family complex with the bond of blood relationship"[96] or "a group of people united by actual or perceived kinship and descent."[97] Patriarchal clan refers to a kinship in which "the father is the supreme authority in the family, and descent is reckoned in the male line."[98]

The traditional Chinese legal culture is deeply rooted in the patriarchal clan. There were two elements that played essential roles in shaping the imperial legal system: one is "family" and the other is the "state." These two elements were linked to the two ruling authorities: father and emperor. In the family, all members must follow the command of the father while in the state everyone is subject to the authority of the emperor. A common saying in Chinese historical literature describing this patriarchy is that when the emperor called a subject to die, the subject had to die, and if the father called a son to die, the son had to die as well.

As noted, the main themes of the patriarchal clan system were loyalty, obedience, and filial piety, reflected in the *Confucian* Three Cardinal Guides. Built on this system were the hierarchical bureaucrats and the totalitarian government. At the center of this administrative structure was the absolute power of the emperor. Any offense to the basic notion of patriarchal clan would be viewed as a serious crime on which a severe punishment would be imposed. This notion was reflected in what the imperial codes called the "Ten Abominations" or "Ten Evils."

The "Ten Abominations" referred to the ten categories of major offenses in imperial China, classified as the most heinous of all crimes, involving mainly violation of loyalty and filial piety. The formation of the "Ten Abominations" took place gradually with the *Confucianization* of the traditional legal system. Beginning in the *Western Han* Dynasty, disrespect, great irreverence, depravity, and violation of filial piety were provided as criminal offenses in the law. In the period of the Three

95 See Oregon State University, *Definitions of Anthropological Terms*, available at https://oregonstate.edu/instruct/anth370/gloss.html.

96 See Na Ning, *Evolution of Clan Culture and Its Contemporary Significance*, 4 Asian Culture and Hist. 122 (2012).

97 See *Tribe*, New World Encyclopedia, available at www.newworldencyclopedia.org/entry/Tribe.

98 See John Stoltenberg, Refusing to Be a Man: Essays on Social Justice, 50 (University College London Press, 2000).

Kingdoms, the *Wei*, *Jin*, Southern and Northern Dynasties, the law was further *Confucianized*. Following the principle of combining "*Li*" and "*Fa*," the Northern *Qin Dynasty* law stipulated ten felonies.[99] From the "ten felonies," there developed the "Ten Abominations" in the *Tang* Dynasty.

The "Ten Abominations" were formally provided in the *Tang* Code. As noted, the *Tang* Code was modeled by all subsequent imperial codes. Thus the application of the "Ten Abominations" formed in the *Tang* Dynasty continued in every dynasty thereafter.[100] Under the *Tang Code*, the "Ten Abominations" included: (a) plotting a rebellion, (b) plotting great sedition – against royal mausoleums and palaces, (c) plotting treason, (d) evil disobedience – premeditated assault and murder of elder kin, (e) inhumanity / depravity, (f) great irreverence, (g) impiety, (h) discord / familial disharmony, (i) unrighteousness, and (j) incest.[101]

The "Ten Abominations" were considered the most serious crimes in China's imperial autocracy. The promulgation of the "Ten Abominations" was the product of the integration of "*Li*" with "*Fa*," and it created a crime and punishment system that was aimed solely at maintaining the imperial power. Among the Ten Abominations, the first three were directly intended to uphold the emperor's controlling authority and autocratic government. The abomination of great irreverence was purposed to protect against any offense to the emperor and disrespect for the imperial authority. The rest of the abominations were mainly to maintain family values and social ethics. The punishment for the Ten Abominations was severe. It not only included the death penalty for the violator himself, but also could result in the death of his entire family up to nine generations.

Therefore, the imperial power, clan-based ethic standard and totalitarian structure of bureaucrats were three essential and indispensable elements in the traditional Chinese legal system. As noted, both imperial power and the clan-based ethic standard were directly associated with the exercise of "*Li*" because they were all in fact a matter of loyalty and obedience which constituted not only an ideological but also a practical basis for the entire society. The top-down bureaucrat structure served as a mechanism to ensure that the central power was not challenged, and the ultimate sovereignty of the emperor was maintained.

The combination of "*Li*" and "*Fa*" implicated these three elements to the extent that the imperial power was unchallenged. More specifically, "*Fa*" in the traditional Chinese legal system primarily functioned as an external force to enforce "*Li*." Because "*Li*" had an explicit focus on the social order and rank of status, "*Fa*"

[99] See Zhongqiu, *supra* note 53, at 50.

[100] The "Ten Abominations" were finally abolished during legal reform in the late *Qing* Dynasty, a few years before the fall of the *Qing* Dynasty.

[101] See Asia for Educators of Columbia University, *Selections from the Great* Tang *Code*, Article 6 "Ten Abominations," available at http://afe.easia.columbia.edu/ps/cup/zhangsun_wuji_great_tang_code.pdf.

operated to help make the order stable and keep the status well respected. Thus, any violation of "*Li*" would necessarily result in a punishment imposed under "*Fa*."

Under the traditional Chinese legal system, the patriarchal clan became the major driving force of the social order, and the imperial power was sacredly inviolable. It is thus not difficult to conclude that the long-lasting clan and imperial culture embedded in the traditional Chinese society diminished the democratic consciousness of the people and seriously constrained the development of individual pursuits and spiritual civilization, which made it inevitable to have a system under which the country was governed by the rule of man.

C. *Criminal Law-Focused Legal Tradition and Subordination of the Judiciary to the Administration*

Another unique characteristic of the traditional Chinese legal system was that the legislative focus was primarily on legal punishments, and civil law was largely overshadowed by criminal law. The concept of civil law as used here refers to the law regulating civil affairs rather than a civil legal system. The focus on criminal law over civil law occurred because the "*Li*" premised legal system was mainly concerned with the relationship between the state and its citizens (or a vertical relationship) and there was little attention given to civil matters (or a horizontal relationship). Consequently, "*Fa*," to a great extent, was synonymous with punishment (*Xing*), and the fundamental role of "*Fa*" was to "stop violence and eliminate evil."[102]

Thus the traditional Chinese legal system was almost entirely a criminal law system. A closer look at Chinese legal history reveals that in almost every dynasty, criminal law constituted the backbone of "*Fa*" and the legal code consisted mostly of the penal code despite the fact that provisions in the code did not necessarily only address criminal offenses. In the traditional Chinese legal system, no separation was made between criminal law and civil law. The same code contained both civil and criminal provisions with criminal punishment as the center.

The judicial structure also had a clear focus on the criminal law function. At the central level, there were three legal branches: the Board of Punishment (*Xing Bu*), the Central Judicial Court (*Da Li Si*), and the Office of Censors or *Censorate* (*Yu Shi Tai*). This "three-branch" format of legal bodies was established in the *Tang* Dynasty and subsequent dynasties largely adhered to it. Although the three branches each had their own role to play, they all took part in legal proceedings.

The Board of Punishment was in charge of drafting and examining laws and regulations and classifying criminal punishment. It functioned more like a legislative body, but it also had the power to review judgments concerning the death sentence and exile. The Central Judicial Court was responsible for adjudicating all

[102] See *id.* at 68.

cases except for the death penalty and exile cases that were subject to the Board of Punishment's review and approval. The Office of Censors mainly dealt with supervision of officials at both the central and local levels, but was also authorized to adjudicate certain cases.[103]

The Board of Punishment was the most powerful of the three legal branches, since it was the top body of criminal law legislation and enforcement. Notwithstanding the three legal branches, final adjudication power in the traditional Chinese legal system rested with the emperor. The emperor was not only the top authoritative force because his words had binding legal effect but also was the final adjudicator of all cases due to his ultimate judicial power. Therefore, the emperor possessed all the powers of the legislature, executive and judiciary. For this reason, the traditional Chinese legal system was viewed as a totalitarian legal system.

In addition, although the Central Judicial Court was much like a supreme court of the nation, there was no independent court system. Rather, the judiciary was in general subordinate to the administration for several reasons. First, under the notion of "law from the emperor," the will of the emperor was the source of law. The emperor held the highest legislative power of the country, and an imperial edict was the supreme law of the land. The emperor, as the top adjudicator, had the final say for all legal cases.

Secondly, the Central Judicial Court was less powerful than the Board of Punishment and was also influenced by the Office of Censors. The so-called joint trial by three branches (*San Tang Hui Shen*) was a common occurrence in judicial proceedings. It referred to the situation where under the specific edict of the emperor, officers from the three legal branches came to sit together to try a case that was regarded as important or had significant impact nationwide.

Finally, there were no local courts. As noted, in the imperial period of China, the government was structured under a prefecture-county administrative scheme. Beginning with the *Qin* Dynasty, the local administration was divided into three levels: province, prefecture and county – all under the direct control of the central government. Unlike the central government that consisted of different branches or departments, the local executive office handled almost everything. The chief executive officer was not only the head of local administration, but also served as the judge. As such, a considerable amount of the local executive officer's daily work involved adjudicating cases, civil and criminal. In Chinese history, the local administrative office was commonly called "*Yamen*," referring to both the executive office and the courtroom.

The combination of executive and judiciary power into one office at the local level was a peculiar system that appeared throughout the feudal period of Chinese history. The underlying rationale was to ensure that the imperial power was not compromised, and the emperor retained control of the reins of the nation's

[103] The Office of Censors was renamed under the *Ming* Dynasty as the Council of Supervision.

judiciary. Unfortunately, as a consequence of such a system, the executive was superior to the judiciary and enjoyed the privilege of being able to interfere with judicial proceedings.[104]

Given his two-fold authority, executive and judiciary, a local chief officer was often nicknamed "parental officer" (*Fu Mu Guan*), meaning that such an officer had the right to determine the life of any person. Many of such officers often took their power for granted. Even at the present time, government officers at various levels, especially at the grassroots level, still consider themselves as, or prefer to be called, "parental officer."

4. CIVIL LAW INFLUENCE

The modern Chinese legal system bears a stronger resemblance to a civil law tradition than the Chinese legal tradition. Nothing here, however, is intended to implicate that the traditional Chinese legal system has no influence in the modern time. On the contrary, the legal philosophy and ideology that developed over the thousand-year history of the nation continues to have strong impacts on today's legal system. But in terms of legal structure as well as conceptual origin, the modern Chinese law does have its parentage from the civil law system.

Historically, China was known as a seclusive and self-sufficient country. Although there were some trade and other relations with foreign countries from dynasty to dynasty, the self-proclaimed "Great China" always regarded itself as the center of the world. Being bathed in that shining glory, emperors never really paid any attention to the world outside China but rather indulged themselves by receiving "tributes" (*Gong Ping* or *Jin Gong*) from foreign countries.

But in the late nineteenth century, the great glory of China was abruptly diminished when its imperial dignity was shattered by the cannons of foreign superpowers emerging from the Western industrial revolution. During the Opium Wars (1839–1842; 1856–1860), foreign invaders were able to infiltrate and occupy Chinese territory, ending the period of peace and isolation. At that time, China lost its capacity to resist foreign invasion and was completely unable to contend with foreign troops. A principal reason for the defeat was that China lagged far behind the Western world both politically and economically.

The end of China's seclusion was an immediate consequence of the Opium Wars, and the door of China was pushed open to the outside world. In defeat, China was left with no leverage to bargain and was essentially forced to sign many "unequal treaties." Eager to take advantage of China's weakened state, the major Western countries, later joined by Japan, established extraterritorial spheres of influence on Chinese soil. In those extraterritorial spheres of influence, Western nations created their own civil and criminal courts and foreign citizens were not subject to Chinese

[104] See Jinfan, *supra* note 9, at 214.

law. In other words, the extraterritoriality allowed these foreign nations to administer "Western justice" in their established "treaty ports" or "spheres of influence" within China.[105]

After the Opium Wars, Western influence began to take hold in China. Encountered with the unpleasant experience of foreign occupation, many in the Forbidden City struggled to find a "cure" to help revitalize the ailing country. As a result there grew an outcry for political and legal reforms. In response to advocacy by a group of reformists, Emperor *Guangxu* in 1902 issued an "Imperial Edict" ordering revision and amendment of the existing "Great *Qin* Codes" (*Da Qing Lv*).

A significant move in the process of law revision was the use of foreign laws as a reference. It was the first time ever in Chinese history that legal revision was made using Western legal models. In fact, many in China even believed that the country should follow the lead of powerful European countries and adopt a constitutional government.[106] For purposes of the reform, the emperor appointed jurists *Shen Jiaben* and *Wu Tingfang* as the commissioners of legal revision.[107] Both of them had great access to Western legal materials.

In addition, as part of the effort to examine foreign laws, many foreign legal books and articles were translated into Chinese. Moreover, scholars who had trained overseas introduced foreign laws and legal culture into China. For example, Wu Tingfang, one of the appointed commissioners in charge of legal revision, was himself a lawyer trained in London. In the meantime, a growing number of students were provided with government grants to study foreign law, and as a result, many of them received their legal education overseas, mainly in Europe.

It should be noted that the penetration of Western culture into Chinese tradition and the opening up of China to the outside world had quite a lot to do with foreign missionaries living in China during this period of time. In 1876, the total number of foreign missionaries was 473. Thirteen years later, in 1889, this figure went up to 1,296. In 1910, there were over 5,000 foreign missionaries throughout the country.[108] Although many of such missionaries were religion-related, their widely spreading presence in China significantly increased the country's exposure to foreign ideologies and social values.

[105] See Jerome A. Cohen, *Forward!* in The Rule of Law: Perspectives from the Pacific Rim, xi (The Mansfield Center for Pacific Affairs, 2000).

[106] Kevin O'Brien, Reform Without Liberalization, 13 (1990).

[107] See Wang Jiafu, Civil Law Obligatio, 17–18 (Law Press, 1999). Also in 1904, Emperor *Guangxu* issued an edict to Tsai Feng (Prince Chun), which stated: "The development of commercial relations, the encouragement to industry have always been the primary duty of the Government, and must be carefully attended to. We hereby order that Tsai Feng, Yuan Chih Kai and Wu Ting Fang be commissioned to compile a commercial code which will constitute the rule to be observed in commercial transactions." See Joseph En-Pao Wang, *China Studies*, in Civil Code of the Republic of China, x–xi, Studies in Chinese Government and Law (Kelly & Walsh, 1930), reprinted by University Publications of America, Inc. (1976).

[108] See Jinfan, *supra* note 9, at 295–296.

The legal reform further infused a movement known as "learning from the West" in China (*Yangwu Yundong*). In 1907, a national body – the Office of Legal Revision – was created to take charge of legal revision and law drafting. The Office of Legal Revision consisted of Chinese students who had returned from studying abroad in Japan, Europe and the United States. More strikingly, illustrating its intent to learn from the West, the Office of Legal Revision hired a Japanese jurist as an adviser on legal drafting for the imperial government. At that time, Japan had completed its civil and commercial codification, which was modeled primarily on the German codes.[109] In December 1910, the first draft of the Civil Code was completed and it was finalized in 1911.

The draft of the Civil Code was based mainly on German and Japanese laws. It contained five chapters, the first three of which were actually drafted by the Japanese jurist in the Office of Legal Revision.[110] In addition, during the drafting of the laws, many civil law concepts were borrowed and incorporated into the draft, and those concepts were also addressed in legal writing and legal textbooks as well. Moreover, Chinese legal scholars translated a number of laws and legal books of foreign countries into Chinese.

Notwithstanding the progress made on the Civil Code, it was never enacted into law. In 1911, the *Xinhai* Revolution (named after the year 1911 in Chinese, *Xinhai*) stormed China. The Revolution brought to an end the *Qing* Dynasty and led to the establishment of the Republic of China. Despite the Civil Code's doomed fate, the Revolution resulted in historic changes in the country. The emperor was dethroned and imperial power was destroyed. And as such, the traditional Chinese legal system that was centered on imperial supremacy ended in the country.

Nevertheless, after the 1911 Revolution, the newly formed government applied many of the provisions from the unfinished Civil Code, and in the meantime, drafting work resumed. The second draft, which was completed in 1925, essentially followed the blueprint of the first draft while enhancing its civil law features. Unfortunately, the power struggle among warlords created considerable political chaos during this period, and the second draft met the same fate as the first, never being completed.[111]

The enactment of a Civil Code in China finally came to fruition in 1930 under the National Government (or *Nanjing* Government because the capital of the country was in Nanjing at that time) led by Chiang Kai-shek (1887–1975), who ruled the country from 1927 to 1949. The 1930 Civil Code consisted of five parts, including "General Principles, Obligations, Rights over Things, Family and

[109] See Wang, *supra* note 107, at x–xi.

[110] The Japanese jurist was Mr. Y. M. Matsuoka. See *id.* at 18. During that reform period, with an anxiousness to follow Japan's experience in emerging from the old feudalism into a modern country, hundreds of Chinese in search of new knowledge went to Japan to study, and a significant number of them went to Japanese law schools. See *id.* at xi.

[111] See *id.* at 19.

Succession."[112] Since the Code was devised on the foundation of the first two drafts, it necessarily inherited the civil law tradition. In addition to its civil law style of division between general principles and specific provisions, the Code was replete with civil law concepts. For example, part III of the Code dealt with property rights, but it used the name "Rights over Things." "Things" is a term for property in civil law countries.

In addition to the 1930 Civil Code, five other major codes were promulgated between 1928 and 1937.[113] All together, these compositions were called "the Six Codes" or the "Code of Six Laws" (*Liu Fa Quan Shu*) and were compiled in the form of a corpus of law. Like the 1930 Civil Code, the other five codes also relied heavily on civil law tradition and contained many legal principles and rules taken from such countries as Germany, France, Italy, and Japan. The major categories of law, both conceptually and structurally, paralleled those commonly used in the civil law countries. For example, even the term "Six Codes" was imitated from the French "Five Codes" enacted after the 1789 French Revolution.[114]

The adoption of the "Six Codes" further altered the Chinese legal tradition in that the legal system shifted from the criminal-law-focused "hotchpotch" to a function-driven separation of laws. Put differently, it was a change from a single-code system to a system of multi-codes, each having a defined and different legal function. Perhaps at this level, the enactment of the "Six Codes" was heralded as the complete reception of civil law tradition in the country. Note, however, that the word "alter," as used here, is to mean that the Chinese legal tradition was changed, but not eliminated, as a result of embracing the civil law system in China.

In fact, the "Six Codes" retained quite a number of legal principles and rules from the *Qing* Code. One example was the use of "forced analogy" (*Bi Fu*) to help determine criminal offenses that were not readily found in the provisions of the code. More importantly, at least in the areas of legal philosophy and jurisprudence, despite the strong impacts of civil law tradition, no clear-cut distinction was ever made or could possibly be made between Chinese legal tradition and the contemporary legal system, especially with respect to the deeply rooted concept of "*Li*."

[112] Part I of the 1930 Civil Code was adopted on May 23, 1929, and took effect on October 10, 1929, parts II and III were promulgated in November 1920 and effective May 30, 1930, and parts IV and V were enacted at the end of 1930. See Joseph En-Pao Wang, Civil Code of the Republic of China, Studies in Chinese Government and Law (University Publications of America, 1976 [1930]).

[113] The Six Codes included "Constitutional Law, Civil Law, Civil Procedure Law, Criminal Law, Criminal Procedure Law, and Administrative Law." At the beginning, there was no Administrative Law, but there was Commercial Law. Later on, Administrative Law was adopted, and then Commercial Law was merged into both Civil Law and Administrative Law.

[114] The French "Five Codes" consisted of "Civil Code," "Commercial Code," "Code of Civil Procedures," "Code of Criminal Procedures," and "Penal Code." Although the French Constitution was adopted later, the name "Five Codes" was not changed. In Japan, when the French Codes were translated into Japanese, they were named the Book of French Laws.

In addition, the clan-based ethic standard and totalitarian structure of bureaucrats remained influential.

As noted, since the *Qin* Dynasty, each dynasty in China followed a pattern of having a highly centralized state power with an expansive reach over every corner of the country and ultimate control of people. After the last emperor was dethroned in 1911, many revolutionaries, including Dr. *Sun Yat-sen* and his followers, still believed that it was necessary to establish a government that had an "all-purpose" function, with each individual under government power, ready to sacrifice their personal interests in order to preserve such power.[115]

In addition, as discussed, Dr. *Sun Yat-sen* premised his idea of revolution on the three basic principles of nationalism, democracy, and people's livelihood. He characterized these principles as the doctrine of "Three Principles of People" (*San Min Zhu Yi*).[116] But what Dr. *Sun* actually tried to promote was a so-called guided democracy. Under this guided democracy, a strong government role was needed in the country because people in China were not ready yet to exercise democracy.[117] Dr. *Sun* believed that the Chinese did not have too much government but rather too little.[118] According to Dr. *Sun*, Chinese people were too backward and undeveloped, and they needed to have a strong government to lead them.[119]

But indeed, between the legal reform in the late *Qing* Dynasty and the adoption of the Six Codes by the Nationalist government in the 1930s, China's legal system evolved, developing traits of civil law tradition. First, the codes or statutes became the primary source of law, while previous case law was not generally recognized to have a binding effect. Although court decisions may constitute an important source to supplement the statutes, such decisions, in order to be binding, must meet two requirements under the system of Six Codes: (a) the decisions must be made by the Supreme Court, and (b) the decisions must be reviewed and approved as "precedent" by the Judicial Council of Central Authorities (*Si Fa Yuan*).[120]

[115] See *id.* at 416–417.

[116] The Three Principles of the People refer to Democracy, Nationalism, and People's Livelihood, see Sun Yat-sen, Three Principles of the People (China Publishing Co., 1963). The three principles were incorporated into the Constitution of the Republic of China, promulgated in 1947.

[117] See Richard Hooker, *Modern China*, available at www.wsu.edu:8080/~dee/MODCHINA/SUN.HTM.

[118] See Paul M. A. Linebarger, The Political Doctrine of Sun Yat-sen: An Exposition of the San Min Chu I, 102 (Johns Hopkins Press, 1937).

[119] See Kerry Brown, Friends and Enemies: The Past, Present and Future of Communist China, 37 (Anthem Press, 2009).

[120] The Judicial Council of Central Authorities (JCCA) was the highest judicial body of the nation and now still exists in Taiwan. Currently, the JCCA, consisting of fifteen judges, is mainly responsible for interpreting the Constitution, laws, and regulations. It also serves as an administrative body in charge of the Supreme Court.

Second, the laws or statutes were enacted in the common pattern of a civil law system. The manifestation of such a pattern related to the structural layout of the laws or statutes and consisted of two major parts: the general provisions and the specific provisions. Although the general provisions appear to be vague, they served a dual function: to set the tone for the law and guidance for its application, and to determine cases as primary legal authority if no specific provision in the law could be readily applied.

5. SOCIALIST LEGAL SYSTEM AND TRADITIONAL HERITAGE

As discussed, the current legal system in China is characterized as a socialist legal system with Chinese characteristics. Although the legal system is a product of modern development, especially the economic reforms after 1979, it retains a great deal of traditions formed in China's thousand-year history. The traditions that are clearly discernible in the current system include the highly centralized government structure, syncretism of family and state, officialdom culture, and obedience and loyalty virtue

The traditional Chinese government was structured as an autocratic system of centralization under which the central government retains all power, leaving the local government with little independence in any respect of governance. As noted, ever since the *Qin* Dynasty, the centralization of power had become a mainstay of government organization in China throughout the entire imperial period. After the People's Republic of China was founded in 1949, the social and political systems in the country changed dramatically, but the centralized government structure stayed mostly unchanged.

It is generally believed in China that the concept of centralization of power was introduced by *Han Fei*. As aforementioned, *Han Fei* was a legalist who helped the King of *Qin* become the first emperor of China. According to *Han Fei*, things are scattered everywhere, but the key to get them under control is in the center; when the sage holds the key in his hand, the meritorious services pour into him from all directions.[121] Thus *Han Fei* believed that the power and authority of the country should be centralized in the hands of the ruler, and the ruler should retain such power and authority in an automatic and unfeeling way.[122]

The centralized power system promoted by *Han Fei* was aimed at ensuring that the emperor had the highest power in the country and control over the government through the state bureaucracy under the prefecture-county administrative scheme. The underlying notion is that the imperial power is supreme and indivisible, and the imperial authority is non-transferable but hereditary.

[121] See *Han Feizi*, Wielding Power (Burton Watson trans.) (Columbia University Press, 2003), available in PDF at https://terebess.hu/zen/mesterek/Han-Feizi.pdf.

[122] See Lee Dian Rainey, Confucius and Confucianism: The Essentials, 84 (2010).

Han Fei and other legalists propelled centralization of state power into the hands of the emperor and established a bureaucratic pattern for Chinese politics that lasted for nearly two thousand years. No subsequent dynasty has ever attempted to dismantle it. State power remains centralized in China at the present time. In other words, centralization of power still dominates the state bureaucratic system.

However, in contrast to tradition, the current government structure possesses several distinctive features. First, it is not a monarchy but has a centralized administrative management under the leadership of the Communist Party of China (CPC). Second, the centralization does not represent a relationship between the emperor and his subjects but mainly deals with central and local governments. Third, the ultimate decision-making power is in the hands of the central government, and all resources of the country are subject to allocation by the central government. Fourth, the unitary system ensures the uniformity of the state and top-down administration.

Ever since the CPC took power, the country has been struggling with the balance of power between the central and local governments. The focal point of the issue is whether the local governments should have autonomous power to decide their own affairs in order to achieve administrative efficiency. In the planned economy era of 1949 to 1978, the state controlled everything through highly centralized plans. During economic reforms, attempts were made to loosen the tight control and allow local governments to share power. But the question never resolved was how much power the local governments may have.

In recent years, there has been a growing tendency in China to strengthen the centralized power of the state government. The tendency is being underscored by the signified role of the CPC in the government. The past few decades have witnessed a strong call in the country for political reform, and a major part of the suggested reform was separating the party from state administration. But the possibility of such reform seems to have significantly diminished with the escalation of control the CPC has over the country.

To justify the power centralization, the current Chinese leadership often uses China's cultural and historical tradition as a reference point. The ideologies from both *Confucian* and legalist philosophers are frequently drawn as models, while emphasizing the governing principle that "east, west, south, north and center, the party is leader of all." In addition, since 2013, the CPC has officially launched a campaign against such Western values as universalism, judicial independence, checks and balances, civil society, and individual liberty, and put in place core socialist values instead. As will be discussed, the core socialist values bear a strong resemblance to Chinese tradition.

The syncretism of family and state is a concept of the homogeneous relationship between home and country. In Chinese traditional culture, family is a fundamental element of the patriarchal society, and the state has the same organizational structure as a family. Under this culture, both family and state are governed by kinship-clan-based paternalism – a social system, as noted, in which the father or eldest male is head of the family and descent is traced through the male line.

The idea of family and state relationship is an important source of ancient Chinese state governance and represents an externalization of the patriarchal hierarchy. As a strong social integration force, it emphasizes stabilization of the social order beginning from individual self-cultivation to the coordination of family ethical relations, and finally to the harmony of the country. In short, under the family and state syncretism, the father is considered the "monarch of the family," while the emperor is the "father of the country," reflecting an intimate relationship between the family and the state.

An important aspect of the family and state syncretism is that equivalent to the responsibility of the father in a family, the ruler of the country has the duty to exercise his authority to instruct and educate his people in order to effectively rule the country. The social consequence of the family and state syncretism is that people are accustomed to being led, and the ruler is obsessed with the desire to take the lead. As discussed, government officials in China are often labeled as "parental officers." The term "parental officer" exemplifies such a syncretic relationship between the family and the state.

The legacy of the Chinese traditional family and state syncretism continues to influence Chinese society today. Many in China still believe that inheriting tradition and reconstructing an idea of home and country isomorphism will help promote the Chinese spirit, enhance the cohesion of all people, and provide a theoretical basis for the construction of a harmonious socialist society.[123] At the present time, China's highly centralized administrative structure and the legal system interwoven with traditional ethics and family values constitute the country's political thread and social fiber.

The officialdom culture is premised on the official-centered or official-oriented ideology that holds government officials more valuable and more esteemed than the common people. A notable feature of the officialdom is that official ranking is the primary standard to determine a person's social status and political elite standing.[124] Originating from *Shang Yang*'s view of "culture valuing officials," the official-centered ideology formed a Chinese traditional social value that focuses mainly on officials – treasuring them, respecting them, and following them. *Shang Yang* divided culture into three types: in the highest antiquity, people loved their relatives and were fond of what was their own; in middle antiquity, they

[123] For a detailed discussion on family and state syncretism, see Shih Yuan-Kang, *The Isomorphism of Family and State and the Integration of Church and State: On the Differences between the Confucian Political Tradition and Democratic Politics*, in Tian Yu Cao, Xueping Zhong, & Liao Kebin, eds., Culture and Social Transformations in Reform Era China, 97–118 (Brill, 2010).

[124] See Gino LaPaglia, The Cultural Roots of Strategic Intelligence, 159–162 (Lexington Books, 2020).

honored talent and talked of moral virtue; and in later days, they prized nobles and respected officials.[125]

After *Qin* adopted *Shang Yang*'s idea to establish the first dynasty unifying China, the official-centered ideology became a value system that deeply penetrated into every level of Chinese society. The centralization of power further enhanced the noble status of officials and developed the official-centered notion into an officialdom culture in which the emperor was the supreme leader of the country and the bureaucratic hierarchy was the ruling force of society. Given the power in their hands, government officials could do whatever they wished, subject only to the likes or dislikes of their superiors.

Closely associated with the officialdom is the traditional virtue of loyalty and obedience. As noted, filial piety is the core value of Confucianism. The centerpiece of filial piety consists of loyalty and obedience. There are three levels where loyalty and obedience are preserved as traditional moral standards. The first level is the national level, at which all ruled must be loyal and obedient to the ruler, and it is not tolerable for anyone to boldly challenge government power. The second level is the family level. Within a family, the father shall always maintain the controlling authority, and it is morally required that all younger members respect and are obedient to the elders. The third level is the social level. In all social activities or settings, the authorities should be redeemed and highly regarded.

It is true that the virtue of loyalty and obedience now is not the same as it should be under the tradition, especially at the family level. But the virtue as such remains strongly influential at both national and social levels. For example, children in China at a very young age are instilled with the idea that the CPC is always and forever correct. Thus, it is vital to become determined to listen to the CPC, follow the CPC, and never deviate from the CPC's line. Another example is that it is rare in China for those at junior levels to openly challenge or question those at senior levels within government or in any other place.

There are at least two distinctive features of officialdom culture. One is that the official position or rank is a social standard of a person's career achievement. Such a position or rank not only means power or authority but also implicates benefits. In other words, holding a government position is an effective shortcut to becoming rich. As a result, it becomes a common scenario for people to seek and preserve official positions by any means, and to rely on their official status to obtain benefits and bring glory to their family and ancestors.

The other feature of officialdom culture is that government officials are not responsible to the people but to their superiors, and ultimately to the top leader. There are several attributes to this feature. The first attribute is the standard of social value. It is quite common in China that the career achievement of a person is not

[125] See The Book of Lord *Shang*, VII, Opening the Blocked, edited and translated by Yuri Pines (Columbia University Press, 2017).

judged by social contribution but by their position in the government. Under this standard, official ranking becomes a key indicator of success in career pursuits because the ranking in a government position not only represents social status but also brings lifetime privileges and other material gains.

The second attribute is the system of government official selection. In history, government officials were mainly selected via an imperial examination system. In most cases, only those who passed the examination might be dispatched to hold government positions at different levels. At the present time, the CPC has a settled process for selecting government officials, and the officers for major government posts are all appointed through an internal selection mechanism. Such an appointment also applies to the presidents of universities and CEOs of all state-owned enterprises. Even for people's delegates in congress, they are either assigned or predetermined, and in almost every case, the election of a delegate is just a formality or a "procedural walk-through." Because the delegates have no constituency, none of them need to be responsible to voters.

Again, for the government officials who are either dispatched or appointed, what really matters is their ability to work to the satisfaction of their superiors. Since both promotion and demotion of government officials largely depend on how the superior views their work performance, to secure faster career growth, nothing is more important than maintaining close ties with the superior.

The third attribute is the lack of civil society. China never really had a civil society that comprised groups or organizations for the interest of the citizens and was independent from the government and businesses. Chinese citizens enjoy no freedom to engage in political advice or launch campaigns outside the realm or control of party rule. Therefore, unless substantial political reform takes place, the official-centered culture inherited from history will continue to dominate Chinese society.

The handling of outbreaks of the 2012 SARS (Severe Acute Respiratory Syndrome) and the 2019 COVID (CO for "corona," "VI" for "virus," and "D" for disease, commonly called coronavirus) in China provide good examples of China's officialdom culture. On November 16, 2002, the first case of SARS was reported in the Guangdong province in southern China. However, due to concern about social stability, which is the key element for their job evaluation, officials asked doctors not to report new cases when SARS spread to Beijing, and censored the doctors to ensure secrecy of the epidemic disease. The cover-up resulted in the rapid spread of the illness. Over the next several months, 8,096 people in 26 countries contracted the new viral illness, leading to 774 deaths.

Similarly, in late 2019, COVID originated in Wuhan in the Hubei province of China. When eight people, including an eye doctor who himself was infected, whistle-blew about the possible spread of the disease, they were immediately admonished or reprimanded by the police under instruction from the city government and were demanded to sign a paper of repentance promising not to disperse any such information in the public. The doctor died from COVID infection weeks later. The spreading COVID soon became a global public health emergency and was declared a global pandemic by the World Health Organization (WHO) in early 2020.

The death of the whistle-blowing doctor generated tremendous public outrage about the government and the country's censorship.[126] When asked at a press conference why they did not disclose the epidemic disease in a timely manner, the Mayor of Wuhan answered: "I had the information, but I was not authorized to disclose it." The implication of the Wuhan Mayor's answer is that as a government officer, his accountability is owed primarily to the leaders above him. The nation-wide lockdowns during the COVID period, as noted, further reflected the mentality of Chinese government officials.

Both the SARS and COVID situations perfectly exemplify the officialdom culture in China. Clearly, the official-centered bureaucratic system has produced two major consequences: the power is highly centralized in the hands of the core leaders, and government officials in general lack any kind of boldness to move forward on their own initiative. Government officials at every level would do anything possible to please their superiors in order to keep their position and rank, because government position ranks are essentially a combination of power, privilege, honor and wealth.

As noted, an ideal government under *Mencius*'s view was one that would put the people first. According to *Mencius*, the common people are the most valuable; next is the national altar of the soil and grain; the ruler is insignificant. Thus, it was *Mencius's* belief that only the person who can gain the hearts of the common people would be the ruler, and those who had the confidence of the ruler could become the bureaucrats.[127] This view, however, was only taken as a ruling strategy and accepted under the condition that the supreme authority of the rulers would not be challenged.

The concept of putting people first is also received by the CPC as a governing strategy. In 2003, when the former Chinese President Hu Jintao introduced his doctrine "Scientific Outlook," "putting people first" became a major policy pursuit in the country. President Xi Jinping, Hu's successor, illustrated his "China Dream" to also include the idea of putting people first. But as a governing policy, putting

[126] See Doug Stanglin, *Death of Doctor Who Warned about the Coronavirus Triggers National Backlash over China's Censorship*, USA Today, February 7, 2020, available at www.usatoday.com/story/news/world/2020/02/07/coronavirus-doctor-li-wenliang-death-china-censors-anger-speech/4688827002/. On March 18, 2020, the Chinese government rescinded Dr. Li's penalty in order to assuage public anger about the government's action to cover up the spread of the disease at the beginning of the pandemic. See Chun Han Wong, *China Rescinds the Penalty for Late Doctor who Warned about the Coronavirus*, The Wall Street Journal, March 19, 2020, available at www.wsj.com/articles/china-rescinds-penalty-for-late-doctor-who-warned-about-coronavirus-11584637545.

[127] See *Mengzi*, "*Jin Xin* (II)," an English translation is in Mencius Selections by A. Charles Muller, available at www.acmuller.net/con-dao/mencius.html.

people first now has little to do with the political power of the people but instead the welfare of people.

According to Xi, people look forward to better education, a more stable job, a more satisfactory income, and expect their children to grow up, work and live better. Thus, to put people first is said to help people realize their dream. Since Xi took the reins of the CPC in 2012, "China Dream" has become a signature slogan of his political ambition. But questions remain as to what the dream as described by Xi actually refers to and how people can really benefit from it. While hanging the banner of "China Dream," Xi firmly emphasizes that the CPC-led one-party totalitarian system must be preserved in China. A mandate is that CPC leadership, with Xi as the core, must be upheld over all forms of work in the country.[128]

[128] See Zheping Huang, *Xi Jinping Says China's Totalitarian System Can Be a Model for the World*, Quartz, March 9, 2018, available at https://qz.com/1225347/xi-jinping-says-chinas-one-party-authoritarian-system-can-be-a-model-for-the-world/.

2

Theoretical Foundation of Modern Chinese Law

INTRODUCTION

Contemporary Chinese law and legal system are established on the basis of Chinese legal tradition, the civil law model, and socialist ideology. Chinese legal tradition, as noted, consists of *Confucian* heritage and legalist thoughts, which significantly shaped Chinese legal culture and remain strongly influential today in many aspects. As discussed, *Confucianism* cast great emphasis on personal cultivation and self-perfection under the "*Li*," but it ignored personal liberty and individual freedom, especially ideological and political freedom. Similarly, the Legalists despised individual thoughts and deprived private property.

In addition, *Confucianism* advocated social harmony that was often achieved at the cost of individual interests. It had been a prevalent rule that when conflicts arose between individuals and society, individuals must always give in to society. A dictate of *Confucianism* was that in order to "govern the country, manage the family, and maintain social stability," individuals must "examine themselves three times a day," which made obedience of subordinates to superiors an established virtue. It is such virtue that becomes the soil for the officialdom to grow in the country.

More generally, the focal point of both *Confucianism* and *Legalism* was the maintenance of absolute authority of imperial power. Thus, the public may act against corrupt officials, but never the ruling authority. A long-lasting sequela produced by this tradition was that people in China always hoped for wise rulers and wise ministers, and had no knowledge or even consciousness that government power or public authority should be limited.

The civil law model mainly refers to the structure of law and basic rules, especially in regulating civil affairs. Socialist ideology comprises the governing legal principles and conceptual underpinnings of social and ethical norms. Premised on the legal tradition, civil law model, and socialist ideology is the concept of the socialist legal system with Chinese characteristics that defines the nature of the current law and legal system in China.

The legal theory or jurisprudence that underlies such a nature determines the operative boundary of legal institutions, the contextual scope of legal reasoning, and ultimately the role and function of law. In the Western atmosphere, several modern legal schools of thought in the study of law have been developed. China, however, takes its own route to address the law in light of Chinese characteristics.

The theoretical foundation of law is concerned with, among others, the basic understanding of law and the essential elements of the legal system. The perception of law in a society affects the governance of the society, including such important factors as the behavioral norms, moral standards, and social justice. The legal system consists of a social environment in which the law exists and functions, and a process in which the law is enacted, interpreted, and enforced.

1. GOVERNING IDEOLOGY

China is a country where ideology plays an important role in the nation's governance. In a society, there is always a dominant ideology representing the basic values, morals, and beliefs held by the majority of people, which reflects the nature and character of the society. China, however, takes a different path. The dominant ideology in China is the ideology adopted by the ruling authority as a means of social and ideological control. Thus, an ideology becomes dominant not because most people share it, but because it is the governing ideology set forth by the government for the country.

As discussed, in the Spring-Autumn and Warring States period, each small state attempted to become strong and powerful so that it could take over others. To that end, the states competed to retain elite scholars or philosophers to work on ruling strategies, which prompted many schools of thought to contend with each other. As a result, there developed such major ideological doctrines as *Confucianism*, *Legalism*, *Taoism*, and *Mohism*. As discussed, since the *Han* Dynasty, *Confucianism* had become the orthodox ideology supplemented by *Legalism* for the entire imperial period in the country's history.

Again, the imperial model of governance that lasted nearly two thousand years in China was a combination of *Confucian* ideology and legalist means. Externally, the system was based on *Confucian* "*Li*," while internally, the country was ruled under the mechanism of legalist "*Fa*." In addition, the *Taoist* doctrine was also employed to help buffer the tension between the ruler and the ruled. To be more specific, under the imperial governance model, *Confucianism* was aimed at constructing the "benevolent government"; *Legalism* was intended to maintain social order so that the imperial authority would not be challenged. The *Taoist* doctrine was used as a lubricant to alleviate social contradictions and promote social harmony and development.

Confucianism as the governing ideology faded away after the Opium Wars. In order to search for a solution to the weakening state of the nation, China started to turn its eyes to the Western countries that arose powerfully after the eighteenth-century industrial revolution. As a result, several waves of learning from the West developed in the nation. The first one was the Westernization Movement, which took place in the 1860s. It was a nationwide initiative to revive the country through Western studies, aiming to introduce Western science, technology, literature, doctrines, and ideology into China. Given its purpose, the Westernization Movement was also called "Self-reliance" or the "Self-strengthening" Movement.

However, the Westernization Movement failed in the end due to the loss of the Beiyang Marine Division in a war against Japanese troops. The Movement, nevertheless, changed China significantly. It brought to China modern industrial systems including banking, postal service, railways, and heavy industry, which helped to reduce the gap between China and the world in many aspects. More importantly, the Western ideas China learned stayed and grew in the country despite the doomed fate of the Westernization Movement. Students who studied abroad acquired both knowledge and skills, and their understanding of Western science and technology became a significant driving force for China's future development.

Following the Westernization Movement was the 1898 Reform Movement. As noted, the reform was led by a group of reformists, including *Kang Youwei* and *Liang Qichao*, with the support of Emperor *Guangxu*. The main purpose of the reform was, through learning from the West, to reshape the country's political as well as educational system. Among its ambitious plans, the reform intended to restructure government institutions, abolish redundant officials, encourage the establishment of private industrial and mining enterprises, open new schools to attract talent, translate Western books and new ideas, establish newspapers, and promote open speech.

As part of learning from the West, reformists put great effort into translating foreign legal and political books and materials, and many of them wrote books and articles on a comparative basis to help boost public awareness of Western civilization. The most notable person is *Liang Qichao*, who was one of the most influential reformists in the late *Qing* Dynasty. In 1899, *Liang* published his famous book *Differences and Similarities of Constitutions in Various Countries*, in which *Liang* illustrated the Western concept of separation of powers from a comparative perspective.[1]

In order to promote legal reform in China, *Liang* also created a biweekly journal known as "*New Citizen*" in 1902. As the chief editor of the journal, *Liang* himself wrote several articles to disseminate the idea of democracy and the notion of a republic. Among the articles, the one entitled "The Doctrine of Montesquieu, a Jurisprudence Scholar," was a major piece in which *Liang* focused on introducing

[1] See Han Xiuqi, Judicial Independence and Modern China, 97 (Tsinghua University Press, 2003).

to the public the essence and meaning of law through Montesquieu's work "The Spirit of Laws."[2]

The Reform Movement, however, lasted only 103 days and aborted after Emperor *Guangxu* was detained by Empress *Dowager Cixi*. The reason why *Cixi* withdrew her support of the reform is a debatable topic for historians, but the goal of the Reform, to develop the capitalist economy and establish a constitutional monarchy in the country, was considered a threat to *Cixi*'s power and to the interests of the conservative bloc around *Cixi*. Nevertheless, a legacy of the Reform Movement was that the Western breeze further touched the country so as to shake the ideological basis of the ruling *Confucian* orthodoxy.

The third wave came after the Reform Movement, represented by the 1911 Revolution (*Xinhai* Revolution). It was the revolution that brought to an end the entire imperial system that existed in China for two thousand years. A revolt against the *Qing* Dynasty, the 1911 Revolution completely overthrew the monarchy and established a republican government in China. A significance of the 1911 Revolution was that it spread democratic ideas throughout the country and laid a foundation for the reconstruction of a new China. Dr. *Sun Yat-sen*'s notion of the "Three Principles of the People" and the "Five-Power Constitution" became the guiding ideology of the nation.[3] This ideology now remains influential in Taiwan, while mainland China has moved in a different direction.

In the early twentieth century, a group of revolutionists, including *Chen Duxiu*, *Li Dazhao*, *Hu Shi*, *Lu Xun*, *Qian Xuantong*, and *Cai Yuanpei*, led a new initiative known as the New Cultural Movement, the fourth wave of learning from the West. Aimed at fighting against tradition, namely centralism and totalitarianism, the New Cultural Movement advocated for democratic republicanism modeled on Eurocentrism (European civilization). The climax of the New Cultural Movement was the May Fourth Movement – an anti-imperialist and anti-feudalist cultural and political movement that grew out of student protests in Beijing on May 4, 1919. The students took to the streets to protest against the treaty signed by the government allowing Japan to retain the territories in Shandong that had been surrendered by Germany.

Among the revolutionists, both *Chen Duxiu* and *Li Dazhao* were also the framers and founders of the Communist Party of China (CPC). In 1915, as part of his effort to boost the *New Cultural Movement*, *Chen Duxiu* created a vernacular publication "*New Youth*" where he published a series of articles promoting the concepts of "Mr. *De*" and "Mr. *Sai*." "Mr. *De*" referred to "democracy," while "Mr. *Sai*" represented

[2] See Complete Works of Liang Chi-chao, Vol. IV, "A *Journey to the New World*," 1039–1044 (Beijing Press, 1999).

[3] Five Powers refers to the five branches of government, namely executive, legislative, judicial, civil service examination, and supervision branches. For general discussion, see Frederick Tse-shyang Chen, *Dr. Sun Yat-sen's Five-Power Constitution: Theory and Practice*, 2011, available at https://aacs.ccny.cuny.edu/2011conference/Papers/Chen,%20Frederick.pdf.

"science." Believing that the young generation should become a fresh impetus for democratic reform in China, *Chen*, in his article entitled "*An Advice to the Youth*," asked Chinese young people to become "independent not submissive; progressive not conservative; outspoken not reserved; cosmopolitan not parochial; practical not formalist; and scientific not imaginative."[4]

Externally, in 1917, the October Revolution led by Lenin took place in Russia. The revolution had significant impacts on China. First, it brought to China *Marxism-Leninism* and proletarian class theory. Second, it changed the direction of the New Cultural Movement from pro-Western democracy to pro-*Marxist* ideology. Third, it paved the way for, and contributed to, the birth of the CPC. Lastly, the 1917 October Revolution shifted the course of China from the practice of the "Three People's Principles" to the pursuit of communism.

Thus, from the 1911 Revolution to the 1919 May Fourth Movement, China experienced dramatic changes both politically and ideologically. In Chinese history, the 1911 Revolution was considered a milestone that marked a new era for the country. Many in China believed that the 1911 Revolution not only summoned the arrival of the New Culture Movement and the May Fourth Movement, but also opened the channel for the dissemination of Marxism in the nation.[5] *Chen Duxiu* and other radical democrats in intellectual circles inherited and developed the fruits of the 1911 Revolution's ideological emancipation movement and ushered Chinese ideological emancipation to a new stage of development. More significantly, the wide spread of *Marxist* theory led to the birth of the CPC, and in the meantime helped form the ideological foundation for the CPC.[6]

After the CPC took control of China in 1949, *Marxism-Leninism* became the official ideology governing all political and social aspects of the nation. In his speech at the first session of the First National People's Congress in 1954, *Mao* in particular made it a creed for the nation that the "core force leading our cause is the Communist Party of China and the theoretical basis guiding our thinking is *Marxism-Leninism*."[7] Ever since, *Marxist* theory has been the fundamental ideology governing the country, although a vast majority of people have little knowledge about *Marxist* theory.

[4] "New Youth" was originally published under the name "Youth Magazine" in the first year. "An Advice to the Youth" was an inaugural introduction Chen wrote himself to the "Youth Magazine" published on September 15, 1915. See Youth Magazine, Vol. 1, No. 1, at www.360doc.com/content/15/0826/23/259476_495062878.shtml.

[5] See Jin Chongji, *The Historic Status of Xinhai Revolution: In What Aspects Did It Change China?* People's Daily, September 13, 2011, available at www.cppcc.gov.cn/2011/09/13/ARTI1315894977638363.shtml.

[6] See He Qiying, *Inheritance and Transcendence: The Chinese Communist Party and the Xinhai Revolution*, 38 J. of Hubei U. (Phil. & Soc. Sci.) 44 (2011), available at https://core.ac.uk/download/pdf/41452325.pdf.

[7] See Mao Zedong, *Speech at the First Session of the First National People's Congress of China*, People's Daily, September 15, 1954, available at https://cn.govopendata.com/renminribao/1954/9/15/1/#114790.

As discussed, *Marxism* is the philosophic doctrine based on the works of Karl Marx, a philosopher and revolutionist in the nineteenth century, and is the founding ideology of communism. With the notion of dialectical materialism, *Marxism* holds a belief that political and historical events result from the conflict of social forces and are interpretable as a series of contradictions and their solutions.[8] Underlying the conflict or contradiction is the theory of class struggle between the proletarian (working class) and the capitalist (exploiting class). According to *Marxism*, social development is a process of class struggle, and revolution is the driving force of social changes.[9]

Leninism is held as *Marxism* in the era of imperialism and the proletarian revolution.[10] During the course of the Russian Revolution, *Leninism* developed the proletarian theory and put in motion the concept of a proletarian dictatorship as part of the efforts of socialist construction.[11] *Mao Zedong* (*Tsetung*) Thought is acclaimed as a product of the combination of *Marxism-Leninism* with Chinese revolutionary practice.[12] *Mao*, however, overly expanded the theory of class struggle, making it a core element of socialist construction.

According to *Mao*, each society is full of contradictions, but there is always one primary contradiction that dominates all others. In the historical period of socialism, there were classes, class contradictions, and class struggle. Class struggle is the primary or major contradiction in the socialist society of China – it is the struggle between the socialist road and the capitalist road.[13] It was *Mao*'s view that as long as class struggle is dealt with properly, all other contradictions would then be resolved. Thus, without proper handling of class struggle, the socialist system of China would turn into its opposite and degenerate, and a capitalist restoration would take place. *Mao* especially emphasized that people must be reminded of class struggle yearly, monthly, and even daily. He made it a mandate to never forget classes and never forget class struggle. It was Mao's strong belief that "class struggle is the key link, everything else hinges on it."[14]

Ever since *Mao* managed to infuse *Marxist* theory with Chinese practices, it has become a general pattern in the country that the application of *Marxist* theory is always associated with the ideas of the CPC leader. In *Mao*'s era, the ruling ideology

[8] See Stanford Encyclopedia of Philosophy, *Karl Marx*, available at https://plato.stanford.edu/entries/marx/. See also, Massalijn, *Marxism-Leninism-Maoism Basic Course*, available at http://massalijn.nl/theory/marxism-leninism-maoism-basic-course/.

[9] See *Karl Marx*, *supra* note 8.

[10] See Massalijn, *supra* note 8.

[11] See *id.*

[12] See the CPC, *Resolution on Certain Historical Issues of the Party since the Founding of the People's Republic of China*, Adopted at the Sixth Plenary Session of the 11th Central Committee of the CPC on June 27, 1981, available at https://special.chaoxing.com/mobile/mooc/tocourse/88888246.

[13] See *id.*

[14] See Jeremy Brown, Maoism at the Grassroots (Harvard University Press, 2015).

was stated as "*Marxism-Leninism and Mao Zedong Thought.*" When the 1982 Constitution was amended in 1999, it was modified as "*Marxism-Leninism, Mao Zedong* Thought and *Deng Xiaoping* Theory." The 2004 Amendment to the 1982 Constitution made *Jiang Zemin*'s "Three Represents" a component of the ruling ideology.[15]

Again, in 2018, the 1982 Constitution was amended to include in the country's ruling ideology the former President *Hu Jintao*'s "Scientific Outlook on Development" doctrine and *Xi Jinping*'s Thought. Now, under the Chinese Constitution as amended in 2018, the ruling ideology of the country is defined as *Marxism-Leninism, Mao Zedong* Thought, *Deng Xiaoping* Theory, the important thought of Three Represents, the Scientific Outlook on Development, and *Xi Jinping* Thought on Socialism with Chinese Characteristics for a New Era.[16]

Deng Xiaoping abandoned *Mao*'s class struggle theory and turned the course of the country to economic development. Unlike Mao, who was fond of mass political campaigns, Deng took a more pragmatic approach to reshape China's move toward economic development. According to Deng, "it doesn't matter if a cat is black or white so long as it catches mice."[17] In pursuit of his "cat" theory, Deng launched vast economic reform in China, which brought the country to the modern stage. *Jiang Zemin*'s "Three Represents" approach is nothing more than an ideological reformulation of Mao's slogan of "Serve the People." In *Jiang*'s own words, the basic requisites for implementing the Three Represents are, "in essence, to advance with the times, maintain the Party's advanced nature and administer the country in the interests of the people."[18]

The Scientific Outlook on Development was an idea introduced by *Hu Jintao* in 2003 for further economic development. The idea was formulated as a political means "against the backdrop of rapid economic growth and a series of problems including excessive consumption of resources, serious environmental pollution and a widening gap between the rich and poor,"[19] and then was escalated to become the

[15] It was the first time in China that an abbreviation appeared in the Constitution. The concept of "Three Represents" was introduced by then President *Jiang Zemin* in 2000 as a guiding social and political theory for the party and then was extended to serve as a guiding principle for the country. According to Jiang, the CPC represents the advanced productive forces, represents the progressive course of China's advanced culture, and represents the fundamental interests of the majority of the people. See the Central Committee of the CPC, *On the Three Represents*, available at https://web.archive.org/web/20040925080450/http://www.idcpc.org.cn/english/policy/3represents.htm.

[16] See 1982 Constitution of China (as amended in 2018), Preamble, available at www.gov.cn/xinwen/2018-03/22/content_5276319.htm.

[17] See Deng Xiaoping, *How to Restore Agricultural Production*, in *Selected Works of Deng Xiaoping*, 322–327 (People's Press, 1994 [1962]).

[18] China Daily, *Three Represents*, July 10, 2007, available at www.chinadaily.com.cn/china/2007-07/10/content_6142053.htm.

[19] See China Daily, *Scientific Outlook on Development Becomes CPC's Theoretical Guidance*, November 18, 2012, available at http://usa.chinadaily.com.cn/2012-11/08/content_15892786.htm.

theoretical guidance of the CPC. The concept, as explained officially in China, contains two basic components: (a) advancement of people's interests and (b) maintenance of comprehensive, coordinated, and sustainable development.[20]

In the post-*Mao* period, the ruling ideology in China has become a moving target and has constantly been updated along with the change of leadership of the CPC. Each update reflected a shift of the propaganda priority at a given time, and more importantly, resulted in an amendment to the Constitution. Interestingly, since *Deng*'s theory was added to the 1982 Constitution, the ruling ideology in China has become more policy-driven, more tediously worded, and more obscure in substance.

A significant part of the 2018 amendment was to enshrine the guiding role of *Xi Jinping* Thought. In making *Xi*'s Thought the mainstay of the ruling ideology of the country, the 2018 Amendment expands the words of the ruling ideology to a total of forty-six Chinese characters.[21] In addition, as noted, the 2018 amendment lifted the two-term limit set by *Deng Xiaoping* for the top leader of the country, paving the way for *Xi* to sit on the top of the country for as long as he wishes. With regard to *Xi*'s Thought, although in essence it does not appear much different from that of his predecessors, a lot of efforts have been made to advocate the novelty of it, signifying that the country is now under the leadership of *Xi*.

Despite the unwavering advocacy for the importance of *Xi*'s Thought, there is not a clear definition of what Xi's Thought is exactly about. An official summary of *Xi*'s Thought states that it includes "Eight Definitenesses and Fourteen Adherences."[22]

[20] See *id.*

[21] It is believed that the CCP under *Xi Jinping* has moved away from the stiff and dull language of Sino-Marxism that characterized party communication for so long. See Kristin Shi-Kupfer et al., *Ideas and Ideologies Competing for China's Political Future: How Online Pluralism Challenges Official Orthodoxy*, Merics Papers on China, October 2017, available at www.merics.org/sites/default/files/201807/171004_MPOC_05_Ideologies_0_web.pdf.

[22] "Eight Definitenesses" refers to (1) development of socialism with Chinese characteristics; (2) belief that the main contradiction of our society in the new era is the contradiction between the people's increasing needs for a better life and unbalanced and inadequate development; (3) clarification that the overall layout of the socialist cause with Chinese characteristics is "five in one" and the strategic layout is "four comprehensives," emphasizing the firm roads of self-confidence, theoretical self-confidence, system self-confidence, and cultural self-confidence; (4) the goal to improve and develop the socialist system with Chinese characteristics, and to advance the modernization of the national governance system and governance capabilities; (5) comprehensive promotion of the rule of law to build a socialist legal system with Chinese characteristics and a socialist country ruled by law; (6) building the People's Army that is capable of winning the battle to become a world-class army; (7) promotion of Great Power diplomacy with Chinese characteristics to enhance the establishment of a new type of international relations and a community of shared future for humanity; and (8) the leadership of the Communist Party of China as the core to ensure that east, west, north, and south, the CPC leads in all areas of the country. The "Fourteen Adherences" means adherence to (a) the party's leadership over all work, (b) the people as the center, (c) comprehensively deepened reforms, (d) the new development concept, (e) the people as the masters of the country, (f) the rule of law in a comprehensive manner, (g) the core value system of socialism, (h) the

A closer look at these "Definitenesses and Adherences," however, reveals nothing more than a string of political slogans or policy banners. Two short terms often used to describe *Xi Jinping* Thought are "China Path" and "China Dream." But, as noted, due to the vagueness of these terms, it seems to be quite hard to figure out what the "China Path" or "China Dream" is about other than *Xi*'s likes or dislikes.

Note also that public acceptance of the ruling ideology in China, as many have observed, never relied on the power of persuasion, but rather, it was always achieved by dramatic measures taken to suppress different opinions or ideas that are considered hostile.[23] Historically, Emperor *Wudi* of the *Han Dynasty* banned all other schools in order to make the *Confucian* school the ideological orthodox. In *Mao*'s era, the nationwide Anti-Rightist Campaign shut the door for intellectuals to freely express their own ideas, and the Cultural Revolution stifled all individual freedoms.

During the past few decades, vast economic reform and the opening-up policy have prompted calls for ideological freedom and independence, and the development of new technology. The use of the internet in particular makes it possible to have a free flow of information across national borders. As a result, public opinions and ideas have become far more diverse than ever before, which has posed a great challenge to the CPC's attempts to build a unifying ideology.[24] Thus, for maintaining the dominance of the ruling ideology, the CPC imposes strict censorship on both traditional and new media, especially the internet, to eliminate any potential subversion of the CPC's leadership.

Since *Xi Jinping* was made the CPC chief in 2012, the effort to establish *Xi Jinping* Thought as the ruling ideology for the country has taken center stage in the nation's political operations. On the one hand, all state media and modern communication channels are being maneuvered to indoctrinate *Xi Jinping* Thought to the public, portraying Xi as the "Almighty Lord" who shows the right direction for all things and whose Thought shines in every sector of society. In the legal area, for example, the rule of law is replaced with the *Xi Jinping* Thought of the Rule of Law, even though *Xi* himself has no legal background at all. On the other hand, additional measures are being taken to step up censorship and suppress dissidents. Most of the measures taken are content-based to entail information control.[25]

Another big move in this regard was the adoption of the *Provisions on Ecological Governance of Network Information Contents* on December 15, 2019 (2019

protection and improvement of people's livelihood in development, (i) the harmonious coexistence of man and nature, (j) the overall national security concept, (k) the party's absolute leadership over the people's army, (l) the "one country, two systems" and promotion of the unification of the motherland, (m) the construction of a community of shared future for mankind, and (n) the strict governance of the CPC itself.

[23] See Shi-Kupfer et al., *supra* note 21.

[24] See *id.*

[25] See *id.*

Provisions).[26] Issued by the Order of the Cyberspace Administration of China, the 2019 Provisions, as stated, are purposed to "create a good network ecology, protect the legitimate rights and interests of citizens, legal persons and other organizations, and safeguard national security and public interests" – in sum, to clean up "the weeds" on the internet.

In contrast with previous internet rules, the 2019 Provisions contain a much broader and more extensive scope of coverage. According to the 2019 Provisions, ecological governance of network information content includes "any activity of promoting positive energy and disposing of illegal and harmful information conducted by the government, enterprises, society, internet users, and other parties based on cultivating and practicing core socialist values and targeted at network information content with the purpose of establishing and improving a comprehensive network governance system, creating a clean cyberspace, and building a sound network ecosystem."[27] Those who are subject to the 2019 Provisions include information content producers, content service platforms, content service users, and industry organizations.

For the purpose stated earlier, the 2019 Provisions make it a top priority for information content producers to focus on publicizing "the *Xi Jinping* Thought on Socialism with Chinese Characteristics for a New Era, and interpreting the path, theory, system, and culture of socialism with Chinese characteristics in a comprehensive, accurate and vivid way," and promoting "the Party's theoretical line, principles and policies, as well as the major decisions and arrangements of the Central Committee."[28] The content service platforms are, in addition to adhering to mainstream values,[29] required to strengthen the platforms' governance of the online information content ecosystem and cultivate an online culture that is positive, healthy, and supportive.[30]

Additionally, information content producers are prohibited from making, copying, or disseminating any information that is considered "illegal." The 2019 Provisions provide a laundry list of illegal information, including, among others, jeopardizing national security, divulging state secrets, subverting state power, or undermining national unity.[31] The 2019 Provisions also mandate content service platforms to take appropriate measures against information content producers for producing, copying, or releasing prohibited information, to promptly eliminate illegal content, document relevant activities, and report such matters to the relevant department.

The 2019 Provisions target mainly online content and impose greater censorship to control the flow of information on the internet. The sweeping terms in the

[26] The 2019 Provisions took effect on March 1, 2020. A full text of the Rules with English translation is available at http://en.pkulaw.cn/display.aspx?cgid=dc8a694ae08ed787bdfb&lib=law.

[27] See *id.*, art. 2.

[28] See *id.*, art. 5.

[29] See *id.*, art. 11.

[30] See *id.*, art. 8.

[31] See *id.*, art. 6.

laundry list of illegal information are not only quite broad but also appear ambiguous in many ways. For example, the rules make it illegal to spread rumors that disturb the economic and social order.[32] But what may constitute a rumor is an open-ended question and could be used to cover any information that the government does not like.[33] All the measures in place are to ensure dominance of the CPC's ruling ideology.

2. CONCEPT OF LAW

Law as a legal concept and social instrument is subject to various interpretations. Although a common understanding has developed that law is a body of rules created and enforced by government institutions or controlling authorities to protect rights and regulate conduct,[34] the nature and social attributes of law are matters of long-standing contest. A major difference among the legal schools of thought are the questions of what law ought to be or how law should be defined.

For example, the classic natural law theory considers law as the rule of nature reflecting human reason.[35] According to natural law theory, there are inherent laws that are common to all societies, whether or not they are written down or officially enacted. Law comes from eternal nature, and it should be consistent with it, especially with natural rationale, or should be based on reason. As determined by nature, natural law is immutable and universally applicable, independent from any human dictates.[36] Under natural law theory, a human law must be reflective of compelling reasons; otherwise it is not properly a "law" at all.[37]

In contrast to natural law theory, legal positivism takes the view that the content of law is dependent on social facts and that a legal system's existence is not constrained by morality.[38] Legal positivism asserts that the legitimate sources of law are those written rules, regulations, and principles enacted, adopted, or recognized by humans through a governmental entity or political institution, and there is no inherent and necessary connection between law and morality.[39]

32 See *id.*

33 Dr. Li Wenliang's whistleblowing of a possible outbreak of coronavirus was labeled as "rumors" disturbing social order by the government in the first place, which not only resulted in the widespread virus outbreak but also took Dr. Li's life.

34 For example, *Black's Law Dictionary* defines law as "a body of rules of action or conduct prescribed by controlling authority and having binding legal force." Thus, "that which must be obeyed and followed by citizens subject to sanctions or legal consequence is a law." (Black's Law Dictionary (6th ed., West, 1990)).

35 See Roscoe Pound, *Theories of Law*, 22 Yale L. J. 114, 126–127 (1912).

36 For a detailed discussion, see John Finnis, *Natural Law Theories*, Stanford Encyclopedia of Philosophy, available at https://plato.stanford.edu/entries/natural-law-theories/.

37 See *id.*

38 See Leslie Green, *Legal Positivism*, Stanford Encyclopedia of Philosophy, available at https://plato.stanford.edu/entries/legal-positivism/.

39 See *id.*, 105.

Within positivist thinking, the analytical school concentrates on the logical structure of law, the meanings and uses of its concepts, and the formal terms and modes of its operation in order to help understand the nature of law. Thus, jurisprudence should provide a clearer conspectus or map of those features of legal concepts and clearly exhibit their distinctive mode of functioning. According to Professor Hart, one of the most influential analytical theorists, what is needed in the law is the "clarification of fundamental notions or concepts which we can master adequately for the purposes of ordinary use in addition to the definitions offered in a textbook dealing with a substantive branch of the law."[40]

As opposed to positivist thinking, the sociological school of legal thought takes a more pragmatic approach by focusing on the actual social effects of legal doctrines and practices. Considering law as a means to an end of social welfare and justice, the sociological theory views law in action and examines the actual effects of law within society and the influence of social phenomena on the substantive and procedural aspects of law. The sociological school believes that the traditional notion of the power of the state being the sole source of law is wrong. As Professor Pound argued, "Realizing that a final answer to the question, 'what is law' is impossible, since the thing to be defined is living and growing and therefore subject to change, the most conspicuous representative of the Social-Philosophical School abandons that question and goes behind it to define the legal order in which law results and for which it exists."[41]

The basic issues that every legal theory attempts to resolve include the nature, source, function, operation, and structure of law. The answer to these issues varies from theory to theory. Take the nature of law, for example. Under the natural school theory, law is determined by nature and exists objectively and independently of human understanding and the power of any state.[42] The positivist school, however, believes that law is a matter of what has been posited or the command of human beings.[43] According to the analytical theory, law is a system of social rules.[44] But the sociological theory views law as a social phenomenon and an instrument of social control.[45] Sociological thinking insists that law has some primary or indirect relation to society.[46]

At the center of all issues is the definition of law, a long-lasting "battle ground of jurisprudence."[47] "What is law" is considered a question concerning human society

[40] See H. L. A. Hart, *Analytical Jurisprudence in Mid-Twentieth Century: A Reply to Professor Bodenheimer*, 105 U. Pa. L. Rev. 153, 165 (1957).

[41] See Pound, *supra* note 35, at 145–146.

[42] See Finnis, *supra* note 36.

[43] See Green, *supra* note 38.

[44] See Max A. Shepard, *Analysis of Analytical School of Jurisprudence*, 4 J. Pol. 371 (1939).

[45] See James Gardner, *The Sociological Jurisprudence of Roscoe Pound (Part I)*, 7 Villanova L. Rev. 1, 9–10 (1961).

[46] See *id.*

[47] See Pound, *supra* note 35, at 116.

that has been asked with persistence and "answered by serious thinkers in so many diverse, strange and even paradoxical ways."[48] It is not because law itself is complicated but because the understanding of law varies. Legal structure aside, the social and cultural traditions in different countries pose great challenges to having law defined in a way acceptable to all.

In China, law evolved with a different definition throughout history. In ancient China, as noted, law was originally seen in the form of *Xing*, meaning "punishment," which originated from the power of the ruling authority and served as social norms that required obedience.[49] Under the legalist philosophy, law was viewed as a legal instrument to maintain social order by regulating conduct and to achieve social justice through equal application. But the *Confucianist* orthodoxy made the law a coercive means to implement "*Li*" and a measure supplementary to virtues or moral standards.[50]

The archaic style of the Chinese character "law" (灋) possesses three components: water, divine beast, and removal. Water means flat, representing levelness and balance. A divine beast is an animal from ancient legends capable of telling right from wrong. Thus, the literal meaning of the word "law" in the original Chinese character is to let the divine beast identify criminals and punish them, because the divine beast would attack the unreasonable person and make them leave.[51] Although it remains debatable as to whether the "water" used as a radical in the word "*Fa*" actually means fairness and justice, it is agreed that the essence of "*Fa*" in ancient China meant punishment.

In addition to its meaning of "*Xing*" (刑), "*Fa*" (法) was also interchangeably used with "Lv" (律) to refer to rules, norms, and standards during the *Qin* and *Han* dynasties.[52] Later, in the *Tang* Code, it was explicitly stated that "*Fa*" means "*Lv*," and thus it is also called "*Lv*." But the use of "*Fa*" and "*Lv*" together as a compound word, "*Falv*" (法律), began in the late *Qing* Dynasty. Since then, "*Fa*" and "*Falv*" have become synonymous with law. It is important to note that when "*Fa*" became "*Falv*," the meaning of "*Fa*" changed completely from "*Xing*" to legal rules.

Also, "*Fa*" in the traditional Chinese legal system was implemented in the form of a "code" after the *Tang* Dynasty. The code constituted the central element of the

48 See H. L. A. Hart, The Concept of Law, 1 (2nd ed., Oxford University Press, 1994).

49 See Yu Xingzhong, *Legal Pragmatism in the People's Republic of China*, in Perry Keller, ed., Chinese Law and Legal Theory, 64 (Ashgate/Dartmouth, 2001).

50 See Xu Zhongmin & Ren Qiang, Legal Spirit of China, 60–64 (Guangdong People's Press, 2007); see also Zhang Jinfan, Evolution of the Chinese Legal Civilization, 1–2 (China University of Politics and Law Press, 2000).

51 According to the book *Shuo Wen Jie Zi* (the first Chinese dictionary), the ancient inscription "Fa" is "灋." The word comes from 廌 to represent the judgment between right and wrong. The "廌" (read zhiyin) is a kind of god beast. It looks like a unicorn, with green hair, a strong body, and great spirituality. It can identify a criminal by turning its horn toward him. Part of the word "灋" is water, a metaphor for flatness – leveling and balancing. The author of the book Shuo Wen Jie Zi, Xu Shen (AD 58–147), created 540 radicals according to the shape of the characters, and classified 9,353 characters into 540 radicals.

52 For example, in his legal reform, Shangyang used "*Lv*" instead of "*Fa*" to describe legal rules.

legal system for all post-*Tang* dynasties.[53] As noted, the *Confucianists* and Legalists considered the role that law might play. But since law was so closed off and associated with imperial power in traditional Chinese society, it was made and understood primarily to govern the behavior of people and to maintain imperial supremacy.[54]

In its recent history, China absorbed the civil law tradition and as a result, European elements were easily identifiable in Chinese law. After the *Qing* Dynasty collapsed in 1911, the Nationalist government adopted a series of laws for the country in the form of "six codes," and all those codes were based on the European civil law model.[55] But until 1949, when the People's Republic of China was founded, China suffered a period of constant political upheaval and foreign occupations. The domestic uncertainty in both political and economic aspects made it impossible to have the enacted codes fully implemented. These laws were then abolished entirely in 1949 when the communist government came to power.[56]

It is worth noting that although law as a legal term appeared in China at a very early stage of the development of the country's traditional legal system, the concept of law in light of jurisprudence was never clearly addressed. In their statements of law, the ancient scholars, both *Confucianist* and Legalist, focused mainly on the annotation of legal rules or statutes and rarely tried to define the law. In the *Han* Dynasty, there emerged a doctrinal study and research in law that was known as "*Lv Xue*" (doctrine of law), but most were merely works of legal annotations.[57]

[53] See William Jones, *Trying to Understand the Current Chinese Legal System*, in Stephen Hsu, ed., Understanding China's Legal System, 9 (New York University Press, 2003).

[54] See Xingzhong, *supra* note 49, at 63–64. See also Wu Zhumo & Li Shuangyuan, A General Introduction to Jurisprudence, 3–4, University Textbook Series (Law Press, 2007).

[55] The Six Codes included "Constitutional Law, Civil Law, Civil Procedure Law, Criminal Law, Criminal Procedure Law, and Administrative Law." See Ji Pomin (Chinese Academy of Social Sciences), *Before and After Abolition of the Six Codes*, available at http://iolaw.cssn.cn/ddyj/200406/t20040603_4590872.shtml; see also, Ralph Folsom et al., Law and Politics in the People's Republic of China, 19, 25 (West, 1992).

[56] In February 1949, the CPC Central Committee issued "Instructions to Abolish the Six Codes of the Nationalist Party and Establish Judicial Principles for the Liberated Areas." According to the Instructions, under the people's democratic dictatorship with the worker-peasant alliance as the principal body led by the proletarian class, the Six Codes of the Nationalist Party should be abolished and people's judicial work should not rely on the Six Codes but on the new laws of the people. The Instructions are available at https://chinacopyrightandmedia.wordpress.com/1949/02/28/instructions-concerning-abolishing-the-six-codes-of-the-guomindang-and-determining-judicial-principles-for-the-liberated-areas/.

[57] In the *Han* Dynasty, there developed a legal discipline that taught and annotated statutes based on *Confucian* principles. It not only elaborates on the text from textual and logical aspects, but also illustrated certain legal principles, such as the relationship between etiquette and law, the boundary between the interpretation of law and preserving the classics, the connection between legal articles and their actual meaning, and the relationship between statutes. See Shen Zonglin & Zhang Wenxian, Jurisprudence, Higher Education Textbook Series, 10 (2nd ed., Higher Education Press, 2004).

Not until the late nineteenth century did the term "jurisprudence" begin to be used in China. As noted, after the Opium Wars, a change that had dramatic influence on the development of law and the legal system in China was that Western legal literature was introduced into China by foreign missionaries and scholars. For example, in 1864, William A. P. Martin, a well-known American Presbyterian missionary to China, translated into Chinese Henry Wheaton's book *Elements of International Law* and introduced to China for the first time such concepts as "natural law" and "rights."[58]

The development of modern legal theory in China was also greatly attributed to the works of returned students who had studied abroad. From 1896 to 1912, some 39,056 students studied in Japan.[59] Before the 1911 Revolution, the number of Chinese students majoring in law who graduated from Hosei University in Japan reached 1,346.[60] Thanks to their research and writing, there was a great increase in public awareness of Western constitutionalism,[61] the modern concept of legislation,[62] criminal justice,[63] and civil law principles.[64]

[58] See Zuo Zeyuan, An Introduction to Law, 193 (Law Press, 2007). From 1863 to 1903, Dr. Martin translated into Chinese several Western law books and published them in China. In addition to Wheaton's Elements of International Law (Little, Brown and Company, 1855), the books translated into the Chinese language also included Theodore D. Woolsey's Introduction to the Study of International Law (Scribner, Armstrong & Co., 1875), and W. E. Hall's Treatise on International Law (Clarendon Press, 1903). During 1875 and 1878, Dr. Martin also edited the Peking *Scientific Magazine*, printed in Chinese.

[59] See Han Xiutao, *The Legal Thoughts of the Jurist Group in the Republic of China*, Renmin University Legal Culture Research Center Platform, available at www.ruclcc.com/article/?id=1957.

[60] See *id.*

[61] During the Republic period, legal scholars, regardless of their political orientation, all advocated for the formulation of the Constitution, the implementation of constitutionalism, and the realization of a democratic republic. As a result, overthrowing the monarchy, abolishing autocracy, and establishing a democratic republic became a major trend in society at that time. See Wang Kai, Constitution Course, 5 (University of International Business & Economics Press, 2010). See also Zhou Wei & Xie Weiyan, Constitution Course, Higher Education Legal Textbook Series, 50–54 (Sichuan University Press, 2012).

[62] Influenced by the theory and practice of the separation of powers since the European bourgeois revolution, many in the early period of the Republic believed that although there was the fact of legislation in ancient China, that legislation was to restrain the people's freedom and to serve the need of autocracy, and therefore, was not really legislation. It was also believed that the term "legislation" was derived from Western constitutionalism and was an activity created by specialized state organs through certain procedures to create laws. See Xiutao, *supra* note 59.

[63] Ancient Chinese law was synonymous with punishment. Traditional Chinese criminal law centered on physical punishment. The punishment was based on the principle of sternness, which reflected the nature of retribution and intimidation or cruelty in the punishment system. There developed a consensus in the late nineteenth and early twentieth centuries that the criminal law system of the Republic of China should be modeled after the Western principle of criminal justice, mainly the principle of "*Nulla Poena Sine Lege*" (no penalty without a law). See in general, Wu Yuxin, Research on the Criminal Law System of the Republic of China (Jiu Zhou Press, 2012).

[64] As noted, since traditional Chinese law was criminal-law-based and the law as such paid little attention to private rights, civil law in China was underdeveloped, and the civil provisions, if

The pursuit of Western-style jurisprudence significantly changed the discourse on the development of law and the legal system in the Republic of China. The democratic ideas, especially the concepts of separation of powers and independence of the judiciary, were well received in the country. Dr. *Sun Yat-sen*'s notion of "Three People Principles" and "Five Constitution Powers" not only reflected a great ambition to transform China from a traditionally autocratic and authoritarian state to a democratic and constitutionalist country, but also implicated both the structure and substance of the legal system to be established in China.

Unfortunately, however, the development of a modern legal system in the country during the Republic period did not move as smoothly as desired. Although the republic government managed to have six codes adopted, those codes, as noted, were not actually enforced in the nation due to internal political chaos and foreign troop occupation. Finally, the codes were abolished in 1949 when the People's Republic of China was founded. The abolishment left the country with a state of legal vacuum.

After 1949, the establishment of a socialist law or people's law became a main pursuit in China. In *Mao*'s era, however, such pursuit turned into a crucial "class struggle." Until 1978, the country never really focused on the development of a socialist law endeavor. Twenty-two years later, in 2010, the CPC-led government declared that a socialist legal system with Chinese characteristics had been established in the country. As discussed, the system consists of three levels and seven branches of law.

However, in modern Chinese jurisprudence, the theoretic underpinnings of law were, and still are, the doctrine of *Marxism*.[65] Although the definition of law given by Chinese scholars looks similar to the one illustrated by A. Y. Vyshinsky, a Soviet legal scholar of the 1930s,[66] many in China are reluctant to discuss the Soviet influence on Chinese law. Instead, they consider Marx's work to be the original authoritative source of their conception of law.[67]

any, were all included in the criminal code. In the late Qing Dynasty, as part of legal reform, the formulation of civil law was an important part of the revision of the law. In the Republic period, civil law legislation thrived, which resulted in the enactment of the first civil code in the country. Even the term "civil law" was actually introduced to China by a Japanese jurist. See Shen Weixing, Civil Law, 2 (Peking University Press, 2013).

65 See Zhumo & Shuangyuan, *supra* note 54, at 5–6; see also Xu Chongde, Constitution, 3–4 (People's University Press, 1999).

66 See Xinzhong, *supra* note 49, at 68–69. Under Vyshinsky's definition, law is

> the aggregate of the rules of conduct expressing the will of the dominant class and established in legal order, as well as of the customs and rules of community life confirmed by the state authority, the application whereof is guaranteed by the coercive force of the state to the end of safeguarding, making secure and developing social relationships and arrangements advantageous and agreeable to the dominant class.

See Soviet Legal Philosophy (Hugh Babb trans.), 336 (Harvard University Press, 1951).

67 Zhumo & Shuangyuan, *supra* note 54, at 5; see also Congde, *supra* note 65 at 3.

According to Vyshinsky, law is a system of rules formulated by the state, which expresses the will of the ruling class and is enforced by the coercive force of the state to protect, maintain, and develop social relations and orders that are acceptable to and beneficial for the ruling class.[68] Vyshinsky's definition of law, which is believed to derive from John Austin's command theory,[69] has two focal points: (a) law is an expression of the will of the ruling class and (b) law is the norms enforced by the coercive force of the state. These points are deeply embedded in the concept of law as understood in China.

In modern China, there is no legislative definition of law, but law is commonly explained and understood as an expression of the will of the dominant or ruling class. This understanding is premised on Marx and Engels' *Manifesto of the Communist Party* in which the bourgeois jurisprudence was criticized for the will of the bourgeois class being made into a law for all.[70] An important notion in the Chinese conception of law is that law comprises a "nature of class," which means that law is dependent on the will of the dominant class and also serves the need of such class.

The class theory forms an ideological foundation for the leading position of the CPC. The basic notion is that the dominant class is the class that retains the power of the state, or the ruling class,[71] and the CPC is the only representative of the ruling class. Thus, since the law expresses the will of the ruling class, it in essence represents the will of the Communist Party.[72] It is officially held in the country that legislation is an important political process that "legalizes and institutionalizes the CPC's ideas and the people's will."[73] With that in mind, it is not difficult to understand why all the work of the National People's Congress (NPC) is aimed at ensuring that the proposition of the CPC becomes the will of the state through the legislative process.[74]

[68] See Enrico Pattaro & Corrado Roversi, *Legal Philosophy in the Twentieth Century: The Civil Law World*, in A Treatise of Legal Philosophy and General Jurisprudence, Vol. 12, 607 (Springer, 2016).

[69] The command theory of law was the product of John Austin, the creator of the school of analytical jurisprudence. According to Austin, commands always involve three things: a desire concerning someone's behavior; an expression of that desire; and a sanction, threatened harm for non-compliance. See in general, B. Bix, *John Austin*, Stanford Encyclopedia of Philosophy, available at https://plato.stanford.edu/entries/austin-john/.

[70] In Marx and Engels' Manifesto of the Communist Party, it was stated: "Your very ideas are but the outgrowth of the conditions of your bourgeois production and bourgeois property, just as your jurisprudence is but the will of your class made into a law for all, a will whose essential character and direction are determined by the economic conditions of existence of your class." See Manifesto of the Communist Party, available at www.marxists.org/archive/marx/works/download/pdf/Manifesto.pdf.

[71] See *id.* at 11. See also Zhongmin & Qiang, *supra* note 50, at 364–370.

[72] See Manifesto of the Communist Party, *supra* note 70; see also Zeyuan, *supra* note 58, at 4–5, 33.

[73] See Huang Haihua, *The Legislative System of China*, 2 J. China People's Cong. (2025), available at www.npc.gov.cn/npc/c2/c30834/202502/t20250218_442863.html.

[74] See Wu Bangguo (current Chairman of the National People's Congress of China), *Stick to the Path of Political Development of Socialism with Chinese Characteristics and Strive to Upgrade the Work of the National People's Congress to a New Level*, Speech at the First Assembly

During *Mao*'s period, the nature of class in the concept of law was overly stressed. As a result, law was crafted to mainly serve the needs of class struggle and was used as a tool to maintain the proletarian dictatorship represented by the CPC. Ultimately, the law was replaced by the party's policies and in most cases by *Mao*'s quotations.[75] In addition, law, if any, took the form of public law, leaving out the law on civil matters.[76] During the decade-long Cultural Revolution, all legislative activities were suspended and the whole judicial system collapsed.

After *Mao*'s death, as noted, China began to shift the focus of the country from class struggle to economic development. Along with economic reform was the effort to restore and rebuild the nation's legal system. It was this effort that brought change to the understanding of law. As a result, law is no longer considered as the means for class struggle. Rather, law is viewed to contain a social nature as well. It has now become a general belief in China that law serves the common need of society, which implicates the common good regardless of class.[77]

In an official Chinese textbook, law is defined as the aggregate of the rules of conduct enacted or approved by the state, expressing the will of the dominant class determined by certain economic conditions and meeting the common need of society, containing rights and obligations, and the application of which is guaranteed by the coercive force of the state.[78] Similarly, another Chinese legal textbook describes law as a system of norms formulated, recognized, and enforced by the state, which reflects the will of the ruling class or people determined by their social and material living conditions, and is purposed to identify, protect, and develop social relations and value goals that the ruling class or people would expect.[79] Moreover, the law is also viewed as a norm for social behavior, including normative documents, formulated or recognized by the state, containing mainly rights and obligations, which are guaranteed for enforcement by the state's coercive power.[80]

Under the Chinese definition, law by its nature is a special type of social norm that is aimed at regulating the behavior of people in society. Like other social norms such as ethic rules, religious canons, and institution regulations, law contains three major attributes: normativity, generalization, and predictability.[81] Normativity means that law is the legal criterion for evaluating people's behavior, by which people can judge what can be done and what cannot, and whether certain action is legal or illegal. Generalization suggests that law, as a general norm, applies to a

Meeting of the 11th National Congress on March 19, 2008. A text of the speech is available at http://politics.people.com.cn/GB/1024/7129950.html.

75 See Xin Chunying, Chinese Legal System and Current Legal Reform, 14–18 (Law Press, 1999).

76 See Tong Rou, Wang Limin, & Ma Junju, Chinese Civil Law, 13–15 (Law Press, 1990).

77 The sociality in this regard includes rules adopted for the management of public facility, protection of the environment, promotion of public health, etc.

78 See Zhumo & Shuangyuan, *supra* note 54, at 16.

79 See Su Guoying & Li Hongbo, Ladder of Jurisprudence, 24 (Tsinghua University Press, 2006).

80 See Zeyuan, *supra* note 58, at 12.

81 See *id.* at 15–16.

certain type of action or person, and its application is not targeted on any individual person or specific thing. Predictability refers to the consequences of violating the law. In other words, from the legal provisions, it can be ascertained as to whether a conduct or action is permissible or prohibited, and what possible legal consequences must be faced if a violation occurs.

But unlike other social norms, law is a norm of coercive nature. According to Chinese legal scholars, law is a body of rules of conduct, which implements the will of the state and is enforced coercively by the state.[82] Note that although the social function of law is now widely recognized in China, the law's class nature remains the centerpiece in the jurisprudence. An official view is that in a class society, law is an embodiment of the will of the ruling class, while in a socialist country like China, law is an expression of the will of the people.[83]

3. THE RULE OF LAW IN A CHINESE CONTEXT

Rule of law is an imported concept in China. An inference from Chinese legal history is that while the country had a legal system in place for thousands of years, the rule of law, as both a legal concept and an actual practice, was alien to it. Conceptually, in traditional Chinese legal literature, nothing implicated the rule of law. Chinese legal culture is rooted deeply in both *Confucianism* and *Legalism*. As noted, *Confucianism* considered good governance as rule by leaders who are benevolent and virtuous, while *Legalism* advocated strict adherence to law intended to maintain authoritarian power. It is true that the Legalist doctrine attached great importance to legal norms, but the legal norms the Legalists advocated functioned primarily as a tool to maintain the totalitarian tructure of society or the *shi* (the imperial power).[84] It is highly noticeable that over Chinese legal history, law always was purposed to govern the governed, namely the people, rather than to place restrictions on government.[85]

In the Western world, the rule of law, though it may be defined differently, is generally considered a principle under which all persons, institutions, and entities are accountable to the law.[86] Under the concept of rule of law, law consists of norms

[82] Zongling & Wenxian, *supra* note 57, at 32–42.
[83] See Zeyuan, *supra* note 58, at 19.
[84] See Wu Shucheng, History of Chinese Legal Thoughts, 143 (Law Press, 2004).
[85] There were three elements that were essential and indispensable to the traditional Chinese legal system: imperial power, clan-based ethical standards, and the totalitarian structure of bureaucrats. Both imperial power and the clan-based ethic standard were directly associated with the exercise of "*Li*" because they were all in fact a matter of loyalty and obedience which constituted not only an ideological but also a practical basis for the entire society. The top-down bureaucratic structure served as a mechanism to ensure that the central power was not challenged, and the ultimate sovereignty of the emperor was ensured. Thus, under this system it is hard, if not impossible, to imagine that there was any room for the rule of law.
[86] See the United States Courts, Review – Rule of Law, available at www.uscourts.gov/educational-resources/educational-activities/overview-rule-law.

that are, among others, (a) publicly promulgated, (b) equally enforced, and (c) independently adjudicated.[87] It is also held that the rule of law contains such universal principles as accountability, just laws, open government, and accessible justice.[88] In addition, the rule of law is viewed as an authority and influence on norms in society, and as the principle whereby all members of a society are considered equally subject to publicly disclosed legal codes and processes.[89]

As a result of the economic reforms, the transition to a market economy in China has been a driving factor in a move toward the rule of law. But the rule of law is not limited to the governance of commercial matters. It in fact has broad coverage, including, for example, the enhancement of prospects for such values as democracy and human rights. During the past few decades, the rule of law in China has been a hotly contested subject discussed and debated among foreigners and within the Chinese legal community. Foreign lawyers and scholars wanted to see the rule of law in China as they see it in their own countries,[90] while their Chinese counterparts were eager to develop a Chinese version of rule of law based on the historical, social, and political context of the Chinese legal system.[91] Thus, the rule of law, as applied in China today, is being adapted into Chinese reality and contains Chinese characteristics.

87 See *id*. Under the United Nations' definition, the rule of law is

> a principle of governance in which all persons, institutions and entities, public and private, including the State itself, are accountable to laws that are publicly promulgated, equally enforced and independently adjudicated, and which are consistent with international human rights norms and standards. It requires, as well, measures to ensure adherence to the principles of supremacy of law, equality before the law, accountability to the law, fairness in the application of the law, separation of powers, participation in decision-making, legal certainty, avoidance of arbitrariness and procedural and legal transparency.

See the United Nations, *What Is the Rule of Law*, available at www.un.org/ruleoflaw/what-is-the-rule-of-law/.

88 See World Justice Project (WJP), *What Is the Rule of Law*, available at https://worldjusticeproject.org/about-us/overview/what-rule-law. According to the WJP, among the rule of law principles, accountability requires that the government as well as private actors be accountable under the law. Just Laws means that the laws are clear, publicized, stable, and applied evenly, and that laws protect fundamental rights, including the security of persons and contract, property, and human rights. Open Government requires that the processes by which the laws are enacted, administered, and enforced are accessible, fair, and efficient. Accessible Justice demands justice be delivered timely by competent, ethical, and independent representatives and neutrals who are accessible, have adequate resources, and reflect the makeup of the communities they serve.

89 See Oxford English Dictionary, *Rule of Law*, online version available at www.oed.com.

90 See Pitman Potter, *The Legal Implications of China's Accession to the* WTO, 167 China Q. 592, 603 (2001).

91 See Zhu Weijiu, *Toward Rule of Law Government*, in Cai Dingjian & Wang Chenguang, eds., China's Journal toward the Rule of Law: Legal Reform 1978–2008, 67–68 (Brill, 2010). See also Randell Peerenboom, *Let One Hundred Flowers Bloom, One Hundred Schools of Thought Contend*, Debating the Rule of Law in China, 23 Mich J. Int'l L., 471, 526 (2002).

From the Chinese government's viewpoint, the lesson learned from the consequence of legal nihilism in the Cultural Revolution is that the building of an effective legal system in the country is a necessity. More importantly, economic reform and an increasingly international presence require China to commit to the rule of law. However, there is a growing concern of undue Western influence on the development of the legal system in China. Thus, it becomes a critical question as to what the rule of law should mean to China, especially in the context of civil liberty *vis-à-vis* government control or individual rights as opposed to government power.

Against this background, the rule of law in China is inevitably driven to take its own path. At first, the rule of law is employed as a benchmark to help differentiate today's China from its ancient image of the rule of man. Opposite the rule of law, the rule of man refers to the legal system that was centered on the imperial power, leading to the lawlessness of *Mao*'s era.[92] Second, the rule of law is primarily considered a legal structure that serves instrumentally to build social order and maintain stability.[93] Third, as will be discussed *infra*, rule of law is widely used as a synonym for "ruling the country by law."[94] But most importantly, a reality in China is that the development of the rule of law is (or must be) strictly tied with the maintenance of the absolute leadership of the CPC.

A. *The Rule of Law from a Chinese Perspective*

Many in China have tried to define rule of law in ways that they believe more accurately reflect its essence. Because of this, the major role of the rule of law has been articulated in various forms, from "constraining the arbitral act of the government from facilitating and ensuring economic development,"[95] and "protecting [the] individual against the state" to "providing [a] fair mechanism for resolving disputes."[96] However, the official meaning that captures the Chinese conception of the rule of law comes from the statement made by *Jiang Zemin* in his report at the 15th National Congress of the CPC in 1997.[97]

According to *Jiang*:

> Ruling the country by law means that the broad masses of the people, under the leadership of the Party and in accordance with the Constitution and other laws,

[92] See Wang Chenguang, *From the Rule of Man to the Rule of Law*, in Cai Dingjian & Wang Chenguang, eds., China's Journal toward the Rule of Law: Legal Reform 1978–2008, at 4 (Brill, 2010). See also Guoying & Hongbo, *supra* note 79, at 283 (Shu described in his book the seeking of rule of law as a hundred-year dream in China).

[93] See Peerenboom, *supra* note 91, at 498.

[94] See Zhumo & Shuangyuan, *supra* note 54, at 53.

[95] See Randell Peerenboom, *Ruling the Country in Accordance with Law, Reflections on the Rule and Role of Law in Contemporary China*, in Perry Keller, ed., Chinese Law and Legal Theory, 182 (Ashgate, 2001).

[96] See *id.*

[97] See Zhumo & Shuangyuan, *supra* note 54, at 53.

> participate in one way or another and through all possible channels in managing state affairs, economic and cultural undertakings and social affairs, and see to it that all work of the state proceeds in keeping with law, and that socialist democracy is gradually institutionalized and codified so that such institutions and laws will not change with changes in the leadership or changes in the views or focus of attention of any leader.[98]

The emphasis of Jiang's statement was the effort to improve the legal system so that the country is to be ruled by law. This statement appears, if obscurely, to express a desire to build a legal system that is consistent in terms of application of law and an attempt to develop a legal scheme ensuring that the government will act under the law. Both legal consistency and law abidance, as many have argued, are the key components of the rule of law.[99]

As a matter of fact, the term "rule of law" itself was not well received in China due to the lack of policy endorsement until 1996. At the beginning of the economic reform in 1979, one task set for the political platform was to strengthen the legal system so that the laws would not change every time when the leadership changes or whenever the leaders change their view.[100] During that period, the center of attention was ensuring legal consistency.

In the early 1980s, there emerged a call from the Chinese legal community for the development of the rule of law in response to the government's practice of reviewing and approving cases handled by the judiciary, a scenario in which the judicial determination of a case would not be final until it was reviewed and approved by the government.[101] Such a call generated a national debate on the rule of law versus the rule of man. One of the key issues was whether the term "rule of law" should be used in the country because it was deemed different from the officially recognized term "legal system."[102]

98 See Jiang Zemin, Report at the 15th National Congress of the CPC,1997, available at http://academics.wellesley.edu/Polisci/wj/308S/Readings/jzm15CCP.htm.

99 Rule of law in Western modern society, according to one view, contains the following core components: constitutionalism, government bound by law, independent judiciary, fair and consistent application of law, transparency and accessibility of law, efficient and timely application of law, protection of property and economic rights, protection of human and intellectual rights, and transparency and accessibility of the established process for the change of law. See Barry Hager, The Rule of Law: A Lexicon for Policy Makers, 19–46 (The Mansfield Center for Pacific Affairs, 1999); see also David Kairy, Search for the Rule of Law, 36 Suffolk U. L. Rev. 307 (2003) for more discussion on the rule of law.

100 See Deng Xiaoping, *Emancipate the Mind, See Truth from the Facts, and Unite as One in Looking to the Future*, Speech at the Closing Session of Central Working Conference (December 1978).

101 A common phenomenon at that time was that any case dealt with by either the people's court or people's procuratorates would need to get approval from the party committee of government at the same level before a decision was made. This practice was repealed in September 1979 under the CPC's Instruction on the Firm Assurance of the Earnest Implementation of Criminal Law and Criminal Procedure Law. See Chenguang, *supra* note 92, at 7.

102 See *id.*

In 1996, thanks to the unremitting efforts of legal scholars, rule of law as a legal concept began to appear in central government documents, finally becoming an official term in China.[103] The acceptance of the term "rule of law" not only brought to an end the debate on what is the rule of law China should pursue but also furthered the country's effort to build a socialist country governed by law, which resulted in a constitutional amendment in 1999, mandating the country to be ruled by law.[104] At that time, the focus was on the development of a legal system to ensure that the country is to be governed by the law.

A significant move echoing the 1999 constitutional amendment was the judicial reform. In 1999, the Supreme People's Court (SPC) initiated its first so-called Five Year Reform program. As noted, the judicial reform programs were taken in five-year segments, and each segment has a different focus. The first segment was aimed at promoting judicial justice and impartiality and restoring public confidence in the judiciary.[105] Following the SPC's lead, both the Supreme People's Procuratorate (SPP) and the Ministry of Justice have all put in place their own five-year reform programs.[106]

There is no question that progress has been made in China toward fulfilling the pledge to rule the country according to law. In fact, the rule of law is becoming a popular and frequently used term. As a commentator has observed, it is now virtually impossible to open any Chinese newspaper without seeing a reference to the rule of law.[107] But given the remarkable impact of both Chinese legal tradition and the ideology of the CPC, it would be unrealistic to expect the rule of law in China to be an exact replica of its Western counterparts.[108] Clearly, there remains a degree of resistance in the country to a purely Western concept of the rule of law.[109]

[103] For example, some leading Chinese scholars strongly advocated for the use of the term "rule of law" in their invited lectures to central government officials in 1996 on the building of the legal system. See *id.*

[104] In 1999, the 1982 Constitution was amended for the third time. The amendment added a new paragraph to article 5 of the 1982 Constitution as the first paragraph, which reads, "the People's Republic of China practices ruling the country in accordance with the law and building a socialist country of law." An English version of the Chinese Constitution (as amended 1999) is available at www.cecc.gov/resources/legal-provisions/1999-amendment-to-the-constitution-of-the-peoples-republic-of-china.

[105] The five-year periods of the SPC's reform programs include: 1999–2003, 2004–2009, 2009–2013, 2013–2019, and 2019–2023.

[106] In 2015, the Supreme People's Procuratorate issued its first five-year reform program, and the second one began in 2018. The Ministry of Justice has also implemented a five-year reform program for the period of 2018–2022.

[107] See Randall Peerenboom, China's Long March toward Rule of Law, 1 (Cambridge University Press, 2002).

[108] It has been acknowledged that the ends served by the rule of law in China may differ from the ends the rule of law serves elsewhere. See Peerenboom, *supra* note 95, at 205.

[109] See Hager, *supra* note 99, at 1 (there is a degree of suspicion or resistance to the rule of law concept among Asian leaders).

Conceptually, however, the rule of law remains a debatable concept in China. A lingering issue is whether the notion of ruling the country according to law, or in short the rule by law, is actually to mean the rule of law. In the early stage of economic reform, the basic requirements for rebuilding the legal system were described in general terms as follows: (a) there are laws to follow, (b) laws must be followed, (c) enforcement of laws must be strict, and violation of laws must be dealt with. Many in China, however, believe that those requirements are essential to the rule by law but may not necessarily constitute the rule of law because the rule of law is not simply a demand for a rule by law.

According to Chinese legal scholars, the rule by law generally means a legal system, a system of doing things under the law, or more broadly a system of promulgation, enforcement, and observance of law.[110] The rule of law, however, is a principle under which accountability to the law is required. A general understanding in the Chinese legal community is that the rule of law is a governing strategy under which a country chooses a law-based approach to control society among various social regulation methods.[111] But there remains a gap between what the rule of law is understood to be in China and how the concept is generally explained elsewhere.

In Chinese legal literature, the rule of law is viewed as a much-needed strategy for the country to move toward modernization with reforms. A prevailing proposition is that the rule of law not only refers to a system of law but also represents a value orientation, making it the highest value and ultimate goal to protect human rights and achieve social justice.[112] Thus, to establish the rule of law, it is important to have a system in which (a) the law is an expression of the will of the people, (b) law recognizes, respects, and protects the rights and freedom of the people, (c) law is equally applied, and (d) law recognizes the diversity of social interests.[113]

Many Chinese legal scholars believe that an essence of the rule of law is to maintain a general obedience to the law.[114] The underlying notion is actually a concern that there is a lack of genuine respect for the rule of law given the absolute power of the ruling political party. In 2012, in his Report at the 18th National Congress of the CPC, Chinese President *Hu Jintao* began to use the words "法治" (a Chinese term deemed equivalent to the rule of law) instead of "法制" (the system of law) to describe China's commitment to the rule of law.[115]

[110] See Zeyuan, *supra* note 58, at 152–153.

[111] See Guoying & Hongbo, *supra* note 79, at 273; see also Zongling & Wenxian, *supra* note 57, at 194.

[112] See Zongling & Wenxian, *supra* note 57, at 196.

[113] See Guoying & Hongbo, *supra* note 79, at 275.

[114] See *id.*

[115] See Hu Jintao, *Unswervingly Advancing along the Road of Socialism with Chinese Characteristics and Striving for a Comprehensive Well-Off Society*, Report at the 18th National Congress of the Communist Party of China, November 18, 2012, available at https://language.chinadaily.com.cn/19thcpcnationalcongress/2017-10/16/content_32684880.htm.

According to *Hu*, the rule of law is the basic way of governing the country. His Report stressed that the rule of law as applied in China would in substance include four elements: scientific legislation, strict law enforcement, fair justice, and universal abidance by the law.[116] Thus, in order for the country to be governed by law, it is important to adhere to the equality of all people before the law, and to ensure that there is law to comply with, that the enforcement of law is strict, and that violation of the law will be handled properly.[117] As noted, in 2014, the CPC issued the Decision on Several Important Issues Concerning the Comprehensive Promotion of Governing the Country by Law. The Decision further endorsed the four elements of the rule of law and made them the goal of development of the rule of law in the country.[118]

Since 2014, the "rule of law" has become a popular term in the official documents in China. As noted, the 1982 Constitution was amended again in 2018. An important change in the 2018 Amendment is the replacement of the phrase "legal system" with the term "rule of law." In the preface of the amended Constitution, it states that the "people of all ethnic groups in China will ... under the leadership of the Communist Party of China ... continue to improve the socialist rule of law." But still, since many in China believe that the rule of law as provided in the 2018 Amendment is derived from the concept of "governing the country in accordance with law," which was introduced by President *Jiang Zemin* in 1997,[119] it basically means the rule by law.

As noted, the rule of law in China is now redefined as *Xi Jinping* Thought of the Rule of Law (though Xi himself received no legal training nor did he have any legal experience). Formally introduced in 2020, *Xi*'s brand of rule of law is illustrated to contain eleven "adherences." More specifically, the eleven "adherences" came from Xi's speech at the CPC Central Committee Comprehensive Work Conference on the Rule of Law on November 17, 2020. According to *Xi*, to practice the rule of law in China is to adhere to: (1) the party's leadership in comprehensively governing the country according to law, (2) the people-centered approach, (3) the path of socialist rule of law with Chinese characteristics, (4) governing and managing the country in accordance with the constitution, (5) promoting the modernization of the national governance system and capabilities, (6) building a socialist legal system with Chinese characteristics, (7) joint advancement of governing and administering the country according to law to build an integrated country, government and society

[116] See *id.*

[117] See *id.*

[118] See the CPC, The Decision on Several Important Issues Concerning the Comprehensive Promotion of Governing the Country by Law, October 23, 2014, available at www.ccps.gov.cn/xytt/201812/t20181212_123256.shtml.

[119] The concept of "governing country according to the law" first appeared in *Jiang Zemin*'s report to the Party's 15th Congress in 1997 and was written into article 5 of the P.R.C. Constitution in 1999.

under the rule of law, (8) comprehensively promoting scientific legislation, strict law enforcement, fair justice, and law-abiding by all people, (9) the overall promotion of domestic rule of law and foreign-related rule of law, (10) building a high-quality legal team with both ability and political integrity, and (11) disciplining the "critically small number" of leading cadres.[120]

Xi's speech was propagandized in China as "a major theoretical innovation [that] emerged in response to the requirements of the era of realizing the great rejuvenation of the Chinese nation, the latest achievement of the Sinicization of *Marxist* rule of law theory, and a comprehensive and fundamental action guide for governing the country according to the law."[121] But still, except for further strengthening the CPC's leadership and control, barely anything in the eleven "adherences" explicitly tells what the rule of law is. Certain universally accepted substances of the rule of law, such as an independent judiciary, checks and balances of government power, and accountability, are clearly missing. Instead, people in China are led to hold that the leadership of the CPC is the most fundamental guarantee for the socialist rule of law.[122] Thus, the development of the rule of law in the country becomes a process of realizing the CPC's will through implementation of the law.

It is interesting to note that in early 2021, the CPC Central Committee issued the "Plan for the Construction of a Rule of Law China (2020-2025)."[123] According to the Plan, by 2025, the socialist rule of law with Chinese realities will be initially formed, and by 2035, a system where a country ruled by law, a government ruled by law, and a society ruled by law will be basically established.[124] The Plan, though quite ambitious, fails to clearly define the rule of law except for a string of empty political slogans. What the Plan emphasizes, however, is the requirement for adherence to the centralized and unified leadership of the Party. According to the Plan, firmly grasping the leadership of the Party is the most fundamental guarantee of socialist rule of law.[125]

Nevertheless, the acceptance of the rule of law in China demonstrated the progress China has made in its effort to establish a sound legal system. But as many

[120] See Xi *Jinping*'s speech, available at www.gov.cn/xinwen/2020-11/17/content_5562085.htm.

[121] See Wang Chen, *Adhere to the Guidance of Xi Jinping Thought on the Rule of Law and Write a New Chapter in Comprehensively Governing the Country According to Law in the New Era*, *Qiushi* Magazine (Seeking Truth), March 2021, available at www.chinalaw.org.cn/portal/article/index/id/29483.html.

[122] See Chen Wenqin, *Improve the Socialist Legal System with Chinese Characteristics (Study and Implement the Spirit of the Third Plenary Session of the 20th CPC Central Committee)*, People's Daily, August 6, 2024, a full text of the article is available at http://sh.people.com.cn/n2/2024/0806/c134768-40935361.html.

[123] See the CPC Central Committee, *The "Plan for the Construction of a Rule of Law China (2020–2025)*," issued in January 2021, available at www.gov.cn/zhengce/2021-01/10/content_5578659.htm.

[124] See *id.*

[125] See *id.*

foreign observers point out, Chinese rule of law differs fundamentally from rule of law as internationally understood.[126] In Western eyes, despite China's extraordinary effort to transform into a country under the rule of law, the Chinese legal system remains an instrument of the CPC.[127] In their view, given China's pragmatic use of law, the rule of law in China is a "cautionary tale for the international community."[128]

B. *Law and Government*

It seems no doubt that no nation has ever produced legislation, in both substance and procedure, more quickly and heavily than China has done in modern history.[129] As discussed, the past decades have witnessed overwhelming legislation and "ballooned" volumes of law in China.[130] The progress is indeed remarkable. But the rule of law means much more than legislation alone. The mass legislation in China only suggests that the country is at the stage of "having law to rely on." The biggest challenge is how to develop a system that strictly and consistently enforces the laws to make the rule of law meaningful in the country. To that end, China would need to further depart from the authoritarian tradition and build the "people's democracy" under the internationally perceived rule of law.

In the West, the heart of rule of law is that the government itself is bound by the law.[131] This notion is derived from concerns about limits on governmental power.[132] Thus, in the Western democratic system, statutes as passed by the legislature bind all of government. When making statutes, the legislature is bound by the limits prescribed by the constitution, a formal document that carries the general consent of the governed or the will of the people.[133] Under this system, a major function of law is to prevent government from abuse of power and from arbitrary and unfair treatment of individual(s).[134] Under the rule of law, government may only act within the boundary of the law or do only what the law allows.

[126] See Paul Gewirtz, *What China Means by "Rule of Law,"* New York Times, October 20, 2014, a full text of the article is available at www.nytimes.com/2014/10/20/opinion/what-china-means-by-rule-of-law.html.

[127] See *id.*

[128] See Ronald T. P. Alcala et al., *China and the Rule of Law: A Cautionary Tale for the International Community*, Just Security, available at www.justsecurity.org/58544/china-rule-law-cautionary-tale-international-community/.

[129] See Jerome A. Cohen, *China's Legal Reform at the Crossroads*, Far Eastern Economic Review, March 2006, available at www.cfr.org/publication/10063/china_legal_reform_at_the_crossroads.html.

[130] See Eric Orts, *The Rule of Law in China*, 34 Vand. J. Transnat'l. L. 43, 64 (2001).

[131] See Hager, *supra* note 99, at 21.

[132] See *id.*

[133] See *id.*

[134] See *id.*

This is not the case in China. Historically, as noted, China was a bureaucrat-centered country with a *Confucian* tradition that relied on the benevolence of the rulers for the good of the country.[135] The law did not function primarily to limit government power but to provide what the governed can and cannot do. It created a strong desire among the public to rely on government rather than on law.[136] Even today, this tradition is still influential in the country. For example, it is a very common belief in China that a good government is the source of a better life for the people, and the traditional concept of "parental officers," whose job is to make decisions for the people, as noted, remains intact in the public's and government's minds.[137] Thus, it is often the case in China that people rely on government offices other than the court to address their grievances and to solve their disputes. It remains a common belief in the country that the administration is more powerful than the judiciary.[138]

People in China are also often led to show how grateful they are to the government. Although the CPC government regards it as their mission to serve the people, in most cases the mission simply becomes nothing more than a political slogan. As a result, to serve the people is not seriously taken as an obligation of the government; on the contrary, people should always express their gratefulness or appreciation to the government and to the CPC for what the government has done. It is also a routine protocol in any speech for acceptance of an award to first thank the leaders in the government even though the award received has had nothing to do with the leaders.[139]

Not surprisingly then, when the COVID epidemic began to show signs of easing in the epicenter of Wuhan, *Wang Zhonglin*, the newly appointed secretary of the CPC Wuhan Municipal Committee, called for a "grateful education" campaign among citizens to thank the top leader *Xi Jinping*, despite the wide criticism of *Xi*'s failure to effectively handle the health crisis at the beginning.[140]

[135] See Weijiu, *supra* note 91, at 66.

[136] It was observed that in the legal tradition in China, "the need for wise and benevolent leaders using law to impose order and achieve the highest good for the whole society was emphasized." See Hager, *supra* note 99, at 12.

[137] See Cai Dingjian, *Toward the Rule of Law Government*, Cai Dingjian & Wang Chenguang, eds., China's Journal toward the Rule of Law: Legal Reform 1978–2008, 87 (Brill, 2010).

[138] In the widely publicized "Chongqing Nail House" case, when the president of the court hearing the case offered to meet the homeowner who was sued by the developer, the homeowner refused but requested to meet with the party chief of the city instead, because in her mind the party chief had all the power to change her situation. For more information about the case, see Mo Zhang, *From Public to Private: The Newly Enacted Chinese Property Law and Protection of Property Rights in China*, 5 Berkeley Bus. L. Rev. 317 (2008).

[139] For example, Li Na, a famous Chinese tennis player, received a lot of criticism because at the end of games, she would always thank many people when standing on the podium, but never thanked the leaders. She was considered a violator of the routine protocol.

[140] BBC, *Pneumonia Outbreak: Chinese Officials Make Wuhan Grateful for Positive Energy Public Opinion*, March 9, 2020, available at https://translate.google.com/translate?hl = en&sl = zh-CN&u = https://www.bbc.com/zhongwen/simp/chinese-news-51800636&prev = search.

This time, *Wang* had to roll his comments back the next day due to great resentment and anger about his "grateful education" speech among the vast majority of people nationwide.

Standing closely in line with *Confucian* tradition was the top-down authoritarian system that served as the backbone of the state administration. In Chinese history, the center of such an authoritarian system was the imperial power. As noted, after the founding of the People's Republic of China, a so-called democratic centralism was adopted as the administrative governing mechanism. Since the focal point of democratic centralism is centralization, the government structured on this basis is still purposed to secure central authority and control.[141]

In addition, democratic centralism shares many elements in common with the traditional authoritarian system. A highly notable commonality is that the government at both central and local levels is very powerful and barely transparent.[142] Because of the authoritarian nature, the accountability of the centralization-structured government inevitably becomes an issue. More disturbing is the complex political entanglement between the government and the CPC at every level in the current system.[143] As a consequence, the government is not separated from the state, and the ruling party becomes an equivalent of state power.

Indeed, after the 2004 Constitutional Amendment calling for the development of the rule of law in the country, there has been an increasing call for a rule-based government, or a government ruled by law. To establish a rule-based government, it is essential that the government should act within the scope of the law. However, given the almost unfettered power of the government at all levels in the country, challenges are enormous to curb it. Since the Chinese judiciary, as noted, does not have the authority to review and judge the constitutionality of the government's acts, a viable option for redress of grievances against government abuse of power is administrative litigation, a process known in China as "people suing the government," meaning that a regular citizen brings a lawsuit in court against a government agency or officer for abuse of power.

China did not have an official channel for a private person to sue a "government official" until 1989 when the first Administrative Litigation Law (ALL) was adopted. The 1989 ALL was amended in 2014 and 2017, respectively. Under the ALL (as amended in 2017), a person, including a citizen, legal person, or any other organization, shall have the right to file a complaint with a people's court if his/her lawful rights and interests are infringed by an administrative action taken by an

[141] Despite the change of name, in light of the administration, the top-down feature of the system stays unchanged. In addition, the single-party controlled system is deemed a sort of neo-authoritarian system. See Peerenboom, China's Long March, *supra* note 107, at 188.

[142] See Chenguang, *supra* note 92, at 29.

[143] The current government structure is based on a system of executive responsibility under the leadership of the committee of the CPC.

administrative agency or any employee thereof, including an administrative action taken by an entity authorized by a law, regulation, or rule.[144]

The enactment of the ALL is viewed by many in China as a significant move toward the rule of law. But the extent to which the ALL is enforced in order to restrain government power is limited. First, the scope of the ALL is prescribed within the listed areas, mainly including administrative measures or administrative agency actions affecting personal and property rights and interests.[145] Second, the courts in administrative litigation are not allowed to hear, among others, cases concerning administrative regulations and rules or decisions and orders with general binding force adopted and issued by administrative agencies.[146] Third, given the ambiguity of the ALL in the determination of the legality of government action and

[144] See Administrative Litigation Law of China (as amended in 2017), art. 2, at www.hongfanglaw.com/wp-content/uploads/2019/10/Administrative-Litigation-Law-of-the-Peoples-Republic-of-China-2017-RevisionENCN.pdf.

[145] Under article 12 of the ALL (2017), ALL cases include (1) a complaint against any administrative punishment, such as administrative detention, suspension or revocation of a license or permit, ordered suspension of production or business, confiscation of illegal income, confiscation of illegal property, a fine, or a warning; (2) a complaint against any administrative compulsory measure, such as restriction of personal freedom or seizure, impoundment, or freezing of property, or administrative enforcement; (3) a complaint against an administrative agency's denial of, or failure to respond within the statutory period to, an application for administrative licensing or any other administrative licensing decision made by the administrative agency; (4) a complaint against an administrative agency's decision to confirm the ownership or the right to use any natural resource, such as land, mineral resources, water, forest, hill, grassland, wasteland, tidal flat, or sea area; (5) a complaint against a decision on expropriation or requisition or a decision on compensation for expropriation or requisition; (6) a complaint against an administrative agency's refusal to perform, or failure to respond to an application for the administrative agency to perform, its statutory duties and responsibilities in respect of protecting personal rights, property rights, and other lawful rights and interests; (7) a complaint claiming that an administrative agency has infringed upon the plaintiff's autonomy in business management, right in the contractual operations on rural land, or right in operations on rural land; (8) a complaint claiming that an administrative agency has abused its administrative power to preclude or restrict competition; (9) a complaint claiming that an administrative agency has illegally raised funds or apportioned expenses or illegally required performance of other obligations; (10) a complaint claiming that an administrative agency has failed to pay consolation money, minimum subsistence, or social insurance benefits according to the law; (11) a complaint claiming that an administrative agency has failed to perform according to the law or as agreed upon, or illegally modified or rescinded, an agreement, such as a government concession agreement or a land and building expropriation compensation agreement; and (12) a complaint claiming that an administrative agency has otherwise infringed upon personal rights, property rights, or other lawful rights and interests. In addition to those as set out in the preceding paragraph, the people's courts shall accept administrative cases that may be filed as prescribed by laws and regulations. See *id.*

[146] See *id.*, art. 13(2). Other cases outside the scope of the ALL are actions taken by the state in national defense and foreign affairs; decisions of administrative agencies on the rewards or punishments for their employees or the appointment or removal from office of their employees; and administrative action taken by an administrative agency as a final adjudication according to the law. See *id.*, art. 13(1)(3)(4).

the extensive government power, it remains very difficult to sue the government in many cases, especially when the maintenance of social stability is at stake.

Take the *Chen Pingfu* case as an example.[147] *Chen Pingfu*, born in 1957, was one of the first generations of students to take the national college-entrance examination when the universities reopened after the Cultural Revolution. He graduated from Northwest Normal University in 1982 and was assigned a teaching job at the vocational school of *Shengli* Machinery Factory of Capital Steels in 1984, where he taught math for over twenty years.

In May 2005, Chen suffered a heart attack and underwent heart surgery. Since his employer was on the brink of bankruptcy, Chen had to pay the $6,000 medical expense out of pocket. At the same time, his son was planning to attend college, adding to his debt woes. To survive, Chen began playing his violin on the streets of *Lanzhou* to earn extra money during his spare time. In 2009, his employer went bankrupt, forcing him to busk full time. While playing violin on the street, he received all kinds of ill treatment from local police, staff of a local homeless shelter management organization, and officers of the local migrant population administration and urban management.

Chen started writing about his story in 2007 and posted a number of articles he wrote online. According to Chen, what drove him to publish his writing online was his desire to seek public support because, in his words, "[the] government didn't help me at all." In one article, he wrote,

> At the hardest time of my life when I had to give up treatment and go home to wait for my death … when I needed relief the most, there was no government to be seen. But when I was deeply in debt, and jobless, and had no choice but to play violin on the street to help myself, the Relief Station of Lanzhou's municipal government came with a barred jail truck.[148]

In a blog article, Chen wrote, "Looking back at my life thus far, I found that I had lived meaninglessly for all these years without doing one worthwhile and meaningful thing. I cannot swallow the humiliation in silence; I have kept thinking and reading to break the cultural dictatorship so that my mind can go to a farther and wider world"[149] (Chen, I Cannot Bear the Humiliation in Silence). Chen also shared his experience with a local government official who said to him: "I'll send you to your death if you dare be a nuisance! Who do you

[147] The details of the case are available at https://zhidao.baidu.com/question/691727999948294404.html.

[148] See Pingfu Chen, *Weasels Serve Chickens*, in Chen Pingfu's Inciting to Subvert State Power by His Blogposts? Available at https://humanrightsinchina.wordpress.com/2012/09/09/chen-pingfus-inciting-to-subvert-state-power-by-his-blogposts/.

[149] See Pingfu Chen, *I Can't Bear Humiliation in Silence*, in Autin Ramzy, Teacher, Violinist, Enemy of the State? Web Posts Spur Free-Speech Debate in China, Time, September 11, 2012, available at https://world.time.com/2012/09/11/teacher-violinist-enemy-of-the-state-web-posts-spur-free-speech-debate-in-china/.

think you are? Making you die is nothing for us! Go with us if you dare and see how we will tidy you up!"[150]

Chen's writing was deemed extremely anti-government. On September 4, 2012, Chen was charged with "inciting subversion of state power," a crime that would face up to five years in prison.[151] The evidence cited in the charge consisted of a long list of blog posts and nothing else. During the trial, Chen was ordered to be "residing under surveillance" until the sentence was announced. Chen's trial met massive criticism in the Chinese legal community and generated great debate on the legal basis of the "inciting subversion" crime.[152] Facing social pressure, the local procuratorate's office dropped the charge before the court's decision was made. Chen's case was not an isolated one. There are many similar cases in which the accused were not as lucky as Chen.[153]

The "inciting subversion" crime was first provided in the criminal law in 1997 to replace the former "counter-revolutionary" crime. Both of them, however, have been widely criticized because of concerns that they would likely become instruments of political repression for the government. One problem is the ambiguity of the provision of "inciting subversion." The target of the provision is speech (oral and written), but it never clearly defines under what circumstances speech would amount to "inciting subversion." Therefore, the determination of such a crime is highly subjective and arbitrary. In addition, as many in China argued, it is very dangerous to make it a crime to criticize or oppose the government.[154]

Like in many other cases, the criminal charges in Chen's case were made based on an expression in public of dissatisfaction with the government and with the Communist Party. Relying on article 150 of the Criminal Law, however, the charges as such consciously ignored the difference between the government and state power, and between the political party and the state. As Chen's lawyer asked, since a state is made up of a certain territory, people, and sovereignty, how could it be incitingly

[150] See *id.*, Pingfu Chen, *Fight against Brutality and Pursue Civilization*, available from Chen's blog at www.zyzc9.com/archives/13103.

[151] Under article 150 of the Criminal Law of China, anyone who uses rumor, slander, or other means to encourage subversion of the political power of the state or to overthrow the socialist system shall be sentenced to a fixed-term imprisonment of not more than five years. However, ringleaders and anyone whose crime is monstrous shall be sentenced to a fixed-term imprisonment of not less than five years.

[152] See Austin Ramzy, *Teacher, Violinist, Enemy of the State? Web Posts Spur Free-Speech Debate in China*, Time, September 11, 2012, available at https://world.time.com/2012/09/11/teacher-violinist-enemy-of-the-state-web-posts-spur-free-speech-debate-in-china/.

[153] For general information, see U.S. Department of State, 2022 Report on International Religious Freedom: China (Includes Hong Kong, Macau, Tibet, and Xinjiang), available at www.state.gov/reports/2022-report-on-international-religious-freedom/china/.

[154] See Chen's lawyer's defense statement, available at https://blog.boxun.com/hero/201209/xszg/3_1.shtml.

subverted by speech?[155] In addition, criticism of the ruling party by no means would implicate a subversion of state power.

Under the leadership of the CPC, an important notion that underlies all work in China is the desire for social and political stability.[156] Therefore, law must serve as a mechanism to achieve stability. This notion has significant impact on what the rule of law in China is seeking. For example, ruling the country by law is taken by the CPC as the basic strategy necessary for a vital guarantee of lasting political stability of the country.[157] In the meantime, stability serves as a pragmatic parameter that is used to judge the government's work at all levels and to evaluate job performance and promotion of government officials.

Apparently, the strategy of ruling the country by law focuses not on how to impose restraint on the government but on how to confine the conduct of people. There are several reasons for this. The first reason is a conviction that the essence of stability is the CPC's leadership or power.[158] Second, stability in China is not viewed in terms of popular control over the government but rather as governmental control over society.[159] As the *Chen Pingfu* case demonstrated, maintaining stability often became political justification for suppressing any civil activity or dissenting voice that is considered a threat to government power. In addition, there is no such tradition in China to challenge the government. As a matter of fact, the power of government, at any level, is not regarded as being given by the people but by a higher level of government authority.

While drafting legislation, China now often turns its eyes to other countries for direction, especially in the country's underdeveloped areas of law. But it would be naive to assume that China would follow a certain legal pattern or theory that is popular elsewhere to develop its legal system under the rule of law. A standard answer in a recent Chinese bar exam question states clearly that "Western capitalist rule of law theory" is not an "origin" of Chinese rule of law.[160] Instead, an official statement says that a fundamental principle of Chinese rule of law is "adherence to the leadership of the CPC."[161]

Therefore, the legal system in China will develop in a Chinese way with Chinese characteristics. Despite the vagueness of Chinese characteristics, the CPC, in

[155] See *id.*

[156] A very popular slogan in China today is "stability overrides everything."

[157] See Zemin, *supra* note 98.

[158] See Hu Kangsheng, *Study Constitution, Be Loyal to Constitution and Preserve Authority of Constitution*,Speech at the Standing Committee Group Study Session of the NPC, February 28, 2009, available at www.npc.gov.cn/npc/xinwen/2009-02/28/content_1476418.htm.

[159] See VOA News, *China's Legislature Stresses Social Stability*, March 6, 2009. A full text of the report is available at www1.voanews.com/english/news/a-13-2009-03-06-voa13-68772437.html.

[160] See selection of Chinese bar examination questions, available at www.ppkao.com/shiti/10491599/.

[161] See the CPC, *supra* note 118.

response to the growing demand in the country for a democratic government,[162] repeatedly forecloses the possibility of following the Western political system in regard to separation of powers.[163] The Central Committee of the CPC has made it clear that the Western separation of powers is not suitable for China because it is nothing but a "rival show."[164] According to the CPC, there are no "rivals" in China because all government branches are uniformly subject to the leadership of the CPC.[165]

But an unavoidable question is how to make the CPC and the CPC-led government accountable so that public power will not be corrupted or abused. The accountability of a government to a great extent depends on a system in which the government may only act within the law, is answerable to the people it serves, and is liable for any wrongdoing it commits. China does not seem to have such a system in place. Instead, the country is led to hold the idea expressed in the so-called Yan'an Cave Dialogue.

The "Yan'an Cave Dialogue" refers to *Mao*'s chat with *Huang Yanpei* in 1945. *Huang*, a well-known educator and co-founder of the Chinese Democratic and Political League, was invited with other famous figures from the republic period to visit *Yan'an*, then the headquarters of the CPC. In his meeting with Mao at Mao's cave dwelling, *Huang* said:

> I have lived for more than 60 years. Apart from what I have heard, what I have seen with my own eyes is truly that "while the rise to prosperity can be rapid, the fall can suddenly come." Nobody in history, including an individual, a family, a group, and even a country, has been able to escape the domination of this "rapid rise and sudden fall" cycle.

Huang then asked Mao if "the CPC has found a new way out of this cycle." *Mao* replied: "We have, and we can jump out of this cycle." He said to Huang: "The new way is democracy," referring to people's democracy (or mass democracy). According to *Mao*, "Only by allowing the people to supervise the government can a lax government be avoided, and only when everyone takes responsibility can a government survive."[166]

Mao's "*Yan'an* Cave Dialogue" has long been regarded by the CPC as a classic statement of political power construction to resolve the historical cycle problem for the country.[167] But the Dialogue contained nothing about how the people's

[162] See Wang Zhenmin, A System of Unconstitutionality Review in China, 1–18 (China University of Political Science & Law Press, 2004).

[163] See Wu Banguo, Working Report of the Standing Committee of the NPC to the Second Annual Assembly Meeting of the 11th NPC on March 9, 2009.

[164] See *id.*

[165] See *id.*

[166] See Du Shangze & Liu Shaohua, *Respondents to Questions in Cave Dwelling*, People's Daily, January 14, 2022, available at https://baijiahao.baidu.com/s?id=1721887865792497556&wfr=spider&for=pc.

[167] See *id.*

democracy is to be achieved in the country. As many have observed, Mao's problem-solving democracy is not the same as the right to vote in the West because it is Mao's belief that the Western-style democracy of free voting is essentially the paralysis and domination of the bourgeoisie over the proletariat and the working masses.[168] In fact, *Mao*, driven by his "class struggle" philosophy, never made the people's democracy a real mechanism to effectively "supervise the government" in the country.

Due to the lack of a meaningful system to restrain the government power, corruption and power abuses have become quite extensive and are getting even worse in many aspects. In response to public outrage, the CPC has taken several measures to clean up corrupted officials at all levels. Those measures are now collectively called the self-revolution of the CPC. The self-revolution was introduced by Xi in 1995 as a measure of internal reform of the CPC for self-improvement. In a recent article published in the CPC-run magazine "*Seeking the Truth*," *Xi Jinping* specifically elevated the "self-revolution" of the CPC to the level of "a new way" to deal with the rise-and-fall cycle.

Xi acknowledges that as the largest Marxist ruling party in the world, "how the CPC can successfully break out of the historical cycle of the rise and fall chaos and ensure that the party never deteriorates or becomes stale" is "a strategic issue before all members in the party." According to *Xi*, "since the 18th National Congress of the CPC, in the great practice of promoting comprehensive and strict governance of the party, we have continued to carry out practical exploration and theoretical thinking." *Xi* then concludes that "based on the first answer given by Comrade Mao Zedong" in the cave dwelling dialogue to "let the people supervise the government," we now have the second answer, that is, to "continuously promote the party's self-revolution."[169]

Self-revolution refers to a "spiritually puritanical self-discipline" that underpins the conduct of all CPC members, which is deemed a useful tool enabling the CPC to recognize its own shortcomings, supervise itself, correct itself, and develop itself.[170] But since the self-revolution focuses on internal regulation, its effectiveness is necessarily in serious doubt because, as a governing party, the CPC cannot possibly overcome by itself the addictive nature and intoxicating effect of power without any external constraints. In fact, given Xi's emphasis that the self-revolution must adhere to the centralized and unified leadership of the CPC, with unified

[168] See Jiang Jiang, *101st Year Anniversary, Mao's Cave-Dwelling Dialogue, and Historical Cycles*, Ginger River Review, July 4, 2022, available at www.gingerriver.com/p/101st-year-anniversary-maos-cave.

[169] See Xi Jinping, *Deeply Promote the Party's Self-Revolution*, "Seeking the Truth," Vol. 24, 2024, available at https://baijiahao.baidu.com/s?id = 1818493455507740592&wfr = spider&for = pc.

[170] See China Daily, *Party's Strong Vitality Originates from Continuous Self-Revolution*, July 2, 2024, available at https://global.chinadaily.com.cn/a/202407/02/WS668349dfa31095c51c50bca2.html.

planning for deployment and advancement,[171] a question inevitably raised is how the self-revolution can actually help solve the "Cave Dialogue" puzzle,[172] especially in dealing with the corruption that has become a feature rather than a bug within the CPC and its led government.[173]

C. Confucian *Impacts*

Although China has made efforts to develop the rule of law, there remains a lack of public confidence in the legal system of the country. The public still doubts that the current Chinese legal system is adequate to provide a just result.[174] People are constantly plagued by lingering misgivings that the system will work as it should. People had hoped that the establishment of the socialist legal system would provide an important legal infrastructure for the development of the rule of law in China.[175] But given the political hurdles associated with the Chinese characteristics that dictate the country, the path toward the rule of law in the country is, and will continue to be, quite thorny, and certain setbacks along the way will conceivably recur from time to time.[176]

One of the hurdles has to do with tradition, or more specifically, *Confucian* impacts. As discussed, China was historically reputed as a country with the rule of man.[177] One major reason for this is that *Confucian* orthodoxy significantly undermined the function of law in favor of moral standards or the "*Li*." Another reason relates to the fact that the traditional Chinese legal system was centralized in the imperial power of one person, the emperor. An additional reason is perhaps the lawlessness, or legal nihilism, created by *Mao*'s unlimited power that penetrated the country for decades.

In efforts to revamp its legal system, since the 1980s China has attempted to depart from the old image of rule of man by assigning an important role to law.[178] A substantial step in this regard was, as noted, the constitutional amendment made in 1999, demanding that the country be governed according to law. In the meantime, China has engaged in extensive legislation, hoping to demonstrate that the country is moving toward the rule of law.[179]

[171] See Jinping, *supra* note 169.

[172] See Arran Hope, *"Self Resolution" Suggests Stronger CCDI Mandate*, 24 China Brief, January 19, 2024, available at https://jamestown.org/program/self-revolution-suggests-stronger-ccdi-mandate.

[173] See *id.*

[174] See Margaret Woo, *Law and Discretion in Contemporary Chinese Courts*, 8 Pac. Rim L. & Pol'y J. 581 (1999).

[175] See the State Council Information Office, *White Paper on the Rule of Law in China* (2008), a full text of the White Paper is available at www.china.org.cn/government/news/2008-02/28/content_11025486.htm.

[176] See Chenguang, *supra* note 92, at 32.

[177] For general comments, see Jones, *supra* note 53; see also Chunying, *supra* note 75, at 22.

[178] See Cohen, *China's Legal Reform at the Crossroads, supra* note 129.

[179] See Peerenboom, *China's Long March, supra* note 107, at ix–x.

Ideologically, however, China is still wrestling with a proper interplay between law and man. As a result of the impact of *Confucianism*, there is a strong belief in the country that law is not enough to govern a society.[180] This belief has at least two implications. First, good moral norms are equally as essential as written law and sometimes play an even more important role in governing behavior. Second, even though laws as written are in place, they cannot execute themselves, and as such, people are needed to implement laws.[181] Therefore, there remains a general holding that good governance depends on the "right" man or a "great" man.[182]

This holding derives from a *Confucian* proposition that law does not work itself.[183] The proposition as such has a clear emphasis on the role of man in making the law work. As between the law and man, a well-stated *Confucian* view was that "there is a ruling man but not a ruling law."[184] This view implies that law could not cover everything nor could it be able to cope with changing situations, and therefore there is a need for the right man.[185] According to *Xunzi*, for example, law cannot stand alone and legal analogy cannot be exercised by itself. Thus, with the right man the law lasts; but without the right man, the law perishes.[186] Also, according to *Xunzi*'s conclusion, there have been cases in which chaos occurred despite a good law, but chaos never ensued with a good man in charge.[187]

Therefore, although the light of the rule of law has been shed in China today, pursuit of the rule of law is being proscribed by the country's long-lasting *Confucian* tradition. In a narrow sense, there exists a belief that the rule of law, in order to be effective, should be supplemented by the rule of man.[188] In a broad sense, maintaining the CPC's absolute leadership, as noted, is entrenched as the prerequisite for the exercise of the rule of law. People in China therefore are driven to conclude that only the CPC may bring a bright future to China.[189]

In ancient China, any word from the emperor was an imperial edict, which must be followed. The impact of this history, however, continues today. The words from the top CPC leader are weighted most heavily because political uniformity is

[180] See Jerome A. Cohen, The Criminal Process in the People's Republic of China 1949–1963: An Introduction, 4 (Harvard University Press, 1968).
[181] See Chenguang, *supra* note 92, at 7.
[182] See Hager, *supra* note 99, at 13.
[183] See Chenguang, *supra* note 92, at 7.
[184] See the *Xunzi*, ch. 12, *Jundao*, vol. book 12, at 175, On the Way of a Lord (it was translated as "There are men who can bring order about, but there is no model that will produce order"), a full text of *Xunzi*'s work is available at www.quanxue.cn/ct_rujia/xunziindex.html. For an English translation, see John Knoblock, Xunzi (Stanford University Press, 1990).
[185] See Sucheng, *supra* note 84, at 154.
[186] See the *Xunzi*, *Jundao*, *supra* note 184.
[187] See *id.*, ch. 9, *Wang Zhi*, book 9, On the Regulation of a King.
[188] See Chenguang, *supra* note 92, at 7.
[189] See Zuo Zeyuan, *Harmonious Society and Rule of Law*, in Li Lin, ed., Ruling Country according to Law and the Building of Harmonious Society, 43–47 (China Legal Publishing House, 2007); see also Congde, *supra* note 65, at 82–86.

required for all government officials. By uniformity, it means that the whole country must keep politically aligned with the CPC Central Committee. Thus, the term "uniform" in China, as observed, is in many cases a euphemism for "central."[190]

4. SOCIAL HARMONY PURSUIT AND UNDERLYING CORE SOCIALIST VALUES

While making an effort to develop the rule of law in the country, China has put great emphasis on fostering its mainstream ideology in order to stay independent of Western influence. To that end, since the early stage of economic reforms, the country has set in motion an ideological cleaning-up movement with a purpose to maintain Marxism as the fundamental governing ideology of the country. The official description of the movement as such is the construction of a socialist spiritual civilization.

In general, spiritual civilization stands for a spectrum of Chinese socialist cultural and ideological values. According to the CPC Central Committee, the construction of a socialist spiritual civilization is aimed at improving the ideological and moral qualities and scientific and cultural qualities of the nation.[191] As explained by the CPC, the construction of a socialist spiritual civilization is divided into cultural construction and ideological construction.[192]

The ideological construction relates to the socialist nature and direction of spiritual civilization, and it focuses on the ideals, morality, and discipline of individuals and the general public. Cultural construction includes development of socialist culture, science and technology, education, and health. Thus, the purpose of the construction of socialist spiritual civilization is to turn the members of society into "good citizens" equipped with socialist ideals, morals, culture, and discipline. In this regard, the socialist spiritual civilization is considered an important feature of socialism in China.[193]

There have been two major moves in China toward construction of the socialist spiritual civilization. The first move was the national campaign for the building of a harmonious society.[194] The campaign was launched in 2004 under the theory of "the scientific outlook on development" (SOOD). As noted, SOOD was set by the CPC as authoritative guidance for the nation in the form of a political ideology in 2003. While the essence of SOOD, according to the CPC, is to "put people first

[190] See Cohen, *supra* note 129.

[191] See the CPC Central Committee, *Resolution on Guidelines for the Construction of Socialist Spiritual Civilization*, adopted on September 28, 1986, available at http://cpc.people.com.cn/GB/64162/64168/64565/65381/4429515.html.

[192] See *id.*

[193] See *id.*

[194] The goal to build a harmonious society was put forward by the CPC in its Fourth Plenary Session of the 16th National Congress in 2004.

with an aim to achieve a comprehensive, coordinated and sustainable development,"[195] the concept of a harmonious society is in fact the continuity of national heritage bestowed by the *Confucian* tradition of promoting "natural ease" or harmony.[196]

In 2006 the CPC adopted a resolution that made it a goal to create a harmonious socialist society in China by 2020.[197] The relevance here is not whether the goal as such was actually achieved as desired, but rather that the concepts of both "putting people first" and "social harmony" are taken as the main themes for the development of the rule of law in China. It is then held by the CPC that the rule of law is the best way for settling social conflicts peacefully and rationally.[198] As a result, it became a popular idea that a harmonious society is a rule-of-law society, and that law is the aggregate of rules of conduct seeking social harmony.[199] In addition, there is a growing trend in China that the concept of putting people first is the basic spirit of law.[200]

The very concept of harmony under the *Confucian* tradition was the promotion of tolerance and conciliation among people with different thoughts and backgrounds, thereby creating peaceful interpersonal relationships. A civil and ethical principle considered *Confucius*'s lifetime motto was "what you do not want done to yourself, do not do to others."[201] This principle was also meant to be a social standard for the judgment of people. From *Confucius*'s viewpoint, a noble man seeks harmony despite differences, while a petty man stays in discord despite agreement.[202] In addition, *Mencius* laid out three essential elements for success, which

[195] See Communiqué of the Third Plenary Session of the 16th Central Committee of the CPC, Xinhua News Agency, October 14, 2003, available at www.people.com.cn/GB/shizheng/1024/2133923.html.

[196] See the Analects of Confucius (Lun Yu), *Xue Er* (Learning). Paragraph 12 of the Learning is translated as "In practicing the rules of propriety, a natural ease is to be prized. In the ways prescribed by the ancient kings, this is the excellent quality, and in things small and great we follow them." The saying "a natural ease is prized" is also translated as "harmony is what matters." An English translation of the Analects is available at www.camcc.org/_media/reading-group/lunyu/lunyu-en.pdf.

[197] The resolution was adopted by the CPC in its Sixth Plenary Session of the 16th National Congress in 2006. See Xinhua News Agency, *China Publishes Resolution on Building Harmonious Society*, October 18, 2006, available at http://english.cri.cn/2946/2006/10/18/176@152257.htm.

[198] See Report on Hi Jintao's meeting with part of the delegates of the 22nd Congress on Law of the World, available at http://politics.people.com.cn/GB/1024/3670020.html. For a report in English, see China Society for Human Rights Studies, Roundup: Human Rights Issue at 22nd Congress on Law of the World, a full text of the report is available at http://211.167.236.236/zt/magazine/200402006215101321.htm.

[199] See Zeyuan, *supra* note 58, at 33; see also Wang Liming, *A Harmonious Society Should be a Rule of Law Society*, in Li Lin, ed., Ruling the Country according to the Law and the Building of Harmonious Society, 211 (China Legal Press, 2007).

[200] See Lv Shilun & Gao Zhong, *Socialist Harmonious Society and the Rule of Law Spirits of Putting People First*, in Li Lin, *id.* at 17.

[201] See the *Analects of Confucius*, *supra* note 196, ch. 15, The Lord of *Weiling*.

[202] See *id.*, ch. 13, *Zhi Lu*.

included "time opportunity," "topographic advantage," and "harmony of people," viewing the harmony of people as the most critical.[203]

Today, the drive to form a harmonious society in China serves multiple purposes. In one respect, it reinforces the need for social order and stability under the leadership of the CPC. The basic notion is that harmony would not be achieved without an orderly and stable society.[204] In another respect, it helps alleviate the tension caused by the increasing disparity between rich and poor economically, and the growing public outrage over unceasing political corruption. More significantly, it helps justify "Chinese characteristics" that support the political system currently in operation.[205]

The building of social harmony seems to have become a strong ideological force that is being grafted onto the development of the rule of law,[206] although at present, there have been more words than actions. The concept of social harmony, though still vague in many aspects, is being incorporated into the legal framework of China. It has become imperative that the rule of law be geared toward creating and enhancing social harmony. Interestingly, in the year 2020, nobody seemed to believe that China had become a harmonious society although the official deadline to reach that goal was 2020.

The doctrine of putting people first also has its origin in *Confucian* philosophy. As noted, *Mencius* placed a high value on the benevolence of a ruler and believed that a benevolent ruler must care about the people.[207] *Xunzi* went even further, warning of the dangers of losing the people's confidence. According to *Xunzi*, "the water that swallows a boat up is the same that bears it."[208] The message both *Mencius* and *Xunzi* intended to send was clear: a ruler should not be too cruel to the ruled. Unfortunately, at most times in the history of China, this message was merely a hope.

Many in China see putting people first as progress toward appreciating the value of people both as individuals and as a social force.[209] It is also considered an

[203] See the *Mengzi*, book two, *Gongsun Chou* II (Opportunities granted by Heaven are less important than terrestrial advantages, which in turn are less important than the harmony among people). For an English translation of *Mengzi*, see Bryan W. Van Norden, Mengzi with Selections from Traditional Commentaries (Hackett, 2008).

[204] See Liming, *supra* note 199, at 211.

[205] For example, the CPC-led People's Congress system is appraised as the "political foundation and institutional safeguard for the socialist harmonious society in China." See Li Lin, *The Role of People's Congress System in the Building of the Harmonious Society*, in Li Lin, ed., Ruling the Country according to the Law and the Building of Harmonious Society, 157 (China Legal Press, 2007).

[206] See *id.* at 1–3.

[207] See the *Mengzi*, *supra* note 203. See Jonathan Ocko, *Using the Past to Make a Case for the Rule of Law*, in Karen G. Turner et al., eds., The Limits of the Rule of Law in China, 72 (University of Washington Press, 2000).

[208] See the *Xunzi*, *Wangzhi*, *supra* note 184.

[209] See Shilun & Zhong, *supra* note 200, at 24–25.

indicator that the country is showing signs of respecting personal liberty and human rights.[210] In reality, however, putting people first is both a pragmatic approach and a political strategy to retain public support for the leadership of the CPC. In this regard, it is fair to say that putting people first does not change the bureaucrat-centered tradition but rather revives the *Confucian* belief in the benevolence of government over people.

For example, in order to spur into motion the doctrine of putting people first, some courts in China initiated reproduction of a trial format known as the "*Ma Xiwu* Trial Method" (*Ma*'s Method) in 2009. *Ma*'s Method was used mainly in CPC-controlled areas in the late 1940s and throughout the whole country in the early 1950s.[211] The highlight of *Ma*'s Method was "trial at the edge of a field," which actually entailed a bench trial at the corner of a farm or in the courtyard of a household.[212]

Ma Xiwu, a non-legally trained and government bureaucrat-turned-judge, strongly believed that the judiciary must serve people and that party policy was the most direct law. He took the position that the best way to conduct a trial was to have the trial outside of a formal courtroom with no legal jargon, because it was easiest for people to understand.[213] In this regard, *Ma* preferred to call his trials mediations rather than adjudications.[214] It was also his view that people's satisfaction was the major criterion to measure the outcome of the trial.[215] *Ma*'s Method was hailed as a model by many top leaders of China, and *Ma* himself was praised by Chairman *Mao* as a person closest to the people.[216]

The initiation received endorsement from the SPC. As a result, a nationwide campaign was launched in the judiciary under the slogan "people's court serves people."[217] In many courts, particularly at the trial level, judges were required to follow *Ma*'s Method by conducting trials in the field to show that the judiciary cares about people.[218] Believing that *Ma*'s Method exemplified how to put people first,

[210] See Li Buyun, *Doctrinal Highlights of the "Social Harmony,"* in Li Lin, ed., Ruling the Country according to the Law and the Building of Harmonious Society, 7 (China Legal Press, 2007).

[211] *Ma Xiwu* (1899–1962), former Vice President of the Supreme People's Court.

[212] See Southern Weekend, *The Biggest Controversy over Judicial Reform – The Revival of Ma Xiwu*, June 11, 2009, p. A8.

[213] See *id.*

[214] See *id.*

[215] See *id.*

[216] See *id.*

[217] "People's court serves people" was a slogan introduced by the President of the SPC as a concrete step to carry out the notion of "putting people first." It is deemed by the SPC as an incarnation of a scientific outlook on development in the judiciary. See the SPC Report, *Vice President Shen Deyong's Written Message to the Conference on "People's Court Serves People,"* July 29, 2009, available at www.court.gov.cn/news/bulletin/release/200907290004.htm.

[218] See Takungpao Newspaper, *The High Court President of Henan Province Actively Pursues the Ma Xiwu Trial Method*, July 24, 2009, available at http://henan.takungpao.com/news/ShowArticle.asp?ArticleID=37747.

some courts even went further by opposing wearing a robe during the trial because, in their view, the robe separated a judge from the people.[219] The advancement of *Ma*'s Method caused a great deal of controversy in the country. Many regarded this practice as a reversal of the ongoing judicial reform that has helped restore judicial professionalism.[220] Facing mounting criticism, this practice faded out in a few years.

The second major move was the promotion of "socialist core values." Initiated in 2006, the formation of a system of socialist core values was considered an indispensable part of the socialist spiritual civilization and also the ideological basis for a harmonious society.[221] It was held that a system of core values, once established, could help establish a harmonious idea, cultivate a harmonious spirit, form harmonious interpersonal relationships, shape a harmonious mentality, create a harmonious atmosphere of public opinion, and form a good moral fashion and common ideals and beliefs.[222]

With the rapid growth of the country's economy, there is increasing concern about spiritual or moral cultivation. Believing that the nation's prosperity is inseparable from spiritual support, the CPC in 2012 reiterated the 2006 initiative to build a system of socialist core values and further materialized the substance of the core values. In the Eighteenth National Conference of the CPC, which was held in November 2012, the socialist core values were defined as twelve values, including prosperity, democracy, civilization, harmony, freedom, equality, justice, the rule of law, patriotism, dedication, integrity, and friendliness.[223] Since then, these twelve values have become the most visible policy guide in China for ideological purification and morality advancement.

The twelve values involve three different levels: nation, society, and individuals. The first four values, namely prosperity, democracy, civilization, and harmony, are at the national level. The next four, freedom, equality, justice, and the rule of law, primarily concern society as a whole. The final four values, comprising patriotism,

[219] See Li Zhen & Huang Xiaozhen, *Upholding the Flag of Ma Xiwu Trial Method Unwaveringly*, available at www.chinacourt.org/html/article/200907/23/366557.shtml.

[220] See Southern Weekend, *Do Not Return to Ma Xiwu Rigidly*, June 11, 2009, p. A3. See also Zhang Weiping (Professor of Law, Tsinghua University School of Law), *What Do We Need to Go Back to Ma Xiwu, Method or Spirit?* Available at http://news.ifeng.com/opinion/200906/0613_23_1201152.shtml.

[221] In October 2006, the Sixth Plenary Session of the Sixteenth Central Committee of the CPC adopted the "Decision on Several Major Issues Concerning the Construction of a Harmonious Socialist Society," in which the major proposition and strategy of "building a socialist core value system" was introduced for the first time. The full text of the Decision is available at www.gov.cn/govweb/gongbao/content/2006/content_453176.htm.

[222] See Guo Jianyu, Basic Contents of the Socialist Core Values – Explanations (People's Press, 2014).

[223] See Hu Jintao, *Unswervingly Advance Along the Path of Socialism with Chinese Characteristics Struggle for Building a Well-Off Society in All-Round*, Report at the 18th National Congress of the CPC, November 8, 2012, available at www.wenming.cn/xxph/sy/xy18d/201211/t20121119_940452.shtml.

dedication, integrity, and friendliness, relate to individuals. Putting all of the values together, all three categories form a uniform and common ideological basis for the country.

In addition, under the CPC's mandate, the socialist core value system must contain four basic elements, including (a) the guiding ideology of Marxism, (b) the common ideal of socialism with Chinese characteristics, (c) the national spirit of patriotism, reform, and innovation, and (d) the socialist view of honor and disgrace.[224]

It is acclaimed that those core values embody the common vision of the contemporary Chinese efforts to achieve the rejuvenation of the nation, and help inspire morale, promote social harmony and invigorate vitality among the public.[225]

To implement the CPC's mandate, the General Office of the CPC Central Committee and the State Council in 2016 issued the "Guiding Opinions on Further Integrating Socialist Core Values into the Construction of the Rule of Law."[226] Two years later, in 2018, the Central Committee of the CPC issued "The Plan of Legislation and Law Amendments for Integrating Socialist Core Values into the Construction of the Rule of Law."[227] Both the "Guiding Opinions" and the "Plan" made it imperative to incorporate the socialist core values into laws and regulations.

In addition, the SPC requires all courts to actively practice and promote the core socialist values and integrate the core socialist values into judicial decisions. According to the SPC, the integration should be made in judicial interpretation, judgment reasoning, and typical (model) cases.[228] In helping promote and justify the integration of the socialist core values into judicial decisions, some argue that the integration is natural because (a) the socialist core values are the legislative reasons behind the court judgments, and (b) promotion of the socialist core values by the courts is the social effect expected from the judgments they make in cases.[229]

The idea of building core values has its roots in Chinese history and culture. As noted, in traditional Chinese society, moral cultivation carried equal weight, if

[224] See *id.*

[225] See Jianyu, *supra* note 222.

[226] See the General Office of the CPC and the State Council, 2016 Guiding Opinions, available at www.gov.cn/zhengce/2016-12/25/content_5152713.htm.

[227] See Central Committee of the CPC, Legislation and Law Amendment Plan 2018, available at www.gov.cn/xinwen/2018-05/07/content_5288843.htm.

[228] See SPC Press Briefing, People's Courts Practicing Core Socialist Values, August 2, 2023. Text of the Briefing is available at www.chinacourt.org/article/detail/2023/08/id/7452160.shtml.

[229] See Yu Fei, *The Function of Socialist Core Values in Civil Adjudication*, Social Science in China, Vol. 1 (2024), available at https://cssn.cn/dkzgxp/zgxp_zgshkx/2024nd1q/202402/t20240226_5734894.shtml. In 2016, the SPC published ten typical cases exemplifying the promotion of socialist core values. See SPC, Socialist Core Value Typical Cases, available at www.court.gov.cn/zixun/xiangqing/408162.html. Following the SPC, many provincial high courts and even local courts also published typical cases as such to show how the socialist core values were implemented in their judicial practices.

not more, than the development of law. According to *Confucius*, for example, while economic development can further improve people's lives, thriving culture and education can cultivate more knowledgeable and responsible citizens, and thus boost social ethics.[230] *Mencius* regarded people learning etiquette, benevolence, and righteousness through education as a symbol of an affluent country.[231]

Similarly, *Wei Zheng*, an influential politician in the *Tang* Dynasty, in his advice to Emperor *Taizong*, explicitly stated that "those who want trees to grow must fix their roots; those who desire to flow far must dredge their sources; and those who think of the country's stability must accumulate virtue."[232] The basic concept was that adequate food and clothing are a necessary but superficial aspect of an affluent life, and cultural richness and spiritual wealth are inevitable demands following economic prosperity. Thus, moral cultivation is considered an effective means to achieve ideological unity, which forms the basis for social stability.

In Chinese history, moral build-up, as discussed, was mostly centered on loyalty and obedience, especially on maintenance of the supremacy of imperial power. Presently, the establishment of a core value system is intended to provide spiritual guidance for the people so that the country will keep to the socialist path under *Marxist* ideology.[233] Put differently, the promotion of socialist core values reflects the consistent desire to maintain communist ideals and the pursuit of socialism with Chinese characteristics. The purpose is to help foster the CPC's dominance in the ideological field and build the Chinese spirit, strength, and power.[234]

Some foreign observers, however, view China's promotion of socialist core values as an effort to accumulate moral capital vis-à-vis economic growth[235] and as a move to tamp down any nascent dissent.[236] Indeed, the current emphasis on the building of prescribed core values is a strategy to ensure that the people remain following the

[230] See the Analects (Lun Yu), Zi Lu 13-9. Confucius went to the country of Wei. Ran You asked, "This country has quite [a] large population, and what else should be done?" Confucius answered, "Make them rich." Ran You asked again, "What else should be done after people get rich?" Confucius replied, "Make them well educated." *Supra* note 186.

[231] See Cao Yaxin, Chinese Values: Traditional Culture and Contemporary Values (Foreign Language Press, 2018).

[232] See Wei Zheng, *Ten Thoughts on Remonstrating with Emperor Taizong*, available at https://wenku.baidu.com/view/1b6d7eb44afe04a1b071de7f.html.

[233] See Xi Jinping, *Secure a Decisive Victory in Building a Moderately Prosperous Society in All Respects and Strive for the Great Success of Socialism with Chinese Characteristics for a New Era*, Report at the 19th National Congress of the CPC, October 18, 2017, available at www.chinadaily.com.cn/china/19thcpcnationalcongress/2017-11/04/content_34115212.htm.

[234] See Liu Yunshan, *Cultivating Core Socialist Values and Putting Them into Practice*, 6 *Qiushi* Journal, July 1, 2014, available at http://english.qstheory.cn/2014-08/14/c_1111962462.htm.

[235] See Michael Gow, *The Core Socialist Values of the Chinese Dream: Towards a Chinese Integral State*, 49 Critical Asian Stud. 1 (2016).

[236] Kerry Brown, *China's New Moral Education Campaign: As Economic Growth Slows, China's Leaders Are Trying Their Hands at Building Moral (Rather Than Economic) Capital*, The Diplomat, September 21, 2015. The full article is available at https://thediplomat.com/2015/09/chinas-new-moral-education-campaign/.

CPC's lead, given the spiral of governmental corruption that has seriously damaged the CPC's image. What is envisaged by the CPC is that the implementation of core values would lead to the unification of thought in the country.[237]

Also, it is interesting to note that while the rule of law is held as one of the core values, the CPC makes it imperative to incorporate the core values into the socialist rule of law through the work of the judiciary in order to achieve an integration of law and morality. This implicates that although judicial independence is an indispensable part of the rule of law elsewhere, it is not the case in China because the Chinese judiciary must serve the needs of the CPC. In other words, judicial independence in China has to be an independence that may only be exercised under the leadership and at the pleasure of the CPC.

[237] Delia Lin & Susan Traveskes, *Creating a Virtuous Leviathan: The Party, Law, and Socialist Core Values*, 6 Asian J. of L. and Soc'y 41–46 (2019).

3

Socialist Legal System

Sources of Law and Legal Hierarchy

INTRODUCTION

A legal system is generally described as a procedure or process for interpretation and enforcement of the law.[1] In comparative law, the legal system is the concept of a legal family that shares the same or similar traditions, principles, and formalities. According to Professor John Merryman, for example, there are three highly influential legal traditions in the world, namely, civil law, common law, and socialist legal traditions.[2] Here, legal tradition is synonymous with legal family, which represents a particular system of law.

In most cases, however, legal system refers to the legal framework consisting of different branches of law in a country. It includes all existing rules, procedures, and enforcement mechanisms. The legal system of each country is determined and shaped by its unique history and tradition, and thus contains individual variations. The current legal system in China, as noted, is defined as a socialist legal system with Chinese characteristics. It bears civil law tradition, but its socialist nature and Chinese characteristics signify its uniqueness.

To understand the Chinese legal system, or a legal system in general, it is necessary to look first at where law comes from. This is a question about the source of law. Related to the source is the basic framework of the legal system, referring to the components that structure and form the system. The source of law also involves the effect of law, because laws from different sources have different authoritative effect. In other words, the hierarchy of law is dependent on its source.

1 See Cornell Law School, ILL, *Legal System*, available at www.law.cornell.edu/wex/legal_systems, accessed August 23, 2025.

2 See John H. Merryman, The Civil Law Tradition: An Introduction to the Legal Systems of Western Europe and Latin America, 1 (2nd ed., Stanford University Press, 1985).

1. SOURCES OF LAW

The source of law has various viewpoints. A law has a historic source if it is viewed from its root. In this regard, the question is about how the law evolved throughout history. If, however, the question concerns the underlying legal theory of a law, the focus is then on the theoretic or ideological source of the law. Similarly, the source of law can be its documentary source or academic source when the citation or scholarly explanation is at issue. Finally, if the law itself is examined, the source of law can either be the nature of law (e.g., natural law, positive law) or the form of law (e.g., statute or precedent).

In a narrow sense, however, the source of law refers to the origin of the law or the authority from which the legal rules are derived. It serves as a legal basis for the best interpretation of a rule, principle, or value in the law.[3] From the viewpoint of Chinese legal scholars, the origin of law includes both the source of the form of the law and the source of the effect of the law. The form of law is the external manifestation of the existence of the law, and the effect of law is the primary basis for the law to become operative.[4] Without a specific form, the law would not exist, and without a certain effect, the law, though it exists, would be useless.[5]

Thus, it is generally held in China that law must be expressed in a certain form by specific government institutions, and only when the law is so expressed can it be known and followed by people and have legal effect.[6] A commonly accepted notion in the country is that like all other things, law itself is a unity of content and form: content is the body of internal elements, while form is an expression of the content.[7] In this context, the particular form of expressing and effecting the law is considered the source of the law. The form of law deals with such questions as whether the law is codified or non-codified, or whether precedent may constitute law. The effect of law mainly concerns the binding force of the law.

Like in many other countries, law in China has two sources: primary sources and secondary sources.[8] In general, the primary source of law is the source where the law is created by the legislature or another law-creating body and can be directly used to resolve legal issues. Since the primary source of law comes from authoritative state organs, reflecting the will of the state, it contains binding effects and can directly regulate the behavior of all participants in their social and business activities.

3 See, in general, John Bell, *Sources of Law*, 77 Cambridge L.J. 40 (2018).

4 See Zuo Zeyuan, An Introduction to Law, The State Higher Education Textbook Series, 45 (Law Press, 2007); see also Wu Zhumo & Li Shuangyuan, A General Introduction to Jurisprudence, The State Higher Education Textbook Series, 17–18 (Law Press, 2007).

5 See Zeyuan, *supra* note 4, at 45.

6 See Zhumo & Shuangyuan, *supra* note 4, at 17.

7 See Shen Zhonglin & Zhang Wenxian, Jurisprudence, 307 (2nd ed., Higher Education Press, 2004).

8 *See generally* Shu Guoying & Li Hongbo, Ladder of Jurisprudence, 39–50 (2006).

The secondary source refers to non-law-making institutions. This source cannot be used as a legal ground necessary and sufficient to deal with legal issues, although it may have a certain influence on legal activities. Unlike the primary source, the secondary source does not produce legal effects, but it nevertheless has a certain degree of persuasion and may be taken as a reference, particularly in the case where the primary source is absent. Since the secondary source, though not binding, is a meaningful source for the development of law, it is called by some scholars in China "the semi-product of law."[9]

Another way to tell whether a source of law is primary or secondary in China is to see if it is a regulatory document promulgated by the state or a government agency. The regulatory document implicates that law in China only takes a codified or statutory form. Therefore, rooted in the civil law tradition, China does not have judge-made law or precedent as a primary source of law. Any source of law other than the regulatory document is a secondary source. Also, it is important to note that scholars' writings or opinions are in general not a source of law, primary or secondary, in the current Chinese legal system.

In Chinese jurisprudence, the regulatory document may broadly refer to the normative legal documents produced by legislative organs with legislative power in accordance with legislative procedures. It may also narrowly mean the normative legal document promulgated only by the National People's Congress (NPC) and its Standing Committee. In terms of the source of law, the law is specifically tailored to its narrow meaning, namely the normative legal document resulting from the legislative action of the NPC and its Standing Committee.

A. *Primary Sources of Law*

Under the 1982 Constitution and the Legislation Law,[10] the primary source of law in the country includes the Constitution, laws, administrative regulations, local regulations, autonomous regulations, specific regulations and rules, and local decrees. As provided in the 1982 Constitution, only the NPC and its Standing Committee have the authority to adopt laws.[11] The power to issue administrative regulations rests with the State Council.[12] The instrumentalities of the State Council, including ministries and commissions, as well as the central bank and the state audit office, may adopt rules within the scope of authority granted.[13] The provincial, autonomous region, or directly governed municipality people's

9 See *id.* at 40.

10 The Legislation Law was promulgated by the NPC on March 15, 2000, and was amended on March 15, 2015. An English translation is available at www.chinalawtranslate.com/2015lawlaw/?lang=en.

11 See *id.*, art. 2.

12 See *id.*, art. 65.

13 See *id.*, art. 80.

congresses and their standing committees may formulate local provisions based on specific situations and the actual needs of the administrative region.[14]

a. Constitution and Laws

Both the Constitution and laws are adopted by the state legislature. As the fundamental law that has the highest legal status, authority, and effect in the country, the Constitution forms the basis for the formulation of all other laws. A settled principle in the Constitution is that all laws, regulations, and local decrees must not be in conflict with the Constitution. Under the Constitution are the laws that govern specific matters and apply uniformly throughout the country.

According to the Chinese Legislation Law, the matters that shall only be governed by law include: (1) issues concerning state sovereignty; (2) the formation, organization, functions, and powers of the people's congresses, the people's governments, the people's courts, and the people's procuratorates at all levels; (3) the regional ethnic autonomy system, the special administrative region system, and the self-government system of people at the grassroots level; (4) criminal offenses and penalties; (5 compulsory measures and penalties involving deprivation of a citizen's political rights or restriction of personal freedom; (6) the establishment of any category of tax, determination of tax rates, tax collection administration, and other basic taxation rules; (7) expropriation and requisition of property not owned by the state; (8) the basic system of civil matters; (9) basic economic rules and basic rules on the treasury, customs, finance, and foreign trade; (10) litigation and arbitration systems; and (11) other matters which must be governed by laws developed by the NPC and its Standing Committee.[15]

The top legislative body of China is the NPC. The legislative power of the NPC rests with the General Assembly and the Standing Committee. Since the General Assembly of the NPC only meets once a year, the Standing Committee of the NPC is in charge of the routine legislative work. Under article 7 of the Legislation Law, the NPC has the sole power to amend the Constitution and to formulate and revise criminal, civil, and state organic laws and other basic laws, while its Standing Committee may only adopt and revise the laws other than those reserved to the NPC General Assembly.[16]

[14] See *id.*, art. 70.

[15] See *id.*, art. 8.

[16] Despite this provision, however, the passage of the Torts Law in December 2009 took an unusual step. Given its status as a basic civil law, the Torts Law is a law that must go through the NPC General Assembly. But in order to meet the timeline the CPC set for the establishment of the socialist legal system with Chinese characteristics in 2010, the Torts Law was enacted by the NPC's Standing Committee instead. This move was challenged by many scholars because they believed that the Standing Committee lacked the power to pass the Torts Law. See Hou Guoyue, *The Standing Committee of the NPC Lacks the Power to Enact the Torts Law*, available at http://civil.law.com.cn/article/defaut.asp?id=47528. See also Xu

I. LEGISLATIVE PROCESS. Pursuant to the Legislation Law, the law-making process in China consists of four steps: bill introduction or proposal, legislative review, vote, and promulgation. In the first step, a legislative bill may be introduced or proposed through various sources. As provided in the Legislation Law, a legislative bill may be introduced to the NPC for review through the Presidium of the NPC, the Standing Committee of the NPC, the State Council, the Central Military Committee, the Supreme People's Court (SPC), the Supreme People's Procuratorate (SPP), or the special committees of the NPC.[17] The bill may also be introduced by a delegation or thirty or more delegates acting jointly.[18]

Meanwhile, a legislative bill can be introduced to the Standing Committee of the NPC by the Council of Chairmen of the NPC, the State Council, the Central Military Committee, the SPC, the SPP, the special committees of the NPC,[19] or by ten or more constituent members of the Standing Committee acting jointly.[20] Note again that only the bills that involve laws not reserved to the NPC may be introduced to the Standing Committee.

However, those who introduce the bill may not necessarily undertake drafting the law. In general, basic laws are normally drafted by a particular office of the Standing Committee of the NPC, while other laws are often drafted by the State Council or by a relevant ministry. In many cases, legal drafting requires the participation of legal experts working together with those who are from particular legislative offices, and from specific government agencies as well.

The introduction of the bills is followed by legislative review. The review can be undertaken either by the NPC or its Standing Committee. The process of review in the Standing Committee requires three readings before the bill may be presented for a vote. The three readings are conducted by the members of the Standing Committee of the NPC. After passing the three readings, the bill is ready for a floor vote either in the NPC or in the Standing Committee. The passage of a law requires a simple majority vote except for an amendment to the Constitution. Under article 64 of the 1982 Constitution (as amended 2018), an amendment to the Constitution can be proposed by the Standing Committee of the NPC or by more than one-fifth of the delegates to the NPC. Adoption of the amendment must cross the threshold of two-thirds of the votes of all delegates to the NPC.[21]

Xianmin, *The Torts Law Should Be Submitted to the NPC's National Conference for Review*, available at www.npc.gov.cn/nc/xnwen/tpbd/cwhhy/2009-12/23/content-1531743.htm.

[17] See the Legislation Law, *supra* note 10, art. 14.

[18] See *id.*, art. 15.

[19] See *id.*, art. 26.

[20] See *id.*, art. 27.

[21] See the 1982 Constitution (amended in 2018), available at https://npcobserver.files.wordpress.com/2018/12/PRC-Constitution-2018.pdf. Also, according to article 64 of the 1982 Constitution, laws and other bills are to be adopted by a majority of all delegates to the NPC.

II. GENERAL LAW V. SPECIAL LAW. In light of its legal effect, laws can be categorized as general laws or special laws. The law of a general nature is a law applicable to any person or thing within the territorial domain of the country, while a special law refers to the law that is effective in a specific region, for a specific period or a specific event, or to specific persons in the country. Normally, a law like the Criminal Law or Civil Law is a general law, and a law such as the Law of Teachers or the Law of Judges would be considered a special law. But there is no clear-cut line between general and special laws. Take contracts, for example: the Civil Law is a general law, while contract law is a special law. However, if sales are involved, contract law will be considered a general law and the statute on sales will then be a special law.

The significance of separating general law from special law does not lie in the coverage of the laws but in their hierarchical effect. Under the doctrine of "*lex specialis derogat legi benerali*" (special law prevails over general law), if two or more norms deal with the same subject matter, priority should be given to the norm that is more specific. The doctrine establishes a rule of interpretation in jurisprudence that a specific provision takes precedence over a general one. In other words, the application of the special law precludes the effect of the general law on the same thing or person. When the special law is repealed, the effect of the general law remains. On the other hand, if the general law is abolished, the special law does not necessarily cease to apply.

Also, law in China is commonly considered to consist of three basic elements: concept, principle, and norm. As an element of law, a concept is the legal category representing certain characteristics of a particular subject in the law. For example, legal person is a concept created by law as a category of legally fictitious persons that have both legal rights and obligations. Another example is the concept of "missing person." A person who is considered missing in law does not necessarily mean that the person in fact is missing, because it is a legal presumption of missing under certain circumstances.[22]

A principle is the theoretical foundation underlying the law and jurisprudence. It functions as the basis of legal rules and governing guidelines. In Chinese contract law, for example, the principles that govern contracts include equality, voluntariness, fairness, good faith, legality, and fulfillment of contractual obligations. These principles have multiple roles: first, they are mandatory and must be followed; second, they are gap-fillers that can help supplement and aid courts in interpreting the contract law provisions; and third, they can be used as the legal benchmark for construction of contract terms or missing content.[23]

[22] Under article 20 of the 1986 Civil Code and article 40 of the 2017 GPCL, if the whereabouts of a natural person have been unknown for two years, an interested person may apply to a people's court for a declaration that the natural person is missing.

[23] For detailed discussion of Chinese Contract Law principles, see Mo Zhang, Chinese Contract Law: Theory and Practice, 93 (2nd ed., Brill, 2020).

A norm refers to the rule that provides rights, obligations, and consequences of violation. Given its substantive nature, a norm is viewed as the core element of the law. Jurisprudentially, legal norms can have different categories. In their effect, norms can be divided into mandatory norms and permissive norms.[24] Mandatory norms make it imperative to do something or not to do something, and they are rules that cannot be derogated from by the parties or anyone else; otherwise, legal liability will be imposed. By contrast, permissive norms allow the relevant parties to freely determine their rights and obligations within the scope permitted by law. Most permissive norms are used in legal areas involving civil and commercial matters.

b. Treaties

Parallel to the law are international treaties. Although in theory, a treaty has the same effect as the law, its application often involves such issues as what effect the treaty should have, especially when there appears to be a discrepancy between the treaty provisions and domestic law, and how the treaty is to be applied in the courts. In essence, these issues concern the relationship between treaties and domestic law, or the status of international treaties in the domestic legal system.

In international law, there are different theories that define the relationship between an international treaty and domestic law. One theory is called monism or the monistic approach, which holds that international treaties are superior to domestic law. Monism emphasizes the supremacy of international law and considers domestic law subordinate to international law.[25] The other theory is known as dualism or the dualistic approach. Under dualism, domestic law and international law are different systems, and neither legal order has the power to create or alter the rules of the other.[26]

Between the two theories mentioned is the mixed doctrine that combines the traits of both the monist and the dualist. Under the mixed approach, the application of a treaty in domestic courts depends on how the treaty is to be interpreted. In the United States, treaties are divided into two categories: self-executing and non-self-executing.[27] A self-executing treaty is a treaty that operates in and of itself without the aid of any legislative provision, while a non-self-executing treaty requires a legislative

[24] In addition, according to the way law regulates social behaviors, legal norms can be divided into authoritative norms, obligatory norms, and prohibitive norms. From their contents, legal norms can be classified as deterministic norms (norms that are directly applicable), appointment norms (norms that authorize the implementation of legislation), and applicable norms (norms that allow an application of another rule by reference).

[25] See Burns H. Westen, Richard A. Falk, & Hilary Charlesworth, International Law and World Order: A Problem Oriented Coursebook, 229–233 (3rd ed., West, 1997).

[26] See *id.*

[27] Carlos Manuel Vazquez, *The Four Doctrines of Self-Executing Treaties*, 89 Am. J. Int'l L. 695, 722 (1995).

act in order to operate as domestic law.[28] Whether a treaty is self-executing or non-self-executing requires a multi-factor analysis. One factor is whether the treaty provisions are suitably precise or obligatory to be capable of judicial enforcement, or if they contemplate implementing legislation or other legal measures.[29]

Thus, how to solve the conflict between an international treaty and domestic law largely depends on how the international treaty stands in the domestic system. Under the general legal principle, if there is a hierarchy between the norms, the superior norm prevails over the inferior norm (*lex superior derogat legi inferiori*). If, however, the two norms are at the same level, the later norm controls (*lex posterior derogat legi priori*).[30] The principle of "later norm controls" is commonly called the "last-in-time" rule, meaning that effect is given to "whichever was enacted later in time."[31]

In China, there is no provision in the Constitution or any statute that prescribes the relationship between a treaty and domestic law. Before the 2020 Civil Code was adopted, a relevant provision on the application of international treaties was article 142 of the 1986 General Principles of Civil Law (1986 Civil Law). Under article 142, if any international treaty concluded or acceded to by the People's Republic of China contained provisions that differed from those in the civil law of China, the treaty provisions applied, except for those to which China had made reservations.[32] Article 142 suggested that treaties would be superior to domestic law when a conflict occurred. But it was unclear whether a people's court may directly apply the treaty. It was also questionable whether the treaty should still prevail if legislation enacted after the treaty appeared to be in conflict with the treaty.

In several other pieces of legislation, the priority of treaty application was provided the same way as article 142 of the 1986 Civil Law.[33] The Civil Procedure Law makes it a general principle that if an international treaty concluded or acceded to by the People's Republic of China has different provisions from the CPL, the provisions of the international treaty shall apply, except for provisions to which the People's Republic of China declares reservations.[34] In judicial practice, the SPC in a

[28] See Restatement (Fourth) of Foreign Relations Law § 310(1)(2) (2018).

[29] See *id.*

[30] See, in general, Erich Vranes, *The Definition of "Norm Conflict" in International Law and Legal Theory*, 17(2) EJIL 395 (2006).

[31] See Julian Ku, *Treaties as Law: A Defense of Last-In-Time Rule for Treaties and Federal Statutes*, 80 Ind. L.J. 319 (2005).

[32] See The General Principles of Civil Law (1986), art. 142. An English translation of the law is available at www.lawinfochina.com/display.aspx?id = 1165&lib = law (hereinafter referred to as 1986 Civil Law).

[33] See, for example, article 95 of the Law of Negotiable Instruments, article 268 of the Maritime Law, and article 148 of the Law of Civil Aviation, which all follow verbatim article 142 of the 1986 Civil Law.

[34] See The Civil Procedure Law of China (1991), art. 238, available at www.asianlii.org/cn/legis/cen/laws/cpl179/.

2000 Notice required all people's courts to give superiority of application to the treaty provisions in cases where a domestic law was inconsistent with the treaty.[35]

The 2018 Foreign Investment Law (FIL), however, alters article 142 of the 1986 Civil Law pertaining to the application of treaties. Under article 4 of the FIL, where international treaties or agreements concluded or acceded to by the People's Republic of China provide for more preferential treatment for the entry admission of foreign investments, the relevant provisions may be applied. Unlike article 142 of the 1986 Civil Law, article 4 of the FIL does not mandate the application of a treaty if the treaty provisions differ from domestic law with regard to the treatment granted to foreign investors.

When the FIL was drafted, article 4 was heavily debated. In an early draft, article 4 simply followed article 142 of the 1986 Civil Law and contained the term "shall apply," which makes application of the treaty mandatory if there is a conflict between the treaty and domestic law. However, many were opposed to the use of mandatory language in article 4. A major concern was that when application of the treaty was made compulsory, it would provide foreign investors with an opportunity to challenge domestic law, which may destroy the uniformity of domestic law regulating foreign investment.[36]

As a result, in the final version of article 4 of the FIL, the term "shall apply" was replaced with the term "may apply." The change is significant because it departs from article 142 of the 1986 Civil Law by making the application of treaties optional rather than mandatory. The problem now is that article 4 of the FIL is not only inconsistent with article 142 of the 1986 Civil Law, but also creates uncertainty about the effect of international treaties, particularly when the treaty provision appears to be in conflict with Chinese domestic law.[37]

The 2020 Civil Code contains no provisions on the application of international treaties, and the 1986 Civil Law was repealed when the 2020 Civil Code took effect on January 1, 2021. In 2023, China adopted its first Law of Foreign Relations (LFR). Aimed at "strengthening foreign related legislative work and developing a rule-based system in foreign affairs,"[38] the LFR provides that the state will take due measures to implement and apply treaties and agreements to which China is a party, but

[35] See the SPC, *The Notice on Several Questions that Deserve Attentions Concerning Adjudication and Handling of Foreign Civil and Commercial Cases* (2000), available at http://luhongxia.chinalawedu.com/falvfagui/fg23079/3093.shtml.

[36] See a report on the scholarly debates over article 4 during the public comment period, available at https://finance.china.com/news/11173316/20190129/35108597_1.html.

[37] Interestingly, in the 2019 version of the Special Administrative Measures for the Entry Admission of Foreign Investment (Negative List), issued by NDRC and MOFCOM on June 30, 2019, the provision for the mandatory application of treaties remains intact. See NDRC and MOFCOM, *The 2019 Negative List*, available at www.gov.cn/xinwen/2019–06/30/content_5404703.htm.

[38] See Law of Foreign Relations of China, art. 29, available at http://en.moj.gov.cn/2023-07/11/c_901729.htm.

implementation and application shall not undermine state sovereignty, national security, and public interests. Again, the LFR does not prescribe how a treaty is to be applied.[39]

In response to growing calls across the country for clarification of treaty application in people's courts, the SPC issued the "Interpretation of Several Issues Concerning the Application of International Treaties and Practices in the Trial of Foreign Civil and Commercial Cases" on December 28, 2023.[40] Under article 1 of the SPC "Interpretation," if there are different provisions in an international treaty and the laws of the People's Republic of China, the provisions of the international treaty shall apply, except for provisions to which the People's Republic of China declares reservations.[41] The SPC "Interpretation" also allows the parties, by agreement, to exclude, in whole or in part, application of a treaty.[42]

With regard to whether a people's court may directly apply a treaty, the SPC "Interpretation" seems to try to go one step further. In addition to reaffirming the priority of applying treaties over domestic law, the SPC "Interpretation" specifically provides that when a foreign-related civil and commercial case involves the application of two or more international treaties, the people's court shall determine the applicable international treaty based on the applicable relationship clauses in the international treaty.[43]

Moreover, under the SPC "Interpretation," if the parties cite in the contract an international treaty that has not yet entered into force for China, the people's court may determine the rights and obligations between the parties based on the contents of the international treaty, unless the application violates the mandatory provisions of the laws and administrative regulations of China or harms the sovereignty, security, or social or public interests of China.[44]

c. Regulations, Rules, and Decrees

Regulations, also named "provisions" or "measures," refer to the administrative norms formulated by the State Council. The Regulations the State Council adopts under the authorization of the NPC or its Standing Committee are called "interim regulations" or "interim provisions."[45] The departments of the State Council or the

[39] See *id.*, art. 31.

[40] See the SPC, *Interpretation of Several Issues Concerning Application of International Treaties and Practices in the Trial of Foreign Civil and Commercial Cases*, available at https://cicc.court.gov.cn/html/1/218/62/84/2430.html.

[41] See *id.*, art. 1.

[42] See *id.*, art. 3.

[43] See *id.*, art. 2.

[44] See *id.*, art. 4.

[45] See the State Council, *Regulations on Procedures for the Formulation of Administrative Regulations*, art. 5, adopted November 16, 2001, available at www.npc.gov.cn/zgrdw/englishnpc/Law/2007-12/14/content_1384236.htm.

local people's governments may formulate normative documents in the form of rules or decrees but not "regulations." The department rules have nationwide effect but only on specific matters or issues. The local rules or decrees may only apply locally.[46]

It is required that all rules and decrees not contradict the provisions of the Constitution, laws, administrative regulations and other higher-level rules.[47] The power to promulgate and interpret administrative regulations belongs to the State Council, while the adoption and interpretation of rules or decrees are the responsibility of the relevant ministries, departments under the State Council, or local governments involved. If a state agency, social group, enterprise, institution, or citizen believes that a rule or decree is in conflict with laws and administrative regulations, a written request may be submitted to the State Council for review.[48]

d. Legislative Interpretations

Another important primary source of law is the interpretation of law by the Standing Committee of the NPC. Under the 1982 Constitution, the Standing Committee of the NPC has the authority to interpret the Constitution and laws.[49] Therefore, the interpretation of law by the Standing Committee has the same effect as law. Note that the SPC also has the power to make interpretations, but its interpretations are limited to the application of law, meaning that the SPC's interpretation may only deal with how the laws are to be applied and implemented. Since the SPC does not have the power to make law, its interpretations, though binding on the courts with respect to the application of law, are not the law.

B. *Secondary Sources of Law*

The secondary sources of law in China are commonly described as including customs and moral standards. In general, it is held that customs and moral standards, though not necessarily binding, have considerable impact on courts' decisions. In other words, they are factors that the courts would have to consider in adjudicating cases.[50] From the legal perspective, custom is a generally accepted practice

[46] See the State Council , *Regulations on Procedures for the Formulation of Rules or Decrees*, art. 6, adopted November 16, 2001, available at www.gov.cn/gongbao/content/2002/content_61556.htm.

[47] See *id.*, art. 3.

[48] See *id.*, art. 35.

[49] See 1982 Constitution, *supra* note 21, art. 67.

[50] See Guoying & Hongbo, *supra* note 8, at 49. *See also* Zongling & Wenxian, *supra* note 7, at 320–321; Sun Guohua & Feng Yujun, Study on the Socialist Legal System with Chinese Characteristics: Concepts, Theories and Structure, 440 (China Democracy and Legal System Publishing House, 2009).

that is repeatedly and continuously followed and accepted as a norm to the point that it becomes the usual way of conduct in given circumstances.

Customs are not law themselves unless they are incorporated into a normative document. The application of customs in most cases is supplementary. According to Article 10 of the Civil Code, a custom may be applied in the courts resolving civil disputes where the law does not specify if the application does not offend the public orders or good morals. In this regard, customs serve as a gap-filler to the law in question. In light of their application, customs can be local customs within a country or international common practices.

Usually, for customs to apply, authorization from the particular provision of the law is required. Put differently, only if the law recognizes its effect can customs be used to supplement law in China. For example, under both the 1982 Constitution and the 1984 Regional Ethnic Autonomy Law (amended in 2001), the local governments of autonomous regions have the power to implement laws and policies of the state in light of their respective actual local situations, and have the power to formulate autonomous regulations and separate regulations in light of the political, economic, and cultural characteristics of the ethnicity or ethnicities in the respective areas.[51] Here, both the "actual local situations" and the "political, economic and cultural characteristics" refer to local traditions and customs.

With regard to international practices, their application is allowed in China only in the case where there are no applicable provisions in the Chinese laws or the treaties to which China is a member. Under article 142 of the 1986 GPCL, international practice may be applied to matters for which neither the law of China nor any international treaty concluded or acceded to by China has any provisions.[52] A similar provision is also contained in Chinese Maritime Law.[53] The 2020 Civil Code, as noted, does not contain any provision pertaining to the application of international practices.

International practices are not defined in Chinese law but usually referred to behavioral rules or customary norms formed through long-term practice in international interactions and generally accepted by the international community.[54] Since international practices are not formulated by the national legislature, they cannot be directly applied by the courts unless otherwise authorized. However, due to their customary nature, international practices often function as important guidance and reference in judicial proceedings.[55]

[51] See the 1982 Constitution, *supra* note 21, arts. 115, 116; The 1984 Regional Ethnic Autonomy Law (as amended 2001), arts. 19–20. An English version is available at www.cecc.gov/resources/legal-provisions/regional-ethnic-autonomy-law-of-the-peoples-republic-of-china-amended.

[52] See the 1986 Civil Law, *supra* note 32, art. 142.

[53] See Maritime Law of China, art. 268, available at www.asianlii.org/cn/legis/cen/laws/mcotproc360/.

[54] See Li Shuangyuan, China and International Unification Process of Private International Law, 134–139 (Wuhan University Press, 1998).

[55] See *id*.

The SPC in its recent interpretation on the application of international treaties and practices further clarifies how international practices are applied in people's courts. According to the SPC, an international practice can be applied in Chinese courts either by the express choice of the parties or for a "fill-in" purpose. Under the SPC "Interpretation," when the parties explicitly choose to apply international practices, the rights and obligations between the parties to the contract can be directly determined based on international practices.[56]

The "fill-in" application of international practice refers to the situation where there is no provision in the law of China or a treaty concluded or acceded to by China, or the parties have not made an express choice. In this situation, the court may apply international practices. The application as such will not be affected when the parties claim to exclude the application of international practice simply on the ground that they have not expressly made a choice of it.[57] But in either case, the application of international practices may not violate China's sovereignty, national security, or public interests.[58]

Moral standards are important social rules of conduct in China. Historically, as noted, the *Confucian* rule of virtue functioned as the governing orthodoxy that controlled people's behavior. As discussed, in ancient Chinese hierarchical society, virtue, like law, was purposed to maintain the imperial power and to ensure monarchical control over the country. A violation of virtue was deemed a serious offense for which a severe punishment would be imposed. Thus, in ancient China, virtue did not simply refer to being good, but like a moral standard, served as a principle of conduct, ethics, and behavior.

Nowadays in China, moral standards remain a significant source of rules of conduct. The socialist core values promoted in the country are held as the centerpiece of such moral standards. Under Chinese jurisprudence, both law and morality are social norms that regulate conduct and behavior. Unlike the law that is a norm of conduct, morality is not only a norm of conduct but also a norm of ideology. Since law and morality are considered mutually supplemental, the rules of morality are deemed just as important as provisions of law. It is held in China that law is based on morality, and at the same time, law is the external maintaining force to effectively protect morality from being impaired.[59]

In many other countries, the secondary sources of law also include publications and opinions that explain, criticize, and discuss the law and regulations, represented by restatements, law review and journal articles, legal treatises, and textbook or norm books. It is, however, not the case in China. First, scholars' opinions are not considered an authoritative source, though they are relevant in the process of

[56] See the SPC, *Interpretation on Application of International Treaties and Practices*, *supra* note 40, art. 5.
[57] See *id.*, art. 6.
[58] See *id.*, art. 7.
[59] See Zeyuan, *supra* note 4, at 78.

drafting law. Second, courts may not cite thesis in law reviews or journals as legal support for their judgments. The judgments are required to be made on the basis of the relevant legal provisions and the facts of the case, while legal thesis are usually regarded as the result of academic research. Third, in certain cases, courts do accept scholars' opinions, but such opinions may only serve as evidence to prove certain facts.

C. *Policies of the CPC*

Closely related to the sources of law are policies. Under generally accepted jurisprudence, policies are not laws, but they may influence how laws are applied or help in understanding the laws. It is also required that policies be consistent with existing law. In China, given the controlling leadership of the CPC, its policies play a unique role in shaping the political and legal landscape of the country. As discussed, law in China is characterized as embodying and reflecting the will of the CPC. In this context, the CPC's policies are deemed to be the core content, the soul, and essence of the law, and the development of the rule of law in the country is viewed as making full use of the law to realize the party's policies.

During *Mao*'s era from 1949–1976, the CPC's policies virtually functioned as the primary source of law.[60] At that time, the CPC's policies replaced all legislation, which resulted in rampant legal nihilism all over the country.[61] Since Mao's death in 1976, the vast economic reform and the shift of the nation's focus from class struggle to economic development led to the abandonment of the conception of "the party policy as the law" and the acceptance of the idea of the rule of law. As a result, it has become a common understanding that no policy may be deemed directly as law. But since law and policy are still closely intertwined in the country, the CPC's policies remain decisively influential in several aspects.

First, the CPC's policies are held conceptually as the forerunner and guiding principle of national laws and regulations, and the laws and regulations are considered to be the fixation and stereotype of the CPC's policies. Despite the public concerns that the CPC's policies may again step into the shoes of the law, people are led to stay with the belief that the development of the rule of law in the country is a process of making full use of the law to realize the party's policies. Thus, the party's leadership of the people in governing the country becomes synonymous with governing the country according to law.

Second, the country's legislation is premised on the will of the CPC. Because, as noted, the CPC is defined as the sole representative of the ruling class of the

60 See Guoying & Hongbo, *supra* note 8 at 48. See also Mo Zhang, *The Socialist Legal System with Chinese Characteristics: China's Discourse for the Rule of Law and a Bitter Experience*, 24 Temple Int'l & Comp. L.J. 1, 38–40 (2010).

61 See *id.*

country, the law must only reflect the will of the CPC. Thus, the CPC's policies determine what laws are to be adopted and what should be provided in the laws. A striking example is the constitutional amendments. Each time an amendment is made, it has been based solely on the proposal introduced by the CPC and passed verbatim by the NPC. Thus, after the party's will as reflected in its policies becomes law, the implementation of the law carries two important implications: (a) an implementation of the party's will, and (b) execution of the CPC's policies.

The third aspect is the policy-driven mechanism in the application and enforcement of law. There has been a common belief in China that in the application of law, it is often necessary to take into consideration the CPC's policies to ensure that the policies are correctly implemented. Take the "strike hard" campaign, for instance. It is a purely policy-based crackdown campaign that targets activities deemed destructive to the social and political stability of the country. During the "strike hard" campaign, tougher measures were usually taken against crimes, and swifter and harsher penalties were imposed out of policy considerations.[62] From 2011, the "strike hard" mechanism was further applied to internet activities, known as the "Special Campaign to Purify the Network Environment."[63] Each time, the Campaign had a special focus.[64] In the "Network Purification 2021," over 110,000 websites were blocked and closed, and more than 103,000 suspects were arrested for criminal charges.[65]

2. HIERARCHY OF LAW

In terms of authoritative force, laws operate in the rungs of a hierarchy. Although such hierarchy may vary from country to country, it defines the rank of laws in their effects. In general, the hierarchy of law serves two important functions. First, it determines the level of legal effect of the law, because the law at different levels

[62] From 1980 to 2010, the country conducted four rounds of "strike hard" campaigns to cope with high crime rates and complicated security situations. Since the campaign was policy-based, it raised a great deal of concern about due process. A quite controversial one was the 2014 "Strike Hard Campaign against Violent Terrorism" in the far west province of Xinjiang as part of the de-extremification measures in the region.

[63] See *Network Purification Campaign*, available at https://baike.baidu.com/item/净网行动/219681?fr=ge_ala.

[64] See *id.*

[65] The 2021 online strike hard campaign was aimed at cleaning up all kinds of information containing pornographic content on literature websites, game websites, audio-visual program websites, mobile smart terminal application platforms, online video playback software, network resource download tools, and online game promotion advertisements. The cleanup covered all pornographic information on forums, post bars, blogs, microblogs, social networking sites, search engines, network hard drives, and instant messaging groups, as well as computer and mobile phone sellers and repair shops that pre-install, copy, and spread pornographic information using network TV sticks, network storage, mobile phone memory cards, and other devices. See *id.*

carries different weight. Thus, the force of a law is subject to its level in the hierarchy, particularly when a discrepancy exists between two competing laws. Second, the hierarchy of law prescribes the scope and authority of the laws at each level. An important rule is that the application of a law must not contradict the principle of a law that is superior to it or the source it derives from.

The rungs of the hierarchy of law are closely related to the legislative system. The more diverse the legislative power is, the more complicated the hierarchy of the law will be. In general, the level of the law in the legal hierarchy is dependent on the rank of the legislative body in the legal system as well as the importance of the law involved. If the rank of the legislative body is more superior or the law is more important in substance, the level of the law in its legal effect will be higher.

In the Chinese legal system, legislative power is vested in different legislative bodies, including (a) the NPC and its Standing Committee; (b) the State Council and its ministries and commissions; (c) provincial people's congresses and their standing committees; (d) autonomous region people's congresses; (e) provincial governments; and (f) Special Administrative Regions (SARs). Among those legislative bodies, the first two are at a national level, and all others are at local levels. The SARs are created under the "One Country, Two Systems" scheme with semi-independent legislative power for the region. In addition, the Central Military Commission also has legislative power to adopt military rules and regulations.

As discussed, China is a country with a unitary system, and centralization remains the mainstay of the country's administrative structure. Except for the SARs and certain autonomous regions, national laws must be strictly followed nationwide in order to maintain legal unification as well as uniformity of application. The local people's congresses and governments, especially at the provincial level, are granted legislative power, but the exercise of such power is limited as a matter of law to (1) the matters for which specific provisions are necessary, based on the actual circumstances of the administrative region, for the implementation of laws or administrative regulations, and (2) the matters of local affairs that require the formulation of local regulations.[66]

Since 2010, China's legal system has been branded as a socialist legal system with Chinese characteristics. In terms of legal hierarchy, the legal system so established consists of one core and three tiers. The core is the Constitution. The first tier under the core is the law, followed by the administrative rules and regulations adopted by the State Council. At the bottom of the tier are local rules and decrees (local regulations). Although treaties are not specified in the tiers, they are considered to have the same status as law in the legal system. Thus, the legal effect of the laws in China is ranked in the following order: the Constitution, laws and treaties, administrative regulations, and local regulations.

[66] See the Legislation Law, *supra* note 10, art. 73.

There are also departmental rules and local government rules. Department rules are the rules adopted by the ministries, commissions, or offices under the State Council. The department rules are purposed to (a) implement laws and administrative regulations, and (b) carry out the orders or decisions of the State Council. Local government rules are rules made by local governments to implement local regulations adopted by the local legislature and to deal with local administrative matters. Although the rules are legal norms, they do not constitute a separate level in the legal system.

The Legislation Law makes it imperative to follow the legal hierarchy of the laws. First of all, the Constitution has the highest legal force, and must not be contravened by any laws, administrative regulations, local regulations, autonomous regulations, special regulations, or rules.[67] Secondly, the force of laws is higher than that of administrative regulations, local regulations, and rules, and the force of administrative regulations is higher than that of local regulations and rules.[68] Lastly, the force of local regulations is higher than that of the rules of local governments at or below the corresponding level.[69] As for the local minority areas, the rules promulgated by the people's government of a province or autonomous region have higher legal authority than local rules adopted by the people's government of a districted-city of autonomous prefecture located in its jurisdiction.[70]

As noted, on October 27, 2011, the Information Office of the State Council of China issued a White Paper on the Chinese Socialist Legal System with Chinese Characteristics.[71] According to the White Paper, as a commitment to building a rules-based legal system, China has made "governing the country by law" a fundamental principle for the nation. The White Paper states that the establishment of a socialist legal system with Chinese characteristics to ensure that there are laws to abide by is the "precondition and foundation to implement the fundamental principle of the rule of law in all respects."[72]

Figure 3.1 is a chart of the system of Chinese law as stated in the White Paper. It shows how laws in the country operate under the structure of "One Core, Three Tiers, and Seven Branches."

The White Paper describes the tiers of Chinese laws with an official explanation of the branches of the laws and relevant legislative bodies within the socialist legal system. For discussion purposes, the following is an excerpt of the White Paper (bold added):

[67] See *id.*, art. 87.
[68] See *id.*, art. 88.
[69] See *id.*, art. 89.
[70] See *id.*
[71] See the Information Office of the State Council of China, *The Socialist Legal System with Chinese Characteristics*, available at www.china.org.cn/government/whitepaper/node_7137666.htm (hereinafter referred to as White Paper).
[72] See *id.*, *Foreword.*

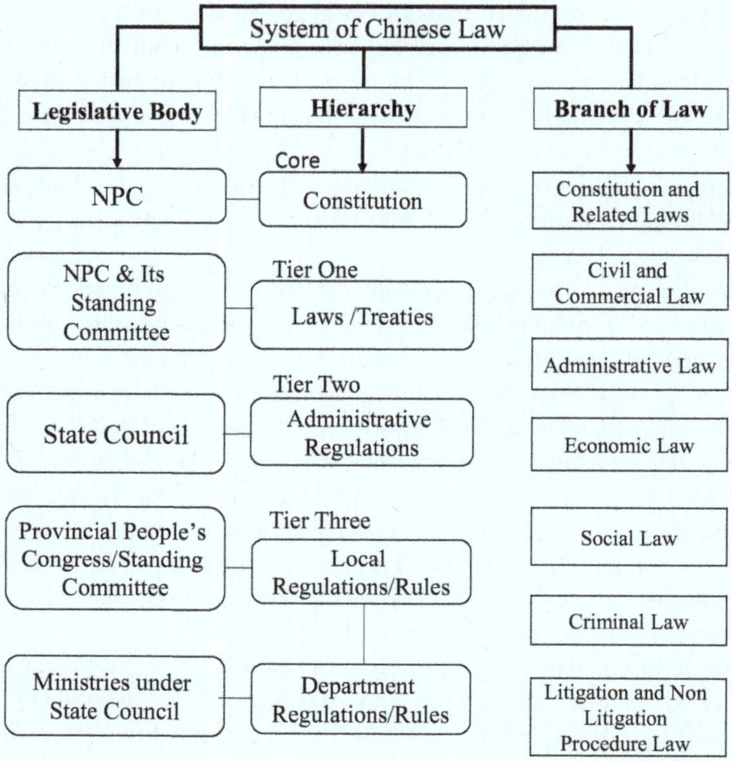

FIGURE 3.1 System of Chinese Law.

II. Composition of the Socialist System of Laws with Chinese Characteristics

1. Tiers of the socialist system of laws with Chinese characteristics

"The **Constitution** is the paramount law of the socialist system of laws with Chinese characteristics. As China's fundamental law, the Constitution assumes the commanding position in the socialist system of laws with Chinese characteristics and is the fundamental guarantee of lasting stability and security, unity of ethnic groups, economic development and social progress. In China, people of all ethnic groups, all state organs, the armed forces, all political parties and public organizations, and all enterprises and institutions in the country must take the Constitution as the basic standard of conduct, and they have the duty to uphold the dignity of the Constitution and ensure its implementation...

The Constitution has supreme legal authority in the socialist system of laws with Chinese characteristics. All laws, administrative and local regulations must be made in accordance with the Constitution and follow its basic principles, and must not contravene the Constitution.

The **laws** are the main body of the socialist system of laws with Chinese characteristics. The Constitution stipulates that the NPC and its Standing

Committee exercise the legislative power of the state. The laws formulated by the NPC and its Standing Committee are the main body of the socialist system of laws with Chinese characteristics, and deal with matters of fundamental and overall importance to national development and those which affect the country's stability and long-term development. The laws are the basis of the nation's legal system, and must not be contravened by administrative or local regulations.

The Law on Legislation ensures exclusive legislative power to the NPC and its Standing Committee. The NPC enacts and amends basic laws governing criminal offences, civil affairs, state organs and other matters; the Standing Committee of the NPC enacts and amends laws other than the ones to be enacted by the NPC. When the NPC is not in session, it may supplement and amend laws enacted by the NPC, but must not contradict the basic principles of such laws. The Law on Legislation also stipulates that the following must be governed by law: affairs concerning state sovereignty; formation, organization, and functions and powers of state organs; the system of regional ethnic autonomy; the system of special administrative regions; the system of primary-level self-governance; criminal offences and their punishment; mandatory measures and penalties involving deprivation of citizens' political rights or restriction of the freedom of the person; requisition of non-state-owned property; basic civil system; basic economic system; basic systems of fiscal administration, taxation, customs, finance and foreign trade; systems of litigation and arbitration; and other affairs.

The laws enacted by the NPC and its Standing Committee establish the important and basic legal systems in the nation's economic, political, cultural, social and ecological civilization construction, are the main body of the socialist system of laws with Chinese characteristics and provide an important basis for the formulation of administrative and local regulations.

Administrative regulations are an important component of the socialist system of laws with Chinese characteristics. The State Council formulates administrative regulations in accordance with the Constitution and laws, which is an important form of the State Council's implementation of its responsibility endowed by the Constitution and laws. The administrative regulations may regulate matters concerning the implementation of the provisions of the laws and performance of the administrative functions and powers of the State Council. For matters that shall be governed by laws to be formulated by the NPC and its Standing Committee, the State Council may enact administrative regulations first in its place with authorization from the NPC and its Standing Committee. The administrative regulations occupy an important position in the socialist system of laws with Chinese characteristics by detailing the related systems stipulated by laws, elaborating and supplementing the laws...

Local regulations are another important component of the socialist system of laws with Chinese characteristics. The people's congresses and their standing committees of the provinces, autonomous regions, municipalities directly under the central government, and the larger cities may, in accordance with the

Constitution and laws, formulate local regulations, which is an important channel and form of the people's participation in the administration of state affairs and promotion of local economic and social development by law.

The people's congresses and their standing committees of the provinces, autonomous regions and municipalities directly under the central government may, in the light of the specific local conditions and actual needs, formulate local regulations, provided that they do not contradict the Constitution, the laws and the administrative regulations. The people's congresses and their standing committees of the larger cities may, in the light of the specific local conditions and actual needs, formulate local regulations, provided that they do not contradict the Constitution, laws, administrative regulations and local regulations of their respective provinces or autonomous regions.

Moreover, they shall submit such regulations to the standing committees of the people's congresses of the provinces or autonomous regions for approval before implementation. The people's congresses of the ethnic autonomous areas have the power to formulate autonomous regulations and separate regulations on the basis of the political, economic and cultural characteristics of the local ethnic group(s). Where certain provisions of the laws and administrative regulations are concerned, adaptation may be made in autonomous regulations and separate regulations, but such adaptation may not contradict the basic principles of the laws and administrative regulations.

However, no adaptation may be made to the provisions of the Constitution and the Law on Regional Ethnic Autonomy, or the provisions in other laws and administrative regulations that are specially formulated to govern the ethnic autonomous areas. The autonomous regulations and separate regulations of the autonomous regions shall be submitted to the Standing Committee of the NPC for approval before they go into effect. The autonomous regulations and separate regulations of the autonomous prefectures or counties shall be submitted to the standing committees of the people's congresses of the relevant provinces, autonomous regions, or municipalities directly under the central government for approval before they go into effect.

The people's congresses and their standing committees of the provinces and cities where special economic zones are located may, upon authorization by the NPC and its Standing Committee and in the light of specific local conditions and actual needs, formulate regulations in accordance with provisions of the Constitution and basic principles of the laws and administrative regulations, and enforce them within the limits of the special economic zones. Local regulations may be formulated to govern matters requiring the formulation of rules to implement the provisions of laws and administrative regulations, and matters pertaining to local affairs.

Except for matters governed by laws exclusively formulated by the NPC and its Standing Committee, local regulations can also be made on other matters which are not yet covered by existing laws and administrative regulations. The local regulations also occupy an important position in the socialist system of laws with Chinese characteristics. They elaborate and supplement the laws and administrative regulations, extend, and improve national legislation and accumulate useful experience for national legislation. . .[73]

The scope and authority of a law are subject to the hierarchical level of the law. Since there are multiple legislative bodies in the country, potential conflicts among the laws in their legal effects at different levels inevitably exist. The conflict in legal effect refers to the discrepancies and contradictions in the application of different forms of law that contain inconsistent provisions. Such conflict may occur between laws of the same level, or between laws at different levels.

China's Legislation Law provides a mechanism to deal with possible conflicts between the legal effects of the laws. The mechanism has four components. The first component is a system of submission for approval in the legislative process, which applies to the regulations and rules adopted by local legislatures. As noted, the local people's congresses and their standing committees may adopt local regulations in certain areas. But such local regulations may only take effect after being submitted to, and approved by, the standing committees of the people's congresses of the relevant province or autonomous region.[74]

Under the Legislation Law, upon receiving a submission, the standing committees of the people's congresses of provinces or autonomous regions shall review the legality of the local regulation submitted for approval. If, after the review, it is determined that the local regulations do not contravene the Constitution, laws, administrative regulations, or the local regulations of that province or autonomous region, an approval shall be made within four months from the date of submission.[75]

Also, the people's congresses of ethnic autonomous areas are empowered to formulate autonomous regulations and special regulations on the basis of the political, economic, and cultural characteristics of the local ethnicities. Such regulations, however, must be submitted to the Standing Committee of the NPC for approval before they are to take effect. Again, the review and approval by the superior legislature is to make sure that the proposed local regulations do not contradict the basic principles of the laws or administrative regulations.[76]

The second component of the mechanism to address conflicts is the procedure of filing. Unlike submission for approval, filing does not require approval. Pursuant to article 98 of the Legislation Law, administrative regulations, local regulations, autonomous regulations, special regulations, and rules shall be filed with the relevant authorities for record within thirty days after their release. A presumption in the filing is that the local regulations filed are made on the basis of, and in no conflict with, the Constitution and the national laws.

[73] See *id.*, II (1) *Tiers of the Socialist Legal System with Chinese Characteristics.*

[74] See the Legislation Law, *supra* note 10, art. 72.

[75] See *id.*

[76] See *id.*, art. 75.

Under article 98, the filing shall follow the following procedures: (1) administrative regulations are filed with the Standing Committee of the NPC; (2) local regulations formulated by the people's congresses of the provinces, autonomous regions, or directly governed municipalities and their standing committees are filed with the Standing Committee of the NPC and the State Council; (3) autonomous and special regulations formulated by the people's congresses of autonomous prefectures or counties are filed with the Standing Committee of the NPC and the State Council through the standing committees of the people's congresses of the provinces, autonomous regions, and directly governed municipalities; (4) departmental or local governmental rules are filed with the State Council, and local government rules are filed concurrently with the Standing Committee of the local people's congress; and (5) regulations adopted upon authorization shall be filed with the authorizing organ stipulated in the authorization decision.[77]

The third component is the process of conflict examination and annulment. As authorized by the Legislation Law, if the State Council, the SPC, the SPP, and the standing committees of the provincial people's congresses consider that administrative regulations, local regulations, autonomous regulations, or separate regulations contradict the Constitution or laws, they may make written requests to the Standing Committee of the NPC for examination. The request for examination may also be made to the Standing Committee of the NPC by other state instrumentalities, public organizations, enterprises and institutions, or citizens if they believe that certain regulations contradict the Constitution or laws.[78]

Upon receipt of the requests, a special committee will be formed to conduct research and examination. If, based on the examination, the special committee or the Standing Committee of the NPC finds that the regulation or provision in question conflicts with the Constitution or laws, the regulation or provision shall be referred to the drafting authority for explanation. The drafting authority must respond within two months. Then, the Law Committee and the special committee of the Standing Committee of the NPC will provide the drafting authority with their comments, based on which the drafting authority shall revise or annul said regulation or provisions.[79]

The revision or annulment of a statute contradicting the Constitution or law may only be made within the scope of legislative power or relevant authorities. Pursuant to article 96 of the Legislation Law, a law, administrative regulation, local regulation, autonomous regulation, special regulation, or rule may be revised or annulled under any of the following circumstances: (a) it exceeds the scope of authority; (b) a

[77] See *id.*, art. 98. In addition, the regulations adopted by the people's congresses of district-cities or autonomous prefectures and their standing committees shall be filed with the Standing Committee of the NPC and the State Council through the standing committees of the people's congresses of provinces or autonomous regions.

[78] See *id.*, art. 99.

[79] See *id.*, art. 100.

lower-level law is contrary to the provisions of a higher-level law; (c) different provisions exist in respect of the same matter among rules, and pursuant to a ruling, one of the provisions shall be revised or repealed; (d) the provision of a rule is found improper and shall be revised or annulled; and (e) it violates legally prescribed procedure.[80]

Article 97 of the Legislation Law further provides specific rules for the revision and annulment of improper statutes or provisions. The rules mainly prescribe the authority of legal revision and annulment at different levels:

(1) The NPC has the authority to revise or repeal any improper law enacted by its Standing Committee, and to annul any autonomous or special regulations approved by its Standing Committee in violation of the Constitution or the law.
(2) The Standing Committee of the NPC has the authority to repeal any administrative regulation that contravenes the Constitution or any law, and to annul any local regulations that contravene the Constitution or any law or administrative regulation.
(3) The State Council has the authority to revise or annul any improper departmental or local government rules.
(4) The provincial People's Congresses and their Standing Committees have the authority to revise or annul any inappropriate local regulations or rules adopted or approved by their Standing Committees.
(5) The Standing Committees of local People's Congresses have the authority to repeal any improper rules enacted by the governments at the same level.
(6) The provincial governments have the authority to revise or annul any improper rules enacted by the lower-level government.
(7) The granting authority has the authority to repeal regulations that have been drafted by a granted authority acting beyond the scope of its authority, or in violation of the authorization, and if necessary, the authorizing authority may revoke the authorization.[81]

The fourth component of the mechanism to address conflicts in China's Legislation Law is a system of ruling on the conflicts of the laws and regulations at the same level. The conflict may occur between the newly adopted laws and regulations and the existing ones on the same matter or issue, and between local regulations. Under Chinese law, if there is conflict, a solution shall be made under the principles of (a) the law of a higher level prevails over the law of a lower level, (b) a new law takes priority over an old law, and (c) special law beats general law.[82]

[80] See *id.*, art. 96.
[81] See *id.*, art. 97.
[82] See *id.*, art. 92. (Where special provisions are inconsistent with general provisions in laws, administrative regulations, local regulations, autonomous regulations, special regulations or rules formulated by the same organ, the special provisions are to be applied; and where new provisions are inconsistent with old provisions, the new provisions are to be applied.)

In certain cases, however, the conflict still cannot be resolved under these principles.

To deal with this situation, there is a special mechanism provided in the law. According to the Legislation Law, if an applicable legal provision could not be determined due to an inconsistency in the laws regarding the same matter between a new general provision and an old special provision, the Standing Committee of the NPC shall make a ruling on the application. When an inconsistency exists in administrative regulations regarding the same matter between a new general provision and an old special provision, the State Council shall rule on which provision should be applied.[83]

In addition, in the case where local regulations and rules are inconsistent, and the applicable provision cannot be determined, a ruling on the conflict would need to be made in the following way as provided in the Legislation Law:

(1) When new general provisions and old special provisions adopted by the same authority are inconsistent, the adopting authority is to make a ruling.
(2) When local regulations and central government department rules have inconsistent provisions on the same matter, and the applicable provision cannot be determined, the ruling on the application shall take two steps: first, the State Council issues an opinion, and second, if the State Council finds that the local regulations shall apply, then the local regulations shall be applied in the given jurisdiction; if, however, the State Council deems that the department rules shall apply, it shall request the Standing Committee of the NPC to make a ruling.
(3) When there are inconsistent provisions on the same matter between department rules, or between departmental rules and local government rules, the State Council is to make a ruling. If, however, the inconsistent provisions exist between regulations made pursuant to authorization and laws, and the applicable provision cannot be determined, the ruling shall be made by the Standing Committee of the NPC.[84]

One last point worth noting is the retroactive effect of the law in China. With regard to a law, the retroactive effect involves ex post facto, referring to whether the law may apply to the actions that were committed, or relationships that existed, before its enactment. If a law has a retroactive effect, it will apply regardless of the time of occurrence of the thing or action involved. As often is the case, the issue of retroactive effect arises when a new law is enacted to replace an old one. There are different rules that are intended to define the retroactive effect.

The first rule is the rule of "following the old." Under this rule, the newly enacted law does not apply to the thing or action that occurred before the law is adopted, but rather the old law remains effective for such thing or action. If this rule applies, the

[83] See *id.*, art. 94.
[84] See *id.*, art. 95.

new law will not have retroactive effect. The second rule is the rule of "following the new." Opposite to the first rule, the second rule gives the new law a retroactive effect and makes the law applicable to the thing or action that already existed before the enactment of the law, even if the new law is more restrictive, or contains a more severe sanction, than the old law. The third rule is the rule of *lex mitior* ("the milder law"). This is the rule that is purposed to apply the version of the law that is more advantageous for or more lenient to the accused, regardless of whether it is the new law or the old one.

In addition, there also developed two mixed rules. One is the rule of following the old but applying the new law if the new law is milder. This rule implies that a newly enacted law has a retroactive effect only if the application of the law would result in a lesser punishment or lighter obligation to be imposed. The other mixed rule is the rule of following the new law but applying the old law if the old law is milder. This rule allows the newly enacted law to apply retroactively, but the old remains effective if the old leads to a lesser punishment or lighter obligation to the defendant.

In many countries, the retroactive effect of law is not allowed if the retroactive application of law would impair the rights acquired under the old or existing law, particularly for criminal laws, or if it interferes with contractual obligations. In the United States, for example, ex post facto laws are prohibited in general at both federal and state levels because of the belief that they are against natural rights.[85] But under the Supreme Court's decision in *Calder v. Bull*, the prohibition applied only to criminal matters, not civil matters.[86] In addition, the Supreme Court classified four categories of ex post facto laws as unconstitutional.[87]

In China, the retroactive effect of a law is handled under a mixed rule. The general principle is that a law does not have retroactive effect unless the provisions in the new law are milder or more advantageous for the accused. Under article 93 of

85 As Thomas Jefferson, one of the Founding Fathers of the United States, wrote,

> The sentiment that *ex post facto* laws are against natural right is so strong in the United States, that few, if any, of the State constitutions have failed to proscribe them. The federal constitution indeed interdicts them in criminal cases only; but they are equally unjust in civil as in criminal cases, and the omission of a caution which would have been right, does not justify the doing what is wrong. Nor ought it to be presumed that the legislature meant to use a phrase in an unjustifiable sense, if by rules of construction it can be ever strained to what is just. (Thomas Jefferson, *Letter to Isaac McPherson*, August 13, 1813, available at https://founders.archives.gov/documents/Jefferson/03-06-02-0322.)

86 Calder v. Bull, 3 U.S. 386 (1798), general overview available at https://en.wikipedia.org/wiki/Calder_v._Bull.

87 See *id.*, the four categories include: (1) the law that makes an action done before the passing of the law, and which was innocent when done, criminal, and punishes such action; (2) the law that aggravates a crime, or makes it greater than it was when committed; (3) every law that changes the punishment and inflicts a greater punishment than the law annexed to the crime when committed; and (4) the law that alters the legal rules of evidence, and receives less or different testimony than the law required at the time of the commission of the offence, in order to convict the offender.

the Legislation Law, the laws, administrative regulations, local regulations, autonomous regulations, special regulations, and rules do not have retroactive force, except where a special provision is made in order to better protect the rights and interests of citizens, legal persons, and other organizations.[88]

There is a particular clause on retroactive effect in the 1979 Criminal Law (as amended 2017).[89] In accordance with article 12 of the 1979 Criminal Law, if an act committed after the founding of the People's Republic of China and before the entry into force of the Criminal Law was not deemed a crime under the laws then in force, those laws shall apply. If the act was deemed a crime under a law then in force, the law shall also apply, unless the act in question is no longer deemed a crime or is subject to a lighter punishment under the Criminal Law.[90]

Another provision that is considered to have retroactive effect is article 60 of the 1990 Copyrights Law (as amended 2010).[91] The provision of article 60 distinguishes the protection of copyrights from infringement in terms of its application. For protection, it provides that the rights of copyright owners, publishers, performers, producers of sound recordings and video recordings, radio stations, and television stations as provided in this Copyrights Law, of which the term of protection specified in the Law has not yet expired on the date of this Law's entry into force, shall be protected in accordance with the Law.[92]

However, any infringements upon copyright and the rights related to copyright or breaches of contract committed prior to the entry into force of this Law shall be dealt with under the relevant regulations or policies in force at the time when the infringement was committed.[93] In other words, the retroactive effect of the Copyrights Law applies only to copyright protection but not to infringement committed prior to its enactment.

3. BRANCHES OF LAW

Within the framework of the socialist legal system with Chinese characteristics, in addition to the one core and three tiers, the laws are further divided into seven branches. In China, the hierarchy of law or legal norm determines the scope and

[88] See the Legislation Law, *supra* note 10, art. 93.

[89] The Criminal Law of China was first adopted in 1979. It was then amended ten times, and the latest amendment was made on November 4, 2017. The latest version of the Criminal Law is available at www.66law.cn/tiaoli/9.aspx.

[90] See *id.*, art. 12.

[91] The Copyrights Law of China was adopted on September 7, 1990, and was amended twice. The latest amendment was made on February 26, 2010. An English translation of the Copyrights Law is available at https://en.wikisource.org/wiki/Copyright_Law_of_the_People%27s_Republic_of_China_(2010).

[92] See *id.*, art. 60.

[93] See *id.*

effect of the law or legal norm, while the branch of law concerns classification or characterization of the laws and legal norms. In general, a classification as such refers to the method under which laws or legal norms are characterized into different categories according to different standards and from different perspectives.

In Chinese jurisprudence, a legal system is composed of two basic components: the contents of legal norms and the classification of legal norms. The contents involve normative documents or laws within the legal system, while classifications divide the legal norms in the system into different branches.[94] The legal branches are categorized according to the specific social relationships the legal norms regulate and the regulatory means. Conceptually then, legal norms regulating the same social relationship and applying the same type of regulatory means belong to the same legal branch.[95] Within the legal system, all legal branches are intended to operate harmoniously and coordinate with each other to avoid repetition, replication, or conflict.[96]

As noted, the socialist legal system with Chinese characteristics is structured on seven different branches of laws. Prescribed in the White Paper, the seven branches are: (a) Constitution and related laws; (b) civil and commercial laws; (c) administrative laws; (d) economic laws, (e) social laws, (f) criminal laws, and (g) litigation and non-litigation procedural laws. In terms of tiers, the Constitution as the supreme law is on the top, followed by laws as the main body of the legal system, and then administrative and local regulations as major components.[97]

Each branch of the law regulates a legal relationship of the same kind or one closely related. According to the White Paper, the laws in all branches together form "a solid foundation for the rule of law and for the construction of a socialist country under the rule of law." The White Paper also asserts that law in China "has become an important means for Chinese citizens, legal persons and other organizations to resolve disputes and conflicts," and it "provides an important basis for the people's courts at all levels to safeguard the lawful rights and interests of citizens, legal persons and other organizations."[98]

The White Paper describes each of the legal branches in the country as follows. Note, however, that there are several new developments after the publication of the White Paper. The most striking development is the adoption of the 2020 Civil Code that consolidates into a single comprehensive code all existing laws regulating civil matters.

94 See Qiao Xiaoyang, *Formation, Characteristics and Contents of the Socialist Legal System with Chinese Characteristics*, A Lecture on Chinese Legal System at NPC Standing Committee Members Group Studies, June 25, 2013, available at www.npc.gov.cn/npc/c541/201306/4f1ffbf3b2054e559ee143e8a35f9949.shtml.

95 See *id.*

96 See *id.*

97 See the White Paper, *supra* note 71.

98 See *id.*

Branches of the socialist system of laws with Chinese characteristics are specified in the White Paper as follows:

> **Constitution and Related Laws.** The laws related to the Constitution are the collection of legal norms supporting the Constitution and directly guaranteeing its enforcement and the operation of state power. These laws regulate the political relationships of the state and mainly consist of laws in relation to the establishment, organization, functions, powers and basic working principles of state organs; laws on the system of regional ethnic autonomy, the system of special administrative regions and the primary-level self-governance; laws in relation to maintaining state sovereignty, territorial integrity, national security and national symbols; and laws in relation to guaranteeing the basic political rights of citizens.
>
> By the end of August 2011, China had enacted thirty-eight laws related to the Constitution, as well as a number of administrative and local regulations. China has formulated electoral laws related to the NPC and local people's congresses at all levels, organic laws of local people's congresses and people's governments at all levels, and developed mechanisms for the election of deputies of the people's congresses and the leadership of state organs, providing an institutional guarantee for the people's exercise of state power and a legal basis for the formation of state organs. It has enacted organic laws of the NPC, the State Council, the People's Courts and the People's Procuratorates, and established systems concerning the organization, function,power and limits of related state organs.
>
> . . .
>
> **Civil and commercial laws.** Civil laws adjust property and personal relationships between civil subjects with equal status, that is, between citizens, between legal persons and between citizens and legal persons, and follow the principles of equal status between civil subjects, autonomy of will, fairness, honesty,credibility and other basic principles. Commercial laws adjust commercial relationships between business subjects and follow the basic principles of the Civil Law and the principles of the freedom of commercial transaction, compensation of equal value, convenience and safety, among other principles. By the end of August 2011 China had promulgated thirty-three civil and commercial laws, as well as a large number of administrative and local regulations concerning commercial activities.
>
> . . .
>
> **Administrative laws.** Administrative laws are a collection of legal norms on the granting, execution, and supervision of administrative power. They regulate the relationships between administrative authorities and subjects of administration, follow the principles of statute-based-authority, statutory procedure, fairness, openness, and effective supervision, and guarantee the discharge of the functions and powers of administrative organs, as well as the rights of citizens, legal persons and other organizations.
>
> China has formulated the Law on Administrative Penalties, established the basic principles of penalty by law, fairness and openness, a corresponding penalty for offence and a combination of penalty and education. China has also standardized the enactment rights of administrative penalties, developed fairly complete procedures of the decision and execution of administrative penalties, and established the

hearing system of administrative penalties, by which an administrative organ, before making a decision on administrative penalty that may have a significance influence on the production and life of the party concerned, shall notify the party the right to request a hearing.

...

Economic laws. Economic laws are a collection of laws and regulations which adjust social and economic relations arising from the state's intervening in, managing and regulating economic activities for the society's overall interests. They provide legal devices and an institutional framework for the state to conduct appropriate intervention in, and macro control of the market economy, thereby preventing malpractice resulting from spontaneous and blind operation of the market economy.

...

Social laws. China's social laws are the collection of laws and regulations with respect to the adjustment of labor relations, social security, social welfare and protection of the rights and interests of special groups. The social laws follow the principles of justice, harmony and appropriate state intervention. By performing their duties, the state and society provide necessary protection for the rights and interests of laborers, the unemployed, those incapacitated for work, as well as other special groups in need of help so as to safeguard social equity and promote social harmony.

...

Criminal Law. This is the law that defines crimes and penalties. It aims to punish crime and protect the people, maintain social order and public security, and safeguard national security through regulating the state's power of punishment. The Criminal Law clearly defines these basic principles: punishment of crimes is defined by law, everyone is equal before the law, and punishment should match the severity of the crime.

The Criminal Law expressly stipulates that any act explicitly stipulated by law as a crime is to be convicted and given punishment by law, and that any act that is not deemed a crime by the explicit stipulations of the law is not to be convicted or punished. The law shall be equally applied to anyone who commits a crime. No one shall have the privilege of transcending the law. The degree of punishment shall be commensurate with the crime committed and criminal responsibility is to be borne by the offender.

...

Litigation and Non-litigation Procedure Laws. These are laws giving standard solutions to various litigation and non-litigation activities arising from social disputes. The litigation system aims to regulate the state's judicial activities in settling social disputes, and the non-litigation system aims to regulate arbitration agencies and people's mediation organizations in settling social disputes.

China's Civil Procedure Law stipulates the following basic principles and system: the parties to civil litigation shall have equal litigation rights; mediation shall be conducted for the parties on a voluntary and lawful basis; the court shall follow the system of public trial and the court of second instance being that of last instance.

It makes clear the litigation rights and obligations of the parties concerned, the use of evidence, the civil trial procedures such as ordinary procedure of first instance, procedure of second instance, summary procedure, special procedure, procedure for trial supervision, and procedure of execution and enforcement execution measures.

...

China's Arbitration Law has provisions for the establishment of domestic arbitration and foreign-related arbitration agencies and stipulates that an arbitration commission shall be independent of any administrative organ, which guarantees its independence. It also specifies that arbitration should be conducted upon a voluntary and independent basis, and that a system of a single and final award shall be practiced for arbitration. It also contains details about arbitration procedures.[99]

4. GUIDING CASES

As noted, in the Chinese legal system, courts do not have law-making power, and the judges generally do not follow precedent. In the past decades, however, a trend has emerged to incorporate common law elements into both legislation and judicial practice. A highly notable phenomenon that represents such a trend is the establishment of a guiding case system in people's courts – a system that focuses on the role of cases in judicial proceedings. The guiding cases are cases selected nationwide and published periodically by the SPC with a stated purpose of helping guide the lower courts in their adjudication of cases in the same or similar situations.

As a matter of fact, case publication by the Supreme People's Court began as early as 1985 when the *Gazette of Supreme People's Court* was first published.[100] At that time, the publication of cases was considered part of China's judicial reform to promote judicial efficiency and transparency, and it was aimed mainly at providing references to the lower courts.[101] As noted, in the late 1990s, to foster reform, the SPC launched a series of five-year reform programs called the Five-Year Judicial Reform Outline. The first outline took effect in 1999.[102]

99 See *id.*

100 The *Gazette of the Supreme People's Court* is an official publication of the Supreme People's Court and is published monthly. Prior to the publication of the *Gazette*, the Supreme People's Court already started compiling cases, but the compilation was issued in the form of internal documents within the courts. In 1983, for example, the Supreme People's Court compiled seventy-five selected criminal cases and sent them to the lower courts for reference. From 1983 to 1989, the total number of compiled cases reached 293. See Hu Yunteng & Yu Tongzhi, *Study on Several Important and Complicated Issues Concerning the System of Case Guidance*, 6 Juris. Rsch. 3 (2008).

101 See Deng Jinting, *The Guiding Case System in Mainland China*, 10 Frontiers L. China, 1, 1–2 (2015).

102 See the Supreme People's Court, *Notice of Issuance of the Five-Year Reform Outline of the People's Court*, October 20, 1999, available at http://sifaku.com/falvfagui/39/zcff03a163ec.html. In the Notice, the Supreme People's Court made it clear that the reform of the people's court was an important component of judicial reform in the country.

In its Second Five-Year Reform Outline that began in 2004, the SPC made a bold move and formally announced that it would employ guiding cases in people's courts. According to the SPC, given the ongoing judicial reform, it was necessary to "put in place a guiding case system to help improve judicial justice."[103] The goal of the SPC was to utilize guiding cases to help "unify the standard of application of law, direct the adjudicative work of the lower courts, and enrich and develop legal theories."[104] The 2004 Outline sent a clear signal that the SPC wanted to create a legal framework for applying guiding cases in the Chinese judiciary.

However, ever since the SPC started to publish cases in the mid 1980s, there have been debates over what legal effect the cases published by the SPC should have. The debates were further intensified by the SPC's efforts to establish a guiding case system. The highly contested issue is whether the guiding cases should have a binding effect on people's courts. In addition, there was also concern about the process by which the SPC selects cases for guiding purposes.

In response to the debates and these concerns, in November 2010 the SPC issued the *Provisions Concerning the Work of Guiding Cases* (Guiding Case Provisions), aiming to systemize the application of guiding cases in the Chinese judiciary.[105] The Guiding Case Provisions were intended to set forth the standards and procedures for the selection of guiding cases. An important effort taken under the Guiding Case Provisions was to select and publish guiding cases periodically. The first set of guiding cases, which consisted of four cases, was published by the SPC on December 20, 2011.[106] As of July2025, the SPC had published a total of 261 guiding cases in 46 batches.[107]

On June 2, 2015, the SPC adopted the Detailed Rules for the Implementation of the Guiding Case Provisions (Detailed Rules) to further direct and manage the use of guiding cases.[108]As noted, the SPC only has the power of judicial interpretation prescribed by the Organic Law of People's Courts, which is deferent to the

[103] See Supreme People's Court, *Notice of Issuance of the Second Five-Year Reform Outline of the People's Courts*. The second reform outline covered the period of 2004 to 2008, but the Notice was issued on October 26, 2005. The Notice is available at www.66law.cn/tiaoli/2915.aspx.

[104] See *id.*

[105] See the SPC, *Provisions Concerning Work on Case Guidance (passed by the Adjudication Comm. of the Sup. People's Ct. Nov. 15, 2010, issued and effective Nov. 26, 2010)*, China Guiding Cases Project, English Guiding Cases Rules, June 12, 2015 ed., available at http://cgc.law.stanford.edu/guiding-cases-rules/20101126-english/. (Hereinafter SPC, *the Guiding Case Provisions.*)

[106] See Notice of Release of the First Set of Guiding Cases (promulgated by Sup. People's Ct.), available at http://gongbao.court.gov.cn/ArticleList.html?serial_no = al.

[107] See the SPC, *Guiding Cases*, available at www.court.gov.cn/shenpan-gengduo-77.html.

[108] See the SPC, *Detailed Implementing Rules on the "Provisions of the Supreme People's Court Concerning Work on Case Guidance" (passed by the Adjudication Comm. of the Sup. People's Ct. Apr. 27, 2015, issued and effective May 13, 2015)*, China Guiding Cases Project, English Guiding Cases Rules, June 12, 2015 ed., available at http://cgc.law.stanford.edu/guiding-cases-rules/20150513-english/. (Hereinafter *Detailed Rules.*)

legislative interpretation vested with the NPC and its Standing Committee. The Detailed Rules are designed to provide the judges with instruction on how to refer to guiding cases in case adjudications. The guiding case system, although requiring much more improvement, both implicates China's move toward utilizing case law and demonstrates a growing expansion of the power of the Chinese judiciary in the development of law.

A. *Criteria of Guiding Cases*

Guiding cases are selected cases. According to the 2010 Guiding Case Provisions, to qualify as a guiding case, two requirements must be met: (1) the judgment of the case has taken effect and (2) the case shall have one of the following values: (a) it is of great social concern; (b) it involves an issue for which the legal provision is relatively general; (c) it is typical; (d) it is difficult, complicated, or of a new type; or (e) it contains another quality of guidance.[109]

The 2015 Detailed Rules further define a guiding case as a case that has such essential factors as follows: (1) the judgment has become effective; (2) the determination of facts is clear; (3) the application of law is correct; (4) the reasoning of judgment is sufficient; (5) its legal and social consequences are positive; and (6) it can provide meaningful and general guidance for the trial of similar cases.[110] For the purpose of guiding case selection, the Detailed Rules focus more on the substance of the case, including fact determination, application of law, legal reasoning, and social impacts.

B. *Selection Mechanism*

With regard to the source of guiding cases, the Guiding Case Provisions and the Detailed Rules provide a three-step selection process. The first step is case recommendation. There is a broad basis for making such a recommendation. Under the Guiding Case Provisions and the Detailed Rules, the recommendation could be made internally or externally. The internal recommendation may come from the adjudication divisions of the SPC, High People's Courts, and military courts. The people's courts at all intermediate and trial levels may also make recommendations through their corresponding High People's Court.[111] Externally, recommenders could be the delegates of the NPC, members of the Chinese People's Political Consultative Conference (CPPCC), experts, scholars, lawyers, and any others who are interested in the adjudication and enforcement work of people's courts.[112]

109 See the SPC, *the Guiding Case Provisions, supra* note 105, art. 2.
110 See the *Detailed Rules, supra* note 108, art. 2.
111 See *id.*, art. 4.
112 See *id.*, art. 5.

The second step consists of case selection and review. In order to implement the Guiding Case Provisions and facilitate the guiding case selection, the Supreme People's Court has created an office that works on guiding cases (the Guiding Case Office). Members of the Guiding Case Office are judges designated within the SPC. Under the Detailed Rules, the Guiding Case Office is in charge of the solicitation of case recommendations and is responsible for collecting, selecting, and reviewing the cases recommended.[113] In addition, the Guiding Case Office has the authority to coordinate the guiding case selection process and provide instruction on guiding cases nationwide.[114] Furthermore, the Guiding Case Office is equipped with the power to publish and compile guiding cases and undertake research in related matters.[115]

The third step is the approval of guiding cases. Upon its review of the recommended cases, the Guiding Case Office makes its selections and then submits the selected cases to the Judicial Committee of the SPC for approval.[116] After approval, the guiding cases will be sent in the form of an SPC notice to all High People's Courts and, in the meantime, will be published in the *Supreme People's Court Gazette*, *People's Court Daily*, and on the SPC website.[117] If, in the Guiding Case Office's view, further discussion or research is needed for certain selected cases, it may send these cases to relevant government entities, social organizations, members of the guiding case advisory committee, or other experts and scholars for opinions and comments.[118]

It should be noted that in contrast with the cases previously published by the SPC, the guiding cases are distinctive in at least two aspects. First, before the guiding case system was initiated, the SPC from time to time published certain cases either on its own or as decided by lower courts. Case publication at that time aimed to serve two functions: a general public function and a judiciary function. The general public function was that the publication of cases would help maintain judicial transparency and justice. With regard to the judiciary function, the cases published were intended to provide lower courts with certain examples.[119] In contrast, the guiding cases have a clear focus on providing a guiding effect with a notion to bind all lower courts.

Second, the cases previously published did not have a formal selection process, and although the cases were edited to meet the needs of publication, there was no unified procedure. The guiding cases are obviously different: not only must selection follow the required procedure, but also the cases selected should all uniformly comply with a particular formality. Under article 3 of the Detailed Rules, a guiding

[113] See the *SPC, the Guiding Case Provisions*, *supra* note 105, art. 3.
[114] See the *Detailed Rules*, *supra* note 108, art. 4.
[115] See *id.*
[116] See *id.*, art. 8.
[117] See *id.*
[118] See *id.*, art. 7.
[119] See Yunteng & Tongzhi, *supra* note 100, at 2–3.

case must contain the following elements: (a) a title, (b) key words, (c) main points of adjudication, (d) relevant legal provisions, (e) basic facts of the case, (f) result of adjudication, (g) judgment reasoning, and (h) the name of the judges appearing on the judgment that has taken effect.[120]

The important part of a guiding case is the reasoning on which its judgment stands. The judgment in Chinese courts used to be very simple and contained no legal reasoning.[121] In 1999, when the SPC issued its first Five-Year Judicial Reform Outline, improving judgment writing became part of judicial reform. The Outline required the addition of legal analysis and reasoning to the judgment in order to make the judgment more rational and persuasive.[122] The reform on judgment writing was further endorsed in the 2012 amended Civil Procedure Law (CPL).

Article 152 of the CPL provides that a judgment shall state the outcome of the judgment and reasoning and shall include (1) the cause of action, claims, and the facts and reasons of disputes; (2) the facts and causes affirmed by the judgment, applicable laws and causes; (3) the consequences of a judgment and the obligation of litigation costs; and (4) the time limit for filing an appeal and the appellate court with which the appeal shall be filed.[123] The guiding cases certainly are intended to serve as a model to guide judges in writing the legal reasoning in their judgments.

C. *Distinctive Features of Guiding Cases*

A guiding case as selected and published has a number of unique features. First, it is an edited version of the original case. Therefore, it looks more like a brief of the case than the case itself. Second, those who edited the case were not judges in the case and therefore took no part in the trial of the case. Under both the Guiding Case Provisions and the Detailed Rules, the final review of a guiding case before it is submitted for approval of publication is the responsibility of the Guiding Case

[120] See the *Detailed Rules*, *supra* note 108; Stanford Law School has an ongoing "China Guiding Cases Project." In one of its online publications, it explains the required elements as follows: 1. "Keywords" (to list keywords that indicate the nature of the dispute etc.); 2. "Main Points of the Adjudication" (to include general principles prepared by the SPC that it expects other courts to refer to); 3. "Related Legal Rule(s)" (to list the legal rule(s) considered in the GC); 4. "Basic Facts of the Case" (to summarize the most important facts of the GC); 5. "Results of the Adjudication" (to report the outcomes of legal proceedings); and 6. "Reasons for the Adjudication" (to summarize the reasons for the final ruling/judgment). *See Stanford Law School: China Guiding Cases Project*, available at https://cgc.law.stanford.edu/guiding-cases-analytics/issue-4/.

[121] In the past, a civil judgment in Chinese courts typically followed a six-part pattern. It began with an introductory paragraph stating the names of the parties and the cause of action, followed by "plaintiff claims that…" and then "defendant argues that…" The fourth part is "it is found by the court that," and the next one is "it is the opinion of the court that." The last part is "it is decided by the court that."

[122] See The SPC, *Five-Year Reform Outline of People's Courts*, issued on October 21, 1999, art. 13 (1999), available at www.chinacourt.org/article/detail/2013/04/id/941425.shtml.

[123] See the CPL, *supra* note 34, art. 152.

Office of the SPC. Third, since the guiding case is selected and published by the SPC, it represents the position that the SPC takes pertaining to the legal issue involved and the application of law to that issue.

Another notable feature of the guiding cases is that not all of the guiding cases are cases that were tried or reviewed by the SPC. In fact, many cases that are selected as guiding cases are those decided by the lower courts, including High People's Courts, intermediate people's courts, and even the basic people's courts at the trial level. But in recent years, the number of guiding cases selected from SPC cases has been on the rise.

For example, before 2017, in the first seventy-seven guiding cases issued by the SPC, there were only sixteen cases that were actually decided by the SPC. All other guiding cases were judgments rendered by lower courts, including twenty-two from the High People's Courts, twenty from the intermediate people's courts, and seventeen from the basic (district) people's courts.[124] More specifically, nearly 80 percent of the guiding cases were picked from lower court decisions.[125]

Between March 2017 and January 2020, the SPC published another 62 guiding cases, bringing the number of guiding cases to a total of 139. Of the sixty-two guiding cases, twenty-eight were SPC cases, more than 45 percent. The rest of them included ten from High People's Courts, seventeen from intermediate people's courts, and only seven from the basic people's courts.[126]

It is worth noting that the publication of guiding cases is also intended to serve a function of guiding the general public or society as a whole in addition to its primary purpose of guiding the people's courts in their future trials. Thus, when reporting the guiding cases, the major media of the SPC, the People's Court Daily, always releases an editorial note addressing the social effect of each of the guiding cases published. For instance, in its report on the No. 64 guiding case, the People's Court Daily pointed out that the judgment and its supporting reasoning possess significant guidance for maintaining a good order of operation in the telecommunication service industry and protecting consumer interests.[127]

The No. 64 guiding case was a contract case decided by the Quanshan District People's Court in Xuzhou, Jiangsu Province in 2011. The case involved a cellphone

[124] The details are as follows: the SPC cases: No. 2, 20, 33, 34, 35, 36, 42, 43, 44, 47, 52, 56, 61, 67, 68, and 75; the High People's Court cases: No. 3, 4, 8, 11, 12, 15, 16, 22, 27, 29, 30, 37, 40, 45, 46, 48, 49, 53, 54, 55, 58, and 72; the intermediate people's court cases: No. 1, 2, 9, 10, 17, 19, 21, 31, 38, 39, 51, 57, 59, 60, 62, 65, 66, 69, 74, and 76; the basic (district) people's court cases: No. 5, 6, 13, 14, 18, 23, 24, 25, 26, 28, 32, 41, 50, 61, 64, 71, and 77.

[125] See *id.*

[126] The SPC cases: No. 78, 79, 81, 82, 84, 85, 88, 100, and 107–126; the High People's Court cases: No. 83, 86, 91–93, 95, 96, 127, 129, and 132; the intermediate people's court cases: No. 80, 87, 90, 97–99, 101, 103, 104, 106, 130, 131, 133–136, and 138; the basic people's court cases: No. 89, 94, 102, 107, 128, 137, and 139.

[127] *See The Supreme People's Court Announces the Thirteenth Set of Guiding Cases*, People's Ct. Daily, June 30, 2016, available at www.chinacourt.org/article/detail/2016/07/id/2011306.shtml.

prepaid card service agreement between *Liu Chaojie*, the Plaintiff, and China Mobile, Xuzhou Branch, the Defendant. On November 24, 2009, the Plaintiff purchased a prepaid cellphone card from the Defendant. After purchase, the Plaintiff could use the card for cellphone use up to the amount on the card. The Plaintiff could continue to use the card by adding money onto it. Under the agreement, the Defendant could suspend or restrict the Plaintiff's use of phone service if (a) the Defendant was unable to receive the Plaintiff's payment for service due to the Plaintiff's bank account being attached or frozen by court order, or insufficient funds in said account or the like; or (b) the prepaid fee was used up and no money was added in a timely manner.

On July 5, 2010, the Plaintiff added RMB 50 to the prepaid phone card. The service, however, was suspended on November 11, 2010, even though there was still unused money on the card. When consulting with the Defendant, the Plaintiff was told that the phone card could not be used because the validity period of the card had expired. According to the Defendant, the prepaid phone card has a fixed period of use, and the period began with the first prepayment. If no additional payment was made before the expiration date, the card would be suspended regardless of the residual amount of money paid to the card.

The Plaintiff brought the case on the ground of breach of contract. The district people's court ruled in favor of the Plaintiff. The Defendant appealed but withdrew it later. In its decision, the district people's court stated that under the provision of article 39 of the Contract Law of China, when a contract is made on the basis of the standard form, the form provider shall define the rights and obligations of the parties in accordance with the principle of fairness, and shall by reasonable means inform the other party of any liability exclusion or restriction.

Applying the provision mentioned earlier to this case, the district people's court held that since the Defendant, at the time the service agreement was made, did not tell the Plaintiff about the fixed period for the use of the prepaid phone card, but then suspended its service to the Plaintiff during performance because of the expiration of the fixed period, the Defendant's conduct constituted a breach of contract for which the Defendant was liable.

In the judgment's reasoning, the district people's court was of the opinion that if a business operation did not explicitly provide limitations or conditions on certain products or services in its standard contract, and could not prove that at the time of contract it had made the consumer informed of the limitations or conditions and had obtained the consumer's consent to them, such limitations or conditions shall have no effect on the consumer.[128]

In the past few years, there appear to have been two changes in guiding case selection and publication. First, the number of selected cases that were decided by the SPC has increased dramatically. Prior to January 2017, seventy-seven guiding

[128] See *id.*

cases were published, among which only fifteen cases were decided by the SPC, representing 20 percent of the guiding cases published. From January 2017 to January 2020, among the sixty-two guiding cases added, twenty-seven cases, or 45.5 percent, were SPC cases.

The second change was that the group of guiding cases published became more subject-centered. For example, guiding cases No. 117 to No. 126 involved civil procedures pertaining to judgment enforcement and enforcement supervision, and all of those cases were decided by the SPC. Guiding cases No. 127 to No. 138 were concerned with environmental protection against pollution and public welfare. Guiding cases No. 113 to No. 115 were intellectual property cases, which all ended in an SPC decision. Note that in guiding case No. 113, the SPC ruled in favor of Michael Jordan, the U.S. basketball legend, in a trademark dispute with a Chinese sportswear company. According to the SPC ruling, the Chinese sportswear company must stop using the characters for Jordan's name, read as *Qiaodan* in Chinese.

D. *Nature and Legal Effect of Guiding Cases*

According to the SPC, building the guiding case system in the people's courts would help unify the application of law, enhance the quality of adjudication, and maintain judicial justice.[129] With regard to the legal effect of the guiding cases, however, the SPC has been very cautious in addressing it, given the constitutional restraint on its power to make law. Under article 7 of the Guiding Case Provisions, the people's courts at all levels shall refer to the guiding cases when adjudicating similar cases.[130]

The issuance of the Guiding Case Provisions is considered a significant step in establishing a guiding case system in the Chinese judiciary because it not only formally makes the compilation of guiding cases routine work of the SPC, but also mandates the use of guiding cases in trials.[131] Unfortunately, since article 7 of the Guiding Case Provisions does not define "shall refer to" and "similar cases," confusion occurs due to the vagueness of these two terms.

The most important provision in the Detailed Rules is article 10, where the SPC intends to deal with the "shall refer to" issue. Under article 10, when referring to the guiding cases during the adjudication of similar cases, the courts at all levels shall cite the guiding cases in their judgment reasoning but may not use the guiding cases as a legal basis for their judgments.[132]

The underlying notion of article 10 is that the guiding cases are to play a unique role in the adjudication of cases at the people's courts. In addition, to emphasize the

[129] See the SPC, *the Guiding Case Provisions*, *supra* note 105, introduction paragraph.
[130] See *id.*, art. 7.
[131] See *id.*
[132] See *id.*, art. 10.

necessity for adopting the guiding case system in the Chinese judiciary, the SPC in the Detailed Rules reiterates that the goal of using guiding cases is to make attainable the uniformity of application of law and the achievement of judicial justice.[133]

The Detailed Rules also require that the guiding cases follow certain formalities.[134] The purpose is to make the guiding cases model cases that contain the typical practices of people's courts in adjudicating similar cases and help apply the law in a way that is desired to achieve uniformity. In this respect, many consider the issuance of guiding cases as an alternative to, and a practical form of, judicial interpretation by the SPC.[135] It is also believed in the Chinese legal community that the requirement of citing the guiding cases in the judgment's reasoning clearly goes beyond the normal scope of reference because it makes citing the relevant guiding cases mandatory.[136]

Despite the SPC's efforts, questions remain widely open in respect to the legal effect of guiding cases. The most troublesome issue is where the guiding cases should stand in the Chinese judicial system. Since citing the guiding cases is required in the judgment's reasoning, it becomes questionable whether a guiding case has the effect of precedent or remains merely as reference. Related to this question is whether a judgment can be deemed erroneous in the application of law and thus be appealable if it differs from an applicable guiding case, because the traditional notion in the country is that a judgment is binding only on the parties involved in the specific case.

In a common law system, precedent is generally defined as "an adjudicated case or decision of a court, considered as furnishing an example or authority for an identical or similar case afterwards arising or a similar question of law."[137] During trials, common law courts "attempt to decide cases on the basis of principles established in prior cases."[138] In contrast, the guiding cases function differently.

In one aspect, a guiding case is not necessarily a prior case decided by the same court or its superior court. As noted, guiding cases are selected from the cases adjudicated by courts at various levels all over the country. In another aspect, both "guiding" and "reference" as the nature of guiding cases do not amount to a degree of being binding. Partly because of the difficulty in positioning the guiding cases, many in China call the guiding case system "the case law with Chinese

[133] See *id.*, art. 1.

[134] See *id.*, art. 3.

[135] See Shen Deyong, *Exploring to Establish the Guiding Case System with Chinese Characteristics under the Truthful, Practical, Reformative, and Innovative Spirits*, in Shen Deyong et al., eds., Studies on the Guiding Case System with Chinese Characteristics, 1 (People's Court Press, 2009).

[136] See Wang Limin, *Study on Several Issues Concerning the Guiding Case System of China*, 1 Legal Sci. 71, 75–76 (2012).

[137] See Black's Law Dictionary, 1176 (6th ed., West, 1979).

[138] See *id.*

Characteristics,"[139] to differentiate guiding cases from common law precedent, even though the term "Chinese Characteristics" itself, as noted, is considerably ambiguous.[140]

The guiding case system is a special product of the Chinese judiciary under the people's congress-centered government infrastructure. It reflects the ambition of the SPC to push toward law-making power, especially in the gray area between the interpretation of law and the interpretation of the application of law. In the meantime, it also represents a new trend of legal development in China – a merger of civil law tradition with common law practice.

The application of guiding cases in the Chinese judiciary indeed implicates a move toward the adoption of case law in the country. But many issues remain to be answered. Among the important issues are (a) whether the guiding cases may become a source of law, (b) how the guiding cases could be effectively applied and, more generally, (c) whether there may develop a power for the SPC to make law de jure through guiding case compilation.

E. *Guiding Cases in Application*

With the lingering question over the legal effect of the guiding cases, their application in Chinese courts faces considerable challenges. First, the legal status of guiding cases remains to be further clarified. As stated in the Detailed Rules, the SPC wants to maximize the directive role of the guiding cases in trials at people's courts.[141] However, due to the vagueness of the "directive role" of the guiding cases, judges in people's courts are struggling with the extent to which the guiding cases may be used in their judgment making.[142]

In addition, although the SPC has emphasized that the guiding cases are binding, it is still unclear as to the scope of their binding force. As discussed, the question is whether the guiding cases may become a source of law. Moreover, there is a concern from the viewpoint of the legislature that the SPC may step out of bounds and virtually exercise law-making power.[143]

[139] See Deyong, *supra* note 135, at 3–4.

[140] In recent years, "Chinese characteristics" has become a popular term to describe and justify whatever is different in China compared with the rest of the world. For example, the socialist system in China is labeled as a socialist system with Chinese characteristics, and the Chinese legal system is called the Chinese legal system with Chinese characteristics, even though the vast majority of people in China may not actually know what the Chinese characteristics really are. With regard to the Chinese characteristics related to case law, one interpretation is that case law in China (a) is based on a statutory tradition, (b) focuses on the main points of adjudication edited and summarized from the original case, and (c) is selected and compiled by the Supreme People's Court only. See Zuo Weimin & Chen Ming-guo, The Research on the Guiding Case System in China, 144–145 (Peking University Press, 2014).

[141] See the *Detailed Rules*, *supra* note 108, art. 1.

[142] See Yunteng & Tongzhi, *supra* note 100, at 11.

Under both the Guiding Case Provisions and the Detailed Rules, the application of guiding cases in the people's courts shall be made (a) by reference and (b) in similar cases.[144] But neither "reference" nor "similarity" is defined or explained. In the Detailed Rules, the SPC seems to infer that "to refer to guiding cases" is to cite the guiding case in the judgment reasoning.[145] Some scholars, however, suggest that "to refer to" shall be understood as "to follow," which would mean to be bound by the guiding case, not simply to take the guiding case as a reference.[146]

With respect to similarity, the SPC is silent about how it should be determined. According to one scholarly opinion, similarity shall include (a) similar facts, (b) similar legal relations, (c) similar disputes, or (d) similar legal issues.[147] The question, however, remains because it is still disputable whether all of the four aspects must be present in order to find similarity or if any one of the four would suffice.

The more difficult issue is again the legal status of the guiding cases. For decades, there have been debates on the role of published cases. The establishment of the guiding case system raises a further question as to whether the guiding cases should be deemed precedent. Under the Detailed Rules, the application of guiding cases as referenced in similar cases is compulsory.[148]

But what compulsory reference would mean to the people's courts inevitably becomes an issue not only for the Supreme People's Court but also for the country in general. The bottom line is whether there is or should be case law in China, which once again relates to the likelihood of the guiding cases constituting a source of law.

Views over the legal effect and role of the guiding cases differ sharply in China. Some believe that guiding cases possess no legal force of law and thus should not be considered a source of law.[149] In their view, because of their role of guiding and reference, the guiding cases have only persuasive effect,[150] and they are no more than a useful tool to help judges conduct legal research and exchange experiences of case adjudication.[151]

Others, however, disagree. They argue that the guiding cases, once issued by the Supreme People's Court, should have an effect by which all lower courts shall

[143] See Lang Guimei, *Study on Certain Fundamental Issues Concerning the Guiding Case System of China*, 17 Shanghai Jiaotong U. J. – Phil. & Soc. Sci., 24, 29 (2009).

[144] See the *Detailed Rules*, *supra* note 108, art. 10.

[145] See *id.*

[146] See Limin, *supra* note 136, at 75.

[147] See *id.*

[148] See the *Detailed Rules*, *supra* note 108, arts. 9–10.

[149] See Zhou Wei, *Interpretation of Law through Cases: Development of the Supreme People's Court Guiding Case System*, 23 Contemp. L. Rev. 134, 139 (2009).

[150] See Yue Zhiyong, *Construction of Guiding Case System of the Country*, 7 Leg. Sys. & Soc. 45 (2009).

[151] See Cui Kai, *Establishment of Guiding Case System in China: A Comparison with the Case Law in the West*, 4 J. of the Postgraduate of Zhongnan U. of Econ. & L. 146–149 (2006); *see also* Zhang Yadong, *Rethinking the Guiding Case System*, 269 J. App. L. 34 (2008).

abide.[152] It is further asserted that the guiding cases should have the same legal status as judicial interpretation by the Supreme People's Court, and therefore their application in judicial proceedings shall be imperative.[153]

In the middle of the spectrum is the argument that the guiding cases are an important supplement to the source of law and have de facto, if not necessarily de jure, binding effect.[154] The idea is that the function of the guiding cases is to guide how the law is to be applied, and taking guiding cases as reference as required by the SPC is purposed to (a) impose duties on the judges to follow the guiding cases and be critical to the legal reasoning in their judgment making; (b) help justify the grounds on which judicial supervision is sought for certain cases; and (c) provide lawyers and other litigation participants with an official channel for better understanding the application of law in their arguments or defenses.[155]

With regard to the binding force of the guiding cases, at least three issues are involved. The first issue is whether the result of adjudication of the guiding cases is binding. The second issue concerns whether the rules derived from the main points of adjudication have any authoritative effect. The third issue relates to whether the judgment reasoning of guiding cases has any force of control.[156] For the first issue, it is generally agreed, as noted, that the judgment of a guiding case is binding only to that case and the parties involved in the case.[157]

Thus, many of the debates on the legal effect of the guiding cases have to do with the second and third issues, namely the main points of adjudication and judgment reasoning. The reason is that in terms of significance, both the main points of adjudication and the judgment reasoning of a guiding case are not necessarily limited to the guiding case itself but are applicable to future similar cases.

A survey conducted by two scholars with regard to the legal effect of the guiding cases revealed very diverse opinions among judges and lawyers in the country.[158] The survey was made in the form of mailing questionnaires. Of 4,521 returned questionnaires, 3,994 were valid and effective, including 1,367 from judges and 488 from lawyers. Among the judges participating in the survey, slightly more than 26 percent (26.26%) considered the guiding cases as having de jure binding effect, and about 47 percent (47.12%) deemed the guiding cases to have de facto binding effect. Some 16 percent (16.24%) thought that the guiding cases had only evidentiary effect, and about 15 percent (15%) believed that the guiding cases have no binding effect. Among the lawyers, the ratio was 26.84%, 43.65%, 13.73%, and 11.48,

[152] See Dong Hao & He Xiaoyu, *Technic Probe into the Guiding Cases in Uniform Application of Law*, 11 Legal Science, 144 (2008).

[153] See Zhu Jianmin, *Several Issues on the Building of Guiding Case System:* A Respective of *Effect Determination*, 7 R. of L. Res. 35 (2008).

[154] See Weimin & Ming-guo, *supra* note 140, at 137–141.

[155] See *id.* at 143–144.

[156] See *id.* at 162–163.

[157] See *id.*

[158] Weimin & Ming-guo, *supra* note 140, at 82.

respectively.[159] What the survey revealed is that the majority would regard the guiding cases as having de facto binding effect.

In fact, as demonstrated in the Detailed Rules, the SPC does intend to make the guiding cases binding although it does not explicitly use the term "binding force." The compulsory reference is widely understood to infuse the guiding cases with legal authority.[160] The requirement of citing guiding cases in the judgment reasoning of a similar case is obviously an indicator of the authoritative force of the guiding cases.[161]

Even though under the Detailed Rules the people's courts may not rely on a guiding case to enter a judgment, the judgment's reasoning that embodies the guiding case suggests the actual force of the guiding case. In addition, it is required under the Detailed Rules that the judges adjudicating a case look up relevant guiding cases during the process of adjudication and shall also explain whether a reference has been made to a relevant guiding case if the parties or their lawyers in the case have cited the guiding case in their arguments or defense.[162]

But, given the debatable nature of the legal status of the guiding cases, the effective application of them in judicial proceedings remains to be tested. According to the SPC report on the judicial application of guiding cases released on March 29, 2018, during the period of January 1, 2012, to July 2, 2017, the total number of cases in which the guiding cases were referred to was about 531, including 489 civil cases, 35 administrative cases, and 7 criminal cases.[163]

This number was quite small compared with the number of cases filed and adjudicated in the people's courts. As revealed in the SPC's working report to the NPC in March 2018, from 2013 to 2017 the number of cases filed with the people's courts of various levels reached over 82 million, of which nearly 77 million cases were adjudicated.[164] During this period, about 82,383 cases were brought to the SPC, and 79,692 of them obtained a final decision from the SPC.[165]

Of the 531 cases applying guiding cases, over 54% took place in the courts of second instance, trial, or in the appellate courts (54% in civil cases, 46% in administrative cases, and 57% in criminal cases).[166] Under the SPC rules, the application of guiding cases may be made upon the parties' request or at the court's initiation. According to the report, the parties' request triggered the application in a majority of

[159] See *id.* Note that about 2.05 percent of judges and 4.30 percent of lawyers did not answer.

[160] See the *Detailed Rules*, *supra* note 108, art. 9.

[161] See *id.*, art. 10.

[162] See *id.*, art. 11.

[163] See the SPC, *An Analytical Report on the Application of the Guiding Cases*, published on March 29, 2018, available at www.court.gov.cn/fabu-xiangqing-88832.html.

[164] See Zhou Qiang, the SPC Working Report to the NPC, March 9, 2018, available at http://gongbao.court.gov.cn/Details/69d3772d9e94aae3ea2af3165322a1.html.

[165] See *id.*

[166] See the SPC, *Report on the Application of the Guiding Cases*, *supra* note 163.

cases. Out of 232 cases in the first instance, 120 cases, or 52 percent, involved application of guiding cases at the request of the plaintiffs.[167]

In all 531 cases, there were only 126 cases in which the application of guiding cases was initiated by the judges, representing 24 percent of the total. In the 126 application cases, 97 occurred in the first instance, accounting for 77 percent of the applications by judges.

Among the 264 second-instance civil cases, there were 176 cases in which the appellants advocated for an application of a guiding case, accounting for 67 percent. In some sixteen administrative litigation cases, parties made requests for guiding case application in eleven cases, as high as 69 percent.[168]

In 2022, another report on the judicial application of guiding cases revealed that out of 221 guiding cases published by the SPC, 149 guiding cases were "cited" in a total of 10,343 cases.[169] According to the report, there are three ways in which the guiding cases were quoted in the courts. The first one is the "express citation." It means that the judge clearly cited the guiding cases for reasoning when making a ruling. The "express citation" includes active citation and passive citation. The former refers to the judge actively citing guiding cases to explain the reasoning for their decision; the latter takes place when a judge is requested to cite guiding cases, and the judge responds to the request in the judgment's reasoning.[170]

The second way is called "implicit citation." This happens in cases in which, during the trial, prosecutors suggest or litigation participants request that the judge cite the guiding cases for judgment. The judge does not respond to the request specifically in the reasoning for the judgment, but the result of the judgment is consistent with the main theme of the guiding cases.[171] In this context, "implicit" means that the judge does not cite the guiding cases as requested but does actually follow the guiding case to reach his or her decision.

The third way is known as "commentary citation." It refers to situations where the guiding cases are not mentioned in the text of the judgment but are mentioned in the comments, analyses, or supplementary opinions of legal experts attached to the case, which constitute a source of the judge's reasoning for the decision.[172] According to the report, out of 10,343 "citation" cases, 4,440 were "express citation" cases, including 2,990 active citation cases and 1,450 passive citation cases. In addition, the number of implicit citation cases was 5,860, while the number of commentary citation cases was only 43.[173]

167 See *id.*

168 See *id.*

169 See Peking University Legal Information Network, 2022 *Annual Report on the Judicial Application of the Supreme People's Court Guiding Cases*, 4 China Applied Juris. J. (2023), the full text of the report is available at https://roll.sohu.com/a/706206599_121123754 (2022 *Annual Report*).

170 See *id.*, footnote 6.

171 See *id.*, footnote 7.

172 See *id.*, footnote 8.

Still, the number of "referring to" guiding cases remained relatively low. Even in cases where a guiding case was cited, the judge ultimately chose not to refer to it. Among 4,440 express citation cases, for example, there were 1,222 cases in which the guiding cases, though cited, were not "referred to." In the passive citation cases, the rate of "referring to" was only about 34 percent. The vast majority of passive citation cases ended without referring to the guiding case.[174]

The reasons attributable to the lack of enthusiasm in the application of the guiding cases might be many. The primary reason, however, is the uncertainty of the legal status of the guiding cases. The ambiguity of "shall refer to" causes a great deal of confusion among the people's courts. It has been found that for many years, "difficulty in reference" of guiding cases has consistently been a problem plaguing trial practice, mainly in finding similarities between the case at hand and the guiding cases, in determining the specific contents to be referred to, and in justifying the reference with sufficient reasoning.[175]

Since the statutory rules are the main source of law on which judgments are made, the people's courts are often quite hesitant to apply the guiding cases without statutory provisions.[176] Thus, there has been a suggestion that in order to get the guiding cases effectively applied, some legislative action would be required.[177] Given the difficulty in finding similarity, some have suggested changing "basic facts," as provided in article 9 of the 2015 Detailed Rules, to "material facts," meaning that the case in adjudication does not have to be similar in all basic facts but only in the important facts relevant to the guiding case for the purpose of "referring to."[178]

In addition, although the SPC requires the judges to refer to guiding cases in similar cases, the Detailed Rules provide no explanation as to the circumstances under which the guiding cases must be applied and the effect that must be given to the guiding cases.[179] Also uncertain is the question of whether an appeal is allowed on the ground that the case decided was in conflict with, or the court failed to cite, the applicable guiding case.

F. *Future Implications*

No matter how the guiding cases are currently applied in the Chinese courts, the establishment of a guiding case system in the Chinese judiciary will certainly have a long-term impact on the Chinese legal system. It is highly likely that the application of guiding cases will bring changes to the Chinese legal landscape in a number of

[173] See *id.*
[174] See *id.*
[175] See *id.*
[176] See the SPC, *Report on the Application of the Guiding Cases*, *supra* note 163.
[177] See *id.*
[178] See 2022 *Annual Report*, *supra* note 169.
[179] See *id.*

ways. First, the guiding cases will play an increasingly important role in Chinese judicial proceedings, with more actions expected from the SPC, and both judges and litigation participants will need to pay great attention to them. More specifically, the main points and judgment reasoning of the guiding cases will, to say the least, become dicta that greatly influence future trials and judgments in cases bearing similarities and even just cases in general.[180]

Second, the introduction of guiding cases into Chinese judicial proceedings will inevitably bring to an end the sole statutory-based trial and will incorporate cases into Chinese judicial proceedings and the legal system as well. It is true that case law does not officially exist in China, but it is hard to deny the legal function of the guiding cases because, under the requirement of compulsory reference imposed by the SPC, guiding cases would constitute the legal basis on which a court opinion would rely. Additionally, the compilation of guiding cases will necessarily become a unique source pertaining to the application of law. Moreover, given their stated purpose to maintain unification of the application of law, the guiding cases would ultimately affect how the laws are to be applied.[181]

Third, by adopting the guiding case system, the SPC has actually moved beyond the normal scope of judicial interpretation and expanded its power from interpreting the application of law to establishing the case-based framework under which the adjudication of people's courts is directed. Fortunately, the move does not seem to have met any objection from the NPC. The recognition of such practice in the judiciary by the legislature would help reinforce the SPC's effort to promote the use of guiding cases. As a matter of fact, both the SPC and the NPC are expected to adopt certain rules to materialize the guiding cases and elaborate their application to cement the status of the guiding cases and ensure their authoritative force.

Fourth, the development of a guiding cases system will result in changes in the content and substance of legal education as well as legal training. From an educational perspective, guiding cases are valuable resources for legal textbooks and class teaching. The reasons are obvious. First, the guiding cases are real cases, and the use of them in the classroom will help bridge the gaps between law on paper and law in motion. In addition, since the guiding cases reflect the legal opinions and holdings endorsed by the SPC, their authoritative force in respect to the application of law goes far beyond the academic field. In addition, the judgment's reasoning contained in the guiding cases will help enhance the type of legal analysis and critical thinking that are essential for legal professionals.[182]

180 See Wang Chenguang, *System Construction and Technique Innovation: Challenges Our Guiding Cases System Is Facing*, Stan. China Guiding Cases Project (February 2, 2015), available at https://cgc.law.stanford.edu/wp-content/uploads/sites/2/2015/09/commentary-2-English.pdf.

181 See Weimin & Ming-guo, *supra* note 140, at 43–44.

182 See Yunteng & Tongzhi, *supra* note 100, at 10–11; see also Fang Wencui & Ding Haihu, *The New Trend of Legal Education Reform: The Guiding Case System*, 6 App. L. J. 81 (2008).

Fifth, the guiding cases would become an influential force that affects the development of law and, to a certain extent, shapes the trend of legal development. Like all other civil law countries, statutes in China are the primary source of law. A notable feature of the statutes is that the provisions in the statutes are not detailed, and they are quite inflexible and very abstract in general, which often creates blanks between the provisions of law and their application to particular cases or cases with unique facts. The guiding cases provide much-needed guidance to help fill in those blanks and thus achieve the outcome intended by the provisions of law. In doing so, the guiding cases would also help the legislature figure out whether a particular provision of law would need improvement and how the improvement should be made.[183]

Thus, it is fair to say that the adoption of the guiding case system in China was a significant step taken by the SPC to promote case law in the country. But nothing here is meant to suggest that the guiding cases are the same as case law in the sense of common law. On the contrary, there are a number of distinctions between the guiding cases and common law cases. First of all, the guiding cases are only the cases selected by the SPC and therefore are not all of the cases decided by people's courts. Secondly, the guiding cases selected are not necessarily the higher courts' decisions, and in fact, many of the guiding cases are decisions made by lower courts. Thirdly, as noted, the guiding cases are not original but edited judgments, and the editors are not the judges who actually tried the cases. Lastly, the guiding cases are standardized under the format prescribed by the SPC.

[183] See Limin, *supra* note 136, at 75–76.

4

Chinese Constitution and Government Structure

INTRODUCTION

In China's socialist legal system with Chinese characteristics, the Constitution is considered the core. According to the State Council's White Paper, the Constitution is the paramount law of the country, and it has supreme legal authority among all other laws or legal norms. The Constitution is also the controlling document that defines the system of the state and prescribes the structure of the government. Put differently, the Constitution is the basis of governance of the state and the source of the government's powers.

However, since law "is particular to the society it operates within,"[1] the Constitution in China is shaped by Chinese tradition, values, and visions. The Confucian spirit, socialist pursuit, and single ruling party's power constitute the combined forces that determine the distinctive features of the nation's Constitution, in contrast to those in other countries. A critical question yet to be answered in China is whether a constitution is purposed primarily to limit government power or to maintain the stability of society with a focus on the governed. An issue that remains unsolved is how the power of the Communist Party of China (CPC) is to be constrained within the law.

In recent years, the CPC has repeatedly vowed that China will never follow the path of Western constitutionalism, separation of powers, or judicial independence.[2] This message on its face is an emphasis that China will take the path it sees fit and proceed following Chinese reality. The underlying notion, however, is that the maintenance of the CPC's leadership is the prerequisite condition. This notion is further strengthened by the 2018 Amendment to the Constitution, where, as noted,

[1] See Wen-Chen Chang et al., Constitutionalism in Asia: Cases and Materials, 69 (Hart, 2014).

[2] See Xi Jinping, *Strengthen the Party's Overall Leadership over the Building of the Rule of Law in the Country*, 4 Qiushi J. (2019), available at www.qstheory.cn/dukan/qs/2019-02/15/c_1124114454.htm.

the leadership of the CPC is signified as the defining feature of the socialist system with Chinese characteristics.[3]

It is on this constitutional ground that the Chinese government is structured. With the CPC's leadership as the defining feature, and socialism as the fundamental system of the country, the organization of the Chinese government bears several distinctions. First, China is prescribed as a state governed by a people's democratic dictatorship. Second, the state power is exercised under the mode of the people's congress led by the CPC. Third, the state operates through a scheme of democratic centralism. Fourth, the whole country is administered under the unified control of the central authorities.

1. CONSTITUTION

As discussed, the current Constitution of China was adopted in 1982. Prior to 1982, several versions of the Constitution were adopted. But after 1982, amendments became the only thing keeping the Constitution afloat. The Constitution consists of four chapters plus a very lengthy preamble. In the preamble, the Constitution specifically addresses the achievements of the CPC, states the governing ideology, and describes the importance of the CPC's leadership. The four chapters include General Principles, Fundamental Rights and Duties of Citizens, Structure of the State, and National Flag, Anthem, Emblem, and Capital.

A. *Conception of Constitution*

Traditional China was not a constitution-structured country, and imperial power played a dominant role in society. Although the term "constitution" is found in some ancient Chinese legal literature, it was used to mean different things. In one place it was used to refer to a statute or code, while in another place, it was used to indicate the system of laws. The term was also used to mean the promulgation of law or certain legal departments. Moreover, the term was employed to describe legal observance or the imposition of punishment.[4] Whatever meaning it might have had in Chinese legal history, the term carried no implication of the constitution in the modern sense.

Thus, the modern constitution is an imported concept in China. According to a Chinese constitution textbook, in the late nineteenth century, *Huang Zhunxian*, a Chinese diplomat missioned in Japan, introduced to China the modern concept of "constitution" from Japanese law. The first constitutional document was the

[3] See 2018 Amendment to Chinese Constitution (adopted by the NPC on March 11, 2018), the full text of the amendment is available at https://npcobserver.com/2018/03/11/translation-2018-amendment-to-the-p-r-c-constitution/.

[4] Zhou Wei & Xie Weiyan, Constitution Textbook, Higher Education Legal Textbook Series, 3 (Sichuan University Press, 2012).

Outlines of Constitution, which was issued in the form of an imperial edict in the late *Qing* Dynasty in 1908. Since then, the modern meaning of constitution has been formally established in China, and constitutionalism has become an evolving movement in the country.

However, despite a common understanding that the Constitution is the basic law of the nation, a well-accepted definition is still absent. In fact, scholars in China have been debating how the Constitution should be defined. Some view the Constitution as an integral part of the law, reflecting the actual relationship of contrast between various political forces while stipulating the fundamental tasks and systems of the state: the social system, the principles of the state system, the organization of state power, and the basic rights and obligations of citizens.[5]

Others focus on the function of the Constitution and describe it as the basic law of the state that regulates the relationship between citizens and the state, stipulates the state organs and their powers, and provides the basic rights and freedoms of citizens.[6] Under this definition, the relationship between the state and its citizens is the center of attention of the constitution. Thus, to achieve a balance of the exercise of state power and the protection of the rights of citizens, it is necessary to set certain boundaries on state power.

Note, however, that the understanding of the Constitution in China has been deeply influenced by the "will theory." As discussed, law in China is commonly held as an essentialized expression of the will of the ruling class. The Constitution is then considered a declaration of the will as such. This notion to a great extent is based on *Lenin*'s "theory of the constitution," which constituted the ideological foundation of the law of the former Soviet Union.[7] According to *Lenin*, the essence of a constitution is that all the basic laws of the country, the laws concerning the electoral power of the representative organs, and the powers of the representative organs show a contrasting relationship between the various forces in the class struggle.[8]

Under the will theory, there are several reasons why the Chinese Constitution is a product of the contrasting relationship between various political forces. First, the Constitution is not representative of the will and interests of the whole people but rather is only a concentrated expression of the will and interests of the class that has won the class struggle. Therefore, the Constitution has a strong class character. Second, the actual balance of various political forces in society determines and affects the specific contents of the Constitution. The contents of the Constitution may vary depending on conditions that affect the balance of the political forces. Third, when the actual contrasting relationship between various political forces

5 See Xu Congde, Chinese Constitution, 27 (Renmin University Press, 1996); see also Wei Dingren, Constitutionology, 15 (2nd ed., Peking University Press, 1994).

6 See Wei & Weiyan, *supra* note 4, at 8.

7 See Yin Xiaohu, Constitutionology, Principle and Application, chapter 4(6) (Shanghai Social Science Academy Press, 2016).

8 See the Complete Works of Lenin, Vol. 15, 146 (People's Publishing House, 1988).

changes, it will inevitably create constitutional changes, and such changes can be fundamental or non-fundamental.[9]

Obviously, the *Leninist* view of the constitution is rooted in class theory under which class struggle was the major driving force in society. In former Soviet constitutionology, class struggle was taken as the base for analyzing the relationship between the constitution and the state, the relationship between the state and the citizens, as well as the role and nature of the constitution. This was also a dominant phenomenon in China during *Mao*'s era. After the economic reforms in the country, as discussed, the notion of class struggle faded and was gradually replaced with the idea of economic development.

There has also been mounting criticism of the class struggle paradigm. The major argument is that because of the class struggle pursuit, the academic value of constitutional science has diminished, constitutional logic has been overshadowed by political logic, the social function of the Constitution has been strictly restricted, and the foundation on which constitutionology as an independent discipline relies has been obstructed.[10] But since the will theory remains the mainstay of the ideological foundation of the law in China, the class nature of the Constitution is still quite noticable in the current Chinese constitutional literature.

For example, in the preamble of the 1982 Constitution (as amended 2018), it is clearly stated that in China, the exploiting classes as such have been eliminated, but the class struggle to a certain extent will continue to exist for a long period of time.[11] The preamble also emphasizes that the Chinese people must fight against those forces and elements, both at home and abroad, that are hostile to China's socialist system and try to undermine it.[12] This statement sets a benchmark for the nation to run under the leadership of the CPC.

Both will theory and class struggle ideology have profound impacts on Chinese constitutionology. When defining the Constitution, scholars in the country struggle with the description of the nature of the Constitution. The traditional view, which is entirely based on class nature, believes in the concept of a contrasting relationship of political forces and considers the Constitution as the manifestation of such a relationship in the class struggle. Under this view, as explained in one Chinese constitution textbook, the nature of the Constitution embodies class struggle in several aspects.

First, the Constitution is formulated by the class that prevails in the class struggle and controls state power. Thus, the whole process of Constitution drafting not only

[9] See Wang Kai, Constitution Textbook, 9–10 (University of International Business and Economics Press, 2010).

[10] See Liu Chunping, *The Impacts of Soviet Constitutionology on the Chinese Constitutionology*, 4 N. Legal Sci. 33–34 (2012).

[11] See 1982 Chinese Constitution (as amended 2018), available at https://npcobserver.files.wordpress.com/2018/12/PRC-Constitution-2018.pdf.

[12] See *id.*

reflects the will of the ruling class but also is guided by the idea of class struggle. Second, in its contents, the Constitution must affirm the basic systems beneficial to the ruling class, and must also prescribe the status and interrelationship of all classes in society according to the will and interests of the ruling class. Third, in light of its development, the Constitution changes or evolves in substance with the changes in the actual contrasting relationships of various political forces in various periods.[13] In other words, changes in politics prompt changes in the Constitution.

The modern view, by comparison, takes a more liberal approach. The modern view argues that class struggle should not be the ideological basis of the Constitution but, on the contrary, the Constitution should focus more on the protection of the rights of citizens as a whole than on the pursuit of class interests.[14] Liberal approach advocates believe that the Constitution, as the fundamental law of the country, is the product of the combined effects of specific social, political, economic, as well as ideological and cultural conditions. Thus, although the Constitution reflects the actual contrasting relationship of various political forces, it provides the fundamental tasks of the nation and defines the systems of society, including the principles of the social and State systems, the structure of state power, and the basic rights and duties of citizens.[15]

B. *Constitutional Legislation*

Again, the Constitution is a matter of modern legislation in China. Constitutional legislation in the country can be divided into two different periods: before 1949, or the Nationalist period, and after 1949, or the socialist period. These two periods witnessed the development of constitutional legislation in China and demonstrated the sharp differences in the structure and content of the Constitution between the Nationalist government and socialist government.

As noted, in 1911, China experienced the Nationalist Revolution known as the *Xinhai* Revolution. Two years earlier, in 1908, the imperial government issued an "Outline of Constitution," aiming to undertake certain reforms to establish a constitutional monarchy for maintaining imperial power. In the meantime, the imperial government provided a nine-year preparation period (later revised to a five-year period) for the Constitution to take effect. In 1911, as a response to the Revolution, the imperial government rushed to adopt the Nineteen Major Constitutional Covenants (Nineteen Covenants), an effort to save the falling imperialist system.[16]

[13] See Kai, *supra* note 9, at 9–10.

[14] See *id.*

[15] See Wei & Weiyan, *supra* note 4, at 16–23.

[16] See *id.* at 51. See also Hongda Chiu, *Constitutional Development and Reform in the Republic of China on Taiwan*, in Bih-Jaw Lin, ed., Contemporary China and the Changing International Community, 3 at 4–6 (University of South Carolina Press, 1994).

In early 1912, however, when the last emperor was dethroned, the *Qing* Dynasty was abdicated, and the entire imperial system in the country ended. With the fall of the *Qing* Dynasty, the "Nineteen Covenants" never became effective. Therefore, although constitutional legislation in China began in the late *Qing* Dynasty, no constitution was ever adopted at that time. More specifically, there was no Constitution in China until 1912 when the Provisional Constitution of the Republic of China was promulgated.

The 1912 Provisional Constitution, consisting of seven Chapters and fifty-six articles, was the first Constitution in modern China. It created a government that was structured on the French cabinet model, where the prime minister is the head of the government and his power is granted by congress.[17] Serving as the fundamental law of the young republic, the 1912 Provisional Constitution affirmed the basic principles of Western democratic republics, such as governance by the people, separation of powers, and equality for all. The significance of the 1912 Provisional Constitution is that it established a democratic republic, ending the feudal monarchy and imperial system that had lasted more than 2,000 years in China.[18]

However, the 1912 Provisional Constitution was replaced in 1914 with the Constitutional Law of the Republic of China, promulgated on May 1, 1914, by the government under *Yuan Shikai*. In contrast to the 1912 Provisional Constitution, the 1914 Constitution changed the government structure from the cabinet system to the presidential system. The change was purposed to provide *Yuan Shikai*, the president, with full power and control, expanding the authority of the president to the level of an authoritarian emperor.[19] *Yuan Shikai* crowned himself as an "emperor" in late 1915 but died eighty-three days after his coronation.

After the death of *Yuan Shikai*, China underwent a twelve-year period of tangled fights between warlords, known as the 1916–1928 Warlord Period.[20] In 1923, when taking the position of the presidency,[21] warlord *Cao Kun* promulgated a "Constitution of Republic of China." Viewed as a "hotch-potch" of the presidential and cabinet systems, the 1923 Constitution lasted only one year and was abandoned after *Cao Kun* was ousted in 1924. On August 3, 1925, warlord *Duan Qirui* appointed

[17] See Chiu, *supra* note 16. The text of the Provisional Constitution is available at https://zh.m.wikisource.org/zh-hans/中華民國臨時約法.

[18] See Wei & Weiyan, *supra* note 4, at 52.

[19] See the 1914 Constitutional Law of the Republic of China, chapter III, President, the full text of the 1914 Constitutional Law is available at https://wenku.baidu.com/view/7561bd2703768e9951e79b89680203d8ce2f6a90.html.

[20] Edward A. McCord, *The Warlords*, in Oxford Bibliographies, available at www.oxfordbibliographies.com/view/document/obo-9780199920082/obo-9780199920082-0154.xml. In China, however, this period is normally called the Northern Warlord Period, dated from 1916 to 1928, including the era of Yuan Shikai.

[21] In between Yuan Shikai and Cao Kun, there were three Acting Presidents in the Republic of China, including Li Yuanhong (1916–1917; 1922–1923), Feng Guozhang (1917–1918), and Xu Shichang (1918–1922).

a committee to draft a new constitution. The draft was completed in December 1925 but was never adopted due to the quick fall of the warlord government.

When the Nationalist government, which was formed in 1925, won the battle against the warlords, China became a politically unified country again. After the Warlord Period in 1928, China entered a six-year period of political tutelage, referring to the period of transition from a traditional monarchy to republicanism. The key framer of the transition was Dr. *Sun Yat-sen*. According to Dr. *Sun*, reconstruction of the Republic of China would take a process consisting of three periods: (a) a period of military operations; (b) a period of political tutelage; and (c) a period of constitutional government.[22] In preparation for transitioning into the third period, the Nationalist government drafted a constitution and published the formal draft on May 5, 1936, which is commonly called the "May 5th Draft."

But due to the Japanese invasion and the anti-Japanese war, promulgation of the Constitution did not take place until 1946. In December 1946, the National Assembly passed the Constitution, which was published on January 1, 1947. Based on the "May 5th Draft," the 1947 Constitution consisted of 14 chapters and 175 articles. It was the first time that *Sun Yat-sen*'s "Five Powers" concept was incorporated into and became the theoretical basis of the Constitution. Under the 1947 Constitution, the government was structured on the format of a presidency and five branches, including the legislature, executive, judiciary, examination, and supervision.[23] As noted, the 1947 Constitution, along with all other laws adopted by the Nationalist government, was abolished in 1949 when the People's Republic of China was founded.[24]

In 1949, the CPC-led government held its first National Political Consultation Conference in which a "Common Program" was adopted for the newly established People's Republic of China. The Common Program served as an interim Constitution to replace the 1947 Constitution. Containing seven chapters and sixty articles, the Common Program defined the nature of the People's Republic as "a New Democratic or a People's Democratic state" carrying out "the people's democratic dictatorship led by the working class, based on the alliance of workers and peasants, and uniting all democratic classes and all nationalities in China."[25] The

22 See Sun Yat-sen, *A Program of National Reconstruction: The Three Stages of Revolution*, the full text of the article is available at http://afe.easia.columbia.edu/ps/cup/sun_yatsen_revolution.pdf.

23 See the 1947 Constitution available at https://en.wikisource.org/wiki/Constitution_of_the_Republic_of_China_(1947).

24 The 1947 Constitution remains effective in Taiwan. It, however, did not begin to serve its intended purpose as the foundation for democratic governance and rule of law until after 1987, when martial law was lifted in Taiwan. Since then, it has undergone seven rounds of revision: in 1991, 1992, 1994, 1997, 1999, 2000, and 2005. More detailed info about the 1947 Constitution is available at www.taiwan.gov.tw/content_4.php.

25 See the 1949 Common Program, art. 1, available at https://sourcebooks.fordham.edu/mod/1949-ccp-program.asp.

Common Program also provided that the organizational form of the political power of the country is the system of the people's congress.[26]

The first Constitution of the People's Republic was adopted in 1954. A significant feature of the 1954 Constitution was that it was drafted predominantly under the will of the CPC. The 1954 Constitution included a preamble, 4 chapters and 108 articles.[27] It established a government structure that remains the main framework of the current governing system in the country. Under the 1954 Constitution, similar to the Common Program, China was defined as "a people's democratic state led by the working class and based on the alliance of workers and peasants."[28] The 1954 Constitution also reaffirmed the people's congress system established under the Common Program as the country's organizational form of government.[29]

In addition, the 1954 Constitution provided for four different ownerships as the country's economic basis: state ownership, collective ownership, individual ownership, and capitalist ownership.[30] It also emphasized that state ownership was the leading force in the nation's economy.[31] Moreover, there were two important articles in the 1954 Constitution that concerned protection of the rights of citizens. The first one was article 85, under which all citizens of the country are equal before the law.[32] The other one was article 87, which granted citizens the rights of "freedom of speech, freedom of the press, freedom of assembly, freedom of association, freedom of procession and freedom of demonstration."[33]

The 1954 Constitution, however, was never fully enforced and virtually ceased to operate after 1957, when the Anti-Rightist Movement was launched nationwide against intellectuals. Not until 1975 did China begin to revive its Constitution. As a result, a new Constitution was adopted in January 1975. The 1975 Constitution significantly altered the 1954 Constitution and reduced the number of articles from 160 to 30. In its substance, the 1975 Constitution adhered to the class struggle theory and was purposed to maintain the legitimacy of the Cultural Revolution. Given its unpopular political nature, the 1975 Constitution was doomed to a short life.

In 1978, after *Mao*'s death and the downfall of the Gang of Four (the name referring to the political group consisting of four powerful CPC party members during the Cultural Revolution), China began to shift the country's focus from class struggle to economic development. Such a shift created an urgent need to replace the 1975 Constitution. Under these circumstances, the third Constitution was

26 See *id.*, art. 12.
27 See the 1954 Constitution of China, available at http://en.pkulaw.cn/display.aspx?cgid=52993&lib=law.
28 See *id.*, art. 1.
29 See *id.*, art. 2.
30 See *id.*, art. 5.
31 See *id.*, art. 6.
32 See *id.*, art. 85.
33 See *id.*, art. 87.

quickly promulgated on March 5, 1978. The 1978 Constitution reinstated several provisions in the 1954 Constitution, particularly those involving the rights and duties of citizens. In late 1978, vast economic reforms began in the country.

Since the 1978 Constitution was adopted before the economic reforms and remained closely tied to the class struggle ideology, there grew a great need for a new constitution. Four years later, in 1982, the fourth Constitution was promulgated. After the 1982 Constitution took effect, revisions to the Constitution started to take the form of amendments. As noted, since its adoption, the 1982 Constitution has been amended five times: in 1988, 1993, 1999, 2004, and 2018, respectively.

The 1982 Constitution takes the 1954 Constitution as its blueprint and significantly revises the government structure established under the 1975 and 1978 Constitutions. The 1982 Constitution downplays class struggle and places top priority on modernization through economic development. While specifically expunging all rhetoric associated with the Cultural Revolution, the 1982 Constitution incorporates the Four Basic Principles introduced by *Deng Xiaoping* as the primary governing rules.

The Four Basic Principles are also known as the four adherences, including (a) adherence to the leadership of the CPC; (b) adherence to *Marxism, Leninism,* and *Mao Zedong* Thought; (c) adherence to the people's democratic dictatorship; and (d) adherence to the socialist road. As noted, *Marxism, Leninism,* and *Mao Zedong* Thought was the ruling ideology of the country and expanded over the years to contain the ideas of the top leaders of the CPC, including *Deng Xiaoping* Theory, *Jiang Zemin's* Three Represents (added in the 1999 Amendment), *Hu Jintao's* Scientific Outlook on Development (added in the 2018 Amendment), and *Xi Jinping* Thought on Socialism with Chinese Characteristics for a New Era (added in the 2018 Amendment). Both the basic principles and ruling ideologies are explicitly stated in the preamble of the Constitution, although their contents are quite vague and confusing.

The 1982 Constitution consists of a preamble and 4 chapters with a total of 138 articles. Like all previous Constitutions, the preamble is a lengthy statement describing, among other things, the CPC's achievements, the ruling ideology and principles, the basic policies of the State, and the legal effect of the Constitution. A highly contested issue concerning the preamble is whether it should have any legal effect.[34] Many argue that since the Preamble is part of the Constitution, it should have the same effect as all other provisions in the Constitution.[35] Some, however, disagree, asserting that the preamble is quite descriptive and can hardly be governing legal norms.[36] In practice, however, as often is the case, there is a

[34] See Wei & Weiyan, *supra* note 4, at 40.
[35] See *id.*
[36] See *id.*

tendency to rely on the ruling ideologies to judge constitutionality if no provision is readily applicable.

Chapters one to three of the 1982 Constitution are the main body, and chapter four contains supplementary provisions. In the main body, there are provisions on the General Principles (chapter one), the Fundamental Rights and Duties of Citizens (chapter two), and the Structure of the State (chapter three). Note that in the 1954, 1975, and 1978 Constitutions, the Chapter of the Fundamental Rights and Duties is provided after the Structure of the State. The 1982 Constitution reversed the order to better incarnate the principle of the CPC-led people's sovereignty.[37]

C. *Constitutionalism*

A painful lesson China learned from the Cultural Revolution is that there must not only be laws but also a sound system to ensure the enforcement of the laws. Thus, since the 1982 Constitution was promulgated, there has been growing public outcry for the establishment of constitutionalism in the country to maintain the supremacy of the Constitution. A common belief is that in order for the Constitution to fully and effectively function as intended, constitutionalism needs to be developed.[38]

A question, then, is what constitutionalism refers to. In the Stanford Encyclopedia of Philosophy, constitutionalism is defined as "the idea, often associated with the political theories of John Locke and the founders of the American republic, that government can and should be legally limited in its powers, and that its authority or legitimacy depends on its observing these limitations."[39] In China, however, there is no generally accepted definition. But as noted, law in China, including the Constitution, is not aimed at limiting government power.

In *Mao*'s era, constitutionalism was rarely discussed in public. *Mao* once viewed it as "democratic politics,"[40] but during *Mao*'s rule democracy in China was virtually nothing more than lip service. Constitutional scholars in the country also struggled to define constitutionalism without cloning the Western concept. *Zhang Youyu*, the late leading Chinese constitution scholar, once termed constitutionalism as a political form using the constitution to stipulate the state system, political power structure, and rights and obligations of the government and the people, so that both the government and the people can enjoy rights and bear obligations under the laws, and nobody may violate or exceed the laws or act arbitrarily.[41]

[37] See *id.* at 41.

[38] See Wang Zhenmin, Chinese Constitutional Review System, 3 (China University of Political Science and Law Press, 2004).

[39] See Stanford Encyclopedia of Philosophy, *Constitutionalism*, available at https://plato.stanford.edu/entries/constitutionalism/.

[40] See Selected Works of Mao Zedong, 735 (People's Press, 1991).

[41] See Zhang Youyu, Constitutional Treatise Series, 97–103 (People's Publishing House, 1986).

In addressing constitutionalism, Chinese scholars at the present time remain quite divided. Some scholars consider constitutionalism as a process of political conduct in creating, implementing, maintaining, and developing the constitution on the basis of the principle of implementing democratic politics and the rule of law, with the purpose of guaranteeing the power of the people and the rights of citizens.[42] Other scholars regard constitutionalism as a political process of governance of the country under the constitution.[43] A similar but short definition describes constitutionalism as constitutional politics, meaning to govern the country through a constitution.[44]

Another scholarly definition holds a different view and refers to constitutionalism as a political system (rather than a process) in which the state is governed by a constitution that fully reflects modern civilization, with a series of democratic principles and systems as the main content, the rule of law as the basic guarantee, and the full realization of the most extensive human rights as the ultimate goal.[45] Under this definition, constitutionalism as a political system is based on a well-structured constitution, and it serves as a guarantee of the rule of law and a legal mechanism to protect human rights.

Despite these differences, many in China agree that to establish constitutionalism in the country, certain criteria must be met. First, there must be a constitution, and the constitution must be real and effective. Second, the principle of the people's sovereignty must be followed, under which state power comes from the people and belongs to the people, and the exercise of such power is under the scrutiny of the people. Third, a representative system must be in place to ensure a democratic system in which people have the right to elect a representative to represent their interests and concerns. Fourth, there must be a system of rule of law so that the constitution is the supreme law, government power is limited, due process is observed, and human rights are protected. Fifth, there must be a mechanism of checks and constitutional review to prevent the abuse of power and maintain constitutionality.[46]

Note, however, that the criteria for constitutionalism as publicly discussed among Chinese scholars do not contain an independent judiciary. The missing element of judicial independence is in part due to the fear of being blamed for offending the CPC, because the CPC repeatedly eliminates judicial independence in the country. More broadly, given the CPC's strong stance against it, the term judicial independence almost becomes a legal taboo. Therefore, in most cases, judicial

[42] See Guo Daohui, The Zeitgeist of Law, 337 (Hunan Press, 1997).

[43] See Wei & Weiyan, *supra* note 4, at 12.

[44] See Xu Congde, Constitution and Democratic Politics, 3 (China Prosecution Press, 1994).

[45] See Li Buyun, *Constitutionalism and China*, in Li Buyun & Zhang Wenxian, eds., Jurisprudence, Comments and Discussions, Vol. 1, 589 (Law Press, 1999).

[46] See Wei & Weiyan, *supra* note 4, at 13–14.

independence is replaced with independence in trial or adjudication in order to be politically correct.

Definition aside, the state attitude toward constitutionalism in the country is strongly driven by the party interests of the CPC. Since 1993, when the 1982 Constitution was amended to adopt the concept of ruling the country according to law, a lot of efforts both in theory and in practice have been made to build a legal system under the rule of law, but the process has never been as smooth as it should be. The institutional defects in the country's political system create significant obstacles to the practice of the rule of law.

A major obstacle is the status of the CPC within the law. The problem is that although the people's congress is the basic system under the Constitution for the exercise of state power, the exercise must be under the control of the CPC. It is such control that virtually makes the people's congress a "rubber stamp." More strikingly, as many critics argue, the CPC is the master of almost all of the important political resources and power but never really operates within the realm of law and the legal system.[47] Therefore, whether the CPC is to be governed by the law has been and remains to be an open question. Given the CPC's dominant force over state power, the rule of law can hardly exist in the country without a constitutional leash on the CPC.

As noted, a prominent feature of Chinese characteristics is the power of the CPC. In order to maintain the supremacy of the leadership of the CPC, some in China directly regard the Constitution as the most important and fundamental form of legalizing the CPC's line, principles, and policies.[48] Thus, in the Constitution, the CPC's party line, principles, and policies must be given the highest legal effect so that they can forever be followed and enforced.[49] The norms and values articulated and provided by the CPC form a substantial basis of the country's Constitution. Largely for that reason, China is viewed as a "single-party constitutional state."[50]

Therefore, it has become a dictum in China that the development of the rule of law in the country must not undermine the CPC's leadership. For example, in the 19th Congress of the CPC held in October 2017, while stressing the need for the development of the rule of law in China, the CPC Central Committee once again set as the primary tone for the country that among the party, government, military, civilians, and academia, and in the east, west, south, north, and middle of the country, the CPC must lead everything – a popular slogan in *Mao*'s era.[51] Further, it

[47] See Ni Wen-ying, *Key Elements Affecting the Construction of Constitutionalism in China*, available at https://wenku.baidu.com/view/cef0191e866fb84ae45c8d8a.html.

[48] See Zhenmin, *supra* note 38, at 15.

[49] See *id.*

[50] See Jiang Shigong, *Chinese-Style Constitutionalism: On Backer's Chinese Party-State Constitutionalism*, 40 SAGE J. 133 (2013), available at https://journals.sagepub.com/doi/abs/10.1177/0097700413511313?journalCode = mcxa.

[51] See Xi Jinping, Report to the 19th Congress of the CPC, October 18, 2017, available at www.qstheory.cn/llqikan/2017-12/03/c_1122049424.htm.

is a rule of thumb that the CPC's leadership is a fundamental guarantee for the rule of law.

Officially, the 19th Congress of the CPC is acclaimed as the beginning of a new era of constitutionalism in China.[52] But the reality is just the opposite. As discussed, in 2018 the 1982 Constitution was amended at the CPC's initiative. A main purpose of the 2018 Amendment was to drop the term limits for the President of China, lifting the constitutional ban on lifetime tenure for the presidency currently held by Xi. The amendment to the term limits has been viewed both at home and abroad as a significant setback in much-needed political reform for the country. In the meantime, in order to justify the non-challengeable leadership position of the CPC, a political campaign was maneuvered in the nation to clean up the Western concept of constitutionalism and its influence.

Therefore, the road to constitutionalism in China remains quite rocky and remote. Although constitutionalism has become a hot topic, especially in the legal community, there are so many minefields lying ahead and each of them is quite explosive. The issues that are considered sensitive include, among others, the political party and the power of the people's congress; the ruling position of the CPC and the supremacy of the Constitution and the laws; congressional supervision and balance of powers; abuse of power and constitutional review; and the people's delegates and their constituents.

D. *Constitutional Amendments*

As noted, since the 1982 Constitution was adopted, all constitutional revisions have been made through amendments. According to article 62 of the 1982 Constitution, only the National People's Congress (NPC) has the power to amend the Constitution.[53] The 1982 Constitution also prescribes a procedure for amending the Constitution. Under article 64 of the 1982 Constitution, amendments to the Constitution are to be proposed by the Standing Committee of the NPC or by more than one-fifth of the delegates to the NPC and adopted by a vote of more than two-thirds of all the deputies to the congress.[54]

However, no amendment has ever been proposed by "one-fifth of the delegates." In fact, all amendments were initiated by the central committee of the CPC. Upon approval of the CPC, draft amendments were introduced as CPC proposals to the

[52] See *id.* (The 19th National Congress of the CPC is a very important conference that is held during the crucial period of fully building a well-off society and entering a new era of socialism with Chinese characteristics); see also Larry Catá Backer, *Chinese Constitutionalism in the New Era: The Emerging Idea and Practice of Constitution in the 19th CPC Congress Report*, SSRN, available at https://papers.ssrn.com/sol3/papers.cfm?abstract_id = 3066974.

[53] See the 1982 Constitution, *supra* note 11, art. 62.

[54] See *id.*, art. 64 (for the laws and NPC decisions, however, only a simple majority vote is needed to pass).

NPC for an assembly vote. Thus, no constitutional amendment proposal would ever reach the assembly floor of the NPC without the CPC's approval. As discussed, since the 1982 Constitution was promulgated, it has been amended five times.

The 1988 Amendments contain two major provisions. One provision is to permit the private sector of the economy to exist with a legal status as a "supplement to the socialist public economy." As noted, the 1954 Constitution recognized "individual ownership" as part of the state economy. The "private sector" as provided in the 1988 Amendments and "individual ownership" as used in the 1954 Constitution, though different in wording, have the same or similar effect of upholding private ownership in the socialist economy. The other provision in the 1988 Amendments is to allow transfers of the right to the use of land under the provisions of law.[55]

The 1993 Amendments focus on redefining the nature of the country's economic system to justify the need for economic reforms. To that end, the Amendments position China in the "preliminary stage of the socialism," meaning that the country remains in a developing period with limited wealth. Under the "preliminary stage" theory, it is necessary for China to open its door to the West and draw foreign capital and advanced technology into the country to modernize the nation's economy. On that ground, the 1993 Amendments formally adopt the concept of a socialist market economy to replace the planned economy that dominated China for decades.[56]

The 1999 Amendments further define the private economy as a non-public economy, including an individual economy and a private economy.[57] There were two major developments in the 1999 Amendments. First, the legal status of the private sector of the economy was changed from "the supplement to [the] socialist market economy" to an "important component of the socialist market economy." In the meantime, the Amendments make it a constitutional duty for the State to protect the legitimate rights and interests of private and individual economies.[58] The second development is the adoption of the concept of the rule of law. The 1999 Amendments add into the 1982 Constitution a new provision that the State "practices ruling the country in accordance with the law and building a socialist country under the rule of law."[59]

The 1982 Constitution was amended again in 2004.[60] Aimed at protecting property rights, the 2004 Amendments contain several provisions to safeguard private

[55] The 1988 Amendment is available at www.cecc.gov/resources/legal-provisions/1988-amendment-to-the-constitution-of-the-peoples-republic-of-china.

[56] The 1993 Amendment is available at www.cecc.gov/resources/legal-provisions/1993-amendment-to-the-constitution-of-the-peoples-republic-of-china.

[57] The 1999 Amendment is available at www.cecc.gov/resources/legal-provisions/1999-amendment-to-the-constitution-of-the-peoples-republic-of-china.

[58] See *id.*

[59] See *id.*

[60] The 2004 Amendment is available at www.cecc.gov/resources/legal-provisions/2004-amendment-to-the-constitution-of-the-peoples-republic-of-china.

property and property rights. First, the Amendments specifically provide that the "lawful private property of citizens is inviolable." Second, it is required that the "State, in accordance with law, protects the rights of citizens to private property and to its inheritance." Third, the State may expropriate or requisition private property but must meet such conditions as (a) being for the public interest, (b) in accordance with the law, and (c) making compensation.[61]

The 2004 Amendments also emphasize that the "State encourages, supports and guides the development of the non-public sectors of the economy."[62] The non-public sectors not only include individual and private economies but also cover foreign investment enterprises. In addition, the 2004 Amendments, for the first time, provide that the "State respects and preserves human rights,"[63] making human rights protection a constitutional mandate in the country.

The 2018 Amendments were the latest revision to the 1982 Constitution.[64] As discussed, the 2018 Amendments, on the one hand, signify the constitutionality of one-party rule, making the leadership of the CPC the "defining feature of socialism with Chinese characteristics,"[65] and, on the other hand, remove the term limit for the presidency of the country. The term limit refers to article 79 of the 1982 Constitution, which provided that the term of the presidency shall be no more than two consecutive terms and each term is five years. The amended article 79 provides that the term of office of the President and Vice President of the People's Republic of China is the same as that of the NPC, which is five years.[66]

As noted, the term limits on the government were initiated by *Deng Xiaoping* in an effort to end the lifelong system of individuals holding government offices. According to *Deng*, the lifelong system is a chronic illness of the rigid socialist model. In 1982, article 38 of the Charter of the CPC was amended to provide that for the leading cadres at all levels of the party, whether elected or appointed, their positions are not permanent and can be changed or removed.[67] When the 1982 Constitution was adopted, the term limits were written into the Constitution, applying to all government offices at various levels of the country.[68]

The removal of term limits in the 2018 Amendments is widely viewed as "an end to the era of collective leadership" and sets the stage for "a return to individual

61 See *id.*
62 See *id.*
63 See *id.*
64 The 2018 Amendment 2018 Amendment to Chinese Constitution.
65 See *id.*
66 See *id.*
67 See the CPC Constitution (as revised 2017), art. 38, available at www.xinhuanet.com//english/download/Constitution_of_the_Communist_Party_of_China.pdf.
68 See the 1982 Constitution of China (as amended 2004), art. 79, available at www.npc.gov.cn/zgrdw/englishnpc/Constitution/2007-11/15/content_1372966.htm.

autocracy."[69] The removal has also met widespread criticism within China. It has become a common belief that the abolishment of life tenure in government offices, as a historic reform of China's political system,[70] was an effective means to prevent "the excessive concentration of government power in the hands of a single individual" and "the rise of personal cults." Both "excessive concentration of government power" and "personal cults" were the major causes of the Cultural Revolution.[71]

E. *Interpretation of the Constitution*

Constitutional interpretation in China involves two major issues. The first issue concerns the nature of interpretation. Generally, constitutional interpretation in China refers to the description or explanation of the content, meaning, and scope of the provisions of the Constitution.[72] But scholars have varied views on the substance of interpretation. Some opine that constitutional interpretation involves the understanding and explanation of constitutional provisions.[73]

Others regard constitutional interpretation as a supplement to, and an explanation of, the specific meaning and scope of the application of constitutional provisions.[74] There is also an argument that constitutional interpretation is a clarification of the contents, meaning, and limits of constitutional norms.[75] Despite the different views, scholars agree that constitutional interpretation has constitutional force, meaning that the interpretations have the same binding effect as the Constitution itself.

The second issue is about who may conduct the interpretation or has the authority to interpret. Under article 67 of the 1982 Constitution, the Standing Committee of the NPC has the power to interpret the Constitution and supervise its implementation.[76] Based on article 67, it is commonly held in China that constitutional interpretation rests solely with the Standing Committee of the NPC. Unlike other countries where constitutional interpretation is made either by the judiciary (regular courts) or by special entities (constitutional court), China leaves constitutional interpretation to the state legislature.

69 See Suzuki Ken, *China's New "Xi Jinping Constitution": The Road to Totalitarianism*, Nippon.com, November 27, 2018, available at www.nippon.com/en/in-depth/a05803/china's-new-xi-jinping-constitution-the-road-to-totalitarianism.html.

70 See Han Dayuan, *The Significance of the Provision on Term System in the Chinese Constitution* – In Commemoration of the 35th Anniversary of the Promulgation of the 1982 Constitution, Journal of Faxue, Vol. 11, 2017, available at https://boxun.com/news/gb/pubvp/2018/02/201802261257.shtml.

71 See *id.* See also Xu Zhangrun, *Our Current Fears and Expectations*, Unirule Institute of Economics, July 24, 2018, available at http://unirule.cloud/index.php?c = article&id = 4625.

72 See the NPC, *What Is the Constitutional Interpretation?* in Qs & As in Studying the Constitution and Amendments, October 15, 2004, available at www.npc.gov.cn/zgrdw/npc/oldarchives/zht/zgrdw/common/zw.jsp@label = wxzlk&id = 329966&pdmc = 1504.htm.

73 See Kai, *supra* note 9, at 58.

74 See *id.* at 59.

75 See *id.*

76 See the 1982 Constitution, *supra* note 11, art. 67.

Therefore, constitutional interpretation in China is a matter of legislative interpretation, which means that the interpretation is conducted in the form of legislation through legislative procedure rather than litigation under judicial procedure. Put differently, legal interpretation in China is divided into legislative interpretation or interpretation by the legislature and judicial interpretation or interpretation by the judiciary. Since constitutional interpretation falls within legislative power, no courts in China may interpret the Constitution.

The constitutional interpretation by the Standing Committee of the NPC is deemed to serve two functions: supplementing legislation and implementing the Constitution. According to Chinese scholars, constitutional interpretation plays several roles, including (a) explaining the meaning of constitutional provisions, (b) filling gaps in the Constitution, (c) adapting to new developments, (d) maintaining the supremacy of the Constitution and the unity of the state legal system, and (e) identifying and preventing possible violations of the Constitution.[77]

Some in China argue that the NPC itself should also have the power of constitutional interpretation. This argument relies on article 62 of the 1982 Constitution, which provides that the NPC has the power to alter or annul inappropriate decisions of the Standing Committee of the NPC.[78] According to the argument, for purposes of legislative interpretation, the "decisions" referred to in article 62 should include both the "decisions" made, "the laws, regulations" adopted, and interpretations conducted by the Standing Committee. Therefore, if the NPC is dissatisfied with the interpretation of the Standing Committee, it may directly make its own interpretations.[79]

There are two questions closely related to constitutional interpretation. One question is how the interpretation should be made, and the other question is when an interpretation shall be made. The former involves the procedures for interpretation, while the latter concerns the circumstances in which a constitutional interpretation is needed. Since the 1982 Constitution contains no provisions on the constitutional interpretation process, some in China suggest adopting unified interpretation procedures to ensure uniformity and avoid confusion.

In November 2015, aimed at providing a blueprint for future legislation, a group of Chinese constitutional scholars drafted a Law of Procedures for the Constitutional Interpretation (the 2015 Draft).[80] Under the 2015 Draft, constitutional interpretation should take four procedural steps: (a) request for the interpretation, (b) acceptance

[77] See Ma Ning, *The Procedural Design of the Constitutional Interpretation in China*, Renmin University online publication on Constitutional Governance, available at www.calaw.cn/article/default.asp?id=10954.

[78] See the 1982 Constitution, *supra* note 11, art. 62.

[79] See Ning, *supra* note 77.

[80] See Han Dayuan et al., *The Law of the People's Republic of China on the Constitutional Interpretation Procedure (Expert Draft) and Its Explanation*, China Consititutionalism Net, November 21, 2015, available at www.calaw.cn/article/default.asp?id=10166.

of the request, (c) examination and review of the request, and (d) adoption of the interpretation.[81]

The 2015 Draft also specifies circumstances under which the Standing Committee of the NPC may interpret the Constitution. According to the 2015 Draft, an interpretation of the Constitution is needed only if (1) the specific meaning of a provision of the Constitution needs to be further clarified; (2) the basis of application needs to be clearly defined for the implementation of the Constitution; (3) regulatory documents such as laws, administrative regulations, or local regulations are in conflict with the provisions of the Constitution, and the meaning of the provisions of the Constitution needs to be clarified; and (4) other circumstances that require the interpretation of the Constitution.[82]

In addition, the 2015 Draft provides that a Constitutional Committee shall be formed under the NPC to conduct research and review bill drafting related to constitutional interpretation.[83] It is further provided that interpretation may be initiated by the Standing Committee of the NPC or by the request of state organs, armed forces, political parties and social organizations, enterprises, institutions, and individuals, depending on the nature of the request.[84] The request can be classified into different categories by its nature, including prevention,[85] general review,[86] specific review,[87] and personal petition.[88]

Interpretation for prevention purposes refers to the interpretation made by a legislating body during the process of adopting such normative documents as laws, administrative regulations, or local regulations to prevent any possible conflict with the Constitution. General review takes place in the situation where a law, administrative regulation, or local regulation is deemed to conflict with the Constitution, which prompts a request by certain entities other than the legislating body to the Standing Committee of the NPC for interpretation. Specific review is an interpretation made upon request by the Supreme People's Court (SPC) pertaining to a specific case during the trial where a possible conflict between a law or regulation and the Constitution is at issue. Personal petition is the case where an individual believes that his or her basic rights have been infringed and there is a need to request a constitutional interpretation because all legal channels are exhausted, but no relief is available.

The 2015 Draft, as a scholarly work, has no legal effect. Nevertheless, it represents the prevalent view of legal scholars in the country and reflects a development in

[81] See *id.*
[82] See *id.*, art. 6.
[83] See *id.*, art. 5.
[84] See *id.*, art. 7.
[85] See *id.*, art. 8.
[86] See *id.*, art. 9.
[87] See *id.*, art. 10.
[88] See *id.*, art. 11.

adopting a formal procedure for constitutional interpretation in the country. Many of the provisions in the 2015 Draft implicate certain expectations for the future. For example, the idea of the formation of a Constitutional Committee implies a constitutional review. The impact of the 2015 Draft is already observable. In the 2018 Amendments, "the Law Committee" under the NPC was renamed the "Constitution and Law Committee."[89] This change was not in the original proposal of the Amendments but was added at the request of a number of delegates during the NPC Assembly Meeting.

F. *Constitutional Review*

China does not have a system of constitutional review. But some in China believe that the 1982 Constitution actually contains provisions that provide both a general and specific legal basis for constitutional review.[90] The general basis derives from certain articles of the 1982 Constitution, including article 2 (all power belongs to the people), article 5 (no organization or individual may be "privileged to go beyond the Constitution or laws"), and article 41 (citizens have the right to criticize and make suggestions regarding any state organ or functionary and the right to compensation for the losses suffered as a result of infringement of their civil rights by any state organ or functionary)."[91]

The belief that the 1982 Constitution has a specific legal basis for constitutional review refers to article 67 of the 1982 Constitution. As noted, under article 67, the NPC has the power to (a) supervise the implementation of the Constitution and (b) alter or annul inappropriate decisions of its Standing Committee.[92] Some individuals then argue that the NPC's power to supervise constitutional implementation under article 67 is, in essence, a power of constitutional review.[93] But still, there is no provision in the Constitution that explicitly authorizes constitutional review.

Three issues remain highly debatable. The first issue is the concept of constitutional review. In many countries, constitutional review is characterized as a process of evaluating the constitutionality of laws, or a system of preventing violations of constitutional rights and assuring the efficacy, stability, and preservation of the Constitution.[94] In the United States, the evaluation of the constitutionality of laws is a judicial function by which the courts examine the actions of all other

[89] See the 2018 Amendments to the 1982 Constitution, available at www.fdi.gov.cn/1800000121_39_4866_0_7.html.
[90] See Zhenmin, *supra* note 38, at 99, 107.
[91] See the 1982 Constitution, *supra* note 11, arts. 2, 5, 41.
[92] See *id.*, art. 62.
[93] See Zhenmin, *supra* note 38, at 107.
[94] See Tom Ginsburg, *Comparative Constitutional Review*, June 30, 2008, available at https://comparativeconstitutionsproject.org/files/cm_archives/constitutional_review.pdf.

government branches to determine whether such actions are consistent with the Constitution.[95]

In China, constitutional review is generally characterized as a review of a violation of the Constitution.[96] The terms often used interchangeably in the Chinese legal community to refer to constitutional review include "constitutionality review," "review on violation of constitution," "judicial review," "constitutionality guarantee," and "constitutional litigation." In a Chinese constitution textbook, constitutional review is described to mean that specific state organs review and decide whether the laws, regulations, or documents with legal significance are compatible with the Constitution through statutory procedures on the basis of the norms, provisions, and principles of the Constitution.[97]

As noted, article 67 of the 1982 Constitution provides the Standing Committee of the NPC with the power to supervise the implementation of the Constitution. Constitutional supervision is considered to have the function of constitutional review because it is purposed to help assure the full implementation of the Constitution. But many in China doubt that constitutional supervision as provided in article 67 may well apply as intended. There are several concerns. First, there is the lack of a mechanism to effectively undertake the supervision. Second, unlike review that requires active action, supervision can be quite passive, meaning to watch without taking action. Third, since the Standing Committee of the NPC itself has lawmaking power, constitutional supervision by the Standing Committee is, in fact, self-supervision.

The second issue concerns the entity that should have the authority to conduct constitutional review. As discussed, the Chinese judiciary does not have jurisdiction over cases involving constitutionality, and the power to determine constitutionality issues is retained by the state legislature. But it has been highly debatable whether the power should be exercised by the NPC, its Standing Committee, or a special body designated by the NPC. Under the 2018 Amendments to the 1982 Constitution, the NPC formed a Constitution and Law Committee. It, however, remains unclear whether such a committee is a designated body to conduct constitutional review in the country.

The argument in favor of the NPC's power of constitutional review argues that although the Constitution contains no provision on constitutional review, the NPC's power to undertake constitutional review can be inferred from the Legislation Law. Under article 88 of the Legislation Law, the NPC has the authority to amend or repeal any inappropriate national law enacted by its Standing Committee, and to invalidate any autonomous decree or special decree approved

95 See *id.*
96 See *id.* at 19.
97 See Kai, *supra* note 9, at 94.

by its Standing Committee in violation of the Constitution.[98] The NPC also has the authority to amend or void any inappropriate administrative rule or local rule.[99]

Relying on the Legislation Law, some argue that the Standing Committee of the NPC should have the power to conduct constitutional review. Authorized by the Legislation Law, the Standing Committee of the NPC may repeal any administrative regulation which contravenes the Constitution or any national law, and invalidate any local decree which contravenes the Constitution or any national law or administrative regulation. The Standing Committee is also empowered to amend or annul any autonomous decree or special decree, approved by the standing committee of the people's congress of any province, autonomous region, or municipality directly under the central government, that is found to have violated the Constitution.[100]

Many, however, believe that the Legislation Law can hardly be seen as an authoritative legal source of constitutional review. In one respect, the Legislation Law is not at the same level as the Constitution and therefore may not constitute the statutory basis for constitutional review. In addition, the Legislation Law is enacted under the Constitution to standardize lawmaking activities, perfect the state legislative institution, and promote governance of the country through legal mechanisms. Thus, the primary concern of the Legislation Law is not the Constitution, but the legislative process of laws and regulations.

In another respect, under the Legislation Law, the local people's congresses, including their standing committees, also have the authority to amend or invalidate any inappropriate local decree enacted by their standing committee or any inappropriate local rule approved by their standing committee, and have the authority to amend or void any inappropriate local rule enacted by a lower-level government. If the Legislation Law is the source of constitutional review, a question necessarily raised then is whether constitutional review could be conducted at both the central level and the local level.

The third issue is how to undertake constitutional review, referring to the process or procedure of constitutionality determination. As many have argued in China, constitutional review would serve three basic functions: (a) to maintain the supremacy of the Constitution, (b) to ensure respect and protection of the fundamental rights of people, and (c) to set a boundary on government power.[101] A government with limited power is considered a prerequisite to the establishment of a system of constitutional review.[102]

98 See the Legislation Law of China (adopted March 15, 2000), art. 88(i). An English version of the Legislation Law is available at www.cecc.gov/resources/legal-provisions/legislation-law-chinese-and-english-text.

99 See *id.*, art. 88(iii).

100 See *id.*, art. 88(ii).

101 See Kai, *supra* note 9, at 97–98; see also Zhenmin, *supra* note 38, at 38–39.

102 See Zhenmin, *supra* note 38, at 38.

Unfortunately, the government in China, as noted, always has a tendency to control everything with no limitation. It seems quite natural in the country that the law is viewed as a device to "rule" people rather than to "rule" government.[103] A bitter experience from the ten-year social upheaval of the Cultural Revolution is that the unbounded power of the state leader would inevitably lead to the chaos of lawlessness. In the past decades, a public awareness has developed that it would be impossible to have a rule-based society without limiting government power.[104] But in reality, a tough question was, and remains to be, how to impose limits on government power. More specifically, the question is whether the power of the CPC is subject to any limits.

What is worth noting in this regard is the Administrative Litigation Law (ALL). As discussed, the ALL was first enacted in 1989 to protect the lawful rights and interests of citizens, legal persons, and other organizations, and oversee administrative agencies' exercise of power according to the law.[105] The ALL authorizes the courts to examine the legality of administrative actions during the trial of administrative cases. When the ALL was amended in 2014, it further granted the courts power to review administrative normative documents.

Under article 53 of the ALL, a citizen, a legal person, or any other organization who files a complaint against an administrative action may request a review of the normative documents adopted by the departments of the State Council or a local government and its agencies if it is believed that the action taken on the basis of such normative documents is illegal. Article 53 is deemed in China as a significant step toward developing the rule of law. But as many argue, the courts' review of the legality of administrative actions is very limited both in scope and in substance[106] because article 53 makes it clear that the court review is limited to the normative documents, excluding administrative rules and regulations.[107] A study shows that a large majority of cases filed under the ALL were denied because the courts seldom and reluctantly scrutinized the substantive contents and merits of the administrative normative documents.[108]

On October 28, 2014, the CPC Central Committee issued the Decision on Major Issues Pertaining to Comprehensively Promoting the Rule of Law. The Decision requires that people of all ethnic groups, all state organs and armed forces, all political parties and public organizations, and all enterprises and institutions must

[103] See *id.* at 36.

[104] See *id.* at 37.

[105] See the Administrative Litigation Law (as amended 2017), art. 1, available at www.hongfanglaw.com/wp-content/uploads/2019/10/Administrative-Litigation-Law-of-the-Peoples-Republic-of-China-2017-RevisionENCN.pdf.

[106] See Shiling Xiao & Yang Lin, *Judicial Review of Administrative Rules in China: Incremental Expansion of Judicial Power*, 17 J. of Comp. L. 2 (2022), available at https://papers.ssrn.com/sol3/papers.cfm?abstract_id=4296692.

[107] The term "administrative normative document" is very confusing. It generally refers to documents that have legal effect but are below rules and regulations in terms of their legal hierarchy.

[108] See Xiao & Lin, *supra* note 106.

take the Constitution as the basic standard of conduct and shall have the responsibility to safeguard the dignity of the Constitution and ensure the implementation of the Constitution. According to the Decision, any act in violation of the Constitution must be investigated and corrected.[109]

The Decision is praised as a historic move for the promotion of the rule of law under the Constitution in China.[110] But it is still doubtful that the rule of law would effectively operate without a leash on the power of the CPC and its leaders. In 2017, in his Report to the 19th Congress of the CPC, *Xi Jinping* called for strengthening the implementation and supervision of the Constitution, promoting the review of constitutionality, and safeguarding constitutional authority.[111]

The Report is viewed in China as official recognition of constitutional review for the first time in China. In response to the Report, the Law Committee of the NPC was renamed the Constitution and Law Committee. But except for the name change, no concrete steps have ever been taken. In fact, both the Decision and the Report make it imperative that the absolute leadership of the CPC must be maintained, emphasizing once again the supreme position of the CPC.

Thus, the development of the rule of law as pledged and the maintaining of the CPC's leadership as mandated create a complex interplay between the ruling force of the CPC and the legal system in China.[112] The CPC's strong position against the Western concepts of universal value, separation of powers, and judicial independence constitutes insurmountable hurdles for China's move toward a rule-based country. With regard to constitutional review, a mere recognition on paper does not necessarily mean that it will be implemented. The lack of a mechanism and the absence of limits on the power of the CPC will eventually render constitutional review an empty call.

G. *Judicial Application of Constitution*

A long unresolved issue in China is whether the provisions of the Constitution may be applied in the courts. Put differently, it is a question of whether a court may

109 See the CPC, *The Decision on Major Issues Pertaining to Comprehensively Promoting the Rule of Law*, available at www.gov.cn/zhengce/2014-10/28/content_2771946.htm.

110 See Qiao Xinsheng, *Party Congress Promotes Rule of Law*, China Daily, October 23, 2017, available at www.chinadaily.com.cn/opinion/2017-10/23/content_33594766.htm.

111 See Xi Jinping, *Secure a Decisive Victory in Building a Moderately Prosperous Society in All Respects and Strive for the Great Success of Socialism with Chinese Characteristics for a New Era*, Report to the 19th Congress of the CPC, October 18, 2017, available at www.xinhuanet.com/english/special/2017-11/03/c_136725942.htm.

112 As pointed out by one commentary, the reality in China now is that "on the one hand, Xi has positioned himself as a champion of the rule of law, in an attempt, some argue, to justify his wide-ranging anti-corruption campaign and reduce resistance to economic reform at local levels"; and on the other hand, "he's made it clear that legal reform can never be allowed to challenge the party's authority." See Zheping Huang, *Xi Jinping Promised Legal Reform in China, but Forget about Judicial Independence*, Quartz, January 18, 2017, available at https://qz.com/886665/xi-jinping-promised-legal-reform-in-china-but-forget-about-judicial-independence/.

decide a case on a constitutional ground or cite a provision of the Constitution when making a judgment. Since the 1954 Constitution was adopted, there has been an unwritten rule in the country that no constitutional provision may be used in the process of adjudication.[113] A decades-long wonder in the Chinese legal community is why the Constitution, the fundamental law of the country, may not be directly applied by the courts in judicial proceedings.[114]

The non-judicial application of the Constitution in China is said to originate from the SPC's 1955 "Reply" to Xinjiang High People's Court concerning the legal source of criminal punishment. In the "Reply," the SPC opined that the Constitution was the fundamental law of the country and the "mother law" of all laws. According to the SPC, "as far as criminal matters are concerned, the Constitution does not stipulate how to deal with criminal punishment . . .," therefore, "the Constitution should not be cited as the basis for the assessment of criminal punishment."[115]

Although the SPC's 1955 "Reply" only involved criminal punishment, it had quite a broad impact on the application of the Constitution in all cases in the courts. On October 28, 1986, when answering the question raised by the Jiangsu High People's Court pertaining to the application of law in formulating court documents, the SPC stated that when the people's courts hear civil and economic disputes and enter judgments, the laws and regulations formulated by the NPC and its Standing Committee, and the administrative regulations formulated by the State Council, may be cited. The SPC, however, particularly mentioned that the rules issued by the instrumentalities of the State Council and by local government may be taken as reference if not in conflict with the Constitution, laws, and administrative regulations, but may not be cited.[116]

The SPC's 1955 Reply and the 1986 Answer are widely considered to mean that the SPC disallowed direct application of the Constitution in the courts. As a result, for many years, there had been no cases in people's courts where the Constitution was applied. Also, in Chinese constitution textbooks, the application of the Constitution in legal proceedings is rarely discussed or not even mentioned.

Many in China, however, disagree, asserting that the non-judicial application of the Constitution is groundless. They argue that since the Constitution is "the fundamental law of the State" and has "the supreme legal authority," there is no statutory basis to the effect that the courts may not apply the Constitution.[117] They

[113] See Zhenmin, *supra* note 38, at 168–169.

[114] See *id.*

[115] See the SPC, *A Letter of Reply Concerning the Matter of Not Citing the Constitution as the Grounds of Criminal Punishment in the Criminal Judgment*, July 30, 1955, available at www.sohu.com/a/160899055_772384 (the Reply was repealed in 2012).

[116] See the SPC, *An Answer on How the People's Court Should Cite Legal Normative Documents in Production of the Court Documents*, October 28, 1986, available at www.cefa123.com/zxdt/426.htm (repealed in 2013).

[117] See Zhenmin, *supra* note 38, at 169–171.

further argue that the SPC's "1955 Reply" and "1986 Answer" should not be interpreted to infer that the Constitution may not be cited as a legal ground in all cases because the SPC did not specifically say so in the "1955 Reply" and "1986 Answer."[118]

Note that under article 5 of the 1982 Constitution, no laws, administrative regulations, or local regulations may contravene the Constitution, and all state organs, the armed forces, all political parties and public organizations, and all enterprises and institutions must abide by the Constitution and other laws, and all acts in violation of the Constitution or other laws must be investigated.[119] But a question that has long been debated is how article 5 of the 1982 Constitution would be effectively enforced without active involvement of the judiciary.

In 2001, the SPC in *Qi Yuling v. Chen Xiaoqi* took a bold move to allow the court to adjudicate the case on the basis of the Constitution.[120] In that case, the Plaintiff, *Qi Yuling*, and the Defendant, *Chen Xiaoqi*, studied in the same middle school in Shandong Province and graduated in the same year. In their examinations for admission to college in 1990, Qi achieved satisfactory scores for admission, but Chen failed. In order to be able to study in college, Chen fraudulently intercepted Qi's notice of admission. Chen's father assisted Chen in falsifying her personal identification and application files and helped Chen steal Qi's identity.

When Chen presented the forged document to the college, the college did not check the authenticity of the document or Chen's identity. Then, under Qi's name and identity, Chen was admitted and began her studies. In 1993, after pretending to be Qi for three years, Chen graduated and got a job at a local bank. Although a number of government institutions were actually aware of the fraud, none of them took any actions to stop it, partly due to the efforts made by Chen's father.

When Qi later discovered what had happened, she sued on the grounds that Chen's conduct violated her constitutional right to her name and to education. The trial court held that under the general rule of the civil law, it is prohibited to interfere with, falsify, or pass oneself off as the name or identity of another. The trial court entered a judgment for Plaintiff Qi but only on the ground of the violation of the right to her name. The difficulty the trial court encountered was that the 1986 General Principles of Civil Law did not explicitly provide for the right to education. Qi was not satisfied with the trial court judgment and appealed.

On appeal, the appellate court faced the same issue pertaining to the right to education. The issue then was submitted through the High People's Court of Shandong to the SPC for clarification. In its reply issued on June 28, 2001, the SPC was of the opinion that based on the facts of this case, *Chen Xiaoqi* and others, via infringing *Qi Yuling's* right to her name, infringed upon the basic right to

[118] See *id.*
[119] See *id.*
[120] For details of the case and the court judgment, see *id.* at 206–213.

education Qi had enjoyed under the provisions of the Constitution, causing specific damages, and therefore should bear corresponding civil liability.[121] The appellate court's final judgment was then made for Qi on the basis of the SPC's opinion.

The significance of *Qi Yuling v. Chen Xiaoqi* is not its judgment but the SPC's opinion about the application of the Constitution. It was the very first case in the country where the SPC explicitly allowed a judgment to be made in reliance on the Constitution. The case was widely considered a breakthrough in the judicial application of the Constitution. More strikingly, the case was hailed both at home and abroad as the beginning of constitutional review in the Chinese judiciary.[122] Some foreign commentators even viewed the case as the Chinese version of *Marbury v. Madison*.[123]

The key drafter of the SPC's opinion in the *Qi* case was the former Vice President of the SPC, Justice *Huang Songyou*.[124] In his article published after the *Qi* case in People's Court Daily, *Huang* explained that the SPC's opinion in the *Qi* case was meant to spark the application of the Constitution in the courts. With a hope to establish a system of constitutional review in China, Huang, taking *Marbury v. Madison* as a reference, believed that the Constitution could be gradually introduced into legal proceedings and allow courts to rely on the Constitution in making their rulings in China.[125] According to Huang, there were various misunderstandings that had kept the courts from applying the Constitution in the past.[126]

But the public excitement about the SPC's opinion in the *Qi* case seemed to make the SPC quite nervous. In the current Chinese legal system, as noted, the SPC does not have the authority to determine constitutionality. On December 18, 2008, the SPC withdrew its 2001 interpretative opinion in the *Qi* case because of concern about "sweeping chaos" and the "complete disintegration of control."[127] The underlying rationale is that the Constitution in China is not subject to judicial interpretation or application. Therefore, the courts should not step outside the boundary to rule on the encroachment of individual rights on the ground of the Constitution.

[121] See the SPC, Fashi (2001) No. 5, *id.* at 196.

[122] See Thomas Kellogg, *Constitutionalism with Chinese Characteristics? Constitutional Development and Civil Litigation in China*, 7 Int'l J. of Const. L., 215 (2009).

[123] See Robert Morris, *China's Marbury:* Qi Yuling v. Chen Xiaoqi – *The Once and Future Trial of Both Education & Constitutionalization*, 2 Tsinghua Chinese L.Rev. 274 (2012).

[124] Huang was appointed the Chief of the Civil Division of the SPC in 1999 and promoted to the Vice President of the SPC in 2002. He was removed from the bench in 2008 on a corruption charge and was sentenced to life imprisonment in 2010.

[125] See Tong Zhiwei, *Comment on the Rise and Fall of the Supreme People's Court's Reply to Qi Yuling's Case*, 43 Suffolk U. L. Rev. 669, 672 (2009).

[126] Huang Songyou, *Judicial Application of the Constitution and Its Significance*, People's Court Daily, August 13, 2001; see also, Thomas Kellogg, *The Death of Constitutional Litigation in China?* China Brief, April 2, 2009, available at https://jamestown.org/program/the-death-of-constitutional-litigation-in-china/.

[127] See Songyou, *supra* note 126.

A criticism of the SPC's opinion on the *Qi* case argued that the SPC's opinion was suspiciously unconstitutional.[128] The criticism viewed the SPC's effort in the *Qi* case as an intent to break free from the restraints that prevent the SPC and all other courts from applying the Constitution.[129] But the vast majority in the Chinese legal community appraised the SPC's move because they believed the issue of whether the Constitution can be directly cited as a legal basis by the court in adjudicating cases had never been, but should be, solved through litigation.[130]

In 2016, the SPC retreated further and issued the Rules on the Production of Civil Judgment Documents in People's Court, where the SPC formally shut the door to the application of the Constitution in judicial proceedings on civil matters. According to the SPC, judgment documents shall not refer to the Constitution as the basis for the judgment, but the principles and spirit embodied in the Constitution could be explained in the reasoning of the judgment.[131] Although the 2016 Rules only prohibit the courts from applying the Constitution in their civil judgments, it is generally understood that the ban applies to all cases.

The SPC, however, provides no reason why the Constitution could not be applied in the courts. Many questioned the appropriateness of the 2016 Rules. An argument is that since the SPC is established under the Constitution, if the SPC in the exercise of its authority granted by the Constitution explicitly prevents the courts from referring to the Constitution as the basis of judgment, the Constitution would be gravely disrespected.[132] Nevertheless, the judicial review of constitutionality, though highly expected, remains inapplicable in China.

2. STRUCTURE OF GOVERNMENT

The structure of government refers to the organizational setup of the state governing system. There are two components that are deemed essential for the government structure. One component is the state system, defining the nature or kind of state, and the other one is the polity system, concerning how the government is organized. As explicitly provided in the Constitution, the cornerstone of the Chinese state system consists of (a) leadership of the CPC, (b) socialism, (c) people's democratic dictatorship, and (d) democratic centralism. The basic polity system of the country is premised on the system of people's congress.

[128] See Zhiwei, *supra* note 125, at 669.

[129] See *id.* at 675.

[130] See Zhenmin, *supra* note 38, at 214.

[131] See the SPC, *The Norms for the Production of Civil Judgement Documents in People's Court*, issued on June 28, 2016, available at www.360doc.com/content/19/0323/14/4375909_823597283.shtml.

[132] See Luo Shuping, *Why Does It Become a Question as to Whether the Constitution Can Be the Basis of Court Judgment?* 32 Democracy & Legal Sys. 50 (2017).

A. *The State System*

The state system involves the very nature of the state. Under the orthodox view in China, the state system is simply a question of the status of various social classes within the state,[133] indicating which class can use the state machinery to achieve class dictatorship. Thus, it is held in China that from the viewpoint of the Constitution, the state system reflects the relationship between the state and the people, and it deals with such questions as who holds the ruling power of the state, what rights the people enjoy, and what authority the state has.[134]

Article 1 of the 1982 Constitution defines China as "a socialist country under the people's democratic dictatorship led by the working class and based on the alliance of workers and peasants." Pursuant to article 1, the power base of China is "the people's democratic dictatorship," and the basic system of the state is a "socialist system." It is further provided that a "sabotage of the socialist system by any organization or individual is prohibited."[135]

In the 1949 Common Program and the 1954 Constitution, the state power base was described as a "proletarian dictatorship," which embodied the concept of class struggle. When the 1982 Constitution was adopted, the proletarian dictatorship was changed to the people's democratic dictatorship. The change was made to signify that China had departed from the ideology of class struggle and turned the focus of the state to economic development.

However, in the preamble of the 1982 Constitution, the people's democratic dictatorship is stated as "in essence the dictatorship of the proletariat."[136] An explanation is that the people's democratic dictatorship and proletarian dictatorship, though they are different, share the similarity in that they are all led by the working class under the alliance of workers and peasants. The major difference is that the proletarian dictatorship is closely associated with the class struggle while the people's democratic dictatorship, at least on its face, is not.

In China, the concept of a people's democratic dictatorship is viewed as a product of *Mao*'s integrating the *Marxist-Leninist* theory with Chinese realities. In June 1949, *Mao* published an article entitled "On the People's Democratic Dictatorship" in commemoration of the twenty-eighth anniversary of the CPC.[137] In that article, *Mao* wrote explicitly that there are "bourgeois republics in foreign lands, but China cannot have a bourgeois republic because China is a country

[133] See Mao Zedong, *On New Democracy*, January 1940, in Selected Works of Mao Zedong, an English translation of the article is available at www.marxists.org/reference/archive/mao/selected-works/volume-2/mswv2_26.htm.

[134] See Kai, *supra* note 9, at 111.

[135] See the 1982 Constitution, *supra* note 11, art. 1.

[136] See *id.*, preamble.

[137] See Mao Zedong, *On the People's Democratic Dictatorship*, June 30, 1949, in Selected Works of Mao Zedong, an English version of the article is available at www.marxists.org/reference/archive/mao/selected-works/volume-4/mswv4_65.htm.

suffering under imperialist oppression. The only way is through a people's republic led by the working class."[138] *Mao* further stated that "all the experience the Chinese people have accumulated through several decades teaches us to enforce the people's democratic dictatorship, that is, to deprive the reactionaries of the right to speak and let the people alone have that right."[139] According to *Mao*, "the combination of these two aspects, democracy for the people and dictatorship over the reactionaries, is the people's democratic dictatorship."[140]

Underlying the people's democratic dictatorship is the idea that under the leadership of the CPC, the state always represents the fundamental interests of the vast majority of the people and can use authoritarian methods to deal with hostile forces to protect the rights of people. More specifically, the people's democratic dictatorship means that the government led by the CPC practices democracy among the people, and exercises dictatorship against hostile forces both at home and abroad.

But the question is how the people's democratic dictatorship is being achieved. In one Chinese constitutional law textbook, the people's democratic dictatorship can be realized when (a) people are the masters of the country, and (b) people directly or indirectly exercise state power through a settled system.[141] But still, it remains unclear what the people's democracy exactly refers to, although dictatorship has a clear meaning of control.

In addition, the socialist public ownership of the means of production is regarded as the economic foundation of the people's democratic dictatorship. Following *Marx*'s doctrine of an economic foundation dictating superstructure,[142] a conventional theory in China is that the status of various social classes in political life reflects their position in the socio-economic structure. Only an economically dominant class can control state power and use the power to maintain its economic dominance.[143] Thus, although China has abandoned *Mao*'s class struggle approach, the class theory remains a powerful driving force in the country.

B. *Form of Government*

There are two major forms of government in today's world: presidential and parliamentary,[144] and most of them are democratically based. In Western countries, as

[138] See *id.*

[139] See *id.*

[140] See *id.*

[141] See Kai, *supra* note 9, at 112.

[142] According to Karl Marx, all economic processes or the totality of all means and relations of economic production of society as the foundation of society determines the superstructure, referring to all other aspects of society. See Olu Oyinlade, David Finch, & Zachary Christo, *The Multi-Institutional Substructure-Superstructure Model of Understanding Causal Relations among Social Structures*, 10 Sociology Mind 3 (July 2020).

[143] See *id.*

[144] See Chang et al., *supra* note 1, at 127.

noted, the primary goal of the constitution is to limit the government, and the system of checks and balance under the separation of powers among government branches provides assurance to avoid abuse of power. This Western style of government structure has been followed in many countries in Asia.[145]

China, however, does not fall within either of the two forms mentioned earlier. Instead, China adopts its own government form known as the people's congress. Article 2 of the 1982 Constitution sets forth the form of government. Under article 2, all power belongs to the people. It is further provided in article 2 that the National People's Congress and the local people's congresses at various levels are the organs through which the people exercise state power. In addition, according to article 2, the people administer state affairs and manage economic and cultural undertakings and social affairs through various channels and in various ways in accordance with the provisions of law.[146]

In Chinese legal literature, the form of government is referred to as the political system of the state. The form of government is defined as a governing system under which the ruling class in a specific society adopts certain principles and methods to form, and represent, the state to exercise power systematically in order to achieve the goal of ruling.[147] The substance of the form of government includes (a) division of the state power under certain standards according to the needs of operation; (b) formulation of state organs and configuration of the power among those organs so as to make the government functional; and (c) stipulation of rules and principles based on the nature of the exercise of power to determine the relationship among various state organs.[148]

As the form of government or political system of China, the people's congress system is proclaimed in the country as "a great creation of the Chinese people in the history of the human political system," and "an inevitable choice for the Chinese people to turn over and take control of their own destiny."[149] Since it was formally introduced as a desired form of government by *Mao* as early as 1940,[150] the people's congress has been appraised as "a good system that conforms to China's national conditions and reality, reflects the nature of a socialist country, guarantees that the people are the masters, and guarantees the great rejuvenation of the Chinese nation."[151]

It was *Mao*'s belief that "without a proper form of the political organ, it cannot represent the country."[152] According to *Mao*, China should have the people's congress

[145] See *id.*
[146] See the 1982 Constitution, *supra* note 11, art. 2.
[147] See Wei & Weiyan, *supra* note 4, at 103–104.
[148] See Kai, *supra* note 9, at 113.
[149] See Xi Jinping, Speech at the Conference Celebrating the 60th Anniversary of the Establishment of the NPC, September 5, 2014, available at www.qstheory.cn/dukan/qs/2019-09/15/c_1124994844.htm (hereinafter referred to as Xi Jinping 2014 Speech).
[150] See Zedong, *supra* note 133.
[151] See Xi Jinping 2014 Speech, *supra* note 149.
[152] See Zedong, *supra* note 133.

at the national, provincial, county, district, and even township level, and governments at all levels should be elected by their respective people's congress.[153] In both the 1949 Common Program and the 1954 Constitution, the people's congress was stipulated as the basic form of the government in the country. Ever since, the people's congress has become the "fundamental political system" of China.[154]

C. *Democratic Centralism*

Democratic centralism is held as "the basic principle of China's national organization and activities."[155] It serves as the core mechanism in China's political system. Originating from *Lenin*'s work "*What Is to Be Done*" in 1902, democratic centralism was initially a set of principles for organizing the revolutionary workers' party, and then became a rule for the voting process for policy making, including electing officers and leaders.[156] Generally, "democratic" means free discussion among all members, while centralism refers to decision-making by a group of people in charge. The basic rule is that before a decision is made, all opinions can be freely expressed, but once the decision is reached by a majority, it is binding on all members.

In China, democratic centralism is employed both as the CPC's rule of discipline and as the constitutional mandate for the whole country. In the 1949 Common Program, it was required that the organs of state power at all levels practice democratic centralism.[157] Under the 1954 Constitution, the NPC, the local people's congresses, and other organs of the state shall all practice democratic centralism.[158] Article 3 of the 1982 Constitution also makes it imperative that the state organs apply the principle of democratic centralism.[159]

In the 1982 Constitution, it is further provided that the NPC and the local people's congresses at different levels are instituted through democratic election, and they are responsible to the people and subject to their supervision.[160] Also under article 3 of the 1982 Constitution, all administrative, judicial, and procuratorial organs of the state are created by the people's congresses, to which they are responsible and under whose supervision they operate, and the division of functions and powers between the central and local state organs is guided by the principle of giving full play to the initiative and enthusiasm of the local authorities under the unified leadership of the central authorities.[161]

[153] See *id.*
[154] See Xi Jinping 2014 Speech, *supra* note 149.
[155] See *id.*
[156] See Lenin, What Is to Be Done, Lenin's Collected Works, Vol. 5, 347–530 (Foreign Languages Publishing House, 1961).
[157] See the 1949 Common Program, *supra* note 25, art. 15.
[158] See the 1954 Constitution, *supra* note 27, art. 2.
[159] See the 1982 Constitution, *supra* note 11, art. 3.
[160] See *id.*
[161] See *id.*

Conceptually, democratic centralism is defined in China as a combination of centralism built on the basis of democracy and democracy exercised under centralized guidance.[162] Although its definition is quite awkward, democratic centralism is explained to contain four "defers": (a) individual defers to organization, (b) minority defers to majority, (c) the inferior defers to the superior, and (d) the whole party defers to the central committee.[163] In the exercise of democratic centralism, "defer" essentially means "obey," and at the core is the centralization of authority. However, there are two fundamental issues that have strong impacts on how democratic centralism is to be implemented.

The first issue involves the relationship between democracy and centralization. In 1945, when explaining democratic centralism, *Mao Zedong* stated that it is both democratic and centralized, that is, democracy-based centralization and guided democracy under centralization.[164] *Mao* later, however, illustrated that a thing like democracy seems to be the goal, but in fact, it is just a means,[165] and that democracy is a method, depending on whom it is used for and what it does.[166] Thus, in Mao's view, the essence of democratic centralization is centralization, and democracy is nothing but a means for centralization. Therefore, during *Mao*'s era, democratic centralism eventually became the centralization of powers in the hands of *Mao*, with no democracy.

Democratic centralism now remains a mechanism in the country's policy-making process. In fact, under the banner of "the Party leads everything," power often is excessively centralized and used abusively. A very common phenomenon is that at almost every level, the party chief has the final say and his authority is rarely challenged, although in theory, all party members are able to participate in the discussion, decision-making, and management of inner-Party affairs, thus playing their role as principal actors. This demonstrates that democracy remains quite superficial in the scheme of democratic centralism.

[162] See Xi Jinping 2014 Speech, *supra* note 149.

[163] In the Charter of the CPC, it is explicitly provided that all members of the party must follow the rules of democratic centralism: (a) individual party members defer to party organizations, (b) the minority defers to the majority, (c) lower-level Party organizations defer to higher-level Party organizations, and (d) all organizations and members of the party defer to the National Congress and the Central Committee of the Party. See the Charter of the CPC (as amended 2017), available at www.xinhuanet.com//english/download/Constitution_of_the_Communist_Party_of_China.pdf.

[164] See Mao Zedong, *On United Government*, April 24, 1945, available at www.marxists.org/chinese/maozedong/marxist.org-chinese-mao-19450424.htm.

[165] See Mao Zedong, *On Correctly Handling the Contradictions Among the People*, February 27, 1957, available at www.marxists.org/chinese/maozedong/marxist.org-chinese-mao-19570227AA.htm.

[166] See Mao Zedong, Speech at the Second Plenary Session of the Eighth Central Committee of the Communist Party of China, November 15, 1956, available at www.marxists.org/chinese/maozedong/marxist.org-chinese-mao-19561115.htm.

What is clearly lacking in the system of democratic centralism is a mechanism to safeguard democracy. According to *Deng Xiaoping*, democratic centralism is the easiest and most rational system. Rationality aside, democratic centralism is indeed easy because the centerpiece of it is centralization. It is the centralization that makes it possible to effectively integrate all resources under the will of the CPC, to efficiently implement the CPC's policies and decisions, and to prevent any unwanted distortion that may occur during the implementation process.

Some democratic centralism advocates in China strongly criticize Western democracy while upholding democratic centralism. They argue that in recent years, "under the impact of the international financial crisis, Western countries have been held to ransom by 'ballot politics,' facing the dilemma of triggering an economic crash if they don't reform, but risking a government collapse if they do."[167] But the criticism fails to demonstrate how democracy under democratic centralism would function well without a meaningful mechanism to ensure that centralization will not turn into a totalitarian device.

The second issue is how democratic centralism functions. A key question at stake is whether the rule of governance should be "let the people choose" or "choose for the people." "Let the people choose" means that people can freely express their wishes without external interference and may directly exercise their rights, while "choose for the people" is the situation where someone addresses the people's wishes and then picks a solution for them.

As discussed, the local officers in China often call themselves "parenting officers," meaning that their relationship with the people in their jurisdiction is like a parent to children. The implication of the term "parenting" is that the officers are the decision makers for the people. A verse often heard in the country is that "it would be better for him to go home selling sweet potatoes if an officer were not able to make [a] decision for the people." Thus, in many cases, democratic centralism virtually became a device by which the government officials dictate the will of the people.

The bureaucratic system in China exemplifies how democratic centralism operates. As noted, under the "officialdom" political culture, the officials at all levels are mainly responsible to their superiors. It has become routine that the promotion or demotion of a local officer mostly depends on the like or dislike of his or her superior. A popular folklore reads: "If your superior says you are capable, you will then be capable, even though you are actually incapable; if, however, the superior says you are not capable, you are then not capable; even though you are in fact capable."[168]

[167] See Wang Chuanzhi, *Democratic Centralism: The Core Mechanism in China's Political System*, 5 Qiushi J., No. 4, October 1, 2013, available at www.qstheory.cn/zxdk/2013/201310/201305/t20130513_230301.htm.

[168] In a 2015 middle school politics course mock exam, this folklore was used in a multiple-choice question as follows: The folklore best illustrates which of the following: (1) "Rule of man" –

Another example is the election. Although it has been a constitutional principle since the 1954 Constitution that the people administer State affairs and manage economic and cultural undertakings and social affairs, China has never had a general election above the county level. Under the 1953 Election Law, the general election was limited to the township level.[169] In 1979, when the new Election Law was adopted, the general election was extended to the county level.[170] An official explanation for not having a general election at higher levels of government in the country is that the people are not used to it.

This explanation first appeared in the speech of the former President *Liu Shaoqi* at the third Beijing Municipal People's Congress in 1951. At that time, *Liu* made clear that the "universal, equal, direct, and secret ballot" election method cannot and should not be adopted under the current situation in China.[171] According to *Liu*, when it came to elections, some people often thought of the old slogan "universal, equal, direct, and secret ballot." This slogan, however, was not quite suitable for the actual situation of the Chinese people because there was a lack of interest and enthusiasm for elections among the majority of people in the country.[172]

Thirty-six years later, in 1987, *Deng Xiaoping* reiterated that in a big country like China, the conditions for higher-level direct elections were still immature mainly due to the insufficiency of the cultural quality.[173] In 2003, when asked by the *Washington Post* whether the general election would advance to a level higher than county, then Premier *Wen Jiabao* replied, "because China is very large, with a large population, an underdeveloped economy, and uneven development, it is impossible to conduct direct elections at higher levels at this stage."[174] *Wen* emphasized that in China "the conditions for a direct election above [the] county level are not yet mature, and first of all, the cultural quality is not high enough."[175]

substituting law with words, which is opposite to "rule of law"; (2) Ruling the country according to law and building a socialist country under the rule of law requires to put an end to the aforementioned abuse of power; (3) "Rule by man," undermining the law and not acting in accordance with the law – it is not conducive to the construction of the rule of law in our country, and damages the fundamental interests of the people; (4) At the initial stage of socialism, under the circumstances that our country's legal system is not yet perfect, it is inevitable. A: (1) and (3); B: (2), (3), and (4); C: (1), (2), and (4); D: (1), (3), and (4). The standard answer is A. The exam is available at http://czzz.cooco.net.cn/testdetail/42088/.

169 See the 1953 Election Law (March 1, 1953), art. 3, available at https://news.qq.com/a/20111206/001250.htm.

170 See the 1979 Election Law (as amended 2004), art. 2, available at www.360doc.com/content/17/0131/20/36432137_625662673.shtml.

171 See Liu Shaoqi, Speech at 3rd Beijing Municipal People's Congress, February 28, 1951, available at http://cpc.people.com.cn/GB/69112/73583/73601/73624/5068363.html.

172 See *id.*

173 See Deng Xiaoping, *The Pace of Reform Should be Accelerated*, in the Selected Works of Deng Xiaoping, Vol. III, 242 (People's Press, 1993).

174 See Report, Premier Wen Jiabao interviewed by the Editor-in-Chief of the Washington Post, November 23, 2003, available at www.china-embassy.org/chn/zmgx/zxxx/t44934.htm.

175 See *id.*

What cultural quality actually means is subject to debate. But the idea behind it appears to be that the people in China are not ready to choose government officials as they wish, and thus the choice has to be made for them under the system of democratic centralism. *Xi Jinping* seems to have a particular fondness for democratic centralism. According to *Xi*, the principle of democratic centralism shall be used to safeguard the authority of the party and the state, and all efforts shall be made to ensure that the CPC's ideas become the will of the country through the legal process.[176]

In the meantime, following *Xi*'s comments, the CPC-controlled media describes the election in the United States as "the choice of political parties" rather than "the choice of the people." While appraising China's democratic centralism, Chinese media asserts that the U.S. elections, both congressional and presidential, are virtually controlled by the political parties, from the nomination of candidates, to the raising of election funds, and to the organization of electoral campaigns.[177]

3. ORGANIZATION OF GOVERNMENT

Chinese government is organized under a centralized top-down structure that has evolved in the country ever since the *Qin* dynasty in 221 BC. On the top is the central government, under which local governments operate at different levels. Currently, the local governments in China are divided into four levels: (a) provinces, autonomous regions, and municipalities directly under the central government; (b) cities with districts and autonomous prefectures; (c) counties, cities without districts, and municipal districts; and (d) townships, including nationality townships and towns.

At the present time, there are thirty-four provincial-level governments in China, including twenty-three provinces, five autonomous regions, four municipalities directly under the central government, and two special administrative regions (SARs).[178] However, the SARs, as noted, are not within the unitary system of the state administration of China. Constitutionally, the SARs are local administrative regions of China and subordinate to the central government, but unlike other provinces, they are granted a high degree of autonomy and self-governance. A significant feature of the SARs is that they each have their own legislature other than the people's congress.

Under the people's congress system, the NPC is the highest organ of the state power,[179] while the local people's congresses are local organs of state power at each of the four levels of local government,[180] except for the SARs. The primary functions of the local people's congresses are to ensure the observance and implementation of

[176] See Xi Jinping 2014 Speech, *supra* note 149.

[177] See Chuanzhi, *supra* note 167.

[178] On the official map of administrative regions in China, the 34 provincial-level governments include Taiwan. In addition, there are some 333 cities with districts and autonomous prefectures, 2,848 counties, and 28,726 townships and towns.

[179] See the 1982 Constitution, *supra* note 11, art. 57.

[180] See *id.*, art. 96.

the Constitution, laws, and administrative regulations in their respective administrative regions, and, within the scope of their authority as prescribed by law, adopt and issue resolutions and review and decide plans for the development of local economy, culture, and public services.[181]

The provincial people's congresses and their standing committees may adopt local regulations not contravening the Constitution, laws, or administrative regulations. The local legislation at the provincial levels must be reported to the Standing Committee of the NPC for record.[182] Similarly, the local people's congresses of the cities and their standing committees may adopt local rules not in conflict with the Constitution, laws, administrative regulations, or the local regulations of corresponding provinces or autonomous regions. The rules so adopted, before taking effect, must be reported to and approved by the standing committees of the people's congresses of the corresponding provinces or autonomous regions.[183]

The administration body sides with the people's congress at each level of government. At the national level is the State Council, the national administrative organ. Defined as "the executive body of the highest organ of the State power" in the 1982 Constitution,[184] the State Council is composed of such members as Premier, Vice-Premiers, the State Councillors, Ministers (ministries and commissions), Auditor-General, and Secretary-General.[185] Under the Chinese Organic Law of the Local People's Congresses and Local People's Governments, the local people's governments at various levels are the local organs of state administration and the executive organs of the local people's congresses at the corresponding levels.[186] It is required that all local governments are under the unified leadership of the State Council and are subordinate to the State Council.[187]

Parallel to the State Council are the SPC and Supreme People's Procuratorate (SPP). Both the SPC and SPP are the top judicial bodies of China. Note that in China, although "judiciary" normally refers to courts, the term "judicial body" is used broadly to include courts, procuratorates, public security bureaus, and justice departments. Thus, at the national level in the country, the judicial bodies consist of the SPC, SPP, Ministry of Justice (MOJ), and Ministry of Public Security (MPC). Unlike the SPC and SPP, which report directly to the NPC, both the MOJ and MPC are under the State Council.

With regard to political parties, China is a single-party-ruled country with the coexistence of multiple parties. The CPC is the only party that holds the reins of

[181] See *id.*, art. 99.
[182] See *id.*, art. 100.
[183] See *id.*
[184] See *id.*, art. 85.
[185] See *id.*, art. 86.
[186] See the Organic Law of the Local People's Congresses and Local People's Governments of The People's Republic of China (adopted in 1979, as amended 2004), art. 54, an English translation of the 1979 Organic Law is available at www.asianlii.org/cn/legis/cen/laws/olotlpcalpgotproc908/.
[187] See *id.*, art. 55.

state power and is cemented as the core force leading the cause of the country. As noted, in the 1982 Constitution (as amended 2018), the leadership of the Communist Party of China is categorized as the defining feature of socialism with Chinese characteristics. The CPC is organized in the form of a general secretary, politburo standing committee, politburo, central committee, and local committees.[188] The general secretary is both the party's chief and the head of the state and military. The members of the politiburo standing committee hold positions as the chief of such key government bodies as the NPC and the State Council.

As noted, there are several minority political parties in China. But all of these political parties are functioning through a political organization known as the Chinese People's Political Consultative Conference (CPPCC). The CPPCC is defined as an organization of the patriotic united front of the Chinese people, but in fact is a CPC-led alliance of all minority parties. The CPPCC is required to operate under the leadership of the CPC. The CPC-led multi-party cooperation and political consultations are considered the basic political system in China. In contrast to the alliance of minority parties in other countries, the CPPCC has two distinctive features.

First, the CPPCC is not an independent political organization or branch. As noted, the CPPCC must work under the leadership of the CPC. In addition, none of the minority political parties may become an opposition party, and any new political party may not be formed without the CPC's approval. Even within the CPPCC, the CPC remains the dominant force: on the one hand, the CPPCC chairman position is always held by a designated member of the Politiburo Standing Committee of the CPC, and on the other hand, more than two-thirds of the CPPCC seats are held by selected CPC members, and many of them are retired ministers, provincial governors, and military generals.

Second, the CPPCC serves only as a political advisory body. According to the Charter of the CPPCC, the major functions of the CPPCC include: (a) conducting political consultations, (b) exercising democratic supervision, and (c) organizing its members from various non-CPC political parties, mass organizations, and public personages from all walks of life to take part in the discussion and management of state affairs.[189] Consisting of the National Committee and local committees, the CPPCC is mandated to uphold the leadership of the CPC[190] and is required to stay with the CPC's party line and to faithfully implement the CPC's basic theory and policy.[191]

Figure 4.1 is a chart of the current government structure of China. It shows how the people's congress system works in the country with an interplay between the CPC and the state. It also reflects the relationship between the central government and local

[188] See the Charter of the CPC, *supra* note 163.

[189] See the Charter of the CPPCC (adopted in 1982, as amended 2018), art. 3, an English version of the CPPCC Charter is available at www.cppcc.gov.cn/zxww/2018/12/27/ARTI1545876942660350.shtml.

[190] See *id.*, art. 2.

[191] See *id.*, art. 5.

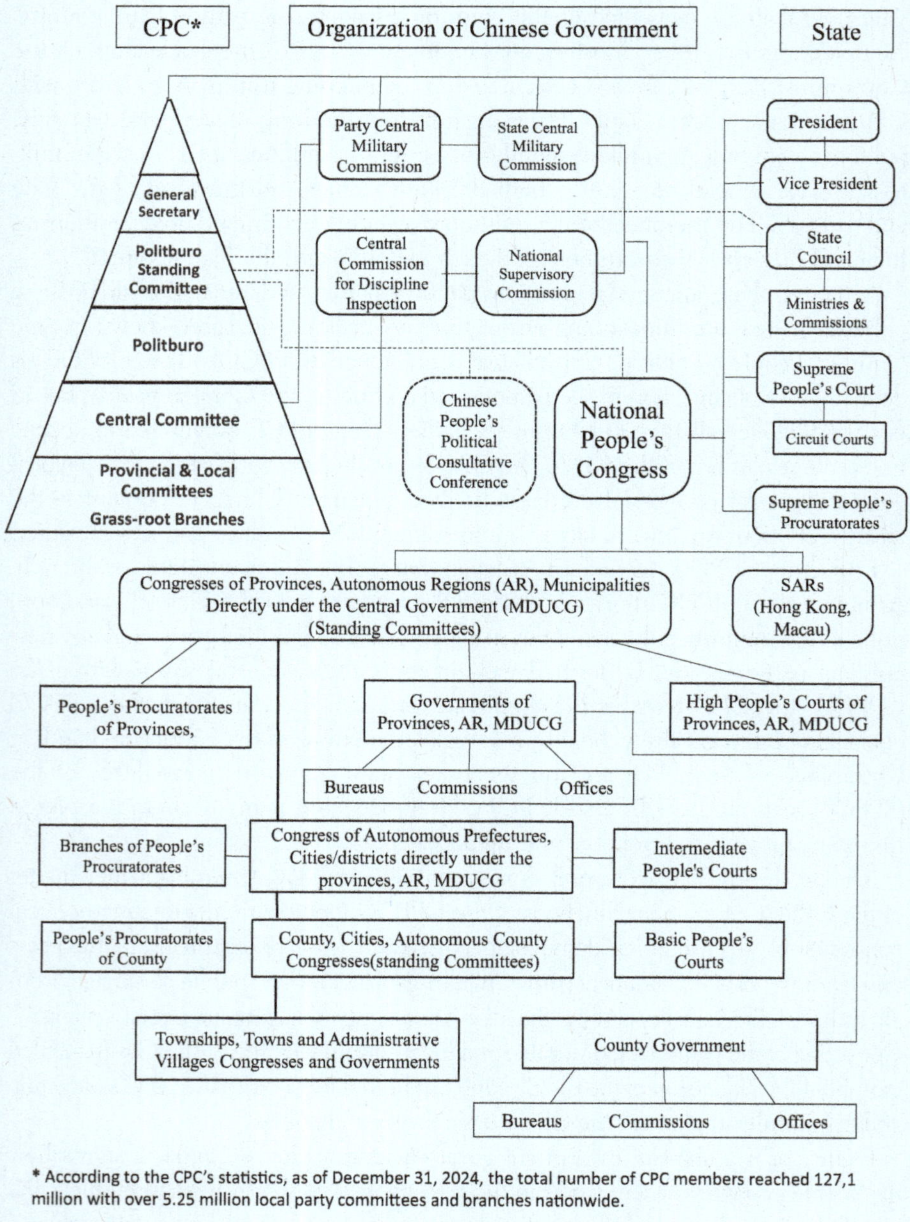

FIGURE 4.1 Organization of Chinese Government.

governments under a unitary system, as well as the "one country with two systems" scheme that applies specifically to the SARs, including Hong Kong and Macau.

Note again that in China, although the people's congresses are the center of power in the government at both the national and local levels, the actual power is in the hands of the CPC, or more specifically the General Secretary and Politburo Standing Committee of the CPC. A general pattern of the organization at every level of government, and in institutions, state-owned enterprises, units, and universities, is that there are two chiefs: an administrative or executive chief and the party chief (secretary of the party committee). In most cases, the party chief has the final say. Also, in the past few years, there developed a new routine under which the NPC, the State Council, the SPC, and the SPP all must report annually to the politburo, and to the General Secretary of the CPC in particular.

A. *The National People's Congress*

Again, under the people's congress system, the NPC possesses the highest state power. As the country's top legislature, the NPC exercises a broad range of powers of the state as prescribed by the Constitution.[192] The NPC is composed of people's delegates elected by the people's congresses of the provinces, autonomous regions,

[192] See *id.*

Article 62 The National People's Congress exercises the following functions and powers:

(1) to amend the Constitution;
(2) to supervise the enforcement of the Constitution;
(3) to enact and amend basic laws governing criminal offences, civil affairs, the State organs and other matters;
(4) to elect the President and the Vice-President of the People's Republic of China;
(5) to decide on the choice of the Premier of the State Council upon nomination by the President of the People's Republic of China, and on the choice of the Vice-Premiers, State Councilors, Ministers in charge of ministries or commissions, the Auditor-General and the Secretary-General of the State Council upon nomination by the Premier;
(6) to elect the Chairman of the Central Military Commission and, upon nomination by the Chairman, to decide on the choice of all other members of the Central Military Commission;
(7) to elect the President of the Supreme People's Court;
(8) to elect the Procurator-General of the Supreme People's Procuratorate;
(9) to examine and approve the plan for national economic and social development and the report on its implementation;
(10) to examine and approve the State budget and the report on its implementation;
(11) to alter or annul inappropriate decisions of the Standing Committee of the National People's Congress;
(12) to approve the establishment of provinces, autonomous regions, and municipalities directly under the Central Government;
(13) to decide on the establishment of special administrative regions and the systems to be instituted there;
(14) to decide on questions of war and peace; and
(15) to exercise such other functions and powers as the highest organ of state power should exercise.

Article 63 The National People's Congress has the power to remove from office the following persons:

and municipalities directly under the central government, and by the People's Liberation Army. The delegates of the NPC only meet once a year. The permanent body of the NPC is its Standing Committee.

The 1982 Constitution provides the Standing Committee of the NPC with quite extensive power.[193] Also, the Standing Committee is a designated body to manage

(1) the President and the Vice-President of the People's Republic of China;
(2) the Premier, Vice-Premiers, State Councilors, Ministers in charge of ministries or commissions, the Auditor-General and the Secretary-General of the State Council;
(3) the Chairman of the Central Military Commission and other members of the Commission;
(4) the President of the Supreme People's Court; and
(5) the Procurator-General of the Supreme People's Procuratorate.

[193] See the 1982 Constitution, *supra* note 11, art. 67 (The Standing Committee of the National People's Congress exercises the following functions and powers: (1) to interpret the Constitution and supervise its enforcement; (2) to enact and amend laws, with the exception of those which should be enacted by the National People's Congress; (3) to partially supplement and amend, when the National People's Congress is not in session, laws enacted by the National People's Congress, provided that the basic principles of these laws are not contravened; (4) to interpret laws; (5) to review and approve, when the National People's Congress is not in session, partial adjustments to the plan for national economic and social development or to the State budget that prove necessary in the course of their implementation; (6) to supervise the work of the State Council, the Central Military Commission, the Supreme People's Court and the Supreme People's Procuratorate; (7) to annul those administrative regulations, decisions or orders of the State Council that contravene the Constitution or other laws; (8) to annul those local regulations or decisions of the organs of state power of provinces, autonomous regions, and municipalities directly under the Central Government that contravene the Constitution, other laws or administrative regulations; (9) to decide, when the National People's Congress is not in session, on the choice of Ministers in charge of ministries or commissions, the Auditor-General or the Secretary-General of the State Council upon nomination by the Premier of the State Council; (10) to decide, when the National People's Congress is not in session, on the choice of other members of the Central Military Commission upon nomination by the Chairman of the Commission; (11) to appoint or remove, at the recommendation of the President of the Supreme People's Court, the Vice Presidents and Judges of the Supreme People's Court, members of its Judicial Committee and the President of the Military Court; (12) to appoint or remove, at the recommendation of the Procurator-General of the Supreme People's Procuratorate, the Deputy Procurators-General and procurators of the Supreme People's Procuratorate, members of its Procuratorial Committee and the Chief Procurator of the Military Procuratorate, and to approve the appointment or removal of the chief procurators of the people's procuratorates of provinces, autonomous regions, and municipalities directly under the Central Government; (13) to decide on the appointment or recall of plenipotentiary representatives abroad; (14) to decide on the ratification or abrogation of treaties and important agreements concluded with foreign states; (15) to institute systems of titles and ranks for military and diplomatic personnel and of other specific titles and ranks; (16) to institute State medals and titles of honor and decide on their conferment; (17) to decide on the granting of special pardons; (18) to decide, when the National People's Congress is not in session, on the proclamation of a state of war in the event of an armed attack on the country or in fulfillment of international treaty obligations concerning common defense against aggression; (19) to decide on general or partial mobilization; (20) to decide on entering the state of emergency throughout the country or in particular provinces, autonomous regions, or municipalities directly under the Central Government; and (21) to exercise such other functions and powers as the National People's Congress may assign to it.)

the election of delegates to the NPC.[194] Given the Standing Committee's authority, there is no such concept as "electoral constituency" or "gerrymandering" in the country. The number of delegates is allocated by the Standing Committee of the NPC to each province, except for Hong Kong SAR and Macau SAR. The number of delegates assigned to the SARs is prescribed separately by the NPC.

Pursuant to the Election Law, the allocation of delegates is based on population and is made under the principle that the same size of an urban or rural population is represented by each delegate to ensure that all regions, nationalities, and other sectors have an appropriate number of representatives.[195] The total number of delegates to the NPC is capped at 3,000 by the Legislation Law,[196] making the NPC the largest legislative body in the world. In 2023, a total of 2,977 people's delegates were elected to the 14th Assembly of the NPC. Among the delegates attending the 2023 annual assembly meeting of the NPC, about 32.55 percent were government officials of various levels, and about 26.54 percent were women.

Each Assembly of the NPC has a term of five years. But there is no term limit for a deputy to be reelected to the congress. Since there is no direct election in China above the county level, the delegates to the NPC are elected by the people's congresses at the provincial level.[197] In many cases, the number of delegates allocated to a particular province includes a certain number of delegates who are "designated," meaning that those delegates are "earmarked" by the central government and must be elected. The designated delegates are normally those who are leaders in the central government. For example, in the 2018 election for the 13th Assembly of the NPC, *Xi Jinping* was a designated delegate to be elected in the Autonomous Region People's Congress of Inner Mongolia, while *Li Keqiang* was elected in Guangxi Zhuang Autonomous Region.

If not designated, all delegates to the NPC are elected from the provinces or regions they belong to. The Election Law provides that the delegate candidates for the national and local people's congresses be nominated on the basis of electoral districts or electoral units. For the purpose of election, a recommendation for a particular candidate may be made by political parties or people's organizations jointly or separately, or by a joint group of at least ten voters or deputies.[198] It is required that the number of candidates for delegate be greater than the number of delegates to be elected.[199]

[194] See *id.*, art. 59.

[195] See the Election Law of China (adopted in 1979, as amended 2015), art. 15, an English translation of the Election Law is available at www.china.org.cn/china/LegislationsForm2001-2010/2011-02/11/content_21898708.htm.

[196] See *id.*

[197] See *id.*, art. 2.

[198] See *id.*, art. 29.

[199] See *id.*, art. 30.

In reality, however, almost every delegate candidate for the NPC is selected by the local party organization. Thus, anyone whose views are at odds with the CPC party officials will not be selected. Those who are loyal to, or trusted by, the CPC party leaders will easily become delegates to the NPC. The same is true for congresses at local levels. Take *Shen Jilan*, a lifelong delegate from *Shanxi* Province, for example. *Shen* was handpicked as the NPC delegate in 1954 and then was reelected every time thereafter at the CPC's recommendation. Known as a "living fossil delegate," *Shen* stayed through all thirteen Assemblies of the NPC and served as an NPC delegate for sixty-six years until she died in 2020.

The reason why *Shen* could be a "forever" delegate is quite simple. In her own words, "The task of a delegate to the NPC is to listen to the CPC." She felt proud of being "very supportive of the CPC" and having "never voted against anything made by the CPC."[200] What she said was true for her, and for many other delegates as well. A critique posted on a blog described her as a delegate "representing the anti-rightist movement, representing the Cultural Revolution, and representing all she was told by the party, but never representing the people."[201] Nevertheless, in 2019, she was awarded a "National Medal" by *Xi Jinping* for her contribution to the state.

Among the powers both the NPC and its Standing Committee exercise under the Constitution, the most important one is legislative power. As discussed, the power to amend the Constitution and to enact laws is exclusively vested with the NPC and its Standing Committee. As noted, the legislative process consists of four major steps: introducing, reading, voting, and promulgating. Of the legislative process, the most significant step is reading. A reading can be either an NPC reading or a Standing Committee reading, depending on the nature and type of the law to be adopted.[202]

Under the Legislation Law, the NPC reading includes delegate deliberation and special committee deliberation,[203] while the Standing Committee reading can take three different forms: a full session deliberation, group deliberation, or joint group deliberation.[204] In addition, in order to help legislative deliberation, the Standing Committee may hold forums, seminars, hearings, or publish the draft to solicit public opinions or comments on certain legislation.[205]

Generally, for a legislative bill to be introduced by the Standing Committee to the Assembly floor of the NPC for a final vote, a process of "three readings" within the Standing Committee is required.[206] Under article 64 of the 1982 Constitution, a vote

[200] See Tencent News, March 11, 2009, available at https://news.qq.com/a/20110303/001237.htm.

[201] See Caixin.com, February 1, 2013, available at http://m.china.caixin.com/m/2013-02-01/100488595.html.

[202] The NPC is responsible for constitutional amendments and enactment of basic laws, while the Standing Committee of the NPC is responsible for the enactment of all other laws.

[203] See the Legislation Law of China (adopted 2000, amended 2015), arts. 14, 18, available at www.law-lib.com/law/law_view.asp?id=490890.

[204] See *id.*, art. 29.

[205] See *id.*, art. 36.

[206] See *id.*, art. 29.

of at least two-thirds of the NPC delegates present is required to adopt an amendment to the Constitution, while only a simple majority vote is needed to pass a law.[207]

Again, as discussed, although the NPC is the supreme organ of state power under the Constitution, its primary mission is to ensure that (a) the will of the CPC is incorporated into the law through the legislative process, (b) all candidates recommended by the CPC for leadership positions in various state organs are appointed, and (c) the CPC's leadership is enforced through state power.[208] Due to the CPC's powerful hand behind the scenes, the NPC virtually becomes the tool of the CPC to exercise its controlling power, or a "rubber stamp" in the eyes of many foreign observers.[209]

B. *The President*

China is not a country with a presidential system but does have a President. The office of the presidency is considered a special government organ with an important state function. Under the 1982 Constitution, the President, as the head of state, has four major powers: promulgation and proclamation,[210] appointment or removal of government officials,[211] diplomatic affairs,[212] and conferral of honors or medals.[213] All of these powers are exercised upon the decision of the NPC and its Standing Committee.[214]

In countries with presidential systems, the president is both the head of state and the chief of the executive branch. In China, however, the President is basically an honorary position in terms of constitutional powers. But since the presidency is held

[207] See the 1982 Constitution, *supra* note 11, art. 64.

[208] See the CPC 2014 Decision, *supra* note 109.

[209] See BBC News, *How China Is Ruled*, available at http://news.bbc.co.uk/2/shared/spl/hi/in_depth/china_politics/government/html/7.stm; see also France24, *China's Rubber Stamp Parliament at a Glance*, available at www.france24.com/en/20190305-chinas-rubber-stamp-parliament-glance.

[210] See the 1982 Constitution, *supra* note 11, art. 80 (The President of the People's Republic of China, in pursuance of the decisions of the National People's Congress and its Standing Committee, promulgates statutes, issues orders of special pardons; proclaims the entering of a state of emergency; proclaims a state of war; and issues mobilization orders).

[211] See *id.* (The President appoints and removes the Premier, Vice-Premiers, State Councilors, Ministers in charge of ministries or commissions, the Auditor-General and the Secretary-General of the State Council).

[212] See *id.*, art. 81 (The President of the People's Republic of China, on behalf of the People's Republic of China, engages in activities involving State affairs and receives foreign diplomatic representatives and, in pursuance of the decisions of the Standing Committee of the National People's Congress, appoints or recalls plenipotentiary representatives abroad, and ratifies or abrogates treaties and important agreements concluded with foreign states).

[213] See *id.* (The President confers State medals and titles of honor).

[214] See *id.*, art. 80. Also, under the 1982 Constitution, the Vice President assists the President, and may exercise such functions and powers of the President as the President may entrust to him. See *id.*, art. 82.

by the General Secretary of the CPC Central Committee, the President is the most powerful person in the country. While serving as President, the General Secretary is also the chairperson of the Party Central Military Commission and the State Central Military Commission.

The President of China is not elected by the public through a general election but by the NPC.[215] Under the 1982 Constitution, any Chinese citizen who has the right to vote, the right to stand for election, and has reached the age of forty-five is eligible to be elected President or Vice President.[216] But in reality, the candidates for the President and Vice President are predetermined, and recommended to the NPC for a vote by the CPC, and there is only one candidate for each position. The term of office of the President and Vice President used to be limited under the 1982 Constitution to a five-year term with a maximum of two consecutive terms. As noted, the term limit was lifted at the request of the CPC through the 2018 Amendment to the 1982 Constitution.

C. *The State Council*

The administrative branch of government in China is the State Council. Article 85 of the 1982 Constitution provides that the State Council is the Central People's Government of China. Defined by the 1982 Constitution, the State Council is the executive body of the highest organ of state power and the highest organ of state administration.[217] The head of the State Council is the Premier. Just like the NPC, the State Council is limited to a five-year term. The Premier, Vice-Premiers, and State Councillors may serve no more than two consecutive terms.[218]

Under the 1982 Constitution, the State Council has quite extensive powers, including both legislative and administrative powers.[219] The legislative power of the State Council involves two aspects: the first aspect is administrative regulation. Under article 89 of the 1982 Constitution, the State Council has the power to adopt administrative measures, enact administrative regulations, and issue decisions and orders in accordance with the Constitution and other laws.

The second aspect is to enact regulations and rules to serve a particular purpose or to implement the law as authorized by the NPC or its Standing Committee. This power may only be exercised under authorization with a limited scope. Authorized legislation may occur when certain legislative matters fall within the power of the NPC or its Standing Committee, but the time for such legislation is not yet ripe, and the NPC or its Standing Committee authorizes the State Council to formulate

[215] See *id.*, art. 79.
[216] See *id.*
[217] See the 1982 Constitution, *supra* note 11, art. 85.
[218] See *id.*, art. 87.
[219] The 1982 Constitution provides a laundry list of the functions and powers of the State Council. See *id.*, art. 89.

administrative regulations for the purpose of testing the waters. After a period of experimentation, the NPC or its Standing Committee will act to make the law in this regard.

The administrative power of the State Council mainly includes (a) exercising unified leadership over the work of the ministries and commissions and directing all other administrative work of a national character that does not fall within the jurisdiction of the ministries and commissions; and (b) exercising unified leadership over the work of local organs of state administration at various levels throughout the country and formulating the detailed division of functions and powers between the central government and the organs of state administration of provinces, autonomous regions, and municipalities directly under the central government.[220]

In addition, the State Council has the authority to make proposals to the NPC or its Standing Committee for review and approval. The State Council proposals as such generally include (a) the national economic and social development plan and plan implementation; (b) the state budget and budget implementation; (c) treaties or important agreements concluded with foreign countries, which must be approved or repealed by the Standing Committee of the NPC; (d) personnel appointments or removals that must be made by the NPC or the Standing Committee; and (e) any other matters that must be provided through laws adopted by the NPC or the Standing Committee.[221]

As noted, under the people's congress system, there is no separation of powers in the Chinese government. All government branches, including the State Council, are responsible to, and subject to the supervision of, the NPC. The relationship between the State Council and the NPC, as provided in the 1982 Constitution, is formed in a way that the State Council serves at the "pleasure" of the NPC. But since the Premier of the State Council and Chairman of the NPC are all members of the Politiburo Standing Committee of the CPC, the State Council, like the NPC, must operate pursuant to the will of the CPC.

First, the Premier of the State Council is nominated by the President and appointed by the NPC. All other members of the State Council, including the Vice-Premier, State Councillor, Ministers, Directors, Auditor General, and Secretary-General, are nominated by the Premier and approved by the NPC.[222] When the NPC is not in session, the decision on the candidates for State Council members nominated by the Premier will be made by the Standing Committee of the NPC.[223] In addition, the NPC has the power to remove the Premier and any other member of the State Council.[224] But the removal of any state government official must obtain the CPC's approval in advance.

[220] See *id.*

[221] See Wei & Weiyan, *supra* note 4, at 183.

[222] See the 1982 Constitution, *supra* note 11, art. 62 (5).

[223] See *id.*, art. 67 (9).

[224] See *id.*, art. 63.

Second, the State Council is responsible to, and reports to, the NPC, or to the Standing Committee of the NPC during the NPC's intersession period. On the one hand, the State Council reports to the NPC and works under the supervision of the NPC. On the other hand, the NPC can hold a hearing to question the Premier and any other State Council members and may recall irresponsible government officers for liabilities.[225]

D. *The Supreme People's Court and Supreme People's Procuratorate*

As noted, the SPC and SPP are the judicial bodies parallel to the State Council in the government structure. Under the 1982 Constitution, the SPC is the highest judicial organ,[226] while the SPP is the highest procuratorate of the country.[227] The presidents of the SPC and SPP are elected by the NPC from candidates designated by the CPC. The removal of the SPC and SPP's presidents is also within the power of the NPC.

There is no life tenure in Chinese judicial bodies. The President of the SPC serves on a five-year term but may not serve more than two consecutive terms. The same limitations apply to the President of the SPP as well. There is, however, a difference between the SPC and SPP in respect to the relationship with the local people's courts and people's procuratorates. As provided in the 1982 Constitution, the SPC supervises the trial work of local people's courts at all levels, and the people's courts at higher levels supervise the trial work of people's courts at lower levels.[228] The SPP leads the work of local people's procuratorates at all levels, and the people's procuratorate at a higher level leads the work of people's procuratorates at lower levels.[229]

Under the 1982 Constitution, the people's courts and the people's procuratorates shall exercise their power independently in accordance with the law, without interference from administrative organs, social organizations, or individuals.[230] It is, however, required in the 1982 Constitution that the SPC and SPP be responsible to the NPC and the Standing Committee of the NPC, and that local people's courts and people's procuratorates at all levels be responsible to the people's congresses at their corresponding level.[231] In addition, a local people's procuratorate at a lower level is also responsible to the people's procuratorate at a higher level.[232]

[225] In reality, however, since both the appointment and removal of all government officials are predetermined by the politiburo of the CPC, the power of the NPC is more procedural than substantive.

[226] See the 1982 Constitution, *supra* note 11, art. 132.

[227] See *id.*, art. 137.

[228] See *id.*, art. 132.

[229] See *id.*, art. 137.

[230] See *id.*, arts. 131, 136.

[231] See *id.*, arts. 133, 138.

[232] See *id.*, art. 138.

E. *The State Supervisory Commission*

The State Supervisory Commission (SSC) is a newly created government branch. Formed under the 2018 Amendment to the 1982 Constitution, the SSC and the local supervisory commission serve as national supervisory bodies. The SSC is the highest state supervisory organ and leads the work of local supervisory commissions at all levels. Note that the concept of state supervisory power is not new in China. As noted, it was part of Dr. *Sun Yat-sen*'s "five-power constitution" theory. Also, prior to the creation of the SSC, there existed a Ministry of Supervision that was established in 1993 under the State Council.

The SSC is a state power organ corresponding to the Central Commission for Discipline Inspection of the CPC (CCDI). The CCDI functions as the inspection and supervision authority of the Central Committee of the CPC. With jurisdiction over all CPC members, the CCDI is responsible for maintaining the party's charter and other internal party regulations, ensuring the implementation of the party's policies and resolutions, assisting the party committee in strengthening party construction, and organizing and coordinating the main tasks of anti-corruption work. The SSC has a similar function but runs at the state level, covering the bureaucrats of the entire country.

Along with the creation of the supervisory commissions was the adoption of the Supervision Law by the NPC on March 20, 2018.[233] The main purpose of the Supervision Law is to deepen the reform of the national supervisory system, strengthen the supervision of all public officials who exercise public authority, achieve comprehensive coverage of national supervision, carry out anti-corruption work in depth, and promote the modernization of the national governance system and governance capabilities.[234]

As provided in the Supervision Law, the primary responsibilities of the supervisory commissions include (a) carrying out education for public employees in clean governance, and oversee and inspect their performance of duties in accordance with law, impartial exercise of power, clean governance, and ethical integrity; (b) conducting investigations into violations and crimes abusing public office, such as suspected corruption, bribery, abuse of power, dereliction of duty, rent-seeking, siphoning benefits, twisting the law for personal gain, and wasting State assets; and (c) making decisions on governmental sanctions for public employees who break the law; holding accountable those leadership personnel who perform their duties ineffectively or who shirk their duties and responsibilities; transfering the investigative conclusions on suspected crimes abusing public office to the people's

[233] See the Supervision Law of China (promulgated by the NPC on March 20, 2018); a full text of the Supervision Law is available at www.xinhuanet.com/politics/2018-03/26/c_1122591453.htm.

[234] See *id.*, art. 1.

procuratorates to initiate public prosecutions in accordance with law; and issuing supervision recommendations to the units of the targets of supervision.[235]

As an organ of state power, the SSC, like all other state organs, is responsible to the NPC and its Standing Committee. The election and removal of the director of the SSC is determined by the NPC with the consent of the CPC. Upon recommendation of the director of the SSC, the Standing Committee appoints or removes the deputy director(s) and member(s) of the SSC. The director of the SSC is also subject to term limits – a five-year term with a maximum of two consecutive terms.[236]

Under the 2018 Amendment, the supervisory commissions shall independently exercise their supervisory power in accordance with the law and shall stay free from any interference by administrative organs, social groups, or individuals.[237] In addition, supervisory commissions should handle and cooperate with the judiciary, procuratorial departments, and law enforcement agencies in dealing with offenses and crimes related to the performance of official duties.

The supervisory commissions have jurisdiction over all public officials and related personnel.[238] Pursuant to article 15 of the Supervision Law, the scope of the authority of the supervisory commissions covers (a) civil servants of party organizations and government agencies; (b) personnel engaged in public affairs authorized by laws or regulations or entrusted by state organs to manage public affairs according to law; (c) managers of state-owned enterprises; (d) personnel engaged in management in publicly run units such as education, scientific research, culture, medical and health, sports, etc.; (e) persons engaged in management in grassroots mass autonomous organizations; and (f) other personnel who perform public duties according to law.[239]

It is important to note that although the supervisory commissions are not judicial bodies, they are granted the power to take certain actions that otherwise may only be taken by judicial bodies. For example, under article 22 of the Supervision Law, if a person under investigation is suspected of having committed a serious crime or crimes such as corruption, bribery, negligence, or dereliction of duty, and the supervisory authority has obtained some of the facts and evidence of the crime(s), and there are still important issues that need further investigation, the person can be detained at a specified time and in a specified place upon approval by the supervisory authority under certain circumstances.

The circumstances under which a person may be detained by supervision authorities include: (a) a serious and complicated case is involved; (b) the person in question may escape or commit suicide; (c) the person may collude with others or

[235] See *id.*, art. 11.
[236] See the 1982 Constitution, *supra* note 11, art. 124.
[237] See *id.*, art. 127.
[238] See *id.*
[239] See *id.*, art. 15.

forge, conceal, or destroy evidence; or (d) other acts that may hinder the investigation. In addition, supervisory detention may not necessarily follow any statutory procedures (fair notice, right to an attorney, etc.). Furthermore, the detention also applies to those who are involved in bribery crimes or join in crimes related to the discharge of public duties.[240]

[240] See *id.*, art. 22.

5

Chinese Judiciary and Judicial Power

INTRODUCTION

Since China is a unitary state, it has a uniform judiciary. However, under the scheme of one country with two systems, the judicial uniformity applies only within the mainland. Hong Kong and Macau, as the Special Administrative Regions (SARs), have their own judicial systems that were formed and developed during the colonial period. Although those two regions were handed over to China in 1997 and 1999, respectively, their judicial systems, which are different from the mainland's, remain unchanged.

The uniformity of the Chinese judiciary has several notable features. First, the establishment, organization, and powers of the people's courts are uniformly governed by the Organic Law of People's Courts. The Organic Law was first adopted by the National People's Congress (NPC) in 1979. Since then, it has been amended four times by the Standing Committee in 1983, 1986, 2006, and 2018.[1] Under the Organic Law, the people's courts try criminal, civil, administrative, and other cases prescribed by law, punish crimes, protect innocent people from criminal prosecution, resolve civil and administrative disputes, and protect the legitimate rights and interests of individuals and organizations. In addition, the people's courts have the duty to supervise administrative organs in exercising their powers in accordance with the law, safeguard national security and social order, safeguard social fairness and justice, safeguard the unity, dignity, and authority of the state's legal system, and ensure the smooth progress of the construction of socialism with Chinese characteristics.[2]

Second, the courts at different levels are horizontally responsible to, and subject to the supervision of, the people's congress at the corresponding level. More

[1] The Organic Law of the People's Courts (as revised 2018), available at www.npc.gov.cn/zgrdw/npc/xinwen/201810/26/content_2064483.htm.

[2] See *id.*, art. 2.

specifically, the appointment of judges in all courts other than the Supreme People's Court (SPC) is made by the local people's congresses at various levels, and the budget of the courts is part of the budget of local governments. In other words, the courts are closely tied to local government in terms of personnel and funds.

Third, the SPC is the highest judicial body of the country, but the SPC exercises no control over the lower courts. As provided in the Organic Law of People's Courts, the SPC oversees the trial work of all the levels of local people's courts, and people's courts of higher levels oversee the trial work of lower-level people's courts.[3] The relationship between the SPC and local courts does not involve leadership, but the trial work only, although the SPC rules and decisions are binding on all people's courts.

In China, the terms judiciary and judicial body are interchangeably used to refer to the courts. But as noted, judicial body has a broad meaning to include the procuratorates, public security departments, national security departments, and justice departments, in addition to the courts, while judiciary generally means courts only. In many cases, the courts are also referred to as adjudicative authorities. In article 128 of the 1982 Constitution, for example, the people's courts are defined as "the State's adjudication organs."[4]

1. ORGANIZATIONAL STRUCTURE OF CHINESE COURTS

Courts in China are called people's courts, suggesting an idea of serving the people. The structure of people's courts contains two parts: internal structure and external structure. Internal structure refers to organization and operation within a court, while external structure involves the levels of the courts and the relationship between the courts at the different levels. The Organic Law of People's Courts provides a statutory basis on which the people's courts of various levels are organized both internally and externally.

According to article 2 of the Organic Law, the people's courts, through hearing criminal, civil, administrative, and other cases, perform the following major functions: (a) punishing crime; (b) ensuring that the innocent are not prosecuted; (c) resolving civil and administrative disputes; (d) protecting the lawful rights and interests of individuals and organizations; (e) overseeing administrative organs' lawful exercise of their authority; (f) safeguarding national security and social order; (g) preserving social fairness and justice; (h) maintaining the uniformity, dignity, and authority of the state's legal system; and (i) ensuring that socialism with Chinese characteristics is smoothly established.[5]

[3] See *id.*, art. 10.

[4] See *id.*, art. 2.

[5] See *id.*

A. *External Structure of Chinese Courts*

Externally, the people's courts are structured with categories and tiers. The category refers to the classification of people's courts. Under categories, the people's courts are divided into: (a) the SPC, (b) local people's courts of various levels, and (c) specialized people's courts.[6] The local people's courts are further divided into higher people's courts, intermediate people's courts, and basic level people's courts.[7] The specialized people's courts include railway courts, military courts, maritime courts, intellectual property (IP) courts, financial courts, and international commercial courts.[8]

The high people's court is a provincial-level court, and it is the highest judicial body in a province, autonomous region, or municipality directly under the central government. The basic level people's courts are the courts located in counties and county level cities. Between the high people's courts and basic level people's courts are the intermediate people's courts that are established in the municipalities under the administration of the province or autonomous region, municipality directly under the central government, autonomous prefecture, or prefecture in a province or autonomous region.

The SPC used to release the number of intermediate and basic level people's courts but has not done so for many years. Under a judicial statistic released by the SPC in 2013, as of 2012, there were some 408 intermediate people's courts and 3,115 basic level people's courts.[9] A new development during recent years in the structure of the Chinese judiciary is the creation of the circuit courts and the establishment of specialized courts. The circuit courts are aimed at helping deal with major cross-region administrative and civil cases. The specialized courts are intended to provide a professional dispute resolution mechanism in specialized areas.

According to the SPC, the formation of circuit courts has far-reaching significance. In one aspect, it is believed that the adjudication of major cross-regional administrative, civil, and commercial cases by the circuit courts is a means conducive to (a) maintaining judicial justice, (b) effectively supervising, guiding, and supporting local courts to exercise judicial power independently and impartially, (c) promoting sound implementation of laws, and (d) safeguarding the uniformity of the national legal system.[10]

In the other aspect, the circuit court provides a convenient channel for the parties to conduct local litigation that otherwise would have to take place before the SPC in

6 See *id.*, art. 12.
7 See *id.*, art. 13.
8 See *id.*, art. 15.
9 See Gao Kui, *The New Thinking of Court Reforms* (Chapter I: The Statistics of Chinese Courts), available at https://wenku.baidu.com/view/fdbc6104a26925c52cc5bf78.html.
10 See the SPC, *Press Release on the Circuit Courts*, January 28, 2015, available at www.court.gov.cn/xunhui1/xiangqing-13539.html.

Beijing. Thus, it is believed that to litigate in a regional circuit court would reduce the parties' litigation burden and protect their legitimate rights and interests more effectively. Another belief is that having disputes resolved in different geographic spots would not only help maintain social harmony and especially stability in Beijing, but also help the SPC focus on formulating judicial policies and judicial interpretations, hearing the cases of great significance to the uniform application of laws, and enhancing the SPC's role in supervising and guiding the trial work of national courts.[11]

In short, the circuit courts are intended to serve a twofold purpose: to solve "cross-regional" and "serious" administrative, civil, and commercial disputes, and to avoid the influence of local interests. It is important to note, however, that the creation of circuit courts does not add any additional level to the current court system of China. Put differently, the circuit courts are not the adjudicative bodies of an independent tier, but merely the dispatched branches of the SPC. The chief judge position of each circuit is held by a vice president of the SPC. Thus, a trial by a circuit court is equivalent to a trial by the SPC, and the judgment made by a circuit is deemed the same as if it were entered by the SPC.[12]

In early 2015, two circuit courts were established in the country. The First Circuit is located in Shenzhen in the South, while the Second Circuit is in Shenyang in the North. The First Circuit covers three provinces: *Guangdong*, *Guangxi*, and *Hainan*. The Second Circuit has jurisdiction over *Liaoning*, *Jilin*, and *Heilongjiang* provinces. In December 2016, four more circuit courts were established in *Nanjing*, *Zhengzhou*, *Chongqin*, and *Xian*, respectively. In terms of jurisdiction, the six circuits cover a total of twenty-six provinces and municipalities in the mainland,[13] while the remaining provinces and municipalities, including *Beijing*, *Tianjin*, *Hebei*, *Shandong*, and *Inner Mongolia*, are directly under the SPC.

The specialized courts are the courts established to hear cases in particular legal areas. In 2014, three IP courts were established in *Beijing*, *Guangzhou*, and *Shanghai* to adjudicate IP cases.[14] In December 2020, a fourth IP court was created in *Hainan* Province. Each IP court has centralized jurisdiction over IP cases in the first instance within the municipality or province. In addition, there are about thirty IP tribunals in the local courts of various cities.[15] Among the specialized people's courts, the financial courts are relatively new. The first financial court was

[11] See *id*.

[12] See *id*.

[13] The Third Circuit covers Jiangsu, Shanghai, Zhejiang, Fujian, and Jiangxi; the Fourth Circuit – Henan, Shanxi, Hubei, and Anhui; the Fifth Circuit – Chongqing, Sichuan, Guizhou, Yunnan, and Tibet; the Sixth Circuit – Shaanxi, Gansu, Qinghai, Ningxia, and Xinjiang.

[14] The three IP courts were formed in Beijing, Guangzhou, and Shanghai on November 6, December 16, and December 28, respectively.

[15] See SPC, *Press Conference*, January 6, 2025, available at https://news.qq.com/rain/a/20250106A07QO300.

established in *Shanghai* in 2018. Under the SPC rules, the *Shanghai* Financial Court mainly deals with financial-related civil and commercial cases, and administrative cases that involve financial matters.[16]

In the past few years, Internet Courts have emerged in the Chinese judiciary. Mainly located in *Beijing*, *Shanghai*, and *Guangzhou*, the Internet Courts are courts that can conduct trials through the internet. Since the use of the internet during the trial does not involve the substance of the cases, the Internet Courts are not considered specialized courts. In other words, the Internet Courts differ from regular courts only in the method of trial. According to the SPC, Internet Courts use online methods to hear cases, meaning that for certain cases, the acceptance, delivery, mediation, evidence exchange, pre-trial preparation, trial, and sentencing of cases can be completed online.[17]

On September 15, 2025, the SPC issued the Rules on the Jurisdiction of Internet Courts (2025 Rules). With adjustment to the adjudication of Intenet-related cases, the 2025 Rules intend to optimize the jurisdiction and trial mechanism of the Internet courts.[18] Under the Rules, the Internet courts shall have centralized jurisdiction over the following first-instance cases within their respective municipalities: (1) Disputes over online data ownership, infringement, and contracts; (2) Disputes regarding online personal information protection and privacy rights; (3) Disputes involving online virtual property ownership, infringement, and contracts; (4) Disputes concerning online unfair competition; (5) Disputes pertaining to online domain name ownership, infringement, and contracts; (6) Disputes arising from the signing or performance of online shopping contracts through e-commerce platforms; (7) Disputes related to online service contracts where the signing and performance of the contracts are completed online; (8) Administrative disputes out of administrative actions taken by administrative agencies involving the supervision of online data, online personal information protection, and online unfair competition, and the managemnt of online transaction and online information service; and (9) Online public interest litigation cases initiated by the people's procuratorate. [19]

In addition, according to the 2025 Rules, the above urisdiction provisions also apply to foreign-related civil cases, as well as civil cases involving the Hong Kong and Macao Special Administrative Regions and Taiwan. In the meantime, with the approval of the SPC, the relevant high people's courts may also designate Internet

[16] See the SPC, *Rules on the Jurisdiction of the Shanghai Financial Court*, adopted July 31, 2018, available at www.chinacourt.org/law/detail/2018/08/id/149788.shtml.

[17] See the SPC, *Provisions on Several Issues Concerning the Trial of Cases by Internet Courts*, issued on September 3, 2018, available at www.chinacourt.org/law/detail/2018/09/id/149799.shtml.

[18] See the SPC, Rules on Jurisdiction of the Internet Courts, adoped on September 15, 2025, effective November 1, 2025, available at https://fzzy.jxfy.gov.cn/law/detail/2025/10/id/151447.shtml.

[19] See *id.*, art. 1.

Courts to have jurisdiction over other specific types of online civil and administrative cases.[20] Moreover, the 2025 Rules allow the parties by agreement to subject their disputes over contracts and other property rights to the jurisdiction of the Internet Court that has a real connection with the disputes.[21]

The international commercial courts are the courts that handle international commercial dispute cases. With the approval of the SPC, some twelve international commercial courts have been established locally in *Suzhou*, *Beijing*, *Chengdu*, *Xiamen*, *Changchun*, *Quanzhou*, *Wuxi*, *Nanning*, *Hangzhou*, *Ningbo*, *Nan*jing, and *Qingdao*. According to the SPC, the local international commercial courts hear the first instance of foreign civil and commercial cases under a cross-region centralized jurisdiction designated by the SPC.[22]

At the national level, there are two kinds of specialized courts established under the SPC: the China International Commercial Court, known as the CICC, and the China Intellectual Property Court (China IP Court). In 2018, the SPC created two CICCs located in *Shenzhen* and *Xian*, respectively. As SPC-dispatched courts, the CICCs are equipped with jurisdiction over certain cases that involve international commercial disputes. The CICCs are directly under the SPC and also are a part of the SPC.

The China IP Court, situated in *Beijing*, was created in 2019. According to the SPC, the China IP Court is a permanent adjudication body dispatched by the SPC and has jurisdiction over appeal cases involving patents, other intellectual properties, and monopoly nationwide that require strong professional and technical knowledge.[23] Since the China IP Court is a part of the SPC, its judgments, rulings, mediation letters, or decisions are those of the SPC.[24] Also, as an appellate division,

[20] See *id.*

[21] See *id.*, art. 2.

[22] See Shen Xiang, *Judicial Safeguard of the "Belt and Road" Initiative in the Past Decade*, 17 Journal of China Adjudication (2003), available at https://cicc.court.gov.cn/html/1/218/149/156/2406.html.

[23] See the SPC, *Provisions on Several Issues of Intellectual Property Court*, adopted December 3, 2019, effective January 1, 2019, art. 1 (2019 *Provisions*), available at www.sohu.com/a/286671589_99921288.

[24] The SPC 2019 Provisions were amended in 2023, in which the jurisdiction of the China IP Court is provided to include: (i) administrative appeals regarding the authorization and confirmation of patents, new plant varieties, and integrated circuit layout designs; (ii) civil and administrative appeals regarding the ownership and infringement of invention patents, new plant varieties, and integrated circuit layout designs; (iii) civil and administrative appeals regarding the ownership and infringement of major and complex utility model patents, trade secrets, and computer software; and (iv) civil and administrative appeals regarding monopoly. In addition, the China IP Court also hears such cases specified above as (i) major and complex first-instance civil and administrative cases nationwide; (ii) cases where the judgments, rulings, and mediation documents of the first-instance civil and administrative cases that have become legally effective are applied for retrial, protest, retrial, and other cases subject to trial supervision procedures in accordance with the law; (iii) cases where disputes over jurisdiction of first-instance civil and administrative cases, applications for reconsideration of conduct preservation decisions, reconsideration of fines and detention decisions, and extension of trial deadlines;

the China IP Court takes appeals from the judgments or decisions made by the high people's courts, local IP courts, and intermediate people's courts on IP disputes.[25]

The tiers of people's courts relate to the hierarchy of the Chinese judiciary. In general, the people's courts operate under four tiers: basic level people's courts, intermediate people's courts, high people's courts, and finally the SPC. The specialized courts, except for the military courts, may either have basic and intermediate levels or intermediate level only. The military courts consist of three levels: basic, intermediate, and high military courts.

The judicial proceedings in people's courts are composed of two instances: trial and appeal. Commonly called two-tier adjudication, the "two-instances"means that in any given case, there is only one appeal. Therefore, a decision made by an appellate court is final, and no more appeal is allowed. If, however, an appellate decision is in error, a retrial may be requested through a trial supervision proceeding. Among the four tiers, the tier of appellate court depends on where the first instance trial begins. In most cases, the first instance trial is held at the basic level people's courts. In certain cases, however, the first-instance trial may take place at the intermediate people's court, high people's court, or even the SPC.

The caseload in Chinese courts is relatively heavy. According to SPC statistics, in 2010, the total number of cases accepted by local people's courts of various levels was 11.70 million, of which about 11 million were adjudicated. In 2019, these numbers reached 31.567 million and 29.02 million, respectively. 15,985 cases were accepted by the SPC in 2015, and the number increased to 38,498 in 2019, while the SPC adjudicated 14,135 cases in 2015 and 34,481 in 2019.[26] From January to September 2023, a total of 25.789 million cases were in the court dockets nationwide, a 9.12 percent increase from the same period in the previous year, and some 23.509 million cases were adjudicated, increasing at a rate of 6.67 percent.[27]

a. The Basic People's Courts

The basic level people's courts are the lowest level courts, situated in the counties and municipal districts. Under the Organic Law of the People's Courts, the basic level people's courts adjudicate cases of first instance, unless otherwise provided by law.[28] Thus, in terms of subject matter jurisdiction, the basic level people's courts exercise general trial competence. For most cases, the first instance starts at the basic level people's courts. Then, the intermediate people's courts will be the appellate courts for appeal.

and (iv) other cases that the SPC believes should be heard by the China IP Court. See SPC, *Decision on Amending the SPC Provisions on Certain Issues Concerning Intellectual Property Court* (2023), art. 1, available at www.chinacourt.org/article/detail/2023/10/id/7599115.shtml.

25 See the SPC, 2019 *Provisions*, *supra* note 19, art. 2.

26 See the SPC, *Judicial Statistics Reports*, available at http://gongbao.court.gov.cn/ArticleList.html?serial_no=sftj.

27 See the SPC, *The Major Data on the Judicial Trial Work from January to September 2023*, available at https://enipc.court.gov.cn/zh-cn/news/view-2605.html.

28 See the Organic Law of the People's Courts, *supra* note 1, art. 25.

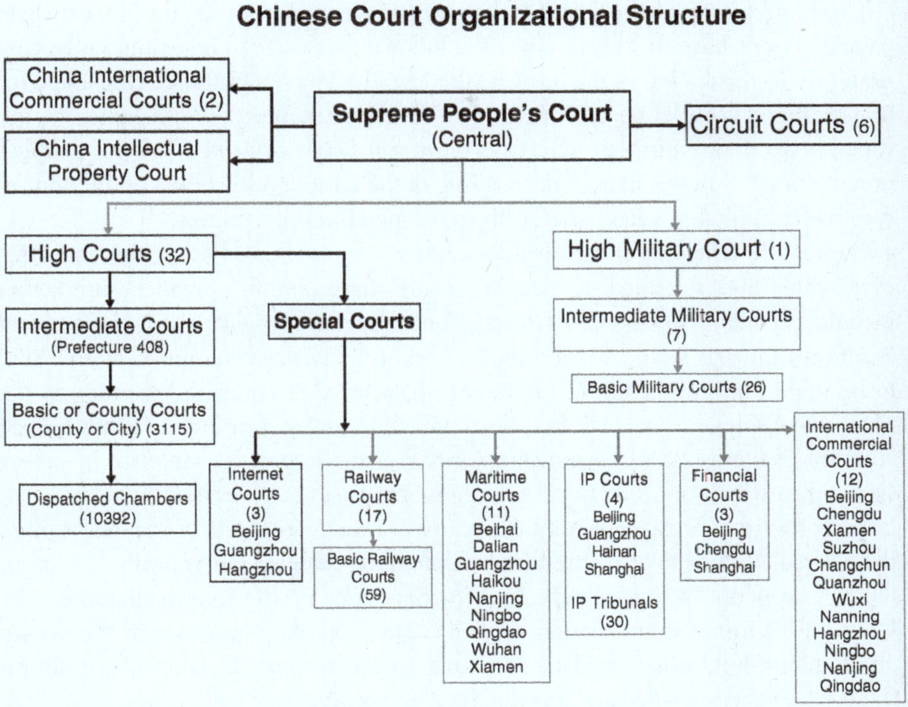

FIGURE 5.1 Chinese Court Organizational Structure.

For purposes of convenience to the litigation at the grassroots level, the basic level people's courts may establish dispatched tribunals based on the region, population, and the nature of cases. The dispatched tribunal is not a separate court but an integral part of the basic level people's court. Therefore, the judgments and rulings of the dispatched tribunals are the judgments and rulings of the dispatching basic level people's courts. In addition to trial cases at the first instance, the basic level people's court is also empowered to provide professional guidance to the mediation work of the local people's mediation committee.

b. Intermediate People's Courts

The intermediate people's courts are one tier up from the basic level. Established in prefectural regions or cities, the intermediate people's courts are both trial courts and appellate courts. Unlike the basic level people's courts, which have jurisdiction over the cases of first instance on a broad basis, the power of the intermediate people's courts to adjudicate at the first instance is limited to the cases prescribed by law or designated by the SPC. Without statutory or SPC authorization, the intermediate people's court may only hear cases of the second instance, meaning the appeals from judgments of the basic level people's courts.

Under article 23 of the Organic Law of the People's Courts, the intermediate people's courts have jurisdiction over the following cases: (a) The first-instance case under their jurisdiction as provided by the law; (b) The first-instance case asked for trial by the basic level people's court; (c) The first-instance case designated by the superior people's court; (d) The case of appeal from, or protest by, the people's procuratorate against a judgment or ruling of the basic level people's court; and (e) A retrial case filed in accordance with trial supervision procedures.[29]

Pursuant to article 19 of the Civil Procedural Law (as revised 2023), the civil cases over which the intermediate people's courts have the first-instance jurisdiction include (a) major foreign cases (cases containing foreign elements); (b) cases of significant impacts within the jurisdiction; and (c) cases as determined by the SPC to be under the jurisdiction of the intermediate people's courts.[30] According to the SPC, major foreign cases refer to cases in which the subject in dispute involves large amounts of money, the facts are complicated, or the impact is significant in such a situation in which one side has a large number of parties concerned.[31]

With regard to local impacts, the amount of money involved in disputes is often determinative Prior to 2021, the threshold amount varied geographically.[32] In 2021, the SPC issued a Notice on Adjusting the Standards for the Intermediate People's Courts' First-Instance Jurisdiction of Civil Cases. The 2021 Notice raised the money amount threshold established in 2015 and, in the meantime, adopted a uniform standard for the intermediate courts across the country.

Under the 2021 Notice, when the parties are all domiciled or not domiciled in the provincial administrative jurisdiction of the court accepting the case, the intermediate people's court shall have jurisdiction over first-instance civil cases if the amount incontroversy exceeds 500 million yuan. But if one of the parties is not domiciled in the provincial administrative region where the court accepting the case is located,

[29] See *id.*, art. 23.

[30] See the Civil Procedural Law of China (as revised 2023), art. 19, a full text of the Civil Procedural Law is available at www.npc.gov.cn/c2/c30834/202401/P020240108541839745616.pdf (CPL).

[31] See the SPC, *Interpretations on the Application of the Civil Procedural Law of China*, issued on January 30, 2015, art. 1, available at www.chinacourt.org/law/detail/2015/01/id/148091.shtml.

[32] Pursuant to the SPC's 2015 Notice Concerning Adjustment of Money Amount for the Civil and Commercial Case Jurisdiction of First Instance, if both of the parties are domiciled in the same province, the intermediate people's courts in such regions as Beijing, Shanghai, Jiangsu, Zhejiang, and Guangdong shall have jurisdiction of first instance over civil and commercial cases in which the money amount in dispute exceeds 100 million RMB. In other regions, the amount is reduced to 30 million, 10 million, and 5 million RMB, respectively. See the SPC, *Notice on Adjusting the Standards of the First Instance Trial of Civil and Commercial Cases under the Jurisdiction of Higher People's Courts and Intermediate People's Courts*, issued on April 30, 2015, available at http://tlzy.chinacourt.gov.cn/article/detail/2018/11/id/3585188.shtml. (Thirty million RMB threshold applies to Tianjin, Hebei, Shanxi, Inner Mongolia, Liaoning, Anhui, Fujian, Shandong, Henan, Hubei, Hunan, Guangxi, Hainan, Sichuan, and Chongqing; 10 million applies to Jilin, Heilongjiang, Jiangxi, Yunnan, Shaanxi, and Xinjiang; 5 million applies to Guizhou, Tibet, Gansu, Qinghai, and Ningxia. If, however, one of the parties is not a local domiciliary, the money amount will be 50 million, 20 million, 10 million, and 5 million.)

the intermediate people's court should have first-instance jurisdiction over the case in which the amount in controversy exceeds 100 million yuan.[33]

In 2022, the SPC issued Several Provisions on the Jurisdiction of First-Instance IP, Civil, and Administrative Cases. Under the 2022 Provisions, the intermediate people's court of the place where the provincial, autonomous region, or municipality government is located (capital city) or the intermediate people's court designated by the SPC shall have the first-instance jurisdiction over IP cases.[34] Therefore, unless there is an IP court in the region, all IP cases shall be filed with an intermediate court in the capital city for the first-instance trial.

c. High People's Courts

The next tier above the intermediate level is the high people's court. There are thirty-one high people's courts situated in the capitals of provinces, autonomous regions, and municipalities directly under the central government, excluding Hong Kong and Macau. As the highest court at the provincial level, the high people's court is responsible for guiding and supervising the trial activities of the intermediate people's courts and the basic level people's court within its jurisdiction. The high people's court hears appeals from the judgments or rulings of the intermediate people's court, but it also takes certain first-instance civil cases.

As provided in the Organic Law of People's Courts, the cases that come under the jurisdiction of the high people's courts include: (a) The first-instance case under their jurisdiction as provided by the law; (b) The first-instance case asked for trial by the lower-level people's court; (c) The first-instance case designated by the SPC; (d) The case of appeal from, or protest against, a judgment or ruling of the intermediate people's court; (e) A retrial case filed in accordance with the judicial supervision procedures; and (f) The death penalty case reported by the intermediate people's courts for review.[35] Under article 20 of the Chinese Civil Procedure Law (as revised 2023), the high people's court may hear first-instance civil cases that have significant impacts within its jurisdictional region.[36]

As a principle, Chinese courts must stay with a two-instance trial rule, namely, a trial and an appeal in the judicial proceeding. In other words, after a trial, only one appeal to the next higher level of the people's court is available.[37] But there is a

[33] See the SPC, *Notice on Adjusting the Standards for the Intermediate People's Courts' First-Instance Jurisdiction of Civil Cases*, issued on October 1, 2021, available at http://hngy.hunancourt.gov.cn/article/detail/2023/01/id/7094568.shtml.

[34] See the SPC, *Several Provisions on the First Instance Jurisdiction of IP, Civil and Administrative Cases*, issued on April 20, 2022, art. 1, available at www.lindapatent.com/cn/law_patent/1707.html.

[35] See the Organic Law of the People's Courts, *supra* note 1, art. 24.

[36] See the CPL, *supra* 26, art. 20.

[37] In China, most cases will begin at the county level trial court as the first instance. But for certain cases that are considered to have significant impacts locally or nationally, the first

special proceeding known as judicial supervision that could break this rule and have the case tried anew.[38] Judicial supervision has been strongly criticized in China because it creates a serious issue regarding the finality of the case involved.[39] Since the criteria for initiating judicial supervision are very broad, literally almost in every case, the party dissatisfied with the judgment made by the court on appeal may make a request for judicial supervision and thus render the final judgment (judgment made in the second instance) virtually non-final.[40]

d. The Supreme People's Court

The SPC, as noted, is the highest judicial organ of the state. Under the two-instance trial system, only a limited number of cases may be brought to the SPC. In accordance with the Organic Law of the People's Courts, the SPC hears the

instance could start at an intermediate people's court, a high people's court, or even the Supreme People's Court.

38 Under the two-instance system, a trial at the first instance may take place at any of the four levels: the basic people's court, the intermediate people's court, the high people's court, and the Supreme People's Court – depending on the nature of the case, but a vast majority of cases start at the trial level. If a party disagrees with the trial court judgment, the party may make an appeal to the next level of higher court. There is only one appeal available. However, when the final judgment takes effect, a party may still file a petition for a retrial at a higher level of people's court through a judicial supervision process. Under article 210 of the Chinese Civil Procedure Law, if the parties concerned believe that there is an error in a legally effective judgment or ruling, they may apply to the people's court at the next higher level for a retrial. If one party to the case comprises a large number of inividuals, or both parties to the case are citizens, they may also apply to the people's court of original instance for retrial. However, the execution of the judgment or ruling shall not be suspended during the application. Article 211 provides a list of circumstances in which a retrial should be conducted, including: (1) There is new evidence that is conclusive enough to overrule the original judgment or ruling; (2) The main evidence used in the original judgment or ruling to find the facts was insufficient; (3) The main evidence used in the original judgment or ruling to find the facts was forged; (4) The main evidence used in the original judgment or ruling to find the facts was not cross-examined; (5) The parties concerned are unable to collect the main evidence of the case by themselves for objective reasons and apply for help to the people's court, but the people's court fails to collect such evidence; (6) There was an error in the application of the law in the original judgment or ruling; (7) The trial organization was unlawfully formed or adjudicators that should have withdrawn did not do so; (8) The person incapable of action is not represented by a legal agent, or the party that should have participated in the litigation failed to do so because of reasons not attributable to himself or his legal agent; (9) The party's right to debate was deprived of in violation of the law; (10) The default judgment in the absence of the party was made whereas that party was not served with summons; (11) Some claims were omitted or exceeded in the original judgment or ruling; (12) The legal document on which the original judgment or ruling was made is canceled or revised; or (13) The judicial officers committed embezzlement, accepted bribes, engaged in malpractice for personal benefit, or perverted the course of law when trying the case. See the CPL, *supra* note 26, art. 211.

39 See generally, Jing Hanchao, *On the Retrial System Reform*, in Cao Jianming, ed., Research on the Theoretic Issues Involving the Reform of Trial Methods in China, 794–801 (China University of Politics and Law Press, 2000).

40 See *id*. at 799–800.

following cases: (a) A first-instance case that is stipulated by law and is deemed to be under its jurisdiction; (b) cases of appeal from, and in protest against, the judgments or rulings of the high people's court; (c) appeal and protest cases filed in accordance with the rules adopted by the Standing Committee of the NPC; (d) A retrial case filed in accordance with trial supervision procedures; and (e) death penalty cases submitted for approval by the high people's courts.[41]

China is one of the few countries in the world that maintains the death penalty. However, in order to control the use of the death penalty, the first-instance trial that involves the death penalty must be handled by the intermediate people's court. Thus, no basic level people's courts may enter a judgment for the death penalty. In addition, all death penalty judgments, except for those made by the SPC, must be reported to the SPC for review and approval before the execution.

In Chinese judicial proceedings, protest is a legal supervision mechanism by which the people's procuratorates request a court to change the judgment or retry the case according to legal procedures. The request is made on the basis of a finding after the people's procuratorates' review of the trial that there is an error in the court's judgment or ruling that has already taken effect. The protest can be launched by the SPP and local procuratorates. It may also be made by people' procuratorates at the petition of the interested party.

Under article 219 of the Chinese Civil Procedural Law (as revised 2023), the SPP may lodge a protest against the effective judgment or ruling made by a court at any level, the higher people's procuratorates may lodge a protest against the effective judgment or ruling made by any court at a lower level, and any local people's procuratorates may lodge a protest against the effective judgment or ruling made by the court at the same level. Protest may also be made against a mediation ruling made by the court if the mediation is found harmful to the State and social public interests.[42]

Allowing the appeal and protest cases to be filed under the NPC's Standing Committee rules is a provision newly added into the Organic Law of the People's Court in 2018. The provision mainly deals with judgments made by the IP courts. In response to the SPC's suggestion for improving the appeal-hearing mechanism of IP cases, the Standing Committee of the NPC adopted the Decision on Several Issues Concerning Litigation Procedures in Patent and IP Cases in October 2018.

The 2018 Decision grants the SPC the jurisdiction to hear the following appeal cases: (a) an appeal against the judgment or ruling of a patent case of the first instance involving an invention, utility model, new plant variety, integrated circuit layout design, technical secrets, computer software, or monopoly, which is highly technical; (b) an appeal against the judgment or ruling of the IP administrative case of the first instance involving a patent, new plant variety, integrated circuit layout design, technical secret, computer software, or monopoly, which is highly technical; or (c) retrial or protest through judicial

[41] Chinese Organic Law of the People's Courts, *supra* note 1, art. 16.

[42] See the CPL, *supra* note 26, art. 219.

supervision against first-instance judgments, rulings, and mediation documents of the cases mentioned earlier that have already become legally effective.[43]

B. *Internal Structure of Chinese Courts*

Internally, the people's courts are organized into three layers. On the top is the administration that consists of a president and several vice presidents. The president is both the chief judge and chief administrator in charge of the overall work of the court. The president supervises the trial work of the court and manages the administrative affairs of the court, while the vice presidents assist the president in performing his or her duties. In most cases, the president of a court is also the chief of the party committee that actually controls the court.

The second layer is the judicial committee. It is required under the Organic Law of the People's Courts that a judicial committee be established at every level of the people's courts.[44] The judicial committee is composed of the president, vice presidents, and several senior judges who normally are the heads of divisions or chambers. If needed, the judicial committee may hold general meetings or professional meetings. The professional meeting is a meeting that focuses on a certain area of law or specific type of case.

The judicial committee is an adjudicatory body within the people's courts, and it has the power of quasi-governance with regard to trial activities in particular. The judicial committee meetings are normally presided over by the president, or the vice president designated by the president. For each judicial committee meeting, a quorum of more than half of the committee members is required. The decision-making process of the judicial committee is based on democratic centralism, meaning that a majority of votes controls.[45]

The major functions of the judicial committee, as provided in the Organic Law of the People's Courts, include (a) summarizing the trial work experience; (b) reviewing and determining the application of law in major, difficult, and complex cases; (c) discussing and deciding whether a retrial is needed for a case in which the judgment, ruling, or judicial mediation has taken effect; and (d) reviewing and making decisions on other major issues related to trial work.[46]

In 2019, the SPC issued the Opinions on Perfecting the Working Mechanism of the People's Court Judicial Committee. In its Opinions, the SPC urged giving full play to the functions of the judicial committee.[47] According to the SPC, the people's

[43] See the Standing Committee of the NPC, *Decision on Several Issues Concerning Litigation Procedures in Patent and Intellectual Property Cases*, October 26, 2018, available at www.npc.gov.cn/npc/c12435/201810/e47a80671d5e4c85b7b531e7e6cbf0e7.shtml.

[44] See the Organic Law of the People's Courts, *supra* note 1, art. 36.

[45] See *id.*, art. 38.

[46] See *id.*, art. 37.

[47] See the SPC, *Opinions on Perfecting the Working Mechanism of the People's Court Judicial Committee*, issued on September 22, 2019, art. 4, available at www.chinacourt.org/law/detail/2019/09/id/149972.shtml.

courts at all levels shall make every effort to optimize the composition of the judicial committee, well position the judicial committee, and improve the operational mechanism of the judicial committee.[48] It is required that the decision made by the judicial committee on the case or matter discussed be followed by the judges, trial panel, or divisions involved.[49]

The third layer is the major workforce of the court, which consists of divisions or chambers. Based on the kinds of cases, Chinese judges in people's courts specialize in different areas of law, and work in different divisions or chambers. Typically, a people's court contains quite a number of divisions, which include, among others, a criminal division, civil division, administrative division, case-filing division, judicial supervision division, and enforcement division. In some larger cities, the court may contain multiple criminal and civil divisions. In the Shanghai No. 1 Intermediate People's Court, for example, there are two criminal divisions and six civil divisions.[50]

It is important to note that the trial in a people's court is conducted by a collegial panel or, in certain cases, by a single judge. The collegial panel is an actual adjudicative body in a particular case and is composed of judges, or judges and people's assessors. Each collegiate panel has an odd number of three or more members. The collegial panel is presided by a judge, but all members have equal rights when hearing the case.[51]

The collegial panel decides the case in accordance with the opinion of the majority, and each member of the collegial panel has one vote. The opinion of the minority is written into the record.[52] Both the transcript of the court hearing and the judgment documents bear the signatures of all members of the collegial panel.[53] When a collegial panel hears a case, the judge is responsible for fact determination and the application of the law of the case,[54] while the people's assessors are required to participate in the court hearing of the case as a matter of law.[55]

2. JUDICIAL POWER AND THE ROLE OF THE SUPREME PEOPLE'S COURT

As noted, the Chinese judiciary is not framed on the notion of separation of powers, but rather under the people's congress system. All courts in China are subject to, and report to, the people's congresses at their corresponding levels. The relationship

48 See *id.*, art. 3.
49 See *id.*, art. 22.
50 For details, see Shanghai No. 1 Intermediate People's Court available at www.a-court.gov.cn/platformData/infoplat/pub/no1court_2802/homepage_13602/index.html.
51 See the Organic Law of the People's Courts, *supra* note 1, art. 30.
52 See *id.*, art. 31.
53 See *id.*, art. 32.
54 See *id.*, art. 33.
55 See *id.*, art. 34.

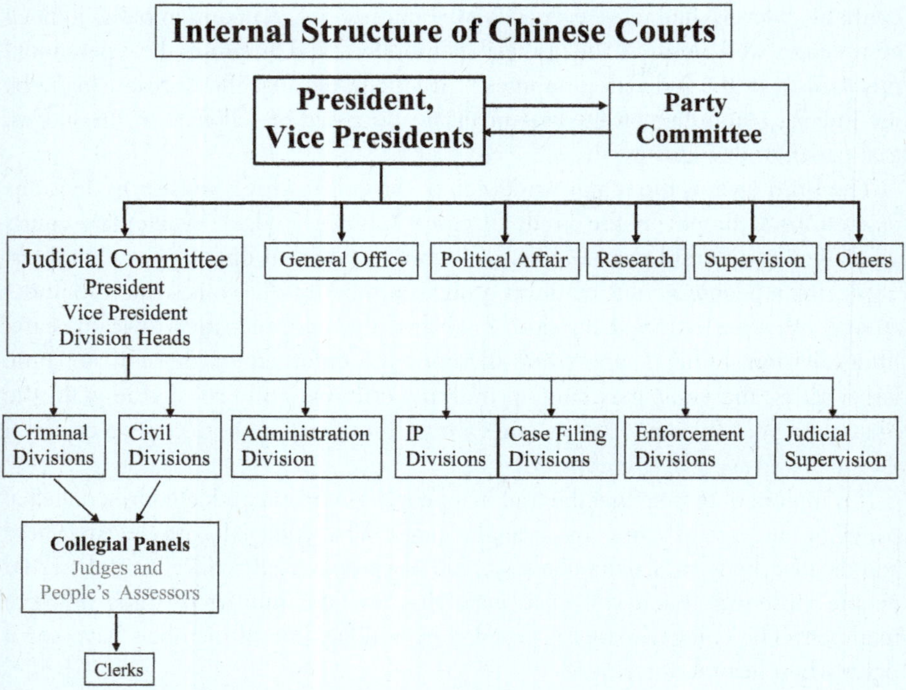

FIGURE 5.2 Internal Structure of Chinese Courts.

between the people's congress and the judiciary is not horizontal but vertical. Consequently, the judicial power in the country mainly focuses on adjudication and does not function as a legal mechanism of checks and balances in government. The people's congress has the constitutional power to check and supervise the work of the judiciary, but not vice versa.

A. *Organization of the Supreme People's Court*

The SPC is organized in the same way as all other people's courts, but on a larger scale. At the administrative level, there is one president and several vice presidents. The president of the SPC is elected by the NPC, and all vice presidents are appointed by the Standing Committee of the NPC upon nomination by the President of the SPC. An authoritative body within the SPC is the judicial committee. In addition to the president and vice presidents, the members of the judicial committee include the heads of divisions and a certain number of full-time members. All members of the SPC judicial committee are appointed by the Standing Committee of the NPC.

At the operational level are the divisions and circuit courts. In addition to the six circuit courts, there are a total of twenty-six divisions and departments in the SPC, of which seventeen divisions are adjudication-related.[56] Among the seventeen adjudication-related divisions are five criminal divisions and four civil divisions. The judges of the SPC are appointed by the Standing Committee of the NPC under the recommendation of the SPC. The SPC judges, though not tenured, have no term limit, except for the president, who, as noted, may only serve two 5-year terms.

Since 2014, as part of the judicial reform, all courts in China, including the SPC, have adopted a judge-quota system, meaning that the number of judges in each court is fixed based on such factors as the caseload, population density, and court settings. In 2018, the total number of judges of the SPC was 367, with an average age of 47 and average legal work experience of 22 years.[57]

B. *Major Functions of the Supreme People's Court*

Again, under the Chinese Constitution, the people's courts are the adjudicatory organs of the State.[58] As the highest adjudicatory body of the country, the SPC has four major functions. The first function is case adjudication. The adjudicatory power of the SPC is exercised mainly on appeals, and most of the appeals are from first-instance judgments made by the high people's courts.

The SPC may also be a court of the first-instance trial, but such a trial has two distinctions. One distinction is that the first-instance trial at the SPC must have a statutory basis and must serve a particular need. The other distinction is that there is no appeal available from a first-instance trial at the SPC. In other words, once a decision is made by the SPC, it is final – the litigation is complete, and the case is closed.

The second function involves supervision of the trial work of the people's courts at all levels, including the specialized people's courts. The supervision authority reflects the relationship between the SPC and all other people's courts. The same is true between the higher-level people's courts and lower-level people's courts within the same geographic jurisdiction. Note again that the SPC's supervision power does not reach the courts in Hong Kong and Macau under the system of one country with two systems.

SPC supervision is undertaken in the following ways: (a) directly taking a case for a hearing or ordering a retrial in the lower court if it is found that an effective

[56] Others are not directly involved in the adjudication of cases, including the general office, foreign affairs bureau, political department, unit party committee, supervision bureau, research office, as well as the retired official affairs bureau.

[57] See the SPC News, *New Guests at Dongjiaomin Lane 27 – Some Foreign Media Chief Reporters in China Walked into the Supreme People's Court*, December 21, 2018, available at www.court.gov.cn/fabu-xiangqing-136751.html.

[58] See the Chinese Constitution 1982 (as amended 2018), art. 128, available at https://english.www.gov.cn/archive/lawsregulations/201911/20/content_WS5ed8856ec6d0b3f0e9499913.html.

judgment or ruling entered by a local people's court or specialized people's court indeed contains an error; (b) correcting an error in the lower court's judgment when hearing the case on appeal or in a protest raised by the procuratorate; (c) hearing the case through judicial supervision proceedings; and (d) correcting illegal and improper conduct in the trial process of the lower people's courts by explaining the specific issues in the application of law.

The third function of the SPC concerns management of the judicial administration of people's courts throughout the country. With this function, the SPC has the authority to establish unified, standardized, and efficient judicial administrative work mechanisms in people's courts for institutional arrangements, duties of leadership, business scope, allocation of responsibilities, and work procedures.[59] Under the people's congress system, the SPC does not have direct control over the lower courts' appointments and budgets. The SPC, however, has the power to adopt rules to maintain judicial uniformity in the nation and to regulate the judicial practice of all people's courts. In this regard, the SPC rules are binding on people's courts at every level.

The fourth function is judicial interpretation. This is the competence of the SPC over the application of law. As explained later, judicial interpretation is an important function of the SPC and also an area that often causes confusion. The interpretation defined as "judicial" not only represents a statutory limit on the power of the SPC pertaining to the application of law, but also signifies the difference between the Chinese judiciary and the judiciary in other countries.

C. *Judicial Interpretation*

Again, under the people's congress system, the Chinese judiciary does not have the power to make law. As noted, the law-making authority in China rests exclusively with the legislative branch, namely the NPC and its Standing Committee. The executive branch is empowered to adopt administrative regulations that are not inconsistent with the law enacted by the people's congress. Under the 1982 Constitution and the Legislation Law, the Chinese judiciary does not have the power to interpret law but to implement and apply the law. A major form of the implementation of law by the judiciary is judicial interpretation.

Given the constitutional limit on judicial power, legal interpretation in China is divided into two different categories: legislative interpretation and judicial interpretation. Legislative interpretation is the interpretation of law by the legislature, while judicial interpretation only concerns the application of the laws. The former is purposed to tell what the law is, and the latter is aimed at making sure the law is to be applied as intended by the legislature.

[59] See the SPC, *Opinions on Several Issues Concerning the Improvement of Judicial Administration to Meet the Requirement of Justice for the People*, issued on December 30, 2003, available at www.chinalawedu.com/falvfagui/fg22598/6461.shtml.

Pursuant to the 1982 Constitution, the power of interpretation of law is exclusively in the hands of the Standing Committee of the NPC. In addition, the Legislation Law of China explicitly provides that the authority to interpret the law belongs to the Standing Committee of the NPC.[60] In accordance with article 45 of the Legislation Law, the Standing Committee of the NPC shall make interpretation of a law if the specific meaning of a provision of such law requires further clarification or a new situation arises after the enactment of such law, requiring clarification on its application.[61]

Article 46 of the Legislation Law further provides that if a need for an interpretation of law arises, the SPC may make a request to the Standing Committee of the NPC for interpretation.[62] The underlying notion of article 46 is that interpretation of law is an exercise of law-making power, and such power is reserved exclusively for the legislature. Thus, judicial interpretation refers only to the interpretation of the application of law. The Legislation Law recognizes the SPC's power to conduct judicial interpretation but does not make judicial interpretation a source of law.

In 1981, a year before the adoption of the 1982 Constitution, the Standing Committee of the NPC adopted a Resolution on Strengthening the Work of Interpretation of Law (1981 Resolution). In the 1981 Resolution, the Standing Committee of the NPC established a framework for the interpretation of law, which allows the SPC to exercise a limited power of interpretation. According to the 1981 Resolution, if the law itself needs to be clarified, the interpretation shall be made by the Standing Committee. But if the issue involves the specific application of law in the adjudication in the courts, the SPC may do the interpretation.[63]

The 1981 Resolution, still effective today, has several implications. First, legislative interpretation and judicial interpretation are two different legal interpretations. Second, legislative interpretation is within the domain of the Standing Committee of the NPC, and judicial interpretation is a function of the judiciary. Therefore, no people's court may interpret the law. Third, the SPC is the only body in the nation that has the authority to make judicial interpretation, and none of the lower courts may do so.

In addition to the 1981 Resolution, the Organic Law of the People's Courts, as noted, also provides the SPC with the power of judicial interpretation. Echoing the 1981 Resolution, article 32 of the Organic Law of People's Courts provides that the SPC conducts interpretation on issues concerning the specific application of laws

60 See Legislation Law of China 2000 (as amended 2023), art. 45, available at http://en.moj.gov.cn/2023-12/15/c_948358.htm.

61 See *id.*

62 See *id.*, art. 26.

63 See the Standing Committee of the NPC, *Resolutions on Strengthening the Work of Interpretation of Law* 1981, available at www.npc.gov.cn/wxzl/gongbao/2000-12/06/content_5004401.htm.

and decrees in judicial proceedings.[64] Article 32 of the Law of Organization of the People's Court, together with the 1981 Resolution, constitutes the statutory basis that limits the power of the SPC's judicial interpretation to the application of law only.

However, what has become problematic is how to differentiate between legislative interpretation and judicial interpretation. Since the line between legislative and judicial interpretation blurs in many cases, confusion always arises. Firstly, it is difficult, if not impossible, to separate interpretation of the application of law from the interpretation of law because, in judicial practice, the issue of application of law often involves what a provision of law actually means and how that provision should be applied.[65]

Secondly, a question commonly encountered is whether judicial interpretation has the same effect as legislative interpretation. Put differently, the question is whether judicial interpretation can be deemed as law in court proceedings.[66] In fact, when adjudicating cases, the people's courts are bound by the SPC's interpretation in their determination of the law to be applied. The determination as such not only involves how the law is to be applied but also concerns what the law is.

Thirdly, from a practical viewpoint, judges sitting on the bench often struggle with the issue of whether their judgment could rely solely on judicial interpretation.[67] In other words, it is an issue whether a court may explain (interpret) the meaning of the law that is to be applied in the way intended by the judicial interpretation without referring to the law. Since the SPC has no law-making power, a dilemma facing courts in judicial proceedings is whether a judgment could be made solely on the basis of the SPC judicial interpretation.

The lack of clarity on the distinctions between legislative interpretation and judicial interpretation often results in a "clash" between the legislature and the judiciary. On the one hand, the ambiguity makes it possible for the judiciary to step into the realm of interpretation of law while making judicial interpretation. On the other hand, the legislature may feel offended by the judiciary, and thus get antagonistic to the possible intrusion by the judiciary into the application of law.[68]

Take the corn seeds case, for example. On May 22, 2001, Plaintiff Yu Yang Seeds Co. claimed that they entered into a contract with defendant Yi Cuan County Seeds Co. Under the contract, the plaintiff agreed to provide the defendant with 4,857 *jin* of parent corn seeds (1 Chinese *jin* is equivalent to 1.1 lb), and

[64] See the Organic Law of People's Courts, *supra* note 1, art. 32.

[65] See Cao Shibing, *The Legal Status of the Judgment and Judicial Interpretation of the Supreme People's Court*, 3 Chinese Sci. L. 175–181 (2006), available at www.iolaw.org.cn/showNews.asp?id = 16296.

[66] See in general, Ji Cheng, Judicial Interpretation of the Supreme People's Court: A Preliminary Study (China University of Political Science and Law, 2007).

[67] See *id.*

[68] See Qian Kun, *The Constitutional Status of the Judicial Interpretation of the Supreme People's Court*, 1 Legal Sys. Soc. Dev. 115–135 (2025).

the defendant agreed to use them to reproduce 200,000 *jin* of hybrid corn seeds with a quality matching the national standard of second grade or above. The defendant defaulted on delivering hybrid corn seeds to the plaintiff, causing the plaintiff to suffer a loss of around RMB 1 million yuan. After several unsuccessful negotiations, the plaintiff brought a lawsuit at Luo Yang Intermediate People's Court, Henan Province.

The defendant argued that its failure to perform the contract was caused by a significant drop in production resulting from severe drought. With regard to the damage calculations, the plaintiff and the defendant disputed which law should be applied. At the time of the contract, there were two effective laws: one was a provincial regulation on the administration of corn seeds, and the other was the national Seeds Law. According to the provincial regulation, the purchasing and selling of seeds must strictly follow the price fixed by the provincial government. Under the national Seeds Law, however, corn seeds did not fall within the category of State-fixed or guided pricing, meaning that the price of corn seeds would have to be determined by market forces.

The judge ruled in favor of the plaintiff and granted relief calculated under the national Seeds Law. In her reasoning for the judgment, the judge held, in particular, that the provincial regulation is a local law which is subordinate to the national law in terms of legal effect, and any of its provisions that are in conflict with the national Seeds Law shall necessarily be void. In reaching the conclusion, the judge carefully examined the local regulations in light of the national law and made rational efforts to maintain the authority of the national law.

Article 79 of the Legislation Law explicitly provides that the legal authority of State law is higher than that of local law and regulations,[69] which means that any existing local law or regulation contradicting the newly enacted national law shall be void. In addition, under the Judge Law of China, judges are required to faithfully implement the Constitution and laws, and it is the obligation of the judges to strictly observe the Constitution and laws.[70]

When the judgment was handed down, however, it was immediately deemed offensive to the local government. The judge's opinion concerning the application of the Seeds Law over local regulations was considered an intrusion into local government power, and even more seriously, a violation of the Chinese people's congress system. On October 13, 2003, both the Office and Legal System Division of the Standing Committee of the People's Congress of Henan Province issued a

[69] The Legislation Law of China regulates the enactment, amendment, and repeal of laws, administrative regulations, local laws and regulations, regulations of autonomous regions, and specific regulations. See Legislation Law, *supra* note 56.

[70] The Judges Law was promulgated by the Standing Committee of the NPC on February 28, 1995, and then amended in 2001, 2017, and 2019, respectively, available at www.sls.org.cn/levelThreePage.html?id=10685, arts. 3 and 7.

notice condemning the judgment and urged the High People's Court of Henan to vigorously look into and handle this "serious matter."[71]

On October 21, 2003, the high people's court circulated a Notice of Criticism among its court system, characterizing the judgment as law-breaking conduct of the court that threatened the authority of local law and regulation as well as the unified legal system. Under tremendous pressure from the local government, the Luo Yang Intermediate People's Court issued a self-criticism notice internally on October 28, 2003, directly blaming the judge and her supervisor for failure to duly perform their duties as judges.

In its notice, the Intermediate Court stated that during trial, the people's court may only apply the law and has no authority to question the validity of local law and regulations. The Intermediate Court further stressed that no judgment shall ever contain anything that would render local law and regulations void.[72] As a punishment, the judge's work at the court was suspended. She was, however, reinstated several months later due to great sympathy nationwide for the judge and strong criticism from the legal community.

The case further sparked serious discussions on the following questions: (1) What law should the judge preserve and follow – national law or local law? (2) What would "unified legal system" really mean? (3) What would judicial power be under the Constitution? (4) Should a judge be held liable for his or her judgment? (5) What would be the real relationship between national law and local law? (6) Would the legislative body have the power to interfere with judicial matters?[73] The centerpiece of all those questions is the role of a judge in the application of law.

[71] See the Official Document of the Office of the Standing Committee of the People's Congress of Henan Province, Yu Fa Chang Ban (2003) No. 78, and Official Document of Legal System Division of the Standing Committee of the People's Congress of Henan Province, Yu Ren Chang Fa (2003) No. 18.

[72] See Official Notice of Luo Yang Intermediate People's Court, Luo Zhong Fa (2003) No. 147.

[73] In November 2003, a roundtable discussion on the Luo Yang case was held at Tsinghua University School of Law in Beijing. Attended by a number of constitutional law scholars, lawyers, and judges, the discussion dealt with several interesting questions arising from the Luo Yang case, and some of them seemed both controversial and sensitive: **Constitutional Questions**: (a) The relationship between legislation and the judiciary – who deals with what? (b) Review of law and constitutionality – should the people's court have any sort of judicial review power? (c) Division between national legislative power and local legislative power, and between central government authority and local government authority. (d) Judicial effect of a constitutionally legal question – what judicial effect should the Legislation Law have? (e) Understanding of the unified legal system – who has the obligation to maintain the unified legal system? **Judicial Questions**: (a) Are the judges state judges or local judges, and what should the judges protect? (b) Should there be legal reasoning in the court judgment, and how should such legal reasoning be written? (c) Is judicial independence the independence of the court or independence of the judge, and should the "trial committee" be abolished? (d) Relationship between a higher people's court and its lower people's courts – should the high people's court be responsible for the conduct of its lower people's courts?

It should be noted that in China, judicial interpretation is actually SPC interpretation because only the SPC has the power to make it. Under the Organic Law of People's Courts, it is the SPC that provides interpretation on the issues pertaining to the specific application of law in trial work.[74] It is also required in the Organic Law that a judicial interpretation by the SPC on the application of law be reviewed and approved by the judicial committee of the SPC before its issuance is released.[75]

In 2007, the SPC adopted the Provisions of Judicial Interpretation Work,[76] and the Provisions were revised in 2021.[77] According to the SPC, judicial interpretation can take five different forms, namely "interpretation," "provision," "rules," "reply," and "decision."[78] Another form considered by scholars to be equivalent to judicial interpretation is the SPC "notice."[79] Since notices mostly deal with announcements to call attention or to disseminate information, they do not carry much weight in substance.

In the 2021 Provisions, the SPC explicitly states that judicial interpretations issued by the SPC have legal effect.[80] But it remains highly debatable what the legal effect refers to, or whether the legal effect may mean a source of law. Some suggest to have the SPC's judicial interpretation defined as "applied legal interpretation."[81] Some NPC members (delegates) also propose to adopt a "law of judicial interpretation" to ascertain the legal status of the SPC's judicial interpretation.[82] Nevertheless, a common understanding is that the SPC's judicial interpretation is binding on all courts in the country, except for the courts in Hong Kong and Macau. In fact, the people's courts at various levels often rely on the SPC's judicial interpretation in their case adjudication, especially when the law at issue is ambiguous or unclear.

74 See the Organic Law of People's Courts, *supra* note 1, art. 18.

75 See *id.*, art. 37.

76 See SPC, *Provisions on the Judicial Interpretation Work* (promulgated March 9, 2007, effective April 1, 2007), CLI.3.89508(EN) (en.pkulaw.cn).

77 See SPC, *Provisions on the Judicial Interpretation Work*, revised on June 8, 2021, a full text available at http://gongbao.court.gov.cn/Details/b1a7af04dadc864fc2b87fd9bbe4dc.html (2021 *Revised Provisions*).

78 See *id.*, art. 6. According to the SPC, "interpretation" is to handle the issue concerning how to specifically apply a certain piece of law or how to apply the law to a specific type of case or matter in judicial practice; "provisions" refer to judicial interpretation made in lieu of regulations or opinions adopted on the basis of the need for judicial work pursuant to the legislative spirit; "rules" are the judicial interpretations regulating trial and execution activities of people's courts; "reply" is an interpretation in response to the request from higher people's courts or military courts for direction on the specific application of laws in the trial; and "decision" is the form employed by the Supreme People's Court to amend or repeal a judicial interpretation.

79 See Zhang Weiping, Civil Procedure Law, 16 (3rd ed., Law Press, 2013).

80 See SPC, 2021 *Revised Provisions*, *supra* note 73, art. 4.

81 See Kun, *supra* note 64, at 115.

82 See *id.*

3. JUDGES

Judges in the people's courts at each level are appointed by the Standing Committee of the people's congresses at the same level of government. The appointing Standing Committee also has the power to remove the judges so appointed. Before 2017, the total number of judges in the people's courts reached nearly 210,000. In 2017, as noted, a judge-quota system was implemented as part of judicial reform, which imposed a cap on the total number of judges in the people's courts.

As a result, there was a significant drop in the number of judges, down to 125,000 in 2018. In the meantime, the quality of judges in terms of educational background and professional credentials increased.[83] In the SPC, for example, the total number of judges was reduced from 642 to 367 in 2018 due to the quota restriction. Among the 367 judges, 119 judges held a doctoral degree, 205 judges held a master's degree, and 43 judges earned a bachelor's degree.

An issue that has faced Chinese courts for many years is judicial professionalism. In the early 1980s, a notorious move in China was to appoint a large number of military veterans to the judgeship in people's courts. The move caused tremendous damage to the image of the Chinese judiciary as a legal profession.[84] Not until 1995, when the Judges Law was adopted, did judicial professionalism become the center of attention. Since then, efforts have been made to improve the quality of judges. In the past decade, judicial reform has had a focus on the promotion of professionalism in the people's courts with a purpose to make the judiciary "regularized, specialized, and professionalized."[85]

A. *Qualification of Judges*

Judges in China are defined as trial personnel who exercise state adjudication powers in accordance with the law. Under the Judges Law, the judges include a president, vice presidents, members of the judicial committee, division heads, deputy division heads, and the adjudicating judges of all people's courts – military, specialized, and regular people's courts alike. Before 2019, the judges also included assistant judges. The 2019 Amendment to the Judges Law eliminated the category

[83] See the SPC, *Judicial Reform in Chinese Courts (2013–2018)*, White Paper, People's Court Press (February 2019), available at www.court.gov.cn/upload/file/2019/02/27/13/55/20190227135543_29566.pdf (hereinafter referred to as the *2019 SPC White Paper*). In 2024, the total number of judges in Chinese courts slightly increased to some 128,000. See Gao Qianqian, How Can the People's Courts Break the Dilemma of too Many Cases and too Few People to Handle Them? People's Court Daily, March 7, 2025.

[84] See He Weifang, *Military Veterans Going to Courts*, The Southern Weekend, January 2, 1998, a full text of the article is available at www.china-judge.com/fnsx3/fnsx2044.htm.

[85] See the 2019 *SPC White Paper*, *supra* note 79; see also Xiong Qiuhong, *The Reform on the Judges Quota System to Promote Judicial Elite*, People's Court Daily, July 7, 2017, available at www.chinacourt.org/article/detail/2017/07/id/2914083.shtml.

of assistant judge. The 2019 Amendment also raised the judge qualification threshold in people's courts.

Under the amended Judges Law, there are three sets of criteria for selecting judges. The first criterion consists of general requirements. In people's courts, a judge must (a) be a Chinese citizen; (b) uphold the Chinese Constitution, the leadership of the CPC, and the socialist system; (c) have good political and professional quality, and good moral character; and (d) be physically capable of performing the duties normally. Note that upholding the leadership of the CPC is a statutory requirement in China to become a judge.[86]

The second criterion concerns legal education and professional background. As provided in the Judges Law, a judge must be (a) a graduate from a law school with a bachelor of law degree or higher; (b) a graduate from an undergraduate college or above with a bachelor's degree in an area other than law, and a master of law (LL.M.) or juris master (J.M.) degree or higher; or (c) a graduate from a college with a bachelor's degree or above in any area other than law but having professional knowledge in law.[87] Simply put, to be a judge, a bachelor's degree is a minimum requirement, but it may not necessarily be in law. A judge could have a bachelor's degree in a non-legal area but must either have a master's degree in law or have professional knowledge in law.

The requirement of professional knowledge in law seems quite ambiguous. It mainly refers to legal work experience or bar membership. In certain places, however, if it is difficult to find someone who meets the legal education or knowledge requirements for being a judge, an exception may apply for a certain period of time upon review and approval by the SPC. In this situation, a simple bachelor's degree from a college would suffice.[88] The places to which the exception applies mostly include remote or minority areas.

The third criterion relates to legal background. Generally, five years of legal work experience is required to become a judge. For those who have obtained a master's degree in law or a Ph.D. degree in law, the required time length of legal work experience is reduced to four or three years, respectively.[89] In addition, under the 2019 amended Judges Law, those who are first appointed to the judgeship must also have passed a bar exam and obtained a lawyer qualification certificate.[90] This provision, however, does not apply to those who became judges before 2019, when the lawyer qualification certificate was not required.[91]

Also, prior to the 2019 Amendment, there was a provision in the Judges Law under which a judge should be at the age of twenty-three or older. This age requirement

86 See the Judges Law, *supra* note 66, art. 12 (1)(2)(3)(4).

87 See *id.*, art. 12 (5).

88 See *id.*, art. 12.

89 See *id.*, art. 12 (6).

90 See *id.*, art. 12 (7).

91 The bar membership requirement was added into the criteria for judges in the 2019 Amendment to the Judges Law.

provision was removed in the 2019 Amendment. But given the newly added education and work experience requirements, the minimum age for a judge now would have to be twenty-seven or older.[92] Another major change in the 2019 Amendment is that people's courts may, on an as-needed basis, openly select judges from those engaged in legal professions, such as lawyers and legal educators or researchers.[93]

In addition, pursuant to the Judges Law, persons not eligible to serve as a judge include: (a) those who have received criminal penalties and have been convicted of a crime; (b) those who have been expelled from public office; (c) those who have been disbarred, disqualified as a notary public, or removed from an arbitration commission; or (d) those in other situations provided for by law.[94] The meaning of "other situations" in category (d) is quite vague, which may cover any circumstance for excluding those who otherwise might be eligible to be a judge.

B. *Rights and Responsibilities of Judges*

As noted, judges in China have no life tenure, and are appointed and removed by the Standing Committee of the people's congress at their corresponding level. But in order to protect judges, the Judges Law provides judges with the following rights: (a) the authority and working conditions necessary to perform their duties; (b) job security and welfare benefits entitled to them for performing their duties; (c) legal protection of the safety of their person, property, and domicile; (d) ability to raise petitions or make accusations; and (e) other rights provided for by law.[95] The 2019 Amendment added a new provision that protects judges from being transferred, removed, demoted, or sanctioned for reasons other than those legally prescribed and without due legal process.[96]

In the meantime, judges are required to bear certain responsibilities. Under article 10 of the Judges Law, judges shall (a) strictly follow the Constitution and laws; (b) handle cases impartially and not bend the law for personal gain; (c) safeguard the procedural rights of parties and other litigation participants in accordance with law; (d) preserve national interests and societal public interests, and preserve the lawful rights and interests of individuals and organizations; (e) protect

[92] This age is calculated on the basis of the Chinese education system: 6 (starting at elementary school) + 12 (elementary, middle, and high schools) + 4 (undergraduate college study) + 5 (legal work experience).

[93] See the Judges Law, *supra* note 66, art. 15. In addition to meeting the requirements for a judge, lawyers participating in open selection shall have at least five years of actual practice, rich practice experience, and a good reputation; legal educators and researchers shall have an academic title of intermediate level or higher, and have been engaged in teaching or research for at least five years, with outstanding capacity for research and corresponding research accomplishments.

[94] See *id.*, art. 13.

[95] See *id.*, art. 11.

[96] See *id.*

state secrets and trial work secrets, and keep confidential the commercial secrets and private information learned during case hearings; (f) be under legal and general public oversight in accordance with law; (g) strengthen the public consciousness of the rule of law through handling cases and using cases to explain the law, and promote the construction of a rule-of-law society; and (h) perform other duties provided for by law.[97]

C. *Ranks and Promotion of Judges*

Judges in people's courts are ranked under categories and levels. The Judges Law divides the judge ranks into three categories and twelve levels. The three categories are justice, senior judge, and judge. The twelve levels include three levels of justices, four levels of senior judges, and five levels of judges. The three-level Justices refer to the Chief Justice, First-grade Justice, and Second-grade Justice. The president of the SPC is the Chief Justice.[98] The executive vice president of the SPC is normally the First-grade Justice, and all other vice presidents of the SPC and the chief judge at the high people's court are justices in the second grade.

The senior judges rank from grade one to grade four, while the judges are graded from one to five.[99] Entry-level judges generally work at the basic level people's courts.[100] The determination of judges' rank is based on such factors as personal integrity and ability, professional skill level, and years of trial practice and work.[101] In general, judges are promoted through a mechanism combining regular periodic promotions and selective promotions. Selective promotion is mainly based on merits. Judges in frontline case-handling positions who are either exceptional or especially needed for specific work can be particularly selected for promotion.[102] In addition, performance in judges' training is also an element for promotion consideration.[103]

As a promotion path, judges are usually to be selected incrementally up through the levels, meaning that promotion should normally be made level by level. The judges working in the SPC or High People's Courts, however, may be selected from the people's courts of two levels below. To be promoted to a higher-level people's court, a judge shall have served a certain number of years in the lower-level people's court and have work experience corresponding to the promoted position.

As noted, the judges in people's courts are all appointed by people's congresses. The selection of judges, however, is conducted through the people's courts.

[97] See *id.*, art. 10.
[98] See *id.*, art. 27.
[99] See *id.*, art. 26.
[100] See *id.*, art. 17.
[101] See *id.*, art. 28.
[102] See *id.*
[103] See *id.*, art. 32.

As required by the Judges Law, new judges should be selected on the basis of tests and assessment, and according to the merits of both ability and integrity, from those who meet the requirements for being a judge.[104] Thus, at the present time, in order to become a judge, the candidate must not only pass the bar exam but also pass the selection test and assessment.

The 2019 amended Judges Law contains a particular provision for the selection of the president, vice presidents, and members of the judicial committee. Under article 14 of the Judges Law, the president of a people's court shall possess legal expertise and experience in legal practice. It is further provided that the vice presidents and judicial committee members shall be chosen from among the judges, procurators, or other persons who are eligible for being selected as a judge.

Note that article 14 does not specify how the president of the people's court should be chosen because, in most cases, the presidents of people's courts are political appointees. Many in China regard article 14 as a provision helping ensure that the position of president or vice president of a people's court is held by a legal professional.[105] Some, however, have expressed concern that the requirement of legal expertise and experience for the president of a people's court might be too ambiguous to be manageable.[106]

D. *Evaluation and Removal of Judges*

Under the Judges Law, judges in people's courts are all subject to routine and annual reviews. The reviews are conducted by a committee of five to nine members in the judges' own courts, led by the court president.[107] The purpose of the reviews is to evaluate the judges in such aspects as actual trial work performance, professional ethics, professional skills, ability to work, as well as trial style. The focus of the evaluation is on the actual trial work performance of the judge.[108] The annual evaluation will be scored as outstanding (exceptional), competent (meets expectations), basic competence (needs some improvement), or incompetent (poor).[109]

Evaluation results are the basis for adjusting judges' rank and salary, and for rewards, punishments, removal, demotion, or dismissal. Judges' salaries are leveled in accordance with their duties and rank and raised periodically on a regular basis. A judge whose job performance is viewed as outstanding or competent in

[104] See *id.*, art. 14.
[105] See Zhou Qiang, *Explanations on the Draft Amendment to the Judges Law*, December 12, 2017, available at www.npc.gov.cn/zgrdw/npc/xinwen/2019-04/23/content_2086166.htm.
[106] See Legal Impression, *Why Was the Mayor Rather Than a Judge Chosen as the President of the County Court? People Are Pondering...*, April 1, 2020, available at www.yidianzixun.com/article/0PokVAyk?s = &appid.
[107] See the Judges Law, *supra* note 66, arts. 38–40.
[108] See *id.*, art. 41.
[109] See *id.*, art. 42.

evaluations may get a pay raise to the next level.[110] A judge who makes notable achievements or contributions in trial work, or has other prominent accomplishments, will be rewarded pursuant to the provisions of the law.[111]

On the other hand, a judge of a people's court can be removed at any time. But the removal may only be made by the appointing people's congress for cause. More specifically, the President of the SPC can be removed by the NPC, while the vice presidents, judicial committee members, division heads, deputy division heads, and other judges of the SPC and circuit courts can be removed by the Standing Committee of the NPC at the request of the SPC President. The president of all levels of local people's courts is removed by the people's congress at the corresponding level, and all other judges of local courts are removed by the Standing Committee of the same level of the people's congress at the request of the respective court president.[112]

The possible causes for removal of a judge need to have a statutory basis. Under the Judges Law, the causes for judge removal include (a) loss of Chinese citizenship; (b) job transfer out of the people's courts; (c) change in position so that the judgeship should not be retained, or personal request for being removed, upon approval, from the judge post; (d) incapability upon evaluation to successfully serve as a judge; (e) inability to perform judge's duties for a long time due to illness; (f) retirement; (g) resignation or discharge in accordance with law; and (h) unsuitability to continue holding the office due to violations of discipline or law.[113]

A judge may resign from the bench upon approval. But, within two years after the resignation, a resigned judge is prohibited from serving as an agent *ad litem* or defender in the capacity of a lawyer. More restrictively, a resigned judge may never serve as an agent *ad litem* or defender handling cases in their previous people's court, except where the resigned judge is the guardian of a party, or the party represented is a close relative.[114] But a judge who is dismissed from the people's court may not serve as an agent *ad litem* or defender at all, unless the judge is the party's guardian or an agent *ad litem* or defender of a close relative.[115]

[110] See *id.*, art. 59.

[111] See *id.*, art. 44. Also, under article 45 of the Judges Law, judges shall be given rewards under any of the following circumstances: (a) outstanding accomplishment in preserving judicial justice; (b) significant achievements in drawing experience from trial practice so as to play a guiding role for trial work; (c) notable achievements and contributions in handling major cases, dealing with emergencies, and undertaking important special work projects; (d) proposal for reforms of trial work that has been accepted with noticeable effect; (e) judicial recommendations that have been adopted, or engagement in increasing public awareness of the rule of law or in guiding mediation organizations to mediate various kinds of disputes with striking results; or (f) other achievements.

[112] See *id.*, art. 18.

[113] See *id.*, art. 20.

[114] See *id.*, art. 36.

[115] See *id.*

4. PEOPLE'S ASSESSORS

People's assessors are not judges, but members of a collegial panel sitting with a professional judge to try cases, both civil and criminal, of the first instance in the people's courts. The mechanism of people's assessors is deemed an important part of the Chinese judicial system. The mechanism was created along with the founding of the People's Republic of China. The underpinning theory is that in a socialist country with a people's democratic dictatorship, all power belongs to the people, and therefore, the judicial power, which is an important part of state power, should also be handled and exercised with the participation of the people.

A. *Governing Rules*

The first legal provision governing the people's assessors was the Provisional Regulations on the Organization of the People's Courts, which was adopted in 1951.[116] Under article 6 of the Provisional Regulations, in order to facilitate the people's participation in the trial, the people's court should have a people's assessor system based on the nature of the case, and the people's assessors should have the right to assist in the investigation, participate in the trial, and express opinions.[117]

Three years later, in 1954, when the Constitution was adopted, it became a constitutional requirement that people's courts adjudicate cases under a people's assessor system in accordance with the law. This requirement, however, was removed in the 1975 Constitution. The 1982 Constitution is also silent about people's assessors. Before 2018, the Organic Law of People's Courts had a provision on people's assessors.[118] The 2018 Amended Organic Law of People's Courts dropped the provision and provides instead that people's courts shall accept oversight of the masses and safeguard the masses' enjoyment of the rights to know of, participate in, and supervise the people's courts' work in accordance with law.[119]

The current legislation of people's assessors is the Law of People's Assessors. Adopted in 2018, the Law of People's Assessors is aimed at ensuring citizens can participate in trial activities in order to promote judicial justice and enhance public confidence in the judiciary.[120] In February 2019, the SPC issued an Interpretation

[116] The Provisional Regulations on the Organization of the People's Courts was promulgated by the Central People's Government on September 4, 1951, available at www.npc.gov.cn/wxzl/wxzl/2000-12/10/content_4254.htm.

[117] See *id.*, art. 6.

[118] Under article 9 of the 2006 Organic Law of People's Courts, cases of first instance in the people's courts shall be tried by a collegial panel of judges or of judges and people's assessors; simple civil cases, minor criminal cases, and cases otherwise provided for by law may be tried by a single judge.

[119] See the Organic Law of People's Courts (as amended 2019), *supra* note 1, art. 11.

[120] The Law of People's Assessors was promulgated by the Standing Committee of the NPC on April 27, 2018, available at www.npc.gov.cn/zgrdw/npc/lfzt/rlyw/2018-04/27/content_2054207.htm.

on Several Issues Concerning the Implementation of the Law of People's Assessors.[121] The SPC's Interpretation provides detailed rules for the people's assessor system to operate.

Under the Law of People's Assessors, all citizens have a duty to serve as people's assessors,[122] and the people's assessors participating in the trial activities of the people's courts shall have the same rights as judges unless otherwise provided by law.[123]

Pursuant to the Law of People's Assessors, selection of people's assessors is made randomly from local residents based on household registration.[124] All people's assessors are appointed by the Standing Committee of the local people's congress upon recommendation by the president of the local people's court.[125]

B. *Selection of People's Assessors*

As a statutory requirement, the pool of candidates selected for people's assessors should be five times more than the number of people's assessors to be appointed.[126] The actual number of people's assessors is determined by the Standing Committee of the local people's congress upon the request of the trial court on needed basis.[127] But the total number of people's assessors may not be less than three times the number of judges in the local court.[128]

As required by the Law of People's Assessors, when people's assessors are needed in the collegial panel for a trial at the trial court, they shall be randomly selected from the roster of people's assessors on the court record.[129] If a case is tried for the first instance by an intermediate or a high people's court, which requires people's assessors to participate in the collegial panel for trial, they shall be randomly selected from the roster of people's assessors at the trial people's courts within the jurisdiction.[130]

To serve as a people's assessor, a candidate must meet the following criteria: (a) support the Chinese Constitution; (b) be at least twenty-eight years old; (c) comply with laws and regulations, have good character, be fair and decent; and (d) possess a good physical condition for normal performance of duties. The minimum

[121] See the SPC, *Interpretation on Several Issues Concerning the Implementation of the Law of People's Assessors*, issued on February 8, 2019, available at www.court.gov.cn/zixun-xiangqing-154792.html.

[122] See *id.*

[123] See the Law of People's Assessors, *supra* note 116, art. 2.

[124] See *id.*, art. 9.

[125] See *id.*, art. 10.

[126] See *id.*, art. 9.

[127] See *id.*, art. 8.

[128] See *id.*

[129] See *id.*, art. 19.

[130] See *id.*

education level for a people's assessor is completion of high school.[131] A college degree is preferred but not required for a people's assessor. The term of a people's assessor is five years and may not be renewed in general.[132]

There are two groups of people who may not serve as people's assessors. One is a "cannot" group, and the other is a "should not" group. Those who cannot serve include: (a) the members of the Standing Committee of the people's congress, the staff of the supervisory committee, people's court, people's procuratorate, public security department, national security bureau, or judicial administrative organ; (b) lawyers, public notaries, arbitrators, and grassroots legal service workers; and (c) other persons unsuitable to serve as people's assessors due to their public duties.[133]

People in the "should not" group are not allowed to serve as people's assessors as a matter of law. This group includes those (a) who have received criminal punishment; (b) who were fired from public office; (c) whose practice license as a lawyer or notary has been revoked; (d) who are listed as a person who lacks credibility; (e) who are dismissed as people's assessors as a result of punishment; and (f) who are in other serious violations of laws and disciplines that may affect public confidence in the judiciary.[134]

C. *Role of People's Assessors*

During the trial, the people's assessors and judges form a collegial panel. The trial should be presided over by a judge. The collegial panel can be a three-person panel or a seven-person panel.[135] If a seven-person collegial panel is formed, there should be three judges and four people's assessors. It is interesting to note that in the three-person collegial panel, people's assessors may independently express their opinions on the determination of facts and the application of the law, and have the right to vote on the judgment,[136] while in the seven-person collegial panel, the people's assessors may vote on the determination of facts, but not on the application of law.[137]

When the collegial panel evaluates a case, the presiding judge is required to provide the people's assessors with necessary explanations and explanations on such

[131] See *id.*, art. 5.

[132] See *id.*, art. 13.

[133] See *id.*, art. 6.

[134] See *id.*, art. 7.

[135] Under the Law of People's Assessors, a seven-person collegial panel shall be formed in any of the following cases: (1) criminal cases involving a sentence of fixed-term imprisonment of more than ten years, life imprisonment, the death penalty, or having significant social impact; (2) public interest litigation cases filed under the Civil Procedure Law and Administrative Procedure Law; (3) cases involving such cases of significant social impacts as land acquisition and demolition, ecological environmental protection, and food and drug safety; or (4) other socially significant cases. See *id.*, art. 16.

[136] See *id.*, art. 21.

[137] See *id.*, art. 22.

matters as fact determination, evidence rules, legal provisions, and other issues that should be noted in the case.[138] In its evaluation of cases, the collegial panel is governed by the rule of majority control. If a people's assessor dissents from the majority, the dissenting opinions shall be taken into the record. If the opinions of the members of the collegial panel differ significantly, the people's assessors or judges may request the collegiate panel to refer the case to the president of the people's court for a decision on whether a judicial committee's action should be called.[139]

5. JUDICIAL INDEPENDENCE: CONCEPT AND REALITY

Judicial independence has long been an issue in China, and the Chinese courts are reputed both at home and abroad as having a lack of independence. In the Western world, judicial independence is deemed a cornerstone of both democracy and the rule of law.[140] Conceptually, judicial independence is defined in various ways. But in essence, it may refer to the "preservation of a separate institution of government that can adjudicate cases or controversies with impartiality."[141] In a narrower sense, judicial independence may mean "the principle that judges must decide cases fairly and impartially, relying only on the facts and the law."[142]

A. *Concept of Judicial Independence*

A theoretical foundation of judicial independence is the doctrine of separation of powers, which "elevates the judiciary to the status of a co-equal branch" of government.[143] According to Montesquieu, "there is no liberty, if the power of judging be not separated from the legislative and executive powers."[144] Thus, it is deemed vitally important in a democracy to make "individual judges and the judiciary as a whole impartial and independent of all external pressures" so that those who appear before

[138] See *id.*, art. 20.

[139] See *id.*, art. 23.

[140] See Courts and Tribunals Judiciary (CTJ), *Independence*, available at www.judiciary.uk/about-the-judiciary/the-judiciary-the-government-and-the-constitution/jud-acc-ind/independence/; see also American College of Trial Lawyers (ACTL), *Judicial Independence: A Cornerstone of Democracy, Which Must Be Defended*, available at www.actl.com/docs/default-source/default-document-library/position-statements-and-white-papers/actl_judicial_independence_a_corner stone_of_ democracy.pdf?sfvrsn = 4; and Mia Swart, *Independence of the Judiciary*, in Oxford Constitutional Law, available at https://oxcon.ouplaw.com/view/10.1093/law-mpeccol/law-mpeccol-e339.

[141] See Irving Kaufman, *The Essence of Judicial Independence*, 80 Columbia L. Rev. 671, 688 (1980).

[142] See ACTL, *Judicial Independence*, *supra* note 136.

[143] See Kaufman, *supra* note 137, at 688.

[144] See Charles de Montesquieu, *The Spirit of the Laws* (1748), Excerpts, available at https://ca01001129.schoolwires.net/cms/lib/CA01001129/Centricity/Domain/270/MontesquieuSpiritLawsTextBioVocab.pdf.

them and the public in general "can have confidence that their cases will be decided fairly" and justly.[145]

It is also believed that judicial independence equips the judges with the freedom "to decide individual cases according to their view of the law as necessary to protect the liberty of" the individual party.[146] By freedom, it means that judges can exercise their judicial powers without interference from anyone, public or private, and without any improper influence. Thus, although the view on the value of individual liberty may vary in different societies, there is a belief that an independent judiciary helps promote the efficient administration of a complex social system.[147]

China, however, was and still is antagonistic toward the Western concept of judicial independence. A major reason is that the maintenance of the CPC's absolute control over the country precludes any idea or approach that might be conceived as a possible force to weaken the CPC's leadership. Another reason is that under the people's congress system led by the CPC, as noted, there is no separation of powers, but merely an allocation of powers among government branches in the country. Consequently, the public conscience and awareness of judicial independence are significantly overshadowed by the extensive power of the CPC-led government.

Nevertheless, there is, at least on paper, a Chinese version of judicial independence in the nation. Under article 78 of the 1954 Constitution, people's courts conduct trials independently and only obey the law.[148] Many in China regard article 78 as a clear constitutional basis for the independent exercise of judicial power by the people's courts.[149] But it is important to note that the provision of article 78 referred only to adjudicatory independence rather than judicial independence. The provision of article 78 was later contained verbatim in the 1954 Organic Law of People's Courts.[150]

In both the 1975 and 1978 Constitutions, the adjudicatory independence clause was removed. The ground for removal was that a socialist country should not allow independence of adjudication because of its bourgeois or capitalist character.[151] The 1982 Constitution reinstates the adjudicatory independence clause but in a modified provision. According to article 131 of the 1982 Constitution (as amended 2018), the

145 See the CTJ, *Independence*, *supra* note 136.

146 See Thomas Plank, *The Essential Elements of Judicial Independence and the Experience of Pre-Soviet Russia*, 5 Wm. & Mary Bill Rts. J. 1, 3 (1996).

147 See *id*.

148 See the 1954 Constitution of China, art. 78, available at http://en.pkulaw.cn/display.aspx?cgid=52993&lib=law.

149 See Han Dayuan, *On the Principle of Adjudication Independence in the 1954 Constitution*, 5 Chinese Juris. 5 (2016).

150 See the 1954 Organic Law of People's Courts, art. 4, available at www.cecc.gov/resources/legal-provisions/1954-prc-organic-law-of-the-peoples-courts-chinese-text.

151 See Han Dayuan, *The Constitutional Function of the Principle of Adjudication Independence*, 1 J. Soochow U. L. Edition 1 (2014).

people's courts exercise adjudicatory power independently in accordance with the provisions of law, and are not subject to interference by any administrative organ, social group, or individual.[152] The same provision is also found in the 2018 Amended Organic Law of People's Courts.[153]

Article 131 of the 1982 Constitution contains two essential elements: adjudicatory independence and being free from interference. Based on these elements, article 131 is deemed by many in China as a judicial independence clause in the Constitution.[154] In their view, article 131 is both a constitutional principle and a judicial activity rule. As a constitutional principle, it confirms the exclusivity and independence of the judicial power of people's courts, while as a rule of judicial activity, it ensures the exercise of the judicial power of the people's courts and their judicial activities are protected from any improper external interference, influence, and control.[155]

But the judicial independence, if any, as provided and understood in China, has several notable features. First, it focuses on the adjudicatory power of the courts, not necessarily the judges. Second, it does not treat the judiciary as a separate and co-equal branch of the government. Third, "free from interference" has a limited scope, leaving the door open to the CPC or CPC-led legislature for possible intervention. Lastly, the independent adjudicatory power is required to be exercised "in accordance with the provisions of law." This requirement not only downgrades the adjudicatory independence from a constitutional power to a statutory power but also provides a legal basis for the legislature to impose limits on the independence.

B. *Chinese Reality*

Thus, theoretically, the people's courts are granted independent adjudicatory power under the Constitution and the law. In reality, however, it remains difficult, if not impossible, for the people's courts to exercise their power independently. There are many obstacles that would jeopardize the independence of the people's courts. One major obstacle is the power of the CPC. As discussed, in the 2018 Amendment to the 1982 Constitution, the leadership of the CPC is held as the defining feature of socialism with Chinese characteristics.[156] Therefore, it has become the preeminent mission for every sector of the country, including the judiciary, to preserve the absolute leadership of the CPC.

[152] See the 1982 Constitution, art. 131, available at https://npcobserver.files.wordpress.com/2018/12/PRC-Constitution-2018.pdf.

[153] See the Organic Law of People's Courts (amended as 2018), *supra* note 1, art. 4.

[154] See Dayuan, *supra* note 147, at endnote 1.

[155] See *id.*

[156] See the 2018 Amendment to the 1982 Constitution, available at www.fdi.gov.cn/1800000121_39_4866_0_7.html.

Take the SPC, for example. Under the Constitution, the SPC is the highest judicial body of the nation. But the SPC is first and foremost viewed as a political institution, and its political nature, according to an official statement, is determined by the country's state and political system, and by the nature and tasks of the people's courts.[157] The SPC must report not only to the NPC but also to the CPC central committee. In addition, all people's courts in the country are required to adhere firmly to the CPC's leadership in judicial work, and to ensure full implementation of the CPC central committee's policies and decisions.[158]

Another obstacle is the relationship between the people's courts and other government branches. As noted, under the people's congress system, people's courts are subordinate to the people's congresses. Thus, the work of the judiciary is all under the supervision and oversight of the people's congresses. Put differently, the people's congresses at all levels do have the power to "interfere" with the judiciary and may do so whenever they see fit or necessary.

Although the judiciary and administration are equal under the people's congresses, the judiciary is often influenced by the administration, especially at local levels. Structurally, at the provincial or lower levels of government, there is always a deputy governor or mayor who is designated to provide oversight of the political and legal affairs that include the work of people's courts, procuratorates, and public security. Therefore, from the administrative viewpoint, the president of a people's court is also responsible to the local administrative officer in charge.

A potential form of control the administration has over the judiciary is administrative authority over the personnel management and operation costs of the people's court. The headcounts of the people's courts, including judges, are subject to the local government's staffing plans and quota. The expenses of operation and the judges' salaries at each court are allocated under the local government budget of the same level. This institutional defect inevitably facilitates local influence and unavoidably affects the independence of the people's courts.[159] As noted, since 2014, in order to avoid local influence, there has been an effort to reform the judicial budgetary system by transferring court fund allocation authority from the local government to the provincial government. But the reform in this regard remains far from completion.

A third obstacle relates to the internal structure of the people's courts that constitutes hurdles affecting the exercise of independence in case adjudication. The most notable hurdle is the judicial committee. As discussed, the judicial

[157] See Zhou Qiang, *Strengthen the Consciousness of Political Organs, Enhance the Party Construction in the Courts, and Better Fulfill the Mission of the People's Courts in the New Era*, in the Party Lecture to the Party Member of the SPC, June 24, 2020, available at www.court.gov.cn/zixun-xiangqing-238251.html.

[158] See *id*.

[159] See Zhou Wei & Xie Weiyan, Constitution Textbook, 230–231 (Sichuan University Press, 2012).

committee is a decision-making body in the court. Any case, if considered sensitive in terms of national security, diplomacy, or social stability, or if deemed significant, difficult, or complex, must be reported to the judicial committee for review before or during the court hearings.[160] In addition, there are some other cases that could be submitted to the judicial committee for opinions.[161]

The problem is that when reviewing the case, the judicial committee makes its decision based only on the collegial panel's presentation in the closed-door meetings. Thus, although the judicial committee is not the trier of a case, it makes the final decision for the case. During its deliberation, the judicial committee may reject the opinion of the collegial panel and enter a different judgment. Once a decision is made by the judicial committee, the collegial panel must accept it even if the panel disagrees with the decision. Many in China have serious doubts that, given the power of the judicial committee, the collegial panel may adjudicate the case independently.[162]

The second hurdle is court administrative interference. The president of a people's court is both the chief judge and the chief executive. The president has the power to influence the promotion and demotion of any judge in the court, and to supervise the trial work of all judges. For certain cases, the judgment made by the collegial panel must be reviewed and approved by the president, or by the division head who directly reports to the president, before the judgment is released.

As noted, the president of a people's court is mostly a political appointee and thus has to listen to the local government. A scenario that often occurs is that the president of a people's court cannot, or would not be able to, resist the intervention

[160] According to the SPC, the following cases tried by people's courts at all levels shall be submitted to the judicial committee for discussion and decision: (1) sensitive cases involving national security, diplomacy, and social stability, as well as major, difficult, and complex cases; (2) judgments, rulings, mediation documents, etc. made by the court that have already taken effect but have been found wrong so as to require a retrial; (3) the people's procuratorate at the same level filed a protest in a criminal case according to the trial supervision procedure; (4) new types of cases where the application of laws is unclear; (5) the case in which the defendant is to be acquitted; and (6) cases where criminal punishment is to be made below the statutory sentence or an exemption from criminal punishment is to be granted. In addition, when a high people's court or an intermediate people's court intends to impose the death penalty, the case shall be submitted to the judicial committee. See the SPC, *Opinions on Perfecting the Working Mechanism of the People's Court Judicial Committee*, *supra* note 43, art. 8.

[161] See *id.*, art. 9 (The following cases may be submitted to the judicial committee: (1) the collegial panel disagrees greatly on the application of law, and it is difficult to make a decision after a professional [presiding] judges meeting; (2) cases where the proposed judgment may conflict with the kind of judgment made by the court or a higher court; (3) people's procuratorates at the same level filed major, difficult, and complicated civil and administrative cases in protest in accordance with the trial supervision procedures; (4) cases involving orders for new trial or remand for retrial; and (5) other cases that need to be submitted to the judicial committee).

[162] See He Weifang, *Amending the Organic Law of Chinese Courts and Judicial Independence*, available at https://carnegieendowment.org/pdf/2005-04-18/he_remarks.pdf; see also Chen Huijing, *An Analysis of Judicial Committee*, available at www.chinacourt.org/article/detail/2012/03/id/476449.shtml.

by external forces during the trial of a case when local interests are at stake or a request comes from a prominent local government official. The *corn seeds* case exemplifies exactly how the president of a people's court acts under the pressure of local government to intervene.

Another hurdle is concerned with the internal reporting and supervision system. The system is designed to deal with the issue of the application of law in cases where the lower court is unclear about the law to be applied or the law in question is subject to different interpretations. The system, however, has always been expanded to the extent that the lower court must ask the superior court for its opinion about how a particular case should be handled. On the other hand, the superior court also from time to time instructs a lower court to adjudicate a specific case in a particular way.[163]

[163] See Wang Liming & Yao Hui, *Research on the People's Court Organizational Format and the Reform of Trial Methods (Part 2)*, 2000, available at www.law-lib.com/lw/lw_view.asp?no = 221; see also Wu Ruyu & Huang Jinbo, *Pros and Cons of the Case Report and Ask System and Its Way Out*, People's Court Daily, August 30, 2013, available at http://rmfyb.chinacourt.org/paper/html/2013-08/30/content_69937.htm?div = -1.

6

Legal Education in China and the Chinese Bar

INTRODUCTION

Effective implementation and sound development of the law would not be possible without legal professionals. The quality and qualification of legal professionals largely depend on legal education and training. Legal education is the tool or vehicle to prepare for career engagement in legal practice as well as enforcement. In order to practice law, however, a professional membership is normally required. The professional membership not only serves as an indicator of qualification or eligibility for a profession, but also demonstrates the minimum level of skills and knowledge that are often required for legal professionals, lawyers in particular.

Legal professionals in China have been in short supply ever since the founding of the People's Republic in 1949. There are several reasons for this. First, as noted, when the Communist Party of China (CPC) took control over the country, it abolished all existing laws. All of a sudden, the legal professionals who had worked under the old legal system found themselves with no role to play in the newly established government. On the other hand, the suspicion about their loyalty and allegiance to the new government substantially prevented those legal professionals from actively being engaged in any legal work.

Second, the abolishment of the old legal system brought the legal infrastructure of the country almost to ground zero on day one of the new government. As a result, the reformation of the legal system had to follow Mao's "plain paper" theory and eventually copied the former Soviet Union. The adoption of the 1954 Constitution at the first assembly meeting of the National People's Congress (NPC) marked the beginning of the legal system being rebuilt under the socialist fiber. In the meantime, an effort was put into place to boost legal education to meet the urgent need for legal professionals. Unfortunately, the effort was interrupted due to the Anti-Rightist Movement and the Great Leap Forward campaign.

Third, during the decade-long Cultural Revolution from 1966–1976, almost every law school was dissolved, and law school faculty members were either dispatched to the countryside for labor-intensive reeducation or transferred to work in non-legal areas. As a result, there were barely any law graduates in that period, which caused a generational gap in legal professionals in the nation. Not until 1977 did legal education start to resume with the restoration of law schools.

1. CHINESE LEGAL EDUCATION

The last four decades have witnessed a revival and rapid development of Chinese legal education. The most striking change has been the exponential growth of law schools and law school enrollment. In addition, since the judicial examination was first administered in 1986, licensed legal professionals not only have expanded significantly in numbers, but also have gradually become major players in the legal arena. But the role of legal professionals in shaping the country's legal system has not reached the level it should. Limitations remain immense.

A. *An Historical Review*

Modern legal education in China can be traced back as early as 1862, when a government school known as *Tong Wenguan* (the School of Combined Learning) was created to teach Western languages and science. The founding of *Tong Wenguan* was part of the effort made by the late Qing government to learn from the West. Among the courses offered in *Tong Wenguan* was international law. William A. P. Martin (*Ding Weiliang* in Chinese), an American Presbyterian missionary to China, who served as a head instructor of *Tong Wenguan*, translated Henry Wheaton's famous book "Elements of International Law" into Chinese. It is believed in China that the norms of modern international relations addressed in the book played a special role in modernizing diplomacy in the late *Qing* Dynasty.[1]

In 1895, the *Qing* government established a new type of school named "*Tianjin Zhongxi* Academy," which offered a four-year higher education program. Included in the course curriculum of the school, among others, was public law. More notably, the school offered special subjects for students in their second year. The special subjects were divided into five different disciplines, including engineering, electricity, mining, machine science, and law.[2] It is commonly held in China that the law course offering and the classification of law as an independent discipline at *Tianjin Zhongxi* Academy marked the beginning of modern legal education in the country.[3]

[1] See Tian Tao, *Ding Weiliang and Elements of International Law*, 5 Soc. Sci. Res. 107 (1999), available at www.ixueshu.com/document/c99e4ff167e446cb318947a18e7f9386.html.

[2] See Li Shi, History of Education in Qing Dynasty, Deep into China Histories (DeepLogic E-book, 2019).

[3] In 2018, Tsinghua University Law School organized a roundtable discussion attended by the deans of Tsinghua University, Peking University, and Renmin University, and the President of

In 1898, the Imperial University of Peking (IUP), now Peking University, was established as the first comprehensive university under the central government. At its inception, the IUP offered legal courses to students in advanced political science. In 1902, the Political Science Department formally started to offer law courses authorized by the *Qing* government. In January 1904, the law section was established within the Political and Legal School.[4]

In 1903, *Tianjin Zhongxi* Academy was restructured and renamed *Peiyang* University, the predecessor of what is now Tianjin University.[5] In 1917, the whole section of law at *Peiyang* University was transferred to the Imperial University of Peking. Two years later in 1919, the Department of Law was officially formed at the Imperial University of Peking.[6] In 1930, the Department of Law was upgraded to the School of Law. At that time, the law school consisted of three departments: political science, economy, and law.[7]

In 1912, *Chaoyang* University was founded in Beijing. It was the first university in China that specialized in law, and soon became a famous institution for legal study and research during the Republic period. Another university that impacted Chinese legal education was Methodist University or *Dongwu* University (also called *Soochow* University), a private university established in 1900 in *Su Zhou*. In 1915, *Dongwu* University created a Comparative Law College of China in Shanghai, which was actually the Law School of *Dongwu* University.[8] There was an old saying about legal study and research in China during that time, which was "*Chaoyang* in the north and *Dongwu* in the south," referring to the two best places for legal pursuits. A more specific description about those two law schools was that "*Chaoyang* produces judges while *Dongwu* makes lawyers."[9]

In addition to *Chaoyang* and *Dongwu* law schools, there were many other law schools or departments operating in the country. In 1928, when the Republic government finally achieved unification of the south and north of the nation, quite

China University of Political Science and Law. The discussion reviewed some major events in the development of legal education in China. The summary of the roundtable discussion was published as China's Legal Education in the Past Forty Years of Reform and Opening Up, 3 China L. Rev., 2018, available at www.iolaw.org.cn/showNews.aspx?id=67920 (hereinafter referred to as 2018 Roundtable Discussion).

4 See Peking University Law School, *Introduction*, PULS Webpage, available at http://en.law.pku.edu.cn/overview/history/index.htm, accessed August 23, 2025.

5 See *Introduction* to Tianjin University, Tianjin U. Webpage, available at www.tju.edu.cn/tdgk/xxjj.htm, accessed August 23, 2025.

6 See Peking University Law School, *supra* note 4.

7 See *id.*

8 See Zeng Tao, *The International Law Education and Soochow University Law School*, 1 China Legal Educ. Res., 2009, available at http://cesl.cupl.edu.cn/upload/201103224081685.pdf. See also He Qinghua, *Inheritance of Huazheng: Legacy of Soochow University Law School*, Legal Daily, February 11, 2020, available at www.legaldaily.com.cn/index/content/2020-02/11/content_8114462.htm.

9 See Qinghua, *supra* note 8.

a large number of law schools experienced a structural change. Take *Tsinghua* University, for example. It was formed in 1911 as an overseas study preparation school. In 1928, the school was expanded and renamed National *Tsinghua* University. During the same year, *Tsinghua* Law School was created. Another example is *Wuhan* University. It was called *Wuchang* University until 1928, when it was restructured.

The 1949 was a turning point in Chinese legal education. The abolishment of the law and legal system operating under the Republic regime resulted in a completely different legal learning environment. In 1949, *Chaoyang* University was changed to China University of Politics & Law, and one year later in 1950, it was merged into *Renmin* University. *Dongwu* University was dissolved in 1944 due to the invasion of Japanese troops, then resumed in 1945 under the name of China Eastern University. In 1949, all foreign faculty members hired by *Dongwu* University were expelled and the Univerity ceased to operate. In 1951, *Dongwu* University was rebuilt in Taiwan under the English name "*Soochow* University."

In order to meet the need for the development of socialism led by the CPC, China reconstructed the nation's education system and shuffled all educational institutions in the country in 1952 (1952 Reconstruction). The purpose was to transform the education system from the Anglo-American style in the Republic of China into the Soviet style focusing on developing engineering universities/colleges and reducing the number of comprehensive universities. During that period, many well-known universities with long histories were dismantled, and the number of comprehensive universities dropped significantly. Instead, many single-discipline and specialized universities across the country were established. In addition, all previous private and church-run universities were eliminated.

As a result, the total number of colleges and universities nationwide was reduced from 211 to 182, including 14 comprehensive universities, 39 engineering colleges, 31 normal (teachers) colleges, 29 agricultural and forestry colleges, 29 medical colleges, 4 politics and law colleges, 6 financial colleges, 15 art colleges, 8 language colleges, 5 sports colleges, and 2 ethnic colleges.[10] The most notorious feature of the 1952 educational reconstruction under the Soviet model was that engineering studies were overly emphasized in contrast to science, humanities, and social sciences. Politics and law were especially weakened.[11]

The four law colleges were Beijing, East China, Central South, and Southwest Colleges of Politics and Law. In addition, there was a law department at *Renmin*

[10] There were 211 colleges and universities prior to 1952, but the number was down to 201 by the end of 1952, and further down to 182 in 1953. See Li Gang, *The End of Universities – "Higher Education Adjustment" in the Early 1950s*, 8 China's Reform, 2003, available at www.aisixiang.com/data/3481.html.

[11] See Chen Hui, *Adjustment of Chinese Colleges and Universities in 1952 – The Consequences of "Following the Soviet Model,"* 3 Mod. China Stud., 2003, available at www.modernchinastudies.org/cn/issues/past-issues/82-mcs-2003-issue-3/1309-1952-.html.

University, *Wuhan* University Law, and Northeast *Renmin* University (now *Jilin* University), respectively. For reconstruction purposes, the law colleges or departments at all other universities were merged into those law colleges and departments.[12]

In 1954, the *Peking* University Law Department was restored, bringing the total number of law departments to four. In 1958, Northwest College of Political Science and Law was formed, becoming the fifth law college. At that time, legal education in China was undertaken mainly in those law colleges and departments, commonly called "Five Colleges and Four Departments." But, due to the Anti-Rightist Movement and particularly the Cultural Revolution, legal education in China was mostly paralyzed until 1977 when the national college entrance examination resumed.

The year 1977 is historical in modern China because it was the year that the higher education in China resumed to normal after the decade-long political chaos in the nation. Along with the normalization, the country's legal education was revived. In 1977, three universities, *Peking* University, *Jilin* University, and *Hubei* College of Finance and Economy, started to offer degree programs majoring in law, and enrolled 182 students in total throughout the nation.

After 1977, legal education in China developed dramatically from recovery to growth and then from growth to stabilization.[13] The recovery was from 1977 to 1992 during which most of the previous law schools (departments) were restored or rebuilt. In 1988, for example, the number of law schools in the country exceeded 80. Following the recovery was the period of growth running from 1992 to 2012. The most remarkable feature of the growth period was that law schools boomed. In 2005, the total number of law schools climbed up to 559.[14] It then kept growing to reach a peak of 639 law schools in the country in 2012.[15]

Since 2012, the development of legal education in the country has entered into a relatively steady period. The center of attention then shifted from quantitative growth to the maintenance of quality and substance of legal teaching and learning. The freshman enrollment (majoring in law) of the law schools nationwide currently is around 80,000. On the one hand, all non-regular legal educational institutions and programs that mushroomed in the growth period were phased out, including self-learning law programs, correspondence law school, television law school, evening law programs, as well as vocational law school.[16] In 2024, there were about

[12] For example, the law schools at both Peking University and Tsinghua University joined Beijing College of Political Science and Law. Chaoyang University became the Law Department of Renmin University. The law departments of nine universities including Fudan University, St. John's University, and Soochow University were merged into East China College of Political Science and Law.

[13] See the 2018 Roundtable Discussion, *supra* note 3.

[14] See Jianfu Chen, Chinese Law: Context and Transformation, 167, footnote 85 (Nijhoff, 2008).

[15] See the 2018 Roundtable Discussion, *supra* note 3.

[16] See *id.*

625 universities and colleges that offer law degrees, but only 313 law schools were listed in a national law school ranking system.

On the other hand, a national effort was made to standardize the legal education and requirements for law schools. The effort led to the issuance of the National Standards for Teaching Quality of Undergraduate Major in Law in Regular Universities and Colleges by the Ministry of Education (MOE) in 2018 (National Standards).[17] The National Standards not only set the minimum standards for the basic legal education, but also establish a mechanism for the formation of law schools or legal programs. Under the National Standards, no new law school may be created without review and approval by the Higher Education Teaching Steering Committee organized by the MOE.

B. *Chinese Higher Education System and Structure*

Higher education in China is primarily run by the State and centrally administered by the MOE.[18] The primary responsibilities of the MOE include the overall planning, coordination, and management of all forms of education at various levels; formulating standards for schools of all types at various levels; guiding the reform of education and teaching methods; providing guidance for the supervision over education nationwide; developing strategies, policies, and plans for educational reform and development; and drafting and implementing relevant rules and regulations.[19]

Most of the universities in China are public universities, and they are either under the direct leadership of the MOE (MOE universities) or administered by provincial governments (provincial universities). Currently, there are seventy-five major universities that are MOE universities. Many of the MOE universities have law schools, but there is only one university specializing in law directly under the MOE.[20]

[17] The National Standards cover all majors in higher education in China. The Standards for the Law Major, which was issued on April 10, 2018, are available at www.calaw.cn/article/default.asp?id=12649.

[18] See the Higher Education Law of China, adopted in 1998 by the Standing Committee of the NPC and amended in 2015 and 2018, available at www.npc.gov.cn/npc/c30834/201901/9df07167324c4a34bf6c44700fafa753.shtml. Under article 29 of the Law of Higher Education, the establishment of colleges and universities offering undergraduate education and above shall be subject to scrutiny and approval by the State Council's education administration. The establishment of colleges and universities engaging in specialized or vocational education shall be subject to examination and approval by the people's governments of the provinces, autonomous regions, and municipalities directly under the Central Government, and shall be reported to the State Council's education administration for the record.

[19] The full list of MOE's responsibilities is available at http://en.moe.gov.cn/about_MOE/what_we_do/.

[20] The MOE university specializing in law is China University of Political Science and Law. A list of MOE universities is available at www.moe.gov.cn/jyb_zzjg/moe_347/201708/t20170828_312562.html.

In addition, universities are further divided into different "bands" based on their strength and quality in certain areas, fields, programs, or disciplines, and on the mission they are expected to accomplish, set by the National Government. The bands are known as "211" universities, "985" universities, and "dual first class" universities.

The term "211" refers to the State education project focusing on construction of 100 colleges and universities and a number of key disciplines in the country during the twenty-first century. Approved by the State Council, the "211" project officially started in November 1995. The "211" project was considered a key construction project by the State in the field of higher education. It was a major part of the Chinese government's initiative to implement their strategy of "rejuvenating the country through science and education." A university on the "211" list not only enjoys "nation favored" status, but also retains eligibility for more fund allocation from the central government.[21] Although the "211" project was intended to include 100 colleges and universities, the actual number on the list reached 116.

The "985" is another major state education project. The purpose of the "985" project is to build world-class universities with world-class standards at the turn of the century, set by the CPC. The project is named "985" because it was declared on May 4, 1998 (98 refers to the last two digits of 1998, and 5 represents the fifth month of the year), by then-President Jiang Zemin. According to Jiang, "in order to achieve modernization, China must have a number of world advanced first-rate universit [ies] of the same level." In 1999, the State Council approved the MOE's "Action Plan for the 21st Century Education Promotion," and the "985 Project" was officially launched. Currently, there are thirty-nine universities selected as "985" universities.[22]

The "dual first class" is an initiative to consolidate the "211" and the "985" projects. On December 30, 2011, believing that the number of universities in both the "211" project and the "985" project had reached the desired level, the MOE decided not to add any more universities into them, attempting to focus more on the curriculum rather than the number of universities, and put in place a competition mechanism to better support national key disciplines. On November 28, 2019, the MOE announced that the "211" project, the "985" project, and other key educational projects would all be integrated into the "duel first-class" initiative.[23]

By definition, the "dual first class" means "the first-class university and the first-class disciplines in the world." The "dual first class" initiative was launched in

[21] See the MOE, *The "211" Project*, available at www.moe.gov.cn/s78/A22/xwb_left/moe_843/tnull_33122.html, accessed August 23, 2025.

[22] See the MOE, *The "985" Project*, available at http://old.moe.gov.cn/publicfiles/business/htmlfiles/moe/s6183/201112/128828.html, accessed August 23, 2025.

[23] See the State Council, *General Plan to Promote the Construction of the World First-Class Universities and Disciplines*, issued on October 24, 2015, available at http://lawinfochina.com/display.aspx?lib = law&id = 20368 (hereinafter referred to as State Council General Plan).

2017 under the decision of the CPC to enhance the comprehensive strength of China's higher education and increase China's international competitiveness. Aimed at helping realize the "China dream" prescribed by the CPC, the initiative is considered in China as an effective development strategy to elevate the nation's higher education to new heights.

The "first-class" universities are divided into two tiers. The first tier consists of thirty-six universities, while the second tier has only six universities.[24] In addition, over ninety-five universities are targeted to develop the "first-class" disciplines and course subjects. The universities that are selected to build first-class disciplines in law include *Peking* University, *Tsinghua* University, *Renmin* University, *Wuhan* University, China University of Political Science and Law, and South-Central University of Economics and Law.

The development strategy under the "duel first class" initiative contains three planned steps. The first step is to make several universities and a number of disciplines highly ranked worldwide, and some disciplines to become the world's top disciplines by 2020. The second step is to have more universities and disciplines to be ranked top in the world by 2030, with several universities in first place, get a batch of disciplines to be at the forefront of world-class disciplines, and improve the overall strength of higher education in the country significantly. The third step is that by the middle of the twenty-first century, the number and strength of first-class universities and disciplines will all reach the top of the world, making China a strong country of higher education.[25]

But the plan and reality do not always match. More realistically, the "first class" is not based on the plan or desire but rather on actual strength and quality developed over a considerable period of time. Feasibility aside, the top-down designed "211" and "985" projects, and the initiative of "duel first class" indeed reflect the country's administrative mentality and managerial style formed under the planned economy.

The backlash of those State-led projects and initiatives is the nationwide race among universities to either be included in or associated with the project or initiative without concentrating on how to effectively and adequately develop or build their real strength and quality. This practice is also criticized as being unfair because it grants special status to particular universities. The argument is that only if all universities are treated fairly and equally will healthy competition for better quality be achieved.[26]

[24] The first tier of "double first class" universities includes all major universities in the country. The universities in the second tier are Northeast University, Hunan University, Zhengzhou University, Northwest Agriculture and Forestry University, and Xinjiang University.

[25] See the State Council General Plan, *supra* note 23.

[26] See the 2018 Roundtable Discussion, *supra* note 3. See also Xu Shirong, *"211" and "598" Projects: Obstacles and Governance Approach*, 3 Chongqin Higher Educ. Rsch. 15 (2015), a full text of the article is available at www.paper.edu.cn/journal/showPdf/MUTGIF4QNRDVEI1eQOAeQeQ.

With regard to their governance, universities in China have several distinctions in contrast to those of the universities elsewhere. First, the CPC's leadership must be maintained. It is required under the Higher Education Law that the state-run institutions of higher education operate under the president responsibility system through the leadership of the grassroots committees of the CPC, and all major decisions must be made by the CPC committee.[27] Therefore, the real governing body of universities in China is the CPC committee. Although the president of a university is the top officer in charge, the person who has the final say is actually the chief of the CPC committee at the university.

Second, the appointment of a university president and vice presidents is in the hands of the government. All universities and colleges in China have no authority to conduct any search for president or vice president. As administrators of a university or college, the president and vice president are either appointed by the MOE or by local government depending on the school's affiliation status (directly under the MOE or not). In addition, the university president, as well as other university-level administrators, not only have a job title but also have an administrative rank. Their rank determines their salary level and related benefits. As a general pattern, the job title has a term limit, but the administrative rank remains for a lifetime.[28]

Third, the degrees awarded by every university or college in China are State degrees, and no university or college may convey its own independent degrees without approval. Under the State Regulation of the Academic Degrees, the academic degree may only be conferred by the colleges, universities, or scientific research institutes authorized by the State Council.[29] Degree-conferring eligibility is reviewed by the State Academic Degree Committee, and a list of eligible universities and colleges is published upon approval by the State Council.[30]

It is interesting to note that almost everything in China now is tied with the country's governing ideology set forth by the CPC, and college degree conferral is no exception. Under the Administrative Measures for the Authorization and Award

[27] Under article 38 of the Law of Higher Education, the responsibilities of leadership are mainly to implement the policies of the CPC, adhere to the socialist orientation of running the institutions, exercise leadership over ideological and political work, and work related to morality in the institutions. They view and decide the internal organizational structures and candidates for the persons in charge, and review and decide such major matters as the reform, development, and basic administrative rules of the institutions. See the Law of Higher Education, *supra* note 18.

[28] For example, the president of major universities such as Peking University and Tsinghua University is a vice minister level government official, while the president of all other universities is bureau level or lower. The administrative rank is normally stated in the appointment letter, and then will stay with the appointee for the rest of his/her life and will not be affected by stepping down from the official position.

[29] See the Regulation of the Academic Degrees, promulgated by the Standing Committee of the NPC on February 12, 1980, and amended in 2004, art. 8, available at www.lawinfochina.com/display.aspx?lib = law&id = 8&CGid.

[30] See *id.*

of Bachelor Degrees issued by the State Council Academic Degrees Office on July 9, 2019 (Administrative Measures of Bachelor Degrees), the conferral of bachelor degrees should (a) be guided by Xi Jinping's socialist ideology with Chinese characteristics in the new era; (b) implement the spirit of the 19th National Congress of the CPC and the spirit of the National Education Conference, fully implement the party's education policy and the fundamental task of establishing a virtue; and (c) firmly grasp the core point of improving the quality of personnel training and cultivate socialist builders and successors with all-around development in moral standards, intellectual level, physical condition, aesthetic view, and working skills.[31]

Under the Law of Higher Education, higher education in China consists of curricula education and non-curricula education. The curricula education is further divided into two-to-three-year specialty (vocational) education, four-to-five-year undergraduate education, and two-to-four-year postgraduate education (two to three years for a master's degree, and three to four years for a doctoral degree).[32] Graduates from curricula education programs will receive two documents: a graduation diploma and a degree certificate. In contrast, those who attend non-curricula education programs will be given only a degree certificate.

The graduation diploma is proof of a college education, while the degree certificate only indicates the degree received. The difference between the curricula education and non-curricula education is not specified in the Law of Higher Education, but a common belief in the country is that the curricula education is more formal and thus more attractive than non-curricula education. Since universities in foreign countries only award one diploma specifying the degree conferred, a diploma earned overseas would need to be verified by the verification institute designated by the MOE in order to be officially recognized in the country.

Fourth, the curriculum and textbooks are subject to government review and approval. No university or college in China may independently compile or select its own curriculum and textbooks without passing government censorship or screening. With regard to certain majors or disciplines that are considered ideologically sensitive, such as law, economics, and journalism, the core curriculum and textbooks must follow the directives of, or be designated by, the government.[33] In some cases, even classroom teaching would have to be under a certain level of scrutiny.

C. *Law School Mission and Academic Standards*

There is no special accreditation agency in China to oversee law schools and evaluate law schools on a regular basis to ensure their compliance with the State

[31] See the State Council Academic Degrees Office, *Administrative Measures for the Authorization and Award of Bachelor Degrees*, art. 2, available at www.moe.gov.cn/srcsite/A22/yjss_xwgl/moe_818/201907/t20190726_392378.html.

[32] See the Law of Higher Education, *supra* note 18, art. 16.

[33] See the 2018 Roundtable Discussion, *supra* note 3.

standards. As noted, oversight is conducted either by the MOE for those law schools that are under the MOE or by the provincial governments for all other law schools. In either case, the compliance is basically dependent on each of the law schools, and there is no statutory requirement for regular on-site inspection.

The general criteria for schools of law, as stated in the National Standards of Legal Education, are quite broad. It is mandated that all law schools adhere to the principle of virtue cultivation, promote the learning of both virtue and law, and adapt to the actual needs of developing a socialist legal system with Chinese characteristics and building a socialist country ruled by law.[34] The management of a law school is under the supervision of the CPC party committee in the law school, although the dean is in charge.

Under the National Standards of Legal Education, the mission of law schools is to cultivate multi-faceted, practical, and creative legal talents and reserve forces who (a) possess integrity in ethics and profession; (b) have a solid professional theoretical foundation and professional skills; (c) are equipped with a reasonable knowledge structure; (d) have the ability to undertake government work according to law, conduct scientific legislation, fulfill administrative obligations according to law, help maintain fair justice, provide efficient and high-quality legal services, or engage in innovation and entrepreneurship; and (e) are familiar with, and adhere to, the Chinese socialist legal system.[35]

In addition, there are special requirements for law school faculty. In accordance with the National Standards of Legal Education, the full-time faculty of a law school "should have strengthened ideals and beliefs, adhere to the correct political direction, have noble moral sentiments, and be a firm believer, active disseminator, and model practitioner of Marxist legal thought and socialist rule of law theory with Chinese characteristics."[36]

It is further required that law school faculty should (a) have extensive professional knowledge; (b) be proficient in professional theories and methods, with the knowledge reserve to complete the teaching tasks of the major; (c) have a deep understanding of the actual situation of the rule of law and promote the combination of theory and practice; (d) have basic humanities and social science knowledge, a practical work style, and the spirit of innovation; (e) have strong teaching and scientific research capabilities, and (f) be able to transform scientific research results into teaching contents.[37]

Given these requirements, one issue that always arises in Chinese law schools is what the teachers may teach on their own. At the heart of the issue is whether teachers may have academic freedom or freedom to express their own independent

[34] See the National Standards, *supra* note 17.

[35] See *id.*

[36] See *id.*

[37] See *id.*

opinions. There is no easy answer, but what often is the case is that a teacher is considered unsuitable to teach simply because of inappropriate speech or the contents of their speech in the classroom.[38] As some in China point out, one of the biggest challenges facing law schools in the country is how to respect academic freedom institutionally.[39]

A closely related issue is the academic autonomy of the university and law school. For the past few decades, there has been an increasing call for universities and educational institutions' right of self-governance. Under the Law of Higher Education, universities and colleges may independently determine such matters as disciplines and specialties, teaching plans, coursebook selection and compilation, research projects, technological development, and exchange cooperation. But the exercise of independence as such is subject to various limitations. What remains as a taboo or minefield for universities and colleges is the pursuit of independent thinking and academic freedom.

D. *Law School Admissions and Curriculum*

Legal education in China is a basic college education. Although law schools are considered professional schools, they are general undergraduate legal studies. There is no special examination for law school admissions. Students who want to study law must take the National Unified Examination for Admissions to General Universities and Colleges (College Entrance Examination). It is the only examination taken by high school graduates or those with the same academic credentials as qualified high school graduates in the country for their college admission application, excluding Hong Kong and Macau.[40]

A law school admission is part of the general admission to the university or college where the law school is situated. The admission is mainly based on the scores of the college entrance examination, although it is generally held that the college admission shall be made upon a comprehensive evaluation of the morality, intelligence,

38 For example, in March 2019, Tsinghua University suspended all teaching and academic work of a law professor and banned enrollment of any graduate student under his supervision because the professor boldly and publicly criticized the policy of the CPC leader and the government. The incident caused widespread repercussions, and many scholars signed an open letter of solidarity urging Tsinghua University to resume the professor's teaching duties.

39 See the 2018 Roundtable Discussion, *supra* note 3.

40 Under article 19 of the Law of Higher Education, graduates of senior secondary school or those with an equivalent education level shall, upon passing the examination, be admitted by institutions of higher learning imparting corresponding curricula education and obtain the qualification for admission as specialty students or undergraduate students. See the Law of Higher Education, *supra* note 18. Take China University of Political Science and Law (CUPSL), the biggest law school in China, for example. In 2018, a total of 2,175 students were enrolled, including 690 males and 1,485 females, with a ratio of 1:2.15. The age of newly enrolled students ranges from 16 to 22. See the CUPSL 2018 Enrollment Data, available at www.zizzs.com/c/201808/28681.html.

and physical fitness of the applicant. The college entrance examination is uniformly administered by the MOE. The enrollment of each university or college is under the enrollment plan approved by the MOE (for those directly under the MOE) or by the local provincial government (for all others).

Undergraduate study at law school is a four-year program. Students are generally required to complete a total of 160 credits, including a minimum of 15 percent on clinical learning. The standard law school curriculum includes doctrinal courses and practical courses. The doctrinal courses consist of ideological and political theory, general law, and professional courses, while the practical courses contain experiments and clinics, professional internships, social practice, and a graduation thesis.[41]

The courses of ideological and political theory refer to such courses as the Introduction to *Mao Zedong* Thought and Theoretical System of Socialism with Chinese Characteristics, Fundamental Principles of Marxism, Basics of Ethics and Law, Policies, and Modern and Contemporary Chinese History.[42] It is required that all majors in law have the ideological and political theory curriculum and fully implement it in accordance with relevant regulations.[43]

The National Standards also set personal quality criteria for law school graduates, which they are expected to acquire through ideological and political course studies. The factors deemed essential to form a good personal quality include, among others, to "love the socialist motherland," "support the leadership of the CPC," "master the theoretical system of socialism with Chinese characteristics," and "have a correct view on the society, life and values."[44]

The professional courses are offered in a format of 10 plus X. The students majoring generally in law are required to take ten mandatory professional courses, including jurisprudence, constitutional law, Chinese legal history, criminal law, civil law, criminal procedure, civil procedure, administrative law and administrative procedure, international law, and legal ethics. The "X" courses refer to other professional courses that can be decided on an individual school basis according to their own teaching plan. Those courses are, among others, economic law, intellectual property (IP) law, commercial law, private international law, international economic law, environmental and natural resources law, labor and social security law, evidence, and taxation. The number of "X" courses to be taken should in general not be less than five.[45]

Students in other specific legal majors follow a different course track. For example, the core courses for students majoring in IP law include jurisprudence,

[41] See the National Standards, *supra* note 17.

[42] Those ideological and political theory courses are mandatory for all law school students throughout the country.

[43] See the National Standards, *supra* note 17.

[44] See *id.*

[45] See *id.*

constitutional law, criminal law, civil law, criminal procedure, civil procedure, administrative law and administrative procedure, general intellectual property rights, copyright law, patent law, trademark law, competition law, intellectual property management, and intellectual property literature, document retrieval, and application.[46]

General courses are the courses arranged according to the major being pursued and actual social needs. The course offering covers a wide range of studies, including foreign language, physical education, and computer programs. There is no specific requirement for the subjects of the general courses to be offered, but official guidance is that the general course curriculum would need to be balanced in terms of humanities, social sciences, and natural sciences.[47] A graduation thesis is required for all senior students at the law schools.

The thesis can be completed in various genres such as an academic paper, case analysis, graduation design, or research report. Students may select thesis topics as they like, but the selection generally would need to be problem-oriented. They are encouraged to write a graduation thesis under the guidance of an instructor according to their own interests, combined with social practice and in consideration of the hot and difficult issues of economic and social reality. Students are also expected to demonstrate in the contents of a graduation thesis their application of the theories and professional knowledge learned in law school.[48]

There is a general rule that the writing of a graduation thesis should abide by academic ethics and academic norms. Each student has an instructor for his or her graduation thesis. The instructor should be a faculty member with an academic title of lecturer or above. An adjunct faculty member from the professional practice department or working unit may be invited to serve as a co-instructor. The instructor has the duty of guiding and supervising the student in their selection, topic affirmation, writing, and other aspects of the graduation thesis to ensure compliance with academic norms.[49]

E. *Law Programs and Degrees*

Chinese law schools offer a variety of degree programs. The conventional degree programs are LL.B, LL.M, and Ph.D. programs.[50] LL.B is an undergraduate legal degree, while both the LL.M and Ph.D. are graduate degrees. Most law school graduates finish their legal studies with an LL.B degree, and only a certain number of law school graduates continue on to pursue graduate study in the LL.M program

46 See *id.*
47 See *id.*
48 See *id.*
49 See *id.*
50 Under article 3 of the Regulation of the Academic Degrees, the academic degrees in China are divided into three levels: bachelor, master, and doctor, *supra* note 29.

or both the LL.M and Ph.D. programs (an LL.M degree is normally a prerequisite to applying for a Ph.D. program).

In addition, many law schools also offer a joint bachelor's degree program. The joint degree refers to study in two majors in different disciplines. According to the Administrative Measures of Bachelor's Degrees, colleges and universities with the right to grant a bachelor's degree may grant a bachelor's degree in a minor program of study to full-time undergraduate students who meet the criteria for a degree. Those who have not obtained a bachelor's degree in their major shall not be granted a bachelor's degree in their minor. The bachelor's degree in a minor is indicated on the certificate of the bachelor's degree in a major, and there is no separate degree certificate for the minor.[51]

A related degree is the second bachelor's degree. In contrast to the joint bachelor's degree, the second bachelor's degree has different features. First, the second degree program may only enroll those who have graduated from a college or university with a bachelor's degree. Second, students graduating from their second bachelor's degree program will have two graduation diplomas and two degree certificates, while the joint bachelor's degree graduates have only one graduation diploma and one degree certificate. Third, after graduation, a second bachelor's degree holder shall be treated as a graduate with a master's degree, but a joint bachelor's degree recipient remains at the bachelor level.

The Master of Law degree program is a graduate program in law, and at present it is in general open only to those who have obtained an LL.B degree or have studied law. In other words, a graduate applying for a Master of Law degree program must have previously studied at a four-year university majoring in law. Those who have completed studies in law either in a three-year college or through a self-taught examination are also eligible to apply.[52] The Master of Law is generally a three-year program.

In the past few decades, many law schools in China have created a different kind of master's program in law, known as a JM (*Juris* Master) program, or Master of Law program for non-law college graduates. Started in 1996, the JM program is modeled after the JD program in the United States and is aimed at providing advanced-level training to professionals already in legal practice. The JM program is divided into two categories: JM for law graduates and JM for non-law graduates.

The JM for law graduates is a graduate program that is open to those who have studied law in a college or university, including three-year college study and those who are self-taught. The JM for non-law students is the graduate program in law available to those who are not law school graduates. Students in the JM programs can be either full

[51] See the *Administrative Measures of Bachelor Degrees*, *supra* note 31, art. 13(b).

[52] The self-taught examination is a self-study-oriented national examination established by the State Council in 1981 mainly for a higher education diploma. It is a form of higher education combining individual self-study, social assistance, and national examination. Upon passing all required exams, the self-taught student will be granted a graduation diploma recognized by the State.

time or part time. Full-time students usually take two to three years to complete the program, while part-time students may take up to four years to finish.

The JM program requires at least forty-five credit hours, of which thirty credit hours are for mandatory courses and the rest are electives. Upon graduation, students will receive both a postgraduate diploma and a Master of Law degree certificate. Currently, there are over seventy-eight universities in the country that offer JM programs. Most of the students enrolled in the JM program have a certain number of years of work experience, and many of them maintain their work relationship with their employers during their period of study.

In comparison with the regular Master of Law program, the JM program has several distinctions. First, the regular Master of Law program is basically a research program. Students major in a certain area of law and have an academic focus on a specific subject under the supervision of a professor or faculty member. The regular Master of Law program is the advanced degree program between the Bachelor of Laws and the Doctor of Laws and is intended for those who already have a bachelor's degree to pursue advanced study in a legal area of their interest and to engage in solid theoretical research.

The JM program, however, is more practically oriented and quite classroom-teaching based. As a professional degree program, the JM emphasizes the practical ability and legal analysis skills of its students. A tutor group in lieu of an academic supervisor is employed to help JM students with their course studies. The students in a JM program are expected to undertake practical work in legislation, judicial justice, administrative law enforcement, legal services, and business management upon their graduation.

Second, the entrance examination for the JM programs is a national examination jointly administered by the universities authorized to enroll JM students. The Master of Law program, however, has two entrance examinations. One is the general examination or examination on general subjects, and the other is the specific examination or examination on a particular area of law depending on the academic focus. The general examination is a national examination, while the specific examination is a university-based examination. The Master of Law program candidates must obtain satisfactory scores on both examinations in order to be considered for admission.

Third, to apply for admission to the Master of Law program, applicants in most cases must have a bachelor's degree but are not limited to majoring in law, although a vast majority of the applicants have a bachelor's degree in law or an LL.B. The JM program applicants, as noted, may have a law or non-law degree with an undergraduate diploma or equivalent. Generally, to be admitted into a graduate program, an applicant with an equivalent undergraduate diploma should have work experience of more than two years, or three years if the applicant has only an equivalent vocational school diploma.[53]

[53] Take Renmin University Law School, for example. Those who are eligible to apply for the JM program include: (a) undergraduates who have received academic qualifications recognized by the state (including regular colleges, adult colleges, and adult higher education graduates held

F. *Law School Graduates' Placement*

Law school placement in China used to be under the State allocation plan. But since 1984, when the State decided to reform the nation's education system, the placement has been the matter dealt with by each individual college or university. Prior to 1984, like all other university graduates, the graduates from law schools were dispatched uniformly by the State to different places according to a predetermined state plan. During that period, the education departments and institutions were not only responsible for training but also responsible for the deployment of graduates to fulfill the State allocation plan.[54]

In 1985, the State Council issued the "Decision on the Reform of the Educational System" (1985 Decision).[55] According to the 1985 Decision, the placement of university graduates would no longer be handled by the State. Instead, it would be made under the guidance of the State plan and undertaken through a combined method of the voluntary application of the graduate, the school recommendation, and the choice of the best candidate by the employer.[56] The 1985 Decision broke the tradition that the placement of university graduates was in the hands of the State and instead gave employers the right to select graduates.[57]

For many decades in the past, when reporting to the work unit or employer, the university graduates would need to show a "dispatch card" issued by the university. In 2000, as part of further reform on university placement, the MOE replaced the "dispatch card" with the "report card." Thus, when a graduate is hired by an employer, the report card will serve as an official certificate of the graduate's employment. The switch from "dispatch card" to "report card" is viewed as a milestone in the State employment policy pertaining to university graduates – a change from the State plan to marketization.[58]

Presently, most university graduates are placed through job offers from employers. Graduates from law schools generally will take the judicial examination before or right after their graduation. In order to help graduates with their

by regular colleges and universities) or through self-study exams or online education programs; (b) undergraduates with a bachelor's degree from a college or university; (c) graduates from vocational colleges who have worked for more than two years and have reached the same academic level as university graduates; or (d) graduates who have obtained undergraduate qualifications recognized by the State. More detailed information is available at www.law.ruc.edu.cn/article/?id = 55328.

54 See Meng Bing, Zhong Xinwen, & Liu Ming, *Evolution of the State Policy for the Employment of College Graduates in 70 Years after the Founding of the New China*, 2 J. Hebei Normal Univ., Educ. Sci. Ed., 17 (2019), available at www.cssn.cn/jyx/jyx_gdjyx/201909/t20190917_4972981.shtml.

55 The Decision was made by the Central Committee of the CPC on May 27, 1985. A full text of the Decision is available at www.huaue.com/fg/fg14.htm.

56 See *id.*

57 See Bing et al., *supra* note 54.

58 See *id.*

placement, each law school has a graduate employment consultation office or personnel with a duty to coordinate the graduates' search for a job based on the need of potential employers and to facilitate employers' on or off campus interviews. But again, after 1985, law schools were no longer directly responsible for the employment of their graduates.

The job market for law school graduates is quite diverse. The general pattern of the career pursuits of law school graduates in China consists of four categories. The first category is graduate study both at home and abroad. The second category is legal work in government offices, including government departments, courts, procuratorates, and public security bureaus. The third category is the legal counsel office in business sectors, state-owned enterprises, and private companies alike. The fourth category is an associate position at a law firm.

In the past decade, however, the job market has not been promising for law school graduates, although the demand for legal talent remained high in the country from several aspects. During the three-year period of 2016–2019, the national average employment rate of law school graduates was the lowest among eleven college majors. On the top was the engineering major with an employment rate of over 93 percent for all three years, while the law school graduate employment rate was in the range of 84.0 percent to 85.3 percent.[59] In a 2020 report, the law major remained "red" in the employment rating, meaning that the unemployment rate is high, and salary and employment satisfaction are low.[60] Take China University of Political Science and Law, the largest law school in the country, for example. In 2022, only 8.3 percent of the undergraduates had a job offer as of their graduation, and the employment rate for those with graduate degrees was 74.12 percent.[61]

There may be many reasons for the low employment rate of law school graduates. Economic parameters aside, growing competition, inadequacy of placement guidance and consultation, as well as a lack of practical skills of the graduates, are all possible attributes. A major reason, as many point out, is the wide disparity between the quantity and quality of the law school graduates.[62] The problem is that the quality of legal talents cannot meet the requirements of social development, and the knowledge structure of many law school graduates appears to be quite narrow.[63]

[59] See Mycos Research Institute, *Chinese College Graduates Employment Annual Report* 2019, a Chinese version of the report is available at www.sohu.com/a/336596717_440518.

[60] See Huaxia Times, *News on the Mycos 2020 Report on Chinese Graduate Employment*, available in Chinese at www.cinic.org.cn/xw/schj/862369.html.

[61] See China University of Political Science & Law, 2022 *Employment Statistics*, available at https://baijiahao.baidu.com/s?id=1753991244784057704&wfr=spider&for=pc.

[62] See Gong Wenhao, *A Research on Employment Dilemma of Law School Graduates*, 8 Higher Educ. F. 7 (2018); see also Kang Lingli, *A Study in the Employment Issue of Law School Graduates in China*, Master of Law thesis, available at http://cdmd.cnki.com.cn/Article/CDMD-10053-1011114285.htm.

[63] See Lingli, *supra* note 62.

G. *Trends of Chinese Legal Education*

The low employment rate facing law school graduates creates a dilemma in Chinese legal education. On the one hand, there is increasing demand for legal professionals, and on the other hand, a growing number of law school students are unable to find a job upon graduation. A critical issue raised in response to the dilemma is where the legal education in the country should head in the near future.

It is now commonly agreed in China that given the complexity of economic activities in the globalized market, law schools now should not only provide students with solid legal expertise but also help students develop practical knowledge and skills in multiple aspects, including international commercial transactions, business management, economic analysis, as well as foreign languages. The desired goal is to produce highly capable legal talents that are practically suitable to the changing social and economic environments.[64]

To meet these challenges, many law schools in China have been exploring a new strategy and methodology of teaching and learning. The changes that have already taken place in the nation's top law schools are discernible from several respects. First, there is a change in the view of legal education from "general education" to "professional education." The change reflects an understanding that legal education is not personal quality education, common education, or specialty education, but a specialized professional education. In other words, a law school should be the place to generate legal professionals rather than regular college graduates.[65]

The second respect is the change in the substance of law school teaching. For many years in the past, law schools mainly focused on doctrinal teaching or the students' understanding of legal doctrines and theories, and ignored the training and cultivation of students' skills and analytical ability. Two causes were blamed for this situation. One cause was the overly emphasized "elite education" of the law schools, which led the students to become quite deficient in actual skills.[66]

The other cause was the traditional mindset that law is a social science, and thus legal education should follow the educational model of philosophy, history and other social sciences. Then, much attention was paid to theoretical teaching, or even simply ideological injection, and the law was deemed an individually delineated discipline that contains only logical deduction from theory to theory without any empirical analysis of social problems. As a result, law school graduates ended up with no practical experience and lacked the ability to apply legal knowledge to actual social problem solving.[67]

64 See the 2018 Roundtable Discussion, *supra* note 3.

65 See *id.*; see also Shen Weixing, *The Development Calls for "Clinical Law" – The Three Major Changes in Chinese Education in Law*, 3 Compar. L. Rsch. 121 (2008).

66 See Weixing, *supra* note 65.

67 See *id.*

To help cope with this situation, many law schools experimented with introducing a clinic legal education into their curriculum. Modeled on American legal clinic courses, the clinic legal education with a concentration on the skills of legal thinking and analysis provides students with the opportunity to be exposed to legal practice through the guidance of experienced teachers or lawyers so as to help narrow the gap between theoretical education and actual legal practice. At the same time, students are given the chance to gain first-hand legal experience by providing legal assistance to socially disadvantaged groups.[68]

The third is a change in the methodology of teaching. The change contains two switches. The one is a switch from subject or theory-oriented teaching to case analyzing and problem-solving focused teaching. The other is a switch from normative or rule analysis to empirical or practical analysis.[69] The whole purpose is to equip students studying in law with both the knowledge and skills needed to handle legal issues in the real world and to become more qualified legal professionals.

2. LEGAL PRACTICE IN CHINA AND THE CHINESE BAR

As noted, a vast majority of law school graduates typically practice law as lawyers or work in government sectors as legal staff. In most law-related work, a license to practice law is required. Those who want to work for the government also need to take an additional examination for civil servants. Obtaining a license to practice law in China requires passing the uniformed national bar examination. The examination is now known as the National Uniform Legal Professional Qualification Examination (LPQE). The LPQE is a qualification exam not only for lawyers but for judges and prosecutors as well.

A. *Lawyers in Modern Chinese History*

The term "lawyer" is an imported concept in China. Historically, the Chinese lawyer system is the product of the reform of the late *Qing* Dynasty to imitate Western rules and regulations.[70] Following the *Qing*'s blueprint of construction of the lawyer system, the *Beiyang* government on September 16, 1912 promulgated the

68 See the 2018 Roundtable Discussion, *supra* note 3.

69 See *id.*

70 In 1906, the Ministers of Law Revision of the Qing government, Shen Jiaben and Wu Tingfang, presided over the drafting of the "Criminal and Civil Procedure Law." The law had a total of 5 chapters and 260 articles, of which the fourth chapter, "General Laws of Criminal Civil," specifically included a "lawyer" section. It had a total of nine provisions dealing with such matters as lawyer qualification, registration, filing, and disciplinary action. See Zhang Weixin, *The Background and Disputes of "Criminal & Civil Procedure Law" in the Late Qing Dynasty*, January 9, 2020, available at https://legalhistory.cupl.edu.cn/info/1034/1351.htm.

"Provisional Regulations for Lawyers" (1912 PRL).[71] It was the first law on lawyers and the legal service industry in China's history and marked the beginning of the formal establishment of a lawyer system in the country. The 1912 PRL was viewed as an important symbol of the modernization of the Chinese legal system.[72]

The 1912 PRL contained seven chapters and a total of thirty-eight articles, covering such matters concerning lawyers as qualification, certificates, duties, obligations, union and discipline. Under the 1912 PRL, the country held its first national bar examination at the end of 1912, and a total of 297 applicants passed the examination and were awarded a lawyer certificate by the Ministry of Justice. One year later in 1913, the number of certified lawyers soared to 2,716.[73]

In 1941, the National Government, after several years of preparation, adopted the Law of Lawyers under which the country's statutory scheme governing lawyers was formally established. The 1941 Law of Lawyers consisted of forty-eight articles and the major provisions included the nature of the profession of lawyers, lawyers' qualification, legal practice procedures, lawyers' obligations, lawyers' union, and discipline. The 1941 Law of Lawyers, together with other regulations concerning lawyers and legal practice, constituted the country's lawyer system that lasted until 1949.[74]

In 1949, all existing laws adopted by the National Government, as noted, were abolished, including the Law of Lawyers. From 1949 to 1954, the new government made attempts to rebuild the lawyer system. For example, in the 1954 Constitution, it was provided that all trials in the people's courts shall be open unless otherwise provided for by the law and the accused has the right to a defense.[75] The 1954 Organic Law of People's Courts further provided that in addition to exercising the right to defend himself or herself, the accused may appoint a lawyer and the people's court may also designate a defender for him or her if necessary.[76]

The attempt, however, was aborted in 1957 when the Anti-Rightist campaign was launched in the nation. Not until 1978 did the construction of the lawyer system resume. In 1979, the legal committee of the Standing Committee of the NPC started drafting the regulation on lawyers. One year later in 1980, the Provisional Regulation

[71] See the *Provisional Regulations for Lawyers of Republic of China*, issued on September 16, 1912, available at www.pinlue.com/article/2019/03/2211/588319188406.html.

[72] See Zhang Zhiming, *Looking Back and Forward: The Development Trajectory of Chinese Lawyers in the Past 100 Years*, 1 Nat'l. Coll. Procuraterates J. 17 (2013), available at www.sohu.com/a/215394937_773108.

[73] See *id.*

[74] See in general Xu Jiali & Wu Yunhao, History of Chinese Lawyers System (China University Political Science and Law Press, 2000); see alsoZhong Bin, A *Review of the Lawyer System in the Republic of China from 1940 to 1949 – Centered on the 1941 Lawyer Law*, available at www.docin.com/p-943639049.html.

[75] See the 1954 Constitution of China, art. 76, available at http://en.pkulaw.cn/display.aspx?cgid = 52993&lib = law.

[76] See the 1954 Organic Law of People's Courts, art. 7, available at www.cecc.gov/resources/legal-provisions/1954-prc-organic-law-of-the-peoples-courts-chinese-text.

of Lawyers was promulgated, which was the first law that governed lawyers in China after 1949. It took more than thirty years to finally establish a legal framework for lawyers in the nation. In 1986, the All China Lawyers Association was formed.[77]

The promulgation of the 1980 Provisional Regulation of Lawyers marked the beginning of the restoration of the lawyer system that had been expected since the early 1950s. During the early stage of the restoration, however, lawyers were defined as state legal workers.[78] As such, all lawyers had to work in a legal institution called the "legal advisory office" under the administration of the Ministry of Justice(MOJ). No lawyers could engage in private practice. The legal advisory office was a non-profit State institution, and its funding and staffing were all within the State budget. Thus, the organization and operations of the legal advisory office were subject to the leadership of the state administrative agency.[79]

In 1984, with a change from a governing budgeting to self-management for the funding of legal services, the legal advisory office started to gradually transform into law firms. In 1988, law firms were allowed on a trial basis to form as partnerships separated from the government. Since then, law firms have shifted structurally from state-owned entities to privately managed cooperatives. In 1993, the State Council approved the Ministry of Justice's "Plan on Deepening the Reform of Lawyers' Work," under which the nature of lawyers formally changed from the "state's legal workers" to "social legal service providers."[80]

In 1996, the Standing Committee of the NPC adopted the Law of Lawyers. Developed from the 1980 Provisional Regulation, the 1996 Law of Lawyers contained detailed provisions on the nature of lawyers, requirements for legal practice, law firms, lawyers' business, the rights and obligations of practicing lawyers, legal aid, lawyers' associations, and the legal responsibilities of lawyers. In order to further improve the lawyer system, the 1996 Law of Lawyers was amended in 2001, 2007, 2012, and 2017, respectively.[81]

77 See Introduction to All China Lawyers Association, available at www.acla.org.cn/home/toMenu?menuIdStr = 1-62.

78 See the Provisional Regulation of Lawyers, adopted by the Standing Committee of the NPC on August 26, 1980, effective January 1, 1981. Under article 1 of the Provisional Regulation of Lawyers, lawyers are the state's legal workers and function to give legal assistance to state organs, enterprises, establishments, mass organizations, the people's communes, and citizens in order to ensure the correct implementation of law and protect the interests of the state and the collectives as well as the legitimate rights and interests of the citizens. A full text of the Regulation is available at www.npc.gov.cn/wxzl/gongbao/2000-12/06/content_5004390.htm; a translated version in English is available at https://repository.law.umich.edu/cgi/viewcontent.cgi?article = 1777&context = mjil.

79 See *id.*, arts. 13, 16.

80 See the MOJ, *Memorabilia of the Development of the Chinese Lawyer Industry*, available at www.moj.gov.cn/subject/content/2019-11/25/1371_3236926.html.

81 The 2017 Amended Law of Lawyers was promulgated on September 1, 2017. A full text of the Amended Law of Lawyers is available at www.fdi.gov.cn/1800000121_23_73981_0_7.html.

B. *Legal Professional Qualification Examination*

The LPQE is a unified national examination for those who pursue legal careers. Prior to 2002, there were separate examinations for lawyers, judges and prosecutors. The lawyers' examination began as early as 1984 when some provinces held their own independent examination for lawyers. At that time, the examination was intended mainly to test the legal knowledge of those who wanted to become lawyers. The examination was held individually at different times on different subjects.

In 1986, the MOJ for the first time organized pilot examinations for lawyers in a dozen of provinces. Two years later, a nationwide lawyers' examination was administered by the MOJ and took place at the same time with unified contents and requirements. In the 1988 lawyers' examination, over 80,000 applicants took the examination. In 1993, with approval by the State Council, the lawyers' examination started to be administrated on a yearly basis. In the 1996 Law of Lawyers, the lawyers' examination became a statutory requirement for engaging in legal practice.[82]

In 2001, the Standing Committee of the NPC amended the Judges Law, the Law of Prosecutors, and the Law of Lawyers. A major part of the amendments was to combine all three existing legal professional examinations into a single judicial examination. For example, under article 5 of the Law of Lawyers (as amended 2001), in order to be qualified to be a lawyer, individuals must pass the unified national judicial examination.[83]

On October 31, 2001, the MOJ in conjunction with the SPC and the Supreme People's Procuratorate (SPP) issued the Implementation Measures of the National Judicial Examination (Provisional). The Measures were formulated to establish and standardize the national uniform examination for legal professionals to ensure the quality of judges, prosecutors, and lawyers. The first national judicial examination was held in 2002.

In 2008, the 2001 Measures were amended, which formed the regulatory scheme for the judicial examination.[84] The 2008 Measures defined the national judicial examination as a uniformly organized national qualification examination for legal professions.[85] Under the 2008 Measures, it is imperative that unless otherwise provided by laws and administrative regulations, all entry-level judges and prosecutors, and those applying to be lawyers and public notaries, must pass the national judicial examination to obtain legal professional qualification.[86]

82 See the 1996 Law of Lawyers, art. 6, available at www.asianlii.org/cn/legis/cen/laws/ll129/.

83 See the 2001 Law of Lawyers, art. 6, available at www.law-lib.com/law/law_view.asp?id = 16820.

84 The 2008 Implementation Measures of the National Judicial Examination was issued by the MOJ, SPC, and SPP on August 8, 2008, available at www.moj.gov.cn/organization/content/2009-05/31/zcfg_19076.html.

85 See *id.*, art. 2.

86 See *id.*

Under the 2008 Measures, the national judicial examination is administered by the MOJ in consultation with the National Judicial Examination Coordinating Committee established jointly by the MOJ, SPC and SPP.[87] The MOJ is also responsible for formulating the rules that govern such examination matters as registration, room setting, discipline, test preparation, proctors, grading, and other related work.[88] In addition, within the MOJ, a functional department is designated to undertake all administrative work for the national judicial examinations. The department is now named the Department of Management of Legal Profession Qualification.[89]

According to the 2008 Measures, the national judicial examination is held once a year. The examination mainly tests legal professional knowledge and the ability to engage in the legal profession. The contents of the examination include theoretical law, applied law, current laws and regulations, legal practice, and professional ethics. The theoretical law mainly refers to legal theories, philosophies, and doctrines, while applied law means specific types of law or legal areas.

In 2018, as part of the reform on the selection of qualified legal professionals, the judicial examination was renamed as LPQE. In addition, there were certain changes in the format and substance of the exam. One change was that the judicial examination was a one-part examination while the LPQE contains two parts. Another change involved exam methods. The judicial examination was basically a paper examination. The LPQE, however, was primarily a computerized examination. Also, the MOJ tightened legal background requirements for LPQE and set the four-year undergraduate diploma as the minimum.

The two parts of the LPQE are the subjective part and the objective part. The subjective part contains short answer or essay questions, and the objective part comprises multiple-choice questions. The objective part is a computerized test while the subjective part can be either computerized or paper-based at the choice of the test taker. For each examination, there is one set of subjective part questions and two sets of objective part questions.

It is important to note that only those who have passed the test on the objective question part may take the test on the subjective question part. The two tests are

[87] See *id.*, arts. 4, 5.

[88] See *id.*, art. 12.

[89] The Department of Management of Legal Profession Qualification (LPQ) is an internal body of the MOJ. Its official duties include: (a) organizing and implementing the national unified legal profession qualification examination, reviewing and formulating the national unified legal professional qualification examination outline and examination questions, and determining collaberately the passage standards; (b) undertaking the national uniform legal professional qualification review, award and qualification certificate management; (c) organizing the formulation and implementation of pre-employment training plans for legal professionals; and (d) participating in the guidance of legal education, and in higher legal vocational education within the system of MOJ. See the description of Department of Management of LPQ available at www.moj.gov.cn/organization/node_570.html.

generally a couple of weeks apart. Only those who passed both parts of the LPQE will be awarded qualification certificates. Those who pass the objective part but fail the subjective part may sign up to take the subjective part test again in the next year and the next year only.

For example, the objective part of the 2020 LPQE had two sets of questions.[90] The first set included theory of the rule of law with Chinese socialist characteristics, jurisprudence, constitutional law, Chinese legal history, international law, judicial system and legal ethics, criminal law, criminal procedure, administrative law, and administrative procedure law. The second set consisted of civil law, IP law, commercial law, economic law, environmental law, labor and social security law, private international law, international economic law, and civil procedure law (including arbitration).[91]

Each set of the test has 100 multiple-choice questions with 150 points – one point each for 50 questions and 2 points each for the remaining 50 questions. The total score of the two sets of objective parts was 300 points. Given the large number of test takers, the 2020 judicial examination was taken in two groups. The test for one group took place on October 31, 2020, and the test for the other group was on November 1, 2020. The time allowed for each set of the test was 180 minutes.[92]

The test for the subjective part was administered on November 28, 2020, and it was a one-set test. The contents covered in the subjective part included socialist rule of law with Chinese characteristics, jurisprudence, constitutional law, criminal law, criminal procedure law, civil law, commercial law, civil procedure law (including the arbitration system), administrative law and administrative procedure law, the judicial system, and legal professional ethics. The full scores of the subjective part were 180 points and the time length for the test was 240 minutes.[93]

To be eligible to take the LPQE, the applicants must meet the following conditions: (a) be a national of the People's Republic of China; (b) support the Chinese Constitution and have the right to vote and to be voted; (c) possess good political and professional standing and moral character; (d) have full capacity for civil conduct; and (e) have the required legal background.[94] Because of the Chinese nationality requirement, no foreigner is allowed to take the LPQE, and thus no foreigner can be a lawyer licensed in China.

In addition, there is a minimum legal background requirement. As stipulated by the MOJ, anyone sitting for LPQE must obtain (a) an undergraduate or graduate diploma in law from a full-time college or university with a bachelor's degree or above; (b) an undergraduate or graduate diploma in any area other than law from a

[90] See the MOJ, *Bulletin of the 2020 National Judicial Examination*, available at www.moj.gov.cn/organization/content/2020-07/02/575_3252006.html.

[91] See *id.*, art. 2.

[92] See *id.*

[93] See *id.*, art. 3.

[94] See *id.*, art. 1.

full-time college or university with a bachelor's degree or above and a master's degree in law; or (c) an undergraduate or graduate diploma in a non-law major from a full-time college or university with a corresponding bachelor's degree or above and having engaged in legal work for more than three years.[95]

In the 2020 LPQE, however, an exception was granted to the four-year college graduates with only an undergraduate diploma but no law degree if they were from an ethnic minority or remote areas. Also note that the four-year college or university students may take the LPQE during their senior year. In other words, the college or university students may sit for the LPQE in advance of receiving their college diploma and degree. The master's degree students may do the same during their graduating year.[96]

The LPQE pass rate is relatively low in the country. From 2002 to 2017, the MOJ administered a total of fifteen national judicial examinations. Of some 4.6 million applicants who took the examination, over 800,000 passed and were awarded the certificate of legal profession qualification. The average pass rate was about 17.4%.[97] Again, according to onestatistic, from 2018 to 2022, the LPQE pass rate was 18.27%, 21.42%, 22.88%, 23.60%, and 19.41%, respectively.[98] In 2023 and 2024, the pass rate was down to 17.89% and 13.8 respectively.[99]

C. *Lawyers and Chinese Law Firms*

Under article 2 of the Law of Lawyers (as amended 2017), a lawyer is defined as a professional who has acquired a lawyer's practice license pursuant to law, and is authorized or designated to provide clients with legal services.[100] According to Article 5 of the Law of Lawyers, a person who upholds the Constitution of the People's Republic of China and meets the required conditions may apply to obtain a lawyer's practice license. The conditions are: (a) hold the qualification certificate; (b) practiced training at a law firm for a full year; and (c) have good character and standing.[101]

Therefore, to become a lawyer in China, both the qualification certificate and practice license must be obtained. The LPQE is only for the qualification. The

95 See *id.*

96 See *id.*

97 See China Legal Information Center, *National Judicial Examination*, available at www.chinadaily.com.cn/m/chinalic/2017-07/07/content_30036163.htm.

98 See Zhao Dacheng, Vice Minister of the MOJ, interview with the reporter from the Voice of China, March 8, 2019, available at www.sohu.com/a/300021511_164794. See also *LPQE Statistic Analysis*, available at https://baijiahao.baidu.com/s?id=1781012542601412418&wfr=spider&for=pc.

99 See Leal Home, 2023 *LPQE Statistic Analysis*, November 30, 2024, available at https://news.sohu.com/a/831832226_121123868; See also Beida Fabao, 2024 LPQE Pass Rate, April 14, 2025, available at https://baijiahao.baidu.com/s?id=1829338931534391926&wfr=spider&for=pc.

100 See the Law of Lawyers, *supra* note 81, art. 2.

101 See *id.*, art. 5.

receipt of the qualification certificate is a condition precedent to the conferment of the practice license. In addition, the one-year legal practice training in a law firm must be fulfilled prior to the filing of an application for the legal practice license.

In the past four decades, the number of lawyers in China has increased dramatically. In 1979, the number of lawyers in the country was only 212.[102] As of 2022, the number of lawyers in China exceeded 651,600, among which there were 504,700 full-time practicing lawyers, representing 77.46% of all lawyers, 14,300 part-time lawyers (2.19%), 95,900 public lawyers – lawyers on government payrolls (14.73%), 29,900 corporate lawyers (4.6%), and 1,500 military lawyers (0.23%).[103] In comparison with 2019 statistics, the number of public lawyers increased from 43,300 (9.17%), and corporate lawyers from 10,900 (2.31%).[104]

According to the MOJ 2022 statistics, more than 107,900 lawyers were under 30 years old (16.56%), over 419,500 lawyers were between the ages of 30 to 49 (64.39%), about 106,300 lawyers were in the range of 50 to 64 years old (16.32%), and nearly 17,700 lawyers were over 65 years old (2.73%). In terms of education level, more than 466,900 lawyers had a four-year college diploma (71.66%), over 130,400 lawyers earned a master's program diploma (20.01%), more than 7,800 lawyers obtained a doctoral diploma (1.21%), and some 46,400 lawyers had a non-four-year college diploma (7.12%). In addition, over 5,727 lawyers received an education and obtained degrees abroad (1.34%).[105]

In January 2019, the MOJ issued the Outline of Comprehensively Deepening the Reform of Judicial Administration (2018–2022). In the Outline, the MOJ set a goal of expanding the number of lawyers to 620,000 by 2022 to achieve a ratio of 4.2:10,000 between lawyers and population. The number was adjusted in 2021 in the MOJ's "2021–2025 Plan," where the number of lawyers was projected to reach 750,000 by 2025 with a lawyer–population ratio of 5.3:10,000.[106] According to the MOJ, the actual number of lawyers already exceeded 830,000 in September 2025.[107]

In addition, as intended in the MOJ 2019 Outline, all government departments and civil organizations at the county level or above will establish public lawyer positions, and the major state-owned and privately owned enterprises should all have

[102] See China Law Journal reporter, *Chinese Bar Works Out 2002–2006 Development Program*, 6 China L. J. 13 (2002), available at www.pkulaw.cn/fulltext_form.aspx?Db=qikan&gid=1510089638.

[103] See the MOJ, *2022 Statistics Analysis of the Work of Lawyers and Grass-root Legal Services*, available at www.moj.gov.cn/pub/sfbgw/zwxxgk/fdzdgknr/fdzdgknrtjxx/202306/t20230614_480740.html (hereinafter referred to as MOJ 2022 Statistics).

[104] The MOJ 2019 Statistics is available at www.moj.gov.cn/government_public/content/2020-06/22/634_3251200.html.

[105] See MOJ 2022 Statistics, *supra* note 103.

[106] See the MOJ, *2021–2025 Plan for the Construction of National Public Legal Service System*, issued on December 30, 2021, available at www.moj.gov.cn/pub/sfbgw/zwxxgk/fdzdgknr/fdzdgknrtzwj/202201/t20220124_446894.html.

[107] See MOJ, News Briefing, September 8, 2025, available at www.moj.gov.cn/pub/sfbgw/sfbxwfbhzb/2025nsfbfbh/202509gzlwcsswgh/.

corporate lawyers.[108] According to the MOJ, by the end of 2022, over 13,000 grassroots legal services entities in the country were established, and the number of grassroots legal service providers reached 56,000.[109]

The law firm, according to article 14 of the Law of Lawyers, is an organization in which lawyers practice law.[110] Under the Law of Lawyers, to establish a law firm, the firm must have: (a) its own name, domicile and articles of association; (b) lawyers who conform to the provisions of the law; (c) a funder who is a lawyer with certain practice experience and has not been punished by suspension of practice within three years; and (d) assets that meet the amount prescribed by the judicial administration department of the State Council.[111]

As required by the Law of Lawyers, an application for creating a law firm shall be submitted to the judicial administrative department of the people's government of a city consisting of districts or of the people's government of district in a municipality directly under the central government. The department accepting the application shall examine the application within twenty days from the date of acceptance and submit the examination opinions and all application materials to the judicial administrative departments of the people's governments of provinces, autonomous regions, and municipalities directly under the central government for approval.[112]

Structurally, there are three types of law firms in China: State-funded law firms, partnership-based law firms, and solo-practice law firms. The State-funded law firm is a law firm established by the judicial administrative authority based on the needs of the state. Featured as a state enterprise legal person, the State-funded law firm is staffed under State personnel policies and its funds are on the state budget. Simply put, the normal operations of a State-funded law firm rely on state financial appropriations.

The State-funded law firms used to be the major form of law firms in China. Beginning in 2001, with the progress of reform, all State-funded law firms were required to be separated from the State, and to bear responsibilities with their own assets. Since then, a vast majority of the State-funded law firms have been dissolved or restructured under a new business form. Currently, the State-funded law firms exist mainly in poor or remote areas.

Prior to 2008, State-funded law firms were regulated under the Measures of Administration of the State Funded Law Firms, adopted by the MOJ in 1996. In 2008, the MOJ adopted the Administrative Measures of Law Firms to govern all law firms regardless of their organizational structure. The 2008 Administrative

[108] Ilawpress report: *The total number of lawyers nationwide in 2022 will reach 620,000: MOJ "Outline" for Judicial Administrative Reform*, February 6, 2019, available at www.ilawpress.com/material/detail/325230759197540864.

[109] See the MOJ 2022 Statistics, *supra* note 103.

[110] See the Law of Lawyers, *supra* note 81, art. 14.

[111] See *id.*

[112] See *id.*, art. 18.

Measures were amended in 2012, 2016, and 2018.[113] Pursuant to article 20 of the Law of Lawyers, a law firm funded by the state shall independently conduct legal services in accordance with the law and shall be liable for its debts with all the assets of the law firm.[114]

Article 14 of the Administrative Measures (as amended 2018) further requires that a law firm funded by the state shall have at least two lawyers who are in compliance with the Law of Lawyers and are capable of full-time practice.[115] In addition, under the Administrative Measures, a law firm funded by the state shall be established by the local county-level judicial administrative agency, and the relevant department of the local county-level people's government must approve the establishment and provide a financial guarantee before applying for the establishment permit.[116]

A solo-practice law firm is basically an individually operated law firm. It is founded with the investment of a single lawyer and the name of the law firm is a combination of the names of the province, city, and the lawyer. Like a single-person-invested enterprise, the founding lawyer of a solo-practice firm bears unlimited external liabilities of the firm. Also, it is required under the Law of Lawyers that to form a solo-practice law firm, the founder shall be a lawyer with more than five years of practice experience in addition to the general conditions for creating a law firm.[117] Further, under article 11 of the Administrative Measures of Law Firms, the founder of a solo-practice law firm should be capable of full-time practice and have assets over RMB 100,000 yuan.[118]

Most of the law firms in China now are formed under the partnership business structure. As provided in article 15 of the Law of Lawyers, formation of a partnership law firm requires three or more partners, and the person intending to establish a partnership law firm shall be a lawyer with at least three years of experience in the profession.[119] It is further provided that the partnership-based law firm can be in the form of either a common partnership or a special common partnership pursuant to the Partnership Law, and all partners in the law firm bear responsibilities according to the type of partnership of the firm.[120]

Under the Partnership Law,[121] a professional service institution, including a law firm, may be organized as a special common partnership. The special common

[113] The Administrative Measures of Law Firms were adopted on July 18, 2008. The 2018 amended version of the Administrative Measures is available at www.66law.cn/tiaoli/165.aspx (hereinafter referred to as Administrative Measures).

[114] See the Law of Lawyers, *supra* note 81, art. 20.

[115] See the Administrative Measures, *supra* note 113, art. 14.

[116] See *id.*

[117] See the Law of Lawyers, *supra* note 81, art. 16.

[118] See the Administrative Measures, *supra* note 113, art. 11.

[119] See *id.*, art. 15.

[120] See *id.*

[121] The Law of Partnership Enterprises was adopted on February 23, 1997, and amended 2006. A full text of the Partnership Law is available at www.npc.gov.cn/wxzl/gongbao/2006-09/26/content_5354975.htm.

partnership means that a partner or several partners shall bear unlimited liabilities or unlimited and joint liabilities for the debts incurred to the partnership on the basis of fault, while other partners shall bear liabilities limited to their respective shares of property in the partnership.[122] In contrast, in a common partnership, all partners generally bear unlimited liabilities.[123]

The Administrative Measures of the Law Firms contain different provisions governing the two types of law firm partnerships. For a common partnership law firm to be established, it must meet such additional conditions as (a) a written partnership agreement; (b) three or more partners as founders; (c) more than three years of practicing experience and founders capable of full-time practice; and (d) more than RMB 300,000 yuan assets.[124] With regard to a special common partnership law firm, the additional conditions for formation include (a) a written partnership agreement; (b) more than twenty partners as founders; (c) more than three years of practice experience and founders capable of full-time practice; and (d) more than RMB 10 million yuan assets.[125]

As of 2022, there were more than 38,600 domestic law firms in China. Among the law firms, partnership-based law firms were 28,200 or 73.16% of the total; individually operated law firms were over 9,777, representing 25.62%, while the State-funded law firms were 604 (down from 970 in 2019), amounting to 1.56% (down from 2.98% in 2019). In terms of law firm size, more than 25,300 law firms had fewer than 10 lawyers, accounting for 65.50%; there were 8,023 law firms with 11 to 20 lawyers, or 20.74%, while more than 4,037 law firms contained 21 to 50 lawyers, or 10.44%. Some 784 law firms had 51 to 100 lawyers, accounting for 2.03%, and nearly 500 law firms consisted of 100 or more lawyers, representing 1.29%.[126] According to the MOJ, by the end of August 2025, the total number of domestic law firms increased to about 45,000, and about 207 overseas branches have established by Chinese law firms in 37 countries and regions around world, with more than 12,000 lawyers engaged in international legal practices.[127]

In addition, as an efford to expand legal service coverage in the country, MOJ in 2023 put in place a "pairing assistance" program to help legal service access in western regions and remote areas such as Tibet, Qinghai, Gansu, Sichuan, etc. Under the program, the MOJ provided funds to the law firms in eastern and central regions for their participating in the program, while local justice bureaus provided administrative support to those law firms for their establishing branches in the regions where lawyering resources are scarce. Pursuant to the MOJ, as of September 2025, with the establishment of law firm branch in 46 "counties with

[122] See *id.*, art. 55.
[123] See *id.*, art. 2.
[124] See the Administrative Measures, *supra* note 113, art. 9.
[125] See *id.*, art. 10.
[126] See MOJ 2022 Statistics, *supra* note 103.
[127] See the MOJ, News Briefing, *supra* note 107.

no lawyers", China has achieved the "full coverage" of legal services at all counties in the country.[128]

D. *Chinese Bar Association and Maintenance of CPC Leadership in Chinese Legal Practices*

The Chinese Bar Association is known as the All China Lawyers Association (ACLA). The ACLA was established in 1985 upon approval by the CPC. The ACLA's inaugural general meeting was held on July 5, 1986. In its Articles of Association, the ACLA is defined as a social group legal person composed of lawyers and law firms, and a national self-regulatory organization for lawyers, which manages the lawyer industry in accordance with the law.[129] In fact, however, it is a semi-government entity under the supervision and guidance of the MOJ.

Like all other semi-government or government-controlled organizations or associations, the ACLA must be loyal to the CPC. As stated in its Articles of Association (as amended 2018), the mission of the ACLA includes, among others, adherence to the guiding ideology of Xi Jinping Thought; adherence to the leadership of the CPC; uniting and leading its members to hold high the great banner of socialism with Chinese characteristics; maintaining firmly the authority and centralized leadership of the Central Committee of the CPC with Xi Jinping as the core; faithfully implementing the duties and mission of the work team of the socialist rule of law with Chinese characteristics; strengthening the ideological and political construction of the lawyer forces; and making the support of the leadership of the CPC and support of the socialist rule of law as the basic requirements of lawyers' practice.[130]

Under the Articles of Association of the ACLA, the primary responsibilities of the ACLA are listed as follows: (a) to ensure that lawyers practice law in accordance with the law and to safeguard the lawful rights and interests of lawyers; (b) to "sort out and promote the exchange of" the work experience of lawyers; (c) to formulate industry norms and disciplinary rules; (d) to organize lawyers' professional training, professional ethics, and practicing discipline education, and assessment of lawyers' practicing activities; (e) to organize and manage internship activities for those who apply to be a practicing lawyer, and to assess the interns; (f) to reward and discipline lawyers and law firms; (g) to hear complaints or reports against lawyers, and mediate disputes arising from lawyers' practice activities; and (h) to undertake other duties stipulated by laws, administrative regulations, and rules.[131]

[128] See *id.* According to China's National Bureau of Statistics, in 2025, there are 1,323 counties in China, including 117 autonomous counties.

[129] See the Articles of Association of the ACLA, adopted in 1999, amended 2002, 2008, 2011, 2016, and 2018, available at www.acla.org.cn/home/toMenu?menuIdStr = 1-63.

[130] See *id.*

[131] See *id.*, art. 6.

Unfortunately, however, the political-slogan centered mission seems to turn the ACLA into more of a political tool of the CPC than a professional association. Although the mission of the ACLA also contains such statements as faithfulness to the Constitution and the law, consciously practicing the core socialist values, and safeguarding the legitimate rights and interests of the parties, the correct implementation of the law, and social fairness and justice,[132] these statements are overshadowed by the political feature of the ACLA, and as a set rule, the operation of the ACLA is subject to the authority and leadership of the CPC.

The ACLA is not alone. Law firms in China must also be under the control of the CPC. As noted, the latest amendment to the 2008 Administrative Measures of the Law Firms was made by the MOJ in 2018. The sole purpose of the 2018 amendment was to strengthen the leadership of the CPC in law firms. The 2018 amendment was related only to three articles, namely articles 3, 4, and 16.

The amended article 3 now reads:

> Law firms should adhere to Xi Jinping's new era of socialism with Chinese characteristics as the guidance; adhere to and strengthen the party's overall leadership over lawyers' work; firmly maintain the authority and centralized leadership of the Party Central Committee with Comrade Xi Jinping as the core; regard the support of the leadership of the Communist Party of China and the socialist rule of law as the basic requirements for the legal professions, and advance the consciousness and firmness of lawyers to follow the path of socialist rule of law with Chinese characteristics.[133]

For that purpose, article 4 now is revised to contain three mandates. First, it is required that law firms strengthen party construction and give full play to the role of the party organization as a "battle fortress" (stronghold for the party's interests), and the pioneer and exemplary role of lawyers who are party members. In other words, the party's leadership must be firmly maintained in every law firm.[134]

Second, the law firms must have a party organization branch. Under the amended article 4, a basic party organization must be established in a law firm that has three or more full party members.[135] If the law firm has fewer than three full

[132] See *id.*

[133] See the Administrative Measures (as amended 2018), *supra* note 113, art. 3. Under the previous article 3 (as amended 2016), law firms should regard supporting the leadership of the Communist Party of China and the socialist rule of law as basic requirements. The 2016 version of the Administrative Measures is available at http://pkulaw.cn/fulltext_form.aspx?Gid=280850&Db=chl.

[134] See the MOJ, *Decision on Amending the "Administrative Measures for Law Firms,"* adopted on December 5, 2018, effective January 15, 2019, at www.moj.gov.cn/government_public/content/2018-12/13/fggz_232477.html.

[135] Under the CPC Constitution, there are two types of the CPC members: full members and probationary members. One year of probationary membership is required prior to obtaining the full membership. See the CPC Constitution, art. 7, available at http://eng.chinamil.com.cn/CHINA_209163/TopStories_209189/10195159.html.

party members, it shall carry on the party's work through the party organization established jointly with another law firm, or a party's work instructor designated by the higher-level party organization. But the party's primary organization must be formed timely once the conditions (more than three full party members) are met.[136]

Third, law firms are required to establish and improve working mechanisms for party organizations to participate in the decision-making and management of law firms, and provide support for party organizations to carry out activities and to facilitate the party's work with needed venues, personnel, and funds.[137] In addition, article 16 is amended to demand an inclusion of this provision as required content into law firms' Articles of Association.[138]

According to MOJ statistics, by the end of 2019, the number of lawyers who were CPC party members reached 163,000, accounting for 34.5 percent of all lawyers in the country. In 1999, there were over 1,900 newly recruited party members who were lawyers. In addition, more than 12,600 party organizations were established among law firms nationwide, and more than 6,300 party's work instructors were dispatched to law firms that had no party members,[139] realizing the CPC's "full coverage" of domestic law firms. Additionally, as of 2022, over 12,017 lawyers were "delegates," including 4,219 delegates to people's congresses at various levels, 7,067 delegates to political consultation conferences at all levels, and 731 delegates to CPC congresses at different levels.[140]

E. *Chinese Legal Ethics and Professional Responsibilities*

Legal ethics have been and continue to be an issue facing Chinese lawyers or, more broadly, the entire Chinese legal profession. A highly notable feature in Chinese culture that undermines legal ethics is the strong appetite for personal relationships. As always is the case, personal relationships constitute a quite influential social force, and are heavily relied upon in individual actions. It is not a surprise to see that personal relationships are "so powerful that connections to the right people and an ability to get the desired results from them rather than possessing legal competence are stressed as the essential ingredient to a successful practice."[141]

In the past few decades, along with the development of legal services in the country, China has made many efforts to establish a regulatory system that governs lawyers in their practice. Both the Law of Lawyers and the Administrative Measures contain a great deal of provisions purposed to ensure that lawyers will act in a

[136] See *id.*
[137] See *id.*
[138] See *id.*
[139] See the MOJ 2019 Statistics, *supra* note 104.
[140] See the MOJ 2022 Statistics, *supra* note 103.
[141] See Leland Benton, *From Socialist Ethics to Legal Ethics: Legal Ethic, Professional Conduct and the Chinese Legal Profession*, 28 UCLA Pac. Basin L.J., 210, 231 (2011).

professional manner. In addition, there are specific ethic rules that streamline the conduct of lawyers and their practices.

As early as 1993, the MOJ promulgated the Lawyers' Profession Ethics and Practice Discipline Standards (Ethic Rules).[142] In 1996, the ACLA adopted a new version of the Ethic Rules (ACLA Ethic Rules). Amended in 2001,[143] the ACLA Ethic Rules are aimed at (a) maintaining the professional reputation of lawyers, (b) improving thoroughly the moral standards of the lawyers, (c) regulating the practice of lawyers, and (d) warranting that lawyers fulfill their mission and responsibilities to society and the public.[144]

The Ethic Rules (2001) consist of seven chapters and forty articles. The seven chapters are (a) general provisions, (b) basic norms of the professional ethics of lawyers, (c) discipline of lawyers in their working institutions, (d) discipline of lawyers in litigation and arbitration activities, (e) discipline concerning the relationship between lawyers and their clients as well as the opposing party, (f) discipline involving the relationships among lawyers, and (g) supplement provisions.[145]

In addition to the Ethic Rules, in 2004 the ACLA formulated the Conduct Code of the Legal Practice of Lawyers (ACLA Code of Conduct). Amended in 2009 and 2017,[146] the ACLA Code of Conduct is intended to serve as (a) a guide to regulate the practice of lawyers, (b) an industry standard for evaluating lawyers' practice, and (c) a norm of conduct for lawyers to self-discipline.[147]

The ACLA Code of Conduct contains 9 chapters and a total of 109 articles. It provides specific rules that govern the conduct of lawyers in such areas as legal practice, business promotion, relations between lawyers and clients or parties, participation in litigation or arbitration, relations among lawyers, relations between lawyers and their law firms, and the relationship between lawyers and lawyer associations.

Literally, the ethical standards and professional responsibilities provided in these regulations and rules for lawyers are quite compatible with, if not the same as, internationally accepted common practices. But the problem, as many have observed, is the level of compliance in the country.[148] The violation of ethics and conduct rules often occurs due to the lack of an effective enforcement mechanism. In many cases, the ignorance of the rules results directly from

142 The MOJ's Lawyers' Professional Ethics and Practice Discipline Standards were adopted on December 27, 1993, available at www.law-lib.com/law/law_view1.asp?id = 10081.

143 The ACLA's Lawyers' Professional Ethics and Practice Discipline Standards were adopted in 1996, amended November 26, 2001, available at www.law-lib.com/law/law_view.asp?id = 17071.

144 See *id.*, art. 1.

145 See *id.*, arts. 1–40.

146 The Conduct Code of Legal Practice of Lawyers was adopted by the ACLA on March 20, 2004. The amended version is available at www.360doc.com/content/17/0820/16/32444430_680639107.shtml (hereinafter referred to as ACLA Code of Conduct).

147 See *id.*, art. 1.

148 See Benton, *supra* note 141, at 231.

conscionable desires to establish or maintain an interpersonal relationship or personal networking.

According to a scholarly study, although prohibited by law, certain conduct in violation of the legal ethics has a high rate of reoccurrence.[149] An example of notable conduct is legal representation with a conflict of interest. The Law of Lawyers explicitly prohibits a lawyer from representing parties on both sides in the same case, and from handling legal affairs that have a conflict with his or her own interests or the interests of his or her close relatives.[150] The ACLA Code of Conduct further requires all law firms to establish a conflict-of-interest review system, and to conduct a conflict-of-interest review before being retained.[151]

In actual practice, however, conflicts of interest still often arise. Common situations include conflicts of interest between lawyers in the same case, conflicts of interest between the same lawyer in different cases, and conflicts of interest between different lawyers in the same law firm in the same case.[152] Also under the ACLA Code of Conduct, a lawyer shall not represent a client and shall take the initiative to recuse himself or herself whenever a relationship of interest or conflict of interest exists between the lawyer and the client.[153] But often, the concerns about potential conflicts of interest were overcome by the desire to generate more income or boost business for the lawyers or the law firms.

Another conduct violation frequently seen is the lack of accountability or breach of fiduciary duty. Both the Law of Lawyers and the ACLA Code of Conduct mandate lawyers to be honest, trustworthy, diligent, and responsible, to protect the legitimate rights and interests of the parties on the basis of facts and laws, to safeguard the correct implementation of the law, and to maintain social fairness and justice.[154] There are, nonetheless, many situations where the clients' interests were seriously damaged as a result of the lawyer's failure to act with reasonable diligence and promptness in representing the client. In some cases, lawyers failed to present the needed evidence. In other cases, lawyers neglected to file an appeal within the time allowed. In commercial transactions, complaints about lawyers often arise in cases where lawyers failed to review contracts or other legal documents diligently, failed to conduct a due diligence study as needed, or even assigned non-lawyers to practice on their behalf.[155]

Also a quite troublesome conduct violation is the improper behavior of lawyers in their case-handling processes. One common phenomenon is the private contact of

149 See Wu Hongqi, *Retrospect and Prospect of the Construction of Lawyers' Professional Ethics*, 2 Shanghai Jiao Tong U. L. Rev. 25, 34 (2018).

150 See the Law of Lawyers, *supra* note 81, art. 39.

151 See the ACLA Code of Conduct, *supra* note 146, art. 49.

152 See Hongqi, *supra* note 149, at 34.

153 See *id.*, art. 50.

154 See the Law of Lawyers, *supra* note 81, art. 2; see also the ACLA Code of Conduct, *supra* note 146, art. 7.

155 See Hongqi, *supra* note 149, at 34.

lawyers with judges or government officials in order to achieve the goal desired, to affect the outcome of the case, or to obtain a favorable action from the government. Other improper behaviors include false propaganda for publicity, false promises to induce clients to retain the service, slander of other lawyers to unfairly compete, establishment of branch offices without authorization, and refusal to cooperate with lawyer associations in investigations.[156]

In a nationwide survey conducted in 2016 on professional ethics of lawyers, among 18,552 entities and 5,848 legal practitioners in 31 provincial-level regions across the country that were interviewed, 22.6% of the respondents believed that their local lawyers were likely or very likely to have false publicity issues, 23.6% expressed concern that local lawyers were likely or very likely to have made false promises, and 22.7% held an opinion that local lawyers were likely or very likely to have an improper connection of interest with judges.[157]

A similar nationwide questionnaire survey in 2016 also revealed that of 6,916 people across the country surveyed on how they view their local lawyers with regard to "no false promises and no false propaganda," less than half responded with an answer of "full trust" (44.13%) or "somewhat trust" (3.48%). Among the majority, 247 people or 3.57% chose "extremely distrustful," 2,209 people or 31.94% chose "not trustful," and the rest were returned with no answers.[158] The two surveys show that the general public in China are not currently satisfied with lawyers' observance of professional ethics.

In terms of Chinese reality, it is important to be mindful that in at least two aspects there are substantial differences between China and elsewhere in legal ethics. The first aspect involves confidentiality. In the United States, for example, the communications between lawyer and client are privileged as a matter of law and thus the lawyer is protected from being forced to reveal them. In addition, the ethic privilege under the rule of confidentiality requires a lawyer not to use the information obtained from representation of a client to the disadvantage of the client without informed consent.

In China, however, such privilege does not seem to exist. Instead, the lawyer must disclose the facts and information learned from the client concerning the crime that they or another person is allegedly preparing to carry out if they will endanger national or public security or seriously endanger the personal safety of others. Confidentiality only applies to the relevant materials or information acquired in the legal representation that the client and others do not want to disclose, including business secrets and personal privacy.[159]

[156] See *id.*

[157] See Zhang Baosheng, Zhang Zhang, & Wu Hongqi., China Judicial Civilization Index Report 2016, 34–37 (Chinese University of Political Science and Law Press, 2017).

[158] See Hongqi, *supra* note 149, at 31.

[159] See the Law of Lawyers, *supra* note 81, art. 38, and the ACLA Code of Conduct, *supra* note 146, art. 9.

The second aspect concerns the loyalty of lawyers. In many other countries, a lawyer, once retained, is obligated to pursue and must also be free to pursue the client's objectives unfettered by conflicting responsibilities or interests. Such loyalty is derived from the principle of agency or the fiduciary duty. By contrast, lawyers in China, as noted, are required to firmly make the adherence to the leadership of the CPC the basic proposition for their careers.

Under the ACLA Code of Conduct, lawyers are prohibited from using their lawyer status or the name of a law firm to speculate on individual cases, and from instigating, abetting, or organizing relevant interest groups to interfere with or disrupt the normal social order. Lawyers must not attack the socialist system, engage in activities that endanger national security, or instruct the parties to collude for false confessions, forged evidence, or interference with normal judicial activities. Evidently, the language used in the ACLA Code of Conduct is so broad and vague that it is very difficult, if not impossible, for a lawyer to put the client's interests first or to effectively protect the client's interests.

In 2014, the MOJ issued the Opinions on Further Strengthening the Construction of Lawyers' Professional Ethics.[160] The MOJ Opinions called for vigorously strengthening the professional ethics of lawyers with "loyalty, serving the people, rule of law, justice, integrity, and dedication" as the main contents.[161] To implement the MOJ Opinions, in the same year the ACLA adopted the Basic Norms of Professional Ethics for Lawyers (ACLA Basic Norms), which contained six articles corresponding to the main contents required by the MOJ to be included in professional ethics.[162]

The ACLA Basic Norms are unfortunately highly political, which makes lawyers even more like party-interest-serving social workers than the licensed practitioner providing legal services to the client as defined in the Law of Lawyers. With regard to loyalty, for example, the ACLA Basic Norms signifies with a mandate that lawyers should stick firmly with the ideals and beliefs of socialism with Chinese characteristics, adhere to the essential attributes of the socialist lawyer system with Chinese characteristics, support the leadership of the party, support the socialist system, and consciously safeguard the dignity of the Constitution and the law.[163]

Nevertheless, according to the ACLA Basic Norms, it is imperative that lawyers always regard practicing for the people as their fundamental purpose, serve the people wholeheartedly, and strive to safeguard the fundamental interests of the people and the legitimate rights and interests of citizens, legal persons, and other

[160] See the MOJ, *Opinions on Further Strengthening the Construction of Lawyers' Professional Ethics*, issued on May 30, 2014, available at www.moj.gov.cn/government_public/content/2014-05/25/fggz_6527.html.

[161] See *id.*, art. 3.

[162] See the ACLA, *The Basic Norms of Professional Ethics of Lawyers*, issued on June 5, 2014. A full text is available at http://en.pkulaw.cn/display.aspx?cgid = 782d442068b02a95bdfb&lib = law.

[163] See *id.*, art. 1.

organizations through practicing activities. Lawyers should also seriously perform legal aid obligations, actively participate in social welfare activities, and consciously assume social responsibilities.[164]

F. *Foreign Law Firms in China*

China's opening-up of its legal service market to foreign law firms began in the early 1990s as part of the country's effort to join the GATS (General Agreement on Trade in Service). On May 26, 1992, the MOJ and the SAIC (State Administration of Industry and Commerce) jointly issued the Interim Provisions for Foreign Law Firms to Establish Offices in China.[165] In July 1992, with approval by the State Council, the MOJ started to allow foreign law firms (including Hong Kong law firms) to open offices in certain pilot cities.

The first group of pilot cities included Beijing, Shanghai, Guangzhou, Haikou, and Shenzhen. On October 20, 1992, the MOJ granted the first twelve foreign and Hong Kong law firms the permits to establish offices in Beijing, Shanghai, and Guangzhou, respectively.[166] At the time, the activities of foreign law firms in the country were strictly limited to three areas: (a) providing clients with consultations on the laws of the country where the law firm has been approved to engage in legal practice and relevant international treaties, international commercial laws, and international practices; (b) being retained by clients or Chinese law firms to handle legal affairs in the country where the law firm has been approved to operate; and (c) retaining, on behalf of foreign clients, Chinese law firms to handle legal affairs in China.[167]

There were 303 representative offices established by foreign law firms in China in 1999. In addition, some thirteen representative offices were operated by Taiwanese law firms. Furthermore, twenty-five Hong Kong and Macao law firms established partnership-type joint law firms with mainland China law firms, and eight foreign law firms established representative offices in the Shanghai Free Trade Zone and formed joint ventures with Chinese law firms.[168] The total number of foreign law firms, however, was down to 282 in 2022, representing a total of 271 foreign law firms from 22 countries and regions, of which there were 205 foreign law firms (225 in

[164] See *id.*, art. 2.

[165] See the MOJ and the SAIC, *The Interim Provisions for Foreign Law Firms to Establish Offices in China*, available at www.fdi.gov.cn/1800000121_23_69599_0_7.html (hereinafter referred to as 1992 Interim Provisions).

[166] See the MOJ, *Notice on the Matters Concerning the Establishment of Offices of Foreign Law Firms in China*, October 30, 1992, available at www.chinalawedu.com/falvfagui/fg22598/28352.shtml. Among the twelve foreign law firms, there were eight Hong Kong law firms, two English law firms, one French law firm, and one American law firm. The first US law firm was Coudert Brothers.

[167] See the MOJ 1992 Interim Provisions, *supra* note 165, art. 15.

[168] See MOJ 2022 Statistics, *supra* note 103.

2019) and 64 Hong Kong law firms.[169] In 2023–2024, some twelve U.S. major law firms closed their branches in China due to concerns about the sour U.S.–China relationship and the changing legal environment in the country.[170]

The presence of foreign law firms is governed by the Regulations on the Administration of Representative Offices of Foreign Law Firms in China, promulgated by the State Council in 2001 (Foreign Law Firm Regulations).[171] Under article 6 of the Foreign Law Firm Regulations, foreign law firms must obtain approval from the judicial administration departments of the State Council to establish representative offices in, and to dispatch representatives to, China.[172]

For the administration of foreign law firms operating in China, the judicial administration departments refer to those of the governments of provinces, autonomous regions, and municipalities directly under the central government. According to the Foreign Law Firm Regulations, upon receiving the required application documents and materials filed by a foreign law firm for establishment of a representative office, the relevant judicial administration department should complete an examination within three months and then submit its examination opinion to the MOJ for review. The MOJ should make a decision within six months. Once approved, a license and certificate will be issued.[173]

The representative office and the representatives of foreign law firms may only conduct certain activities that do not encompass Chinese legal affairs. In addition to those provided in the Interim Provisions, the foreign law firm's activities allowed in China include: (a) to maintain through contract a long-term retaining relation with Chinese law firms for legal affairs and (b) to provide information on the impact of the Chinese legal environment.[174] But it is unclear what constitutes "China legal affairs."

The representative office of foreign law firms may, under a retainer agreement, directly instruct the lawyers in the retained Chinese law firms, as agreed between both parties. A representative office and its representatives are, however, prohibited from conducting any legal service activities or other for-profit activities other than those provided in the law.[175] Moreover, no representative office of foreign law firms

[169] With more US law firms to pull out of China recently, the number of foreign law firms in the country declined further. See John Roemer, *US Firms Are Closing Their China Offices*, ABA J., October 1, 2024, available at www.abajournal.com/magazine/article/us-law-firms-are-closing-their-china-offices; see also Pak Yiu & Echo Wong, *U.S. Law Firms Hasten Retreat from Mainland China*, NIKKEI Asia, July 8, 2024, available at https://asia.nikkei.com/Business/Business-trends/U.S.-law-firms-hasten-retreat-from-mainland-China.

[170] See Maisy Mok, *Flight or Fight*, China Bus. L. J., October 7, 2024, at https://law.asia/us-law-firms-exit-china-causes-trends/.

[171] See the State Council, *Regulations on Administration of Foreign Law Firms' Representative Offices in China*, issued on December 22, 2001, effective January 1, 2002, at www.china.org.cn/english/DAT/214778.htm (hereinafter referred to as *Foreign Law Firm Regulations*).

[172] See *id.*, art. 6.

[173] See *id.*, art. 9.

[174] See *id.*, art. 15.

[175] See *id.*

may hire Chinese practicing lawyers, and no supporting staff employed in the representative office may provide legal services to clients.[176]

As part of an administrative measure, it is required that the representative offices file an annual report for review. Under article 22 of the Foreign Law Firm Regulations, the representative office of a foreign law firm shall, before March 31 of each year, submit to the provincial judicial administration department where the office is located a copy of its license and its representatives' certificates and other materials as required by the law.[177] After their examination, the resulting opinions will be submitted to the MOJ for record.

In September 2002, the MOJ issued the Rules for the Implementation of the Foreign Law Firm Regulations (Implementation Rules).[178] The Implementation Rules on the one hand further refine procedural matters concerning the establishment of representative offices, and on the other hand clarify certain issues that appear to be vague in the provisions of the Foreign Law Firm Regulations. According to the MOJ, the Implementation Rules intend to help the judicial administrative department perform administrative duties to manage foreign legal service activities in China.[179]

The Implementation Rules define a foreign law firm as a legal service entity duly established outside of China that is composed of foreign practicing lawyers, engages in legal service activities other than Chinese legal affairs, and independently assumes external civil liabilities by all or some of its members. Excluded from the definition of a foreign law firm are (a) legal service departments in foreign governments, commercial organizations, and other institutions and (b) a practice association of two or more foreign practicing lawyers or law firms that does not share profits or risks.[180]

Pursuant to the Foreign Law Firm Regulations, a representative of the representative office must be a practicing lawyer and must have practiced for not less than two years outside of China, without being punished for a criminal offense or a

[176] See *id.*, art. 16. As a matter of fact, many foreign law firms hire Chinese lawyers to work in their representative offices. But once hired, the Chinese lawyer does not work as a lawyer but as a legal consultant or legal assistant.

[177] See *id.*, art. 22. For the purpose of filing the annual report, the following materials from the previous year are required: (1) information on the performance of legal services, including the legal affairs retained to Chinese law firms; (2) the annual financial statement audited by an accounting firm, and documents certifying that the accounts have been settled within the territory of China and taxes have been paid according to law; (3) information on the change of the firm's representatives and the employment of Chinese support staff; (4) information about the residence of the representatives in the territory of China; (5) information concerning the registration of the office and its representatives; and (6) other information on the performance of the duties provided for by the law.

[178] See the MOJ, *Rules for the Implementation of the Regulations on the Administration of Representative Offices of Foreign Law Firms in China*, July 4, 2002, available at www.cctv.com/news/china/20020731/190.html (hereinafter referred to as *Implementation Rules*).

[179] See *id.*, art. 1.

[180] See *id.*, art. 2.

violation of the professional ethics or practice discipline. The chief representative must have practiced for more than three years outside of China and be a partner or equivalent of the firm.[181] A foreign practicing lawyer, under the Implementation Rules, refers to a person who has legally obtained a foreign lawyer's practicing qualification and has obtained a legal practice license in a country where the qualification is obtained.[182]

In order to avoid ambiguity and confusion, the Implementation Rules explicitly address, among other things, three major issues arising from the provisions of the Foreign Law Firm Regulations. One issue was the scope of China legal affairs that may not be touched by foreign law firm representative offices. Article 32 provides a list of matters that fall within China legal affairs.[183] In addition, article 33 makes it clear that the representative office of a foreign law firm may not give any specific opinion or judgment with respect to the application of Chinese law when providing information about the environmental impact of Chinese laws.[184] Moreover, under article 38 of the Implementation Rules, foreign law firm representatives and their supporting staff may not provide Chinese legal services to clients in the name of a Chinese legal consultant.[185]

The China legal affairs as listed in article 32 include (a) participating in litigation activities in China as a lawyer; (b) providing opinions or verification on specific issues concerning the application of Chinese law in contracts, agreements, articles of association, or other written documents; (c) providing opinions and evidence on actions or incidents in which Chinese laws are applicable; (d) offering opinions or comments in arbitration; and (e) on behalf of the client, handling the registration, modification, application, filing, and other procedures with Chinese government agencies or other organizations of administrative functions authorized by laws and regulations.

The next issue concerns whether a foreign law firm may establish more than one office in China. The Foreign Law Firm Regulations are silent in this regard. The Implementation Rules permit a second office with certain conditions. In accordance with article 10 of the Implementation Rules, to apply for an additional representative office, two conditions must be met: (1) the recently established representative office in China has been practicing for three consecutive years and (2) the established representative office and representatives abide by Chinese laws, regulations, and rules, abide by the professional ethics and discipline of lawyers, and have not been held accountable for various legal responsibilities stipulated in the law.[186]

[181] See the *Foreign Law Firm Regulations*, *supra* note 171, art. 7.
[182] See the *Implementation Rules*, *supra* note 178, art. 2.
[183] See *id.*, art. 32.
[184] See *id.*, art. 33.
[185] See *id.*, art. 38.
[186] See *id.*, art. 10.

The third issue was related to hiring Chinese lawyers. As noted, the Foreign Law Firm Regulations forbid the representative office of a foreign law firm from hiring Chinese practicing lawyers. Pursuant to article 40 of the Implementation Rules, in any of the following circumstances, the representative office of a foreign law firm shall be deemed as hiring a Chinese practicing lawyer: (a) entering into an employment or labor agreement with a Chinese practicing lawyer; (b) forming *de facto* employment or labor relations with a Chinese practicing lawyer; (c) reaching an agreement with a Chinese practicing lawyer to share profits, share risks, or participate in management; (d) making payment for remuneration, expenses or business shares to a Chinese practicing lawyer; and (e) retaining a Chinese practicing lawyer to engage in external business activities in the name of the law firm or representative office of the law firm.[187]

[187] See *id.*, art. 40.

PART II

Chinese Civil Law and Civil Code

Civil law may refer to a branch of law or a family of legal tradition. As a branch of law, civil law is the law regulating civil matters. In terms of legal tradition, civil law means a system of law that originated from Europe and relies on written statutes. Civil law as a legal tradition is often referenced in comparison with common law, which is derived from judicial precedents or case law rather than statutes. Both civil law and common law are considered highly influential legal traditions in the contemporary world.

As noted, the two Opium Wars in the 1840s and 1850s broke up China's clan-based traditional legal culture and brought the Chinese legal system into the civil law family. Ever since, China has been characterized as a civil law country. Although the 1949 power shift in the country resulted in China pursuing socialism under the leadership of the Communist Party of China (CPC), the civil law nature of the Chinese legal system remained intact. In fact, the effort to build the socialist legal landscape was modeled on the former Soviet Union after the abolishment of all existing codes by the Nationalist Government, which further enhanced the civil law distinctions in the country.

In contrast to common law, a striking distinction of the civil law tradition is legal codification or code of law. One of the most significant codes in major civil law countries is the civil code – a codification of private laws regulating civil affairs relating to persons, things, obligations, family relations, and successions. Historically, the 1804 French *Napoleonic* Code (Code Civil) and the 1881 German BGB (Civil Law Books) not only best represented the civil law codification, but also set a model followed by many other countries.

As discussed, China in its history had a criminal law focused legal culture. There was barely any civil legislation until the early 1900s. In 1907, the Office of Legal Revision under the imperial government was established to revise existing laws and draft new laws. Influenced by scholars who were educated abroad, the legal drafting targeted primarily the civil code. The first draft of the civil code was completed in

December 1910. Although it was finalized in 1911, the draft never became law due to the fall of the Qing Dynasty that year.[1]

The first draft of the civil code, which was mainly based on the German model, consisted of 5 parts, 36 chapters, and a total of 1,569 articles. The five parts included general principles, rights of *obligatio*, property rights, domestic relations, and inheritance. Despite its doomed fate, the first draft of the civil code provided a blueprint for later civil law legislation. For example, the draft for the first time adopted the civil law concept of *obligatio* in the country to describe civil rights and obligations. Since then, the law of *obligatio* has become an important component of the nation's civil legislation.

The first enactment of a civil code in China took place in 1930, when the Civil Code of the Republic of China was adopted. Consisting of 1,225 articles, the 1930 Civil Code had 5 parts (Books), referring to General Principles, *Obligatio*, Right Over Things, Family, and Succession. Prior to the adoption of the 1930 Civil Code, there was an attempt to pass a civil code in the 1920s. A draft of civil code was completed, but eventually aborted due to political chaos in the country under warlord governments.[2]

Note, however, that during the process of drafting the 1930 Civil Code, the different parts were promulgated separately at different times. The first part (Book I) was promulgated on May 23, 1929, effective the same year. Books II and III were adopted on November 15, 1929 and November 30, 1929, respectively, effective at the same time on May 5, 1930. The last two Books were enacted on December 26, 1930, effective May 5, 1931.[3] The 1930 Civil Code ceased to operate in mainland China in 1949, when it was abolished together with the other five codes, but it remains operative today in Taiwan.

From 1949 to 1979, there were two failed attempts to draft a civil code to fill in the hole left by the annulment of the 1930 Civil Code. The first drafting work began in 1954 and was completed in 1956, with a draft containing 525 articles that covered general provisions, ownership, *obligatio*, and inheritance. The 1956 draft basically followed the 1922 Soviet Civil Code. Unfortunately, the Anti-Rightist Movement against intellectuals that started in 1957 eliminated all legislation in the country, and the drafting of the civil code came to a complete stop.[4]

1 See Wang Jiafu, *Civil Law Obligatio*, 16 (Law Press, 1991). See also Joseph En-Pao Wang (ed.), *Civil Code of Republic of China*, in China Studies, Studies in Chinese Government and Law, x–xi (Kelly & Walsh Ltd., 1930) (Reprinted by Univ. Pubs. of Am., Inc. 1976).

2 See Wang, *supra* note 1, at 19.

3 See Ching-Lin Hsia, James Chow, and Yukon Chang, The Civil Code of the Republic of China, (Kelly & Walsh Ltd. 1930), available at https://archive.org/details/civilcodeofrepuboo chin/page/n9/mode/2up.

4 See Huang Lansong, *The Brief History of the Compilation of the New China Civil Code*, Chinese Social Science Net, November 23, 2016, available at www.cssn.cn/sf/bwsf_fx/201611/ t20161123_3287568.shtml. See also People's Daily, *The Historical Evolution of the Civil Code of New China*, October 26, 2016, available at www.npc.gov.cn/npc/c10134/201610/ b1efb07c9bb 14b4f99253ef07b1a3d53.shtml.

Drafting work resumed in 1962, which resulted in the second draft of the Civil Code in 1964. Compared to the first draft, the second draft was much shorter and had only three parts: general provisions, ownership, and property transfer, with 262 articles in total. What was interesting about the second draft was that it tried to depart from the former Soviet model on the one hand, and was determined to stay away from the civil code of capitalist countries on the other. As a result, the second draft appeared to be neither fish nor fowl, despite its embedded civil law characteristics.[5]

The fate of the second draft of the civil code was no better than that of the first draft. The Cultural Revolution, launched in 1966, paralyzed the country for a decade, and the second draft of the civil code was never on the legislative agenda. It was the economic reform that prompted the third attempt to draft the civil code. As early as August 1979, the Standing Committee of the NPC formed a group for civil code drafting. An initial draft was completed in May 1982, which contained 8 parts, 43 chapters, and 465 articles.[6]

However, due to the difficulty in reaching a consensus on various issues, the focus of the drafting work was then shifted from adoption of a comprehensive civil code to the enactment of each specific part, with a plan to consolidate the enacted parts into a single code when the time was ripe. Consequently, a series of significant legislations in the civil field were made, including the 1986 General Principles of Civil Law, 1999 Contract Law, 2007 Property Law, 2009 Torts Law, and 2017 General Provisions of Civil Law (GPCL). All these laws paved the way for the final enactment of the Civil Code in 2020.

[5] See Lansong, *supra* note 4.

[6] See *id.*

7

General Provisions of the Civil Code

INTRODUCTION

The drafting of the Civil Code officially started in 2015. As a matter of fact, the Standing Committee of the National People's Congress (NPC) once tried to push through an enactment of a civil code in 2001 when drafting the Property Law, and a draft containing 1,209 articles was even submitted to a formal meeting of the Standing Committee for hearing in 2002. But the effort was suspended until 2015 due to a need both in theory and in practice to focus on legislation in specific civil areas.

The 2020 Civil Code was enacted in two steps. The first step was the enactment of the general provisions, which resulted in the 2017 General Provisions of Civil Law (GPCL). The second step was the promulgation of all specific parts on the basis of previously adopted laws. On May 28, 2020, the NPC passed the final draft of the Civil Code, marking the beginning of the era of the comprehensive Civil Code in China.[1] Effective January 1, 2021, the Civil Code is hailed in the country as a basic law of the socialist market economy and an encyclopedia of social life.[2]

The laws incorporated into the Civil Code include the 1981 Marriage Law, the 1985 Succession Law, the 1986 General Principles of the Civil Law, the 1991 Adoption Law, the 1995 Guarantee Law, the 1999 Contract Law, the 2007 Property Law, the 2009 Tort Liability Law, and the 2017 GPCL. It should be noted that all of these laws were repealed upon the effectiveness of the 2020 Civil Code.[3] Therefore, there is no separate contract law, property law, torts law, or marriage law but a general Civil Code in China.

[1] See the Civil Code of China (2020). A full text is available at www.npc.gov.cn/npc/c30834/202006/75ba6483b8344591abd07917e1d25cc8.shtml (hereinafter the 2020 Civil Code).

[2] See Liu Dong, *This Encyclopedia Is for You*, edited from Xinhua Net, May 28, 2020, at www.npc.gov.cn/npc/c30834/202005/070c47d5666143fd8df8b8ce805bd43d.shtml.

[3] See the 2020 Civil Code, *supra* note 1, art. 1260.

1. OVERVIEW OF THE CIVIL CODE

Promulgation of the 2020 Civil Code is the first ever comprehensive civil law legislation in China after 1949. It codifies the basic rules that govern all civil and commercial matters and is expected to strengthen the protection of civil rights and promote fulfillment of civil obligations. As a primary source of law regulating civil and commercial affairs, the Civil Code constitutes the fundamental legal framework under which the country operates in every dimension of civil and commercial relationships.

The Civil Code consists of 7 parts and 1,260 articles. Each part contains several chapters that are numbered independently. The seven parts include General Provisions, Right to Things, Contracts, Rights of Personality, Marriage and Family, Succession, and Tort Liabilities. Note that unlike the civil code in other countries, China's 2020 Civil Code does not make *obligatio* an independent part, but rather singles out Contracts and Torts from the *obligatio* and provides them in separate parts.

A. *Structure of the Civil Code*

Structurally, the Civil Code, like all other laws based on the civil law tradition, is divided into two sections: general provisions and specific provisions. The General Provisions, which constitute part I of the Civil Code, mostly incorporate the 2017 GPCL. Provided in the general provisions are mainly the basic principles and general rules that govern all civil relationships and activities. The specific provisions containing parts II to VII cover particular types of civil relationships and activities.

A notable feature of the Civil Code is that it signifies the rights of personality (the inherent civil rights that are exclusively enjoyed by the person in civil law, referring to such rights as the right to life, name, portrait, honor, reputation, privacy, etc.) and makes them an independent part of the Code. During the drafting process, there were debates on whether the rights of personality should be a separate part of the Civil Code. The views differed mainly in the relationship between personality and personality rights and the difference between personality rights and other civil rights. A major concern was that it would be difficult to define the scope of the rights of personality and hard as well to prescribe liability for infringement upon the rights.

Scholars in favor of having separate provisions for the rights of personality believe that personality rights are independent civil rights and thus should be stipulated parallel to other civil rights. In addition, according to those scholars, the rights of personality are purposed to protect personality interests rather than the personality that refers mainly to the qualification of legal subjects. Scholars taking the opposite view, however, argue that personality rights are inseparable from personality, and although personality rights are different from other civil rights, they should not be provided separately but should be included in the general provisions.

Related to the scholarly debate were the arguments about the specific model for personality rights to be provided in the Civil Code. There were three options on the table: (a) to formulate separately the law of personality rights as an independent part of the Civil Code; (b) to provide the personality rights in the general provisions, as the Swiss Civil Code does; or (c) to follow the German Civil Code, having the personality rights provided in the torts law provisions. The drafters of the Civil Code took the first option.

B. *Concept of Civil Law*

Civil law as a legal concept was originated from *jus civile*, a part of Roman law that exclusively applied to Roman citizens.[4] In Roman jurisprudence, there were three major parts of private law: *jus civile*, *jus gentium*, and *jus naturale*.[5] Consisting of the enacted or customary law governing the relations of Roman citizens among themselves, *jus civile* was referred to as "the law peculiar to one state or people."[6] In contrast, *jus gentium*, or the law of nations, was the law applicable to all people within Roman jurisdiction regardless of their citizenship, and it was devised as a system of equity applying to cases between foreigners and Roman citizens. *Jus naturale*, meaning natural law, was a category of law based on "the principles shared by all living creatures."[7]

Derived from *jus civile*, civil law, through the process of codification, soon developed into a legal source that provided a comprehensive written collection of all private laws. Both the French Civil Code and German Civil Law Books not only signified such development but also laid a foundation for the modern civil law in terms of both the body of law and the family of legal tradition. As a body of law, as noted, civil law is defined as the law concerned with civil or private rights and remedies.[8]

In China, the term "civil law" is a foreign concept, although the Chinese words equivalent to "civil law" were once used in the Book of Documents (*Shang Shu*), a classical history book in the *Spring and Autumn* period during 772 BC to 476 BC.[9] A common belief in the country is that the notion of civil law was introduced to China by Japanese jurists at the time when the *Qing* Civil Code was drafted in the early twentieth century.[10] But the official use of the term "civil law" began with the enactment of the 1930 Civil Code by the Nationalist government.[11]

4 For general information, see George Mousourakis, Roman Law and the Origins of the Civil Law Tradition, 27–94 (Springer, 2015).

5 See Gordon Sherman, *Jus Gentium* and International Law, 12 Am. J. Int'l L. 56, 57 (1918).

6 See Black's Law Dictionary, *Jus Civile*, 858 (6th ed., West, 1990).

7 See Berkeley Law, *Roman Legal Tradition and the Compilation of Justinian*, available at www.law.berkeley.edu/wp-content/uploads/2019/08/romanlaw.pdf, accessed August 23, 2025.

8 See Black's Law Dictionary, *supra* note 6, at 246.

9 See Shen Weixing, Theory of Civil Law, 1 (Peking University Press, 2013).

10 See *id.* at 2. See also Tong Rou, Chinese Civil Law, 2 (Law Press, 1989).

11 See Weixing, *supra* note 9.

Conceptually, civil law as a body of law is commonly understood in China as the legal norms regulating property and personal relations between civil subjects with equal legal status.[12] It is used as a general term for, or a conglomeration of, the laws formulated and enforced by the state that govern civil relationships and activities.[13] In the 1986 General Principles of Civil Law, civil law was defined as the law that regulates the property and personal relationships between citizens and legal persons as civil subjects of equal status.

The 2017 GPCL modified the civil law definition from the 1986 General Principles of Civil Law. Under article 2 of the 2017 GPCL, civil law is the law that regulates property and personal relationships between natural persons, legal persons, and non-legal person organizations being civil subjects with equal status.[14] There are two major changes in the 2017 GPCL definition. First, citizens are replaced with natural persons. One reason is that the term citizen appears more political than civil. Second, the non-legal person organizations are added as civil subjects for purposes of civil law. The 2017 GPCL definition is adapted verbatim in the 2020 Civil Code.

The civil law as a Chinese concept as prescribed in the 2020 Civil Code has a clear focus on two relationships between civil subjects of equal status. The two relationships are property and personal relationships. The equal status refers to the standing of the participants (civil subjects) in civil activities.[15] The property relationship denotes a relationship containing economic values formed by civil subjects during the process of production, distribution, exchange, and consumption, and it mainly includes property ownership and transactions.[16] Given the equal status of the parties, the creation, modification, and extinguishment of certain property relationships should all be on a voluntary basis and determined by the free will of the parties.[17]

The personal relationship stands for a social relationship created or formed on the basis of personality or status of person.[18] Personality is a right attached to a person, including, for example, the right to life, health, name, portrait, honor, etc.[19] Status implicates the position a person holds in society or in connection with others. For the purpose of civil law, status is often associated with marriage or family relations.[20] In this sense, civil status represents a social relationship that contains the specific interests of personal identity.[21]

[12] See Rou, *supra* note 10, at 1.

[13] See Weixing, *supra* note 9, at 3–4.

[14] See the 2017 General Provisions of Civil Law, art. 2, available at www.npc.gov.cn/npc/c12435/201703/7944f166a8194d788c63cc6610aebb4a.shtml (hereinafter 2017 GPCL).

[15] See Weixing, *supra* note 9, at 4–5.

[16] See Rou, *supra* note 10, at 4.

[17] See Weixing, *supra* note 9, at 4.

[18] See Rou, *supra* note 10, at 5.

[19] See *id.*

[20] See *id.*

[21] See Weixing, *supra* note 9, at 5.

There are two important distinctions between the property relationship and the personal relationship. The first distinction is the personal relationship's non-property nature of contents. In the personal relationship, both the rights of the obligee and the obligations of the obligor do not directly reflect property interests.[22] The personal relations are not based on an exchange of equal values between people, nor are their social relations formed by people in pursuit of certain economic interests and material needs, although they are related in a certain way to the property relationships.[23]

The second distinction between the two relationships is inseparability, meaning that the personal relationship is inseparable from the person. The notion is that a personal relationship in civil law is exclusive to the person, and it may not arise or exist without attaching to the person. Therefore, unless otherwise provided by law, the personal rights enjoyed by a person as a civil subject may not be transferred, nor can they be inherited. In addition, absent provisions of law, a personal right may not be waived or deprived arbitrarily.[24]

C. *General Principles of Civil Law*

In Chinese civil law literature, the general principles of civil law refer to the principles that run through the entire civil legal system and underscore all civil legislation. It is held in China that, given their nature of general application, civil law principles represent the essence of civil relations and reflect the basic characteristics of civil activities.[25] Thus, in regard to the creation and regulation of civil relations, the civil law principles significantly shape both the structure and substance of civil legislation.[26]

Like many other civil law countries, China attaches great importance to the general principles in both legislation and application of law. In their application, the civil law principles serve several functions. First, the civil law principles set the tone for civil legislation. They determine the basic value orientation of civil legislation and lay the foundation for formulating specific rules governing civil activities. More significantly, the civil law principles not only are a legal reflection of the country's civil philosophy and policy, but also constitute the basis on which the civil system stands.

Second, the civil law principles are the authoritative source for the interpretation of law. An important role of the civil law principles is gap-filling. When a provision of law or regulation is ambiguous or not quite clear on a particular issue, an interpretation shall be made in light of the principles. On the other hand, if a rule or provision of law is subject to two conflicting interpretations, the interpretation

22 See *id.*

23 See Rou, *supra* note 10, at 5.

24 See Weixing, *supra* note 9, at 5.

25 See Rou, *supra* note 10, at 21.

26 Internal structure of civil law refers to the subjects, contents, and basic rules of civil law, while the external structure relates to the relationship between civil law and other laws.

that better conforms to the principles should prevail. Any interpretation that conflicts with the civil law principles shall be invalid.[27]

Third, the civil law principles establish the basic norms of conduct that govern all parties in civil relations and activities. It is required that, when forming, modifying, or terminating their civil relationships, the parties – natural persons, legal persons, and all other civil entities alike – are bound by the general principles in addition to the specific provisions of law or regulation that apply.[28] In the absence of a governing provision in the law or regulation, the parties must follow the norms set under the general principles.

The civil law principles in Chinese civil legislation were first provided in the 1986 General Principles of the Civil Law. The principles stipulated in the 1986 General Principles of the Civil Law included (a) equal status of civil subjects, (b) compensation for equivalent value, (c) voluntariness and fairness, (d) honesty and credibility, (e) legality compliance, and (f) social ethics and public interests.[29] Note that the principle of compensation for equivalent value was based on the concept of a commodity economy that was widely used in the beginning stage of economic reform in the country.

In the 2017 GPCL, the civil law principles were restated as (a) equality, (b) voluntariness, (c) fairness, (d) good faith and honesty, (e) legality, and (f) green environment.[30] Compared with the 1986 General Principles of Civil Law, the 2017 GPCL removes the principle of compensation for equivalent value but adds green environment as a new principle that reflects China's commitment to the protection of the environment. The civil law principles provided in the 2017 GPCL are all incorporated into the Civil Code.

In addition, As noted the Civil Code contains a specific provision on the use of customs in dealing with civil disputes. Under article 10 of the Civil Code, in the case where there is no provision of law, a custom may be applied without violating public order or good morals. According to the Supreme People's Court (SPC), customs referred to in the article include folklores, common practices, etc. that are generally observed by ordinary people when engaging in civil activities within a certain region and industry for a long time. It is required by the SPC that, when the application of a custom is claimed, the claimant should provide evidence to prove the custom and its contents. But if necessary, a court may find it out *ex officio*. The SPC also emphasizes that the application of customs must not violate the core socialist values.[31]

[27] See Weixing, *supra* note 9, at 37.

[28] See *id.* at 38.

[29] See the 1986 General Principles of Civil Law, arts. 3–7, available at www.china.org.cn/china/.LegislationsForm2001–2010/2011-02/11/content_21898337.htm.

[30] See the 2017 GPCL, *supra* note 14, arts. 4–9.

[31] See SPC, *Interpretation on Several Issues Concerning Application of the General Provisions of the Civil Code*, issued on February 24, 2022, art. 2, at http://gongbao.court.gov.cn/Details/2dfca1b19663c57f990410a8a60795.html (hereinafter 2022 *Interpretation on the Application of Civil Code*).

a. Equality

The principle of equality is the requirement concerning the status of participants in civil activities (commonly called civil subjects). Under article 4 of the 2020 Civil Code, all persons of the civil law shall enjoy equal status in civil activities.[32] Under the principle of equality, all participants in civil activities shall have equal status regardless of their gender, education level, residential area, or ethnicity. In civil activities, nobody shall be affected or treated differently on the basis of administrative rank or official status. In addition, equality of status requires that the lawful rights and interests of civil entities, however different, be equally protected.

Some in China believe that equality of status also includes equality in a civil rights capacity. Unlike the civil conduct capacity that may vary based on the age or mental health of a person, the civil rights capacity of a natural person is with the person upon birth. A settled rule in civil law is that all natural persons have equal capacity for civil rights. Under this rule, everyone enjoys the same right as others in terms of capacity in civil law, and such right may not be arbitrarily restricted or deprived of.[33]

b. Voluntariness

The voluntariness principle focuses on the free will of the parties. According to article 5 of the Civil Code, in civil activities, the voluntariness of participants must be maintained, meaning that creation, modification, or termination of a civil relationship must be made according to the will of the parties.[34] Voluntariness refers essentially to the respect for the inner wishes of participants in their civil engagements. Under this principle, the parties, when dealing with their civil rights and obligations, should not only be able to fully express their own true wishes, but also respect each other. The voluntariness principle is aimed at ensuring that nobody in a civil relationship be forced by or force the other to do anything.

c. Fairness

The fairness principle mainly concerns a just and equitable process and outcome of civil activities. Article 6 of the Civil Code provides that civil activities shall observe the principle of fairness.[35] In simple terms, fairness is judged by looking at whether the rights and obligations of all parties are reasonably determined and allocated in civil activities. More specifically, determination of fairness requires a factor-based

[32] See the 2020 Civil Code, *supra* note 1, art. 4.
[33] See Weixing, *supra* note 9, at 38.
[34] See *id.*, art. 5.
[35] See the 2020 Civil Code, *supra* note 1, art. 4.

analysis. Factors essential to fairness consideration include equal opportunity in conducting civil acts, balance of rights and obligations among all parties, and liability matching the level of fault committed.

In many cases, the fairness principle is used by the courts as a benchmark to adjudicate disputes when there is no specific provision in the law, or the provision is unclear, and the parties are unable to reach an agreement. The fairness principle also applies to liability allocation in the case where the plaintiff suffers injury by the possible conduct of multiple defendants, but it is difficult to identify which defendant should be blamed.

d. Good Faith

The good faith and honesty principles are the civil law principles based on moral and ethical standards. According to article 7 of the Civil Code, the parties, when engaging in civil activities or exercising civil rights and fulfilling civil obligations, are required to act in good faith, abide by promises, and be honest with no intent to deceive.[36] It is also required that, when pursuing their own interests, the parties must not harm the interests of others or society.

The principles of good faith and honesty aim to help ensure that all civil activities and transactions take place in an orderly fashion and a reasonable expectation of the parties will be realized justly. Although good faith and honesty may be defined in different ways, they are usually judged by commonly accepted norms embedded in social and cultural tradition as well as general practices. Relying on these principles, the courts exercise a wide range of discretionary power to determine liabilities in civil disputes on a case-by-case basis.

e. Legality

Legality is a principle expressed in the Civil Code as "no violation of law," referring to legal compliance. Under article 8 of the Civil Code, when conducting a civil activity, nobody may violate the law or offend public order or good morals.[37] The legality principle as provided in article 8 has a twofold effect. On the one hand, any civil act not in compliance with the law must be void. On the other hand, in conducting civil activity, no one may harm the public interest for personal gains.

Note, however, that compliance under the legality principle is limited to mandatory provisions of law because in the law regulating civil affairs, most norms or rules are non-mandatory or optional. Therefore, legality becomes an issue only if a mandatory norm is violated. But, when evaluating the legality of a civil act, the court will look at mandatory provisions not only in private law but also in public law.

[36] See *id.*, art. 7.
[37] See *id.*, art. 8.

Also in China, public order generally refers to the basic values and fundamental concepts of politics, the economy, and culture that are related to the overall interests of the country and society. Good morals, also known as social public morality, are the traditions or practices representing the mainstream moral concepts of society.

f. Green Environment

The green environment is a newly established principle that governs civil activities in light of environmental protection. Known as the green principle, it intends to maintain a legal equilibrium between respect for civil autonomy and preservation of the ecological environment. According to article 9 of the Civil Code, when engaged in civil activities, all parties shall act in the manner conducive to the conservation of resources and protection of the ecological environment.[38] The green principle is considered essential in China because of the country's pressing need for the sustainable use of national resources and maintenance of ecological balance.

D. *Civil Legal Relationship*

The legal relationship is an important concept in Chinese law. It is a relation that arises upon certain legal fact or by provision of law. Legal fact refers to any occurrence, action, event, or situation that creates, alters, or terminates a legal relation. Once a legal relation is created, the parties involved will enjoy certain legal rights and bear corresponding obligations. Within the legal relation, the parties are obligated to fulfill their obligations respectively to each other.

a. Definition

A civil legal relationship is defined in China as the relation formed between parties of equal footing.[39] Under article 2 of the Civil Code, the civil legal relationship can be either a personal relation or property relation that is established under the law between natural persons, legal persons, and non-legal person organizations of equal status.[40] Take a contract of sale, for example. The formation of a contract constitutes a legal fact. Based on that fact, a creditor–debtor relation is created between the buyer and the seller. Under the legal relationship so created, the buyer (creditor in terms of receiving delivery) has the right to receive performance from the seller (the debtor), and, on the other hand, the buyer (debtor in terms of making payment) has the obligation to pay the contract price to the seller (creditor).

[38] See *id.*, art. 9.
[39] See Weixing, *supra* note 9, at 46.
[40] See the 2020 Civil Code, *supra* note 1, art. 2.

b. Components

As commonly understood in China, a civil legal relationship contains three components: the subject, the object, and the contents. The subject refers to a party who is a player in the civil legal relation, enjoying civil rights and undertaking civil obligations. As a civil subject, the party could be a natural person or an entity, including a legal person or a non-legal person organization. The act of a civil subject in performing obligations can be active or passive depending on the nature of the obligations.

The civil object is the target of civil rights and obligations or the purpose to be achieved. Without an object, the realization of civil rights and performance of obligations would be meaningless. There are debates among Chinese scholars on what may constitute a civil subject, but a general understanding is that a civil object may include a thing, an action or omission, or an intellectual achievement. Some argue that civil object should also include personal interests, referring to the interests of personality or status.[41]

A thing is an item or object that can satisfy human needs and can be dominated or controlled by humans. Unlike an object in the concept of physics, the civil object is required not only to be in existence (objective reality) but also to contain dominability (to be dominated and disposed of) and utility (to be useful, functional, and beneficial). Things are of great significance in civil law, and in many cases are closely related to the civil legal relation. A civil legal relationship may have things as objects, such as ownership and security rights, or may focus on performance but still rely on things as realized benefits. In a sale contract, for example, the primary goal is delivery of goods or performance, but the benefit sought is "goods" – things.

Acts, including omissions, as civil objects mainly refer to the conduct or performance of a debtor to meet the expectation of a creditor by satisfying the debts owed. Payment is an example in many cases. As noted, *obligatio* is a civil relationship. Under the concept of *obligatio*, the right of a creditor is the right to claim. To satisfy such right, the creditor may request the debtor for the benefits of the creditor to make such performance as delivery of the goods, completion of the work, or making of a payment. The creditor, however, may not directly control the debtor's thing or property.

Intellectual achievements are the knowledge, products, or spiritual wealth created by human mental work. As the object of intellectual property rights, an intellectual achievement has the characteristics of creativity, immateriality, and objectivity, and is accessible in the form of literature, art, scientific and technological work, invention, utility model, design, or trademark. Note, however, intellectual property protection is not about the carrier or external appearance of intellectual achievements (e.g., the physical book), but the information contained (e.g., the contents in

[41] See Weixing, *supra* note 9, at 55.

the book). The carrier itself is a matter of property rights (e.g., the book itself as property of the owner).

The contents of the civil legal relationship are the actual rights and obligations that are created upon the formation of such legal relation. For example, a personal injury creates a civil legal relation under torts law between the tortfeasor and the injured person. The contents of this legal relation refer to the rights the injured person has against the tortfeasor and the liabilities imposed on the tortfeasor for his/her wrongful conduct. Note that in China, a civil relation is considered a part of social relations. Thus, the contents of a civil legal relationship are deemed the legal embodiment of the contents of social relations regulated by civil law.

2. PERSONS IN CIVIL ACTIVITIES

Again, persons are the subjects of the civil legal relationship. In civil law, a person is a participant in, or player of, the civil activity in which the person could be a holder of civil rights, a performer of civil obligations, or a bearer of civil responsibilities. As civil subjects, persons may be categorized differently under different laws. In the 1986 General Principles of Civil Law, persons were defined to include citizens and legal persons.[42] According to the Civil Code, however, persons are divided into natural persons, legal persons, and non-legal person organizations. Despite the difference in categorization, the most notable feature of civil law persons is that they are equal in civil relations regardless of their status.

A. *Natural Person*

A natural person is an individual human being who has his or her own personality. A natural person can be a citizen of a country, a foreigner, or a stateless person. In the 1986 General Principles of Civil Law, a natural person was narrowly defined as a citizen, referring to a person of Chinese nationality. The 2017 GPCL changed "citizen" to "natural person," expanding the civil subjects to include not only citizens but also foreigners and stateless persons. The Civil Code keeps the term "natural person" intact.

Note that the natural person under Chinese law also includes self-employed industrial or commercial households (SICH) and rural land lease-holding households (RLLH). As defined in the Civil Code, the SICH is a household-run business lawfully registered and operated by a natural person.[43] The RLLH is a rural household that is engaged in land management by the members of rural economic collectives under a contractual right and lawfully obtained.

[42] See the 1986 General Principles of Civil Law, *supra* note 29, art. 2.

[43] See the 2020 Civil Code, *supra* note 1, arts. 54–55.

a. Civil Capacity of a Natural Person

The civil capacity of a natural person consists of their civil right capacity and their civil conduct capacity. The civil right capacity, or capacity for civil right, refers to the eligibility or qualification of a natural person to enjoy civil rights and assume civil liabilities in accordance with the law. Under article 13 of the Civil Code, a natural person shall have a civil right capacity from the time of birth until the time of death. Since the civil right capacity is a right for a person, it may not be deprived of by anyone, and it is also nontransferable.[44]

The time of birth or death of a natural person is the time recorded on the person's birth or death certificate. In the absence of either certificate, the time recorded as such in the natural person's household registration or other valid identity certificate shall be the time of the person's birth or death. If there is sufficient evidence overturning the time recorded on the aforementioned documents, the time that is established by such evidence shall prevail.

There are two important rules concerning the civil right capacity. The first rule is the equality rule. article 14 of the Civil Code provides that all natural persons are equal in their capacity for enjoying civil rights.[45] The second rule is the fetus protection rule. Under article 16 of the Civil Code, a fetus shall be deemed as having the capacity for civil right pertaining to such matters as inheritance or reception of donations that involve the protection of the interests of a fetus. However, such capacity shall be deemed non-existent *ab initio* if the fetus is stillborn.[46]

In addition, in its 2021 Interpretation on Several Issues Concerning the General Provisions of the Civil Code, the SPC further emphasizes the protection of the interests of a fetus. According to the SPC, when it comes to the protection of such interests of the fetus as inheritance and acceptance of gifts, if parents act as agent *ad litem* to make claim for corresponding rights of the fetus before the birth of the fetus, the claim should be granted.[47]

The civil conduct capacity means the ability of a natural person through his/her own conduct to participate in a civil legal relation, exercising civil rights and undertaking civil obligations. Unlike the civil right capacity that exists with the life of a natural person, the civil conduct capacity is associated with the maturity, intelligence, and mental health of a person. In this context, the civil conduct capacity can be a full capacity, limited capacity, or no capacity as prescribed by law.

Pursuant to article 18 of the Civil Code, a natural person who is eighteen years or older is an adult, and an adult has full capacity for civil conduct and can undertake

[44] See *id.*, art. 13.
[45] See *id.*, art. 14.
[46] See *id.*, art. 16.
[47] See the SPC, *2022 Interpretation on the Application of Civil Code*, *supra* note 31, art. 4.

civil legal acts independently. Those who are under eighteen years old are minors. However, a natural person who is over sixteen but under eighteen years old will be deemed as having a full capacity for civil conduct if his/her primary source of living is the income earned from his/her own work. Anyone who is under eight years old or is unable to comprehend his/her own conduct has no capacity for civil conduct.[48]

Natural persons who have limited capacity for civil conduct include (a) minors over eight years old and (b) adults who cannot fully comprehend their own conduct. A person with limited capacity for civil conduct may undertake civil activities only through or upon the consent or ratification of his/her agent *ad litem*. A guardian can be a legal guardian or a designated guardian. The legal guardians of minors are their parents.

The parents of a minor may enter into an agreement with another person who has guardianship qualification to the effect that the person will serve as the guardian when the minor's parents lose their guardianship capacity. If, however, the agreement so entered is aimed at exempting the parents with guardianship capacity from their guardianship responsibilities, the agreement will be null and void. The guardianship capacity of a natural person is determined by a court based on age, physical and mental health, and the economic conditions of the person.[49]

The designation of a guardian is governed by the principle of the best interests of the ward (person under the guardianship), with full respect to the true wishes of the ward. As required by the SPC, when designating a guardian or guardians, the courts shall take into account the following factors: (a) the closeness of the life and emotional connection with the ward; (b) the sequential order of guardianship of the eligible persons; (c) illegal or criminal records affecting the performance of guardianship duties; and (d) the guardianship ability, willingness, and moral conduct of the eligible person.[50]

A person with limited civil capacity may be deemed as being able to perform a civil act independently if such act is purely beneficial to him/her or is appropriate for the person's intelligence and mental status. The determination of appropriateness, according to the SPC, shall be made in consideration of the extent to which the act is related to the person's life, the status of intelligence and mental health of the person, the level of the person's understanding of his/her conduct and its foreseeable consequences, and other factors such as the subject matter, quantity, price, or remuneration of the act.[51]

Note that in most cases, the agent *ad litem* of a limited capacity person refers to the person's guardian. In China, the agent *ad litem* could be a spouse, adult child,

48 See the 2020 Civil Code, *supra* note 1, arts. 21–22.

49 See the SPC, 2022 *Interpretation on the Application of Civil Code*, *supra* note 31, art. 6 (For an organization or entity, the determination of its guardianship capacity will be made in consideration of its qualification, credibility, and financial status).

50 See *id.*, art. 9.

51 See the SPC, 2022 *Interpretation on the Application of Civil Code*, *supra* note 31, art. 5.

parents, relatives, another person or entity, or a local government agency. Eligible relatives include grandparents and siblings.[52] Another person or entity refers to an individual or organization that (a) is willing to serve as a guardian and (b) receives consent from the residents' committee, villagers' committee, or the civil affairs department of the place where the person at issue is domiciled.[53]

b. Domicile of a Natural Person

Domicile is an important factor connecting a natural person with a particular place or legal seat that affects the legal interests of such person. From the viewpoint of conflict of laws, for example, domicile is considered to be the place with which "an individual's life has the most significant continuing relationship" and is determinative in ascertaining both jurisdiction and choice of law.[54] In civil law, domicile is commonly defined as a person's permanent place of dwelling and is characterized as a legal relationship between a person and a locality. In China, domicile is a decisive factor in determining such matters as guardianship, declaration of missing person or death, place of debt performance, place of jurisdiction, and applicable law in foreign cases.

Under article 25 of the Civil Code, the domicile of a natural person is the residence recorded in the household registration or other valid identification document. Article 25 also provides that if a natural person's habitual residence and domicile are different, the habitual residence is deemed as his/her domicile. In contrast to the domicile provision in the 1986 General Principle of Civil Law, the Civil Code contains two major changes. First, it replaces "citizen" with "natural person" to better reflect the civil nature. Second, it uses "residence" instead of "place of residence registered" to define domicile and extends the concept of domicile to include the place of residence as shown on the person's personal ID card.[55]

The Civil Code attaches great importance to the habitual residence and prioritizes it over domicile in the situation where the place of habitual residence differs from the place of domicile. However, the Civil Code does not specify how the habitual residence is to be determined. According to the SPC's opinion, for a residence to be "habitual," it must meet two conditions: (a) it is the person's last continuous residence and (b) the continuity of residence is more than one year.[56]

[52] For a minor, the guardian can be his/her parents, or, absent parents, grandparents or elder brother or sister, or other individuals or entities. See *id.*, art. 27.

[53] See *id.*, art. 28.

[54] See Peter Hay, Patrick J. Borchers, & Symeon C. Symeonides, Conflict of Law, 286, Hornbook Series (5th ed., West, 2010).

[55] Under article 15 of the 1986 General Principles of Civil Law, the domicile of a citizen shall be the place where his residence is registered. If his habitual residence is not the same as his domicile, the habitual residence shall be regarded as his domicile.

[56] See SPC, 1988 *Opinions on Several Issues Concerning the Implementation of the General Principles of the Civil Law*, art. 9, issued by the SPC on April 2, 1988, available at www.lawinfochina.com/display.aspx?id = 3700&lib = law&SearchKeyword = civil%20law&

In practice, when determining habitual residence, the courts often make subjective inquiries to help ascertain (a) whether the residence of a person in a particular place is based on the person's true will and (b) whether the person's act of residence carries any intention of settlement. In addition, based on the SPC's interpretation, to determine habitual residence, the rule of continuous residence does not apply to the situation where a residence is taken for the purpose of medical treatment, labor dispatch, or business affairs.

B. *Household-Based Individual Entity*

As discussed, a natural person as defined in the Civil Code also includes two individual entities that operate on a household basis, namely the SICH and RLLH. Again, the SICH is a household that registers to operate industrial or commercial businesses, while the RLLH is a household engaged in rural land contractual management.[57] More specifically, the SICH is a civil entity legally registered by a natural person who uses his/her personal or family property as operating capital to engage in industrial and commercial operations within the scope permitted by law. RLLH, on the other hand, is an entity operating a piece of land on a household basis under a land management contract with the collectives who own the land.

As a natural person, the SICH can have a trade name to independently conduct civil or business activities. But note that when registering a SICH, the household members do not lose their natural person status pertaining to their civil right ability and civil conduct capacity. Instead, they acquire additional ability and capacity for the SICH to engage in certain commodity production and business activities.

A key feature of the SICH and RLLH is the personal liability of their members for the entity's debts. Under article 56 of the Civil Code, the debts of a SICH shall be collected from the assets of the individuals who operate the business in his/her own name or from their family's assets if the business is operated in the name of the household. In addition, if it is impossible to determine whether the business is operated in the name of the individual or in the name of the individual's household, the debts shall be paid from the individual's family assets.[58] Thus, unlike a corporation, a SICH as a business entity does not shield its members from being held personally liable for the SICH's debt.

SearchCKeyword = ; See also the SPC, 2012 *Interpretation of Several Issues Concerning the Application of the Law of the People's Republic of China on the Application of the Law of the People's Republic of China on Foreign-related Civil Relations* (I), art. 15, adopted by the SPC on December 10, 2012, amended December 23, 2020, available at https://english.court.gov.cn/2021-10/19/c_761776.htm.

[57] See the 2020 Civil Code, *supra* note 1, art. 54.

[58] See *id.*, art. 56.

The RLLH, as noted, is an entity engaging in the operation of land on a household basis under a contract to manage the land.[59] As provided in article 56 of the 2020 Civil Code, the debts of RLLH shall be paid from the assets of the household operating the contracted rural land or from personal assets of those family members who actually participate in the land operation of the RLLH.[60]

C. *Legal Person*

Legal person is defined in the Civil Code as an organization that has the capacity for civil rights and conduct and can independently enjoy civil rights and bear civil liability in accordance with the law.[61] Under this definition, a legal person has the following three features: (a) it is an organization or human or nonhuman entity, (b) it has the capacity for civil rights and conduct, and (c) it can act independently to enjoy civil rights and assume civil liabilities. As an independent civil entity, a legal person has the same civil status as a natural person.

a. Categories of Legal Person

The Civil Code divides legal person into three categories: for-profit legal person, non-profit legal person, and special legal person. A for-profit legal person is a legal person incorporated for the purpose of making profits and distributing the profits among its shareholders and other capital contributors. According to article 76 of the Civil Code, for-profit legal persons include limited liability companies, joint stock companies limited by shares,[62] and other enterprises that have legal person status.[63]

Non-profit legal person refers to a legal person that is established to provide public welfare or for other non-profit purposes and distributes no profit to its capital contributors, incorporators, or members. As provided in article 87 of the Civil Code, non-profit legal persons include public institutions, social organizations, foundations, social service institutions, and the like.[64] Put differently, non-profit legal persons consist of public-interest legal persons serving the interests of the general public or unspecified majority, and legal persons established for other non-profit purposes.

59 See *id.*, art. 55.
60 See *id.*, art. 56.
61 See *id.*, art. 76.
62 Under article 3 of Chinese Company Law (as amended 2021), a limited liability company is a company in which shareholders assume liability toward the company to the extent of the capital contributions subscribed respectively by them, while a joint stock company refers to a company where shareholders assume liability toward the company to the extent of the shares subscribed respectively by them.
63 See the 2020 Civil Code, *supra* note 1, art. 76.
64 See *id.*, art. 87.

Special legal person is a new term in the Civil Code to cover those entities that are neither for profit nor non-profit but are granted legal person status. Included in this category are state-organ legal person, rural economic collective legal person, urban and rural cooperative economic organization legal person, and grassroots-level self-governing legal person.[65] Note, however, that the special legal person status of the rural economic collective legal person and urban and rural cooperative economic organization legal person may only be obtained in accordance with the law. If law or administrative regulation provide otherwise for these entities, such law and administrative regulation shall be followed.[66]

b. Requirements for Legal Person

In China, a legal person must meet four requirements: (a) it is established according to the law; (b) it has the necessary assets or funds; (c) it has its own name, organizational structure, and domicile; and (d) it is capable to independently bear civil liabilities. In addition, if an approval by a relevant government authority is required under the law or administrative regulation for the establishment of a legal person, such approval must be obtained. Take Sino-foreign joint ventures in China, for example. A government approval is required for its formation.

Under article 59 of the Civil Code, a legal person's capacity to enjoy civil rights and to perform civil acts is acquired at the time the legal person is established and ends when the legal person is dissolved. In addition, to register, a legal person must have a domicile, which is the place where the legal person's principal administrative office is located.[67] As a general requirement, when registering, a legal person must list the place of its principal administrative office as its registered domicile.[68]

D. *Unincorporated Organizations*

Unincorporated organizations in China are commonly called non-legal persons and refer to an organization or unit that does not have legal person status but may engage in civil activities in its own name in accordance with the law. Under the 2020 Civil Code, unincorporated organizations include sole proprietorships, partnerships, and professional service institutions.[69] The formation and registration of an unincorporated organization would be subject to approval by the relevant authority if required by the law.[70]

[65] See *id.*, art. 96.
[66] See *id.*, arts. 99–100.
[67] See *id.*, art. 59.
[68] See *id.*, art. 63.
[69] See *id.*, art. 102.
[70] See *id.*, art. 103.

In contrast to the legal person, a notable distinction of the unincorporated organization is that when an unincorporated organization becomes insolvent, its capital contributors or promoters shall assume unlimited liability for the debts of the organization unless otherwise provided by law. For purposes of assuming debt liability, the assets of unincorporated organizations include two parts: the unincorporated organization's own property, that is, the property contributed by the contributors or promoters to the unincorporated organization, and the personal property of the contributors or promoters.

E. *Agency*

Agency in China is described as a civil relationship in which one party independently undertakes legal acts with a third party on behalf of another person under the consent, and subject to the control, of such person, within the scope of their authorization, with the resulting legal effects directly attributable to the other person.[71] The one for whom an act is to be undertaken is the principal, while the one who is to undertake the act is the agent. Under article 161 of the Civil Code, a person in civil law may perform a civil act through his/her agent.[72] Article 162 further provides that a civil act performed by an agent in the name of the principal within the scope of authorization shall be binding on the principal.[73]

a. Types

Agency as provided in the Civil Code includes an entrusted agency, or agency by agreement, and statutory agency, or agency by the operation of law.[74] In an entrusted agency, the agent acts in accordance with the principal's authorization, while in the situation of a statutory agency, the agent shall act according to law.[75] However, if an act must be performed by the principal as required by law, agreed by the parties, or based on the nature of the act, such act may not be undertaken through an agent.[76]

Under article 64 of the 1986 General Principles of Civil Law, in addition to entrusted agency and statutory agency, an agency also included an appointed one.

[71] See Weixing, *supra* note 9, at 121.
[72] See the 2020 Civil Code, *supra* note 1, art. 161.
[73] See *id.*, art. 162.
[74] Before the Civil Code was adopted, the types of agency also included designated or appointed agency, which refers to an agent performing the act designated by a court or relevant authority for the interests of a particular person (a minor, for example). Relevant authority means the organization that is obliged to protect the interests of the principal, such as the residents' committee and the villagers' committee in the place where the minor lives. The Civil Code drops the designated agent from the category of agency.
[75] See the 2020 Civil Code, *supra* note 1, art. 163.
[76] See *id.*, art. 161.

An appointed agency refers to the situation where the agent is designated by a people's court or an appointing unit.[77] The 2020 Civil Code does not contain the appointed agency, making the entrusted agency and statutory agency the only two types of agencies in the country. The idea is that the appointed agency is in fact a kind of statutory agency.

In China, agency can be used in all civil acts concerning the establishment, modification, and elimination of a civil relation that contains civil rights and obligations. The civil acts could be (1) the legal acts of two or more persons in such transactions as buying and selling, leasing, lending, contracting for work, as well as insurance; (2) unilateral legal acts, such as acting on behalf of others to exercise the right of ratification, revocation, etc.; or (3) other acts, such as acting on behalf of others to conduct an invitation for an offer, withdrawal of an offer, withdrawal of an acceptance, assertion and recognition of the creditor's rights, etc.[78] In addition, agency is often seen in such civil activities as application (e.g., application for trademark registration), filing (e.g., tax filing), and litigation (in both civil and criminal cases).

According to article 135 of the 2020 Civil Code, the entrusted agency may be created in writing, orally, or in any other form.[79] Article 165 of the Civil Code further provides that for an entrusted agency, if the authority is conferred in writing, the name of the agent, the authorized matters, as well as the scope and duration of the authority shall be clearly stated in the letter of authorization, signed or sealed by the principal.[80] If, however, an agent knows or should have known that conducting the authorized matter is in violation of law but still acts as authorized, or, if a principal knows or should have known that an act of the agent is in violation of law but raises no objection thereto, the principal and the agent shall bear joint and several liability.[81]

b. Restrictions

As a fundamental rule of agency, the 2020 Civil Code explicitly prohibits self-dealing or multiple representations of an agent. According to article 168 of the 2020 Civil Code, an agent shall not, in the principal's name, perform a civil act with the agent himself/herself, unless it is consented to or ratified by the principal. In addition, an agent who has been designated by two or more principals shall not, in the name of

77 See the 1986 General Principles of Civil Law, *supra* note 29, art. 64.

78 See Yang Lixin & Li Yiwen, Key Points of the New Provisions in the Chinese Civil Code, 148 (Law Press, 2020).

79 Under article 135 of the Civil Code, a civil act may be done in writing, orally, or in any other form. Where a specific form is required by law or administrative regulation, or agreed to by the parties, a civil act shall be done in such a form. See the 2020 Civil Code, *supra* note 7, art. 135.

80 See *id.*, art. 165.

81 See *id.*, art. 167.

one principal, perform a civil juristic act with another principal whom the agent concurrently represents unless it is consented to or ratified by both principals.[82] In addition, no multiple representation is allowed without consent of or ratification by the principals involved, regardless of whether those principals are in competition.

c. Authority

Under the Civil Code, the authority of an agent can be either an actual authority or an apparent authority. Actual authority is an authority expressly or impliedly conferred to the agent by the principal, while apparent authority refers to an authority of the agent in the mind of a third party, based on the principal's conduct, that the agent has the authority to act on behalf of the principal. In either situation, the principal can be held liable for the conduct of the agent.

In accordance with article 171 of the Civil Code, an act performed by a person on behalf of a principal without authority, beyond authority, or after the authority is terminated has no effect against the principal unless ratified by the principal.[83] However, an act as such will be effective against the principal if the other party affected has reason to believe that the person performing the act has been authorized by the principal.[84] Under the SPC's interpretation, the other party's belief will be ascertained under the following two circumstances: (a) there appears agency power, and (b) the other party did not know without fault that the agent had no agency power.[85]

d. Termination

The Civil Code also contains provisions under which an agency relationship is terminated. For an entrusted agency, termination occurs when (a) the term of agency expires or the authorized tasks have been completed; (b) the principal revokes the agency or the agent resigns; (c) the agent loses the capacity for performing civil juristic acts; (d) the agent or the principal becomes deceased; or (e) the legal person or unincorporated organization who is the agent or the principal ceases to operate.[86]

In addition, an act performed by an agent under agreement after the principal becomes deceased remains valid if (a) the agent does not know or should not have known of the death of the principal; (b) the act is ratified by the heirs of the principal; (c) it is clearly stated in the letter of authorization that the agency ceases only upon completion of the authorized tasks; or (d) the agent has started the act

[82] See *id.*, art. 168.
[83] See *id.*, art. 171.
[84] See *id.*, art. 172.
[85] See the SPC, 2022 *Interpretation on the Application of Civil Code*, *supra* note 31, art. 28.
[86] See the 2020 Civil Code, *supra* note 1, art. 173.

before the principal becomes deceased and continues to act in the interests of the heirs of the principal.[87] Under the Civil Code, those provisions also apply *mutatis mutandis* when the principal, who is a legal person or an unincorporated organization, is dissolved.[88]

For a statutory agency, the agency relationship may be terminated under any of the following circumstances: (a) the principal obtains or regains full capacity for performing civil juristic acts; (b) the agent loses the capacity for performing civil juristic acts; (c) the agent or the principal becomes deceased; or (d) any other circumstance as provided by law exists.[89]

3. CIVIL RIGHTS

Civil rights, along with civil activities and liabilities, are major components of the general provisions of the Civil Code. For purposes of the Civil Code, civil rights refer to the interests that the law entrusts to civil subjects, being achieved under the will of the civil subjects through action or non-action, which include the interests directly enjoyed by the rights holder (e.g., personal rights), and the interests obtained (e.g., property rights).[90] When such interests are infringed or harmed, the civil subjects affected may make claims to the relevant state authority against the infringer for remedies.

More broadly, civil rights are the freedoms guaranteed by law to realize or maintain specific interests of civil subjects. In its nature, a civil right can be an active right or passive right. An active civil right is, in essence, a freedom of self-determination. For example, civil right holders may create, modify, or terminate certain legal relationships with each other at their own will. In contrast, a passive civil right is a freedom from infringement. The right of personality, for example, is typically a passive civil right. Between active and passive rights is a right with combined features. A property right, for instance, possesses such a combined nature.

A. *Nature of Civil Rights*

Under the Civil Code, civil rights are divided into personal rights and property rights. In addition, under article 126 of the Civil Code, persons of civil law also enjoy other civil legal rights and interests as provided by law. By its nature, article 126 is considered a "catch-all" clause. Many believe that, as a matter of civil law protection, other rights and interests should include a natural person's sexual right, the

[87] See *id.*, art. 174.
[88] See *id.*
[89] See *id.*, art. 175.
[90] See Li Shuangyuan & Wen Shiyang, Comparative Civil Law, 79–80 (Wuhan University Press, 2016).

personality interests of the deceased, pure economic loss, and environmental rights and interests.[91]

Personal rights mainly include rights of personality and status (family right, spousal right, parental right, etc.). Property rights under the Civil Code, as understood in China, mainly consist of right to things and right of *obligation*. In a broader sense, it also includes right of succession, intellectual property rights,[92] equity, and other investment rights. Rights of *obligatio* are defined in article 118 as the right of an obligee to request a specific obligor to do or not do a certain act, as arising from a contract, a tortious act, a *negotiorum gestio*, or unjust enrichment, or otherwise arising by operation of law.[93] Under the civil law concept, a right to things is an absolute right that could be asserted against anyone, while a right of *obligatio* is a relative or limited right that can only be claimed against a specific person.

In Chinese civil law literature, a civil right is described to contain two distinct traits. The first trait is equality. As noted, under equality, all civil subjects are of equal footing in terms of civil status and enjoy equal civil rights regardless of their age, gender, ethnicity, religious belief, or occupation. The second trait is continuity. The civil rights of a natural person begin from the birth of such person and continue until the person dies, while a legal person's civil rights exist from the establishment of the legal person to its extinction.[94]

B. *Components of Civil Rights*

In addition, a civil right is considered in the country as having four major components, namely control, claim, defense, and formation. Control refers to the power of the right holder to dominate and determine every aspect of the right directly and exclusively. The right of control could either be the right of domination over things, for example, property rights, or the right of domination over intellectual achievements, that is, intellectual property rights.[95] But, under certain circumstances, an

[91] See the SPC Leading Group, Understanding and Application of Civil Code (General Provisions), 650–651 (People's Court Press, 2020) (Sexual right refers to the right of sexual autonomy, meaning that a person has the right to control his/her own sexual interests free from any interference, harassment, or offense. The personality interests of a deceased are the interests of reputation, name, or portrait of the deceased. Pure economic interests mean the economic losses beyond the losses resulting from personal and property damages. Environmental rights and interests refer to the rights and interests enjoyed by persons of civil law in good environmental quality).

[92] According to article 123 of the Civil Code, intellectual property rights are the exclusive rights enjoyed by the right holders in accordance with law over the following subject matters: (a) works; (b) inventions, new utility models, or appearance designs; (c) trademarks; (d) geographical indications; (e) trade secrets; (f) layout designs of integrated circuits; (g) new plant varieties; and (h) other subject matters as provided by law. See the 2020 Civil Code, *supra* note 1, art. 123.

[93] See *id.*, art. 118.

[94] See Weixing, *supra* note 9, at 56–57.

[95] See *id.* at 58.

exercise of the right of control is subject to limitation. An example is easement, which is a nonpossessory right granted by the property right holder to allow another party to use the property for his/her own benefit.

Claim is a right to request others to do or not do a certain act. Depending on the nature of the right it relies on, the claim can be a claim made on a creditor's right, property right, intellectual property right, personality right, or even personal status.[96] A claim based on the creditor's right is a right arising from the creditor–debtor relation to request a specific person (the debtor) to perform a specific obligation (pay the debt). The property right claim is a claim premised on the property right to request return or restoration of the property when the owner's right to the property has been or is likely to be infringed. It also includes a possessor's claim for protection of possession of the property.

Defense is the right against all others. It refers to a right to defend against the claim made by others. In a broader sense, it is the right to prevent all others from making a claim or other assertions against the right holder. For example, under article 20 of the Guarantee Law of China, for purposes of debt performance, the right of defense means a debtor's right to exercise the right of claim on a legal basis against a creditor when the creditor seeks to enforce his/her rights.[97]

Formation is a right to create, alter, or terminate a civil legal relationship according to the will of the right holder. The right of formation, also called the right of alteration, can arise based on agreement or by the operation of law. Examples of the right of formation include the right to create a creditor's right, right to rescind, to revoke, to ratify, or to modify. In a contract, for example, rescission of a contract due to a material mistake is the right of formation under the provision of law. On the other hand, the rescission of a contract pursuant to the terms as agreed by the parties is the right of formation by agreement.

Under the Civil Code, a civil right can be a property right or a personal right based on property interests. A property right is a right that directly reflects property interests, including right to things, creditor's right, inheritance right, as well as intellectual property right. Personal right includes the right of personality and the right of personal identity.

In addition to personal and property rights, a person in civil law may also enjoy such investor rights as an equity right[98] and other civil-law rights and interests as provided by law.[99] A new provision in the 2020 Civil Code is that where there are laws particularly providing for the protection of data and online virtual assets, such provisions shall be followed.[100]

96 See *id.*
97 See Guarantee Law of China (1995), art. 20, available at www.npc.gov.cn/zgrdw/englishnpc/Law/2007-12/12/content_1383719.htm.
98 See the 2020 Civil Code, *supra* note 1, art. 125.
99 See *id.*, art. 126.
100 See *id.*, art. 127.

C. *Acquisition of Civil Rights*

A civil right can be acquired either through original acquisition or by succession. An original acquisition of a civil right means that the right is not inherited from others. Acquisition of a civil right by succession implicates that the right is given by or transferred from the previous right holder. Under article 129 of the Civil Code, a civil right may be acquired through the performance of a legal act, the occurrence of an act de facto, the occurrence of an event as prescribed by law, or by other means provided by law.[101]

Some in China, however, argue that article 129 of the Civil Code has a loophole because it fails to provide for acquisition of a civil right by the lapse of time. The lack of such provision in the Civil Code is deemed to be at odds with the civil law legislation in many other countries where the lapse of time is recognized as a means of civil right acquisition. It is also argued that since the Civil Code contains the provisions of statute of limitations concerning litigation affecting civil rights, the acquisition of civil right by lapse of time should be provided as well.[102]

To protect civil rights, the Civil Code makes it clear that persons in civil law may exercise their civil rights according to their own will under the law and free from any interference. At the same time, the Civil Code imposes certain conditions on the exercise of civil rights. First, when exercising civil-law rights, a person shall perform his/her obligations as provided by law or as agreed with the other parties.[103] Second, no person in civil law shall abuse his/her civil-law rights and harm the interests of the state or public, or the lawful rights and interests of others.

4. CIVIL ACTS

As defined in the Civil Code, a civil act is an act expressing an intent that creates, alters, or terminates a civil relationship.[104] A core feature of a civil act is that it derives from the expressed intent and produces the legal effect so intended. In Chinese civil law books, civil act is commonly categorized as a legal fact or conduct that causes changes of a civil legal relationship.[105] The occurrence of such legal fact or conduct results from the expression of intent.

A. *Expression of Intent*

For purposes of the Civil Code, the expression of intent refers to an action that transforms what the parties have in their minds to an external act or conduct that has

[101] See *id.*, art. 129.
[102] See Lixin & Yiwen, *supra* note 78, at 115–116.
[103] See *id.*, art. 131.
[104] See *id.*, art. 133.
[105] See Cui Jianyuan et al., General Theory of Civil Law, 152 (3rd ed., Tsinghua University Press, 2019).

legal effect. Take an offer, for example. When making an offer, the offeror expresses an intent to make a deal with the offeree. In this regard, what is in the offeror's mind is to make a deal through extending an offer – an act that produces legal effect. Thus, making an offer is the external action of the offeror, which is the result of an expression of the offeror's intent.

The 2020 Civil Code attaches great significance to the expression of intent because intent has direct impact on the validity of a legal act. In the 1986 General Principles of Civil Law, legal act is narrowly tailored to lawful acts. Under article 54 of the 1986 General Principles of Civil Law, a civil act shall be the lawful act of a citizen or legal person to establish, change, or terminate civil rights and obligations.[106] The Civil Code, however, does not require lawfulness for a civil act. Thus, in the context of the Civil Code, a civil act can be a valid act, a rescindable act, or an invalid act.

Pursuant to the Civil Code, a civil act can be accomplished through an expression of common intent of two or more parties, or through one party's unilateral expression of intent.[107] Unless otherwise provided by law or agreed by the parties, a civil act takes effect at the time it is accomplished.[108] For example, when a legal person or an unincorporated organization makes a resolution, its resolution-making act is accomplished at the time when the resolution is adopted in accordance with the procedure and voting method provided by law or stipulated in its articles of association.[109] In addition, a person who performs a civil act may not change or revoke the act without authorization, unless doing so is in compliance with law or consented to by the other party.[110]

An expression of intent can be ascertained under a subjective or objective standard. A subjective standard refers to the inner meaning of the intent or the state of mind standard. An objective standard, however, determines the intent from the standpoint of a reasonable person under the same or similar circumstances.[111] In both situations, the intent must be communicated or expressed externally. If an intent is kept in the party's heart, it will have no legal effect. Therefore, an important factor affecting the effect of an expression of intent is the way of communication or formality.

The Civil Code is quite flexible about a formality requirement. According to article 135 of the Civil Code, a civil act can be done in writing, orally, or in any other form. The other form, under the SPC's interpretation, can be conduct of

[106] See the 1986 General Principles of Civil Law, *supra* note 29, art. 54.
[107] See the 2020 Civil Code, *supra* note 1, art. 134.
[108] See *id.*, art. 136.
[109] See *id.*, art. 134.
[110] See *id.*, art. 136.
[111] Chinese courts normally follow a mixed approach in the determination of intent, looking at intent subjectively first, and then making an objective inquiry if the party's intent cannot be ascertained subjectively.

performance.[112] If, however, a specific form is required by law or administrative regulation, or agreed to by the parties, such requirement must be met.[113] In other words, a civil act can take any form unless a particular form is called for either by the agreement of the parties or by provisions of the law.

B. *Effectiveness of Civil Acts*

Since expression of intent is essential to a civil act, the time when the expression of intent becomes effective is determinative to the effectiveness of the civil act. Under the provisions of the Civil Code, an expression of intent may take effect in different ways depending on how the expression is made. First, if an expression of intent is made in a real-time communication, it becomes effective from the time the person to whom the intent is expressed is aware of its content. If, however, an expression of intent is made in non-real-time communication, it takes effect at the time it reaches the person to whom the intent is expressed.[114]

Second, where an expression of intent is made through an electronic data message and the person to whom the intent is expressed has designated a specific data-receiving system, it becomes effective from the time such a data message enters that system. If no data-receiving system is specifically designated, it becomes effective from the time the person to whom the intent is expressed knows or should have known that the data message has entered the system. On the other hand, if the parties have agreed otherwise on the effective time of the expression of intent made in the form of an electronic data message, such an agreement shall prevail.[115]

Third, when an expression of intent is not made to any specific person, it becomes effective when the expression is completed, unless otherwise provided by law.[116] In addition, if an expression of intent is made through public notice, it becomes effective upon the time the public notice is posted.[117] Moreover, an expression of intent can be made either expressly or implicitly. But silence will be deemed as an expression of intent only when it is so provided by law, agreed to by the parties, or in accord with the course of dealing between the parties.[118]

Pursuant to the Civil Code, an expression of intent, when made, can be withdrawn by way of notice. As provided in article 141 of the Civil Code, for an effective withdrawal of the expression of intent, the notice shall reach the other party prior to

[112] See the SPC, *2022 Interpretation on the Application of Civil Code*, *supra* note 31, art. 18 (If the party does not use written or oral form, but the act itself shows that the intention has been expressed and meets the conditions for the establishment of a civil legal act, the people's court may hold that the parties' intention falls within other forms).

[113] See the 2020 Civil Code, *supra* note 1, art. 135.

[114] See *id.*, art. 137.

[115] See *id.*

[116] See *id.*, art. 138.

[117] See *id.*, art. 139.

[118] See *id.*, art. 140.

or at the same time with the other party's receipt of the expression of intent.[119] Thus, a withdrawal occurs before the expression of intent takes effect. Once effective, the expression of intent may only be revoked, not withdrawn. Also, withdrawal does not apply to an expression of intent made to a non-specific person because the expression of intent as such becomes effective when made.

C. *Ascertainment of Intent*

To ascertain the meaning of an intent expressed, article 142 of the Civil Code provides a twofold interpretation rule. In one aspect, if an expression of intent is made to a specific person, the meaning of the expression shall be interpreted according to the words and sentences used, with reference to the relevant terms, the nature and purpose of the civil juristic act, custom, and the principle of good faith.[120] In the other aspect, if an expression of intent is not made to any specific person, an interpretation of the intent shall be made along with the relevant terms, the nature and purpose of the civil act, custom, and the principle of good faith, but not solely on the words and sentences used.[121]

Thus, under the provision of article 142, an interpretation of expression of intent can be made on the basis of plain language, context, purposes, industrial customs, or the good faith principle. For example, when the parties dispute over terms related to the expression of intent, the meaning of the terms shall first be interpreted under the standard of an ordinary person's reasonable understanding of the terms. If the meaning of the terms in dispute cannot be ascertained by the plain language, interpretation shall be made according to the context or purposes of expression of the intent, or industrial customs. If a gap remains in the interpretation, the principle of good faith will apply.

D. *Validity of a Civil Act*

The effectiveness of a civil act is an issue concerning whether the civil act has taken effect. But taking effect itself does not necessarily mean that the civil act is legally valid. The validity of a civil act not only determines the legal consequences of the civil act, but also affects the civil relationships' creation, modification, and termination. The Civil Code on the one hand sets forth certain conditions for a civil act to become valid, and on the other hand provides the circumstances under which the civil act will become void or voidable.

Under article 143 of the Civil Code, a civil act is valid if the following conditions are satisfied: (a) the person performing the act has the required capacity for

[119] See *id.*, art. 141.
[120] See *id.*, art. 142.
[121] See *id.*

performing civil juristic acts; (b) the intent expressed by the person is true; and (c) the act does not violate any mandatory provisions of law or administrative regulation, nor offend public order or good morals.[122] Note that in comparison with the 1986 General Principles of Civil Law, the Civil Code has made a significant change to the legality requirements.

Pursuant to article 55 of the 1986 General Principles of Civil Law, a civil act shall not violate the law or social public interests. Article 143 of the 2020 Civil Code narrows the scope of illegality and limits violation to the mandatory provisions of law only. In accordance with article 143 of the Civil Code, if a provision of law or administrative regulation is not mandatory in nature, a failure to follow it may not make a civil act invalid. In addition, article 143 of the Civil Code adds to the legality requirement the non-violation of public order or good morals as new components.

Thus, under the Civil Code, a civil act will be held invalid and thus void in such situations as (a) the civil act is performed by a person who has no capacity;[123] (b) a civil act is performed by a person and his/her counterpart under a false expression of intent;[124] (c) a civil act is performed in violation of the mandatory provisions of laws or administrative regulations unless such mandatory provisions do not lead to invalidity of such a civil act; (d) performance of a civil act offends the public order or good morals;[125] or (e) a civil act is conducted through malicious collusion between the person who performs the act and a counterparty thereof and thus harms the lawful rights and interests of another person.[126]

With regard to a civil act conducted by a person with limited civil act capacity, the Civil Code provides two conditions for its validity. First, the civil act will be held valid if it is purely beneficial to the person with limited civil act capacity or appropriate given the person's age, intelligence, or mental status. Second, any other civil act performed by such a person will also be held valid if consent or ratification is obtained from his/her agent *ad litem*.[127]

The other party who is involved in the civil act performed by a person with limited civil act capacity may request the agent *ad litem* of the person to ratify the act within thirty days from receipt of the notification. Inaction of the agent *ad litem* is deemed as refusal to ratify. If the other party is a *bona fide* party, the party, before such an act is ratified, may revoke the act upon notice of the revocation.[128]

A civil act is voidable and thus may be revoked if it is performed (a) based on material misunderstanding;[129] (b) by fraudulent means inducing the other party to

[122] See *id.*, art. 143.
[123] See *id.*, art. 144.
[124] See *id.*, art. 146.
[125] See *id.*, art. 153.
[126] See *id.*, art. 154.
[127] See *id.*, art. 145.
[128] See *id.*
[129] See *id.*, art. 147.

perform a civil act against the party's true intent;[130] (c) by a party as a result of a third person's fraudulent act against the former's true intent, of which the other party knows or should have known;[131] (d) by a party who performs a civil act against the party's true intent under duress by the other party or a third person;[132] or (e) in a situation where one party takes advantage of the other party who is in a desperate situation or lacks the ability to make a sound judgment, rendering the performance of such civil act obviously unfair.[133]

Under the SPC's interpretation, a material mistake occurs when a party misunderstood the nature of the act, the other party, or the variety, quality, specification, price, quantity, etc., of the subject matter, if, based on a common understanding, the party would not have made the corresponding expression of intention without the mistake.[134] The SPC also opines that fraud is committed when a party deliberately presents false information or deliberately conceals true information in violation of a duty to inform, causing the other party to express his/her intention based on false information.[135]

The Civil Code does not specify what may constitute the lack of ability to make sound judgment so as to make a civil act voidable. In its 2023 Interpretation on Several Issues Concerning the Application of the General Principles of Contracts of the Civil Code, the SPC illustrates the situations in contract in which a party may be found to lack judgment ability. According to the SPC, if it can be determined that a natural person to a contract, based on the person's age, intelligence, knowledge, experience, and the complexity of the transaction, does not have the proper cognitive ability to understand the nature of the contract, the legal consequences of the conclusion of the contract, or the specific risks existing in the transaction, the person will be deemed as lacking judgment ability under the Civil Code.[136]

E. *Consequences of Void or Voidable Civil Acts*

When a civil act is void or revoked, certain legal consequences will follow. The Civil Code contains several rules that govern voidance and revocation. The first rule is the invalidation rule. Under article 155 of the 2020 Civil Code, a void or revoked civil act becomes invalid and does not have any legal effect *ab initio* (from the very beginning).[137] The reasoning is that an invalid civil act is illegal in nature and thus

[130] See *id.*, art. 148.
[131] See *id.*, art. 149.
[132] See *id.*, art. 150.
[133] See *id.*, art. 151.
[134] See the SPC, 2022 *Interpretation on the Application of Civil Code*, *supra* note 31, art. 19.
[135] See *id.*, art. 20.
[136] See the SPC, *Interpretation on Several Issues Concerning the Application of the General Principles of Contracts of the Civil Code*, issued on December 4, 2023, art. 11, at www.court.gov.cn/fabu/xiangqing/419382.html.
[137] See the 2020 Civil Code, *supra* note 1, art. 155.

unenforceable. In addition, once a civil legal act is held invalid, the invalidity will have retroactive effect.

The second rule is the partial voidance rule. In accordance with article 56 of the Civil Code, if a civil act is partially void and the voided part does not affect the validity of the other part, the other part of the act will remain valid. This rule is derived from a Latin maxim known as "*Utile Per Inutile Non Vitiatur,*" meaning "a useful thing is not vitiated by a useless one."[138] The reasoning of this maxim is that one which is otherwise useful is not rendered invalid by something useless.[139]

The third rule is the rule of restitution. Article 157 of the Civil Code provides that when a civil act is void, revoked, or determined to have no legal effect, the property thus obtained by a person as a result of the act shall be returned. If it is impossible or unnecessary to return the property, compensation shall be made based on the appraised value of the property. It is further provided in article 157 of the 2020 Civil Code that unless otherwise provided by law, the loss thus incurred upon the other party shall be compensated by the party at fault, or by the parties proportionally if both parties are at fault.[140]

A major difference between a void civil act and a voidable civil act is that in a voidable situation, the civil act may only be avoided upon request by the party affected. The request, however, must be made timely. As provided in the Civil Code, a party adversely affected in a civil act has the right to request the court or an arbitration institution revoke the act. For example, under article 148 of the Civil Code, where a party fraudulently induces the other party to perform a civil act against the other party's true intention, the defrauded party has the right to ask the court or an arbitration institution to revoke the act.

On the other hand, the Civil Code imposes certain time limits on the exercise of the right to request revocation of a civil act. According to article 152 of the Civil Code, a party's right to revoke a civil act will be extinguished under either a specific time limit or a general time limit. The specific time limit contains a particular time period that applies to a specific situation, while the general time limit sets a maximum time limit that governs any other situation.[141]

Under article 152 of the Civil Code, the right to request revocation is extinguished under any of the following circumstances: (a) a party has failed to exercise the right to revocation within one year from the date when the party knew or should have known of the cause for revocation, or within ninety days from the date when the party who has performed the act with serious misunderstanding knows or should have known of the cause for revocation; (b) the party under duress has failed to exercise the right to revocation within one year from the date when the duress

[138] See Black's Law Dictionary, *supra* note 6, at 1546.
[139] See Jianyuan, *supra* note 105, at 212.
[140] See the 2020 Civil Code, *supra* note 1, art. 157.
[141] See *id.*, art. 152.

ceases; or (c) the party who becomes aware of the cause for revocation waives the right to revocation expressly or through its own conduct. If none of these apply, the right to revoke is extinguished if the party involved fails to exercise it within five years from the date when the civil act has been performed.[142]

F. *Civil Act with Conditions or Terms*

Under the Civil Code, a condition may be attached to a civil act unless the nature of the act denies such an attachment.[143] The Civil Code does not contain a definition of condition. In Chinese civil law books, however, condition is described as a fact or event that may or may not occur in the future but must occur so that the civil act will be affected.[144] For the purposes of civil acts, a condition under the provisions of the 2020 Civil Code is divided into an entry-into-effect condition and a dissolving condition.

The entry-into-effect condition refers to a condition that will cause a civil act to take effect. Under article 158 of the Civil Code, a civil act subject to an entry-into-force condition becomes effective when the condition is satisfied.[145] In contrast, the dissolving condition is the condition under which a civil act will cease to be effective. As provided in article 158, a civil act subject to a dissolving condition becomes invalid when the condition occurs.[146]

But note that although a civil act subject to an entry-into-force condition will not take effect until the condition is satisfied, it does not necessarily mean that before the condition is fulfilled, the act taken does not possess any binding effect on the parties involved. According to the SPC opinion, once a valid civil act is completed, a binding force will be created between the two parties under the good faith principle, and none of the parties may change or rescind it unilaterally.[147] The reason is that after a condition is satisfied, its effect mainly involves performance, that is, a party can request the other party to perform as agreed, and the other party may not refuse to perform without legal grounds.[148]

On the other hand, in order to prevent a party from manipulating a condition for his/her own interests in violation of the good faith principle, the Civil Code provides a rule of constructive fulfillment of condition. According to article 159 of the Civil Code, when a condition is attached to a civil act, the condition will be deemed as

[142] See *id.*

[143] See the 2020 Civil Code, *supra* note 1, art. 158.

[144] See Jianyuan, *supra* note 105, at 213.

[145] See the 2020 Civil Code, *supra* note 1, art. 158.

[146] See *id.* (Compared with the condition as defined in U.S. law, the entry-into-force condition is equivalent to the condition precedent, while the dissolving condition is the same as or similar to the condition subsequent).

[147] See SPC Leading Group on Implement of the Civil Code, General Provisions, *supra* note 91, at 795.

[148] See *id.*

having been fulfilled if a party, for the sake of its own interests, improperly obstructs the fulfillment of the condition, or the condition will be deemed as not having been fulfilled if a party improperly facilitates the fulfillment of the condition.[149]

A civil act can also be performed based on terms. Under article 160 of the 2020 Civil Code, a term may be attached to a civil act unless the act by nature does not permit a term. Like a condition, the term can affect a civil act in two different ways. First, the parties can attach a term to the effectiveness of their civil act. Article 160 provides that a civil act subject to a term of effectiveness becomes effective when the term begins.

Second, the parties can base the termination of their civil act on a certain term. According to article 160, a civil act subject to a term of termination ceases to be effective upon expiration of the term.[150] Unlike the condition, which is a fact or event uncertain to occur in the future at the time the civil act takes place, a term refers to a fact or event that is certain to occur in the future. Thus, a term attached to a civil act is something that is sure to happen. A fact or event, if not certain to happen, may only be a condition.

5. CIVIL LIABILITIES

A civil liability is understood in China to mean the unfavorable legal consequences that a civil subject should bear for failure to fulfill civil obligations.[151] Thus, non-performance or breach of a civil obligation is a prerequisite for civil liability imposition. In a contract, for example, under the Civil Code, the legal consequences facing a non-performer or breaching party include both continuing performance of the obligation as agreed and other legal remedies of compensatory nature.[152]

A. *Functions of Civil Liabilities*

In one Chinese civil law book, a civil liability is described to have multiple functions: (1) a legal consequence of breach of civil obligations; (2) a necessary measure of remedies for damage to civil rights; and (3) a direct means to realize the expected interests and protect civil rights of a grieved party.[153] The main characteristics of a civil liability include (a) a legal liability premised on civil obligations, (b) a legal liability of a property nature, and (c) a legal liability that is compensatory, though it may also be punitive.[154]

[149] See the 2020 Civil Code, *supra* note 1, art. 159.
[150] See *id.*, art. 160.
[151] See Lixin & Yiwen, *supra* note 78, at 163.
[152] See SPC Leading Group, General Provisions, *supra* note 91, at 877.
[153] See Lixin & Yiwen, *supra* note 78, at 163–164.
[154] See *id.*

Under article 176 of the Civil Code, a civil legal person shall perform civil obligations and bear civil liability in accordance with the law or an agreement of the parties.[155] Article 176 carries two important notions. First, any breach of civil obligation creates a civil liability. In one aspect, a civil liability arises where a person has an obligation but fails to perform it. In the other aspect, when a person enjoys a civil right, any other person has the obligation not to infringe upon it. Otherwise, a civil liability will be imposed.

The second notion is that the civil obligation from which the civil liability derives can be created by agreement between the parties and by the operation of law. Generally, the liability arising from the breach of an agreement between the parties is a contractual liability, and the liability for infringement of civil rights and interests stipulated by law is a tort liability. In terms of liability nature, a statutory liability is mainly mandatory, while contractual liability is basically compensatory. The difference is that the mandatory provisions of the law leave no room for the parties to derogate from, but the contractual provisions can be replaced by the parties with a supplementary agreement or even a new agreement.[156]

B. *Joint Civil Liabilities*

Once again, a civil liability is a liability imposed on the party who breaches his/her civil obligation. In many cases, however, there is more than one person who is liable for the breach of a civil obligation. In civil law, if a liability is shared by two or more persons, the liability is a joint one. Based on liability allocation, joint liability can be joint, several, or joint and several. Joint liability is a liability where the parties are each liable up to the full amount of the obligation in question. Several liability, also called proportionate liability, is a liability under which the parties are liable only for their respective obligation. Joint and several liability is a liability where each party is independently liable for the full extent of the obligation.

The 2020 Civil Code contains two specific provisions on joint liabilities: one is joint liability by proportion or proportional joint liability, and the other is joint and several liability. Under article 177 of the Civil Code, where two or more persons assume shared liability in accordance with the law, each person shall bear the liability proportionally if the portion of liability can be determined, or equally if the specific portion cannot be determined.[157] In addition, civil liability can be imposed proportionally under an agreement of the parties if there is such an agreement where the parties stipulate the corresponding liability arising from a failure to perform the agreed obligations.[158]

[155] See the 2020 Civil Code, *supra* note 1, art. 167.
[156] See the SPC Leading Group, General Provisions, *supra* note 91, at 879–880.
[157] See the 2020 Civil Code, *supra* note 1, art. 177.
[158] See the SPC Leading Group, General Provisions, *supra* note 91, at 882.

Pursuant to article 178 of the Civil Code, where two or more persons assume joint and several liability in accordance with law, the right holder has the right to request some or all of them bear the liability.[159] Article 178 further provides that the persons subjected to joint and several liability shall each bear the liability in proportion to their respective share of liability, or in equal share if such share cannot be determined. A person who has assumed the liability more than his/her share has the right to ask for indemnity from other person(s) subject to the joint and several liability.[160] Again, the joint and several liability can be either imposed by law or stipulated by the parties in their agreement.[161]

C. *Statutory Forms of Civil Liabilities*

Again, a breach of civil obligation results in civil liability. The imposition of the liability, however, depends on the nature of the breach. Depending on the nature of the breach, a different method of compensation will apply. The method of compensation refers to the specific means or forms by which a party will undertake corresponding to his/her legal or contractual obligation to compensate the other party who suffers injury due to the former's failure to fulfill his/her obligation.

The Civil Code provides a list of compensation methods or the forms of civil liabilities. There are several points worth noting in respect to the imposition of civil liabilities. First, the forms of civil liabilities as provided in the Civil Code are all statutory. Therefore, a civil liability must have a statutory base, and its imposition must be made under the provision of law. Second, the forms of civil liabilities provided in the list may be applied separately or concurrently. Third, in contrast to the previous civil law legislation, the 2020 Civil Code not only makes "continuing performance" a type of civil liability, but also contains a new provision on punitive damages.

According to article 179 of the Civil Code, the main forms of civil liabilities include: (1) cessation of infringement; (2) removal of the nuisance; (3) elimination of danger; (4) restitution; (5) restoration; (6) repair, redoing, or replacement; (7) continuance of performance; (8) compensation for losses; (9) payment of liquidated damages; (10) elimination of adverse effects and rehabilitation of reputation; and (11) extension of apologies.[162] Also under article 179, where punitive damages are provided by law, such provisions shall apply.[163]

The forms of civil liabilities as listed can be divided into four categories. The first category is action based, which requires particular conduct from the actor. This category includes the first three forms on the list. Cessation of infringement requires

[159] See the 2020 Civil Code, *supra* note 1, art. 178.
[160] See *id.*
[161] See *id.*
[162] See *id.*, art. 179.
[163] See *id.*

the perpetrator to immediately stop the ongoing infringement, while removal of the nuisance applies in the situation where the conduct of the perpetrator makes it impossible for others to exercise, or normally exercise, personal or property rights and interests, and then the grieved party may request the perpetrator remove obstacles that hinder the former's exercise of his/her rights and interests. In addition, elimination of danger refers to the civil liability arising in the situation where the conduct of the actor or the object under his/her control threatens the person and property of others, or there is the possibility of infringing upon the person or property of others, which requires an effective removal of such danger.

The second category is the liability that involves property interests, including return of property, restoration, and repair, redoing, or replacement. Return of property is a basic form of restitution, which is a civil liability sought to prevent unjust enrichment. To return property generally means to send back the original property either illegally appropriated or obtained under an agreement that is invalid or has been rescinded. Restoration means a recovery of property in its original state or the state before the rights were violated, and is commonly used for damaged properties. Repair, redoing, or replacement applies to the case in which the delivered item does not meet the agreed quality standards, and the debtor is liable for having it fixed.

The third category is compensation specific, which contains continuing performance, compensation for losses, and payment of liquidated damages. Continuing performance is a liability imposed when a party fails to perform contractual obligations or does not perform contractual obligations as agreed, but is requested by the other party for continuance of performance in accordance with the contract. Compensation for losses is deemed in China as the most basic civil liability and applies whenever damages are caused by breach of contract or tortious conduct. Payment of liquidated damages is a liability agreed by the parties in advance, referring to a contractual remedy independent of the act of performance after the breach of contract occurs.

The fourth category covers liability associated with reputation or moral harms. There are two liability forms in this category: elimination of adverse effects and rehabilitation of reputation, and extension of apologies. Elimination of adverse effects and rehabilitation of reputation are the liability mechanisms by which the court, at the request of the victim, orders the perpetrator to take appropriate measures to eliminate the negative impact on, and to restore, the victim's reputation. Extension of apologies is a liability under which the tortfeasor is required to admit his/her fault to the victim, to express his/her apology, and to seek the victim's forgiveness. The apologies can be made either orally or in writing.

D. *Special Civil Liabilities*

In addition to the general provisions, the Civil Code also contains several special civil liabilities. Those liabilities are special because they are imposed in specific situations. The first one is liability for harms to the personality right and interests of a hero or martyr. Under article 185 of the Civil Code, any person who infringes the name, likeness, reputation, or honor of a hero or martyr and thus harms the social public interests shall bear civil liability.[164] For purposes of article 185, heroes or martyrs are those who meet the standards set forth in the state regulations.

The second special liability involves the combination or overlapping of contractual and tort liabilities. Legal liabilities are combined in a situation where the same conduct of a person gives rise to two or more legal liabilities of different natures, and thus should bear multiple legal liabilities. Article 186 of the 2020 Civil Code provides that where a party's breach of contract causes harm to the other party's personal or proprietary rights and interests, the latter party may elect to request the former to bear liability either for breach of contract or for commission of tort, but not both.[165]

Under article 186, if two or more liabilities overlap, the party whose rights are adversely affected has the right to choose how to proceed. For example, in a case that involves both torts and contract liabilities, the plaintiff may elect to pursue a cause of action either on torts or on contract. Article 186 is intended to serve a twofold purpose: on the one hand, it helps better balance the interests of the parties, and on the other hand, it helps promote judicial efficiency and save judicial resources.

The third special liability is a liability imposed under the liability priority rule. According to article 187 of the Civil Code, where a person shall concurrently bear civil, administrative, and criminal liabilities as a result of the same act he/she has conducted, the assumption of administrative or criminal liabilities by the person shall not affect the civil liability he/she should bear.[166] If, however, the assets of the person are insufficient to pay for all the liabilities, the civil liability shall be paid first.[167]

E. *Civil Liability Exemptions*

Civil liability can be exempted under certain circumstances. The parties may provide by agreement the grounds for exemption, but in most cases the exemptions are to be made on a statutory basis. Under either basis, exemption serves as a defense for a defendant to assert against the plaintiff's claim. The Civil Code contains several exemption provisions, which can be divided into two categories: justifiable reason and external cause.

Justifiable reason is a statutory ground on which the defendant will be protected from civil liability that otherwise would be imposed. It applies in the situation where the defendant's conduct causes damages, but because of the legitimacy and

[164] See *id.*, art. 185.
[165] See *id.*, art. 186.
[166] See *id.*, art. 187.
[167] See *id.*

justification of the conduct, the defendant should not be held liable as a matter of law. Under the 2020 Civil Code, justifiable reasons include justifiable defense, response to an emergency, protection of others' rights and interests, and voluntary rescue.

Justifiable defense is not defined in the Civil Code. In its 2022 Interpretation, the SPC holds that justifiable defense shall refer to an action taken against a person who is committing infringement to stop the person from causing further harm to national interests, social public interests, or personal, property, and other legitimate rights and interests of oneself or others.[168] It is generally understood in China that justifiable defense is a protective measure taken within the limits necessary to safeguard public interests, or personal or others' legitimate interests from imminent harm or damage.[169]

Under article 181 of the Civil Code, a person who causes harm out of a justifiable defense bears no civil liability.[170] Article 181, however, also provides that a person who, when acting out of justifiable defense, exceeds the necessary limit and thus causes undue harm to the aggressor shall bear appropriate civil liability.[171]According to the SPC, to determine whether a justifiable defense is excessive, the courts should look at such factors as the timing, means, intensity, and consequences of damage caused by the defense in light of the nature, means, intensity, and degree of harm by the unlawful infringement.[172]

The implication of article 181 is that to justify a protective measure causing harm, the following conditions must be met: (a) existence of unlawful harm, (b) eminence of ongoing harm, (c) done for the purpose of protecting lawful interests, (d) the measure was taken against the aggressor, and (e) the measure did not exceed necessary limits. If the protective measure is taken excessively, causing undue harm, a liability for additional damage caused by excessive force will be imposed.

Response to an emergency refers to measures taken under unavoidable circumstances causing a manageable amount of loss done for the sake of social public interests and to avoid greater damage to the legitimate interests of oneself or others. In accordance with article 182 of the Civil Code, where a person, when seeking to avoid a peril in response to an emergency, causes harm to others, the person who creates the peril shall bear civil liability.[173]

Article 182 further provides that where the peril is caused by natural forces, the person who causes harm to others by seeking to avoid the peril bears no civil liability. But the person may make appropriate compensation. In addition, if the measures taken by a person seeking to avoid a peril in response to an emergency are improper

[168] See the SPC, 2022 *Interpretation on the Application of Civil Code, supra* note 31, art. 20.
[169] See the SPC Leading Grou, General Provisions, *supra* note 91, at 909–910.
[170] See the 2020 Civil Code, *supra* note 1, art. 181.
[171] See *id.*
[172] See the SPC, 2022 *Interpretation on the Application of Civil Code, supra* note 31, art. 31.
[173] See the 2020 Civil Code, *supra* note 1, art. 182.

or exceed the necessary limit, causing undue harm to others, the person shall bear appropriate civil liability.[174] Under the SPC's interpretation, the appropriateness of the responsive measures is to be determined by the courts based on an analysis of multiple factors, including the nature of the danger, the degree of urgency, the rights and interests protected, and the consequences of the damage.[175]

Protection of others' rights and interests is a conduct endorsed and encouraged under the law for righteousness. More specifically, it is a brave act of a person who has no legal or consensual obligation to stop various tortious acts or to prevent accidents to protect the personal or property rights and interests of others. Pursuant to article 183 of the 2020 Civil Code, where a party is injured for protecting the rights and interests of another person, the tortfeasor shall bear civil liability.

In addition to the tortfeasor's liability, article 183 also provides that when a person protecting the rights and interests of others is injured during his/her action, the beneficiary may make appropriate compensation to the person for the injury. Moreover, under article 183, in the absence of a tortfeasor, or if the tortfeasor flees or is incapable of assuming civil liability, upon request of the person who suffers the injury, the beneficiary shall make appropriate compensation.[176]

Voluntary rescue is an effort timely made in response to an emergency to rescue a person who is experiencing difficulty. As provided in article 184 of the Civil Code, a person who voluntarily engages in rescuing another person in a situation of emergency and thus causes harm to the rescued person bears no civil liability. To qualify as a voluntary rescue, three factors are required. First, the rescue situation must be urgent. Second, the rescue effort must be made on a voluntary basis. Third, the exemption from liability must be made for the damages caused by the rescue to the recipient but not to others.

The external cause is the case in which attribution of the damage is a cause other than the defendant's own act or conduct, mainly *force majeure*. Under article 180 of the Civil Code, a person who is unable to perform his/her civil-law obligations due to *force majeure* bears no civil liability, unless otherwise provided by law.[177] Force majeure is defined in the 2020 Civil Code to mean objective conditions which are unforeseeable, unavoidable, and insurmountable.

6. STATUTE OF LIMITATIONS

The statute of limitations is defined in China as the rule that sets a statutory period producing certain legal effect with the passage of time. The legal effect so produced is based on a factual state and the continuity of such factual state within the

[174] See *id.*

[175] See the SPC, 2022 *Interpretation on the Application of Civil Code, supra* note 31, art. 33.

[176] See the 2020 Civil Code, *supra* note 1, art. 183.

[177] See *id.*, art. 180.

prescriptive period.[178] Ultimately, upon expiration of the statutory period, a claim, though valid, will be time-barred.

A. *Application*

In civil law, there are two kinds of statute of limitations: one deals with litigation and the other applies to acquisition. The former is based on the factual state of non-exercise of the right to claim, which sets a deadline for making a claim. The latter is conditioned on the factual status of possession, which allows the possessor of others' property to acquire title to the property after a sufficient time period lapses. An acquisition under a statute of limitations is commonly called in many other countries an "adversary possession."

For purposes of the Civil Code, the statute of limitations is a time restriction on the exercise of a right – the time within which a legal proceeding may be brought or a claim can be filed. The time limitation varies depending on the type of legal claim. As provided in the General Provisions of the 2020 Civil Code, the statute of limitations consists of three types: a general statute of limitations, a special statute of limitations, and a maximum statute of limitations.

The general statute of limitations has a general application to various legal relationships, while the special statute of limitations applies to certain legal relationships specially stipulated by the law. Under article 188 of the Civil Code, the limitation period for a person to request the people's court to protect his/her civil-law rights is three years, unless otherwise provided by law. Article 188 has two meanings: first, the general statute of limitations for civil claims is a period of three years, and second, the special statute of limitations covers any civil claim that falls within "otherwise provided by law."

The maximum statute of limitations is the longest time period allowed by law. Pursuant to article 188 of the Civil Code, no protection to a right is to be granted by the court if twenty years have lapsed since the date when the injury occurred, unless the limitation period is extended by the court under special circumstances. Thus, under the 2020 Civil Code, the maximum civil law statute of limitations in China is twenty years.

B. *Calculation*

The limitation period in both general and special statutes of limitations begins from the date when the right holder knows or should have known that his/her right has been harmed, unless the law provides otherwise. Under the SPC's interpretation, if the rights of a person without capacity or with limited capacity for civil conduct are harmed, the statute of limitations shall be calculated from the date when the agent

[178] See the SPC Leading Group, General Provisions, *supra* note 91, at 946.

ad litem knows or should know that the right is damaged and who the obligor is, unless otherwise provided by law.[179] However, the maximum statute of limitations starts to run from the time the harm occurs. More importantly, the maximum statute of limitations is not subject to interruption or suspension. In other words, the limitation period provided in the maximum statute of limitations is absolute.

Note that there are certain situations in which the limitation period will be calculated differently. The first one is about installment payments of debt. Under article 189 of the Civil Code, where the parties agree on payment of a debt by installment, the limitation period begins from the date when the last installment is due.[180] The second situation concerns a person who lacks capacity or has limited capacity. Article 190 of the Civil Code provides that the limitation period for a person with no or limited capacity for a civil act to bring a claim against his/her agent *ad litem* begins from the date when the agent *ad litem* is terminated.[181] The third situation involves minors who have been sexually assaulted. According to article 191, the limitation period for a minor to bring a sexual molestation claim against the offender begins from the date when the minor reaches the age of eighteen.[182]

The statute of limitations is mandatory in nature, meaning that the prescriptive period may not be altered by the parties through agreement. Article 197 of the Civil Code explicitly provides that the limitation period, its counting methods, and the grounds for its suspension or interruption are all provided by law, and any arrangement otherwise agreed by the parties is void. In addition, any in-advance waiver of interests by the parties related to the statute of limitations is also void.[183]

C. *Interruption*

As noted, in general and special statutes of limitations, the limitation period may be suspended or interrupted upon occurrence of certain events. In accordance with article 194 of the Civil Code, the limitation period is suspended if, within the last six months of the limitation period, a right holder is unable to exercise the right to bring a claim owing to the existence of such obstacles as (a) *force majeure*; (b) no agent *ad litem* for a right holder with no or limited capacity for civil acts, or the death or loss of capacity of an agent *ad litem*, or loss of the right as an agent *ad litem*; (c) no identified heir or appointed administrator of estate after a succession begins; (d) the right holder is controlled by the obligor or another person; and (e) other obstacles that cause the right holder to be unable to exercise the right to claim.[184] Under

[179] See the SPC, 2022 *Interpretation on the Application of Civil Code*, *supra* note 31, art. 36.
[180] See the 2020 Civil Code, *supra* note 1, art. 189.
[181] See *id.*, art. 190.
[182] See *id.*, art. 191.
[183] See *id.*, art. 197.
[184] See *id.*, art. 194.

article 194, in any of the situations mentioned earlier, the limitation period shall expire six months after the date when the cause for suspension is removed.[185]

Interruption of the limitations period occurs in the case, where during the limitations period, upon the existence of certain statutory events, the limitation period will be recalculated after the statutory event ceases to exist. According to article 195, a limitation period is interrupted under any of the following circumstances: (a) the right holder requests the obligor to perform the obligation; (b) the obligor agrees to perform the obligation; (c) the right holder initiates a lawsuit or arbitration proceeding against the obligor; or (d) there exists any other circumstance that has the same effect as initiating a lawsuit or arbitration proceeding by the right holder.[186] When the limitation period is interrupted, it shall run anew when the time of the interruption or the time for the relevant proceeding is completed.[187]

The last point worthy of noting is that there are also certain circumstances under which the statute of limitations is not applicable. Pursuant to article 196 of the Civil Code, the statute of limitations does not apply to the following claims: (a) a claim for cessation of the infringement, removal of the nuisance, or elimination of the danger; (b) a claim for return of property of a person who has a real right in an immovable or a registered movable property; (c) a claim for payment of child support or support for other family members; or (d) any other claims to which the limitation period is not applicable in accordance with law.[188]

[185] See *id.*
[186] See *id.*, art. 195.
[187] See *id.*
[188] See *id.*, art. 196.

8

Property Law

INTRODUCTION

Like in other civil law countries, the property law in China resembles the law of real rights.[1] In Chinese history, although provisions on land ownership can be seen as early as the Shang Dynasty (1600–1046 BC), the concept of property, and private property in particular, was never really developed in the country. The first modern legislation on property in China was the 1930 Civil Code adopted by the Republic Government. As noted, the 1930 Civil Code consisted of five parts, and part III covered "Rights over Things" (a civil law concept for "property").[2] Unfortunately, the 1930 Civil Code was not actually applied due to Japanese occupation, followed by China's eight-year war against Japan and then the country's three-year civil war. In 1949, as discussed, when the Communist party came into power, the 1930 Civil Code, along with five other Codes, were entirely annulled.[3]

From 1949 to 1976, following the former Soviet Union model and socialist ideology, Mao strongly pushed for a system that would diminish both private ownership and individualism. Consequently, private interests and private property rights became synonymous with capitalism and the bourgeoisie. The ten-year Cultural Revolution further diminished private property and property rights for

[1] See Wang Liming, The Law of Real Rights, 1 (Wells, 2017).

[2] The Five Parts in the 1930 Civil Code were: General Principles, Obligations, Rights of Things, Family, and Succession. Part I was adopted on May 23, 1929, and took effect October 10, 1929. Parts II and III were promulgated in November 1929 and effective May 30, 1930, and parts IV and V were enacted at the end of 1930. See Joseph An-Pao Wang, The Civil Code of the Republic of China (Studies in Chinese Government and Law) (Praeger, 1976).

[3] The 1930 Civil Code and other five codes were known as the "Six Codes." In addition to the Civil Code, the Six Codes included the Constitution, Commercial Code, Criminal Law, Criminal Procedure, and Civil Procedure. The Six Codes were repealed by the Communist Party in February 1949.

people in the country, if not completely stripped them away.[4] After 1978, following the "opening-door" policy and vast economic reforms, China entered into a stage of transition, shifting from its rigid planned economy to a market economy.

Ever since, the shift has dramatically changed the way people think about property rights, and the concept of private ownership and property interests is no longer taboo in the country. In the nearly three decades since the economic reform, people in China have started to regain consciousness of their private property rights and have sought further protection of these rights. On March 16, 2007, China finally had its first Property Law pass the National People's Congress (NPC) after a fourteen-year legislative marathon.[5]

Effective on October 1, 2007, the Property Law was hailed in the country as a milestone of modern Chinese legislative history. A significant piece of legislation granting legal protection to private property rights, the Property Law filled in the country's "legal blank" in property regulation, private property in particular. It helped enhance the legal infrastructure of the country by establishing a long-awaited legal framework regulating and protecting property rights and interests.

More importantly, the Property Law reinforces the "inviolable" nature of private property in China, a concept that was constantly denied in the country until 2004. In 2004, the 1982 Constitution was amended for the fourth time to make the protection of private property and property rights a constitutional mandate. In 2020, the Property Law was incorporated into, and became part II of, the Civil Code. Entitled "Right to Things," part II of the Civil Code is composed of 5 Sections, 20 Chapters, and 258 Articles. Based on the Property Law, the Civil Code not only refines the provisions of the Property Law, but also improves the rules that govern property rights and interests in the country.

1. GENERAL PROVISIONS

Part II of the Civil Code contains comprehensive provisions of the rights to things. The five sections in part II of the Civil Code include "General Provisions," "Ownership," "Usufructuary Right," "Right of Security Interest," and "Possession." The "General Provisions" section comprises the basic principles intended to safeguard property rights and interests. It also provides major rules that apply to the creation, alteration, transfer, and termination of property rights.

[4] As has been observed, the Anglo-American conception of "rights" is basically associated with individuals and is often linked with defying state authority, while in China "rights" are more commonly related to the public or collectives. See Neil Diamant, Engaging the Law in China, State, Society, and Possibilities for Justice, 14 (Stanford University Press, 2005).

[5] The drafting of the Property Law started in 1993 and the draft was submitted in 2002 to the National People's Congress for the first reading.

A. *The Concept of Real Rights*

In China, as in many other civil law countries, the term "res" (things) is commonly used to refer to property and as such property rights are normally called "real rights" (*jura in re*). One possible reason for this is that the term "property" is considered overly broad, which could potentially include anything of value,[6] while the term "things" generally has a narrower definition, referring to tangible and intangible things of certain economic value.[7] In this context, a more restrictive definition limits the thing to tangibles or *corporeal res*.[8] Although some argue that the use of the term "things" rather than "property" is merely a matter of Chinese tradition,[9] it is important to note that under this definition of "thing," creditor rights would not be regarded as a "thing" or "res," but such rights may be deemed as a kind of "property."[10]

Again, under the civil law tradition, a civil relationship involves a civil subject or person and a civil object or civil matters. The law regulating civil matters has two major components: one dealing with "things" and the other concerning "*obligatio*" (often referring to obligations in common law countries). The law of things is to protect the rights over property against any other person, while the law of *obligatio* functions to secure the right of a person against another specific person, namely a creditor against a debtor. In common law countries, no bright line seems to exist as to the law regulating property and obligations. Despite the difference, however, it is commonly understood that "thing" refers to property, and "real right" is a property right. In this context, the terms "property law" and "real rights law" are used in China interchangeably to mean the law that governs property and related rights and interests.

As defined in article 114 of the Civil Code, a property right is the right to control a specific thing directly and exclusively by the right holder in accordance with law, which consists of the ownership, right to usufruct, and security interests in the property. Article 144 further provides that persons in the civil law enjoy property rights in accordance with law. Also pursuant to article 205 of the Civil Code, the property law regulates the civil relationships arising from the attribution and utilization of things.

6 For example, in the United States, property may denote everything that is the subject of ownership. This can be objects that are corporeal or incorporeal, tangible or intangible, visible or invisible, real or personal, or that which has exchangeable value or which makes up wealth or an estate. Black's Law Dictionary, 1216 (8th ed., West, 2004).

7 See Jiang Ping, A Course in Chinese Real Rights Law, 1 (Intellectual Property Right Press, 2007).

8 See *id.* at 2.

9 See *id.* at 60.

10 See Wang Liming, Study on Crucial and Difficult Problems of Chinese Civil Code, 258–259 (Law Press, 2006).

More specifically, for purposes of the Civil Code, the law of property governs the following relationships: (a) the relationship arising from the establishment or acquisition of a property right; (b) the relationship arising from a change or extinguishment of a property right; (c) the relationship arising from the transfer of a property right; and (d) the relationship arising from affirmation of, or infringement upon, a property right.[11] Again, in contrast to the creditor's right, which is the right against a relevant or specific person (debtor), a property right is an absolute right against everyone.

There is also a concept of "quasi-real rights." In civil law, quasi-real rights refer to the rights of real property that are acquired under the law outside the normal spectrum of real rights. More specifically, a quasi-real right is the right obtained within the scope of an administrative authorization to possess, utilize, and benefit from the use of natural resources, free from interference by others. Essentially, it is the right within legal limits to exclusively dominate the use of natural resources.

Under article 329 of the Civil Code, the right to explore and mine minerals, to draw water, and to use waters and mudflats to engage in aquaculture or fishing that are acquired in accordance with law are protected by law.[12] Thus, for the purposes of the Civil Code, the quasi-real rights include (a) the right of exploration of minerals and mining, (b) water rights or riparian rights, (c) aquaculture rights, and (d) fishing rights. The significance of quasi-real rights is that the right holder may bring a property right claim against an infringement of any of the quasi-real rights.

B. *Socialist Economic System*

The Civil Code contains a special provision that defines China's economic system, which forms the foundation of the property law. Under article 206 of the Civil Code, China upholds and improves the fundamental socialist economic systems, including (a) the ownership system under which diverse forms of ownership co-develop with public ownership as the pillar, (b) the distribution system under which multiple forms of distribution co-exist with distribution according to work as the mainstay, and (c) the system of a socialist market economy.[13]

The socialist economic system specified in article 206 has three major components: public ownership, distribution according to work, and a market economy. Public ownership is the leading force of the Chinese economy. But given the co-existence of multiple ownerships and the need for economic growth, article 206 explicitly provides that the State encourages, supports, and guides the

[11] See the SPC Leading Group, Understanding and Application of the Civil Code: Law of Property, 18–19 (People's Court Press, 2020) (hereinafter referred to as SPC Leading Group, Property Rights).

[12] See the 2020 Civil Code, art. 329, available at www.wipo.int/wipolex/en/text/586681.

[13] See *id.*, art. 206.

development of the non-public sector of the economy.[14] Public ownership in China includes state ownership and collective ownership (rural collectives), while the non-public sector mainly refers to private ownership.

The distribution system refers to the scheme under which products or income are divided and allocated among civil subjects (persons). The concept of "distribution according to work" is derived from the socialist distribution ideology known as "from each according to his ability to each according to his work." A prevailing theory in China is that the mode of production determines the mode of distribution, and the ownership structure of the means of production dictates the distribution structure. Thus, corresponding to the co-existence of different ownerships in the Chinese economy, the distribution system is also structured in a way that different distribution methods co-exist with "distribution according to work" as the main body. It is believed in the country that the combined distribution mechanism can help mobilize the enthusiasm of all people, promote the improvement of economic efficiency, and foster the development of productive forces.

China has endeavored to build a market economy as its economic framework through the country's decades-long economic reforms. The adoption of the market economy evidenced China's departure from a planned economy and signified a shift from state control to voluntary engagement in the process of economic decision-making. To help promote the market economy, the Civil Code is purposed to ensure that all economic entities have equal footing and enjoy equal rights in their business interactions. Under article 206 of the Civil Code, the State implements a socialist market economy and protects the equal legal status and development rights of all market participants.[15]

C. *Principles of Property Law*

There are several principles in the Civil Code that govern property rights and interests. As noted, principles not only serve as the grounds for other provisions to rely on, but also have practical significance for courts in applying the property law, especially when some provisions are ambiguous or there appears to be a gap. In the Civil Code, some of the principles are explicitly provided while some are implied in the provisions of law.

a. Equal Protection

Again, the property law in China covers rights and interests of the State, collectives, and individuals, but the realm of private law remains the law that governs relationships among individuals and entities of equal status. A significant characteristic of

[14] See *id.*
[15] See *id.*

private law is that the relationship governed by the law is horizontal and all parties concerned should be protected equally. Applied to property rights, equal protection requires that owners of property be treated in an equal manner, regardless of the form of ownership. Equal protection is vitally important in China because of the country's long-term bias against private ownership and the government's overreaching power, especially when public interest is involved.

Many in China believe that without equal protection, public confidence in creating social wealth would be dampened and the very purpose of property law provisions in the Civil Code would be frustrated.[16] The underlying notion is that a market economy demands equal protection of different property owners and that without equal protection the market economy would fail.[17] In China, equal protection was first provided in the 1986 General Principles of Civil Law as a general principle that governed civil relationships. In contrast, a more specific provision on the protection of property rights and interests was article 4 of the 2007 Property Law.

Under article 4 of the Property Law, the property rights of the State, collectives, or any other right holder shall be protected by law and shall not be infringed by any entity or individual.[18] The Civil Code modifies article 4 of the Property Law by adding the word "equally" to emphasize equal protection. Pursuant to article 207 of the Civil Code, the property rights of the State, collectives, private individuals, and other right holders shall be equally protected by law and free from infringement by any entity or individual.[19]

Like article 4 of the Property Law, article 207 of the Civil Code grants no special status to public property, state or collective. The implication of article 207 is that private property is protected in the same manner as public property and any violation of property rights is prohibited, regardless of the type of property owner. For the purposes of article 207, equal protection includes at least three elements: equal status of property owners, application of the same rules, and equal liability.

Equal status means that as far as property rights are concerned, nobody shall be discriminated against based on the status of the property owner. Application of the same rules provides a surety that if a dispute over property occurs between the state and an individual, each party has the same right of claim, the same access to legal redress, and is subject to the same rules.[20] Equal liability refers to a situation where a property right is infringed, and ensures that the infringer shall bear the same

[16] See Liming, *supra* note 10, at 247–250. *See also* Hu Kangsheng, Explanations to the Property Law of the People's Republic of China, 7–9 (Law Press, 2007) (Hu serves as the head of Legislative Affairs Committee of the Standing Committee of NPC).

[17] See Ping, *supra* note 7, at 173. *See also* Kangsheng, *supra* note 16, at 7–8.

[18] See Property Law of China (March 16, 2007), art. 4, available at www.bjreview.com.cn/document/txt/2007-07/26/content_70481.htm.

[19] See the 2020 Civil Code, *supra* note 12, art. 207.

[20] See Liming, *supra* note 10, at 246.

liability, no matter whether the infringer is the state or an individual.[21] But it is required that the application of the equal protection principle not belittle public ownership.

b. Leading Position of Public Ownership

As noted, public ownership is the core element of the socialist economy.[22] But for decades in Mao's era, the dominance of public ownership was overly stated to the extent that public ownership was maintained and defended against any non-public ownership.[23] Consequently, the whole country was led to believe that public ownership was superior to all other forms of ownership.[24] From a legal perspective, the superiority of public ownership was first stressed in the 1954 Constitution. Under article 6 of the 1954 Constitution, ownership by the whole people, represented by the state-run economy, was "the leading force in the national economy and the material foundation of the socialist transformation." The state was determined to ensure "the priority of the development of the State-run economy."[25]

The 1975 Constitution not only emphasized the "leading force" of the state-run economy, but also added the principle that "socialist public property is inviolable."[26] This principle was then carried over verbatim into the 1978 Constitution.[27] The 1982 Constitution further emphasized this principle by adding the word "sacredly."

21 See Huang Songyou, Understanding and Application of Property Law of China, 245 (People's Court Press, 2007).

22 See Mario Ferrero, A *Rational Theory of Socialist Public Ownership*, 16 Sage J. 371, 371–372 (November 2004).

23 A typical example is the "Great Leap Forward" campaign from 1958–1960, aimed at eliminating all private elements in the countryside by bringing (if not forcing) millions of farmers into people's communes, the basic forms of public ownership, where the farmers would not work for themselves but for the communes to ensure that everyone would follow the party's policy to "speedily run into communism." A direct result of the "Great Leap Forward" was the disaster of severe famine in the early 1960s that led to millions of people dying of starvation. See Stanley B. Lubman, Bird in a Cage: Legal Reform in China after Mao, 80 (Stanford University Press, 1999).

24 In China, public ownership includes state ownership and collective ownership. State ownership, also called ownership by the whole people, controls both industry and commerce. Collective ownership is used to mean ownership held in rural people's communes through a three-level structure including communes, the production brigade, and the basic level called the production team. Constitution of China (1975) art. 7, available at http://chr.sagepub.com. Now it is used to refer to ownership by rural collective economic organizations through the household-based output-related contracted responsibility system. Chinese Constitution (1982), art. 7, available at https://china.usc.edu/constitution-peoples-republic-china-1982.

25 See 1954 Constitution of China, art. 6, available at www.lawinfochina.com/display.aspx?lib = law&id = 14754&CGid.

26 See 1975 Constitution of China, art. 8, available at https://china.usc.edu/1975-constitution-peoples-republic-china.

27 See 1978 Constitution of China, art. 8, available at https://china.usc.edu/1978-constitution-peoples-republic-china.

Under article 12 of the 1982 Constitution, socialist public property was sacredly inviolable.[28]

Although the reason for the change was not given in the official report on the draft revision of the Constitution, it is clearly an indication of a more serious stance toward the protection of public property. This stance can also be seen in the 2004 Amendment, in which protection of private property became a constitutional mandate. While article 13 of the 1982 Constitution (as amended 2018) held lawful private property of citizens as merely "inviolable,"[29] article 12 remains to hold socialist public property "sacredly inviolable."[30]

The Civil Code does not use the word "sacredly" to describe the inviolable nature of public property rights; instead, it attaches great significance to the equality of protection – private and public properties alike. Under article 206 of the Civil Code, the State implements a socialist market economy and protects the equal status and development rights of all market participants. But it is easily perceptible that public ownership remains in a prominent position in the country's economic system.

First, the Civil Code does not take the "single term" approach to simply using "property rights" to cover all properties, but instead uses a "separate term" mechanism to differentiate the state or collective property rights from individual or other holders' property rights. Second, the Civil Code emphasizes the leading role of public ownership by providing public ownership as the mainstay in the country's ownership system. In addition, as noted, under the Civil Code, the State consolidates and develops the public sector of the economy. By contrast, the State encourages, supports, and guides the development of the non-public sector of the economy.[31] Third, there is in general a consensus in China that equal protection does not necessarily mean an equal role for public property and that the leading force of public ownership must be maintained.[32]

c. The *Numerus Clausus*

A well-known civil law principle that governs property is that property rights must be prescribed by law and may not be created by or between the parties. This principle is widely stated in civil law countries as the "*Numerus Clausus*," a classic Roman concept meaning that "the number is closed."[33] As applied to property, the "*Numerus Clausus*" is aimed at excluding the "autonomy" of the property owner

[28] See 1982 Constitution of China, *supra* note 24, art. 12.

[29] See 1982 Constitution (as amended 2018), art. 13, available at https://english.www.gov.cn/archive/lawsregulations/201911/20/content_WS5ed8856ec6d0b3f0e9499913.html.

[30] See *id.*, art. 12.

[31] See the 2020 Civil Code, *supra* note 12, art. 206.

[32] See Kangsheng, *supra* note 16, at 7, 28. See also Yao Hong, Detailed Explanations to the Property Law of the People's Republic of China, 8 (People's Press, 2007).

[33] See John Merryman, *Policy, Autonomy, and the Numerus Clausus in Italian and American Property Law*, 12 Am. J. Comp. L. 224 (1963).

to "invent" any property interest that is not named or provided by the law.[34] This principle also affects how property is to be defined.[35] In common law systems, the concept of the "*Numerus Clausus*" is understood to mean that property rights must conform to certain standardized forms.[36]

The notion behind "*Numerus Clausus*" is the absoluteness of the property, meaning a right against all others.[37] Thus, if an owner is allowed to create a property right or interest at will, the creation would affect all other people.[38] This notion is also accepted in common law to the extent that the "*Numerus Clausus*" serves to prevent situations in which too many individuals have a veto right over the use or disposition of a resource.[39] One of the reasons to maintain the "*Numerus Clausus*" is to ensure the safety of property transactions because the principle has the effect of creating a clean title to the property.[40] Another reason is that "*Numerus Clausus*" can help reduce ascertainment costs of property rights.[41]

The "*Numerus Clausus*" principle is provided both in the Property Law and the Civil Code. Under article 5 of the Property Law and article 116 of the Civil Code, the kinds and contents of property rights shall be prescribed by law. In other words, without statutory prescription, nothing may be deemed a property right or property interest, and the legal dimensions of property must be within the boundary clearly stated by law.[42] In this context, the provisions concerning property rights are generally compulsory and may not be varied by the conduct of any right holder[43]

d. One Thing, One Right

"One thing, one right" is a doctrine under which property is held as a "thing" containing an exclusive right of ownership.[44] In other words, no two conflicting

[34] See *id.*

[35] See Thomas W. Merrill & Henry E. Smith, *Optimal Standardization in the Law of Property: The Numerus Clausus Principle*, 110 *Yale. L. J.* 1, 4 n.6 (2000).

[36] See *id.* at 4. [Article actually says that in contrast to civil law systems, where *numerus clausus* is recognized explicitly, "[i]n the common law, the principle that property rights must conform to certain standardized forms has no name."]

[37] See Kangsheng, *supra* note 16, at 30. A similar concept in U.S. property law is the "fee simple absolute," meaning that ownership lasts forever. See Joseph Singer, Introduction to Property Law, 308 (Aspen, 2005).

[38] See Ping, *supra* note 7, at 129.

[39] See Merrill & Smith, *supra* note 35, at 6.

[40] See Liming, *supra* note 10, at 266.

[41] See Merrill & Smith, *supra* note 35, at 8. ("When property rights are created, third parties must expend time and resources to determine the attributes of these rights, both to avoid violating them and to acquire them from present holders.")

[42] As described in an English case, "incidents of a novel kind cannot be devised and attached to property at the fancy or caprice of any owner." Keppell v. Baily (1834) 39 Eng. Rep. 1042, 1049 (Ch.).

[43] See Liming, *supra* note 10, at 265.

[44] See Ping, *supra* note 7, at 116.

property rights may exist over any "one thing" and, as such, the subject of property rights must be specific and ascertainable.[45] In civil law theory, property rights can be divided into two major categories: *plena in re potestas* (complete and absolute property rights) and *jura in re aliena* (certain property rights to the property owned by others).[46] It is commonly understood that the *plena in re potestas* basically denotes ownership or dominium, while the *jura in re aliena* mainly refers to other property rights such as usufructuary rights and rights on securities.[47]

A practical matter in China concerning the "one thing, one right" doctrine is the likely conflict between the independent civil status of state-owned enterprises and state ownership. As players in the market, state-owned enterprises must be able to act independently, including having the ability to dispose of property they control. But the state-owned enterprises are not the actual owners of property and have no right to dispose of it.[48] Many then argue that the "one thing, one right" doctrine is inapplicable to state-owned property. Some suggest an approach of "dual ownership," under which the state owns the value of the property, while state-owned enterprises own the value of the use of the property.[49]

Some in China argue that the "one thing, one right" doctrine is both the core and the very foundation of property rights. The reason is that given the absolute and exclusive feature of the property right, it is impossible to establish two ownerships on any given property. In addition, it is believed that the "sole" or "unique" nature of property rights gives rise to the necessity to have a singular right only to any one thing.[50]

On its face, the Civil Code, like the Property Law, does not specifically state the "one thing, one right" principle, but instead it defines property rights as the exclusive right of control over a specific thing.[51] There is belief in the country that the "exclusive right" to "a specific thing" actually means "one thing, one right."[52] An opposing argument, however, is that both the Property Law and the Civil Code only address the exclusivity of the property right, which does not necessarily lead to the assertion of "one thing, one right."[53]

45 See Songyou, *supra* note 21, at 43.

46 See Luigi Miraglia, Comparative Legal Philosophy Applied to Legal Institutions, 523–524 (John Lisle trans., Boston Book Company, 1912).

47 See Liming, *supra* note 10, at 264.

48 Ownership is considered to comprise a bundle of rights, including the right to possession, the right to use, the right to interest, and the right to disposition. Among these rights, the right to disposition is deemed the most crucial one. See Singer, *supra* note 37, at 2–3.

49 By analogy, the State and a state-owned enterprise are deemed a shareholder and a company, where a shareholder owns equity of the company but does not have ownership of the value he/she contributed to the company, and the company is the owner of the property of the company. See Xu Diyu, Lectures on Hot Topics of Property Law, 32 (China Legal Publishing House, 2007).

50 See Ping, *supra* note 7, at 115–116.

51 See Property Law, *supra* note 18, art. 2.

52 Ping, *supra* note 7, at 121–122.

53 See Songyou, *supra* note 21, at 47–49.

D. *Creation and Change of Property Rights*

Creation of a property right refers to the acquisition of the right as such, which could be done either by agreement or by operation of law. Change of a property right includes alteration, alienation, and extinguishment of the right to the property, and the change can involve the subject, object, as well as the contents of the property right. To be effective, both creation and change of a property right must have a statutory basis and must also meet the formality requirements.

a. Nature of Property: Movable vs. Immovable

Under article 115 of the Civil Code, a thing in property law includes movable property and immovable property.[54] The Civil Code, however, provides no definition of these two kinds of properties. In concept, moveable property and immovable property are mainly used in civil law countries, and correspond to personal property and real property in common law countries. The difference between movable property and immovable property generally depends on whether the property can be moved, whether the move is economically reasonable, and whether the property is attached to a piece of land.

Also, according to article 115, if the law provides that a right shall be treated as property, such provisions shall be followed.[55] Thus, the object of a property right under the Civil Code has three components: movable property, immovable property, and a right possessing the nature of property. It is important to note that to be treated as property, the right must be specifically provided by the law. Once again, under the "*Numerus Clausus*" principle, any property and property right or interests must have a statutory basis.

In Chinese civil law literature, the object of a property right refers to the specific object directed, dominated, and controlled by the property right. Specifically, an object of a property right must be a specific thing that (a) exists objectively, (b) can be controlled by human power, (c) has a certain value, and (d) can meet the needs of human production and living.[56] Moreover, a thing that could be the object of a property right is considered in China to have at least four distinctive features.

The first feature is oneness, which means that as an object of a property right, the thing in its form can exist individually or in unity. The second feature is called independence. It is the feature that means the object of a property right is physically, conceptually, and legally capable of being distinguished from other things and staying independent. The third feature is specificity, meaning that a thing has its

[54] See the 2020 Civil Code, *supra* note 12, art. 115.

[55] See *id.*

[56] See the SPC Leading Group, Understanding and Application of the Civil Code (General Provisions), 577 (People's Court Press, 2020).

uniqueness and cannot be replaced. The last feature is tangibleness In general, the object of a property right should be a thing that is tangible, especially the object of ownership. Thus, a non-tangible thing may not be an object of a property right but a right only.[57]

b. Mechanism for the Creation and Change of Property Rights

As noted, both creation and change of a property right can be made either by agreement or by operation of law. The process of creation and change, however, differs depending on the nature of the property. Under article 208 of the Civil Code, the creation, alteration, alienation, or extinguishment of a property right in immovable property shall be registered, while the creation and alienation of a property right in movable property shall be subject to delivery. Thus, the creation or change of the property right in an immovable property will not be legally complete until registration is made, and the creation or change of a property right in movable property takes effect upon delivery.

I. REGISTRATION OF IMMOVABLE PROPERTY. Registration is known as a system of publicity for creation or change of a right in immovable property.[58] A failure to register adversely affects the property acquired and the right of owners to their property. In addition, publicity as required by the law functions to ensure the safety of property transactions and the certainty of property ownership. In civil law countries, there are two major registration systems: "effective by registration" and "against third party."

The "effective by registration" system can be found in countries such as Germany and Switzerland, where registration is a prerequisite to the acquisition of ownership in land.[59] Under the "effective by registration" system, the acquisition or change of property rights in land would not take effect without valid registration. The system of "against third party" is employed in countries like Japan, where registration may not necessarily affect the acquisition or change of property rights but may serve as a defense against a third party. Under the Japanese Civil Code, for example, acquisition, loss, or alteration of rights in immovable property may not be made against a third party without registration, which renders registration essential to property rights against third parties.[60]

57 See *id.* at 577–578.

58 The term "publicity" is popular in China to refer to the formalities for the change of property. See Liming, *supra* note 10, at 306.

59 Under §891 of the German Civil Code, the registration of a property right in the land register is required for obtaining ownership of the land. See Michael Wendler, Bernd Tremml, & Bernard Buecker. Key Aspects of German Business Law, 121–130 (3rd ed., Springer, 2006). According to §656 of Swiss Civil Code, the entry thereof in the land register is necessary to the acquisition of ownership in land. See the Swiss Civil Code, 155 (Boston Book Company, 1915).

60 See Kazuo Hatoyama, *The Civil Code of Japan Compared with the French Civil Code*, 11 *Yale L. J.* 354, 362 (1902).

By contrast, in common law countries, a common mechanism for land registration is called the "Torrens" system. Introduced by Sir Robert Torrens of Australia in 1858, the "Torrens" system established a legal procedure whereby property is transferred by registration instead of deed and the state guarantees the owner's indefeasible title to the property registered.[61] In the United States, a comparable system called "recording" is used instead of registration.[62] But in most US states, recording is not required to validate the transfer of the property interest, although it is deemed "essential to both provide an official record of the state of the title and to protect the buyers against any competing claim that may be created by the grantor in others."[63]

China follows civil law practice. At first, it makes registration a basic mechanism of publicity for the acquisition and change of property rights. Under Article 209 of the Civil Code, the creation, alteration, alienation, or extinguishment of the rights to immovable property shall become effective upon registration according to the law. Unless otherwise provided by law, the property right acquisition or change will have no effect absent registration.[64]

(a) Effect of Registration Article 209 of the Civil Code has several implications on the property right registration: (1) registration only applies to immovable property, (2) no acquisition or change of property right in immovable property becomes effective unless registered, and (3) the registration is subject to exceptions provided by the law. The significance of registration is that it determines the effectiveness of transactions on immovable property. Any exception to the registration must have a statutory ground.

A notable exception is the *proviso* in the second paragraph of article 209 under which an ownership registration is not required for state-owned natural resources.[65] In addition, there are certain situations in which the effectiveness of a change of property rights is not dependent on registration. One situation is the change caused by a legal document issued by a court, arbitration body, or a government decision of expropriation.[66] Another situation is the acquisition of property rights by inheritance.[67] Also, if a change of property rights results from such a *de facto* act as construction or demolition, the change becomes effective upon completion of the act.[68]

The exception to registration also applies to the change of rights to certain use of land. As discussed, no individual in China may own a piece of land, only the right to

[61] See Jesse Dukeminier et al., Property, 615–623 (6th ed., Espen, 2006).
[62] Today, only a few states in the United States use registration for the title of land. See *id.* at 617.
[63] See Singer, *supra* note 37, at 545.
[64] See the 2020 Civil Code, *supra* note 12, art. 209.
[65] See *id.*
[66] See *id.*, art. 229.
[67] See *id.*, art. 230.
[68] See *id.*, art. 231.

use the land. Land use under Chinese law is divided into different categories, including the right to the contracted management of land, the right to undertake construction on land, and the right to use house sites. Among the land use rights, the right to use house sites would need approval by a certain authority, and thus its effectiveness does not depend on registration but onby approval.

Similarly, the right to contracted management of land is created when the contract is made rather than at the time of registration.[69] Note, however, that although registration is optional for the right of contracted management of land, such a right may not be asserted against a bona fide third party without registration.[70] The same rule also applies to such property interests as easements.[71]

Under article 210 of the Civil Code, immovable property registration shall be handled by the registration authority at the place where the property is located, and a unified registration system shall be employed nationwide.[72] Also under article 210, the scope, authorities, and measures for the registration are to be specified by laws and administrative regulations.[73]

Pursuant to article 213 of the Civil Code, the authority of immovable property registration is prohibited from engaging in the following acts: (a) requiring an appraisal of the immovable property; (b) conducting repeated registration in the name of annual inspection, and the like; and (c) undertaking other acts that exceed the scope of its responsibilities for registration.[74] Article 213 is purposed to prevent abuse of power by the registration authority and ensure a smooth process of registration.

(b) Registration vs. Property Contract Registration is a process of publicity required to effectuate the acquisition or change of an immovable property right. The transaction that results in the acquisition or change of such property right, however, relies on a contract. The Civil Code separates property contracts from property registration so that the registration affects only the effectiveness of the acquisition or change but not the property contract itself. According to article 215 of the Civil Code, a contract concluded by the parties on the creation, alteration, alienation, or extinguishment of an immovable property right becomes effective upon its formation, unless it is otherwise provided by law or agreed upon by the parties, and the validity of the property contract would not be affected without property registration.[75] Thus, under the Civil Code, a failure to register, standing

69 See *id.*, arts. 333, 363.
70 See *id.*, art. 335.
71 See *id.*, art. 374.
72 See *id.*, art. 210.
73 See *id.*
74 See *id.*, art. 213.
75 See *id.*, art. 215.

alone, will not render the underlying contract of the immovable property transaction invalid or unenforceable.

(c) Advance Registration Advance registration as provided in the Civil Code is a mechanism that aims to protect the right holder for realization of the property right in the future. It mainly applies to the presale of a newly built house where a buyer can register the unfinished house in advance to prevent the developer from reselling or mortgaging the houses before delivery of the house. Pursuant to article 221 of the Civil Code, where the parties enter into a contract for the sale of a house or on any other immovable property right, they may apply for an advance registration to ensure the realization of the immovable property right in the future.[76]

The effect of advance registration is that upon registration, the immovable property involved may not be transferred without the consent of the right holder. According to the Supreme People's Court (SPC), absent the consent of the holder of the property right registered in advance, a transfer of such property right as ownership of an immovable property, establishment of a right of the use of construction land, right of habitation, easements, or mortgages shall be held invalid.[77] In China, advance registration serves multiple purposes: (a) to help ensure a future realization of the property right; (b) to maintain the exclusivity of the property right; (c) to establish an order of priority in the property; and (d) to protect the right holder from anyone else's claim on the property.[78]

(d) Register and Ownership Certificate Registration of an immovable property produces two documents: a register and an ownership certificate. A register is a document of the official record, while the ownership certificate is conclusive and official proof of the right on the property. Under article 216 of the Civil Code, the register of immovable property is the basis for determining the attribution and contents of the rights in immovable property.[79] Also, article 216 requires that the register of immovable property be kept by the registration authority.[80]

In addition to its official record function, the register also determines the time at which the transaction of immovable property takes effect. As specified in article 214 of the Civil Code, the creation, alteration, alienation, or extinguishment of a property right of the immovable property, if a registration is required under the law, becomes effective when the register of such property is established. Thus, under

[76] See *id.*, art. 221.

[77] See the SPC, *Interpretation on the Application of the Property Rights Provisions of the Civil Code (I)*, issued on January 1, 2021, art. 4, available at www.bjgzc.com/gzal/202103/20212111452386.html.

[78] See the SPC Leading Group, Property Rights, *supra* note 11, at 118–119.

[79] See the 2020 Civil Code, *supra* note 12, art. 216.

[80] See *id.*

articles 209 and 214, an immovable property transaction takes effect upon registration, and registration is complete at the time of the establishment of a register.

The ownership certificate for an immovable property is proof of a right holder's entitlement to said property. Pursuant to article 217, all items recorded in the ownership certificate for immovable property shall be consistent with those recorded in the register of the property. If, however, a discrepancy between the register and ownership certificate appears, the register shall prevail, unless there is evidence establishing a clear error in the register.[81]

(e) **Liability for Registration Error** Given the legal significance of immovable property registration, if an error in the registration causes harm to the right holder or a bona fide third party, a civil liability to compensate will be imposed under the Civil Code. The cause of error may have two possible attributes. One possible attribute is false information provided by the party seeking registration. In this situation, a civil liability will be imposed if damage occurs. Under article 222 of the Civil Code, a party who provides false materials for registration, which causes damage to another person, shall be liable for compensation.

The other possible attribute is clerical error. A clerical error is an error caused by the registration authority. Article 222 further provides that where damage is caused to another person due to a clerical error upon registration, the registration authority shall be liable for compensation. Also, in accordance with article 222, after compensation is made, the registration authority has the right to indemnification against the person who made the error. What is unclear, however, is the extent to which compensation should be made.

II. DELIVERY OF MOVABLE PROPERTY. Unlike the immovable property transaction for which registration is required, an acquisition or transfer of the right to movable property is subject only to "delivery." According to article 224 of the Civil Code, the creation or alienation of property rights to movable property shall come into effect upon delivery unless otherwise provided by the law.[82] Thus, delivery is a condition precedent to the effectiveness of the transaction involving movable property.

Note that under Chinese law, vessels, aircraft, and vehicles are all classified as special properties for which the rules governing movable property apply. However, pursuant to article 225 of the Civil Code, no property right claim may be made against a bona fide third party if the creation, alteration, alienation, or extinguishment of the property rights in vessels, aircraft, motor vehicles, and the like is not

[81] See *id.*, art. 217.

[82] See *id.*, art. 224. (The easement shall be established at the time when the easement contract comes into effect. Where the related parties request to have the easement registered, they may apply to the registration agency for registration. Without being registered, no easement shall be made against a bona fide third party.)

registered,[83] although the transaction of such properties will take effect upon delivery.

For purposes of movable property transactions, delivery under the Civil Code may take two additional forms. The first one is called invisible delivery or implied delivery. Deriving from the traditional concept of shorthand delivery or *traditio brevi manu* in Latin, invisible delivery refers to the act of a person, to whom an item is transferred, who is not the owner but is already in possession of the item. The purpose is to prevent "double delivery" for a party to take ownership of an item already in their possession.

Under article 226 of the Civil Code, where a right holder is already in possession of a movable property before a right in the movable property is created or alienated, the right becomes effective at the time when the civil act for the transaction is effected. The idea is that when the owner transfers the right of a movable property to a person who has possessed said property, an actual delivery of the property would not be needed because the property is already in the control of that person.

To illustrate, suppose that a person already possesses a movable property through an entrustment, lease, use, or loan, etc. before ownership of the movable property is transferred. When the owner transfers the moveble property to the person, the delivery is deemed as having been completed from the time when the contract for transferring the ownership of the movable property becomes effective. In this situation, an agreement for the transfer of the property would have the same effect as actual delivery of the property.

The second delivery form is called constructive delivery. It applies when the owner of a movable property transfers the right of the property to a person, but because the property is being possessed by a third party, the owner then assigns the right of claim for return against the third party to the person in lieu of actual property. Upon the assignment, the property will be deemed delivered. In this context, constructive delivery is also considered a subrogation of the right to return.

According to article 227 of the Civil Code, where a third person is in possession of a movable property before the property right in the movable property is created or alienated, the person obligated to deliver the movable property may transfer his/her right to the return of such property against the third person as substitute for delivery.[84] The prerequisite to the application of article 227 is that the transferor of movable property rights does not physically nor directly possess and control the property transferred, but rather the possession and control are in the hands of a third party.[85]

In addition, there is a situation where the owner of movable property and the buyer agree that after the movable property is transferred, the movable property will

[83] See the 2020 Civil Code, *supra* note 12, art. 225.
[84] See *id.*, art. 227.
[85] See the SPC Leading Group,Property Rights, *supra* note 11,, art. 227.

remain in the possession of the original owner, and the buyer as a new owner will obtain an indirect possession of the movable property. Different from direct possession, indirect possession means that the owner of the movable property does not have actual possession of the movable property, but controls and manages the movable property based on a certain legal relationship with the possessor.

In China, indirect possession is known as transfer of ownership with no change of possession. Since there is no delivery involved in the property transaction, an issue then is when the transaction shall take effect. The Civil Code takes the "time of contract" approach. Under article 228 of the Civil Code, if, upon alienation of a property right in movable property, the parties agree that the transferor continues to be in possession of the movable property, the acquisition of the property right in such property becomes effective at the time when the agreement enters into effect.[86]

c. Property Right Protection

Protection of a property right is the remedy device provided under the law to the person whose property right and interest are infringed. The infringement on the property includes, among others, possession without proper grounds, obstruction to the exercise of property rights, and damage or loss of the property. According to article 233 of the Civil Code, where a property right is infringed upon, the right holder may seek protection through settlement, mediation, arbitration, or litigation. Under the Civil Code, in the case of property right infringement, the form of remedies varies depending on the type of infringement, including confirmation of property rights, restitution, removal of nuisance or elimination of danger, repair, reworking, replacement, restoration to the original condition, or compensation for damages. The Civil Code further provides that the forms of property right protection may be applied either separately or concurrently according to the circumstances of the infringement of a right.[87]

I. CONFIRMATION OF PROPERTY RIGHT. Confirmation of property rights is a remedy available to a person whose property right is contested. According to article 234 of the Civil Code, where a dispute arises over the attribution or contents of a property right, an interested person may request confirmation of the right.[88] For the purposes of article 234, the interested person making a request does not necessarily have to be the right holder because in the dispute over a property right, the parties involved may all have the right to make a request for property right confirmation.

When seeking property right confirmation, the interested party may make the request only to the relevant authority, and such authority could be a court,

[86] See the 2020 Civil Code, *supra* note 12, art. 226.
[87] See *id.*, art. 239.
[88] See *id.*, art. 234.

arbitration institution, or an administrative agency. The property right in dispute may involve right of ownership, usufructuary right, or a security interest. When confirming, the relevant authority will rely on provisions in the Civil Code concerning the creation, alteration, transfer, as well as extinguishment of the property right.

One practical issue relating to property right confirmation is whether the request for confirmation is subject to the statute of limitations. A general holding is that the statute of limitations does not apply to property right confirmation because the right to request confirmation is not considered a right of claim in substance but rather a right of claim in procedure. Thus, it is believed that when the interested party requests confirmation of a property right, the opposing party's defense on the statute of limitations shall not be accepted.[89]

II. RESTITUTION. Restitution is a right of the property owner to request a return of the original property from a person who does not have the right to possess the property or has improperly taken away the property. Under article 235 of the Civil Code, where an immovable or movable property is possessed by a person who is not entitled to the property, the right holder may request restitution.[90] Note that an exercise of the right to request the return of the original property is premised on the existence of such property and related property rights. Therefore, if the original property no longer exists, the return of the property would be impossible. In this situation, the right holder may only seek such remedy as compensation for damages.

There are several issues concerning restitution. The first issue is whether the restitution also includes accrued interest. Under article 460 of the Civil Code, when requesting restitution, a person holding a right in the property, in addition to a request for the return of the original property, may also demand a return of the fruits and proceeds deriving from the property.[91] However, if a bona fide possessor is involved, the necessary expenses incurred for the maintenance of the property shall be paid by the person seeking restitution.

The second issue relates to compensation. The question is whether the property right holder, while making a request for restitution, may ask for compensation if the property has been damaged by the possessor. In other words, it is an issue about the possible combination of restitution and compensation as a remedy to the right holder. Although there is no clear indication in the law, the general practice is that if the original property and related property right are damaged, in addition to restitution, compensation shall be allowed if requested.

The third issue concerns the burden of proof. Since the existence of original property is required for restitution, when making a request for restitution, the interested party must prove that he or she is the owner or right holder of the original

89 See the SPC Leading Group, Property Rights, *supra* note 11,, at 187.

90 See the 2020 Civil Code, *supra* note 12, art. 235.

91 See *id.*, art. 460.

property. However, the interested party need not prove that the possessor of the original property has no right to possess it. In addition, since the right to claim restitution in China is considered a property right rather than a creditor's right, the question of whether the possessor was at fault when infringing the property and property right would be irrelevant. Thus, when claiming restitution, the property owner need not prove that the unauthorized possession of the property was caused by the possessor's fault. Simple proof of infringement on the property and property right would be sufficient.

III. REMOVAL OF NUISANCE OR ELIMINATION OF DANGER. Nuisance refers to an illegal or unjustified obstruction of the right holder's exercise of their property right, which includes an obstruction that (a) has not yet occurred but is bound to occur, (b) is occurring, or (c) has already occurred. For the nuisance that has not yet occurred but is bound to occur, the right holder can request elimination of the danger. With regard to ongoing nuisances or nuisances that have already occurred, the right holder may request removal of the nuisance.

Under article 236 of the Civil Code, if there is a nuisance or a potential nuisance against a property right, the right holder may request for removal of the nuisance or elimination of the danger. The request can be made by the property owner, the person exercising the ownership function according to the law, or the holder of the right over the property of another (*jus in re aliena*). For purposes of article 236, the property owner includes the co-owner, executor of the estate, and the owner's agent *ad litem*.

To make a request for either removal of the nuisance or elimination of the danger, two elements are considered essential. One element is the fact that the property right involved is obstructed or may be obstructed. The other element is the act of obstruction or possible obstruction that makes the right holder unable to exercise the property right normally.[92] In addition, for the right holder to possibly exercise the right to make the request, the property in question must exist. On the other hand, it must be possible to have the nuisance removed. If the nuisance is objectively impossible to remove, it would be meaningless to request removal.[93]

IV. REMEDIES FOR DAMAGED PROPERTY. If the property in question was damaged while in the possession of another person, the right holder is entitled to remedies as provided by the law. In accordance with article 237 of the Civil Code, where an immovable or movable property is destructed or damaged, the right holder may request for the repair, reworking, replacement, or restoration to the original condition.[94] These remedies are intended to provide adequate protection to

[92] See the SPC Leading Group, Property Rights, *supra* note 11, at 195.

[93] See *id.*

[94] See the 2020 Civil Code, *supra* note 12, art. 237.

the right holder, especially for property that is irreplaceable to the right holder or owner.

Repair is a remedial method that is aimed at restoring the damaged property to its original condition. Reworking means to reproduce or remake the property as it was originally made, and it is usually used in the situation where repair is not possible. Replacement refers to a substitute of the original property that is damaged with an identical or similar property when repair or reworking is not possible. Different from restitution that requires the return of property, restoration mainly involves damage to the property, aiming to bring the damaged property back to the state as it was before the damage.

In addition, under article 238 of the Civil Code, if a property right is infringed, and damage is thus caused, the right holder may request that the infringer compensate them for the damage and bear other civil liabilities as well.[95] For purposes of article 238, compensation could be either a monetary payment or a substitute property. In the meantime, the right holder may also seek other civil remedies against the infringer. Article 238 does not specify what other civil remedies are, but the general understanding is that the other civil remedies are the liabilities suitable for disputes over property rights pursuant to article 179 of the Civil Code.[96]

d. "Taking" of Private Property

Under article 13 of the Chinese Constitution (as amended after 2004), the state may, for the public interest and in accordance with law, expropriate or requisition private property for its use and shall make compensation for the property expropriated and requisitioned.[97] Since article 13 is quite vague on the compensation required in the case of a taking, it generates great concern about whether there should be a standard of compensation as a prerequisite for the taking. By simply providing "compensation," article 13 does not seem to curb government power over private property, and does not ensure that proper compensation is guaranteed because there is no safeguard against excessive interference from the government and the overreaching authority of government agencies.

1. MAJOR ISSUES. Based on the Property Law, the Civil Code contains several provisions on government expropriation of property. According to article 243 of the

[95] See *id.*, art. 238.

[96] As noted, under article 179 of the Civil Code, the main forms of civil liability include: (1) cessation of the infringement; (2) removal of the nuisance; (3) elimination of the danger; (4) restitution; (5) restoration; (6) repair, redoing, or replacement; (7) continuance of performance; (8) compensation for losses; (9) payment of liquidated damages; (10) elimination of adverse effects and rehabilitation of reputation; and (11) extension of apologies. See *id.*

[97] 1982 Constitution (as amended 2018), *supra* note 29, at art. 13.

Civil Code, for the need of the public interest, collectively owned land, houses and other immovable property of an organization or individual may be expropriated within the scope of authority and pursuant to procedures provided by law. Both the Property Law and the Civil Code intend to set certain limits on taking, but there are at least three issues that require further clarification.

The first issue is the purpose of the taking. Under article 243 of the Civil Code, a taking is allowed "for the need of public interest." But like previous property law legislation, the Civil Code does not explain what may constitute public interest. Many in China have suggested that the "public interest" should be well defined in order to help prevent abuse.[98] Others, however, preferred to have a generalized provision for various reasons, including, among others, that (a) it is impossible to make a complete list of public interests; (b) public interests shall have broad content in order to meet different public needs in a constantly changing environment; and (c) the law in many other countries does not limit public interests within certain categories.[99]

Nevertheless, in order to help identify public interests, some scholars have proposed a factor-based approach under which the following factors would need to be considered to determine public interests: (a) scope of beneficiaries, (b) burdens on general public, (c) priority of interests involved, and (d) availability of alternatives.[100] As a practical matter, courts will have to determine the "public interest" on a case-by-case basis. A thorny question is how to differentiate the need for public interests from the need for commercial use, because in many cases the two are closely tangled.

The second issue is the process of taking. At the heart of the issue is the standard or requirement to guarantee a fair and just process for the taking. Article 243 of the Civil Code simply requires that a taking be conducted "within the scope of authority and pursuant to the procedures provided by law." Still, the door is wide open as to whether due process should be followed and what must be done to make the process fair and just. In fact, there are certain laws and regulations involving taking in which due process is neither addressed nor specifically required. Take the Urban House Regulation, for example. Adopted by the State Council in 2001, the regulation is criticized for having a bias against household owners because it lacks a clear focus on a fair process for the taking.[101]

[98] For example, one scholar proposed defining the public interest to include public roads and transportation, public health, disaster prevention and treatment, courses of science, culture, and education, environmental protection, preservation of cultural and historical relics and national scenery, protection of water sources and land for water channeling and draining, protection of forests, and other public interests as provided by law. See Liang Huixing, Articles, Explanations, Rationing, and Legislative References of Proposed Draft Property Law, 191–192 (Social Science Archive Press, 2000).

[99] See Songyou, *supra* note 21, at 162–163.

[100] See Liming, *supra* note 10, at 420.

[101] See *Regulation of Administration of Demolishment and Relocation of Urban Houses*, art. 6 (promulgated by Standing Comm. Nat'l People's Cong., June 6, 2001, effective November 1,

The third issue is compensation. In China, all laws related to taking provide for compensation, but none of them define compensation. It then seems that in the case of taking, as long as compensation is made, the level of the compensation in terms of reasonableness would be irrelevant. The underlying notion in this regard is that compensation is a matter of local concern.[102] It is often asserted that since actual compensation is provided by the local government in consideration of local needs and development level, it is difficult to establish a general or uniform standard nationwide.[103]

II. RULES OF COMPENSATION. In response to public outrage at the inadequate compensation in cases of taking or expropriation, the Civil Code ties the means of compensation to the type of property expropriated. More specifically, the Civil Code, like the Property Law, treats collectively owned property and private property differently for the purpose of compensation in the case of taking. In addition, the Civil Code prohibits any organization or individual from embezzling, misappropriating, secretly distributing, intercepting, defaulting on payment of the compensation for expropriation, or the like.[104]

For collectively owned property, article 243 of the Civil Code provides that in the case of expropriation of collectively owned land, land compensation fees, resettlement subsidies, and compensation fees for rural villagers' dwellings and other ground attachments as well as young crops shall be paid in full in a timely manner in accordance with law, and social security premiums of the farmers whose land has been expropriated shall be arranged, their lives secured, and their lawful rights and interests safeguarded.[105]

Given the shortage of arable land in the country, the Civil Code imposes certain restrictions on the taking of collectively owned land. It is provided in article 244 that the State will provide special protection to cultivated land, strictly restrict the conversion of agricultural land into land used for construction purposes and control the overall volume of the land used for construction purposes. Also, it is required

2001), www.law-lib.com/law/law_view.asp?id=15353 (P.R.C.). Under the Urban Houses Regulation, a developer may not undertake demolishment and relocation without obtaining a license from an administrative agency of the local government, but the license may be issued without any knowledge of the owner of the household affected. In addition, as soon as the license is issued, the owner of the household is obligated to enter into a contract with the developer for demolishment and relocation. Moreover, if the owner and developer fail to reach an agreement, the developer may seek a decision by the local administrative agency. If the house's owner disagrees with the administrative decision, the owner may file a lawsuit with a people's court. During the legal proceeding, demolishment and relocation shall not be halted if monetary compensation is made or a relocation house is provided. Finally, if the owner of the household refuses to move, a forced demolishment and relocation may be imposed.

[102] See Hong, *supra* note 32, at 71.

[103] See Kangsheng, *supra* note 16, at 102–103.

[104] See the 2020 Civil Code, *supra* note 12, art. 243.

[105] See *id.*

that collectively owned land not be expropriated in a way that exceeds the scope of authority or in violation of the procedures provided by law.[106]

When an expropriation affects houses or other immovable property of organizations or individuals, the Civil Code requires compensation. Under article 243 of the Civil Code, in order to safeguard the lawful rights and interests of the person whose immovable property has been expropriated, compensation for the expropriation shall be made in accordance with law. In the case of expropriation of individuals' dwelling houses, the living conditions of such individuals shall also be guaranteed.[107] Again, there is no requirement for reasonable and just compensation in the Civil Code. The lawful rights and interests as well as the living condition as stated in article 243 remain too vague to be measurable.

In accordance with the Civil Code, a "taking" may also take place in the case of an emergency. Under article 245 of the Civil Code, in response to an emergency such as providing disaster relief and preventing and controlling pandemics, the property, moveable or immoveable, of an organization or individual may be requisitioned within the scope of authority and pursuant to the procedures provided by law.[108] It is, however, required that the requisitioned property be returned to the affected organization or individual after use, and compensation be made for the requisition, or in the situation where the property is destructed, damaged, or lost after being requisitioned.

2. OWNERSHIP

The primary component of a property right is ownership. Under article 240 of the Civil Code, a property owner is entitled to possess, use, benefit from, and dispose of his/her own immovable or movable property in accordance with law. The gist of article 240 is that ownership under Chinese law consists of four basic ownership rights: the right to possess, the right to use, the right to benefit, and the right to dispose. Full and complete ownership means that the property is directly controlled by its owner through the owner's effective exercise of those ownership rights.

As understood in China, a distinctive feature of ownership is its integral nature or wholeness. Wholeness means that ownership is not a quantitative synthesis of possession, use, benefit, and disposal, but a whole right. Ownership as a whole right is unique in two aspects. First, ownership is the right to fully control the property, not a simple addition of various property rights. Even if some property rights are exercised or restricted by others according to the will of the right holder, the nature of ownership will not be affected. Second, ownership is not divisible in content or

[106] See *id.*, art. 244.
[107] See *id.*, art. 243.
[108] See *id.*, art. 245.

time. For example, an establishment of usufruct or security interest on ownership is not a transfer of a part of ownership, but rather the creation of a new independent property right.

On the other hand, although ownership has an integral nature or wholeness, some ownership rights may be exercised by someone other than the owner. For example, the owner of a property may have another person possess and use the property without a change of ownership. The owner may also allow another person to retain the benefits accrued from the property. In other words, as long as the owner retains the right of disposal, an alienation of any other property right would not affect ownership.

A. *Types of Ownership*

As noted, there are three basic ownerships in China: State ownership, collective ownership, and private ownership. In contrast to private ownership, both State ownership and collective ownership are public ownership. Under the Civil Code, State ownership covers such property as (a) mineral deposits, waters, and sea areas;[109] (b) uninhabited islands;[110] (c) urban land;[111] (d) natural resources, such as forests, mountain ridges, grasslands, unreclaimed lands, and mudflats, other than those provided by law to be collectively owned;[112] (e) the wild animal and plant resources provided by law to be owned by the State;[113] (f) radio-frequency spectrum resources;[114] (g) the cultural relics provided by law to be owned by the State;[115] (h) assets for national defense; and infrastructure such as railways, roads, electric power facilities, telecommunication facilities, as well as oil and gas pipelines provided by law to be owned by the State.[116]

Collective ownership consists of immovable and movable property, including (a) the land, forests, mountain ridges, grasslands, unreclaimed land, and mudflats provided by law to be owned by collectives; (b) the buildings, production facilities, and farmland water conservancy facilities that are owned by collectives; (c) the educational, scientific, cultural, public health, sports, and other facilities that are owned by collectives; and (d) any other immovable and movable property that is owned by collectives. Collective ownership can be either a farmer collective or an urban-town collective. A notable feature of collective ownership is that the members of the collective cannot exercise their rights over collective property alone and cannot request the division of collective property when they leave the collective.

[109] See *id.*, art. 247.
[110] See *id.*, art. 248.
[111] See *id.*, art. 249.
[112] See *id.*, art. 250.
[113] See *id.*, art. 251.
[114] See *id.*, art. 252.
[115] See *id.*, art. 253.
[116] See *id.*, art. 254.

For example, under article 261 of the Civil Code, the immovable and movable properties of a farmer collective are collectively owned by the members of the collective. The matters that require a decision by the collective's members include (1) land contracting schemes, and the subcontracting of land to any organization or individual outside the collective; (2) adjustment to the contracted land among the persons who have the right to contractual management of land; (3) methods for the use and distribution of funds such as land compensation fees; (4) matters such as changes in the ownership of enterprises invested in by the collective; and (5) other matters as provided by law.

Private ownership refers to the right of a private person to possess, use, benefit from, dispose of, and exclude others from interfering with legally acquired real and movable properties. For purposes of the Civil Code, private person not only includes Chinese citizens but also covers foreign nationals and stateless persons who lawfully own property in China. On the other hand, the private person can also be a natural person, an economic household, or a non-state-owned enterprise. Economic households mainly refer to individually run industrial and commercial households and rural land contractual management households. Non-state-owned enterprises include such entities as sole proprietorships as well as partnerships.

Pursuant to article 266 of the Civil Code, a private person has the right to own his/her lawful income, houses, articles for daily use, production tools, raw materials, as well as other immovable and movable property.[117] Also, as noted, under article 127 of the Civil Code, the data and online virtual assets lawfully owned by a private party will also be protected if so provided by the law. The key word defining the nature of private ownership is "lawful," which means that the Civil Code only protects private property that is considered lawful or is lawfully acquired. A question necessarily raised then is what would constitute lawfulness or what is the standard under which lawfulness is to be determined.

Also, under article 268 of the Civil Code, the State, collectives, and private individuals may establish companies with limited liabilities, joint stock companies limited by shares, or other enterprises through making capital contributions in accordance with law. Where the immovable or movable property of the State, collectives, and private individuals is invested in an enterprise, the investors are, in accordance with their agreement or in proportion to their investment, entitled to receive returns on assets, make major decisions, and select business managers, and in the meantime are obligated to perform their duties.

B. *Management of Public Property*

Public property in China is controlled and managed under a scheme provided by the law. According to article 255 of the Civil Code, a State organ has the right to

[117] See *id.*, art. 266.

possess and use the immovable and movable property directly under its control and to dispose of such property in accordance with law and the relevant regulations made by the State Council. In other words, state-owned property is managed by government agents at different levels designated by the State.[118]

For example, under article 256 of the Civil Code, a public institution established by the State has the right to possess and use the immovable and movable property directly under its control, and to benefit from and dispose of such property in accordance with law and the relevant regulations made by the State Council.[119] With respect to enterprises invested in by the State, article 257 of the Civil Code further provides that the State Council and the local people's governments shall, on behalf of the State, perform investors' duties and enjoy investors' rights and interests, respectively, in accordance with laws and administrative regulations.[120]

The property owned by collectives is managed based on the type of collective ownership. According to article 262 of the Civil Code, ownership of collectively owned land, forests, mountain ridges, grasslands, unreclaimed land, mudflats, and the like shall be exercised on behalf of collectives in the following way: (a) where they are owned by the farmer collective of a village, the ownership shall be exercised collectively by the collective economic organization of the village or the villagers' committee; (b) if they are owned by two or more farmer collectives within a village, the ownership shall be exercised by the respective collective economic organizations or the villagers' groups; and (c) where they are owned collectively by the farmer collective of a rural town, the ownership shall be exercised by the economic organizations of the town.[121]

C. *Ownership Protection and Liabilities*

The Civil Code prohibits any organization or individual from misappropriating, looting, or destructing property owned by the State, collectives, or private persons. For property owned by the State, the prohibition also extends to any secret distribution or interception of the property, while for property owned by collectives, the extension of prohibition covers secret distribution.

The Civil Code also imposes liabilities on certain conduct. Under article 259 of the Civil Code, the institutions and their staff with the duties of administration and supervision over the state-owned property shall, among other things, strive to preserve and increase the value of such property and prevent any loss thereof. Any institution and its staff shall assume legal liabilities if losses are caused to state-owned property as a result of their abuse of powers or dereliction of duties.[122]

[118] See *id.*, art. 255.
[119] See *id.*, art. 256.
[120] See *id.*, art. 257.
[121] See *id.*, art. 262.
[122] See *id.*, art. 259.

In addition, pursuant to article 269 of the Civil Code, a person who causes losses to the state-owned property by transferring it at low prices, secretly distributing it in conspiracy with other persons, creating a security interest on it without authorization, or by other means in the course of enterprise restructuring, merger or division, affiliated transactions, and the like, in violation of the provisions on the administration of the state-owned property, shall bear legal liability in accordance with law.[123]

D. *Adjacent Relationship*

Adjacent relationship in China refers to the relationship between the owners or users of properties adjacent to each other for exercising ownership or the right to use their properties, involving such matters as ventilation, lighting, water, drainage, traffic, etc. Under article 288 of the Civil Code, the persons entitled to adjacent rights in immovable property shall properly deal with adjacent relationships in accordance with the principles of facilitating production, convenience for daily lives, solidarity and mutual assistance, and fairness and reasonableness.[124]

In dealing with adjacent relationships, article 289 of the Civil Code requires that where there are laws and regulations providing for adjacent relationships, those provisions shall be applied, and if there are no such provisions, local customs may be followed.[125] Customs, as used in China, refer to the generally recognized code of conduct gradually formed in long-term social practice. The application of customs is subject to two conditions. First, it applies only in the case where there is no applicable provision of law. Second, whether a customary rule is to be applied or which customary rule is to be applied is within the discretionary power of the court.

The provisions in the Civil Code governing adjacent relationships require the holder of a real property right to provide a person entitled to an adjacent right with necessary convenience (a) for the use of water or drainage,[126] (b) for the use of the property for passage,[127] and (c) for constructing or maintaining a building, or for laying electrical wires, cables, or pipelines for water, heating, or gas.[128] With regard to the use of water and drainage, the Civil Code further requires that the right to utilization of natural flowing water shall be reasonably allocated among the persons entitled to the adjacent rights of the immovable property, and when discharging the water, the direction of the natural water flow shall be respected.[129]

[123] See *id.*, art. 269.
[124] See *id.*, art. 288.
[125] See *id.*, art. 289.
[126] See *id.*, art. 290.
[127] See *id.*, art. 291.
[128] See *id.*, art. 292.
[129] See *id.*, art. 290.

The Civil Code also imposes restrictions on the use of land in respect to adjacent relationships. Under article 293 of the Civil Code, for example, the construction of a building should not obstruct the ventilation, lighting, or sunlight of the adjacent buildings.[130] In addition, according to article 294 of the Civil Code, a person entitled to property rights in immovable property should not, in violation of the regulations of the State, discard solid waste or emit harmful substances such as atmospheric pollutants, water pollutants, soil pollutants, noises, light radiation, or electromagnetic radiation.[131]

Furthermore, article 295 of the Civil Code prohibits the holder of a property right from endangering the safety of the adjacent immovable property when excavating land, constructing buildings, laying pipelines, or installing facilities.[132] Also, under article 296 of the Civil Code, a person entitled to a property right in immovable property who utilizes the adjacent immovable property for the purpose of using water, drainage, passage, laying pipelines, and the like, shall spare no effort to avoid causing damage to the person entitled to the property right in the adjacent immovable property.[133]

E. *Co-Ownership*

Co-ownership is the ownership rights and interests among two or more co-owners of the same property. Pursuant to article 297 of the Civil Code, immovable or movable property may be jointly owned by two or more organizations or individuals. In China, co-ownership can be either ownership by shares or joint ownership. In ownership by shares, the owners jointly own immovable or movable property according to their shares, while under joint ownership, the owners own immovable or movable property together, each with equal rights and responsibilities to the property.

However, according to article 308 of the Civil Code, if there is no agreement among the co-owners or the agreement is unclear as to whether the co-owned immovable or movable property is under ownership by shares or joint ownership, the property shall be deemed to be under ownership by shares, unless the co-owners are in a relationship such as a familial relationship.[134] In other words, the co-ownership of property among family members is generally joint ownership.

In addition, under article 309 of the Civil Code, if, for ownership by shares, there is no agreement on the allocation of shares, or the agreement is unclear, the shares of co-owners in the immovable or movable property shall be determined according to each person's capital contribution. But if it is impossible to determine the amount

[130] See *id.*, art. 293.
[131] See *id.*, art. 294.
[132] See *id.*, art. 295.
[133] See *id.*, art. 296.
[134] See *id.*, art. 308.

of each capital contribution, the co-owners shall be entitled to an equal number of shares.[135] Article 309 has two implications. First, the co-owners can arbitrarily set the proportion of shares by their unanimous consent, regardless of their capital contributions or their contributions to the common property. Second, the presumption of equal shares shall be used only when the co-owners have not agreed, or the agreement is not clear.

a. Governance of Co-Owned Property

It is required under article 300 of the Civil Code that the co-owners manage the co-owned immovable or movable property in accordance with their agreement. If, however, there is no agreement or the agreement is unclear, each of the co-owners has the right and duty to manage the property.[136] Article 301 of the Civil Code further provides that unless otherwise agreed by the co-owners, any disposition of the co-owned immovable or movable property, or any major repair or change of the nature or intended use of the co-owned immovable or movable property, shall be subject to the consent of the co-owners whose shares account for two thirds or more of the total shares, or to the consent of all joint co-owners.[137]

If there are expenses incurred as a result of the co-owned property management or other burdens arising therefrom, the co-owners, under article 302 of the Civil Code, shall bear the expenses according to their agreement. Absent such agreement, the expenses or burdens shall fall on the shoulders of the co-owners proportionally in the case of co-ownership by shares or jointly borneby the co-owners in the situation of joint ownership.[138]

b. Partition and Alienation of the Co-Owned Property

The co-owned property may be partitioned. But if the co-owners have agreed not to partition in order to maintain co-ownership, the agreement shall be followed.[139]An exception is that if there is a compelling reason for partition, a co-owner may make such request. In the case of partition, if there is no agreement to that effect, or the agreement is unclear, a co-owner in the ownership by shares may request partition at any time. But a co-owner in a joint ownership may request partition when the basis for the joint ownership ceases to exist (e.g., divorce) or there is a compelling reason for partition (e.g., special need for medical or educational payments).[140] Note that if

[135] See *id.*, art. 309.
[136] See *id.*, art. 300.
[137] See *id.*, art. 301.
[138] See *id.*, art. 302.
[139] See *id.*, art. 303.
[140] See *id.*

partition causes damage to the other co-owners, compensation shall be made accordingly.[141]

When partitioning, the co-owners may negotiate to determine a method of partition. If no agreement can be reached, the co-owned property, immovable or movable, may be divided among the co-owners if the property is divisible and its value is not diminished upon division. After a partition, if the property acquired by a co-owner in partition is proven to be defective, the other co-owners are required to share the losses.[142] However, if it is difficult to divide the co-owned property or the value of the property would be impaired upon division, partition shall be made by dividing the proceeds based on appraisal or obtained from auction or sale of the property.[143]

Under article 305 of the Civil Code, a co-owner in ownership by shares may transfer his/her shares, but the other co-owners have the right of first refusal to buy the shares under equivalent conditions.[144] In addition, when a co-owner in the ownership by shares transfers his/her shares, notice is required to be given to the other co-owners in a timely manner concerning the conditions of transfer.[145] With regard to their right of first refusal, the other co-owners must exercise it within a reasonable period of time. Also, if two or more co-owners assert their right of first refusal, they shall determine by agreement the proportion of shares each may purchase. Absent such agreement, their right of first refusal shall be exercised in proportion to the shares they each own at the time of transfer.[146]

c. Rights and Liabilities among Co-Owners

The co-owners of a property under co-ownership are entitled to the rights created out of the property, and in the meantime are liable for the obligations arising from the property. Note that under the concept of *obligatio*, the rights, in contrast to the obligations, are normally referred to as creditor's rights. In terms of co-ownership, the form of right entitlement and the obligation bearing for the co-owners is dependent on whether the relation involved is an internal relation or an external one. An internal relation means a relation among the co-owners, while an external relation refers to the one between the co-owner(s) and a third party.

Externally, the co-owners are jointly and severally entitled to rights and also are jointly and severally obligated to perform obligations arising from the co-owned property, unless otherwise provided by law, or if the third person is aware that the co-owners are not in a relationship of joint and several rights and obligations. As provided in the Civil Code, joint and several creditor rights arise when there

[141] See *id.*
[142] See *id.*, art. 304.
[143] See *id.*
[144] See *id.*, art. 305.
[145] See *id.*, art. 306.
[146] See *id.*

are two or more creditors and any of the creditors has the right to request the debtor perform the whole obligations.[147]

For internal relations, unless otherwise agreed by the co-owners, the co-owners in the ownership by shares are entitled to rights and obligated to perform obligations in proportion to the shares they each own, while the co-owners in joint ownership are jointly entitled to claims and obligated to perform obligations. If a co-owner in the ownership by shares has performed an obligation exceeding his or her share, the co-owner has the right of indemnity against the other co-owners.

F. *Acquisition of Ownership*

As noted, transfer of a property right in China must meet certain statutory requirements in order for the transferee to acquire the title of the property being transferred. For property ownership, there are special provisions in the Civil Code that govern its acquisition. The provisions apply to such cases as the property being transferred by a party who has no right to transfer, lost property, fruits from the use of the property, as well as property resulting from the processing, attaching, or mixing of a thing. Also, for the purposes of property transfer, when a principal property is transferred, all accessory parts attached thereto shall be transferred concomitantly, unless otherwise agreed by the parties.[148]

The issue arising from the transfer of a property without the right is whether the owner of the property may claim its return. Put differently, it is an issue of whether the transferee may acquire the ownership of the property transferred. Article 311 of the Civil Code provides that where a person with no right to dispose of a property transfers it to another person, the owner has the right to recover it.[149] The owner's right to recover, however, is subject to certain statutory exceptions. A typical rule of exception is bona fide acquisition.

Under article 311, unless otherwise provided by law, the transferee acquires the ownership of the immovable or movable property under the following circumstances: (1) the transferee is bona fide at the time when the property is transferred to him or her; (2) the transfer is made at a reasonable price; and (3) the transferred property has been registered as required by law or has been delivered to the transferee where registration is not required.[150] Article 311 sets forth a rule that in bona fide acquisition, the original owner may not reclaim ownership of the property. But as provided in article 311, the original owner has the right to claim damages against the person who disposes of the property without a right.

The Civil Code does not define what bona fide is. In its interpretation of the Civil Code, the SPC opines that when accepting the immovable property or movable

[147] See *id.*, art. 518.
[148] See *id.*, art. 320.
[149] See *id.*, art. 311.
[150] See *id.*

property, the transferee does not know, without gross negligence, that the transferor has no right to dispose of the property, the transferee shall be deemed to acquire ownership of the property bona fide. According to the SPC, if the property owner claims that the transferee is not a bona fide transferee, the owner bears the burden of proof.[151] The SPC's opinion creates a rule for bona fide acquisition, which is known as the rule of presumption of bona fide acquisition. Pursuant to article 311, the bona fide acquisition rule also applies *mutatis mutandis* to a property right other than ownership. In addition, under article 313 of the Civil Code, after a bona fide transferee acquires the movable property, the original right in the movable property is extinguished, unless the transferee knows or should have known of such right at the time of the transfer.[152]

There are several provisions in the Civil Code that govern lost property. It is worth noting that the lost property provisions, unless otherwise provided by the law, also apply to a drifting property that is found or a property buried underground or hidden that is discovered.[153] In accordance with article 312, an owner or any other right holder has the right to recover lost property. If the lost property is possessed by another person by way of a transfer, the right holder has the right to claim damages against the person who disposes of the thing without the right to disposition, or to request the transferee return the original thing within two years from the date on which the right holder knows or should have known of the transferee.[154]

If, however, the transferee has acquired the lost property at an auction or from a qualified business operator, the right holder shall, at the time of requesting the return of the original property, reimburse the expenses that have been paid by the transferee. The right holder, after having reimbursed the expenses paid by the transferee, has the right to indemnification against the person who disposes of the thing without the right to disposition.[155]

As is normally required in China, article 314 of the Civil Code provides that when lost property is found, it shall be returned to its right holder, and the finder shall, in a timely manner, notify its right holder or hand it over to the relevant departments such as the department for public security.[156] Also, under article 315, when the relevant department receives lost property and knows who its right holder is, the department shall, in a timely manner, notify the right holder to collect the lost property. If, however, the department does not know who the right holder is, a notice of lost and found shall be issued timely.[157]

[151] See the SPC, *Interpretation on Several Issues Involving Application of the Property Law of the People's Republic of China (1)*, issued on February 23, 2016, art. 15.

[152] See the 2020 Civil Code, *supra* note 12, art. 313.

[153] See *id.*, art. 319.

[154] See *id.*, art. 312.

[155] See *id.*

[156] See *id.*, art. 314.

[157] See *id.*, art. 315.

Further, article 316 requires the finder to have the lost property kept safe before it is delivered to the relevant department, and the relevant department shall keep it safe before it is collected by the right holder.[158] Thus, a person who, intentionally or by gross negligence, causes the lost property in his/her custody to be destructed, damaged, or lost shall bear civil liability. If costs for the keeping of lost property incur to the finder or relevant department, the right holder, when collecting the lost property, will be held liable for the costs.[159]

The Civil Code also contains other provisions concerning lost property. First, when a right holder has offered a reward for finding the lost property, the right holder shall, at the time of collecting the lost thing, perform what has been promised.[160] Second, if a finder misappropriates the lost property, the finder is neither entitled to request reimbursement of expenses associated with the lost property, nor entitled to request the right holder perform the obligations as promised.[161] Third, when lost property has not been claimed by anyone within one year from the date the lost-and-found notice is publicized, the lost property is to be escheated to the State.[162]

The fruits from the use of property consist of two kinds of fruits: natural fruits and civil fruits. Natural fruits are products naturally grown or produced on the property while civil fruits are revenues derived from a property by operation of law, or income received from a right pursuant to the purpose of the right or due to a legal relationship. A question often encountered is the ownership of the fruits as such because the property in question can be possessed and used by the owner or by another person with a usufructuary right.

Under article 321 of the Civil Code, unless otherwise agreed by the parties, the natural fruits of a property shall be acquired by the owner of the property. If, however, there is both an owner and a usufructuary of the property, the natural fruits shall belong to the usufructuary. On the other hand, according to article 321, the civil fruits of a property shall be acquired as agreed by the parties. If there is no agreement or the agreement is unclear, the ownership of the civil fruits shall be determined by the course of dealing.[163]

A property created as a result of processing, attaching, or mixing with another thing or things shall be owned in accordance with the agreement between the parties involved, or under the provision of law in cases where there is no agreement between the parties or the agreement between them is not clear. Absent any applicable provision of law, ownership of such property shall be determined to be in compliance with the principles of making full use of the property and protecting

[158] See *id.*, art. 316.
[159] See *id.*, art. 317.
[160] See *id.*
[161] See *id.*, art. 318.
[162] See *id.*, art. 319.
[163] See *id.*, art. 321.

the party without fault. If, due to a party's fault or the determination of the attribution of the property, damage is caused to the other party, a compensation or indemnity shall be made.[164]

3. POSSESSION

As noted, possession is an indispensable property interest in ownership. Given the legal significance of possession, there is a special chapter in the Civil Code that governs possession. Although possession is not defined in the Civil Code, it is generally understood in China as a right to control and dominate the property factually and physically. In the context of possession, control means that the property involved is under the management or influence of the possessor, and domination refers to the capability of the possessor to use the property in a certain way.[165]

There is a debate in China on whether possession is a fact or a legal right. A common holding is that possession is a fact but has certain legal effects because possession reflects the relationship of domination of a person over a thing, not a relationship of rights between the person and the thing.[166] In fact, in many cases, possession can simply be based on the fact of domination and management of a property regardless of the legality of domination and management conduct, especially in the situation where the possessor has no right to possess.

A. *Categories of Possession*

Possession can be divided into different categories. First, depending on the legal cause, possession can be either possession with the right to possess or possession without the right to possess. The former is possession on the basis of such property rights as ownership as well as usufructuary rights, while the latter means possession that has no legal cause. Examples of possession without the right to possess include possession of stolen property by a thief, possession of lost property by the person who found the property, the lessee's possession of the leased property after the termination of the lease contract, and the like.

Second, in terms of whether the property is actually possessed, possession can be divided into direct possession and indirect possession. Direct possession is possession that has de facto dominance over the property. For example, a lessee is a person with direct possession over the rented property. Indirect possession means possession in which the person who does not have direct possession has the right to request return based on a certain legal relationship, and thus indirectly has de facto control over the

[164] See *id.*, art. 322.
[165] See the SPC Leading Group, Property Rights, *supra* note 11, at 1325–1326.
[166] See the 2020 Civil Code, *supra* note 12, art. 326.

property. In contrast to the lessee, a lessor, for instance, is a person who does not directly possess the property rented out but has the right to request a return of the property after the lease agreement expires.

Third, in light of possession without authorization, the possession may be a bona fide possession or *mala fide* possession. Bona fide possession takes place when the possessor honestly believes that he/she has the right to possess but in fact the possession is not authorized. *Mala fide* possession on the other hand is the possession in which the possessor takes the possession with knowledge that he or she has no right to possess or with a doubt about the right to possess. The standard is whether the possessor has an honest belief about having the right to possess.

B. *Rules of Possession*

The provisions of the Civil Code on possession mainly focus on such matters as the scope of the possession, liabilities for damages in the case of no right to possess, return of the original and accrued interests, and protection of the possession. There are some other cases in which possession may become an issue. Therefore, the Civil Code provides a set of rules that govern possession in specific cases. Those rules are special because they are intended to deal with the issues not covered by the provisions of ownership.

The first rule concerns the legal sources of possession. Under article 458 of the Civil Code, possession of a property can be based on a contractual relationship. If there is a contract, matters such as the use of the property, the benefits therefrom, and the default liability shall be subject to the agreement in the contract. If there is no agreement thereon in the contract or the agreement is unclear, the relevant provisions of law shall be applied.[167] The underlying concept of article 458 is the principle of party autonomy, meaning that with regard to possession involving the use of property, the benefits therefrom and the default liability, the contractual agreement takes priority over the provisions of law. In other words, the provisions of law will apply only if there is an absence of agreement.

The second rule is the rule of compensation. The rule serves a twofold purpose. In one aspect, if damage is caused to a property by its possessor as a result of use of the property, a *mala fide* possessor shall be liable for compensation.[168] In the other aspect, when a property is in the possession of another person, a person holding a right in the property may request the possessor to return the original property and its fruits and proceeds, but the necessary expenses incurred, if any, by a bona fide possessor for the maintenance of the property shall be paid.[169]

[167] See *id.*, art. 458.
[168] See *id.*, art. 459.
[169] See *id.*, art. 460.

The third rule is the liability rule. According to article 461 of the Civil Code, where a property in another person's possession is destructed, damaged, or lost, and a person holding a right in the property requests compensation, the possessor shall return to the right holder the amount of insurance payment, compensation or indemnity received for the property destructed, damaged, or lost. If the right holder has not been fully compensated, a possessor *mala fide* shall also compensate for the loss.[170]

In addition, under article 462, where a property is trespassed or converted, its possessor has the right to request restitution. If there is a nuisance against the possession, the possessor may request the removal of the nuisance or elimination of the danger. If damage is caused as a result of the trespass, conversion, or nuisance, the possessor is entitled to request compensatory damages in accordance with law.[171] The possessor's right to request restitution must be exercised within one year from the date the trespass or conversion occurs.

4. RIGHTS OF USUFRUCT

Usufruct is the right to use and benefit from the property of another person. Unlike a property right, which is the right to own property – a complete right with the power to possess, use, benefit from, and dispose of the property – usufruct is the right to use and benefit from a property not owned by the user. The person who enjoys the usufruct is called the usufructuary. According to article 323 of the Civil Code, a usufructuary has the right to possess, use, and benefit from the immovable or movable property owned by another person in accordance with law.[172] In China, rights of usufruct mainly include the right to the use of land, the right of habitation, and easement.

A. *The Right to the Use of Land*

Bear in mind that a property right in China does not necessarily mean the right to own a piece of land. As discussed, there is no privately owned land in China and all lands in the country are either owned by the State or by the collectives. Under the Chinese Constitution, land in urban areas is owned by the state, and land in the rural and suburban areas is owned by collectives, except for those that belong to the state according to law.[173] Since no private ownership of land exists in China, the right to the use of land constitutes the most important usufructuary right in the country.

[170] See *id.*, art. 461.
[171] See *id.*, art. 462.
[172] See *id.*, art. 323.
[173] Chinese Constitution (1982) (as amended 2018),art. 10, available at https://english.www.gov.cn/archive/lawsregulations/201911/20/content_WS5ed8856ec6d0b3f0e9499913.html.

Under the provisions of the Civil Code, the land use right is divided into three categories: the right to the contractual management of land, the right to the use of construction land, and the right to the use of house sites. Given the usufructuary nature, the right to the use of land means that the user of the land has the right to possess and use the land, and the right to gain interest from the land, but has no right to dispose of or sell the land.[174] In addition, as a property interest, the right to the use of land is inheritable in certain cases (e.g., commercial housing).

Similarly, the owner of a house in China is the holder of the right to use the respective land. Thus, the ownership of a house may reach everything affixed to the house, but not the land on which it is built. Additionally, for each household, the right to use land is on a term basis, and acquisition of such a right has an economic value which is included in the purchase price of the house. Under the 1990 State Council Interim Provisions for the Granting and Transferring of Land Use Rights on State-owned Land in Cities and Towns, the maximum term of the use of land for residential purpose is seventy years.[175]

Pursuant to article 324 of the Civil Code, organizations and individuals may, in accordance with law, possess, use, and benefit from the natural resources owned by the State, the state-owned natural resources that are used by collectives, and the natural resources that are owned by collectives as provided by law. In addition, under article 325, the use of natural resources shall be paid use, unless otherwise provided by law. It should also be noted that the right to use natural resources under the Civil Code includes the right to use the sea areas,[176] to explore and mine minerals, to draw water, and to use waters and mudflats to engage in aquaculture or fishing, that are acquired in accordance with law.[177]

a. Right to Contractual Management of Land

There are three rights that are associated with land, namely ownership, contracting rights, and management rights. These three rights are exercised through land contractual management under a separation rule, meaning that each of the three

[174] Article 10 of the Chinese Constitution explicitly prohibits organizations or individuals from appropriating, buying, selling, or in any other ways unlawfully transferring land. See *id.*

[175] The Provisions put the right to use land into different categories and each category has a different term. Under article 12 of the Provisions, the maximum term for each category is as follows: Residential: seventy years; Industrial: fifty years; Education, Science and Technology, Culture, Public Health, or Athletic Facilities: fifty years; Commercial, Tourist, or Recreation: forty years; Combined or other purposes: fifty years. A full text of the Provisions in Chinese is available at www.jincao.com/fa/law19.95.htm; Temporary Regulation for Transfer of the Right to Use the State Owned Land, Order No. 55 by St. Council of China. *See also* Patrick Randolph & Lou Jianbo, Chinese Real Estate Law, 127–128 (Kluwer, 2000).

[176] See the 2020 Civil Code, *supra* note 12, art. 328.

[177] See *id.*, art. 329.

rights can be separated and exist independently of each other. A combination of the contracting right and the management right constitutes the right to land contractual management, separated from land ownership.

Resulting from the land use reform in the country, the right to land contractual management is a system employed for farmers to collectively use land owned by the collectives or the State. Under article 330 of the Civil Code, the land contractual management system applies to the use of cultivated land, forestland, grassland, and other land owned collectively or by the State for agricultural, forestry, animal husbandry, fishing, and other production and business activities.[178] The rules of right to the land contractual management also apply *mutatis mutandis* to state-owned land used for agricultural purposes.[179]

The holder of the right to land contractual management is called the rural collective economic organization. Pursuant to article 330, a rural collective economic organization is a two-tier management system with household contractual management as the base, integrating with collective management.[180] The two tiers refer to two operation levels: the family-based individual level and the collective unified level. A member of a rural collective economic organization who obtains the right to the land contractual management is called the person with the right to the contractual management of land.

1. CREATION OF THE RIGHT TO CONTRACTUAL MANAGEMENT OF LAND. A person who is entitled to contractual management of land shall meet two requirements. First, the person must be a member of a rural collective economic organization, namely a household situated in a local collective community. Second, the right obtained for land management is based on a contract with local collectives. Under article 333 of the Civil Code, a right to contractual management of land is created at the time when a contract on the right to contractual management of land takes effect.[181]

The right to contractual management of land, once created under the contract, shall be registered with the local government authority. Article 333 of the Civil Code requires that the registration authority issue a certificate, such as a certificate of the right to contractual management of land, a certificate of the right to forestry, or the like, to the person entitled to the respective right to contractual management of land.[182] For the purpose of recording and confirming the land contractual management right, a register shall be established within the registration authority.[183]

[178] See *id.*, art. 330.
[179] See *id.*, art. 343.
[180] See *id.*, art. 330.
[181] See *id.*, art. 333.
[182] See *id.*
[183] See *id.*

II. CONTENTS AND TERMS OF THE RIGHT TO CONTRACTUAL MANAGEMENT OF LAND. Under article 331 of the Civil Code, a person who has the right to contractual management of land is, in accordance with law, entitled to possess, use, and benefit from the cultivated land, forestland, and grassland contracted and managed by him, and to engage in agricultural production such as crop cultivation, forestry, and animal husbandry.[184] An important implication of article 331 is that the right to the land contractual management is considered a right of a property nature rather than a contractual nature. It is also the reason why the right to land contractual management is provided in the Civil Code as a right of usufruct.[185]

The right to the land contractual management is exercised on a term basis and the length of the term depends on the type of land. Under article 332 of the Civil Code, the contractual management for arable land has a term of thirty years, while for grassland the term ranges from thirty to fifty years. The contractual management for forest land has the longest term, from thirty to seventy years.[186] The term, however, is renewable. Upon expiration of the term, the person with the right to contractual management of land may renew the contract in accordance with the provisions of laws on rural-land contracting.[187]

The parties to the land management contract are individual family households and the village collective economic organizations or the village committees. The latter is also called the party issuing the contract. Pursuant to article 340 of the Civil Code, within the term as agreed in the contract, the person with the right to management of land is entitled to possess the rural land, to carry out agricultural production and operation on his/her own, and to benefit therefrom.[188] In order to protect the right to the land contractual management, the Civil Code contains certain restrictions that apply to the party offering the contract.

One restriction is that within the term of the contract, the party issuing the contract may not adjust the contracted land. As an exception, an appropriate adjustment might be made under special circumstances if necessary. An example of circumstances as such is severe deterioration on the contracted land caused by natural disasters.[189] The other restriction is the limitation on the right of the person issuing the contract. Under the Civil Code, during the term of contract, the party issuing the contract may not take back the contracted land, unless otherwise provided by law.[190]

[184] See *id.*, art. 331.

[185] There has been an argument in China that the right to land contractual management is a right deriving from *obligatio*. The argument holds that the rural land contractual management is essentially a contractual relationship of joint production, and the contents of the land contractual management are determined by contract, which may only bind the contractual parties and may not be used against a third party.

[186] See the 2020 Civil Code, *supra* note 12, art. 332.

[187] See *id.*

[188] See *id.*, art. 340.

[189] See *id.*, art. 336.

[190] See *id.*, art. 337.

Also, according to the Civil Code, when the contracted land is expropriated, the affected person with the right to contractual management of land is entitled to corresponding compensation.[191] In the process of compensation, however, an issue is how to determine the qualified person with the right to contractual management of land when the status of such person is in dispute. According to the SPC's opinion, determination shall be made under the household registration in consideration of the time length of the person's living and working in the local collective economic organization.[192]

The SPC further opines that when hearing a dispute over the allocation of land compensation fees, the status of the person in question shall be determined under such considerations as the production and living conditions of the person, the household registration status, the basic living security function of rural land, and more importantly, the other alternative basic living security the person affected may receive. Other factors to be considered include protection of the legitimate interests of women and children.[193]

III. TRANSFER OF THE RIGHT TO CONTRACTUAL MANAGEMENT OF LAND. Given the separability of the three rights arising from the use of land, the person with the right to land contractual management may transfer to another person the right to land management while keeping the right to the contracted land. Thus, under the Civil Code, the right to contractual management of land is transferable, subject to certain conditions. According to article 334 of the Civil Code, a person with the right to the land contractual management is entitled to exchange or transfer the land management right in accordance with law.[194]

The exchange or transfer of land management rights requires a written transfer contract between the land management contractor and the land contractual management right holder. It is also required that in either an exchange or a transfer, the contracted land should not be used for non-agricultural construction purposes without approval.[195] In addition, the parties may at their choice seek to have the exchange or transfer of the right to the land management registered. Without registration, no claim may be asserted against a bona fide third person.[196]

The exchange or transfer of the right to land management may take different forms. The Civil Code allows the person with the right to contractual management

[191] See *id.*, art. 338.

[192] See the SPC Leading Group, Property Rights, *supra* note 11, at 691.

[193] See SPC, *The Minutes of the 8th National Civil and Commercial Trial Work Meeting of the People's Courts*, issued on November 21, 2016, art. 23, available at www.court.gov.cn/zixun/xiangqing/199691.html

[194] See the 2020 Civil Code, *supra* note 12, art. 334.

[195] See *id.*

[196] See *id.*, art. 335.

of land to decide on his or her own to transfer the right to management of land to others by leasing, contributing it as shares, or other means in accordance with law.[197] On the other hand, if the rural land is contracted by such means as bidding, auction, or open negotiation, and the title certificate is obtained through registration, the right to manage such land may then be transferred by way of leasing, contributing it as shares, mortgaging, or in other forms.[198]

Pursuant to article 341 of the Civil Code, for transfer of the land management right with a period of more than five years, the contractor will obtain the right when the transfer contract takes effect.[199] However, as noted, the transfer of a right in immoveable property in general shall not take effect without registration. But, under article 341, registration is not needed for the effectiveness of a transfer of a right to land management, although the land contract management right, as a usufructuary right, is a right in immoveable property.[200]

b. Right to the Use of Land for Construction

As discussed, a notable feature of the Chinese socialist system is the public ownership of land. Given its public nature, the ownership of land is not transferable and may not be retained by any individual or organization. However, the state and collectives, as the owners of land, can grant individuals or organizations a right to use the land as prescribed by the law. One important use as such is the use of land for development, and the right so granted is commonly called the right to the use of land for construction.

The holder of the right to the use of land for construction is subject to certain restrictions, depending on the type of land ownership. As discussed, the holder of the right to the use of collectively owned land must be a member of a rural collective economic organization. For state-owned land, however, the holder of the right to the use of the land can be a company, enterprise, other organization, or individual, unless otherwise provided by the law. It is worth noting that the holder of the right to use state-owned land for construction purposes is not necessarily limited to Chinese citizens. In other words, the right as such can be granted to a foreigner, business entity, or individual alike.

According to article 344 of the Civil Code, a person with a right to the use of state-owned land for construction purposes is entitled to possess, use, and benefit from the land, and to use it to construct buildings, structures, and auxiliary facilities.[201] Among those entitlements, the most important is to use the land for the construction of buildings, structures, and auxiliary facilities. For the purposes of article 344,

[197] See *id.*, art. 339.
[198] See *id.*, art. 342.
[199] See *id.*, art. 341.
[200] See *id.*
[201] See *id.*, art. 344.

buildings include residences, offices, and factory buildings, while structures refer to such constructions as roads, bridges, tunnels, pools, etc. that do not serve residential or business production functions.[202]

I. ACQUISITION OF THE RIGHT TO THE USE OF LAND FOR CONSTRUCTION. In China, the right to use the land for construction purposes may be acquired in two different ways: government grant or commercial transfer. A government grant is an allocation of land by the government for a designated use. There are two notable features of the land grant: it is free of charge and provides indefinite time for use. More importantly, allocation of land via government grant requires an approval by the government at or above the county level. In addition, the land, once allocated, shall not be transferred, leased, or mortgaged.

Under article 345 of the Civil Code, the right to use land for construction purposes may be extended to the surface, above, or below the land.[203] In addition, article 346 mandates that acquisition of the right to use land for construction purposes shall be in conformity with the requirements for conservation of resources and protection of the ecological environment, and in compliance with the provisions of laws and administrative regulations on the planned use of the land.[204] Moreover, the use may not impair the rights to usufruct already created thereon.

Unless it is granted, the right to the use of land for construction purpose is transferable. If the land is used for such business purposes as industrial, commercial, tourism, recreational, and commercial residential purposes, or if there are two or more intended users competing for the right to use the same land, the transfer must be made through a means of public bidding, including bidding and auction. In addition, a contract in writing is required for the transfer of the right to use land for construction purposes.[205]

To transfer the right to use the land for construction, the contract entered into shall generally contain the following clauses: (1) the name and address of each party; (2) the metes and bounds and area of the land; (3) the space occupied by the buildings, structures, and the auxiliary facilities thereof; (4) the planned use and zoning conditions of the land; (5) the term of the right to use the land for construction purposes; (6) the transfer fee and other fees, and the mode of payment thereof; and (7) the means of dispute resolution.[206]

In addition, the holder of the right to the use of land for construction may transfer, exchange, offer as capital contribution, give away as a gift, or mortgage the right, unless otherwise provided by the law. Under article 354, when transferring, exchanging, offering as capital contribution, giving away as a gift, or mortgaging the right to the use of land for construction, the parties shall enter into a contract in writing. But

[202] See *id.*
[203] See *id.*, art. 345.
[204] See *id.*, art. 346.
[205] See *id.*, art. 347.
[206] See *id.*, art. 348.

the term of the use agreed by the parties may not exceed the remaining term of the right allowed to the use of land for construction.[207]

II. REGISTRATION AND APPROVAL. It is required that to obtain a right to the use of land for construction, application for registration must be filed with the registration authority. Pursuant to article 349 of the Civil Code, only upon registration will the right be acquired. After registration, a title certificate will be issued by the registration authority. Registration is also required when the right to the use of land for construction is transferred, exchanged, offered as capital contribution, or given away as a gift.

Under article 356 of the Civil Code, in the case where a right to the use of land for construction is transferred, exchanged, offered as capital contribution, or given away as a gift, the buildings, structures, and auxiliary facilities thereof attached to the land shall go with the land concomitantly. On the other hand, according to article 357 of the Civil Code, in a transaction where a building or structure and auxiliary facilities thereof are transferred, exchanged, offered as capital contribution, or given away as a gift, the right to the use of land for construction on the land on which the building, structure, and auxiliary facilities stand shall automatically be included in the transaction.

III. TERMS OF USE. As noted, the right to the use of land for construction has a term limit unless granted otherwise. As provided in the laws and regulations, the term limit varies depending on the purpose of the use of land for construction. In general, the use of land for residential purposes (land for commercial housing) is limited to a term of seventy years, while the land used for industrial purposes has a period of fifty years. The fifty-year term also applies to the use of land for such public welfare as education, science and technology, culture, health, sports, as well as for other purposes. If the land is used for commerce, tourism, and entertainment, the term of use is shortened to forty years.

A notable issue concerning the term of land use is whether the term is renewable. Another issue is how a renewal is to be made. The Civil Code treats the use of land for residential housing differently from the use of land for other purposes. Under article 359 of the Civil Code, the right to use a piece of land for construction of residential buildings is automatically renewed upon expiration of the term. The payment, reduction, or exemption of the renewal fees shall be dealt with in accordance with the provisions of laws and administrative regulations. Thus, for residential housing, the right to the land use has an automatic renewal when the statutory term of use expires. But the conditions and fees for the renewed period are subject to change.

[207] See *id.*, art. 353.

On the other hand, pursuant to article 359, the renewal of the right to use a land for construction of buildings other than residences shall be handled in accordance with the provisions of the laws, upon expiration of the term. The ownership of the buildings and other immovable property on such land shall be determined in accordance with the agreement, or, where there is no agreement or the agreement is unclear, in accordance with the provisions of laws and administrative regulations.[208]

In addition, as the owner of land, the State may take back the land used for construction purposes. According to article 358 of the Civil Code, when a right to use the land for construction purposes needs to be taken back prior to expiration of its term, two conditions shall be met. First, the taking-back must be made for public interest purposes. Second, compensation shall be made for the houses and other immovable property on the land according to the provisions of law, and the portion of the unused transfer fee shall be refunded.[209]

c. Right to the Use of a House Site

The right to the use of a house site is a unique usufructuary right in China. It is a right to possess and use the land owned by the collective, and to utilize such land to build a dwelling and auxiliary facilities. A distinctive feature of such right is that the holder of the right to the use of a house site must be a member of a rural economic organization. Thus, nobody other than a member of the rural economic organization may obtain the right to use the land for a house site.

Article 363 of the Civil Code provides that acquisition, exercise, and transfer of the right to use a house site are governed by the laws on land administration and the relevant regulations of the State. Due to the requirement of membership in a rural economic organization, urban residents are prohibited from purchasing the right to the use of the house site. Put differently, the right to the use of the house site may not be transferred outside the rural economic organization.[210]

[208] See *id.*, art. 359.

[209] See *id.*, art. 258.

[210] There have been intense debates on the transferability of the right to the use of the land house site in China. One argument is that the right to the use of the land for a house site shall be freely transferable between and among the members of the rural economic organization. The reasoning is that it is meaningless to differentiate between rural housing and urban housing because the substance in terms of ownership is the same regardless of the location of the housing. An opposite opinion is that the right to the use of land for a house site should not be transferred, since such right is the foundation of farmers' basic living security. In addition, the non-transferability of the right to the use of the land for a house site is determined by the fact that the house site is allocated. Between the two extremes is the argument that the right is transferable, but the transfer must meet certain conditions. The conditions include, among others, (a) the transferor and transferee should both be members of the rural economic organization; (b) the transferee should not have an existing house site, and should also meet

The primary purpose of the right to the use of the house site is to meet the living needs of rural villagers. Therefore, the use of a house site may not violate residential needs. For example, the house site shall not be used to engage in production and business activities, and the purpose of the use of house site shall not be arbitrarily changed. On the other hand, given the importance of the house site to villagers, article 364 of the Civil Code explicitly provides that where a house site is destroyed as a result of natural disasters or for other reasons, the right to the use of the house site is extinguished, and a new house site shall be allocated to the villagers who have lost their house site.

B. *Right of Habitation*

The right of habitation refers to a right to possess and use another person's dwelling as agreed in the contract to meet his or her needs of habitation. It is a usufructuary right obtained by a natural person according to a contract or a will to live in a house owned by another person. It is important to note that the right of habitation is not an ownership right, and the right to live in someone else's dwelling is not transferable or inheritable. The right of habitation also differs from a leasehold, although both rights involve possession and use of another person's house. The differences between the right of habitation and leasehold can be further illustrated from the following aspects.

First, the right of habitation is a usufruct, which is a property right, while the leasehold falls within "*obligatio*," or a creditor's right. Put differently, the former is a right against anyone, but the latter is a right that can only be asserted against a particular person (the debtor). Upon the establishment of the right of habitation, the holder of the right has the usufructuary right to live in the other's house under a contract or as provided by the law.

Second, the right of habitation is generally free of charge, and the holder of the right of habitation does not need to pay the owner. Under article 368 of the Civil Code, a right of habitation shall be created free of charge, unless otherwise agreed by the parties.[211] In contrast, under a leasehold, the lessee contracts with the lessor for the right to possess and use the property in exchange for a series of scheduled payments over the term of the lease. Therefore, unlike the right to live in a leased place, the right of habitation stipulated in the Civil Code generally has a nature of support, friendliness, and assistance.

Third, the right of habitation cannot be transferred, but the right of lease can be transferred with the consent of the owner of the property. As provided in article 369 of the Civil Code, a right of habitation may not be transferred or inherited.

the conditions for the application for allocation of the right to the use of the house site; and (c) the transfer must obtain consent from the rural economic organization involved.

[211] See the 2020 Civil Code, *supra* note 12, art. 368.

In addition, no leasehold may be created on a dwelling in which a right of habitation is created, unless otherwise agreed by the parties.[212] Thus, different from a lease, a right of habitation is not transferable or leasable.

Fourth, registration is required for creation of a right of habitation while no registration is needed to establish a leasehold. Pursuant to article 386 of the Civil Code, to create a right of habitation, an application for the registration of the right shall be filed with the registration authority.[213] The right of habitation is created upon registration, and when a right of habitation is extinguished, a deregistration shall be made in a timely manner. According to article 370 of the Civil Code, a right of habitation is extinguished when the term of the right expires, or when the person entitled to the right deceases.[214]

Under article 367 of the Civil Code, creation of a right of habitation shall be made by a written contract between the parties. In addition, a contract so entered generally contains the following clauses: (1) the name and address of each party; (2) the location of the dwelling; (3) the conditions and requirements for the habitation; (4) the duration of the right of habitation; and (5) the means of dispute resolution.[215]

C. *Easement*

Easement as a usufruct is a non-possessory right to the use of another's real property either for the benefit of the user or for the public interest (e.g., public utilities). According to article 372 of the Civil Code, a person who has an easement right is entitled to utilize the real property of another person to enhance the efficiency of his or her own immovable property. The property of another person as used in the easement is called servient land, while the property of the person entitled to the easement is referred to as dominant land.[216]

a. Contents of Easement Rights

In Chinese property literature, easement rights are considered to contain such rights as building support, lighting, viewing, water intake, and road access. Since no private person may own land in the country, the easement in many cases involves another person's land use right. Thus, easement holders include not only landowners but also land contract management right holders, construction land use right holders, and homestead use right holders.

In addition, based on its source, an easement in China can be divided into contractual easements and statutory easements. A statutory easement is a

[212] See *id.*, art. 369.
[213] See *id.*, art. 386.
[214] See *id.*, art. 370.
[215] See *id.*
[216] See *id.*, art. 372.

usufructuary right to another's land as provided by the law. A major reason why the law stipulates an easement is that it would be impossible or inconvenient for a person to use his/her own land if he/she were not given such an easement. By granting an easement, an effective and efficient use of the two pieces of land involved will be ensured. However, when there is no legal obligation to provide an easement, it may only be made on the basis of a contract.

b. Contractual Easement

Pursuant to article 373 of the Civil Code, to create an easement, the parties shall enter into an easement contract in writing. The easement contract generally contains the following clauses: (1) the name and address of each party; (2) the location of the servient land and the dominant land; (3) the purposes and methods of utilizing the servient land; (4) the duration of the easement; (5) the fees and the mode of payment; and (6) the means of dispute resolution.[217]

For a contract easement, the easement is created upon the effectiveness of the easement contract. In other words, a contractual easement takes place at the time when the easement contract enters into effect. In addition, if the parties request registration, an application shall be filed with the registration authority. According to article 374 of the Civil Code, without registration, an easement created under a contract may not be asserted against a bona fide third person.[218]

Under an easement contract, the holder of the right to the use of the servient land shall allow the person entitled to an easement to utilize the real property as agreed in the contract and may not interfere with the right of the easement holder to exercise such right.[219] The person granted with an easement is required to utilize the servient land in accordance with the purposes and methods of utilization as agreed in the contract, and to minimize restrictions imposed under the easement on the property rights of the holder of the right to the use of the servient land.[220]

Also, the term of contractual easement is subject to the agreement of the parties on the easement. But whatever term the parties provide in their agreement, it may not exceed the remaining term of the right to usufruct, such as the right to contractual management of land or the right to the use of land for construction purposes.[221] In addition, when a landowner holds the right of or is encumbered with an easement, if a right to usufruct, such as a right to contractual management of land or a right to use a house site, is created on the land, the usufructuary shall

[217] See *id.*, art. 373.
[218] See *id.*, art. 374.
[219] See *id.*, art. 375.
[220] See *id.*, art. 376.
[221] See *id.*, art. 377.

continue to be entitled to or be encumbered by the easement thereon that has already been created.[222]

As provided in the Civil Code, the holder of the right to servient land may terminate the agreement under any of the following circumstances: (1) abuse of the right to easement in violation of the provisions of laws or the contract; or (2) in the case of unpaid use of the servient land, failure to pay the fees upon receipt of two warning notices within a reasonable period of time after the payment is due under the agreement.[223] The Civil Code further provides that when a registered easement is altered, transferred, or extinguished, registration of the change or deregistration shall be made in a timely manner.[224]

c. Restrictions

The Civil Code imposes certain restrictions on the right of easement. First, when a right to usufruct, such as a right to contractual management of land, a right to use the land for construction purposes, or a right to use a house site has already been created on the land, no easement may be created on the land without the consent of the usufructuary. Second, an easement may not be transferred separately. If a right to contractual management of land, a right to use a piece of land for construction purposes, or similar rights are transferred, the easement shall be transferred concomitantly, unless otherwise agreed in the contract. Third, an easement may not be mortgaged separately. When a right to contractual management of land, a right to use the land for construction purposes, and the like are mortgaged, the easement shall be transferred concomitantly with the mortgage.

Also, if a right to easement is involved when the dominant land and a right to contractual management of land, a right to use the land for construction purposes, and the like thereon are partially transferred, the transferee is simultaneously entitled to the easement.[225] In the case where a right to easement is involved when the servient land and a right to contractual management of land, a right to use the land for construction purposes, and the like thereon are partially transferred, the easement is legally binding on the transferee.[226]

5. SECURITY INTERESTS

In Chinese property literature, a security interest is described as a right in the property of another or *jus in re aliena*. More specifically, it is the right established on property owned by, or rights of, the debtor or a third party to ensure the

[222] See *id.*, art. 378.
[223] See *id.*, art. 384.
[224] See *id.*, art. 385.
[225] See *id.*, art. 382.
[226] See *id.*, art. 383.

realization of the creditor's right. Under article 386 of the Civil Code, when a debtor fails to perform his or her obligation that is due, or an event upon which a security interest is to be realized as agreed upon by the parties occurs, the person entitled to the security interest has priority to be paid from the collateral, unless otherwise provided by law.[227]

Unlike ownership, the basic nature of the security interest is the right to control the collateral, not the right of the claim. But, since the priority of payment of the security interest is based on the exclusivity of the property right, it is the right to a thing, not to a person. In addition, although the security interest also takes the right as its object, it is the right to the value of the thing or right given by the debtor as security. Under the Civil Code, the security interest includes a mortgage, pledge, or lien.

A. *Creation and Extinguishment of Security Interests*

A security interest is created on the basis of a contract. According to article 388 of the Civil Code, to establish a security interest, a security contract shall be entered into under the provision of law. A security contract is a contract secondary to the principal contract or the contract of the principal claims and obligations. When a principal contract becomes void, the security contract secondary to it is also void, unless otherwise provided by law. With regard to the liabilities, when a security contract is determined to be void, if the debtor, the security provider, and the creditor are all at fault, they shall each bear civil liability in proportion to their fault.[228]

A security interest may also apply to non-property transactions. Under article 387 of the Civil Code, if a creditor needs to secure his/her claims in a civil activity such as lending, buying, or selling, he/she may create a security interest in accordance with the provisions of this Code and other laws. In addition, if a third person provides security to the creditor for the debtor, the debtor may be requested to provide a counter-security for the third person.[229] Also, unless otherwise agreed by the parties, the scope of a security interest includes the principal claim and the interests accrued therefrom, liquidated damages, compensatory damages, and the expenses arising from safekeeping the collateral and enforcing the security interest.[230]

Moreover, when a claim is secured by both a collateral and a surety under an agreement, the creditor may enforce the claim in accordance with the agreement if the debtor fails to perform his/her obligations due or any event upon which a

[227] See *id.*, art. 386.
[228] See *id.*, art. 388.
[229] See *id.*, art. 387.
[230] See *id.*, art. 389.

security interest is to be realized as agreed occurs. In a case where there is no agreement or the agreement is unclear, if the collateral is provided by the debtor, the creditor shall first enforce the claim against the collateral. If, however, the collateral is provided by a third person, the creditor may elect to enforce the claim against the collateral or request the third party assume liability.[231]

There are two provisions in the Civil Code that are aimed at protecting the interests of the third party who provides security or serves as a guarantor. First, a third party, after assuming liability upon the request by the creditor, has the right of indemnification against the debtor.[232] Second, when a third person provides security but the creditor allows the debtor to transfer all or part of the secured obligations without the third person's written consent, the third party is no longer liable for securing the part of the obligations so transferred.[233]

Under article 393 of the Civil Code, a security interest is extinguished under any of the following circumstances: (a) the claim under the principal contract is extinguished; (b) the security interest is realized; (c) the creditor waives his or her security interest; or (d) there exists any other circumstance in which the security interest is extinguished as provided by law. If, however, during the duration of security a collateral is destructed, damaged, or lost, or is expropriated, the person entitled to a security interest has priority to be paid from the insurance payment, compensation, or indemnity received on the collateral. If the collateral is destructed, damaged, or lost, or is expropriated prior to the due date of performance of the secured claim, the insurance payment, compensation, or indemnity may also be placed in escrow.

B. *Mortgage*

A mortgage is provided in the Civil Code as a security interest under which a debtor or a third person, in order to secure the performance of an obligation, gives his/her property as collateral to the creditor without relinquishing possession of the property, and the creditor has priority to be paid from the collateral if (a) the debtor fails to perform his or her obligation due or (b) an event upon the occurrence of which the security interest in the collateral is to be realized as agreed by the parties occurs. The property used as collateral to secure the creditor's right is called the mortgaged property.[234]

a. Basic Requirements

As commonly held in China, a property that may be mortgaged shall meet two requirements. First, the property must be one of which the debtor or a third party is

[231] See *id.*, art. 292.
[232] See *id.*
[233] See *id.*, art. 391.
[234] See *id.*, art. 394.

entitled to dispose. Second, the property must be mortgageable.[235] According to Chinese scholars, for a property to be capable of being mortgaged, the property must possess the nature of negotiability, independence, and open-endedness.[236] Negotiability means that the property can be freely transferred, while independence refers to the separability of the mortgaged property from other property. Open-endedness implicates that unless prohibited by the law, any property can be mortgaged as long as it is legally transferable and can exist independently.

b. Mortgageable Property

Under article 395 of the Property Law, the property capable of being mortgaged includes: (a) buildings and other things attached to the land; (b) the right to use the land for construction purposes; (c) the right to use the sea areas; (d) production equipment, raw materials, semi-finished products, and finished products; (e) buildings, vessels, and aircraft under construction; (f) vehicles for transport; and (g) other property not prohibited by laws or administrative regulations from being mortgaged. For the purposes of a mortgage, the property listed in article 395 can be divided into three categories: immoveable property, moveable property, and the right to the use of property.

Among the categories of mortgageable property, the most notable is the moveable property. Borrowed from the concept of floating charge, the Civil Code allows a mortgage to be created on the moveable property of a debtor to secure realization of a creditor's rights. "Floating charge" is known in the Western economy as a security interest over a group of current or non-constant assets that may change in quantity and value.[237] Current assets refer to business possessions, including, among others, the accounts receivable, inventory, and marketable securities that can be quickly liquidated for cash. The floating charge may convert to a fixed charge (assets become fixed) when there is a default or similar event. The process of conversion is called crystallization.

The Civil Code, however, imposes certain limitations on the use of a floating charge. First, pursuant to article 396 of the Civil Code, the person who may mortgage moveable property is limited to an enterprise, an individual-run industrial and commercial household, or an agricultural production operator. Second, the movables capable of mortgage only include production equipment, raw materials, works in process, and finished products that are currently owned or thereafter acquired. Third, under article 396, if the debtor fails to perform his/her obligations due or any event upon which a security interest in the mortgaged property is to be

[235] See the SPC Leading Group, Property Rights, *supra* note 11, at 1039–1040.

[236] See *id.*

[237] For more discussion, see Sarah Worthington, *Floating Charges: An Alternative Theory*, 53 Cambridge L.J. 81 (1994).

enforced as agreed by the parties occurs, the creditor has priority to be paid from the movable property determined at the time when the mortgaged property is ascertained.

The Civil Code also provides certain situations in which a floating charge crystallizes, or a conversion takes place. Under article 411 of the Civil Code, after a mortgage on a moveable property is created, the mortgaged property shall be ascertained at the time when one of the following circumstances occurs: (1) the claim is not satisfied upon expiration of the term of performance of the obligation; (2) the mortgagor is declared bankrupt or dissolved; (3) an event upon which the mortgage is to be enforced as agreed upon by the parties occurs; or (4) any other circumstance that seriously affects the enforcement of the claim.[238]

c. Governing Rules

There are several rules provided in the Civil Code that govern mortgages. The first one is the rule of *pactum commissorium*, a civil law concept that refers to an agreement in a mortgage under which the mortgagee can appropriate or dispose of the mortgaged property if the mortgagor cannot fulfill his or her obligation. In some countries, *pactum commissorium* is recognized on the basis of party autonomy. In many other countries, however, an agreement as such is prohibited due to the concern that unfairness might occur.

China takes a mixed approach. It does not explicitly outlaw *pactum commissorium* but limits it to a right of priority to be compensated in case of the mortgagor's failure to perform. According to article 401 of the Civil Code, if prior to the due date of performance of an obligation, the mortgagee reaches an agreement with the mortgagor under which the mortgaged property belongs to the mortgagee in the event that the mortgagor fails to perform the obligation due, the mortgagee may only have priority to be paid from the mortgaged property in accordance with law.

The second rule is the rule of collateral mortgage that governs the relationship between the land and the building attached. Note that in China, all land is publicly owned – either by the state or by the collectives – and individuals or entities may only have the right to the use of land. Therefore, when a mortgage is created on a right to the use of land or on a building, a question that necessarily arises is how to deal with the land when the building on it is mortgaged, or how to handle the building when the right to the use of the land underneath it is mortgaged.

Pursuant to article 397 of the Civil Code, when a building is mortgaged, the right to the use of land in the area occupied by the building for construction purposes shall be mortgaged concomitantly. Where a right to use a piece of land for construction purposes is mortgaged, any building on the land shall be mortgaged concomitantly. If, however, a mortgagor fails to concomitantly mortgage the

[238] See the 2020 Civil Code, *supra* note 12, art. 411.

property as provided, the unmortgaged property in question shall be deemed to have been concomitantly mortgaged.[239]

The third rule is the rule of formality. Under article 400 of the Civil Code, to create a mortgage, the parties shall enter into a mortgage contract in writing. It is also required that a mortgage contract generally contain such terms as (1) the type and amount of the secured claim; (2) the term during which the debtor shall perform obligations; (3) the name and quantity of the mortgaged property; and (4) the scope of the security interest.[240]

The fourth rule is the rule of registration. When a mortgage is created on an immoveable property as well as a building under construction, registration is mandated for the mortgage to become effective. In contrast, a mortgage on movable property is created and takes effect at the time when the mortgage contract enters into effect. Simply put, to place a mortgage on movable property, registration is not required. However, a mortgage as such without registration may not be asserted against a bona fide third person.

The fifth rule is the rule of transfer. As provided in article 406 of the Civil Code, a mortgagor may transfer the mortgaged property to another person during the term of the mortgage unless otherwise agreed by the parties. But the transfer of the mortgaged property may not affect the mortgage. When a transfer is made, a notice shall be sent to the mortgagee in a timely manner. The mortgagee may request the mortgagor to apply the proceeds of the transfer to pay off the obligation before it is due, or to place such proceeds in escrow if it is established that the transfer of the mortgaged property may impair the mortgagee's right to the mortgage.[241]

In addition, if the portion of the proceeds obtained from the transfer exceeds the amount of the obligation owed, it will belong to the mortgagor, while any deficiency shall be satisfied by the debtor. Further, a mortgage may not be transferred separately from the underlying claim or be used as security for another claim. When a claim is transferred, the mortgage securing the claim shall be transferred concomitantly with it, unless otherwise provided by law or agreed by the parties.[242]

The sixth rule is the waiver of priority. The priority in a mortgage refers to the order of payment among the mortgagees when a mortgagor establishes two or more mortgages on the same property. In accordance with article 409 of the Civil Code, a mortgagee may waive his/her right to the mortgage or waive his or her priority order. In addition, a mortgagee and a mortgagor may reach an agreement to change such things as the mortgagee's priority order and the amount of the secured claim, provided that any change to the mortgage may not adversely affect the other mortgagees without their written consent.[243]

[239] See *id.*, art. 397.
[240] See *id.*, art. 400.
[241] See *id.*, art. 406.
[242] See *id.*, art. 407.
[243] See *id.*, art. 409.

On the other hand, where a debtor creates a mortgage on his/her own property, and the mortgagee waives his/her right to the mortgage and his/her priority order in the line of mortgagees, or changes the mortgage, the other security providers shall be exempted from the security liability.

But the exemption shall be limited to the rights and interests of the mortgagee that are forfeited owing to the waiver of his/her priority to be paid from the mortgaged property, unless the other security providers are still committed to providing security.[244]

Furthermore, when a debtor fails to perform his/her obligation due or an event upon which a mortgage is to be enforced as agreed upon by the parties occurs, the mortgagee may, upon agreement with the mortgagor, have the priority right to appraise and accept the mortgaged property, or apply the proceeds obtained from an auction or sale of the mortgaged property to satisfy his/her claim against the mortgagor.

If, however, the agreement mentioned earlier is detrimental to the interests of other creditors, the other creditors may request that a people's court rescind it. When a mortgagee and a mortgagor fail to reach an agreement on the methods of enforcing the mortgage, the mortgagee may request the people's court to have the mortgaged property sold at auction or in a sale. The appraisal or sale of the mortgaged property shall be based on the market price thereof.

d. Exclusions

There are certain properties on which no mortgage may be created. As provided in article 399 of the Civil Code, the property or property rights that are not subject to mortgage include: (1) land ownership; (2) the right to use the land owned by a collective, such as house sites, land, and hills retained for household use, unless otherwise provided by law; (3) educational facilities, medical and health facilities, and other public welfare facilities of non-profit legal persons established for public welfare purposes, such as schools, kindergartens, and medical institutions; (4) property of which the ownership or right to use is unclear or disputed; (5) property that has been seized, detained, or placed under custody in accordance with law; and (6) other property that may not be mortgaged as provided by laws or administrative regulations.

e. Maximum Mortgage

The Civil Code divides mortgages into general mortgages and maximum mortgages. In contrast to general mortgages, the maximum mortgage is a special kind of mortgage. It is established by the debtor or a third party to provide mortgages within

[244] See *id.*

the limit of the maximum creditor's rights in order to guarantee the creditor's rights will occur continuously in a certain period of time in the future.[245] The major differences between the maximum amount mortgage and the general mortgage lie in the number of secured claims, the time when the claims occurred, the certainty of the amount of the claims, and the conditions for the transfer and extinction of the mortgage.

In the process of legal establishment, the maximum amount mortgage and the general mortgage are also different. When establishing a maximum amount mortgage, a maximum amount mortgage contract needs to be submitted, while a general mortgage only needs to submit an ordinary mortgage contract. The registration of the maximum mortgage right is based on the contract of claims that occur continuously over a period of time, while the registration of the general mortgage right is based on the contract of specific claims. Unlike the general mortgage, a maximum mortgage has a number of distinctions.

First, the creditor's right in a maximum mortgage is not specific because it is a future creditor's right. Second, the number of claims under the creditor's right is capped in a maximum mortgage, referring to the maximum number of claims to be received by way of priority. Under the maximum mortgage, the value of the mortgaged property is certain at the time of the mortgage, although the creditor's right is yet to be specified. Third, a maximum mortgage is not premised on the existence of a creditor's right. Fourth, the mortgage as such would not be extinguished upon extinguishment of individual claims. Fifth, only after the creditor's rights secured by the maximum mortgage are determined,[246] and if all the creditor's rights are extinguished, will the maximum mortgage right be extinguished. In other words, a maximum mortgage is not subordinate to the creditor's right the same way a general mortgage is.[247]

[245] To illustrate, suppose that A wants to borrow money from a bank and asks B as guarantor. B then mortgages his own property worth $1 million with the bank for the benefit of A, but limits the maximum mortgage amount to $700,000 for a one-year term. Under this arrangement, A can get money from the bank multiple times at A's choice but with the total amount not exceeding $700,000.

[246] Under article 423 of the Civil Code, the claims of the mortgagee are ascertained under any of the following circumstances:

> (1) the agreed period of time for the claims to be ascertained expires; (2) the mortgagee or the mortgagor requests for ascertainment of the claims after the lapse of two years from the date of the creation of the mortgage when there is no agreement on the period of time for the claims to be ascertained or the relevant agreement is unclear; (3) it is impossible for a new claim to arise; (4) the mortgagee knows or should have known that the mortgaged property has been sealed up or detained; (5) the debtor or the mortgagor is declared bankrupt or dissolved; or (6) there exists any other circumstance under which the claims are to be ascertained as provided by law. (See *id.*, art. 423.)

[247] In general mortgages, if the creditor's rights guaranteed are eliminated, the mortgage is also eliminated. In a maximum mortgage, however, the mortgage will not be eliminated due to the elimination of individual creditor's rights. After the creditor's rights guaranteed by the

Under article 420 of the Civil Code, when a debtor or a third person provides a collateral for future claims that will arise consecutively within a certain period of time to secure performance of the obligations, if the debtor fails to perform an obligation due or an event upon which such a mortgage is to be enforced as agreed upon by the parties occurs, the mortgagee has the priority to be paid from the mortgaged property up to the maximum amount of his/her claim. Also, pursuant to article 420, a claim that exists prior to the creation of the maximum mortgage may, upon consent of the parties, be included in the claims secured by such a mortgage.[248]

The Civil Code permits a change made by the parties to the maximum mortgage. In accordance with article 422, before the claims secured by a maximum mortgage are ascertained, the mortgagee and the mortgagor may change by agreement the period for the ascertainment of the claims, the scope of the claims, and the maximum amount of the claims. The change so made, however, may not adversely affect other mortgagees.[249] In addition, before the ascertainment of the claims secured by the maximum mortgage, if part of the claims are transferred, the mortgage may not be transferred unless otherwise agreed by the parties.[250]

C. *Pledge*

A pledge is a security interest in which the debtor or a third party hands over their own property to the possession of the creditor or creates a pledge on their own property rights as a guarantee for debt performance. In a pledge, the debtor or the third person is called the pledgor, while the creditor is the pledgee. The movable property delivered is the pledged. In China, a pledge is also divided into a pledge on property and a pledge on the right to property. Unlike the pledge on property, the pledge on the right to property refers to the pledge establishing any transferable property rights other than ownership or usufructuary rights.[251]

Under article 425 of the Civil Code, when a debtor or a third person pledges his/her movable property to the creditor for possession in order to secure the performance of an obligation, if the debtor fails to perform the obligation due or an event

maximum mortgage are ascertained, the mortgage is eliminated only if all the creditor's rights are eliminated.

[248] See the 2020 Civil Code, *supra* note 12, art. 420.

[249] See *id.*, art. 422.

[250] See *id.*, art. 421.

[251] According to article 440 of the Civil Code, the following rights, of which a debtor or a third person has the right to dispose, may be pledged: (1) drafts, promissory notes, and checks; (2) bonds and certificates of deposit; (3) warehouse receipts and bills of lading; (4) transferable fund shares and equity; (5) transferable proprietary rights contained in such intellectual property as the right to the exclusive use of registered trademarks, patent rights, and copyrights; (6) existing and future accounts receivable; and (7) other proprietary rights that may be pledged in accordance with the provisions of laws and administrative regulations. See *id.*

upon the occurrence of which the pledge is to be enforced as agreed upon by the parties occurs, the creditor has priority to be paid from the movable property as pledged.[252] It is further provided in article 426 that a non-transferable movable property under the law or administrative regulations may not be pledged.[253]

In China, a pledge is considered a typical security interest. The most notable characteristics of a pledge include: (a) the establishment and continuation of a pledge is based on the transfer of possession of the property involved; (b) the subject of a pledge is moveable property; and (c) the pledgee enjoys a priority of being compensated in case of the pledgee's failure in performance or occurrence of event agreed by the parties to realize the pledgee's rights.

a. Creation of Pledge

Creation of a pledge is based on contract. Article 427 of the Civil Code mandates that to create a pledge, the parties shall enter into a pledge contract in writing. A pledge contract generally contains such clauses as follows: (1) the type and amount of the secured claim; (2) the time period for the debtor to perform the obligation; (3) such particulars as the name and quantity of the pledged property; (4) the scope of the security coverage; and (5) the time for, and the mode of, the delivery of the pledged property.[254]

In general, a pledge is created upon delivery of the pledged property by the pledgor.[255] But for the property rights pledged, the pledge may be created either by delivery or by registration depending on the type of property. If a pledge is made on a draft, promissory note, check, bond, certificate of deposit, warehouse receipt, or bill of lading, it is created at the time when the certificate of such a right is delivered to the pledgee or, in the absence of such a certificate, at the time when the pledge is registered, unless otherwise provided by the law.

If, however, a pledge is made on fund shares or equity, an intellectual property right, or on receivables, the creation of it will be upon registration. One restriction is that once a pledge is placed, those property rights become non-transferable unless otherwise agreed by the pledgor and pledgee. But if the pledged property rights are transferred as agreed, the proceeds obtained by the pledgor from the transfer shall be applied to pay to the pledgee to discharge the obligation before it is due or be placed in escrow.[256]

b. Issues Involved

There are several issues that are worth noting. One issue involves the doctrine of liquidity. In a pledge contract, liquidity is often called a compensation clause. It is

[252] See *id.*, art. 425.
[253] See *id.*, art. 426.
[254] See *id.*, art. 427.
[255] See *id.*, art. 429.
[256] See *id.*, arts. 443, 444, 445.

an agreement between the parties when establishing a pledge as a security interest to the effect that when the pledgor fails to perform the debt, the pledgee will obtain the ownership of the pledged property. Under the 2007 Property Law and the 1995 Guarantee Law, a pledgor and a pledgee may not stipulate in their contract that the ownership over the property pledged would be transferred to the pledgee if the pledgee is not fully compensated and paid upon the expiration of the term for performance of the debt.[257]

The Civil Code, however, reverses this. Under article 428 of the Civil Code, if, prior to the due date of performance, the pledgee reaches an agreement with the pledgor that the pledged property will belong to the creditor in the event that the pledgor fails to perform the obligation due, the pledgee may have priority to be paid from the pledged property in accordance with law.[258] Thus, under article 428, liquidity is allowed but only under the provisions of law. The Civil Code further provides that a pledgee has the right to collect the fruits and proceeds accrued from the pledged property unless otherwise agreed in the contract. But the said fruits and proceeds shall first be applied to offset the expenses of collection of them.[259]

Another issue is the liability of the pledgee pertaining to the property pledged. Article 431 of the Civil Code provides that a pledgee who, during the effective period of the pledge, uses or disposes of the pledged property without the consent of the pledgor and thus causes damage to the latter, shall be liable for compensation.[260] In addition, pursuant to article 432 of the Civil Code, a pledgee is obligated to keep the pledged property safe, and shall be liable for compensation if the pledged property is destructed, damaged, or lost due to his/her improper custody. Where the pledgee's act is likely to cause the pledged property to be destructed, damaged, or lost, the pledgor may request the pledgee place the pledged property in escrow, or request the pledgee discharge the obligation before it is due and return.[261]

The third issue concerns re-pledge. A re-pledge refers to an action of transferring a pledge by which the pledgee establishes the pledge right for a third party with the pledged property he/she owns in order to guarantee his/her own debt during the period of the pledge. Under article 434 of the Civil Code, a pledgee shall be liable for compensation where he/she, during the effective period of the pledge, re-pledges the pledged property without the consent of the pledgor to a third person and thus causes destruction, damage, or loss to the pledged property.[262]

If, however, due to a cause the pledgee is not responsible for, the pledged property is likely to be damaged or significantly diminished in value that suffices to jeopardize the pledgee's rights, the pledgee has the right to request the pledgor provide

[257] See article 211 of the Property Law (2008) and article 66 of the 1995 Guarantee Law.
[258] See the 2020 Civil Code, *supra* note 12, art. 428.
[259] See *id.*
[260] See *id.*, art. 431.
[261] See *id.*, art. 432.
[262] See *id.*, art. 434.

additional security. On the other hand, if the pledgor fails to do so, the pledgee may have the pledged property sold at auction or in a sale and may, by agreement with the pledgor, apply the proceeds obtained from the auction or sale to discharge the obligation before it is due or place such proceeds in escrow.[263]

The fourth issue is related to waiver. Since a pledge is a right of security interest, a right as such is waivable. According to article 435 of the Civil Code, a pledgee may waive his or her right to the pledge. If a debtor creates a pledge on his/her own property and the pledgee waives his/her right to the pledge, the other security providers shall be exempted from the security liability. The exemption is limited to the extent of the rights and interests of the pledgee that are forfeited owing to the waiver of his/her priority to be paid from the collateral, unless the other security providers are committed to still provide security.[264]

The fifth issue is about the pledgor's fulfillment of their obligation required under the pledge. Article 436 of the Civil Code explicitly provides that a pledgee shall return the pledged property after the debtor has performed his/her obligation or the pledgor has paid the secured claim before it is due. It is further provided that if a debtor fails to perform an obligation due, or an event upon the occurrence of which the pledge is to be enforced as agreed upon by the parties occurs, the pledgee may, by agreement with the pledgor, appraise based on the market value and accept the pledged property as satisfaction of his/her claim, or have priority to be paid from the proceeds obtained from auction or sale of the pledged property.[265]

After a pledged property is appraised and accepted by the pledgee as full or partial satisfaction of his/her claim, or is sold at auction or in a sale, if the value of the pledged property as appraised or the proceeds obtained from auction or sale is in excess of the amount of the obligation owed, the excessive portion shall belong to the pledgor, while any deficiency shall be satisfied by the debtor.[266] In addition, a pledgor and a pledgee may create a maximum pledge by agreement. Similar to a maximum mortgage, the maximum pledge is to ensure that when the debtor or a third party providing a pledge guarantee fails to perform, or the agreed event triggering the pledge occurs within a certain period of time, the pledgee has the priority to receive payment for the secured interest within the limit of the maximum pledge.[267]

The last issue rests with the obligation of the pledgee. The Civil Code provides the pledgor with a right to request the pledgee enforce the pledge in a timely manner after expiration of the period for performance of the obligation. If the pledgee fails to do so, the pledgor may request the people's court have the pledged property sold at auction or in a sale. Also, the pledgee will be liable for

[263] See *id.*, art. 433.
[264] See *id.*, art. 435.
[265] See *id.*, art. 436.
[266] See *id.*, art. 438.
[267] See *id.*, art. 439.

compensation if, upon the pledgor's timely request for enforcement of the pledge, the pledgee is indolent in performing so that damages to the pledgor are caused.[268]

D. *Lien*

In China, a lien is the right of a creditor created according to the law to keep the moveable property of a debtor in the possession of the creditor under a certain legal relationship until the debt is discharged. Under a lien, if the debtor fails to perform their contractual obligation, the creditor has the right to dispose of the possessed property. The creditor in a lien relationship is called the lienholder, and the movable property possessed by the lienholder is the property under lien. It should be noted that when a lien is created on a movable property on which a mortgage or pledge has already been placed, the lienholder takes priority in compensation.[269]

As provided in article 447 of the Civil Code, in the case of a debtor's failure to perform his/her obligation that is due, the creditor may retain the debtor's movable property which is already in the lawful possession of the creditor and has priority to be paid from the movable property.[270] In addition, pursuant to article 452 of the Civil Code, a lienholder has the right to collect the fruits and proceeds accrued from the property retained under a lien. But the fruits and proceeds as such shall first be applied to offset the expenses for collecting them.[271]

a. Lien vs. Pledge

A lien differs from a pledge in several aspects. First, a lien may only be created on a statutory basis, while a pledge, as noted, may be made either under the law or by agreement. Second, when establishing a lien, the property is already in the possession of the creditor, but the possession of the pledged property is transferred to the creditor at the time of creation of the pledge. Third, the subject matter of a lien may only be moveable property. By contrast, the property for pledges includes moveable property and property rights. Fourth, a lien would be extinguished where the lien property is lost, the creditor abandons the lien, or the debtor provides another guarantee. A pledge can be extinguished by the loss of the pledged property but will not be affected by the transfer of ownership of the pledged property.

b. Creation

Thus, to create a lien, three requirements must be met. First, the subject of a lien is moveable property. Second, the property is already in the possession of a creditor

[268] See *id.*, art. 437.
[269] See *id.*, art. 456.
[270] See *id.*, art. 447.
[271] See *id.*, art. 452.

based on a certain legal relationship between the creditor and debtor. And third, the debtor fails to fulfill his/her legal obligations when the allowed debtor repayment period expires. Also, it is important to note that unlike a mortgage or pledge, which is a contractual-based security interest, a lien is a statutory rather than contractual creation. In other words, a lien is a statutory right – not a contractual right based on the agreement of the parties.

c. Distinctions

In addition, compared with other security interests, a lien, by its statutory nature, has its own distinctions. First, the movable property retained under a lien by the creditor is in the same legal relationship as the underlying claim. Note, however, that the same legal relationship may not apply to the lien between two enterprises or a commercial lien. The reason is that given the complexity of a commercial relationship, it is often hard to identify the direct connection between the property under a lien and a particular transaction.[272]

Second, although a lien may not be created by contract, the parties may by agreement exclude the application of a lien. In accordance with article 449 of the Civil Code, the movable property that is not subject to retention under a lien as provided by law or as agreed by the parties should not be retained.[273] Therefore, when the parties agree in advance that a lien is not applicable, no lien may be created. Put differently, if the parties do not want to have a lien in their relationship, they can exclude it through an agreement ahead of time.

Third, when the property retained under a lien is divisible, the value of the retained property shall match the amount of the obligation. The idea is that since the purpose of retaining the lien property is to satisfy the lienholder's creditor right, as long as the value of the property retained is equivalent to the amount of the debt, the realization of the lienholder's creditor right will be guaranteed.[274] On the other hand, a lienholder is obligated to keep the retained property safe and shall be held liable for compensation if the retained property is destructed, damaged, or lost due to improper storage.[275]

Fourth, as noted, a lienholder has the right to dispose of the lien property upon the debtor's failure to perform the obligation as agreed. In general, the terms of performance are provided in the agreement between the parties. If, however, there is no agreement or the agreement is unclear, article 453 of the Civil Code requires that the lienholder give the debtor a period of at least sixty days to perform unless the retained movable property is perishable.[276]

[272] See *id.*, art. 448.
[273] See *id.*, art. 449.
[274] See *id.*, art. 450.
[275] See *id.*, art. 451.
[276] See *id.*, art. 453.

When the debtor defaults upon expiration of the performance period, the lienholder may, based on agreement with the debtor, appraise and accept the retained property to satisfy the claim, or be paid with priority from the proceeds obtained from auction or sale of the retained property.[277] Also, it is provided in article 453 that the appraisal or sale of the retained property shall be based on the market price.[278]

Fifth, the debtor in a lien has the right to request a lienholder exercise the lien right timely. In accordance with article 454 of the Civil Code, a debtor may request the lienholder to enforce the lien after expiration of the term of performance. In case the lienholder fails to do so, the debtor may request the people's court have the retained property sold at auction or in a sale.[279]

After the property retained under a lien is appraised and accepted by the lienholder, or is sold at auction or in a sale, if the value of the retained property or the proceeds obtained from auction or sale of the retained property exceeds the amount of the obligation owed, the excessive portion shall belong to the debtor, but any shortfall must be covered by the debtor.[280] In addition, as noted, a lien is extinguished when the lienholder loses possession of the retained property or accepts another form of security provided by the debtor.[281]

[277] See *id.*
[278] See *id.*
[279] See *id.*, art. 454.
[280] See *id.*, art. 455.
[281] See *id.*, art. 457.

9

Contract Law

INTRODUCTION

In Chinese history, a contract was commonly called an agreement or "*Qi Yue*" in Chinese.[1] The written form of "*Qi Yue*" in the country can be found as early as in the Western Zhou period (1100 to 770 BC).[2] During the Western Zhou period, "*Qi Yue*" was used to record the consent of two parties to their exchange of goods or purchase of land, and it was also employed to document other civil activities between parties such as loans and leases. On certain occasions where the exchange was deemed especially important, the process and the terms of the exchange were inscribed in a bronze tripod (bronze cauldron often used in rituals or to record major events or things) as evidence of the exchange. A written form of "*Qi Yue*" was called "*Qi Juan*" (documented agreement) or "*Pan Shu*" (half-half or split document), including "*Fu Bie*" (loan), "*Yue Ji*" (land), and "*Zhi Ji*" (sales).[3]

Ever since the Western Zhou period, "*Qi Yue*" had become a major form representing the consent of the parties in their civil activities and serving as evidence of the agreement entered into by the parties concerned. Under the Tang Code, for example, a "*Qi Yue*" was required for the sale of a homestead or livestock, and anyone who completed such sale without a "*Qi Yue*" would be punished.[4] During the Republic period from 1911 to 1949, "*Qi Yue*" was the major form used for civil obligations in the Civil Code, one of the Six Codes that made up the main body of the law of the Republic.[5]

[1] See Wang Liming, Contract Law of China, 2 (Hein Wells, 2016).

[2] For general information, see Zhang Jinfan, Evolution of the Chinese Legal Civilization, 55–56 (China University of Political Science and Law Press, 1999).

[3] See *id. Zhi Ji*, for example, is an agreement written on a bamboo slip divided into two pieces, with each party holding one piece.

[4] See generally Geoffrey MacCormack, *The Law of Contract in China under the T'ang and Song Dynasties*, 32 Revue Internationale des Droits de l'Antiquité 17 (1985).

[5] See 1929 Civil Code, available at http://ishare.iask.sina.com.cn/f/25306726.html.

However, the contract did not play any active role after the founding of the People's Republic of China in 1949 until the 1980s. During that period, contract regulation, if any, was made basically in lieu of government policies. There were many factors attributive to this phenomenon. The most notable one was the planned economy that dominated the country. Another significant factor was the ideology that private interest should unconditionally be subordinated to the public interest – a rigid rule that profoundly governed the nation for decades.

Contract law legislation formally began in China in 1980 with the adoption of the Economic Contract Law (ECL). The ECL regulated contracts that were entered into for business purposes between legal persons, other economic organizations, individual businesses, and rural business households.[6] Under the ECL, a contract was called an "economic contract" because at that time contracts were still viewed as the legal means to realize economic goals as stipulated by state plans.[7] In the ECL, natural persons were excluded from making economic contracts, and thus no individual may be a contractual party. The ECL was amended in 1993 to reflect China's ongoing economic reform. The most striking change in the amended ECL was that contracts were no longer defined as the means to ensure the implementation of the state plans.

The second important piece of contract legislation was the Foreign Economic Contract Law (FECL), which was promulgated by the National People's Congress (NPC) on March 21, 1985. The FECL was designed to apply to contracts in which a foreign party or foreign element was involved. Under article 2 of the FECL, foreign economic contracts referred to the contracts entered into between enterprises or other economic organizations of the People's Republic of China and foreign enterprises, other foreign economic organizations, or individuals.[8] Once again, no Chinese citizen was allowed to enter into a foreign economic contract. In addition, the FECL did not apply to contracts of international transportation.

On June 23, 1987, the Technology Contract Law (TCL) was adopted with a stated purpose of providing an impetus for scientific and technical development in China. The application of the TCL, however, was limited to contracts between two legal persons, between legal persons and citizens, or between two citizens, and which were entered into for the purpose of establishing civil rights and obligations in technical development, technology transfer, and technical consulting and services. Promulgation of the TCL signified the first time that Chinese contract law legislation permitted Chinese individuals to enter into contracts. Due to the law's intended domestic nature, however, the TCL did not apply to contracts involving a foreign

6 See *Economic Contract Law of the People's Republic of China*. An English translation is available at www.qis.net/chinalaw/prclaw19.htm.

7 See Wang Shengming, Introduction to the Contract Law of China and Important Drafts of the Contract Law, 3 (Law Publishing House, 2000).

8 See *Foreign Economic Contract Law of the People's Republic of China*. An English translation is available at www.qis.net/chinalaw/prclaw20.htm.

party, regardless of whether the foreign party was an enterprise, organization, or individual.[9] Moreover, the application of the TCL was limited to technology contracts.[10]

The enactment of the TCL marked the beginning of China's "triarchy" period of contract law legislation, in which three contract laws simultaneously operated to govern contracting in different legal areas. The concurrent operation of three contract laws caused a great deal of confusion and legal inconsistency. Prior to its adoption of the TCL, the NPC passed the 1986 General Principles of Civil Law, which contained ten articles on contracts. In 1999, the first unified Contract Law was promulgated. The Contract Law was then incorporated into the Civil Code in 2020 with modifications in both substance and structure.

By comparison, there are over 300 changes made in the Civil Code to the 1999 Contract Law, and many of them are either newly added provisions or substantive amendments to the existing rules. More specifically, the Civil Code deletes 37 articles from the 1999 Contract Law, modifies 153 articles, and adds 136 new articles. The current contract law in China is part V of the Civil Code, which contains 525 articles in total, nearly half of the total 1,260 articles of the Civil Code. With all the changes, the Civil Code is considered to further cement party autonomy in contracts.

The major changes to the Contract Law in the Civil Code include the rules of contract performance under the concept of "*obligatio*," the provisions of quasi-contract, obligations of the parties in preparing to make a contract, formation of contract by performance, status of a non-effective contract, third-party interests, green performance requirements, and electronic contracts. In addition, the Civil Code expands specific contracts from fifteen types in the 1999 Contract Law to nineteen types.

Two other changes to the 1999 Contract Law are deemed significant. First, the Civil Code formally adopts the doctrine of *Rebus Sic Stantibus* (things thus standing) pertaining to contract performance. For many years, even before the 1999 Contract Law was adopted, there had been a widespread call in the country for allowing a contractual party to be excused from performing a contract if the circumstances surrounding the contract and its execution had changed so dramatically that injustice would occur should the performance continue. Under the Civil Code, *Rebus Sic Stantibus* becomes a statutory ground for discharging the duty of performance without incurring liability to the non-performing party for breach of contract.

Second, the Civil Code establishes a rule of compulsory contracting under the state purchasing order or mandatory task. Both the state purchasing order and mandatory task were provided in the 1999 Contract Law as devices to implement state plans through the means of contract. The Civil Code makes it an obligation for

9 See *Technology Contract Law of the People's Republic of China*. An English translation of the law is available at www.qis.net/chinalaw/prclaw21.htm.

10 The Technology Contract Law was not supposed to supersede any part of the Economic Contract Law.

the parties to enter into a contract necessitated by a state purchasing order or mandatory task, or under the operation of law.

In addition, the Civil Code defines the grounds for issuing a state purchasing order or mandatory task to include rescue and disaster relief, epidemic prevention, and other needs. Moreover, in contrast to the 2009 Contract Law, the Civil Code expands those who are subject to a state purchasing order or mandatory task from a "relevant legal person or other organization" to all "relevant civil subjects," including individuals.

Through the changes and modifications, the Civil Code integrates existing contract legislation, judicial practices, and new developments into a refined legal framework that governs contract in the nation. As a civil law tradition, the provisions of contract in the Civil Code are divided into general provisions and specific provisions. The general provisions provide basic rules that govern contract formation, modification, performance, rescission and termination, breach and liability, as well as third-party interests. The specific provisions cover particular contracts, including sales, utility supplies, gifts, loans, suretyships, leases, financing leases, factoring, work-for-hire, construction projects, transportation, technology, storage, warehousing, commission/entrustment, property management services, brokerages, intermediaries, and partnerships.

Note that the Civil Code for the first time in the country adopts the quasi-contract concept in the law of contract, and contains a special section that applies specifically to quasi-contracts, referring to *negotiorum gestio* and unjust enrichment. As discussed, under article 118 of the Civil Code, a right to request fulfillment of an obligation can be created by contract, tort, *negotiorum gestio*, or unjust enrichment.[11] Pursuant to the Civil Code, in addition to contracts and torts, *negotiorum gestio* and unjust enrichment each can be an independent cause of action. For example, a person may request a return of money paid in error to another person under the provisions of unjust enrichment.

1. CONTRACT IN GENERAL

Once again, the most well-known term equivalent to "contract" in China is "*Qi Yue*." In the Chinese language, "*Qi Yue*" consists of two words: "*Qi*" and "*Yue*." "*Qi*" means "carved character," indicating a formal record of consent. "*Yue*," as noted, denotes an agreement to be bound.[12] According to Chinese legal history scholars, the term "contract" (*He Tong*) actually appeared in ancient China 2,000 years ago, but was soon replaced by the term "*Qi Yue*." At that time, a contract was regarded as a form of *Qi Yue*, and therefore, the contract itself was not a *Qi Yue*;

[11] See the Civil Code of China (2020), art. 118, available at https://english.www.gov.cn/archive/lawsregulations/202012/31/content_WS5fedad98c6d0f72576943005.html.

[12] See Liming, *supra* note 1, at 1–2.

rather, it was used as a mark or symbol evidencing the existence of the *Qi Yue* between the parties.[13] In that sense, therefore, "contract" was once translated in Chinese as "*Qi Ju*" – a certificate or written document of *Qi Yue*.

Although the concept of *Qi Yue* was used in China for many centuries, it was never clearly defined.[14] In many cases, as a normal practice, a signed *Qi Yue* would be torn in half, and each party kept a half as evidence of the agreement that existed between them. A *Qi Yue*, once made, would implicate a legal relationship under which an obligation was created.[15] In addition, when the term "*obligatio*" was initially used in the country, it was often to mean contractual obligation, referring mostly to the monetary obligation under which a debtor was responsible for paying a creditor.[16]

In modern China, the term "contract" was not used independently to refer to an agreement reached by the parties until the late 1970s, when Western contract literature was introduced into the nation. For many years before that, the term "contract," when used, was always associated with "*Qi Yue*" and thus was phrased as "*He Tong Qi Yue*" (contractual agreement). Scholars in China have debated the difference between *He Tong* (contract) and *Qi Yue* (agreement),[17] but most now believe that differentiating the terms bears no practical significance.[18]

A. *Concept of Contract*

There was no clear definition of "contract" in China until 1986, when the 1986 General Principles of Civil Law was adopted. Nonetheless, prior to 1986, a commonly held notion was that "contract in essence is an agreement." For example, the 1981 Economic Contract Law described the economic contract as "an agreement between legal persons to ascertain their mutual rights and obligations for purposes of achieving a certain economic goal."[19] This description had at least two flaws. First, it limited the purpose of a contract to the achievement of a "certain economic goal," a discernible *sequela* of the decades-long planned economy.

[13] See He Weifang, *Analytical Differentiation between "Contract" and "Agreement,"* 2 Chinese J. L. 36 (1992).

[14] In 1955 and 1956, the drafters of the proposed Civil Code tried to define "*Qi Yue*" as "an agreement made between two or more people in order to create, modify, or terminate the *obligatio* relation of right and liability." Many drafters argued against adopting this definition, however. See He Qinghua et al., An Overview of Civil Code Drafts of New China, vol. I, 175 (Law Press, 2003).

[15] See Jinfan, *supra* note 2, at 287.

[16] See Wang Jiafu, Civil Law Obligatio, 16 (Law Publishing House, 1991).

[17] Some scholars argued that "contract" refers to the meeting of minds in the same direction of the parties involved, while "agreement" means the declaration of wills between the parties, which includes a meeting of the minds but not necessarily in the same direction. See Zhou Linbing, Comparative Contract Law, 80–81 (Lanzhou University Press, 1989).

[18] See Wang Liming, Contract Law, Fundamentals and Case Analysis, 7 (People's University Publishing House, 2001).

[19] See Economic Contract Law of China (1981), *supra* note 6, art. 4.

Second, it excluded natural persons from the pool of those capable of making a contract, which rendered the Contract Law a piece of "broken" legislation.

The 1986 General Principles of Civil Law provided a formal definition of contract. Under article 85 of the 1986 General Principles of Civil Law, a contract is defined as an agreement establishing, modifying, or terminating the civil relations between the parties. Following that concept, article 2 of the 1999 Contract Law further defines a contract as an agreement establishing, modifying, or terminating the relations of civil rights and obligations between natural persons, legal persons, or other organizations of equal status. The Civil Code revises article 2 of the Contract Law and simply defines a contract as "an agreement that establishes, modifies, or terminates a civil legal relationship between persons of civil law."[20]

Under the Civil Code definition, a contract generally contains the following legal characteristics: (a) a "civil legal act" performed by civil law persons, including natural persons, legal persons, and other organizations of equal status; (b) a mutual consent manifesting the will of the parties to be bound by what they mutually consented to; and (c) an agreement that creates, modifies, or terminates a legal relationship between the parties concerning their civil rights and obligations.

As a "civil legal act," a contract signifies the parties' expression of their will for civil and economic benefits. In the meantime, the contract must serve a lawful purpose. Scholars in China try to differentiate a "legal act" from a "de facto act." In their view, a "legal act" is premised on the expectation of actors (parties) and produces anticipated results, while a "*de facto* act" does not lead to any mutually expected outcomes. Therefore, a contract, as a legal act, requires the mutual assent of parties. By contrast, a "*de facto* act," such as a tort or an act resulting in unjust enrichment, does not demand such mutuality.[21]

To qualify as an enforceable contract, the agreement reached by the parties must serve a lawful purpose. Thus, only if the expression of the will of the parties is made for a lawful purpose, without violating any law or social morals, may a contract so concluded become binding and enforceable. For this reason, a contract is also described as a "lawful civil act." If an agreement is made for the purpose of achieving an illegal goal, that agreement, despite being based on "mutual consent" or "expression of wills," does not have the binding effect of a contract.

Since a contract is a civil legal act, all participants in such an act shall be equal regardless of their respective statuses. As noted, under the equality principle set forth in the Civil Code, all persons of civil law are equal in their legal status when conducting civil activities.[22] As applied to contracts, the equality principle is meant to uphold an idea that a contract is the result of free bargaining, without coercion or

[20] See the 2020 Civil Code, *supra* note 11, art. 464.

[21] See Wang Liming, Study on Contract Law, 7–14 (People's University Press, 2002); see also Jiafu, *supra* note 16, at 15–18.

[22] See the 2020 Civil Code, *supra* note 11, art. 4.

fear on the basis of social or other status, between the parties. Equal status is vitally important, particularly in contract dispute cases where a governmental entity is involved. In such cases, equal status ensures that the governmental entity and the private party are treated in the same manner and to the same extent.

Most Chinese contract scholars describe American contract law as a typical common law contract system where a contract is defined as "a promise or a set of promises."[23] They believe that the defining distinction in contract theory between civil law and common law systems is that a contract is promise-based in a common law system, while it is agreement-based in a civil law system.[24] From the viewpoint of Chinese contract law scholars, a "promise" is not a mutual act, and it, at least on its face, does not necessarily require mutual assent. Chinese contract law does not focus on "why a promise or a set of promises should be enforced," but rather emphasizes "what constitutes an agreement and how an agreement should be enforced." Also, as discussed, a contract in China is generally regarded as an act to create, modify, or terminate civil relations through an agreement between the parties.[25]

But note that under article 464 of the Civil Code, an agreement on establishing such personal a relationship as marriage, adoption, guardianship, or the like shall be governed by the provisions of law regulating such relationship. Only in the absence of the applicable provisions may the contract provisions of the Civil Code be applied mutatis mutandis according to the nature of the agreement as such. In addition, labor contracts remain outside the realm of the contract law provided in the Civil Code. Although labor contracts are subject to the general principles of civil law, they are governed separately and specifically by the Labor Contract Law and other regulations applicable to labor and employment relationships. Under article 11 of the Civil Code, if other laws have special provisions on civil relations, those provisions shall apply.[26]

B. Obligatio *and Contractual Relationship*

As noted, in Chinese contract law, an important concept that defines the contractual relationship between the parties is "*obligatio*." Again, the *obligatio* represents a legal relationship in which one party (obligor) is obligated to the other (obligee). An "*obligatio*" that is created by an agreement of the parties is known as a contract. Under the agreement-based *obligatio*, an obligee (creditor) has the right to request an obligor (debtor) perform the obligor's obligation, and an obligor (debtor) is liable for a failure to fulfill what the obligor has promised to an obligee (creditor) under a contract.

[23] The Restatement defines a "contract" as "a promise or a set of promises for the breach of which the law gives a remedy, or performance of which the law in some way recognizes as a duty." *Restatement (Second) of Contracts* § 1 (Am. L. Inst., 1981).

[24] See Jiafu, *supra* note 16, at 254–258.

[25] See Li Guoguang, Explanation and Application of the Contract Law, 11 (Xinghua Press, 1999).

[26] See the 2020 Civil Code, *supra* note 11, art. 11.

a. Theory of *Obligatio*

In the civil law system, the term "*obligatio*," a Roman law concept alien to many common law lawyers, is commonly used to refer to both rights and obligations in civil aspects. In the Institutes of Justinian, the sixth-century codification of Roman law ordered by the Byzantine emperor Justinian I, "*obligatio*" was characterized as "a bond of law by which we are under a necessity of releasing (*solvendae*) something according to the laws of our state."[27] Roman jurist Gaius divided "*obligationes*" into three major categories based on their origin, including obligations *ex contractu* (obligations arising out of contracts), ex delicto (obligations incurred in torts), and *ex variis causarum figuris* (obligations by other causes or an unclassifiable miscellaneous group).[28] The *ex variis causarum figuris* was understood to contain *obligationes quasi ex contractu* (quasi-contractual obligations) and *quasi ex delicto* (quasi-delictual obligations).[29]

Today, in countries with a civil law tradition, civil obligations are generally classified into contractual obligations and non-contractual obligations. The former deals with consensual obligations, and the latter covers non-consensual obligations. Conceptually, non-contractual obligations are further classified into obligations that arise out of tort and non-tort obligations. Non-tort obligations refer to, particularly, unjust enrichment and *negotiorum gestio* (agency without due authority). In addition, there also developed a doctrine of *culpa in contrahendo* (faulty in contract negotiating) to impose a liability arising out of contract negotiations prior to the formation of the contract.

b. *Obligatio* in Chinese Civil Legislation

Compared with previous contract law legislation, a distinction of the Civil Code is that it incorporates the concept of *obligatio* into contract and equips the law of contract with the function of *obligatio* so as to establish primary rules that govern the legal relationship arising from *obligatio*. The Civil Code rules not only govern contractual relationships but also apply through a reference clause to non-contractual relationships. The idea is to maintain the entirety of *obligatio* while making the law of contract the center of *obligatio*. Note that unlike civil legislation in other countries, the Civil Code in China is not structured so as to place both contractual and non-contractual obligations under the umbrella of *obligatio*.

Obligatio as a legal concept was first introduced to China in the late nineteenth century. As noted, it formed part of the 1907 *Qing* draft Civil Code. Since then, the

[27] See Thomas C. Sanders, The Institute of Justinian, 319 (7th ed., The Lawbook Exchange Ltd., 1917); see also William Smith, A Dictionary of Greek and Roman Antiquities, 817–821 (John Murray, London, 1875).

[28] See Smith, *supra* note 27, at 818; see also Max Radin, *The Roman Law of Quasi-Contract*, 23 Va. L. Rev. 241, 242 (1937).

[29] See Smith, *supra* note 27.

term *obligatio* has been widely accepted in China and has become an important system regulating civil rights and obligations in the country. In Chinese civil law, *obligatio* serves as the legal basis that separates creditor's rights from property rights and determines the cause of action as to whether a particular claim is a matter of obligation or an issue of the right to things.

In the 1986 General Principles of Civil Law, *obligatio* was defined as "a relationship of specific rights and duties between parties, arising either from terms of a contract or by the operation of law."[30] Under that definition, the party who enjoys a right is the obligee, while the party who bears the duty is the obligor. In the relationship arising out of obligatio, the obligee has the right to demand that the obligor perform his/her duty according to the terms of the contract or the provision of law. Thus, an *obligatio*, as defined in the 1986 General Principles of Civil Law, includes both creditor's rights and debtor's obligations.

As discussed, in contrast to the property right, which is a right against anyone, *obligatio* mainly refers to the relationship between specific parties. By "specific," it refers to a civil relationship that focuses primarily on the debtor or obligor. In other words, in order to realize the creditor's right, the debtor must be specific. The underlying theory is that the *obligatio* creates a right to make a claim against a specific person. Therefore, the satisfaction of a creditor's right depends on fulfillment of the obligation that requires the obligor's action.

The Civil Code structures the law of both contractual and non-contractual obligations under the concept of *obligatio*. As noted, under article 118 of the Civil Code, the right arising from *obligatio* is the right of an obligee or creditor to request a specific obligor to or not to engage in certain performance, as arising from a contract, a tortious act, *negotiorum gestio*, unjust enrichment, or another provision of the law.[31]

Article 118 of the Civil Code is a replica of article 118 of the 2017 General Provisions of Civil Law (GPCL), where the *obligatio* was provided primarily from the perspective of the creditor's right. Also, similar to the 1986 General Principles of Civil Law, the Civil Code makes the agreement and the operation of law two legal sources of *obligatio*. One refers to contracts, while the other includes torts, unjust enrichment, and *negotiorum gestio*. Note, however, that under the Civil Code, both unjust enrichment and *negotiorum gestio* are provided under quasi-contracts, which are covered by the law of contracts.

c. *Obligatio* under the Civil Code

In the Civil Code, the *obligatio* is further divided into selective *obligatio* and joint *obligatio* when more than two obligees/creditors or debtors/obligors are involved in

[30] See the General Principles of Civil Law, adopted in 1986, art. 84, available at www.npc.gov.cn/zgrdw/englishnpc/Law/2007-12/12/content_1383941.htm.

[31] See the 2020 Civil Code, *supra* note 11, art. 118.

an *obligatio* relationship. The selective *obligatio* refers to the *obligatio* in which there are two or more subject matters of obligation and the obligor may choose to perform any of them to satisfy the creditor's rights. According to article 515 of the Civil Code, when an obligation has multiple subject matters and the debtor only needs to perform one of them, the debtor has the right to choose which to perform unless otherwise provided by law, agreed upon by the parties, or specified by transaction practices.[32]

If, however, the party who has the right to choose does not make a choice within the agreed upon time limit or before the expiry of the performance time period, and fails to choose within a reasonable time limit after being urged, the right to choose shifts to the other party. When making a choice, the party is required to provide timely notice. Under article 516 of the Civil Code, when a party exercises its right to choose, a timely notice should be provided to the other party, and only if the notification reaches the other party will the subject matter to be performed be ascertained. Once ascertained, the targeted subject matter for performance should not be changed unless agreed to by the other party. However, if any of the subject matters available for choice become impossible to fulfill under certain circumstances, the party with the right to choose shall not choose the impossible subject matter unless the impossible situation is caused by the other party.[33]

Joint *obligatio* includes joint *obligatio* and joint and several *obligatio*. Under the Civil Code, a joint *obligatio* may refer to either joint creditors' rights or joint debtors' liability. In cases where there are more than two creditors and the subject matter involved can be divided, the creditors' right will be the joint creditors' right if the right of each of the creditors is based on the portion to which the creditor is entitled.[34] On the other hand, if there are two or more debtors, and each of the debtors is liable for a part of the debts, the debtors will be joint debtors or debtors with joint liability. For both joint creditors and joint debtors, if the portions of credits or debts among the creditors or debtors are difficult to identify, they each will be deemed to have an equal portion.[35]

A joint and several *obligatio* covers the "one for all" situation. As provided in article 518 of the Civil Code, if there are two or more creditors, and some or all of the creditors can request the debtor to perform the debt, the creditors' right will be considered joint and several. Likewise, if there are two or more debtors, and the creditor can request that some or all of the debtors perform the entire debt, the debtors bear joint and several debt liability. Under article 518, the joint and several creditors' right or debtors' liability may only be created by operation of law or by agreement of the parties.[36]

[32] See *id.*, art. 515.
[33] See *id.*, art. 516.
[34] See *id.*, art. 517.
[35] See *id.*, art. 518.
[36] See *id.*

The complexity in joint and several *obligatio* lies with the determination of indemnity between or among joint and several creditors or debtors. Pursuant to article 519 of the Civil Code, a joint and several debtor who assumes more than their own share of debt shall have the right to recover the excess portion from the other joint and several debtors within their unfulfilled share and enjoy the rights of the creditor accordingly. But the joint and several debtors' exercise of that right shall not harm the interests of the creditor. The defense available to the other joint and several debtors against the creditor may be claimed against the joint and several debtor who sues to recover the excess portion. If, however, a joint and several debtor against whom the indemnity is sought is unable to perform its portion of debt, the other joint and several debtors shall share it proportionally.[37]

With regard to joint and several debtors, the Civil Code also contains the rules that govern the allocation of liability in different situations. First, if some of the joint and several debtors perform so as to offset the debts or deposit the subject matter of debts, the debts of other debtors to the creditor shall be extinguished correspondingly and those joint and several debtors may recover from the other debtors. Second, if the debts of some joint and several debtors are forgiven by the creditors, the debts of other debtors to the creditors shall be eliminated within the scope of the liability shares that such joint and several debtors should bear. Third, when the debts of certain joint and several debtors and the creditor's rights are combined and belong to the same person, the creditor's rights to other debtors continue to exist after deducting the debtor's share combined.

In addition, the Civil Code requires that a joint and several creditor who actually receives payment based on the creditor's rights repay other joint and several creditors in proportion to their creditors' rights. If the actual shares of creditors' rights are difficult to ascertain, the joint and several creditors shall be deemed to have equal shares. The same rule also applies to joint and several debtors. The portion of the debts among the joint and several debtors will be considered equal if the actual portion for each debtor is unable to be determined.

Also, under article 520 of the Civil Code, if the creditor's acceptance of the payment made by some of the joint and several debtors is delayed, the legal effect of such delay shall be applicable to other joint and several debtors.[38] The idea is that when the debtor is fulfilling the obligation to pay, the creditor's delay in acceptance may cause loss to the debtor. It then would be unfair to have the debtor bear the loss resulting from the delay by the creditor.

Since the purpose of establishing joint and several debts is to realize the creditor's right, when the creditor accepts the full performance from a joint and several debtor, the debt liability of all joint and several debtors will be discharged. If, however, the creditor delays in accepting performance, it will affect not only the performing

[37] See *id.*, art. 519.

[38] See *id.*, art. 520.

debtor but also other debtors who are jointly and severally liable for the debt. Therefore, in its delay in accepting performance, the creditor should be responsible for possible loss incurred to both the joint and several debtor fulfilling the obligation and other joint and several debtors involved.

C. *Preliminary Contract*

A notable feature of contract law under the Civil Code is the concept of preliminary contract that makes the parties' agreement to enter into a contract a contractual obligation. Under article 495 of the Civil Code, the agreement by the parties to execute a contract within a certain period of time in the future, in the form of subscription, form of orders, form of reservation, and the like, constitutes a preliminary contract[39] – an agreement to enter into a contract or an agreement to agree. The legal effect of the agreement as such creates an obligation to make a contract between the parties. Therefore, as article 495 provides, if one of the parties fails to perform the obligation to make the contract as promised, the other party may hold him/her liable for breach of the preliminary agreement.

Previously, the obligation arising from a preliminary agreement to contract was handled under pre-contractual liability. Pursuant to article 42 of the 2009 Contract Law, a party shall be liable for losses caused to the other party if, during the formation of the contract, it (a) disguises and pretends to conclude a contract and negotiates in bad faith; (b) deliberately conceals the important facts relating to the conclusion of the contract or purposefully provides false information; or (c) engages in other acts in violation of the principle of good faith.[40]

In its 2012 Interpretation on the Issues Involving Application of Law in Adjudicating Disputes over sales contracts, the Supreme People's Court (SPC) for the first time used the term "preliminary contract" to describe pre-contractual obligations arising during contract negotiation.[41] According to the SPC, when the parties sign a preliminary contract – such as a letter to prescribe, letter of order, letter of booking, letter of intent, or memorandum – under which they agree to conclude a contract of sales at a specified time in the future, and one party fails to fulfill the obligation to enter into the contract, the other party may bring a suit against him/her for breach of preliminary contract or for rescission of preliminary contract and seek compensation for damages.[42]

Compared with the SPC's interpretation, article 495 of the Civil Code more directly defines the preliminary contract and emphasizes the liability for the breach

[39] See the 2020 Civil Code, *supra* note 11, art. 495.
[40] See 1999 Contract Law, art. 42, available at www.asianlii.org/cn/legis/cen/laws/clotproc376/.
[41] See the SPC, *Interpretation on the Issues Concerning Application of Law in Adjudicating Disputes over Sales Contracts*, issued on May 10, 2012, available at www.64365.com/zs/671442.aspx.
[42] See *id.*, art. 2.

of such a contract. But in substance, both the SPC's interpretation and article 495 of the Civil Code are premised on the view that the preliminary contract is a mutually independent contract from the main contract, and that the liability for breach of the preliminary contract is not based on negligence but rather an independent contractual obligation.

Article 495 of the Civil Code is significant because it extends the preliminary contract obligation to all contracts and creates a statutory claim by which a party may be held liable for failure to perform. As a practical matter, when making a promise to enter into a contract in a certain written form during negotiations, the parties may subject themselves to contractual liability if they fail to reach the final deal. Put differently, article 495 of the Civil Code provides a legal ground on which a party may make a claim against the other party for breach of preliminary contract under this circumstance.

In practice, however, debates remain as to whether the letter of intent or memorandum may constitute a preliminary contract. According to the SPC, as a type of contract, a preliminary contract should have the essential elements forming a contract – that is, the content is specific and definite and the parties intend to be bound by it. Thus, since the letter of intent or memorandum normally only indicates that the parties intend to enter into a contract, it does not constitute a preliminary contract. However, if the letter of intent or memorandum is specific enough to contain essential elements of a contract, it will be deemed as a preliminary contract.

More specifically, the SPC is of the opinion that a preliminary contract shall be deemed to have concluded in the situation where the parties agree to conclude a contract within a certain period of time in the form of a subscription letter, order book, reservation letter, etc., or pay a deposit to guarantee the conclusion of a contract within a certain period of time in the future, and the contents such as parties and subject matter, etc., of the contract to be concluded in the future can be ascertained.[43] But if the parties only express their intention to make a deal by signing a letter of intent or memorandum, etc., without agreeing to conclude a contract within a certain period of time in the future, or although there is an agreement, it is difficult to determine the parties and subject matter of the contract to be concluded in the future, no preliminary contract shall be considered to have been formed.[44]

Nevertheless, if the subscription letter, order, or reservation form signed by the parties contains their consent on the main contents of the contract, such as the subject matter, quantity, price, or remuneration, so as to meet the conditions for the conclusion of the contract, a preliminary contract shall be held to have been

[43] See the SPC, *Interpretation on Several Issues Concerning Application of the Provisions of Contract in the Civil Code*, December 4, 2023, art. 6, available at www.court.gov.cn/fabu/xiangqing/419382.html (hereinafter referred to as 2023 *Interpretation on Contract Provisions*).

[44] See *id.*

established even though there is an absence of the parties' clear agreement to conclude the contract separately within a certain period of time in the future, or there is an agreement, but one party has performed and the other party has accepted the performance.[45]

Moreover, pursuant to the SPC, after a preliminary contract takes effect, if one party refuses to conclude the contract or violates the principle of good faith when negotiating to conclude the contract, resulting in failure to conclude the contract, the party shall be held liable for breach of the preliminary contract. In determining whether a party has violated the principle of good faith when negotiating and concluding the contract, a court shall take into consideration such factors as whether the terms or conditions proposed by the party during the contract negotiation clearly deviate from the contents of the preliminary contract, and whether reasonable efforts have been made to negotiate.[46]

The SPC also holds that if one party fails to perform its obligations in entering into a contract as required under the preliminary contract, the other party may request compensation for the resulting losses. The compensation shall be determined as agreed by the parties if there is an agreement between them. Absent such agreement, the compensation shall be assessed by the court in consideration of the factors such as the completeness of the contents of the preliminary contract and the level at which the conditions for entering into the contract are met.[47]

Another issue that often causes dispute is whether a form of subscription, order, or reservation may have the effect of preliminary contract if there is lack of required signatures by the parties. Since a written form is required, signatures by parties must be affixed to the form in order for a preliminary contract to be found. But in cases where a deposit for the future conclusion of a contract has been paid, a preliminary contract will be deemed to have been established between the parties even though a party or the parties failed to sign the form.

D. *Quasi-Contracts*

Quasi-contract is a new system in the law of contract under the Civil Code. As a legal concept, quasi-contract is not a native product of China. Historically, quasi-contract originated from the Roman concept of *obligationes quasi ex contractu* (quasi-contractual obligations).[48] Due to the fact that it was not a mutually agreed obligation, quasi-contract was considered as a statutory obligation resting not upon the consent of the parties.[49] Now, in American contract law theory, quasi-contract is

45 See *id.*
46 The SPC, the 2023 *Interpretation on Contract Provisions*, *supra* note 43, art. 7.
47 See *id.*, art. 8.
48 See Smith, *supra* note 27, at 819.
49 See William Keener, *Quasi Contract, Its Nature and Scope*, 7 Harv. L. Rev. 57, 68 (1893).

used as a synonym of contract implied in law, meaning that it is not really a contract at all but a legal fiction.[50]

The Civil Code provides no definition of quasi-contract. Instead, it divides quasi-contract into two categories: *negotiorum gestio* and unjust enrichment. In many other countries, both *negotiorum gestio* and unjust enrichment are considered non-contractual obligations, and each of them is an independent source of *obligatio* by the operation of law.[51] In China, however, they are grouped together under quasi-contract and constitute part of the law of contract, although many believe that they are not the obligation arising from contract.[52]

Under article 979 of the Civil Code, *negotiorum gestio* occurs where a person without statutory or consensual obligations manages the affairs of others in order to avoid loss in the interests of others.[53] In case of *negotiorum gestio*, the managing person may request the beneficiary repay the necessary expenses incurred in the management of affairs, and if the managing person suffers losses due to the affair management, he/she may request the beneficiary to make appropriate compensation.[54]

Article 979 also contains certain requirements for the managing person in order to make *negotiorum gestio* actionable for compensation. First, the management of affairs must conform to the real intention of the beneficiary, unless the real intention of the beneficiary violates the law or public order and good morals.[55] Second, the methods used to manage the affairs of others shall be beneficial to the beneficiary, and the managing work may not be interrupted if that interruption is detrimental to the beneficiary.[56] Third, whenever possible, the beneficiary shall be promptly notified of the managed affairs. If the managed affairs need not be dealt with urgently, the managing person shall wait for the instruction from the beneficiary.[57] And fourth, after the managing work is complete, the managing person shall report

[50] See Edward A. Farnsworth, Contract, 101 (3rd ed., Aspen, 1999); Jeff Ferriell, Understanding Contracts, 4 (2nd ed., LexisNexis, 2009); David Epstein et al., Making and Doing Deals: Contracts in Context, 955 (LexisNexis, 2006). For general discussion of quasi contract as used in the common law system, *see* Timothy Sullivan, *The Concept of Benefit in the Law of Quasi Contract*, 64 Geo. L.J. 1 (1975).

[51] Under the 2007 EU Regulation on the Law Applicable to Non-Contractual Obligations, for example, *negotiorum gestio* and unjust enrichment, together with torts and *culpa in contrahendo* (pre-contractual liability), are categorized as non-contractual obligations. See Regulation (EC) 864/2007, 2007 O.J. (L 199/40).

[52] See Shen Weixing, Civil Law, 500, 508 (Peking University Press, 2013) (where *negotiorum gestio* and unjust enrichment are termed statutory *obligatio* in contrast to the contractual *obligatio*). *See also*Cui Jianyuan et al., General Theory of Civil Law, 283, 315 (Tsinghua University Press, 2019).

[53] See 2020 Civil Code, *supra* note 11, art. 979.

[54] See *id.*

[55] See *id.*

[56] See *id.*, art. 981.

[57] See *id.*, art. 982.

to the beneficiary on the status of the managed affairs, and any property acquired during the affair management shall be timely transferred to the beneficiary.[58]

Unjust enrichment in the United States is viewed basically as an equitable principle under which restitution is sought in order to prevent a person from being enriched at the expense of another.[59] Although the debates on how unjust enrichment should be defined and applied never rested at ease over the development of the concept, the most recent contract law literature has interpreted unjust enrichment as an "enrichment that lacks adequate legal basis."[60] The legal basis in this context is understood to refer to such legal sources as contracts, trusts, gifts, and so on.[61] In many cases, the discussion of unjust enrichment is closely related to quasi-contract.[62]

In China, like many other civil law countries, unjust enrichment is a statutory claim. Under article 92 of the 1986 General Principles of Civil Law, unjust enrichment refers to the benefits that are acquired improperly and without a legal basis. In case of unjust enrichment, restitution shall be made if the enrichment results in loss to the other party.[63] The Civil Code follows the provision of article 92 of the 1986 General Principles of Civil Law but makes certain exceptions to the restitution.

In accordance with article 985 of the Civil Code, no restitution shall be granted if (a) a payment is made to fulfill moral obligations; (b) repayment of debts is made before maturity; and (c) a debt repayment is made with knowledge that there is no obligation to pay.[64] The rationale underlying article 985 is that in any of those three situations, no unjust enrichment occurs. Article 985 then constitutes a legal basis on which the receipt of payments is justified. In the first situation, for example, if a payment is made to support elder relatives, no restitution is allowed on the basis of unjust enrichment due to moral obligations.

In addition, the Civil Code sets forth three particular rules on restitution in case of unjust enrichment. The first one is the non-return rule. Pursuant to article 986, if a recipient does not know and should not have known that the benefits obtained have no legal basis, and the benefits obtained no longer exist, the recipient has no obligation to return the benefits.[65] The second rule is the rule of compensation. In accordance with article 987, if a recipient knows or should have known that the benefits obtained have no legal basis, the person who has suffered losses may request the recipient to return the benefits obtained and to compensate for the losses under

58 See *id.*, art. 983.
59 See Farnsworth, *supra* note 50, at 103.
60 See HLR, *The Intellectual History of Unjust Enrichment*, 133 Harv. L. Rev. 2077, 2099 (2020).
61 See *id.*
62 See Epstein et al., *supra* note 50, at 956–998.
63 See the 1986 General Principles of Civil Law, *supra* note 30, art. 92.
64 See 2020 Civil Code, *supra* note 11, art. 985.
65 See *id.*, art. 986.

the law.[66] The third rule is the rule of claim against third parties. It is provided in article 988 that if the recipient has transferred the benefits obtained to a third party gratis, the person who has suffered losses may request the third party to bear the obligation of return to the corresponding extent.[67]

2. FORMATION OF CONTRACTS

Formation of a contract requires mutual assent between the parties. Under the 1999 Contract Law, to form a contract, mutual assent between the parties is required, and that mutual assent is manifested and materialized through offer and acceptance.[68] The Civil Code expands contract formation to include "other means" in addition to offer and acceptance. The Civil Code does not specify what constitutes "other means." In a scholarly interpretation, "other means" refers to a process in which a contract is formed in cases where there is either lack of a clear external form of offer and acceptance or no identifiable process of offer and acceptance can be ascertained.

It seems difficult to understand how a contract could be made without offer and acceptance because offer and acceptance manifest the mutual assent of the parties. But the Civil Code appears to try to avoid unwanted debates or disputes over the finding of offer and acceptance in certain contracts and attempts to provide a more practical way than the conventional offer–acceptance scheme to ascertain the existence of a contract. The concept is that the "other means" could serve as a useful device to help prescribe and maintain a contractual relationship that would otherwise be uncertain between the parties.

Nevertheless, the formation of a contract is generally made through a process of offer and acceptance. It is important to note that like in other civil law countries, contract formation in China does not require consideration, a key element for making a binding contract in common law systems. Therefore, a contract under Chinese law is normally formed when the acceptance to an offer takes effect.

A. *Offer*

Formation of a contract begins with an offer. In article 472 of the Civil Code, an offer is defined as "a manifestation of intent showing the desire to enter into a contract with others."[69] Under this definition, there are two elements that an offer must contain: (a) manifestation of intent and (b) desire to make a contract with

66 See *id.*, art. 987.
67 See *id.*, art. 988.
68 See the 1999 Contract Law, *supra* note 40, art. 13.
69 See the 2020 Civil Code, *supra* note 11, art. 472. In comparison, under article 14 of the 1999 Contract Law, offer was defined as "a proposal hoping to enter into a contract with other party." See *id.*, art. 14.

others. In addition, to constitute an offer, the intent manifested must meet two requirements that are set forth in article 472: (a) the contents must be concrete and definite and (b) the offeror must be bound by his/her manifestation of intent upon acceptance by the offeree.[70]

"Concrete and definite" mainly involves the certainty of the offer. To be certain, an offer must contain the contents necessary for making a contract. The Civil Code does not specify the essential contents of a contract, but provides a list of contents that are generally included in a contract. According to article 470 of the Civil Code, the contents of a contract shall be agreed by the parties, which include in general (a) name or designation and domicile of each party; (b) subject matters; (c) quantity; (d) quality; (e) price or remuneration; (f) time period, place, and manner of performance; (g) default liability; and (h) dispute resolution.[71]

To be binding, the offeror's manifestation of intent must be made either orally or in writing to the offeree. The Civil Code is not explicit whether the offeree should be a specific person. The majority opinion in China, however, favors the "specific person" requirement, though the person specified need not necessarily be just one person. An underlying reason is that, unless the offeree is specific, it would be hard to predict who is the intended person to whom the offer is made. In addition, if an offer is allowed to be made to a non-specific person, it may result in a situation where the offeror faces multiple contracts if acceptances are made by several non-specific persons that are unknown to the offeror.[72]

a. Invitation for an Offer

Under the Civil Code, an offer is "a manifestation of intent." However, not every manifestation of intent constitutes an offer. To become an offer, manifestation must be made to the effect that it is understood by the other party that the intent so manifested is to ask for a deal. If a party's manifestation of intent does not clearly indicate that the party is intending to make a contract, or if it is simply to pass on business information or to advertise products or services, the manifestation will not be considered an offer.

A manifestation of intent that is not sufficient to constitute an offer is often labeled as an invitation for an offer. Article 473 of the Civil Code defines an invitation for an offer as a manifestation of intent indicating a desire to receive offers from others. According to article 473, an invitation for an offer includes an auction announcement, bidding announcement, stock prospectus, bond prospectus, fund prospectus, commercial advertisement and promotion, mailed price catalog, and the like. But as

[70] See 2020 Civil Code, *supra* note 11, art. 472.
[71] See *id.*, art. 470.
[72] See Liming, *supra* note 21, at 208–209.

an exception, a commercial advertisement or promotion would constitute an offer if its content meets the requirements for an offer.[73]

A long-debated issue is whether a reward advertisement constitutes an offer. One argument considers reward advertisement as unilateral act, while another argument deems it an offer made to an unspecified person. In its 2009 Interpretations on Contract Law, the SPC recognizes the legal effect of a reward made to the public. According to the SPC, when the offeror of a reward publicly announces an offer to pay a person who has performed certain acts, and then that person completes the act and requests the payment, the People's Court shall grant the request, unless fraud, coercion, or other illegality is involved.[74] Apparently, the SPC regards a reward advertisement as an offer to form a reward contract.

The Civil Code recognizes the enforceability of the reward offer without specifying its nature. In accordance with article 499 of the Civil Code, when a person promises via public announcement to pay a reward to anyone who has completed a particular act, the person who has completed the act may request payment from the former.[75] It is through article 499 that the Civil Code brings the reward into the domain of contracts, and provides the person who has performed the act sought by the reward with the right to make a claim.

b. Effectiveness of an Offer

An issue concerning offers is when an offer takes effect. As a general rule, an offer, once made, is not effective until it is received. Under article 137 of the Civil Code, an offer may take effect in several ways: (a) when an offer is made orally, it becomes effective from the time the offeree is aware of it; (b) if an offer is made in writing, it takes effect at the time it reaches the offeree; and (c) in the case where an offer is made electronically, it becomes effective when such a data message enters that system, or at the time the offeree knows or should have known that the data message has entered the system if the data-receiving system is not specifically designated, unless the parties have agreed otherwise.[76]

An offer can be withdrawn before it reaches the offeree. As noted, pursuant to article 141 of the Civil Code, an expression of intent can be withdrawn when the notice of withdrawal reaches the other party prior to or at the same time the other party receives the expression of intent. Since an offer is an expression of intent, a withdrawal of it is permissible before the offer takes effect. The Civil Code contains no specific requirement for the formality of withdrawal of an offer, but the

[73] See the 2020 Civil Code, *supra* note 11, art. 473.

[74] See the SPC, *Interpretation on Several Issues Concerning the Application of the Contract Law* (2), issued on April 24, 2009, art. 3, available at http://gongbao.court.gov.cn/Details/7100a86f0aec21e6f9eb6c813cd081.html (2009 Contract Interpretation).

[75] See the 2020 Civil Code, *supra* note 11, art. 499.

[76] See *id.*, art. 137.

withdrawal, if intended, must be made timely. The key element is the offeree's knowledge of the withdrawal notice prior to acceptance.

An offer, once effective, may not be withdrawn but can be revoked. Revocation is an act to cancel an effective offer before the offer is accepted. Since a contract is a voluntary engagement, any offer can be revoked unless it is irrevocable. According to article 476 of the Civil Code, an offer is revocable unless (a) the offeror has explicitly indicated that the offer is irrevocable by specifying a time limit for acceptance or in any other manner; or (b) the offeree has reasons to believe that the offer is irrevocable and has made reasonable preparations for performing the contract.[77]

The Civil Code does not require the revocation of an offer to be made in a manner comparable to the way the offer was made. Instead, article 477 of the Civil Code simply provides that to be effective, an expression of intent to revoke the offer, if made by way of conversation, shall be known to the offeree before the offeree makes an acceptance, or shall reach the offeree prior to acceptance if made in another form. In both situations, the revocation of an offer is effective only when the offeree is informed of the revocation before acceptance.[78]

c. Voidance of an Offer

An offer, though effectively made, may become null and void. A void offer means that the offer has lost its legal effect and the offeree's power to accept the offer no longer exists. Therefore, when an offer is null and void, it is terminated. A terminated offer produces no contract, so its acceptance, even if timely made, does not result in a contract. Simply put, the voidance of an offer deprives the offeree of the power or ability to accept the offer.

As stipulated in the Civil Code, there are certain situations in which the effect of an offer will be adversely affected. Under article 487 of the Civil Code, an offer becomes invalid under any of the following circumstances: (a) the offer is rejected, (b) the offer is legally revoked, (c) the offeree makes no acceptance prior to the expiration of the time limit for acceptance, or (d) the offeree has materially altered the contents of the offer. An invalid offer invites no acceptance.

Rejection of an offer means that the offeree declines the offer or does not accept the terms and conditions stated in the offer. Since article 137 of the Civil Code requires a notice either through conversation or by other means to effectuate an expression of intent, it is generally believed that rejection of an offer must be made expressly. In addition, because a rejection, if made in a form other than conversation, takes effect only after it has reached the offeror under article 137, some scholars argue that a rejection may be withdrawn before or at the same time the offeror receives the rejection notice.

[77] See *id.*, art. 476.

[78] See *id.*, art. 477.

A revocation of an offer also brings the offer to an end. As discussed, under article 477 of the Civil Code, an offer may be revoked before the offeree's acceptance unless the offer is irrevocable. Upon revocation, an offer becomes null and void. An acceptance made after the offer is effectively revoked will not constitute an acceptance but a new offer. Thus, when "after revocation" acceptance is made, the offeree takes the place of the offeror, and acceptance of the new offer falls into the hands of the former offeror.

A lapse of time in accepting an offer terminates the offer if the offer has specified a time limit for acceptance. For the purposes of article 478 of the Civil Code, the offeree's failure to accept the offer within the allowed time period will be deemed a rejection of the offer.[79] Note, however, that like many other civil law countries, China applies the "arrival rule" rather than the "mailbox rule" to acceptance in the context of the formation of a contract. Then, it is essential that the acceptance reaches the offeror before the expiration date of the offer.

Material alteration is a substantial change to the term or content of the offer. Under article 488 of the Civil Code, any material alteration to the content of the offer constitutes a new offer. Article 488 defines a material change as a change concerning the subject matter, the quantity, quality, price or remuneration, time period of performance, place and manner of performance, default liability, the methods of dispute resolution, or the like.[80] When a material alteration is made to an offer, the offeree's power to accept the offer is terminated.

B. *Acceptance*

The concept of acceptance is provided in article 479 of the Contract Law, which defines acceptance as an expression of intent of the offeree to accept an offer.[81] Again, in China, both offer and acceptance are the expression of intent to make a deal. Since a contract is a mutual agreement, it is important that the intent of one party is expressed to the other party in the way legally required, and the acceptance must match the offer in order for a contract to be formed. Under Chinese law, a valid acceptance results in the conclusion of a contract and no consideration is needed. In addition, for certain contracts, their effectiveness is contingent upon administrative approval after they are formed.

a. Requirements for an Acceptance

Pursuant to article 479, acceptance signifies that the offeree agrees to the terms and conditions contained in the offer and wants to enter into a contract with the offeror

79 See *id.*, art. 478.
80 See *id.*, art. 488.
81 See *id.*, art. 479.

accordingly. Article 483 further provides that a contract is concluded at the time acceptance takes effect, unless otherwise provided by the law or agreed by the parties.[82] Under the Civil Code, an effective acceptance must meet the following requirements.

1. ARRIVAL RULE. The first requirement is the "arrival" requirement. In contrast to the "mailbox" rule that governs acceptance under the common law system, China follows the "arrival rule" under which an acceptance takes effect upon arrival in the place of the offeror. In general, an acceptance should be made by means of notice. Acceptance can also be made through conduct under certain circumstances.

As provided in article 480, if there exists a transaction practice or if the offer allows the acceptance to be made through an act or conduct, the performance of such act will then constitute an acceptance.[83] Under article 484, when an acceptance is made by means of notice, it takes effect when the other party knows of the contents of the acceptance in the case of conversation, or becomes effective when the acceptance reaches the offeror in all other cases.[84] If, however, notice is not required, the acceptance becomes effective when an act of acceptance is performed according to the parties' course of dealing or as indicated by the offer.[85]

Timely arrival of an acceptance notice is an important factor in the application of the "Arrival Rule." Article 481 of the Civil Code requires that an acceptance reach the offeror within the time limit specified in the offer in order for the acceptance to take effect. If, however, no time limit for acceptance is specified in the offer, the acceptance shall be made promptly if the offer is made via conversation or shall reach the offeror within a reasonable period of time if the offer is made in any other form.[86]

The Civil Code does not define what a reasonable period of time is. In their determination, courts often look to industrial usages or transaction customs, previous dealings, or the nature of a particular business.

The Civil Code, however, does specify when the time period for acceptance starts to run. According to article 482 of the Civil Code, the time period for acceptance is to be calculated in three different ways. First, if an offer is made in the form of a letter or telegram, the time limit for acceptance commences from the date shown on the letter or from the date the telegram is handed in for dispatch. The "date shown on the letter" refers to the time the offer letter is dated while the "date for dispatch" means the time the telegram is given to a post office or another office engaged in the telegram business of sending telegrams, which is normally indicated in the official receipt of such office. Second, if the letter is not dated, the time limit for an

[82] See *id.*, art. 483.
[83] See *id.*, art. 480.
[84] See *id.*, art. 137.
[85] See *id.*
[86] See *id.*, art. 481.

acceptance begins on the date shown on the envelope that contains the offer. Third, if the offer is made by means of instantaneous communications such as by telephone, facsimile, or email, the time limit for an acceptance starts at the moment the offer reaches the offeree, meaning the moment at which the offeree answers the phone or receives the fax or email.[87]

II. CONSISTENCE RULE. The second requirement is "contents in consistence" with the offer, which is called the consistence rule. Article 488 of the Civil Code requires that the contents of the acceptance match the contents of the offer. Thus, an alteration to the contents of an offer might affect the effect of the acceptance.[88] As noted, when an alteration is material, the original offer is terminated and the acceptance becomes a new offer. If, however, the alteration is non-material, under article 489, the acceptance shall be effective and the content of the contract shall be as altered by the acceptance, unless the offeror objects in a timely manner, or the offer indicates that an acceptance may not make any alteration to the contents of the offer.[89]

III. COMMUNICATION RULE. The third requirement is that the acceptance must be communicated by the offeree to the offeror. Since acceptance is an expression of the offeree's assent to an offer, only the offeree has the ability and power to accept the offer. But an acceptance may not have to come from the offeree personally because it can be made by an authorized agent of the offeree. On the other hand, an acceptance may not necessarily be made by just one offeree. It could be made by several offerees if the offer is made to more than one specified person. If, however, an acceptance is made by a third party, a non-intended offeree, it will be regarded as an offer.

It is unclear under the Civil Code whether an acceptance should comply with the format required by the offer. A general holding is that if the offeror stipulates in the offer a specific method for acceptance, as long as the method is not objectively impossible, acceptance must comply with the method specified by the offeror. For example, if an offer states that the acceptance must be made through telegram, a mailed acceptance of that offer will be deemed unacceptable. Therefore, a failure to follow the format specified in the offer for an acceptance may render the acceptance ineffective.[90]

As noted, under article 480 of the Civil Code, an acceptance can be made through an act according to the parties' course of dealing or as indicated in the offer. A question then is whether an acceptance can be implied, or more precisely,

[87] See *id.*, art. 482.
[88] See *id.*, art. 488.
[89] See *id.*, art. 489.
[90] See the SPC Leading Group, Understanding and Application of Civil Code, Contracts, 107 (People's Court Press, 2020).

whether an offeree's acceptance of an offer can be manifested by silence. According to article 140 of the Civil Code, silence is deemed as an expression of intent only when it is so provided by the law, agreed to by the parties, or accords with the course of dealing between the parties.[91] Thus, silence in general does not constitute an acceptance unless it can be proved that silence as an acceptance is permitted under the law, is specifically agreed to by the parties, or is allowed in the course of dealing between the parties.

b. Withdrawal of an Acceptance

Since under the "arrival rule" an acceptance does not become effective until it reaches the offeror, it follows that an acceptance may be withdrawn before such arrival. Pursuant to article 485 of the Civil Code, an acceptance may be withdrawn by way of notice.[92] However, under article 141 of the Civil Code, a withdrawal notice must reach the offeror before or at the same time that the acceptance notice reaches the offeror in order for a withdrawal of an acceptance to be effective.[93]

Therefore, to withdraw an acceptance, timing is a critical factor. When a withdrawal notice is timely dispatched but arrives late, though it should have arrived on time in a normal situation, the offeree should under the good faith principle notify the offeror that the acceptance cannot be withdrawn because it arrived late. If, however, the offeror fails to notify the offeree, the arrival of the withdrawal notice will be deemed to have been timely and then the withdrawal is considered effective.

c. Late Acceptance

As noted, under article 478 of the Civil Code, an offer becomes void if it is not accepted within the time limit specified in the offer. There are two situations wherein no acceptance is made before the time for acceptance expires. One situation is that the offeree does not agree to the terms and conditions in the offer and has no desire to enter into a contract with the offeror. In this situation, there will never be an acceptance. The other situation is that an acceptance is not made until after the expiration of the time required for acceptance. The acceptance that is made after the fixed time for acceptance is labeled as "late acceptance."

The Civil Code takes an "up-to-offeror" approach to deal with late acceptance, but requires that notice be timely made to the offeree. As provided in article 486, when an offeree accepts the offer beyond the time limit for acceptance, or the acceptance is made within the time limit but the notice of acceptance cannot reach the offeror on time under normal circumstances, such an acceptance constitutes a

[91] See the 2020 Civil Code, *supra* note 11, art. 140.

[92] See *id.*, art. 141.

[93] See *id.*

new offer, unless the offeror timely notifies the offeree that the acceptance is effective.[94]

The effect of article 486 is that late acceptance has no effect unless the offeror accepts the late acceptance with a timely notice to the offeree. If, however, the offeror chooses not to act, the late acceptance becomes a new offer, which the offeror may decide whether to accept within a reasonable period of time. Thus, an offeror's silence with respect to a late acceptance does not lead to the effectiveness of the acceptance. Since the focus of article 486 is on when an acceptance is made, not the time at which the acceptance is received, a late acceptance means that the acceptance is made after the lapse of the fixed time.

d. Late Arrival of Acceptance

The late arrival of an acceptance refers to the situation wherein the acceptance was made within the time limit, but it reached the offeror after the acceptance deadline. Unlike late acceptance, the late arrival of an acceptance creates a "half good and half bad" dilemma. In many cases, the late arrival of an acceptance is caused by a problem during transmission. Thus, it would appear to be unfair to handle late arrival the same way as late acceptance.

Given the difference between late acceptance and late arrival of acceptance, the Civil Code applies a rule of presumption under which an acceptance arriving late is presumably effective unless the offeror clearly indicates otherwise. Under article 487, if an offeree dispatches acceptance within the time limit and the acceptance would have reached the offeror in time under normal circumstances, but due to other reasons it reaches the offeror beyond the time limit, the acceptance shall be effective unless the offeror timely notifies the offeree that the acceptance is not accepted as it exceeds the time allowed.[95] Thus, an acceptance that was timely sent but arrived late will generally be presumed effective absent the offeror's prompt rejection.

Questions remain as to what constitutes "normal circumstances" and "other reasons" for the delay in the arrival of acceptance. As a practical matter, "normal circumstances" refer to those that are commonly accepted pursuant to the customs or usages of business dealings or of particular industries, and their determination largely depends on evidence proving customs or usages that support a timely arrival of acceptance. The "other reasons," though they might be construed differently from case to case, are generally interpreted as the events that usually would not happen and do not involve the offeree's fault.[96]

94 See *id.*, art. 486.

95 See *id.*, art. 487.

96 See Economic Law Chamber of the SPC, Contract Law Explanation and Application, 149 (Xinghua Publishing Press, 1999).

C. *Acceptance and Conclusion of Contract*

Conclusion of a contract is viewed in China as a prerequisite to (a) the establishment, modification, or termination of a contractual relationship between the parties involved, (b) the ascertainment of a contract's effectiveness, and (c) the determination of contractual liability.[97] Under article 483 of the Civil Code, a contract is concluded when acceptance becomes effective unless otherwise provided by the law or agreed by the parties.[98] Thus, the conclusion of a contract is dependent upon the effectiveness of the acceptance.

For purposes of the Civil Code, the conclusion of a contract means that the parties have reached mutual assent and agree to be bound by the contractual terms and conditions. In addition, the conclusion of the contract signifies the institution of the parties' respective contractual rights and obligations. There are two factors that are important to the effectiveness of acceptance.

The first factor is effective time of acceptance. The effective time is important because it determines when the contract is made or at which point the contract is formed. The general rule is in article 483 of the Civil Code, under which a contract is concluded when acceptance takes effect. Article 490 further provides that written contracts are concluded at the time both parties sign, stamp, or put their fingerprints on the contract.[99] Although article 490 does not specify whether the signature or the stamp controls if the two are both put on the contract but at different times, the courts normally follow the doctrine of "first in time."

If, however, prior to signing, stamping, or fingerprinting, one of the parties has already performed the principal obligation and the other party has accepted the performance, the contract is formed at the time of acceptance of the performance.[100] This performance rule also applies where completing a contract in writing is required by law, administrative regulation, or the agreement of the parties and the parties fail to make the contract in writing, but one of the parties has already performed the principal obligation and the other party has accepted the performance.[101]

In addition, under article 491, if the parties conclude a contract in the form of a letter, data message, or the like, and a confirmation letter is required to be signed, the contract is formed upon the signature of the confirmation letter.[102] Moreover, if the information about goods or services published by a party via information network, such as the internet, conforms to the conditions for an offer, a contract is

[97] See Second Civil Division of the SPC, Adjudication Guide of Contract Cases, 5 (Law Press, 2014).
[98] See the 2020 Civil Code, *supra* note 11, art. 483.
[99] See *id.*, art. 490.
[100] See *id.*
[101] See *id.*
[102] See *id.*, art. 491.

formed at the time the other party chooses such product or service and successfully submits the order, unless otherwise agreed by the parties.[103]

The second factor is the location of the contract's conclusion or the place of contract. The place where a contract is made is an essential element in the determination of jurisdiction and governing law over the contract. Generally, as set forth in article 492 of the Civil Code, the place where an acceptance becomes effective is the place where the contract is formed.[104] Thus under the arrival rule, the place of contract in most cases is the place where the offeror is located.

But if a contract is concluded in the form of a data message, unless otherwise agreed by the parties, the recipient's principal place of business is the place of contract; in the absence of a principal place of business, the recipient's domicile is the place where the contract is formed. Article 493 further provides that if the parties conclude a contract in the form of a written booklet, the place where the contract is finally signed, stamped, or fingerprinted is the place where the contract is formed, unless the parties have agreed otherwise.[105]

D. *Effectiveness of Contract*

A common view in contract theory is that effective acceptance of an offer results in a contract.[106] It follows under this view that a contract takes effect upon its conclusion. In China, however, the conclusion of a contract and the effectiveness of a contract are different matters, and a contract that is concluded does not necessarily mean that it is effective. Thus, a contract will take effect at the time it is concluded if its effectiveness is not impacted by internal or external factors. An internal factor refers to a condition imposed by the parties in the contract, while an external factor is a requirement provided in the law.

In addition, according to the SPC, the effectiveness of a contract falls within the scope of review by the court *ex officio*. Thus, when hearing contract dispute cases, even if the effectiveness of a contract is not an issue raised by the parties, the court may still examine it. Upon its examination, the court shall differentiate between invalidity and such matters as revocability, ineffectiveness, and pending effectiveness, and then determine civil liability based on the circumstances that may affect the effectiveness of the contract along with the parties' litigation requests.[107]

Under article 502 of the Civil Code, a contract formed in accordance with the law becomes effective upon its formation unless otherwise provided by law or agreed

[103] See *id.*
[104] See *id.*, art. 492.
[105] See *id.*, art. 493.
[106] See Ferriell, *supra* note 50, at 189.
[107] See the SPC, *Minutes of the National Court Civil and Commercial Trial Work Conference*, November 8, 2019, Section III(a) Effectiveness of Contracts, available at www.huixiaolaw.cn/page7?article_id=83.

upon by the parties. Compared with the Contract Law, the Civil Code contains more specific rules in ascertaining the effect of a contract. One rule is the rule concerning the effect of an exculpatory clause in a contract. Article 506 of the Civil Code explicitly provides that an exculpatory clause in a contract is void if it aims to exempt (a) the liability arising from physical injury inflicted on the other party; or (b) the liability arising from losses caused to the other party's property due to an intentional act or by gross negligence.[108]

Another rule that is worth noting is article 507, which provides that when a contract has no effect, or is void, revoked, or terminated, the validity of a clause in the contract concerning dispute settlement is not affected.[109] Under article 507, the validity of the dispute settlement clause is independent from the validity of the underlying contract. Therefore, a claim against the validity of the dispute settlement clause, including jurisdiction and choice of law, must be made specifically. A claim against the contract in general would not affect the validity of the dispute settlement clause.

A third rule involves the effect of a signed empty contract. This rule applies to the case where a party signs and seals a contract that either does not have any contents (blank contract) or leaves certain blank spaces in the contents (partial blank contract). According to the SPC, if one party hands over a contract with blank content to the counterparty, the contract should not necessarily be held invalid but shall be deemed to contain unlimited authorization to the counterparty who can fill in the corresponding contents in the blank for the matter the contract is intended to deal with.[110]

a. Presumption of Effectiveness

Again, a contract in China is legally characterized as a civil act. As noted, under article 143 of the Civil Code, a civil act is valid and effective as a matter of law if (a) the person performing the act has the corresponding civil capacity, (b) there is a genuine expression of intent, and (c) it does not violate mandatory provisions of law or administrative regulation nor offend public order or good morals.[111]

Also, according to article 502 of the Civil Code, a lawfully formed contract is effective upon its formation absent any obstacle to its effectiveness under the law or agreement.[112] The implication of article 502 is that a contract will be presumed to become effective when concluded. The notion underlying this presumption is that a

[108] See the 2020 Civil Code, *supra* note 11, art. 506.
[109] See *id.*, art. 507.
[110] See the SPC decisions, Gaofa Min Shen No. 1889 (2023), Gaofa Min Shen No. 5986 (2020), Gaofa Min Shen No. 5948 (2020), Gaofa Min Shen No. 1111 (2020), Gaofa Min Shen No. 3112 (2018), and Minshen Zi No. 1654 (2015), etc.
[111] See the 2020 Civil Code, *supra* note 11, art. 143.
[112] See *id.*, art. 502.

court shall uphold the effectiveness of a contract, unless otherwise proven to be ineffective.

b. Government Approval

In China, there are certain contracts that need government approval before taking effect. For these contracts, effectiveness is separate from formation, which means that such a contract, when formed, will not take effect until approved by the government. Currently, there are four areas in which government approval is required for a contract to become effective, including finance and insurance, transfer of state-owned property, foreign investment, and transfer of prospecting and mining rights. Foreign investment mainly involves joint ventures.

Under the Contract Law, if a contract is subject to approval or registration as provided for by the laws or administrative regulations, the provisions of such laws or regulations shall be followed. The Civil Code scraps the registration requirement and provides a number of rules concerning approval. The first rule is about the effect of contract. Under article 502 of the Civil Code, a contract formed in accordance with law becomes effective upon its conclusion, unless otherwise provided by law or agreed by the parties. It is further provided that if a contract is subject to approval as required by the law or administrative regulation, a failure to obtain the approval will render the contract ineffective. Thus, absent government approval, the contract for which the approval is required will not be deemed invalid but ineffective.[113]

According to the SPC, for example, if a contract for the establishment or change of a foreign-invested enterprise requires approval by the relevant government authority in order to take effect, it shall take effect from the date of approval. Absent the approval, the contract will have no effect. But the ineffectiveness due to the lack of approval is not grounds for the court to hold the contract invalid. In addition, the ineffectiveness will not affect the enforceability of the clause in the contract that obligates a party to obtain an approval, and other relevant clauses related to the fulfillment of such obligation.[114]

The other rule deals with the right to make a claim. Pursuant to article 502 of the Civil Code, if the party obligated to file an application for approval or undertake other procedures fails to do so, the other party may request that the former continue fulfilling the obligation to obtain the approval or bear the liability for breach of such obligation.[115] The practical significance of this rule is that if an approval is required for a contract, a failure to obtain the approval, although the contract would not take

[113] See *id.*

[114] See the SPC, *Provisions on Several Issues Concerning the Trial of Dispute Cases of Foreign-Invested Enterprises (I)*, issued on May 17, 2010, art. 1, at http://gongbao.court.gov.cn/Details/7c45c46f5b4ec4e81e9d043b78b05c.html.

[115] See the 2020 Civil Code, *supra* note 11, art. 502.

effect, creates a right for the other party to make a claim. In general, upon request, the court will direct the obligated party to fulfill the obligation of filing. If the obligated party takes no action, the other party may rescind the contract and ask for damages stemming from breach of contract.[116]

The third rule involves approval for modification, assignment, or dissolution of the contract. It is provided in article 502 of the Civil Code that if under the provisions of the laws or administrative regulations, modification, assignment, or rescission of a contract is subject to approval, such provisions shall be followed.[117] Thus, article 502 of the Civil Code not only applies to a contract itself, but also governs modification, assignment, or dissolution of the contract if government approval is legally required. The purpose is to help maximize the effectiveness of a contract freely entered into by the parties.

However, according to the SPC, when a party claims a contract to be valid on the grounds that the contract has been filed with the relevant administrative department for record or has been approved by the approval authority, or a registration has been made on changes or transfers of property rights based on the contract, if the contract is void or revocable, the claim will not be granted by the court.[118]

c. Contract by Agent without Due Authorization

Under Chinese law, a contract made by an agent, if duly authorized to act on behalf of the principal, will bind the principal. In many cases, however, authorization becomes problematic. The situations in which an agent is considered to lack due authorization include: (a) there is no authorization, (b) authorization has been revoked or held ineffective, (c) the scope of authorization has been exceeded, or (d) the authorization has expired or terminated. The issue then is whether a contract entered into by an agent in any of these situations would have a binding effect on the principal.

Under the Contract Law, a contract made by an agent without due authorization will not bind the principal unless and until the principal ratifies it or the other party has reason to believe that the agent has been duly authorized.[119] The former refers to actual authority of the agent, while the latter implicates the apparent authority of the agent. The Contract Law, however, is silent on how ratification should be made, particularly in the case where the principal has performed under a contract entered into by the unauthorized agent.

The Civil Code fills this gap by providing a rule of implied ratification. According to article 503 of the Civil Code, if a person without authority concludes a contract in

[116] See the SPC, the 2023 *Interpretation on Contract Provisions*, *supra* note 43, art. 12.
[117] See the 2020 Civil Code, *supra* note 11, art. 502.
[118] See the SPC, the 2023 *Interpretation on Contract Provisions*, *supra* note 43, art. 13.
[119] See the 1999 Contract Law, *supra* note 40, art. 44.

the name of a principal, and the principal has already started performing the contractual obligations or accepted the performance of the other party, the contract is deemed ratified.[120] Article 503 is premised on the notion that to maintain the free will and equal status of the parties, it is important for the parties to recognize their own performing acts in the process of contract performance, as well as the performance of the other party. Thus, under article 503, the principal's ratification could be made either expressly or implicitly.

Also, under article 504, in a case where the legal representative of a legal person or the responsible person of an unincorporated organization acts *ultra vires* to conclude a contract, the act is effective and the contract so concluded is binding on the legal person or the unincorporated organization unless the other party knows or should have known that the legal representative or the responsible person acted *ultra vires*.[121] In addition, if the parties conclude a contract beyond their scope of business, the contract may not necessarily be invalid solely on the grounds that it is beyond the business scope.[122]

However, in the case where a contract was stamped with a company's official seal but not signed by the company's legal representative, the effectiveness of such contract would depend on whether there was due authorization by the company. In *Liaoning Litai Industrial Co., Ltd. v. Fushun Pacific Industrial Co., Ltd.* over a Corporate Loan Dispute (2019), the SPC held that the official seal is an important external manifestation of the company's intention. However, the law does not stipulate that a person other than the legal representative can directly represent the company's will simply by virtue of the fact that he/she holds the company's official seal, because holding the official seal does not necessarily mean that the person possesses authority, actual or apparent, to act on the company's behalf.[123]

E. *Standard Contracts*

Standard contract is defined in article 496 of the Civil Code as the contract consisting of the terms that are prepared by one party in advance for repeated use and are not negotiated with the other party in concluding a contract.[124] In many cases, standard terms refer to standard contracts. The Civil Code recognizes the legal effect of the standard terms but imposes certain conditions. First, under article 39 of the Contract Law, for example, the party who supplies the standard terms is required to abide by the principle of fairness in defining the rights and obligations

[120] See the 2020 Civil Code, *supra* note 11, art. 503.
[121] See *id.*, art. 504.
[122] See *id.*
[123] Liaoning Litai Industrial Co., Ltd. v. Fushun Pacific Industrial Co., Ltd., SPC Minshen 2898 (2019), available at www.court.gov.cn/fabu/xiangqing/202441.html.
[124] See the 2020 Civil Code, *supra* note 11, art. 496.

between the parties, and to provide notice to the other party in a reasonable manner with regard to a liability exclusion or alleviation clause.

In contrast to the 1999 Contract Law, the Civil Code imposes more stringent conditions on standard terms. The purpose of this is to ensure that the standard terms will not be abused, and rights and obligations between the parties will be balanced. To that end, the Civil Code altered the Contract Law in several aspects. First, under article 496 of the Civil Code, the standard terms of which the other party must be made aware were expanded from the liability exclusion or alleviation clause to include clauses involving significant interests or concerns of the other party. Article 496 provides the courts with discretionary power to determine whether the interests and concerns of the other party are significant. As a practical matter, however, the main terms of a contract, or other terms that are related to the purpose of the contract or may affect the balance of rights and obligations of the parties, are normally considered significant to the interests of the other party.

Under the SPC's interpretation, the notice obligation will be deemed to have been fulfilled if (a) the party providing the standard terms uses words, symbols, fonts, and other obvious signs, which are usually sufficient to attract the attention of the other party when concluding the contract, to remind the other party to pay attention to such abnormal clauses aimed at exempting or reducing the former's responsibilities, excluding or restricting the rights of the other party that involve significant interests of the other party, or (b) the party providing the standard terms, at the request of the other party, provides the other party with a generally understandable explanation in writing or orally of the concept, content, and legal consequences of the abnormal terms that have significant impacts on the interests of the other party.[125]

However, according to the SPC, the party who provides the standard terms shall bear the burden of proof that it has fulfilled its notice obligation. For electronic contracts concluded through information networks such as the internet, a mere claim of fulfillment of notice obligation by the party providing the standard terms on the grounds of having taken such measures as check boxes, pop-up windows, etc. will not be considered sufficient, unless the measures taken are proven to have reached the level described in above (a) or (b).[126]

Second, the Civil Code specifies the legal consequences of the standard terms provider's failure to fulfill its obligation to provide prompt notice. Unlike the Contract Law, which is silent about what happens when the party providing the standard terms violates its notice duty, the Civil Code gives the other party an option to reject the standard terms if the required notice was not given. Pursuant to article 496, where the party providing the standard terms fails to make the other party aware of the terms that involve its significant interests and concerns, the other party may

[125] See the SPC, the 2023 *Interpretation on Contract Provisions*, *supra* note 43, art. 10.
[126] See *id*.

bring a claim to exclude the terms from the contract. According to the SPC, when such a claim is made, the people's courts shall rule in favor of the claimant.

Third, the Civil Code strengthens the review of reasonableness of the standard terms and invalidates terms that restrict the main rights of the other party in a more specific way than the Contract Law. Under article 497 of the Civil Code, in addition to the situation where a civil act is considered invalid, a standard term will become void if the term (a) unreasonably exempts or alleviates that party from liability, imposes a heavier liability on the other party, or restricts the major rights of the other party; or (b) deprives the other party of its main rights. These two invalidation situations are also seen as the legal consequences of the standard terms provider's violation of the principle of fairness in determining the rights and obligations between the parties.[127]

Lastly, the Civil Code provides an interpretation rule for the standard terms. According to article 498 of the Civil Code, where a dispute arises over the understanding of a standard clause, the clause shall be interpreted under its commonly understood meaning. In addition, if there are two or more interpretations of a standard clause, the clause shall be interpreted against the party providing the standard clause. Furthermore, when a standard clause is inconsistent with a non-standard clause, the non-standard clause shall prevail.[128]

The SPC also opines that when the parties claim that a contract clause is not a standard clause on the grounds that the contract was made based on the model contract text or the parties have clearly agreed that it is not a standard clause, the court will rule against the claim if the contract clause meets the standards set forth in article 496 of the Civil Code. In addition, if a party engaged in business activities asserts that the contract terms, though drawn up in advance and not negotiated with the other party, are not standard terms because the terms have not been actually reused, the court will not uphold the assertion unless there is evidence that the terms were not pre-drafted for reuse.[129]

F. *Formality of Contracts*

Contract formality is about how a contract should be formed. Both the 1999 Contract Law and the Civil Code take a more flexible approach to the formality requirement than previous contract legislation.[130] The underlying notion

[127] See the 2020 Civil Code, *supra* note 11, art. 497.

[128] See *id.*, art. 498.

[129] See the SPC, the 2023 *Interpretation on Contract Provisions*, *supra* note 43, art. 9.

[130] All previous contract legislation in China emphasized the need for contracts to be in writing and made writing a general requirement for every contract, with the exception of those made and executed instantly. For example, under article 3 of the Economic Contract Law, an economic contract, if not made and executed instantly, must be in writing. The rigid writing requirement is said to comport with the idea that a contract is a tool to implement the State economic plan.

is that a contract is an agreement between the parties, and it is therefore up to the parties, within the boundaries of statutory requirements, to choose the format they see fit for the contract. The formality provisions reflect the belief that flexibility in contract formality requirements has such benefits as (a) better serving the parties' needs in different transactions, (b) convenience, and (c) facilitating quick adaptation to new technological developments.

There are two points that require further discussion in regard to formality. First, there is no equivalent in Chinese contract legislation to the statute of frauds, pertaining to the writing requirement, which exists in a country like the United States. In China, if writing is required for a particular type of contract, that requirement will be set forth in a specific provision of the law. Second, although contract formality requirements under the 1999 Contract Law and the Civil Code are not restrictive, writing is still generally preferred, and in some cases is required. This practice is consistent with China's reservation made to article 11 of the United Nations Convention on Contracts for the International Sale of Goods (CISG). Under article 11 of the CISG, writing is not required for contracts for the sale of goods.[131]

Article 469 of the Civil Code defines writing as any form that contains the contents capable of being represented in a tangible form, such as a written agreement, letter, telegram, telex, or facsimile. In addition, a data message in any form, such as electronic data interchange and e-mails, if capable of being represented in a tangible form and accessible for reference and use at any time, will be deemed as writing.[132]

Like the 1999 Contract Law, the Civil Code does not make contract formality mandatory. Instead, it allows parties to make decisions as they see fit. In addition, even if writing is required for a contract either by law or by the parties, the transaction covered by the contract might be affected but the conclusion of the contract under certain circumstances would remain intact. Moreover, under article 490 of the Civil Code, when writing for a contract is required by law, administrative regulation, or under the agreement of the parties, but the contract is not made in writing, the contract will remain effective if one of the parties has already performed the principal obligation and the other party has accepted the performance.[133]

G. *Compulsory Contracting*

In China, as noted, the parties have the right, under the principle of voluntariness, to determine whether to enter into a contract. The right, however, is limited in the

[131] Article 11 of the CISG provides that a contract of sale need not be concluded in or evidenced by writing and is not subject to any other requirements as to form. Such a contract may be proved by any means, such as by witnesses.

[132] See the 2020 Civil Code, *supra* note 11, art. 469.

[133] See *id.*, art. 490.

situation where government mandatory tasks or purchase orders are involved. State mandatory tasks are issued by the State for the needs of the national economy and social development, while the State purchase orders are the form of government procurement under the State plan to be fulfilled by particular business entities or enterprises.

According to article 38 of the 1999 Contract Law, when the State issues a mandatory task or purchase order on the basis of necessity, the relevant legal persons or other organizations shall enter into contracts accordingly.[134] Article 38 serves two purposes: on the one hand, the parties involved are required to enter into a contract to implement the State mandatory task or fulfill the State purchase order, and on the other hand, a contract would be considered invalid if it fails to follow such mandatory task or purchase order.

Article 38 is widely viewed as a residual of the planned economy that used to dominate the country. The Civil Code revises article 38 of the Contract Law and creates a rule of compulsory contracting. Under article 494 of the Civil Code, where the State issues mandatory tasks or purchase orders, the civil subjects (i.e., persons) concerned shall conclude the contracts in accordance with the rights and obligations provided by the relevant laws or administrative regulations.[135] In contrast to article 38 of the Contract Law, article 494 of the Civil Code is distinctive in several aspects.

First, article 494 expands the coverage of State mandatory tasks and purchase orders from "legal persons" or "other organizations" to "civil subjects" – a general term referring to all persons participating in civil activities. Second, article 494 defines the term "necessity" and limits the application of mandatory contracting to such events as "emergency and disaster relief, pandemic prevention and control, or the like." What is unclear, however, is whether "the like" would also include the need for national defense, state key construction, as well as national strategic reserves.

The third and more striking aspect is that in article 494, there is a new provision of mandatory offer and acceptance, which constitutes the core of compulsory contracting. Pursuant to article 494, the party that has an obligation to make an offer in accordance with the provisions of laws and administrative regulations shall make a reasonable offer in a timely manner, and likewise, the party that has an obligation to make an acceptance shall not reject the reasonable request of the other party to conclude a contract.[136] Thus, in light of article 494, compulsory contracting is a process in which a contract is made where a party is required to make an offer to the other party, or a party is obligated to enter into a contract with the other party. In either case, it is an obligation for one party to enter into a contract with the other.

[134] See the 1999 Contract Law, *supra* note 40, art. 38.
[135] See the 2020 Civil Code, *supra* note 11, art. 494.
[136] See *id.*

H. *Contents of a Contract*

Contents refer to the terms and conditions agreed by the parties for a contract. There are two major issues pertaining to the contents: One issue concerns the terms that should be included in a contract, and the other issue relates to missing or vague terms. As noted, article 470 of the Civil Code contains a list of terms that are considered to be normally included in a contract. Since the terms listed in article 470 are not mandatory, the parties may choose whatever terms they see fit for their contract. It is not unusual that certain terms be left out during the conclusion of the contract, or the parties may attach different meanings to the same term.

Under article 510 of the Civil Code, after a contract takes effect, if no agreement has been made on such contents as the quality, price or remuneration, or the place of performance of the contract, or the agreement is unclear in this regard, the parties may make a supplementary agreement to that effect.[137] An implication of article 510 is that missing such term as the price, quality, or performance place in a contract does not necessarily render the contract ineffective. Article 511 further provides that if the parties fail to reach a supplementary agreement, the contents of those missing terms can be determined according to the relevant clauses of the contract or the course of dealing.[138]

According to the SPC, when the parties dispute whether a contract is formed, if the names of the parties, the subject matter of the contract, and quantity can be ascertained, the contract shall generally be deemed to have formed, unless otherwise provided by law or agreed upon by the parties.[139] Once the formation of a contract is so established, other missing terms of the contract can be determined in accordance with articles 510 and 511 of the Civil Code.[140]

In addition, the Civil Code provides a gap-filling rule that applies to a contract with missing terms absent parties' supplementary agreement or which governs the contents of the contract pertaining to the missing or unclear terms absent the parties' supplemental agreement or course of dealing. Pursuant to article 511 of the Civil Code, the gap-filling rule consists of several provisions that govern quality, price or remuneration, place of performance, time and manners of performance, and allocation of costs for performance.[141] The ultimate purpose of article 510 is to

[137] See *id.*, art. 510.

[138] See *id.*

[139] See the SPC, the 2023 *Interpretation on Contract Provisions*, *supra* note 43, art. 3.

[140] See *id.*

[141] See the 2020 Civil Code, *supra* note 11, art. 511. Under article 511 of the Civil Code, if an agreement between the parties concerning the contents of their contract is unclear and such contents cannot be determined, the following provisions shall be applied:

(1) Where the quality requirements are not clearly stipulated, the contract shall be performed in accordance with a mandatory national standard, or a recommendatory national standard in the absence of a mandatory national standard, or the standard of the industry in the absence of a recommendatory national standard. In the absence of any

encourage transactions and ensure as much as possible that legally made contracts continue to be performed.

I. *Interpretation*

As discussed, article 142 of the Civil Code sets forth the basic rules for interpretation of the meaning of the parties' expression of their intent. Article 466 further requires that when the parties dispute over a contract term, the meaning of the disputed term be determined in accordance with article 142.[142] Also, under article 466, when a contract is concluded in two or more languages with the same legal effect, the words and phrases used in each version are presumed to have the same meaning. If, however, the words and phrases used in each version are inconsistent, interpretation shall be made in accordance with the relevant terms, nature, purpose of the contract, and the principle of good faith.[143]

In its 2023 opinions, the SPC reiterates that the court's interpretation of contract terms shall be based on the ordinary meaning of the words and phrases, together with the relevant terms, the nature and purpose of the contract, trade practices, and the principle of good faith. The SPC also emphasizes that when making interpretation of disputed terms of a contract, reference shall be made to such factors as the contracting background, negotiation process, and performance conducts.[144]

According to the SPC, if it is evident that the common understanding of the contract terms by the parties differs from the ordinary meaning of the words and phrases, the courts shall strike down the claim by any party that the contract terms

national or industrial standard, the contract shall be performed in accordance with the general standard or a specific standard conforming to the purpose of the contract.

(2) Where the price or remuneration is not clearly stipulated, the contract shall be performed in accordance with the market price in the place of performance at the time the contract is concluded. Where a government-set or government-guided price shall be applied as required by law, the contract shall be performed at such a price.

(3) Where the place of performance is not clearly stipulated, the contract shall be performed at the place of the party receiving money where payment of money is involved, or, where real estate is to be delivered, at the place where the real estate is located. For other subject matters, the contract shall be performed at the place where the party performing the obligation is located.

(4) Where the period of performance is not clearly stipulated, the debtor may perform the obligation at any time, and the creditor may request the debtor perform at any time, provided that he give the debtor a period of time necessary for preparation.

(5) Where the manner of performance is not clearly stipulated, the contract shall be performed in a manner conducive to realizing the purpose of the contract.

(6) Where the allocation of expenses for performance is not clearly stipulated, the expenses shall be borne by the party performing the obligation. Where the expenses for performance are increased due to the creditor's reason, the creditor shall bear the increased part of the expenses.

[142] See the 2020 Civil Code, *supra* note 11, art. 142.

[143] See *id.*, art. 466.

[144] See the SPC, the 2023 *Interpretation on Contract Provisions*, *supra* note 43, art. 1.

shall be reviewed under the ordinary meaning of the words and phrases.[145] In the meantime, the SPC signifies that if there are more than two interpretations of a contract clause, which may affect the validity of the clause, the People's Court shall choose the interpretation that is conducive to the validity of the clause. But if it is a gratuitous contract, the court shall choose the interpretation that imposes a lighter burden on the debtor.[146]

The SPC also specifies what may constitute the trade practices for purposes of interpretation of contract terms. In accordance with the SPC, if no mandatory provisions of laws and administrative regulations or public order and good morals is violated, the trade practices may refer to (a) the usual practices in transaction activities between the parties, or (b) the practices that are commonly adopted, known, or ought to be known to the other party at the time of contract, in the place where the transaction occurs or in a certain field or industry. The SPC further requires that when claiming trade practices, the claimant bears the burden of proof.[147]

In addition, the SPC makes it clear that a determination of the right and obligation relationship between the parties should not be limited to the name used in the contract, but instead it should be made on the basis of the contents of the contract as agreed by the parties. Thus, when the rights and obligations claimed by the parties are inconsistent with those determined under the contents of the contract, the court shall figure out the actual civil relationship between the parties based on the contracting background, transaction purpose and structure, performance acts, as well as the possibility of sham transactions made between the parties.[148]

3. VALIDITY OF CONTRACTS

Validity of a contract is an issue that determines whether the contract will be effective and legally binding as to the contractual parties. In China, if a contract lacks an element that is essential to its effectiveness or validity, the contract will not be enforceable as a matter of law.[149] On the other hand, when part of a contract becomes invalid, the validity of the contract's remaining terms will not be affected if the invalidated part can be isolated. Also as noted, an invalidation of a contract has no impact on the effect of the dispute settlement provisions in the contract.

Issues affecting the validity of a contract involve several aspects. Under the Civil Code, a contract that has a validity issue may become void or voidable. In addition, the Civil Code recognizes a special category of contracts that are not necessarily void

145 See *id.*
146 See *id.*
147 See *id.*, art. 2.
148 See *id.*, art. 15.
149 See Jiang Bixin et al., Understanding and Application of the Adjudication Rules of the Guiding Cases of the SPC (Contract, Vol. I), 100–101 (China Legal Publishing House, 2012).

or voidable but require further determination as to their validity. Such a contract, in China also called an effect-to-be-determined contract, has two distinctions: first, the effectiveness of the contract is uncertain, and second, the defect that affects the effectiveness is curable.[150] Since contracts are civil acts, their validity is equally subject to the general provisions of the Civil Code on the legal effect of civil acts.

Moreover, the Civil Code subjects contracts to administrative supervision. Under article 534 of the Civil Code, the market regulatory authority and other relevant administrative agencies are empowered to supervise contracts and handle cases where the parties take advantage of a contract to commit an act that endangers the State's interests or public interests.[151] In the Contract Law, there is a provision under which a criminal charge can be made if the act constitutes a criminal offense. This provision, however, is deleted in the Civil Code.

A. *Effect-to-be-Determined Contracts*

The term "effect-to-be-determined" in China signifies that it is uncertain, before certain acts or facts are ascertained, whether an already-concluded contract is effective.[152] Thus, the doctrine of effect-to-be-determined is premised on the notion that the contract itself is good, but there is a problem with respect to the capacity of one or more party to the contract. In other words, the effect-to-be-determined does not affect the contract's conclusion or its contents, but rather involves the capacity of a party to the contract.

Contracts that are subject to further determination of the effect include (a) a contract that is concluded by a person with limited civil capacity, (b) a contract that is entered into by an agent in the name of the principal without authorization, and (c) a contract concerning a property transfer that is made by a person without the right of disposition to the property. In any of these cases, the contract, although it is concluded, will have no effect unless and until further action as required has been taken.

A person with limited capacity can be either a minor or an intellectually disabled person. A contract concluded by such a person has no effect unless and until ratified by the person's agent *ad litem*.[153] Ratification can take the form of approval, affirmation, or acknowledgment. Note that in China, ratification is deemed to be civil conduct empowering agents *ad litem* to protect the legitimate interests of those who have limited civil capacity, and the power of ratification rests with the agent *ad*

[150] See Liming, *supra* note 1, at 96–102.

[151] See the 2020 Civil Code, *supra* note 11, art. 534.

[152] See Liming, *supra* note 21, at 540–541. But others insist that an effect-to-be-determined contract shall specifically refer to a contract where one party's capacity is limited and the contract's effectiveness therefore requires a relevant third party's affirmation. See Cui Yunling, General View on Contract Law, 139–140 (China University of People's Public Security Press, 2003).

[153] See the 2020 Civil Code, *supra* note 11, art. 145.

litem. In one contract book, ratification is explicitly defined as a manifestation of intent of the agent *ad litem* to acknowledge and accept the effect of the contract for a person with limited civil capacity made with other people.[154]

But a pure profit-making contract or a contract concluded appropriate to the person's age, intelligence, or mental health conditions need not be ratified by an agent *ad litem* of such person. The term "pure profit-making" means to enjoy all of the benefits without bearing any responsibility or liability, which include receipt of reward, donation, or payment. The concept of "appropriate to age, intelligence, or mental health conditions" refers to conduct of which a minor or mentally ill person fully understands the nature of the contract in accordance with the person's given age, intelligence, and mental health condition.

When making a contract, an agent without due authorization exists when (a) there is no authorization, (b) the scope of the authorization is exceeded, or (c) the authorization is terminated or expires. In those cases, the contract will have no binding effect upon the principal without the principal's ratification, and the person who lacks the due authorization shall be held liable.[155] Thus, before the principal ratifies such a contract, the contract's effectiveness is still pending. A principal's ratification can be made either by words or through conduct.

"No-right-to-dispose" refers to the situation where a person who disposes of the other person's property through a contract has no right to do so. Since no-right-to-dispose involves the status of the person in question, it is treated as a capacity issue. Thus if a person who has no-right-to-dispose of another person's assets disposes of such assets through a contract, the contract will only be valid if the holder of the right to the assets ratifies the contract or the person that initially lacked the right of disposal acquires the right after the conclusion of the contract.

Disposal refers to legal disposal, which means the determination of the fate of the property (e.g., whether the property will be sold or given away as a gift, or whether a mortgage will be taken against the property). As noted, full ownership encompasses such rights as the rights to possession, use, receipt of benefits, and disposal of the property. Under the civil law ownership doctrine, except for the right of disposal, all ownership rights may be separated from ownership. Because of this, the right to dispose is regarded as the core of full ownership, without which full ownership does not exist.

In 2012, the SPC explicitly addressed validity issues with respect to sales contracts. The SPC instructed the courts not to uphold any claim that a contract is void because the seller did not have full ownership or the right to dispose of the subject matter at the time of the contract.[156] However, in the SPC's opinion, when a seller fails to obtain full ownership or the right to dispose of the subject matter of the

[154] See Su Haopeng, Conclusion and Effectiveness of Contracts, 251 (China Legal System Press, 1999).

[155] See the 2020 Civil Code, *supra* note 11, art. 145.

[156] See the SPC, *Interpretation on the Issues Concerning Application of Law in Adjudicating Disputes over Sales Contract*, *supra* note 41, art. 3.

contract, such that ownership of the subject matter cannot be transferred to the buyer on the basis of the contract, the buyer may ask the seller to bear liability for its breach of the contract or request a rescission of the contract in addition to compensation for damages.[157]

When handling contract cases involving no-right-to-dispose, the courts in China normally use two criteria to determine the validity of the contract. The first criterion looks to whether the third party is a bona fide party, or whether the party knows or ought to know that the person he or she is dealing with lacks the right to dispose of the assets concerned in the contract. The second criterion focuses on whether the transfer of the assets in question is made for value. If the third party in good faith acquires the assets through a purchase, the ownership of the property is transferred regardless of the original owner's ratification. If, however, the third party receives the assets without paying its value, the original owner has the right to reclaim the assets regardless of whether or not the third party acted in good faith.[158]

B. *Void Contracts*

A contract will not be enforced if it is void, and the voidness retroactively applies to the contract from the date the contract was made. Generally, a void contract is a contract that is concluded but that violates the law or regulations or that does not meet the requirements for the contract to be valid. Therefore, if a contract is void, it has no legal effect. Under article 155 of the Civil Code, a contract that is null and void has no legally binding force from its inception.

Based on the provisions of the Civil Code on the effect of civil acts, a contract is null and void in any of the following situations: (a) false expression of intent; (b) a party with no capacity for civil acts, (c) violation of a mandatory provision of law or administration regulation, (d) offense to public order or good morals, and (e) malicious collusion damaging the lawful rights and interests of other person.

The voidness provisions serve a twofold purpose: to help maintain the business transaction in good order, and to prevent the power to invalidate contracts from being abused so that the parties' reasonable expectations will be protected. Thus, unless the law provides otherwise, all contracts are assumed to be valid.[159] Since decisions on nullity and voidness of contracts must be made on a statutory basis, no contract may be deemed null and void except as pursuant to a provision of law.

Note, however, under article 153 of the Civil Code, a civil act in violation of mandatory provisions of law or administrative regulation may not become void if application of the mandatory provisions does not lead to invalidity of such an act.[160]

[157] See *id.*

[158] See Guoguang, *supra* note 25, at 216–218.

[159] See Yunling, *supra* note 152, at 112.

[160] See the SPC, the 2023 *Interpretation on Contract Provisions*, *supra* note 43, art. 16.

According to the SPC, a court may hold a contract to remain valid under any of the following circumstances even if the contract has violated the mandatory provisions: (a) if the mandatory provisions involved are intended to maintain social and public order, the actual performance of the contract has a significantly slight impact on social and public order and invalidation of the contract at issue will cause the unfair and unjust outcome; (b) when the mandatory provisions are intended to safeguard the government's taxation, land transfer fees, and other national interests or the legitimate interests of other civil subjects rather than the civil rights and interests of the parties to the contract, maintaining of the validity of the contract will not affect the realization of the purpose of the provisions involved; (c) if the mandatory provisions are intended to require a party to strengthen risk control, internal management, etc., and the other party has no ability or obligation to review whether the contract violates the mandatory provisions, invalidation of the contract will cause the party to bear adverse consequences; (d) in the case where one party violated the mandatory provisions when entering into the contract, after the conclusion of the contract, the party was able to correct the violation but failed to do so in contravention with the principle of good faith; or (e) other situations stipulated in laws and judicial interpretations.[161]

On the other hand, the SPC through its interpretation has expanded the application of article 153 to void contracts. In accordance with the SPC, a contract shall be held invalid though it does not violate any mandatory provisions if (a) it affects political security, economic security, military security, and other national security; (b) it affects social stability or the order of fair competition, or it harms public interests or violates social and public order; (c) it deviates from social morality or family ethics, or it damages personal dignity or other good customs.[162]

The SPC also holds that to determine whether a contract violates public order and good customs, the court should, under the guidance of the core socialist values, thoroughly consider and provide a full reason in the judgment the parties' motivations and transaction purposes, the intensity of supervision by government departments, the frequency of similar transactions by the parties within a certain period, the social consequences of the behavior, and other necessary factors. If, however, the parties make a contract for their daily needs and their contractions do not have a significant impact on social and public order, nor do they affect national security or violate good customs, the contract as such shall not be held invalid.[163]

C. *Voidable Contracts*

A contract, though not necessarily void, may become voidable under certain circumstances. The major difference between void contracts and voidable contracts

[161] See *id.*
[162] See *id.*, art. 17.
[163] See *id.*

is that when a contract is void, it will take no effect without any action of the parties, but if a contract is voidable, the party seeking to void the contract must make a request. When a contract is voidable, the injured party has two alternatives: to modify or to rescind the contract. In either case, the injured party must make a request. But if the parties have chosen to modify the contract, the contract may not be rescinded.

Under the Civil Code, a contract is voidable in the case of fraud, duress, exploitation of the other party's precarious position, or material misunderstanding. Note that under the 1999 Contract Law, a contract is void if it involves fraud or duress that causes harm to a State interest. The Civil Code makes a contract voidable in all fraud or duress cases, treating the State, collective, and private interests equally. Also, the same as in a void contract, a voidable contract does not have legal effect *ab initio*. But for a voidable contract, its effectiveness is not affected until the contract is voided, and if voided, the voidance takes effect retroactively.

The issue that follows the voidance in either a void or voidable contract is the restitution or compensation that can be made to one party or to each of the parties.

Pursuant to article 157 of the Civil Code, there are three remedy rules in cases where a contract becomes void unless otherwise provided by the law.[164] The first rule is restitution. It requires the property obtained as a result of the contract to be returned. The very purpose of restitution is to restore the parties to the position they would be if there had been no contract. The second rule is compensation. If it is impossible or meaningless to return the property, compensation shall be made based on the appraised value of the property. The third rule deals with damages. When a party is at fault, causing the other party to suffer losses, damages are warranted. If both parties are at fault, each party shall be respectively liable.

Article 157 of the Civil Code establishes a fault standard for determining damages when a contract is void or voidable. First, the fault must occur in the process of making a contract. Second, the fault that leads to the voidance of a contract can be either unilateral or bilateral. Third, if the fault is bilateral, damages can be offset. Fourth, damages should be calculated in proportion to the degree of the fault committed.

D. *Conditions*

When making a contract, the parties may agree to certain conditions on which the contract will be affected. In China, conditions attached to a contract are considered a matter of effectiveness, meaning that upon the occurrence or non-occurrence of the agreed conditions, the contract may take effect or become null and void. In this context, a condition is also deemed a limitation on the validity of the contract.

[164] See the 2020 Civil Code, *supra* note 11, art. 157.

As noted, a condition in civil law is generally defined as an uncertain future fact. As far as contracts are concerned, a condition is an auxiliary clause that is based on the occurrence of an uncertain fact to determine the effectiveness of the contract. Thus, for a fact to become a condition, it is required that (a) at the time of contract the occurrence of the fact was uncertain (i.e., a past or existing fact is not a condition), (b) the occurrence of the fact is possible (i.e., a fact that will never occur or will definitely occur is not a condition), (c) it is unpredictable or uncertain as to when the fact will occur, (d) the fact is chosen by the parties, not provided by law, and (e) the fact is legal.[165]

As discussed, conditions as provided in the Civil Code are divided into two categories: effecting (or entry-into-force) conditions and dissolving (or come-to-a-stop) conditions.[166] A contract with an effecting condition takes effect when such condition is satisfied. By contrast, a contract that has a dissolving condition becomes null and void when such condition takes place.

Also, the parties may not abuse conditions. As noted, under article 159 of the Civil Code, if a party, for its own benefit, prevents a condition from occurring without justification, the condition shall be deemed to have occurred. Conversely, if a party unjustly makes a condition occur, the condition shall be regarded as having not occurred.[167] Moreover, for certain transactions, if the attached condition would harm the legitimate interest of a party, such condition should not be attached. For example, if a condition is attached to the endorsement of a check, the check may not be accepted for payment.

In addition to conditions, the Civil Code also allows the parties to subject the effectiveness of the contract to a time period. In a contract to which a time period is attached, the effectiveness of the contract will be affected by the expiration of the time period. Under article 160 of the Civil Code, a time limit may be attached to a civil act. But article 160 also provides an exception under which no time limit should be attached if it is against the nature of the civil act.[168]

Like conditions, time periods are also split into effecting time periods and dissolving time periods. In accordance with article 160 of the Civil Code, a contract subject to an effecting time period shall be effective when the period expires, while a contract subject to a dissolving time limit will become ineffective when the period

[165] See Jiang Ping, A Detailed Explanation of the Contract Law of China, 36 (China University Political Science and Law Press, 1999).

[166] In American contract law, conditions are classified as condition precedents, concurrent conditions, and conditions subsequent. As Professor Rosett pointed out, a condition precedent is an event that must exist or occur before a duty of immediate performance of a promise arises. Where the occurrence of an event extinguishes an existent immediate duty to perform, the condition is said to be subsequent. A condition is concurrent if a party's duty to perform is conditional upon a simultaneous tender of performance by the other. See Arthur I. Rosett & Daniel J. Bussel, Contract Law and Its Application, 693–695 (6th ed., Foundation Press, 1999).

[167] See the 2020 Civil Code, *supra* note 11, art. 159.

[168] See *id.*, art. 160.

comes to an end.[169] Both time periods and conditions affect the effectiveness of contracts. But the concepts are different in that a condition is an uncertain fact at the time of contract, while a time period is a certain fact at the time of contract. The certainty of the time period means that when concluding the contract, the parties know that the time would come at a particular point.

Note also that the time period attached to a contract is different from the time period for performance. As discussed, the time period attached to a contract concerns the effectiveness of the contract because the contract may become effective or ineffective upon the expiration of the time period as agreed by the parties. The time period provided for performance, however, deals with the party's tender of duty to each other after the contract takes effect.

4. PERFORMANCE OF CONTRACTS

Contract performance concerns fulfillment of legal duties or obligations that become due as agreed upon by the parties under the contract. In China, contract performance is defined as conduct that executes contractual duties or obligations. When such performance is completed, the parties are discharged from any further obligations. Performance is considered to be the core of contract law because it involves the achievement of a contract's purpose and the realization of the expected interests of the parties to a contract. Under the Civil Code, a contract, once effective, must be properly and completely performed.

A. *Principles of Performance*

There are three major principles in the Civil Code that govern the performance of contracts: complete and adequate performance, good faith performance, and green performance. The very purpose of the first two principles is to assure that a contract will be performed as agreed by the parties and the performance will be undertaken in a proper manner. Green performance is a principle newly provided in the Civil Code, which aims to help protect the environment and maintain sustainable development. In addition, there are a number of rules that are purposed to safeguard contract performance.

a. Complete and Thorough Performance

Article 509 of the Contract Law requires that parties to a contract perform their obligations as agreed completely and thoroughly.[170] Complete and thorough performance means that the parties accomplish what they promised or agreed upon in

[169] See *id.*
[170] See *id.*, art. 509.

the contract to the extent that all legal duties are completely fulfilled and all legal rights are satisfied. Performance is considered complete and thorough when the parties have performed the contractual obligations they respectively assume exactly in accordance with the terms and conditions of the contract. Scholars in China have suggested that complete and thorough performance also means proper performance, which refers to the way in which a contract is performed. Performance is proper if a contract is performed by the right party at the right time at the right place with the right contents.[171]

Because of the requirement for complete and adequate performance, the doctrine of substantial performance does not apply in China. Therefore, damages for breach of contract will be imposed if performance is found to be defective. There are two articles in the Civil Code that directly deal with defective performance. One is article 530, which relates to advance performance, and the other is article 531, which concerns partial performance.

Advance performance is performance that is made ahead of the agreed time to perform. Advance performance may occur either at the request of the obligee or at the initiative of the obligor. Under article 530, the obligee may reject an advance performance of the contract by the obligor, except where advance performance causes no damages to the interests of the obligee. This exception is intended to help facilitate transactions and maintain the business relationship between the parties. However, if advance performance causes additional costs to the obligee (e.g., warehouse fees), the obligor shall bear those costs.[172]

Partial performance is also deemed defective performance because it violates the principle of complete and thorough performance. According to article 531, the obligee may reject the partial performance of the contract by the obligor, except where the partial performance does not cause damages to the obligee's interests.[173] In most cases, partial performance of a contract is permissible when the contract itself is divisible and can be performed separately. Partial performance is also acceptable if the parties agree to have a contract performed in different parts. However, the obligor shall be responsible for any additional costs that the obligee may incur during the course of the partial performance.

b. Good Faith Performance

Good faith performance is based on moral values and standards. In the context of contract performance, good faith means to perform the contract according to the nature and purpose of the contract as well as transaction usages. Since complete and

[171] See SPC Leading Group, Understanding and Application of Civil Code, Contracts, *supra* note 90, at 340–341.

[172] See the 2020 Civil Code, *supra* note 11, art. 530.

[173] See *id.*, art. 531.

thorough performance is the primary requirement for performing contractual obligations, good faith performance is used as a secondary and supplementary means to ensure that the performance is made completely and thoroughly. The requirement of good faith performance has particular significance in the case where the parties' agreement concerning performance contains ambiguities or has loopholes.

In accordance with article 509 of the Civil Code, the parties shall abide by the principle of good faith and perform such duties as notice, assistance, and confidentiality on the basis of the nature and purpose of the contract or under transaction practices.[174] More explicitly, the good faith performance under article 509 mainly involves two basic duties associated with contract performance, in China commonly called the "attached duty" and the "other related duty."

The attached duty is the duty subordinate to the main duties of the contract, and it entirely depends on the existence of the contractual relationship between the parties. The performance of the attached duty is not to increase the burden of either party because it involves the natural duty embedded in the performance of the contract. Under article 509, the attached duties include notice, assistance, and confidentiality. The duty of notice necessarily occurs when a contractual relationship is established between the parties. The duty to assist is an inherent obligation of the parties to a contract. Since a contract is a product of cooperation, the parties are obligated to assist each other in performing the contract and to facilitate the completion of the contract's performance.

The duty to maintain confidentiality is in fact an extension of the duty that arises at the time of contract negotiation. When making a contract, the parties have the opportunity to learn each other's business secrets, and it is critical that the parties maintain the confidentiality of the business information they obtain during the process of contract formation as well as performance. Confidentiality is also required by the mutual trust on which the parties make the contract between one another. A breach of the duty to maintain confidentiality implicates bad faith, for which contractual liability, and in many cases tort liability, will be imposed.

Other related duties cover all other obligations necessary to facilitate performance of a contract, though the obligations as such may not be clearly stated in the contract. For example, after conclusion of a contract, each party has the duty to be prepared, or to get ready, for performance. A failure to prepare may constitute bad faith, particularly when the failure to prepare is made intentionally, because it would affect the performance.

c. Green Performance

As noted, it is the Civil Code that makes the "green" rule a civil law principle. But, unlike other principles provided in the Civil Code, the "green" rule is more like

[174] See *id.*, art. 509.

guidance than a mandate, meaning that it is a legal norm advocating, promoting, and guiding all civil actors to adopt specific behavior patterns. According to the SPC, the "green" rule, though not mandatory, plays a unique role in different aspects.[175]

First, it guides future civil legislation and helps formulate relevant laws and regulations in the civil area to achieve the "green" goal. Second, it sets standards for civil behavior in environmental protection and establishes basic compliance for people in their civil engagements. Third, it provides certain standards for case adjudication.[176] In other words, under the "green" rule, the conservation of resources and eco-environment protection become important factors the court should consider when adjudicating relevant cases.

As applied to contracts, the "green" rule operates as a directive that imposes certain obligations on the parties in different aspects of the contract. In one aspect, the "green" rule may create additional obligations for the contractual parties because, in making a contract, a duty to protect the environment could arise. In another aspect, the "green" rule may affect the performance of the contract since the obligee could refuse to accept the performance if such performance is considered inconsistent with environmental protection. Furthermore, the "green" rule may also influence the validity of a contract because a contract could be held void if the contract or the performance of it is deemed harmful to the environment.

With regard to green performance, it is required under article 509 of the Civil Code that the parties avoid wasting resources, polluting the environment, or damaging ecology during performance of the contract.[177] Article 619 further provides that in sales, when there is no agreement between the parties on the packaging method or the agreement is unclear, if the packaging method cannot be determined and if there is no generally accepted method for the packaging, a manner that is sufficient to protect the item and is also conducive to preserving resources and protecting the ecological environment shall be used.[178]

B. *Right of Defense to Non-Performance*

The right of defense to non-performance of contract is a civil law concept that is aimed at protecting the obligor from being harmed by the abuse of the right of the obligee. By definition, the right of defense is the right to defend against the claim of the other party or to deny the right asserted by the other party. To the extent the

[175] See the SPC Leading Group, Understanding and Application of Civil Code, Contracts, *supra* note 90, at 343.

[176] See the SPC Leading Group, Understanding and Application of Civil Code – General Provisions, 78 (People's Court Press, 2020).

[177] See the 2020 Civil Code, *supra* note 11, art. 509.

[178] See *id.*

obligor may refuse to honor the obligee's request, the right of defense is also called the right of opposition.

Note, however, that the right of defense to non-performance is not a denial of contractual obligations or a discharge of contractual duties. Rather, it provides the obligor with a legal ground on which the obligor may refuse the obligee's request for performance. The underlying notion is that in a contract, the rights and obligations between the parties are reciprocally connected and mutually dependent. One party's performance is a prerequisite to the other party's performance, and each party, when enjoying its rights under the contract, correspondingly bears contractual obligations. Thus, in order to realize their contractual rights, the parties must each perform their respective obligations. Without one party's performance, the other party's performance will not occur.

Therefore, the right of defense to non-performance is a self-protection right that is created by the law in order to help maintain the balance of interests of the parties in the course of contract performance. Based on such right, a suspension of contractual performance by one party, where that party wants to ensure that the other party will properly perform, is not a breach of contract. In this regard, many Chinese contract law scholars regard the right of defense to non-performance as a guarantee of contractual rights.[179]

The right of defense to non-performance did not appear in Chinese contract legislation until the adoption of the Contract Law in 1999. In the past, a concept of "mutual breach" was widely used in judicial practice because at that time it was overly emphasized that a contract involves mutual obligations between the parties, and that whoever did not perform the contract would be held liable regardless of the reason for non-performance. The enactment of the Contract Law reversed this practice and made it possible for parties to protect their contractual interests through exercise of their right of defense without litigation. Following the Contract Law, the Civil Code divides the right of defense to non-performance into two types of defenses: fulfillment plea and unrest defense.

a. Fulfillment Plea

A fulfillment plea is the right granted to a party in a bilateral contract to refuse to perform or to reject the request of the other party for performance before the other party diligently or properly performs the contract. Under the fulfillment plea, since the parties to a contract are mutually responsible to each other and each bears a duty to the other to perform contractual obligations, any non-performance or non-conforming performance of one party will constitute grounds for the other party to refuse to perform.

[179] See Dong Ling, Performance, Modification, Assignment and Termination of Contracts, 62 (China Legal System Publishing House, 1999).

A practical importance of the fulfillment plea is that it helps a court or arbitration body draw a line between breach and non-breach of the contract, especially when a contributory breach defense is asserted, because the non-performance by the party exercising the fulfillment plea is not a breach of contract. There are two categories of fulfillment pleas under the Civil Code: simultaneous fulfillment pleas and orderly fulfillment pleas.

A simultaneous fulfillment plea occurs where the contractual obligations of the parties are mutually implicative. As provided in article 525 of the Civil Code, if the parties have obligations toward each other and there is no order of priority in performance, the parties shall perform the obligations simultaneously.[180] Under the simultaneous fulfillment plea, a contracting party has the right to reject the other party's performance request before the other party performs, and also to reject the other party's corresponding performance request if the other party's performance does not meet the terms or conditions of the contract.[181]

An orderly fulfillment plea is a defense that can be asserted against a party that is required to perform first under a contract but fails to do so. In accordance with article 526, where the parties have mutual obligations and the performance of those obligations takes an order of priority, the party who should perform second has the right to reject the performance request of the party who should perform first if that latter party fails to make timely performance.[182] In addition, if the performance by the party who has the duty to perform first does not meet the contract requirements, the other party has the right to reject the corresponding performance request.

The orderly fulfillment plea is intended to protect the interest of the party whose performance is subsequent to the performance of the other, and to urge the party who is supposed to perform first to fulfill his or her obligations. The orderly fulfillment plea applies where the first performing party does not perform or the performance is defective. It should be noted that the orderly fulfillment plea, like the simultaneous fulfillment plea, gives a party the right to withhold his or her performance until the other party performs.[183]

Therefore, when the first performing party performs after the assertion of the orderly fulfillment plea, the asserting party must then perform. In the case where the orderly fulfillment plea is made, the first performing party may be held liable for any

[180] See the 2020 Civil Code, *supra* note 11, art. 525.

[181] The Principles of International Commercial Contracts of UNIDROIT contains a similar provision. Article 7.1.3(1) of the Principles provides: "Where the parties are to perform simultaneously, either party may withhold performance until the other party tender[s] its performance."

[182] See the 2020 Civil Code, *supra* note 11, art. 626.

[183] The term "fulfillment plea" is not used in the Principles of International Commercial Contracts of UNIDROIT; rather, "withholding performance" is used instead. With regard to orderly performance, article 7.1.3(2) provides: "Where the parties are to perform consecutively, the party that is to perform later may withhold its performance until the first party has performed."

delay in its performance. No liability, however, will be imposed on the other party for not being able to timely perform due to the first performing party's delay.

b. Unrest Defense

The defense of unrest allows the party who should perform first to, under certain circumstances, suspend its performance until the other party's performance is ascertained. This defense provides the performing party with the right to hold off its performance if the party believes with certainty that the other party will not be able to perform at the time agreed upon for performance. As a result of the performing party's exercise of the unrest defense, that party's performance is suspended unless and until the other party's performance is guaranteed or is proven to be certain.[184]

Under article 527 of the Civil Code, the party who shall perform first may suspend its performance if it has conclusive evidence to prove: (1) the other party's business conditions are seriously deteriorating, (2) the other party diverted its property or took out its capital to evade debts, (3) the other party lost its business credibility, or (4) other circumstances show that the other party has lost or is likely to lose its capacity to perform.[185]

The very purpose of the unrest defense right is to protect the interest of the party who is under the obligation to render its performance first in the case where it is clear that the other party's subsequent performance is uncertain. The unrest defense differs from the orderly fulfillment plea in that the former intends to maintain the interests of the party who is the first to perform, while the latter is just the opposite, being concerned about the protection of the interest of the subsequent performing party.

Like the fulfillment plea, the unrest defense is available only in bilateral contracts. In addition, the unrest defense must also be made on the basis of privity of contract. This privity requirement means that the unrest defense becomes applicable only between the parties to the contract. In the SPC's opinion, the breach of contract by a third party should not be grounds for application of the unrest defense.[186]

Two factors are essential to the assertion of the unrest defense. First, the party who asserts the unrest defense must be obligated to perform first under the contract, with the other party being obligated to perform thereafter. It is the consecutive

[184] Some scholars compare the doctrine of the unrest defense to the concept of implied anticipatory repudiation as used in the United States and believe that these two are substantially the same. Implied anticipatory repudiation refers to the "prospective inability" stated in UCC §2-609. See Ling, *supra* note 179, at 79.

[185] See the 2020 Civil Code, *supra* note 11, art. 527.

[186] Yu Chaixin v. Fujian Huachen Real Estates Co. Ltd & Wei Chuanrui, the SPC (2010) Min Yi Zhong Zhi No. 13.

performances between the parties that necessitate a mechanism for protecting the preceding performing party's expectation of receiving due performance from the other party.

Second, there must exist definite evidence that the other party's ability or capacity to perform has been impeded so seriously that the performance is unlikely to take place. To justify an exercise of the right of the unrest defense, the impediment must be caused by any of the statutory reasons. If, however, a party asserts the unrest defense to suspend its performance without conclusive evidence, the asserting party, under article 527 of the Civil Code, shall be liable for breach of contract.

Exercise of the unrest defense is subject to certain limits as delineated in article 528 of the Civil Code. First, the party who suspends performance shall notify the other party of the suspension in a timely manner. Second, the performance shall be resumed if the other party provides an appropriate assurance.[187] Therefore, without notice, the first performing party may not suspend its performance. An unreasonable suspension of performance after an appropriate assurance is provided may make the first performing party liable for breach of contract.

After a party suspends performance, where the other party fails to restore its ability to perform the obligation and fails to provide an appropriate assurance within a reasonable period of time, the other party is deemed to implicate by its conduct that it will not perform the principal obligation, and the party that suspends the performance may rescind the contract and may request that the other party bear default liability. The right to rescind the contract resides with the preceding performing party as a remedy in the case where the other party's inability to perform continues.

C. *Protective Measures for Performance*

Protective measures refer to the mechanism to ensure the realization of the contractual rights of a party (creditor) in a situation where the other party (debtor) purposefully reduces its property, increases its liability, or neglects to exercise its own creditor's right in order to evade its debt liability. Under the Contract Law, the protective measures consist of two rights: the right of subrogation and the right of cancellation. The Civil Code consolidates those two rights under the preservation of contracts.

a. Right of Subrogation

The right of subrogation is a civil right aimed at protecting the creditor right of the obligee. It allows the obligee, in his own name, to exercise the obligor's credit right against a third party who is a debtor of the obligor. As provided in article 73 of the 1999 Contract Law, if the obligor is indolent in exercising its due creditor right so as

[187] See the 2020 Civil Code, *supra* note 11, art. 528.

to damage the interest of the obligee, the obligee may ask the court for subrogation to exercise in its own name the obligor's creditor right, except that the credit right exclusively belongs to the obligor.[188]

The Civil Code reformulates the right of subrogation. First, it expands the subrogation right to also apply to rights collateral to the obligor's creditor right. Under article 535 of the Civil Code, the right of subrogation may be exercised upon the obligee's request when a debtor is indolent in exercising its creditor right or a collateral right related thereto so that the realization of the obligee's due creditor right would be adversely affected. Article 535 limits the scope of the right of subrogation to the obligee's creditor right that has become due.

Second, despite the limited scope prescribed in article 535, the Civil Code further provides a rule that expands the application of subrogation to the obligor's creditor right not yet due. According to article 536 of the Civil Code, prior to the due date of the obligee's creditor right, where there exists a circumstance under which the statute of limitations for the debtor's principal right or a collateral right related thereto is to expire, or the debtor fails to timely declare his right in a bankruptcy proceeding, and the enforcement of the obligee's creditor right is thus adversely affected, the creditor may, by subrogation, request the debtor of the obligor to perform his obligation to the obligor, declare the debtor's right to the bankruptcy administrator, or take other necessary action.

Third, the Civil Code signifies the legal effect of the right of subrogation. Article 537 of the Civil Code provides that where the People's Court determines that the right of subrogation is granted, the debtor of the obligor shall perform the obligation to the obligee.[189] Article 537 further provides that, after performance is accepted by the obligee, the corresponding rights and obligations between the obligee and the obligor, and between the obligor and the obligor's debtor, are terminated.[190] In addition, when the debtor's creditor right or a collateral right related thereto against its debtor is subject to preservation or enforcement measures, or when the debtor becomes bankrupt, it shall be dealt with in accordance with the provisions of the relevant laws.

b. Right of Cancellation

Similar to the right of subrogation, the right of cancellation is also purposed to protect the obligee's creditor right and to ensure that the contract will be fully performed. Unlike the right of subrogation, the right of cancellation applies when the obligor's gratuitous disposition or unreasonably priced transaction leads to a reduction in his property rights or to an improperly aggravated liability burden so

[188] See the Contract Law, *supra* note 40, art. 73.
[189] See the 2020 Civil Code, *supra* note 11, art. 537.
[190] See *id.*

that the realization of the obligee's creditor rights would be impaired. In this situation, the obligee, as the creditor of the obligor, may request that a court cancel the obligor's transaction at issue or revoke the obligor's actions.

The right of cancellation, as a statutory right, was first provided in article 74 of the 1999 Contract Law. The Civil Code differs from the Contract Law in that it separately provides more detailed rules for the gratuitous transfer of property and transactions at unreasonable prices. Under article 538 of the Civil Code, if an obligor gratuitously disposes of his proprietary rights and interests by renouncing his creditor's right, disclaiming the security for such right, or transferring his properties gratis, and the like, or if the obligor maliciously extends the period of performance of due obligations so that the enforcement of the obligee's creditor right is adversely affected, the obligee may request that the People's Court revoke the obligor's transactions involved.[191]

Pursuant to article 538 of the Civil Code, to exercise the right of cancellation, three conditions must be met. First, the creditor's right of the obligee must be valid and effective against the obligor; second, the obligor must have done something resulting in a gratuitous transfer of property or related rights; third, the transactions involved must be harmful to the realization of the obligee's creditor rights. In addition, in the situation where the obligor extends the period of performance of the debts owed to him, malice is a prerequisite. Note that in the Contract Law, the renounced creditor right must be the right that is due already, while the Civil Code simply requires a "creditor right," regardless of whether the right is due or not.

Article 539 of the Civil Code deals with the obligor's transfer of property at an unreasonable price, and it also includes a situation in which the obligor provides a guarantee for others. Under article 539 of the Civil Code, when the obligor transfers his property at an obviously unreasonably low price, takes another's property, or provides security for another's obligation at an obviously unreasonably high price so as to adversely affect the realization of the obligee's creditor right, the obligee may request that the People's Court revoke the obligor's act if the other knows or should have known of such circumstance.[192]

To determine whether the price in the involved transaction is reasonable or not, the SPC developed a "transaction time and place" rule. According to the SPC, the reasonableness of the transaction price shall be determined on the basis of the price prevalent at the time and location of the transaction. In addition, the SPC sets forth a 30 percent standard to help judge reasonableness. More specifically, if a transaction price is 30 percent lower than the local fair price at the time of the transaction, the transaction price will generally be considered "unreasonably low." Conversely, if a transaction price is 30 percent higher than the fair price, the transaction price will

[191] See *id.*, art. 538.
[192] See *id.*, art. 539.

be deemed "unreasonably high." For the purpose of price determination, the fair price could be either the guided price or the market price.[193]

Article 542 of the Civil Code further provides that when an act of an obligor adversely affecting the creditor's right to the obligee is canceled, the act shall have no effect *ab initio*.[194] This provision is premised on article 155 of the Civil Code, which states a general rule that a void or revoked civil act does not have any legal effect from the very beginning.[195] Also, under the Civil Code, the right of cancellation must be exercised within one year of the time when the obligee knows or should have known the cause for cancellation. The maximum period for the exercise of the creditor's right of the obligee is limited to five years from the date on which the act of the obligor takes place.[196]

D. *Change of Circumstances during the Performance*

Change of circumstances refers to the situation when, during the performance of a contract, the basic presumption on which the contract was formed changes so dramatically that continuing performance of the contract as originally agreed upon will be obviously unfair and unreasonable. The changed circumstance then prompts a need to modify or rescind the contract. The theoretical basis justifying the modification or rescission of a contract when circumstances change is the doctrine of *rebus sic stantibus* (things thus standing).

This doctrine, as noted, was not legislatively accepted in China until the adoption of the Civil Code, although in their practice, courts recognized it for many years before that. Under article 533 of the Civil Code, after a contract is formed, where a fundamental condition upon which the contract is concluded is significantly changed, which is unforeseeable by the parties upon conclusion of the contract and which is not one of the commercial risks, if continuing performance of the contract is obviously unfair to one of the parties, the party that is adversely affected may re-negotiate with the other party, or request that a court or an arbitration body rectify or rescind the contract if an agreement cannot be reached within a reasonable period of time.[197]

Pursuant to article 533, an application of *rebus sic stantibus* must meet certain conditions. First, the change must involve the basic condition upon which the contract was made; second, the change must be objective and unforeseeable at the time of contract; third, the change must not fall within any of the commercial risks; and fourth, continuing performance of the contract must result in obvious unfairness to one of the parties. It is required under article 533 that, upon request by the

[193] See the SPC, 2009 Contract Interpretation, *supra* note 74, art. 19.
[194] See the Contract Law, *supra* note 40, art. 542.
[195] See *id.*, art. 155.
[196] See *id.*, art. 541.
[197] See *id.*, art. 533.

parties, the court or arbitration body shall modify or rescind the contract under the principle of fairness, taking into account the actual circumstances of the case.[198]

5. MODIFICATION OF CONTRACTS AND ASSIGNMENT

Once a contract is formed, a need may develop during the performance to make a change to the contract. Such a change may be effectuated in two different ways: a change to the contents of the contract or a change to the parties to the contract. In Chinese contract literature, the former involves contract modification, while the latter refers to contract assignment, including both assignment and delegation. In the Civil Code, modification and assignment are provided in the same chapter.

A. *Modification*

Under the Civil Code, a contract modification may be made by an agreement of the parties or by the operation of law. When a modification is sought under the provision of law without an agreement, it must be made through a court or by an arbitration body. Article 543 of the Civil Code provides that a contract may be modified upon mutual assent of the parties through consultation.[199] Article 543 has several implications. First of all, the parties are free to modify their contract. Secondly, a modification shall be made by an agreement of the parties. Thirdly, the agreement to modify the contract shall be reached by mutual consent of the parties through consultation. Most notably, given the civil law tradition, no consideration is needed for the modification.

The Civil Code contains no specific requirements for the formality of contract modification. Like a contract itself, a modification can be made orally, in writing, or in another form. Written form is preferred in practice because writing obviously has an evidentiary effect to prove the modification,[200] and in certain cases, an oral modification is accepted only if both parties agree to it. On the other hand, if writing is required for modification under the agreement of the parties, a modification made orally may not be enforced unless the written requirement is waived or the parties agree otherwise.

However, modifications are also subject to certain restrictions. One restriction is legality, which means that a modification must not violate the legality requirement of the contract. To be more specific, a contract modification cannot render the contract itself illegal. In other words, legality is a matter of limits imposed on the parties to ensure that the enforceability of the existing contract will not be adversely

[198] See *id.*
[199] See *id.*, art. 533.
[200] See the SPC Leading Group,, Contracts, *supra* note 90, at 557–558.

affected by the modification. Otherwise, the modification will be invalid and unenforceable.

The other restriction is that the agreement to modify a contract must be unequivocal. Since modification involves changes that may result in a mutual adjustment of rights and obligations between the parties, it is essential that a modification made to the existing contract be clearly stated. According to article 544 of the Civil Code, if an agreement between the parties to modify the contents of a contract is unclear, the contract is assumed to have not been modified.[201]

For the purpose of contract modification, unequivocal change is a matter of burden of proof. According to the SPC, in a contract dispute, the party claiming that the contractual relationship has changed bears the burden to prove with evidence the facts of the change as such.[202] Ambiguity in contract modification mainly occurs in two situations: (a) the agreed change itself is ambiguous, or (b) the parties have different understandings of the contents of the change.

The primary legal effect of a valid modification is that performance shall be made based on the modified contract. Since the contents of the contract have changed as a result of modification, a failure to perform the modified obligations will constitute a breach of the contract for which the breaching party will be held liable. In addition, modification will only affect subsequent performance and thus has no retroactive effect on the obligations already performed. By the same token, the parties may not avoid previous performance on the grounds that the contract has been modified.

A debatable question arising from the modification of a contract is whether the modification will affect the right of the parties to seek damages. The question mainly involves the damages caused by one party to the other before the contract was modified. There are two different approaches: the independent claim approach and the waiver approach. The independent claim approach argues that the party's right to the recovery of damages is an independent claim and thus shall not be affected by modification. Thus, the aggrieved party may seek damages regardless of the modification agreement.[203] The waiver approach asserts that if not mentioned in the modification agreement, the right of a party to seek to recover the damages should be deemed to have been waived.[204]

Although proponents of the waiver doctrine believe that the way in which the modification agreement is made will lead to a different effect of the modification with regard to prior damages, they take the view that the modification shall not affect

[201] See the 2020 Civil Code, *supra* note 11, art. 544.

[202] See the SPC, *Several Provisions on the Evidences of Civil Litigation* (2001), art. 5, an English translation is available at https://seafarersrights.org/wp-content/uploads/2018/03/CHN_LEGISLATION_EVIDENCE-IN-CIVIL-PROCEDURES_2001_ENG.pdf, accessed August 26, 2025.

[203] See *id.*

[204] See Liming, *supra* note 21, at 206–208.

the liability for breach of contract that occurred before the contract was modified.[205] Their belief seems to suggest that the modification, depending on the parties' agreement, may affect the damages but not the liability for the breach of contract.

B. *Assignment*

An assignment in China is deemed as a change that involves the contractual parties or a transfer of contractual rights or obligations. Under the Civil Code, an assignment may take three different forms: transfer of contractual rights, transfer of contractual obligations, and transfer of both the rights and obligations of a contract. The former two refer to assignment and delegation, while the third concerns the replacement of a party so as to create a new contractual relationship. In Chinese contract textbooks, the replacement of a party is often called comprehensive assignment.

a. Assignment of Rights

Under article 545 of the Civil Code, the obligee may assign, in whole or in part, its *obligatio* rights to a third party.[206] In the 1999 Contract Law, the rights assigned are termed "contractual rights" or "rights under the contract." The Civil Code changes "contractual rights" to "*obligatio* rights," implicating that the rights assigned could be any rights arising from an *obligatio* relationship. Therefore, the application of article 545 is not necessarily limited to the assignment of contractual rights.

1. WHOLE OR PARTIAL ASSIGNMENT. As a result of assignment, the assignor's interests in the *obligatio* are transferred to the assignee. But in a whole assignment, the status of the assignee remains subject to debate. One opinion is that if the *obligatio* rights are assigned in whole, all the creditor's rights are transferred, and the original debt relationship is eliminated. Thus, upon an assignment in whole, the assignee then acquires the status of assignor, and a new debt relationship is established upon the assignment. Consequently, the obligor is obligated to make performance to the assignee.[207]

Others, however, disagree. They argue that, even if all of the creditor rights are transferred, the assignor may still be under an obligation to perform the obligations it is supposed to perform. The notion is that although a full assignment of creditor rights terminates the rights of the assignor, it does not necessarily extinguish the assignor's *obligatio* relationship with the obligor. Rather, it only conveys to the assignee the assignor's right to receive the performance from the obligor.[208]

[205] *id.* at 207–208.
[206] See the 2020 Civil Code, *supra* note 11, art. 545.
[207] See the SPC Leading Group, Understanding and Application of the Civil Code, Contracts, *supra* note 90, at 562.
[208] See Yang Lixin, Implication and Application of the Contract Law, 153 (Jilin People's Publishing House, 1999).

Indeed, the status of the assignor is of practical significance when a dispute arises between the assignee (the third party) and the other party (obligor) of the contract over contract performance. A question often raised involves whether the other party (obligor) may have a claim against the assignor. Put differently, the question is whether the assignor may remain liable when the assignee breaches the contract.

As noted, under Chinese contract literature, the parties to a contract assume mutual obligations. Based on this mutuality, a party in the contract is an obligee in one respect and an obligor in the other, depending on the nature of performance. The point is whether a full assignment necessarily breaks the mutuality of the contractual obligations between the parties to the contract.

If the creditor's rights are partially assigned, the assignee will join the existing debt relationship as a third party and share the creditor's rights with the assignor. But there has been concern that partial assignment may increase the burden of performance on the obligor because the obligor has to deal with more than one obligee after a partial assignment. One suggestion is that if a dispute arises, the increased burden on the obligor arising from the partial assignment should be a factor for the court to consider.

Also, the Civil Code contains no provision concerning multiple assignments of the same right. Since the Civil Code does not prohibit multiple assignments, many suggest that a contract right can be assigned more than once. In addition, if an assignment results in an increase of expense for performance, under article 550 of the Civil Code, the increased amount shall be borne by the assignor.[209]

II. FORMALITY OF ASSIGNMENT. Since assignment is a manifestation of the intent of the obligee to transfer its creditor's rights to a third party, there must be an agreement for an assignment. But the Civil Code does not impose a writing requirement on the assignment, nor is there any special formality the parties must follow to make an assignment. Therefore, the creditor's rights in China may be assigned in the way both the assignor and the assignee see fit. In most cases, assignment takes the form of writing.

However, the Civil Code mandates notice to the obligor as a prerequisite to the effectiveness of an assignment of the creditor's rights. Under article 546 of the Civil Code, if an obligee assigns his creditor's rights but fails to notify the obligor, the assignment will have no effect as to the obligor.[210] Since the Civil Code does not dictate the means of notice, it may be made orally or in writing, as long as the obligor is informed of the assignment.

Note that an assignment without notice to the obligor has no effect to the obligor, but the absence of notice does not affect the validity of the assignment agreement. In *Taibao Investment Management Co. Ltd. of Shunde District of Foshan City*

[209] See the 2020 Civil Code, *supra* note 11, art. 550.
[210] See *id.*, art. 546.

v. Guangdong Zhong Ding Group Co. Ltd., the parties disputed the validity of the assignment of creditor rights because of the lack of required notice. The SPC held that when assigning its creditor rights, the assignor should inform the obligor of the assignment; without such notice, the assignment shall not take effect as to the obligor. Thus, the obligor has a right against the claim of the assignee, but the validity of the assignment agreement reached by the assignor and assignee shall remain intact.[211]

Given the determinative force of notice to the effectiveness of an assignment, a related issue is whether an assignment notice, once sent, is revocable. Article 546 of the Civil Code further provides that notice of the assignment of the rights may not be revoked unless the assignee agrees.[212] Thus, once the assignment notice is dispatched, the revocability of the assignment is in the hands of the assignee.

III. NON-ASSIGNABLE RIGHTS. Generally, an assignor may assign all of its rights arising from an *obligatio* relationship. However, there are certain circumstances under which the creditor's rights are not assignable. Under article 545 of the Civil Code, the creditor's rights may not be assigned if the rights are non-assignable (a) according to the nature of the *obligatio*, (b) based on the agreement between the parties, or (c) as provided by law.[213] Thus, other than those listed in article 545 of the Civil Code, all rights in an *obligatio* relationship are assignable in China.

The nature of an *obligatio* relationship mainly refers to the contractual rights created based on the status of a specific party or in reliance upon a specific person's qualifications and ability. A contractual right is not assignable by nature if the contract is made between the parties with a distinctive personal feature or particular relations, and if the performance will be materially altered or the value of the performance will be substantially reduced if any of the contractual rights are assigned to a third party.

The contractual rights that are considered non-assignable by nature include: (1) rights that are based on personal trust and credibility, such as employment or agency; (2) rights arising from personal service contracts, such as entertainment performance; (3) subordinate rights, namely the rights dependent on the main rights of the contract, such as rights in a guaranty contract.

The creditor's rights may also not be assigned if the parties by agreement prohibit the assignment. The effect of an anti-assignment agreement is that any intended assignment will be ineffective unless the obligor consents to the assignment. In China, as long as the agreement prohibiting assignment does not violate mandatory provisions of the law or public policy, it will be held to be valid and enforceable.

[211] Taibao Investment Management Co. Ltd of Shunde District of Foshan City v. Guangdong Zhong Ding Group Co. Ltd., see the SPC (2004) Min Er Zhong Zhi No. 212.

[212] See *id.*

[213] See the 2020 Civil Code, *supra* note 11, art. 545.

In addition, non-assignment, if agreed, would mean to prohibit both the assignment of rights and the delegation of duties. The prohibition of assignment must be clearly stated in the agreement.

When a party breaches an anti-assignment agreement and assigns its rights in a contract to a third party, there is a question about the effectiveness of the assignment if the assignee is a third party. The Civil Code differentiates the assigned rights in violation of a non-assignment agreement into money-related or non-money-related rights pertaining to a third party. According to article 545 of the Civil Code, if a non-pecuniary claim is involved, the non-assignment agreement may not be asserted against a bona fide third person. If, however, the non-assignment agreement concerns a pecuniary claim, it may not be asserted against any third person.

Non-assignment as provided by the law mainly includes three rights. The first one is a right that is dependent on personal status or relation, such as family relation. A typical right that relates to personal status and therefore is not assignable is the right of claim for alimony, child support, or maintenance.[214] The second one is a right created and protected by the law for public policy concerns. Such a right includes the right to claim a pension fund, retirement fund, and labor insurance payment. The third right that is statutorily not assignable is a civil law claim right. The most common civil law claim is a tort claim. The right to a claim for an award arising from personal injury or dignitary damages may not be assigned.

IV. EFFECT OF ASSIGNMENT. A valid assignment has two effects. First, after the assignment, as noted, the assignee will take the place, in part or in whole, of the assignor and enjoy the creditor's rights accordingly. Generally, an assignment will make the assignee a new obligee (if it is a whole assignment) or a co-obligee (if it is a partial assignment). But, as noted, the obligor must be notified of the assignment by the assignor in order to effectuate the assignment.

When making an assignment, the assignor also has an implied duty to guarantee that the rights assigned are free from any claims. If there exist defects in the assigned rights that cause damages to the assignee, the assignor shall be held liable unless the assignee knew the defects at the time of assignment. In addition, the assignor has the obligation to provide the assignee with all documents necessary to prove the assigned rights.

Second, an assignment makes the obligor responsible for performance under the *obligatio* relationship. If the assignment is made in full, the assignor's right to demand performance ends. On the other hand, the obligor must perform the

[214] In China, alimony refers to mutual support between spouses, and maintenance concerns the support provided by adult children to their parents (old parents in particular). Under Chinese law, children have the obligation to support their parents. For example, article 49 of the 1982 Chinese Constitution (as amended in 2004) explicitly states that parents have the obligation to raise and educate their children who are minors, and adult children are obligated to support and assist their parents.

obligations to the assignee. If the performance is made to the assignor after the assignment (except for a partial assignment), the obligations will be deemed to have not been performed. Also, the assignor may be liable for unjust enrichment if it continues to accept the obligor's performance after the right to performance has been assigned.

An important matter involved in assignment is the right subordinate to the assigned rights, including the right to security interest and accrued interest, claim for stipulated damage, and claim for remedies. The subordinate right itself is not assignable independently, but will be transferred to the assignee when the creditor's rights are assigned.

Under article 547 of the Civil Code, when a creditor's right is assigned, the assignee acquires the accessory right related to the assigned right unless the accessory right belongs exclusively to the assignor.[215] Article 547 further provides that failure to register the assignment of the accessory right or failure to change the possession thereof does not affect the acquisition of the accessory right by the assignee.[216] Article 547 mainly applies to the situation where the right to after-sale services is assigned to the new owner in a transfer of real property.

V. RIGHT OF DEFENSE IN ASSIGNMENT. After assignment, the right of defense that the obligor has against the assignor remains unaffected but may be exercised against the assignee. According to article 548 of the Civil Code, after an obligor receives a notice of assignment of the creditor's rights, the obligor's defenses against the assignor may be asserted against the assignee.[217] The purpose is to protect the obligor's rights from being impaired as a result of the assignment. If, however, the assignor assigns all of its creditor's rights to the assignee, the obligor's defense based on the *obligatio* relationship with the assignor may only be asserted against the assignee.

Under the Civil Code, the obligor may also offset with the assignee the creditor's right that the obligor has against the assignor. Pursuant to article 549 of the Civil Code, an obligor may claim a set-off against the assignee if the obligor receives the notice of assignment of the creditor's rights, the obligor has a claim against the assignor which becomes due prior to or at the same time as the due date of the assigned rights, or the obligor's claim and the assigned creditor's right are created under the same contract.[218]

b. Delegation of Obligations

In China, delegation is generally defined as a transfer of debt obligations under a contract from the obligor to a third party without affecting the substance of the

[215] See the 2020 Civil Code, *supra* note 11, art. 547.
[216] See *id.*
[217] See *id.*, art. 548.
[218] See *id.*, art. 549.

original obligations. In Chinese contract law literature, delegation may take the form of assumption of the debts or a substitute of the obligor to perform. Assumption of debts means a transfer of debts by an agreement among the obligee, obligor, and third party, and the transfer may be made in whole or in part. Substitute of obligor refers to the situation where a third party offers to take the place of the obligor to perform contractual duties without an agreement for the transfer of debts. In the context of the Civil Code, delegation mainly refers to a transfer of debts by agreement.

I. DELEGATION AS A TRANSFER OF OBLIGATIONS IN WHOLE OR IN PART. The Civil Code allows for the transfer of debts. As a general rule, the obligor may delegate its obligations if the following conditions are met: (a) a valid *obligatio* relationship exists, (b) the obligor and the third party agree to the delegation, (c) the obligee makes no objection to the delegation, and (d) the obligations are delegable. In addition, under article 551 of the Civil Code, if the obligor delegates, in whole or in part, its obligations to a third party, it must obtain the obligee's consent.[219] Therefore, without valid consent from the obligee, no delegation will be permitted.

Chinese law distinguishes between a delegation in whole and a delegation in part. Delegation in whole is deemed to be a complete transfer of contractual obligations from the obligor to a third party. After such a transfer is complete, the original obligor is "exempted" from its contractual obligations and is replaced by a third party, the new obligor. A partial delegation is defined as a co-assumption of debts. When the obligor delegates some of its contractual obligations to a third party, the obligor and the third party become jointly responsible for the performance of the contract.

With regard to the consent of the obligee in the delegation of contractual obligations, there are no formality requirements in the Civil Code. Thus, the consent may be made in writing or orally, and may also be implied from the conduct of the obligee. Under article 551 of the Civil Code, the debtor or the third person may demand that the creditor give his or her consent within a reasonable period of time. If, however, the creditor makes no indication, it shall be deemed that no consent has been given.[220]

II. SUBORDINATE DUTIES. When an obligor delegates its obligations to a third party, the duties attached to the delegated obligations shall also be transferred along with the delegation. The duties that are deemed subordinate to the principal obligations include the duty to pay interest, the duty to pay stipulated damages or earnest money for breach of contract, and the duty arising from the guaranty that the obligor provided to ensure the performance of the obligations.

[219] See *id.*, art. 551.
[220] See *id.*

Because of the importance of subordinate duties in a delegation, the Civil Code requires a transfer of such duties in the delegation. In accordance with article 554 of the Civil Code, when a debtor delegates his obligation, the delegate shall assume the obligations subordinate to the principal obligation, unless the subordinate obligations belong exclusively to the original debtor. For example, if the parties agree that the obligor may paint a portrait for the obligee as a payment for the interest accrued from the contractual obligations, the duty to paint the portrait will be regarded as personally exclusive to the obligor and may not be delegated without the obligee's specific consent.

If, however, contract performance is under a guaranty provided by a third-party guarantor, the duty of guaranty will not be included in the delegation unless the guarantor expressly agrees to the continuance of the guaranty after the delegation. Otherwise, the guaranty ends with the delegation. According to article 23 of the Guaranty Law of China, if during the term of guaranty the obligee allows the obligor to delegate duties, the guarantor's written consent must be obtained in order for the said guaranty to remain effective. Thus, if the duties are delegated without the guarantor's consent, the guarantor will no longer be responsible for the guaranty.

III. NON-DELEGABLE OBLIGATIONS. The Civil Code in general imposes no restrictions on the delegability of contractual obligations. Thus, as long as the obligee agrees, all contractual obligations are delegable unless the obligations may not be delegated either because of the nature of the debts or because of the provisions of relevant laws. Also, if the contract contains a provision that explicitly prohibits delegation of obligations, no delegation shall be made unless otherwise waived by the obligee.

But for specific contracts, certain obligations may not be delegated to a third party. For example, under article 791 of the Civil Code, which concerns construction contracts, the general contractor for a construction project is prohibited from delegating its duty to any subcontractor on the construction of the mainframe of the project.[221] In addition, obligations that are normally deemed personal, such as obligations for child support or alimony, are also not delegable. Moreover, the obligor may not delegate to anyone his obligations arising from civil liabilities imposed by the operation of law. Such obligations include, for example, rehabilitation of another's reputation, elimination of ill effects, or apology to others.

IV. TRANSFER OF OBLIGOR'S DEFENSES AGAINST OBLIGEE. When an obligor delegates its obligations to a third party, any defense that the obligor has against the obligee will be transferred to the third party. Consequently, the third party may exercise the defense to the extent that the obligor is entitled to make it. A rule provided in article 553 of the Civil Code is that if an obligor delegates his obligation

[221] See *id.*, art. 781.

to a third party, the delegate may assert a defense the original debtor would have against the obligee.[222]

Note, however, that in order to effectuate such transfer, the right of defense that belongs to the original obligor in relation to the delegated obligations must accrue before the delegation is made. In other words, the third party or the delegate may not assert any defense that the original obligor may not have against the obligee before the delegation but acquired thereafter. In addition, as article 553 provides, if the original obligor has a credit right against the obligee, the delegate may not claim a set-off against the obligee.[223]

The transfer of the obligor's defenses also depends on the validity of the delegation. If the delegation is invalid or has not taken effect, the obligor's defenses will not be transferred. For instance, if the delegation requires the obligee's consent, a transfer of the obligor's defenses will not take effect unless the obligee agrees to the delegation of the contractual obligations. The simple reason is that without the obligee's consent, no delegation will be effective. Consequently, without an effective delegation, there will be no basis for the transfer of the obligor's defenses.

c. Comprehensive Assignment

In China, a comprehensive assignment occurs when there is both an assignment of contractual rights as well as a delegation of contractual obligations with regard to a particular contract. Under article 555 of the Civil Code, the party to a contract may assign its rights and obligations together under the contract to a third party with the consent of the other party.[224] Accordingly, then, a comprehensive assignment of the contract is permissible, but the consent of the other party is required.

A comprehensive assignment may be made by agreement. To assign a contract by agreement on a comprehensive basis, two agreements are needed. One is the agreement between the original parties, in which a party's request for a transfer of all of its rights and obligations under the contract to a third party is agreed to by the other party. The other agreement needed is the agreement entered by the assignor and assignee, under which the assignee agrees to take over the rights the assignor has under the contract, and in the meantime to assume all obligations that the assignor is required to perform.

Under the Civil Code, for a comprehensive assignment to be valid, four elements are required. First, there must be a valid contract. The existence of a valid contract is a prerequisite to assignment. Second, there must be mutual assent between the assignor and assignee to the assignment. Third, express consent must be obtained from the other party to the contract. And fourth, there must be no violation of law

[222] See *id.*, art. 553.
[223] See *id.*
[224] See *id.*, art. 555.

with regard to the assignment. For example, the contractual rights must be assignable, and the obligations must be delegable.

6. RESCISSION AND TERMINATION OF CONTRACTS

A legally formed contract must be performed, and any non-performance or incomplete performance of a contract will result in liability for breach of contract. If a breach occurs, remedies will follow under the terms of the contract, a provision of the law, or both. Non-performance, however, may be excused under certain circumstances. Excusal of non-performance leads to an alteration of the contract or a discharge of all contractual obligations. With an alteration, the contract is modified and performance continues on the modified basis. Discharge means that the contract is rescinded or terminated. Both rescission and termination bring the contractual relationship to an end.

In China, however, there have been debates over the difference between the rescission of a contract and the termination of a contract. One argument is that rescission and termination are the same, and rescission in essence refers to an advance termination of the contract by agreement of the parties or by operation of law.[225] The other opinion, however, regards rescission as one of the elements of contract termination. Under this opinion, rescission differs from termination in several aspects.

First, rescission may be followed by restitution in order to avoid unjust enrichment, but termination ends with the discharge of the contract. Second, rescission may retroactively affect past rights and obligations under the contract, while termination only deals with the present and future effect of the contract. Third, rescission is often used as a means to punish the breaching party. Termination, by contrast, is mainly used in situations where there is no breach of contract.[226]

In response to these debates, the Civil Code provides rescission separately from termination. The former deals with dissolution of contracts specifically, while the latter brings to an end the *obligatio* relationship in general. In both situations, the duty to perform a contract is discharged and the contractual relationship between the parties is extinguished. But in the case of rescission, the duty to perform a contract may be discharged without triggering liability for a breach of the contract, and the discharge may have a retroactive effect, meaning restitution.

A. *Rescission*

Rescission of a contract is a mechanism provided by the parties or by the law to nullify the binding force of the contract. The legal effect of rescission is to reinstate the original position of the parties prior to the contract. Under article 557 of the Civil

[225] See Liming, *supra* note 21, at 273.
[226] See *id.*

Code the relationship of rights and obligations under a contract is terminated upon rescission.[227] After the rescission, the parties will no longer be bound by the contract, and thus none of the parties have the right to ask the other party to perform the contract.

Under the Civil Code, a contract may be rescinded either by an agreement or pursuant to a provision of law. The statute requires that the rescission of a contract comply with the agreement or the provision of law. According to the SPC, if rescission by a party is made on grounds that do not meet the condition as agreed for the rescission or does not fall within any of the categories as provided in the Contract Law to trigger the rescission, the rescission, though it is requested by the party, has no effect and thus the performance of the contract will not be interrupted.[228]

a. Rescission by Agreement

Pursuant to the provisions of the Civil Code, a consensual rescission of a contract can be made (a) by an agreement, or (b) upon agreed conditions to rescind. Article 562 of the Civil Code provides that the parties may rescind the contract upon agreement through consultation. Article 562 further provides that the parties may agree on the causes for a party to rescind the contract, so that when a cause for rescission of contract arises, the party with the right to rescission may rescind the contract.[229]

A rescission agreement refers to mutual consent voluntarily reached by the parties to bring their contract relationship to an end after the contract is concluded but before the contract is performed or the performance is complete. An agreement on rescission has three distinctions. First, it is an agreement that is aimed at ending the existing contractual relationship. Second, the agreement is made after the conclusion of the contract and before the performance or completion of the contract's performance. Third, the agreement must be made voluntarily and reflect the true intention of the parties.

The effect of a valid rescission agreement is to extinguish the contract. The parties may, however, set forth a date on which their contractual relationship will cease to exist in the rescission agreement. If there is such a day in the parties' agreement for the rescission to take effect, the contract will remain in effect and the performance will continue until the date as agreed comes.

Rescission upon agreed conditions involves events agreed upon by the parties in a contract. An occurrence of any of the events enables a party to rescind the contract.

[227] See the 2020 Civil Code, *supra* note 11, art. 557.

[228] Sichuan Jufeng Real Estate Development Co. Ltd. v. Dazhou University of Broadcast and Television, the SPC (2013) Min Yi Zhong Zi, No. 18.

[229] See *id.*

Based on article 562 of the Civil Code, the notable feature of agreed conditions is that the conditions are contractually provided to give a party the right to end the contract upon satisfaction of the conditions as agreed by the parties. Satisfaction means the occurrence or non-occurrence of a certain event. In addition, the agreed conditions should be events that may happen in the future.

As discussed, there is a concept of a dissolving condition concerning a civil act. If a contract contains a dissolving condition, the occurrence of the condition will necessarily terminate the contract. The common character of a dissolving condition and an agreed condition is that both are provided in the contract and are the agreed-upon events that may affect the effectiveness of the contract. They, however, differ from each other in that the dissolving condition deals with automatic dissolution of the contract upon the occurrence of the condition, while the agreed condition may affect the contract only if the party having the right to rescind chooses to exercise the right.

b. Rescission by Provision of Law

Absent agreement by the parties, a contract may also be rescinded if certain events as set forth in the law occur. Rescission by operation of law takes place where the law allows a party to choose to cancel a contract when certain conditions are met. To compare, the rescission of a contract by agreement is a bilateral dissolution requiring both parties' consent, while rescission by operation of law is a unilateral dissolution that does not need consent from the other party.

Also, unlike rescission by agreement, rescission by operation of law is a statutory right that enables a party to dissolve a contract under specific conditions. The right is intended to effectively protect the legitimate interests of a contractual party by permitting the party to decide whether or not to stay in the contract. Note, however, that an affirmative action on behalf of the interested party is required to exercise the right to rescind a contract. In other words, the party able to rescind the contract under a provision of law must act to that effect in order to have the contract rescinded.

The Civil Code provides five circumstances in which a contract may be rescinded unilaterally. Each of the circumstances stands as the legal ground for the rescission of a contract. But for a contract under which the debtor is required to continuously perform an obligation for an indefinite period of time, the parties to the contract may rescind the contract at any time, provided that the other party is notified within a reasonable period of time.[230]

According to article 563 of the Civil Code, a party may rescind the contract when: (a) the purpose of the contract cannot be realized due to *force majeure*; (b) one party to the contract, before the expiry of the performance period, explicitly expresses or

[230] See the 2020 Civil Code, *supra* note 11, art. 563.

indicates through its conduct that it will not perform the principal obligations; (c) one party to the contract defaults in performing its principal obligations under the contract and, after being urged, fails to perform such obligations within a reasonable period of time; (d) one party to the contract defaults in performing its contractual obligations or commits other acts in breach of the contract so that the purpose of the contract cannot be realized; or (e) other situations as stipulated by law.[231]

As noted, *force majeure* is defined in article 180 of the Civil Code as objective circumstances that are unforeseeable, unavoidable, and insurmountable.[232] Such objective circumstances include natural disasters, abnormal social or political changes, and government action.[233] In addition, change of law is regarded as an objective circumstance for the purpose of dissolving a contract.[234] For instance, if a contract were to become invalid under a newly adopted law, the new law would be the cause of the contract's dissolution since the adoption of the new law would make it impossible to continue performing the contract.

Anticipatory repudiation is a concept borrowed from the common law that gives a party a legal right not to go forward with performance of a contract when the other party disclaims any intention to perform before the performance of the contract is due. Under article 563 of the Civil Code, three elements are required in order to find anticipatory repudiation: (a) manifestation of intent not to perform, (b) expiry of the time period for performance, and (c) non-performance of principal obligations.

Unreasonable delay in performance encompasses two situations: delay in delivery (including making a payment) or delay by the obligor, and delay in acceptance or delay by the obligee. Article 563 of the Civil Code deals only with delay in delivery because it is basically concerned with performance of obligations, while delay in acceptance mainly involves improper cooperation of the obligee with regard to the obligor's performance. In this context, delay in delivery is generally called delay in performance. Delay in performance occurs when the obligor fails to timely perform the contract as agreed.

When a delay in performance occurs, the obligee is required to "urge" the obligor to perform. To "urge" means to send a notice of performance to the obligor. The notice can be made either in writing or orally. After the notice, the obligor is allowed a reasonable period of time to prepare for the performance. A reasonable period of time is the time necessarily needed for the preparation according to the nature and customary practice of the particular transactions. In general, according to the SPC, a reasonable period of time after the notice and before the exercise of the right to rescind shall be no more than three months.[235]

[231] See *id.*
[232] See *id.*, art. 186.
[233] See Bixin et al., *supra* note 149.
[234] See *id.* at 268–269.
[235] See the SPC, *Interpretation of Several Legal Issues on the Application of Law in Adjudication of the Cases Involving Disputes over the Contracts of Sales of Residential Housing*, art. 15 (2003)

Thus, to rescind a contract based on delay in performance, the following elements are required: (1) delay in performance, (2) of principal obligations, (3) without just reason, and (4) failure to perform, (5) within a reasonable period of time, (6) after a notice to urge is given. Obviously, the requirement of impact on principal obligations serves a twofold purpose: to assure that the aggrieved party gets what he has bargained for, and to avoid undue hardship on the non-performing party arising from the possible rescission of the contract.

Frustration of purpose of a contract as a result of delay in performance or other conduct resulting in a breach of contract is centered on the consequences of non-performance of the contract. Rescission in this case can be triggered by two different causes: delay in performance and other breaches of contract. In either case, the key is whether the purpose of the contract is frustrated or destroyed.

A delay in performance itself, without more, would suffice to rescind a contract if the delay frustrates the purpose of the contract. For example, if the time of performance is critical or essential to the contract and any late performance would render the contract meaningless, the delay will give rise to the right of the aggrieved party to rescind the contract regardless of principal obligations or notice to urge performance.[236]

"Other conduct resulting in breaches of contract" as the cause to rescind a contract refers to all other situations where the purpose of the contract cannot be realized due to violation of statutory or contractual obligations and obligations under the principle of good faith. The situations as such include, among others, refusal to perform, defective performance, partial performance, and improper performance, as well as violation of such ancillary obligations as assistance, attention, care, and faithfulness under the good faith principle.

"Other reasons provided by the law for rescission" under article 563 is deemed a catchall provision under which a contract may be rescinded. The provision, on the one hand, requires a cross-reference to the relevant provision contained in another part of the Civil Code or any other existing laws, and on the other hand, leaves certain room for later legislation. For example, under article 528 of the Civil Code, a contract may be rescinded by a party if the other party, after the performance is suspended, fails to reinstate its capacity of performance and to provide proper assurance for the performance within a reasonable period of time.[237]

(absent legal provisions or agreement by the parties, the reasonable period of time for exercise of the right of dissolution is limited to three months after the notice to urge), available at http://gongbao.court.gov.cn/Details/56d4bed82d352fa9a0cdc850e97778.html, accessed August 26, 2025.

[236] A similar concept in this regard in U.S. contract law is the doctrine of "time is the essence of contract." But the difference is that in order to assert this doctrine to hold the other party who delays in performance liable, it must be specified in the contract (i.e., there must be a phrase in the contract stating that time is of the essence).

[237] See the 2020 Civil Code, *supra* note 11, art. 528. Other examples in the Civil Code include articles 610 (defective quality of contracted goods), 632 (defective item among many items), and 634 (failure to pay in installment payments).

For purposes of article 563, a question is whether "other laws" include lower-level regulations – for example, regulations adopted by the State Council, rules issued by various ministries, ordinances passed by local legislative bodies, or even government policies, as well as unpublished government directives. According to the SPC's interpretation, when determining the validity of a contract, the people's courts shall only follow the laws passed by the NPC and its Standing Committee, and the administrative regulations adopted by the State Council. Thus, in this context, the State Council regulations are a part of the law, but local ordinances are not.

c. Rescission Notice

Pursuant to article 565 of the Civil Code, if one of the parties requests to rescind the contract, the other party shall be duly notified. The contract is rescinded at the time the notice reaches the other party, or, where the notice states that the contract is to be automatically rescinded if the debtor fails to perform his obligation within a specified period of time, the contract is rescinded when the debtor fails to perform the obligation upon expiration of the specified period of time. In the meantime, article 565 gives either of the parties a cause of action to ask the court or arbitration body to affirm the validity of the rescission made under the contract or the provision of the law if the other party disagrees therewith.[238]

In addition, when the law or an agreement provides a time limit for exercising the right to rescind the contract, if the party with the right to rescission has not exercised the right upon expiration of the period, such right is extinguished. However, in the case where no such time limit is provided, the right is extinguished if not exercised within one year after the party with the right to rescission knows or should have known the causes for rescission, or within a reasonable period of time after being urged to perform by the other party.[239]

d. Effects of Rescission

When a contract is rescinded, the contract relationship between the parties ends. Under the Civil Code, a rescission not only terminates the contract but also retroactively affects part of the contract that has been performed. According to article 565 of the Civil Code, the rescission of a contract may have certain effects. First, after a contract is rescinded, if a contractual obligation has not yet been performed, the performance shall be terminated.

Second, if the contract has already been performed, the parties may, depending on the state of performance and the nature of the contract, request restoration to the original status, restitution, or other remedial measures, and if damages occur, the

[238] See *id.*, art. 565.
[239] See *id.*, art. 564.

parties have the right to seek compensation.[240] Restitution is aimed at restoring the parties to the position they were supposed to be in if the contract had not been performed, while compensation is made for losses.

Third, if a contract is rescinded due to a breach of contract, the party with the right to rescind the contract may request that the breaching party bear liabilities for the breach, unless otherwise agreed by the parties. In addition, when the principal contract is rescinded, a security provider shall still be obligated to secure the debtor's liability, unless otherwise agreed in the security contract.

The damages related to restitution are described by some scholars in China to include: (a) necessary expenses spent for the conclusion of the contract, (b) costs for the preparation for the performance of the contract, (c) opportunity costs, (d) losses caused by the failure to return the original items, and (e) other additional costs incurred to the aggrieved party as a result of the dissolution.[241] Non-performance damages normally refer to expectation interest and reliance interest.

In addition, when a party asks for damages while rescinding a contract under either the agreement or a provision of the law, the people's courts will normally require the presence of the following elements before a decision is made: (a) the other party has acted in breach of the contract; (b) the requesting party has chosen to rescind the contract; (c) the requesting party has suffered losses or damages; (d) there is causation between the damages and the conduct of the breach of the contract; and (e) the requesting party is not at fault.[242]

B. *Termination*

As noted, the Civil Code separates termination from rescission and applies the provisions of termination to the *obligatio* relationship in general. Under article 557 of the Civil Code, an *obligatio* relationship is terminated under any of the following situations: (a) the obligation has been performed; (b) the obligations are offset against each other; (c) the debtor has placed the subject matter in deposit in accordance with law; (d) the creditor has exempted the obligation; (e) the claim and obligation are merged to be held by the same person; or (f) there exists any other circumstance under which the claim or obligation is terminated as provided by law or agreed by the parties.[243]

The legal effect of termination is to discharge all duties under the *obligatio* and extinguish the *obligatio* relationship. However, there are at least two major post-termination issues. The first issue is the right to seek damages. Termination will not

[240] Keep in mind that the retroactive effect of dissolution only affects the contract or the part of the contract that has been performed. Where the contract or part of the contract has not yet been performed, retroactivity is not an issue.

[241] See Bixin, *supra* note 149, at 218.

[242] See *id.* at 400–401.

[243] See the 2020 Civil Code, *supra* note 11, art. 557.

abrogate the right of a party to seek damages resulting from the breach of contract caused by the other party.

The second issue concerns after-termination obligations. As provided in article 558 of the Civil Code, after *obligatio* rights and obligations are terminated, the parties shall, under the principle of good faith, perform such obligations as providing notice, rendering assistance, keeping confidentiality, and retrieving used items according to the course of dealing.

The Civil Code also contains certain rules that apply to the termination of *obligatio* relationship. One rule is the "settlement and clearance independence" rule. Under article 567 of the Civil Code, the termination of the rights and obligations of a contract may not affect the settlement and clearance clauses in the contract.[244] The same rule also applies to a dispute resolution clause, as to both litigation and arbitration, agreed upon by the parties.

The other rule is the rule of auxiliary obligations. Article 559 of the Civil Code explicitly provides that upon termination of the *obligatio* rights and obligations, the rights subordinate to the *obligatio* rights are extinguished concomitantly, unless otherwise provided by law or agreed by the parties. In contract, for example, when a contractual right is terminated, the right that relies on the contractual right – including such right as a security right, interest right, the right to claim liquidated damages, etc. – will also be extinguished.

a. Performance

An obligation is discharged after it has been fully performed. Once all obligations arising out of an *obligatio* relationship are fulfilled as agreed, the relationship between the parties under the *obligatio* comes to an end. As noted, pursuant to the complete and thorough performance principle, for obligations to be discharged, the performance would need to be appropriate, correct, and complete.

"Appropriateness" means that the contract is being performed according to the conditions and terms agreed upon by the parties. It also means that the performance complies with the good faith principle or provisions of law where certain terms of the contract are not clearly defined. For example, if there exists ambiguity as to the place of performance or the time of performance, the ambiguity needs to be clarified under the good faith principle or a provision of law absent agreement of the parties.

"Correctness" requires that there be no defects in the performance. Normally, a contract is to be performed by the obligor to the obligee. In certain cases, the performance can be made by a third party as long as the terms and conditions of the contract are met. To assure that performance is correct, the obligations should

[244] See *id.*, art. 98.

be cleared off by the delivery of the same item or services as agreed or a substitute item if it has the same value as the agreed item and is agreed by the obligee.[245]

"Completeness" means the satisfaction of the debts or realization of creditor's rights, since performance is geared toward satisfying the creditor's rights in order to accomplish the purpose of the *obligatio* relationship so created. Only if the creditor's rights are satisfied will the obligations be discharged. Therefore, for an *obligatio* relationship to be terminated via performance, the performance must be fully complete.

b. Offset

Offset applies where the parties are mutually obligated to each other, and their obligations may be discharged to the amount that can be offset. An advantage of offsetting is the efficacy in clearing off obligations the parties owe to each other.[246] As a mechanism and a statutory ground for the termination of an *obligatio* relationship, an offset can be made by law or under agreement.

Offset by law, also referred to as statutory offset, is one that meets the requirements of law and may be exercised through the operation of law. Under article 568 of the Civil Code, when the parties mutually owe obligations to each other, and the subject matter of the obligations are of the same kind and quality, any party may offset its obligation against the obligation of the other party that becomes due, unless the obligations cannot be offset by virtue of their nature, or in accordance with the agreements by the parties or the provisions of law.[247]

In addition, there are two requirements for making debt offset. The first requirement is notice. According to article 568, a party who claims a set-off shall notify the other party, and the notice becomes effective when it reaches the other party. The second requirement is that no conditions or time limit may be attached to the set-off.[248] A major change the Civil Code has made to the Contract Law in the statutory offset is that the Civil Code does not require debts to be offset if they are mutually due.

An offset may also be made by the agreement of the parties. According to article 569 of the Civil Code, if the parties mutually owe obligations to each other and the subject matter of the obligations are not of the same kind or quality, the obligations may also be offset upon agreement by the parties through consultation. Obviously, consensual offset is less restrictive than statutory offset.

[245] See Ling, *supra* note 179, at 179–180.

[246] In China, some scholars view an offset as having the function of guaranteeing performance of the contract. The reason for this is that since the parties are both obligee and obligor to each other, the creditor right of one party would be safeguarded by his obligations owed to the other party, and vice versa.

[247] See the 2020 Civil Code, *supra* note 11, art. 568.

[248] See *id*.

Consensual offset differs from statutory offset in several aspects. First, a statutory offset may be requested at the choice of a party unilaterally, but consensual offset requires mutual assent of the parties. Second, in a statutory offset, the subject matter of the obligations would need to be the same kind and quality, while the subject matter can be different in type and quality in a consensual offset. Third, for a statutory offset, the debts of the party requesting an offset must be due. A consensual offset, however, applies to any mutually owed debts regardless of whether they are due or not. Fourth, a statutory offset takes effect upon notice, but a consensual offset relies on the agreement of the parties.[249]

c. Deposit

For purposes of termination of an *obligatio* relationship, deposit – also called escrow – is a legal device by which an obligor may have its obligations discharged by submitting or delivering the unperformed obligations or the subject matter of the obligations to designated government authorities. Deposit is deemed necessary because in certain cases, for reasons beyond its control, an obligor may encounter difficulties in fulfilling its obligations.

The primary purpose of depositing the debt obligation or the subject matter of the contract with government agencies is to protect the legitimate interest of the obligor. Without such a device, the obligor would always be liable for unperformed obligations even when performance becomes extremely difficult for a cause attributable to the obligee. Since completion of the deposit directly results in the termination of the *obligatio* relationship, the use of the deposit is limited to the situation in which the obligor is left with no meaningful way to complete performance.

Under article 570 of the Civil Code, when it is difficult to perform an obligation under any of the following circumstances, a debtor may place the subject matter in deposit: (a) the creditor refuses to accept the performance without just cause; (b) the creditor cannot be located; (c) the creditor dies and his heirs or estate administrator have not been determined, or the creditor loses his capacity for performing civil juristic acts with no guardian determined; or (d) there exists any other circumstance as provided by law.[250]

Article 570 further provides that if the subject matter is not suitable for being placed in deposit or the expenses therefor are excessively high, the debtor may sell the subject matter through auction or sale, and place the proceeds in deposit.[251] According to article 571 of the Civil Code, the subject matter or the proceeds obtained from auction or sale of the subject matter are deposited when the debtor

[249] See the SPC Leading Group, Understanding and Application of Civil Code, Contracts, *supra* note 90, at 676.

[250] See the 2020 Civil Code, *supra* note 11, art. 570.

[251] See *id.*

delivers the subject matter or proceeds thereof to the deposit authority. Once the subject matter or its proceeds have been placed in deposit, the debtor is deemed to have performed to the extent of deposited subject matter.[252] In other words, after a valid deposit, the obligee will have no claim against the obligor with regard to the obligations involved.

The other circumstances under which a deposit can be made refer to the situations authorized by the law. One example is the Guaranty Law, where a number of provisions permit a deposit. For instance, under article 49 of the Guaranty Law, the proceeds obtained by the mortgager through transfer of the mortgaged property shall first be used to liquidate the claim secured by the mortgage, or it shall be deposited with a third party agreed upon by the mortgagee. Another example is the Rules of Notarization of Deposit adopted by the Ministry of Justice on June 2, 1995. One of the situations where a deposit may be notarized under the Rules is when the parties agree in their contract to make payment in the form of a deposit.

The Civil Code does not specify the authority with which the deposit should be made. Under article 2 of the Rules of Notarization of Deposit, deposit notarization is an activity to take care of or take custody of the object of the debts or guarantees (including substitutes) submitted by the obligor or guarantor for the benefit of the obligee, and to return them to the obligee when required conditions are met.[253] Relying on article 2 of the Rules, it is generally believed that the notary public office is the authority designated for the deposit. Some, however, argue that despite the Rules, deposit authority includes those appointed by the court, such as a bank, trust institution, or warehouse.

To make a deposit, the obligor needs to make the first request with all of the supporting documents. When approved by the deposit authority, the obligor shall submit what will be deposited. After the submission, the obligor will obtain a certificate of deposit. The certificate will have an evidential effect that releases the obligor from its debt obligations.

However, in order to make the deposit effective, the obligor must satisfy the requirement of notice. In accordance with article 572 of the Civil Code, after a subject matter is deposited, the debtor shall promptly notify the creditor or the creditor's heirs, estate administrator, guardian, or custodian for his property.[254] In addition, under article 573 of the Civil Code, after the deposit, the risk of destruction, damage, or loss of the subject matter shall be assumed by the creditor. Also, during the period of the deposit, although the accrued proceeds of the subject matter belong to the creditor, the expenses incurred should be borne by the creditor.[255]

[252] See *id.*, art. 571.

[253] See the MOJ, Deposit Notarization Rules, issued on June 2, 1995, art. 2, available at www.gov.cn/zhengce/1995-06/02/content_5713692.htm.

[254] See the 2020 Civil Code, *supra* note 11, art. 572.

[255] See *id.*, art. 573.

But the deposit made under the Civil Code shall by no means deprive the obligee of the rights to or interests in the deposited subject matter. Article 574 of the Civil Code provides that a creditor may collect the subject matter deposited at any time from the deposit authority. But if an obligation owed by the creditor to the debtor becomes due, the collect request may be rejected at the demand of the debtor before the creditor performs such obligation or provides security therefor.[256]

Although the obligee's right to claim the deposited object remains after the deposit, the right will be lost if not exercised after a certain period of time. Under article 574 of the Civil Code, the creditor's right to collect the subject matter placed in deposit is extinguished if such right is not exercised within five years from the date of deposit, and the subject matter shall then be escheated to the State, minus the deposit authority's expenses. If, however, a creditor fails to perform his overdue obligation to the debtor, or if the creditor waives his right to collect the deposited subject matter in writing to the deposit authority, the debtor has the right to take back the subject matter after paying the deposit expenses.[257]

d. Exemption

The obligations under an *obligatio* relationship may be exempted by the obligee in whole or in part, and after the exemption, the obligations are discharged with regard to the amount that has been exempted. Article 575 of the Civil Code provides that if the obligee exempts the obligor from its debt obligations wholly or partially, the whole or part of the rights and obligations shall be terminated, unless the debtor objects within a reasonable period of time.[258] Note that in contrast to article 105 of the 1999 Contract Law, article 575 adds a proviso clause to the debt exemption, aiming to provide the debtor with a choice to accept or reject the exemption.

There are certain conditions that must be met for an exemption. First of all, an exemption must be voluntarily manifested by the obligee eligible to dispose of the right to the performance of the obligations. Secondly, the manifestation of exemption must be made to the obligor. The legal effect of exemption is that the obligee forgives the obligor's obligations. Thus, if exemption is manifested to a third party, it will have no effect on the obligor and the obligor shall remain liable for the fulfillment of the obligations. In addition, an expression of intent for debt exemption, once made, may not be withdrawn. Thirdly, an exemption may not be made as a bargain with the obligor. To exempt the debt obligations, the obligee may not ask the obligor for something in return. Fourthly, the exemption may not affect the interests of a third party.

[256] See *id.*, art. 574.
[257] See *id.*
[258] See *id.*, art. 575.

e. Merger

A merger takes place when the *obligatio* rights and obligations are assumed by the same person as a result of consolidation of the parties or combination of the obligee's rights with the obligor's obligations. Under article 576 of the Civil Code, where a creditor's rights and an obligor's obligations are merged to be held by the same person, both the rights and the obligations are terminated unless the termination is detrimental to the interests of a third person.

As a result of a merger, the *obligatio* relationship comes to an end. It is a common view that a merger kills the creditor right because nobody may have a creditor right against himself. Also, under the doctrine of mutuality, there must be at least two parties in an *obligatio* relationship, and each has rights or obligations to the other. But if a third-party interest is at stake, a merger of rights and obligations will not result in a termination of the *obligatio* relationship.[259]

f. Other Circumstances

The other circumstances under which the obligation to perform may be exempted include those as agreed by the parties and those as provided by the law. The agreement-based circumstances refer to the situations where the parties agree on the termination of contract. As noted, the parties may agree to attach a dissolving condition or time period to a contract. When the condition is satisfied or the period expires, the contract is terminated.

Statutory-based circumstances are the grounds or facts as provided by the law for termination of a contract. For example, under article 934 of the Civil Code, an entrustment contract is terminated where the principal dies or is dissolved, or the agent dies, loses capacity for performing civil acts, or is dissolved, unless otherwise agreed by the parties or if it is inappropriate to terminate the contract based on the nature of the entrusted matter.[260]

C. *Debt Settlement*

Debt settlement or clearance refers to the act by which the debtor performs its debt obligations as agreed by the parties or under the provisions of the law so as to relieve the *obligatio* relationship. Therefore, when obligations are fully performed, the *obligatio* relationship between the parties is terminated. In many cases, however, when a debtor owes several debts to a creditor, if the payment made by the debtor is

[259] For example, if the creditor right of the contract is pledged to a third party as the security for a debt, the pledged creditor right shall remain intact despite the integration. In addition, a merger may also not affect the contractual obligations if so provided by law.

[260] See the 2020 Civil Code, *supra* note 11, art. 934.

not sufficient to settle all the debts, questions will necessarily arise as to which debts have been satisfied by the payment and which debts should be satisfied first in the situation where more than one debt has already become due.

The Civil Code establishes a mechanism to help determine the satisfied debts when the debtor's payment is insufficient to pay off the entire debt in the case where the debtor bears similar debts to the same creditor, or agrees to pay the same debt in installments. The mechanism consists of three settlement methods: under agreement, through designation, and by operation of law.

According to article 560 of the Civil Code, if a debtor owes a creditor multiple obligations of the same kind, and the debtor's payment is not sufficient to discharge all of the obligations, upon making performance, the debtor shall designate which obligation is to be discharged, unless otherwise agreed by the parties.[261] The implication of article 560 is that when a payment is insufficient to clear up entire debts, the debt settlement shall first be made as agreed by the parties. Absent an agreement as such, the debtor's designation controls.

If, however, there is no agreement or debtor's designation, the settlement shall then be made in an order as provided by the law. Under article 560 of the Civil Code, the order of debt settlement is as follows: (a) where the debtor fails to make a designation, the obligation that has become due shall be performed first; (b) where multiple obligations have become due, the obligation not secured or with the least security shall be performed first; (c) where none of the obligations are secured or the obligations are equally secured, the obligation with which the debtor assumes the heaviest burden shall be performed first; (d) where the burdens are the same, the obligations shall be performed in the priority order of their due dates; and (e) where the due dates are the same, the obligations shall be performed on a *pro rata* basis.[262]

Article 561 of the Civil Code further provides that in addition to performing the principal obligation, a debtor shall pay to the creditor interests and other expenses related to the enforcement of the obligation. If the payment is not sufficient to discharge all of the obligations, unless otherwise agreed by the parties, the debtor shall perform the obligations in accordance with such an order of priority as (a) the relevant expenses incurred by the creditor for enforcing the claim, (b) the interests, and (c) the principal obligation.[263]

7. BREACH OF CONTRACTS AND REMEDIES

The parties to a contract that is legally enforceable are mutually obligated to perform their respective obligations arising from the contract. A failure to perform without justification will constitute a breach of the contract for which the breaching party

[261] See *id.*, art. 560.
[262] See *id.*
[263] See *id.*, art. 561.

will be held liable. In the case of a breach, damages will be assessed and legal remedies available to the aggrieved party will be applied against the damages. Although remedies for breach of contract can be a broad topic, the basic forms of remedies include monetary compensation and non-monetary relief. In either form, there are also different types or categories, depending on the nature of the breach.

A. *Liability for Breach*

Liability for breach is defined in China as civil liability that is derived from a violation of a contractual obligation or a failure to render the performance that is due under a contract. Thus, once a breach occurs, liability arises. Defined as a consequence that requires a party who has failed to fulfill its obligations to either continue performing or take other remedial action,[264] liability is the legal ramification facing the breaching party in case of breach of contract or failure to perform.[265]

There are four liabilities related to contracts under the Civil Code: pre-contractual liability, liability after voidance, rescission or termination of a contract, liability arising from anticipated repudiation, and liability for breach of contract. As noted, pre-contractual liability involves an obligation resulting from the violation of a preliminary agreement to contract, while the liability in post-voidance, rescission, or termination concerns restitution and compensation. Anticipatory repudiation and breach of contract are the two major failures to performance in contracts as agreed by the parties for which the breaching party will be held liable.

The ground on which liability for breach of a contract is imposed has long been a contested issue in China. The center of the issue is whether the liability for breach of contract is imputed on a basis of fault or non-fault. Fault-based liability means that a breach may not necessarily result in liability unless the breaching party is found at fault. In other words, the liability imposition is contingent upon the presence of fault of the breaching party rather than the fact of breach. The non-fault-based liability focuses on whether there is a proven breach regardless of the underlying fault of the party in breach.

Under article 577 of the Civil Code, if a party fails to perform his contractual obligation or his performance does not conform to the agreement, he shall bear liability for breach.[266] Article 577 does not require a finding of fault on the breaching party in order to impose liability. Based on article 577, non-fault liability forms a general foundation for liability imputation in contracts. It is believed that in contrast to fault-based liability, strict contractual liability will better help protect the

[264] See Cui Jianyuan, Studies on Contractual Liabilities, 3 (Ji Lin People's Publishing House, 1992).

[265] See Liming, *supra* note 21, at 381.

[266] See the 2020 Civil Code, *supra* note 11, art. 577.

legitimate rights and interests of the parties and more effectively regulate the behavior of the parties.

The Civil Code, however, recognizes certain exceptions. For example, according to article 776 of the Civil Code, in a work contract, a contractor shall promptly notify the ordering party if the contractor finds that the drawings or technical requirements provided by the ordering party are unreasonable. But if losses to the contractor are due to indolence in reply by the ordering party, the ordering party shall be liable for providing compensation. In this case, the ordering party's fault (failure to timely reply) is required for the imposition of liability.[267]

In certain cases, the obligor's failure to perform is due to the obligee's fault. The question then is whether the obligor shall still be held liable for breach in this situation. Based on fairness considerations, the Civil Code imputes liability onto the obligee, rather than the obligor, when the obligee is found at fault. A notable provision to this effect is article 832 of the Civil Code, under which a carrier shall not bear liability for compensation for any destruction, damage, or loss of goods occurring in the course of transport if said destruction, damage, or loss is caused by the negligence of the consignor or the consignee.[268]

B. *Breach*

A common holding in China is that any failure to perform the contract without justification constitutes a breach, which includes (a) refusal to perform, (b) inability to perform, (c) delay in performance, and (d) incomplete performance. Under the Civil Code, a breach can take the form of anticipatory repudiation or actual breach. The former, as noted, refers to a situation where one party to a contract, before the performance is due, explicitly expresses or indicates through conduct that the contract will not be performed. The latter, however, is the case in which one party to a contract fails to perform its obligations under a contract or the performance fails to satisfy the terms or conditions of the contract.

a. Anticipatory Repudiation

Pursuant to article 578 of the Civil Code, anticipatory repudiation occurs when a party explicitly expresses or indicates by his actions that he will not perform his contractual obligation before expiration of the time period for performance. In its external form, an anticipatory repudiation may be expressed by language or implied from conduct. In either case, to find the repudiating party liable, the repudiation must be unequivocal.

[267] See *id.*, art. 776.
[268] See *id.*, art. 832.

As article 578 provides, when an anticipatory repudiation by a party occurs, the other party may request the former to bear liability for breach before the expiry of the time period for performance.[269] There are two options provided in the Civil Code pertaining to anticipatory repudiation. One option is to rescind the contract and the other is to sue for breach of contract. Note, however, that in order for a contract to be rescinded, an anticipatory repudiation must involve a principal obligation; whereas in seeking liability for breach of contract, the involvement of a principal obligation is not a prerequisite.

b. Actual Breach

Actual breach is a failure to perform a contract after the contract's performance is due. Failure to perform can be either a non-performance of contractual obligation or a non-conforming performance. Non-performance refers to a complete failure to perform the contract's obligations, and non-conforming performance is a partial failure to render performance. In many cases, an actual breach also includes delayed performance.

Based on its scale, a breach of contract is further divided into fundamental breach and non-fundamental breach. "Fundamental breach" is a concept contained in the United Nations Convention on Contracts for the International Sale of Goods, known as CISG. Under article 25 of the CISG, a breach of contract is fundamental if it results in such detriment to the other party as to substantially deprive him of what he is entitled to expect under the contract.[270]

In China, the test to ascertain whether the breach is fundamental is whether the purpose of the contract has been destroyed or whether the aggrieved party has suffered substantial damages.[271] If the breach is fundamental, the aggrieved party may either dissolve the contract or refuse to accept the performance.[272] If, however, the purpose of the contract is still attainable despite the breach, the breach is non-fundamental, and the aggrieved party may not terminate the contract or refuse to accept the goods, but may seek damages suffered therefrom.

Non-conforming performance occurs where the obligor has performed the contract but the performance is either incomplete or improper because it does not conform to the requirements of the contract. Performance will be deemed incomplete if only partial obligations of the contract have been performed during the

[269] See *id.*, art. 578.

[270] See the United Nations Convention on Contracts for the International Sale of Goods (1980), art. 25, available at https://uncitral.un.org/sites/uncitral.un.org/files/media-documents/uncitral/en/19-09951_e_ebook.pdf.

[271] See Xing Ying, Liabilities for Breach of Contract, 86–95 (China Legal System Press, 1999).

[272] One of the most commonly cited provisions in the Civil Code to support this argument is article 610, according to which if the quality of the goods fails to satisfy the quality required by the contract such that the purpose of the contract cannot be realized, the buyer may refuse to accept the goods or may dissolve the contract.

required time for performance. Complete and proper performance requires that the contract be performed to the extent that the quality, quantity, time, location, as well as manner of the performance, match the terms and conditions as agreed upon by the parties to the contract.

C. *Remedies*

Remedies, as provided in article 577 of the Civil Code, take three forms: continuing performance, remedial measures, and damages. Thus, when breach of contract occurs, the non-breaching party may seek either of the three remedy forms, depending on the nature and scale of the breach. Continuing performance possesses the character of compulsory performance and is available regardless of whether the legal or monetary remedy is adequate. Remedial measures generally mean the measures taken to help cure the defects in the performance. Damages refer to the remedy to compensate the losses resulting from the breach.

There is no preferential emphasis on any particular remedy; all remedies are optional to the aggrieved party,[273] and the remedies for breaches of contract are basically compensatory rather than punitive in nature.[274] In addition, according to article 583 of the Civil Code, if as a result of non-performance or non-conforming performance, the aggrieved party suffers other losses, the breaching party shall, after performing its obligations or taking remedial measures, compensate for the losses.[275]

a. Continuing Performance

Continuing performance requires that in the case of a breach, the breaching party, upon the demand of the aggrieved party, must continue to perform its contractual obligations if performance is possible. Since continuing performance is intended to effectuate the contract's performance as agreed, there should be no substitute performance. The ultimate goal of continuing performance is to help achieve what the parties have bargained for in their contract. Under the Civil Code, continuing performance may apply to both monetary and non-monetary obligations.

For the purposes of the Civil Code, a claim for continuing performance must meet certain conditions. First, there must be a breach of contract, because continuing performance is a remedy that is available only in the case of breach. Second, the performance as requested must be possible to continue. If performance becomes impossible either as a matter of fact or as a matter of law, there will be no basis suitable for continuing performance. Third, continuing performance must not be made at the court's initiative but rather be requested by the aggrieved party.[276]

273 See Wang Liming, *China's Proposed Uniform Contract Code*, 31 St. Mary's L.J. 7, 15–16 (1999).

274 See the Research Department of the General Office of the NPC Standing Committee, A Practical Guidance of Contract Law, 105–106 (Huawen Press, 1999).

275 See the 2020 Civil Code, *supra* note 11, art. 583.

276 See Han Shiyuan, The Law of Contracts, 603 (3rd ed., Law Press, 2001).

Monetary obligations are the obligations based on the payment of a certain amount of money. Continuing performance in most cases deals with monetary obligation. In accordance with article 579 of the Civil Code, where a party fails to pay the price, remuneration, rent, or interests required, or fails to perform another pecuniary obligation, the other party may request such payment or performance. It is commonly held that continuing performance for monetary obligations does not have to be specific.

However, there are two issues that concern monetary obligations. One issue is whether monetary obligations may be discharged by exemption. In general, a monetary obligation may not be exempted because of the highly fungible nature of money. On this ground, the performance of monetary obligations may not be excused on the grounds of *force majeure*, because a lack of money does not render the performance of a monetary obligation objectively impossible. In most cases, the difficulty in paying money can be overcome through other payment alternatives such as installments or extension of the payment period.

The other issue is whether the aggrieved party is entitled to other remedies when requesting the continuing performance of a monetary obligation. As noted, under the Civil Code, continuing performance and other types of remedies are not mutually exclusive. Therefore, while seeking continuing performance, an aggrieved party may still claim other remedies to which he is entitled.

Non-monetary obligations refer to any obligations other than the payment of money. As provided in article 580 of the Civil Code, if a party fails to perform a non-pecuniary obligation or the performance does not conform to the agreement, the other party may request continuing performance.[277] In addition, under article 581 of the Civil Code, if the continuing performance is not available due to the nature of the obligation, the non-breaching party may seek a substitute performance by a third party and ask the breaching party to bear the expenses that incur in this regard.[278]

But the court may not grant a request for continuing performance if (a) the performance is impossible either *de jure* or *de facto*; (b) the object of the obligation is not suitable for compulsory performance or the expenses for performance are excessively high; or (c) the creditor fails to request performance within a reasonable period of time. Pursuant to article 580 of the Civil Code, in the case where the purpose of the contract cannot be achieved, the court or arbitration body may terminate the contractual relationship upon request by a party, without affecting the liability for breach.[279]

It is important to note that for the purpose of article 580 of the Civil Code, "a party" includes both the breaching party and the non-breaching party. Therefore,

[277] See the 2020 Civil Code, *supra* note 11, art. 580.
[278] See *id.*, art. 581.
[279] See *id.*, art. 580.

when the purpose of the contract cannot be achieved, the breaching party also has the right to seek termination of the contract. However, to exercise the article 580 right to terminate a contract, certain conditions must be met: (a) the performance is non-monetary, (b) continuing performance is excused on any of the statutory grounds, (c) the contract's purpose cannot be realized, (d) the termination must be made by a court or an arbitration body upon request, and (e) the breaching party's liability for breach of contract shall remain.

b. Remedial Measures

Remedial measures are the remedies that are purposed to cure any defects in performance and simultaneously prevent further losses or damages that may incur in the breach of contract. Under the Civil Code, as discussed, measures that are remedial mainly include repair, reworking, replacement, return of goods, or reduction of price or remuneration. Given their focus on defective performance, remedial measures mostly apply to non-conforming performance in quality or performance that does not meet the standard, specification, or terms as agreed upon in the contract.

In accordance with article 582 of the Civil Code, the aggrieved party may seek remedial measures from the other party under the agreement between the parties as to the liability for non-conforming quality of performance. Absent such agreement, or if the agreement is unclear, and if the liability cannot be determined by a supplementary agreement, contract provisions, or transaction practices, the measures to be taken will be based on the nature of the subject matter and the degree of the losses.[280]

Again, though remedial measures mainly deal with defective performance, they may also be applicable to continuing performance when non-conforming performance is involved. Also, in order to make the application of remedial measures meaningful, two factors are considered important: (a) the defective performance is remediable, and (b) the breaching party has the ability to take the remedial measures.

c. Damages

Damages in contract law are basically the monetary remedy to compensate the losses that the aggrieved party suffers from the breach of contract. In certain cases, damages may take the form of "in kind," meaning other goods or items of the same quantity and quality used as a substitute for performance.[281] Compared with other

[280] See *id.*, art. 582.

[281] But if "in kind" damages are awarded, they must be something different from the object of the contract; or otherwise, the "in kind" would not be the damages but specific performance.

remedies provided in the Civil Code, damages have at least two unique distinctions. The first distinction is the nature of general application. Damages are applicable to any case where other remedies are not suitable, available, or adequate. The second distinction refers to the function of the supplement. Damages always function to fill in the gap left by other remedies or to supplement losses that cannot be recovered under other remedies.

Under the Civil Code, damages consist of direct losses and indirect losses. As provided in article 584 of the Civil Code, in the case of breach of contract, damages shall include the interests expected from the performance of the contract.[282] In its 2012 Interpretation on the 1999 Contract Law, the SPC explicitly states that when a party in a sales contract breaches the contract, causing damages to the other party, and the other party claims the interests it expected to receive, the court shall, on the basis of the claim, determine such interests in accordance with relevant provisions of law.[283]

The Civil Code also imposes a ceiling on damages. According to article 584, the total damages awarded shall not exceed the probable losses as a result of a breach that was, or ought to have been, foreseen by the breaching party at the time of the contract.[284] Since foreseeable damages include both direct and indirect damages, it can be inferred from article 584 that indirect damages, though not defined, must also be foreseeable at the time of contract.

To claim damages for breach of contract, the aggrieved party must prove (a) the fact of breach, (b) losses, and (c) the connection between the breach and the losses. Which damages are foreseeable is a matter for the court to determine. The standard generally employed is whether the damages are the reasonable and natural outcomes of the breach and whether the damages are those that would be contemplated by an ordinary person in the same or a similar situation at the time of contract. If the aggrieved party asks for additional damages, it must be proven that there are additional damages and the damages were foreseeable under the special circumstances known to the parties.

Under the Civil Code, there are four kinds of damages available for a breach of contract: compensatory damages, liquidated damages, punitive damages, and earnest money. As noted, contract remedies are in general compensatory by nature. Therefore, punitive damages are available only in very special and limited cases, and the imposition of such damages must have a statutory basis.

1. COMPENSATORY DAMAGES. The most significant damages provided for in the Civil Code are compensatory damages. Damages are deemed compensatory if their

282 See the 2020 Civil Code, *supra* note 11, art. 584.

283 See the SPC, *Interpretation on the Issues Concerning Application of Law in Adjudicating Disputes over Sales Contracts*, *supra* note 41, art. 29.

284 See the 2020 Civil Code, *supra* note 11, art. 584.

purpose is to place the aggrieved party in the same position that the aggrieved party would have been in if the contract had been performed as agreed upon by the parties. As noted, according to article 584 of the Civil Code, the breaching party shall be liable for damages that are caused to the aggrieved party, and the amount of damages shall be equal to the losses caused by the breach of contract, including the interest that would have accrued if the contract were performed properly.[285]

Article 584 of the Civil Code is the basic law of damages of a compensatory nature. But the determination of compensatory damages is subject to the rule of foreseeability. As noted, article 584 limits compensatory damages to the amount of probable losses caused by the breach of contract. The probable losses for the purpose of article 584 are the losses that were foreseen or should have been foreseen when the contract was made.

In addition, the Civil Code contains several special rules that govern damage compensation for breach of contract. The first one is the rule of mutual breach. According to article 592 of the Civil Code, where both parties are in breach of contract, each shall bear the corresponding liability. If, however, one party's breach causes losses to the other party, and the other party also has fault that contributes to such losses, the amount of compensation may be reduced accordingly.[286]

The second rule is the rule of mitigation. It is required under article 591 of the Civil Code that when a party is in breach of a contract, the other party shall take appropriate measures to prevent further loss. If no appropriate measures are taken so that the loss is aggravated, no compensation shall be made for the aggravated part of the loss.

In addition, the reasonable expenses incurred by a party in preventing the aggravation of the loss shall also be borne by the breaching party.[287]

The third rule is the rule of the obligee's liability for refusing to accept the obligor's performance. Pursuant to article 589 of the Civil Code, when an obligor performs his obligation in accordance with the agreement and the obligee refuses to accept the performance without just cause, the obligor may request that the obligee compensate him for any additional expenses.[288] Article 589 imposes liability on the obligee and gives the obligor the right to make a request for compensation. The trigger of article 589 is the obligee's refusal without justification.

In certain cases, however, the obligee does not necessarily refuse to accept the performance but delays in making its acceptance when the obligor performs. Under these circumstances, unless the delay makes it impossible to achieve the purpose of the contract, the obligor remains liable for performance. But in order to protect the obligor, article 589 provides a safety valve under which the debtor may not only be

[285] See *id.*
[286] See *id.*, art. 592.
[287] See *id.*, art. 591.
[288] See *id.*, art. 589.

able to claim additional expenses but also does not need to pay interest for the period of delay.

II. LIQUIDATED DAMAGES. Liquidated damages, also known as stipulated damages, are the damages provided in the contract that the breaching party must pay to the aggrieved party in the case of breach. One major aspect of liquidated damages is that such damages are agreed upon by the parties in advance and take effect when the breach occurs. Another notable aspect of liquidated damages is that such damages are not determined on the basis of actual losses but rather on an estimation of the losses as set forth in the parties' agreement. Liquidated damages may be made in the form of a specific amount of money or as calculated pursuant to a particular formula agreed upon by the parties.

Under article 585 of the Civil Code, the parties to a contract may agree that, in the event of a breach of the contract, the breaching party shall pay liquidated damages of either a certain amount or an amount calculated by a certain method agreed upon by the parties.[289] The liquidated damages so provided may become punitive when the actual amount of damages is less than the agreed-upon amount. A common understanding in China is that an important function of liquidated damages is to deter breaches of contract. Thus, by providing a liquidated damages amount or formula in the contract, the parties agree to accept economic punishment if either party fails to perform its obligations under the contract.

The Civil Code allows a justification to be made for the liquidated damages if the amount turns out to be unreasonably higher or lower than the actual damages. According to article 585, when the agreed-upon amount of liquidated damages is lower than the losses caused, the amount of liquidated damages may be increased upon request from one party. On the other hand, if the agreed-upon amount of liquidated damages is excessively higher than the losses caused, the amount may be appropriately reduced upon request from one party. In addition, when the contract provides liquidated damages for delayed performance, the breaching party shall continue to perform the obligation after paying the liquidated damages.[290]

The Civil Code provides no standard for the adjustment of liquidated damages. According to the SPC, when a party requests an increase in the amount of liquidated damages, the total amount after the increase must not exceed the actual losses.[291] On the other hand, if a party seeks to reduce the amount of the liquidated damages, the court shall make a decision in light of fairness and good faith principles on the basis of actual losses, with consideration of (a) the performance situation, (b) the degree of fault of the party, and (c) the expected interests of the

[289] See *id.*, art. 585.

[290] See *id.*

[291] See the SPC, Interpretation on Several Issues Concerning Application of Contract Law (II), issued by the SPC on April 24, 2009, arts. 27, 28.

party.[292] The standard for reduction is whether the stipulated damages are excessively higher than the actual losses. If the amount of stipulated damages is 30 percent higher than the amount of actual losses, the stipulated damages will be considered excessively high.[293]

III. PUNITIVE DAMAGES. Punitive damages are in general not available in contract claims because their primary purpose is to punish willful and wanton conduct in order to deter the wrongdoer or any other person from the same or similar conduct in the future.[294] In China, the award of punitive damages is not eliminated in contract cases, but the use of such damages is strictly limited. In other words, punitive damages may not be granted in contract claims unless otherwise provided by the law.

A provision in the Civil Code that contains punitive damages is article 587, in which a party receiving a deposit who fails to perform their obligation is required to refund double the amount of the deposit to the other party.[295] Another provision is article 49 of the Consumers Protection Law, which provides that if a business operator is found to have committed fraudulent conduct in providing goods or services, the damages for losses so caused to consumers shall be multiplied upon the demand of the consumers. The increased amount of damages shall be equal to double the amount of the price of the goods purchased or services received.[296]

IV. EARNEST MONEY. Under the Civil Code, the parties to a contract may agree to provide a sum of money as security to guarantee the performance of a contract. The sum of money so provided is labeled in China as earnest money. According to article 586 of the Civil Code, an earnest money contract is formed upon actual delivery of the sum. Article 586 further provides that the amount of earnest money shall be agreed upon by the parties but may not exceed 20 percent of the value of the underlying contract, and any excessive amount will not be considered earnest money.

If, however, the amount of the earnest money actually delivered is more or less than the agreed amount, the agreed amount of the earnest money is deemed to have been modified.[297] After a debtor has performed the obligation, the earnest money shall be deducted from the total price or be refunded. When a party paying the earnest money fails to perform the obligation or fails to perform it in conformity with

[292] See *id.*, art. 29.
[293] See *id.*
[294] See Joseph M. Peillo, Contract, 513 (7th ed., West, 2014).
[295] See the 2020 Civil Code, *supra* note 11, art. 587.
[296] See the Consumer Protection Law of China, promulgated by the Standing Committee of the NPC on October 31, 1993, art. 49, available at www.npc.gov.cn/zgrdw/englishnpc/Law/2007-12/12/content_1383812.htm.
[297] See the 2020 Civil Code, *supra* note 11, art. 586.

the agreement so that the purpose of the contract cannot be achieved, the party forfeits the earnest money. On the other hand, as noted, if a party receiving the earnest money breaches the contract, the party shall refund twice the amount of the earnest money.[298]

The contractual parties may agree on both liquidated damages and earnest money, but if a party defaults, the other party may only choose either liquidated damages or earnest money. However, under article 588 of the Civil Code, where the amount of earnest money is insufficient to compensate the losses caused by one party's default, the other party may request compensation for the losses in excess of the amount of the earnest money.[299]

D. *Statutory Exemption of Liability*

The only legal exemption of contractual liability under the Civil Code is the exemption on the grounds of *force majeure*. Pursuant to article 590 of the Civil Code, when a party is unable to perform the contract due to *force majeure*, the party shall be exempted from liability in whole or in part according to the impact of the *force majeure*, unless otherwise provided by law.[300] Upon the occurrence of *force majeure*, a party's obligation to perform the contract will be excused and the liability for breach will be exempted.

But there are two exceptions to the application of *force majeure*. The first exception is where the law provides otherwise. For example, under article 34 of the Post Law, *force majeure* may not exempt the liability of the post office for the loss of money remittances or insured postal articles. The second exception involves delayed performance. Article 590 of the Civil Code provides that if *force majeure* occurs after one party has delayed in performance, the liability shall not be exempted.[301]

Quite often, parties to a contract prefer to negotiate into their contract a *force majeure* clause in order to better protect their respective interests. Note that in China, absence of a *force majeure* clause does not deprive a party of the right to claim an exemption upon the occurrence of *force majeure* because of the statutory nature of the *force majeure* exemption. But if there is a *force majeure* clause in the contract, the clause will be regarded as a supplement to the legal exemption and may be used to help allocate risks and ascertain the scope or coverage of the *force majeure*.

In addition, it is required under article 590 that the party unable to perform the contract due to *force majeure* promptly notify the other party to mitigate the losses that may be caused to the other party, and shall provide proof of the *force majeure*

[298] See *id.*, art. 587.
[299] See *id.*, art. 588.
[300] See *id.*, art. 590.
[301] See *id.*

within a reasonable period of time.[302] To be exempted from liability for breach of contract on the grounds of *force majeure*, the breaching party bears the burden of proving that the circumstance leading to the failure to perform meets the standard of "unforeseeable, unavoidable and insurmountable."[303]

8. THIRD PARTIES

In the area of contract, a third party is a person who is not the party but is related to the contract or has interests in the contract. A broad definition of a third party also includes a person who has an impact on the performance of the contract. The very basic assumption in the contract literature is that a valid contract has an effect on, or produces consequences only for, the parties themselves, and does not externally affect others.[304] But the third-party theory penetrates the internality of the contract affairs and brings non-party interests into the center of discussion by looking at external effects created by the contract.

In China, third-party interests in contracts are handled in a way that is different from many other countries. First, there is no particular section but only scattered provisions in the Civil Code dealing specifically with third-party interests. Second, almost none of the contract books make third-party interests a separate issue or discuss them in a specific way. Thirdly, there is a lack of systematic rules that govern the relations between the parties and non-parties.[305]

The provisions in the Civil Code that involve third parties can be divided into different categories. Based on their role or status, the third parties under the Civil Code include: a third party who receives performance; a third party who performs the contract; a third party who causes a breach of contract; a third party who joins in the debt obligations; and the *bona fide* third party.

A. *Third Party Receiving Performance*

Under the Civil Code, the parties to a contract may agree to have the contract performed to a third party. In China, the third party who is designated to receive performance could be either the person upon whom the benefits of the contract will be conveyed through performance or the person who will not benefit from the performance but will receive the performance on behalf of the obligee for the benefit of the obligee. In the former situation, the third party is called the

[302] See *id.*

[303] See *id.*, art. 180.

[304] See Robert Scott & Jody Kraus, Contract Law and Theory, 1127 (3rd ed., LexisNexis, 2002).

[305] A predominant doctrine in China that precludes non-parties from a contract is the relativism of contract. Under this doctrine, only the parties may claim the rights and bear the obligations arising from the contract. In this sense, relativism may actually mean or bear a great resemblance to "privity," though the term "privity" is not commonly used in China.

beneficiary, but in the latter case, the third party is actually an agent of the obligee for the purpose of receiving the performance.

According to article 522 of the Civil Code, where the parties agree that the obligor performs the obligation to a third person, if the obligor fails to perform or the performance does not conform to the agreement, the obligor is liable to the obligee for breach of contract.[306] Three points can be inferred from article 522. First, it is permissible that a contract be performed to a third party upon the agreement of the parties. Second, a contract to be performed to a third party is enforceable, and failure to perform constitutes a breach of contract. Third, in the case of a breach, the obligee remains entitled to make a claim against the obligor for remedies.

Also, according to article 522, when it is provided by law or agreed by the parties that a third person may directly request that the obligor perform the obligation to him, and the third person does not explicitly reject it within a reasonable period of time, if the obligor fails to perform or the performance does not conform to the agreement, the third person may request that the obligor bear the liability for breach. But the obligor may assert against the third party any defenses that the obligor has against the obligee.[307]

The performance to a third party under article 522 is believed to possess three distinctive features. First, the contract will not be performed to the obligee but to the third party because the obligee has agreed that the third party will be the recipient of the performance. Second, the third party acquires directly from the agreement of the parties the right to request performance from the obligor, and then both the obligee and the third party have a right to the performance. Third, the performance to a third party is not premised on the consent of the third party.[308]

B. *Third Party Performing the Contract*

Third party performance, by Chinese definition, is different from delegation or novation in that third party performance involves no transfer of debt or change of party but only a substitute of the obligor for performance of the contract. The substitute of the obligor means that a third party agrees to render the performance of the contract to the obligee on behalf of the obligor. The substitute may occur in two situations: one is the situation where there is an agreement and contractual relationship between the obligor and the third party; and the other is the case in which a third party voluntarily performs for its own interests.

In accordance with article 523 of the Civil Code, where the parties agree that a third party performs the contract obligations for the obligee, if the third party fails to

[306] See the 2020 Civil Code, *supra* note 11, art. 522.
[307] See *id.*
[308] See Sun Lihai, A Practical Explanation to the Contract Law of China, 86–87 (Industry and Commerce Publishing House, 1999).

perform or the performance does not satisfy the terms of the contract, the obligor shall be liable to the obligee for breach of contract.[309] The provision of article 523 implicates a number of factors essential to third party performance.

First, third party performance is based on the consent of the parties to the contract. Second, the third party, when completing the performance, does not acquire the status of a party to the contract. Third, the third party may refuse to perform, and the obligee has no claim against the third party. Fourth, the debt obligations under the contract are borne by the obligor, not the third party. Fifth, the obligor remains liable to the obligee until its obligations are fully performed.

Voluntary performance by a third party is a situation where, absent a contractual agreement between an obligee and obligor, a third party voluntarily performs contractual obligations to the obligee on behalf of the obligor. According to article 524 of the Civil Code, if an obligor fails to perform an obligation and a third person has a lawful interest in the performance of the obligation, the third person has the right to make performance to the obligee on behalf of the obligor, unless the obligation may only be performed by the debtor based on the nature of the obligation, as agreed by the parties, or as provided by law.[310]

In contrast to third party performance under article 523, article 524 cases have several distinctive features. According to the SPC, the third party's voluntary performance occurs when (a) the contract does not stipulate that the third party has an obligation to perform; (b) the obligor fails to perform his obligations; (c) the third party has legitimate interests in the performance of the operations at issue, and (d) performance by the third party is not prohibited by the nature of the obligations, the parties' agreement, or the law.[311] Also, pursuant to article 524, after the obligee accepts the performance done by the third person, his claim against the obligor is transferred over to the third person, unless otherwise agreed by the obligor and the third person.[312]

C. *Third Party Causing Breach of Contract*

It is not uncommon that a contract is breached not because of the fault of either of the parties but due to the conduct of a third party. There can be different situations in which the breach of a contract is caused by a third party. In one situation, the third party is a secondary performer of the contract, meaning that the third party is assisting the obligor in performing the contract. The other situation involves a third party who is a subcontractor, responsible for performing the contract in whole or in part. A third situation is that the third party is the superior or parent company of a party to the contract.

[309] See the 2020 Civil Code, *supra* note 11, art. 523.

[310] See *id.*, art. 524.

[311] See the SPC Leading Group, Understanding and Application of the Civil Code, Contracts, *supra* note 90, at 421–423.

[312] See the 2020 Civil Code, *supra* note 11, art. 524.

Also, it is quite typical in China that a party, a state-owned enterprises for example, breaches a contract as a result of the conduct of a government authority, most of which occurs when the party is asked to change production plans or to accommodate local needs. As often is the case, the breaching party tries to avoid its liability for breach by citing the government action as an excuse.

Like the Contract Law, the Civil Code separates the claim for contract liability from other claims. According to article 593 of the Civil Code, a party who breaches a contract due to a third person's action shall bear liability to the other party for the breach under the law. The dispute between the breaching party and the third person shall be resolved separately in accordance with the provisions of law or the breaching party and the third person's agreement. For purposes of article 593, the government is treated the same as a third party.

The notion underlying article 593 is the doctrine of relativism of contract. Under relativism, a third party's conduct constitutes no breach of contract because the contract is only a matter between the contracting parties. But relativism does not mean that the third party is free from any liability for its conduct that is the cause of the breach of a contract. On the contrary, a third party will be liable to the breaching party when the third party's conduct is the direct cause of the breach of contract.

Article 593 is clear on two points: First, if a contract is breached due to the action of a third party, the breaching party is liable for the breach and the aggrieved party may not make, and does not need to make, any claim against the third party. Second, the breaching party may seek redemption from the third party, and if there is an agreement between the breaching party and the third party, the dispute over the redemption shall be settled according to the agreement.

D. *Third Party Joining of the Debt Obligations*

In a contract, once a creditor–debtor relationship is created, the relationship exists only between the parties, and thus the debtor is normally a party to the contract. In certain cases, however, a third party may voluntarily join in, or make accession to, the debts that incur between the parties under the contract. This joining in or accession is called debt assumption, which can be made independently by the third party or jointly with the existing debtor.

The joining in of the debt obligations by a third party under the provisions of the Civil Code refers to the situation in which a third party voluntarily joins in the debts and performs the contract along with the original debtor. With the third party's joining in the debts, the creditor is further secured to realize his rights and interests through the contract performance. In this case, the original debtor remains liable for the contractual obligation. The difference between the debt joining in and delegation is that, unlike delegation, the debt joining in does not require the consent of the creditor.

Under article 552 of the Civil Code, where a third person agrees with the obligor to join in the obligation and notifies the obligee of it, or a third person indicates to the creditor his willingness to join in the debt obligations, if the creditor does not explicitly make a rejection within a reasonable period of time, the creditor may request that the third person assume the obligations jointly and severally with the obligor to the extent of the obligation the third person is willing to assume.[313]

The SPC construes article 552 as consisting of four elements: (a) there exists an original credit–debt relationship under the contract; (b) a third party agrees to join in the debt as a new debtor; (c) the debt owed by the original obligor is not reduced or exempted; and (d) consent of the creditor is not needed as long as the creditor is notified or the creditor does not expressly object within a reasonable period of time.[314] A key feature of the debt joining in is that upon the third party's joining in the debt, the third party and the debtor are jointly and severally liable for the contractual obligations.

E. Bona Fide *Third Party*

A *bona fide* third party is generally understood in China as someone who is not a party to a contract but is related in good faith to one of the parties in the contract. There are several articles in the Civil Code that are aimed at protecting the *bona fide* third party in good faith. In contract, article 545 of the Civil Code provides that a contract may not be assigned if the parties have an agreement prohibiting the assignment; however, an agreement that involves a non-pecuniary claim may not be asserted against a *bona fide* third party.[315]

The protection of *bona fide* third parties is purposed to maintain the fairness of transactions. Thus, to identify a *bona fide* third party, two conditions must be met: (a) the third party has no knowledge or has no reason to know about any issue in the transaction involved, and (b) the third party has not acted inappropriately or negligently in the transaction. Innocence is the key for the third party to be qualified as *bona fide*.

[313] See *id.*, art. 552.

[314] See the SPC Leading Group, Understanding and Application of Civil Code, Contracts, *supra* note 90, at 581–582.

[315] See the 2020 Civil Code, *supra* note 11, art. 545. The other provisions of the Civil Code that protect *bona fide* third parties include article 311, concerning good faith acquisition of a property from a person who has no power to dispose of the property, and article 312, involving a return of lost property from a *bona fide* third party. In addition, in each of the following cases, no claim may be made against a *bona fide* third party: (a) establishment, change, transfer, and elimination of property rights in ships, aircraft, motor vehicles, etc. without registration, (b) change or transfer of land contract management rights without registration, (c) establishment of an easement without registration, and (d) establishment of a mortgage right over moveable property without registration.

10

Law of Personality Rights

INTRODUCTION

In civil law, as noted, rights can generally be divided into three major categories: personal rights, property rights, and *obligatio* rights (creditor's rights). Personal rights refer to those that a person has over his or her body, or those appertaining to the person, which includes rights of personality, personal identity, and status. In contrast to property rights, personal rights do not directly involve property interests and in principle may not be transferred or abandoned because the rights as such exclusively belong to, and are inseparable from, the person – natural persons as well as legal persons. Different from the *obligatio* rights, which are relative rights, personal rights, like property rights, are absolute in their nature.

In the Civil Code, the rights of personality are provided in part Four. The significance of part Four is that it constitutes an independent part of the Civil Code specifically governing the rights of personality. In many countries, the rights of personality are traditionally not provided separately in a single law but are scattered in various provisions of different laws. In the United States, personality rights are generally referred to as tort-based rights, including the right to privacy and the right of publicity.[1] For that reason, part Four of the Civil Code is viewed in China as a breakthrough from tradition in civil legislation.

In Chinese civil law literature, the rights of personality are stated as the very basic and important rights of the civil law person because the rights not only affect the personal freedom and dignity of a person, but also form the basis for the exercise of all other rights.[2]

[1] See Case Western Reserve Univ. School of Law, IP Law Guide, available at https://lawresearchguides.cwru.edu/IP/personality-rights, accessed August 26, 2025 (The right of publicity is a state law-based right addressed in torts. The matters involved include (a) intrusion upon physical solitude, (b) public disclosure of private facts, (c) depiction in a false light, and (d) appropriation of name and likeness).

[2] See the Supreme People's Court Working Group, Understanding and Application of the Civil Code of China – Law of Rights of Personality, 13 (People's Court Press, 2020).

Conceptually, the rights of personality can be general or specific. The general rights of personality consist of such rights as individual freedom and personal dignity, while the specific rights of personality involve a wide range of rights related to the person. A striking distinction is that the general rights of personality apply only to natural persons.

Article 990 of the Civil Code defines the rights of personality as the rights enjoyed by the person of civil law, which consist of the right to life, corporeal integrity, health, personal name, trade name, personal portrait, reputation, honor, privacy, and the like. In addition, under article 990, a natural person also enjoys other personality rights and interests arising from personal liberty and human dignity. Again, the rights arising from personal liberty and human dignity are the general rights of personality, and all other rights fall within the specific rights of personality. Moreover, unlike the property rights that require a statutory basis, the rights of personality can be created either on a statutory basis or on a non-statutory ground.

Personality rights in China are further divided into material personality rights and spiritual personality rights. The former refers to the personality interests embedded in the human body, including rights to life, body, and health. The latter means personality interests pertaining to the person with spiritual attributes, including the right of portrait, reputation, honor, privacy, and other related rights. The differentiation between material and spiritual personality rights is of significance in the determination of the type of remedies available in case of infringement.

The legislation on the rights of personality in China began with the adoption of the 1986 General Principles of Civil Law. Under article 99 of the 1986 General Principles of Civil Law, legal persons, individual businesses, and individual partnerships shall enjoy the right of name, and enterprises as legal persons, individual businesses, and individual partnerships shall have the right to use and lawfully assign their own names.[3] Article 101 of the 1986 General Principles of Civil Law further provided that citizens and legal persons shall enjoy the right of reputation, and the personality of citizens shall be protected by law. Any insult, libel, or other means damaging the reputation of citizens or legal persons shall be prohibited.[4]

It is held in China that although the 1986 General Principles of Civil Law did not use the term "rights of personality," it in fact recognized the rights as such, including the rights to name, reputation, and honor.[5] In 2001, the SPC in its Interpretation on Several Issues Concerning Determination of the Liability for Mental Damages Compensation in Torts for the first time referred to personal dignity and personal liberty rights as rights of personality.[6] In 2017, when the 2017 General Provisions of

[3] See General Principles of Civil Law of China (1986), art. 99, available at www.china.org.cn/china/LegislationsForm2001-2010/2011-02/11/content_21898337.htm.

[4] See *id.*, art. 101.

[5] See Wang Liming, The Law of Personality Rights, 28 (Renmin University Press, 2009).

[6] According to the SPC, if a natural person suffers illegal infringement of the following personality rights and files a lawsuit in a people's court for compensation for mental damage, the people's court shall accept the case according to law: (1) right to life, right to health, and

Civil Law (GPCL) was adopted, the rights of personality were signified as basic civil rights. The 2017 GPCL, as claimed in the country, laid a foundation for the rights of personality to become an independent part of the Civil Code.

Part IV of the Civil Code contains 6 chapters and 51 articles in total. The provisions in part IV include the rules that govern rights of personality in general, and the rules that apply specifically to different aspects of personality rights. Premised on the civil rights section of the General Provisions of the Civil Code, part IV stipulates the personality rights with particularities, aiming at establishing a mechanism for protection of the rights of personality. In addition, the provisions in part IV have integrated relevant liability rules of torts.

1. GENERAL PROVISIONS OF THE RIGHTS OF PERSONALITY

In contrast to other civil rights, a distinctive feature of the rights of personality is their inherent nature. Inherent here means that acquisition or extinguishment of the personality rights occurs automatically upon the birth or death of a natural person, or upon the creation or dissolution of a legal person. Because the rights of personality are so closely related to the person, they can be exercised by a person in the way that would best serve the person's own personal interests.

The Civil Code provides a set of general rules that apply to the rights of personality. The rules govern such issues as, among others, (a) the exercise of the personality rights and limitations; (b) protection of the rights of personality; (c) remedies available in case of infringement of the personality rights; and (d) expanded protection. More specifically, the general rules consist of one principle and several basic rules that govern the rights of personality.

A. *Principle of Non-Infringement*

According to article 991 of the Civil Code, the personality rights of a person are protected by law and are free from infringement by any organization or individual. Non-infringement under article 991 means that any person has the right to prohibit others from illegally interfering with or infringing upon his or her personality rights.[7] In China, personality rights are viewed as rights against all, meaning that an exercise of personality rights resists any interference from any other person. Therefore, when the right of personality of a person is interfered with or harmed, the person is entitled to a claim against the infringer for torts liability.

right to body; (2) right to name, portrait, reputation, and honor; and (3) right to personal dignity and personal liberty. See the SPC, *Interpretation on Several Issues Concerning Determination of the Liability for Mental Damages Compensation in Torts* (2001), art. 1, available at www.lawtime.cn/article/lll8897898948830016009.

7 See the Civil Code of China, art. 991, available at https://regional.chinadaily.com.cn/pdf/CivilCodeofthePeople%27sRepublicofChina.pdf.

The provision of article 991 is based on article 38 of the 1982 Constitution. Under article 38, the personal dignity of citizens of the People's Republic of China is inviolable, and any insult, libel, false accusation, or false incrimination directed against citizens by any means is prohibited.[8] As noted, article 109 of the Civil Code makes personal liberty and dignity basic civil rights that are protected by law. It is then held that articles 109 and 991 of the Civil Code transform the personal liberty and dignity provided in the Constitution for citizens into rights of personality to which a person is entitled under civil law.

B. *Non-Alienability*

The basic rules set forth in the Civil Code are the statutory norms under which the rights of personality are exercised and maintained. The first one is the rule of non-alienability. Article 992 of the Civil Code makes it imperative that the rights of personality should not be waived, transferred, or inherited.[9] As noted, a distinctive feature of the rights of personality is exclusivity. The substantial elements of exclusivity include (a) non-separability, (b) non-transferability, (c) non-inheritability, and (d) non-waiverability. Because of their exclusivity, the rights of personality are not alienable.

The non-alienability of personality rights, however, does not prohibit others from using parts of such rights. On the contrary, under article 993 of the Civil Code, a person in civil law may by way of authorization allow others to use his name, identity, likeness, or the like, unless the authorization is not allowed by law or the nature of the right.[10] In other words, the personality right of a person may be used by others through authorization of the person. Authorized use is widely considered an exception to the non-alienability of the rights of personality.

C. *Protection of the Deceased*

The second rule is the rule that extends the protection of the personality rights to the deceased. Again, a settled proposition is that the rights of personality of a person go with the person. An issue that necessarily arises, however, is whether the rights of personality may exist before the birth, or after the death, of the person. As discussed, an unborn baby under the Civil Code will be deemed to have the capacity of civil rights, but only for the protection of interests in inheritance, acceptance of gifts, or the like.[11] Then, an extension of the protection of the rights of personality mainly involves the deceased.

[8] See 1982 Chinese Constitution, art. 38, available at www.npc.gov.cn/zgrdw/englishnpc/Constitution/2007-11/15/content_1372964.htm.

[9] See the Civil Code, *supra* note 7, art. 992.

[10] See *id.*, art. 993.

[11] See *id.*, art. 16.

According to article 994 of the Civil Code, where the name, likeness, reputation, honor, privacy, remains, or the like of the deceased is harmed, the spouse, children, and parents of the deceased have the right to request that the actor bear civil liability in accordance with law. If the deceased has no spouse or children, and the parents of the deceased have already died, other close relatives of the deceased may make such request under the law. Thus, the beneficiary of the extended protection of a deceased's rights of personality could be the spouse, children, parents, or close relatives of the deceased.

The provision of article 994 involves two basic questions. The first question is which of the rights of personality of a deceased person should be protected. Article 994 is clear that the personality rights of a deceased that should be protected include his/her name, likeness, reputation, honor, privacy, and remains. There are three interests embodied in the personality rights of a deceased: personal interests of the deceased, family interests of the deceased, and social interests. The notion underlying extended protection is that the personality rights of the deceased have spiritual value that can turn into commercial or property value. The effect of the spiritual value as such signifies that the deceased person should be respected, and his/her good reputation or honor should be protected.

The commercial or property value refers to the gains or benefits obtained from the use of the deceased's personality rights for commercial purpose. Those who benefit from the use of the deceased's personality interest include the family members or close relatives of the deceased, the public or the state, and developers. The family members or close relatives of the deceased are the primary beneficiaries of the property interests derived from the use of the deceased's personality interests. The public or state becomes the beneficiary only if the personality interests of the deceased belong to the public or the state.[12] "Developer" refers to the person who utilizes the personality interests of the deceased to pursue commercial development when such personality interests are not protected and thus become public resources.

An issue concerning the rights of personality of a deceased person is whether their protection is subject to a term limit. The Civil Code is silent in this regard. In practice, Chinese courts seem to take the liberty of using their discretionary power to make the determination on a case-by-case basis. Generally, if property interests such as the deceased's portrait and name are highly commercialized, the courts would apply the Copyright Law by analogy, allowing a fifty-year limit after the death of the deceased. For all other interests, the length of protection varies depending on the specific circumstances and social reality.

[12] In general, for public figures, the civil law no longer protects their personality interests after death, and thus the property interests of their personality rights belong to the public. In certain cases, the personality interests of the deceased belong to the state, such as state leaders as well as historical figures whose personality interests are protected by the state. See the SPC Working Group, *supra* note 2, at 67.

When the period of legal protection expires, the personality interests of the deceased will become public domain. It is held in China that after passing the protection period, the personality interests of the deceased may be utilized to meet the needs of the public and create social value.[13] It is, however, required that the utilization of the personality interests of the deceased should abide by public order or good customs and should not violate social morals.[14] The second question is who may make claims for compensation when the rights of personality of the deceased are infringed. Pursuant to article 994 of the Civil Code, given their beneficiary status, the spouse, children, parents, or other close relatives of the deceased are eligible to make the claim.[15]

A related question is whether the use of the portrait or likeness of the deceased requires the consent of the deceased's family members or close relatives. One argument is that because the portrait of a deceased has specific spiritual, emotional, and economic value to the family members and close relatives of the deceased, the right to use the portrait of the deceased should belong to the family members or close relatives of the deceased. Based on this argument, it will be considered illegal to use the portrait of the deceased without the consent of the family members or close relatives of the deceased, unless the use has been pre-authorized by the deceased.[16]

The counterargument holds that the use of portrait rights of the deceased does not require the consent of the family members or close relatives of the deceased. The reasoning is that use of the portrait of the deceased without the consent of the family members or close relatives of the deceased, even if the use is for the purpose of making a profit, does not constitute infringement as long as the use does not harm the reputation or personal dignity of the deceased's family members or close relatives and does not violate moral standards.[17] For example, it is believed that a mere use of a deceased portrait does not necessarily constitute a tort unless the use violates good morals.

D. *Remedies*

The rule of remedies refers to the civil liability for the infringement of the rights of personality. Under article 995 of the Civil Code, a person whose personality rights are infringed upon has the right to request that the infringer bear civil liability and is entitled to civil remedies.[18] Under article 995, the remedies for infringement of the rights of personality include cessation of the infringement, removal of the nuisance,

[13] See *id.* at 68.
[14] See *id.*
[15] See the Civil Code, *supra* note 7, art. 994.
[16] See the SPC Working Group, *supra* note 2, at 69.
[17] See *id.*
[18] See the Civil Code, *supra* note 7, art. 995.

elimination of the danger, elimination of adverse effects, rehabilitation of reputation, and extension of apologies. Note, however, that an extension of apologies is not subject to the statute of limitations.

In addition, the Civil Code provides the person whose personality rights are infringed with the right to request a restraining order from a court to stop the infringement. The issuance of a restraining order is at the discretion of the court but must meet two requirements. First, there must be clear evidence to prove that the infringer is committing or is about to commit an illegal act that infringes upon the personality rights of the claimer. Second, it must beproven that failure to timely stop the infringing act will cause irreparable harm to the lawful rights and interests of the claimer.

Under article 998 of the Civil Code, in the determination of civil liability for infringing upon another's personality rights, factors that should be considered include the occupations of both the infringer and the infringed, the scope of impact, the degree of fault, as well as the purposes, methods, and consequences of the infringing conduct.[19] But this factor-based consideration does not apply to infringement upon another's right to life, to corporeal integrity, or to health.

The civil liability imposed on personality rights infringement may arise from torts or contract. As noted, article 186 provides that if a party's breach of contract causes harm to the other party's personal or proprietary rights and interests, the other party may elect to request the breaching party bear liability either for breach of contract or for commission of tort.[20] In a torts case, the injured may claim both property and mental damages, while in a contract case, mental damages are in general not permitted. But for a contract-based claim against personality rights infringement, the Civil Code allows mental damages to be awarded.

In accordance with article 996 of the Civil Code, when the personality rights of a party are harmed by the other party's breach of contract and the injured party thus suffers severe emotional distress, if the injured party chooses to request the other party bear liability based on breach of contract, the right to claim compensation for pain and suffering will not be affected.[21] In China, article 996 is viewed as a provision that governs liability and compensation for mental damages in the situation of concurrent liabilities between torts and contract.[22]

The Civil Code also contains two specific provisions. The first is the provision of matching. In the case of personality rights infringement, the remedies available under the law are mostly non-property based, and some of the remedies are difficult to measure. For that reason, article 1000 of the Civil Code explicitly provides that when a civil liability such as elimination of adverse effects, rehabilitation of

[19] See *id.*, art. 998.
[20] See *id.*, art. 186.
[21] See *id.*, art. 996.
[22] See the SPC Working Group, *supra* note 2, at 80.

reputation, or extension of apologies is imposed for infringing upon other's personality rights, the imposition shall be commensurate with the way the infringing act is committed and the scope of its impacts.[23]

The second provision is compulsory enforcement. According to article 1000, if an infringer refuses to bear civil liability for the infringement of the other's personality rights, the court may take such measures as making an announcement, publishing the final judgment, or the like, through media, such as newspapers, periodicals, or online websites. In this case, the infringer will be required to bear any expenses thus incurred.[24]

E. *Fair Use*

The rule of fair use constitutes an exception to the infringement of personality rights. The essence of personality rights is the right to control personal interests under the law and to prevent others from infringing with the purpose of realizing and maintaining personal dignity and liberty. But in certain cases, personality rights may be reasonably used to serve certain public interests. In other words, the use of personality interests of a person without the person's consent does not necessarily constitute an infringement if the use is reasonable and for public interests.

Pursuant to article 999 of the Civil Code, the name, identity, likeness, personal information, and the like of a person may be fairly used by those engaged in news reporting, public opinion supervision, or the like, for public interests.[25] A civil liability shall be imposed only if the use unreasonably harms the personality rights of the person. In the application of article 999, however, there are two issues subject to debate. The first issue is what may be considered a fair use,[26] and the second issue is what the scope of the public opinion supervision should be. The second issue is more controversial than the first one because the public opinion supervision seems very vague and overly broad as well.

2. RIGHTS TO LIFE, CORPOREAL INTEGRITY, AND HEALTH

Among the rights of personality, the most significant is the right to life. With life safety and dignity as essential components, the right to life is not only an important personality right of natural persons, but also constitutes the very basis of all other personality rights. A fundamental notion is that personality rights would not exist without the right to life. Thus, when a conflict occurs between the right to life and

23 See the Civil Code, *supra* note 7, art. 1000.

24 See *id.*

25 See *id.*, art. 999.

26 According to the SPC Working Group, fair use has at least two meanings: (a) the contents of the use are fair and (b) the means to obtain the personal information are reasonable. See the SPC Working Group, *supra* note 2, at 112–113.

all other rights, the right to life prevails in all aspects. Closely related to the right to life are the rights to corporeal integrity and health.

A. *Contents and Scope of the Right to Life*

The Civil Code makes the right to life paramount to all other rights of personality. It is signified in article 1002 of the Civil Code that a natural person enjoys the right to life. Article 1002 mandates that a natural person's life safety and dignity be protected by law and be free from infringement by any organization or individual.[27] Life safety is purposed to maintain the continuity of life. It is a general holding in China that the maintenance of life safety is made mainly in the form of defense, including protection for life interests and defense against infringement.

Under articles 1003 and 1004 of the Civil Code, a natural person enjoys the rights to corporeal integrity and health, and the person's corporeal integrity, freedom of movement, and physical and mental health are protected by law and free from infringement by any organization or individual. As noted, the rights to corporeal integrity and health, together with the right to life, of a natural person are collectively referred to as material personality rights on which the spiritual personality rights depend.

The right to corporeal integrity, or the bodily right of a natural person, is the right to maintain and control corporeal integrity, including limbs, organs, and other bodily tissues. Therefore, if any of the components of a person's body are forcibly controlled and used against the person's will, the person's right to maintain and control his or her body is violated. In the case of violation, the injured person is entitled to legal remedies, including both property and mental damages, in addition to such other remedial measures as cessation of the infringement, removal of the nuisance, and elimination of the danger.

The Civil Code also imposes an obligation to rescue when a person's right to life, body, or health is in danger. Such obligation, however, is imposed only upon those who are legally obligated to assist. Article 1005 of the Civil Code explicitly provides that where a natural person's right to life, corporeal integrity, or health is infringed upon or otherwise in peril, the organization or individual who is legally obligated to aid shall promptly extend rescue.[28] The significance of article 1005 is that it makes the obligation to rescue a statutory requirement.

B. *Protection of the Right to Life*

The Civil Code contains specific provisions that are aimed at effectively protecting a person's rights to life, corporeal integrity, and health. A highly notable one is the

[27] See the Civil Code, *supra* note 7, art. 1001.
[28] See *id.*, art. 1005.

provision on organ donation. In China, organ donation refers to the act of a natural person voluntarily giving away his own organs, blood, bone marrow, corneas, and other body parts, or even his body after his death, free of charge. Although organ donation in the country began in the 1960s, there were no regulations on it until the State Council adopted the Regulations of Human Organ Transplant in 2007, where voluntariness is required for organ donation. The Civil Code is the first national legislation that governs organ donation.

The Civil Code reinforces the voluntary principle for human organ donation. In accordance with article 1006 of the Civil Code, a person with full capacity for performing civil acts has the right to make a voluntary decision in accordance with law to donate his cells, tissues, organs, and remains. Article 1006 prohibits any organization or individual from forcing, deceiving, or inducing a person to make such donation. In addition to the requirement that the person making the organ donation should have full civil capacity, article 1006 also requires the consent of the person for organ donation purposes to be made in writing or through a will.[29]

Thus, according to the provisions of the Civil Code, an organ donation must meet four conditions: (a) the person making the donation must have full civil capacity, (b) the donation must be made on a voluntary basis, (c) the donation must be made free of charge, and (d) the person's consent to donate must be expressed in writing. Note that to encourage organ donation, the expression of consent to donate under the Civil Code can be made either by the donor or by the donor's family members or close relatives.[30] It is provided in article 1006 that where a natural person has not been opposed to being an organ donor during his life, his spouse, adult children, and parents may, upon his death, jointly decide to make the donation. Again, the decision so made shall be in writing.[31]

Another provision is article 1007, which prohibits any form of purchase or sale of human cells, tissues, organs, or remains.[32] Since article 1007 is mandatory, it may not be derogated from by the parties through their agreement. Put differently, any contract for an organ transaction will violate article 1007 and therefore be void. The underlying concept is that the selling or buying of human cells, tissues, and organs destroys the integrity of a natural person's body and thus damages the person's right to their body. The very purpose of article 1007 is to protect the right to the body of natural persons.

A related provision concerns human body-related study and research. The Civil Code allows medical and scientific research activity involving human genes, embryos, and the like.[33] But such research, under article 1009 of the Civil Code, is subject to two requirements. First, the research must follow relevant provisions of

[29] See *id.*, art. 1006.
[30] See *id.*
[31] See *id.*
[32] See *id.*, art. 1007.
[33] See *id.*, art. 1009.

the state laws, administrative regulations, and rules. Second, the research shall not endanger human health, offend ethics and morals, or harm public interests.[34]

The Civil Code also contains a provision that regulates clinical trials. Article 1008 of the Civil Code has specific requirements for conducting clinical trials in the country. First, there must be a need for developing new drugs and medical devices or developing new prevention and treatment methods. Second, the conduction of clinical trials must be approved by the relevant competent authorities and also must pass examination and approval of the ethics committee. Third, participants in the clinical trials, or the guardians thereof, shall be informed of the details of the study, including the purposes, methods, and possible risks of the trial. Fourth, for the purposes of clinical trials, written consent must be obtained from the participants or their guardians. In addition, no fees may be collected from the participants in the clinical trials.[35]

There are two protective provisions in the Civil Code that are purposed to safeguard the right to corporeal integrity and dignity of a person: one is the rule against sexual harassment, while the other is the rule of civil liability imposition on the conduct of illegal search and detention. Sexual harassment in China has long been a widespread social issue that raises serious concerns in the nation, especially in workplaces. The lack of effective measures against sexual harassment prompts public demand for an anti-sexual harassment mechanism.

In 2005, China revised the 1992 Law of the Protection of Women's Rights and Interests (Women Protection Law) to include a provision that prohibits sexual harassment of women and grants women victims the right to file complaints with their working units and relevant authorities. This is the first legislation in the country that clearly stipulates against sexual harassment.[36] However, the Women Protection Law contains no provisions of civil obligations and responsibilities arising from sexual harassment. The Civil Code cures this deficiency and clearly defines sexual harassment as an act of infringing on a person's personality rights.

Under article 1010 of the Civil Code, a person who has been sexually harassed against his/her will by another person through oral words, written language, images, physical acts, or the like, has the right to request that the actor bear civil liability in accordance with law.[37] In addition, it is required that State organs, enterprises, schools, and other organizations take reasonable precautions, accept and hear complaints, investigate and handle cases, and take other measures to prevent and stop sexual harassment conducted by a person taking advantage of his or her position, power, or a superior–subordinate relationship.[38]

[34] See *id.*

[35] See *id.*, art. 1008.

[36] The Law of the Protection of Women's Rights and Interests was adopted on April 3, 1992, by the NPC and revised on August 28, 2005, available at http://gongbao.court.gov.cn/Details/45412fdb12dd405d68004o694bd425.html.

[37] See *id.*, art. 1010.

[38] See *id.*

Thus, when encountering sexual harassment, the victim has the right to request the perpetrator stop. The request may be made either directly to the perpetrator or to a court. In addition to the right to make a request, the victim is also entitled to remedies if harm occurs. The remedies include property compensation and compensation for mental damages. The property compensation mainly covers medical expenses, nursing fees, loss of wages, or other financial damages resulting from wrongful termination of employment. Also, the victim may seek other remedies, including elimination of ill effect and extension of apologies.

The provision against illegal search and detention is article 1011 of the Civil Code. Derived from article 37 of the Constitution that prohibits unlawful detention or search of a person, article 1011 provides that a person whose freedom of movement has been deprived of or restricted by illegal detention or similar measures, or whose body has been illegally searched, has the right to seek civil remedies against the actor.[39] The application of article 1011 requires such essential elements as (a) unlawfulness of the conduct of detention or search, (b) harm, (c) causation between the conduct and harm, and (d) fault of the actor.[40] The civil remedies include cessation of the infringement, removal of the nuisance, damage compensation, elimination of adverse effects and rehabilitation of reputation, as well as extension of apologies.

3. RIGHT TO NAME

The right to name refers to the right to choose, use, and change the name of a person in accordance with the law. In civil law, the name of a person can be the name of a natural person or the name of an entity, namely a legal person or an unincorporated organization. For a natural person, the right to name is an indispensable right of the person. A distinctive attribute of the right to name is its absoluteness, meaning that the right may be exercised against all others for purposes of infringement.

Under the Civil Code, the right to name is prescribed as a right of personality. Although the right to name involves not only personal interests but also family interests as well as property interests, it is not characterized in China as a property right, an intangible property right, or a family right. The main argument is that despite its property nature, the right to name cannot be transferred or disposed of as a property. In addition, the name of a natural person is associated more closely with personal identification than family ties, though it derives from and reflects the family relation.[41]

A. *Legal Significance of a Person's Name*

An individual name is an identification of a natural person, which distinguishes one from another. The name of a natural person, like gender, age, birth, or domicile,

[39] See *id.*, art. 1011.
[40] See *id.*
[41] See Liming, *supra* note 5.

constitutes a determinative factor for individualization and personalization of the person. Additionally, a person's name may possess certain economic value to the person. In one situation, when a person uses his or her name in the commercial field, generating economic gains, the name itself becomes an asset to the person. In another situation, if a person is a prominent or public figure, the person may authorize others to use his name for commercial purposes and get paid for it through an agreement.

Given the significance of names, article 1012 of the Civil Code provides that a natural person enjoys the right to their name, and is entitled to determine, use, change, or allow others to use his or her name in accordance with law. Under article 1012, an exercise of the right to name, however, shall not violate public order or offend good morals.[42] Article 1012 is understood in China to also implicate that a natural person has the right to keep his own name and may not be forced to give up or change the name without his consent.

The limitations on the use of a name by a person under the "public order or good morals" provision are described in China to include several aspects. First, the composition of a person's name shall comply with the laws and relevant administrative regulations. Second, a personal name shall be used on the household registration card, and the name so used shall be identical to the name appearing in all personal identification cards. Third, the right to the use of a person's name shall not be abused. Abuse is considered to occur when a person (a) allows others to use his name in a way that violates public order and good morals, (b) illegally transfers his name, or (c) changes his name for such purpose as committing bigamy or tax evasion.[43]

B. *Name Right Infringement*

The infringements of the right to name vary. In most cases, however, the infringements fall within three major categories. The first category is the case where a person's right to determine, use, or change his or her name is interfered with. The interference often seen is in the situation where an adopted child or person under guardianship attempts to change his or her family name but meets resistance from their adoptive parents or guardian. Another situation in which an interference occurs is that a person prevents others from using the same surname as that of the person.[44]

The second category refers to the case in which a person misappropriates or fraudulently uses the name of another person. In either situation, the use of a person's name is made without the person's authorization or consent. A major

[42] See Civil Code, *supra* note 7, art. 1012.
[43] See the SPC Working Group, *supra* note 2, at 192–194.
[44] See Liming, *supra* note 5, at 194–195.

distinction between the two, according to Chinese scholars, is that misappropriation often directly damages the interests of the victim, while fraudulent use is purposed at obtaining illegal personal gains by using the name of another person to undertake civil or business activities.[45]

The third category includes all other situations where the right to name is infringed. In one case, for example, in order to retaliate against the plaintiff, the defendant used the plaintiff's name for the character in his novel to vilify and humiliate the plaintiff. Many in China take the view that the use of the other person's name, or a name similar to the other person's name, may constitute an infringement of the right to name if it can be determined that the name is used to refer to the person specifically.[46]

An entity name is a symbol and mark used by a legal person and other unincorporated organizations to identify and represent itself and to distinguish it from others.[47] Under article 110 of the Civil Code, a legal person or an unincorporated organization enjoys the right to entity name, the right to reputation, and the right to honor.[48] Article 1013 of the Civil Code explicitly provides that a legal person or an unincorporated organization enjoys the right to an entity name, under which it is entitled to decide, use, change, transfer, or allow others to use its entity name in accordance with the law.[49]

As noted, a business entity in China can be formed as a legal person or unincorporated person, and a legal person can be a for-profit legal person, non-profit legal person, or special legal person. Under the Civil Code, an entity has the right to choose its own name, but the establishment of an entity name is subject to certain legal requirements. One requirement is registration. If registration is required for a legal person to be formed, the name of such legal person will not be established until registration is complete. In China, except for some special legal persons, registration must be made for a legal person to be formed.

The other requirement concerns the components of an entity name. According to 2012 State Council Regulations on the Administration of Enterprise Name Registration (as amended 2021), the name of an enterprise shall be composed of the name of the administrative division, the trade name, the industry or operating

45 See *id.* at 196.

46 See *id.*

47 The symbol or mark used as the entity name differs from the trademark, if any, of the entity. First, the right to name is a right of personality, while a trademark is a property right. Second, a trademark must be distinctive to avoid public confusion, but the entity name need not have such attributes. Third, from a legislative viewpoint, the right to name is mainly to maintain the independence and integrity of the person's personality. In contrast, the trademark right mainly reflects the economic interests of the right holder in the goods or services it provides. See *id.* at 203–204.

48 See Civil Code, *supra* note 7, art. 110.

49 See *id.*, art. 1013.

characteristics, and the form of organization.[50] It is further required that the trade name contained in the enterprise name consist of two or more Chinese characters.[51]

A significant difference between the name of a natural person and the name of an entity is that the latter is transferrable while the former may not be transferred. Unlike a natural person's name, an entity name is considered an intangible asset that possesses logo value, advertising value, as well as goodwill value. The transfer of an entity name means that the transferor gives all the rights to name to the transferee, and after the transfer, the original name right holder no longer has the right to the name. It is mandated that when transferring an enterprise name, the transferor and transferee sign a written contract and agreement, and file it with the original registration authority for approval.

Compared with the name of an entity, the name of a natural person is more dependent on the person. Normally, a natural person's name in China is composed of two parts: a surname and a given name. The surname is also known as the family name. In traditional Chinese culture, a family name embodies blood inheritance and ethical order. Therefore, the choice of a family name involves public morals. On that ground, the Civil Code contains a special provision that governs both acquisition and selection of a family name.

C. *Rules Governing the Right to Name*

Under article 1015 of the Civil Code, the general rule of naming is that a natural person shall take the family name of either his or her father or mother. The natural person, however, may take a surname other than his father's or mother's if the chosen name is (a) the family name of a senior lineal relative by blood; (b) the family name of a non-statutory foster parent who provides care thereto; or (c) a particular family name with other legitimate reasons that do not offend public order and good morals.

In China, statutory foster liability lies between parents and children, between grandparents and grandchildren, and between elder sister or brother and younger sister or brother. But, as for grandparents or elder sister and brother, their foster liability arises only when (a) the parents die or are incapable of raising children, and (b) the grandparents or elder sister and brother are able to foster. Note, however, that an adoption of the family name of a non-statutory foster parent requires the mutual consent of both the child and the non-statutory foster parent.

Non-violation of public order or good morals is a catch-all clause that allows a person to have ample freedom to choose a surname. The whole idea is that in all

[50] See the State Council, *Regulations on the Administration of Enterprise Name Registration*, adopted in 2012, art. 6, amended 2021, available at www.gov.cn/zhengce/content/2021-01/19/content_5581091.htm.

[51] See *id.*, art. 8.

other situations, there is no need to impose harsh restrictions on the right of a person to choose a surname if public order and good morals are not violated. The underpinning theory is personal autonomy, meaning that a person should be allowed to select a surname based on his or her own values or interests. In other words, the selection of a surname can be made by a natural person according to his or her personal desire or preference.

One practical issue from which a dispute often arises is whether the selection of a child's surname requires parental consent. In many cases, it is a question whether a remarried mother may unilaterally change, or a marital mother may unilaterally determine, the surname of her child. Under Chinese tradition, a child normally takes his or her father's family name as his or her surname. It is true especially when the child is male, because in Chinese society a boy is considered the person who should carry the paternal (father) family name.

There is no readily available answer in Chinese law. One argument is that selection of the surname of a child shall follow the principle of mutual determination by parents. If, however, the parents have divorced or are not married, the parent who lives with and raises the child may unilaterally determine the child's surname. The other argument takes the view that selection or change of the surname of a person shall vary depending on such factors as (a) personal preference if the person is able to make an independent judgment, (b) the best interests for physical and mental growth if the person is a minor, and (c) possible impacts on the person.[52]

It is held in China that selecting, changing, or transferring the name is a manifestation of a person's independent decision, but the name itself also involves the state and other public interests. Thus, it is required under the Civil Code that a natural person who decides to take or change his name, or a legal person or an unincorporated organization who decides to take, change, or transfer its entity name, should file for registration with the relevant authority unless otherwise provided by law. In addition, after the name change, the person involved shall remain bound by the acts performed prior to the change.

D. *Protection of Famous Names*

The Civil Code contains a provision that is aimed at protecting the name of famous people. According to article 1017 of the Civil Code, with regard to a pseudonym, stage name, screen name, translated name, trade name, abbreviation of a name, or entity name of social popularity, if the use of which by others will cause public confusion, the relevant provisions for the protection of the right to the name of a natural person or an entity shall be applied *mutatis mutandis*.[53] Article 1017 is a reference clause that enables other laws to apply for the purpose of protecting a famous name.

[52] See the SPC Working Group, *supra* note 2, at 214.

[53] See the Civil Code, *supra* note 7, art. 1017.

Application of article 1017 may only be triggered when (a) the person concerned is of social popularity, and (b) public confusion occurs as a result of the use of the person's name. The Civil Code provides no definition of social popularity. As a practical matter, however, the popularity is judged under two tests. One test is the degree of public knowledge of the name at issue, while the other test is the level of public recognition of it. In China, the popularity of a person can generally be divided into some popularity, relatively high popularity, and extremely high popularity. For article 1017 to be applied, only some popularity would suffice if public confusion could be caused by the use of the name of the person involved.

4. RIGHT TO LIKENESS

The likeness or portrait of a person is defined in article 1018 of the Civil Code as an external image of a specific natural person contained in or reflected by video recordings, sculptures, drawings, or other media by which the person can be identified. Article 1018 explicitly signifies that a natural person enjoys the right to likeness and is entitled to make, use, publicize, or authorize others to use his or her image in accordance with law.[54]

The implication of article 1018 is that the right to likeness rests only with a natural person. Thus, legal persons and unincorporated organizations do not have a right to likeness. A common belief in China is that, as an external image of a specific natural person, the likeness reflects the external image characteristics of the person. For that reason, likeness is considered a basic element of personality that is closely related to personal dignity and the social evaluation of a natural person.[55]

For purposes of article 1018, the external image refers to, but is not necessarily limited to, the facial image of a natural person. Therefore, any external feature of a natural person can become part of the likeness of the person as long as it presents the external image so clearly that the external feature, in the eyes of others, belongs to a specific natural person. It is important to note, however, that likeness is not merely an external image of a particular person but one that is identifiable.[56] More specifically, if a claimed misappropriation of the image of a claimer does not clearly reflect the claimer's personal characteristics and thus is not identifiable, there would be no infringement of the claimer's right to likeness.

A. *Protection of the Likeness Rights*

Given its significance as a basic right of personality to a natural person, the right to likeness is protected under the Civil Code in two specific ways. One is positive and

[54] See *id.*, art. 1018.
[55] See the SPC Working Group, *supra* note 2, at 236.
[56] See *id.* at 237.

the other is negative. Article 1018 of the Civil Code is considered the positive aspect of protection. Under article 1018, a natural person is statutorily entitled to make, use, or allow others to use his image. Article 1019, on the other hand, is held as the negative aspect of protection. Article 1019 prohibits any organization or individual from infringing upon others' right to likeness by vilifying or defacing the image thereof, or through other means such as falsifying another's image by utilizing information technology.[57]

In addition, under article 1019, unless otherwise provided by law, no one may make, use, or publicize the image of another person without that person's consent.[58]Article 1019 also contains a provision imposing restrictions on the person who has the right to the works of the image of others. Pursuant to article 1019, without the consent of the person having the right to likeness, a person holding a right in the works of the image of the former shall not use or publicize the said image by way of publishing, duplicating, distributing, leasing, or exhibiting it.[59]

The provision of article 1019 involves two persons: the likeness right holder and the likeness works right holder. The latter refers to the person who is the author in the works of the image of another person or the holder of copyright in the image works. If the author wants to use or publish his image work, he must obtain the consent of the likeness right holder. Otherwise, the use or publication would constitute an infringement for which the author will be held liable.

The trigger of article 1019 liability is "without consent." To justify the use or publication of the works of another person's image, consent from that person is required. The consent can be obtained from the image right holder himself or from the holder's legal guardian if the holder has limited civil capacity. The form of the consent can be an authorization of, or an agreement with, the image right holder. The agreement as such is normally named "contract for the use of image (portrait)."

B. *Extended Protection*

There is an argument in China that the protection of the right to likeness should be extended to certain identifiable personal interests. The reason is that, although many personal interests related to likeness do not belong to likeness rights, they are closely related to such rights. According to the argument, the personal interests that should also be covered by likeness right protection include voice, art of body, right of publicity, and group portrait. Among those interests, the right of publicity and group portrait are worth further discussion.

The right of publicity is a right that protects the name and likeness of a person, a celebrity in particular, from unauthorized exploitation or misappropriation of other

[57] See Civil Code, *supra* note 7, art. 1019.
[58] See *id.*
[59] See *id.*

indicia of the person's identity for commercial purposes. The primary target of the protection of a person's publicity right is the commercial value of the image that the person has cultivated. On its face, the right of publicity shares certain similarities with the right to likeness. They, however, differ from each other in several aspects.

First, the right of publicity is basically a property right, while the right to likeness is a right of personality. Second, the right of publicity concerns the commercial value of a person's likeness. The right to likeness, however, involves a personality right that contains the spiritual and material interests embodied in the image of a person. Third, the right of publicity is protected by intellectual property law or contract law, but the right to likeness is governed by the law of personality.[60] Despite the differences, it remains a belief among Chinese scholars that the right of publicity can be regarded as an extension of the right to likeness because it entails the image of a natural person.

Group portrait, also called collective portrait, refers to the portrait of multiple individuals appearing on a carrier to form a complete portrait. A distinctive feature of the group portrait is that the portraits of several individuals coexist in a single portrait independent of the individuals. Put differently, the portraits of multiple individuals in a group portrait do not stand separately and independently, but only as part of the whole group portrait, and the individual portraits together constitute a collective and independent portrait. On this ground, some suggest that the protection of the right to likeness should be extended to group portraits.

But the Civil Code does not seem to recognize the group portrait right. As noted, article 1018 defines likeness as an external image of a specific natural person. Under this definition, the right to portrait belongs only to a specific individual. The right of group portrait, on the other hand, is not a single but collective right enjoyed by two or more natural persons. The essence of the group portrait right is the right to produce, use, disclose or allow others to use, and obtain benefits from, the independent portraits of two or more natural persons in the group. Therefore, for the use of a group portrait, the respective authorizations of these natural persons for their respective portrait rights must be obtained.

C. *Issues in Debate*

There are several issues arising from article 1019 that generate debate among Chinese scholars. The first issue is whether an infringement of the right to likeness must be premised on property damage. The general holding is that property damage is not a prerequisite for seeking compensation for infringement of the right to likeness.[61] As noted, when a person's personality rights are infringed, the person, under article 995 of the Civil Code, has the right to request that the infringer bear

60 See Liming, *supra* note 5, at 216–217.

61 See the SPC Working Group, *supra* note 2, at 244.

civil liability. Since the right to likeness is a right of personality, an infringement of it will give rise to civil liability regardless of the occurrence of any property damage. If the infringement involves breach of a contract, in addition to contractual liability, the infringer may also be asked to compensate for mental damages.

The second issue concerns whether imposition of civil liability for infringement of the right to likeness is based on fault. One argument is that infringement of the right to likeness is a strict liability, and the infringer is liable as long as infringement occurs. Others argue that likeness right infringement is a fault liability, and a person who infringes the likeness right of others may only be held liable if the person is found at fault. But many believe that by making "without consent of the likeness right holder" the condition for imposing liability for infringement, article 1019 in fact implicates the fault requirement, because a failure to obtain consent is nothing but a fault.[62]

The third issue involves whether the extent of fault may affect the compensation liability. Article 1019 is unclear in this regard. In practice, however, courts often determine the compensation liability arising from the infringement of the right to likeness in consideration of such factors as the extent of the infringer's fault, the circumstances of the infringement, as well as its consequences and impacts. From the courts' viewpoint, since the degree of fault differs in each case of likeness right infringement, the determination of the liability for compensation shall take it into account.[63]

There is a "reasonable use" exception to the application of article 1019. Under article 1020 of the Civil Code, the use of another person's likeness may be made without the person's consent if the use is made in a reasonable way and falls within the following categories:

(a) Using publicly available images of another person to the extent necessary for personal study, art appreciation, classroom teaching, or scientific research;
(b) Making, using, or publicizing the image of another person, which is inevitable for conducting news reporting;
(c) Making, using, or publicizing the image of another person to the extent necessary for a State organ to perform its responsibilities in accordance with law;
(d) Making, using, or publicizing the image of another person, which is inevitable for demonstrating a specific public environment (e.g., a photo taken from a public event or tourist site) (note added); and
(e) Performing other acts of making, using, or publicizing the image of another person for protecting the public interests or the lawful rights and interests of said person.[64]

62 See *id.* at 245.
63 See *id.* at 245–246.
64 See the Civil Code, *supra* note 7, art. 1020.

With regard to the use of a person's image by the media, the reasonableness is to be determined through two inquiries: the first inquiry is whether the use is related to social and public interests, and the second inquiry involves whether the facts in the report are true, and comments made are fair and appropriate. A question often raised, however, is what may constitute social and public interests. A common understanding in China is that the social and public interests shall be the common interests of the vast majority of members in the society, the maintenance of which can benefit the work, study, production and life of the public in general.

As noted, consent to the use of a natural person's image can be made by contract. In respect to the contract for authorized use of a person's image, several issues are worth mentioning. One issue concerns the contractual terms for use. This issue is relevant because the parties to the contract often attach different meanings to terms, so interpretation is needed to resolve disputes arising therefrom. To deal with this issue, the Civil Code has a special rule of interpretation. According to article 1021 of the Civil Code, when the parties dispute over a term relating to the authorized use of the image of another person, interpretations shall be made in favor of the person holding the right to likeness over his image.[65]

The other issue involves rescission of a contract for authorized use. Like other contracts, a contract for authorized use can have a term limit or no term limit. As provided in article 1022 of the Civil Code, if the parties have expressly agreed on a term of authorized use of the image, the person holding the right to likeness over the image may rescind the contract with just cause, but notice shall be given to the other party within a reasonable period of time. If, however, the rescission causes loss to the other party, compensation shall be made, unless the loss is caused by a reason not attributable to the person holding the right to likeness over the image.[66]

On the other hand, if the parties have not agreed on a term limit of authorized use, or the agreement is unclear in the contract, either party may rescind the contract at any time under article 1022 of the Civil Code, provided that the other party is notified within a reasonable period of time.[67] The rescission of an authorized use contract in this situation is also called rescission at will. A rescission as such does not have any conditions attached nor is it based on any cause. Therefore, when the rescission is made, no question will be raised as to whether there is a breach of contract, and whether exercise of the right to rescind the contract is timely made.

The third issue is the extent to which the protection of the right to likeness might be applied to other personality rights. As noted, there is a suggestion from Chinese scholars that the likeness right protection be extended to other areas. In response, the Civil Code provides a rule of application by reference. According to article 1023 of the Civil Code, for an authorized use of another person's name or the like, and for

[65] See *id.*, art. 1021.
[66] See *id.*, art. 1022.
[67] See *id.*

the protection of a natural person's voice, the relevant provisions on the protection of the right to likeness shall be applied *mutatis mutandis*.[68]

The authorized use of another person's name or the like under article 1023 is characterized as the commercial use of personality rights. The implication of article 1023 is that the name as a personality right is suitable for commercial use. Like the right to likeness, the right to name reflects the personality interest embodied in the external representation of the person, and thus can be used for commercial purposes. In the Chinese legal community, the personality right representing a person externally is characterized as a representative personality right.[69]

5. RIGHTS TO REPUTATION AND HONOR

The right to reputation is the right of civil subjects to maintain their reputation from being harmed by others, while the right to honor is the right of civil subjects to enjoy titles of honor and related privileges. The right to reputation focuses on social opinion or evaluation of a civil subject. Under article 1024 of the Civil Code, reputation is a social evaluation of the moral character, prestige, talent, and credit of civil subjects. As discussed, for purposes of the Civil Code, civil subjects include natural persons, legal persons, or non-incorporated business entities.

A. *Distinctions of Right to Reputation*

A natural person's reputation right normally includes the person's social evaluation, personal privacy, and individual integrity. A legal person's reputation right, though containing no direct economic content itself, often has a significant impact on the

[68] See *id.*, art. 1023.

[69] In China, based on the contents of the personality interests involved, personality rights can be divided into material personality rights, representative personality rights, evaluative personality rights, and free personality rights. The material personality right is the right containing the personality interests closely related to the physical body of a natural person, including the rights to life, body, and health. Since the material personality right has a great impact on the existence and life of a natural person, it cannot be used for any commercial purpose. The representative personality right is the right based on the personality interests embodied in the external representation of the subject, including the right of name, title, portrait, etc., and its objects are external, controllable, and commercially exploitable. The representative personality right brings economic benefits to the right holder and is the main type of personality right that can be used commercially. The evaluative personality right is the personality right with the content of evaluating the interests of the person, including the right of reputation and the right of honor. This kind of personality right mainly involves personal evaluation and reputation in society, which may not be used commercially. The right of free personality is the right of personality with the content of personal freedom and interests, including the right of privacy. Whether the right of privacy may be commercialized is a question subject to debate, though it is generally held that the personality right as such involves human freedom, and the value of that freedom contains certain commercial interests. See the SPC Working Group, *supra* note 2, at 264.

social and economic benefits of the legal person's activities. More specifically, the damage to the reputation of a corporate legal person would adversely affect its production, operation, and sales. Similarly, harm to the reputation of a non-incorporated business entity, institution, or even government agency may lower its social prestige and hinder its work.

According to Chinese legal scholars, the right to reputation of a civil subject has several distinctions. The first distinction is the statutory feature. The right to reputation is not an inherent but a statutory right, meaning that the right to reputation must be provided by law. The provisions of law not only govern the contents of the reputation right, but also regulate the scope and protection of, as well as limitations on, the reputation right. In other words, without legal stipulation, no reputation right would exist.[70]

The other distinction is the non-property nature. The right to reputation is not a property right, although it may be related to property interests. Reputation is an important personality right, but reputation itself is not a property. In essence, the right to reputation embodies important spiritual interests. Although the right to reputation does not directly reflect any property interest, nor can it be valued remuneratively or by money, since the reputation has impacts on the gain or loss of certain property rights, an infringement of the right of reputation would necessarily affect property interests.[71]

The third distinction is the exclusivity of reputation. The right to reputation arises with the birth of a natural person or the establishment of a legal person or other entity and ends only with the death of the natural person or the dissolution of the legal person or other entity. Because the right to reputation, once created under the law, becomes inseparable from the person, it is neither transferable nor can it be deprived of. In addition, as noted, the right to reputation may not be abandoned by the person at will. Thus, the right to reputation is always with a person during the lifetime of the person.[72]

The fourth distinction is specificality. The right to reputation is considered the right of specific people to ask to be evaluated objectively and fairly, and to exclude others from derogating the person's own reputation. Because of the specific nature of the right to reputation, infringement on the right to reputation must be committed against a specific person. In other words, only when damage is caused to a specific person's reputation can liability for infringement be imposed.[73]

B. *Infringements upon the Right to Reputation*

Under the Civil Code, infringement of the reputation right of a person mainly consists of insults, defamation, and the like. Article 1024 of the Civil Code provides

[70] See Liming, *supra* note 5, at 233.
[71] See *id.*
[72] See *id.* at 234.
[73] See *id.*

that no organization or individual may infringe upon the other's right to reputation by way of insulting, defaming, or the like. Thus, any harm to the reputation of others by means of insult or slander, including publicizing the privacy of others in written or oral form or fabricating facts to blatantly smear the personality of others, should be deemed an infringement of the others' right to reputation for which the infringer will be held liable.

A person whose reputation is injured can be a natural person, legal person, or unincorporated organization. The reputation right of a natural person, however, differs from that of a legal person or unincorporated organization in several aspects. First, the contents of reputation differ from each other. For a natural person, reputation mainly involves moral character and talents of the person, while the reputation of a legal person or unincorporated organization is related primarily to its credibility, production capacity, as well as its condition of operation, which are all more closely connected with property than with personal interests.

Second, the interests affected by the injury to reputation differ. An injury to the reputation of a natural person affects the interests of the person with no commercial contents, because the reputation of a natural person only involves the integrity of the person. In contrast, an injury to the right to reputation of a legal person or unincorporated organization is often associated with damage to its business credibility or product reputation. In addition, conduct infringing on the right to reputation of a legal person may also constitute unfair competition stipulated in the Anti-Unfair Competition Law.[74]

Third, the consequences of injury to reputation differ. A notable consequence of an injury to the reputation of a natural person is that the person may suffer mental damage as a result of the injury. The mental damage, however, does not apply to an injury to the reputation of a legal person or unincorporated organization. As noted, the reputation damage of a legal person or unincorporated organization is mainly measured by commercial or property loss, although the right to reputation of a legal person or unincorporated organization may not be defined as a property right.[75]

C. *Determination of Injury to the Reputation Right*

Generally, a finding of infringement upon a person's reputation right in Chinese courts depends on several factors: first, the perpetrator has committed insults, slander, or another act of defamation. In China, a civil insult refers to the act of deliberately degrading the personality of others or damaging the reputation of others through violative or other means, while slander consists of fabricating false facts, orally or in writing, to vilify the personality of another person and injure the person's

[74] See the SPC Working Group, *supra* note 2, at 275–276.
[75] See *id.*

reputation.[76] The other act of defamation includes such acts as news reports or artistic work. For example, if a media publication made false reports, or failed to conduct reasonable verification of the facts, leading to false reports, it may be found to have committed an infringement upon the other's right to reputation.

Second, the act of defaming reputation has a specific target. In other words, to constitute an infringement of a reputation right, the defamatory act must be directed at a specific person. Thus, if the act of the perpetrator does not point to a specific target, but only involves ordinary people or people in a certain sector randomly so that the person at whom the defamatory act is directed cannot be ascertained, no infringement will be found even if the plaintiff is among the people affected. In addition, to determine whether the perpetrator's conduct was directed against a specific person, a determinative factor to consider is whether the perpetrator acted with malicious intent, meaning that the perpetrator acted willfully or intentionally to fabricate facts or disseminate false information to damage the reputation of the targeted person.[77]

Under article 1027 of the Civil Code, for instance, if a literary or artistic work published by an author depicts a real person and event or a specific person, which contains insulting or defamatory content and infringes upon the person's right to reputation, the person has the right to request that the author bear civil liability. If, however, the literary or artistic work does not depict a real or specific person, but only some patterns of the story are similar to the situation of such person, the author shall bear no civil liability.

Third, the infringing conduct or act must be known to a third party. The direct consequence of an infringement upon the right of a person's reputation is the damage caused to the reputation of the person. But whether damage has occurred is determined by the social impact on the specific person, which is assessed by knowledge of the third party about the infringing activities. Since the Civil Code, as noted, defines reputation as a social evaluation, the harm to a person's right to reputation may only take place when the perpetrator's infringing conduct has affected the social evaluation of the person. Therefore, to judge the injury resulting from the infringing activities, the test is whether the social evaluation of the person has been hurt.[78]

D. *Liability Exemption Rules*

Under the Civil Code, the liability for an infringement of the reputation right of a person may be exempted under certain circumstances. Pursuant to article 1025 of the Civil Code, a person who makes a news report or acts as supervision by public

[76] See Liming, *supra* note 5, at 241–242.
[77] See *id.* at 246.
[78] See *id.* at 246–248.

opinion purposed for public interests, adversely affecting the other's reputation, shall not bear civil liability.[79] A news report is defined in China as the reports made by newspapers, news agencies, radio or TV stations, and other news organizations on current political or social events.[80] Supervision by public opinion refers to the process in which the public uses different methods to discover and disclose unhealthy phenomena and misbehavior in society through the news media, and to urge the social problem to be resolved.[81]

The liability exemption, however, is subject to certain exceptions. As provided in article 1025, the liability exemption does not apply if one of the following situations occurs: (a) the actor has fabricated or distorted the facts; (b) the actor has failed to fulfill the obligation to reasonably verify the seriously misrepresented information provided by others; or (c) the actor has used insulting words and the like to degrade the other's reputation.[82]

Making reasonable verification is an obligation imposed by the law to help ensure the authenticity of facts. Under article 1026 of the Civil Code, to determine whether the obligation to reasonably verify has been fulfilled, the factors to be considered include (a) the credibility of the source of the information; (b) whether the information that is clearly controversial has been fully investigated; (c) the timeliness of the information; (d) the relevance of the information with public order and good morals; (e) the likelihood that the victim's reputation would be degraded; and (f) his ability to verify and the cost for verification of the information.

E. *Specific Remedies*

When the right to reputation of a person is damaged by an untruthful news report or improper personal credit evaluation, the person is entitled to make a request for specific remedies under the Civil Code. Unlike the general civil remedies, the specific remedies do not necessarily rest on torts.[83] It is held in China that a claim on personality right differs from a claim for damages caused by tortious conduct, because the tort-based claim is premised on the occurrence of tortious conduct and resulting damages, while in the case of infringement of the right to reputation,

79 See the Civil Code, *supra* note 7, art. 1025.
80 See Liming, *supra* note 5, at 277.
81 See *id.*
82 See *id.*, art. 1025.
83 As noted, under article 179 of the Civil Code, the general remedies in the forms of civil liability include: (1) cessation of the infringement; (2) removal of the nuisance; (3) elimination of the danger; (4) restitution; (5) restoration; (6) repair, redoing, or replacement; (7) continuance of performance; (8) compensation for losses; (9) payment of liquidated damages; (10) elimination of adverse effects and rehabilitation of reputation; and (11) extension of apologies. Also, pursuant to article 995, a person whose personality rights are infringed upon has the right to request that the actor stop the infringement, remove the nuisance, eliminate the danger, eliminate the adverse effects, rehabilitate his/her reputation, or extend apologies.

the right holder may still make a claim against the actor even if no actual damages are caused and the action does not amount to the level of a tort.[84]

According to article 1028 of the Civil Code, when a person has evidence to prove that the content of a media report, such as a newspaper, a periodical, or an online website, is inaccurate and thus harms the person's reputation, the person so affected has the right to request that the media take necessary remedial measures, including making a correction of or deleting the content in a timely manner.[85] The very purpose of article 1028 is to minimize to the greatest extent the possible damage to the reputation right of the person affected and to prevent any further expansion of the negative consequences of the report at issue.

As a general practice in Chinese courts, the standard to grant the article 1028 request is materiality. More specifically, only when the contents in the media report are materially inconsistent with the facts can it be deemed to be untrue. Thus, if the issue addressed in an article published by media is basically accurate and contains no insult to the personality of a person, no infringement of the right to reputation should be found. However, if the basic contents of the article are inaccurate and are damaging to the reputation of a person, the infringement of the right of the person's reputation will be deemed to have occurred.

With regard to a personal credit evaluation, the person involved may check his own credit report and has the right to raise an objection and request correction, deletion, or other necessary measures to be taken when the credit report is found incorrect. Upon the request, the credit evaluation entity shall examine the report and take necessary measures in a timely manner if the report is confirmed to contain error or false information.[86] In China, the credit of a person represents the credibility of the person, referring to the person's ability to fulfill what they have promised and the social evaluation of the person. Some scholars characterize the credit of a person as an all-around evaluation of the economic capacity of the person, including their economic condition, production capacity, product quality, as well as debt performance ability.[87]

Like the right to reputation, the right to honor of a person is also a statutory right granted to the person. The right to honor, as noted, is the right to obtain and keep honorary title in accordance with the law. As an independent right of personality, the right to honor is legally protected. Article 1031 of the Civil Code prohibits any organization or individual from unlawfully depriving others of their honorary titles or defaming or degrading their honors thereof.[88] Thus, for the purpose of protection, if an awarded honorary title of a person should have been but has not been recorded,

[84] See the SPC Working Group, Rights of Personality, *supra* note 2, at 304.
[85] See the Civil Code, *supra* note 7, art. 1028.
[86] See *id.*, art. 1029.
[87] See Liming, *supra* note 5, at 257–258.
[88] See the Civil Code, *supra* note 7, art. 1031.

the person may request that it be so recorded. On the other hand, if an awarded honorary title is incorrectly recorded, the person may request to have it corrected.[89]

6. RIGHT TO PRIVACY AND PROTECTION OF PERSONAL INFORMATION

As noted, the government in China possesses extensive power in every aspect, including information access, and often exercises such power excessively on the ill-defined ground of national security. Therefore, the protection of privacy and personal information is always a public concern. In the Chinese Constitution, privacy is provided as a basic right associated with the right of correspondence. Under article 40 of the 1982 Constitution, freedom and privacy of correspondence of citizens of the People's Republic of China are protected by law. No organization or individual may, on any ground, infringe upon citizens' freedom and privacy of correspondence.[90]

Article 40, however, can hardly be a constitutional ground for the right to privacy. First, article 40 does not explicitly make privacy a constitutional right, though it protects the privacy of correspondence. Second, even for matters involving correspondence privacy, article 40 protection does not apply in the case where public security or procuratorial organs censor and examine individuals' private correspondence for the interest of state security or for the purpose of criminal investigation.[91]

The Civil Code is the first legislation in the country that categorizes the right of privacy and personal information protection as the right of personality. Under article 1032 of the Civil Code, a natural person enjoys the right to privacy, and no organization or individual may infringe upon another's right to privacy by prying into, intruding upon, disclosing, or publicizing others' private matters.[92] The Civil Code also, for the first time, defines privacy as the private peaceful life of a natural person and the private space, private activities, and private information that a natural person does not wish to be known by others.[93]

After enactment of the Civil Code, China adopted the Personal Information Protection Law (PIPL).[94] Effective November 1, 2021, the PIPL establishes a mechanism for personal information protection in the country and provides a set of rules for processing personal information, including rules for processing sensitive personal information and special rules that govern state agencies in handling personal

89 See *id.*

90 See 1982 Chinese Constitution, *supra* note 8, art. 40.

91 See *id.*

92 See the Civil Code, *supra* note 7, art. 1032.

93 See *id.*

94 The PIPL was adopted by the Standing Committee of the National People's Congress on August 20, 2021. An English version of the PIPL is available at www.china-briefing.com/news/the-prc-personal-information-protection-law-final-a-full-translation/.

information. The PIPL also provides the rights of individuals in the activities of personal information processing, and obligations of the personal information processor.

A notable provision of the PIPL is article 28, which addresses sensitive personal information. Under article 28, sensitive personal information is defined as the personal information that can easily lead to the infringement of personal dignity of natural persons or the harm of personal or property safety once leaked or illegally used, including such information as biometrics, religious belief, specific identities, medical health, financial accounts, and whereabouts, and the personal information of minors under the age of fourteen.[95]

A. *Contents of Privacy*

Privacy is a relatively new term to the general public in China because ever since the founding of the People's Republic of China in 1949, it has become common belief that all should be dedicated to the cause of the Communist Party and socialism. Therefore, to be loyal to the Party, nothing from an individual perspective may be considered private. Not until the Tort Liability Law was enacted in 2009 was privacy provided as a right in civil legislation. Article 2 of the Tort Liability Law defines the right to privacy as part of civil rights, referring to personal and property rights and interests.[96] The significance of article 2 of the Tort Liability Law is that it recognizes privacy as a basic civil right.

The Civil Code takes one step further and makes the right to privacy a right of personality to be protected together with personal information. Under article 1032 of the Civil Code, the right to privacy consists of four major aspects, namely, tranquility in private life, private space, private activities, and private or personal information. All these aspects are considered basic elements of human rights that must be protected. It is understood in China that the right to privacy has two distinctive features: first, it may only be enjoyed by natural persons, and second, it is an absolute right. By absolute, it means that nobody may infringe upon the right to privacy of the other.

In addition, it is held in China that the right to privacy of a natural person has three major components: privacy enjoyment, privacy maintenance, and use of privacy. Privacy enjoyment is the right of a person to have his or her privacy protected from illegal disclosure or publicity by any other person. Put differently, no individual or organization may disclose the privacy of others without legal justification. Privacy maintenance means the right of a person to make a claim for legal remedies or ask the infringer to bear corresponding liability when the right to

95 See *id.*, art. 28.

96 See Tort Liability Law of China (2009), art. 2, available at www.npc.gov.cn/zgrdw/englishnpc/Law/2011-02/16/content_1620761.htm.

privacy of the person is infringed upon. Use of privacy refers to utilization by a person of his or her privacy to meet the person's material or spiritual needs. Publication of a personal biography or memoir, and being a painting model, are examples in this regard.

B. *Conducts Infringing upon the Right to Privacy*

For the purposes of article 1032 of the Civil Code, tranquility in private life refers to the right of a natural person to a peaceful life and restfulness, or the right to be left alone. Thus, any illegal stalking, snooping, or harassing via telephone of a person, as well as stuffing a person's mailbox with junk mail, will be deemed a violation of the peace of the private life of the person. Conduct as such results in civil liability under the Civil Code for infringement of the personality right because it not only obstructs the normal life of a person, but also causes mental anguish of the person.[97]

Private space implicates both space and places that are controlled or dominated by individuals for private use, including physical and virtual space. The typical private space is a person's residence. Other places, such as a dormitory, hotel room, telephone booth, or locker room, if used by a person, are also considered private space. To protect a person in their private space, nobody may peep, secretly record, or photograph without permission, private acts of the person in a place under the person's own control.[98]

Private activities mean all personal activities of a person that involve no public interests, including the person's daily life, social interaction, or spousal relationship. If the person is unwilling to make his or her personal activities known to others, no one should film, record, disclose, spy on, or eavesdrop on the person's private activities. Thus, an intrusion on the seclusion of a person, such as the use of electronic surveillance or other means to keep a lookout over the person's activities, or interference with a person's daily activities, will constitute an infringement on the right to privacy of the person.[99]

Private information of a person is considered quite a broad term in China: it covers any information of an individual person that the person does not want to make public. More specifically, any personal information that an individual wants to keep private may fall within the scope of the right to privacy, as long as the information does not become public domain or is not required under law for public access, and the person is unwilling to disclose it, regardless of whether the disclosure of such information has a positive or negative impact on the person, or whether the information has commercial value.[100]

[97] See the SPC Working Group, Rights of Personality, *supra* note 2, at 339.
[98] See *id.* at 340.
[99] See *id.* at 341.
[100] See *id.* at 341–342.

An indispensable part of private information is personal information. As defined in article 1034 of the Civil Code, personal information refers to the information recorded electronically or in other ways that can be used, by itself or in combination with other information, to identify the person, including their name, date of birth, identification number, biometric information, residential address, telephone number, email address, health information, and the person's whereabouts.[101]

The Civil Code further provides a list of conduct that is prohibited for the purpose of protecting the right to privacy. Under article 1033 of the Civil Code, unless otherwise provided by law or expressly consented to by a person, no organization or individual may (a) intrude upon the person's private life by making phone calls, sending text messages, using instant messaging tools, sending emails and flyers, and the like means; (b) enter into, take photographs of, or peep into a person's private spaces such as their residence or hotel room; (c) take photographs of, peep into, eavesdrop on, or disclose the private activities of a person; (d) take photographs of or peep at the private parts of a person's body; (e) process the person's private information; or (f) infringe upon the person's privacy through other means.[102]

In addition, to constitute an infringement upon a person's right to privacy, the following elements must be present: (a) the perpetrator has committed an illegal act that violates the right to privacy of the other. An illegal act refers to an act that is listed in article 1033 of the Civil Code; (b) there must be a fact of infringement – in other words, the right of privacy of the other has indeed been infringed; (c) causation must exist between the infringing conduct and the fact of infringement; and (d) the perpetrator must be at fault subjectively (with knowledge).[103]

C. *Rules Governing Personal Information*

Given the significance of personal information in the right to privacy, the Civil Code contains certain provisionss that apply specifically to personal information. In 2021, one year after the Civil Code was promulgated, the Standing Committee of the NPC adopted the Personal Information Protection Law (PIPL).[104] The Civil Code and the PIPL form a legal framework in the country to protect personal information rights and interests, regulate the processing of personal information, and promote the reasonable use of personal information.[105]

For purposes of the Civil Code and PIPL, personal information is defined as the information recorded electronically or in other ways that can be used, by itself or in combination with other information, to identify a natural person, including his

[101] See the Civil Code, *supra* note 7, art. 1034.
[102] See *id.*, art. 1033.
[103] See the SPC Working Group, Rights of Personality, *supra* note 2, at 350–351.
[104] The PIPL was adopted by the Standing Committee of the NPC on August 20, 2021, available at https://personalinformationprotectionlaw.com/PIPL/hello-world/.
[105] See *id.*, art. 1.

name, date of birth, identification number, biometric information, residential address, telephone number, email address, health information, whereabouts, and the like, except for the information processed after being anonymized.[106] Information anonymization refers to the process in which the personal information is processed in the way that makes it impossible to identify a certain natural person and unable to be recovered.[107]

Under article 1034 of the Civil Code, any natural person's personal information is protected by law.[108] Article 10 of the PIPL further provides that no organisation or individual may illegally collect, use, process, or transmit other people's personal information, or illegally trade, provide, or disclose other people's personal information, or engage in the processing of personal information that endangers the national security or public interests.[109]

There are several rules in the Civil Code and the PIPL that govern the use of personal information. The first rule is the rule of personal information processing, which sets forth the basic principles and conditions for handling information that is personal. Under article 1035 of the Civil Code, the processing of personal information includes the collection, storage, use, refinement, transmission, provision, disclosure, and the like, of the personal information.[110] Article 4 of the PIPL has a similar provision with an expanstion to include "easure of perspnal information."[111] Pursuant to article 1035, the processing of personal information shall comply with three principles, namely, lawfulness, justification, and necessity. Lawfulness means that the collection and processing of personal information must follow legal norms. Justification requires that the purpose of the collection and use of the personal information must be justified. Necessity refers to the limit on the collection and processing of personal information, meaning that no personal information shall be processed excessively.

The processing of personal information must also meet the following conditions: (a) consent has been obtained from the natural person or his/her guardian, unless otherwise provided by laws or administrative regulations; (b) the rules for processing information are open and transparent; (c) the purpose, method, and scope of the information processing are clearly indicated; and (d) it is not in violation of laws or administrative regulations or against the agreement of both parties.[112]

The second rule is the rule of exceptions. Under article 1036 of the Civil Code, when dealing with the personal information of another person, no one should be held liable if: (a) the act is reasonably conducted and limited to the extent that the natural person or his/her guardian consents to; (b) the information processed is only

[106] See the Civil Code, *supra* note 7, art. 1034. See also the PIPL, *supra* note 104, art. 4.
[107] See the PIPL, *supra* note 104, art. 73 (IV).
[108] See the Civil Code, *supra* note 7, art. 1034.
[109] See the PIPL, *supra* note 104, art. 10.
[110] See *id.*, the Civil Code, art. 1035.
[111] See the PIPL, *supra* note 104, art. 4.
[112] See the Civil Code, *supra* note 7, art. 1035.

that which is disclosed by the natural person himself or has already been legally disclosed, unless the said person explicitly refuses or the processing of the information infringes upon a significant interest of the person; and (c) other acts are reasonably conducted to protect the public interest or the lawful rights and interests of the person.

In short, no civil liability shall be imposed for the use of personal information if effective consent is obtained from the right holder or his/her agent *ad litem* if (a) the right holder has no civil capacity or has limited civil capacity, (b) the personal information in question is legally disclosed to the public, or (c) the public interest or the lawful right of the person involved is at stake. Note that, as a general practice in China, the processing of personal information must meet the principles of legality, justification, and necessity even if the processing is done on the basis of public interest. Thus, any personal information, if it does not fall within the scope necessary to achieve the purpose of protection of public interests, must not be collected and processed.

The third rule is the rule of protective request. In accordance with article 1037 of the Civil Code, a natural person has the right to make a protective request when his/her personal information is at issue. First, a natural person may by request retrieve or make copies of his or her personal information from the information processors. Second, if it is discovered that his/her personal information is incorrect, the person has the right to raise an objection and request corrections or other necessary measures to be taken in a timely manner. Third, if it is found that an information processor has violated the provisions of laws or administrative regulations or has breached the agreement between the parties while processing his/her personal information, the person has the right to request the information processor delete such information in a timely manner.

The fourth rule is the rule of non-disclosure. To protect the personal information of a person, the rule of non-disclosure imposes two duties: the duty not to disclose the personal information of a person to anyone without consent of the person, and the duty to keep such personal information confidential. In addition, under the Civil Code, the non-disclosure rule applies to both the personal information processor and the state agencies, including their staff handling the personal information. Under the PIPL, a personal information processor refers to organization or individual that independently determines the purpose and method of processing in personal information processing activities.[113]

In accordance with article 1038 of the Civil Code, an information processor shall not disclose or tamper with the personal information collected and kept, and shall not provide others with the personal information of a natural person without the person's consent.[114] However, the article 1038 rule of non-disclosure does not apply if

[113] See the PIPL, *supra* note 104, art. 73 (I).
[114] See the Civil Code, *supra* note 7, art. 1038.

the information processed could not be used to identify any specific person and cannot be restored to its original condition.[115]

It is also required that an information processor take technical and other necessary measures to ensure the security of the personal information collected and saved, and shall prevent the information from being leaked, tampered with, or lost. If, however, a person's personal information has been or is likely to be leaked, tampered with, or lost, the information processor shall take remedial measures in a timely manner and, in the meantime, shall notify the person concerned and report to the relevant competent authorities.[116]

It is further provided in article 1039 that the state agencies, legal entities of administrative functions, and their staff therein shall keep confidential the private and personal information of a natural person known to them during the execution of their official duties.[117] Article 1039 also prohibits the state agencies, legal entities of administrative functions, and their staff from disclosing to or sharing with others the personal information of a person they have obtained.[118]

Note that the PIPL applies to both the processing of the personal information of natural persons within the territory of China and the activities carried out outside the territory of China that have domestic impacts. Under Article 3 of the PIPL, the PIPL applies to extraterritorial activies if (a) the purpose of the activites is to provide products or services to domestic natural persons; (b) the actities are purposed to analyze and evaluate the activities of domestic natural persons; or (c) in other circumstances provided by laws and administrative regulations.[119]

[115] See *id.*
[116] See *id.*
[117] See *id.*, art. 1039.
[118] See *id.*
[119] See PIPL, *supra* note 104, art. 10.

11

Marriage, Family Relations, and Succession

INTRODUCTION

Marriage and family are the essential elements of society. Marriage is a union between spouses recognized by a specific social system, while family is a kinship group and living unit formed by marriage and blood ties. In China, marriage and family are collectively described as a kinship consisting of personal and property relationships between husband and wife, and among family members and other close relatives.[1]

A personal relationship refers to relationships that arise based on marriage, birth, and adoption, and are extinguished due to divorce, death, or termination of adoptive relation. By contrast, a property relationship in marriage and family is premised on the existence of specific kinship inseparable from personal tie or status, which does not reflect direct economic purposes, but signifies the need to live together.[2]

Unlike the general civil law property relationship to which the principles of equal value, fairness, and voluntariness apply in the process of transactions, the property relationship in marriage and family focuses primarily on maintaining spousal needs, supporting the elderly, and raising children. The focus is not necessarily to be fair and equal among members, but to embody strong ethical and clan values. The rights and obligations arising from marriage and family property relationships are not only based on, but also subordinate to, the specific status of the person(s) involved.

In China, marriage and family are deemed to have two attributes: natural attributes and social attributes. Natural attributes are reflected in physiological factors and blood relationships. Social attributes refer to the essential nature attached to marriage and family relationships under the social system. More precisely,

[1] See the SPC Leading Group, Understanding and Application of the Civil Code – Marriage, Family Relations and Succession, 13 (People's Court Press, 2020) (the SPC Leading Group, Marriage and Family Relations).

[2] See *id.*

marriage and family form a social relationship, which is an integral part of human society and represents a certain society's mode of reproduction and lifestyle.

Prior to the adoption of the Civil Code, the basic law that governed marriage and family relations was the Marriage Law, adopted in 1950 and amended in 1980 and 2001.[3] In 1991, the Adoption Law was promulgated to specifically protect the legal relationship of adoption and safeguard the rights and interests of the parties involved. The Adoption Law was then amended in 1998.[4] Both the Marriage Law and the Adoption Law are now merged into the 2020 Civil Code under the title Marriage and Family.

Succession in essence is an entitlement to the legal patrimonial relationships of a deceased person or the legal inheritance of the property or assets left by the deceased. The right of inheritance is an important civil right that enables the successors, heirs, or beneficiaries to inherit property rights from the deceased either at the will of the deceased or under provisions of the law. The right of inheritance as such has dual characteristics of property and status. Property means the value in the things inherited, while status implicates that the right of inheritance belongs only to a specific type of person in a given relationship, especially a marriage and family relationship.

China's Succession Law was enacted in 1985.[5] The Civil Code incorporates it with several major changes. First, the provisions are expanded from thirty-seven articles in the Succession Law to forty-seven articles in the Civil Code. Second, the rights of succession are refined to not only include such traditional rights as property rights, creditor's rights, and intellectual property (IP) rights, but also new types of property rights such as equity rights, digital property rights, and virtual asset rights. Third, the inheritable properties or estates are broadly defined to cover all lawful personal properties.[6]

Literally, inheritance can be prescribed in a broad and narrow sense. Inheritance in a broad sense includes property inheritance and identity inheritance. Identity inheritance means that the living heir inherits the personal title of the deceased. An inheritance in the narrow sense refers only to property inheritance. For the purpose of the Civil Code, inheritance involves no personal title but only the distribution of the personal property left behind by a natural person after his/her death.[7]

1. MARRIAGE AND FAMILY RELATIONS

In the Civil Code, the provisions that govern marriage and family relations consist of two parts: a general part and a specific part. The general part contains principles and

[3] Marriage Law of China as amended 2001, available at www.npc.gov.cn/zgrdw/englishnpc/Law/2007-12/13/content_1384064.htm.

[4] Adoption Law of China as amended 1998, available at www.npc.gov.cn/zgrdw/englishnpc/Law/2007-12/12/content_1383868.htm.

[5] Succession Law of China, 1985, available at www.asianlii.org/cn/legis/cen/laws/losotproc426/.

[6] See the SPC Leading Group, Marriage and Family Relations, *supra* note 1, at 473–475.

[7] See *id.* at 575.

rules of general application. The specific part includes marriage, family relations, divorce, and adoption. Under article 1040 of the Civil Code, the law of marriage and family relations regulates and governs all civil relationships that arise from marriage and family.[8]

In China, the marriage and family law is considered to have several distinctions, in contrast to the laws that govern other civil relationships. First, the marriage and family law is extremely extensive in its application and applies to everyone. Since marriage and family relationships are ubiquitous social relationships in human society, and families based on marriage are cellular organizations in society, everyone, regardless of gender, age, and other circumstances, is the subject of a legal relationship of marriage and family.[9]

Second, the marriage and family law has a unique ethical nature. Applied to marriage and family relations, ethics refers to the principles, values, concepts, and codes of conduct defining and affecting the relationship between husband and wife and between parents and children, which are formed and developed in a historical process and are observed by the public. In a society, ethics are closely associated with the society's cultural tradition and social moral standards.[10]

Third, the provisions of marriage and family law are mostly mandatory. Unlike other civil law provisions that are primarily based on the autonomy of the parties, the marriage and family law contains many mandatory legal norms, and the extent to which the parties may choose or decide as they wish is quite limited. In the field of marriage and family law, the requirements for the formation and termination of specific legal relationships and their contents are all statutory based. When certain legal facts occur, the corresponding legal consequences will inevitably follow. The legal consequences as such are pre-specified and strictly stipulated by the law, and thus may not be altered or derogated from by the parties involved.[11]

A. *General Principles and Rules*

The Civil Code sets forth several basic principles that govern marriage and family relations, and also certain prohibitive rules that are purposed to protect marriage and the rights of family members. Also, the Civil Code, for the first time in the country's marriage and family legislation, prescribes the scope of family relatives. Under article 1045 of the Civil Code, family relatives include spouses, relatives by blood,

8 See the Civil Code of China (2020), art. 1040, at https://english.www.gov.cn/archive/lawsregulations/202012/31/content_WS5fedad98c6d0f72576943005.html.

9 See Fang Shaokun et al., Marriage, Family and Succession, 7–8 (2nd ed., Renmin University Press, 2010).

10 See *id.* at 8. See also Xue Ninglan, *Positioning of Marriage and Family Law and Its Ethical Connotation*, 6 Jianghuai Tribune, 2015, available at http://iolaw.cssn.cn/zxzp/197001/t19700101_4639769.shtml.

11 See Shaokun et al., *supra* note 9, at 8.

and relatives by marriage.[12] Also under article 1045, spouses, parents, children, siblings, paternal and maternal grandparents, and paternal and maternal grandchildren are considered close relatives, while spouses, parents, children, and other close relatives living together are family members.[13]

Note, however, marriage in China is, and continues to be, defined as a union between a man and a woman for the purpose of living together for life. It is commonly held in the country that a marriage has three essential elements: (a) a union of men and women; (b) for the purpose of living together; and (c) with the identity known as husband and wife. Under this definition, same-sex marriage is not recognized as a matter of law in China.

Although in recent years there has been a growing call for the recognition of same-sex marriage, a general belief underlying the strong opposition in the country is that same-sex marriage is manifestly repugnant to the nation's traditional values and long-standing moral ethos. Nevertheless, courts in their practices do not reject cases that involve property and/or child custody disputes arising from same-sex cohabitation. Also, both the Marriage Law and the Civil Code do not prohibit a transgender person from marrying another person as long as they are of the opposite sex.

Pursuant to article 1041 of the Civil Code, marriage and family are protected by the State. The principles provided in the Civil Code that govern marriage and family relations include freedom of marriage, monogamy, equality between men and women, and protection of the lawful rights and interests of women, minors, the elderly, and persons with disabilities.[14] In addition, according to article 1044 of the Civil Code, adoption shall be in compliance with the principle of acting in the best interest of the adoptee, and the lawful rights and interests of both the adoptee and the adopter shall be protected.[15]

a. Freedom of Marriage

Freedom of marriage refers to the freedom of the parties to independently decide their own marriage according to their wishes without external interference or coercion. In its substance, freedom of marriage includes the freedom to marry and the freedom to divorce. The freedom to marry requires that marriage be fully voluntary and genuine between men and women. To that end, no one may force, deceive, or take advantage of the other person in marriage, and no third party may arrange or illegally interfere with a marriage.

[12] See the Civil Code, *supra* note 8, art. 1045.

[13] See *id.*

[14] See *id.*, art. 1041. (Pursuant to article 1401, the country's marriage system is premised on freedom of marriage, monogamy, and equality between men and women. Article 1041 mandates that the lawful rights and interests of women, minors, the elderly, and persons with disabilities are protected.)

[15] See *id.*, art. 1044.

Freedom to divorce is supplemental to the freedom to marry, which allows the married couple to dissolve the marital relationship at their own choice. More to the point, based on the freedom to divorce, the spouses have the right to jointly make the decision to divorce and reach a divorce agreement to end the marital relationship, or, if an irreconcilable difference occurs between the spouses and the marriage can no longer be meaningfully maintained, either spouse has the right to seek divorce.

Under article 49 of the Chinese Constitution, nobody may violate the freedom of marriage.[16] To protect the freedom of marriage, article 1042 of the Civil Code explicitly prohibits any arranged marriage, mercenary marriage, and other acts interfering with marriage.[17] In addition, any exaction of money or other property by way of marriage is also prohibited. These provisions are aimed at safeguarding the freedom of marriage so as to make marriage free from any interference.

The freedom of marriage, however, is not absolute, but rather is subject to certain limitations. First, both marriage and divorce must meet legal requirements in substance and follow the procedures and required formalities. Second, the married couple must bear legal obligations during marriage, especially in a divorce where a child's interests are at issue. Third, when exercising the right to freedom of marriage, no one may abuse the right to cause harm to the legitimate interests of others or to damage social and public interests.

b. Rule against Bigamy

It is legally imperative in China that nobody shall have more than one spouse at any given time. Article 1042 of the Civil Code explicitly prohibits bigamy.[18] The principle of prohibition of bigamy operates in two ways: (a) a married person is prohibited from remarrying before the death of, or divorce from, his or her spouse, and (b) an unmarried man or woman is forbidden from marrying two or more people at the same time. In addition, under article 1042, no one who is married may cohabit with a person other than his/her spouse.[19] According to the Supreme People's Court (SPC), cohabiting with another person refers to the situation where a married person lives with a person of the opposite sex outside of marriage, though not as a couple, but in a continuous and stable manner.[20]

A violation of monogamy in China is a criminal offense, which may result in up to two years in prison, or up to three years in prison if the spouse of a serviceperson

[16] See Constitution of the People's Republic of China, adopted by the NPC in 1982, as amended 2018, art. 49, available at https://english.www.gov.cn/archive/lawsregulations/201911/20/content_WS5ed8856ec6d0b3f0e9499913.html.

[17] See the Civil Code, *supra* note 8, art. 1042.

[18] See *id.*

[19] See *id.*

[20] See the SPC, *Interpretation on the Application of the Marriage and Family Relations of the Civil Code (I)*, issued on April 3, 2021, art. 2, available at www.court.gov.cn/zixun/xiangqing/282071.html (SPC, Marriage and Family Relations Interpretation I).

on active duty is involved.[21] Bigamy refers to the situation where a person who is still lawfully married registers for marriage again with another person. Bigamy can also be a *de fecto* one, which occurs when a married person lives with another person and holds themselves out as a married couple though no marriage registration is made, making the people around them believe that they are in a marital relationship.[22]

c. Equality between Men and Women

Equality between men and women is a constitutional principle in China. Article 48 of the Chinese Constitution mandates that women enjoy equal rights with men in all spheres of political, economic, cultural, social, and family life.[23] Applied to marriage and family relations, the equality principle on the one hand intends to ensure that men and women enjoy equal rights and bear equal obligations in marriage and family, and on the other hand demands that family members, when enjoying civil rights, not be treated differently based on gender.

In its substance, the equality principle consists of several aspects. The first aspect concerns marital relationships. The equality principle focuses on the equal right of men and women to enter into marriage and to seek divorce. The second aspect goes to the marriage itself. During marriage, the equality principle applies in the way that the husband and wife enjoy rights and bear obligations equally, especially in claiming damages and compensation, and in repaying common debts. The third aspect involves divorce. The equality principle operates as a basic standard for partition of community property, determination of child custody, and allocation of visitation rights.

For example, under article 1050 of the Civil Code, after a marriage has been registered, based on mutual consent, the wife may become a member of the husband's family or vice versa.[24] According to the principle of equality between men and women, after a man and a woman register their marriage, how to arrange their family's residence and family structure is a matter that should be decided freely

[21] See Chinese Criminal Law (as amended 2020). (Article 258 provides that whoever with a spouse commits bigamy, or whoever knowingly marries a person who has a spouse, shall be sentenced to fixed-term imprisonment of not more than two years or short-term custody. According to article 259, whoever knowingly cohabits with or marries a person who is the spouse of a serviceperson on active duty shall be sentenced to fixed-term imprisonment of not more than three years or short-term custody.) Available at http://en.npc.gov.cn.cdurl.cn/2020-12/26/c_921604_12.htm.

[22] According to the SPC, bigamy is committed if (a) one party legally married registers marriage again with a third party; (b) one party to a registered marriage enters into a de facto marriage with a third party; (c) one party to a de facto marriage registers for marriage with a third party; or (d) one party to a de facto marriage enters into a new de facto marriage with a third party. See the SPC, *Several Opinions on People's Courts Hearing Cases of Cohabitation as Husband and Wife without Marriage Registration*, issued on December 13, 1989. A text of the Opinions is available at https://wenku.baidu.com/view/ed7f382a4b73f242336c5f01.html.

[23] See Chinese Constitution, *supra* note 16, art. 48,

[24] See the Civil Code, *supra* note 8, art. 1050.

by the parties concerned.[25] Article 1055 specifically emphasizes that husband and wife have equal footing in their marriage and family.[26]

In the context of families, the equality principle governs three relationships. First, in the husband–wife relationship, each has an independent right to name, personal freedom, and inheritance, and has equal ownership of the community property. As husband and wife, they have equal rights and obligations to raise and educate their children, and equal rights and obligations to support each other. Second, in the parents–children relationship, each of the parents has equal rights and obligations to look after the children, and at the same time has equal rights to receive support and assistance from the children. Both parents and children have equal inheritance rights. Third, in the relationship with other family members, grandparents have equal obligations to raise grandchildren and have equal rights to receive support from the grandchildren. Among sisters and brothers, they have equal obligations to raise and support each other.

d. Protection of the Lawful Rights and Interests of Women, Minors, the Elderly, and Persons with Disabilities

In Chinese culture, "respect the elderly and love the young" is considered a traditional moral norm that governs family relations.[27] But the tradition also has its dark side toward women. For thousands of years, women in China were bound by the three obediences (obedience to father before marriage, to husband when married, and to son in widowhood) and four virtues (morality, proper speech, modest manner, and diligent work), which were perceived as crucial for womanly behavior.[28] A resulting notion discriminating against women was the concept of male superiority and female inferiority.

Since the fall of the Qing dynasty, women's status in Chinese society has improved dramatically. When the Marriage Law was first adopted in 1950, it purposefully contained a special provision abolishing "the feudal marriage system of arranged marriages, male superiority over women, and disregard for the interests of children."[29] But because of the deeply rooted tradition, women in many cases remain the victims of discrimination both inside and outside the family.

[25] See the SPC Leading Group, Marriage and Family Relations,*supra* note 1, at 78. There is a well-settled tradition in China against a man becoming a member of a woman's family after marriage.

[26] See the Civil Code, *supra* note 8, art. 1055.

[27] See Shaokun et al., *supra* note 9, at 17.

[28] The Three Obediences and Four Virtues, which first appeared in the Book of Etiquette and Ceremonial and the Rites of Zhou, were the fundamental norms and moral standards applied for women in Confucian ideology.

[29] See the Marriage Law (1950), art. 1. A full text is available at www.npc.gov.cn/zgrdw/npc/lfzt/rlys/2014-10/24/content_1882723.htm.

The Civil Code not only enhanced the principle of protection of lawful rights and interests of women, minors, the elderly, and persons with disabilities, but also prohibited domestic violence and maltreatment or desertion of family members.[30] In addition, the Civil Code contains several provisions offering protection in more specific ways, especially for matters that involve pregnant women, division of property in divorce, and child custody and support.

e. Guiding Norms

In addition to the principles, the Civil Code also provides certain guiding rules that are aimed at helping maintain healthy marriages and family relations and promoting harmony among all family members. Premised on the commonly held moral norms and the core socialist values advocated by the State, the guiding rules are purposed to deal with situations outside the provisions of law and to further protect the legitimate rights and interests of every family member.

Under article 1043 of the Civil Code, families shall establish good family values, promote family virtues, and enhance family civility. Husband and wife shall be loyal to each other, respect each other, and care for each other. Family members shall respect the elderly, take care of the young, help each other, and maintain a marital and familial relationship of equality, harmony, and civility.[31]

Article 1043 is deemed as the provision legalizing marriage and family ethics. It is believed in the country that an integration of moral standards into legal norms in the form of legislation demonstrates the kind of marriage and family relationships the State advocates and endorses.[32] But, given its guiding nature, the provision of article 1043 creates no cause of action, meaning that a violation of any of the guiding rules does not give rise to the legal claim for which judicial relief may be sought.[33]

B. *Marriage*

Marriage in China is characterized as a legal act for a man and a woman to establish a marital relationship. For a marriage to be legally effective and protected, it must be

[30] See the Civil Code, *supra* note 8, art. 1042.

[31] See *id.*, art. 1043. Under article 4 of the 1980 Marriage Law (as amended 2001), husband and wife shall be loyal to each other, respect each other, and care for each other. Family members shall respect the elderly, take care of the young, help each other, and maintain a marital and familial relationship of equality, harmony, and civility. When incorporating the Marriage Law, the Civil Code adds a new paragraph, which reads: families shall establish good family values, promote family virtues, and enhance family civility.

[32] See the SPC Leading Group, Marriage and Family Relations,*supra* note 1, at 36.

[33] This issue was addressed by the SPC in its 2001 *Interpretation on Several Issues Concerning Application of Marriage Law* (I), art. 3, available at http://gongbao.court.gov.cn/Details/ea9abc5cd273b7091a762bd99fod5a.html. According to the SPC, if a party files a lawsuit based only on article 4 of the Marriage Law, the People's Court shall not accept the case; if the case has already been accepted, the People's Court shall rule to dismiss the lawsuit.

entered into between the parties in accordance with the conditions and procedures prescribed by law. Under the Civil Code, the conditions for marriage include required conditions and prohibitive conditions.

a. Requirements for Marriage

To get married, two prerequisite conditions must be met. First, there must be an assent or true willingness between a man and woman on a voluntary basis to live together as spouses, that is, both parties agree at their own choice to establish a husband–wife relationship. It is required under article 1046 of the Civil Code that a man and a woman enter into marriage freely and voluntarily.[34] Article 1046 also provides that neither party may compel the other party to enter into marriage against his will, and no organization or individual may interfere with the freedom of marriage.[35] For the purpose of article 1046, no interference includes parents' interference with children's marriage and children's interference with a parent's remarriage.

Second, the parties must reach the legal age for marriage. The legal age refers to the full age, which means to have passed the birthday of the required age. Under Chinese tradition, the age of a person is often calculated under a nominal age system, meaning that a person is deemed as one year old on the day of birth and becomes one year older each year, on the day of the New Year under the Chinese lunar calendar. Therefore, in China, it is quite common to count a person's age one or even two years older than actual age.[36]

Pursuant to article 1047 of the Civil Code, to enter into a marriage, a man shall reach the age of twenty-two, and a woman shall reach the age of twenty.[37] The legal age for marriage is mandatory, meaning that a person has the right to marry only once they have reached the legal age. A marriage under the legal age is illegal and thus invalid.

b. Prohibitive Conditions

Prohibitive conditions are the conditions under which a marriage is barred. According to article 1048 of the Civil Code, those who are lineal relatives by blood, or collateral relatives by blood up to the third degree of kinship, are prohibited from being married.[38] An important change in the Civil Code is that it lifts the ban on marriage for men and women who suffer from any disease which is regarded by

[34] See the Civil Code, *supra* note 8, art. 1046.

[35] See *id.*

[36] See Z. Wang et al., *Age Validation of Han Chinese Centenarians*, in Validation of Exceptional Longevity, available at www.demogr.mpg.de/books/odense/6/12.htm.

[37] See the Civil Code, *supra* note 8, art. 1047.

[38] See *id.*, art. 1048.

medical science as making him or her unfit for marriage. The change is premised on the notion of protection of the freedom of marriage and the belief that with the development of modern science and technology and the improvement of medical and health care levels, many diseases can now be cured or effectively treated.[39]

Lineal relatives by blood include parents, grandparents, children, and grandchildren. The marriage prohibition in this category is also extended to legally constructed lineal relatives, which refer to adopted children and adopting parents, stepchildren and stepparents. But in the case of adoption, the prohibition will no longer apply if the adoption relationship is legally dissolved.

Collateral relatives within three generations refer to the relatives who are not related by blood but are descended from the same grandparents, including brothers and sisters, half brothers and sisters, uncles and nieces, aunts and nephews of different generations who are descended from the same grandparents, and cousins (children of maternal and paternal aunts or uncles). The collateral relatives within three generations who are prohibited from marrying each other are limited to those who have the same blood relationship, excluding collateral relatives legally constructed (i.e., adopted brother or sister).

c. Formality Mandates

A marriage is valid and effective in China only after it is legally registered. It is required under article 1049 of the Civil Code that a man and a woman intending to enter into a marriage file registration of the marriage in person with a marriage registration authority.[40] The marriage will be registered if it is found to conform to the provisions of the law, and a marriage certificate will be issued. Upon completion of marriage registration, a marital relationship between the man and woman will be established.

Thus, marriage registration is a statutory procedure for marriage and also a formal requirement for the establishment of marriage. China generally does not recognize the legal effect of marriage *de facto* but urges those who have failed to file a marriage registration to complete the registration.[41] According to the SPC, if a man and a woman go through the process to make up for their lack of marriage registration, the validity of the marriage relationship will be calculated from the time when both parties met the essential requirements for marriage as stipulated in the Civil Code.[42]

The marriage registration authority is a government agency at various levels. Pursuant to the Marriage Registration Ordinance issued by the State Council in 2003, the authority for marriage registration for mainland residents is the civil affairs

[39] See the SPC Leading Group, Marriage and Family Relations, *supra* note 1, at 65–66.
[40] See the Civil Code, *supra* note 8, art. 1049.
[41] See *id.*
[42] See the SPC, Marriage and Family Relations Interpretation I, *supra* note 20, art. 6.

departments of county-level people's governments or township (town) people's governments. The people's governments of provinces, autonomous regions, and municipalities directly under the Central Government may determine the specific organs for marriage registration for rural residents in accordance with the principle of convenience for the people.[43]

For marriages between Chinese citizens and foreigners, and between Chinese mainland residents and residents of the Hong Kong or Macao Sepecial Administrative Region (SAR), residents of Taiwan, or overseas Chinese, the registration authorities are the civil affairs departments of the people's governments of provinces, autonomous regions, and municipalities directly under the Central Government or the organs determined by the civil affairs departments of the people's governments of provinces, autonomous regions, and municipalities directly under the Central Government.[44]

d. Void and Annullable Marriage

A void marriage is a marriage that is invalid and thus has no legal effect. It refers to an illegal union between a man and a woman that violates the essential requirements for marriage. Under article 1051 of the Civil Code, a marriage is void if (a) either party to the marriage commits bigamy, (b) the parties to the marriage fall within the relative relations prohibited by law from marrying each other, or (c) either party to the marriage is under the statutory age for marriage.[45]

A marriage in violation of article 1051 becomes void at the time of the marriage. According to the SPC, when a request to void a bigamous marriage in accordance with article 1051 of the Civil Code is made against a defendant, but at the time of litigation, the legally married spouse has divorced the defendant or the spouse in the defendant's legal marriage has died, if the defendant relies on the dissolution of the legal marriage or the death of the legally married spouse to argue that the subsequent marriage at issue should become valid due to the occurrence of the circumstances, the argument shall be denied.[46]

Several points pertaining to void marriages are worth noting. First, only a court may void a marriage upon the request of a particular party. According to the SPC, those who have the right to request that a court determine the validity of a marriage are either the parties to the marriage or interested parties. The interested parties can

[43] See the State Council, *Marriage Registration Ordinance*, issued on July 30, 2003, art. 2. A full text of the Ordinance is available at www.gov.cn/gongbao/content/2003/content_62350.htm.

[44] See *id.*

[45] See the Civil Code, *supra* note 8, art. 1051.

[46] See the SPC, *Interpretation on the Application of the Marriage and Family Relations of the Civil Code (II)*, issued on November 25, 2024 (effective February 1, 2025), art. 1, available at https://content-static.cctvnews.cctv.com/snow-book/index.html?item_id=2519158674031523353 (SPC, Marriage and Famility Relations Interpretation II).

be (a) the close relatives and grassroots organizations of the parties in the case of bigamy, (b) the close relatives of the person who has not reached the legal age for marriage in the case of not reaching the legal age for marriage, or (c) the close relatives of the parties with regard to a prohibited relationship of kinship.[47]

Second, the avoidance of a marriage must be based on statutory grounds. As required by the SPC, if a party requests that a marriage be declared invalid pursuant to circumstances other than those stipulated in article 1051 of the Civil Code, the court shall rule to dismiss it.[48] In addition, if a party seeks to void a marriage in accordance with article 1051 of the Civil Code, but the situation rendering the marriage invalid no longer exists when the request is made, a denial will be issued.[49] Also, after the death of one or both spouses, the surviving spouse or an interested party may seek a court judgment to declare the marriage invalid if there are statutory grounds.[50]

The avoidance of marriage often involves those who are underage for marriage. But in many cases, the age of the parties actually was not too far below the minimum age at the time of marriage. Thus, by the time the validity issue is raised, the parties have already reached the minimum age, which makes the case moot. Therefore, if the voidance of a marriage is sought on the grounds of being underage, the request must be made to the court before the parties involved reach the legal age for marriage. The standard to determine the validity of marriage based on age is the actual age at the time when the request is filed with the court.

Third, mediation does not apply to the adjudication on the validity of a marriage. But mediation may be conducted for matters involving property division and child support. If an agreement is reached through mediation, a mediation agreement shall be entered in lieu of a judgment.[51] Also, after the court accepts the case seeking a decision on the validity of a marriage, the plaintiff may not apply to withdraw it. The court then must rule on the case.[52]

An annullable marriage is a marriage in which the law allows one or both parties to request the annulment of the marriage through legal procedures under certain conditions.

The difference between an annullable marriage and an invalid marriage is that the former concerns a marriage, though not necessarily invalid, contained a defect in the formation of the marital relationship, while the latter usually involves a violation of the marriage conditions stipulated by law. In an annullable marriage, the affected party has the right to request that the court nullify the marriage for protecting the party's legal rights and interests.

[47] See the SPC, Marriage and Family Relations I, *supra* note 20, art. 9.
[48] See *id.*, art. 17.
[49] See *id.*, art. 10.
[50] See *id.*, art. 14.
[51] See *id.*, art. 11.
[52] See *id.*

Under the Civil Code, there are two situations in which a marriage may be annulled upon the interested party's request. The first situation is marriage under duress. If one party marries under duress, such as physical coercion or mental control, resulting in a marriage against the party's true will, the party under duress can request that the court nullify the marriage.[53] Under the SPC's interpretation, duress can be found if a party faces a threat of damage to the life, body, health, reputation, or property of the party or his/her close relatives, and is forced to marry the other party against his /her true will. Note, however, that only the party who was under duress may request that the marriage be annulled.[54]

The second situation is if one party suffers from a serious illness but fails to disclose it to the other party at the time of marriage. If one party suffers from a serious illness prior to the marriage but conceals it from the other party before marriage registration, the party who was not informed of the illness can request that the court annul the marriage.[55] Serious illness usually refers to diseases that require expensive treatment and seriously affect the individual's normal work and life for a long period of time, including, among others, serious hereditary diseases, specified infectious diseases, or certain mental illnesses.[56]

e. Consequences of Marriage Avoidance and Annulment

A marriage, once avoided or annulled, has no legal effect *ab initio*, and neither party to such a marriage shall have any rights or duties arising from the marital relationship.[57] According to the SPC, an avoided or annulled marriage having no legal effect *ab initio* means that when a marriage is confirmed to be void or annulled according to law, the marriage as such enjoys no protection of law from the very beginning.[58]

Both avoidance and annulment of a marriage proceeding often involve property partition. Under article 1054 of the Civil Code, the properties acquired during the cohabitation periods shall be treated as jointly owned and be disposed of by mutual agreement, unless there is evidence proving that the property belongs to one of the parties. Absent such an agreement, the court shall make a determination under the principle of favoring the no-fault party. The disposal of property acquired during a marriage that has been voided due to bigamy may not harm the proprietary rights and interests of the parties to the lawful marriage. In addition, when a marriage is made void or annulled, the no-fault party has the right to request damages.[59]

[53] See the Civil Code, *supra* note 8, art. 1052.
[54] See the SPC, Marriage and Family Relations Interpretation I, *supra* note 20, art. 18.
[55] See the Civil Code, *supra* note 8, art. 1053.
[56] See the SPC Leading Group, Marriage and Family Relations, *supra* note 1, at 100.
[57] See the Civil Code, *supra* note 8, art. 1054.
[58] See the SPC, Marriage and Family Relations Interpretation I, *supra* note 20, art. 20.
[59] See the Civil Code, *supra* note 8, art. 1054. See also *id.*, art. 22.

A request to annul a marriage, however, is subject to a one-year statute of limitations. The one-year time limit runs from the date the coercive behavior ends or from the date when the party knows or should have known the cause for the annulment.[60] In the case where a coerced party whose personal freedom is illegally constrained wishes to annul the marriage, the request to annul the marriage shall be made within one year from the date when the party's personal freedom is regained.[61] For the one-year period, the provisions on suspension, interruption, or extension of the statute of limitations do not apply.[62]

f. Foreign-Related Marriage

In China, foreign-related marriage refers to the marriage between a citizen of one country and a citizen of another country (including stateless persons), covering both marriage and divorce. Foreign-related marriage to the extent of its validity is a matter of application of law. Under Chinese law, conditions of marriage are governed by the law of the parties' common habitual residence. Absent common habitual residence, the law of their common nationality shall be applied. In the case where there is no common nationality, the law of the place where the marriage is concluded shall be applied if the marriage is concluded in a party's habitual residence or in the country of a party's nationality.[63] In addition, the formalities of a marriage shall be deemed valid if they conform to the law of the place where the marriage is concluded, or the law of a party's habitual residence or nationality.[64]

C. *Family Relations*

Family in China is considered to bear two characteristics. First, family is a kinship unit consisting of relatives, tied by marriage, blood, or adoption, who are related to each other under certain rights and obligations.[65] In Chinese law as noted, the family members who are bound by legal rights and obligations include spouses, parents and children, siblings, grandparents, and grandchildren. Simply put, a family is a group of relatives who as members live together and share legal rights and bear obligations with each other.

Second, the family is a living unit with common consumption and spending. As a fundamental cell of society, the family provides comfort, support, care, and love to

[60] See *id.*, the Civil Code, arts. 1052, 1053.

[61] See *id.*, art. 1052.

[62] See the SPC, Marriage and Family Relations Interpretation I, *supra* note 20, art. 19.

[63] See the *Law of China on the Application of Law Concerning Foreign-related Civil Relations*, adopted on October 28, 2010, art. 21, available at https://wipolex-res.wipo.int/edocs/lexdocs/laws/en/cn/cn173en.html (hereinafter referred to as Choice of Law Statute).

[64] See *id.*, art. 22.

[65] See Wang Liping et al., Family Law and Succession, 3 (Peking University Press, 2010).

each other in economic needs, moral life, religion, education, and many other aspects.[66] It is commonly held in China that the functions of family include, among others, production, reproduction, daily life, emotion sharing and communication, support, education, and entertainment.

Under the provisions of the Civil Code, family relations, also called domestic relations, are composed of marital relations, parent–child relationships, and relationships among close relatives. The legal rights and obligations that each family member should have constitute the substantial components of family relations. The core, however, is the marital relation.

a. Marital Relation

The marital relation is explained in China as the legal relation consisting of the rights and obligations between husband and wife.[67] As noted, the marital relation involves both a personal relationship and a property relationship. The former refers to the rights and obligations that are related to the identities of husband and wife but do not contain any economic contents, while the latter focuses on the economic content-based rights and obligations between husband and wife.

1. PERSONAL RELATIONSHIP OF SPOUSES. A common holding in China is that the personal relationship between husband and wife determines their property relationship. Put differently, the property relationship between husband and wife is subordinate to their personal relationship.[68] Under the provisions of the Civil Code, the personal relationship between husband and wife mainly involves the right to name, work, study, and join social activities, as well as the rights and obligations to raise children.

There are a set of rules in the Civil Code that govern the personal relationship between husband and wife. First, under article 1056, both husband and wife have the right to use their own family name.[69] China used to have a tradition that the wife takes the husband's family name after marriage. This tradition, however, has been legally abandoned ever since the first Marriage Law was adopted in 1950. It is believed in China that there is no personal dependency between husband and wife, and an important indicator of having no personal dependency is the right for them to keep their own family names.[70]

Second, it is provided in article 1057 that the husband and wife both enjoy the freedom to engage in production and other work, to study, and to participate in

66 See *id.*
67 See *id.* at 61.
68 See *id.*
69 See the Civil Code, *supra* note 8, art. 1056.
70 See the SPC Leading Group, Marriage and Family Relations, *supra* note 1, at 117.

social activities.[71] Article 1057 explicitly prohibits a party in a marital relation from restraining or interfering with such freedom of the other party.[72] The essence of article 1057 is the personal freedom of each of the spouses – the freedom to choose a career, receive an education, and participate in social activities without interference.

Third, according to article 1058 of the Civil Code, both husband and wife have both equal rights and joint duties to raise, educate and protect their minor children.[73] Article 1058 is a newly added provision emphasizing, from the perspective of the rights and obligations of the spouses, that raising, educating and protecting minor children is the common and shared responsibility of both spouses. Article 1058 also replaces the previous provision in the Marriage Law that stressed the obligations of the married couple to implement family planning, given China's lifting of the "one child for a couple" limit in 2015.

II. PROPERTY RELATIONSHIP OF SPOUSES. The spousal property relationship concerns the rights and obligations between husband and wife regarding property arising from their status as spouses. The property relationship as such mainly involves property ownership, mutual support, property division, liabilities allocation, and property inheritance between husband and wife during their marriage.

The nature of spousal property ownership depends on the type of property. As provided in the Civil Code, the property between husband and wife is divided into community property and individual property. Community property refers to the common property acquired by the one or both spouses during the marriage, which is either statutory based or specified under the agreement of the couple. Individual property can be premarital property or postmarital property. Individually owned postmarital property is the property that is retained by husband or wife under his or her personal ownership according to the law or by an agreement between them.

According to article 1065 of the Civil Code, a man and a woman may agree in writing that their premarital property and the property to be acquired by them during their marriage be owned by them separately, jointly, or partially owned separately and partially owned jointly. The agreement as such, once made, is legally binding on the married couple. If there is no agreement or the agreement is unclear, the statutory rules that govern the marital property shall apply.[74] Also, as noted, the Civil Code mandates that husband and wife have equal rights in disposing of community property.[75]

The statutory rules of marital property are articles 1062 and 1063 of the Civil Code. Under article 1062, the property acquired by the spouses during their marriage that constitutes community property and are jointly owned by the spouses includes: (a)

[71] See the Civil Code, *supra* note 8, art. 1057.
[72] See *id.*
[73] See *id.*, art. 1058.
[74] See *id.*, art. 1065.
[75] See *id.*, art. 1062.

salaries and wages as well as bonuses and other remuneration received from services rendered; (b) proceeds obtained from production, business operation, and investment; (c) proceeds arising from intellectual property rights; (d) except as otherwise provided in the will or the gift contract, property acquired from inheritance or given as a gift; and (e) other property that shall be jointly owned by the spouses.[76]

According to the SPC, the community property during the marriage as prescribed in article 1062 shall include (a) the income obtained by one party from investing personal property; (b) the housing subsidies and housing provident funds actually obtained or which should be obtained by both husband and wife; and (c) the basic pensions and bankruptcy insurance actually obtained or that should be obtained by both husband and wife.[77] In addition, when a marriage is determined to be ineffective or annulled, the property acquired by the parties during their cohabitation shall be deemed as community property unless there is evidence that the property is owned by one of the parties.[78]

The SPC also opines that if a house is rented by one party before marriage and purchased with a joint fund after marriage in the name of one party, it shall be deemed common property of the couple.[79] In addition, if one party sells a house jointly owned by the couple without the consent of the other party, and a third party purchases it in good faith, pays a reasonable price and has completed property registration, the other party's claim to recover the house will not be granted by the court.[80] But, if one spouse disposes of a jointly owned house without authorization and causes losses to the other spouse, and the other spouse requests compensation for the losses during divorce, the court should rule to grant the request.[81]

Individual property qualified as separate property of one of the spouses is defined in article 1063 of the Civil Code to include (a) premarital property of one spouse; (b) compensation or indemnification received by one spouse for injury inflicted upon him or her; (c) property that belongs to only one spouse as provided in a will or gift contract; (d) articles exclusively used by one spouse for daily life; and (e) other property that shall be owned by one spouse.[82]

Pursuant to the SPC's interpretation, the individual property of one spouse if identified under article 1063 shall not become community property of the spouses with the continuation of the marriage relationship, unless otherwise agreed by the parties.[83] In addition, for the purposes of article 1063, casualty insurance, disability

[76] See *id.*
[77] See the SPC, Marriage and Family Relations Interpretation I, *supra* note 20, art. 19.
[78] See *id.*, art. 22.
[79] See *id.*, art. 27.
[80] See *id.*, art. 28.
[81] See *id.*
[82] See the Civil Code, *supra* note 8, art. 1063.
[83] See the SPC, Marriage and Family Relations Interpretation I, *supra* note 20, art. 31.

allowance, as well as medical and living allowance of military personnel shall all fall within individual property.[84]

The SPC also makes it clear that when either spouse's parents contribute money toward the purchase of a house for a couple before the couple gets married, the contribution shall be deemed a gift to their own child, except where the parents clearly indicate that the gift is for the married couple.[85] However, when the parents' contribution to the purchase of a house for a couple is made after the couple's marriage, the nature of the contribution shall be determined under the agreement entered for that purpose. If there is no such agreement or the agreement is unclear, the property shall be deemed as community property of the married couple.[86]

During the marriage, one of the spouses may apply to the court for partition of their community property in two different situations. The first situation is if the other spouse has concealed, transferred, sold, destructed or damaged, or squandered the community property, created a false community debt, or committed other acts that seriously harm the interests of the community property. The second is if a person, whom one of the spouses has a statutory obligation to support, is suffering from a serious disease and needs medical treatment, but the other spouse does not agree to pay the relevant medical expenses.[87]

III. COMMON DEBTS OF HUSBAND AND WIFE. Once married, while having equal ownership rights to community property, the couple will be jointly liable for common debts. As defined in article 1064 of the Civil Code, the common debts of a couple include (a) the debts incurred via the manifested intent of both spouses, which are jointly signed by both spouses or are signed by one spouse but subsequently ratified by the other spouse, and (b) debts incurred by one of the spouses in his or her own name during the marriage to meet the daily needs of the family.[88]

However, if a debt incurred by one of the spouses in his or her own name during the marriage exceeds the family's daily needs, it will not be considered a common debt. An exception is if the exceeding debts are taken for both spouses' daily life or joint business production and operation of the spouses, or made under the common expression of intent of the spouses. Under article 1064 of the Civil Code, the creditor bears the duty of proof that the exceeding debts meet the exception as such.[89]

In the case where the spouses agree that the property acquired during the marriage is to be owned separately, a debt incurred by one of the spouses shall be paid off with his or her separate property to the extent that the third person concerned is aware of such an agreement. The notion is that only if a third party

[84] See *id.*, art. 30.
[85] See *id.*, art. 29.
[86] See *id.*
[87] See the Civil Code, *supra* note 8, art. 1066.
[88] See *id.*, art. 1064.
[89] See *id.*

is aware of the agreement between the married couple on their property arrangement will the agreement have an effect to the third party. Thus, if the agreement is unknown to the third party, a payment for the debt incurred by one of the spouses shall be made out of the couple's common property.

b. Relationship among Family Members

The relationship among family members includes the relationship between parents and children and the relationship among close relatives. As noted, close relatives mainly consist of sisters, brothers, and grandparents. Under the provisions of the Civil Code, the relationship among family members involves primarily the obligations of mutual support as well as maintenance, and the emphasis is on the protection of the legitimate interests of both children and the elderly.

For the purpose of protection, the Civil Code dictates that children born out of wedlock have equal rights as children born in wedlock, and no organization or individual may harm or discriminate against them.[90] In addition, according to the SPC's interpretation, a child born as a result of artificial insemination shall be treated as a child born in wedlock if the couple has mutually agreed to the insemination during the marriage.[91]

Moreover, it is required under the Civil Code that a biological parent who does not have physical custody of his or her out-of-wedlock child pay child support for such child who is a minor or who is an adult but incapable of supporting him/herself.[92] The same protection is also extended to stepchildren. Article 1072 of the Civil Code imposes an obligation on stepparents and the stepchild as well, with a provision that stepparents shall not maltreat or discriminate against a stepchild, and vice versa.[93]

1. PARENTS AND CHILDREN. Pursuant to the Civil Code, parents are obligated to raise their minor children and have the rights and obligations to educate and protect them. According to article 1067 of the Civil Code, if parents fail to fulfill their duty to raise their children, a minor child or an adult child who is incapable of supporting him/herself has the right to claim child support payments against his/her parents. In addition, under article 1068 of the Civil Code, where a minor causes damage to others, the minor's parents shall bear civil liability in accordance with law. Furthermore, those who refuse to fulfill their duty to raise their child and maliciously abandon him or her may face criminal charges.[94]

90 See *id.*, art. 1071.
91 See the SPC, Marriage and Family Relations Interpretation I, *supra* note 20, art. 40.
92 See the Civil Code, *supra* note 8, art. 1071.
93 See *id.*, art. 1072.
94 See *id.*, art. 1068.

According to the SPC, an adult child incapable of supporting him/herself shall include a child who is receiving education at the high school level or below, or is unable to maintain normal living due to such non-subjective reasons as total or partial loss of the ability to work.[95] Support payments shall cover living, education, and medical expenses, and the like.[96] If, during the existence of a marital relationship, any of the parents refuse to fulfill the duty to raise a minor child or adult child who is incapable of living independently, when the child files claims with the court asking for support payments, the court shall grant the claims.[97]

On the other hand, adult children have a duty under the law to support their parents. As provided in article 1067 of the Civil Code, parents who lack the capacity to work or who are in financial hardship have the right to claim support payments against the adult child. In China, to support elderly parents is not only a moral requirement but also a legal duty imposed on their children.

Note that the child's duty to support his/her parents is not based on the support the child has received from his/her parents. In other words, lack of support from parents is not an excuse for a child not to support his/her parents. Also, under the Law of the Protection of the Interests of the Elderly, a child may not refuse to support his/her parents on the grounds of giving up his/her rights of inheritance or for any other reason.[98] In addition, children are required to respect their parents' right to marriage and may not interfere with their parents' divorce, remarriage, or their marital life thereafter. Thus, the children's duty to support their parents shall remain intact even with changes to their parents' marital relationship.[99]

Moreover, pursuant to the Civil Code, parents and children have the right to inherit each other's estates.[100] If, however, a parent challenges the maternity or paternity with just cause, the parent may file a lawsuit with a court for affirmation or denial of such maternity or paternity. Likewise, if an adult child challenges the maternity or paternity with just cause, he/she may also file a lawsuit with a court for affirmation of the maternity or paternity in question.[101]

II. RELATIONSHIP AMONG CLOSE RELATIVES. The relationship among close relatives is in fact a matter of the duty to provide support. According to article 1074 of the Civil Code, either paternal or maternal grandparents, if financially capable, have a duty to raise their minor grandchildren whose parents are deceased or are incapable of raising their children. Conversely, either paternal or maternal

[95] See the SPC, Marriage and Family Relations Interpretation I, *supra* note 20, art. 41.

[96] See *id.*, art. 42.

[97] See *id.*, art. 43.

[98] See the *Law of the Protection of the Rights and Interests of the Elderly*, adopted by the Standing Committee of the NPC in 1996, available at www.chinalawtranslate.com/prc-law-on-protection-of-the-rights-of-the-elderly/.

[99] See the Civil Code, *supra* note 8, art. 1069.

[100] See *id.*, art. 1070.

[101] See *id.*, art. 1073.

grandchildren, if financially capable, have the duty to support their grandparents whose children are deceased or are incapable of providing such support.[102]

In addition, under article 1075 of the Civil Code, the elder brothers or sisters, if financially capable, have the duty to raise their minor siblings whose parents are deceased or are incapable of raising them. Also, the younger brothers or sisters who have been brought up by their elder siblings and who are financially capable have the duty to support such elder siblings who lack both the capacity to work and the means to support themselves.[103]

2. DIVORCE

Again, freedom of marriage includes the freedom to divorce. In China, divorce is defined as a civil legal act that dissolves the marital relationship between husband and wife through agreement or litigation so as to terminate the rights and obligations between the couple. The legal consequences of divorce include property division, determination of child custody, etc. In addition, the rights and obligations terminated after divorce include the rights and obligations to live together and the obligation to support each other financially.

A. *Mutual or Unilateral Divorce*

A divorce can be made mutually (via an agreement) or unilaterally (through litigation). The mutual divorce is also called uncontested divorce because the divorce is based on mutual consent, while the unilateral divorce is usually a contested one since it allows a marriage to be dissolved based on the request of one of the spouses. Like marriage, a mutual divorce in China can take place through registration. Under article 1076 of the Civil Code, when the husband and the wife both agree to divorce, they shall enter into a divorce agreement in writing and file a divorce registration in person with the marriage registration authority. The divorce agreement shall include the expression of intent of both parties to voluntarily divorce and their mutual agreement on such matters as child support, property division, and allocation of debts.

It is important to note that after a filing of mutual divorce, there is a thirty-day cooling-off period during which either party may withdraw the divorce registration application. Pursuant to article 1077 of the Civil Code, upon expiration of the cooling-off period, both parties shall, within thirty days, personally visit the marriage registration authority to apply for the issuance of a divorce certificate. Failure to do so will cause the divorce registration application to be deemed as having been withdrawn.[104]

[102] See *id.*, art. 1074.
[103] See *id.*, art. 1075.
[104] See *id.*, art. 1077.

The "cooling-off period" for divorce is deemed as an important provision in the Civil Code to help reduce impulsive or hasty divorces so as to protect marriages. But the reaction to its application is mixed. One criticism is that the imposition of a cooling-off period for divorce ignores the protection of women's rights in cases where domestic violence is the main reason for divorce. Also, since the provision is designed in a one-size-fits-all manner, it undermines the substantive equality between men and women.[105] In reality, the cooling-off requirement indeed reduced the number of consensual divorces, but the number of unilateral divorces or divorces through litigation was on the rise.[106]

In the case of mutual divorce, the marriage registration authority is required to ascertain that the divorce is voluntary and that the two parties have reached agreement on such matters as child support, property partition, and allocation of debts. Upon the ascertainment, the marriage registration authority will register the divorce and issue a divorce certificate. For the purposes of mutual divorce, the marriage registration authority is generally the place where one of the parties has permanent residence (the place of permanent household registration).

In bilateral divorce, the divorce agreement has binding effect on the parties for all matters prescribed in the agreement. But some provisions in the divorce agreement may be modified due to changes in circumstances. According to the SPC, a stipulation in the divorce agreement that one party will directly raise minor children or adult children who cannot live independently, and that the other party will bear no obligation of support, is legally binding.[107]

However, after their divorce, if the economic situation of the party directly raising the children changes, resulting in a significant decrease in the original living standard or a significant increase in the necessary and reasonable expenses for the children's living, education, medical care, etc., and the minor children or adult children who cannot live independently request the other party to pay for child support, the court shall grant the request and determine the amount of support in consideration of the overall divorce agreement, the actual needs of the children, the other party's affordability, local living standards, and other factors.[108]

Unilateral divorce is a process in which a party requests a divorce without the consent of the other party. The major difference between mutual divorce and unilateral divorce in China is that the former relies on mutual consent of the married couple while the latter is made by a court order. Under article 1079 of the

[105] See Lu Wei, Has the Four-Year Implementation of Divorce Cooling-Off Period Reduced the Divorce Rate? Caijing Magazine, March 4, 2025, available at https://baijiahao.baidu.com/s?id=1825677433289985178&wfr=spider&for=pc.

[106] According to national civil affairs statistics, the number of divorces in China was 2.839 million in 2021, 2.879 million in 2022, and 3.6053 million in 2023, respectively. During the period from 2021 to 2023, the number of mutual divorces decreased from 75.4% to 71.9%, while cases of unilateral divorce increased from 24.6% to 28.1%. See *id.*

[107] See the SPC, Marriage and Family Relations Interpretation II, *supra* note 46, art. 16.

[108] See *id.*

Civil Code, when one of the spouses wants a divorce, a relevant organization may offer mediation, or the party may file a divorce suit directly with a court.[109] Note that mediation by a relevant organization, as a non-judicial mediation, is not a required process for divorce. Thus, in a unilateral divorce, any of the parties involved may bypass mediation and directly seek a court order.

B. *Jurisdiction over Divorce*

Since a court order is required, unilateral divorce is also called divorce by judgment. To file a unilateral divorce, the court seized must have jurisdiction. In general, a divorce action shall be filed with the court at the place where the defendant is domiciled. If, however, both spouses have left their place of domicile for more than one year and one spouse files for divorce, the case shall be under the jurisdiction of the people's court at the defendant's habitual residence; if there is no habitual residence, the people's court at the defendant's residence at the time of the plaintiff's lawsuit shall have jurisdiction.[110] If one spouse leaves their place of residence for more than one year and the other spouse files for divorce, the court at the place of the plaintiff's domicile shall have jurisdiction.

C. *Grounds for Divorce*

Under Chinese law, a consensual divorce shall in general meet the following requirements: (a) the parties must be legally married; (b) the parties must have full civil capacity; (c) the parties must have a true intention to divorce; and (d) the matters concerning the custody and support of the children, partition of the property, and settlement of joint debts have been properly dealt with.

Unilateral divorce can be either fault-based or non-fault-based. The ground to grant a divorce based on non-fault is the irreconcilable differences or irretrievable breakdown of the marital relationship between the parties.[111] The SPC, in its Opinions on the Determination of Breakdown of Marital Relationship, provides a list of circumstances as guidance for the courts to make determinations on irreconcilable differences.[112]

[109] See the Civil Code, *supra* note 8, art. 1079.

[110] See the SPC, *Interpretation on the Application of the Civil Procedural Law of China* (as amended 2022), art. 12, available at http://ayzy.hncourt.gov.cn/public/detail.php?id=17731.

[111] See the Civil Code, *supra* note 8, art. 1079.

[112] See the SPC, *Opinions on the Determination of Breakdown of Marital Relationship*, issued on November 21, 1989, available at http://gongbao.court.gov.cn/Details/eeof781acf12e66oo44c99dfca52b9.html. The Opinions, though already repealed by the SPC, are still relevant and influential in courts' decisions. According to the Opinions, the factors to consider included: (a) one party suffers from a disease that is prohibited by law from marriage, or one party has a physical defect or other reasons that prevent sexual intercourse, and the disease is difficult to cure; (b) there was a lack of understanding before marriage, a hasty marriage, failure to establish a marital relationship after

To determine whether the relationship between the couple has broken down, the courts need to consider such factors as the foundation of marriage, the relationship after marriage, the reason for divorce, the current state of the relationship between the couple, and whether there is a possibility of reconciliation. A divorce will also be granted if (a) the spouses have been separated for no less than two full years due to marital discord; or (b) other circumstances exist under which mutual affection no longer exists between the spouses.[113]

Fault-based divorce is a divorce granted due to a fault committed by one of the parties in the marriage. The grounds for fault-based divorce include: (a) one spouse commits bigamy or cohabitates with another person; (b) one spouse commits domestic violence or maltreats or deserts a family member; and (c) one spouse habitually commits acts such as gambling, drug abuse, or the like, and refuses to correct such behavior despite repeated warnings.[114]

In either fault-based or non-fault-based divorce, a court is required to conduct mediation before a divorce judgment is entered. Unlike the non-judicial mediation, a mediation presided over by a court is binding, and a mediation agreement reached by the parties will be incorporated into the court judgment. Only if the mediation fails may a divorce be granted.[115] In addition, if one spouse is declared to be missing

marriage, and difficulty living together; (c) mental illness was concealed before marriage and failed to be cured after marriage, or knowing that the other party suffers from mental illness before marriage, a party married him/her, or one party suffered from mental illness during the period of living together as a couple, and the disease cannot be cured for a long time; (d) one party deceived the other party or committed fraud during the marriage registration to obtain a "marriage license"; (e) after registering for marriage, the parties have not lived together and there is no possibility of reconciliation; (f) in the marriage that was arranged or made for money, one party immediately filed for divorce after marriage, or although living together for many years, no marital relationship has been established; (g) the parties have separated for three years due to emotional discord, and there is no possibility of reconciliation, or they have separated for one year after a court's ruling not to divorce, and failed to perform marital obligations; (h) one party has committed adultery or illegal cohabitation with another person, and has not shown repentance after education, the innocent party or the guilty party has filed for divorce while the other party does not agree to divorce, but after being criticized, educated, or punished, or after the court has ruled not to allow divorce, the guilty party has filed for divorce again, and there is no possibility of reconciliation; (i) one party has committed bigamy and the other party has filed for divorce; (j) one party is lazy and hates work, has bad habits such as gambling, or does not fulfill family obligations, and has made no changes after being repeatedly educated, making it difficult for the couple to live together; (k) one party has been sentenced to long-term imprisonment, or the party's illegal and criminal behavior has seriously damaged the relationship between the couple; (l) one party has been missing for two years, and the other party has filed for divorce, and it is confirmed that there are no whereabouts after a public notice; (m) one party is being abused or abandoned by the other party, or abused by the other party's relatives, or the party's relatives are being abused by the other party, but the situation remains unchanged after the other party is educated, and the abused or abandoned party chooses not to forgive the other party; or (n) the relationship between the couple has indeed broken down due to other reasons.

[113] See *id.*

[114] See *id.*

[115] See *id.*

and the other party files for divorce, the divorce shall be granted.[116] Furthermore, if after a judgment has been made against divorce, the spouses have been separated for another year, a divorce shall be granted when one of the spouses files for divorce again with the court.[117]

D. *Special Restrictions on Divorce*

There are two situations in which a divorce is subject to certain restrictions. First, when the spouse of military personnel on active service requests a divorce, the consent of the spouse who is military personnel on active service shall be obtained unless the latter is at serious fault.[118] Second, a husband may not file for divorce during his wife's pregnancy, within one year after his wife delivers, or within six months after termination of her pregnancy, unless the wife applies for divorce, or the court deems it necessary to hear the divorce request made by the husband.[119]

In a fault-based divorce, damages may be assessed upon request. Under article 1091 of the Civil Code, a spouse who is not at fault has the right to claim compensation where divorce is caused by one of the following acts done by the other spouse: (a) committing bigamy; (b) cohabitating with another person; (c) committing domestic violence; (d) maltreating or deserting a family member; or (e) conducting other serious faults.[120]

E. *Child Custody and Support*

In a divorce proceeding, matters related to the dissolution of the marital relationship are those concerning child custody, child support, visitation rights, community property partition, elder support, alimony, and common debts. Each of these matters is governed by a specific provision in the Civil Code. It is mandated under the Civil Code that after divorce, parents continue to have the rights and duties to raise, educate and protect their children.[121]

Child custody is provided in article 1084 of the Civil Code, under which a mother shall, upon divorce, have physical custody of a child under the age of two. In other cases, child custody will be determined under an agreement reached by the parents upon divorce. Absent such an agreement, child custody will be decided by the court under the principle of the best interests of the child, taking into account the actual situations of both parents. But when a child has reached the age of eight at the time

[116] See *id.*
[117] See *id.*
[118] See the Civil Code, *supra* note 8, art. 1081.
[119] See *id.*, art. 1082.
[120] See *id.*, art. 1091.
[121] See *id.*, art. 1084.

of the parents' divorce, the child's true wishes shall be respected in the determination of custody.[122]

According to the SPC, there are two exceptions to article 1084 concerning the custody of a child under the age of two. First, if the mother is in any of the following situations, the father may request to have direct custody of the child: (a) suffering from a long-lasting infectious disease or other serious disease so that it is not suitable for the child to live with her; (b) failure to fulfill the obligation to raise the child though capable of raising him/her; or (c) other reasons for which it is not suitable for the child to live with her.[123]

The SPC also opines that when both parents seek the custody of a child who is over two years old, priority shall be given to the parent: (a) who has undergone sterilization or has lost fertility due to other reasons; (b) who has lived with the child for a long time so that a change of living environment would be obviously detrimental to the healthy growth of the child; (c) who has no child, if the other parent already has other children; or (d) whose living with the child is beneficial for the child to grow, while the other parent suffers from an infectious disease that cannot be cured after receiving treatment for a long time or other serious illness, or in other situations so detrimental to the physical and mental health of the child that it is not appropriate for him or her to live with the child.[124]

In its 2023 interpretation, the SPC further specifies the situations for the determination of child custody in divorce cases. According to the SPC, in divorce proceedings, when both parents request direct custody of their minor children who have reached two years of age, if a parent is found to fall within any of the following circumstances, the other parent shall have the priority in obtaining direct custody under the principle of best interest of the minor children: (a) committing domestic violence or abusing or abandoning family members; (b) having bad habits such as gambling and drug abuse; (c) committing bigamy, cohabitating with others, or having other serious violations of spousal fidelity obligations; (d) robbing or hiding minor children and the other party does not commit any serious infringement of the legitimate rights and interests of minor children; or (e) other situations detrimental to the physical and mental health of minor children.[125]

For matters of child support, visitation rights, property partition, elder support, and alimony, determination shall be made according to the agreement of the parties at the time of the divorce. A court judgment will be entered only if the parties fail to reach an agreement. When making a judgment, the court is required to follow certain rules. The ultimate goal is to maintain to the greatest extent the autonomy of

[122] See *id.*
[123] See the SPC, Marriage and Family Relations Interpretation I, *supra* note 20, art. 44.
[124] See *id.*, art. 46.
[125] See the SPC, Marriage and Family Relations Interpretation II, *supra* note 46, art. 14.

both spouses in handling their private matters fairly, with the protection of the legitimate interests of children, women, and the elderly.

In its interpretation, the SPC also provides specific guidance for the determination of child support. In accordance with the SPC's interpretation, the amount of child support can be determined based on the actual needs of the child, both parents' ability to pay, and the local living standards. For those who have a fixed income, the amount of child support will generally be paid at a rate of 20 to 30 percent of their total monthly income. If there are two or more children, the percentage can be increased proportionally, but generally should not exceed 50 percent of the total monthly income.[126]

If neither parent has a fixed income, the amount of child support can be determined based on their total yearly income or the average income in the same industry, with reference to the above ratio. Under special circumstances, the above proportion may be appropriately increased or reduced.[127] In addition, it is required that the child support be paid regularly, but it may be paid in one lump sum if conditions permit. If a parent has no financial income or the parent's whereabouts are unknown, his/her property can be used to offset the child support. Under the SPC's interpretation, the period of payment of child support is generally until the child turns 18. However, if a child between 16 and 18 years old has his or her own work income as the main source of living, and can maintain the general living standards of the local area, the parents may stop paying child support.[128]

If, after divorce, a party who does not have direct custody of the children fails to pay child support in accordance with the divorce agreement or commitments made in other ways, the court shall grant the request made by the minor children or adult children who are unable to live independently for the payment of arrears of the support. In the case where the child has reached adulthood and can live independently, if the party having direct custody of the child requests the other party to pay the outstanding sum of child support, the court shall uphold the request.[129]

F. *Property Partition*

The most difficult and also complicated issue in divorce proceedings is the property partition. Under article 1087 of the Civil Code, upon divorce, the community property of the spouses shall be partitioned through agreement. If no such agreement is reached, the partition shall be adjudicated by a court in light of the actual state of the property and pursuant to the principle of favoring the rights and interests of the children, the wife, and the no-fault party.[130]

[126] See the SPC, Marriage and Family Relations Interpretation I, *supra* note 20, art. 49.
[127] See *id.*
[128] See *id.*, art. 53.
[129] See the SPC, Marriage and Family Relations Interpretation II, *supra* note 46, art. 17.
[130] See the Civil Code, *supra* note 8, art. 1087.

If, however, one spouse conceals, transfers, sells off, destructs or damages, or squanders the community property, or creates a false community debt in an attempt to unlawfully seize the property of the other spouse, said spouse may receive less or no property upon partition of the community property in the case of divorce. Where one of the aforementioned acts committed by one spouse is discovered after the divorce, the other party may file a lawsuit with the court for re-partition of the community property.[131]

With respect to the common debts of a married couple, pursuant to article 1089 of the Civil Code, upon divorce, the husband and wife shall jointly pay off their common debts. If the value of the community property is insufficient to pay off the debts, or each spouse owns the property separately, such debts shall be paid off by the spouses through agreement or under the decision of a court when no such agreement is reached.[132]

In 2023, the SPC, based on judicial practices, clarified several rules that apply to the property partition in divorce cases. First, when a married couple, before or during their marriage, agreed to transfer and register the house owned by one party to the other party or to both parties, if at the time of divorce proceedings the ownership of the house has not yet been transferred and registered, but the couple disputes the ownership or division of the house and the negotiation fails, the court may decide to allocate the ownership of the house to one party, and also determine whether the party who obtains the house should compensate the other party and what the specific amount of compensation should be. When making the decision and determination, the court shall take into consideration such factors as the parties' requests in litigation, the purpose of the agreed transfer, the duration of the marriage, the situation of living together and raising their children, fault for the divorce, the size of contribution to the family, and the market price of the house at the time of divorce.[133]

If, however, the house has been transferred and registered to the other party or both parties, and the parties during the divorce proceedings have a dispute over the ownership or division of the house but cannot reach an agreement through negotiation, the court then may restore the ownership of the house to the transferor upon request if the marriage relationship only exists for a short period of time and the transferor does not commit any major fault. In the meantime, the court may determine whether the other party should be compensated and what the specific amount of compensation should be. The factors to be considered for the determination are the same as in the situation mentioned earlier. But if there is evidence that the other party has committed fraud or coercion, has seriously infringed upon the legitimate rights and interests of the transferor or their close relatives, or has failed to

[131] See *id.*, art. 1092.
[132] See *id.*, art. 1089.
[133] See the SPC, Marriage and Family Relations Interpretation II, *supra* note 46, art. 5.

fulfill support obligations for the transferor, the court may revoke the transfer and related act upon request of the transferor.[134]

Second, in the case where one spouse takes such action as giving *gratis* the common property to others or disposing of the common property at an obviously unreasonable price for purposes of committing bigamy, cohabiting with others, or other violations of the marital fidelity obligation, the court shall void the action if the other spouse claims that the action is invalid due to violation of public order and good morals. When the other spouse requests to divide their common property during the marriage or asks the court to allocate to the other party less or no common property in divorce on the grounds that the other spouse has transferred or sold the common property, thereby seriously damaging the common property interests, the court shall grant the request.[135]

Third, when the purchase of a house by a couple during the marriage is fully funded by one spouse's parents, if there is an agreement clearly stipulating that the house is given as a gift only to the spouse, the agreement shall be followed. If, however, there is no such agreement or the agreement is unclear, when partitioning the property in divorce, the court may allocate the house to the spouse. But at the same time, the court shall determine the necessity to compensate the other spouse and the possible amount of compensation. The factors to be considered include the duration of the couple's living together and raising their children, the fault for the divorce, the size of the contribution to the family, and the market price of the house at the time of the divorce.[136]

If, however, a couple during their marriage purchases a house with part of the capital contributed by one or both parties' parents, and there is an agreement clearly providing that the corresponding capital contribution will only be given to their own child, the property partition in divorce shall abide by the agreement. Absent such an agreement, or if the agreement is unclear, the court may, in partitioning the common property, grant the ownership of the house to one spouse and reasonable compensation to the other, taking into consideration the factors mentioned earlier.[137]

Fourth, if one spouse transfers the equity of a limited liability company invested with the couple's common property but registered in his or her own name, and the other spouse requests a court to invalidate the equity transfer contract on the grounds that the transfer infringes upon the interests of the couple's common property without their consent, the court shall deny the request, unless there is evidence that the transferor and the transferee maliciously colluded to harm the other spouse's legitimate rights and interests.[138]

[134] See *id.*
[135] See *id.*, art. 7.
[136] See *id.*, art. 8.
[137] See *id.*
[138] See *id.*, art. 9.

When a couple invests in a limited liability company with their common property and both are registered as shareholders, but there is no agreement or the agreement is unclear on the ownership of the corresponding equity, if during divorce one spouse requests to determine the equity division ratio based on the amount of their respective capital contributions recorded in the shareholder list or the company's articles of association, the request will be denied.[139]

The SPC also adopts a rule on the property partition in cohabitation cases. According to the SPC, in a case of property settlement disputes between parties who are unmarried but live together, if there is an agreement on the property acquired during the cohabitation period, their disputes over the property shall be resolved under the agreement. When there is no agreement and the parties in dispute fail to negotiate a solution, the court shall handle the dispute in the following ways: (a) each party takes his or her own wages, bonuses, labor remuneration, intellectual property rights income, property inherited or donated by each, and income from independent production, operation, investment, etc., and (b) property purchased with joint capital or income from joint production, operation, investment, and other indistinguishable property is divided on the basis of the proportion of respective capital contributions and other factors such as the joint living situation, the presence of their children, and the size of the contribution to the property.[140]

G. *Foreign-Related Divorce*

Foreign-related divorce is a divorce that involves a foreign national or a party living abroad. There are two issues essential to a foreign-related divorce. One issue is jurisdiction, meaning which court is competent to hear a foreign-related divorce case. As discussed *infra* in Chapter 13, Chinese courts generally follow the rule of "defendant domicile" in civil litigation, which means that a court at the place where the defendant is domiciled has general jurisdiction over a civil case.[141] An exception to this rule is the case that involves status of a person, including divorce.

In its Interpretation on the Application of Civil Procedural Law, the SPC set forth certain jurisdiction rules for foreign-related divorce cases. First, for a divorce filed with a people's court by overseas Chinese who married in China and settled abroad, if the court of the country of settlement refuses to accept the divorce lawsuit on the ground that litigation for divorce should be under the jurisdiction of the court of the place of the marriage, the court of the place of the marriage or the place of last residence of one party in China shall have jurisdiction.[142] If, however, the divorce is

[139] See *id.*, art. 10.
[140] See *id.*, art. 4.
[141] See the Civil Procedural Law of China 1991 (as amended 2023), art. 22, available at www.npc.gov.cn/npc/c2/c30834/202401/P020240108541839745616.pdf.
[142] See the SPC, CPL Interpretation, *supra* note 110, art. 13.

filed by overseas Chinese who married abroad and settled abroad because the court of the country of settlement refuses to take the case on the groundsfor the reason that the divorce lawsuit shall be filed with the court of the country of nationality, the court of the original place of domicile or the last place of residence of one party in China shall have jurisdiction.[143]

Second, if one Chinese citizen lives abroad and the other lives in China, no matter which party files a divorce case with a people's court, the court of the place of domicile of the domestic party has jurisdiction.[144] But, in the case where the foreign party sues for divorce in the court of the country of his or her residence and the Chinese domestic party sues in a people's court, the court that receives the lawsuit has jurisdiction. In this case, the domestic party may file a divorce suit in any relevant court he or she chooses.[145]

Third, when both Chinese citizens are abroad but not settled, and one of them sues for divorce with a people's court, the court of the place of the original domicile of either party has jurisdiction.[146] In addition, if divorced Chinese citizens both reside abroad and file a lawsuit solely for the division of domestic property, the jurisdiction rests with the court where the main property is located.[147]

The other issue is the governing law. As provided in article 26 of the 2010 Choice of Law Statute of China, the parties in a consensual divorce may, by agreement, choose to apply the law of one party's habitual residence or the law of either party's country of citizenship. Absent such an agreement, the law of their common habitual residence shall apply. If there is no common habitual residence, the law of the country of their common citizenship shall apply. Without common citizenship, the law of the place where the institution is processing the divorce shall apply.[148] Article 27 of the Choice of Law Statute further provides that a foreign-related divorce by litigation shall be governed by the law of the place of the forum.[149]

3. ADOPTION

Adoption in China is generally defined as a civil act in which a person or couple adopts the child of another person as their child in accordance with the conditions and procedures stipulated by law, thereby establishing a parent–child relationship between the adopter(s) and the adoptee.[150] Under this definition, adoption is legal conduct that involves personal identity, because an effective adoption results in changes in relative identity as well as the rights and obligations arising therefrom.

[143] See *id.*, art. 14.
[144] See *id.*, art. 15.
[145] See *id.*
[146] See *id.*, art. 16.
[147] See *id.*, art. 17.
[148] See the Choice of Law Statute, *supra* note 63, art. 26.
[149] See *id.*, art. 27.
[150] See Liping et al., *supra* note 65, at 175.

After the adoption, a parent–child relationship arises between the adopter and the adoptee, while such relationship between the adoptee and his or her biological parents is eliminated, although the blood relationship between them remains.

Prior to the promulgation of the Civil Code, the legal framework that governed adoption in China was the Adoption Law, enacted by the Standing Committee of the National People's Congress (NPC) in 1991 and amended in 1998. The Civil Code incorporates the Adoption Law with several changes. The major changes include: (a) loosening the conditions for adopters and the number of minors who can be adopted; (b) expanding the scope of minors who can be adopted; (c) lowering the age of the minors whose consent is needed for adoption from 14 to 8; (d) expanding the "forty-year age difference" between adopter and adoptee to cover both single male and female adopters; (e) adding "no criminal record that is detrimental to the healthy growth of the adoptee" as a condition for adopters; and (f) making an adoption evaluation a new requirement, changing the government review of adoption from *pro forma* review to substantive review.

Under Chinese law, adoption can be domestic or foreign. The former refers to an adoption between Chinese citizens, and the latter concerns an adoption between foreign adopting parents and Chinese adopted children. China allows foreigners to adopt children in the country but stipulates strict procedural conditions for foreign adoptions that are different from domestic adoptions. In other words, a foreign adoption must not only follow the general rules on adoption, but also comply with the special provisions on foreign adoptions.

The basic principle that governs adoption as provided in the Civil Code is the principle of voluntariness. Under article 1104 of the Civil Code, both adoption and placing up for adoption shall be based on mutual consent. In addition, when a minor adoptee is eight years old or older, the adoptee's consent shall be obtained.[151] For a child who is under the age of eight, the consent of the child's agent *ad litem* is required. For the purpose of adoption, the agent *ad litem* of a child is the legal guardian of the child.

A. *Requirements for Adoption*

Under the Civil Code, adoptions in China must meet certain requirements. First, only minors may be adopted. According to article 1093 of the Civil Code, the minors who are eligible to be adopted include: (a) an orphan bereaved of parents; (b) a minor whose natural parents cannot be traced; or (c) a minor whose biological parents are incapable of raising him or her due to unusual difficulties.[152] As noted, under the Civil Code, a minor refers to a person who is under the age of 18.

[151] See the Civil Code, *supra* note 8, art. 1104.
[152] See *id.*, art. 1093.

Second, the person who may place a minor up for adoption can be either a natural person or an organization. As provided in article 1094 of the Civil Code, to place a minor up for adoption, the individual or organization could be (a) the guardian of an orphan; (b) a children's welfare institution; or (c) the minor's biological parents who are incapable of raising the minor due to unusual difficulties.[153] In addition, according to article 1095 of the Civil Code, if neither of the parents of a minor has full capacity for performing civil acts, and the minor is likely to be seriously harmed, the guardian of the minor may place such minor up for adoption.[154] Put differently, unless neither of the parents of a minor is fully capable of conducting civil acts and there is likelihood that the minor will be seriously harmed, the guardian of the minor may not put the minor up for adoption.

However, it is required under article 1096 of the Civil Code that when a guardian intends to place an orphan under his guardianship for adoption, the consent of the person who has the duty to raise the orphan must be obtained.[155] When the biological parents intend to place their child up for adoption, they shall act in concert. But if one of the biological parents is unknown or cannot be found, the other parent may place the child up for adoption alone.[156]

Third, the adopter must satisfy certain conditions for adoption. The conditions set forth in article 1098 of the Civil Code for the adopter are: (a) having no child or only one child; (b) capable of raising, educating, and protecting the adoptee; (c) no disease deemed serious enough to make him/her medically unfit to be an adopter; (d) no criminal record unfavorable to the healthy growth of the adoptee; and (e) over the age of 30.[157]

There are also two restrictions that apply to adopters. One restriction is about the number of children to be adopted. Pursuant to the Adoption Law, an adopter can adopt only one child.[158] This restriction, as noted, is relaxed under article 1100 of the Civil Code to allow an adopter who has no child to adopt two children, and an adopter with one child to adopt one more.[159] Also, when a couple makes an adoption, it shall be a joint adoption.[160] The other restriction concerns the age of the adopter. Under article 1102 of the Civil Code, if a person with no spouse intends to adopt a child of a different gender, the prospective adopter shall be at least 40 years older than the adoptee.[161]

[153] See *id.*, art. 1094.

[154] See *id.*, art. 1095.

[155] See *id.*, art. 1096. (But, according to article 1096, if the person obligated to raise the orphan does not consent to the adoption and the guardian is unwilling to continue exercising guardianship, a successive guardian shall be appointed.)

[156] See *id.*, art. 1097.

[157] See *id.*, art. 1098.

[158] See the Adoption Law of China (1991), art. 8, available at www.asianlii.org/cn/legis/cen/laws/alotproc376/.

[159] See the Civil Code, *supra* note 8, art. 1100.

[160] See *id.*, art. 1101.

[161] See *id.*, art. 1102.

B. *Adoption Procedures*

For domestic adoption, there is no statutory requirement for an adoption agreement. In accordance with article 1105 of the Civil Code, the parties to an adoptive relationship may enter into an adoption agreement on a voluntary basis. Also, upon request of the parties or one of the parties to an adoptive relationship, an adoption may be notarized. But under article 1105 of the Civil Code, to form an adoptive relationship, a three-step procedure must be followed.

The first step is the application. When making an adoption, the prospective adopter shall apply for registration with all required supporting materials to the civil affairs department of the government at or above the county level. Upon receipt of the application, the civil affairs department shall evaluate the adoption application in accordance with law. After evaluation, registration will be made, and the adoptive relationship is established upon registration. But it is required that in the case of adopting a minor whose parents cannot be found, the civil affairs department for adoption registration should make public notice prior to registration.[162] Upon establishment of an adoptive relationship, the public security department shall facilitate household registration for the adoptee.[163]

It should be noted that the Civil Code provides the parents of the deceased spouse with the right of priority to raise the child in an adoption. According to article 1108 of the Civil Code, if one spouse is deceased and the surviving spouse intends to place their minor child up for adoption, the parents of the deceased spouse shall have priority in raising the child.[164]

One issue involving adoption is confidentiality. Given the private nature of adoption and the need to protect the right of an adopted child to know his or her own personal identification and biological parents, the Civil Code, like the Adoption Law, follows the principle of respecting the will of the relevant parties. Under article 1110 of the Civil Code, if the adopter or the party placing a child up for adoption requires that the adoption be kept confidential, the other persons shall respect his or her will not to disclose it.[165]

[162] See *id.*, art. 1105.
[163] See *id.*, art. 1106.
[164] See *id.*, art. 1108.
[165] See *id.*, art. 1110. Pursuant to the SPC's opinion, the confidentiality of adoption shall be interpreted and understood from the following aspects: First, if the adopter and the person placing the child up for adoption request to keep the adoption secret, no other person may disclose it. Second, if the adopter and the person placing the child up for adoption do not request that the adoption be kept secret but do not explicitly agree to disclose the adoption, no one else may disclose it, since the privacy of adoption is based on the consent of all parties involved. Third, when the adopter and the person placing the child up for adoption have explicitly agreed to disclose the adoption information, the other person may disclose it in an appropriate manner within the scope of the disclosure agreed by the adopter and the person placing the child for adoption. Fourth, "adoption secret" refers to keeping the establishment of an adoption relationship secret and all other information involving the adoption secret during

C. *Foreign-Related Adoption*

Foreign-related adoption refers to the adoption in which at least one party involved is a foreigner. In the Civil Code, however, a foreign adoption is tailored to the adoption in which foreign adopters adopt Chinese children. It is provided in article 1109 of the Civil Code that foreign nationals may adopt children from China in accordance with law. But despite the civil law provision allowing foreign adoption, the country in September 2024 significantly altered its foreign adoption policy to limit foreign adoption to the adoption of a child or stepchild of blood relatives of the same generation who are within three generations of the adopting foreigners, shutting the door for foreign adoption of children in China in all other cases.[166] Nevertheless, the allowed foreign adoptions remain subject to special provisions of law in addition to the laws that apply to adoption in general. The issues facing foreign adopters include, among others, application of law, the adoption agreement, and adoption procedures.

a. Governing Law

Since foreign adoption involves more than one country, the very first issue is which law governs the adoption. In the determination of applicable law in foreign adoption, the primary connecting factor is the habitual residence of the relevant parties. Under article 28 of the Choice of Law Statute, the law of the habitual residence of the adopter or adoptee governs the conditions and formalities of the adoption. The law of the adopter's residence at the time of adoption determines the effect of adoption, while the law of the adoptee's habitual residence at the time of adoption or the law of the forum governs the termination of the adoptive relationship.[167]

b. Procedures

Given the foreign nature of foreign adoption, the Civil Code requires that the adoption of a child by a foreign national be subject to the review and approval of

its existence, including the identity and conditions of the adopter, the fact of adoption, the identity and conditions of the person placing the child up for adoption, etc. Fifth, for the purposes of keeping the confidentiality of adoption, "all other persons" include child welfare institutions, public security organs, adoption registration authorities and their staff, and anyone who comes into contact with and knows the adoption information during the adoption process. And sixth, if the adoption information is leaked without their consent, the adopter and the person placing the child up for adoption have the right to demand that the person who leaked the information bear tort liability on the grounds of privacy infringement. See the SPC Leading Group, Marriage and Family Relations, *supra* note 1, at 427.

166 See Farah Master, *China Stops Foreign Adoptions of Its Children after Three Decades*, Reuters, September 6, 2024, available at www.reuters.com/world/china/china-stops-foreign-adoptions-its-children-after-three-decades-2024-09-06/.

167 See the Choice of Law Statute, *supra* note 63, art. 28.

the competent authorities of the foreign national's country of residence in accordance with the law of that country. In addition, the foreign adopter shall submit documents issued by the competent authorities of his country of residence certifying such personal information as his age, marital status, occupation, financial situation, physical condition, and history of criminal record, if any.[168] The documents so certified shall be authenticated by the diplomatic authorities of the country in which the foreign national resides or by an agency authorized by said diplomatic authorities, and then authenticated by the embassy or consulate of China in the said country unless otherwise provided by the State.[169]

c. Adoption Agreement

Unlike domestic adoption, in which an adoption agreement is optional, foreign adoption requires an adoption agreement. Under article 1109 of the Civil Code, in a foreign adoption, the foreign adopter shall conclude a written agreement with the person who places the child up for adoption.[170] It is also required that the agreement be made in triplicate when the application for adoption is filed. The adopter and the person placing the child up for adoption shall each hold one copy of the agreement, and the third copy shall be kept on record at the adoption registration authority.[171]

d. Registration

Upon conclusion of the adoption agreement, an adoption registration shall be made with the civil affairs department of the government at the level of provinces, autonomous regions, or municipalities directly under the State Council.[172] Foreigners who adopt Chinese children must come to China in person for the

[168] See the Civil Code, *supra* note 8, art. 1109.

[169] See *id.* Under the *Methods of Registration for Adopting Children by Foreign Nationals in China*, adopted by the Ministry of Civil Affairs on May 25, 1999, the authenticated documents to be submitted from the adopter include: (a) Application for multinational adoption; (b) Birth certificate; (c) Proof of marital status; (d) Proof of occupation, income and property status; (e) Health certificate; (f) Proof of any criminal punishment; (g) Approval of foreign adoption by the competent authority of the adopter's country; and (h) Family situation reports, including the identity of the adopter, the qualifications and appropriateness of adoption, the family condition and medical history, the adoption motivation, and the characteristics suitable for taking care of children. For a foreigner who works or studies in China for more than one year, the documents submitted shall also include proof of marital status, profession, income, or financial status, and non-criminal record issued by the unit the foreigner works with or relevant department, as well as a health certificate issued by a medical institution at or above the county level. See the Ministry of Civil Affairs, *Methods of Registration for Adopting Children by Foreign Nationals in China*, art. 4. A full text of the Methods is available at www.gqb.gov.cn/news/2019/0604/46269.shtml (hereinafter Methods of Foreign Adoption Registration).

[170] See the Civil Code, *supra* note 8, art. 1109.

[171] See the Methods of Foreign Adoption Registration, *supra* note 169, art. 9.

[172] See the Civil Code, *supra* note 8, art. 1109.

registration. When a foreign couple adopts a child in China, they shall come together for the purpose of registration. If, however, one party cannot come to China, the party must authorize the other party to make the registration in writing. The power of attorney must be notarized and authenticated in the country where the parties reside.[173]

During the registration, the adopter(s) shall submit the adoption agreement along with such supporting materials as: (a) a notice of adoption issued by the Chinese adoption organization, and (b) the identification document and photo of the adopter. In addition, the person who places the child up for adoption shall provide the following materials: (a) a notice issued by the civil affairs department that the adoptee has been approved for adoption, and (b) the household registration book and resident identification card of the person who places the child up for adoption, and a photo of the adoptee. If the social welfare institution is the person who places the child up for adoption, the identification card of the person in charge shall be presented.[174]

D. *Effect of Adoption*

Upon registration, an adoptive relationship is established. In China, the establishment of an adoptive relationship produces two legal effects: a constructive effect and an eliminative effect. Constructive effect means that, based on the adoption, a constructive lineal blood relationship is formed between the adopter and the adoptee by operation of law. As a result of adoption, the adoptive parents obtain the status of agent *ad litem* and guardian of the adopted child, and the adopted child obtains the same status as the adoptive parents' own legitimate children. Both parties enjoy the rights of parents and children and bear the obligations of parents and children as stipulated by law.[175]

Eliminative effect refers to the legal consequence of an adoption: although the biological relationship remains between the adopted child and his/her biological parents after adoption, the legal rights and obligations between the adopted children and their biological parents are eliminated. Thus, due to adoption, the biological parents no longer have the obligation to support, educate, and protect the child who has been adopted, nor are they legal representatives or guardians of the adopted child. The biological parents and the adopted child will have no right to inherit each other's property.[176] In addition, the rights and obligations between the adopted child and other close relatives of the biological parents are also eliminated as a matter of law.[177]

[173] See Methods of Foreign Adoption Registration, *supra* note 169, art. 8.
[174] See *id.*, art. 10.
[175] See the SPC Leading Group, Marriage and Family Relations, *supra* note 1, at 429.
[176] See *id.* at 430–431.
[177] See the Civil Code, *supra* note 8, art. 1111.

Under article 1112 of the Civil Code, an adopted child may take the surname of his adoptive father or mother or may retain his original surname upon consent of all the parties to the adoption.[178] Note, however, that during the adoption process, even if no consensus is reached on the adopted child's surname, it does not affect the adoption registration. Since the ascertainment of an adopted child's surname is not a condition for the adoption to be effective, the adopter can always apply for a change of the adopted child's name after the adoption.

E. *Dissolution of Adoptive Relationship*

Once an adoptive relationship is established, it may not be dissolved by the adopter before the adoptee has reached adulthood unless there is an agreement between the adopter and the party who placed the child up for adoption to the effect of dissolution. In the case that the adoptive relationship is dissolved under such an agreement, if the adoptee is eight years old or older, the adoptee's own consent shall be obtained.[179]

But when an adopter fails to perform the duty of raising the adoptee or commits maltreatment, desertion, or other acts infringing upon the lawful rights and interests of the minor adoptee, the person who placed the child up for adoption has the right to request that the adoptive relationship be dissolved. If the party placing the child up for adoption cannot reach an agreement with the adopter for dissolution, either party may file a lawsuit with the court.[180] On the other hand, once the adopted child is an adult, if the relationship between the adoptive parents and the adopted child deteriorates to the extent that they are unable to live together, the adoption may be dissolved by agreement, or through litigation if no agreement can be reached.[181]

Under article 1116 of the Civil Code, when an adoptive relationship is dissolved under an agreement, the dissolution shall be registered with the civil affairs department.[182] For litigation, the request to dissolve an adoptive relationship shall be filed with the court that has jurisdiction under the provisions of the Civil Procedural Law. However, if there is a choice of court agreement in the adoption or dissolution agreement, the choice may only apply to actions involving property partition, child support claims, and requests for compensation of damages after the adoptive relationship has been dissolved.[183]

Upon dissolution of an adoptive relationship, the rights and duties between an adoptee and his adoptive parents, as well as the latter's other close relatives, are terminated. In the meantime, the rights and duties between the adoptee and his/her

[178] See *id.*, art. 1112.
[179] See *id.*, art. 1114.
[180] See *id.*
[181] See *id.*, art. 1115.
[182] See *id.*, art. 1116.
[183] See the SPC Leading Group, Marriage and Family Relations, *supra* note 1, at 455.

biological parents, as well as the latter's other close relatives, are automatically restored. The restoration, however, may be made through consultation with an adopted child who has become an adult. Also, after dissolution of an adoptive relationship, the adoptee who has been raised by the adoptive parents and has now become an adult is required to provide living expenses to his adoptive parents if they lack both the capacity to work and the means to support themselves.[184]

If the adoptive relationship is dissolved because the adopted child maltreats or deserts his adoptive parents after he has become an adult, the adoptive parents may request that the adoptee compensate them for the expenses incurred to raise the adoptee during the adoption period. But if the dissolution is made upon the request of the biological parents of the adoptee, the adoptive parents may ask the biological parents of the adoptee to appropriately compensate the expenses incurred to raise the adoptee during the adoption period, unless the dissolution is necessitated due to the adoptive parents' maltreatment or desertion of the adoptee.[185]

4. SUCCESSION

For the purpose of the Civil Code, succession refers only to the inheritance of property, without involving any personal identity of the decedent. It is a legal process through which the property of a person is distributed among, and inherited by, those who have a certain relationship, mainly kinship, with the person after his or her death. Under article 1120 of the Civil Code, the State protects a natural person's right to inheritance.[186]

The property to be inherited under the law is called the estate, which is defined in the Civil Code as the lawfully owned property left by a natural person upon his or her death.[187] By definition, an estate in Chinese law means assets, which refers only to the positive property or property rights, and excluding negative property or property liabilities. The Civil Code also provides that an estate may not be inheritable either under the provisions of law or if the nature of the estate makes it so it may not be inherited.[188]

In China, a non-inheritable estate includes non-inheritable rights and non-inheritable property. The non-inheritable rights under the provisions of law include the right to the use of natural resources, the right to the use of a rural homestead, others' property rented or borrowed by the decedent during his/her lifetime, insurance money for designated beneficiaries, etc. Under the law, these rights or money may not be categorized as the estate.[189]

[184] See the Civil Code, *supra* note 8, art. 1117.
[185] See *id.*, art. 1118.
[186] See *id.*, art. 1120.
[187] See *id.*, art. 1122.
[188] See *id.*
[189] See the SPC Leading Group, Marriage and Family Relations, *supra* note 1, at 499–500.

What is unclear in the law is whether the right to compensation for the death of the decedent is inheritable. The SPC, however, rules death compensation out of the scope of the estate. According to the SPC, although death compensation originates from the death of the decedent, it is generated after the death of the decedent for the purpose of comforting and compensating the decedent's immediate family members, and therefore should not be contained in an inheritance.[190]

Non-inheritable property by nature mainly refers to exclusive creditor's rights related to the person of the decedent. Examples of such rights are the right of children to claim support from their parents, the right of parents to claim support from their children, the right of spouses to claim alimony, the right of the decedent to claim personal injury compensation, and property rights based on personal trust, such as the property rights arising from service and entrustment contracts. Since these rights are closely related to the person of the decedent, they end upon the decedent's death and cannot be transferred or inherited.[191]

Note that there are two issues concerning estate that remain subject to debate in China. One debate is whether rural land contract management rights may become estate.[192] According to the Law of the Rural Land Contract Management and the SPC's interpretation, the individual right to land contract management that is inheritable includes: (a) the right to forest-land contract management, and (b) the right to contract management of barren hills, gullies, hills, or beaches acquired through such means as bidding, auction, or open negotiation. The right to all other rural land contract management is renewable.[193] But it is unclear if the inheritable individual right or the renewable right to rural land contract management may be deemed an estate in the case of succession.

The other debate focuses on virtual assets, including email accounts, online accounts, financial management accounts, social accounts, online games, game equipment, virtual items, online currency, and online electronic information. Since these virtual assets may likely be converted into real products under certain circumstances, the question that arises is whether virtual assets as such can constitute estate.[194] Because of the uncertainty involving the virtual assets' disposability, price, and use value, and due to the fact that the virtual assets are often affected by the agreement between the user and the provider of the platform on which the virtual assets operate, no consensus has been reached on which virtual assets can be inherited and how.

In the process of succession, an important issue is the time of death, especially in cases where multiple deaths are involved. To deal with this issue, the Civil Code provides a rule of presumption of the time of death. Under article 1121 of the Civil

[190] See *id.* at 501.
[191] See *id.* at 500.
[192] See *id.* at 502.
[193] See *id.*
[194] See *id.* at 503.

Code, succession begins upon the death of the deceased. However, in situations where two or more persons with the right to inherit each other's estate die in the same incident, if it is difficult to determine the time of each person's death, the time of death for each of the decedents will be assumed.[195]

According to article 1121, presumption of the time of death shall be made as follows: (a) a person with no successor is presumed to have predeceased the person with successors; (b) when the deceased persons are in different generations and all of them have successors, the person of the elder generation is presumed to have predeceased the person of the younger generation; and (c) where the deceased are in the same generation, they are presumed to have died simultaneously, and no succession occurs between or among them.[196]

Since succession is a legal right, it can be waived. Under article 1124 of the Civil Code, a successor, after the succession opens, may waive the inheritance by manifesting his/her intention to renounce the inheritance in writing before the estate is disposed of. Absent such a manifestation, the successor is deemed to have accepted the inheritance.[197] According to the SPC, however, the right to inherit may not be waived if the waiver would affect the successor's ability or capacity to perform his or her legal obligations.[198] For example, if the debts owed by the deceased for living or medical expenses are caused by the successor's failure to fulfill the legal obligation of support, the successor may not abandon the inheritance to evade liability for debt repayment.[199]

On the other hand, under certain circumstances, the right to inheritance may be denied by operation of law. Pursuant to article 1125 of the Civil Code, a successor will be disinherited if the successor has committed any of the following acts: (a) intentionally killing the now decedent; (b) killing any other successor in fighting over the estate; (c) abandoning or severely mistreating the now decedent; (d) seriously forging, tampering with, concealing, or destroying the will; or (e) through serious fraud or duress, compelling the testator to write, alter, or revoke a will, or interfering with such acts. However, a successor who has committed one of the acts listed from (c) to (e) above may not be disinherited if he demonstrated true repentance and was forgiven by the now decedent or was thereafter appointed as one of the successors in the decedent's will.

Succession in China is divided into intestate and testate succession. There are also two other forms, known as bequests and the *inter vivos* support agreement. In accordance with article 1123 of the Civil Code, upon the death of the decedent,

[195] See the Civil Code, *supra* note 8, art. 1121.

[196] See *id.*

[197] See *id.*, art. 1124.

[198] See the SPC, *Several Opinions on the Implementation of the Inheritance Law*, issued on September 11, 1985, art. 46, available at http://gongbao.court.gov.cn/Details/34cc8a7e72700c00c08c7b7efc73f9.html.

[199] See the SPC Leading Group, Marriage and Family Relations, *supra* note 1, at 515.

the succession shall be processed as an intestate succession, or, if there is a will, as a testate succession or a bequest, or be processed under an *inter vivos* support agreement when there is such an agreement.

A. *Intestate Succession*

Intestate succession is succession in which there is no will left by the decedent, and the estate is then distributed under the scope of inheritance, order of priority, and principles prescribed by law. For that reason, intestate succession is also called statutory inheritance. The most common intestate succession is the case where there is no will, meaning that the deceased did not leave a will during his life dictating how the property under his name is to be distributed after his death.

In addition, under article 1154 of the Civil Code, intestate succession also occurs when (a) the testamentary successor renounces the inheritance; (b) the testamentary successor is disinherited; (c) the testamentary successor predeceases the testator or is terminated prior to the decedent's death; (d) part of the will affecting a portion of the estate is invalidated; or (e) a portion of the estate is not disposed of by the will.[200]

Under the Civil Code, intestate succession must follow the principle of equality between men and women in their right to inheritance,[201] and proceed with the statutory order of priority. In accordance with article 1127 of the Civil Code, the estate of a decedent shall be succeeded in the following order of priority: (a) first in order: spouse, children, and parents; (b) second in order: siblings, paternal grandparents, and maternal grandparents.[202]

It is further provided in article 1129 of the Civil Code that widowed daughters-in-law or sons-in-law who have made predominant contributions in supporting their parents-in-law are regarded as successors first in order in relation to their parents-in-law.[203] Note that succession begins with the successor first in order, excluding successors second in order. Only if there is no successor first in order may the successor second in order inherit the estate.[204]

In the context of intestate succession, "children" as referred to in article 1127 includes children born in or out of wedlock and adopted children, as well as stepchildren who were raised by the decedent. "Parents" include natural parents, adoptive parents, and stepparents who raised the decedent. In addition, "siblings" include siblings of whole and half blood, adopted siblings, and stepsiblings who supported or were supported by the decedent.[205]

[200] See the Civil Code, *supra* note 8, art. 1154.
[201] See *id.*, art. 1126.
[202] See *id.*, art. 1127.
[203] See *id.*, art. 1129.
[204] See *id.*, art. 1127.
[205] See *id.*

The Civil Code also contains two special rules for inheritance. The first is the rule of subrogation of inheritance. Pursuant to article 1128 of the Civil Code, when a child of a decedent predeceases the decedent, the lineal descendants of the predeceased child shall inherit in subrogation. Similarly, if a sibling of the decedent predeceases the decedent, the children of the predeceased sibling shall inherit in subrogation.[206] In inheritance subrogation, the right of a substitute to inherit the estate on behalf of the person being replaced is called the right of subrogation of inheritance.

Under Chinese law, successors who inherit in subrogation may generally take only the share of the estate *per stirpes* (by roots), meaning the share of estate to which the person being replaced was entitled.[207] The reason is simple: since a substitute successor inherits the estate in place of the person being substituted, the substitute successor can only obtain the share that the person being substituted should have received.

The second rule is the rule of inheritance transfer. Pursuant to article 1152 of the Civil Code, if, after a succession opens, a successor who does not renounce the inheritance dies before the estate is partitioned and distributed, the shares that the successor should have inherited will be transferred to, and inherited by, the successor's heirs, unless otherwise provided in the will.[208] Inheritance transfer applies to both testate and intestate succession. It differs from inheritance subrogation in that the former is inheritance in which the heirs of the decedent's successor directly inherit the estate of the decedent, while the latter refers to substitute inheritance where a substitute successor inherits the estate of the decedent.[209]

When a dispute over succession arises, litigation may take place. An issue in succession litigation is the jurisdiction of the court. Note again that a lawsuit involving succession is subject to a special jurisdiction rule. Under article 34 of the Civil Procedural Law, any dispute over succession shall fall within the exclusive jurisdiction of the court of the place of domicile of the decedent whose property is inherited at the time of death or the place where the major portion of the estate is located.[210] If the court of the place of the decedent's domicile and the court of the place of the estate both have jurisdiction, the party (plaintiff) may choose either court for litigation.

B. *Testate Succession*

Testate succession, or testamentary inheritance, is a succession in which the heirs or beneficiaries inherit the estate of the decedent according to the legal and valid will

[206] See *id.*, art. 1128.
[207] See *id.*
[208] See *id.*, art. 1152.
[209] See the SPC Leading Group, Marriage and Family Relations, *supra* note 1, at 658–660.
[210] See the CPL, *supra* note 141, art. 34.

made by the decedent during his lifetime. Testate succession in China is considered to possess two characteristics: (a) it must satisfy two factual conditions, namely the decedent's death and the legality of the will, and (b) the choice of beneficiaries or heirs, the share and amount of the inheritance to be distributed, and the order of inheritance are all based on the will of the testator him/herself.[211]

Under article 1133 of the Civil Code, a natural person, by making a will in accordance with the law, may dispose of his estate, designate one or more of his statutory successors to inherit his estate, donate his estate to the State or a collective, or an organization or individual other than his statutory successor, or create a testamentary trust.[212] Thus, testate succession can be made as inheritance, bequests, or a trust. It is also required that a necessary portion of an estate be reserved in a will for an heir who has neither the ability to work nor a source of income.[213]

In the case of bequests, the beneficiary must, within 60 days after learning of the testamentary gift, manifest his/her decision to accept or renounce the gift. Absent such a manifestation within the specified period, the beneficiary will be deemed to have renounced the gift.[214] Also, if a beneficiary has committed any of the acts mentioned in article 1125 as grounds for a successor to be disinherited, the beneficiary will have no right to receive the testamentary gift.

As noted, bequests may also be made in the form of an *inter vivos* support agreement. According to article 1158 of the Civil Code, a natural person may enter into an agreement on bequests for *inter vivos* support with an organization or individual other than a successor. Under the agreement, the organization or individual assumes a duty to support the testator during his/her lifetime and attends to the testator's interment after death, in return for the right to receive the testamentary gift.[215]

A will, to be valid for probate, must meet statutory formality requirements. First, a will can be made in writing, in video or audio recording, orally, or in notarized form. A written will can be made autographically or non-autographically. An autographic will is one written by the testator him/herself, while a non-autographic will refers to a will in which the testator verbally dictates the contents of the will and someone else writes it down on the testator's behalf, and the testator confirms and signs the will. In terms of a written will, it can be made in handwriting or printed form.

Second, a will made in any form must satisfy particular conditions. More specifically, (a) an autographic will must be written by the testator in hand, bearing the testator's signature with the year, month, and day of its making;[216] (b) a non-autographic will shall be attested by two or more witnesses, of whom one writes the will, specifying the year, month, and day of its making, and signs it along with

[211] See the SPC Leading Group, Marriage and Family Relations, *supra* note 1, at 505.
[212] See the Civil Code, *supra* note 8, art. 1133.
[213] See *id.*, art. 1141.
[214] See *id.*, art. 1124.
[215] See *id.*, art. 1158.
[216] See *id.*, art. 1134.

the other witnesses and with the testator;[217] (c) a will in printed form shall be attested by two or more witnesses, and the testator and the witnesses shall sign and specify the year, month, and day on each page;[218] (d) a will made in the form of an audio or video recording shall be attested by two or more witnesses, and the testator and the witnesses shall record their names or likeness in the recording and specify the year, month, and day of its making,[219] (e) a notarized will shall be made by a testator through a notary public agency.[220]

Third, for an oral will, article 1138 of the Civil Code specifically provides that when facing emergent situations, a testator may make an oral or nuncupative will, attested by two or more witnesses. But when the imminent danger is removed and the testator is able to make a will in writing or in the form of an audio or video recording, the oral will thus made becomes invalid.[221] Under article 1138, an oral will is valid only if the testator is encountering emergencies.

According to the SPC, for the purpose of making an oral will, an emergent situation refers to a sudden and unexpected natural disaster, accident, war, or sudden life-threatening illness that makes it objectively impossible for the testator to make a will in any other way.[222] It is important to note that an oral will is only a temporary measure in case of an emergency. Thus, after the emergency is over, if the testator is able to make a will in other forms, such as written or audio or video recordings, the oral will should be replaced by one made in other forms as soon as possible; otherwise, it shall become invalid under the law.

The Civil Code also sets forth certain restrictions on the witnesses of a will. Under article 1140 of the Civil Code, a person who is not eligible to witness a will includes (a) a person with no or limited capacity for performing civil acts, or a person otherwise incompetent to attest to a will; (b) a successor of the decedent or a beneficiary of bequests; and (c) a person who has an interest with the successor of the decedent or the beneficiary of bequests.[223] A person otherwise incompetent to attest to a will refers to a person who has full civil capacity but whose ability is impeded for various reasons. One example is an illiterate adult. Another example is a person who does not understand the local dialect the testator speaks.[224]

A will, once made, may be revoked or altered by the testator. Under certain circumstances, a revocation can be implied. Pursuant to article 1142 of the Civil Code, when a testator who, after making a will, acts inconsistently with the contents of the will, the pertinent part of the will is deemed to have been revoked.

[217] See *id.*, art. 1135.
[218] See *id.*, art. 1136.
[219] See *id.*, art. 1137.
[220] See *id.*, art. 1139.
[221] See *id.*, art. 1138.
[222] See the SPC Leading Group, Marriage and Family Relations, *supra* note 1, at 578–579.
[223] See the Civil Code, *supra* note 8, art. 1140.
[224] See the SPC Leading Group, Marriage and Family Relations, *supra* note 1, at 591.

In addition, if a testator has made multiple wills with inconsistencies in their contents, the will that is made last in time prevails.[225]

An important aspect in will probate is the validity of the will. In general, a will made in compliance with the formality requirements is valid and enforceable. But under article 1143 of the Civil Code, a will becomes void in any of the following situations: (a) the will is made by a person with no or limited capacity for performing civil acts; (b) the will is made under fraud or duress in violation of the genuine intention of the testator; (c) the will is forged; and (d) any part of the will that has been tampered with.[226]

In China, a will or bequests may have certain obligations attached, which means that a testator may require in his/her will conditions for the beneficiary to do or not do certain things according to his instructions. Article 1144 of the Civil Code provides that if a testate succession or a testamentary gift is conditioned upon performance of an obligation, the successor or beneficiary shall perform the obligation accordingly. If, however, the successor or beneficiary fails to perform without just cause, a court may, upon request by an interested person or a relevant organization, deprive the successor or beneficiary of the right to inherit the portion of the estate to which performance of the obligation is attached.[227]

C. *Disposition of Estate*

After the succession opens, all the property that originally belonged to the decedent belongs to the heirs and/or beneficiaries (successors). However, at the beginning of succession, there are many uncertain issues. First, the successors do not necessarily possess the estate at the outset of the succession, and even if a successor possesses the estate, he/she may give up the right of inheritance. Second, since the estate has not yet been divided, the amount of the estate that each successor or beneficiary may get is yet to be determined. Third, as is often the case, an estate is associated with the debts owed by the decedent prior to his/her death.

a. Estate Administration

Estate administration refers to the actions taken under the law to manage and liquidate the estate after the inheritance begins but before the estate is distributed, with a purpose to maintain the value of the estate and the legitimate interests of those entitled to the estate. In many cases, the administrator of an estate is the executor of the estate appointed by the decedent. In other cases, the administrator is the person under the provision of law to manage the estate of a decedent.

Under article 1145 of the Civil Code, the administrator of an estate is to be determined in the following way: (a) upon the opening of a succession, the executor

[225] See the Civil Code, *supra* note 8, art. 1142.
[226] See *id.*, art. 1143.
[227] See *id.*, art. 1144.

of the will is the administrator of the estate; (b) if there is no executor designated in the will, the successors shall elect an administrator in a timely manner; (c) when the successors fail to select an administrator, all of the successors are co-administrators; or (d) where there is no successor or where all of the successors renounce the inheritance, the civil affairs department or the villagers' committee in the place where the decedent was domiciled at the time of his death shall serve as the administrator.[228] If, however, a dispute arises over the determination of an administrator of the estate, any interested person may request that the court appoint an administrator.[229]

As provided in the Civil Code, the administrator of an estate is required to perform the duties prescribed by the law, and shall bear civil liability for damages caused by his intentional act or gross negligence to the successor, beneficiary, or creditor of the decedent.[230] But the administrator of an estate may receive remuneration in accordance with the law or based upon agreement.[231] The duties to be performed include (a) verifying and making an inventory of the estate; (b) reporting the inventory of the estate to the successors; (c) taking necessary measures to prevent the estate from being destructed, damaged, or lost; (d) settling the decedent's claims and debts; (e) partitioning the estate in accordance with the will or the law; and (f) any other act necessary for managing the estate.[232]

The executor or administrator has a duty to properly keep and maintain the estate before the estate is distributed. The duty as such is also extended to the person who actually possesses or controls the estate. Article 1151 of the Civil Code mandates that anyone who has in their possession the property of a decedent properly keep such property. Further, article 1151 prohibits any organization or individual from misappropriating or fighting for the estate.[233]

Misappropriation of an estate refers to conduct that secretly or by means not easily found by others takes the estate and keeps it as one's own. Fighting for the estate is the act of openly scrambling to take ownership of the estate. The SPC has clearly opined that if a successor deliberately misappropriates or fights for the estate in order to get a larger share, the court may, at its discretion, proportionally reduce the amount of estate the successor should inherit.[234]

b. Estate Partition and Distribution

An estate partition is a process of dividing the estate among multiple successors according to the respective shares they are entitled to after the succession opens. Following partition is the distribution by which the rights and obligations of the

[228] See *id.*, art. 1145.
[229] See *id.*, art. 1146.
[230] See *id.*, art. 1148.
[231] See *id.*, art. 1149.
[232] See *id.*, art. 1147.
[233] See *id.*, art. 1151.
[234] See the SPC, Opinions on the Inherentance Law, *supra* note 198, art. 59.

estate are allocated to each successor respectively. Before the partition and distribution, all successors and the persons who are entitled to part of the estate have common ownership of the entire estate, and such common ownership ends when the estate is partitioned and distributed among the successors.

There are several rules that govern estate partition and distribution. The foremost is the rule of equal share, premised on the principle of equality. Under article 1130 of the Civil Code, the successors in the same order or priority shall generally inherit equal shares of the estate.[235] The rule of equal share, however, is subject to certain exceptions. First, in the distribution of an estate, due consideration should be given to a successor who has special financial difficulties and is unable to work.[236] Second, for a successor who has made predominant contributions in supporting the now decedent or who has been living with the now decedent, the distributed shares may be proportionally larger. In contrast, for a successor who had the ability and was in a position to support the now decedent but failed to fulfill the duty of support, a smaller or even no shares may be distributed.[237] Third, successors may take unequal shares if there is an agreement reached among them.[238]

Another rule refers to the notice rule. Under article 1150, upon opening the succession, a successor who has knowledge of the death of the decedent shall notify the other successors and the executor of the will in a timely manner. Where none of the successors knows about the death of the decedent or is able to make the notification upon learning of the death of the decedent, the organization to which the decedent was employed at the time of his death, or the urban residents committee or the villagers' committee in the place where the decedent was domiciled at the time of his death shall make the notification.[239]

The third rule is the rule of discretionary allocation, which applies mainly to those other than successors in the estate partition and distribution. As stipulated in article 1131 of the Civil Code, an appropriate share of the estate may be given to a person, other than a successor, who has been depending on the now decedent for support, or to a person, other than a successor, who has made considerable contributions in supporting the now decedent.[240] An example is the decedent's sister or brother who is not the successor first in order but has either received support from or provided support to the now decedent. In this situation, the sister or brother may be given certain shares of the estate along with other successors first in order.

The fourth rule is the rule of protection of the interests of a fetus. It is required under article 1155 of the Civil Code that, when partitioning and distributing an estate, an inheritance share shall be reserved for a fetus. If the fetus is stillborn, the

[235] See the Civil Code, *supra* note 8, art. 1130.
[236] See *id.*
[237] See *id.*
[238] See *id.*
[239] See *id.*, art. 1150.
[240] See *id.*, art. 1131.

reserved share shall be disposed of in an intestate succession.[241] In the case where the fetus results in multiple births, the inheritance share should be reserved according to the number of fetuses. When the fetus dies after birth, the reserved share becomes the estate and is inherited by his/her heirs via intestate succession.

The fifth rule concerns estate utility, based on the principle of the best use of the estate. According to article 1156 of the Civil Code, the partitioning of a decedent's estate shall be conducted in a way beneficial to production and the need for livelihood without diminishing its efficacy. It is further provided that if an estate is unsuitable for partitioning, it may be disposed of by such means as money conversion, appropriate compensation, or establishment of co-ownership.[242]

The sixth rule is the rule of negotiation and mutual concession for dispute settlement. Under article 1132 of the Civil Code, any issue arising from succession shall be dealt with through consultation by and among the successors in the spirit of amity, unity, mutual understanding, and accommodation.[243] Pursuant to article 1132, the time and mode for partitioning the estate and the shares to be distributed shall first be determined by the successors through negotiation. If no agreement can be reached through negotiation, the successors may apply to a local mediation committee for mediation or file a lawsuit with a court.[244]

As noted, the property acquired during the marriage is considered common property of the married couple. Estate may only be the personal property left behind by a decedent upon his/her death. When partitioning an estate that involves community property of husband and wife, unless otherwise agreed upon, under article 1153 of the Civil Code, half of the community property shall be allocated first to the surviving spouse as separate property, while the remaining property becomes part of the decedent's estate. By the same token, if the decedent's estate is a portion of common property of the family, the portion of the property belonging to the other family members shall first be separated from the decedent's estate.[245]

In addition, the estate allocated under the law to a surviving spouse may not be used as leverage to prevent the surviving spouse from getting remarried. Article 1157 of the Civil Code explicitly grants a surviving spouse who remarries the right to dispose of the property the surviving spouse has inherited, and prohibits any organization or individual from interfering with it.[246] The main theme of article 1157 is that a surviving spouse has the right to remarry at his or her own choice after inheriting the deceased spouse's estate.

In certain cases, however, there is an estate that no one may inherit. It occurs when (a) no testate successor, intestate successor, or beneficiary of bequests can be

[241] See *id.*, art. 1155.
[242] See *id.*, art. 1156.
[243] See *id.*, art. 1132.
[244] See *id.*
[245] See *id.*, art. 1153.
[246] See *id.*, art. 1157.

identified; (b) there are intestate and/or testate successors, but all of them renounce the inheritance and give up the right to inherit; and (c) there are no testate or intestate successors but bequest beneficiaries, and the beneficiaries decline to accept the bequests or the right of the beneficiary to accept the bequests is lost.[247]

According to article 1160 of the Civil Code, if there is neither a successor nor a beneficiary to inherit an estate, the estate shall be escheated to the State to be used for public interest purposes. If the decedent was a member of a collective organization at the time of his death, the estate shall then fall within the collective ownership organization.[248] As discussed, in China, the collective ownership organization includes rural collective economic organizations and urban collective economic organizations.[249]

c. Estate Debt Clearance and Settlement

Upon the opening of a succession, the debts or liabilities out of an estate must be cleared and settled before the partition and distribution of the estate. The questions that necessarily arise are: (a) who is responsible for the clearance and settlement, and (b) to what extent the debt liabilities as such are cleared and settled. As noted, estate to be inherited in China does not include liabilities, meaning that the successor or beneficiary is not liable for the outstanding debts and tax liability of the decedent.

In succession theory, there are two different approaches dealing with estate debts clearance and settlement. One approach is known as universal succession (*succession per universitatem*), under which an estate is transferred in its entirety directly to the heirs or beneficiaries, including the deceased's assets and liabilities.[250] Pursuant to the universal succession approach, after the death of the deceased, the property rights and liabilities of the deceased shall be inherited by the successors. Each successor shall obtain the estate rights and bear the estate liabilities to the successor's respective share. The successor is fully responsible for repaying all the estate debts, even if the debts in the estate exceed the value of the estate.

The other approach is termed a limited succession. By "limited," it means that all debts or outstanding obligations of an estate need to be cleared and settled before the estate is inherited. In other words, under a limited succession, an estate is distributed among successors or beneficiaries not by the entirety of the estate but from the

[247] See the SPC Leading Group, *supra* note 1, at 695.

[248] See the Civil Code, *supra* note 8, art. 1160.

[249] A rural collective economic organization refers to the economic organization formed by farmers at the township, village, and group levels, while an urban collective economic organization is an organization collectively formed in an urban area to engage in such economic activity as handicrafts, industry, construction, transportation, commerce, and service.

[250] For general discussion of the universal succession approach, see Jan Peter Schmidt, *Transfer of Property on Death and Creditor Protection: The Meaning and Role of "Universal Succession,"* Max Planck Private Law Research Paper No. 18/3, March 19, 2018, at https://papers.ssrn.com/sol3/papers.cfm?abstract_id=3132995.

remainder after paying off debts. Thus, when inheriting the estate, the successors or beneficiaries are only responsible for paying off the debts of the deceased's estate up to the actual value of the estate, and bear no liability for the debts exceeding the value of the estate.[251]

The Civil Code follows the limited succession approach. Under article 1159 of the Civil Code, when an estate is partitioned, the taxes and debts payable or owed by the decedent in accordance with law shall be paid out of the estate. Article 1161 further provides that a successor is responsible for paying the taxes and debts legally payable or owed by the decedent only to the extent of the actual value of the portion of the estate the successor inherits, unless the successor pays voluntarily in excess of such limit.[252]

But for a successor who has neither the ability to work nor a source of income for living, a necessary portion of the estate should be preserved. Therefore, in the estate debts' clearance and settlement, even if the actual value of the estate is not enough to pay off the debts, an appropriate amount of estate must be reserved for the successor who is in special needs living. Also, according to article 1161, a successor who renounces inheritance assumes no responsibility for the settlement of the decedent's taxes and debts liabilities.[253]

In the case of bequest, article 1162 of the Civil Code stipulates that execution of a bequest may not affect the payment of taxes and debts legally payable or owed by the decedent.[254] Thus, as between bequests and estate debts, debt repayment takes precedence over bequest execution. Only after the estate debts are paid off can bequests be executed. Put differently, if the value of an estate is not enough to pay off debts out of the estate, the bequests based on said estate cannot be executed.[255]

Furthermore, when intestate succession, testate succession, and bequests exist concurrently, the taxes and debts out of the estate should be paid by the intestate successor(s). If such taxes and debts are in excess of the actual value of the portion of the estate inherited by the intestate successor(s), the exceeded part is then to be paid by the testamentary successor(s) and bequest beneficiary in proportion to the shares of the estate that each of them has received.[256]

D. *Foreign-Related Succession*

As noted, under article 1123, succession in China can be a testate succession if there is a will or intestate succession absent a will. In a foreign-related inheritance, the testate succession also takes priority over intestate succession or statutory

[251] See Shaokun et al., *supra* note 9, at 294. See also Liping et al., *supra* note 65, at 361.
[252] See the Civil Code, *supra* note 8, art. 1161.
[253] See *id.*
[254] See *id.*, art. 1162.
[255] See the SPC Leading Group, Marriage and Family Relations, *supra* note 1, at 702–704.
[256] See the Civil Code, *supra* note 8, art. 1163.

inheritance. In addition, if there is an *inter vivos* support agreement or a bequest, it shall be followed prior to intestate succession. In other words, in case of existence of a will, *inter vivos* support agreement, or bequest, an intestate succession will take place only if there is any residual value of the estate.

Since foreign-related succession contains foreign elements, a critical issue is the governing law. Under article 31 of the Choice of Law Statute,[257] in foreign-related statutory inheritance, the law of the habitual residence of the decedent at the time of death shall apply. However, if the estate involves real property, the law of the location of the real property shall apply. Thus, pursuant to article 31, the law applicable to foreign-related statutory inheritance, depending on the nature of the estate, can be either the law of the decedent's habitual residence or the law of the place where the estate is located.

With regard to testamentary inheritance, the validity of a will is under the control of the law of the testator's habitual residence at the time of the creation of the will or the testator's death, or the law of the testator's country of citizenship.[258] According to article 32 of the Choice of Law Statute, a will is deemed effective if the form of the will complies with the law of the habitual residence of the testator at the time of making the will or at the time of death, the law of the country of nationality, or the law of the place where the will is made.[259]

In addition, under article 34 of the Choice of Law Statute, the administration of estates and related matters are subject to the law of the place where the estates are located.[260] Article 35 of the Choice of Law Statute further provides that the disposition of an estate without an heir is governed by the law of the place where the estate is situated at the time of the decedent's death.[261]

[257] See the Choice of Law Statute, *supra* note 63, art. 31.
[258] See *id.*, art. 33.
[259] See *id.*, art. 32.
[260] See *id.*, art. 34.
[261] See *id.*, art. 35.

12

Law of Torts

INTRODUCTION

"Torts," as a legal concept, does not have a Chinese origin. As noted, in Chinese legal history, criminal law dominated both legislation and judicial practice, and civil matters were never the center of attention.[1] It is the same for torts. Nevertheless, it is held in China that, as a social phenomenon, torts began to gain legislative attention in the country as early as the *Qin* Dynasty (221 BC). It was not until the *Tang* Dynasty that tortious conduct was formally regulated. In the *Tang* Code (AC 651), the first codified law in China, there were about twelve articles that dealt with or were related to torts. At that time, however, no definition or conceptual description of torts existed. Instead, the provisions that resembled tort law were simply seen as a way of compensating the harm inflicted upon a thing or person.[2]

The term "torts" was first used in the early twentieth century when the *Qing* Civil Code was drafted. In the draft code, tort was phrased as "*Qing Quan Xing Wei*," meaning conduct infringing upon civil rights.[3] The first torts law legislation in the country was the 1930 Civil Code, promulgated by the Nationalist Government. The 1930 Civil Code contained five parts.[4] In part II, Obligations, there were fifteen articles (articles 184 to 198) on torts. Those articles were further divided into two

[1] See Zhang Jinfan, The Tradition and Modern Transition of Chinese Law, 23 (Law Press, 2005).

[2] The residual value exclusion rule was provided in the *Song*, *Ming*, and *Qing* Codes respectively.

[3] In the first draft of the Qing Civil Code, article 945 provided that a person who unlawfully inflicts harm on another's right, intentionally or negligently, shall be liable for compensating the damage caused thereby. See Jiang Ping, Study on Torts Law, 60 (China Democracy and Legality Press, 2004); see also Zhang Xinbao, Study on the Legislation of the Torts Liability Law, 143 (People's University Press, 2009).

[4] The first part of the 1930 Civil Code was promulgated in May 1929, and the last two parts (Family Relations and Succession) were promulgated in December 1930.

categories: general torts and special torts. As discussed, the 1930 Civil Code was abolished in 1949 when the People's Republic of China was founded.

Not until 1986, when the General Principles of Civil Law was adopted, did China have any major civil law legislation. The 1986 General Principles of Civil Law had a special section on torts. The 2009 Tort Liability Law was the first torts law ever enacted in the country after 1949. Eleven years later, in 2020, the Tort Liability Law was incorporated into part VII of the Civil Code with certain changes. Entitled "Torts Liabilities," part VII contains ten chapters with ninety-five articles in total.

The ten chapters in part VII of the Civil Code consist of two parts: general provisions and special torts. The general rules consist of general provisions, damages, and special provisions of liability assumption. Special torts include product liability, liability for motor vehicle accidents, liability for medical malpractice, liability for environmental pollution and ecological damage, liability for ultrahazardous activities, liability for harm by domesticated animals, and liability for damage by buildings or objects. The focus of this chapter is on the general provisions on torts in the Civil Code.

1. TORTS AND DETERMINATION

What is a tort? Although many believe that a really satisfactory definition of torts is yet to be found,[5] a tort is basically defined as a civil wrong for which law recognizes a legal remedy on behalf of a private individual. In most tort cases, the legal remedy takes the form of monetary damages. In certain cases, other remedies may also be available.[6] It is also argued that "torts" is a deceptively simple subject because there is only one question in each case: who should pay for damages, the plaintiff or the defendant? In other words, should the defendant be held liable, or should the loss be left to the plaintiff?[7] The whole issue involved is who is liable for what and on which basis.

A. *Concept of Torts*

In China, a tort is generally understood as conduct of a civil wrong.[8] Since the term "civil wrong" is itself very vague and broad, and in some cases may be misleading (e.g., a breach of contract may also be deemed a civil wrong), many efforts have

[5] See Page Keeton et al., Prosser and Keeton on Torts, 1 (5th ed., West, 1984).

[6] See Russell Weaver et al., Torts, Cases, Problems, and Exercises, 1 (Anderson, 2003).

[7] Frank Vandall & Ellen Wertheimer, Torts, Cases and Materials, 1 (Michie, 1997).

[8] See Wang Jiafu & Liang Huixing, The Obligatio in Civil Law, 407 (China Law Press, 1998). It has been observed that the word "tort" derives from the Latin "tortus," meaning twisted or crooked, and it has found its way into the English language as a general synonym for "wrong." See also André Tunc, *Introduction* to XI/1 International Encyclopedia of Comparative Law: Torts, 71, 7 (Mohr, 1983).

been made in the country in searching for a definition of torts or a Chinese version of torts. But scholars and legislators have long been struggling with two questions.

The first question is whether there should be a difference between rights and interests. Some assert that rights are created by law, and anyone who infringes upon rights shall be held liable, while interests are not necessarily legally provided and therefore harm to interests may not fall within torts.[9] Others disagree, arguing that interests are the substance of rights because without a protectable interest, there would be no protectable right. They argue further that even if rights and interests are not the same, the difference between them is often too obscure to determine.[10]

The second question is whether "unlawfulness" should be an element of a tort.[11] The debate is mainly between an unlawfulness approach and fault theory. Under the unlawfulness approach, to hold someone liable for a tort, his/her conduct causing harm must also be unlawful even if he is proved to be at fault.[12] But the fault theory takes the position that since the fault itself already infers something unlawful, there is no need to make unlawfulness an additional criterion for a tort.[13] On the other hand, the fault theory argues that given the multiple facets of civil matters, it is very difficult, if not impossible, to define exactly what is lawful and what is unlawful concerning particular conduct.[14]

In the 1986 General Principles of Civil Law, "torts" was not defined but termed a civil liability. Under article 106 of the 1986 General Principles of Civil Law, citizens or legal persons who, through their fault, encroach upon state or collective property, or the property or person of other people, shall bear civil liability.[15] Article 106 implied that a tort would be faulty conduct that infringes upon others' property and personal rights. It can also be inferred from the 1986 General Principles of Civil

[9] Liu Shiguo, A Study in the Major Knotty Issues of the Tort Liability Law, 1 (China Legal Publishing House, 2009).

[10] See Wang Shengming, Explanations to the Tort Liability Law of the People's Republic of China, 10 (China Law Press, 2010).

[11] See Ping, *supra* note 3, at 88–93.

[12] See *id.* at 61; see also Jiafu & Huixing, *supra* note 8, at 61. Historically, unlawfulness as an element of torts originated from the *Lex Aquilia*, in which the term "*iniuria*," meaning "unlawfully," was used to define torts. The *Lex Aquilia* was concerned with damages done from *dammum iniuria datum*, "damages unlawfully inflicted." See William Smith, A Dictionary of Greek and Roman Antiquities, Obligation, 383 (John Murray, 1875); see also Jean Limpens et al., *Liability for One's Own Act*, in René David, ed., International Encyclopedia of Comparative Law: XI, Part II, Torts § 2-15, 9 (Mohr, 1979)

[13] See Wang Liming, Study in the Principles of Liability Imputation of Torts Law, 398 (China University of Political Science and Law Press, 1992).

[14] *id.*

[15] See General Principles of the Civil Law of the People's Republic of China (promulgated by the Nat'l People's Ct., April 12, 1986, effective January 1, 1987), art. 106 (China), www.lawinfochina.com/display.aspx?lib = law&id = 1165.

Law that unlawfulness was not a required element for tort liability imposition.[16] But it remained unclear as to whether civil interests would be included.

Both the 2009 Tort LiabilityLaw and the Civil Code contain no definition for torts either. Under article 2 of the 2009 Tort Liability Law, those who infringe upon the civil rights and interests of another shall be subject to tort liability.[17] Article 1164 of the Civil Code simply provides that the law of torts regulates civil relations arising from infringement of civil rights and interests.[18] What is clear is that article 2 of the 2009 Tort Liability Law and article 1164 of the Civil Code do not base tort liability on the unlawfulness of the tortious conduct. But the two provisions grant protection to both civil rights and civil interests in tort cases. As noted, pursuant to article 3 of the Civil Code, civil rights and interests are the personal rights, property rights, and other lawful rights and interests of civil law persons.[19]

Despite the lack of a tort definition in the law, it can be inferred from Civil Code provisions that torts in China refer to civil conduct that infringes upon the rights and interests of others. In the common law system, a tort consists of such elements as duty, breach, causation, and damages.[20] Civil law countries normally use the term "conduct" instead of duty and breach. Conduct can either be fault-based or non-fault-based. Fault, as used in torts law, indicates the state of mind of the actor at the time a tort was committed, including both intention and negligence.

B. *Determination of Torts*

In China, there are two major doctrines for the finding of a tort. The first is called the "three elements" doctrine, and the other is named the "four elements" doctrine. The agreement between the two doctrines is that a tort should consist of "conduct," "damages," and "causation." The disagreement between the two is the requirement of unlawfulness. The "four elements" doctrine insists that to constitute a tort, the conduct involved must be unlawful, and the unlawfulness of the conduct is critical for the determination of a tort. The Civil Code, however, does not require a showing of unlawfulness. Therefore, for a tort liability to be imposed under the Civil Code, three elements must be present: (1) conduct, (2) damages, and (3) causation.

[16] Before the 1986 Civil Law was adopted, a tort was commonly defined in China as "an *obligatio* relationship between actor and victim that occurred by the operation of law as a result of the actor's unlawful harm to the property right and personal right of the victim, thereby causing property damages to the latter." See Liming, Liability Imputation, *supra* note 13, at 398.

[17] Tort Liability Law of the People's Republic of China (promulgated by the Standing Comm., Nat'l People's Cong., December 26, 2009, effective July 1, 2010), art. 2, available at www.gov.cn/flfg/2009-12/26/content_1497345.htm..

[18] See the Civil Code, art. 1164, at https://regional.chinadaily.com.cn/pdf/CivilCodeoftthePeople%27sRepublicofChina.pdf.

[19] See *id.*, art. 3.

[20] See Joseph Glannon, The Law of Torts, 129 (2nd ed., Aspen, 2000).

a. Conduct

A tort is conduct, but not all conduct constitutes a tort. Under a general pattern, a prerequisite for finding a tort is fault that either derives from the conduct or can be pinned on the person committing the conduct. Thus, an alleged tortfeasor will not be held liable unless he is proved to be at fault. On the other hand, in certain cases, fault will be assumed when harm is caused. It is true that in modern torts law, tort liability may be imposed on a non-fault basis. But non-fault tort liability must be explicitly provided by the law.

For the purposes of torts, conduct can be an act or omission. As discussed, an act in civil law refers to active or affirmative action toward another person, while an omission is a passive action or non-action. When a person fails to perform a certain duty or exercise a certain degree of care that is legally required to protect another person or the public in general, the person may be held liable under the law of tort. Also, in committing a tort, the act or omission could be either intentional or negligent.

Normally, a person will be held liable for his/her own negligent or intentional tortious conduct. In certain cases, however, a person may be required to bear tort liability for conduct committed by another person. An example is vicarious liability. A distinctive feature of vicarious liability is the requirement of a particular legal relationship between the actor and the liable person. The Civil Code also imposes tort liability upon a vicariously liable third person but characterizes the liable person as a special tortfeasor.

b. Damages

Damages are the harm caused to the injured person. As a general principle, when tortious conduct is committed, remedies will not be made without the existence of damages. It is commonly held that the imposition of liability rests upon the harm done. The rule of thumb is "no harm, no remedy." In this regard, the terms "damages," "injuries," and "harms" are often used interchangeably to mean the suffering experienced by the tort victim.

As noted, damages under the Civil Code include the harm caused by a person to the personal rights, property rights, or other legally recognized rights and interests of another. Harm can be losses, injuries, or both. There are two controversial issues related to damages. One issue is about mental damage. Questions involved are what may constitute mental damage and how to measure it. The other issue is what should be considered the legally recognized rights and interests. A question often disputed is whether opportunity losses should be counted as damages for the purpose of compensation.

Generally, damages, for the purposes of compensation, shall meet at least three requirements. First, the damages are compensable or remediable. A common notion is that civil liability for the harm incurred to a person or property of another may arise only if it is legally possible and necessary to be compensated. Therefore, not all civil harm is entitled to compensation. Certain harm, such as lost profits due to market forces or mental suffering below the statutory threshold, may not be legally compensable.[21]

Second, the damages are not speculative. Under the rule of certainty, to be compensable, damages need to be factually certain and measurable. The underlying rationale of the certainty rule is that damages, once incurred, become facts, and determination of the damages should then be based on such facts. To deem damages as facts implicates that to justify compensation, the existence of damages must be real, identifiable, and measurable.[22]

Third, the damages result from the harm caused to the lawful rights and interests of another. A key element for compensation under tort liability is that the harmed interests must be lawful interests. The requirement of lawfulness involves the very purpose of torts law.[23] Since torts law is purposed to protect the lawful interests of the injured, damages can be compensable only in the situation where the lawful interests of another are harmed. Although the tort provisions under the Civil Code are structured to protect a broad range of rights and interests, protection is not extended to any interest that is unlawful.

c. Causation

Causation is the necessary and reasonable connection between the act or omission of the tortfeasor and the damages that the victim has suffered. Causation is further divided into factual cause (cause-in-fact) and legal cause (proximate cause). A general holding in China is that without causation, no tort liability arises. It has become a rule that an act or omission may not be regarded as a cause of harm if the harm would have occurred without it.

Normally, causation is determined on the basis of the cause related to the particular injury or harm. In some cases, however, more than one cause can be attributed to the injury or harm involved. This is the situation where there are concurrent causes or there exists a supervening cause. Concurrent causes occur where the injury or harm was caused by two or more people acting independently. A supervening cause is the case where two acts were committed consecutively and independently, and the later act was the ultimate cause of the injury or harm.

In identifying causation in the tort case where the injury or harm was the result of multiple acts, an approach of presumption of causation has developed. Under this approach, when causation is hard to identify due to the existence of multiple

[21] See Wang Liming, Studies on the Torts Liability Law, Vol. One, 310–313 (Remin University Press, 2010) (hereinafter Studies on Torts).

[22] See *id.*

[23] See *id.*

possible causes, it will be presumed on the basis of fairness and for the best protection of the victim. In the Civil Code, this approach applies to such cases as environmental pollution and ultrahazardous activities. But note that pursuant to the Civil Code, presumption of causation may apply only if the obstacle to the proof of causation is considerably high. It is also required that the presumption of causation be authorized by a specific provision of law.

C. *Functions of Torts Law*

In China, torts law is considered to serve four major functions: (1) to protect the legitimate rights and interests of parties in civil relations, (2) to clarify and allocate tort liability, (3) to prevent and punish tortious conduct, and (4) to promote social harmony and stability. Among the four functions, social harmony and stability promotion has more of a political meaning than a legal meaning. Therefore, from the legal viewpoint, the key functions of torts law are compensation, prevention, and punishment.

Protection is basically the function of redress. Its purpose is to protect one from being harmed by the conduct of another and, in the meantime, to compensate those who suffer a loss or harm as a result of another's conduct. Therefore, redress in the form of compensation is considered the core value of torts law. On this basis, it is deemed vitally important to ensure adequate compensation to tort victims.[24]

Prevention and punishment are aimed primarily at future loss and harm. The main purpose of torts law is not simply to punish the tortfeasor, but to prevent tortious conduct.[25] The intended effect of prevention and punishment is deterrence. The legislative consideration in making both prevention and punishment functions of torts law is that the two are complementary. It is believed that without punishment, future harm may not be effectively prevented; without prevention, punishment would be meaningless.[26]

D. *Scope of Torts Law*

In civil law countries, there are two kinds of major tort legislation models. One is the German model, which enumerates specific rights that must be protected. This model is also called the "list" model.[27] The other is the French model, under which no specific rights or interests are specifically mentioned. Instead, a general scope is provided to cover all tort liabilities. Torts legislation in China follows the "list" model. As noted, the 2009 Tort Liability Law provides a laundry list of protected

[24] *id.*

[25] See Wang Liming, Textbook of the Tort Liability Law of China, 53, 81 (People's Court Press, 2010) (hereinafter referred to as Textbook).

[26] *id.*

[27] See J. Zekoll & M. Reiman, Introduction to German Law, 209 (Kluwer, 2005).

rights and interests. Article 2 of the Tort Liability Law explicitly provides that civil rights and interests shall include the right to life, right to health, right to name, right to reputation, right to honor, right to portrait, right of privacy, marital autonomy, guardianship, ownership, usufruct, security interest, copyright, patent right, exclusive right to trademark use, right to discovery, equities, and right of succession and other personal and property rights and interests.[28]

The Civil Code does not have a "list" as such in the torts provisions but provides those rights and interests in different parts of the Code. In either case, the rights and interests to be protected under torts law can be grouped into five categories: (1) rights and interests of personality, (2) rights and interests of personal status, (3) rights and interests in things, (4) intellectual property rights and interests, and (5) rights and interests in equities and succession. The "other lawful rights and interests" clause is an open-ended provision intended to cover rights and interests that are either not ready to be listed or are yet to emerge.

Note that torts law does not cover contractual liability, and thus no claim may be brought in a tort action on the basis of a breach of contract. But an issue that often arises is the liability of a third party for the harm caused by the third party's conduct to the contractual rights of the parties to the contract. Though it is unclear whether torts law should govern such third-party liability, many in China regard it as a tort liability on the grounds that it falls within economic harm.[29]

2. TORT LIABILITY IMPUTATION

A threshold question concerning the imposition of tort liability is how the liability is imputed. The question not only affects the extent to which tort liability is sought but also dictates allocation of the burden of proof. Since liability imputation forms the basis on which tort liability is to be ascertained, the rules on liability imputation are considered in China to be the cornerstones of the tort system. It is believed that the imputation rules set forth general criteria for determining the tortfeasor's liability and the compensation for the damages caused thereby.

Following the 2009 Tort Liability Law, the Civil Code makes "fault," "presumption of fault," "liability without fault," and "liability on the basis of fairness" the principal rules for imputing tort liability. The significance of these imputation rules is that they provide the legal cause without which no tort liability would arise. In addition, each imputation rule governs a different type of tort and prescribes the factors that constitute that specific tort. Moreover, the imputation rules affect the defenses available to the claim of tort liability because certain defenses may only be asserted under a particular rule of imputation. Also, the imputation rules may impact compensation, since different liability results in different damage allocation.

28 See Torts Law, *supra* note 17, art. 2.

29 See Liming, Textbook, *supra* note 25, at 76.

A. *General Rule of Fault*

Under the Civil Code, fault is the primary legal basis for the imposition of tort liability, and this rule of fault is the most important rule that governs tort liability imputation. According to article 1165 of the Civil Code, a person who, due to his/her fault, infringes upon the civil rights or interests of another, causing damages, shall bear tort liability.[30] Therefore, the basic rule is that no tort liability will be imposed without a requisite finding of fault. It is commonly held in China that fault-based liability is the default rule in torts. Note that, different from the 2009 Tort Liability Law, the Civil Code makes damage a required element for fault-based tort liability. Therefore, the imposition of tort liability is generally based on the presence of fault that causes damages.

Under the fault rule, to hold a person liable for a tort, the person must be found to be at fault by taking an action or omission. Thus, unless otherwise provided by law, the existence of fault is a determinative factor for tort liability. In addition, the level or degree of fault is decisive in defining the scope of liability and assessing compensation for damages. In certain cases, the extent of fault also affects liability reduction or even exemption.

The Civil Code does not define fault. In general tort literature, there are two major approaches. The first is known as the "objective approach," which considers fault as the breach of a duty or conduct that would not have been committed by a prudent person in the same "external" circumstances. The second is called the "subjective approach," under which fault is defined as a state of mind that, with reference to a particular kind of damage, can be blameworthy.

Countries in the civil law system are generally in favor of the objective approach.[31] A common standard adopted in those countries to determine fault is the so-called good family father standard.[32] A good family father is a man who is careful, diligent, and mindful of others.[33] Under this standard, a deviance from what would have been, under the same situation, the behavior of a good family father will constitute a fault.[34] In China, scholars advocate a mixed approach, under which fault is determined from both subjective and objective perspectives.[35]

According to the mixed approach, fault is both a state of mind and an overt act.[36] The state of mind is the mentality of a person toward his or her own conduct, and

30 See the Civil Code, *supra* note 18, art. 1165.

31 See Tunc, *supra* note 8.

32 *id.*

33 *id.*

34 *id.* Translated from a Roman law principle, "deviance" is a failure to act with the expected level of diligence and care. The original Latin term for this concept is *diligentia diligentis patris familias*.

35 Liming, Textbook, *supra* note 25, at 203.

36 See *id.*

liability arises from the impropriety and unjustness of such mentality.[37] But since the law cannot regulate the state of mind, only conduct,[38] a judgment on the state of mind can only be made through the overt conduct of a person.[39] Thus, the intolerance and blamefulness of the conduct are not decided by what the person in question would think, but by what a reasonable person in the same situation would do, or what society would require the person in question to do.[40]

Definition aside, it has become a consensus that fault may be an intentional act or omission, or negligence.[41] Intentional fault directly involves the knowledge of the tortfeasor. The key is the intent, which is defined in Chinese tort law textbooks as "knowing and willing."[42] It is held that the intent of a person is determined when the person has foreseen the consequences of his/her conduct and still wants to see it happen – or does not act to stop it. From the Chinese viewpoint, the focal point of intent is the state of mind of the actor.[43] The fundamental questions are whether the actor has foreseen the outcome of his/her conduct, and whether the outcome is what the actor either hoped for or to which the actorturned a blind eye.[44] In their hearing of tort cases, the courts often infer intent from the conduct of the tortfeasor.[45]

Note that the Civil Code does not particularly separate intentional torts from negligence, but in certain provisions of the torts law in the Civil Code, intent is a critical factor in finding an actor liable. For example, under article 1160 of the Civil Code, a person who abets or assists another person in committing a tort shall be liable jointly and severally.[46] Obviously, such abetment or assistance as such may only be made intentionally. But it is not clear in the Civil Code whether "intent" also includes transferred intent for the purpose of determining tort liability. Transferred intent occurs when the tortfeasor desires to inflict harm on party A, but instead inadvertently harms party B. In fact, the concept of transferred intent does not seem to be well received in China.

Among Chinese scholars, there has been debate on whether it is necessary to differentiate intentional torts from negligence. A traditional view is that the distinction between intention and negligence is significant in criminal law, in terms of determining the degree of guilt and level of sentencing, but in civil law, liability is based on the fact of damages – and thus the legal consequence would be the same

[37] See *id.*
[38] See *id.*
[39] See *id.*
[40] See *id.*
[41] See Shengming, *supra* note 10, at 41.
[42] See Liming, Textbook, *supra* note 25, at 207.
[43] See *id.* at 41.
[44] See Yang Lixin, Detailed Explanations to the Tort Liability Law of the People's Republic of China, 59–60 (Intellectual Property Rights Press, 2010).
[45] See Shengming, *supra* note 10, at 41.
[46] See the Civil Code, *supra* note 18, art. 1160.

pertaining to compensation regardless of intention or negligence of the tortfeasor. Many, however, argue that in certain tort cases – for example, contributory fault – the weight of fault significantly affects the outcome with respect to liability and compensation.[47]

In fact, a vast majority of tort cases arise from negligence. But in China, negligence is rarely used as a tort cause of action; rather, it is deemed as an indication of fault. Further, negligence is understood in China to consist of neglect and slackness.[48] Neglect refers to a failure to foresee something that is or should be foreseeable, while slackness is an absent-minded credence or belief in the avoidance of a certain outcome that has been foreseen.[49] Thus, civil negligence is viewed in China as a fault where a person should have foreseen or is able to foresee the consequences of his/her conduct, or has foreseen such consequences but carelessly believes they can be avoided.[50]

Negligence is not defined in the Civil Code. A prevailing opinion in the country is that negligence is conduct that violates a duty of care that a reasonable person should normally exercise.[51] It is further held that the reasonable person's duty of care is the level of care most people would have exercised under the same or similar circumstances.[52] Some suggest that the duty of care should also meet requirements set forth by law.[53] Another suggestion takes into consideration certain factors such as industry norms or business ethics in the application of the reasonable person standard when the case involves professionals as opposed to laypersons.[54]

Depending on the degree of seriousness, negligence can be further divided into general negligence and gross negligence. Normally, if a person has not only failed to exercise the duty of care that a reasonably prudent person would have exercised, but has also failed to reach the minimum level of care that a regular person should have, the person is found to be grossly negligent.[55] The Civil Code recognizes the concept of gross negligence[56] but limits the application of gross negligence to the situation of contributory negligence of the plaintiff, where the defendant's liability may be reduced because the principle of fault is premised on general negligence.[57]

[47] See Lixin, *supra* note 44, at 60.
[48] See *id.*
[49] See *id.*
[50] See Liming, Textbook, *supra* note 25, at 211; see also Shengming, *supra* note 10, at 41.
[51] See Shengming, *supra* note 10, at 41–42.
[52] See *id.*
[53] See Liming, Textbook, *supra* note 25, at 217–218.
[54] See *id.*
[55] See *id.* at 222.
[56] See *id.*
[57] For example, under article 1245 of the Civil Code, where a domestic animal causes harm to another person, the keeper or manager of the animal shall assume the tort liability, but may assume no liability or reduced liability if it can be proved that the harm is caused by the victim intentionally or by the gross negligence of the victim. See the Civil Code, *supra* note 18.

B. *Presumption of Fault*

The second tort liability imputation rule under the Civil Code is the presumption of fault. As an exception to the general rule of fault that requires proof of fault, in certain cases a fault may be presumed or constructively determined. The presumption may only be made under the provision of law. The presumption of fault was first provided in article 106 of the 1986 General Principles of Civil Law. Under article 106 of the General Principles of Civil Law, civil liability shall be assumed, even in the absence of fault, if the law so stipulates.[58] In the 2009 Tort Liability Law, presumption of fault was set as a rule of tort liability imputation. As a secondary tort liability basis, the presumption is supplemental to the general principle of fault, and its application is limited to cases prescribed by law.

According to article 1165 of the Civil Code, a person who is presumed to be at fault according to the law and cannot prove otherwise shall be subject to tort liability.[59] The presumption of fault under the Civil Code has several distinctions. First, it is a statutory fault. No fault may be presumed unless specifically allowed by law. Second, the presumption is factually based, meaning that it is made based on facts, or "prima facie" evidence, of injuries or damages. Third, the presumption is rebuttable. To defeat the plaintiff's claim, the defendant may offer evidence to prove that he or she has committed no fault.

Note that fault and the presumption of fault are both based on fault. In either case, if it is shown that fault does not exist, no liability will arise.[60] A major difference between fault and presumption of fault lies with the burden of proof. In the case of fault, the plaintiff bears the burden of proof to show that the defendant is at fault. Under the presumption of fault, however, the burden of proof is reversed, and the defendant is presumed to be at fault. Then the defendant must rebut the presumed fault with evidence in order to avoid liability.[61] The very purpose of presumption of fault is to protect the tort victim by shifting the burden of proof over to the defendant.[62] Under the Civil Code, the presumption of fault applies mostly to cases where the victim is in a weak position.[63]

Given the statutory nature of the presumption of fault, the courts would have no discretionary power to presume fault without authorization of law. A practical issue, however, is whether a court has the discretion to make the presumption in cases where the law is not clear. In China, as noted, the courts do not have the power to

58 See 1986 General Principles of the Civil Law, *supra* note 15, art. 106.
59 See the Civil Code, *supra* note 18, art. 1165.
60 See Liming, Textbook, *supra* note 25, at 140–143.
61 *id.* at 141–142.
62 See Shengming, *supra* note 10, at 45.
63 The cases in which the presumption of fault applies involve, for example, the liability of educational institutes to the person who lacks civil capacity, liability of certain medical malpractice, liability for injury caused by the animal of a zoom, or liability arising from a falling object. See the Civil Code, *supra* note 18, arts. 1199, 1120, 1218, 1248, and 1253.

interpret law. Under the 1982 Constitution (as amended 2018), the authority of the interpretation of law rests with the National People's Congress (NPC) and its Standing Committee.[64] But the Supreme People's Court (SPC) does have the power to interpret the application of law by which all lower courts are bound.[65] However, since it is often hard to clearly distinguish between the interpretation of law and the interpretation of the application of law, courts in many cases may step over the boundary, particularly when a gap in the application of law arises that needs to be filled.

C. *Liability without Fault*

Liability without fault or non-fault liability is the third liability imputation rule provided in the Civil Code, under which tort liability can be imposed regardless of the fault of the tortfeasor. In accordance with article 1166 of the Civil Code, a person who causes harm to a civil right or interest of another person, whether at fault or not, shall bear civil liability if so provided for by law.[66] The thrust of article 1166 is liability without fault. In an article 1166 case, when the tortfeasor's conduct injures the personal or property rights or interests of another person, the tortfeasor is tortiously liable even though he is not at fault, unless an exception under the law applies. But article 1166 requires that imposition of tort liability without fault be made on a statutory ground.

In China, liability without fault is considered a special tort liability. Obviously, by placing a much heavier burden on the tortfeasor than in other tort cases, the liability without fault rule focuses on the risk or danger the tortfeasor creates rather than the faultiness of the tortfeasor. Seen as an exception to the general fault principle in China,[67] the rule of liability without fault aims to make the tortfeasor *prima facie* liable for activity that poses unjustifiable risk or danger to others, especially to the public in general.[68] In many other countries, liability without fault is categorized as strict liability.[69]

Except for terminology distinctions, no major difference exists between strict liability and liability without fault. In fact, these two terms are often used

64 Under article 67(4) of the Constitution of China, the Standing Committee of the National People's Congress exercises the power to interpret laws. See Xianfa art. 67 (1982) (China), www.gov.cn/gongbao/content/2004/content_62714.htm, *translated in* Constitution of the People's Republic of China (1982, as amended 2004), available at www.usconstitution.net/china.html.

65 See Organic Law of People's Court of China (as amended 2006) (China), available at www.novexcn.com/organc-law.html. Article 33 of the Organic Law provides that the Supreme People's Court gives interpretations on questions concerning the specific application of laws and decrees in judicial proceedings.

66 See the Civil Code, *supra* note 18, art. 1166.

67 See Shengming, *supra* note 10, at 46–47; see also Lixin, *supra* note 44, at 49–52.

68 See Shengming, *supra* note 10.

69 See Edward Kionka, Torts in a Nutshell, 37–39 (West, 1999).

interchangeably to mean the same thing.[70] In China, liability without fault has become a liability basis and been applied to special types of tort cases ever since it was first adopted in article 106 of the 1986 General Principles of Civil Law. Under article 106 of the 1986 General Principles of Civil Law, civil liability shall still be borne, even in the absence of fault, if the law so stipulates.

Article 7 of the 2009 Tort Liability Law revises article 106 of the 1986 General Principles of Civil Law by emphasizing that tort liability will be imposed on someone whose conduct has caused injury or harm to another person. The Civil Code stays with the same approach. Thus, under the Civil Code, imposition of tort liability without fault requires the presence of four elements: (a) conduct, (b) injury, (c) causation, and (d) a statutory ground. Like presumption of fault, liability without fault may not be imposed without a statutory basis. The requirement of a statutory basis has several implications.

First, tort liability without fault must be imposed within the provision of law. Pursuant to the Civil Code, liability without fault mainly applies to such cases as product liability, liability for environmental pollution, liability for ultrahazardous activities, and liability for injury caused by a domesticated animal. Second, courts are given no power to expand the scope of such liability. Thus, no court may use its discretion to determine non-fault liability without authorization of law.[71] Third, there are certain statutory exceptions under which the liability could either be exempted or reduced. Therefore, in its determination of liability without fault, a court must take into account any applicable exception.[72]

D. *Rule of Fairness*

Another important rule that also constitutes a liability basis under the Civil Code is fairness. As a rule for proper damages allocation, fairness applies mainly in the cases where injury or damage occurs, yet none of the parties involved are found to be at fault or can be legally blamed. As provided in article 24 of the 2009 Tort Liability Law, if neither the victim nor the actor is at fault for the occurrence of damages, both may share the damages based on the actual situation.[73] An equivalent provision in the Civil Code is article 1186. But the Civil Code deletes the phrase "based on the actual situation" and replaces it with "according to the provisions of the law."[74]

70 See Lixin, *supra* note 44, at 49–52.

71 See Shengming, *supra* note 10, at 50.

72 See Liming, Textbook, *supra* note 25, at 166.

73 See Tort Liability Law, *supra* note 17, art. 24. Article 24 of the Tort Liability Law is based on article 123 of the 1986 Civil Code, under which the parties may share civil liability according to the actual circumstances if none of them are at fault in causing damage. See 1986 General Principles of the Civil Law, *supra* note 15, arts. 24 and 123 (noting that article 24 changes "share civil liability" to "share the damage").

74 See the Civil Code, *supra* note 18, art. 1186.

The change in article 1186 is deemed significant. Under article 24 of the 2009 Tort Liability Law, the determination of damages under the fairness rule is entirely discretionary because it authorizes courts to determine the fair share of damages "based on the actual situation." Article 1186 places limits on the courts' discretion and requires the courts to make damage allocation based on a provision of law. The very purpose of the fairness rule is to ensure that the damage will be fairly shared, and compensation will be properly made in certain cases where special consideration is required.

Most cases in which the fairness principle may apply involve damages that are caused by a person who lacks civil capacity (e.g., minors or the mentally impaired), or by a falling object from a building, for which no one may be found responsible. Other cases where the fairness principle becomes applicable involve the damages caused by conduct taken out of necessity in an emergency. In these cases, the source of damages comes from fault that cannot be traced to anyone, or from someone who shall bear no civil liability under the law. If, however, the damages were to go uncompensated, it would be unfair to the victim.

Under the Civil Code, the trigger of the fairness rule is damage resulting from a fault for which no tortfeasor can be identified or accused. The goal is to determine tort liability in such a way that the damage may be fairly shared, because even though it is impossible to identify who is at fault, damage indeed occurred and the victim needs to be compensated.[75] Since the fairness rule applies to cases where certain damages may not be covered and compensated in regular torts, it functions as a gap-filler in order to achieve social justice.[76] For the same reason, the fairness rule is also considered supplementary in nature.[77]

In the application of the fairness rule, the factors that the courts would consider mainly include the type of conduct that has occurred, the surrounding circumstances, the degree of damages, the relation of the parties, the knowledge of the parties, the social impacts, as well as the financial status of the parties.[78] In some cases, courts also take into consideration the benefits received by one party or both parties.[79] For example, a person volunteers to help his friend do some yard work and is injured during the work. In an action for damage, the court may order the friend to pay a fair amount, although the damage was not caused by the friend's conduct or fault, because the friend benefited from the person's work.[80]

[75] *id.*

[76] See Lixin, *supra* note 44, at 96.

[77] See Liming, Textbook, *supra* note 25, at 125.

[78] See *id.* at 167–170; see also Lixin, *supra* note 44, at 97–98.

[79] Shengming, *supra* note 10, at 116.

[80] See *Opinions on Several Questions Concerning Implementation of the General Principles of Civil Law of the People's Republic of China* (1988), art. 157 (China), available at www.dffy.com/faguixiazai/msf/200311/20031110212524-6.htm.

In addition, under article 1190 of the Civil Code, when a person with full civil act capacity is at fault for causing damage to another person due to a temporary loss of consciousness or loss of control, the person shall bear tort liability. But if the person is found not to be at fault, he shall make appropriate compensation to the victim according to his/her financial situation.[81] In the latter case, the court is given certain discretionary power to determine the damage amount or liability level in consideration of the person's financial conditions.

The Civil Code also provides certain tort liabilities that may be imposed on a preventive basis. Under article 1167 of the Civil Code, when a tortious act endangers another person's personal or property safety, the person affected has the right to request that the tortfeasor bear tort liability such as cessation of the infringement, removal of the nuisance, or elimination of the danger.[82] Article 1167 is similar to article 21 of the 2009 Tort Liability Law. But in article 21, the person facing the danger "may make [a] request," while article 1167 changes it to "has the right to request," emphasizing the "right" granted.

3. TORT LIABILITY ALLOCATION

In a tort action, a plaintiff may have claims against more than one tortfeasor for the same cause of action. This is the situation where the tort liability arises from multiple tortfeasors who have either jointly or individually contributed to causing the plaintiff's injury.[83] A tort where multiple defendants are involved is also called a joint tort.[84] A joint tort may occur in different ways. The actors may act in agreement to commit a tort, the independent conduct of two or more actors may combine to inflict the injury, or the actors may have a shared responsibility for a tort by operation of law.[85] When vicarious liability is imposed, the normal remedy is shared liability.[86]

One important distinction of the joint tort in contrast to the regular tort is that in the joint tort there is an issue of liability allocation among the actors. Since a joint tort involves an injury caused by multiple tortfeasors, determination of the liability among the tortfeasors becomes important. The whole issue is how to get the plaintiff compensated if his/her personal or property rights or interests are harmed by the conduct of several defendants. From both legal and practical perspectives, it is the issue of whether the plaintiff should deal with every defendant individually, or if the plaintiff could seek full compensation from any one of the defendants.

[81] See the Civil Code, *supra* note 18, art. 1190.
[82] See *id.*, art. 1167.
[83] See Glannon, *supra* note 20, at 357.
[84] See Keeton et al., *supra* note 5, at 322.
[85] See Glannon, *supra* note 20, at 357–358.
[86] See Richard Epstein, Cases & Materials on Torts, 221 (Aspen, 2004).

A. *Joint Torts*

The concept of joint tort was first used in China in 1986 when the General Principles of Civil Law was promulgated. Under article 130 of the 1986 General Principles of Civil Law, the joint tort is defined as two or more persons jointly infringing upon another person's rights, causing damage.[87] But the 1986 General Principles of Civil Law does not specify what would constitute a joint tort. In 2003, when the SPC issued an Interpretation to Several Questions on the Application of Law in Adjudicating Personal Injury Compensation Cases,[88] the joint tort was further illustrated as a situation where two or more persons with a joint intention or joint negligence cause injury to another person, or the harmful conduct of two or more persons together causes injury to another even in the absence of joint intention or negligence.[89]

Based on the 1986 General Principles of Civil Law and the 2003 SPC interpretation, the 2009 Torts Law and the Civil Code divide joint torts into three categories: (1) joint conduct, (2) joint danger, and (3) joint cause. Under article 1168 of the Civil Code, two or more persons who jointly commit a tortious act causing damage to another person shall bear joint and several liability.[90] In addition, the Civil Code also holds jointly and severally liable those who abet or assist another person in committing a tort.[91] Moreover, the Civil Code establishes vicarious liability for those who have a special relationship with the tortfeasor when a tort occurs and classifies them as the peculiar tortfeasors.

a. Joint Conduct

Under the Civil Code, a joint tort is committed when two or more people act together to cause injury to another person. Note, however, that unlike the 1986 General Principles of Civil Law, the Civil Code does not use "joint torts" but rather "joint commission of a tort," placing more emphasis on the act committed. The change is intended to signify the "in common" character of the joint tort. Although the joint tort involves multiple tortfeasors, the joint commission suggests that the tortfeasors share each of the tort elements of "fault," "conduct," and "damages caused." The most striking feature in a joint conduct case is that the defendants act together in committing the tort.[92]

[87] See General Principles of the Civil Law of the People's Republic of China, *supra* note 15, art. 130.

[88] See the SPC, *Interpretation to Several Questions on the Application of Law in Adjudicating Personal Injury Damage Cases*, available at www.law-lib.com/law/law_view.asp?id = 81918 (hereinafter SPC 2003 Interpretation).

[89] See *id.*, art. 3.

[90] See the Civil Code, *supra* note 18, art. 1168.

[91] See *id.*, art. 1169.

[92] See Shengming, *supra* note 10, at 51.

For joint conduct in torts, a difficult issue is how conduct or action can be identified as "joint." In theory, "joint conduct" may be simply referred to as "acting in concert." But a question is whether "joint" should be judged by looking at the state of mind of the tortfeasors or the connection between the injury and the tortfeasors' conduct. Another question is whether the joint tort may be committed by negligence. In Chinese torts law, there are at least four different theories that attempt to address the "joint" issue.

The first is the "joint mind" theory, which holds that the prerequisite condition for a joint tort is the concerted desire or motive of multiple tortfeasors.[93] Under the joint mind theory, because two or more tortfeasors agree to engage in a course of tortious action, they are regarded as having joint intent to commit a wrong and to injure another person. Therefore, in the view of the joint mind theory, the term "joint" means thinking and acting together.[94] Since the joint mind theory bases joint torts on the tortfeasors' actions in concert or intent to act, it is considered a subjective theory.[95]

The joint mind theory considers the intent or mental status of the tortfeasors in a joint tort case to be determinative. Under this theory, a joint tort occurs when two or more tortfeasors have "communicated" their minds and taken an action in agreement. The focal point is that in the minds of joint tortfeasors, they know and desire the consequence of injury or harm that their conduct would cause. Therefore, because of the joint intent requirement, a joint tort under the joint mind theory may only be committed intentionally. Since it precludes negligence, the joint mind theory is criticized as defining a joint tort too narrowly.[96]

The second theory is also subjective but views joint torts in the light of fault rather than the mental status of the tortfeasors, and is therefore called the joint fault approach.[97] According to the joint fault approach, the joint mind theory is lopsided because it fails to include negligence in defining a joint tort.[98] Contrary to the joint mind theory, the joint fault approach argues that the commission of a joint tort can take place either intentionally or negligently.[99]

A joint tort by negligence is the case where an injury is caused by the joint conduct of tortfeasors who should have known or should have predicted but failed to know or predict the consequences of their conduct.[100] Joint tort by negligence also includes the situation in which no joint intent of the tortfeasors can be ascertained

[93] See *id.* at 55.
[94] *id.*
[95] *id.*
[96] See Liming, Textbook, *supra* note 25, at 352–353.
[97] See *id.* at 354.
[98] *id.*
[99] *id.* at 355.
[100] See Shengming, *supra* note 10, at 55.

with respect to their joint conduct causing injury to the other person, but it can be inferred from the facts of the case that the tortfeasors were jointly negligent.[101]

Under the joint fault approach, a joint fault occurs where several people, when committing a tort, have common knowledge of, or have failed to exercise reasonable care with regard to, their conduct or the consequences of the conduct. Common knowledge implicates the joint intent of the people involved, while the failure to exercise reasonable care implies joint negligence. In either case, a joint tort may take place if it results in injury or harm to another person. Thus, in contrast to the joint mind theory, the joint fault approach is broader in its scope.

The third theory is the doctrine of conduct in concert, or the objective doctrine. This doctrine holds that neither joint mind nor joint fault is a prerequisite for a joint tort, because the standard on which the joint tort is based should not be subjective but objective.[102] Therefore, as long as the tortfeasors act together to cause injury to another person, a joint tort is committed, and it is unnecessary to inquire into the tortfeasor's state of mind.[103] The objective doctrine rests on a belief that it is difficult to prove that the multiple tortfeasors in a joint tort share a common intent, because each may pursue a different motive.[104] Thus, under the objective theory, to constitute a joint tort, the decisive factor is whether the conduct of the alleged tortfeasors, viewed objectively, is in concert.

The focal point of the conduct in concert doctrine is that a joint tort shall be viewed and determined from the conduct itself, because a joint tort is indispensably related to joint conduct that causes harm or injury. On the other hand, the rationale underlying the conduct in concert doctrine is that a tort is a civil liability, which is aimed at compensating damages, not punishing an evil mind. On this ground, if harm is caused by the joint conduct of multiple tortfeasors, a joint tort will be found even if the tortfeasors did not share a common mind.

Conversely, in the case where harm is not caused by the joint conduct of the tortfeasors, it may hardly sustain a joint tort, though the tortfeasors actually think alike, except in the situation in which one acts as a helper to the person who commits the tort.[105] Under the objective doctrine, a focus on conduct does not mean that the joint mind is totally irrelevant to the finding of a joint tort, but that joint conduct is determinative.

The fourth theory is an approach that combines both subjective and objective theories. To the extent that a joint tort is formed, this combined theory advocates that the court should consider not only the internal mind of the alleged tortfeasors but also their external conduct when making a determination.[106] Internally, there

[101] *id.* at 56.
[102] See *id.*; see also Liming, Textbook, *supra* note 25, at 354.
[103] See Liming, Textbook, *supra* note 25.
[104] See *id.*
[105] See *id.*
[106] See Liming, Textbook, *supra* note 25, at 355; see also Shengming, *supra* note 10, at 55.

should be a fault that the tortfeasors can be blamed for, either intentional or negligent; externally, the tortfeasors' conduct should be in concert and interrelated.[107] Some scholars argue that the SPC actually endorsed this mixed approach rather than the objective theory in its 2003 interpretation, because the SPC takes into consideration the joint intent of the tortfeasors for the finding of a joint tort.[108]

It remains unclear what theory the Civil Code adopts in respect to the joint tort. But it is generally held that at least four elements are essential to the determination of joint torts. The first element is the plurality of tortfeasors, which means that there must be two or more tortfeasors. The tortfeasors can be either natural persons or legal persons. The second element is a joint act. For the purposes of torts law, a joint act refers to (a) the act committed jointly and intentionally, (b) the act committed jointly but negligently, or (c) several acts combined, causing damages.[109]

The third element is causation. To hold joint tortfeasors liable, a causation between the infringing act and the damages must exist. In a joint tort, the liabilities to be imposed are twofold. Externally, all tortfeasors bear joint and several liability. Internally, the liability would have to be divided proportionally among the tortfeasors, because the portion of damage caused by each infringing act can be different. Then, it is critical that the damage portion is causally related to the particular infringing act. If there is no causal relationship between an infringing act and the damage, the actor will not be found to be a joint tortfeasor.

The fourth element is damage. Damage is a basic element for the victim to request that the tortfeasor bear liability in a tort action. As noted, under article 1168 of the Civil Code, joint tortfeasors are liable jointly and severally for the damages jointly caused. But the liability may arise only when damages occur. Therefore, the basis on which the joint and several liability is to be imposed on the joint tortfeasors is the common damage or the damage resulting from the joint conduct. If there is no common damage, joint tort liability will not be found.

The liability ground of a joint tort is joint fault. Since fault includes intentional fault and negligence, joint fault can be committed either with joint intent or by joint negligence. Joint intent exists when multiple tortfeasors have shared a common mind at the time the tort is committed. Joint negligence occurs if, when jointly committing a tort, the tortfeasors should know or foresee that each of their conduct may cause a common harm, but due to their neglect or carelessness, the harm is caused. In the joint negligence case, the tortfeasors do not have joint intent.

Two factors are deemed critical in the determination of negligence. The first factor is the foreseeability of the occurring harm. The foreseeability factor concerns whether the actor, when taking an action, should know or ought to know the

[107] See Liming, Textbook, *supra* note 25, at 355.
[108] See the SPC, 2003 Interpretation, *supra* note 88.
[109] See the SPC Leading Group, Understanding and Application of the Civil Code, Torts, 54 (People's Court Press, 2020) (the SPC Leading Group, Torts).

harmful consequences of his/her action. In torts, the finding of negligence requires that the consequential occurrence or harm was foreseeable and could be foreseen based on the actor's knowledge. The second factor is how avoidable the harm caused was. If harm that could have otherwise been avoided is caused by the actor's conduct because the actor neglects to take any necessary preventive measures, or is neglectful about avoiding the harm, the actor is guilty of negligence.

Related to the joint tort is the liability of the person who abets or assists another in committing a tort. The 1986 General Principles of Civil Law contain no provision about the liability of the abettor or helper in a tort. The SPC, in its role of gap-filling, opined in a 1988 interpretation that the person who abets or assists another person in committing a tort is considered a joint tortfeasor.[110] The liability imposed on the abettor or assistor, however, varies depending on the civil act capacity of the primary tortfeasor.

Based on article 9 of the Torts Law, article 1169 of the Civil Code provides that a person who aids or abets an actor in the commission of a tortious act shall assume joint and several liability with the actor. In addition, under article 1169, a person who aids or abets a tortfeasor who has no or limited civil act capacity in the commission of a tortious act shall assume tort liability. Furthermore, a guardian of the tortfeasor who has no or limited civil act capacity shall also assume corresponding liability if the guardian fails to fulfill the duties of guardianship.[111]

b. Joint Danger

Joint danger refers to the conduct of two or more persons engaged in an action that endangers the body or property safety of another. Tort liability will be imposed if the conduct of the person or persons causes injury to another. In the joint danger case, the group conduct poses high potential danger to the body or property of the other person. But it is often challenging to determine who causes the injury because it is difficult, and even impossible in certain cases, to identify the connection between the injury and the danger-bearing conduct of a particular tortfeasor in the group.

In China, joint danger is also called *quasi*-joint conduct.[112] Compared with joint conduct, joint danger focuses on the source of the danger rather than the act of the tortfeasors. Article 1170 of the Civil Code provides that when two or more persons engage in conduct that endangers the personal or property safety of another person, if only the conduct of one or several of them causes harm to another person and the specific tortfeasor can be determined, the tortfeasor shall be liable; but if the specific tortfeasor cannot be determined, all of them shall be jointly and severally liable.

[110] See the SPC, *Opinions on Several Issues Concerning Implementation of the General Principles of Civil Law of China (Provisional)* 1988, art. 148.
[111] See the Civil Code, *supra* note 18, art. 1169.
[112] See Liming, Textbook, *supra* note 25, at 378; see also Lixin, *supra* note 44, at 65.

Thus, under article 1170, a joint tort arising from joint danger should have the following four elements: (1) two or more persons, (2) engagement in dangerous conduct, (3) injury to a victim caused by the conduct of some of the persons, and (4) inability to identify the person whose conduct results in the injury Compared with other tort cases, the distinction of joint danger is that joint intent of the tortfeasors to commit a tort is not required, but the conduct of two or more persons creates danger that may cause injury to another person, and liability cannot be assigned to an individual person.

Also note that to find joint danger, joint fault need not be present under the Civil Code. There are two considerations. First, the purpose of the joint danger rule is to prevent the frustration of the plaintiff's claim when the plaintiff who suffered injury from a joint dangerous conduct of multiple defendants is unable to tell exactly who caused the injury. Second, under the SPC's interpretation, in a joint danger case, the burden of proof is reversed, and the fault of the defendant is presumed. In addition, the joint danger rule may apply to cases where liability is imposed even without fault.

The term "joint" in joint danger essentially means "the same." To apply the joint danger rule in a tort case, a prerequisite condition is that the defendants must be involved in the same dangerous conduct. And the dangerous conduct of multiple defendants must happen at the same time in the same location. Thus, if defendants each act at a different time or in a different place, no joint danger will be found. One last point is the proof of causation. Given the particularity of joint danger, a reversed burden of proof is required; that is, the defendant must prove that the causation between his/her conduct and the plaintiff's injury does not exist.[113]

c. Joint Cause

A joint tort arising from joint cause occurs when two or more persons commit torts respectively but cause the same harm.[114] The major difference between joint cause and other joint torts is that the injury in a joint cause tort is caused by the separate and independent conduct of each tortfeasor. Additionally, among the tortfeasors involved in a joint cause case, there must be no common plan or joint fault, nor may they be related to each other in committing tortious conduct. In other words, joint cause deals with the same injury caused by multiple, unrelated tortious conducts. Given the individual nature of the conduct of the tortfeasors, the tortfeasors in the joint cause tort are also called "mentally unrelated tortfeasors."

Another feature of joint cause is that the harm caused by two or more tortfeasors may be either divisible or indivisible. Divisible harm occurs where the injury is

[113] See the SPC, *Several Provisions of Evidence Concerning Civil Litigation*, issued in 2020, available at www.law-lib.com/law/law_view.asp?id=16829.

[114] See the Civil Code, *supra* note 18, arts. 1171 and 1172.

caused by multiple conducts combined, while indivisible harm involves a situation in which each tortious conduct is sufficient to cause the entire harm. The Civil Code differentiates divisible harm from indivisible harm by imposing different types of liability on defendants. Under article 1171 of the Civil Code, if each of the joint tortious acts is sufficient to independently cause the entire damage, the joint tortfeasors shall assume joint and several liability.[115] Otherwise, under article 1172, each of the joint tortfeasors shall bear liability in proportion to their respective share of fault if it can be determined, or in equal share if it cannot be determined.[116]

B. *Joint Tort Liability*

In a joint tort case, the Civil Code imposes two different liabilities upon tortfeasors. The more common one is joint and several tort liability, which makes each of the multiple defendants accountable for the entire result. Article 178 of the Civil Code explicitly provides that if two or more persons assume joint and several liability in accordance with law, the right holder has the right to request that some or all of them bear the liability.[117] In other words, the right holder may choose to make a claim against an individual person for the payment of all the damages.

Under article 178, joint and several liability can be either imposed by law or stipulated in the agreement of the parties. In torts, however, joint and several liability is statutory and may only be provided by law. The imposition of joint and several liability in a joint tort may result in a single defendant being required to pay for the full amount of the plaintiff's damages. When the full amount is paid by a single defendant, an indemnity or reimbursement of proportionate shares from other defendants will inevitably become an issue.

To deal with the indemnity issue, the Civil Code provides a rule of contribution that grants the overpaying tortfeasor a right of recourse to recover against its fellow tortfeasors. Under article 178 of the Civil Code, a person who has assumed more liability than his/her share of fault has the right to contribution against the other person(s) subjected to the joint and several liability.[118] To ensure proper allocation of liability and fair contribution of damage payment, the right of recourse serves a twofold goal: providing adequate compensation to the tort victim and avoiding unjust enrichment among the liable tortfeasors.

The second kind of joint tort liability is shared liability or liability according to the share of fault. As provided in article 177 of the Civil Code, the persons assuming shared liability in a joint tort shall each bear liability in proportion to their respective share of fault, or in equal share if such share cannot be determined.[119] Premised on

[115] See *id.*
[116] See *id.*, art. 1172.
[117] See *id.*, art. 178.
[118] See *id.*
[119] See *id.*, art. 177.

article 177, article 1172 of the Civil Code, as noted, further provides a rule of liability sharing for the tortious acts committed by two or more persons respectively causing the same damage to another person.[120]

The primary standard to determine the seriousness or level of a tortfeasor's liability is the degree of the tortfeasor's fault.[121] Also, although joint and several liability in torts may only be imposed by the operation of law, contribution proportions may be determined under an agreement reached among the tortfeasors to bypass the seriousness standard.[122] Moreover, there is a consensus that the right of recourse for indemnity will be vested with a tortfeasor under two conditions: (1) the tortfeasor has paid in whole or in part the amount of compensation and (2) the payment is in excess of the contribution the tortfeasor is supposed to bear.[123]

Although the seriousness of a tortfeasor's liability is mainly affected by the degree of fault, many in China suggest that in addition to the degree of fault, courts should also consider the cause each party contributed to the damage.[124] The idea is that since determination of the joint tort on the basis of joint causes heavily depends on the source of the damage, a greater portion of damages should be assigned to the source with a greater causal link to the resulting harm.[125] It is further suggested that in consumer-related cases, if both the degree of fault and level of cause are unidentifiable, the determination of seriousness shall be made in consideration of the market share of the manufacturers to allocate a proper portion of liability before the equal share is imposed among all tortfeasors.[126]

C. *Peculiar Tortfeasors and Liability*

In most tort cases, the victim may only be able to hold the person or persons who committed torts liable. In certain cases, however, a tort victim may seek liability from someone who has a certain relationship with the tortfeasor or is legally obligated to act for the tortfeasor. The liability imposed on such a person other than the tortfeasor is commonly called vicarious liability. One underlying theory of such liability is the classic concept of *respondeat superior* (let the master answer).[127] The imposition of vicarious liability is normally based on "imputed negligence," meaning that the negligence of the tortfeasor is to be charged against the other person who has a special relationship with the tortfeasor.[128]

[120] See *id.*, art. 1172.
[121] See Shengming, *supra* note 10, at 75.
[122] See Liming, Textbook, *supra* note 25, at 407.
[123] See *id.* at 408.
[124] See Liming, Textbook, *supra* note 25, at 411.
[125] See Shengming, *supra* note 10, at 70.
[126] See Liming, Textbook, *supra* note 25, at 411.
[127] See Keeton et al., *supra* note 5, at 499.
[128] See *id.*

Traditionally, vicarious liability is a liability that arises from a master–servant or employer–employee relationship, under which the master or employer is held liable for the tort committed by the servant or employee. In general, to hold a master or employer liable, two factors are considered determinative: (1) the degree of control by the master or employer over the servant or employee and (2) the scope of the servant's or employee's employment. A theoretic basis of vicarious liability is the doctrine of agency, especially in employment relationships, because an employee is deemed a kind of agent of the employer.[129]

With the development of torts law, the application of vicarious liability has extended to other relationships, such as the relationship between an employer and an independent contractor. The extension even reaches the guardian of the tortfeasor. As a result, the agency doctrine seems to be obsolete, at least in these newly developed areas, since unlike the employment relationship, the degree of control becomes irrelevant in cases where the liable person and the tortfeasor are not actually related. In the guardianship situation, although there is an agent issue, the agency relationship is reversed because the guardian, as a matter of law, would be considered the agent of the person under guardianship.

In China, vicarious liability is recognized, but imposition of such liability is not limited to the employment relationship. In fact, the coverage of vicarious liability is quite extensive in the country. Partly because of this extensive coverage, the Civil Code does not use the term "vicarious liability," but instead refers to "peculiar tortfeasors" or persons of special status who will be held liable for the torts committed by another person. Based on their status, these peculiar tortfeasors are divided into three categories: (1) special relationship tortfeasor, (2) limited capacity tortfeasor, and (3) internet-related tortfeasor.

In most cases, a peculiar tortfeasor is a person who has a special relationship with the person directly causing the injury, or with the victim, and is liable for the injury under the law on the ground of that relationship. In certain cases, however, it is highly questionable whether the liability imposed is vicarious. An example is the school's liability for a tortiously injured student on campus. Nevertheless, the Civil Code uses the term "peculiar tortfeasor" to include all of the aforementioned.

Note, however, that one peculiar tortfeasor under the Civil Code is the person whose capacity, though full, is impeded. Under article 1190 of the Civil Code, a person with full capacity for conducting civil acts shall be held liable if the person is at fault for causing damage to another person due to temporary loss of consciousness or loss of control. If, however, no fault is found, the person may not be held liable for torts, but appropriate compensation shall be made to the victim according to the person's financial situation.[130] Moreover, if the temporary loss of consciousness or

[129] See *id.* at 263.

[130] See the Civil Code, *supra* note 18, art. 1190.

loss of control is a result of intoxication or abuse of narcotic or psychotropic drugs, tort liability shall be imposed.[131]

a. Special Relationship Tortfeasors

A special relationship tortfeasor involves such a person as a guardian, employer, public facility manager, mass activity organizer, or educational institute. Based on the distinction of each type of special relationship tortfeasor, the Civil Code imposes tort liability on two different grounds. With respect to guardian and employer, liability arises from the doctrine of *respondeat superior*, under which the guardian or employer is held vicariously liable for injury to a third person. For other relationship tortfeasors, tort liability is imposed for failure to act, which is further divided into failure to exercise the duty of safety protection and failure to perform the duty of education and management.

I. GUARDIANSHIP AND EMPLOYMENT. Guardianship or employment establishes a special relationship between particular persons. The commonality in the relationship so established in each case concerns representation and control. In an employment relationship, representation and control lie with employee and employer respectively, while in a guardianship, the guardian normally retains both. Thus, the guardian not only represents but also has control over the person under guardianship. When a person under guardianship or an employee is involved in a tort, the question will be whether the guardian or the employer is liable.

(a) Guardian. A guardian is a person who under the law has the authority as well as the duty to care for the personal or property interest of another person whose civil act capacity is impeded for various legal reasons. Under article 1188 of the Civil Code, if a person with no or limited capacity for civil conduct causes damage to another person, the guardian of the said person shall assume tort liability.[132] It is believed that the liability imposed by article 1188 on a guardian is vicarious liability, making a guardian liable for the torts committed by a person under guardianship.

In addition, the tort liability as provided in article 1188 may also apply to the case in which a guardian has fulfilled the duties of guardianship. In that case, however, the guardian's tort liability may be mitigated. Furthermore, pursuant to article 1188, a guardian shall remain liable for any deficiency of payment in the case where a person under guardianship, who causes damage to another person, does not have sufficient assets to compensate the victim.[133]

[131] See *id.*

[132] See *id.*, art. 1188.

[133] See *id.*

A question subject to debate is the imputation basis on which the guardian's tort liability is imposed. Apparently, the guardian's liability is not based on fault because the victim is under no burden to prove that the guardian was at fault when the tort was committed. One argument is that the guardian's liability will be presumed as long as the harm is caused by the conduct of the person under guardianship.[134] This argument, however, does not seem persuasive because a guardian would still be held liable even if the guardian did not breach a duty or was not at fault. Others suggest that the guardian's tort liability should be deemed a no-fault liability because under article 1188 of the Civil Code, the guardian is liable for the torts committed by the person under guardianship regardless of the guardian's fault.[135]

Between the two ends of the spectrum is an assertion that the liability basis under article 1188 combines presumption of fault and non-fault. First, a guardian may not be exempted from liability even if there is proof of no fault. It differs from presumption of fault in that a person will not be held liable if he is proved faultless. Second, the Civil Code does not make a guardian absolutely liable, but rather allows the guardian's liability to be mitigated in the case where the guardian has fulfilled his/her guardianship duties.[136] In contrast, the SPC takes a simpler approach, making the liability of a guardian a non-fault liability supplemented by the principle of fairness.[137]

(b) Employer. As used in the tort provisions of the Civil Code, the term "employer" is quite broad in coverage, consisting of the employing unit, labor dispatcher, and individual labor service recipient. The employing unit is the entity that hires employees. For the purposes of tort liabilities, the employing unit includes enterprises, institutions, government agencies, social organizations, and individual business entities. An employee may be either a permanent or temporary employee. However, it is important to note that in China, the relationship between a government agency and its staff is not an employment relationship. Therefore, the Civil Code uses a content-neutral term "employing unit" in lieu of employer. For the same reason, the term "employee" is replaced with the term "working staff" or "worker."

The Civil Code places vicarious liability on the employing unit for the torts committed by its workers. Article 1191 of the Civil Code makes it imperative that where a worker of an employing unit causes any harm to another person during the execution of his or her work duties, the employing unit shall assume tort liability.[138] A change the Civil Code made to the 2009 Torts Law is that under article 1191 of the Civil Code, the employing unit may, after assuming tort liability, seek

[134] See Lixin, *supra* note 44, at 141.
[135] See Liming, Textbook, *supra* note 25, at 456.
[136] See Shengming, *supra* note 10, at 161.
[137] See the SPC Leading Group, Torts, *supra* note 109, at 221.
[138] See the Civil Code, *supra* note 18, art. 1191.

indemnification against the employee who acted wrong intentionally or with gross negligence.[139]

A difficult issue in applying article 1191 is what constitutes "during the execution of [a] work duty." According to the SPC's interpretation, the execution of a work duty includes two situations: (1) business operation or other work activities that are within the scope of authorization or instruction of the employing unit, and (2) although a work act exceeded the scope of authorization or instruction, the act apparently appears to be the performance of a work duty or is intrinsically related to such performance.[140] Although the SPC's interpretation primarily deals with private-sector employing units, it is believed that the interpretation is applicable by reference to cases involving public-sector employing units.

To determine whether an act is done "during the execution of a work duty," some suggest making the following inquiries: (a) whether the act is conducted in the name of the employing unit, (b) whether the act is objectively sufficient to be considered an execution of work duties, and (c) whether, based on common social experience, it is enough to conclude that the act is closely related to the position of the staff member in question.[141] A general belief is that an employing unit may not be held liable for the act of its staff member unless (1) the act is committed by a staff member of the employing unit, (2) within the time period during which the staff member performs his or her duties, (3) at the place where the staff member performs his or her duty, and (4) the damage or harm is caused by the act as such.[142]

Since the employing unit includes government agencies, a tort committed by a government worker during the performance of his/her duty is also governed by article 1191 of the Civil Code. The duty of a government worker can be either official-affairs-related (*ex officio*) or non-official-affairs-related. The former refers to an act on behalf of the government or a government act, while the latter involves general civil matters (e.g., purchasing office supplies). If a tort occurs during the performance of an official act on behalf of the government, the state is liable, and compensation shall be made in accordance with the State Compensation Law (1994). On the other hand, when tortious conduct arises from the engagement in general civil matters, the government agency at issue is liable under the provisions of the Civil Code.

A labor dispatcher is the unit that sends laborers or service workers to another unit for work on an as-needed basis. The 2007 Labor Contract Law requires that for a labor dispatch, a minimum two-year contract shall be formed between the dispatcher and the dispatched, and a work contract be established between the dispatcher and the unit accepting the dispatched. One notable feature of labor

[139] See *id.*
[140] See the SPC, 2003 Interpretation, *supra* note 88, art. 9.
[141] See the SPC Leading Group,Torts, *supra* note 109, at 239.
[142] See *id.*

dispatch is that the labor dispatcher usually does not manage the dispatched nor is involved in any job assignment for the dispatched. After the dispatch, the dispatched works as assigned and instructed by the unit receiving the dispatched.

Therefore, in the labor dispatch, the dispatched is contractually related to both the dispatcher and the unit receiving the dispatched. Then, if during the dispatch, the dispatched causes harm to another person, an issue necessarily raised is who should be held liable. Pursuant to article 1191 of the Civil Code, if, during the period of labor dispatch, the dispatched causes any harm to another person in connection with the performance of his/her work, the unit receiving the dispatched shall assume the liability.[143] Note that under article 34 of the 2009 Tort Liability Law, the labor dispatcher, if at fault, shall bear the corresponding supplementary liability for the harm caused by the dispatched. The provision of article 34 is incorporated into article 1191 of the Civil Code with a deletion of the word "supplementary," requiring the labor dispatcher at fault to bear the liability correspondingly.

While aiming at allocating liability between the unit using the dispatched and the labor dispatcher, article 1191 of the Civil Code attaches more liability to the former. As a principle, the unit using the dispatched is vicariously liable regardless of fault for the harm caused by the dispatched to another person. In contrast, the labor dispatcher may only be held liable when at fault. In addition, the compensation a labor dispatcher is required to make to the victim is proportionate to its fault. Put differently, the labor dispatcher's liability for a tort committed by the dispatched is limited to the extent of the labor dispatcher's fault.

An individual labor service refers to a labor relationship created by two individuals through an agreement in which one is to provide service to the other at a negotiated rate. The major characteristic of the individual labor service is that both parties in the labor relationship are individuals. Perhaps for that reason, the individual labor service is commonly characterized in China as individual-based private hiring.[144] Common examples of such private hiring include a family tutor, baby-sitter or nanny, house cleaner, handyman services, and minor home repair workers. A contract for individual labor service could be made in writing, orally or in other forms.

Tort liability in individual labor service arises when the hired worker causes harm to another person while performing the service. The issue is whether the hiring person shall bear the liability for the harm caused to another person. A related issue is whether the hiring person is liable for the harm the hired worker suffered when providing the service. According to article 1192 of the Civil Code, in a labor relationship formed between individuals, if the party providing labor services causes damage to another person in connection with the labor services, the party receiving labor services shall assume tort liability.

[143] See the Civil Code, *supra* note 18, art. 1191.

[144] See Lixin, *supra* note 44, at 159.

With regard to harm to the hired person himself, the Civil Code adopts a fair share approach and divides the liability between the service provider and service recipient on the basis of fault. According to article 1192, if the labor services provider injures himself during the service performance, both parties shall each assume the liability corresponding to their respective fault.[145] The relevant factors to determine the shares of liability are the fact and degree of the fault on each side. In theory, if not at fault, the service recipient would not be liable for the service provider's harm. But in practice, the service recipient often ends up making a certain payment on the grounds of humanitarian concern rather than his fault.

Article 1192 of the Civil Code is based on article 35 of the 2009 Tort Liability Law. But article 1192 differs from article 35 in two aspects. First, article 1192 provides an indemnification provision that allows the service-receiving party, after assuming tort liability, to claim indemnification against the service-providing party who acts wrongly intentionally or with gross negligence. Second, article 1192 creates a claim against a third party. Under article 1192, where an act of a third person causes damage to the service-providing party when such services are provided, the service-providing party has the right to request that the third person bear tort liability, or to request that the service-receiving party make compensation. The service-receiving party may, after making the compensation, request indemnification from the third person.

Tort liability in the individual labor service is analogically derived from the doctrine of *respondeat superior*. The idea is that when hiring a private labor service, the hiring person is under the duty by operation of law to properly instruct and supervise the hired person. On the other hand, to impose tort liability on the hiring person, it is important that the act causing harm to another person is within the scope of service. Therefore, if the act at issue occurs outside the scope of the services, the hiring person is free from liability.

The Civil Code also contains a provision that governs the liability of a contractor. Pursuant to article 1193 of the Civil Code, if a contractor causes damage to a third person or to himself while performing the contracted work, the ordering party shall not assume tort liability. If, however, the ordering party is at fault in placing the order, giving instructions, or selecting the contractor, the ordering party shall assume corresponding liability.[146]

II. OTHER TORTFEASORS. Other tortfeasors with special relationships involve those who manage public facilities or events or operate educational institutes for minors. A public facility is any place open to the general public for certain business purposes. In addition to hotels, shopping centers, banks, stations, entertainment places, etc., public facilities also include such places as airports, ports, parks as well

[145] See the Civil Code, *supra* note 18, art. 1192.
[146] See *id.*

as restaurants. Public events literally refer to mass gatherings, including sports games, performances, exhibitions, sales promotions, and the like. At these places or events, public safety is always a concern. The same concern also arises with regard to educational institutes such as kindergartens and other schools.[147]

When injury or harm occurs in a public facility or during a public event, tort liability will be imposed. In common law tort theory, the customer in a store or the patron in a restaurant is considered an invitee of the store or restaurant, and the store operator or the restaurant owner is under an affirmative duty to protect the customer, not only against known dangers but also against those discoverable with reasonable care.[148] Chinese law does not use the concept of invitee, but the protection of public safety is a judicially recognized duty of a person engaged in the business of lodging, dining, entertaining, or other social activities. The "person" as such is defined by the SPC to include natural persons, legal persons, or other organizations.[149] The duty of public safety is also called the "duty to act," and failure to act will constitute legal grounds for tort liability imposition.

(a) Management of Public Facilities and Events. Under Chinese law, the duty to act concerning public safety is further divided into the duty of safety protection and the duty of education and management. The former applies to public facilities and public events, while the latter deals with educational institutes. According to article 1198 of the Civil Code, the operators or managers of business or public premises such as hotels, shopping malls, banks, bus or train stations, airports, stadiums, and places of entertainment, or the organizers of mass activities, shall bear tort liability if they fail to fulfill the duty of maintaining safety and cause damage to another person.

Article 1198 of the Civil Code also provides that if the damage to another person is caused by a third person, the third person shall bear tort liability, and the operator, manager, or organizer who fails to fulfill the duty of maintaining safety shall assume the corresponding supplementary liability. In addition, under article 1198, after assuming the supplementary liability, the operator, manager, or organizer may seek indemnification against the third person.

Article 1198 is self-evident. First, the primary persons liable for safety in public facilities are the facility operators or managers, or event organizers. Second, the duty of safety protection serves a twofold purpose: (1) to prevent any injury caused to another person by the faulty conduct of the public facility manager or the public event organizer and (2) to protect another person from being harmed by a third party. What is unclear, however, is whether "another person" would necessarily mean any person. Some suggest that "another person" should be the one who is

[147] See Shengming, *supra* note 10, at 201.
[148] See Keeton et al., *supra* note 5, at 419–420.
[149] See the SPC, 2003 Interpretation, *supra* note 88, art. 1.

lawfully present at the premises in question. Others prefer to describe "another person" as a customer or participant.[150] The Civil Code does not define "another person" and thus leaves it to the courts to decide under the circumstances of each case.

A prerequisite condition to impose tort liability upon a public facility operator, manager, or public event organizer is that the operator, manager, or organizer fails to perform the duty of safety protection. The violation of safety protection duty, as many believe, is fault-based liability. Hence, to file a tort action against a public facility manager or a public event organizer, the plaintiff usually has the burden to prove that the defendant was at fault, namely through a failure to act or an omission.[151]

An issue concerning the application of article 1198 is the extent to which a public facility operator, manager, or public event organizer can be held liable in torts. In *Li Qiuyue v. Hongshan Village Committee* (2017), the plaintiff's father climbed a tree without permission to pick bayberries in the *Hongshan* Village Scenic Area, a national AAA-rated tourist attraction with no entrance fee. After accidentally falling from the tree, the plaintiff's father was fatally injured and died in a local hospital. The plaintiff sued *Hongshan* Village, claiming that the defendant should bear responsibility for her father's death because the defendant failed to fulfill its safety protection obligations and failed to take timely and necessary rescue measures after the accident. The plaintiff requested the court to order the defendant to pay for 70 percent of the personal injury liability of 631,346.31 yuan.[152]

The trial court granted the plaintiff's request but ordered the defendant to pay a reduced sum of 45,096.17 yuan. On appeal, the appellate court affirmed. The plaintiff then challenged the court's order through the proceeding of judicial supervision. After a retiral, the appellate court vacated its previous decision and denied the plaintiff's request entirely. The case was selected by the SPC and published on October 9, 2020 as Guiding Case No. 140.[153] Stated as the key point of the case, the rationale for the denial was that the safety assurance obligations of public facility operators or managers should be confined within reasonable limits and consistent with their management and control capabilities. Thus, no claims shall be granted against a public facility manager on tort liability for the death of a person who with full capacity for civil conduct climbed a fruit tree in a scenic area to pick fruits without permission and accidentally fell.[154]

It is generally held in Chinese courts that "reasonable limits" should be determined on a case-by-case basis. Factors to consider generally include: (a) whether the

[150] See Shengming, *supra* note 10, at 201–202.
[151] See Liming, Textbook, *supra* note 25, at 430.
[152] See Li Qiuyue et al. v. Hongshan Village Committee (2019) Yue 01 Min Zai No. 273.
[153] See the SPC, *Guiding Case No. 140*, available at www.dlhsfy.gov.cn/court/html/2020/zdxal_1019/1959.html.
[154] See *id.*

actual fulfillment of the safety protection obligations, judged objectively, has reached the level of care required by laws, regulations, or industry norms (b) whether the danger could reasonably be foreseen; and (c) whether the party involved should have been required to take corresponding measures to prevent it. The basic notion is that the price paid for a failure to perform the obligations as required by law should not exceed the benefits obtained from fulfilling such obligations.[155]

In addition, as noted, the tort liability of an operator, manager, or organizer arising from a failure to act also applies to harm caused by a third party. However, the difference in the third-party tort is that the manager or organizer's liability to compensate is complementary, which means that the manager or organizer will assume liability only when the third-party tortfeasor cannot be found or is unable to pay for the damage.[156] It is also worth noting that in such third-party tort cases, the operator, manager, or organizer may – under article 1198 of the Civil Code – claim indemnification from the third person after assuming the supplementary liability.[157]

(b) Educational Entity. The duty of education and management concerns educational entities such as kindergartens, schools, or other educational institutions (e.g., training centers). The imposition of this duty is aimed at protecting students, especially children. The focus is on minors who have no or limited civil act capacity. Protection also extends to those who are mentally incapable of cognizing the consequences of their conduct.

In its 2003 Interpretation, the SPC adopted a special damage rule for injuries to minors in schools. According to the SPC, if a school, kindergarten, or any other educational institution that is under the legal duty to educate, manage, and protect minors fails to perform this duty, causing personal injury to a minor or causing a minor to inflict harm on another person, it shall assume liability for compensation corresponding to its fault. If a third party caused the injury, the third party is liable, but if the school or kindergarten was at fault, it shall correspondingly bear supplementary liability for the compensation.[158]

There are three articles in the Civil Code that concern tortious injury in schools, which are in part based on the SPC's 2003 Interpretation. The first is article 1199, which deals with personal injury sustained by a person without civil act capacity during a period of studying or living in a kindergarten, school, or any other educational institution. Under article 1199, a kindergarten, school, or any other

[155] See AterSoft, Legal Database, *Adjudication Rules on the Safety Obligations Disputes as Applied in the Courts across the Country*, available at https://baijiahao.baidu.com/s?id=1798555467033177918&wfr=spider&for=pc.

[156] See *id.* at 201–202.

[157] See the Civil Code, *supra* note 18, art. 1198.

[158] See the SPC, the 2003 Interpretation, *supra* note 88, art. 7.

educational institution shall assume tort liability where a person with no capacity suffers personal injury while studying or living there.

The liability basis of article 1199 is the presumption of fault. The kindergarten, school or other educational institution is presumed to be at fault when injury occurs to a student on campus, unless sufficient evidence proves otherwise. Therefore, if it can be proved that the kindergarten, school, or educational institution has fulfilled its responsibilities in education and management, no tort liability shall be imposed. Under the presumption of fault, the burden of proof is on the educational entity.

The second article is article 1200, which provides that if a person with limited civil act capacity sustains any personal injury during the period of studying at or living in a school or any other educational institution, the school or other educational institution shall assume liability if it fails to fulfill its duties of education and management. A major difference between articles 1199 and 1200 is that article 1199 focuses on persons without civil act capacity, while article 1200 handles those whose civil act capacity is limited. Because of this difference, article 1200, unlike article 1199, does not presume fault, and thus the plaintiff has the burden to prove the defendant's fault.

The third article, article 1201, covers the injuries caused by a third party to a school student with no or limited civil act capacity. Under article 1201, where, during the period of his/her studies or residence in a kindergarten, school, or any other educational institution, a person with no or limited civil act capacity sustains any personal injury caused by an outsider, the outsider causing the harm shall assume tort liability – and in the meantime, the kindergarten, school, or other educational institution shall assume the corresponding complementary liability if it fails to fulfill its duties of management. In addition, after assuming the supplementary liability, the kindergarten, school, or the educational institution may request indemnification from the outsider.

However, the duties of education and management appear to be very broad and ill-defined. Under the Civil Code, there are two duties: duty of education and duty of management. But the Civil Code does not define what these duties are. For the duty of education, one interpretation regards it to mean the duty to educate and supervise students. Under this interpretation, if one student injures another student during school, the school is presumably negligent and liable.[159] But the distinction and interplay between education and supervision remain unclear. In addition, it is difficult to determine the scope of the duty of education. Some suggest that the determination be made by referring to provisions of other laws or regulations, based on the facts of specific cases.

The duty of management is understood to include school facility maintenance, student activity guidance, school safety measures, and other preventive actions.[160]

[159] See Liming, Textbook, *supra* note 25, at 447–448.
[160] See *id.*

In the case of food poisoning at school, for example, the school would be liable for the harm caused to the poisoned students. In the case of an injury inflicted upon students by an intruder, the victim has a tort cause of action against the school for damage if the school is found to have failed to exercise its duty of management. However, since the intruder case involves a third-party tortfeasor, the school's liability would be based on fault. Under this situation, the plaintiff has the burden to prove the school's fault.

Some scholars favor a more general "duty of care" term to describe the duty of education and management. Their argument is that determination of the educational entity's liability for student injuries is dependent on, among others, the educational entity's fault. Thus, whether the educational entity is at fault is a question of whether it has fulfilled its duty of care. According to this argument, to impose tort liability on an educational entity, it must be determined whether the educational entity (1) owes a duty of care, (2) has fulfilled the duty of care, and (3) is able to or should be able to exercise the duty of care.[161] In practice, the threshold issue to determine the fault of an educational entity is whether it has violated any of its duties provided by laws, regulations, rules, or decrees. Any violation would serve as *prima facie* evidence of the education entity's fault.

b. Capacity-Impeded Tortfeasors

A capacity-impeded tortfeasor concerns a type of tort that relates to the tort liability of someone who is fully capable of civil conduct but temporarily loses consciousness or control of his/her own conduct so as to cause harm to another person. Not until the adoption of the Torts Liability Law in 2009 did China have rules in tort applicable to this type of tort. The lack of legislation in this regard was largely due to the difficulty in determining whether and how a person who suffers a temporary loss of consciousness or control should be held liable for tortious conduct committed during the period in which his/her capacity was impeded. Both the 2009 Torts Law and the Civil Code treat the person of this kind as a capacity-impeded tortfeasor to whom certain specific rules apply.

1. CAUSES OF CAPACITY IMPEDIMENT. The Civil Code prescribes three causes for the loss of consciousness or control: (1) with fault, (2) without fault, and (3) intoxication or drug use. Loss of consciousness and loss of control are closely related to each other. In most cases, loss of control is a consequence of loss of consciousness. But loss of consciousness can be either the result of the tortfeasor's own negligence or the outcome of other intervening situations. If, for example, a driver loses control of his/her car, causing personal injury to a pedestrian, the loss may be caused by a variety of factors: the driver's intoxication, malfunction of the car, or

[161] See Lixin, *supra* note 44, at 183–184.

being hit by a flying rock. Some of these causes could be attributed to the fault of the driver, while others might be related to an intervening situation.

(a) With Fault. Under article 1190 of the Civil Code, if a person with full civil act capacity is at fault for causing damage to another person due to temporary loss of consciousness or loss of control, the person shall bear tort liability. When civil liability is based on fault, a question is how to assign blameworthiness to the capacity-impeded tortfeasor. A puzzle is evident. On the one hand, the tortfeasor who lost consciousness can hardly be blamed for any fault because he had no cognizable capacity during the commission of the tort. On the other hand, if no liability is imposed, the innocent victim's damage would go uncompensated, resulting in an unfair and unjust outcome.[162]

To deal with this issue, the country's legislation in torts follows a fault-in-advance approach for the determination of the capacity-impeded person's liability based on fault. Fault-in-advance refers to the neglect or negligence that leads to the loss of consciousness or control.[163] As is often the case, neglect is associated with the tortfeasor's health situation or mental condition. Under the fault-in-advance approach, if the loss of consciousness or control is caused by the fault of the person himself, the person is liable for the tortious conduct committed during the period of such loss. To illustrate: if a person who must take medication to control a muscular problem in his/her arm forgets to take the medicine before riding a bicycle and consequently loses control and hits a pedestrian, he will be considered at fault in advance and thus liable.

(b) Without Fault. Pursuant to article 1190 of the Civil Code, if the temporary loss of consciousness or control of a person with full civil act capacity that causes injury to another person does not result from his/her fault, the person shall make appropriate compensation to the victim according to his financial situation. For example, when a driver loses control due to an unknown sickness while driving, which causes injury to another person, the driver may bear no tort liability but should make proper compensation to the injured. In this situation, what the person concerned may bear is liability for compensation rather than damages. In addition, the compensation so made is based on the person's own financial situation.

For the purposes of article 1190, compensation differs from damages in several respects. First, the nature of compensation is supplementary, while damages are punitive. Second, compensation is made based on fairness when no fault can be found, but damages involve fault liability. Third, compensation is mostly the payment of a certain amount of money. In a contract, damages include monetary

[162] See Shengming, *supra* note 10, at 163.
[163] *id.* at 164.

compensation, supplemented by such other means as restoration to the original condition, return of property, and the like.

(c) **Intoxication/On Drugs.** It is provided in article 1190 of the Civil Code that where a person with full capacity for performing civil acts causes damage to another person due to temporary loss of consciousness or loss of control as a result of intoxication or abuse of narcotic or psychotropic drugs, the person shall bear tort liability. Here, liability is imposed as a result of the fault of the person at issue. The notion is that a person with full capacity for civil conduct should foresee that drinking alcohol or abusively using narcotic or psychotropic drugs will very likely make it difficult to control his or her actions. Therefore, if a person still drives or undertakes other acts after drinking alcohol or abusing narcotic drugs or psychotropic drugs, causing damage to the personal rights and property rights of others, the person shall bear tort liability for what he has done.

In China, intoxication mostly concerns drunk driving. Driving under the influence (DUI) is punishable under Chinese traffic safety laws and may become a criminal offense if it causes injury.[164] Under Chinese DUI laws, a driver may be found guilty of a DUI if the consumption of alcohol was enough to impair his or her ability to safely operate a motor vehicle, or the consumption of alcohol results in a blood/breath alcohol concentration (BAC) above the legal limit. At present, the legal limit of BAC is 0.02. Note, however, that in China, DUI is divided into two categories: after-drink driving and drunk driving. After-drink driving occurs when an individual has a BAC ranging from 0.02 to 0.08. Drunk driving occurs when the driver's BAC exceeds 0.08.

To impose tort liability in a drug-related loss of consciousness or control, two conditions must be met. First, the drug used must be considered a narcotic or psychoactive drug that directly affects the central nervous system. The second condition is that the use of the drug must be abusive. Since abuse of narcotic or psychoactive drugs is illegal conduct in China, a person who loses consciousness or control due to abusive use of such drugs is deemed to have committed two wrongs: fault and illegality. Thus, the tortfeasor's conduct in the abusive drug use case is necessarily deemed more dangerous.[165]

II. FAIRNESS IN COMPENSATION. In the past, courts in intoxication cases often ordered the defendant to compensate the plaintiff to the extent of his/her financial ability.[166] The 2009 Torts Law made fairness a general rule for damage allocation in

[164] See article 91 of the 2003 Road Traffic Safety Law of China (as amended 2007), an English text is available at www.gov.cn/english/laws/2005-09/07content.29966.htm. See also article 133 of the 1979 Criminal Law of China (as amended 2009), available at www.dffg.com/faguixiazhai/xngfa/200311/200311102.13247-6.htm.

[165] See Shengming, *supra* note 10, at 166–167.

[166] See *id*. at 166.

intoxication cases. The Civil Code follows the same approach. Under article 1190 of the Civil Code, when a person with full civil conduct capacity causes harm to another person as a result of his/her temporary loss of consciousness or control of his/her conduct, if not at fault, the person should compensate the victim appropriately according to his/her economic condition.[167] The compensation so made is based on fairness.

In general, a capacity-impeded tortfeasor is liable for the injuries or damages he causes during his/her temporary loss of consciousness or control of conduct because of his/her fault. But in certain cases, a person's temporary loss of consciousness or control does not result from his/her fault. It then would be improper to hold the person liable for a fault-based tort. Under these circumstances, the fairness principle plays a twofold role. On the one hand, the victim will be compensated for the injury sustained in a case where the tortfeasor is found faultless. On the other hand, the compensation made to the victim is assessed in accordance with the tortfeasor's financial condition.

Note that the compensation based on fairness under article 1190 is complementary, which is considered "make-up."[168] In torts, the very purpose of compensation is to restore the victim to his/her pre-injury condition,[169] and therefore, the tortfeasor is normally required to pay for as much damage as the plaintiff has sustained, and in certain situations, punitive damages will be imposed as well. But under the "make-up" mechanism, payment is made merely on the basis of the financial ability of the tortfeasor, not necessarily the full amount of the damage. More importantly, as far as article 1190 is concerned, the "make-up" is applied not on the grounds of legal obligation but on the principle of fairness. In this situation, a court will usually follow a moral standard rather than a legal norm to determine the level of compensation.

c. Internet-Related Tortfeasors

As a new area in torts law, a tort committed on the internet differs from a conventional tort in that (a) an internet-related tort may not take place at any easily identified physical location, and (b) the identity of the tortfeasor is often invisible and thus hard to be ascertained. Although it is arguable that with respect to the liability basis, required elements, and allocation of damages, an internet-related tort may look similar to a conventional tort, the intangible nature of the internet environment changes the way a tort is to be determined and liability is to be specified. The borderless internet poses great challenges in many areas of law based strongly on territoriality, especially in torts. For this reason, the Civil Code categorizes the internet-related tort as a peculiar tort and provides a special set of rules.

[167] See the Civil Code, *supra* note 18, art. 1190.
[168] See Shengming, *supra* note 10, at 165.
[169] See Kionka, *supra* note 69, at 346.

I. INTERNET-RELATED TORTS. Torts committed on the internet may vary, including, among others, such cases as infringement of intellectual property rights, invasion of privacy, infringement of the right of reputation, as well as unfair competition. The online infringement of intellectual property rights mostly involves copyrights and trademarks. The right of privacy concerns the right to freedom from unwanted publicity or the right to seclusion. The right to reputation is a right of personality, which, as noted, is referred to as the right to obtain, enjoy, and maintain personal honor and reputation.

Unfair competition on the internet concerns abusive web conduct such as spamming, domain name grabbing, manipulation of search engines, and the misleading use of hyperlinks for the purposes of gaining unfair advantages against, or attacking, competitors. The common practices of unfair competition on the internet include, for example, offering products that are incompatible with competitors' products without reasonable grounds or authority, disturbing competitors' business operations, or blocking the information of competitors' products or services.

II. LIABILITY RULES. The 2009 Tort Liability Law provides special legal recourse under article 36 that may be sought for internet-related tort liabilities. The Civil Code not only reiterates the special recourse but also materializes it through more detailed rules. This special legal recourse contains one general rule and several subrules. The general rule is the liability rule. According to article 1194 of the Civil Code, which is the revised version of article 36 of the 2009 Tort Liability Law, an internet user or service provider who infringes upon the civil rights or interests of another person through the internet shall bear tort liability.[170] Unlike article 36 of the 2009 Tort Liability Law, article 1194 of the Civil Code contains an exception to the general liability rule, referring to the application of the law that provides otherwise.

Under article 1194, the general liability rule applies to both the internet user and the internet service provider (ISP). The civil rights or interests of a person infringed upon over the internet include, but are not limited to, the right of personality, property interests, and intellectual property rights. Infringement upon the right of personality covers such conduct as the unauthorized use of another person's name or portrait, dissemination of defamatory materials, and invasion of privacy by illegally hacking and downloading another person's personal information. Property interest infringement involves such conduct as compromising and stealing funds from another person's bank accounts. Damages to intellectual property rights mostly relate to the infringement of copyrights and trademarks.[171]

Internet service, as provided in article 1194, includes both internet technical support and internet content supply.[172] Technical support means the service made

[170] See the Civil Code, *supra* note 18, art. 1194.
[171] See Shengming, *supra* note 10, at 189.
[172] See *id.* at 189–190.

for internet access, cache memory, information storage space, search, or link, etc., while supply of the content is the service that makes information and materials available and accessible to internet users. Under the general rule of liability, tort liability will arise when the civil rights or interests of a person are harmed by the internet activity of either the internet user or the ISP.

The subrules include the notice rule, the rebuttal rule, and the knowledge rule. The notice rule operates as a warning to the ISP about the occurrence of infringement and requires certain action from the ISP. In accordance with article 1195 of the Civil Code, when an internet user commits a tort through internet services provided by an ISP, the right holder (victim) has the right to notify the ISP to take necessary measures such as deletion, blocking, or disconnection. Under article 1195, the notice shall contain preliminary evidence establishing the tort and true information of the right holder's identity.[173]

After receiving the notice, the ISP shall timely forward the notice to the relevant internet user and take necessary measures based on the tort and the type of service asserted in the preliminary evidence. A failure to take necessary measures in a timely manner will render the ISP jointly and severally liable with the internet user for the resulting aggravated damage. If, however, a right holder provides an erroneous notice that causes damage to the internet user or the ISP, the right holder shall bear tort liability, unless otherwise provided by the law.

Simply put, the article 1195 notice rule is essentially a process of "notifying" (by the victim) and "taking down" (by ISP). In China, the notice rule is viewed to have a double-facet function. First, it serves as a safe harbor to shelter the ISP from liability when the ISP has taken certain necessary measures at the request of the right holder. Second, it provides legal grounds for the right holder to hold the ISP jointly and severally liable if the ISP ignores the right holder's request. But the ISP's joint and several liability is limited to the additional harm that was caused by the ISP's failure to take any action after the notice.

The rebuttal rule is the device for the internet user to defend upon receiving the right holder's notice of infringement. Pursuant to article 1196 of the Civil Code, after receiving the notice, the internet user may submit a declaration of non-infringement to the ISP, which shall include the preliminary evidence of non-infringement and the information of the internet user's identity. Upon receipt of the declaration, the ISP shall forward it to the right holder with notice that the right holder may file a complaint with the relevant government agency or initiates a lawsuit in court. If a notice of the right holder's filing a complaint or initiating a lawsuit is not received within a reasonable period of time, the ISP must timely terminate the measures already taken.[174]

[173] See the Civil Code, *supra* note 18, art. 1195.

[174] See *id.*, art. 1196.

The knowledge rule applies when the ISP knows or ought to know that the internet user is using the ISP's service to commit infringement. According to article 1197 of the Civil Code, if the ISP has knowledge that an internet user is infringing upon a civil right or interest of another person through its internet services but fails to take the necessary measures, the ISP shall be jointly and severally liable with the internet user for the infringement.[175] Note that when the knowledge rule applies, the ISP bears joint and several liability and thus may be held liable for the entire damage caused to the victim, rather than the "additional harm" under the notice rule.

The Civil Code provides no standard for the determination of knowledge. In practice, however, courts have been following the SPC's 2020 Rules on Several Issues concerning the Application of Law in Civil Disputes concerning Infringement of Personal Rights and Interests Through the Use of Information Networks.[176] Under article 9 of the Rules, the factors for determining whether an ISP "knows" or "ought to know" include: (a) the ISP's use of manual or automatic methods to process the infringing information by way of recommending, ranking, selecting, editing, organizing, modifying, etc.; (b) the ISP's ability to manage information, the nature and method of services provided, and the possibility of infringement; (c) the type and obvious degree of infringement of personal rights and interests by the information in question; (d) the scale of social influence of the information or the number of views within a certain period of time; (e) the technical possibility of the ISP's taking measures to prevent infringement and the corresponding reasonable means taken; (f) the ISP's corresponding reasonable measures against repeated infringements by the same network user or the same infringing information; and (g) other factors related to the case.[177]

4. DEFENSES TO TORT LIABILITY

The defenses to tort liability in the Civil Code include general defenses and specific defenses. General defenses are the defenses provided in the General Provisions of the Civil Code, which, as discussed, include (1) *force majeure*, (2) justifiable defense, (3) response to emergency, (4) protection of others' rights and interests, and (5) voluntary rescue. Under the Civil Code, the general defenses apply to civil liability in general and to tort liability in particular. In addition, according to article 1178 of the Civil Code, if other laws provide otherwise on the circumstances under which tort liability will be exempted or reduced, such provisions shall be followed.[178]

[175] See *id.*, art. 1197.
[176] The SPC's Rules were issued in 2014 and amended in 2020, available at https://zhuanlan.zhihu.com/p/441239533.
[177] See *id.*, art. 9.
[178] See the Civil Code, *supra* note 18, art. 1178.

Specific defenses in the Civil Code to tort liability consist of (1) concurrent fault of the plaintiff, (2) the intentional conduct of the plaintiff, (3) conduct of a third party, (4) presumption of risk, and (5) self-help. These defenses are further divided into two major categories: reasonable grounds and external forces. The former refers to situations where the defendant's conduct can be justified, while the latter concerns causes unrelated to the tortious conduct – including the intentional conduct of the victim and the conduct of a third party. A successful defense will result in no liability, reduced liability, or liability exemption.

A. *Concurrent Fault of the Plaintiff*

Concurrent fault of the plaintiff is the circumstance where the plaintiff was also at fault in the occurrence of the injury caused by the tortious conduct of the defendant. The notion is that since the plaintiff's fault also contributes to the injury, it would be unfair to require the defendant to pay the entire amount of compensation. For that reason, article 1173 of the Civil Code provides that where the harmed person is at fault for the occurrence or aggravation of harm, the liability of the tortfeasor may be reduced.[179] In its nature, article 1173 operates as a provision for the reduction of the defendant's liability in a tort action.

The reduction is purposed to offset the defendant's liability with the concurrent fault of the plaintiff so that the defendant's liability will be reduced up to the level of the plaintiff's fault. In this context, article 1173 is also called the rule of fault offset.[180] The offset concept is similar to the comparative negligence doctrine used in other countries, but they differ in that comparative negligence is a defense to negligence liability, while the offset is premised on mutual fault, including both negligence and non-negligence.

Factors for the application of the fault-offset rule include (1) the fault of the plaintiff (victim), (2) lack of justifiable reason, and (3) causation between the fault and the harm caused. Note that in a concurrent fault case, the defendant bears the burden to prove that the plaintiff has done something wrong that contributes to the harm, and that the plaintiff's fault could not be justified. In the light of fault, the plaintiff's conduct could either be an act or an omission. In an omission situation, the defendant must prove that the plaintiff was under a duty to act but failed to do so.

In terms of compensation, the fault offset functions as damage allocation because to offset his/her fault, the plaintiff has to share the damages in proportion to his/her own fault. As a practical matter, however, there is a question about how to determine the allocation. The issue is whether the allocation shall be made on the basis of the degree of fault or the reason underlying the fault. In many cases, the courts take a mixed approach: to look at the cause first, and take the degree of fault as an additional factor.

[179] See *id.*, art. 1173.

[180] See Lixin, *supra* note 44, at 107.

Another question concerns the coverage of the fault-offset rule. The question is whether the fault-offset rule applies to fault liability only or if it may also apply to non-fault tort liability as well. A general holding is that the fault-offset rule as provided in the Civil Code primarily applies to fault liability, but it may also apply to non-fault cases under certain circumstances. But, unlike in the fault case, the application of the fault-offset rule in a non-fault case requires specific authorization by the law.[181]

B. *Intentional Conduct of the Plaintiff*

In a tort case, if the harm or injury to the plaintiff was caused by the plaintiff's intentional conduct, an issue then will be whether the defendant should remain liable. Article 1174 of the Civil Code explicitly provides that the actor shall not be liable for any harm that is caused intentionally by the victim.[182] There are also several specific provisions in the Civil Code that exempt the defendant from any tort liability. Under article 1238 of the Civil Code, for example, where a civil aircraft causes harm to a person, the operator of the civil aircraft shall bear tort liability unless it can be proven that the damage was intentionally caused by the person.[183]

The main theme of article 1174 is the plaintiff's intent when taking an action. Inferred from intentional tort, intent in article 1174 is understood to mean that the plaintiff knows that his/her conduct will cause harm to himself but still wants to see it happen, or leaves the occurrence of the harm alone. To "see it happen" is viewed as direct intent, while to "leave alone" is considered indirect intent. In both situations, the plaintiff is liable for his/her own harm and, as a result, the defendant is exempted from tort liability. Again, in applying article 1174, the defendant has the burden to prove that the harm is caused by the plaintiff's own intentional conduct.

Confusion, however, remains pertaining to the application of article 1174. One such confusion is its relationship with article 1173. It is believed that the plaintiff's fault that constitutes a ground for reduction of the defendant's tort liability under article 1173 could be an intentional wrong or negligence.[184] Confusion arises when the damage is related to the plaintiff's intentional conduct. The issue is how to differentiate article 1174 from article 1173 with regard to the defendant's liability, since article 1174 exempts the defendant from tort liability, while article 1173 is only to reduce the defendant's liability.

No distinction in this regard is made in the Civil Code. Some, however, argue that the application of article 1173 or article 1174 depends on whether the plaintiff's wrong is the sole cause of the damage.[185] More specifically, if the wrong that caused damage is associated with the defendant's fault, article 1173 applies and the defendant

[181] See SPC Leading Group, Torts, *supra* note 109, at 92–94.
[182] See the Civil Code, *supra* note 18, art. 1174.
[183] See *id.*, art. 1238.
[184] See Shengming, *supra* note 10, at 139–140. See also Lixin, *supra* note 44, at 111.
[185] See Shengming, *supra* note 10, at 141.

remains liable, but the defendant's liability may be reduced due to the conduct of the plaintiff; if, however, the plaintiff's intentional conduct was the sole cause of the damage, then article 1174 applies and the defendant's liability is extinguished.[186]

A difficult situation is a case where the plaintiff acts intentionally, causing damage, and the defendant is also found to have had a minor fault. Some suggest that article 1174 should apply in this case because the primary focus of article 1174 is the intentional conduct of the plaintiff. Therefore, the defendant's negligence, if not material, should not trigger the application of article 1173.[187] Others, however, insist that the application of article 1173 is based on a presumption that the plaintiff's intentional conduct was the sole cause of the damage.[188] If the harm was caused by the intentional conduct of the plaintiff, but there is sufficient evidence that the defendant's intentional or grossly negligent conduct also contributed to the harm, it is generally agreed that article 1174 applies.

Confusion also arises from the issue of whether the intentional conduct of the plaintiff under article 1174 could be interpreted to also include the plaintiff's gross negligence. A concern is that damages could be caused by the plaintiff's gross negligence, absent any fault of the defendant.[189] In China, intentional conduct is often divided into direct or willful conduct and indirect or wanton conduct.[190] Since the lines between wanton misconduct and gross negligence are difficult to articulate, many consider them equivalent to each other and thus view gross negligence as *quasi*-intentional conduct.[191]

Opponents insist that intentional conduct should not include negligence, gross or not. They argue that article 1174 should not cover the plaintiff's gross negligence because the Civil Code tends to treat negligence differently from intentional torts.[192] Under this argument, the plaintiff's gross negligence may only serve as a ground to mitigate the defendant's liability, not as a reason to exempt the defendant from liability.

C. *Act of a Third Party*

The tort liability of a defendant may also be exempted if the plaintiff's injury actually resulted from the conduct of a third party. According to article 1175 of the Civil Code, if the harm is caused by a third party, the third party shall assume tort liability.[193] It is generally understood in China that article 1175 refers to a third party's fault causing injury to the plaintiff, and the fault can be either intentional misconduct or negligence.[194] The defendant bears the burden of proving the third party's fault.

[186] See SPC Leading Group,Torts, *supra* note 109, at 101.
[187] See Lixin, *supra* note 44, at 118.
[188] See Shengming, *supra* note 10, at 141.
[189] See Lixin, *supra* note 44, at 117–118.
[190] See Shengming, *supra* note 10, at 140–141.
[191] See Liming, Textbook, *supra* note 25, at 223.
[192] See *id.* at 224.
[193] See the Civil Code, *supra* note 18, art. 1175.
[194] See Lixin, *supra* note 44, at 119.

To assert an article 1175 defense, the defendant must prove that (1) the harm was caused by the tortious conduct of a third party, (2) the third party's conduct was the sole cause of the plaintiff's harm, and (3) causation exists between the third party's conduct and the plaintiff's harm. Since article 1175 is centered on the third party's sole conduct, it becomes applicable only if the defendant is not a joint tortfeasor.

It is then clear that the assertion of a defense under article 1175 is restricted to cases in which the fault of the third party was the "but for" cause of the plaintiff's injury.[195] Therefore, if the third party was at fault for only part of the plaintiff's injury, the third party will be a joint tortfeasor, and the defendant will remain liable. In addition, there should be no special relationship or affiliation between the defendant and the third party. Otherwise, the defendant may be held vicariously liable.

Article 1175 holds a third party liable for injury caused by fault to the plaintiff. In both fault and presumption-of-fault situations, the defendant will assume no liability as long as it can be proven that the plaintiff's injury resulted exclusively from the fault of a third party. In a non-fault situation, however, the law provides the plaintiff with different compensation options based on the nature of the case. One option is to have the defendant pay first even if the injury was solely due to the third party's fault.[196] The other option is to allow the plaintiff to choose who will pay them first – the defendant or the third party.[197]

But in a third-party conduct case, the issue of whether the third party's conduct causing injury should be unpredictable and unforeseeable is left open. One argument is that since article 1175 applies to cases where the third party's fault is the only cause of the plaintiff's injury, the third party's conduct should be unpredictable and unforeseeable to the defendant. Thus, if the defendant could have foreseen the harmful third party's conduct, the defendant will also be deemed at fault.[198] Another argument focuses on causation between the plaintiff's injury and the third party's conduct. The underlying reason is that, since article 1175 is intended to determine whether the third party is fully liable so that the defendant can be discharged from liability, the foremost concern is what indeed caused the plaintiff's injury.[199]

D. *Assumption of Risks*

Assumption of risk is a common defense to tort liability in many other countries.[200] The 2009 Tort Liability Law did not specifically make assumption of risk a defense

[195] See *id.* at 120.

[196] This option applies to damage caused by an extraordinary incident such as a nuclear accident.

[197] An example of this is article 68 of the Tort Liability Law concerning damage as a result of environmental pollution. Another example is article 83, pertaining to injury caused by domestic animals. See the Tort Liability Law, *supra* note 17.

[198] See Lixin, *supra* note 44, at 120.

[199] See the SPC Leading Group,Torts, *supra* note 109, at 104–107; see also Liming, Textbook, *supra* note 25, at 276.

[200] In the United States, for example, presumption is a defense to negligence, and consent of the victim constitutes a defense to an intentional tort. See Kionka, *supra* note 69, at 131, 180.

to tort liability but contained a provision to that effect. Under article 76 of the Tort Liability Law, when harm is caused by entry into an area of ultrahazardous activities or an area where ultrahazardous materials are stored, if the managing person has taken safety measures and fulfilled the duty of warning, the person's liability may be mitigated, or the person may assume no liability.[201]

The lack of a clear provision on assumption of risk caused confusion in defining the intentional conduct of a plaintiff. One question necessarily raised was whether the intentional conduct of a plaintiff may be inferred from the plaintiff's assumption of risk.[202] The Civil Code takes a step forward, making presumption of risk a defense to tort liability. Under article 1176 of the Civil Code, when a person voluntarily participates in a recreational or sports activity with certain inherent risks and thus suffers damage due to another participant's act, the person may not request that the other participant bear tort liability unless the damage is caused by the other participant's intentional act or gross negligence.[203]

The assumption of risk in article 1176, however, has a narrow scope of application. On the one hand, article 1176 confines the assumption of risk defense to recreation- or sports-related activities. On the other hand, the assumption of risk may be asserted as a defense only by co-participants in the activities at issue. In addition, article 1176 does not govern the liability of the activity organizer but rather leaves it to cross-reference with other provisions of the Civil Code.[204]

To assert assumption of risk as a defense,[205] several conditions must be met. The conditions include, among others: (a) the activity a person participates in or undertakes has an uncertain risk, meaning the possibility of causing harm to the person taking the risk, (b) the person taking the risk has foresight or knowledge of the risk and the possible damage that could be caused, (c) the person is willing to take the chance or voluntarily takes the risk, and (d) the person's taking the risk is not motivated by a legal or moral obligation.

E. *Action of Self-help*

In civil remedies, relief can be either public or private. Public relief refers to the use of public power by state agencies to protect personal or property rights at the request of the right holder. Private relief involves the private efforts on which a party relies to protect certain rights and interests without assistance from state agencies. Private relief can be further divided into self-defense and self-help. Self-defense typically involves protecting oneself or others from wrongdoing. More specifically, it is an

[201] See the 2009 Tort Liability Law, *supra* note 17, art. 76.

[202] See Liming, Textbook, *supra* note 25, at 273–274.

[203] See the Civil Code, *supra* note 18, art. 1176.

[204] See *id*. The organizer's liability is governed by the provisions of articles 1198 through 1201 of the Civil Code.

[205] See the SPC Leading Group, Torts, *supra* note 109, at 116.

action taken to protect the country, public interests, the person, property, and other rights of oneself or others from ongoing harm or infringement.

In contrast, self-help is action taken mainly to restore one's rights after his or her rights have been violated. In the case of self-help, the right holder relies on his or her own efforts to seize or restrain the property of others, or take other corresponding measures, in order to preserve or restore his or her rights or interests after being infringed upon in situations so urgent that state assistance could not be sought in a timely manner.

In the modern legal system, self-help is a legally recognized alternative to judicial remedies. As permissible conduct undertaken by a private person without legal compulsion or the involvement of government, self-help is an effort to protect oneself from or remedy a legal wrong.[206] In the Civil Code, self-help is a newly provided statutory defense for a person to protect his/her legal rights and interests in an emergency situation. The 2009 Tort Liability Law did not make self-help a defense in tort actions due to concern about the unwanted consequences of "fighting violence with violence." The Civil Code for the first time recognizes self-help as a tort remedy.

Under article 1177 of the Civil Code, if a person's lawful rights and interests are infringed upon and irreparable harm may occur if no action is immediately taken due to an urgent situation, and absent immediately available protection from the government, the person may take reasonable measures such as seizing the property of the tortfeasor to the extent necessary for protecting against the infringement.[207]

While allowing self-help, the Civil Code also imposes certain limitations on its exercise. First, when taking an action of self-help, the person shall immediately thereafter request that the relevant state agency handle the situation. Second, the measures taken in self-help must be appropriate to the extent of the possible damages to be suffered. If, however, the self-help measures are improperly taken by a person so that damage is caused to another person, the person shall bear tort liability.[208] In addition, it is required that the rights and interests sought by the action of self-help be those that can be restored or enforced in nature.

For the purposes of article 1177, in order to avoid incurring tort liability for an exercise of self-help, as explained by the SPC, the following requirements must be met. First, there exists ongoing illegal harm. Self-help action is needed only if an infringement causing harm has occurred. No relief will be granted without harm. Second, the self-help action is purposed to protect one's own legitimate rights and interests. Unlike justifiable defenses or responses to emergencies, self-help does not apply to an action taken to protect others' rights and interests. Third, the situation is

[206] See, in general, Douglas Brandon, et al., *Self-Help: Extrajudicial Rights, Privileges and Remedies in Contemporary American Society*, 37 Vand. L. Rev. 845 (1984).

[207] See the Civil Code, *supra* note 18, art. 1177.

[208] See *id.*

so urgent that time does not permit requesting assistance from state agencies. If certain action is not taken for self-help, irreparable harm may be caused thereby. Fourth, the measures undertaken may not exceed the limit necessary for protection. Fifth, the conduct of self-help must be legally permissible and in compliance with the public order and good morals.[209]

F. *Other Defenses*

Defenses available under other provisions may also be asserted in a torts action if applicable. Included in those provisions are the defenses as provided in the General Provisions of the Civil Code, referring to, as noted, *force majeure*, justifiable defense, response to emergency, protection of others' rights and interests, and voluntary rescue. Another defense, for example, is fair use, which applies to the claim on infringement of the right of publicity. Among those defenses, *force majeure*, self-defense, and response to emergency are worth further illustration.

a. Force Majeure

As discussed, the Civil Code recognizes *force majeure* as a statutory defense against civil liabilities, including torts. In essence, *force majeure* refers to an act of nature that is not within the foresight or control of the parties involved in a civil relationship. Under article 180 of the Civil Code, if the harm to another person is caused by an event of *force majeure*, the tortfeasor shall not be liable, except as otherwise provided for by law.[210] The idea is that, when a natural force or disaster causes harm, no tort liability shall be imposed because not only was the defendant not at fault but there was also no causation between the defendant's conduct and the harm. But in order for *force majeure* to be properly claimed as a defense, it is critical that the defendant does not play any role in causing or aggravating the plaintiff's harm.[211]

Based on article 153 of the 1986 General Principles of Civil Law, the Civil Code defines *force majeure* as an objective circumstance or event that is unforeseeable, unavoidable, and insurmountable.[212] Under this definition, *force majeure* shall be viewed from both external and internal perspectives. Externally, *force majeure* is considered an occurrence that is totally beyond the control of any human being. Internally, determination of *force majeure* is based on the ability and capacity of a reasonable person to foresee the event. Therefore, in order to gauge *force majeure*, "unforeseeable" means a lack of ability or capacity to foresee on the basis of the best available technical means, and "unavoidable and insurmountable" suggests an

[209] See the SPC Leading Group, Torts, *supra* note 109, at 127–128.
[210] See the Civil Code, *supra* note 18, art. 180.
[211] See Liming, Textbook, *supra* note 25, at 282. See also Lixin, *supra* note 9, at 124.
[212] See the Civil Code, *supra* note 18, art. 189. See also the 1986 General Principles of the Civil Law, *supra* note 15, art. 153.

occurrence that cannot be prevented or avoided after an exhaustion of all efforts and measures.

As in the 1986 General Principles of Civil Law, the definition of *force majeure* in the Civil Code remains quite vague. It has long been an issue whether such incidents as war, riots, and strikes may be construed as unforeseeable and insurmountable circumstances to assert *force majeure* as a defense.[213] Some believe that, because war, riots, and strikes are social forces beyond the control of the parties, they should fall within *force majeure*.[214] Others, however, regard *force majeure* as an event pertaining only to natural forces, not social forces. This rationale rests on the doubt that a social force is unforeseeable and insurmountable.[215]

A more controversial issue is whether the defendant may assert an order or action of the government as a *force majeure* defense. Some argue that, given the situation of non-transparency in exercising government authority or power in China, it is quite common that certain governmental actions or orders are indeed unforeseeable, unavoidable, and insurmountable to the defendant. Thus, under these circumstances, the defendant should be allowed to apply *force majeure* as a defense in certain cases that involve intervening government authority or power.[216] Many, however, seem to be cautiously reluctant to broaden the coverage of *force majeure* to include governmental actions.[217]

b. Self-Defense

Self-defense can be asserted as a defense to a tort liability under the Civil Code. As a criminal law concept, self-defense is used analogically in civil cases as a justifiable defense to civil liabilities. The first provision of self-defense in China was article 128 of the 1986 General Principles of Civil Law. Under article 128, a person who causes harm in exercising a justifiable defense shall not bear civil liability; however, if the act of justifiable defense exceeds the limits of necessity and causes undue harm, the actor shall assume an appropriate amount of civil liability.

In accordance with article 30 of the 2009 Tort Liability Law, if the harm is caused by self-defense, no liability should be imposed. But if the act of self-defense exceeds necessary limits and causes any undue harm, the person exercising self-defense shall assume proper liability.[218] The Civil Code contains a similar provision. As noted, under article 181 of the Civil Code, no civil liability shall be assumed for harm caused out of self-defense. If, however, the exercise of self-defense exceeds the

[213] See Liming, Textbook, *supra* note 25, at 282.
[214] See *id.* at 282.
[215] See Shengming, *supra* note 10, at 148.
[216] See *id.*
[217] See *id.*
[218] See the Tort Liability Law, *supra* note 17, art. 30.

necessary limit and causes undue harm, the self-defender shall bear appropriate civil liability.[219]

But neither the Civil Code nor previous tort legislation specifies the conditions under which self-defense may be exercised. As a practical matter, it is generally held in China that self-defense may only be taken under the following conditions: (1) occurrence of unlawful harm, (2) in the presence of harm, (3) harm is unlawfully inflicted to the personal or property interests of the self-defender or another person, (4) defense that presupposes infliction of harm, (5) defense that is made against the aggressor himself, (6) defense that is necessary to repel an actual or imminent threat of harm, or (7) the level of defense corresponds to the degree of harm.[220]

As noted, self-defense in civil cases is generally construed in China as a protective measure taken by a defender against ongoing unlawful conduct facing the defender to prevent the harm to personal or other rights of the defender or another person.[221] In this context, self-defense applies only to ongoing unlawful conduct causing harm. Also, given the required condition, self-defense is rebuttable. A failure to meet any of the conditions would make the defense unjustifiable, for which civil liability may be sought.

A question that often arises is whether a defender remains privileged when the defender mistakes or misjudges the threat of harm or real danger, causing harm to the alleged aggressor. Chinese tort law literature rarely discusses the defendant's reasonable belief with respect to the required elements for self-defense. Nevertheless, one suggestion is that a mistake or misjudgment of the threat of harm or real danger should be deemed as fault, to which general tort liability would apply.[222]

c. Response to Emergency

Response to emergency as a defense in a tort action is a matter of necessity. In general, necessity arises when there is no other option but to cause injury or harm to a person or the property of another in order to remove an actual or imminent danger threatening the person or property of the defender, or another person.[223] Unlike self-defense, in the case of necessity, the threatened harm may come from some force of nature, or some other independent cause not connected with the victim.[224] In other words, an action of necessity may be taken to protect both private and public interests.

In many countries, necessity is deemed a privilege by which the defender may inflict harm to the other's person or property without being held liable in torts. This

[219] See the Civil Code, *supra* note 18, art. 181.
[220] See Liming, Studies on Torts, *supra* note 21, at 447–448.
[221] See Liming, Textbook, *supra* note 25, at 284.
[222] See *id.* at 287.
[223] See Limpens et al., *supra* note 12, at 83.
[224] See Keeton et al., *supra* note 5, at 145.

privilege is also recognized under certain conditions in China. According to article 182 of the Civil Code, when harm is caused by conduct taken out of necessity, the person causing the occurrence of danger shall be liable. If the danger is the result of a natural cause, the person causing harm under necessity shall not be liable or shall make proper compensation.[225] Article 182 focuses on two kinds of people: (1) the person who causes the danger that calls for the action of necessity, and (2) the person who takes action out of necessity.

Article 182 of the Civil Code is taken from article 31 of the Tort Liability Law. There are two major issues related to article 182. The first issue involves circumstances under which the necessity defense will be justified. In Chinese legislation, it remains an open issue. Some suggest that necessity may be asserted as a valid defense to tort liability under the following circumstances: (1) a legitimate interest facing imminent threat of harm, (2) absence of any other alternative option or course of action, and (3) reasonableness of the action taken.[226]

The second issue concerns compensation for the harm caused by the act of necessity. The provision of article 182 of the Civil Code is actually a short version of article 129 of the 1986 General Principles of Civil Law. Under article 129, where damages are caused by an action taken to avoid danger in an emergency, the person who caused the danger shall bear civil liability; where the danger was due to natural causes, the person who took action to avoid the danger shall assume no civil liability or shall bear appropriate civil liability. If the action taken to avoid the danger was improper or exceeded the necessary limits, causing unnecessary loss, the person who took the action shall bear appropriate civil liability.[227]

Based on article 129 of the 1986 General Principles of Civil Law, necessity involves danger not only from forces of nature but also from other causes. It is also clear that the necessity defense does not entirely release the defender's liability, even if the danger is caused by an act of nature. The purpose is to ensure fair compensation for the losses incurred by the innocent person who sacrificed his/her interest for a good reason.[228] Moreover, under article 182 of the Civil Code, if improper measures of necessity are taken or an action of necessity exceeds certain limits, causing undue harm, the defender shall bear proper liability.[229] Normally, when the damages do not appear to be alleviated after a necessity action is taken, or the damages caused by the necessity action are more severe than the interests to be protected, the act of necessity would be considered excessive.

Note that in China, no emphasis is ever made on the clean hands of the plaintiff with respect to the danger for which the necessity measure is taken. In the United

225 See the Civil Code, *supra* note 18, art. 182.

226 See Liming, Studies on Torts, *supra* note 21, at 452–453; see also Shengming, *supra* note 10, at 155.

227 See the 1986 General Principles of the Civil Law, *supra* note 15, art. 129.

228 See Liming, Textbook, *supra* note 25, at 290–291.

229 See the Civil Code, *supra* note 18, art. 182.

States, for example, it is required that necessity arises from some independent cause not connected with the plaintiff.[230] The decisive factor of necessity in China, however, is whether there is a need for protection of a public interest or the interest of the defendant or another person. Nevertheless, under article 182 of the Civil Code, the person who caused the danger that necessitated the emergent action must pay for the associated damages.

5. DAMAGES AND COMPENSATION

The goal of tort compensation is to remedy damages. In this sense, the scheme of damages is the core of the tort system. Like the 2009 Tort Liability Law, the Civil Code does not use the jargon of pecuniary and non-pecuniary damages or general and special damages to address compensation. Instead, the Civil Code divides damages into four categories: personal damages, property damages, mental damages, and punitive damages. For each of these damages, the Civil Code contains the rules by which the compensation is to be made. All the compensation rules are premised on three fundamental ideas.

First, compensation must be made for damages. The very basic concept held in China is that there would be no compensation without damages. For compensation to be made, damages must occur and should be measurable. Therefore, no speculative damage may be included in the compensation. But the tort damage is not necessarily limited to bodily and property damages. Mental damages are also compensable under certain circumstances.

Second, the damage remedy is mainly compensatory damages. The purpose of tort damages is to restore the plaintiff to his/her pre-injury condition, in money or in kind. Hence, when sustaining damages, the plaintiff should be compensated for his/her economic loss and his/her non-economic damage as well. Generally, the amount of compensation to which the plaintiff is entitled should be the difference between his/her then-unharmed interests and his/her now harmed interests. Although the plaintiff may make damage claims as he wishes, it is the duty of the court to determine the ultimate amount based on the facts of the harm caused.

Third, all damages must be fully compensated. A general holding is that compensation for tort damages should be adequate. Thus, the requirement for full compensation not only addresses the adequacy of the compensation but also stresses the notion of actual harm; that is, the plaintiff who sues in tort for the harm he suffered is entitled, as a matter of law, to the recovery of all the damages from that harm. But, since the claim for damages is a disposable right, the plaintiff may, at his/her choice, accept a lesser amount of damages or even exempt the defendant's liability for property damages.

[230] See Kionka, *supra* note 69 at 194.

A. *Personal Damages*

Personal damages are the most contested subject of torts in China because opinions are so divided over who is entitled to compensation and how much they are entitled to. As commonly understood in the country, personal damages are the damages caused by an infringement of the right or interests of the life or health of another person, resulting in bodily injury, disability, or death.[231] It is generally agreed that personal damages not only include physical pain, impairment, and loss of life but also cover economic loss and mental distress. But compensation for the damages varies substantially pertaining to the particular personal damage, especially in cases where disability or death is involved.

a. General Standards of Compensation

As provided in article 1179 of the Civil Code, in a tort causing personal injury to another person, the tortfeasor shall compensate the victim for the reasonable costs and expenses for treatment and rehabilitation, including medical, nursing, transportation, and nutrition expenses, as well as food allowances during hospitalization and lost wages. Article 1179 further provides that if the victim suffers any disability, compensation shall also include the costs of living assistance equipment and disability indemnity. If the injury results in the death of the victim, the tortfeasor shall, in addition, pay for funeral expenses and death compensation.[232]

Attempting to scale in equilibrium, article 1179 adopts a three-level format of compensation for personal damages on the basis of the seriousness of the damage: compensation for personal damages in general, disabilities, and death. Under the three-level format, the compensation at the first level seems less controversial because most of the costs at this level are measurable. The issue that may arise at the first level is whether the costs are reasonable. Normally, when determining reasonableness, the court will rely on the costs or expenses actually incurred. Whoever challenges the reasonableness of costs or the need for certain treatment bears the burden of proof.[233]

In 2003, the SPC issued a Judicial Interpretation on Adjudication of Cases Involving Personal Injury Damages (Personal Injury Damages Interpretation).[234] According to the SPC, in order to compensate for personal damages, in addition to the costs for medical treatment expenses, nurse fees, travel expenses, and lost

[231] See Shengming, *supra* note 10, at 8.

[232] See the Civil Code, *supra* note 18, art. 1179.

[233] See Shengming, *supra* note 10, at 85.

[234] See the SPC, *The Interpretation on the Adjudication of Cases Involving Personal Injury Damages*, 2003 (amended 2022), available at http://news.sina.com.cn/c/2003-12-29/15361453464s.shtml. The Interpretation was amended in 2022 with no substantial changes. The amended Interpretation is available at https://law.pkulaw.com/chinalaw/5116216.html.

wages, the tortfeasor is also liable for such costs as (a) inpatient meal allowance, (b) nutrition fee, and (c) lodging. The meal allowance is to cover the costs exceeding the normal expenses for meals at home, while the nutrition fee is the cost for the nutriments needed for the body to recover from the injury. Lodging in general means the hotel cost associated with the medical treatment. The SPC's interpretation now remains applicable for damage calculation.

b. Compensation for Disability

Compensation at the level of disability encounters certain difficulties. The cost for disability life assistance equipment may only be a matter of reasonableness, but disability indemnity is considerably knotty. First, it is still highly disputable as to what constitutes a disability. According to article 2 of the 1990 Law on the Protection of Disabled Persons (as amended 2008), a disabled person is defined as one who suffers from abnormalities or loss of a certain organ or function, psychologically or physiologically, or in anatomical structure, and who has lost wholly or in part the ability to engage in activities in a normal way. It is further provided that disabled persons include those with visual, hearing, speech, or physical disabilities, mental retardation, mental disorder, multiple disabilities, and/or other disabilities.[235] But how to determine the disability remains unclear.

Second, the range of disability indemnity is subject to debate. In China, the indemnity for disability is in general understood to mean the compensation for the total or partial loss of working ability caused by harm to the body or health of a person. The problem, however, is what "disability" may implicate in specific cases. For example, would "working ability" equally apply to those who do not have a job or any income at all? Another example involves the dependents of the victim. The issue is whether the indemnity should also cover the financial need to support these dependents.

Third, it remains questionable what the appropriate standard would be for the determination of the amount of disability indemnity. Many are wondering if there even should be a standard. Some tend to treat the disability indemnity as a compensation for mental suffering. They argue that there is no need to set any standard, and the actual amount of the indemnity shall be decided by the court on an individual case-by-case basis. Others deem the disability indemnity as the payment necessary to make up for the loss of anticipated future income and believe that there should be a standard for the courts to follow.[236] In the middle is the view that

[235] See the Law of the People's Republic of China on the Protection of Disabled Persons, art. 2., adopted by the Standing Committee of the NPC in 2008, available at http://english.cdpf.org.cn/2016-03/01/c_914835.htm.

[236] See Shengming, *supra* note 10, at 87.

the disability indemnity is compensation for both the loss of future income and for mental suffering.

But all those views struggle with how to determine the appropriate amount of compensation. There are three approaches. The first approach is the loss of income. Under this approach, the disability indemnity should be equal to the loss of income between the pre-disability and post-disability of the victim. The second approach is termed as the loss of living resource, which advocates for a living allowance to be included in the compensation in order to help maintain the living standard of the victim. The third approach is the "loss of ability to work." Under this approach, the indemnity aims to compensate the loss of the ability to work because when the plaintiff is disabled, hisher ability to work is impaired. Thus, compensation is assessed on the degree of the impairment that the plaintiff has suffered, regardless of his/her loss of future income.

In its 2003 Personal Injury Damages Interpretation, the SPC introduced a formula for the disability indemnity assessment. According to the SPC, disability indemnity shall be calculated based on the victim's degree of incapacity to work or disability level in reference to the per capita disposable income of urban residents or the per capita net income of rural residents in the previous year where the court with which the lawsuit is filed is located for a period of twenty years from the date of disability determination.[237]

However, under the SPC formula, for those over sixty years old, the calculation period will be reduced by one year for every year exceeding sixty, and for those over seventy-five years old, the period will be five years in total. In addition, if the victim becomes disabled due to injury but his/her actual income does not decrease, or if the disability level is relatively minor but causes occupational hindrance that seriously affects his/her employment, the amount of disability indemnity may be adjusted accordingly. Since the 2009 Tort Liability Law and 2020 Civil Code contain no provision on how disability indemnity should be determined, courts in their practice continue to follow the SPC's formula.[238]

c. Death Compensation

The third-level compensation for the victim's death is perhaps the most debated issue. All disputes in this regard are about compensation for death damages. Two fundamental issues are at the center of debates. The first issue is who is supposed to be compensated, the deceased or his/her surviving family members? This issue involves the nature of death damages. One argument is that since death is a fatal injury to the deceased, damages should be made to the deceased, and then become

[237] See the SPC, 2003 Interpretation, *supra* note 88. In the 2022 amended Interpretation, the "the per capita net income of rural residents in the previous year" was deleted.

[238] See the SPC Leading Group, Torts, *supra* note 109, at 149.

inheritance for the deceased's survivors. The other argument holds that the death of the deceased is in fact damage to the survivors because the civil status of the deceased does not survive the death, and therefore the compensation can only be made to the survivors.[239]

The Civil Code does not address the nature of death damages. Nevertheless, it grants the close relatives of the deceased the right to make a claim against the tortfeasor. According to article 1181, if a tort causes the victim's death, the victim's close relatives are entitled to require the tortfeasor assume tort liability. Article 1181 also provides that in the case of the victim's death, those who have paid for the victim's medical treatment, funeral services, and other reasonable expenses have the right to demand reimbursement from the tortfeasor.[240] In many cases, payment for the victim's medical expenses and funeral services was made first by someone close to the victim. It is then reasonable to require that the payment be reimbursed by the tortfeasor.

In certain cases, a tort victim is not a natural person. A term used in the Civil Code for a non-natural person is "organization," referring to a legal person, or other organization or entity. The Civil Law has a special rule that applies to a unit in case of the unit's structural change. Under article 1181 of the Civil Code, if the unit tort victim is split or merged, the new unit that succeeds the rights of the victim is entitled to require the tortfeasor assume tort liability.[241] Since a merger or split may result in the dissolution of the civil status of such entity, the compensation for tort damages must be claimed by the succeeding entity because the non-existing entity has no legal standing to make any claim.

The second issue is how to determine the amount of death damages. For many years, death damages in tort have been calculated under the formula adopted by the SPC in its 2003 Personal Injury Damages Interpretation. Under that formula, the calculation for death damages in a personal injury case was based on the previous year's average annual disposable income per capita in the city or the previous year's average net income per capita in the countryside in the locale of the forum. That figure is then multiplied by 20 (years). The same as in disability indemnity, in calculating the amount of death damages, if the deceased was over 60 years old, for each year exceeding 60 years, one year will be subtracted from the maximum of 20 years. If the deceased was over 75 years of age, the multiplier will be reduced to 5 (years).[242]

The SPC formula has faced intense criticism ever since its adoption. Because the formula bases death damages on the residence location and age of the deceased, it is denounced as unjust based on the concern that it would result in "the same life but

[239] See Xinbao, *supra* note 3, at 386.
[240] See the Civil Code, *supra* note 18, art. 1181.
[241] See *id.*
[242] See SPC, *Personal Injury Damages Interpretation*, *supra* note 234, art. 29 (China).

different prices."[243] During the drafting of the 2009 Tort LiabilityLaw and the Civil Code, some suggested replacing the SPC's formula with a detailed provision for death damages.[244] But due to an inability to reach any consensus, this issue is ultimately left open, which makes the determination of death damages highly uncertain.

The Civil Code, like the Torts Law, does, however, clarify a compensation standard for the case where tortious conduct causes multiple deaths. Under article 1180 of the Civil Code, if the same tort causes the deaths of several persons, the same amount of death damages may be applied to each of the deaths.[245] The rationale of article 1180 is that no matter what standard is to be used to determine the death damages, to be fair, the amount of the damages received by the close relatives of each deceased should be the same.

B. *Property Damages*

Compensation for property damages in torts mainly involves the value of the property that has been damaged. Under the Civil Code, there are two kinds of property damages: general property damages and personal right-related property damages. General property damages are damages to the property only, including movables (personal property) and immovables (real property). Personal right-related property damages are the economic losses associated with the infringement upon the personal rights and interests. An example is the loss of commercial income as a result of damage to the plaintiff's reputation.

a. Remedies

Property damage may be compensated either by physical restoration of the damaged property or by monetary compensation. As noted, the major forms of civil liability are provided in article 179 of the Civil Code, including return of property and restitution. Here the focus is on monetary compensation. As a general principle, monetary compensation is aimed at, or limited to, furnishing the victim with a monetary equivalent of the property loss.[246] The primary issue concerning monetary compensation is how to determine the proper monetary amount for the damaged property.

For general property damages, article 1184 of the Civil Code requires that in case of harm inflicted on another person's property, the amount of loss shall be calculated according to the market price at the time the damage occurs or by other

[243] See Xinbao, *supra* note 3, at 383.
[244] See Shengming, *supra* note 10, at 89–91.
[245] See the Civil Code, *supra* note 18, art. 1180.
[246] See *id.*, art. 179.

reasonable methods.[247] Thus, the market price is the general means for monetary compensation, and the point of time for it is the time of loss or the time of damage. "Other means" refers to situations where no market price is available or in the circumstance when the market price is not fair or inapplicable given the victim's unique condition. For example, if the damage is the loss of a precious family album. In the former situation, damages may be assessed by an expert's appraisal or evaluation. In the latter situation, the court may determine the amount on the basis of fairness.[248]

As a practical matter, the "other means" mainly include the statutory standard, the non-statutory standard, and appraisal. The statutory standard is the compensation standard provided in the law for certain torts. For instance, under article 56 of the Trademark Law of China (as amended 2001), where it is difficult to determine the profit that the infringer has earned, the People's Court shall impose an amount of damages of no more than RMB 500,000 according to the circumstances of the infringement. The non-statutory standard is the standard of actual loss. It applies when the damages the plaintiff has suffered are difficult to assess under a market price. The appraisal is relevant in the situation where the value of a property has no applicable market price due to its uniqueness.

It is commonly held that property damages comprise damages to both tangible and intangible property. Tangible property refers to property that has a physical form. Note, however, that since no individual may own a piece of land in China, interference with the individual right over land has nothing to do with the ownership of the land but the right to the use of the land. Intangible property primarily consists of intellectual property rights.[249] Because the laws governing intellectual property rights have special provisions for damages, courts normally look for these provisions when making a judgment.[250] In addition, the infringement of equity rights or the interests of another person will also give rise to tort liability for property damages.

One problem with property damages is whether the damages should include indirect damages, meaning the loss of future interest. Scholars disagree regarding what exactly the future interest is and how to compensate the future interest. To define the future interest, some suggest that it should be limited to what is reasonably predictable and expected. Others, however, assert that this limitation is unnecessary because as soon as the future interest is retainable, it should all be compensated.[251] With regard to future interest compensation, one opinion supports complete compensation, while the other stands for reasonable compensation.[252]

[247] See the Civil Code, *supra* note 18, art. 1184.
[248] See Liming, Textbook, *supra* note 25, at 334.
[249] See Lixin, *supra* note 44, at 83.
[250] See Shengming, *supra* note 10, at 99–101.
[251] See *id.* at 97–98.
[252] See Lixin, *supra* note 44, at 86.

b. Compensation Rules

Property damages related to personal rights are dealt with differently from general property damages under the Civil Code. There are two rules that govern such damage compensation. The first rule is the rule of determination. According to article 1182 of the Civil Code, if an infringement upon the personal rights and interests of a person causes property damage, compensation shall be determined on the basis of the damage suffered by the infringed person or the interests gained by the tortfeasor.[253] The Civil Code changes the 2009 Tort Liability Law, where the compensation determination was primarily based on the victim's actual loss, but if the victim's loss was hard to ascertain, compensation would then be determined according to the benefit the tortfeasor received from his/her tortious conduct.[254]

The second rule is the rule of adjudication. Under article 1182, if it is difficult to determine the actual damage suffered by the victim and the interests gained by the tortfeasor, and the victim cannot reach an agreement with the tortfeasor on the amount of compensation, the victim may file a lawsuit with a court. The court shall then determine the amount of compensation under the circumstances of the case. The adjudication rule provides the victim with the last resort for a determination of compensation. This rule may also apply to a case where the defendant committed a tort that caused damage to the plaintiff but received no benefit from it.

The rule of adjudication in its application has three implications. First, in the situation where the tortfeasor did not benefit from his/her tortious conduct or the benefit is hard to calculate, the parties may consult with each other to negotiate the amount of compensation. Second, a tort victim is entitled to the right to claim compensation, and the tortfeasor cannot escape liability for damages on the grounds of not receiving any benefit or difficulty in determining the benefit. Third, the ultimate amount of compensation is to be determined by the court. In making the determination, the court will consider such factors as the seriousness of the tortfeasor's fault, the actual conduct committed, the way the conduct was committed, the consequences of the tortious conduct, and the impacts as well.[255]

Also, as discussed, under article 183 of the Civil Code, when a person sustains harm while preventing or stopping an infringement upon the right or interest of another person, the tortfeasor bears liability for the harm.[256] This is the rule that intends to protect and encourage Good Samaritan activity.[257] With regard to the payment of compensation, the Civil Code allows the parties to negotiate payment methods. Pursuant to article 1187 of the Civil Code, if the negotiation fails, the compensation shall be paid in a lump sum. However, if it is difficult to make a lump

[253] See the Civil Code, *supra* note 18, art. 1182.
[254] See the Tort Liability Law, *supra* note 17, art. 20.
[255] See Shengming, *supra* note 10, at 104.
[256] See the Civil Code, *supra* note 18, art. 1187.
[257] See Shengming, *supra* note 10, at 104.

sum payment, the payment may be made in installments, but the victim has the right to request that proper security for the payment be provided.[258] In terms of compensation, article 1187 equally applies to mental damages.

C. *Mental Damages*

Compensation for mental damages in China is new in law, though it has been recognized in judicial practice for many years. It was the 2009 Tort Liability Law that, for the first time in Chinese legislation, made mental damages a major form of damages in tort. The Civil Code reinforces the Torts Law provision with a change from "the victim may" to "the victim has the right to." Under article 1183 of the Civil Code, when the harm inflicted upon the personal rights or interests of a natural person causes serious mental suffering, the tort victim has the right to request compensation for mental damages.[259]

a. Basic Requirements

Article 1183 further provides that if, due to a tortfeasor's intentional or grossly negligent act, a specific subject that has personal significance to a natural person is harmed, which causes serious mental distress to the person, the person has the right to request compensation for pain and suffering. Under article 1183, a claim for mental damages shall meet three requirements: (a) there is mental suffering, (b) the mental suffering results from the harm to a personal right or interest, and (c) the mental suffering is serious. An implication from article 1183 is that mental damages include both damages in conjunction with actual physical harm and damages for emotional distress without physical contact.

But article 1183 only provides a general rule for a mental damages claim. It remains unclear what may be included in the mental damages or what the scope of mental damage should be.[260] In 2001, the SPC issued the Explanations to Several Questions Concerning the Determination of the Liabilities for Compensating Mental Damages Caused by the Torts, where the SPC provided a list of cases in which mental damages might be claimed.[261] In 2020, the SPC revised its

[258] See the Civil Code, *supra* note 18, art. 1187.

[259] See *id.*, art. 1183. Note that the Civil Code replaces the term "another person" in the Torts Law with "natural person" pertaining to personality rights and interests. Since "another person" does not necessarily mean "natural person," scholars are divided into two groups. One group opposes an entity's standing for mental damage claims since the entity has no "feelings." The other group asserts that an entity may suffer mental distress because the "feelings" of the managerial team of the entity are actually the feelings of the entity. To avoid confusion, the Civil Code narrows it down to natural persons.

[260] A question, for example, is whether the right to personality should be included as well. See Lixin, *supra* note 44, at 90.

[261] See the SPC, *Explanations to Several Questions Concerning the Determination of the Liabilities for Compensating Mental Damages Caused by the Torts*, issued on February 26,

2001 Explanations with a simplified list, aiming to refine the scope of mental damages.[262]

Under the SPC's Explanations (as revised 2020), mental damages may be claimed in the following cases: (a) encroachment of personal rights and interests or specific things bearing personal significance; (b) illegal removal of a ward from custody, resulting in serious damage to the parent–child relationship or the relationship between close relatives; and (c) infringement of a deceased's name, portrait, reputation, honor, privacy, body, or remains.[263] Also, according to the SPC, mental damages do not apply to a claim filed by a legal person or unincorporated organization for infringement of the right to reputation, honor, or name.[264]

b. Outstanding Issues

An issue that arises is whether compensation for mental damages is to be awarded to the tort victim only, or may also be made to a third party. In other words, the issue is whether a family member of the tort victim may claim mental damages, or more precisely, whether a husband who loses his wife, or vice versa, as a result of a tort, may make a claim against the tortfeasor for mental damages. Under article 1183 and the SPC's Explanations (as revised 2020), those who may file a claim for mental damages include the tort victim, close relatives of the tort victim, and the guardian of a ward. But what remains unclear is the bystander situation and whether a bystander who suffers a so-called nervous shock from witnessing serious physical injury to a family member may be actionable for mental damages.[265]

2001. (According to the SPC, compensation for mental damages may be claimed in the following cases: (a) infringement of the right to life, health, body, name, portrait, reputation, honor, dignity, or personal freedom; invasion of the privacy or other personality interest of another person in violation of public policy or social morals; (b) illegal separation of a ward from guardianship or custody that results in serious damage to the relationship between parents and children or among close relatives; (c) emotional distress of the deceased's close relatives inflicted by the infringement of the deceased's name, portrait, reputation, or honor through conduct such as humiliation, slander, disparagement, defamation, or other means in violation of public interests or social morals, or by the invasion of the decedent's privacy through illegal disclosure of the deceased's privacy, or use of the deceased's privacy or other means, or by the intrusion upon the deceased's body or remains by illegal use or damage of such body or remains, or any other means; (d) permanent loss of or damage to a unique memento of personally symbolic significance as a result of tortious conduct). A full text of the SPC's Explanations is available at www.npc.gov.cn/zgrdw/huiyi/lfzt/qqzrfca/2008-12/21/content_1462862.htm.

[262] See the SPC, *Explanations to Several Questions Concerning the Determination of the Liabilities for Compensating Mental Damages Caused by the Torts*, revised on December 3, 2020, available at http://gongbao.court.gov.cn/Details/87b471350704bf50ce1f5e0f9a0e21.html?eqid=b8754b0b000153a700000006647fec70.

[263] See *id.*, arts. 1–3.

[264] See *id.*, art. 4.

[265] See Liming, Textbook, *supra* note 25, at 347; see also Lixin, *supra* note 44, at 91.

Another issue is the seriousness of mental suffering or distress. As noted, article 1183 requires a showing of serious mental suffering in order to claim mental damages. But the Civil Code and judicial interpretations contain no guidance on this matter. One scholarly suggestion is the "social tolerance" theory, under which the seriousness depends on whether the suffering or distress exceeds the minimum levels of societal tolerance.[266] Some propose an exclusion method, requiring that serious mental suffering not extend to occasional pain or sadness.[267] Another view endorses a reasonable person standard, by which the seriousness is to be judged by the degree of pain and suffering that a reasonable person could have endured in the same or a similar situation.[268]

Nevertheless, despite the troublesome term "serious," it is generally agreed that isolated pain or occasional unhappiness is not serious mental suffering. Thus, what amounts to seriousness sufficient for a mental damage claim is a matter of fact to be determined by the court on a case-by-case basis. For example, in body- or health-related injury cases, the courts generally look at whether the injury has caused disability to the victim when determining the seriousness of mental suffering.[269]

c. Assessment of Suffering

Since mental suffering or distress is largely immeasurable, determining appropriate compensation is always a tough issue. In practice, the courts follow a factor-analysis approach adopted in the SPC's 2001 Explanations. According to the SPC, the factors to consider include (a) the degree of fault of the tortfeasor; (b) the details of the means, place and method of the tort committed; (c) the consequence of the tortious conduct; (d) the benefit the tortfeasor obtained; (e) the financial ability of the tortfeasor to assume liability; and (f) the average living standard of the place of the court.[270] In addition, some provinces and major cities have imposed limitations on the total amount of compensation. The present cap ranges from RMB 50,000 to RMB 100,000.[271]

266 See Liming, Textbook, *supra* note 25, at 346.

267 See Shengming, *supra* note 10, at 111.

268 See Wu Gaoheng & Xing Baojum, Explanations to the Tort Liability Law of the People's Republic of China, 61 (China University of Political Science and Law Press, 2010).

269 See the SPC Leading Group Torts, *supra* note 109, at 178.

270 See the SPC, *2001 Explanations*, *supra* note 262, art. 10 (Article 10 is kept intact in article 5 of the 2020 revised Explanations).

271 See *id.* at 112. It is interesting to note that in 2021, the SPC promulgated an Interpretation on Mental Damage Compensation in State Compensation Cases, in which the SPC set forth standards for the determination of the seriousness of mental damage and amount of compensation. However, the nature of state compensation and how it relates to the Civil Code remains a highly debated issue among Chinese scholars. Under article 8 of the Interpretation, if mental damages result in serious consequences, the amount of compensation for the mental damages shall generally be capped at 50 percent of the total amount of personal liberty compensation and life and health compensation combined. However, the court may discretionarily

D. *Punitive Damages*

Prior to the enactment of the Civil Code, punitive damages as statutory damage were applied only in cases where consumers' rights and interests were affected. For example, under article 49 of the 1993 Consumer Rights and Interests Protection Law, business operators found to have committed fraud in providing goods or services shall, upon the consumer's request, compensate the consumer with a sum doubling what the consumers have paid for such commodities or services.[272] When the 1993 Consumer Rights and Interests Protection Law was amended in 2013, the payment amount was increased to three times the price paid by the consumer for the goods or services purchased.[273]

Punitive damages are understood in China as the damages imposed on the infringer that exceed the actual amount of damage caused to the infringed party in order not only to compensate the infringed but also to punish the infringer. The functions of punitive damages include compensation, deterrence, and punishment. Due to their nature of punishment, punitive damages may only be applied as provided by the law both in the scope of application and in scale.

The Civil Code makes punitive damages a major form of tort damages. While recognizing punitive damages, the Civil Code limits the application of punitive damages to the infringement of intellectual property rights. Under article 1185 of the Civil Code, in case of an intentional infringement of another person's intellectual property rights, the infringed person has the right to request corresponding punitive damages if the circumstances are serious.[274] Pursuant to article 1185, an imposition of punitive damages must meet three requirements: (a) infringement of an

determine an amount exceeding the cap when the consequences are particularly serious and the capped amount is proven insufficient.

In addition, the SPC opines that any of the following circumstances may be deemed to have resulted in "serious consequences": (a) a person who is not guilty or whose criminal responsibility has been terminated is detained for more than six months; (b) the victim is identified as suffering more than minor injuries or is disabled; (c) the victim has been diagnosed and identified as having a mental disorder or mental disability, which is related to the tort; or (d) the victim's reputation, honor, family, career, education, etc., have suffered serious damage related to the infringement.

The particularly serious consequences include: (a) the victim has been detained for more than ten years without charge; (b) the victim dies; (c) the victim is identified as seriously injured or has a disability of level one to level four, and is unable to take care of himself; or (d) the victim is diagnosed and identified as having a severe mental disorder or a mental disability of level one to level two, which are related to the infringement, and is unable to live on his/her own. See the SPC, *Interpretation of Several Issues Concerning the Application of Law in Determining Liability for Mental Damage Compensation in State Compensation Cases*, available at www.chinacourt.org/law/detail/2021/03/id/150252.shtml.

[272] See the Law on the Protection of Consumer Rights and Interests (1993), available at https://faolex.fao.org/docs/pdf/chn47424.pdf.

[273] See the Law on the Protection of Consumer Rights and Interests (as amended 2013), available at www.chinalawtranslate.com/en/consumer-protection-law-including-2013-amendments/.

[274] See the Civil Code, *supra* note 18, art. 1185.

intellectual property right, (b) intentional tortious conduct, and (c) seriousness of the circumstances.

The Civil Code, however, does not specify what may constitute seriousness for the purpose of punitive damages. In general, when determining seriousness, the courts will take into account such factors as the means of infringement, duration of infringement, frequency of infringement, and the repetition of infringement after being punished administratively. In addition, the courts will also look at the level of impact of the infringement on the infringed.

With regard to the amount of punitive damages, it would require a case-by-case analysis to determine the damages "corresponding" to the harm. The SPC has issued two interpretations on the application of law to the disputes involving intellectual property rights infringement: one deals with copyrights, and the other applies to trademarks. For copyright infringement, when determining the amount of compensation, according to the SPC, the courts should consider the type of work, reasonableness of royalties, nature of the infringement, consequences, and other circumstances.[275] Similarly, in the case of trademark infringement, consideration shall be made to such factors as the nature, duration and consequences of the infringement, reputation of the mark, amount of royalties, trademark use license category, duration, scope, and reasonable expenses incurred for stopping the infringement.[276]

[275] See the SPC, *Interpretation on Several Issues Concerning the Application of Law in Adjudication of Civil Disputes over Copyrights*, issued in October 2002 (revised 2020), art. 25, available at https://zhuanlan.zhihu.com/p/608004667.

[276] See the SPC, 2002 *Interpretation on Several Issues Concerning the Application of Law in Adjudication of Civil Disputes over Trademarks* (revised 2020), art. 16, available at http://gongbao.court.gov.cn/Details/93ca0d509275338b498e7bef849830.html.

PART III

Civil Dispute Settlement and Legal Process

Legal process in a narrow sense means a writ or formal notice issued by a court, including summons, warrant, mandate, or the like. In a broad sense, however, it refers to proceedings or mechanisms under which disputes are resolved. For civil disputes, the process can be judicial or non-judicial. The basic law that governs the judicial process for the settlement of civil disputes in China is the Civil Procedure Law (CPL). The CPL was adopted in 1991 and then amended in 2007, 2012, 2017, 2021, and 2023.[1] Supplemental to the CPL are the Supreme People's Court (SPC) interpretations.

Under Chinese law, non-judicial process of civil dispute settlement mainly includes negotiation, mediation, and arbitration. Negotiation is the means by which the parties consult with each other for purposes of dispute settlement. As provided in article 53 of the CPL (as amended 2023), the parties may reach a settlement on their own for the disputes between them. Among the non-judicial dispute settlement methods, negotiation between the parties is the most desired but in one many cases may also be the most difficult one because the differences between the parties are hardly reconcilable.

Mediation refers to a method in which the parties to a civil dispute agree to have a neutral and impartial person assist them in resolving their differences after the dispute occurs. The purpose of mediation is to help the parties resolve their disputes quickly and efficiently without getting into a long and often complicated litigation process, thus saving judicial resources. But note that there are two kinds of mediation in China: judicial mediation and non-judicial mediation. The former is conducted under the auspices of a court, while the latter means a mediation undertaken by a third party who can be an individual or local community.

The major difference between the two mediations is that a judicial mediation agreement, once effective, is binding. Under article 96 of the CPL, a people's court,

[1] The Civil Procedural Law of China was adopted by the NPC on April 9, 1991, and was amended five times in 2007, 2012, 2017, 2022, and 2023, available at www.npc.gov.cn/npc/c2/c30834/202401/P020240108541839745616.pdf.

while hearing a civil case, shall conduct mediation according to the will of the party and on the basis of clear facts.[2] Article 100 of the CPL further provides that the court shall make a written mediation statement when the parties have reached a mediation agreement. The mediation agreement shall become legally binding upon the parties' signatures.[3] Under the CPL, a judicial mediation settlement agreement has binding effect, though it is not a court judgment. In this context, "binding" means that if one party fails to perform the obligations specified in the judicial mediation agreement, the other party may apply to the court for an order to enforce.

Non-judicial mediation generally does not have binding effect. A quite common non-judicial mediation in the country is known as people's mediation, undertaken by the people's mediation committee. Defined in the People's Mediation Law (PML), people's mediation refers to the activity in which the people's mediation committee uses methods such as persuasion and guidance to encourage the parties to voluntarily reach a mediation agreement on the basis of equal consultation to resolve civil disputes.[4] In accordance with the PML, the people's mediation committee is a mass organization established in villages, neighborhood communities, enterprises, or institutions in accordance with the law to mediate civil disputes.[5]

Litigation and arbitration are the most common devices employed for civil and commercial dispute settlement, especially in cases that contain foreign elements. The word "foreign" as used to define foreign cases generally refers to a foreign country or foreign country related. But for purposes of dispute settlement, Hong Kong and Macao, though part of China, are both considered foreign. Thus, a civil case related to Hong Kong or Macao is dealt with differently from a domestic case – that is, a case containing Mainland elements only. As noted, cases that have foreign elements are subject to special provisions in the laws. Presently, there are over 50 special foreign-related laws in the country, and more than 150 laws that contain foreign-related clauses.

According to the SPC, a civil or commercial case is considered a case with foreign elements, or foreign case, if (a) one or more parties are foreigners, stateless persons, or foreign enterprises or organizations; (b) the habitual residence of one or more parties is located outside the territory of China; (c) the subject matter of the dispute is situated outside the territory of China; (d) the legal facts that create, modify, or terminate a civil relationship take place outside the territory of China; or (e) other situations in which a case might be classified as a foreign civil case.[6]

2 See *id.*, art. 96.

3 See *id.*, art. 100.

4 See the People's Mediation Law, adopted by the Standing Committee of the NPC on August 28, 2010, art. 2, available at www.gov.cn/flfg/2010-08/29/content_1691209.htm.

5 See *id.*, art. 7 and 8.

6 See the SPC, Interpretation on the Application of Civil Procedural Law, adopted in 2014, amended 2022, available at http://gongbao.court.gov.cn/Details/d6a2b69e70910361e42fbfc00a258a.html.

Thus, the determinative factors of foreign cases include nationality, habitual residence, location of the subject matter, and place of occurrence of the legal facts. The "other circumstance" is a clause that allows the court to make determinations on a case-specific basis. Normally, a civil action with foreign elements involves a foreigner. In many cases, however, a civil action in which the parties are all Chinese nationals may also be categorized as foreign because the habitual residence of the party or parties, the location of the subject matter, or the place of occurrence of legal facts is outside China.

13

International Civil Litigation in Chinese Courts

INTRODUCTION

A civil dispute may happen anywhere for a variety of reasons. The issue that often arises is not why the dispute occurs but how to get it resolved. Of course, the parties involved may always work together to resolve their disputes amicably through negotiation. In reality, however, the parties may hardly reach a consensus on their respective rights and obligations, particularly when one party is allegedly liable for compensating the other, or the parties are from different countries.

Arbitration is an alternative method of resolving civil or commercial disputes, especially in foreign-related commercial transactions or civil activities. But arbitration has its own limitations. First, it relies on an arbitration agreement, without which no arbitration body will have jurisdiction over the disputes. Second, even if there is an arbitration agreement, the agreement might be held to be invalid or set aside on various grounds. Therefore, in many cases, a civil action may have to be sought in order to get the disputes ultimately resolved by an impartial judicial authority.

A civil action has several characteristics. First, it is a process of civil dispute resolution, and such a process is undertaken under the law through particular procedures. Second, it is a course of determining the rights and obligations of the parties involved, and the determination is to be made by a judicial body. Third, it is initiated by an aggrieved party through a request for an adjudication of a claim that the party alleges against the other party, and the adjudication is conducted on the basis of fact finding, presentation of evidence, and arguments of the parties. Fourth, it relies on state power to maintain effectiveness and authoritativeness. The state power is exercised through the compulsory nature of answering a suit and the mandatory character of enforcing a judgment.

For civil proceedings in Chinese courts, one point worth noting is the inquisitorial tradition. As discussed, the Chinese legal system bears a strong civil law tradition. Under the concept of function *ex officio*, the courts play an active and dominant role in the trial. The Civil Procedural Law (CPL) mandates that the people's courts, when adjudicating civil cases, take the facts as the basis (based on the facts) and the law as the criterion (guided by the law).[1] The CPL also requires that the people's courts thoroughly and objectively examine and verify evidence according to the law.[2] Under the CPL, a people's court also has the authority to investigate and collect evidence from any entity or individual.[3]

International civil litigation in China is known as litigation that contains foreign elements or simply foreign litigation. Under article 5 of the CPL, all civil litigation undertaken within China is subject to the CPL.[4] It is further provided that foreigners, stateless persons, foreign enterprises, and organizations in Chinese court proceedings shall be treated the same as their Chinese counterparts.[5] In addition, given its foreign nature, international civil litigation is also governed by the special provisions on cases containing foreign elements or foreign actions. Under article 270 of the CPL, international civil litigation in China must not only follow the special provisions on foreign actions, but also abide by other provisions of the CPL whenever applicable.[6]

There are three major issues facing international civil litigation. The first issue is where to litigate. The "where to" is essentially a matter of jurisdiction because the question involved is whether a court is competent or has the power to adjudicate the disputes brought to it. The second issue involves which law applies. The determination of governing law or the law applicable to the case or controversies requires a choice-of-law analysis and application of choice-of-law rules. The third issue concerns how to enforce a judgment. Enforcement of the judgment is the ultimate goal of the litigation. In many cases, enforcement may have to be sought outside the jurisdiction in which the judgment is entered.

As noted, the CPL was amended again in 2023. The 2023 amendments to the CPL substantially enhance the foreign litigation provisions with the following major changes:

(a) The term "contract disputes or other property rights disputes" is replaced with "foreign-related civil disputes" to define the scope of the jurisdiction in foreign cases, including "property rights disputes" and "non-property rights disputes" (article 276).
(b) The "appropriate connection" is provided as a jurisdiction principle to cover all foreign civil dispute cases for which the jurisdiction basis is not specified (article 276).

1 See The Civil Procedural Law of China (adopted by the NPC on April 9, 1991, and amended five times in 2007, 2012, 2017, 2022, and 2023), available at www.npc.gov.cn/npc/c2/c30834/202401/P020240108541839745616.pdf, art. 7.
2 See *id.*, art. 67.
3 See *id.*, art. 70.
4 See *id.*, art. 4.
5 See *id.*, art. 5.
6 See *id.*, art. 270.

(c) New provisions are added as the rules of consensual jurisdiction (article 277), jurisdiction based on non-objection or counterclaim (article 278), parallel litigations (articles 280, 281, and 302), *foreign non-conveniens* (article 282), and foreign sovereign immunity (article 305).
(d) The exclusive jurisdiction of Chinese courts is expanded to cases involving the validity of decisions as well as the dissolution of Chinese legal persons or other entities, and the validity of interllectual property rights (IPR) (article 279).
(e) The provisions governing the service of process abroad are revised with more detailed rules on foreign discovery (articles 283, 284).
(f) The grounds for denial of recognition and enforcement of foreign judgment are specified, including the situations in which the foreign courts are considered to have no jurisdiction (articles 300, 301).
(g) A review procedure is provided as a remedy mechanism for the denial of recognition and enforcement of foreign judgments (article 303).

1. PROCEEDINGS OF INTERNATIONAL CIVIL LITIGATION

The basic legal framework that governs international civil litigation in China is part IV of the CPL, which contains provisions applying specifically to any civil litigation that involves foreign elements. If, however, there is any matter in the foreign civil litigation that is not dealt with in part IV, other relevant provisions of the CPL shall be applied. Thus, international civil litigation in China follows not only the provisions of part IV of the CPL, but also all other provisions of the CPL whenever applicable.

There are thirty-six articles in the special provisions of the CPL on international civil litigation, which cover such matters as jurisdiction, service abroad, foreign discovery and evidence collection, recognition and enforcement of a foreign judgment, and arbitration-related litigation. The choice of law is a matter to which the Statute of Application of Law to Foreign Civil Relations (Choice of Law Statute) applies. Adopted in 2010, the Choice of Law Statute contains the rules that govern applicable laws and their determination, and is aimed at ascertaining the application of law concerning foreign civil relations.[7]

Under article 274 of the CPL, a foreigner, stateless person, or foreign enterprise or organization that needs to be represented by a lawyer as an agent *ad litem* in a civil action in a people's court shall appoint a Chinese lawyer.[8] It is further provided in article 275 that when a Chinese lawyer is retained by a foreign party who does not

[7] See the Law of China on the Law Applicable to Foreign Civil Relations, promulgated by the Standing Committee of the NPC on October 28, 2010, available at https://wipolex-res.wipo.int/edocs/lexdocs/laws/en/cn/cn173en.html (hereinafter referred to as Choice of Law Statute).

[8] See the CPL, *supra* note 1, art. 274.

reside within the territory of China, the retainer agreement sent or forwarded from outside of China shall have no effect until it has been notarized by a notary public of his own country, and has been authenticated by the Chinese embassy or a consulate in that state, or certified under the procedures provided for in the relevant treaty between China and that state.[9]

A. *Civil Proceedings in Chinese Courts*

Civil litigation in a Chinese court may take on different proceedings. Pursuant to the CPL, there are three proceedings, namely the general, simple, and special proceedings, depending on the complexity of the case and the subject matter of the disputes. The general proceeding is a regular proceeding, and most civil cases are tried for the first instance under this proceeding. Unlike other proceedings, the general proceeding contains formal and comprehensive procedures and applies to first-instance cases not only at the trial courts but also at the higher-level courts. It also applies to remanded cases as well as cases for which a new trial is granted.

The simple proceeding is actually a simplified version of the general proceeding. For example, in a simple proceeding, the plaintiff may file the complaint orally. Under article 160 of the CPL, the simple proceeding is mainly used to adjudicate simple civil cases in which the facts are clear, the relations of rights and obligations are definite, and disputes are minor.[10] In addition, the CPL also allows the parties to choose by agreement to apply the simple proceeding to their case.

After the CPL was revised in 2012, the simple proceeding could include small claim cases. Under article 165 of the CPL (as amended 2023), a small claim is a claim in which the amount in controversy does not exceed 50 percent of the average salary of local employees. Therefore, the actual amount of money for small claims varies from place to place. But pursuant to article 167 of the CPL, the small claim proceeding does not apply to a case with foreign elements.[11]

There are certain cases that are excluded by the Supreme People's Court (SPC) from the use of the simple proceeding. According to article 257 of the SPC *Explanations*, the cases to which the simple proceeding is not applicable are that

[9] See *id.*, art. 275.

[10] According to the Supreme People's Court (SPC), the facts shall be deemed clear if the parties make basically the same statements on the facts of the disputes and are able to provide appropriate evidence, and as a result, the facts can be ascertained without the court's investigation and collection of evidence. Definite relations refer to situations where the party who is liable and the party who is entitled to certain rights are easily distinguishable. The disputes shall be considered minor when the parties do not disagree in principle with regard to the right and wrong involved, the assumption of liabilities, and the subject matter in dispute. See the SPC, *Interpretation on the Application of the Civil Procedural Law*, adopted in 2014, amended 2022, available at http://gongbao.court.gov.cn/Details/d6a2b69e70910361e42fbfc00a258a.html, art. 256.

[11] See the CPL, *supra* note 1, art. 167.

(a) the whereabouts of the defendant are unknown at the time the case is filed, (b) the case is remanded for a retrial, (c) one side to the case has a large number of parties, (d) the judicial supervision procedures are being applied to the case, (e) the case involves a national or public interest, (f) the case is filed by a third party to change or revoke a judgment that is already effective, a ruling or a mediation agreement, and (g) any other case that is found unsuitable for the simple proceeding. Although the simple proceeding normally applies to domestic cases, it may also be applicable to international cases, especially in small claims or on the basis of the parties' choice.

The special proceeding is the proceeding that deals with non-civil dispute cases. Non-civil dispute means that the case does not involve issues of civil matters or any substantial rights or obligations between the parties. The categories of the cases covered in the special proceeding include eligibility of votes, declaration of missing or death of a person, determination of the civil capacity of a citizen, determination of ownerless property, confirmation of a mediation agreement, and realization of a right of security interest in property. Because no civil disputes are present in the special proceedings, the cases are generally handled by the judge *ex officio* and on the basis of papers submitted only.

As far as foreigners are concerned, the special proceeding might become relevant when the security interest in property is at stake. Under the *Chinese Property Law* (2007), the security interest in property is a property right and includes mortgages, pledges, and liens. Article 170 of the *Property Law* provides that unless otherwise stipulated by law, the holder of security interests shall have priority in having his claim paid if a debtor defaults or if the conditions for enforcement of the said interests, as agreed upon by the parties concerned, arise.[12] To realize the security interest in property is to exercise the right of priority for payment. Also relevant to foreigners in special proceedings is the confirmation of a mediation agreement. The confirmation by a people's court is to provide the mediation agreement with a fully binding effect.

Note that when the CPL was revised in 2012, civil litigation cases could be filed in court for promotion of the public interest. In China, public interest litigation is generally understood as the litigation initiated by a relevant government agency, social group or organization, or individual not for the purpose of obtaining personal relief but for maintaining social and public interests in general.[13] Under article 58 of the CPL, the relevant bodies or organizations prescribed by the law may bring a lawsuit to a people's court against such acts that undermine the public interest as environmental pollution or harm of the legitimate rights and interests of a vast number of consumers.[14] It is unclear whether article 55 actually opens the door in

[12] Property Law of the People's Republic of China, adopted on March 16, 2007, effective October 1, 2007.

[13] See Zhang Weiping, Civil Procedural Law, 327 (Law Press, 2013).

[14] See the CPL, *supra* note 1, art. 58.

China for class actions, but public interest litigation will definitely target both domestic and foreign defendants.

B. *Two Instances System: Trial and Appeal*

As noted, there are four tiers in the Chinese court system, namely, the basic trial courts, intermediate courts, provincial high courts, and the SPC. Under the CPL, judicial proceedings in China take place in two instances: trial and appeal. Termed as "two trials with the second one as final," the two instances constitute the basic trial system in China. In a normal proceeding, the judgment made by an appellate court in the second instance is final and no appeal therefrom is permitted.

The adoption of the two instances trial system was originally premised on the factors of (a) convenience to litigants, (b) judicial efficiency, and (c) the need for the higher courts to focus more on their role of judicial administration, guidance, and supervision. But due to the low level of the final court under the two-instance trial (most appeal cases ended at intermediate courts), there has always been a concern about the quality of adjudication and local protection that would affect the effective delivery of justice. It is this concern that prompts a call in the country to add another layer of appeal to judicial proceedings in order to better maintain judicial justice and fairness and also help promote uniformity in the application of law.[15]

The first instance usually occurs in the basic trial court. But in certain cases, the first instance may start at a higher level, or even at the SPC. The cases that are qualified for the first instance at a court of a higher level are provided in the CPL and can also be specified by the SPC as needed through its function of judicial interpretation. Under the CPL, the jurisdiction of courts over certain cases at the first instance varies depending on the nature of the case and the monetary amount in controversy involved. Since there is only one appeal in Chinese judicial proceedings, it is critical to know where the first instance begins if an appeal to a higher level of court is desired.

However, there are two categories of cases for which no appeal is available, which are categorized as "one instance only" cases. The first category contains the cases that are tried for the first instance at the SPC.[16] As provided in article 20 of the CPL, the civil cases that fall within the first-instance jurisdiction of the SPC include the cases having significant national impact and the cases that the SPC believes it should adjudicate.[17] Cases in the second category include small claim cases under article 166 of the CPL and cases of special proceedings under article 185 of the CPL.[18]

[15] See Weiping, *supra* note 13, at 61–63.

[16] Some in China strongly oppose the idea of having the Supreme People's Court take cases at the first instance because they believe that it would unfairly deprive the litigants of their right to appeal. See Weiping, *supra* note 13, at 62.

[17] See the CPL, *supra* note 1, art. 20.

[18] See *id.*, arts. 166 and 185.

Keep in mind that the Chinese legal system, as discussed, bears a strong civil law tradition. In court proceedings, judges take the lead and play an active and dominant role. Under the notion of function *ex officio*, the courts in general possess the power to control the proceedings, the authority to investigate facts and collect evidence, the discretion to question witnesses, the power to verify and ascertain the facts, as well as the right to interpret and clarify ambiguities (also phrased as the "duty to make information known to litigants"). As noted, under the CPL, in trial proceedings, the people's courts are required to base on the facts and abide by the law.[19] The CPL also requires that the people's courts examine and verify evidence according to the law.[20] Pursuant to the CPL, a people's court has the authority to investigate and collect evidence from any entity or individual.[21]

Therefore, Chinese lawyers in court proceedings do not possess the same function as their counterparts in common law countries. Although the lawyers representing their clients in the court may frame each of their clients' cases in light of the client's best interests, their authority to discover and gather evidence, call and question witnesses, and control the process is very limited. The skills and resources of lawyers are relevant and important, but the court's decision is not necessarily made on the basis of the lawyer's presentation. Partly because of the decisive role of the court in litigation, legal representation could fall on the shoulders of someone other than a lawyer. In recent years, as a result of the judicial reform, a trend has developed to add adversarial elements into judicial proceedings. Reflected in this trend is the debate on an evolution from the functionalism of the court *ex officio* to the centralism of litigants.

C. *Trial Supervision Proceedings*

Trial supervision in civil cases refers to the proceedings in which a judgment, ruling, or mediation settlement agreement that has already taken legal effect is retried if it is found that it contains errors. It allows the courts to take a second look at the judgments or rulings that are final but contain obvious errors, and to grant a trial anew. As a remedial procedure, trial supervision is aimed at correcting the court's erroneous judgment, ruling, or other case settlement document that has already taken legal effect via retrial of the case. But trial supervision is neither a required procedure of adjudication nor the same as, or similar to, first and second instance trials. It is a unique and independent proceeding in the Chinese trial system.

Some in China believe that trial supervision is a handy vehicle to correct the possible mistakes made both in law and in fact during the trial. The underlying notion is the concept of "seeking truth from facts and correcting mistakes."

[19] See the CPL, *supra* note 1, art. 7.
[20] See *id.*, art. 64.
[21] See *id.*, art. 67.

A general holding for trial supervision is that the retrial of the case is not because the judgment or ruling lacks the legitimacy of res judicata, but because the judgment or ruling is wrong and should be corrected.[22]

On the other hand, however, trial supervision has met considerable criticism. The major argument against it is that trial supervision proceedings have negative impacts on the finality of judgments.[23] First, when the retrial of a case is pending in the trial supervision proceeding, the judgment of the case, though effective already, can hardly have a *res judicata* effect.[24] Second, since the CPL does not specify how many "retrial" requests may be made via trial supervision, the proceeding can very likely be abused, which will render the case endless.[25]

In their practice, the courts seem to have been quite cautious in dealing with trial supervision cases. Based on the SPC's statistics, in 2018, the total number of requests for retrial via trial supervision in civil cases was 220,356, and the number of retrials actually taken was 44,211. In 2023, there were 344,060 requests for retrial and 52,576 retrials granted.[26] Although the number of retrial requests and retrials increased from 2018 to 2023, the rate of retrial cases granted actually declined from 20.06 percent in 2018 to 15.28 percent in 2023.

Under the CPL, a trial supervision proceeding may be initiated in three ways. First, a retrial can be launched by the original court or by the order of a superior court. According to article 209 of the CPL, when the president of a court at any level finds that a judgment, ruling, or mediation document of the court that has already taken legal effect contains real errors and believes that a retrial is necessary, the case shall be submitted to the trial committee for discussion and decision. In addition, the SPC has the right to bring up for trial or order a court of every level to conduct a retrial of a case if it finds that a judgment, ruling, or mediation document of a local court at any level that has already taken legal effect contains real errors. A higher court has the right to do the same with respect to an effective judgment, ruling, or mediation document of a lower people's court that contains real errors.[27]

Second, a retrial can be conducted upon the request of a party. Pursuant to article 210 of the CPL, any party who believes a legally effective judgment or ruling to be wrong may apply to the immediate superior court for retrial. If one party comprising

[22] See Weiping, *supra* note 13, at 345.

[23] See Chen Xiangyang, *The Flaws and Improvement of Civil Trial Supervision Proceedings*, 2009, available at http://bsxfy.sxfywcourt.gov.cn/article/detail/2009/11/id/4245112.shtml. See also Yu Yanhui, *Defects in the Civil Trial Supervision Procedure and Proposal for Improvement*, Legal System Review, 262 (August 2019), available at https://wenku.baidu.com/view/09812204a6517 7232f60ddccda38376bae1fe046.html.

[24] See Yanhui, *supra* note 23.

[25] See *id.*

[26] See the SPC, National Court Judicial Statistics Bulletin, published annually. The 2018 Statistics Bulletin is available at http://gongbao.court.gov.cn/Details/c70030ba6761ec1 65c3c2f0bd2a12b.html. The 2023 Statistics Bulletin is available at http://gongbao.court.gov .cn/Details/a3e86176b272dc94a05d9cb012c2d5.html.

[27] See the CPL, *supra* note 1, art. 209.

a large number of individuals or both parties thereto are Chinese citizens, the parties may apply for retrial of the case to the original court. In a party-requested retrial, however, the application for retrial will not stop the enforcement of the judgment or ruling that has already taken effect.[28] In order to ensure the party-requested retrial is handled properly, article 211 of the CPL provides a laundry list of circumstances under which a retrial should be granted.[29] The parties are prohibited from applying for retrial of a case where a legally effective judgment or mediation statement has been made to dissolve a marital relationship.[30]

Third, a retrial may take place upon judicial protest by procuratorates. As provided in article 219 of the CPL, when the Supreme People's Procuratorate, or a superior people's procuratorate, finds that a legally effective judgment or ruling made by a court at any level, or by a subordinate people's court, falls under any of the circumstances described in the laundry list of article 21, or if they find that a mediation statement is repugnant to the interests of the state or the public, they shall launch a judicial protest for retrial. A judicial protest may be made by an immediate superior procuratorate upon a request by the procuratorate at the same level as the court involved.[31]The CPL also allows a party to apply to the competent procuratorate for a judicial protest under any of the following circumstances: (a) the court

[28] See *id.*, art. 210.

[29] See *id.*, arts. 200 and 201. Under article 200 of the CPL, where an application for retrial by a party falls under any of the following circumstances, the court shall conduct a retrial: (a) there is new evidence that is sufficient to overturn the original judgment or ruling; (b) the evidence used as a basis for ascertaining the essential facts in the original judgment or ruling was insufficient; (c) the main evidence used as a basis for ascertaining the facts in the original judgment or ruling was falsified; (d) the main evidence used as a basis for ascertaining the facts in the original judgment or ruling was not cross-examined; (e) with regard to the main evidence necessary for the trial, if the party concerned is unable to collect the evidence personally due to objective reasons, and the court fails to investigate or collect such evidence after the party submits a written application to the court to investigate and collect such evidence; (f) an error was found in the application of the law in the original judgment or ruling; (g) the judicial organization was not composed in accordance with the law or a member of the judicial officers who should have withdrawn in accordance with the law did not do so; (h) in the event that the statutory agent of a party with no capacity to bring a case failed to act as an agent in the relevant case, or a party required to participate in the case failed to do so for reasons for which the party or his or her litigation agent is not responsible; (i) the party was deprived of his or her right to argue the case in breach of the law; (j) a default judgment was entered without serving a summons; (k) the original judgment or ruling omitted or exceeded the claims sought in the case; (l) the legal documentation on which the original judgment or ruling is based has been canceled or amended; or (m) any member of the judicial officers committed malpractice in trying a case, such as embezzlement, bribery, engaging in malpractice for personal benefit, or rendering a judgment that perverts the law. In addition, article 201 provides that for a legally effective mediation statement, a party may apply for a retrial if it can present evidence that the mediation violated the principle of voluntary participation or that the content of the mediation agreement violates the law. If the court finds the evidence to be true upon examination, a retrial shall be granted.

[30] See *id.*, art. 213.

[31] See *id.*, art. 219.

rejects the party's retrial application, (b) the court does not issue a ruling on the retrial application within the specified time limit, or (c) the judgment or ruling of the retrial is obviously erroneous. Upon receipt of the application, the procuratorate is required to examine it within three months and decide whether a judicial protest should be made.[32]

D. *Trial Organization*

Under the CPL, civil trials in China shall be conducted by a panel consisting of judges and people's assessors. Only in simplified proceedings may a civil case be heard and decided by a single judge. There are certain procedures for the formation of the panel and the selection of people's assessors. With regard to trial organization, a unique entity in the Chinese courts, as noted, is the judicial committee, an internal adjudicative body with vast authorities.

a. Collegial Panel

As discussed, the basic trial organization in Chinese courts is the collegial panel. In its 2022 "Opinions on Regulating the Operating Mechanism of Collegial Panels," the SPC defines the collegial panel as the basic trial organization of the People's Court where the members consisting of the panel participate equally in the review of case files, trial, deliberation, adjudication and other trial activities; independently express opinions on issues such as the acceptance of evidence, fact finding, application of law, litigation procedure and adjudication, and thereby bear corresponding responsibilities.[33]

As required under the CPL, except otherwise provided by the law, all civil cases of first instance shall be tried by a collegial panel. According to the SPC, the collegial panel can be formed by appointment or generted randomly with a combination of judges and people's assessors or judges only.[34] As noted, in civil cases of the first instance, it is required that at least one-third of the members of the collegial panel be people's assessors. The second instance trial may only be conducted by a collegial panel, but only judges may be on that panel. In both instances, there must be an odd number of members of the panel. Thus, there should be at least three members on any collegial panel. A new collegial panel shall be formed for remanded cases as well as cases that are granted a retrial.[35]

[32] See *id.*, art. 220.

[33] See the SPC, *Opinions on Regulating the Operating Mechanism of Collegial Panels*, issued on October 26, 2022, art.1, available at www.court.gov.cn/zixun/xiangqing/378721.html.

[34] See *id.*, art. 2.

[35] For a retrial case, if the case was originally tried at the second instance or removed *ex officio* to a higher-level people's court, the new collegiate panel shall be formed under the second instance procedure. Otherwise, the formation of the panel applies to the first instance procedure. See *id.*, art. 218.

An important function of the collegial panel is to deliberate over the case after the court hearing and arguments. As discussed, at the end of deliberation, a decision is made by a vote of the collegiate panel, and if there are differences of opinion during the deliberation of the collegial panel, the decision shall be made in accordance with the majority opinion.[36] It is required that the panel deliberations be kept in writing for the record, and the dissenting opinions shall be truthfully included in the deliberation transcript.[37] However, the dissenting opinions are generally not shown or mentioned in the judgment.[38]

Under the CPL, the collegial panel shall be presided over by a judge, and the presiding judge shall be designated by the president of the court or the chief judge of the division. In 2007, the SPC issued a directive that requires the president, vice president, division chief, and deputy division chief of all lower courts to be member of collegial panel in a certain number of cases.[39]

In the common law system, a juror mainly functions as a fact finder, and the judge decides all questions of law and gives instructions to the jury on the law as well. In China, a people's assessor is a member of the collegial panel and thus has rights equal to all other members of the panel, including the judges. During the trial, the people's assessor participates in the hearing and makes a determination on both the facts and the law. In other words, a people's assessor plays the role of a judge in the trial and exercises his or her right to vote independently. The only restriction is that a people's assessor may not serve as the presiding or chief judge in any given case.

The whole idea of having people's assessors is that their participation in the trial helps maintain the transparency of the adjudication process and the independence of courts in the exercise of judicial power. But the concern is that people's assessors may not properly apply the law because they lack professional legal training. Also, a dilemma may appear when two people's assessors who are in the majority disagree with the presiding judge in a three-member collegiate panel. It might not be a problem if the disagreement does not involve the application of law, but it will raise a serious issue if the application of law is the center of the disagreement.

According to the SPC, if the collegial panel cannot reach a majority opinion, the presiding judge shall, in accordance with relevant regulations and procedures, recommend that the court president refer the case to a professional judges' conference for discussion, or to the judicial committee for discussion and decision. The

[36] See the SPC 2022 Opinons, *supra* note 33, art. 7.

[37] See *id.*

[38] The Shanghai No. 2 Intermediate People's Court in 2002 and the Beijing No. 1 Intermediate People's Court in 2005 tried to release dissenting opinions in the judgment in particular cases.

[39] See the SPC, *Several Opinions on Improvement of the Participation of the President, Vice President, Division Chief, and Deputy Division Chief at All Levels of Lower Courts in a Certain Number of Cases as a Member of Collegial Panel*, issued on March 30, 2007, available at www.055110.com/law/1/14770.html.

opinions reached by the professional judges' conference shall be provided for the collegial panel's consideration during its review, but if the case is referred to the judicial committee, the collegial panel shall follow the committee's decision.[40]

b. Judicial Committee

Again, a very unique and also very controversial body in the Chinese court system is the judicial committee (also known as the adjudication committee). As noted, it is a powerful decision-making body formed internally in the court in order to ensure that all trials are conducted appropriately and all judgments are made properly, especially for the cases that are politically sensitive or involve tremendous local social or economic interests. An important feature of the judicial committee is its authority to review and discuss major and difficult cases, supervise and advise on trials, and initiate the judicial supervision process for cases in which obvious errors are found. The collegial panel is also under the supervision of the judicial committee. Since the collegial panel is required to follow the decision made by the judicial committee, the judgments in a considerable number of cases are actually made through the judicial committee rather than the collegial panel alone.

As required by the SPC, under certain circumstances, the collegial panel will need to ask the president of the court to submit the case to the judicial committee for decision. According to the SPC, such circumstances include: (a) the opinions among the members of the collegial panel are so divided that a decision can hardly be made, (b) the provision of law is unclear as to a particular matter or there is a clear difficulty in the application of law, (c) the outcome of the case may generate significant social impacts, (d) it is a new type of case that has merits to provide meaningful guidance to judicial practices, or (e) there are other difficult, complicated or important cases that require the attention of the judicial committee.[41]

There has long been a debate on whether it is necessary and proper to have a judicial committee. Supporters argue that the judicial committee functions as a think-tank in the court and helps more appropriately apply the law and better achieve optimal results for trials. Opponents counter that the judicial committee should be abolished because it has become an obstacle to the collegial panel and its ability to conduct trials independently. Opponents further contend that by acting as a decision maker behind the scenes, the judicial committee actually interferes with the independence of the collegial panel and seriously damages judicial transparency.[42]

40 See the SPC 2022 Opinions, *supra* note 33, art. 7.

41 See the SPC, *Implementing Opinions on the Reform and Improvement of Trial Committee*, issued on January 11, 2010.

42 See Chen Huijing, *A Brief Analysis of Judicial Committee*, China Court Org., March 28, 2012, available at www.chinacourt.org/article/detail/2012/03/id/476449.shtml. See also Chen Ruihua, *The Prospects of the Judicial Committee System*, July 28, 2024, available at www.bilibili.com/

To many foreign litigants, the judicial committee is indeed a mysterious entity. The committee does not hear any case for trial but retains the ultimate authority to decide cases. At any rate, the existence of the judicial committee casts serious doubt on the fairness of trials and judicial justice. But since the judicial committee is a useful and effective tool for court leadership to control trials, it may not be practical to get rid of it any time soon; still, many hope that the power of the judicial committee can be minimized over time.

2. JURISDICTION IN INTERNATIONAL CIVIL LITIGATION

Jurisdiction in the law refers to the legal authority of a court to hear and determine cases. In civil litigation, the jurisdiction of a court involves the competence of the court and the power of the court. The competence of a court defines the types of cases a court may take as prescribed by law, which is also called subject matter jurisdiction or jurisdiction *ratione materiae*. The power of a court means the authority of the court to exercise jurisdiction over particular persons or personal jurisdiction. In a broad sense, the personal jurisdiction of a court includes jurisdiction *in personam* (over a person), jurisdiction *in rem* (over a property), and jurisdiction *quasi-in-rem* (over a person based on property).

For a court to be legally capable of adjudicating civil controversies, it must possess both subject matter jurisdiction and personal jurisdiction. In China, subject matter jurisdiction determines the scope of the court's authority to accept cases, and its determination clarifies which disputes fall within the court's jurisdiction and which disputes do not. Only if a court has subject matter jurisdiction may a case be brought to it for adjudication. A lack of subject matter jurisdiction is always a defense to the eligibility of a court to enter a judgment on the case in question.

Under article 3 of the CPL, the provisions of the CPL apply to civil actions arising from disputes on property and personal relations between and among citizens, legal persons, or other organizations. Article 3 is based on whether the substantive legal relation where the dispute occurs is a civil relation as a criterion to delineate the subject matter jurisdiction of Chinese courts in civil litigation. In addition, the tier of a court also affects the subject matter jurisdiction of the court in certain cases.

Personal jurisdiction of the courts in China depends on various factors and can be established either under the agreement of the parties or by the provision of law absent the parties' choice. The jurisdiction over a foreign defendant must have a statutory ground, and in most cases is territorially based, meaning that the defendant must have a physical presence within China – in person, by its conduct, or by owning property. Chinese courts will have no jurisdiction over a person or controversy that has no connection with China.

read/cv36465478/. For a more general discussion of the judicial committee, see Zuo Weiming, An Empirical Study on the Adjudicative Committee System (Peking University Press, 2018).

A. *Jurisdiction of Chinese Courts*

Under the provisions of the CPL, the jurisdiction of Chinese courts is divided into four major categories, including tiers jurisdiction, territorial jurisdiction, consensual jurisdiction, and exclusive jurisdiction. In addition, the jurisdiction of a court could be designated by the superior court or transferred as a result of a venue change. Both designated jurisdiction and transferred jurisdiction are subject to specific requirements.

Designated jurisdiction takes place when a superior court orders an inferior court to hear a certain case over which it otherwise would not have jurisdiction. According to the CPL, jurisdiction may be designated to an inferior court if (a) a case is transferred to a court that lacks jurisdiction,[43] (b) a court with jurisdiction over the case is unable to exercise jurisdiction due to special reasons (e.g., natural disaster, recusal, etc.),[44] or (c) two or more competent courts dispute over their jurisdiction, and the dispute cannot be resolved by agreement between or among the disputing courts.[45]

Transferred jurisdiction refers to the situation where the case has to be removed from a non-competent court to a competent one. Under article 37 of the CPL, if a court discovers that a case it has accepted is not within its jurisdiction, it shall transfer the case to a court that has jurisdiction. Upon transfer, the transferee court shall take the case. However, if the transferee court believes that it also does not have jurisdiction, it shall refer the case to a superior court for jurisdiction designation.[46]

Pursuant to the CPL, for a valid transfer of jurisdiction, three conditions must be met. First, the transferring court has accepted the case. Second, the transferring court lacks jurisdiction. Third, the case is being transferred to a competent court. For the purpose of transfer, the jurisdiction of the transferring court shall be determined from the time when it accepts the case.

a. Tier Jurisdiction

As noted, the trial system in China consists of four tiers and two instances. At the bottom of the tiers are the trial courts at the county level. In general, the trial courts have jurisdiction over the first-instance trial of all civil or commercial controversies unless otherwise provided by law. The first-instance trial, however, may begin at an intermediate court, high court, or even the SPC, depending on the nature of the case and authorization under the law.

Since in any given case there is only one appeal available under the two-instance trial scheme, the level of the court for the first-instance trial is of practical

[43] See the CPL, *supra* note 1, art. 37.
[44] See *id.*, art. 38.
[45] See *id.*
[46] See *id.*, art. 37.

significance because it determines whether an appeal could reach a higher court or go up to the SPC. But in most cases, the appeal ends at an intermediate court. Although, as noted, there is a judicial supervision proceeding after the second instance appeal, the proceeding must meet specific requirements and is also not available for every case.

As discussed, tiers involve the subject matter jurisdiction of the court at various levels, and thus, an exercise of jurisdiction in violation of tier jurisdiction will render the jurisdiction invalid. Under article 19 of the CPL, an intermediate people's court has jurisdiction as the court of first instance over such civil cases as (a) major foreign cases; (b) cases with significant impact within its jurisdiction; and (c) cases determined by the SPC to come under the jurisdiction of the intermediate people's courts.[47]

According to article 20 of the CPL, a civil case may go to a higher people's court for the first-instance trial if the case has a significant impact in the areas over which the higher people's court possesses jurisdiction.[48] In addition, it is provided in article 21 of the CPL that the SPC may exercise jurisdiction as the court of first instance over (a) cases that have a significant impact nationwide and (b) cases that the SPC sees fit to try itself.[49] Note, however, if a case is tried by the SPC for the first instance, the ruling is final.

Based on the provisions of the CPL on tier jurisdiction, the SPC quantifies the "significant impact" in a monetary amount for the courts to exercise first-instance jurisdiction over foreign cases. In 2022, the SPC adopted the Rules on Several Issues Concerning the Jurisdiction over foreign civil and commercial cases, where the SPC stipulated in detail the authority of lower courts to adjudicate foreign cases at the first instance.[50] According to the SPC, the trial courts have the jurisdiction of the first-instance trial on all foreign cases unless otherwise provided by the law or judicial interpretation.[51]

Under the SPC's 2022 Rules, an intermediate court may have the first-instance jurisdiction over foreign cases when (a) the amount of controversy involved is large, (b) the case is complex, or has a large number of parties, or (c) the case has a significant impact within its jurisdiction. For the purpose of first-instance jurisdiction of the intermediate court, the amount in controversy is currently considered large when the money amount is RMB 40 million or more in the four municipalities directly under the central government, including *Beijing*, *Tianjin*, *Shanghai*, and *Chongqing*, and the five coastal provinces of *Jiangsu*, *Zhejiang*, *Fujian*,

[47] See *id.*, art. 19.

[48] See *id.*, art. 20.

[49] See *id.*, art. 21.

[50] See the SPC, *The Rules on Several Issues Concerning the Jurisdiction over Foreign Civil and Commercial Cases*, issued on November 4, 2022, available at http://gongbao.court.gov.cn/Details/5fdec7c5a7coccb27598fd487c521e.html.

[51] See *id.*, art. 2.

Shandong, and *Guangdong*. In all other areas, the threshold of a large amount is set at RMB 20 million or more.[52]

For a high court to exercise jurisdiction of first instance over foreign cases, the amount in controversy shall be RMB 5 billion or more, or the case must be considered to have a significant impact within the province.[53] Pursuant to the SPC's 2022 Rules, if necessary based on the actual conditions within its jurisdiction, a high court may, upon the SPC's approval, designate one or more trial courts or intermediate courts to handle the cross-region foreign cases of the first instance.[54]

The so-called cross-region centralized jurisdiction over foreign cases is part of an effort to enhance the quality and credibility of the trial and intermediate courts in handling the first-instance foreign civil cases. In fact, prior to its adoption of the 2022 Rules, the SPC had approved the establishment of international commercial courts in the intermediate people's courts of *Suzhou*, *Beijing*, *Chengdu*, *Xiamen*, *Changchun*, *Quanzhou*, *Wuxi*, and *Nanning* to exercise cross-region centralized jurisdiction over the first instance of foreign civil and commercial cases.[55]

The SPC also required under their 2022 Rules that foreign civil and commercial cases be handled by a specialized tribunal or collegial panel of the competent court.[56] In addition, according to the SPC, the 2022 Rules do not apply to foreign maritime dispute cases, foreign intellectual property dispute cases, foreign ecological environmental damage compensation dispute cases, or foreign environment-related civil and public interest litigation cases.[57]

b. Territorial Jurisdiction

Unlike the tier jurisdiction that concerns the competence of a court in taking on cases with foreign elements, the territorial jurisdiction of a Chinese court relates to the power of the court over foreign defendants. It is determined on the basis of the relations between the court and the parties, disputes, or legal facts. To be precise, territorial jurisdiction dictates personal jurisdiction, jurisdiction over property, as well as the venue for the trial.

The factors that affect territorial jurisdiction include, among others, place of domicile or habitual residence, place of registration, place of business, location of property, place of injury, and place of conduct. Based on the cause of action, territorial jurisdiction can be further divided into general territorial jurisdiction

52 See *id.*
53 See *id.*
54 See *id.*, art. 4.
55 See the answers of the Fourth Civil Division Chief of the SPC to reporters' questions on the SPC's 2022 Rules, available at http://sishilawyer.com/content/?3526.html.
56 See *id.*, art. 5.
57 See *id.*, art. 6.

and specific territorial jurisdiction. In either case, an exercise of territorial jurisdiction must have a statutory ground.

I. GENERAL TERRITORIAL JURISDICTION. General territorial jurisdiction is based on the defendant's domicile or habitual residence. Under article 22 of the CPL, a civil action shall generally be instituted in the court at the place where the defendant is domiciled; if the defendant's place of domicile is different from the place of his or her habitual residence, the court in the place of his or her habitual residence shall have jurisdiction.[58] In the case where the places of domicile or habitual residence of several defendants in the same lawsuit are located in the jurisdiction of two or more people's courts, the courts involved shall all have jurisdiction.[59]

For purposes of determining jurisdiction, the domicile of a natural person is the place of their household registration. The domicile of a legal person or other organization shall be the place where the principal office of the legal person or other organization is located, or the place of registration if the place of principal office cannot be ascertained.[60] In China, household registration is a system under which the population and migrants are controlled and managed. Registration provides each household with access to all resources, benefits, and privileges available only to local residents.

Habitual residence means the place in which a person has been continuously living for one year or more prior to the litigation, excluding hospitalization for medical treatment.[61] A suit against a partnership or a partnership-based consortium that has no office shall be filed with the court in the place where the defendant is registered. If, however, there is no registration and the defendants are not in the same jurisdiction, the courts in the places in which the defendants are each domiciled have jurisdiction pertaining to each individual defendant.

The defendant's domicile-based territorial jurisdiction rests with the jurisdiction doctrine commonly referred to in China as "plaintiff following defendant," meaning that the plaintiff accommodates the defendant in the establishment of a court's jurisdiction. However, there are certain exceptions, most of which apply to issues that involve the personal status (relationship status) of the parties. Under article 23 of the CPL, a court of the place where the plaintiff is domiciled or has habitual residence shall have jurisdiction when (a) a suit concerning a personal relationship is instituted against a person not residing within the territory of China; (b) a suit concerning a personal relationship is filed against a person whose whereabouts are unknown or who has been declared missing; (c) an action is initiated against a

[58] See the CPL, *supra* note 1, art. 22.

[59] See *id.*

[60] See *id.*; see also the SPC, *Interpretation on the Application of the Civil Procedural Law*, *supra* note 10, art. 3.

[61] See the SPC, *supra* note 60, art. 4.

person who is undergoing compulsory correction; and (d) an action is brought against an imprisoned person.[62]

The SPC further specifies several cases over which the court of the place where the plaintiff is domiciled has jurisdiction. First, in the case of a claim for maintenance, alimony, or child support, if multiple defendants involved are domiciled in different jurisdictions, the court of the place of the plaintiff's domicile may assert jurisdiction.[63] Second, to claim against designating or changing guardianship, the case may be filed with the court in the place of the ward's domicile.[64] Third, a Chinese plaintiff may sue his or her spouse in a court of his or her own domicile for divorce if the spouse resides in a foreign country.[65]

II. SPECIFIC TERRITORIAL JURISDICTION. In international civil litigation, there are many cases that involve a foreign defendant who is not domiciled or residing in China. In those cases, a Chinese court has jurisdiction if the defendant has established certain connections with China. Note, however, that the defendant's mere presence in China may not constitute a ground for jurisdiction. Therefore, for jurisdiction purposes, a foreign defendant's connections with China must be so meaningful that they provide a sufficient ground to warrant the court's exercise of jurisdiction.

Under article 276 of the CPL, when a lawsuit for foreign civil disputes other than personal status is filed against a defendant who is not domiciled within China, if the contract is signed or performed in China, the subject matter of the lawsuit is located in China, the property available for seizure is situated in China, the tortious conduct is committed in China, or the representative office is located in China, then a Chinese court may have jurisdiction. If the court of the place of contract is in China, the place of performance is in China, the place of the subject matter in dispute is in China, the place of the property is in China, the place of torts committed is in China, or the place of office is in China, then a Chinese court shall respectively have jurisdiction. In addition, if the disputes involved have other appropriate connections with China, a Chinese court may also have jurisdiction.[66]

The SPC expands the place of tort to include the location of the computer and other information equipment for online torts. According to the SPC, the place where a tort is committed online is the place where the computer or other information equipment is located.[67] In addition, when a lawsuit is filed against a property

[62] See the CPL, *supra* note 1, art. 23.
[63] See the SPC, *Interpretations on the Application of the Civil Procedural Law*, *supra* note 10, art. 9.
[64] See *id.*, art. 10.
[65] See *id.*, art. 15.
[66] See the CPL, *supra* note 1, art. 276.
[67] See the SPC, *Interpretations on the Application of the Civil Procedural Law*, *supra* note 10, art. 25.

or personal damages caused to others due to an interior product or service quality, the courts that have jurisdiction include those at the place where the product was manufactured, the place where the product was sold, the place where the service was provided, the place where the infringement was committed, and the place of the defendant's domicile.[68]

For cases arising from other causes of action, the court's jurisdiction can be determined with reference to other provisions of the CPL. For example, under article 25 of the CPL, a case involving insurance contracts shall be adjudicated by the people's court at the place of the defendant's domicile or the place where the insured subject matter is located.[69] Pursuant to article 26, jurisdiction over disputes concerning negotiable instruments is proper at the place where payment was made.[70]

c. Consensual Jurisdiction

Consensual jurisdiction can be established either by the choice of the parties or under the consent of the defendant to the jurisdiction that a court otherwise may not have. The defendant's consent to the jurisdiction of a court can be expressly made or implied by the defendant's failure to timely object to the court's jurisdiction. Pursuant to article 130 of the CPL, an objection to the jurisdiction of a court shall be raised during the time limit for filing an answer to the complaint. A failure to make an objection or file a counterclaim will be deemed as consent to the court's jurisdiction, unless there is a violation of the provisions of the tier or exclusive jurisdiction.[71]

Jurisdiction by the choice of the parties refers to a consensual choice of court. Premised on party autonomy, consensual choice of law is an agreement under which the parties designate a particular court or courts to adjudicate disputes that may arise, or that have arisen, between the parties. Deriving from the freedom of the parties to select a mutually desired forum for dispute settlement, a valid and enforceable choice of court agreement constitutes a legal ground on which the chosen court is empowered to exercise its jurisdiction over the disputes and the parties involved.

As an alternative to territorial jurisdiction, the CPL allows the parties to choose a court they like through mutual agreement. Under article 277 of the CPL, when the parties to foreign civil disputes have chosen a Chinese court in writing, the court may exercise jurisdiction.[72] According to article 35 of the CPL, the court chosen by the parties in disputes involving a contract or other property rights and interests shall

68 See *id.*, art. 26.
69 See the CPL, *supra* note 1, art. 25.
70 See *id.*, art. 26.
71 See *id.*, art. 130.
72 See *id.*, art. 277.

be the court at the place of the defendant's domicile or residence, the place of contract, the place of performance, the place of the subject matter of the claim, or any other places that have an actual connection with the disputes.[73]

The SPC further requires that the choice of a foreign court by the parties also meet the actual connection requirement as provided in article 35, including the place of tortious conduct.[74] In addition, both articles 35 and 277 of the CPL mandate that the choice of court agreement must not violate the tier or exclusive jurisdiction provisions of the CPL.[75] The SPC also prohibits the parties from choosing a foreign court for cases that fall under the exclusive jurisdiction of the courts of China.[76] Thus, for a choice of court agreement to be valid in China, three conditions must be met: (a) the agreement is made in writing, (b) the court chosen has an actual connection with the disputes, and (c) there is no violation of the tier or exclusive jurisdiction.

A valid choice of court agreement not only forms the legal basis for the chosen court to exercise jurisdiction but also serves as an affirmative defense to the jurisdiction of a non-chosen court. There are, however, several issues often encountered in the ascertainment of the validity of a choice of court agreement. One issue is whether the choice of court agreement is exclusive or non-exclusive pertaining to the jurisdiction of the chosen court.

China follows the Hague Choice of Court Convention approach, which deems a choice of court agreement exclusive unless the parties expressly indicate otherwise in the agreement.[77] According to the SPC, in disputes involving a foreign contract or other property rights or interests, if the parties have an agreement clearly stipulating that the court of a country shall have jurisdiction, but do not specify that the jurisdiction as agreed is non-exclusive, the exclusive jurisdiction of the chosen court shall be presumed.[78]

The other issue concerns the so-called asymmetric choice of court agreement. A choice of court agreement is asymmetric when the agreement allows one party to bring a suit against the other party in any jurisdiction but limits the other party to sue in only one exclusive jurisdiction. The main concern is whether a choice of court agreement as such is enforceable. In China, an asymmetric choice of court agreement is generally held to be enforceable but is subject to certain exceptions.

[73] See *id.*, art. 35.

[74] See the SPC, *Interpretations on the Application of the Civil Procedural Law*, *supra* note 10, art. 531.

[75] See the CPL, *supra* note 1, arts. 35, 277.

[76] See the SPC, *Interpretations on the Application of the Civil Procedural Law*, *supra* note 10, art. 529.

[77] See 2005 Convention on Choice of Court Agreements, art. 3 (a choice of court agreement that designates the courts of one Contracting State or one or more specific courts of one Contracting State shall be deemed to be exclusive unless the parties have expressly provided otherwise), available at https://2009-2017.state.gov/s/l/releases/2013/211153.htm.

[78] See the SPC, *Minutes of the Symposium on Foreign-related Commercial and Maritime Adjudication in All Courts of the Nation*, issued on January 24, 2022, §1(1), available at http://cicc.court.gov.cn/html/1/218/62/409/2172/html.

Under the SPC's opinion, in a choice of court agreement, if the parties explicitly provide that when disputes in the foreign contract or other property rights or interests occur, one party can choose a court from more than one country to file a lawsuit, while the other party can only file a lawsuit in a court in a specific country, the agreement shall not be held invalid simply because a party claims that the agreement is unfair due to its asymmetric nature. An exception is where the agreement involves the rights and interests of consumers and employees, or violates the exclusive jurisdiction provisions of the CPL.[79]

The third issue involves the enforceability of the choice of court agreement contained in cross-border consumer online shopping contracts. In online shopping cases, it has become routine for e-commerce platforms to use a standard contract with their consumers. As noted, under article 496 of the Civil Code, where a standard clause is used, the party providing the standard clause shall, in a reasonable manner, call the other party's attention to the clause concerning the other party's major interests and concerns.[80]

Based on article 496, the SPC holds that when the standard online shopping contract contains a choice of court clause, if the e-commerce platform user fails to take reasonable measures to remind consumers of the choice of court clause, the clause will not be enforced upon the consumer's request. In addition, even if the platform user has issued a reasonable reminder, if under the choice of court clause the litigation shall be conducted in a court of a country other than the country where the consumer is domiciled, and litigation in that court unreasonably increases the cost of seeking relief for the consumer, the choice of court clause will be held invalid upon a request by the consumer.[81]

In the determination of a choice of court agreement, a dispute often arises when the primary contract and secondary contract select different courts. This is quite typical in guarantee contracts. In accordance with the SPC, if the main contract and the guarantee contract respectively stipulate the jurisdiction of courts in different countries or regions, jurisdiction shall be determined under the choice of court agreements depending on the type of contract, as long as there is no violation of the exclusive jurisdiction provisions of the CPL.[82]

d. Exclusive Jurisdiction

Exclusive jurisdiction refers to the jurisdiction that rests only with the Chinese courts. A violation of exclusive jurisdiction will incur consequences. First, a choice of court agreement will be null and void if the choice violates the exclusive

[79] See *id.* §1(2).

[80] See the Civil Code of China, adopted in 2020, art. 496, available at https://english www.gov.cn/archive/lawsregulations/202012/31/content_WS5fedad98c6d0f72576943005.html.

[81] See the SPC, *Minutes of the Symposium*, *supra* note 78, §1(3).

[82] See *id.* §1(4).

jurisdiction of the Chinese courts. Second, a judgment made by a foreign court on a matter that falls within the exclusive jurisdiction of Chinese courts will not be recognized and enforced in China. Note, however, the exclusive jurisdiction provisions do not apply to arbitration agreements.

There are two provisions in the CPL that prescribe the exclusive jurisdiction of Chinese courts. Article 34 of the CPL specifies three cases that are subject to the exclusive jurisdiction of a particular court: (a) if an action involves a dispute over immovable property, the court of the place where the property is located shall have exclusive jurisdiction; (b) if a lawsuit concerns a dispute arising from port operations, it shall be under the exclusive jurisdiction of the court of the port; and (c) for a dispute over an inheritance, the exclusive jurisdiction is with the court of the place where the deceased was domiciled at the time of death or where the major estate is located.[83]

Article 279 of the Civil Code dictates that the following cases must come under the exclusive jurisdiction of the Chinese courts: (a) litigation filed due to disputes over the establishment, dissolution, or liquidation of a legal person or other organization established within the territory of China, as well as the validity of resolutions made by such legal person or other organization; (b) lawsuits over disputes relating to the examination of the validity of intellectual property rights (IP Rights) granted in the territory of China; and (c) an action for disputes over the performance of Sino-foreign joint venture contracts, Sino-foreign cooperative joint venture contracts, and Sino-foreign cooperative exploration and development of natural resources contracts within the territory of China.[84] In those cases, foreign jurisdiction is excluded.

As noted, under article 130 of the CPL, if a party to a civil action objects to the jurisdiction of a court, the objection must be raised within the time period prescribed for the filing of answers. After receiving the objection, the court shall examine it and order that the case be sent to a competent court if the objection is tenable, or overrule the objection if it is untenable.[85] Again, the Chinese court will be deemed to have jurisdiction if no objection to the jurisdiction is timely made.[86]

B. *Concurrent Jurisdiction and Jurisdiction Conflict*

Concurrent jurisdiction refers to the situation where two or more courts have valid jurisdiction over the same case (same disputes between the same parties) at any given time. When courts have concurrent jurisdiction, a jurisdiction conflict may occur if the courts involved all exercise jurisdiction without yielding to the other(s). In addition, concurrent jurisdiction, if exercised by multiple courts, may result in inconsistent or conflicting judgments.

[83] See the CPL, *supra* note 1, art. 34.
[84] See *id.*, art. 279.
[85] See *id.*, art. 130.
[86] See *id.*, art. 278.

Under the CPL, when two or more Chinese courts have jurisdiction over an action, the plaintiff may institute his or her action in any of those courts. If, however, the plaintiff brings the suit in two or more Chinese courts that have jurisdiction over the action, the court that first puts the case on its trial docket shall have jurisdiction.[87] Note that if the case is filed with two or more competent courts, the priority to take the case rests with the court in which the case is first docketed for trial rather than the court first seized.

When concurrent jurisdiction exists between a Chinese court and a foreign court, two special provisions of the CPL apply. First, under article 280, for the same dispute between parties, if one party files a lawsuit in a foreign court and the other party files a lawsuit in a Chinese court, or one party files a lawsuit in both a foreign court and a Chinese court, the Chinese court may take the case if it has jurisdiction. When the parties have an exclusive choice of court agreement to choose a foreign court, if the choice does not violate the exclusive jurisdiction of Chinese courts and the case does not involve the sovereignty, security, or social public interests of China, the Chinese court may rule not to take the case. If the case has been accepted, the court may rule to dismiss it.[88]

Second, pursuant to article 281 of the CPL, for litigation in a Chinese court, if the party concerned asks in writing for the court to suspend the litigation on the grounds that a foreign court has accepted the case before the Chinese court has, the litigation in China may be suspended unless (a) the parties have agreed to choose the Chinese court, or the dispute falls under the exclusive jurisdiction of the Chinese court; or (b) it is obviously more convenient to have the case adjudicated in China.[89]

If, however, after suspension of the case, the foreign court fails to take necessary steps to adjudicate the case, or fails to conclude the case within a reasonable period of time, the litigation proceedings in the Chinese court shall resume upon the written request of the parties.[90] In addition, when a foreign judgment has been recognized in whole or in part by a Chinese court, and the party files a lawsuit on the same issue in China, the lawsuit will not be accepted. If already accepted, the case will be dismissed.[91]

C. *International Commercial Court under the SPC*

As noted, China created the International Commercial Court (known as the China International Commercial Court, or CICC) in 2018 to deal with certain international commercial disputes. As noted, in addition to the CICC, there are several local international commercial courts. According to the SPC's 2018 Provisions on

87 See *id.*, art. 34.
88 See *id.*, art. 280.
89 See *id.*, art. 281.
90 See *id.*
91 See *id.*

Several Issues Concerning the Establishment of International Commercial Tribunals (as amended 2023), the CICC is an adjudication body of the SPC (SPC 2018 Provisions).[92] By contrast, the local international commercial courts are those approved by the SPC to exercise cross-region centralized jurisdiction over the first instance of foreign civil and commercial cases.

Unlike the local international commercial courts that are within the intermediate people's courts of specific cities (*Suzhou*, *Beijing*, *Chengdu*, *Xiamen*, *Changchun*, *Quanzhou*, *Wuxi*, and *Nanning*), the CICC is part of the SPC. Pursuant to the Procedural Rules of International Commercial Tribunal (Provisional), issued by the SPC in 2018, the CICC is aimed at providing parties with an international commercial dispute resolution mechanism, integrating litigation with such other means as mediation and arbitration, to resolve disputes fairly, efficiently, conveniently, and at low cost (SPC 2018 CICC Procedural Rules).[93]

According to article 2 of the 2018 Provisions (as amended 2023), the CICC has the jurisdiction over the following cases of first instance: (a) the parties have chosen by agreement the SPC and the controversy amount exceeds RMB 300 million; (b) the High People's Court requests to have the first-instance international commercial cases under its jurisdiction to be heard by the SPC, and the request is granted by the SPC; (c) first-instance international commercial cases that have significant national impact; (d) application for arbitration preservation, revocation, or enforcement of an international commercial arbitration award; or (e) other international commercial cases that the SPC deems should be heard by the CICC.

It is important to note that no appeal is available to the first-instance case tried by the SPC because the SPC has the final say to all cases. However, pursuant to article 16 of the 2018 Provisions, the parties litigating in the CICC may, through a judicial supervision proceeding, apply to the SPC for retrial if any of them disagree with the legally effective judgments, rulings, and mediation documents rendered by the CICC. Once the retrial application is granted, a separate collegial panel shall be formed to conduct the retrial.[94]

The 2018 Provisions further define the international commercial cases. Under article 3 of the 2018 Provisions, a commercial case that falls under any of the following circumstances may be deemed as an international commercial case: (a) one or both parties are foreigners, stateless persons, foreign enterprises, or organizations; (b) the habitual residence of one or both parties is outside the territory of China; (c) the subject matter is outside the territory of China; and (d) the legal facts

[92] See the SPC, *2018 Provisions on Several Issues Concerning the Establishment of International Commercial Tribunals*, amended December 2023, available at http://gongbao.court.gov.cn/Details/26f41d00009ec973d5c70c2c82ca86.html.

[93] See the SPC, *The Procedural Rules of International Commercial Court (Provisional)*, issued on November 21, 2018, available at https://cicc.court.gov.cn/html/1/218/19/278/1122.html.

[94] See the SPC *2018 Provisions*, *supra* note 92, art. 16.

that create, change, or eliminate the commercial relationship occur outside the territory of China.[95] This definition is consistent with the definition of foreign cases in Chinese courts.

The 2018 Provisions set requirements for the judges sitting in the CICC. According to article 4 of the 2018 Provisions, the CICC judges shall be selected by the SPC from senior judges who have rich trial work experience, are familiar with international treaties, international practices, and international trade and investment practices, and are proficient in using both Chinese and English as working languages.[96] It is also required that when hearing the case, the CICC shall form a collegial panel composed of three or more judges, and the decision of the panel shall be made by a majority vote, but the minority opinions can be stated in the judgment.[97]

The proceeding of the CICC trial includes a process of mediation. Under article 12 of the 2018 Provisions, within seven days after accepting a case, the CICC may, upon the consent of the parties, entrust a member of the International Commercial Expert Committee organized by the SPC or an international commercial mediation agency to mediate.[98] It is further provided in article 13 that when the parties reach a mediation agreement, the CICC may issue a mediation decision, or a judgment if so required by the parties.[99]

In addition, in order to facilitate the trial before the CICC, the SPC's 2018 Procedural Rules allow parties to conduct pre-trial activities, including case filing, service, exchange of evidence, mediation, and trial preparations, and even trials online via the internet.[100] The parties may also submit materials to the CICC through the litigation platform on the official website of the CICC (www.cicc.court .gov.cn). If there are indeed difficulties, the parties can submit materials by (a) email, (b) mailing, (c) on-site submission, or (d) other methods approved by the CICC.[101]

As discussed, the CICC is a product of China's "Belt and Road" initiative. It is considered as an inevitable choice for China to promote comprehensive opening up to the outside world and participating in international competition. In the meantime, it also serves as a mechanism of judicial resolution for commercial disputes in response to the growing international commercial activities and engagement. But given China's lack of competitive advantages and the limited resources of the SPC in handling international commercial disputes, there are real dilemmas that face the CICC.

95 See *id.*, art. 3.
96 See *id.*, art. 4.
97 See *id.*, art. 5.
98 See *id.*, art. 12.
99 See *id.*, art. 13.
100 See the SPC, 2018 CICC Procedural Rules, *supra* note 93, art. 4.
101 See *id.*, art. 5.

One dilemma involves the accessibility of the CICC. Although the contractual choice of court is allowed under Chinese law, the choice, however, is restricted by the substantial connection requirements, namely the connection between the chosen court and the parties, as well as their transaction and disputes. Therefore, a choice of the CICC may become invalid due to the lack of a required connection.[102] Another dilemma concerns the selection of judges. Under the current rules, the judges are chosen from the ranking judges of the SPC. Those judges not only sit on the bench of the CICC on a case-by-case basis (no permanent judges in the CICC), but also generally lack professional background, experience, and skills in international settings, which renders the CICC to be short of internationally competitive advantages.[103]

Perhaps the most noticeable dilemma is the gap between the rapid growth of international commercial transaction activities and the commercial law built on the system bearing strong traits of the planned economy.[104] As scholars in China have pointed out, the strong administrativization of, and state intervention in, the resolution of commercial disputes often suffocate the vitality and creativity of the commercial transactions and the whole economy as well, which causes the lag in commercial law regulations.[105] Thus, despite the growing calls for an internationally compatible commercial law in the country, the overall development still trails behind the international trend. All those dilemmas, if not dealt with properly, would seriously affect the effectiveness and competitiveness of the CICC in the international commercial arena.

In addition, since the CICC is relatively new in the Chinese judicial system, there are many specific issues that require further clarification. An example is the legal status of the International Commercial Expert Committee (ICEC). According to the SPC, the SPC will retain Chinese and foreign legal experts who are proficient in international law and Chinese domestic law, and have rich practical experience as well as a high international reputation to form the ICEC. A major task of the ICEC is to provide advisory opinions on specialized legal issues involved in cases handled by the CICC. The ICEC also provides international commercial dispute resolution services upon request by the parties. But the questions that remain include, among others: (a) What is the nature of the ICEC? (b) Do the members of the ICEC exclusively serve the CICC, or can they also serve the parties? and (c) How do the ICEC maintain neutrality?[106]

[102] See Jiang Lili, *Choice of the Future of the International Commercial Court*, 10 People's Justice Journal (2019), available at www.chinaarb.org/Information/Details/caa350373cd348bda403be3cb42b9e52.

[103] See *id.*

[104] See *id.*

[105] See *id.*

[106] See Du Tao & Ye Shanshan, *International Commercial Court: A New Type of International Commercial Dispute Resolution Institution*, People's Court Daily, July 1, 2018, available at https://cicc.court.gov.cn/html/1/218/149/156/828.html.

D. *Forum Non-Conveniens*

Forum non-conveniens is a common law doctrine that allows a court, under certain circumstances, to remit the parties to a trial in another available forum.[107] The doctrine provides the courts with discretionary power to decline jurisdiction they have. Courts in civil law countries, however, generally do not have such discretionary authority to refuse to exercise jurisdiction because the jurisdictional power of civil law courts is statutory-based and thus may not be given up without specific statutory authorization.

Although the *forum non-conveniens* doctrine has gained judicial recognition in China in the past few years, it was not accepted into the law as a legal provision until the CPL was amended in 2023. The 2023 amendments to the CPL added a new provision as article 282 that makes *forum non-conveniens* a legal ground for a court to yield its jurisdiction to a foreign court. Its application, however, is subject to certain conditions and may only be triggered by a foreign defendant's objection to the jurisdiction of a Chinese court.

Under article 282 of the CPL, in a foreign-related civil case accepted by a Chinese court, if the defendant raises an objection to the jurisdiction, the Chinese court may dismiss the suit and advise the plaintiff to litigate the case in a more convenient foreign court.[108] But dismissal on the grounds of *forum non-conveniens* may only be made under the following circumstances: (a) the basic facts of the disputes in the case do not occur in China, and it is obviously inconvenient for the Chinese court to hear cases and for the parties to participate in litigation in the Chinese court; (b) there is no agreement between the parties to choose the Chinese court; (c) the case does not fall under the exclusive jurisdiction of the Chinese court; (d) the case does not involve the sovereignty, security, or public interests of China; and (e) it is more convenient for a foreign court to adjudicate the case.[109]

Article 282 of the CPL provides Chinese courts with discretionary authority to decline jurisdiction on statutory grounds. At the same time, article 282 requires Chinese courts to take the case when filed again by the parties if, after the dismissal, the foreign court refuses to exercise jurisdiction over the dispute, fails to take necessary steps to adjudicate the case, or fails to decide the case within a reasonable time period.[110]

E. *Service of Process Abroad*

To establish a Chinese court's jurisdiction over a foreign defendant or a defendant who is not domiciled within the territory of China, the service of process on the

[107] See Peter Hay, Patrick J. Borchers, & Symeon Symeonides, Conflict of Laws, 551 (5th ed., West, 2010).

[108] See the CPL, *supra* note 1, art. 282.

[109] See *id.*

[110] See *id.*

defendant must be proper and sufficient. The CPL, as amended in 2023, prescribes a list of means for extraterritorial service of process. Under article 283 of the CPL, the Chinese party may use any of the prescribed methods to serve the process on the parties who do not have domicile within the territory of China.[111]

The listed means for service of process abroad under article 283 of the CPL include: (a) the methods stipulated in the international treaty concluded or jointly acceded to by the country where the addressee is located and China; (b) delivery through diplomatic channels; (c) the embassy or consulate of China in the country where a recipient of Chinese nationality is located serves process on the recipient; (d) service on the litigation agent entrusted by the recipient; (e) service on the recipient's wholly owned enterprise, representative office, branch established within the territory of China, or a business agent authorized to accept service; (f) service on such legal person or other organization established in China in which the recipient is a foreigner or stateless person who is the legal representative or main person in charge and is also a co-defendant with the legal person or other organization; (g) service on its legal representative or principal person in charge if the recipient is a foreign legal person or other organization, and its legal representative or the principal person in charge is within the territory of China; (h) by mail if the law of the country where the recipient is located permits; (i) by electronic means that can confirm receipt by the addressee, unless prohibited by the laws of the country where the addressee is located; or (j) other means agreed to by the recipient, except where prohibited by the laws of the country where the recipient is located.[112]

Note that when the service of process is made by mail, if, after three months from the date of mailing, the delivery receipt has not been returned, but various circumstances are sufficient to determine that it has been delivered within the three-month timeframe, the delivery of the service shall be deemed completed.[113] In addition, if a service of process cannot be conducted through any of the listed means, it can be made by publication, and the service of process shall be deemed to have been delivered sixty days after the date of publication.[114]

For purposes of foreign civil litigation in the Chinese courts, the CPL also contains a provision on the collection of evidence abroad. Pursuant to article 284 of the CPL, if the evidence needed for the litigation is located outside the territory of China, the Chinese court, upon a party's request, may investigate and collect it in accordance with the methods stipulated in the international treaties concluded or jointly participated in by the country where the evidence is located and China, or through diplomatic channels.[115]

[111] See *id.*, art. 283.
[112] See *id.*
[113] See *id.*
[114] See *id.*
[115] See *id.*, art. 284.

Article 284 further provides that unless prohibited by the laws of the country where the evidence is located, the Chinese court may investigate and collect: (a) through the embassy or consulate of China in the country where the party or witness is located if the parties and witnesses are Chinese nationals; (b) through instant messaging tools with the consent of both parties; or (c) in other ways agreed by both parties.[116]

3. APPLICATION OF LAW IN INTERNATIONAL CIVIL LITIGATION

Application of law is a matter of choice of law, which refers to the law applicable to cases that contain foreign elements. The applicable law can be the law chosen by the parties through a choice-of-law clause or agreement, or the law determined by the court under the choice-of-law rules absent the parties' choice. Choice of law in China takes place in both contexts. In either case, the law applied by the Chinese courts in international civil litigations can be Chinese law, foreign law, or international treaties.

As noted, China is a unitary country where the central government has ultimate power over all administrative regions, and China's national law applies uniformly to the country as a whole. But the unitary system operates only within the Mainland, excluding Hong Kong and Macao because they possess a special status as Special Administrative Zones under the "One Country, Two Systems" scheme, though they are part of China. For purposes of civil litigation, all cases involving Hong Kong or Macao are dealt with differently from those containing Mainland elements only.

Choice-of-law rules barely existed in China prior to 1986, when the General Principle of Civil Law was adopted. But a clause in the *Tang* Code, known as the *Yong Hui* Code during the *Tang* Dynasty (618–907), is widely considered by Chinese scholars as the earliest choice-of-law legislation in the country.[117] The *Tang* Code provided that if a case involves persons who are subjects of the same foreign sovereignty, the law of said sovereignty should govern; however, if the persons involved belong to different sovereignties, the *Tang* Code shall apply.[118] Another piece of choice-of-law legislation in China was the "Rules of Application of Foreign Law," adopted by the nationalist government in 1918.[119] That legislation, however, did not have much impact in China because of the social disorder in the country in the 1920s and 1930s. In addition, as discussed, all laws enacted during the period of the nationalist government were abolished when the Communist Party rose to power in 1949.

[116] See *id.*

[117] See Han Depei, Private International Law, Textbook Series for 21st Century, 7–9 (Higher Education Press and Peking University Press, 2000).

[118] See *id.*

[119] See Max Habicht, *The Application of Soviet Law and the Exception of Public Order*, 21 Am. J. Int'l. L. 238, 242 n.18. (1927).

From 1949 to 1986, the choice of law in China was addressed only in a few consular treaties between China and other countries and mainly involved the law that governed property. An example is the 1959 Sino–Soviet Consular Treaty.[120] Article 20 of the Treaty provided that any property, including both movables and immovables, left by a citizen of one country in the territory of another country after the citizen's departure shall be governed by the law of the country where the property is located.[121]

The 1986 General Principles of Civil Law marked the beginning of choice-of-law legislation in modern China. Although there are only nine articles in the 1986 General Principles of Civil Law that are aimed at dealing with the law applicable to foreign civil relations, these articles constitute very basic choice-of-law rules in China that cover a wide range of conflict-of-law issues, including, *inter alia*, civil capacity, property, contract, torts, marriage and divorce, family support, succession, and certain escape devices such as the public policy exception.

Two years later, in 1988, the SPC issued the Opinions Concerning Implementation and Application of the General Principles of the Civil Law of (Provisional).[122] The 1988 Opinions further addressed how the law applicable to foreign civil cases is to be determined under the rules of the 1986 General Principles of Civil Law.[123] Thereafter, the 1986 choice-of-law provisions, together with the SPC's 1988 Opinions, formed the basic scheme of choice of law in China. In addition, there are some other choice-of-law provisions scattered in particular areas of law.[124]

The major choice-of-law legislation in China is the 2010 Choice of Law Statute. The significance of the Choice of Law Statute is that it unifies all of the choice-of-law rules in China and establishes an integrated framework under which all choice-of-law issues are to be handled. More importantly, the Choice of Law Statute signifies an era of codification of choice-of-law rules in the country.

The Choice of Law Statute consists of eight chapters and fifty-two articles.[125] Many of the provisions in the statute are modeled after choice-of-law rules in other jurisdictions, including European countries and international conventions such as the conventions of the Hague Conference of Private International Law. Certain concepts from American conflict of laws principles are also incorporated into the

[120] See Consular Treaty between the People's Republic of China and the Union of Soviet Socialist Republics, art. 20, available at www.gov.cn/gongbao/shuju/1959/gwyb195929.pdf.

[121] See *id.*

[122] See the SPC's 1988 *Opinions Concerning Implementation and Application of the General Principles of the Civil Law (Provisional)*, available at www.chinacourt.org/law/detail/1988/04/id/7626.shtml (SPC 1988 Opinions).

[123] See *id.*

[124] For example, Contract Law, Law of Succession, Law of Adoption, and Law of Negotiable Instruments all contain choice-of-law provisions. *See generally id.* at 290–291 (describing legal rules as being more settled in contracts, family relations, and property).

[125] See the Choice of Law Statute, *supra* note 7.

Choice of Law Statute. The stated purpose of the Choice of Law Statute is to ascertain the application of law concerning foreign civil relations, properly solve foreign civil disputes, and maintain the legitimate rights of the parties.[126]

Purposed to ascertain the law applicable to cases involving foreign civil relations, to resolve foreign civil disputes reasonably, and to safeguard the lawful rights and interests of the parties, the Choice of Law Statute has a wide range of coverage. The legal areas to which the choice-of-law rules apply include, among others, civil subjects, marriage and family relations, succession, property, *obligatio*, and IP Rights.[127] Again, as noted, *obligatio* consists of both rights and obligations, created under contract, torts, unjust enrichment, or *negotiorum gestio* (voluntary services).

One issue worth mentioning is the application of international treaties. As noted, according to article 142 of the 1986 General Principles of Civil Law, if there is a conflict between an international treaty to which China is a member state and the civil law provisions of China, the international treaty prevails, except for those provisions in the treaty to which China has announced reservations.[128] This provision is now incorporated into article 271 of the CPL. But a question remains as to whether a court in China may apply the treaty directly.[129]

A. *Choice-of-Law Principles*

In its general provisions, the Choice of Law Statute sets forth several principles that govern the choice of law in determining the rights, duties, and liabilities of parties in foreign civil cases. The function of the principles is twofold: it serves as the very basis on which the choice of law is to be made, and it dictates the primary approaches for the determination of the law to be applied in a particular case that involves two or more jurisdictions.

a. Party Autonomy

Party autonomy is a choice-of-law doctrine that permits parties to choose the law of a particular country to govern their legal relationship if the relationship has connections with multiple different countries.[130] Since its origins in the writings of the French scholar Charles Dumoulin in the sixteenth century,[131] the principle of party

[126] See *id.*, art. 1.

[127] See *id.*

[128] See 1986 General Principles of Civil Law, art. 142, available at www.asianlii.org/cn/legis/cen/laws/gpotclotproc555/.

[129] See Mo Zhang, Chinese Contract Law: Theory and Practice, 412–419 (2nd ed., Brill, 2020).

[130] See J. H. C. Morris, The Conflict of Laws, 321 (David McClean ed., 5th ed., Stevens, 2000).

[131] See Ole Lando, *Contracts,* in Kurt Lipstein ed., III-24 International Encyclopedia of Comparative Law, 6 (Mohr, 1976); see also Ernest Lorenzen, *Validity and Effects of the Contracts in the Conflict of Law*, 30 Yale L. J. 565, 572–575 (1921).

autonomy has been widely accepted by many countries.[132] It now belongs to the common core (general standard) of legal systems.[133] Today, a general consensus among the international legal community is that parties have the right to choose the law applicable to an international contract.[134] In Europe, parties' freedom to choose the applicable law is now considered to be "one of the cornerstones of the system of conflict-of-law rules in matters of contractual obligations."[135]

The Choice of Law Statute follows this international trend and makes party autonomy a general principle in choice of law. Under article 3 of the Choice of Law Statute, the parties may expressly choose the law that is to be applied to the foreign civil relation.[136] Article 3 is significant in at least two aspects. In one respect, it is the first time in China that party autonomy is provided in the law as a general principle.[137] In the other respect, application of party autonomy is not merely limited to contracts or contractual obligations, but rather extends to the whole area of foreign civil relations.[138]

b. The Closest Connection

The "closest connection" principle concerns the determination of applicable law absent a choice of law by the parties. In China, "closest connection" as a choice-of-law rule was first evidenced in the 1985 Foreign Economic Contract Law.[139] One year later, in the 1986 General Principles of Civil Law, application of the closest connection principle was expanded to not only contracts but also family maintenance.[140] The 1999 Contract Law also explicitly provided that where the parties have

[132] See Lando, *supra* note 131, at 3.

[133] See *id.*

[134] See International Institute for the Unification of Private Law (UNIDROIT), Principles of International Commercial Contracts (1994), 34 I.L.M. 1067 (1995).

[135] See Regulation (EC) No. 593/2008, of the European Parliament and of the Council of 17 June 2008 on the Law Applicable to Contractual Obligations (Rome I), 2008 O.J. (L 177) 6, 6.

[136] See Choice of Law Statute, *supra* note 7, art. 3.

[137] Both the 1986 General Principles of the Civil Law and the 1999 Contract Law allow parties to choose the law applicable to settling disputes arising from a foreign contract; however, neither explicitly provides for party autonomy in their general provisions. The 1999 Contract Law is available at https://english.cnipa.gov.cn/transfer/lawpolicy/relatedawsregulations/915598.htm.

[138] See Choice of Law Statute, *supra* note 7, art. 3.

[139] Under China's 1985 Foreign Economic Contract Law, parties to a contract could choose the law to be applied when settling disputes arising from the contract. In the absence of such a choice made by the parties, the law of the country that had the closest connection to the contract would apply. Foreign Economic Contract Law (promulgated by the Standing Comm. Nat'l People's Cong., March 21, 1985, effective July 1, 1985), arts. 5, 3 China L. Rep. 207, 207 (1985) (China).

[140] Under article 148 of the 1986 General Principles of Civil Law, maintenance shall apply the law of the country to which the fostered child is most closely connected. See 1986 General Principles of Civil Law, *supra* note 128, art. 148. According to the Supreme People's Court, maintenance is to mean the mutual fosterage between the parents and children, the mutual

not chosen a law to apply in the settlement of contractual disputes, the law of the country to which the contract is most closely connected shall be applied.[141]

In contrast to the previous choice-of-law legislation in China, the Choice of Law Statute raises the level of importance of the closest connection rule from a specific provision to a principle of general application.[142] According to article 2 of the Choice of Law Statute, in the case where statutes or other laws contain no provisions that govern a foreign civil relation, the law to which the foreign civil relation has the closest connection shall apply.[143] It is important to note, however, that as provided in article 2, the closest connection is not a default but a residual principle, meaning that it only covers the application of law to the foreign civil relations where there is no choice of law by the parties or when no statute or other law readily applies.[144]

In addition, under the Choice of Law Statute, the closest connection principle also serves as a basic conflict-of-law rule to deal with interstate or interregional law conflicts.[145] Pursuant to article 6 of the Choice of Law Statute, when foreign law is to be applied to the foreign civil relation in question, yet different laws are in place in the different regions of the foreign country, the law of the region that is most closely related to the foreign civil relation shall be applied.[146]

c. Mandatory Rules

In the conflict of laws, the "mandatory rules" principle functions to exclude the law chosen by the parties in certain circumstances to safeguard the interest of relevant countries.[147] In general, mandatory rules refer to rules that may not be contracted out of by the parties or by the application of a conflict-of-law rule.[148] In the former situation, if the choice of law by the parties violates a mandatory provision of the forum law (*lex forum*) or the law of the state that would be applied without the parties' choice (*lex causae*), the parties' choice will be discarded. In the latter case, the mandatory rule of a country's law overrides the law that would apply under a choice-of-law rule.[149]

Under Europe's 1980 Rome Convention on the Law Applicable to Contractual Obligations (now known as Rome I), when applying the law of a country, effect may

support between spouses, and the mutual support between others having a relationship of support. See 1988 Opinions, *supra* note 122, art. 189.

[141] See 1988 Opinions, *supra* note 122.

[142] See Choice of Law Statute, *supra* note 7, art. 2.

[143] See *id.*

[144] See *id.*

[145] See *id.*

[146] See *id.*, art. 6.

[147] See Morris, *supra* note 130, at 346–349.

[148] See *id.* at 346–347.

[149] See Russell J. Weintraub, *The Choice-of-Law Rules of the European Community Regulation on the Law Applicable to Non-Contractual Obligations: Simple and Predictable, Consequence-Based, or Neither?*, 43 Tex. Int'l L. J. 401, 406 (2007).

be given to the mandatory rules of the law of another country with which the situation has a close connection, if under the law of the other country these rules must be applied to the contract.[150] Nothing shall restrict the application of the law of the forum in a situation where these rules are mandatory, irrespective of a law that would otherwise be applicable to the contract.[151] The European Regulation on the Law Applicable to Contractual Obligations, known as Rome I,[152] was adopted in 2008. It replaced the Rome Convention and defines the mandatory rules to include simple mandatory rules and overriding mandatory rules.[153]

In accordance with Rome I, simple mandatory rules are the provisions of law that "cannot be derogated from by agreement" and apply to both "domestic cases" and "intra-community cases."[154] The overriding mandatory rules are the "provisions the respect for which is regarded as crucial by a country for safeguarding its public interests, such as its political, social, or economic organization, to such an extent that they are applicable to any situation falling within their scope, irrespective of the law otherwise applicable to the contract."[155] The application of overriding mandatory rules is also supposed to protect the forum state in the state where the contract is to be performed.[156]

The mandatory rules in China do not seem to be as complicated as those in Europe. Within the Choice of Law Statute, mandatory rules are the provisions contained in Chinese law that must be applied regardless of the choice by the parties.[157] Article 4 of the Choice of Law Statute makes it imperative that if the law of China has provided a mandatory rule with regard to certain foreign civil relations, such mandatory rules must be applied directly.[158] Although the Choice of Law Statute gives no definition for these mandatory rules, a rule is considered mandatory if the application of it is necessarily required based on the language of the law.[159]

Article 476 of the Civil Code, formerly article 126 of the 1999 Contract Law, provides an example of China's mandatory rules.[160] Under both provisions, for contracts such as Sino-foreign equity joint venture enterprise contracts, Sino-foreign

[150] See Rome I, *supra* note 135, art. 7.

[151] See *id.*

[152] See *id.*

[153] Overriding mandatory provisions are distinguished from "provisions which cannot be derogated from by agreement." See *id.*, arts. 3, 9.

[154] The domestic state case is a case "where all other elements relevant to the situation at the time of the choice are located in a country other than the country whose law has been chosen," while the intra-community case refers to the case in which "all other elements relevant to the situation at the time of the choice are located in one or more Member States." *id.*, arts. 3, 4.

[155] *id.*, art. 9(1).

[156] See *id.*, arts. 9(2), 9(3).

[157] See Choice of Law Statute, *supra* note 7, art. 4.

[158] *id.*

[159] See Morris, *supra* note 130, at 346–347.

[160] See 1999 Contract Law, *supra* note 137, art. 126.

cooperative joint venture enterprise contracts, and exploration and development of natural resources contracts to be performed within the territory of China, the laws of China apply.[161] Therefore, as a principle, application of any foreign law is excluded for these contracts (collectively referred to as FIE contracts).[162] In addition, the SPC, through judicial interpretation, expanded the application of the mandatory rules to other FIE-related contracts as well.[163]

d. Public Policy

Public policy is a device to avoid or deny the application of a foreign law that would otherwise be applied either by the choice of the parties or under applicable choice-of-law rules. In the United States, it is commonly called an "escape device" because it permits judges to escape applicable law where the law would produce an undesirable outcome.[164] Thus, if the application of foreign law were found incompatible with the public policy of the forum country, the application of the law would be excluded and the forum law will be applied instead.[165]

In China, public policy is termed "social and public interests." The principle was provided in the 1986 General Principles of Civil Law to exclude the application of foreign law that is found to violate the social and public interests of China.[166] The SPC describes public policy as the fundamental principles of law and social public

161 *id.*

162 See *id.*

163 In article 8 of its interpretation, the Supreme People's Court in 2007 added the following contracts to which the application of Chinese law is mandatory: the contract of transfer of shares of Chinese-foreign equity joint ventures, Chinese-foreign contractual joint ventures, or wholly foreign-owned enterprises; contract for operation by a foreign natural person, legal person, or other organization of Chinese-foreign equity joint ventures or contractual joint ventures formed within the territory of China; contracts to purchase by a foreign natural person, legal person, or other organization the equity rights of the shareholders of non-foreign investment enterprises within the territory of China; contract to purchase by a foreign natural person, legal person, or other organization the newly issued shares of a non-foreign-invested limited liability company or company limited by shares within the territory of China; and contract to acquire by a foreign natural person, legal person, or other organization the assets of non-foreign-invested enterprises within the territory of China. See the SPC, *Rules of the Supreme People's Court on Related Issues Concerning the Application of Law in Hearing Foreign-Related Contractual Dispute Cases Related to Civil and Commercial Matters*, promulgated by the Judicial Comm. Sup. People's Ct., June 11, 2007, effective August 8, 2007, art. 8, available at www.fdi.gov.cn/pub/FDI_EN/Laws/GeneralLawsandRegulations/JudicialInterpretation/P020070905634447818232.pdf.(SPC2007 Rules].

164 See David Vernon et al., Conflict of Laws, Cases, Materials and Problems, 278 (2nd ed., LexisNexis, 2003).

165 See Monrad G. Paulsen & Michael I. Sovern, *"Public Policy" in the Conflict of Laws*, 56 Colum. L. Rev. 969, 981 (1956).

166 "The application of foreign laws or international practice in accordance with the provisions of this chapter shall not violate the public interest of the People's Republic of China." 1986 General Principles of Civil Law, *supra* note 128, art. 150.

interest, and holds that when a foreign law is excluded on the grounds of public policy, the applicable law shall be Chinese law.[167]

The Choice of Law Statute modifies the 1986 public policy provision. Under article 5 of the Choice of Law Statute, if the application of foreign law would harm the social and public interests of China, the law of China shall be applied instead.[168] On one hand, to the extent of the public policy exclusion, article 5 of the Choice of Law Statute focuses more on the consequences of the application of foreign law than on the contents of the foreign law. The notion is that the difference in the contents of a foreign law does not necessarily warrant the public policy exclusion, but the consequence of the application matters because in the case of applying a foreign law the difference in content may not lead to an undesirable outcome nor result in harm. On the other hand, pursuant to the Choice of Law Statute, a consequence of public policy exclusion will be the direct application of Chinese law rather than merely excluding the foreign law.

However, the Choice of Law Statute does not state what may constitute public policy. One scholarly interpretation in China is that the social and public interest includes not only the very principles of law, but also social morals and public order principles.[169] In certain cases, the public policy exclusion may also be applied if the application of a foreign law would adversely affect state ownership in a Chinese company, or if application would be considered detrimental to consumer interests.[170]

B. *Threshold Issues in Choice of Law*

In the choice of law, there are a number of issues that would affect the application of the law to be chosen.[171] In conflict-of-law theory, these issues are addressed in different ways. In Europe, these issues are considered the institutions in the foundation of the European choice of law.[172] In the United States, they are grouped into the "escape devices," including public policy. These issues are regarded as "escape devices" because, as noted, the devices serve as manipulative techniques that allow courts to avoid applying the law mandated by the specific choice-of-law rule.[173] In China, these issues are collectively called preliminary matters of the conflict of

[167] See the SPC Answers, 1987 Sup. People's Ct. Gaz. 3 (1987) (China) (SPC 1987 Answers).
[168] See Choice of Law Statute, *supra* note 7, art. 5.
[169] See Liu Xiangshu, Study on Basic Problems of Private International Law, 158–160 (Law Press, 2001).
[170] See Zhang, *supra* note 129, at 320.
[171] See Willis L. M. Reese & Maurice Rosenberg, Cases and Materials on Conflict of Laws, 384–436 (8th ed., Foundation Press, 1984).
[172] See Ralf Michaels, *The New European Choice-of-Law Revolution*, 82 Tul. L. Rev. 1607, 1616 (2008).
[173] See *id.* at 121 n. 53.

laws since they are the primary concerns in the conflict of laws that must be addressed and resolved before the applicable law is ascertained.

a. Characterization

Characterization, also known as categorization or classification, is the process by which the court decides the nature of a case or the nature of an issue in order to determine which law is going to apply.[174] The former involves essentially the cause of action and sometimes even the terms used,[175] while the latter goes to the substantive–procedural distinction. When facing a choice-of-law matter, courts must characterize the issue or the case before determining the applicable law.[176]

Since the line between the causes of action in such cases as contracts, torts, and property is often obscure, while the law applied to each of them varies, defining the nature of the case can determine the outcome of the case.[177] Similarly, the question of whether a particular issue is substantive or procedural can determine the law to be applied because, as a general rule, the law of the forum will apply if a particular issue is classified as procedural in nature.[178]

Characterization in conflict-of-law cases is often an issue due to the fact that the same or similar terms or concepts as used in different jurisdictions involved may mean or refer to different things.[179] A question that necessarily arises, then, is which law shall govern the characterization. Put differently, it is the question about which law determines the type of cause of action (torts or contract), the nature of subject matter (real property or personal property), or the kind of issue (procedure or substance).

In the conflict-of-law literature, there have developed two major approaches in dealing with how a characterization is made. The first approach is the *lex causae* (law of the cause) or *ex lege causae*, which suggests that the characterization shall be

[174] See Lea Brilmayer & Jack Goldsmith, Conflict of Laws, Cases and Materials, 114 (5th ed., Aspen, 2002).

[175] Characterization was first introduced by Prof. Ernest Lorenzen in 1920 to address the problem of differing characterizations that may arise due to the differences in meaning of concepts used and countries differing in their definition of various terms; according to Prof. Lorenzen, the question presented is what law is to determine the meaning of the terms. See Ernest G. Lorenzen, *Theory of Qualification and the Conflict of Laws*, 20 Colum. L. Rev. 247 (1920); see also A. H. Robertson, *A Survey of the Characterization Problem in the Conflict of Laws*, 52 Harv. L. Rev. 747, 747–748 (1938).

[176] See Luther L. McDougal III, *Codification of Choice of Law: A Critique of the Recent European Trend*, 55 Tul. L. Rev. 114, 126 (1980).

[177] See Vernon et al., *supra* note 164, at 286–293.

[178] See Dicey, Morris & Collins on the Conflict of Law, 177 (14th ed., Sweet & Maxwell, 2006); see also Brilmayer & Goldsmith, *supra* note 174, at 129.

[179] See David P. Currie, et al., Conflict of Laws, Cases, Comments, Questions, 43 (7th ed., West, 2006).

made in accordance with the law applicable to the dispute at issue.[180] The argument is that if a foreign law were to govern while not applying its characterization, it would be tantamount to not applying it at all.[181] In contrast, the second approach relies on the *lex fori*, which holds that the law of the forum determines characterization.[182] The idea is that if the foreign law is allowed to determine the situations in which it is to be applied, the law of the forum (*lex fori*) would lose all control over the application of its own conflicts rules and would no longer be master in its own home.[183]

China takes the *lex fori* approach and applies it to all characterization problems.[184] Article 8 of the Choice of Law Statute provides that the law of the forum governs the characterization in a foreign civil relation.[185] The Choice of Law Statute mandates that all characterization problems be solved under the forum state's law. Thus, when adjudicating foreign civil cases as the forum, Chinese courts are required to handle the characterization under Chinese law, except for matters concerning the statute of limitations.

b. Statute of Limitations

The statute of limitations is an issue of characterization because there is always a lingering question as to whether the statute of limitations is substantive or procedural.[186] Traditionally, in common law countries, the statute of limitations has been characterized as procedural so that the limitation periods prescribed by the forum state's laws govern, despite its substantive effect of determining which party wins the lawsuit.[187] In some civil law systems, however, the limitation law is treated as substantive, to which the *lex causae* doctrine would apply.[188]

[180] See Roberto Baratta, *The Process of Characterization in the EC Conflict of Laws: Suggesting a Flexible Approach*, 6 Y.B. Priv. Intl L. 155, 168 (2004).
[181] See Dicey, Morris & Collins, *supra* note 178, at 40.
[182] See *id.*
[183] See *id.* at 39.
[184] See Choice of Law Statute, *supra* note 7, art. 8.
[185] See *id.*
[186] See Currie et al., *supra* note 174, at 50.
[187] See 51 Am. Jur. 2d *Limitation of Actions* § 22 (Thomson Reuters, 2011).
[188] See 193rd Report on Transnational Litigation, Conflict of Laws, Law of Limitation, 2005, Law Commission of India 2, available at http://lawcommissionofindia.nic.in/reports/Report193.pdf (India). Not until recent years has there been a change in common law countries in bringing the limitation law up to par with civil law countries. In the United Kingdom, under the 1984 Foreign Limitation Periods Act, the law was amended to treat the foreign limitation law as substantive, and therefore the law of that other country relating to limitation shall apply in respect of that matter for the purposes of the action or proceedings. The amendment, as such, also took place in other commonwealth countries. In the United States, following the 1983 Uniform Conflict of Laws Limitation Act, several states have adopted a rule that treats the foreign law of limitation as substantive and applies it directly in lieu of the "borrowing statute" practice.

In China, before the adoption of the Choice of Law Statute, the matter of statutes of limitation in foreign civil cases was adjudicated in the Chinese courts under a rule established by the SPC in 1988.[189] According to the SPC, statutes of limitation in a foreign civil relation shall be determined under the proper law of such relation.[190] In conflict of laws literature, the "proper law" refers to the law that should be applied as determined by the choice-of-law rules. Apparently, the SPC's opinion in this regard was premised on a civil law tradition.[191]

The Choice of Law Statute affirms the judicial practice in respect to statutes of limitation but alters the SPC's wording.[192] Article 7 of the Choice of Law Statute provides that the statute of limitations applies the law that the given foreign civil relation would apply.[193] The doctrine on which both the SPC's opinion and the Choice of Law Statute stand is *lex causae*.[194] But the Choice of Law Statute does not use the term "proper law" because the term "proper law" itself is a highly contested term that could be interpreted in several ways.[195]

c. Renvoi

As a result of the choice of law applicable to a civil dispute, or in general to a foreign civil relation, a foreign law or "law of the country" may be applied in the forum court.[196] However, in the context of conflict of laws, the term "law of country" is ambiguous because it is unclear whether the law so chosen is referred to as "internal law," or substantive law of the country, or if it means the "whole law," including the choice-of-law rules of the country.[197] If the choice-of-law rules are included in the "law of country," a problem of *renvoi* may arise during the application of the law chosen.[198]

Renvoi, a French word meaning "sending back" or "remitting,"[199] occurs when a forum's choice-of-law rule refers to the law of a foreign country, but the conflict rule of that foreign country redirects the question to the law of a third country (transmission) or back to the law of the forum (remission).[200] The approach toward the *renvoi*

[189] See the SPC 1988 Opinions, *supra* note 122, art. 195.
[190] See *id.*
[191] See *id.*
[192] See Choice of Law Statute, *supra* note 7, art. 7.
[193] See *id.*
[194] See *id.*; see also the SPC 1988 Opinions, *supra* note 122.
[195] See Chen Weizhuo, *On the Applicable Law and the "Proper Law,"* 3 Tsinghua L. Rev. 121 (2009).
[196] See Dicey, Morris & Collins, *supra* note 178, at 71.
[197] See *id.* at 70.
[198] See Erwin Griswold, *Renvoi Revisited*, 51 Harv. L. Rev. 1165, 1166–1167 (1938).
[199] See Luther McDougal III, Robert Felix & Ralph Whitten, American Conflicts Law: Cases and Materials, 130 (4th ed., Lexis Law Pub., 2004).
[200] See Dicey, Morris & Collins, *supra* note 178, at 71.

problem varies from country to country.[201] Given the complexity of *renvoi* and the goal of achieving certainty in choice of law, there is a growing trend to reject *renvoi* by excluding the choice-of-law rule when applying a foreign law in the forum.[202]

In Europe, for example, article 20 of Rome I defines the application of the law of any country to mean the "application of the rules of law in force in that country other than its rules of private international law, unless provided otherwise."[203] Article 24 of Rome II, which regulates the law applicable to non-contractual obligations, contains a similar provision, but it deletes the phrase "unless provided otherwise," thus completely rejecting *renvoi*.[204]

In China, the judicial attitude toward *renvoi* has been negative. As early as 1987, the SPC expressly rejected *renvoi* in foreign contract cases.[205] Some Chinese scholars suggested recognizing *renvoi* in cases involving personal or family status where the law being referred to is Chinese law.[206] However, the Choice of Law Statute takes the Rome II approach and rules out *renvoi* in all foreign civil cases.[207] Under article 9 of the Choice of Law Statute, the law of a foreign country applicable to foreign civil relations shall not include the choice-of-law rules of that country.[208]

d. Ascertainment of Foreign Law

In applying foreign law, the first issue the court and the parties face is what the foreign law is about.[209] The issue is in essence a functional one, determining whether the foreign law should be deemed as a fact or be considered as the law.[210] Hence, the

[201] In Germany, remission is accepted, but transmission is allowed only insofar as it does not contradict the meaning of the *renvoi*. Swiss law, on the other hand, rejects *renvoi* in general, but accepts remission for matters of civil status. In the United Kingdom, the *renvoi* doctrine applies only in limited cases. In American conflict of laws, the Second Restatement recognizes *renvoi* when the objective of the particular choice-of-law rule is that the forum would reach the same result on the very facts involved as the courts of another state would. See Einführungsgesetz zum Bürgerlichen Gesetzbuche [BGBEG] [Introductory Law to the Civil Code], September 21, 1994, Bundesgesetzblatt [BGBI] I 2494, as amended, art. 4 (Ger.) (hereinafter BGBEG]; see also 1987 Swiss Federal Code of Private International Law, December 18, 1987, RS 291, art. 14.

[202] See generally Rome I, *supra* note 130 (rejecting the doctrine of *renvoi*); see also Regulation (EC) No. 864/2007, of the European Parliament and of the Council of 11 July 2007 on the Law Applicable to Non-Contractual Obligations (Rome II), 2007 O.J. (L 199) 40.

[203] See Rome I, *supra*, note 135, art. 20.

[204] See Rome II, *supra* note 202, art. 24.

[205] See the SPC, *Answers to the Matters Concerning the Application of Foreign Economic Contract Law*, 1987 SPC Gaz 3 (1987), art. 5.

[206] See Chinese Society of Private Int'l Law, *Model Law of Private International Law of the People's Republic of China*, art. 8 (2000) (hereinafter Model Law).

[207] See Choice of Law Statute, *supra* note 7, art. 9.

[208] *id.*

[209] See Dicey, Morris & Collins, *supra* note 178, at 48–55.

[210] See *id.*

center of the issue is eventually a matter of burden of proof.[211] China used to regard the determination of a foreign law primarily as a function of the court, and it is thus the judge's role *ex officio* (by virtue of the office) to determine the law and apply it.[212]

Over the years, however, there has been an attempt in the country to reduce the burden of the court by introducing a less *ex officio* approach to get the parties more involved in the proof of foreign law.[213] In this context, the Choice of Law Statute adopts a mixed approach under which the court, arbitral authority, or administrative organ shall ascertain the foreign law applicable to a case of foreign civil relation, but if the parties choose to apply a foreign law, they shall provide the law as such.[214] The statute further provides that if the law of a foreign country cannot be ascertained, or if its law contains no provision relevant to the case, the law of China shall apply.[215]

In 2023, in its Interpretation on Several Issues Concerning Application of the Choice of Law Statutes (II), the SPC set forth detailed rules for the ascertainment of applicable foreign law in Chinese courts, including the general rule, channels to obtain foreign law, proof of foreign law, and determination.[216] The SPC's interpretation is purposed to tackle the difficulty facing the Chinese courts in ascertaining foreign laws in foreign litigations and to provide unified norms and standards for ascertainment and application of foreign law.[217]

According to the SPC's 2023 Interpretation, when a foreign country's law is to be applied in Chinese courts in foreign-related civil and commercial cases, the law of that country shall be ascertained under the following rule: (a) if the parties choose to apply a foreign law, they should provide the law of that country, and (b) absent the

[211] As a well-established tradition, "[c]ommon law courts [have] treated foreign law as a matter of fact to be pleaded and proved by the party whose cause of action or defense depend[s] upon foreign law." In civil law countries, an accepted maxim is known as *jura novit curia*, meaning that the court knows the law, and therefore determination of foreign law is by and large a judicial function. But as it has been observed, a change has occurred in this regard largely as a result of statute, which concentrates on providing a flexible and fair procedure for the determination by the court of the law of other jurisdictions. See Currie et al., *supra* note 174, at 85; Imre Zajtay, *The Application of Foreign Law*, in Kurt Lipstein ed., III-14 International Encyclopedia of Comparative Law, 3 (Mohr, 1972); Weintraub, *supra* note 149, at 113.

[212] See Zhang, *supra* note 129, at 326.

[213] See *id.*

[214] See Choice of Law Statute, *supra* note 7, art. 10; see also SPC 1988 Opinions, *supra* note 122, art. 193 (addressing several channels employed to help determine foreign law, which include (a) the central authority of the country that has a judicial assistance treaty with China, (b) a Chinese embassy or consulate in a particular country, (c) a foreign embassy or consulate in China, and (d) legal experts).

[215] See Choice of Law Statute, *supra* note 7, art. 10.

[216] See the SPC, *Judicial Interpretation on Several Issues Concerning Application of the Choice of Law Statutes (II)*, issued on November 30, 2023, at http://gongbao.court.gov.cn/Details/190e38dd05e8f28d8e14a7bdadd93d.html (SPC 2023 Interpretation).

[217] The SPC, *Announcement of Judicial Interpretation on Several Issues Concerning Application of the Choice of Law Statutes (II)*, November 30, 2023, available at https://nyzy.hncourt.gov.cn/public/detail.php?id=32658.

parties' choice, the court shall ascertain the law of that country.[218] Under this rule, the courts have the responsibility to ascertain foreign law, and parties also have the duty to provide foreign law when they choose to apply foreign law.

To facilitate the ascertainment of foreign law, the SPC provides seven channels for the courts to obtain foreign law, and those channels can be used individually or in combination. Pursuant to article 2 of the SPC's 2023 Interpretation, the court may ascertain a foreign law by such means as: (a) provided by the parties; (b) provided by the other country's central authority or competent authority through judicial assistance channels; (c) SPC's request to the Chinese embassy or consulate in the foreign country or the foreign country's embassy or consulate in China; (d) provided by the participating party in the mechanism of law ascertainment cooperation established or joined by the SPC; (e) provided by experts in the International Commercial Expert Committee formed by the SPC; (f) provided by legal ascertainment service agencies, or Chinese and foreign legal experts; and (g) by other appropriate ways.[219]

Note that under the SPC's 2023 Interpretations, the parties may still be asked by the courts to provide foreign law even if the parties do not make a choice of foreign law. In this situation, however, the duty of ascertainment of foreign law is mainly on the court, and the parties' providing foreign law is supplementary. For this reason, the SPC makes it clear that when asking the parties to assist in providing foreign laws, the court shall not rule out the foreign law solely on the grounds that the party has not provided assistance.[220]

To prove that foreign law shall rule the case, certain formalities and procedures must be followed. First, if the parties provide the foreign law, they should submit the specific provisions of the law of that country and explain how to access the law, the effectiveness of the law, and the relevance of the law to the disputes in the case. If the foreign law so provided is case law, the full text of the case should also be submitted.[221]

Second, if a law ascertainment service agency or legal expert provides the foreign law, in addition to the submission of the law or cases, the qualification certificate of the law ascertainment service agency, or the identity and qualifications certificate of the legal expert, shall be submitted to the court together with a written declaration of no conflict of interest in the case.[222]

Third, all relevant materials found to be related to foreign laws must be presented in court. The court shall hear the opinions of all parties on the content of foreign law, their understanding, and the application of the law. The court may convene a

[218] See the SPC 2023 Interpretation, *supra* note 216, art. 1.
[219] See *id.*, art. 2.
[220] See *id.*
[221] See *id.*, art. 3.
[222] See *id.*, art. 4.

pre-trial conference or use other appropriate methods to determine the scope of foreign laws that need to be ascertained.[223]

Fourth, if necessary or upon the request of the parties, the court may ask the law ascertainment service agency or a legal expert who provides foreign laws to appear in court for questioning. If, however, it is difficult for the law ascertainment service agency or legal experts to appear in court, they can be questioned online, unless the online cross-border judicial questioning or inquiry is prohibited under the law of the country where the legal identification service agency or legal experts are located. In addition, the law ascertainment service agencies or legal experts who appear in court may only express their opinions and understanding of the foreign laws, and do not participate in other court proceedings.[224]

When determining the applicable foreign law, the courts may identify the contents of the foreign law as well as the understanding and application of it in the following way: (a) if the parties have no objection to the content, understanding, and application of foreign law, the people's court may confirm it; (b) in the case that the parties make objections, they shall explain the reasons, and then if necessary, the court may make additional inquiries or require the parties to provide additional materials. If the parties continue to object thereafter, the court shall make a determination upon its review; or (c) if the contents of a foreign law have been determined in an effective Chinese judgment, the court shall confirm it, unless there is contrary evidence sufficient to overturn it.[225]

In addition, the court is required to set a time limit for the parties to provide foreign laws based on the time needed to complete the relevant procedures. The parties, however, may request an extension if they are unable to provide the foreign law within the time limit for specific reasons. Moreover, if the parties choose to apply foreign law but fail to provide the foreign law within the time limit without justifiable reasons, the court may determine that the foreign law cannot be ascertained.[226]

It is also required that when the court applies foreign law to a case, it shall state in the judgment the process of ascertaining the law and the content of the foreign law. In the situation where the court determines that the foreign law to be applied cannot be ascertained, it shall state the reasons why the foreign law is unascertainable.[227] With regard to the fee arrangement for foreign law ascertainment, if the parties have agreed to that effect, their agreement shall control; if there is no such agreement, the court may make a determination based on reasonableness.[228]

[223] See *id.*, arts. 5–6.
[224] See *id.*, art. 7.
[225] See *id.*, art. 8.
[226] See *id.*, art. 9.
[227] See *id.*, art. 10.
[228] See *id.*, art. 11.

C. *Choice of Law by the Parties*

Permitting the parties to select by agreement the law to govern their civil relationship under the principle of party autonomy does not have a long history in China.[229] Not until 1985, when the Foreign Economic Contract Law was promulgated, was the concept of party autonomy first officially recognized in the country, so that the parties to a contract may choose the law applicable to the settlement of contract disputes.[230] Choice of law by the parties was further provided as a choice-of-law rule in the 1986 General Principles of Civil Law and the 1999 Contract Law, respectively.[231]

a. Party Autonomy in Contractual Choice of Law

In 2007, the SPC issued a set of rules that serve as discretionary guidance for determining the applicable law in contracts and in the application of party autonomy in the courts.[232] The Choice of Law Statute reinforces party autonomy for the selection of governing law. First, the Choice of Law Statute sets party autonomy as a principle for the choice of law that applies to foreign civil relations in general, and second, the Choice of Law Statute allows the application of party autonomy not only in traditional contractual obligations, but also in non-contractual obligations.[233] The expansion of the application of party autonomy as such to a great extent is influenced by Rome II, and reflects the developing modern trend of the party autonomy doctrine.[234]

Under the Choice of Law Statute, in addition to the general provision that grants the parties the power to select the law governing a foreign civil relation,[235] the parties may also choose by agreement the governing law for matters such as entrustment of agency (*per procurationem*),[236] trust,[237] arbitral agreement,[238] spousal property relations,[239]

[229] See Zhang, *supra* note 129, at 313.

[230] See Foreign Economic Contract Law, adopted in 1985 (repealed when the Contract Law was adopted in 1999), *supra* note 139, art. 5.

[231] See 1986 General Principles of Civil Law, *supra* note 128, art. 145; see also 1999 Contract Law, *supra* note 137, art. 126.

[232] See SPC 2007 Rules, *supra* note 163.

[233] See Choice of Law Statute, *supra* note 7, art. 3.

[234] See generally Mo Zhang, *Party Autonomy in Non-Contractual Obligations: Rome II and Its Impacts on Choice of Law*, 39 Seton Hall L. Rev. 861 (2009) (discussing Rome II's treatment of conflict-of-law situations regarding non-contractual obligations subject to the laws of more than one EU member state).

[235] See Choice of Law Statute, *supra* note 7, art. 3.

[236] *id.*, art. 16.

[237] *id.*, art. 17.

[238] *id.*, art. 18.

[239] *id.*, art. 24.

divorce by agreement,[240] property right of movables,[241] change of rights over movables during transportation,[242] contract,[243] torts,[244] unjust enrichment and *negotiorum gestio* (voluntary services),[245] and transfer or licensed use of IPR.[246]

The application of party autonomy within the framework of the Choice of Law Statute is extensive and goes far beyond the traditional boundary of contracts with respect to the choice of law by parties.[247] What then follows is that the parties on a voluntary basis may not only decide which law is to govern their contract, but may also agree to subject their agreement or legal relationship to the law of a particular country. This is perhaps the reason why the Choice of Law Statute generalizes the scope of the parties' choice of applicable law on an abstract level, and why the Choice of Law Statute uses the generic term "foreign civil relations."[248]

b. Features of Contractual Choice of Law

There are several notable features of contractual choice of law under Chinese law. First, a connection between the place of the law chosen and the disputes, transactions, or the parties is not required. The parties by agreement may select whatever law they like regardless of their relationship with the law. In other words, the parties to a contract may subject themselves to a neutral law as long as the choice does not violate the public policy or mandatory rule of China.

Second, the parties may choose a treaty as governing law, including a treaty that has not yet entered into force for China, unless it violates the mandatory provisions of the laws and administrative regulations of China or damages China's sovereignty, security, and public interests.[249] In addition, as noted, the parties to a foreign civil or commercial contract may expressly choose to apply international practices to determine the rights and obligations between them.[250]

Third, the time for the parties to make their choice is quite flexible. The SPC has been taking a liberal stance toward the choice of law by the parties.[251] In many

[240] *id.*, art. 26.
[241] See Choice of Law Statute, *supra* note 7, art. 37.
[242] *id.*, art. 38.
[243] *id.*, art. 41.
[244] *id.*, art. 44.
[245] *id.*, art. 47.
[246] *id.*, art. 49.
[247] The Choice of Law Statute establishes the extensive circumstances under which parties may, by agreement, choose the governing law. See *id.*
[248] *id.*, art. 3.
[249] See the SPC, *Interpretation of Several Issues Concerning Application of International Treaties and Practices in the Trial of Foreign Civil and Commercial Cases*, 2023, available at https://cicc.court.gov.cn/html/1/218/62/84/2430.html.
[250] See *id.*
[251] See generally SPC 2007 Rules, *supra* note 163, art. 4 (allowing parties to choose applicable law up to the end of debate in court).

countries, the parties shall make the choice at the time of contract; otherwise, the parties shall be deemed to have not chosen the applicable law unless some other manifestation of their intention of the choice can be ascertained.[252] In China, however, the parties may choose the governing law or change the governing law they have already chosen any time before the end of the argument in the first court trial (trial of first instance).[253]

Fourth, an express choice may be inferred under certain circumstances.[254] According to the SPC, if the parties have made no choice of which law to apply in contractual disputes, but both of them invoke the law of the same country or region without any objection to its application, the parties shall be deemed to have selected the law of the country or region as the governing law.[255] This interpretation suggests that although the concept of tacit choice is rejected in the country, the SPC seems to try to define express choice in a broader sense so as to include indirect choice or choice by inference in certain cases.

c. Limitations on Contractual Choice of Law

Indeed, the Choice of Law Statute grants the parties ample freedom in selecting the applicable law.[256] But the choice is not unlimited.[257] Statutorily, there are certain restrictions on how the choice is to be made.[258] The first restriction is the express choice rule, which requires that the choice of law by the parties be made expressly.[259] Under article 3 of the Choice of Law Statute, the contractual choice of law shall be made expressly.[260] Thus, no tacit choice is recognized in China.

Put differently, the parties' intention with regard to the governing law of their contract may not be implied from the terms of the contract or from the course of dealing between the parties. As a matter of fact, although both the 1986 General Principles of Civil Law and the 1999 Contract Law contain no requirement of express choice of law by the parties,[261] it has become a well-settled rule in practice

[252] See Morris, *supra* note 130, at 328.

[253] See the SPC 2007 Rules, *supra* note 163, art. 4; see generally Mo Zhang, *International Civil Litigation in China: A Practical Analysis of the Chinese Judicial System*, 25 B.C. Int'l & Comp. L. Rev. 59 (2002) (discussing the Chinese judicial system, which takes place in only two instances: trial and appeal).

[254] See the SPC 2007 Rules, *supra* note 163, art. 4.

[255] See *id.*

[256] See *generally id.* (allowing certain circumstances in which the parties may choose, by agreement, which law will apply).

[257] See *id.*, art. 3.

[258] *id.*

[259] Choice of Law Statute, *supra* note 7.

[260] *id.*

[261] See 1986 General Principles of Civil Law, *supra* note 128, art. 145; see also 1999 Contract Law, *supra* note 137, art. 126.

since 1987, when the SPC interpreted the application of the 1985 Foreign Economic Contract Law.[262]

The other restriction is the exclusion provision.[263] Under the Choice of Law Statute, the choice of law by the parties will be excluded in two situations: where public policy is at stake and where a mandatory rule applies.[264] As discussed, public policy and mandatory rule are two general principles that preempt the application of any foreign law in Chinese courts.[265] Therefore, the exclusion here actually imposes a restriction on the application of foreign law. In other words, if the parties agree to have Chinese law govern their contract, such a choice would not be affected by the exclusion provision.

Based on party autonomy, the parties may choose the law governing the disputes that may arise or that have arisen between them. Put differently, the parties may choose a governing law by an agreement entered into after the event giving rise to the disputes occurred (*ex post* agreement) or by an agreement freely negotiated before the event giving rise to the disputes occurred (*ex ante* agreement).

The Choice of Law Statute, however, limits the parties' choice of governing law to the *ex post* agreement with regard to torts.[266] Under article 44 of the Choice of Law Statute, if the parties choose the applicable law by agreement after a tort takes place, the agreement shall control.[267] But this limitation does not apply to choice-of-law agreements for claims concerning unjust enrichment and *negotiorum gestio*.[268]

d. Unsettled Issues

A relevant but unsettled issue is the application of *dèpeçage* in the choice of law.[269] The doctrine of *dèpeçage* allows the rules of different states to be applied to determine different issues in a single case.[270] With regard to the contractual choice of law, this doctrine permits the parties to select the law applicable to their contract in whole or in part.[271] If in part, different laws may be selected to govern different parts of the contract.[272] In China, the application of *dèpeçage* is included in

262 See the SPC 1987 Answers, *supra* note 167.
263 See Choice of Law Statute, *supra* note 7, arts. 4–5.
264 *id.*
265 *id.*
266 See Choice of Law Statute, *supra* note 7, art. 44.
267 *id.*
268 See *id.*, art. 47.
269 See Morris, *supra* note 128, at 561–563 (addressing the problems that may arise when "two chosen laws cannot logically be reconciled").
270 See Willis L. M. Reese, *Dèpeçage: A Common Phenomenon in Choice of Law*, 73 Colum. L. Rev. 58, 58 (1973).
271 See Morris, *supra* note 128, at 329.
272 See *id.*

choice-of-law legislation or in judicial practice.[273] The Choice of Law Statute, however, contains no provision on *dèpeçage*.

Nonetheless, the doctrine of *dèpeçage* is well accepted in the legal texts in China.[274] The Model Law of Private International Law is both exemplary and illustrative.[275] Under article 100 of the Model Law, the parties may choose the law that will govern the whole contract, or may choose the law that will govern only part or several parts of the contract.[276] It has been argued that, because under the Choice of Law Statute the parties may agree to choose the law applicable to the contract, nothing indicates that the parties may not choose different laws to govern different parts of the contract.[277] On the other hand, as many have noted, the choice of law by the parties is specified in the 1999 Contract Law to only concern the settlement of contract disputes.[278] It actually separates the matters of capacity and formality from other matters of the contract, which has resulted in subjecting the different parts of the contract to different laws.[279]

D. *Determination of Applicable Law Absent the Parties' Choice*

There are two situations in which the parties are deemed to have not made a choice of applicable law. One situation is when the parties do not select any governing law, fail to reach an agreement on the choice of law, and nothing in the contract may infer their choice.[280] The other situation is when the parties have made a choice of applicable law, but the choice is found to be invalid or is set aside for different reasons.[281]

Absent parties' choice, the law to apply has to be determined by the court or an arbitration body.[282] To determine the law to apply, difficulties especially arise in contract cases because a contract requires a high degree of predictability as to the law to be applied in order to protect the expectations of the parties.[283] Approaches employed to solve the choice-of-law issue in this regard are so different that the

[273] See generally Choice of Law Statute, *supra* note 7 (including no recognition of the doctrine of *dèpeçage*).

[274] See Model Law, *supra* note 206, art. 100.

[275] The Model Law was published in 2000 by the Chinese Institute of Private International Law and was intended to serve as a restatement of the law. See *id.*

[276] See *id.*

[277] See Choice of Law Statute, *supra* note 7, art. 41.

[278] See Li Shuangyuan, The Trend of Private International Law in the 21st Century, 527 (Law Press, 1999).

[279] See *id.*

[280] See generally Hay et al., *supra* note 107, at 1131 (discussing the conditions under which an agreement on the choice of law might bind parties to a contract).

[281] See *id.* at 1156–1158.

[282] See *id.* at 1158.

[283] See *id.* at 1158–1159.

applicable law determination becomes a matter of great complexity.[284] In many cases, factors that connect or link the legal issues to the laws of relevant states appear to be determinative.[285]

a. The Closest Connection

As discussed, China requires a connection in the determination of foreign law. In 1985, the rule of the closest connection was first embodied in the Foreign Economic Contract Law,[286] and one year later it was adopted in the 1986 General Principles of Civil Law for the ascertainment of applicable law without the parties' choice.[287] In addition, based on the closest connection rule, the SPC adopted the concept of characteristic performance and incorporated it into the standards for the judicial determination of applicable law in particular cases.[288] The Choice of Law Statute formulates the closest connection rule on a two-layer pattern.[289] In the first layer, the closest connection rule, as noted, is stated as a principle of general application, and in the second layer, the rule is specifically applied to a particular legal relation.[290]

In applying the closest connection rule in China, the determination of the connection is discretionary.[291] Since no legislation has ever prescribed what would be the closest connection, thereby leaving the rule in obscurity, the courts normally follow the guidance provided by the SPC.[292] With regard to contracts, the determination is based on the characteristic performance.[293] In other cases, the courts have to weigh the relevant connecting factors on a case-by-case basis to determine which place or locale has the closest connection for the purpose of the application of law.[294]

As a general practice, before making a determination of applicable law, the courts in China would need to make two inquiries. One inquiry is whether the parties have made a choice of governing law and whether the choice so made is valid, because an effective choice of law by the parties will exclude the judicial determination of the law.[295] The other inquiry is whether the parties are willing to make any choice

[284] See *id.* at 1158–1176.
[285] See *id.* at 1163–1165.
[286] See Foreign Economic Contract Law, *supra* note 139, art. 5.
[287] See 1986 General Principles of Civil Law, *supra* note 128, art. 145.
[288] See the SPC 1987 Answers, *supra* note 167; see also the SPC 2007 Rules, *supra* note 163, art. 5.
[289] See Choice of Law Statute, *supra* note 7, arts. 2, 39, 41.
[290] See *id.*
[291] See Yu Shuhong et al., *Doctrine in the Conflict of Laws in China*, 8 Chinese J. Int'l L. 439 (2009) ("For other international contracts, the court exercised broad judicial discretion in deciding the country of closest connection.").
[292] See *id.* at 430, 432.
[293] See *id.* at 430.
[294] See *id.* at 431.
[295] See *id.*

with respect to the applicable law if there has been no choice-of-law clause or agreement yet.[296] This second inquiry may take place even before the end of the court argument in the first-instance trial.[297]

In contrast to the previous legislation and legal practice in which the closest connection was supplemented by the characteristic performance, the Choice of Law Statute subordinates the closest connection rule to the approach of characteristic performance in its application to contracts.[298] In other words, to determine the applicable law to contracts absent the parties' choice, the closest connection rule will be applied as an alternative when the characteristic performance is not readily applicable.[299] Under article 41 of the Choice of Law Statute, if the parties make no choice of applicable law, the law of the habitual residence of the party whose fulfillment of obligations best reflects the characteristics of the contract, or another law that has the closest connection with the contract, shall apply.[300]

I. CONNECTING FACTORS. In choice of law, the connecting factor serves as a link between a particular type of legal issue and the applicable law. It refers to the "factors that relate to a place where the event or fact occurs: the place where an object is situated, where an obligation is to be performed, or where an (legal) act takes place."[301] In torts, for example, the place of wrong is an important connecting point that determines the law applicable to the tort committed.[302] More generally, the closest connection is also determined by the use of such factually geographical factors.[303]

In choice of law, a connecting factor of great significance is the domicile.[304] The domicile not only represents a personal relationship between an individual and a governmental unit or geographic area, but also an enduring and persistent relationship.[305] Domicile is "often viewed as the most significant personal relationship an individual has to a place."[306] Although it is commonly held that "every person has a domicile at all times and no person may have more than one domicile at a time,"[307] the difficulty is in determining the domicile, because different jurisdictions define the domicile differently.

As a matter of fact, "in modern choice of law, the place of habitual residence or the principal place of business of the parties have become important connecting

[296] See *id.*
[297] See *id.*
[298] See *id.* at 428.
[299] See *id.*
[300] See Choice of Law Statute, *supra* note 7, art. 41.
[301] Mireille van Eechoud, Choice of Law in Copyright and Related Rights, 32 (Kluwer, 2003).
[302] See *id.* at 206.
[303] See *id.*
[304] See Hay et al., *supra* note 107, at 286.
[305] See *id.*
[306] See *id.*
[307] See Restatement of Conflict of Laws (Second), § 11(2) (1971).

factors because these factors generally reflect the closest connection from a factual-geographical perspective."[308] Habitual residence is generally deemed less demanding than domicile, and the focus is more on past experience than future intention; habitual residence is the geographical place usually considered "home" for a reasonably significant period of time.[309] In Europe, habitual residence has been used "in various Hague conventions on the reform of private international law," and has been adopted by the European Commission as a connecting factor for choice of law.[310]

In China, domicile used to play an important role in identifying the geographical location, as well as the political and economic connection, of a person. It was also a main connecting factor in the choice of law with regard to the matters pertaining to personal status. In many cases, domicile was used in conjunction with nationality and habitual residence for the purpose of determining applicable law. In recent years, however, there has been a trend in which habitual residence overtakes domicile in the ascertainment of the legal relationship between a person and a particular place. The development is due, to a large extent, to economic growth and increasing mass migration.

Under the 1986 General Principles of Civil Law, "if the habitual residence of a person is not the same as his domicile, his habitual residence shall be regarded as his domicile."[311] But it is not clear what constitutes a habitual residence. According to the SPC, habitual residence of a person is the place where the person has last resided for more than one year after leaving his/her domicile.[312] Therefore, for a residence to be considered habitual, the length of residence shall be at least one year.

As noted, the domicile of a legal person is the place of its registration, and such place also determines its nationality.[313] Under the SPC's interpretation, a foreign legal person shall have as its national law the law of the country where it is registered.[314] The place of registration of a legal person is also regarded as the place of the legal person's formation.[315] If, however, the place of registration differs from the place of principal business, the latter may be used for choice-of-law

[308] See van Eechoud, *supra* note 301, at 32.

[309] See Pippa Rogerson, *Habitual Residence: The New Domicile?*, 49 Int'l & Comp. L. Q. 86, 87 (2000) ("[habitual residence] has been deliberately not defined in any of the statutes or Conventions in order to prevent the rigidity associated with the alternative concepts of domicile and nationality").

[310] See *id.* at 86.

[311] See *id.*

[312] See the SPC 1988 Opinions, *supra* note 122, art. 9.

[313] See *id.*

[314] See *id.*, art. 184.

[315] See 1986 General Principles of Civil Law, *supra* note 128, art. 39 ("A legal person's domicile shall be the place where its main administrative office is located.").

purposes, but the former will remain as the place of nationality of that legal person.[316]

II. PLACE OF HABITUAL RESIDENCE. The Choice of Law Statute makes habitual residence the rudimentary connecting factor for the choice of law.[317] It alters the previous choice-of-law rules that were based on domicile, and also takes a step further toward making habitual residence a determinative factor for the applicable law in many other areas.[318] More precisely, the Choice of Law Statute abandons the concept of domicile pertaining to the choice of law and replaces it with the concept of habitual residence.[319]

Under the Choice of Law Statute, habitual residence becomes the primary connecting factor in determining the applicable law concerning the status of "civil subjects," including civil capacity, declaration of a missing person or the death of a person, and the right of personality.[320] As discussed, civil capacity consists of the capacity for rights and capacity to act.[321] A general rule of the Choice of Law Statute is that the civil capacity of a natural person is governed by the law of the place of its habitual residence.[322] But if there is a conflict between the law of the place of habitual residence and the law of the place of conduct with regard to the capacity to act, the latter controls, except for the matters involving marriage, family, or succession.[323]

With regard to a legal person, its habitual residence is the place of the legal person's principal business.[324] According to the Choice of Law Statute, the law of the place of registration governs civil capacity, as well as the obligations and shareholders' rights of a legal person's business organization and its branches.[325] However, if the place of registration differs from the place of principal business, the law of the place of principal business may be applied.[326] Thus, if a foreign registered company does business mainly in China, it would be subject to Chinese law in

[316] Under article 184 of the 1988 Opinions of the Supreme People's Court, if a legal person has two or more business places, the place of business that is most closely related to the dispute shall control. See the SPC 1988 Opinions, *supra* note 122, art. 184.

[317] See Chen Weizhuo, *Ten Highlighted Points of the Statute of Application of Law in Foreign Civil Relations*, China Legal Daily, November 2, 2010, at http://news.sohu.com/20101102/n276959905.shtml.

[318] See Choice of Law Statute, *supra* note 7 (allowing for both the "law of the current residence of the person" to apply if habitual residence does not apply, and for the use of habitual residence to determine the law governing a natural person's civil rights); see also 1986 General Principles of the Civil Law, *supra* note 128.

[319] See Choice of Law Statute, *supra* note 7, art. 2.

[320] See *id.*, arts. 11–15.

[321] See 1986 General Principles of Civil Law, *supra* note 128, ch. 2, § 1, ch. 3, § 1.

[322] See Choice of Law Statute, *supra* note 7, arts. 11, 12, 14.

[323] See *id.*, art. 12.

[324] See *id.*, art. 14.

[325] See *id.*

[326] See *id.*

respect to its civil capacity, business organization, and the rights and obligations of its shareholders.

As provided in the Choice of Law Statute, the law of habitual residence also applies in situations where the law of nationality should be applied but the person has dual nationalities, is stateless, or has an unknown nationality.[327] In addition, if the law of the place of habitual residence of a person should apply, but the habitual residence of the person is uncertain, the law of the place of his current residence will be applied instead.[328]

The law of the place of habitual residence is also applied to marital law, family law, and the law of succession. Furthermore, it determines the governing law in instances of marriage, adoption and will formalities, personal and property relations between spouses, personal and property relationships between parents and children, consensual divorce, and guardianship.[329] Additionally, the law of the place of habitual residence is applicable to statutory succession except in real estate succession.[330] It also applies to the determination of the method and validity of a will.[331]

The choice of law based on place of habitual residence is extended to non-contractual obligations as well. Under article 44 of the Choice of Law Statute, for example, the law of the place of a tort shall govern the liabilities for that tort.[332] However, if the parties have common habitual residence, the laws of the common habitual residence shall apply instead.[333] To the extent that the choice of law is involved, two parties have a common habitual residence when their habitual residences are located in the same jurisdiction.[334] Article 47 further provides that for unjust enrichment and *negotiorum gestio*, the law chosen by the parties shall apply; absent the parties' choice, the law of the common habitual residence of the parties shall be applied.[335]

b. Characteristic Performance

The doctrine of characteristic performance originated from Switzerland in the early 1970s in a case involving a contract of agency.[336] The very concept of the doctrine essentially attaches "the contract to the social and economic environment of which

[327] See *id.*, art. 19.
[328] See *id.*, art. 20.
[329] See *id.*, arts. 21–30.
[330] See *id.*, art. 31.
[331] See *id.*, arts. 32, 33.
[332] See *id.*, art. 44.
[333] See *id.*
[334] See *id.*, arts. 12, 23–26, 44, 47 (detailing when the law of common habitual residence will apply in different situations).
[335] See *id.*, art. 47.
[336] See Hans Ulrich Jessurun d'Oliveira, *"Characteristic Obligation" in the Draft EEC Obligation Convention*, 25 Am. J. Comp. L. 303, 304–305 (1977).

it will form a part."[337] The doctrine does not "see a connection of an all-embracing nature, but inquire[s] in respect of each type of contract what is the characteristic content of that contract."[338] The idea is that the performance of the contract refers to the function that the legal relationship fulfills in the economic and social life of any country.[339] Thus, the characteristic performance is considered the one that "usually constitutes the center of gravity and the socio-economic function of the contractual transaction."[340]

In Europe, the characteristic performance doctrine became an important choice-of-law rule in 1980 through the Rome Convention.[341] Since then, the characteristic performance doctrine has been used as the presumption under which the closest connection is to be established.[342] It is presumed that the contract is most closely connected with the country where the party who is to effect the performance, which is characteristic of the contract.[343] The country determination is based on the party's habitual residence, or in the case of a corporate body, its central administration at the time of conclusion of the contract.[344] Furthermore, under article 4(5) of the Rome Convention, the characteristic performance does not apply if it "cannot be determined," or "if it appears from the circumstance as a whole that the contract is more closely connected with another country."[345]

Rome I is more specific than the 1980 Rome Convention in defining characteristic performance in particular contracts in the context of determining applicable law. For example, article 4(1)(a) of Rome I states that, "a contract for the sale of goods shall be governed by the law of the country where the seller has its habitual residence."[346] And the closest connection rule will only apply when (a) "the contract is manifestly more closely connected with" another country;[347] or (b) the applicable

337 See Morris, *supra* note 128, at 333 (quoting Mario Giuliano & Paul Lagarde, *Report on the Convention on the Law Applicable to Contractual Obligations*, 1980 O.J. (C 282) 20).

338 See d'Oliveira, *supra* note 336, at 306.

339 See Anthony Jaffey, *The English Proper Law Doctrine and the EEC Convention*, 33 Int'l & Comp. L. Q. 531, 546 (1984). To illustrate, for a sales contract the characteristic performance is the performance for which payment is due; in other words, the characteristic performance is the delivery of goods, not the payment of money. See also Nicky Richardson, *The Concept of Characteristic Performance and the Proper Law Doctrine*, 1 Bond L. Rev. 1, 2 (1989).

340 See Morris, *supra* note 130, at 333–334.

341 See Shuhong et al., *supra* note 286, at 423–424 (stating that the Hague Convention and the European Parliament adopted the Rome I regulations).

342 See 1980 Rome Convention, art. 4, available at https://eur-lex.europa.eu/legal-content/EN/TXT/HTML/?uri=CELEX:41998A0126(02); see also Rome I, *supra* note 135, art. 4(2).

343 See Rome Convention 1980, *supra* note 342, art. 4 (3).

344 *id.*

345 *id.* art. 4(5).

346 Article 4(1) of Rome I lists eight specific types of contracts and makes express provisions for determining the law governing those types of contracts in the absence of choice. The types of contracts specified are those involving sales, services, immovable property, immovable property for temporary use for less than six months, franchise, distribution, auction, and interest in financial instruments. Rome I, *supra* note 135, art. 4(1)(a)–(h).

347 See *id.*, art. 4(3).

law is unable to be determined under the characteristic performance doctrine.[348] In those two cases, the law of the country in which the contract is most closely connected will apply.[349]

In China, the characteristic performance doctrine was first accepted by the SPC in 1987 as guidance for courts to determine the closest connection.[350] The SPC redefined the application of the doctrine in 2007.[351] Although the 2000 Model Law strongly advocated for the characteristic performance doctrine,[352] the doctrine was not formally adopted into legislation until the promulgation of the Choice of Law Statute.[353]

Article 41 of the Choice of Law Statute generally provides that the law of the country where the habitual residence of the party whose fulfillment of obligations can best reflect the characteristics of the contract is to be applied.[354] Unfortunately, article 41 of the Choice of Law Statute does not define any situation where the characteristics of the contract would be best reflected in terms of the obligation fulfillment.[355]

Therefore, in the application of article 41, the courts would need to refer to the SPC's 2007 Rules in order to determine the applicable law under the characteristic performance doctrine.[356] In its 2007 Rules, the SPC listed seventeen major contracts in which the applicable law is specified on the basis of characteristic performance.[357] But according to the SPC, since the characteristic performance is set in the Choice of Law Statute as the default rule absent the parties' choice, it may be displaced if another jurisdiction has a closer connection with the contract.[358] Thus, if a contract to which the characteristic performance doctrine is applicable is "manifestly more closely connected to another country or region, the law of that country or region shall be applied."[359]

Article 41 of the Choice of Law Statute permits the option of applying the closest connection rule in order to fill in the gap left by the non-application of the characteristic performance doctrine.[360] The presumption is that the choice-of-law rule for the different contract types under the characteristic performance doctrine is "designed to refer the court to the law of the State with which" the contract or a

[348] See *id.*, art. 4(4).
[349] See *id.*
[350] Shuhong et al., *supra* note 291, at 428.
[351] See the SPC 2007 Rules, *supra* note 163, art. 4.
[352] See Model Law, *supra* note 206, art. 101.
[353] Choice of Law Statute, *supra* note 7.
[354] See *id.*
[355] See *id.*
[356] Shuhong et al., *supra* note 291, at 428.
[357] See the SPC 2007 Rules, *supra* note 163, art. 5(1)–(17).
[358] See *id.* at 429.
[359] See *id.*
[360] See *id.*

particular issue is most closely connected.[361] It is believed that the presumption as such will help achieve "legal certainty and predictability" regarding the applicable law because the determination of the governing law under the characteristic performance doctrine will make "the judicial task and process easier," and more attainable.[362]

E. *Choice-of-Law Rules in Special Areas*

The Choice of Law Statute intends to provide a complete set of choice-of-law rules to govern foreign civil relations in China.[363] It contains not only the provisions of general application, but also the specific rules that apply in particular cases or legal relations.[364] In addition, the statute signifies some areas through specially focused rules.[365] One such area is the protection of the interests of weak parties, which includes consumers, employees, and tort victims.[366] Another area is the protection of IPR, the area that has long been neglected in choice of law.[367] Furthermore, the Choice of Law Statute focuses on the area of internet-related torts, which poses great challenges to the existing choice-of-law mechanisms.[368]

a. Property Rights

The Choice of Law Statute contains a set of rules that determine the law applicable to the rights to property. First, the Choice of Law Statute follows the *lex rei sitae*, the universally accepted "*situs*" rule applicable to the rights and interests of real property. Under article 36 of the Choice of Law Statute, a right to an immovable property shall be governed by the law of the place where the immovable property is located, including creation, modification, transfer, or extinction of such property right.[369]

With regard to right to a movable property, the Choice of Law Statute, as noted, allows the parties to choose by their agreement the governing law. Absent the parties' choice, the law of the place in which the movable property is situated at the time the legal fact occurs applies.[370] For purposes of choice of law, the legal fact refers to the situation where the movable property right is established, changed, transferred, or extinguished. Also, under article 38 of the Choice of Law Statute, the parties may through their agreement choose the law to govern the change of the right over a

361 See *id.*
362 See *id.*
363 See *id.*, art. 1.
364 See *id.*
365 *id.*
366 See *id.*, arts. 42–44.
367 See *id.*, arts. 48–50.
368 See *id.*, art. 46.
369 See the Choice of Law Statute, *supra* note 7, art. 36.
370 See *id.*, art. 37.

movable property while in transit. In the case where the parties make no choice of law, the law of the place of the transit destination applies.[371]

In addition, the Choice of Law Statute specifies the law that governs rights of negotiable instruments as well as the rights of pledge. According to article 39 of the Choice of Law Statute, a negotiable instrument shall be subject to the law of the place in which the rights of the negotiable instrument realize, or the law that has the closest connection with the negotiable instrument.[372] Pursuant to article 40 of the Choice of Law Statute, the law of the place where a right of pledge is created governs the right as such.[373]

b. Interests of Weak Party

In modern business transactions, the parties in the course of dealing often possess unequal bargaining power due to factors like asymmetry in market conditions and disparate allocation of resources and information.[374] To combat this problem, many countries have put in place certain norms that are aimed at protecting the weaker party in the stream of commerce.[375] In the conflict of laws area, attention has been drawn to the adoption of rules that are supposed to protect the interests of weak parties.[376] As a result, the choice-of-law rule for consumer contracts has emerged, because it is considered undeniable that consumers are typically in a weaker bargaining position.[377]

The Choice of Law Statute places great emphasis on the protection of the interests of weak parties. Several of the choice-of-law rules provided in the Choice of Law Statute are directly related to the protection of weak parties, and their coverage ranges from family relations to tort victims.[378] In those cases, the applicable law should be the law in favor of protecting the weak, which is chosen from the laws of related places. The most prominent place is the habitual residence of the plaintiff.

In family relations, article 25 of the Choice of Law Statute provides that the personal and property relations between parents and children shall be governed by the laws of their common habitual residence. But if there is no common habitual residence, the laws of one party's habitual residence or the laws of the country of one

[371] See *id.*, art. 38.
[372] See *id.*, art. 39.
[373] See *id.*, art. 40.
[374] See generally Daniel D. Barnhizer, *Inequality of Bargaining Power*, 76 Colo. L. Rev. 139 (2005) (discussing the prevalence of unequal bargaining power and its causes).
[375] See, for example, Rome I, *supra* note 135, recital 23 (citing the protection of weaker parties to a contract as an aim of Rome I).
[376] See *id.*
[377] See Antonio Boggiano, *International Standard Contracts: A Comparative Study*, in 170 Recuiel Des Cours: Collected Courses of the Hague 11, 55 (Brill, 1981).
[378] See Choice of Law Statute, *supra* note 7, arts. 21–30, 42–44.

party's citizenship, whichever better protects the rights and interests of the weaker party, shall apply.[379]

Also, according to article 29, family support shall apply "whichever [law] best protects the rights and interests of the supported."[380] Thus, either the law of the habitual residence, the state of the nationality of a party, or the place of principal properties shall be applied.[381] The same concept is seen in article 30, under which the guardianship shall be governed by the laws of a party's habitual residence or the laws of a party's country of citizenship, whichever better protects the rights and interests of the person under the guardianship.[382]

With regard to contractual obligations, both consumer and labor contracts are subject to the special choice-of-law rules.[383] For consumer contracts, it is required that the law of habitual residence of the consumer be applied.[384] The only exception is that if the business operator does not have any business engagement in the place of habitual residence of the consumer, or, if the consumer so chooses, the law of the place where the goods or services are provided may be applied.[385] But the default rule is the application of law of the habitual residence of the consumer.

The choice-of-law rule for labor contracts is formulated in a way that the parties' choice is excluded.[386] In accordance with article 43 of the Choice of Law Statute, a labor contract is subject to the law of the employee's place of work.[387] If it is difficult to ascertain the working place of a laborer, the laws of the principal place of business of the employer shall apply.[388] If the contract is for labor dispatch, the law of the dispatching place may apply.[389] The driving force behind article 43 is the better protection of the interests of those who provide labor services.

The weak party in torts is usually the victim of tortious conduct. Prior to the adoption of the Choice of Law Statute, the general rule was that the law of the place of tortious conduct applies to torts, and, as an alternative, if both parties are citizens of (or are domiciled in) the same country, the law of their own country or the country of their domicile may be applied.[390]

The Choice of Law Statute turns the focus of the rule more onto the protection of the injured party in two ways.[391] First, it prioritizes the application of the law of the

[379] See *id.*, art. 25.
[380] See *id.*, art. 29.
[381] See *id.*
[382] See *id.*, art. 30.
[383] See *id.*, arts. 42–43.
[384] See *id.*, art. 42.
[385] See *id.*
[386] See *id.*, art. 43.
[387] See *id.*
[388] See *id.*
[389] See *id.*
[390] See 1986 General Principles of Civil Law, *supra* note 128, art. 146.
[391] See Choice of Law Statute, *supra* note 7, arts. 44–45.

place of common habitual residence of the parties in the tort case.[392] Under article 44 of the Choice of Law Statute, torts liability shall be governed by the laws of the place of the tortious act. If, however, the different parties of the tortious act have a common habitual residence, the laws of the common habitual residence shall apply.[393]

Second, the Choice of Law Statute separates product liability from general torts and provides a special choice-of-law rule for product liability.[394] According to article 45 of the Choice of Law Statute, product liability shall be governed by the laws of the victim's habitual residence.[395] If the injured party chooses to make it applicable, or the tortfeasor does not have any business operation in the victim's habitual residence, the laws of the tortfeasor's principal place of business or the laws of the place where the damage occurs shall apply.[396] Once again, the law of the habitual residence of the injured party takes priority in the application.

c. Intellectual Property Rights

In the conflict of laws landscape, protection of IPRis a more recent subject.[397] Information-rich products have long crossed borders, prompting interested countries to pursue some intellectual property policymaking at an international level.[398] However, not until the early 1990s did questions about the need for conflict-of-law rules to deal with intellectual property matters come into the spotlight of discussion.[399]

At the national level, courts in different countries have attempted to apply the territorially based choice-of-law rules such as *lex loci protectionis* (law of the country of protection), *lex fori* (law of the forum), or *lex loci delicti* (law of the place where the tort was committed).[400] Internationally, at least on a restrained concept of

[392] See *id.*, art. 44.

[393] See *id.*

[394] See *id.*, art. 45.

[395] See *id.*

[396] See *id.*

[397] See Graeme B. Dinwoodie, *Developing Private International Intellectual Property Law: The Demise of Territoriality?* 51 Wm. & Mary L. Rev., 711, 713 (2009).

[398] Since the birth of the Paris Convention for the Protection of Industrial Property in 1883, various bilateral and multilateral treaties that were adopted thereafter have formed a body of international substantive law which provides an international legal framework for the protection of intellectual property rights. See Paris Convention for the Protection of Industrial Property, March 20, 1883, 38 Stat. 1811, 155 L.N.T.S. 179, available at www.wipo.int/treaties/en/ip/paris/pdf/trtdocs_wo020.pdf.

[399] See Dinwoodie, *supra* note 397, at 713 n.2.

[400] See Richard Fentiman, *Choice of Law and Intellectual Property*, in Josef Drexl and Annette Kur, eds., 24 Studies in Industrial Property and Copyright Law, Intellectual Property and Private International Law – Heading for the Future, 129, 147–148 (Cambridge University Press, 2005).

territoriality, some countries are exploring the possibility of developing a private international intellectual property law.[401]

In Chinese conflict-of-law literature, IPR protection has long been deemed as covered by the rules of international substantive law.[402] In many Chinese conflict-of-law books, IPR issues are discussed with the application of the international conventions of IPR protection, and those conventions are generally categorized as substantive law rules.[403] The Choice of Law Statute takes an unprecedented step into the area of IPR by providing two basic rules that govern the applicable law for the infringement of IPR.

The first rule is the rule of *lex loci protectionis*.[404] Under article 48 of the Choice of Law Statute, the ownership and contents of the IPR shall be governed by the law of the place where protection is claimed.[405] In addition, as provided in article 50, the rule of *lex loci protectionis* also applies to the determination of tort liabilities for the infringement of IPR.[406]

The second rule is the rule of party autonomy, which is applicable in two situations.[407] One situation is IPR infringement, in which the parties, as an alternative to the *lex loci protectionis*, may agree to make a choice of applicable law.[408] However, there are two restrictions with respect to the choice by the parties.[409] First, when making a choice, the parties must choose the law of the forum.[410] Second, the choice may only be made after the infringement has occurred.[411] The other situation concerns the transfer and licensed use of an IPR.[412] In this case, the parties may, by agreement, choose the applicable law.[413] But absent the parties' choice, the choice-of-law rules applicable to contracts shall be applied.[414]

d. Internet-Related Torts

The development of the internet poses great challenges to conflict of laws. As growing activities on the internet diminish the significance of national

[401] See Dinwoodie, *supra* note 397, for a general discussion of private international intellectual property law.
[402] Cf. Zhang, *supra* note 129, at 307–309 (explaining that, in contrast to conflict of law rules which deal primarily with resolving questions of which law should be applied, substantive law rules directly apply to and affect the rights and obligations of the parties involved).
[403] See Huang Jin, Private International Law, 714 (Law Press, 1999).
[404] See Choice of Law Statute, *supra* note 7, arts. 48, 50.
[405] See *id.*, art. 48.
[406] See *id.*, art. 50.
[407] See *id.*, arts. 49–50.
[408] See *id.*, art. 49.
[409] See *id.*, art. 50.
[410] See *id.*
[411] See *id.*
[412] See *id.*, art. 49.
[413] See *id.*
[414] See *id.*

boundaries, debate increases over whether the nature of conflict of laws has changed and whether conventional choice-of-law rules remain applicable to internet-related conflict-of-law cases.[415] Confronted with a dramatic change in the digital environment, countries must refine their choice-of-law rules.[416]

Much of the discussion about the impact of the popularization of the internet on the conflict of laws in China was initially on jurisdictional issues rather than on choice of law.[417] The SPC has looked into jurisdiction over online copyright infringement three times since 2000 and established a jurisdictional rule that is based on the place of infringement or the place of the defendant's residence.[418] The 2009 Torts Law imposes tort liabilities on any internet user or provider who infringes upon the civil rights or interests of another through the internet,[419] but contains no provision regarding choice of law.

The Choice of Law Statute is the first legislation in China that provides a choice-of-law rule for internet-related torts.[420] The provision implicates the development of Chinese conflict of laws pertaining to online activities, but unfortunately, the applicable rule applies only to infringement upon the rights of personality.[421] Under article 46 of the Choice of Law Statute, if personal rights such as the right to name, right to portrait, right to reputation, right to privacy, or other similar rights are infringed upon via the internet or other means, the laws of the infringed party's habitual residence shall apply.[422] Once again, the habitual residence of the injured party controls for the purpose of choice of law.[423]

4. JUDICIAL ASSISTANCE AND FOREIGN JUDGMENTS

In international civil litigation, it is often the case in which a judicial order or request would need to be recognized or enforced in another jurisdiction. The process of

[415] See Ansgar Ohly, *Choice of Law in the Digital Environment – Problems and Possible Solutions*, in 24 Studies in Industrial Property and Copyright Law, Intellectual Property and Private International Law – Heading for the Future, *supra* note 400, at 241, 241–243; see also Lawrence Lessig, Code and Other Laws of Cyberspace, 190–198 (Basic Books, 1999).

[416] See Ohly, *supra* note 415, at 192–194.

[417] See Michael Bristow, *China Defends Internet Censorship*, BBC News (June 8, 2010, 09:21 AM), http://news.bbc.co.uk/2/hi/americas/8727647.stm (explaining China's assertion that "[w]ithin Chinese territory the internet is under the jurisdiction of Chinese sovereignty.").

[418] See the SPC, *Interpretation on the Matters of Application of Law to the Cases Involving Disputes over Computer Network Related Infringement of Copyrights* (promulgated by the Judicial Comm. Sup. People's Ct., November 20, 2006, effective December 8, 2006), available at www.court.gov.cn/qwfb/sfjs/201006/t20100604_5810.htm. According to the SPC, the place of infringement includes the place of such equipment like the internet servers, computer terminals, etc.

[419] See the 2009 Tort Law, available at www.procedurallaw.cn/english/law/201001/t20100110_300173.html.

[420] See Choice of Law Statute, *supra* note 7, art. 46.

[421] See *id.*

[422] See *id.*

[423] See *id.*

mutual recognition and enforcement as such is known as judicial assistance. In international civil litigation, judicial assistance is to be carried out either under bilateral or multilateral treaties or on the basis of reciprocity absent a treaty.

A. *Judicial Assistance*

In China, judicial assistance in international civil litigations operates under the provisions of the CPL. According to article 293 of the CPL, Chinese and foreign courts may request that the other serve documents, investigate and collect evidence, and conduct other litigation activities according to international treaties concluded or acceded to by China, or based on the principle of reciprocity.[424] But if the matter for which assistance has been requested by a foreign court is detrimental to the sovereignty, security, or social and public interests of China, the Chinese court will not accept it.[425]

Article 294 further provides that judicial assistance shall be conducted through the channels stipulated in the international treaties concluded or acceded to by China, or through diplomatic channels if there is no treaty.[426] In addition, foreign embassies and consulates in China may serve documents to citizens of that country and investigate and collect evidence without violating the laws of China and without taking compulsory measures (to compel).

The CPL also contains two special rules. One is the prohibitive rule under which no other foreign agency or individual may serve documents, investigate, or collect evidence within the territory of China without the permission of the competent authority of China.[427] The other is the procedural rule, which requires Chinese courts to provide judicial assistance under the procedures prescribed by the laws of China. But as an exception, if a foreign court requests using a particular method, the request may be honored if using that method does not violate the laws of China.[428]

B. *Recognition and Enforcement of Foreign Judgment*

Recognition and enforcement of a judgment in international civil litigation involves two kinds of judgments: (a) a judgment made by a domestic court to be enforced in a foreign country, and (b) a judgment made by a foreign court to be enforced in a domestic court. Given the territorial nature of judicial power, the focus here is on the recognition and enforcement of a foreign judgment in a domestic court. By the end of November 2023, there were a total of seventeen foreign court judgments seeking recognition and enforcement in China, of which four were refused

[424] See the CPL, *supra* note 1, art. 293.
[425] See *id.*
[426] See *id.*, art. 294.
[427] See *id.*
[428] See *id.*

recognition and enforcement by Chinese courts.[429] During the same period, Chinese courts applied for recognition and enforcement in foreign countries of twenty-two judgments, of which three were denied by foreign courts.[430]

For a foreign judgment, recognition is a prerequisite to enforcement. In other words, without being recognized first, no foreign judgment will be enforced. But in certain cases, a judgment may only need to be recognized without an action for enforcement. Take a foreign divorce decree, for example: it does not need enforcement but only recognition of its effect if the divorce decree only involves the dissolution of a marriage. Upon recognition, the marital status of the parties at issue will cease in the country where the recognition is sought.

a. Legal Grounds for Recognition and Enforcement

Since China is not a member of any multilateral treaties in cross-border recognition and enforcement of judgments, there are currently two legal bases for Chinese courts to recognize and enforce foreign judgments or to make requests for recognition and enforcement of Chinese judgments in foreign courts: (a) bilateral judicial assistance treaties concluded between China and other countries, and (b) the principle of reciprocity. As of 2023, China had signed bilateral agreements on civil or commercial judicial assistance with thirty-nine countries, thirty-five of which include mutual recognition and enforcement of court judgments.[431] The reciprocity principle applies only if there is no treaty or there is no applicable provision in a treaty.

According to the SPC, if a court of a country does not have a judicial assistance treaty or reciprocal relationship with China, judicial assistance may be provided through diplomatic channels. Otherwise, the request for judicial assistance will be returned without action.[432] It is required by the SPC that when returning the request, the court shall explain the reason for inaction.[433] Also, under the SPC's interpretation, if the party only applies for recognition but not enforcement at the same time, the Chinese court will only rule on whether to recognize the application.[434]

Pursuant to article 297 of the CPL, for a legally effective judgment or ruling made by a Chinese court, if the judgment debtor or its property is outside the territory of

429 Dacheng Law Firm, *The White Paper on the Judicial Practice of Mutual Recognition and Enforcement of Civil and Commercial Judgments between Chinese and Foreign Courts*, 2023, at 4. Full text is available at https://shanghai.dachenglaw.com/dcdt/info_itemid_4375_lcid_218.html.

430 See *id.*

431 See *id.* at 3.

432 See the SPC, *Interpretations on the Application of the Civil Procedural Law*, *supra* note 10, art. 549.

433 See *id.*

434 See *id.*, art. 546.

China, the judgment creditor may apply directly to a foreign court with jurisdiction for recognition and enforcement. A Chinese court may also request that a foreign court recognize and enforce a Chinese judgment or ruling under the treaty concluded or acceded to by China or based on the principle of reciprocity.[435]

b. Rules Governing Recognition and Enforcement

When a judgment is obtained from a foreign court and needs to be recognized and enforced in China, certain rules must be followed. First, the request for recognition and enforcement must be filed with a competent intermediate people's court. Under article 298 of the CPL, for recognition and enforcement of an effective foreign judgment in China, the party concerned may directly apply to the intermediate people's court with jurisdiction over the judgment, or the foreign court may apply to a people's court in accordance with the treaty between that country and China or an international treaty to which both are parties, or under the principle of reciprocity.

For purposes of recognition and enforcement of a foreign judgment, the competent intermediate court refers to the intermediate court in the place where the judgment debtor is domiciled or the judgment debtor's property is located. If there is no intermediate people's court in such a place, the party concerned may apply to the local higher court for recognition and enforcement. Under Chinese law, a valid foreign judgment shall have the same effect as a domestic court judgment and be enforced according to domestic enforcement procedures.

When making a request for recognition and enforcement of a foreign judgment in a Chinese court, in addition to submitting the application, the requesting party shall also provide the original or a certified copy of the effective judgment issued by the foreign court with a Chinese translation,[436] or the documents stipulated under the treaty concluded or acceded to by China.[437] If the judgment of the foreign court is a default judgment, the document certifying that the foreign court has legally summoned the defendant should also be submitted, unless the judgment has clearly stated the service of process.[438]

Second, there must be a treaty or reciprocal relationship between China and the requesting foreign country. According to the SPC, when a party applies to the competent intermediate court of China for the recognition and enforcement of a foreign judgment or ruling, if the country where the court is located and China have not concluded or jointly participated in international treaties, nor have they had a reciprocal relationship, the application shall be denied, except for recognition of a

[435] See the CPL, *supra* note 1, art. 297.
[436] See the SPC, *Interpretations on the Application of the Civil Procedural Law*, *supra* note 10, art. 543.
[437] See *id.*
[438] See *id.*

legally effective divorce judgment made by a foreign court.[439] But if an application for recognition and enforcement is rejected, the party concerned may bring a lawsuit to a Chinese court.[440]

Third, the request for recognition and enforcement is subject to review by a Chinese court. Upon receiving the request, the court will conduct a review and make a decision on whether to recognize and enforce it. As instructed by the SPC, when handling the recognition and enforcement of effective foreign judgments or rulings, the Chinese court shall form a collegial panel to review the cases. For the purpose of review, the court shall serve the judgment enforcement application on the respondent, who may state his arguments.[441]

Under article 290, the review of a foreign judgment seeking recognition and enforcement shall be made under the provisions of a treaty concluded or acceded to by China, or the principle of reciprocity. If the review reveals that the foreign judgment does not violate the basic laws of China nor harm China's national sovereignty, security, or social and public interests, the court shall rule to recognize its effect, and if enforcement is needed, shall issue a ruling to enforce it under the relevant provisions of the CPL.[442]

The ruling made after review takes legal effect once served.[443]

The review of the foreign judgment is not on the contents of the judgment but rather on the conditions under which a foreign judgment will not be recognized and enforced. In this context, recognition and enforcement of a foreign judgment is regarded as a matter of conditions. The conditions as such may vary from country to country, but whether a foreign judgment is to be recognized and enforced is to be determined under the conditions provided in the law of the country where the recognition and enforcement are sought.

c. Grounds for the Denial of Recognition and Enforcement

Recognition and enforcement of foreign judgments are subject to certain conditions set forth in the CPL. It is required under the CPL that a foreign judgment must be a legally effective judgment in order to be recognized and enforced in China. An effective judgment refers to the judgment that is final and made on the merits. A judgment is final when there is no pending appeal and generally is not subject to modification. Put differently, a final judgment brings the litigation to an end and leaves nothing further in the proceedings except for the execution of the judgment.

439 See *id.*, art. 544.
440 See *id.*
441 See *id.*, art. 548.
442 See the CPL, *supra* note 1, art. 290.
443 See the SPC, *Interpretations on the Application of the Civil Procedural Law*, *supra* note 10, art. 548.

In addition, pursuant to article 300 of the CPL, for a legally effective foreign judgment or ruling, the Chinese court, after review, shall rule not to recognize and enforce it if it falls within any of the exclusions provided in the law. As provided in article 300, the exclusions include: (a) the foreign court has no jurisdiction over the case; (b) the respondent has not been legally summoned or has been legally summoned but not given any reasonable opportunity to make statements and arguments, or the party without litigation capacity has not been properly represented; (c) the judgment or ruling was obtained through fraud; (d) the Chinese court has made a judgment or ruling on the same dispute, or has recognized the judgment or ruling made by a third country's court on the same dispute; and (e) the judgment or ruling violates the basic principles of the laws of China or damages China's national sovereignty, security, or social and public interests.

For the purpose of recognition and enforcement of a foreign judgment or ruling, a foreign court will be considered to have no jurisdiction if it is found that: (a) the foreign court has no jurisdiction over the case under its laws; or, although it has jurisdiction in accordance with its laws, (b) the foreign court has no appropriate connection with the disputes involved in the case, (c) there is a violation of exclusive jurisdiction of Chinese courts, or (d) the exclusive choice of court agreement between the parties is violated.

Note that under the CPL, connection and choice of court agreement are two decisive factors to determine whether a foreign court has proper jurisdiction over the case at issue. The connection factor implicates that the Chinese courts do not recognize the jurisdiction of a neutral court. The connection requirement also applies to the contractual jurisdiction because, as noted, it is required by the SPC that when the parties agree to choose a foreign court to resolve disputes involving foreign contracts or other property rights, the court shall have a certain actual connection with the parties or disputes.[444]

The choice of court agreement may be exclusive or non-exclusive. As discussed, to determine the exclusivity of a choice of court agreement, China follows the doctrine of presumption of exclusivity. Under this doctrine, a choice of court clause or agreement, once made, is presumed to be exclusive unless otherwise clearly stated by the parties. Thus, any party that challenges the exclusive nature of such a clause or agreement bears the burden of proof to the contrary.

Pursuant to article 302 of the CPL, in the case where a party applies to a Chinese court for recognition and enforcement of a foreign judgment or ruling, and the dispute involved in the judgment or ruling is the same dispute that is being adjudicated in a Chinese court, the court, upon receiving the application, may rule to suspend the suit. After the suspension, the court may proceed in one of two ways. First, if the foreign judgment or ruling is found to have failed to meet the

[444] See *id.*, art. 531.

recognition conditions, the court shall rule not to recognize and enforce it, and then the suspended suit shall resume.

Second, if the foreign judgment or ruling meets the recognition conditions, the court, after its review, shall rule to recognize its effect and enforce it if needed. In the meantime, for the suit that has been suspended, the court shall rule to dismiss it with prejudice. In addition, under article 303 of the CPL, if a party is dissatisfied with the court's ruling to recognize or not to recognize and enforce the foreign judgment or ruling, the party may, through a review process, apply for reconsideration to the court at the next higher level within ten days from the date of service of the ruling.

14

International Commercial Arbitration in China

INTRODUCTION

Arbitration in China is divided into two categories: domestic arbitration and international arbitration. International arbitration, commonly called foreign arbitration in the country, includes arbitration by Chinese arbitration institutions that contains foreign elements (foreign arbitration or foreign related arbitration), and arbitration by foreign arbitration institutions where the enforcement of the arbitral awards is sought in China (foreign country arbitration). Under current law of arbitration in China, foreign arbitration generally takes the form of institutional arbitration. Under certain circumstances, *ad hoc* arbitration can also be an option.

There was no formal arbitration system in China prior to the enactment of the Arbitration Law of China in 1994,[1] although a scholarly study suggests that arbitration legislation in the country actually started as early as 1913, when the Republic government adopted the Rules of Commercial Arbitration Bureau.[2] Before 1994, arbitrations did take place in the country (after the founding of the People's Republic of China). At that time, however, the arbitrations had two distinctions: first, the arbitrations primarily focused on contractual disputes between enterprises, mostly state-owned.[3] Second, the arbitrations had a strong administrative nature because they were all conducted by the relevant government agencies.[4]

[1] See the Arbitration Law, promulgated Aug. 31, 1994, effective Sept. 1, 1995, available at http://np.china-embassy.gov.cn/eng/78085/zchfl/200410/t20041027_1998190.html.

[2] See Jiang Wei and Xiao Jian Guo, The Arbitration Law, 40 (Renmin Univ. Press ed., 3rd ed. 2016); see also John Shijian Mo, Arbitration Law in China 1 (2001).

[3] Before the Contract Law of China was adopted in 1999, the Economic Contract Law generally precluded individuals from making contracts under the law. Chen Xuebin, *China Enacts a New Contract Law for the New Millennium*, INT'L REL. (2000), www.international-relations.com/cm4-1/WbChineseLaw.htm [http://perma.cc/5HK5-B5LH].

[4] See Jiang Wei and Xiao Jian Guo, *supra* note 2 at 41.

In 1956, the State Council adopted the Interim Rules of Arbitration Procedure of the Foreign Trade Arbitration Commission. The adoption of the 1956 Rules was considered the beginning of foreign arbitration in China because the 1956 Rules established a legal domain for foreign trade arbitration in the country. But not until 1982, when the Civil Procedural Law (Provisional) was adopted (CPLP), was there a legal provision that governed the enforcement of foreign arbitral awards. Under Article 204 of the CPLP, enforcement of foreign arbitral awards must satisfy two conditions: (a) the enforcement should be examined in accordance with the international treaty China concluded or acceded to, or on the principle of reciprocity; and (b) the enforcement should not violate the fundamental principles of the law or national and social interests of China.[5]

In 1987, China joined the Convention on the Recognition and Enforcement of Foreign Arbitral Awards ("New York Convention"). In order to implement the New York Convention, the SPC in the same year issued the Notice of Application of Convention on the Recognition and Enforcement of Foreign Arbitral Awards (1987 Notice).[6] The 1987 Notice, which remains effective, specifies how the Convention is to be applied in Chinese courts. It also prescribed a definition of "contractual and non-contractual relationship[s] of [a] commercial nature" under the commercial reservation China made to the Convention. In addition, the 1987 Notice designated the intermediate people's courts to handle the requests for recognition and enforcement of foreign arbitral awards.[7]

In 1991, China enacted the Civil Procedure Law (1991 CPL) to replace the CPLP of 1987.[8] Under the 1991 CPL, the interested party was able to directly apply to a court for recognition and enforcement of the foreign arbitral award obtained.[9] In 1995, the SPC issued the Notice on Several Matters Concerning the Handling of Foreign Arbitration and Foreign Arbitral Awards in the People's Courts (1995 Notice).[10] An important feature of the 1995 Notice was the establishment of an internal reporting system in Chinese courts. Pursuant to the 1995 Notice, the

5 See Civil Procedure Law (Provisional), promulgated by the Standing Comm. NPC, Mar. 8, 1982, effective Oct. 1, 1982, art. 204.

6 See the SPC, Notice of Application of Convention on the Recognition and Enforcement of Foreign Arbitral Awards. The Notice was issued to all local courts except trial courts on April 10, 1987 (hereinafter referred to as 1987 Notice), available at http://gongbao.court.gov.cn/Details/e4defa983a153b314590d73e5a0c60.html.

7 See *id.*, art. 3. In China, the people's courts have four levels: at the top is the SPC, then the Provincial High People's Court, followed by intermediate people's courts. Trial or county courts are at the basic level and have preliminary jurisdiction over most cases.

8 See the Civil Procedure Law (CPL), promulgated on Apr. 9, 1991, effective Apr. 9, 1991.

9 See *id.*, art. 269.

10 See the SPC, Notice on the Relevant Issues of the People's Court Dealing with Foreign Arbitration and Foreign Arbitration, promulgated by the SPC on Aug. 28, 1995, effective Aug. 28, 1995 (hereinafter referred to as 1995 Notice).

reporting system equally applies to the filing of a case seeking to invalidate the arbitration clause or agreement.[11]

The CPL and the Arbitration Law are the basic legislation that form the framework of international commercial arbitration in China. Compared with the arbitration provisions in the CPL, which mainly deal with recognition and enforcement of foreign arbitral awards, the Arbitration Law has a broad coverage of arbitration that is aimed at (a) ensuring fair and timely arbitration of economic disputes, (b) protecting the legitimate rights and interests of the parties, and (c) assuring the healthy development of the socialist market economy.

The 1991 CPL was amended four times: in 2012, 2017, 2022, and 2023, respectively. In the CPL (as amended 2023), there are seven articles (Articles 288–292, 297, and 304) that specifically govern foreign arbitration.[12] In its Interpretation Concerning Application of the Civil Procedural Law issued on January 30, 2015 (2015 CPL Interpretation), the SPC took an extraordinary step and explicitly addressed several issues that were quite controversial and also caused confusion with regard to foreign arbitration.[13]

The SPC's 2015 CPL Interpretation is considered an important judicial interpretation on foreign arbitration not only because it incorporates opinions of the court stated in prior cases, but also because it restates common practices accepted by the court.[14] The SPC amended its 2015 CPL Interpretation in 2020 and 2022 with no major changes to the foreign arbitration provisions.

On December 26, 2017, the SPC adopted two sets of rules pertaining to the judicial review of arbitration: Provisions on Several Issues Concerning Adjudication of Requests for Judicial Review of Arbitration (2017 Rules of Arbitration Review)[15] and Provisions on the Issue of Reporting for Examination and Approval of the Cases Requesting Judicial Review of Arbitration (2017 Reporting Rules).[16] These rules further addressed issues pertaining to the review of the validity of an arbitration agreement, review of foreign arbitral awards, application of law, and the internal

[11] See *id.*, art. 1.

[12] See the CPL (as amended 2023), at www.npc.gov.cn/npc/c2/c30834/202401/P020240108541839745616.pdf.

[13] See the SPC, Interpretation on the Application of the CPL, issued by the Jud. Comm. Sup. People's Ct., Jan. 30, 2015, effective Feb. 4, 2015, www.cietac.org.cn/Uploads/201612/58678e45783ae.pdf.

[14] See Yan Yang and Hua Zhang, *Annual Review on Commercial Mediation in China* (2016), *in* Commercial Dispute Resolution in China: An Annual Review and Preview (2016) 53, 55-56 (China Legal Publ'g House, 2016).

[15] See the SPC, Provisions on Several Issues Concerning the Trial of Arbitration Judicial Review Cases, promulgated by the Jud. Comm. Sup. People's Ct., Dec. 26, 2017, effective Jan. 1, 2018, SUP. PEOPLE'S CT. NETWORK (2017 Rules of Arbitration Review).

[16] See the SPC, Provisions on the Issue of Reporting for Examination and Approval of the Cases Requesting Judicial Review of Arbitration, issued on December 26, 2017, amended on December 24, 2021, available at www.court.gov.cn/zixun/xiangqing/338601.html (SPC 2017 Reporting Rules).

reporting process pertaining to the denial of recognition and enforcement of foreign arbitral awards.

The 1994 Arbitration Law was amended in 2009 and 2017, respectively, but nothing changed substantially.[17] Given the rapid increase in the number of arbitration institutions and arbitration cases, and the country's eagerness to expand foreign arbitration practices, the current arbitration scheme is widely regarded as incompatible with current international mainstream arbitration practices. Thus, there had been a growing public outcry for revising the 1994 Arbitration Law to integrate with internationally accepted rules and enhance the credibility and international competitiveness of Chinese arbitration. It was believed that if the Arbitration Law was not revised to meet the need for the development of arbitration, it would hinder the further professionalization and internationalization of China's arbitration industry.

The outstanding issues facing the 1994 Arbitration Law were multifaceted.. First, the scope of arbitration was too narrow. Many new types of disputes accompanying the emergence of new economies and new business formats, as well as disputes in the more mature international investment and sports fields, were not covered. Second, the nature, position, and governance structure of arbitration institutions were ill defined, which was un-conducive to the improvement and development of arbitration. Third, the judicial interpretations developed from arbitration practice were not reflected in the 1994 Arbitration Law, so conflicts between the actual practice and provisions of the Arbitration Law inevitably occurred. Fourth, the judicial review standards for domestic and foreign-related arbitral awards were inconsistent, and so were the two judicial supervision methods of setting aside and denying enforcement of arbitral awards. Fifth, the arbitration provisions in many respects were disconnected from the common practices and general rules of international arbitration.[18]

The 1994 Arbitration Law was then revised in 2025. The revision work began in 2019 when the General Office of the CPC Central Committee and the General Office of the State Council jointly issued the "Several Opinions on Improving the Arbitration System and Enhancing the Credibility of Arbitration."[19] The Ministry of Justice (MOJ) initiated the drafting of the revision. In July 2021, the Draft Revision (2021 Draft) was published by the MOJ for public review and comment.[20] On July 31, 2024, the State Council approved in principle the Draft Revision of the Arbitration Law. On November 4, 2024, the Draft Revision was submitted to the

17 The Arbitration Law was amended in 2009 and 2017. The 2017 amended version is available at www.chinajusticeobserver.com/law/x/arbitration-law-20170901.

18 See the MOJ, Explanations on the Draft Revision of the Arbitration Law (for public comment), July 30, 2021, available at www.moj.gov.cn/pub/sfbgw/lfyjzj/lflfyjzj/202107/t20210730_432967.html (MOJ 2021 Draft).

19 The Opinions, issued April 16, 2019, are at www.gov.cn/zhengce/2019-04/16/content_5383424.htm.

20 See the MOJ 2021 Draft, *supra* 20.

Standing Committee of the NPC for its first reading. Four days later, on November 8, 2024, the Standing Committee of the NPC published the Second Draft for public opinion (2024 Draft).[21]

The 2021 Draft was hailed in the country as a bold step toward improving the arbitration system in the country. It took the UNCITRAL's Model Law of International Arbitration as a major reference. The changes include, among others, (a) expanding the scope of application of arbitration, (b) relaxing the requirements for the validity of arbitration agreements, (c) broadening the rule of presumptive validity of arbitration agreements, (d) accepting the concept of place of arbitration, (e) clarifying the competence–competence rule for arbitration tribunals, (f) providing the arbitral tribunal with the power to issue interim measures, (g) optimizing the method of appointing the chief arbitrator, (h) establishing the *ad hoc* arbitration system for foreign-related arbitration, (i) improving the system for revocation of arbitral awards, and (j) altering the process of denial of recognition and enforcement of arbitral awards to exclude parties' petition for non-enforcement.[22]

The 2024 Draft, however, was widely considered as a huge step back from the 2021 Draft. The 2024 Draft on the one hand restored several provisions of the Arbitration Law that were deleted or modified in the 2021 Draft, but also added certain controversial new provisions. The most controversial provisions are the "party leadership" clause and the "government supervision" clauses. Article 2 of the 2024 Draft requires that arbitration work adhere to the leadership of the Communist Party of China, implement the party and the country's opinions, policies, decisions, and arrangements, serve the country's opening and development strategy, and play a role in resolving social conflicts and disputes.[23]

With regard to government supervision, Article 23 of the 2024 Draft requires the strengthening of administrative power to supervise and punish the work of the arbitration committee and its staff for their conducts found to be in violation of law.[24] These provisions met strong criticism because they would raise great concerns

[21] See the Standing Committee of the NPC, Draft Revision of Arbitration Law (for public opinion), available at www.china-arbitration.com/index.php/index/news/detail.html?id=2395 (2024 Draft).

[22] See Xie Lijing, Commentary on the Ten Highlights of the Draft Revision of the Arbitration Law (2021), available at www.dehenglaw.com/CN/tansuocontent/0008/022286/7.aspx?MID=0902&AID=.

[23] See the 2024 Draft, *supra* note 23, art. 2.

[24] Article 23 of the 2024 Draft provides: "The judicial and administrative departments of the State Council shall guide and supervise the arbitration work nationwide in accordance with the law, improve the supervision and management system, and make overall plans for the development of arbitration. The judicial and administrative departments of the people's governments of provinces, autonomous regions, and municipalities directly under the Central Government shall guide and supervise the arbitration work within their respective administrative regions in accordance with the law, and shall deal with those who violate the provisions of this Law. The arbitration committee and its members and staff shall be ordered to make corrections, and depending on the seriousness of the case, they shall be given a warning, a notice of criticism, a

among foreign arbitrators who come to China for arbitration if they would have to accept the indirect management and supervision of the Chinese government.

As many observed, the 2024 Draft failed to adhere necessarily to the principle essential to arbitration, that is, the autonomy of the parties. Since arbitration is a private dispute resolution process that deals primarily with private rights, the arbitral tribunal or arbitrators as chosen by the parties are fully empowered under the will of the parties to dispose of the rights and obligations involved in the dispute between the parties. Given the private nature of arbitration, the public color of arbitration will be disenchanted.[25] Both the party leadership clause and administrative interference under the government supervision clause would eventually destroy the neutrality and impartiality of arbitration.[26]

Responding to the criticism, the Standing Committee softened the party leadership clause by replacing "arbitration work" with "arbitration industry" after its second reading of the draft on April 27, 2025.[27] The final version of revised arbitration law was adopted on September 12, 2025 after the Standing Committee's third reading. In the revised Arbitration Law (Arbitration Law), the party leadership clause is kept but is rephrased more like a policy statement. Under Article 2 of the Arbitration Law, the development of arbitration is to implement the lines, principles, policies, decisions and deployments of the Communist Party of China and the state, serve the country's high-quality development and high-level opening up, create a market-oriented, law-based and internationalized business environment, and play a role in resolving economic disputes.[28] In the meantime, it drops the punishment provision in the government supervision clause provided in the 2024 draft though keeping the government supervision intact.

The Arbitration Law consists of eight chapters and ninety-six articles in total (expanded from previously 78 articles). In addition to the party leadership clause, the Arbitration Law contains several major changes to the country's arbitration landscape. First, the Arbitration Law replaces arbitration commission with

fine of not less than 1 percent but not more than 10 percent of the fees charged in the previous year, and the confiscation of illegal property, as well as penalties such as suspension of arbitration activities within a time limit, revocation of registration certificate, etc." See *id.*, art. 23.

[25] See Fei Lin and Zhao Fang, Reply to the Draft Revision of the Arbitration Law (for public opinion), a full text of the reply is available at https://mp.weixin.qq.com/s?__biz=MzI4NzEyNTY2OA==&mid=2247507894&idx=2&sn=45d7caa45fbc9d3b52a53-9fb d1e8fcf&chksm=ea313067b270c5b14e1e85e290b5b90ba75f692eeaf5aa09ee2f1fe2caf13bb43 3f4dcedeff4&scene=27.

[26] See *id.*

[27] See the Second Draft of Revised Arbitration Law, published by the Standing Committee of the NPC for comments on April 27, 2025, available at www.lg.gov.cn/attachment/1/1581/1581541/12172060.pdf.

[28] See Arbitration Law of China (2025), adopted by the Sanding Committee of the NPC on September 12, 2025, art. 2, available at www.npc.gov.cn/npc/c2/c30834/202509/t20250912_447762.html. (Arbitration Law).

arbitration institution to refer to arbitration body and specifically defines arbitration institution as a public welfare non-profit legal person.[29] The Arbitration Law further categorizes arbitration institutions to include arbitration commissions, arbitration courts, or other institutions established in accordance with the law.[30]

Second, the Arbitration Law recognizes ad hoc arbitration in the country for certain cases. Prior to adoption of the revised Arbitration Law in 2025, China did not recognize *ad hoc* arbitration within the country, but nevertheless allowed to be enforced a foreign *ad hoc* arbitral award under treaties. In 2016, the SPC issued the Opinions on Providing Judicial Protection for the Development of Free Trade Zones (FTZs). Article 9 of the Opinions authorizes Chinese courts at all levels to recognize an arbitration agreement between enterprises in the FTZs that submits disputes to arbitration by a "specific person" in a "specific place" in accordance with the "specific arbitration rules." The Opinions are considered in China as a breakthrough in recognizing the validity of *ad hoc* arbitration agreement in the country, though within the FTZs only.[31]

The Arbitration Law codified the above practice towards the *ad hoc* arbitration. Pursuant to article 82 of the Arbitration Law, for foreign-related maritime disputes or disputes between enterprises established and registered in the pilot free trade zones approved by the State Council, the Hainan Free Trade Port, or other areas prescribed by the State, the party may choose arbitration in China under the agreed arbitration rules with an arbitration tribunal composed of persons who meet the conditions prescribed in the law.[32]

Third, the Arbitration Law adds as a new format of arbitration an Internet-based arbitration system to adapt to the development of information technology. Article 11 of the Arbitration Law provides that arbitration proceedings may be conducted online, unless the parties explicitly disagree, meaning that absent explicit objection, an agreement to online arbitration will be assumed. Article 11 further provides that an arbitration proceeding conducted online shall have the same legal effect as the conventional or offline arbitration proceeding.[33]

Fourth, the Arbitration Law expands the scope of arbitration agreement determination to exclude the finding of arbitration agreement by assumption. According to Article 27 of the Arbitration Law, in the case where one party claims the existence of an arbitration agreement when applying for arbitration and the other party does not deny it before the first hearing, it shall be deemed that an arbitration agreement

[29] See *id.*, art. 13.

[30] See *id.*, art. 89.

[31] See the SPC, Opinions on Providing Judicial Protection for the Development of Free Trade Zones, available at https://fgw.sh.gov.cn/cmsres/eb/eb6066ba691a4a9c912e66b247d139db/0060837c1779058339757305341ce74a.pdf.

[32] See the Arbitration Law, *supra* note 31, art. 82.

[33] See *id.*, art. 11.

exists between the parties upon a notice and being recorded by the arbitration tribunal.[34]

Fifth, the Arbitration Law sets forth a seat-based arbitration rule to align the country's arbitration framework with international practices. The rule makes the seat of arbitration an important basis for determining the applicable law of the arbitration procedure, the rules of evidence, the nationality of the arbitral award, and the jurisdiction of the court. Under article 81 of the Arbitration Law, the parties may agree in writing on the seat of arbitration. Unless the parties have otherwise agreed on the applicable law of the arbitration procedure, the seat of arbitration shall serve as the basis for determining the applicable law of the arbitration procedure and the jurisdiction of the court. The arbitral award shall be deemed to have been made at the seat of arbitration.[35]

Sixth, the Arbitration Law incorporates article 291 of the CPL on the conditions for denial of recognition and enforcement of foreign arbitral awards, and applies those conditions to the annulment of foreign related arbitral awards as well (awards made by Chinese arbitration institutions in foreign related arbitration cases).[36] In the meantime, it adds a new clause encouraging the parties to choose an arbitration institution of the China (including its special administrative regions) and make China the seat of arbitration.[37] Moreover, the Arbitration Law explicitly allows arbitration institutions or tribunals to handle international investment arbitration cases in accordance with the provisions of relevant international investment treaties and agreements on submitting investment disputes to arbitration and in accordance with the arbitration rules agreed upon by the disputing parties.[38]

Seventh, the Arbitration Law supports Chinese arbitration institutions to establish branches and conduct arbitrations overseas.[39] In the meantime, it opens the door for foreign arbitration tribunal to conduct arbitration in China. It is explicitly provided in Article 86 of the Arbitration Law that for the needs of economic and social development and reform and opening up, overseas arbitration institutions may be allowed to have business establishment under relevant national regulations in free trade pilot zones, Hainan Free Trade Port and other areas approved by the State Council to carry out foreign-related arbitration activities.[40]

Lastly, the Arbitration Law provides judicial administrative authorities with a supervision power. According to article 26 of the Arbitration Law, the judicial administrative department of the State Council guides and supervises arbitration work nationwide in accordance with the law, improves relevant work systems, and

34 See *id.*, art. 27.
35 See *id.*, art. 81.
36 See *id.*, art. 83.
37 See *id.*, art. 87.
38 See *id.*, art. 94.
39 See *id.*, art. 86.
40 See *id.*

makes overall plans for the development of arbitration. Article 26 also requires the judicial administrative department of local governments to guide and supervise arbitration work within their respective administrative regions under the law.[41]

1. LEGAL FRAMEWORK OF FOREIGN ARBITRATION

The legal framework that governs foreign arbitration in China consists of three components. The first component is legislation, referring to the laws passed by the NPC and its Standing Committee. The second component contains treaties, including the New York Convention and various bilateral judicial assistance agreements. The third component is the opinion of the SPC in the form of an interpretation, notice, reply, or decision. As discussed, under the Chinese legal structure, the first two components represent the primary sources of law, while the third component concerns only the application of the law. Once again, the Chinese judiciary does not have a function of making laws, although the SPC's opinions are considered to have binding effect on all people's courts.[42]

A. *Foreign Arbitration Legislation*

As noted, before the Arbitration Law was adopted in 1994, China did not have independent arbitration legislation, and the provisions that governed arbitration were scattered in the CPL and other regulations.[43] After the Arbitration Law was enacted, arbitration legislation in China began to take a two-track format: the CPL and the Arbitration Law. The former is the general law on all civil matters, while the latter is the special law on arbitration. As an established principle, if there is any discrepancy between a general law and a special law, the special law takes priority unless otherwise indicated in the law.

Arbitration legislation in China follows the country's tradition to handle domestic and foreign cases differently, or under a dual system. The general pattern is that there are special provisions in the law intended to apply specifically to cases classified as "foreign," while all other provisions apply to all cases in general. Under this pattern, both the Arbitration Law and the CPL contain special provisions that regulate foreign arbitration. Chapter Seven of the Arbitration Law has eleven articles, collectively called "Special Provisions on Foreign Related Arbitration."[44] The CPL, as previously noted, contains seven articles under the title of Special

[41] See *id.*, art. 26.

[42] For more information about sources of law in China and the function of Chinese courts, see Mo Zhang, *Pushing the Envelope: Application of Guiding Cases in Chinese Courts and Development of Case Law in China*, 26 WASH. INT'L L.J. 269, 282-288 (2017).

[43] See, for example, Civil Procedure Law (1982), *supra* note 5, arts. 192-195, 203.

[44] See Arbitration Law, *supra* 31, arts. 78-88.

Provisions on Foreign Related Civil Litigation, which are applied explicitly to foreign arbitration.

The provisions in the CPL and the Arbitration Law deal with foreign arbitration in China, including, as noted, foreign-related arbitration made by Chinese arbitration institutions and the recognition and enforcement of foreign arbitral awards. Under both the CPL and the Arbitration Law, recognition and enforcement of foreign arbitral awards in China is mainly governed by treaties, or under the principle of reciprocity absent a treaty. The most influential treaty is the New York Convention.

B. *New York Convention and Its Application in Chinese Courts*

Since China became a member of the New York Convention in 1987, the New York Convention has been the primary source of legal rules that govern the enforcement of foreign arbitral awards in the country. When joining the New York Convention, China made two reservations. The first is called a "reciprocity reservation," which requires that the Convention apply only to recognition and enforcement of awards made in the territory of another contracting state.[45]

The second reservation is known as a "commercial matters reservation," under which the application of the Convention is to be made only to the differences arising out of legal relationships, whether contractual or not, that are considered "commercial" under the national law.[46] These two reservations impose constraints on the extent to which the New York Convention is to be applied in the country.

There are two major issues often raised with respect to the application of the New York Convention. The first issue is the relationship between treaties and Chinese domestic law. More specifically, this issue is determining which one prevails if a conflict between Chinese domestic law and the New York Convention occurs. In essence, the issue concerns the status of a treaty in Chinese law. The second issue is whether the New York Convention can be applied directly in Chinese courts.

As noted, the Chinese Constitution does not contain any provision specifying the status of treaties in domestic law. Instead, the application of treaties is provided in the law of particular areas. As discussed, under Article 271 of the CPL, a general principle is that if an international treaty concluded or acceded to by China has different provisions from the CPL, the provisions of the international treaty shall prevail, except for the provisions to which China declares reservations.[47]

There is no provision in the law, however, that clarifies whether the provision of a treaty still applies if it appears to be in conflict with a law that is adopted at a later time. It is an issue of whether the "last in time" doctrine applies when the provision

45 See the SPC, 1987 Notice, *supra* note 6, art. 1.

46 See *id.*, art. 2.

47 See the CPL, *supra* note 12, art. 271.

of an existing treaty is at odds with a newly promulgated law. A general assumption in China is that latter legislation would not contradict the treaty obligations that the country has assumed.[48] The SPC has also made it clear that when there is a treaty to which China has joined or acceded, its application shall take priority in the courts, except for the reserved provisions.[49]

The issue concerning application of the New York Convention in the courts involves the judicial authority to apply the treaty. In its practice, the SPC takes a pragmatic position and applies the treaties on the basis of substance.[50] Under the SPC's interpretation, if a treaty involves substantial or specific rights and obligations of the civil parties, the courts may apply it directly.[51] On the other hand, if a treaty is mainly concerned with policies or principles, its application requires an action from the NPC or its Standing Committee.[52]

With regard to the New York Convention, its application in the courts is governed by the rules specified in the SPC's 1987 Notice. Under the 1987 Notice, the courts are required to follow the New York Convention and apply the Convention provisions.[53] But, according to the SPC, application of the New York Convention shall occur under two conditions pursuant to the reservations China has made to the Convention. First, the provisions of the New York Convention apply only to those

[48] See generally Wan Exiang, *Part IV: Application of International Law in China, in* RESEARCH IN THE RELATIONSHIP BETWEEN INTERNATIONAL LAW AND DOMESTIC LAW (Peking Univ. Press, 2011); see also the SPC, Provisions of the Supreme People's Court on Several Issues Concerning the Trial of International Trade Administration (promulgated by Jud. Comm. Sup. People's Ct., Aug. 27, 2002, effective Oct. 1, 2002), art. 9, MINISTRY OF COMM. (stating that if there are two or more reasonable interpretations of the specific provisions of law or administrative regulations applicable in the people's court adjudication, and one of the interpretations is in line with the relevant provision of an international treaty to which China has concluded or joined, such interpretation shall be chosen except for those provisions that China has made reservation).

[49] See the SPC, Notice on Several Issues that Should Be Paid Attention to in the Trial and Implementation of Foreign-related Civil and Commercial Cases, Apr. 17, 2000, effective Apr. 17, 2000, art. 2.

[50] See Cao Jianming et al., The WTO and China's Judicial Adjudication 250-58 (Law Press 2001).

[51] A typical example is the UN Convention on Contracts for the International Sale of Goods (CISG). According to the SPC and judicial practice, the provisions of the CISG have an effect of application in Chinese people's courts, and absent the parties' choice otherwise, the CISG shall be directly applied. See the SPC, Circular on the Publication of the Symposium on the Economic Trials of Foreign Affairs Involving Hong Kong and Macao (promulgated by the SPC, June 12, 1989, effective June 12, 1989). In many cases, the SPC has repeatedly held that people's courts may directly cite the CISG provisions, except for those to which China has made reservations. See Liu Ying, *Direct Application of the CISG in Chinese Courts*, 5 WUHAN U. L. REV. 83 (2009).

[52] According to the SPC, when adjudicating international trade administrative cases, people's courts shall apply Chinese laws and administrative regulations. See the SPC Provisions on Several Issues Concerning the Trial of International Trade Administration, *supra* note 51, arts. 7-8 (having the effect of excluding the direct application of the WTO).

[53] See the SPC, 1987 Notice, *supra* note 6, art. 1.

arbitral awards made in the territory of another contracting state.[54] Second, the New York Convention may only be applied to controversies arising from contractual or non-contractual commercial legal relationships under Chinese law.[55]

In its 1987 Notice, the SPC explicitly stated that if the New York Convention is applicable and its provisions differ from those in the CPL, the courts should apply the Convention.[56] From a general reading of the 1987 Notice, application of the New York Convention in the Chinese courts does not require any transformative legislation from the state legislature. Therefore, the New York Convention itself is an authoritative legal source in China.[57]

The 1987 Notice has a twofold implication: on the one hand, a court may directly apply the Convention or cite it as the legal grounds on which the court's decision is based.[58] On the other hand, the parties may ask the court to follow the Convention or may cite the Convention as a defense if there is a discrepancy between the Convention and Chinese law.

C. *Judicial Interpretation*

Once again, the Chinese judiciary does not have the power to make law, or even to interpret the law. Under the Chinese Constitution, the judiciary has only the power to implement and apply the law. Thus, the implementation of law as a judicial function is mostly seen in judicial interpretations. As noted, under the Chinese legal system, only the SPC has the power to make judicial interpretations.[59] Although the SPC's interpretations are not a primary sourse of law, the courts in China often rely on them in adjudication proceedings, especially where the law is unclear.[60]

It is without doubt that the 1987 Notice serves as the primary guide for Chinese courts in implementing the New York Convention. Eight years later, in 1995, the SPC issued the Notice on Several Matters Concerning the Handling of Foreign Arbitration and Foreign Arbitral Awards in the People's Courts (1995 Notice).[61] An

54 See *id.*

55 See *id.*, art. 2.

56 See *id.*, art. 1.

57 Wan E'xiang and Xia Xiaohong, *Reasons for the Denial of Recognition and Enforcement of Some Foreign Country Arbitral Awards by Chinese Courts: An Analysis of New York Convention Related Cases*, 13 WUHAN U. INT'L L. REV. 1, 11 (2010). Note that Wan E'xiang was the Vice President of the SPC at the time of this publication, and according to his opinion therein, the New York Convention need not be transformed into domestic law in order for it to be applied in the people's courts.

58 See *id.*

59 See the Standing Committee of the NPC, Resolution of the Standing Committee of the National People's Congress Providing an Improved Interpretation of the Law, promulgated by the Standing Comm. Nat'l People's Cong., June 10, 1981, effective June 10, 1981 CLI.1.1006 (EN).

60 See *id.*

61 See the SPC, 1995 Notice, *supra* note 10.

important feature of the 1995 Notice was the establishment of an internal reporting system in Chinese courts.

Under the 1995 Notice, an internal report to the SPC for review and approval is required for a denial of foreign arbitral award enforcement.[62] The very purpose of the 1995 Notice is to ensure proper implementation of the New York Convention in China. Pursuant to the 1995 Notice, the reporting system equally applies to the filing of a case seeking to invalidate the arbitration clause or agreement.[63]

As noted, the SPC in 2017 adopted both the Rules of Arbitration Review and Reporting Rules. Those two 2017 rules further addressed issues pertaining to the review of the validity of an arbitration agreement, review of foreign arbitral awards, application of law, and the internal reporting process. Pursuant to the SPC 2017 rules, all decisions purporting to invalidate arbitral agreements or deny enforcement of foreign arbitral awards may only be made after the SPC's review and approval.[64]

2. ARBITRATION WITH FOREIGN ELEMENTS IN CHINA

Different from domestic arbitration, foreign arbitration refers to arbitration that contains foreign elements. Since the CPL and Arbitration Law do not define what may constitute "foreign" in arbitration, the SPC's definition of foreign civil cases remains prevalent in the country.[65] There are concerns, however, that the SPC's definition does not appear to match the commonly accepted term "international" as defined in UNCITRAL's Model Law of Arbitration, because the terms "foreign" and "international" are interchangeably used in China to mean the same thing. The former relies on nationality, habitual residence, and location of subject matter or cause of action, while the latter simply focuses on the place of business.[66]

62 See *id.*

63 See *id.*, art. 1.

64 See the SPC, 2017 Rules of Arbitration Review, *supra* note 15, art. 2.

65 According to the SPC, if a civil relationship has any of the following circumstances, the people's court may determine it to be a foreign-related civil relationship: (a) One or both parties are foreign citizens, foreign legal persons, other organizations, or stateless persons; (b) The habitual residence of one or both parties is outside the territory of the People's Republic of China; (c) The subject matter is outside the territory of the People's Republic of China; (d) The legal facts that give rise to, change, or eliminate the civil relationship occur outside the territory of the People's Republic of China; (e) Other circumstances that can be determined as foreign-related civil relations. See SPC, Interpretation on Several Issues Concerning the Implementation of the Law of China on the Application of Laws to Foreign-Related Civil Relations (I), art. 1. A full text of the interpretations is available at http://gongbao.court.gov.cn/Details/cd2e8428c4de894455038e760c6472.html.

66 According to UNCITRAL's Model Law, an arbitration is international if (a) the parties to an arbitration agreement have, at the time of the conclusion of that agreement, their places of business in different states; or (b) one of the following places is situated outside the state in which the parties have their places of business: (i) the place of arbitration if determined in, or pursuant to, the arbitration agreement; (ii) any place where a substantial part of the obligations of the commercial relationship is to be performed, or the place with which the subject matter

Compared with domestic arbitration, foreign arbitration in China has several distinctions. First, foreign arbitration is governed by special rules, and only if there is no applicable special rule may the general provisions that govern arbitration apply. Also, foreign arbitration is treated differently with respect to such matters as time periods, service, evidence collection, and protective measures. Second, foreign arbitration is subject to international treaties to which China is a member and is also affected by the reciprocity principle. Third, foreign arbitration often involves application of foreign law.

A. *Arbitration Institutions*

Arbitration in China used to be administrative arbitration, meaning that arbitration was conducted under the auspices of an administrative agency, and the arbitrators were the working staff of the agency. At that time, arbitration was actually an exercise of administrative power by administrative agencies to adjudicate disputes.[67] Not until the Arbitration Law was adopted in 1994 did arbitration in China become a mechanism for resolution of a dispute between parties by a third-party panel through an arbitration known as an arbitration commission.

Under Article 24 of the Arbitration Law, an arbitration institution shall be independent from administrative agencies, and there shall be no subordinate relationship between an arbitration commission and any administrative agency, or between different arbitration institutions.[68] It is believed in the country that the Arbitration Law made a fundamental change to the nature of the arbitration institution in the country, turning it from an arbitration agency of an administrative nature to an independent, non-governmental arbitration body.[69]

In addition, the Arbitration Law further prescribes arbitration as the means to resolve disputes arising out of contracts, and other disputes relating to rights and interests in property between citizens, legal persons, and non legal person organizations of equal status.[70] Given its civil and commercial nature, arbitration under the Arbitration Law does not apply to (a) disputes arising from marriage, adoption, guardianship, support, and inheritance; or (b) administrative disputes that, according to law, should be handled by administrative authorities.[71]

According to Article 13 of the Arbitration Law, an arbitration institution may be formed in the capital city of a province, autonomous region, or municipality directly

of the dispute is most closely connected; or (c) the parties have expressly agreed that the subject matter of the arbitration agreement relates to more than one country. See UNCITRAL, Model Law on International Commercial Arbitration (as amended 2006), art. 1(3), available at https://uncitral.un.org/en/texts/arbitration/modellaw/commercial_arbitration.

67 See Jiang Wei and Xiao Jianguo, Arbitration Law, *supra* note 2, at 85.

68 See the Arbitration Law, *supra* note 31, art. 24.

69 See Jiang Wei and Xiao Jianguo, Arbitration Law, *supra* note 2, at 85.

70 See the Arbitration Law, *supra* 31, art. 3.

71 See *id.*

under the Central Government, and also in other cities divided into districts if the circumstances require, but not necessarily at every administrative level. For its formation, an arbitration institution shall be registered with the local judicial administrative authority (namely, the local bureaus of justice).[72]

The formation of an arbitration institution shall also meet certain statutory requirements. Under Article 15 of the Arbitration Law, an arbitration commission must have (a) its own name, domicile, and constitution; (b) necessary property; (c) legally qualified members; and (d) appointed arbitrators.[73] An arbitration institution shall be composed of one Chairman, two to four Vice-Chairmen, and seven to eleven members, and shall draw up rolls of arbitrators according to different professions.[74] It is further required that the members of an arbitration institution shall be experts in law, economics, trade, science, and technology, as well as individuals with practical work experience, and the number of experts shall not fewer than two-thirds of the total members of the arbitration institution. In addition, the Arbitration Law imposes a five-year term limit on the arbitration institution members and demands a replacement of at least one-third of the members upon expiry of each five-year term.[75]

There are two types of arbitration institutions in China that conduct foreign-related arbitration. The first type is the arbitration commission established especially for foreign-related arbitration. Included in this type are the China International Economic and Trade Arbitration Commission (CIETAC) and China Maritime Arbitration Commission (CMAC). CIETAC was established in 1956 and functions as a permanent arbitration institution to arbitrate economic and trade matters, as well as investment disputes,[76] while CMAC was formed in 1959 to conduct arbitration on disputes involving admiralty, maritime, transport, logistics, and other commercial disputes as agreed by the parties.[77] Both CIETAC and CMAC are under the China Council for the Promotion of International Trade (CCPIT).

Since 2000, CIETAC has adopted another name: the Arbitration Court of the China Chamber of International Commerce (CCOIC). In addition to its headquarters in Beijing, CIETAC currently has thirteen satellite commissions in major cities across the country, and four overseas arbitration centers in Hong Kong, Vancouver, and Vienna, respectively. According to CIETAC, it has conducted arbitration concerning international commercial disputes that involve parties from 166 countries and regions around the world. In 2019, the cases accepted by CIETAC

[72] See *id.*, art. 13.
[73] See *id.*, art. 15.
[74] See *id.*, art. 18.
[75] See *id.*
[76] See CIETAC's introduction at www.cietac.org/index.php?m=Page&a=index&id=34&l=en.
[77] See CMAC's introduction at www.cmac.org.cn/en/index.php?catid=10.

exceeded 3,000 yearly, and by 2024, the number of accepted cases increased to 6,000.[78]

The other type of arbitration institution that may conduct foreign-related arbitration are the arbitration commission created under the Arbitration Law. As noted, the Arbitation Law allows local arbitration commission to be established in provincial capitals or major cities. By September 2025, there have been a total of 285 arbitration institutions in China, with more than 60,000 arbitrators, including 3,400 foreign arbitrators.[79] During 2020-2025, the number of foreign related arbitration cases reached 16,000, involving some 730 billion *yuan* in value. In 2024, there were over 4,373 foreign related arbitration cases and the amount in controversy exceeded 197.8 billion *yuan*, increasing 100% and 136% respectively compared with 2020.[80]

The Arbitration Law does not clearly stipulate whether the arbitration institutions so established may handle foreign-related arbitrations. Nevertheless, in its 1996 Notice on Clarification of Several Issues in the Implementation of the Arbitration Law of China, the General Office of the State Council resolved the ambiguity left in the Arbitration Law concerning the eligibility of other arbitration institutions to handle foreign arbitration. According to the Notice, the main responsibility of the newly established arbitration commission is to accept domestic arbitration cases, but if the parties voluntarily choose to do so, the newly formed arbitration commission can undertake foreign-related arbitration.[81]

The State Council General Office's 1997 Notice gave the green light for all other arbitration commissions established under the Arbitration Law to engage in foreign-related arbitration. In 2022, China launched an initiative to build international commercial arbitration centers and designated Beijing, Shanghai, Guangzhou, Shenzhen, and Hainan as pilot areas.[82] There are now eight arbitration institutions

78 See CIETC introduction, *supra* note 81.

79 See the MOJ, News on the Symposium on Foreign-Related Arbitration, August 31, 2025, available at www.gov.cn/lianbo/bumen/202508/content_7034767.htm.

80 See See the MOJ News Briefing, September 9, 2025, available at www.moj.gov.cn/pub/sfbgw/sfbxwfbhzb/2025nsfbfbh/202509gzlwcsswgh/202509gzlwcsswgh_mtgz/202509/t20250908_524830.html. See also China Report, *Foreign-Related Laws To Be Enhanced*, China Daily, September 7, 2024, available at www.china.org.cn/china/2024-09/07/content_117414084.htm.

81 See the State Council's General Office, Notice on Clarification of Several Issues in the Implementation of the Arbitration Law of China, issued June 8, 1996, available at www.66law.cn/tiaoli/133226.aspx.

82 In 2019, The CPC Central Committee's General Office and the State Council's General Office jointly issued "Several Opinions on Improving Arbitration System and Enhancing the Public Credibility of Arbitration," calling for a major overhaul of the arbitration system in the country. Following the Opinions, the Ministry of Justice put in place a "China Arbitration 2022 Plan" in which the establishment of nationally and internationally influential arbitration centers was listed as one of the top priorities. See China Report, *supra* note 66. See also Ministry of Justice of China, *Build a New Global International Commercial Arbitration Platform*, www.moj.gov.cn/pub/sfbgw/fzgz/fzgzggflfwx/fzgzggflfw/202404/t20240422_497786.html.

in the country that considered the major arbitration institutions engaged in foreign-related arbitration, including CIETAC, CMAC, Beijing Arbitration Commission, Shanghai International Arbitration Center, Shanghai Arbitration Commission, Guangzhou Arbitration Commission, Shenzhen Arbitration Commission, and Hainan International Arbitration Court.

B. *Appointment of Arbitrators*

The Arbitration Law contains several rules that govern arbitrator appointments. The first one is the rule of integrity. Article 21 of the Arbitration Law mandates that arbitrators appointed by arbitration institution be fair and upright, possess good professional qualities, be diligent and responsible, stay honest and upright, and abide by professional ethics.[83] In addition, article 25 of the Arbitration Law requires the country's arbitration association, the self-regulatory body of arbitration institutions to supervise arbitrators in their arbitration activities in accordance with the association's charter.[84]

The second rule is the rule of qualification. Under article 22 of the Arbitration law, only those who meet one of the following conditions may serve as an arbitrator: (a) recipient of the legal professional qualification upon passing the National Unified Legal Professional Qualification Examination (LPQE) with at least eight-year experience in arbitration; (b) a lawyer for at least eight years in practice; (c) a prior judge or prosecutor for at least eight years; (d) a legal researcher or faculty member with a senior professional title in research or teaching; or (e) a person who has legal knowledge, engages in professional work such as law, economics and trade, maritime affairs, science and technology, and has a senior professional title or equivalent professional level.[85] Article 22 of the Arbitration Law also provides that arbitration institutions may appoint arbitrators from overseas persons with expertise in law, economics and trade, maritime affairs, science and technology.[86]

The third rule is the rule of removal. Article 23 of the Arbitration Law requires arbitration institutions to establish an open roster of arbitrators according to different professions.[87] It is further provided in Article 23 of the Arbitration Law that an arbitrator shall be removed from the roster if the arbitrator (a) is dismissed from public office; (b) has his lawyer's practicing license revoked; (c) has his senior professional title taken away, or (d) is no longer qualified to serve as an arbitrator.[88]

[83] See the Arbitration Law, *supra* note 31, art. 21.
[84] See *id.*, art. 25.
[85] See *id.*, art. 22.
[86] See *id.*
[87] See *id.*, art 23.
[88] See *id.*

C. *Foreign Arbitration Proceedings*

Both the CPL and the Arbitration Law contain special provisions that apply to foreign arbitration. But as noted, with regard to certain issues, if there are no applicable special provisions, the general provisions will apply. First, under Article 288 of the CPL, for disputes arising in foreign economic and trade matters or transportation and maritime affairs, the parties shall not file a lawsuit in a court if they have agreed to submit their disputes to a foreign-related arbitration institution of China or another arbitration institution for arbitration.[89]

Article 288 is an exclusion clause, which excludes the court's jurisdiction and bars the parties from bringing a lawsuit if there is a valid arbitration agreement. Pursuant to Article 288, only if the parties do not have an arbitration clause in the contract or a written arbitration agreement afterwards may they file a lawsuit in a Chinese court.[90] The basic notion of the exclusion rule is that an arbitration agreement, if valid, trumps the court's jurisdiction.

Second, in foreign-related arbitration, if a party applies for preservation of the evidence, the foreign-related arbitration commission shall submit the application to the intermediate people's court in the place where the evidence is located.[91] In addition, the foreign-related arbitration tribunal may enter the details of the hearings in written records or make written minutes thereof. The written minutes may be signed or sealed by the parties and other participants in the arbitration.[92]

Third, as noted, the Arbitration Law recognizes *ad hoc* arbitration, but limits it to foreign arbitration in certain location under the written arbitration agreement of the parties. Under Article 82 of the Arbitration Law, if an *ad hoc* arbitration takes place in China, after its formation, the *ad hoc* arbitral tribunal shall within three working days file the names of the parties, the place of arbitration, the composition of the arbitral tribunal, and the arbitration rules with the Arbitration Association.[93] Pursuant to article 25 of the Arbitration Law, China's Arbitration Association is a social organization legal person and the arbitration institutions are its members.[94]

In addition, the Arbitration Law provides special judicial supports to the *ad hoc* arbitration. According to Article 82 of the Arbitration Law, during the arbitration proceeding, if a party applies for property or evidence preservation, or requests to order the other party to perform certain acts or prohibit it from performing certain acts, the arbitral tribunal shall submit the party's application to a court in accordance

89 See the CPL, *supra* note 12, art. 288.
90 See *id.*
91 See the Arbitration Law, *supra* note 28, art. 79.
92 See *id.*, art. 80.
93 See *id.*, art. 82
94 See *id.*, art. 25.

with the law, and upon its receipt of the application, the court shall take prompt action.[95]

With regard to arbitration rules, the Arbitration Law gives priority to the parties' choice. As noted, under article 81 of the Arbitration Law, the parties may agree in writing on the applicable rules of the arbitration proceedings. Absent such an agreement, the seat of arbitration shall be the basis for determining the applicable rules of the arbitration proceedings as well as the jurisdictionally competent court.[96] The Arbitration Law does not define the seat of arbitration. A general understanding is that arbitration seat is the legal place of arbitration and in many cases not necessarily the physical place of arbitration, namely the location where the arbitration hearings actually take place.[97]

Given the importance of arbitral seat in foreign arbitration, the Arbitration Law provides a seat determination rule. In accordance with article 81 of the Arbitration Law, (a) the parties may by written agreement select the seat of arbitration; (b) if, however, the parties could not agree on the seat of arbitration or the agreement is unclear, the seat of arbitration shall be determined in accordance with the arbitration rules agreed upon by the parties, and (c) if there is no relevant provision in the arbitration rules, the seat of arbitration shall be determined by the arbitral tribunal based on the circumstances of the case and in accordance with the principle of convenience to dispute resolution.[98]

D. *Foreign Arbitration Rules*

Foreign arbitration rules refer to the rules and procedures that apply during the process of foreign arbitration or govern the proceedings of foreign arbitration. Since each arbitration institution has its own rules governing the arbitration, the specific contents of foreign arbitration rules may vary between different arbitration institutions. Therefore, before choosing an arbitration institution for foreign-related arbitration, the parties should be aware of the arbitration rules of the institution, because the procedures and requirements set forth in the rules must be followed for the arbitration.

Under Article 91 of the Arbitration Law, arbitration institutions may formulate arbitration rules in accordance with the relevant provisions of the Arbitration Law and the CPL, with reference to the model arbitration rules published by the Arbitration Association of China.[99] Currently there are two major sets of foreign arbitrations rules: the CIETAC's Arbitration Rules and the CMAC's Arbitration

[95] See *id.*, art. 82.
[96] See *id.*, art. 81.
[97] See Jiang Wei and Xiao Jianguo, *supra* note 2, at 67-68.
[98] See the Arbitration Law, *supra* note 31, art. 81.
[99] See *id.*, art. 91.

Rules. In the CIETAC's Arbitration Rules, there is a section that applies to domestic arbitration. The other arbitration commissions in China also have their own arbitration rules but those rules primarily govern domestic arbitration.

In Beijing Arbitration Commission's Arbitration Rules (BAC Rules), for example, the focus is on domestic arbitration with some special rules for international commercial arbitrations. The matters covered by the special rules include interim measures, appointment of an emergency arbitrator, composition of the arbitral tribunal, defenses and counterclaims, notice of hearing, mediation by the tribunal, time limit for rendering the award, and applicable law.[100]

3. ARBITRATION AGREEMENTS

In China, an arbitration agreement is generally described as "a manifestation of the consent of the parties to resolve their disputes through an arbitral body."[101] Also under Article 27 of the Arbitration Law, an arbitration agreement is prescribed to include an arbitration clause stipulated in the contract and agreement of submission to arbitration concluded in other written forms before or after disputes arise.[102] The provision of Article 27 carries at least two basic notions. First, an arbitration agreement is an agreement to submit for arbitration the disputes that have occurred or may occur between the parties. Second, an arbitration agreement can be a contract clause or take another written form.

In addition, an arbitration agreement can be made through a written reference clause. According to the SPC, if the contract stipulates that valid arbitration clauses in other contracts and documents shall be applied to resolve disputes, when a contract dispute occurs, the parties shall submit to arbitration in accordance with the arbitration clause.[103] Also, if there are arbitration provisions in relevant international treaties to which a foreign contract is subject, when a dispute occurs related to the contract, the parties shall submit a request for arbitration in accordance with the arbitration provisions in the treaty.[104]

A valid arbitration agreement is held in China as having both positive and negative effects. The positive effect refers to an obligation of the parties to arbitrate in good faith, while the negative effect implicates a duty of either party not to litigate. In addition, an arbitration agreement, if enforceable, serves as the sole legal basis for arbitration, and in the meantime operates to exclude a court jurisdiction. As

[100] See Beijing Arbitration Commission/Beijing International Arbitration Center Arbitration Rules (2022), available at www.bjac.org.cn/english/page/zc/guize_en2022.html.

[101] See Jiang Wei and Xiao Jianguo, *supra* note 2, at 55-56.

[102] Arbitration Law, *supra* note 31, art. 27.

[103] See the SPC, Interpretation Concerning Some Issues on Application of the Arbitration Law of China (2006), art. 11, at https://flk.npc.gov.cn/detail2.html?NDAyODgxZTQ2MDAwZTI3OTAxNjAwMWI0NjkzZjA5NjI (SPC 2006 Interpretation on Arbitration Law).

[104] See *id.*

provided in article 288 of the CPL, where there is a valid arbitration agreement in foreign related cases, the parties shall not file a lawsuit in the court. Absent an arbitration clause in the contract or a written arbitration agreement reached afterwards, the parties may litigate their disputes in a court.[105]

Under Article 4 of the Arbitration Law, when a party applies for arbitration, the arbitration institution shall not take the case absent a valid arbitration agreement.[106] Article 5 of the Arbitration Law further provides that when the parties have reached an arbitration agreement and one party files a lawsuit with a court, the court shall dismiss the case, unless the arbitration agreement is invalid or otherwise provided by law.[107] In addtion, in the case where the parties have reached an arbitration agreement, but one party files a lawsuit in a court without stating the existence of an arbitration agreement, and after the court accepts the case, if the other party submits the arbitration agreement before the first hearing, the court shall dismiss the lawsuit, unless the arbitration agreement is invalid or otherwise provided by law. If, however, the other party does not raise an objection to the court's acceptance of the case before the first hearing, the party shall be deemed to have waived the arbitration agreement, and the trial shall continue.[108] Moreover, the validity of an arbitration agreement also affects the enforceability of the arbitral award involved.

A. *Formation of Arbitration Agreement*

Again, under the Arbitration Law, an arbitration agreement could be formed as an arbitration clause in a contract, as a separate arbitration agreement, or in other written forms. For an arbitration agreement to be valid and enforceable, it must meet certain requirements of both formality and substance. In regards to formality, an arbitration agreement must be in writing. As for the substance, a valid arbitration agreement shall contain the essential factors as required by the law.

A recent development is the recognition of the deemed arbitration agreement. Arbitration Law contains a new provision to the arbitration agreement. Under article 27 of the Arbitration Law, as noted, if one party claims that there is an arbitration agreement when applying for arbitration, and the other party does not deny it before the first hearing, it shall be deemed that an arbitration agreement exists between the parties after being prompted and recorded by the arbitral tribunal.[109] Again, this provision is a reflection of the actual practice already taking place in the country.

[105] See the CPL, *supra* note 12, art. 288.
[106] See the Arbitration Law, *supra* note 31, art. 4.
[107] See *id.*, art. 5.
[108] See *id.*, art. 37.
[109] See *id.*, art. 27..

a. Writing

Since an arbitration agreement is a manifestation of the parties' consent for arbitration, it shall be made expressly made in a written form. "Expressly made" means that the intentin to arbitrated is the manifested by the parties. Under certain circumstance, however, existence of arbitration agreement may be presumed under Article 27 absent an objection by one party to the other party's asserting such an agreement. "Written form" refers to a form that can show the described contents visibly, such as a written contract, letters, and data-telex, including telegram, telefax, fax, electronic data exchange, or email.[110] With the emergence of new technology and communication methods, the written form may be subject to further interpretation in certain cases.

For example, in *GS Global Corporation v. Shanghai Zhenxu Petroleum Co. Ltd.* (2016),[111] the petitioner, a Korean company, entered into a sales contract with the respondent via email. The contract contained an arbitration clause providing that all disputes concerning the contract shall be subject to arbitration in Seoul by the Korean Commercial Arbitration Court (KCAC). When the parties had a dispute over the performance of the contract, the petitioner took the case to the KCAC for arbitration pursuant to the arbitration agreement. After obtaining an award from the KCAC in its favor, the petitioner requested that the Shanghai No. 1 Intermediate People's Court recognize and enforce the award against the respondent.

The respondent contended that the award should not be enforced because the arbitration agreement was invalid. Among the respondent's arguments was that the sales contract bearing the arbitration clause was made via email, and email was not considered a written form as required under the New York Convention. Shanghai No. 1 Intermediate People's Court rejected the respondent's arguments. In its decision to enforce the award, the court held that since "writing" in the New York Convention is referred to as an exchange of letters or telegrams, emails, though not predicted at the time the New York Convention was adopted, should be regarded as a form of writing under the term "telegrams" for purposes of the Convention. The court made it clear that an agreement made via email was an agreement in writing.

Thus, in terms of arbitration agreement, "writing" in China includes (a) an arbitration agreement reached by the parties before or after their disputes, (b) an arbitration clause included in the contract, (c) all other documents exchanged via different means between the parties, including letters, telegrams, telexes, faxes, electronic data interchange and emails, etc., and (d) the arbitration clause involved in the document referred to by the parties.[112] An arbitration agreement reached by

[110] See the SPC, 2006 Interpretation of Arbitration Law, *supra* note 115, art. 1.

[111] See Shanghai No. 1 Intermediate People's Court, (Hu 01 Xiewairen No. 12), court judgment available at www.lawxp.com/case/c32875207.html.

[112] See Jiang Wei and Xiao Jianguo, *supra* note 2, at 63-64.

the parties by reference means that the parties did not directly enter into an arbitration agreement, but quoted the contract, bill or other written document including the arbitration clause in the contract as the basis for arbitration.[113]

To determine writing, the term "exchange of letters or telegrams" as provided in the New York Convention has generated controversies. From a practical viewpoint, the issue is a matter of interpretation. There are three questions frequently raised in China. The first question is what would constitute an "exchange." In Chinese courts, a proof of acknowledgment of receipt of the letter or telegram bearing the arbitration agreement, or a reply expressly indicating acceptance of the agreement, is required.[114] The second question is whether the signatures or seals of the parties are needed on the document. As a common practice in China, signatures and seals are essential for formal documents.[115] The third question is whether silence by the recipient counts as acceptance. Under Chinese law, acceptance must be made expressly as far as an arbitration agreement is concerned.[116] or if there is an objection to a claimed existence of an arbitration agreement, it must be made timely.

b. Essential Contents

As required under Article 27 of the Arbitration Law, for an arbitration agreement to be valid, it must contain three items: (a) expression of the parties' intention to arbitrate; (b) the matters subject to arbitration; and (c) a designated arbitration institution.[117] It is further provided in Article 29 that if the subject matter for arbitration or designation of arbitration institution is missing from an arbitration agreement or unclear, the parties may make a supplementary agreement to that effect.[118] As a matter of law, each of the three items prescribed in Article 27 is decisive in determining the validity of an arbitration agreement. The intention concerns the willingness of parties to arbitrate, and must be ascertained in order to find a valid arbitration agreement. The subject matter defines the scope of arbitration while the designated arbitration institution involves a choice of arbitration body.

The contents requirement for arbitration agreement, however, has not been received favorably among many commentators. Some argue that as compared with international common practice, this requirement imposes "stricter requirements on

[113] See *id.*

[114] See *id.*; see also Int'l Trade and Bus. Research Council, *Legal Practice Guide of Shanghai Lawyers Handling Recognition and Enforcement of Foreign Arbitral Awards*, at 11, www.lawyers.org.cn/info/cca1ac552671499a8f24ea8eec585c9c.

[115] See Huang Yaying, *On the Form of the New York Convention and Arbitration Agreement*, 2 Juris. J. 13 (2004).

[116] See Wan E'xiang and Xia Xiaohong, *supra* note 43, at 12-13.

[117] See the Arbitration Law, *supra* note 31, art. 27.

[118] See Arbitration Law, *supra* note 31, art. 29.

the content of an arbitration agreement,"[119] and as a result, it may lead to unattainability of arbitration.[120] Another argument is that the requirement, along with provision (now article 29 of the Arbitration Law) that allows the parties to designate an arbitration body in a supplementary agreement,[121] may have at least a *de facto* effect of disqualifying "international arbitration insitutions from operating in China."[122] In fact, in the MOJ's first draft of arbitration law revision, the contents requirement provision was deleted entirely,[123] but was restored in the subsequent drafts and thus remains in the Arbitration Law.

I. INTENTION TO ARBITRATE. Since arbitration is based on an agreement, the mutual assent of the parties to the arbitration must be present.[124] To determine assent, two questions must be answered. The first question is whether there is a contract by which the contractual relationship between the parties has been established.[125] The second question concerns whether the parties have intended to submit the disputes to arbitration.[126] Therefore, if a contract has never been reached, the arbitration agreement would not exist. Additionally, even if there is a contract, an expression of intention by the parties to arbitrate must be found in case of dispute.

Since writing is required for an arbitration agreement, evidence of a writing that proves the parties' intention for arbitration becomes critical for the arbitration as well as the enforcement of the arbitral award. It is generally held in China that the expression of intent to request arbitration shall comply with the general conditions for a valid contract: first, it must be the expression of mutual intention of both parties; second, it must be the true expression of the intention of the parties; and third, it must be the expression of intention of the parties themselves, not that of any other person.

In *Singapore Yimande Asia v. Wuxi Huaxin Cocoa Food*, the petitioner obtained an arbitration award from Cocoa Association of London Ltd and asked Wuxi Municipal Intermediate People's Court to enforce the award against the respondent.[127] Upon review, the court found that the petitioner relied on fax exchanges between the parties, but since the parties were bargaining over the price and quality

[119] See Jingzhou Tao and Von Wunschheim, Articles 16 and 18 of the PRC Arbitration Law: the Great Wall of China for Foreign Arbitration Institutions, 23 ARB. Int'l, 309, 324 (2007).

[120] See *id.*

[121] See Arbitration Law, *supra* note 3 (referring to Article 18, whereas an agreement for arbitration fails to specify or specify clearly matters concerning arbitration or the choice of arbitration commission, parties concerned may conclude a supplementary agreement. If a supplementary agreement cannot be reached, the agreement for arbitration is invalid).

[122] Tao and Von Wunschheim, *supra* note 131 at 309.

[123] See the MOJ, Explanations on the Draft Revision of the Arbitration Law, *supra* note 17, art. 21.

[124] See Jiang Wei and Xiao Jianguo, *supra* note 2, at 56.

[125] See *id.*

[126] See *id.*

[127] *Singapore Yideman Asia Pte Ltd. v. Wuxi Huaxin Cocoa Food Co., Ltd*, CHINESE CT. DECISION SUMMARIES ON ARB. (Sup. People's Ct. 2001) (China).

of the cocoa via the exchange of offers and counter-offers, no purchase agreement was actually reached.[128] It was also found that the purchase contract that the petitioner claimed was the "final version" had no signature of the respondent.[129]

On the basis of its findings, the court concluded that since there was a lack of mutual assent, no contract was ever concluded between the parties, and that the arbitral award made on the non-existing contract should not be recognized nor enforced.[130] In its reply approving the denial, the SPC held that a prerequisite for a valid arbitration clause is mutual assent by the parties of their intent to arbitrate.[131] Since the parties in this case never reached consent to arbitration during their fax exchanges, the arbitral award lacked both factual support and a legal basis, and therefore, its recognition and enforcement were denied.[132]

In *Voesalpine USA Corp v. Jiangsu Foreign Trade Co.*, the representatives of the parties, during contract negotiation, discussed the contents of the contract but did not reach any agreement.[133] Later, the petitioner sent the respondent a letter confirming the sales contract, but the respondent did not sign it. In the contract, there was an arbitration clause making Singapore the place of arbitration and Singapore law the governing law on the issue of validity of the arbitration clause. Before the arbitration took place, the local attorney retained by the petitioner sent a letter to inform the respondent of arbitration, and received no reply from the respondent.[134]

During the arbitration, the SIAC was of the opinion that the respondent's failure to respond and to object to the arbitration agreement within a reasonable period of time implicated the existence of such agreement. The SIAC then entered an award at the request of the petitioner. When the petitioner brought the award for enforcement in China, it was found that the respondent replied to the second letter from the petitioner's attorney rejecting the petitioner's claim of the arbitration agreement.

[128] *Id.*
[129] *Id.*
[130] *Id.*
[131] *Id.*
[132] *Id.*; see also Wan E'xiang and Xia Xiaohong, *supra* note 60, at 6 n.4 (internal citations omitted) (discussing another case where the parties made a series of contracts and arbitration was conducted under the arbitration clause contained in contract No. 623. The enforcement of the arbitral award was denied for lack of mutual assent. During the enforcement of the arbitral award, it was found that the disputes resolved by the arbitration body actually arose out of contract No. 624, and contract No. 623 had already been replaced by contracts No. 622 and 624, each of which had its own arbitration clause. The SPC affirmed the decision to deny recognition and enforcement of the arbitral award on the grounds that, absent the parties' agreement, the arbitration clause in contract No. 623 may not be used to resolve the dispute related to contract No. 624).
[133] *Voest-Alpine Int. Trade Co. v. Jiangsu Prov. Foreign Trade Corp.*, Chinese Ct. Decision Summaries on Arb. (Sup. People's Ct. 2008) (China).
[134] See *id.*

Based on the reply, the respondent argued that there was no express mutual assent to the arbitration.[135]

In affirming the lower court's decision to deny the petitioner's request for enforcement of the award, the SPC regarded the SIAC's finding of the existence of an arbitration agreement as having no legal ground. The reasons stated were, among others: (a) there was no guarantee that the respondent would timely receive the petitioner attorney's letter; (b) respondent rejected the arbitration agreement in its reply to the second letter from the petitioner's attorney; and (c) the petitioner attorney's letter did not specify a deadline for reply and there was no provision in Singapore law imposing a "reasonable period of time."[136]

When determining whether the parties intend to submit their disputes for arbitration, the courts will normally make a three-step inquiry. At first, the court will determine if there is any clause in the contract or separate agreement between the parties pertaining to dispute settlement. If yes, the court then will determine whether the parties have agreed in the clause or agreement to seek arbitration if disputes occur. Third, to ascertain the parties' intention to arbitrate, the court will determine whether the clause or agreement clearly results from the true intention of the parties without any unwanted influence externally.

Generally the determination of intention is based on the language of the contract clause or agreement. If, however, there is a dispute over the meaning of particular language or even the existence of an arbitration clause or agreement, the reasonable person standard and certain circumstantial evidence may be used to identify the actual intention of the parties. However, in the deemed arbitrton agreement case as provided in Article 27 of the Arbitration Law, the parties' intention may be assumed or implied from a party's non objection.

III. MATTERS SUBJECT TO ARBITRATION. Under the Arbitration Law, it is required that the parties in their agreement unequivocally address the matters to be submitted for arbitration.[137] In general, the matters agreed upon for arbitration shall meet two conditions. First, the matters in disputes must be arbitrable, meaning that the matters should not exceed the scope of arbitration stipulated by the law. Second, disputes to be arbitrated shall be clear. Since arbitration bodies only resolve disputes to the extent agreed upon by the parties, disputes to be submitted for arbitration should be specified in the arbitration agreement.

The matters could be stated in general terms, such as "all disputes arising out of this contract," or refer to particular issues that the parties would take to arbitration. Under the SPC's interpretation, if the parties' agreement provides a general term for arbitration based on all contract-related disputes, the term shall be understood to

[135] See *id.*
[136] See *id.*
[137] See Arbitration Law, *supra* note 31, art. 27.

include any contractual dispute involving such matters as formation, validity, modification, transfer, performance, liability for breach, interpretation, or dissolution of the contract.[138]

Note, however, that a defect in providing or addressing matters for arbitration in the agreement between the parties is curable as a matter of law. Thus, if in an arbitration clause or agreement, the parties fail to state the matters eligible for arbitration, or the statement is ambiguous, they may, under Article 29 of the Arbitration Law, enter into a supplementary agreement to clarify.[139] Under Article 29, only if a supplementary agreement cannot be reached by the parties may the arbitration agreement be deemed invalid.[140]

But an issue that often arises is whether a non-contractual claim that is related to the performance of the contract could also be included if a general term is used in the arbitration clause or agreement. This issue is relevant because it may affect the option of a party to pursue litigation rather than arbitration. Article 5 of the Arbitration Law mandates that the People's Court not take the case if the parties involved had a valid arbitration agreement.[141] Thus, no party may seek litigation if the non-contractual claim is not excluded from the general term of arbitration. Therefore, it is important that the matters for arbitration are clearly stated in the arbitration agreement and include or exclude certain issues that might arise.

The scope of the matters for arbitration would also affect the enforcement of the arbitral award. Under Article 83 of the Arbitration Law, a party in a foreign arbitration may request a court to annul an arbitral award if the matters arbitrated are out of the scope of arbitration agreement.[142] In accordance with the SPC, upon the request of a party, if it is clearly found that an arbitral award contains certain matters exceeding what the parties have agreed upon for arbitration, the excessive part will be removed and become unenforceable.[143] If, however, the exceeded part is indispensable from the rest of the arbitral award, the whole award will be set aside by the people's court.[144] In actual cases, the people's courts often look at the "exceeding" issue quite broadly.

In *Gerald Metals Inc. (GMI) v. Wuhu Smelter and Refinery Plant*,[145] the parties entered into a sales contract which provided that any dispute arising out of, or related to, the contract should be subject to arbitration in London in accordance with London Metal Exchange Rules. In December 2001, the petitioner filed a request for arbitration with the arbitration panel of London Metal

[138] See the SPC, 2006 Interpretation on Arbitration Law, *supra* note 115, art. 2.
[139] See the Arbitration Law, *supra* note 31, art. 29.
[140] See *id.*
[141] See *id.*, art. 5.
[142] See *id.*, art. 83.
[143] See the SPC, 2006 Interpretation on Arbitration Law, *supra* note 115, art. 19.
[144] See *id.*
[145] *Gerald Metals Inc. v. Wuhu Smelter and Refinery Plant*, CHINESE CT. DECISION SUMMARIES ON ARB. (Anhui People's Ct. May 23, 2002) (China).

Exchange on the grounds of breach of contract. In its request, the petitioner listed both the respondent and Wuhu Metallurgical Plant (WHMP) as co-parties. The respondent and WUMP neither answered the petitioner's claim nor attended the arbitration.[146]

A default arbitration award was entered in May 2002. Petitioner then took the award to China for enforcement. The respondent asked the People's Court to deny the enforcement of the award on the grounds that the petitioner and respondent (1) never had any business contacts or sales disputes; (2) the respondent never participated in any part of the arbitration; and (3) the respondent was not related to WHMP in terms of property or equity ownership. Upon its review, the High People's Court of An Hui Province found that the respondent was not a party to the arbitration agreement in question, and thus held that the arbitral award exceeded the scope of the arbitration agreement.[147] The court then reported the case to the SPC for approval of the denial.[148]

In its reply, the SPC opined that since the respondent was not involved in the sales contract between the petitioner and WHMP, the arbitral award based on the alleged dispute between the petitioner and the respondent obviously exceeded the underlying arbitration agreement, and therefore, the exceeded part shall be invalid. The SPC also concluded that because the arbitral award did not separate the respondent from WHMP in light of the liabilities claimed, and that since there was no meaningful way to differentiate the non-exceeded part from the award, the award as a whole should not be recognized and enforced.[149]

III. DESIGNATED ARBITRATION INSTITUTION. Again, Article 27 of the Arbitration Agreement requires that an arbitration agreement contain a designated arbitration institution.[150] In foreign arbitration, the parties may choose in their arbitration agreement a Chinese arbitration institution, foreign arbitration institution, or international arbitration tribunal such as the International Chamber of Commerce Arbitration Court. Absent such designation, the agreement would be regarded invalid.

It is important to note that the Arbitration Law does not make the seat of arbitration an essential term in the arbitration agreement. This seems to be at odds with the general practice in international commercial arbitration. One interpretation in Chinese arbitration literature is that since the Arbitration Law does not list the place of arbitration as a basic content of the arbitration agreement, when the

146 See *id.*

147 See *id.*

148 See *id.*

149 See *id.*; see also *Gerald Metals Inc. v. Wuhu Smelter and Refinery Plant*, PEKING U. L. Sup. People's Ct. Nov. 12, 2003.

150 See the Arbitration Law, *supra* note 31, art. 27.

parties choose a permanent arbitration institution, if there is no other agreement, the place where the arbitration commission is located shall be the arbitration seat.[151]

For purposes of the arbitration institution designation, the Arbitration Law allows the parties to cure the defect on this issue retroactively. As discussed, under article 29 of the Arbitration Law, when the designation of an arbitration institution is unclear in the arbitration agreement, the parties may enter into a supplementary agreement to specify the institution. Otherwise, the arbitration agreement will become invalid.[152]

The SPC has also shown certain flexibility in determining whether an arbitration institution is being designated in an arbitration agreement. There are a number of situations in which the arbitration agreement will be deemed to have designated the arbitration body despite certain flaws in the agreement. The first situation is that the arbitration agreement does not accurately state the name of the arbitration body. Under this circumstance, according to the SPC, if the arbitration body can be ascertained, the designation should be considered as having been made.[153]

The second situation refers to the case where the parties have only agreed on the arbitration rules that will be applied if arbitration is sought, but have failed to mention the arbitration body. Although in general, such an agreement would be deemed as containing no designated arbitration body, the agreement will nevertheless be considered valid if (a) the parties reach a supplementary agreement for this purpose, or (b) if the arbitration body could be ascertained via the agreed upon arbitration rules.[154]

The SPC's 2017 Rules of Arbitration Review contains a broader provision in this regard. Under Article 15 of the 2017 Rules of Arbitration Review, if an arbitration institution or place of arbitration is not specified in the arbitration agreement, but can be determined under the applicable arbitration rules chosen by the parties in the arbitration agreement, the arbitration agreement shall be deemed to have contained the arbitration institution or the place of arbitration.[155] Article 15 implicates that the designation of arbitration body can be inferred from the choice of arbitration rules of a particular arbitration institution.

The third situation is the case in which two or more arbitration bodies were provided in the arbitration agreement. If this happens, under the SPC's interpretation, the parties may agree to choose any one of them.[156] However, if the parties fail to reach consent as to the choice, the arbitration agreement will be nullified for lack

[151] See Jiang Wei and Xiao Jianguo, *supra* note 2, at 67.
[152] See the Arbitration Law, *supra* note 31, art. 29.
[153] See the SPC, 2006 Interpretation on Application of the Arbitration Law, *supra* note 115, art. 3.
[154] See *id.*, art. 4.
[155] See the SPC, 2017 Rules of Arbitration Review, *supra* note 15.
[156] See SPC 2006 Interpretation on Arbitration Law, *supra* note 115, art. 5.

of a designated arbitration body.[157] In this situation, none of the arbitration bodies will be regarded as having jurisdiction over the dispute between the parties.[158]

The fourth situation involves the selection of the arbitration institution in a particular place without specifying the name of the arbitration institution. It occurs when the arbitration agreement states only something like, for example, "subject to arbitration in London." Because of the ambiguity in the agreement with regard to the arbitration body, its validity is dependent on whether the arbitration body may be identified.

Two possibilities may be present in this scenario: (a) there is one and only one arbitration institution in the specified place, or (b) the place has two or more such institutions. In the former case, the arbitration body can readily be ascertained.[159] In the latter case, however, the parties would have to make a choice by mutual consent.[160] If no consent can be reached, the arbitration agreement will be held invalid.[161]

In *Changzhou Donghong Packing Materials Co. v. France DMT*, the contract entered into by the parties had the following provision: "Any dispute arising from the contract shall be resolved through amicable consultation. If however, no agreement can be reached by the consultation, the dispute shall be submitted to arbitration. The place of arbitration is Beijing, China. The arbitration shall be conducted under the related rules of the ICC. . . ."[162] When a dispute occurred and consultations failed, the plaintiff brought the case to He Bei High People's Court for litigation, claiming that the arbitration agreement in the contract was invalid.[163]

In their arguments, the parties disputed the arbitration body. The defendant contended that since the arbitration agreement pointed to the ICC rules, the ICC should have the power to arbitrate the dispute.[164] The plaintiff challenged the ICC's jurisdiction, arguing that the arbitration agreement had designated Beijing as the place of arbitration. But since Beijing has multiple arbitration institutions, the court held that due to its lack of a specified arbitration body, the arbitration agreement in question would be deemed invalid under Articles 16 and 18 of the Arbitration Law unless the parties had reached a supplementary agreement.[165] In its decision to annul the arbitration agreement, the court took the position that because there was no supplementary agreement ever reached by the parties, the arbitration agreement

[157] See *id.*
[158] See *id.*
[159] See *id.*, art. 6.
[160] See *id.*
[161] See *id.*
[162] *Cangzhou Donghong Packing Material Co. v. France DMT*, PEKING U. L. (Sup. People's Ct. Apr. 26, 2006) (China).
[163] See *id.*
[164] See *id.*
[165] See *id.*

had to be held invalid.[166] The SPC approved the decision of invalidation on the same grounds.[167]

B. *Validity of Arbitration Agreement*

Like a contract, an arbitration agreement is also subject to scrutiny for validity, and the defenses available to the formation of a contract may also be asserted against the arbitration agreement. But, in Chinese courts, only a party to an arbitration agreement may challenge the validity of the agreement.[168] Therefore, unless a party raises an argument, the court never questions the validity of an arbitration agreement. The underlying notion is the presumption of validity under which no arbitration agreement is considered invalid unless proven otherwise. In other words, an arbitration agreement would be presumptively valid without being challenged on statutorily defined grounds.

There are two principles set forth in the Arbitration Law that may also affext the validity of an arbitration agreement. The first principle is voluntariness. It is required under article 4 of the Arbitration Law, when choosing arbitration to resolve disputes, the parties involved should follow the principle of voluntariness and reach a consent for arbitration.[169] The second principle is good faith. Article 8 of the Arbitration Law demands that arbitration should follow the principle of good faith.[170] As applied to arbitration agreement, arbitration in good faith is aimed at preventing fraud, coercion and other improper conducts to ensure the authenticity and validity of the arbitration agreement.

a. Requirements of Validity

For an arbitration to take place, there must be a valid and enforceable arbitration agreement. Under Article 28 of the Arbitration Law, an arbitration agreement is be null and void if (a) the agreed upon matters to be submitted to arbitration exceed the scope of arbitrable matters as specified by law; (b) one party that concluded the arbitration agreement has no capacity for civil conduct or has limited capacity for civil conduct; or (c) one party coerced the other party into concluding the arbitration agreement.[171]

[166] See *id.*
[167] See *id.*
[168] See the SPC, Several Provisions on the Handling of Foreign-related Arbitration and Foreign Arbitration Cases by the People's Court (Proposal) (promulgated by the Sup. People's Ct., Dec. 31, 2003), art. 3, CHINACOURT.ORG, www.chinacourt.org/article/detail/2003/12/id/98431.shtml (hereinafter referred to as the SPC 2003 Proposal).
[169] See the Arbitration Law, *supra* note 31, art. 4.
[170] See *id.*, art. 8.
[171] See the Arbitration Law, *supra* note 31, art. 28.

For the determination of validity of an arbitration agreement, the SPC more explicitly addressed the situations under which an arbitration agreement may not be enforced. According to the SPC, an arbitration agreement may be set aside by the courts upon the request of a party if (a) the arbitration agreement is reached by a party who has no or limited civil capacity; (b) the arbitration agreement is made by fraud or coercion; (c) the subject matter agreed upon for arbitration exceeds the scope prescribed by law; (d) the agreement allows the parties the option to either apply for arbitration or pursue litigation; (e) the agreement provides only one party with the right to apply for arbitration; (f) the arbitration body specified in the arbitration agreement does not exist and the parties fail to reach a supplementary agreement; (g) the domestic parties agree to submit non-foreign-related matter to a foreign arbitral body for arbitration; or (h) there is another situation in which the agreement would be annulled by law.[172]

Of the SPC's list mentioned above, the issue of capacity requires more discussion. The issue of capacity involves two questions. The first question is whether a party is capable of making a contract. The second question, which is closely related to the first one, involves which law should be used to determine the capacity of the party. In China, a person's capacity includes their capacity for civil rights and capacity for civil conduct.

As noted, under Articles 11 and 12 of the Choice of Law Statute of China, the law of the place of the person's habitual residence determines both the capacity of the person's civil rights and their civil conduct.[173] However, if a natural person is deemed to lack civil capacity for civil conduct under the law of his or her habitual residence, but has such capacity according to the law of the place of conduct, the law of the place of conduct controls.[174]

In Chinese Contract Law, as discussed, the capacity of a party may become an issue in three different settings: (a) where an agreement was made by a person with limited civil capacity; (b) where an agreement was entered into by an agent on behalf of a principal without due authorization; and (c) where a person with no right to dispose of property entered into an agreement involving a transfer of that property.

In the case where an agent is involved in international business transactions, the most common issue is whether the agent is duly authorized. What happens frequently is that the agent makes himself appear to have full authority from the principal (a Chinese domestic entity), but when disputes arise, the principal denies any relationship with such agent. In this situation, without hard evidence to prove otherwise, it would be difficult for a foreign party to hold the Chinese principal

[172] See the SPC 2003 Proposal, *supra* note 200, art. 20.

[173] See Law on the Application of Law Concerning Foreign-Related Civil Relations of the People's Republic of China, promulgated by the Standing Comm. Nat'l People's Cong., Oct. 28, 2010, effective Apr. 1, 2011, arts. 11-12, available at www.gov.cn/jrzg/2010-10/28/content_1732871.htm (Choice of Law Statute).

[174] See *id.*, art. 12.

liable. For an arbitration agreement, its validity can be directly affected by the capacity of the agent.

The case of *British Glencore Co., Ltd. v. Chongqing Machinery and Equipment Import and Export Co. Ltd.* is quite exemplary. In 1996, a salesperson of the respondent contacted the Beijing representative office of the petitioner via a fax requesting to purchase one thousand tons of electrolytic copper priced at about $2.5 million from the petitioner.[175] The representative of the petitioner responded by fax confirming the purchase, and also informed the respondent's salesperson that a formal contract from the petitioner would be sent to the respondent. A few days later, the petitioner sent the contract already signed by the petitioner to the respondent's salesperson for signature. Upon receipt of the contract, the respondent's salesperson signed it and sent it back with his own signature.[176]

The contract provided, *inter alia*, that any dispute or remedy arising out of or relating to the contract, or any alleged breach of the contract, should be subject to arbitration according to the rules of the London Metal Exchange (LME). It was also provided that the validity and interpretation of the contract should be governed by British law. Shortly after the contract was signed, the respondent asked to cancel the contract.[177]

According to the respondent's salesperson, he did not have authorization from the respondent company when he signed the contract, and therefore, the respondent company would not recognize any effect of the contract. The petitioner replied challenging the cancellation, and stated that if the respondent failed to perform the contract, the petitioner would suffer damages for which the petitioner may take legal action against the respondent.[178]

Facing the respondent's refusal to proceed with the contract, the petitioner applied to the LME for arbitration under the arbitration clause in the contract. A notice of arbitration was sent to the respondent, but the respondent did not respond or attend the arbitration. In the respondent's absence, the LME entered a default arbitral award in favor of the petitioner in February 1997. The petitioner then took the LME's arbitral award to Chongqing No. 1 Intermediate People's Court for recognition and enforcement.[179]

In 2000, after its review of the petitioner's request, Chongqing No. 1 Intermediate People's Court held that the arbitration agreement was invalid due to the incapability of the respondent's salesperson.[180] His incapability was found on the grounds that (a) the contract in question did not have the respondent's official seal on it, which

[175] *Glencore International v. Chongqing Machinery and Equipment Imp. and Exp. Co.*, CHINESE CT. DECISION SUMMARIES ON ARB. (Chongqing High People's Ct. Dec. 29, 2000) (China).
[176] See *id.*
[177] See *id.*
[178] See *id.*
[179] See *id.*
[180] See *id.*

should have put the petitioner on alert because, as a general practice in China, the official seal is legally required on all commercial transaction documents; (b) the respondent notified the petitioner that the contract would not be recognized promptly two days after the contract was signed by its salesperson, which implicated that the respondent's representative did not have the authority to make such a contract, nor did the respondent ratify its salesperson's action on the matter; and (c) the respondent's salesperson did not have actual or apparent authority, therefore he had no power to enter into the contract, including the arbitration agreement by which the respondent was alleged to be bound.[181]

The Chongqing No. 1 Intermediate People's Court's decision of denial was endorsed by both the Chongqing High People's Court and the SPC.[182] In its approval, the SPC held that the arbitration agreement was invalid because the salesperson and the respondent lacked a formal agency relationship on the basis of the facts that: (a) the salesperson was not authorized by the respondent, (b) the contract did not bear the official seal of the respondent, and (c) the respondent disapproved the salesperson's act on its behalf.[183] It was also held by the SPC that pursuant to Article V, paragraph (1), subparagraph (a) of the New York Convention, the capacity of the respondent's salesperson should be determined by the law to which he is subject; in this case, the law of China.[184]

In addition to capacity, another issue affecting the validity of the arbitration agreement is whether the existing arbitration agreement applies to the party who is not a party, but is related, to the contract underlying the arbitration agreement. This issue may arise in two different situations: transfer of obligations under the contract or delegation and merger of documents.

Under Chinese Contract Law, the parties may transfer by agreement (wholly or in part) the rights and obligations of a contract to a third party.[185] In delegation, the question is whether the delegatee has the ability to utilize this defense against an arbitration clause not mentioned when the delegation to the delegatee of the contractual obligation is made. One argument is that since the arbitration clause is independent from the contract, a delegatee shall not be bound by the clause unless the delegatee has specifically assented to it.[186]

The SPC, however, takes the view that the arbitration clause remains binding when a contract is transferred, unless the parties have agreed otherwise. According to

[181] See *id.*

[182] *Glencore International v. Chongqing Machinery and Equipment Imp. and Exp. Co.*, Chinese Ct. Decision Summaries on Arb. (Sup. People's Ct. Apr. 19, 2001) (China).

[183] See *id.*

[184] See *id.*

[185] See Chinese Contract Law, promulgated in 1999, arts. 79 and 84, available at www.gov.cn/banshi/2005-07/11/content_13695.htm.

[186] See Qu Guanqing et al., *Examining and Rethinking the Impact of Contract Assignment on the Validity of Arbitration Clause*, 1 China Arb. Consulting 28, 29 (2005) (China), www.docin.com/p-101702663.html [https://perma.cc/R6E7-44XC].

the SPC, when a party transfers, either wholly or in part, its contractual rights or obligations to a third party, the arbitration clause in the contract shall not be adversely affected except when each of the transferor, transferee, and the other contractual party have reached an agreement to the contrary.[187] It is now commonly held in Chinese courts, at least in practice, that the delegation of a contract does not by itself adversely affect the arbitration clause.

The merger of documents is more complicated. Cases in this regard typically involve maritime situations, where the provisions of the charter party and the bill of lading are merged for the purpose of shipping. The provisions of the charter party create a contract between the owner of a vessel and the shipper of goods for the use of the vessel, while a bill of lading is a document necessary for most imports and exports throughout the world.

The question is whether the arbitration clause in the provisions of the charter party would control any disputes arising from the bill of lading. As a general practice, it is required that the arbitration clause in the charter party not have an effect in the bill of lading unless it is clearly stated that all clauses, including the arbitration clause in the charter party shall be merged or incorporated into the bill of lading.[188]

In *Hanjin Shipping Co. Ltd. v. Guangdong Fuhong Oil Products Co. Ltd*, the SPC approved the lower court's decision to deny recognition and enforcement of a British arbitral award.[189] The SPC denied recognition since the petitioner failed to prove that the charter party's arbitration clause was effectively incorporated into the bill of lading.[190] In 2004, the petitioner obtained a British arbitral award and asked Guangzhou Maritime Court to enforce it.[191]

During the court's review, it was found that in front of the bill of lading there was a note stating the bill of lading was to be used together with the charter party provisions. Also, the back of the bill of lading contained a provision requiring all terms and conditions, including application of law and arbitration articles in the charter party provisions, to be merged into the bill of lading.[192]

However, when submitting the shipping contract as evidence to the court, the petitioner was unable to prove that the shipping contract included the same charter party provisions specified in the bill of lading.[193] In response, the respondent argued

[187] See SPC, 2003 Proposal, *supra* note 200, art. 29.

[188] See E'xiang and Xiaohong, *supra* note 60, at 29. Additionally, according to the SPC, only under the following conditions should the arbitration clause in the charter party be considered to have merged into the B/L: (a) there is a note on the front of the bill of lading specifying that the arbitration clause is incorporated into the bill of lading; and (b) the arbitration clause so incorporated is valid. Proposed Rules on Foreign Arbitration Cases art. 30.

[189] *Hanjin Shipping Co., Ltd. v. Guangdong Fuhong Oil Co., Ltd.*, PEKING U. L. (Sup. People's Ct. June 2, 2006) (China).

[190] See *id.*

[191] See *id.*

[192] See *id.*

[193] See *id.*

that the shipping contract actually covered the shipping arrangement between other parties and thus had nothing to do with the charter party provisions mentioned in the bill of lading.[194]

Based on these findings, the Guangzhou Maritime Court denied the petitioner's request for enforcement of the British arbitral award.[195] In its approval of that ruling, the SPC held that since the petitioner failed to prove that the shipping contract is identical to the one referenced in the bill of lading, the shipping contract was not incorporated into the bill of lading. Therefore, the arbitration clause contained in the shipping contract was invalid.[196]

Practically, there are two situations where the validity of an arbitration agreement may become an issue. One situation is that the arbitration agreement contains an option of arbitration or litigation. According to the SPC, if the parties agree that a dispute may be submitted to an arbitration institution for arbitration or be filed with a people's court for litigation, the arbitration agreement shall be invalid, except if one party submits a dispute to an arbitration institution, and the other party does not raise an objection.[197] Under Article 20 of the Arbitration Law, a party's challenge of the validity of the arbitration agreement shall be raised prior to the arbitration tribunal's first hearing.

The other situation refers to the case in which the arbitration agreement provides the parties with an option to litigate after arbitration. In China, this arrangement is also called the clause of arbitration first and litigation later. In the SPC's view, the parties' agreement to "arbitrate first and then litigate" does not constitute the factor that would render the arbitration agreement invalid. The SPC further held that since the Arbitration Law prohibits the parties from bringing the same dispute to a court after an arbitration award is made, the agreement on litigation in the situation of arbitration first and litigation later is invalid, but the validity of the arbitration agreement shall not be affected.[198]

b. Escalation Clauses

An escalation clause, also known as a tiered dispute settlement clause, refers to the provision in an arbitration agreement that requires the parties to resolve disputes through such means as negotiation and/or mediation before resorting to arbitration.[199] The purpose of the escalation clause is to require the parties to try to settle

[194] See *id.*
[195] See *id.*
[196] See *id.*
[197] See SPC 2006 Interpretation on Arbitration Law, *supra* note 115, art. 7.
[198] See the SPC, Minutes of the National Courts' Symposium on Foreign-Related Commercial and Maritime Trial Work (2021), art. 94, available at www.zhcourt.gov.cn/article/detail/2024/06/id/7998025.shtml.
[199] See Klaus Peter Berger, *Law and Practices of Escalation Clauses*, 22 Arbitration International 1 (2006).

their disputes as "preconditions" to arbitration. The question then is whether a clause as such in an arbitration agreement is enforceable. In other words, it is an issue whether a failure to satisfy the "preconditions" as agreed by the parties will affect the arbitration.[200]

There are two approaches in the arbitration jurisprudence to the effect of the escalation clause. One approach rests on the theory that no arbitration may be commenced until the agreed preconditions are met. The other approach is to allow arbitrators to determine the preconditions issue on the basis of the arbitration agreement. The former treats the non-compliance with the preconditions as a matter of jurisdiction, while the latter deems it as a matter of admissibility.[201] The major difference between the two approaches is whether the arbitral tribunal may determine the issue of non-compliance, because if under the jurisdiction approach, the arbitral tribunal is lack of competence with regard to the violation of preconditions.[202]

In China, there are currently no clear laws, regulations, or rules on escalation clause. Scholars are debating on the effect of a clause as such. One view is that the escalation clause, in its effect, is about whether the arbitration tribunal should take the case, and therefore, it is up to the arbitration tribunal to decide. The other view considers the escalation clause as a matter of whether the arbitral tribunal has an authority to take the case, which should be decided by the court. The former actually concerns admissibility of the case for arbitration, while the latter involves the jurisdiction of the arbitral tribunal.

In their practices, Chinese courts in general deem the escalation clause as a matter that does not involve arbitral jurisdiction, and thus leave it for the arbitration tribunal to decide. In *Runfa Development Co., Ltd.'s Application for non-enforcement of arbitration award*,[203] the parties in their arbitration agreement provided that any dispute arising out of or related to their contract should be resolved first through amicable negotiation, and arbitration would take place only after their negotiation fails. *Runda* sought for denial of recognition and enforcement of the arbitral award on the ground that disputes without the parties' negotiation first for resolution do not fall within the scope of the agreed arbitration, because negotiation and failure of negotiation are the prerequisites for submission to arbitration.[204]

In its review on the lower court report on the application for denial of the award enforcement, the SPC opined that although the parties agreed in the arbitration

[200] See Gary Born and Marija Šćekić, *Pre-Arbitration Procedural Requirements, "A Dismal Swamp"* in David D. Caron, Practicing Virtue: Inside International Arbitration, 227-228 (Oxford University Press, 2016).

[201] See *id.*, at 243-247.

[202] See *id.*, at 247-250.

[203] See the SPC, Reply to the Report for Review on *Runhe Development Co., Ltd.'s Application for Non-enforcement of the Arbitration Award* (2008), available at www.055110.com/law/1/14598.html.

[204] See *id.*

agreement that disputes should be resolved through negotiation, they did not clearly stipulate the negotiation period.[205] According to the SPC, when the content of the agreement is relatively general, which may lead to ambiguity in understanding how the clause should be implemented and defined, the true meaning of the agreement should be judged in combination with the purpose of the parties in entering into the arbitration agreement.[206] In this case, the two conditions agreed upon by the parties, namely "friendly negotiation" and "failure of negotiation," were a procedural requirement for negotiation and a result of negotiation. The SPC then held that when it was difficult to define the performance standard for "friendly negotiation," the arbitration tribunal had the right to accept the case based on the arbitration agreement, because the fact that one party initiates arbitration was itself a sign of "failure of negotiation," and thus the prerequisite of failure of negotiation was met.[207]

Chinese courts generally were not inclined to set aside or refuse to enforce an arbitral award when dealing with violation of procedural requirements contained in arbitration agreement. In one case, a court took the position that violation of pre-arbitration procedures, standing alone, was not sufficient to constitute a situation where "the correct adjudication of the case" or "the fair adjudication of the case" would be affected, and therefore did not constitute a legal ground for revoking or refusing to enforce the arbitration award.[208]

In another case, a court was of the opinion that pre-arbitration procedures referred to dispute resolution procedures prior to arbitration, not procedural matters during the arbitration process. Simple violation of pre-arbitration procedures did not constitute a violation of the parties' "special agreement on arbitration procedures," and therefore did not constitute a statutory ground for annulment or non-enforcement of an award.[209] Also, a court in a third case held that if one party relies on the failure to satisfy the preconditions as a reason for annulment or non-enforcement of an arbitral award, a relaxed validity and recognition standard will be employed, that is, to caculate the negotiation period from the date on which one party makes the claim so as to help maintain the enforceability of the effective arbitration award as much as possible.[210]

[205] See *id*.

[206] See *id*.

[207] See *id*.

[208] Beijing No. 4 Intermediate People's Court, *Beijing Weiying Times Co., Ltd. Application for Annulment of the China International Economic and Trade Arbitration Commission's Award* (2021), Jing 04 Minte 936 (2021), available at https://iidps.bit.edu.cn/gatsw/133f96db45614c429a08aa145a83d08e.htm.

[209] Shanghai No. 1 Intermediate People's Court, *Cui Ming v. Shanghai Guochun Venture Capital Co., Ltd. Applying for Annulment of the Arbitration Award*, Hu 01 Minte 250 (2019), at www.sohu.com/a/359449223_120058819.

[210] Beijing No. 4 Intermediate People's Court, *Shanghai Xuandu Entertainment Co. Ltd. Applying for Annulment of the CIETAC Award No. 0894 [2018]*, available at https://

Echoing the judicial practices, some arbitration institutions in China have amended their arbitration rules to contain a provision on escalation clause compliance. The CIETAC, for example, revised its Arbitration Ruls in September 2023. Under article 12 of the revised Rules, where it is agreed in the arbitration agreement that negotiation or mediation shall be conducted before arbitration, the Claimant may apply for arbitration after conducting negotiation or mediation. However, failure to negotiate or mediate shall neither prevent the Claimant from applying for arbitration nor prevent the Arbitration Court from accepting the case, unless the applicable law to the arbitral proceedings or the arbitration agreement expressly provides otherwise.[211]

c. Rule of Independence

An issue in determining the validity of an arbitration agreement is whether the determination would be affected by the validity of the contract of which the arbitration agreement is a part. A commonly accepted rule that governs this issue is the rule of independence, also known as the doctrine of separability. Independence means that the arbitration clause, though a part of the contract, is severable from the contract, and the effect of the arbitration clause does not depend on the effect of the underlying contract. In China, an arbitration clause is considered different from the underlying contract both in nature and in effect.

In its nature, the contract is an agreement that stipulates the substantive rights and obligations of the parties, which is substantive; whereas the arbitration clause is an agreement of the parties to choose arbitration for the settlement of their disputes, which is procedural. In effect, although the arbitration clause is contained in the contract, its effect does not depend on the effect of the contract. Thus, rescission or termination of a contract does not necessarily affect the effectiveness of the arbitration clause contained therein.

The rule of independence is well accepted in Chinese law. According to Article 30 of the Arbitration Law, an arbitration agreement shall exist independently, and whether or not the contract itself is formed, modified, ineffective, terminated, revoked or invalid shall not affect the validity of the arbitration agreement.[212] Also, under Article 507 of the Civil Code, if a contract does not take effect, or is void, revoked, or terminated, the validity of a clause concerning dispute settlement shall not be affected.[213]

arbitrationblog.kluwerarbitration.com/wp-content/uploads/sites/48/2021/09/Multi-tiered-Clauses-in-China-04.pdf.

211 See CIETAC, Arbitration Rules, amnded in September 2, 2023, effective Janurary 1, 2024, art. 12, available at www.cietac.org/sfs/cms/dd4ca1bb9e9d4a6d91ffafd87164e480.pdf.

212 See the Arbitration Law, *supra* 31, art. 30.

213 See the Civil Code of the People's Republic of China, adopted by the NPC in 2020, art. 507. A full text of the code is available at https://regional.chinadaily.com.cn/pdf/CivilCodeofthePeople%27sRepublicofChina.pdf.

In addition, under the rule of independence, if the parties reach an arbitration agreement when entering into a contract, a failure to form the contract will not affect the validity of the arbitration agreement. The purpose of making the arbitration agreement independent from the underlying contract is to ensure the validity of the arbitration agreement notwithstanding the defects in the underlying contract so that the disputes will be resolved in the way agreed upon by the parties.

In Chinese courts, the independence rule that shelters the arbitration agreement also applies to the governing law of the arbitration agreement. This practice is important, especially when the dispute involves a Sino-foreign joint venture. In accordance with Chinese law, Sino-foreign joint venture contracts are exclusively governed by the law of China, excluding the parties' choice of any foreign law.[214] But for arbitration of disputes concerning a joint venture contract, application of Chinese law is not exclusive.

In *Zhang Jia Gang Electronics Co. Ltd. v. Brose Int'l GmbH*, the parties signed a joint venture contract in 1995 to produce auto parts.[215] Under the contract, the conclusion, effect, interpretation, and enforcement of the contract would be subject to Chinese law. The contract also provided that all disputes arising from the contract shall be resolved first through friendly consultation, but if within sixty days after conclusion of the consultations the parties cannot reach an agreement, the disputes should be submitted for arbitration in Zurich, Switzerland. The joint venture contract did not contain a choice of law clause for arbitration.[216]

After the dispute occurred, the plaintiff brought a suit against the defendant in Su Zhou Intermediate People's Court.[217] The defendant used the arbitration clause in the joint venture agreement as a defense, and asked the court to dismiss the case. The plaintiff argued that since the arbitration clause did not specify the arbitration body, it should be held invalid under Chinese law. Su Zhou Intermediate People's Court rejected the plaintiff's argument, upholding the validity of the arbitration clause.[218] On appeal, Jiangsu High People's Court, however, opined that the arbitration clause was unenforceable because: (a) the validity of the arbitration clause in the joint venture contract should be governed by Chinese law and (b) the arbitration clause was invalid under Chinese law for its failure to contain an arbitration body.[219]

The SPC disagreed. In its reply to Jiangsu High People's Court's request for opinion, the SPC held that under well-accepted practice, the law chosen by the parties to govern their contractual disputes shall not be used to determine the

[214] See Chinese Contract Law, *supra* note 225, art. 126.

[215] *Zhangjiagang Xinggang Electronics Co. v. Brose International Co.*, SHANGHAI B. ASS'N (Su Zhou Interm. People's Ct. 2005) (China), www.lawyers.org.cn/info/cca1ac552671499a8f24ea8eec585c9c [https://perma.cc/NX2A-F4MB].

[216] See *id.*

[217] See *id.*

[218] See *id.*

[219] See *id.*

validity of the arbitration clause in the contract, and when the parties did not choose the law governing the arbitration but specified the place of arbitration, the law of such place shall be applied to the validity of the arbitration clause.[220] Thus, in this case, according to the SPC, Swiss law should be the governing law with regard to the arbitration agreement, and under Swiss law, the arbitration agreement was valid. The SPC then affirmed the Su Zhou Intermediate People's Court's decision to dismiss.[221]

The SPC's holding in this case implicates that the law chosen by the parties to govern their contract does not have the effect of governing arbitration unless the parties state otherwise in the contract. What could be reasonably inferred from the SPC's holding is that, when choosing the law applicable to arbitration, the parties may select the same law that governs the contract itself, or pick a different law to be applied to arbitration only. Thus, it is important that the parties make a specific selection in the arbitration clause or agreement if they wish to have the arbitration be subject to a particular law.

The SPC's 2017 Rules of Arbitration Review restates the rule of choice of law for arbitration: Article 13 of the 2017 Rules emphasizes that, when choosing the law via contract to govern the validity of the arbitration agreement, the parties shall unequivocally manifest their intent in this regard.[222] Article 13 also makes it clear that if the parties only agree on the choice of law for the contract, the law so chosen shall not apply to the determination of the validity of the arbitration agreement.[223] Further, under article 14 of the 2017 Rules, absent the parties' choice, if the law of the place of arbitration and the law of the place where the arbitration body is located differ in respect to the validity of the arbitration agreement, the law that would render the arbitration agreement valid shall be applied.[224]

Therefore, once a contract containing an arbitration clause is made, even if the contract later is found invalid, the arbitration clause survives under the rule of independence.[225] What is significant here is that if a party challenges the validity of a contract as a whole, the validity of the arbitration clause would not be affected. Thus, in order to effectively challenge the validity of an arbitration clause, the challenge must be made specifically to the arbitration clause.

d. Doctrine of Competence–Competence

The validity of an arbitration agreement determines the jurisdiction of the arbitration body, because no arbitral authority may be established on an arbitration

[220] See *Zhangjiagang Xinggang Electronics Co. v. Brose International Co.*, *supra* note 206.
[221] See *id.*
[222] See SPC, 2017 Rules of Arbitration Review Rules, *supra* note 15, art. 13.
[223] See *id.*
[224] See *id.*, art. 14.
[225] See *id.* at 57-62.

agreement that is invalid. A question then is who has the authority to determine the validity of an arbitration agreement. At the center of the question is whether the arbitration body itself may determine the validity issue. In other words, it is a question of whether an arbitration body may have the competence to determine its own jurisdiction.

In the modern law of arbitration, a rule of competence–competence has developed. Under this rule, an arbitral tribunal is considered to be competent to decide its own jurisdiction,[226] and to have the power to adjudicate disputes regarding its own competence.[227] According to the Model Law of UNCITRAL, an arbitral tribunal may rule on its own jurisdiction, including any objections with respect to the existence or validity of the arbitration agreement.[228] In the United States, the Supreme Court recognizes the competence–competence rule, but limits its application to matters of procedure, such as waiver, delay, time limits, notice, and other conditions precedent to an obligation to arbitrate.[229]

In China, the competence–competence rule is also accepted, but the parties have the right to decide whether the arbitration body may exercise the rule. Under article 19 of the 1994 Arbitration Law (as amended 2017), the arbitration tribunal has the right to affirm the validity of an arbitration agreement.[230] Under Article 20 of the 1994 Arbitration Law, however, if the validity of an arbitration agreement is disputed, the parties may request the arbitration commission or a court make a decision on its validity.[231] If one party makes a request to the arbitration commission, while the other party refers the matter to a court, the decision shall be made by the court.[232]

In their practice, the arbitration insititutions in Chian reserve the right of determining the validity of arbitration agreement to the arbitration commission rather than arbitral tribunal. For example, pursuant to Article 6, paragraph (1) of the Arbitration Rules of CIETAC (as amended 2015), CIETAC has the power to determine the existence and validity of an arbitration agreement and its jurisdiction over an arbitration case. Such power is delegated to the arbitral tribunal once it is formed.[233]

The provisions of 1994 Arbitration Law and the practices had invited criticism. First, there existed inherent inconsistence between article 19 and article 20. The

[226] Amokura Kawharu, *Arbitral Jurisdiction*, 23 N.Z. U. L. Rev. 238 (2008).

[227] See Gary B. Born, International Commercial Arbitration: Commentary And Materials 853 (2nd ed. 2001).

[228] U.N. Comm'n On Int'l Trade Law, UNCITRAL Model Law On International Commercial Arbitration, art. 16, U.N. Doc. A/61/17, U.N. Sales No. E.08.V.4 (amended 2006), www.uncitral.org/pdf/english/texts/arbitration/ml-arb/07-86998_Ebook.pdf [https://perma.cc/U6RX-3LT3].

[229] BG Group plc v. Republic of Arg., 572 U.S. 25, 26 (2014).

[230] See the 1994 Arbitration Law (as amended 2017), *supra* note 1., art. 19.

[231] See *id.*, art. 20.

[232] See *id.*

[233] See CIETAC Arbitration Rules, amended on November 4, 2014, effective January 1, 2015, art. 6, available at www.arbiter.com.sg/pdf/rules/CIETAC%20Arbitration%20Rules%202015.pdf.

former provided the arbitral tribual with the right to affirm the validity of an arbitration agreement, while the latter gave arbitration commission the decision makin power, which virtually made the arbitral tribual's right meaningless. In addition, many argued that allowing the arbitration commission, rather than the arbitral tribunal (the "judges" who will actually hear the arbitration), to decide the competence issue has several serious drawbacks.

First, it violates the parties' free will in forming the arbitral tribunal, because when picking arbitrators, the parties will give the arbitrator, rather than the arbitration commission, the authority to make the decision. Second, it destroys the efficiency of arbitration, because the arbitration commission is not the body conducting the arbitration. Third, it contradicts the function of the arbitration commission, because the commission is not an arbitral tribunal but an administrative body.[234]

As a response, the Arbitration Law modifies the previous provisions. On the hand, it keeps it unchanged that the arbitral tribual has the right to affirm the validity of an arbitration agreement unless one party refer it to a court for determination.[235] On the other hand, it relaces "the parties may ask arbitration commission," with "the parties may ask arbitration commission or arbitration tribunal" to make decision on the dispute over the validity of arbitration agreement. [236] Thus, under the Arbitration Law, an arbitral trinual now also has a final voice on the validity of arbitration agreement in disputes. What is worth noting is that in its 2023 revised Arbitration Rules, the CIETAC modifies the article 6 to directly deligate its power to determine the validity of arbitration agreement to the arbitration tribual upon the tribunal's formation.

C. *Law Governing Arbitration Agreement*

An arbitration agreement will not be enforced if invalid. When the validity of an arbitration agreement becomes an issue, a question then is under which law the validity of the arbitration agreement should be determined. In conflict of laws, a general approach is to follow the principle of party autonomy, under which the parties may select the governing law to their contract, subject to certain restrictions.[237] Absent the parties' choice, the governing law shall be determined under the prevalent choice of law rules of the forum.[238]

a. Determination of Governing Law

The determination of law applicable to arbitration agreements often encounters two possible laws: the law that governs the arbitration agreement and the law that applies

[234] See Jiang Wei and Xiao Jianguo, *supra* note 2, at 133-134.
[235] See the Arbitration Law, *supra* note 31, art. 30.
[236] See *id.*, art. 31.
[237] See Peter Hay *et al.*, Conflict of Laws 1085-1086 (6th ed. 2018).
[238] See *id.* at 1158-1159.

to the underlying contract. Those two laws might refer to the same law, or they might be different laws in cases where the parties have separately chosen the law that specifically governs the arbitration agreement. If the arbitration agreement is subject to a particular law under the parties' choice, its validity shall be determined under the chosen law.

In China, the agreed upon law applicable to the contract is separated from the governing law for the validity of the arbitration agreement. In its Minutes of the Second National Foreign-related Commercial and Maritime Trial Work Conference issued in 2005, the SPC made it clear that the governing law agreed upon by the parties in the contract to be applicable to the resolution of contract disputes cannot be used to determine the validity of foreign-related arbitration clauses.[239]

In its 2017 Rules of Arbitration Review, the SPC once again clarified that the parties' agreement to the applicable law for confirming the validity of a foreign-related arbitration agreement shall be clearly stated. An expression of intention that merely agrees on the law applicable to the contract cannot be used as the law applicable to confirm the validity of the arbitration clause in the contract.[240] Judicial practice also follows this provision. For example, in the (2018) Tianjin Minzhong No. 264 case, the agreement at issue stipulated that the agreement should be interpreted in accordance with English law. The Tianjin High Court determined that "the agreement did not stipulate the law applicable to the arbitration clause."

In addition, the law of the arbitral seat or the law of the place where the arbitration body is located, and the law of the place where the recognition and enforcement of a foreign arbitral award is sought, are also relevant to the determination of the validity of an arbitration agreement. The former applies when there is no parties' choice of law that applies to the arbitration agreement, while the latter is operative when the validity of the arbitration agreement is at issue during the enforcement of foreign arbitral awards.

In China, when reviewing the validity of an arbitration agreement, the courts will first determine the law that should be applied. Under Chinese choice of law rules, the contractual parties have the freedom to choose the law applicable to the arbitration.[241] If, however, the parties have failed to choose the governing law but have specified the place of arbitration in their agreement, the court will apply the law of the place of arbitration or the law of the place where the arbitration body is located to determine the validity of the arbitration agreement.[242] When the parties

[239] See the SPC, 2005 Minutes of the Second National Foreign-related Commercial and Maritime Trial Work Conference, available at www.pkulaw.com/chl/326819c3f1e219cdbdfb.html.

[240] See the SPC, 2017 Rules of Arbitration Review, *supra* note 15, art. 13.

[241] See the Choice of Law Statute, *supra* note 205, art. 18.

[242] See *id.*

make no agreement on either the applicable law or the place of arbitration, Chinese law (the forum law) will then be applied.[243]

For example, in *Changzhou Donghong Packing Materials Co. v. France DMT*, He Bei High People's Court held the arbitration agreement invalid in accordance with Chinese law or the law of the forum.[244] In this case, the Chinese party and its French counterpart entered into a contract in which Beijing was selected as the place of arbitration, but there was no agreement on the choice of law.[245] Absent the choice of law by the parties, the court applied Chinese law – the law of the forum and the place of arbitration.[246] As discussed, an arbitration agreement is invalid in China if it lacks a choice of arbitration body.[247]

As mentioned, to select the governing law, the freedom of the parties is subject to two major restrictions under the Chinese Choice of Law Statute. First, the selection must be made expressly.[248] China does not recognize any tacit choice or choice by inference.[249] Second, the application of the law selected shall not violate the public policy of China or mandatory rules of Chinese law.[250] As discussed, however, under Chinese law, it is not required that the choice of law by the parties bear a certain relationship with the parties, transactions, or disputes.[251] Therefore, the parties may choose the law of any place, regardless of their connection to the place.[252]

b. Doctrine of Delocalization

In international commercial arbitration, an important issue is which law, both procedurally and substantively, governs the arbitration. In essence, it is a question of whether the parties have the power or freedom to choose procedural and substantive rules for an arbitral proceeding.[253] Under the classic approach of *locus regit actum* (meaning, an act is to be governed by the law of the place of the act), arbitration is subject to the law of the place where the arbitration occurs, or the *lex loci arbitri*.[254] The doctrine of delocalization, however, holds that arbitration shall

[243] See SPC 2006 Interpretation on Arbitration Law, *supra* note 115, art. 16.

[244] Cangzhou Donghong Packing Material Co. v. France DMT, PEKING U. L. (Sup. People's Ct. Apr. 26, 2006) (China).

[245] See *id.*

[246] See *id.*

[247] See the Arbitration Law, *supra* note 31, art. 27.

[248] See the Choice of Law Statute, *supra* note 205, art. 3.

[249] See *id.*

[250] See *id.* Art. 5.

[251] See Mo Zhang, *Codified Choice of Law in China, Rules, Process and Theoretic Underpinnings*, 37 N.C.J. Int'l. and Com. Reg. 83, 118 (2011).

[252] See *id.*

[253] See Theodore C. Theofrastous, *International Commercial Arbitration in Europe: Subsidiary and Supremacy in Light of the De-Localization Debate*, 31 CASE W. RES. J. INT'L L. 455, 456–458 (1999).

[254] See *id.* at 460-464.

follow the rules and procedures chosen by the parties under the principle of party autonomy – these rules are those other than the rules of the place of arbitration.[255]

The core of the doctrine of delocalization is to free the parties from the restriction of the national law of the place of arbitration,[256] allowing the arbitration tribunal to "be guided by the agreement of the parties, or failing such agreement, by its own judgment."[257] With regard to the choice of law by parties, it has become an internationally accepted choice of law principle that the parties are permitted to select as they wish the substantive law of a particular country to govern their contractual and even non-contractual obligations.[258] The law of the forum always controls as far as procedural law is concerned, given its public nature.[259] The theory of delocalization breaks this tradition and provides the parties with the power to choose the procedural rules irrespective of where the arbitration takes place.[260]

For example, under the Model Law of International Arbitration published by the United Nations Commission on International Trade Law (known as UNCITRAL), the parties are generally free to agree on the procedure to be followed by the arbitral tribunal in conducting the proceedings.[261] It is further provided that, failing such agreement, the arbitral tribunal may conduct the arbitration in such manner as it considers appropriate.[262] Obviously, the Model Law does not intend to limit the parties' power to choose only the arbitration rules of the place of arbitration. According to UNCITRAL's status report, the Model Law has now been adopted in 75 states in a total of 106 jurisdictions.[263]

[255] See *id*. at 464-466.

[256] See *id*. at 457.

[257] See *id*. at 456.

[258] See generally Mo Zhang, *Party Autonomy and Beyond: In International Perspective of Contractual Choice of Law*, 20 EMORY INT'L L. REV. 511 (2006); Mo Zhang, *Party Autonomy in Non-Contractual Obligations: Rome II and Its Impacts on Choice of Law*, 39 SETON HALL L. REV. 861 (2009) (discussing party autonomy and choice of law). Under Chinese law, the parties may select a law to govern their civil relations by agreement, but the law so chosen refers only to the substantive law of the particular country or region, excluding any conflict of law rule or procedural law. See the SPC, Rules on Related Issues Concerning the Application of Law in Hearing Foreign-Related Contractual Dispute Cases Related to Civil and Commercial Matters (promulgated by the Jud. Comm. Sup. People's Ct., July 23, 2007, effective Aug. 8, 2007), P.R. C. MINISTRY OF COMM., July 23, 2007, art. 1.

[259] See Peter Hay, Patrick J. Borchers and Symeon C. Symeonides, Conflict of Laws 1137-41 (5th ed. 2010).

[260] See Pippa Read, *Delocalization of International Commercial Arbitration: Its Relevance in the New Millennium*, 10 AM. REV. INT'L ARB. 177, 185 (1999).

[261] See UNCITRAL Model Law on International Commercial Arbitration, art. 19(1) (U.N. COMM'N ON INT'L TRADE LAW 1985) (amended 2006), www.uncitral.org/pdf/english/texts/arbitration/ml-arb/07-86998_Ebook.pdf [https://perma.cc/U6RX-3LT3].

[262] See *id*., art. 19(2).

[263] See Status of UNCITRAL Model Law on International Commercial Arbitration, UNCITRAL.ORG, www.uncitral.org/uncitral/en/uncitral_texts/arbitration/1985Model_arbitration.html (last visited Jan. 28, 2025) [https://perma.cc/XE5T-ENU4].

In China, the doctrine of delocalization did not gain recognition in either legislation or judicial practice prior to the revision of the 1994 Arbitration Law. From a legal perspective, there was no provision in the law that allows the parties to choose the arbitration rules other than those governing the place of arbitration. Under the SPC interpretation, the choice of law by the parties shall be regarded as invalid if there is no legal provision that expressly authorizes such choice.[264]

There is also a skeptism from Chinese legal community about the delocalization due to the concern that it would make international commercial arbitration beyond the control of the legal system of the place where arbitration is conducted.[265] Some Chinese scholars describe the theory of delocalization as purposing to establish an arbitration system not subject to the law of the place of arbitration nor the national law of any particular country.[266] There is also a belief in China that delocalization would lead to a situation where the legal effect of an arbitration award is not governed by the law of the place of arbitration.[267]

CIETAC, however, seems to have taken a flexible approach toward delocalization. Under Article 4 of the CIETAC Arbitration Rules (as revised 2023), where the parties agree to refer their dispute to CIETAC for arbitration but have agreed on the application of other arbitration rules, the parties' agreement shall prevail unless such agreement is inoperative or in conflict with a mandatory provisionof the law applicable to the arbitral proceedings.[268] In addition, Article 4 of the CIETAC Arbitration Rules requires that CIETAC perform the relevant administrative duties when the parties have agreed on the application of other arbitration rules.[269] Because Article 4 of the CIETAC Arbitration Rules permits the use of the non-Chinese arbitration rules, it is considered a limited acceptance of delocalization.[270]

The 2013 ICA arbitration of *Anhui Long Li De Packaging and Printing Co., Ltd. v. BP Agnati S. R. L.* in Shanghai raised an interesting question pertaining to the recognition of delocalization in China. As discussed, the case was arbitrated by ICA in Shanghai under the arbitration rules of the ICA, which were selected by the parties. When affirming the enforceability of the ICA's arbitral award in that case, the SPC made no inquiry into the appropriateness of the use of the ICA arbitration

264 See the SPC, Interpretation on Several Issues Concerning the Application of the Law on the Application of Foreign-related Civil Relations Law (1), art. 6, available at https://cicc.court.gov.cn/html/1/219/199/201/679.html.

265 See Liu Xiaohong, A Monographic Study on International Commercial Arbitration Law 466 (2009).

266 See Dèng Jié, Law of Commercial Arbitration 259 (Tsinghua Univ. Press, 2008).

267 See Zhao Xiuwen, *Non-Domestic Arbitration, in* Chen An, Collected Essays on International Economic Law, 541 L. Press (2002).

268 See CIETAC Arbitration Rules (2024), *supra* note 251, art. 4.

269 See *id.*

270 See Chen Yanhong, The Theory of Delocalization and its Integration Effect on International Arbitration 104 (China U. of Pol. Sci. and L. Press 2015).

rules for an arbitration conducted within the territory of China or the place of arbitration. It is therefore reasonable to wonder if the Supreme People's Court actually gave the "green light" to use of the doctrine of delocalization.[271]

The newly adopted the "seat rule" in the Arbitrtion Law appears to take a further step toward the recognition of delocalization in the country. As noted, under article 81 of the Arbitration Law, unless the parties have otherwise agreed on the applicable law of the arbitration proceure, the seat of arbitration shall be determinative factor for ascertaiment of the law as such.[272] Although this provision may need further clarification, it apparently carries two implications. First, the parties may choose the applicable law of the arbitration procedures, which is not nessarily the law of arbitral seat. Second, absent the parties' choice, the applicable law of arbitraton procedures is to be determined by arbitral seat. Since article 81 does not say that absent the parties' choice, the law of arbitral procedures of the arbitral seat shall apply, the law determined by the arbitral seat may also not necessarily be the law of arbitral seat.

4. RECOGNITION AND ENFORCEMENT OF FOREIGN ARBITRAL AWARDS

To get a foreign arbitral award enforced in China, a request must be made for a court action. In general, the foreign country arbitration cases filed with Chinese courts can be divided into three categories. The first category concerns the requests for confirmation of the effect of foreign arbitration agreements. The second category includes requests for setting aside arbitral awards issued by foreign arbitration institutes of China. The third category involves applications for recognition and enforcement of foreign country arbitral awards (recognition and enforcement).

Thus, arbitral awards in foreign related arbitration may refer to the awards entered by Chinese arbitration institutions or to the awards made by foreign arbitral institutions. In the former case, the enforcement generally will not become an issue unless the arbitral award is annulled by a court order. As a commonly accepted rule and also under the New York Convention, only the court situated in the country in which the award was made may have the power to annul an arbitral award under conditions prescribed by the law of the place where the award was made.[273]

With regard to the arbitral awards made by foreign arbitral tribunals, their recognition and enforcement in China must meet specific statutary requirements. According to CIETAC's Annual Report, in 2015 Chinese courts took a total of 117 foreign arbitral award cases for review, including eighteen cases seeking

[271] See generally Zhāng Jiàn, *Challenges to the Internationalization of Commercial Arbitration in China*, 1 Shanghai C. of Pol. Sci. and L. Rev. 64 (2016).

[272] See Arbitration Law, *supra* note 30, art. 81.

[273] See New York Convention (1958), arts. V(1)(e) and VI, available at www.newyorkconvention.org. See also, Gary Born, International Arbitration, Cases and Materials (2nd ed.), 1099 (Kluwer, 2015).

confirmation of the validity of foreign arbitration clauses, fifty-nine cases requesting to set aside foreign-related arbitral awards, and forty cases applying for enforcing foreign-related arbitral awards.[274] In 2023, the number of foreign arbitral review cases filed with the Chinese courts increased to 203, among which some 75 cases involved recognition and enforcement of foreign arbitral awards.[275]

A. *Enforcement Mechanism*

To recognize and enforce a foreign arbitral award in Chinese courts, the procedure established by the SPC must be followed. Under the SPC's 1987 Notice, enforcement requires three steps: (1) filing with the court that has jurisdiction, (2) ascertaining the applicable law, and (3) obtaining the court's review and examination.[276] The 1995 Notice and 2017 Rules on Reporting added a fourth step: (4) reporting internally in case of denial.[277] Now, all foreign arbitral awards seeking recognition and enforcement in China are handled in the Chinese courts under this four-step framework.

a. Jurisdiction

A request for confirmation of the validity of an arbitration agreement or for recognition and enforcement of a foreign arbitral award will both be handled by an intermediate people's court. But not every intermediate people's court has jurisdiction. According to the SPC's 2017 Rules of Arbitration Review, the cases for confirmation of the validity of an arbitration agreement shall be under the jurisdiction of the intermediate people's court or specialized people's court in the place where the arbitration institution as agreed is located, where the arbitration agreement is signed, where the applicant is domiciled, or where the respondent is domiciled.[278]

Under Article 304 of the CPL, if a legally effective arbitration award made outside the territory of China needs to be recognized and enforced by a people's court, the parties may apply directly to the intermediate people's court where the person subject to the enforcement is domiciled or where his property is located. If the

[274] See the CIETAC, Annual Report on International Commercial Arbitration in China (2015-2016), at 24. In addition, courts concluded sixty-four cases related to Hong Kong, Macau, and Taiwan, including thirty-six confirmation cases, twenty-four cancellation cases, and four enforcement cases. A full text of the CIETAC report is available at www.cietac.org/sfs/cms/202201/61e671866bd11.pdf.

[275] See the CIETAC's Annual Report (2022-2023), at 204, available at www.cietac.org/sfs/cms/202310/Annual%20Report%20On%20International%20Commercial%20Arbitration%20In%20China(2022-2023)-en.pdf. See also the SPC, 2023 Annual Report on Judicial Review of Commercial Arbitration, available at https://www.court.gov.cn/zixun/xiangqing/442471.html.

[276] See the SPC, 1987 Notice, *supra* note 6.

[277] See the SPC, 1995 Notice, *supra* note 10; the SPC 2017 Rules of Arbitration Review, *supra* note 15.

[278] See the SPC, 2006 Interpretation on Arbitration Law, *supra* note 115.

person subject to enforcement is not domiciled or his property is not within the territory of China, the party concerned may apply to the intermediate people's court at the applicant's domicile or a place that has appropriately connection with the arbitrated disputes. The people's courts shall handle cases in accordance with international treaties concluded or acceded to by China, or in accordance with the principle of reciprocity.[279]

The Arbitration Law also contains a provision concerning overseas enforcement of Chinese arbitral awards. In accordance with article 85 of the Arbitration Law as newly revised, when a party seeks for enforcement of a legally effective arbitral award made within the territory of China, if the person subject to enforcement or the person's property is not within the territory of China, the party may directly apply to a foreign court with jurisdiction for recognition and enforcement.[280] Article 85 of the Arbitration Law and article 304 of the CPL do not seem consistent with regard to the enforcement of arbitral award when the person subject to enforcement or the person's property is not within the territory of China, which would require an interpretation from the SPC to clarify.

The 2017 Rules of Arbitration Review further provide that if the arbitration award for which the party is seeking enforcement is related to a case pending in a people's court, and neither the domicile nor the location of the property of the respondent is within China, the request for enforcement shall be filed with the people's court handling the case.[281] If the court involved is a trial court, the enforcement request shall be filed with the people's court in the next level (namely the intermediate people's court).[282] If the court involved is a High People's Court or the Supreme People's Court, the High People's Court or the Supreme People's Court may review the request itself or designate an Intermediate People's Court to deal with the request instead.[283]

Moreover, pursuant to Article 3 of the SPC 2017 Rules, if the foreign-related arbitration is conducted by a Chinese arbitration body, the Intermediate People's Court of the place where the arbitration body is located should have jurisdiction over the enforcement.[284] If the petitioner files the request with two or more competent people's courts, the court with which the request is first docketed shall have jurisdiction.[285]

b. Application of Law

The application of law is an issue either in the case in which the validity of an arbitration agreement is in dispute or in the situation where an application for

[279] See the CPL, *supra* note 12, art. 304.
[280] See the Arbitration Law, *supra* note 31, art. 85.
[281] See the SPC, 2017 Rules of Arbitration Review, *supra* note 15, art. 3.
[282] See *id.*
[283] See *id.*
[284] See *id.*
[285] See *id.*, art. 4.

recognition and enforcement of a foreign arbitral award is challenged. For the determination of the validity of an arbitration agreement, under Article 18 of the Choice of Law Statute, the parties may by agreement choose the law applicable to their arbitration agreement. The law so chosen will also govern the validity of the arbitration agreement.

Absent the parties' choice, under the SPC's interpretation, the law of the place where the arbitration institution is located or the law of the place of arbitration may be applied. If, however, there is a conflict between the two laws in the determination of the validity of the arbitration agreement, the law that confirms the validity of the arbitration agreement shall be applied.[286]

In addition, when a Chinese court reviews a party's application for recognition and enforcement of a foreign arbitral award under the New York Convention, and the respondent raises a defense on the grounds that the arbitration agreement is invalid, the court shall comply with Article V(1)(a) of the New York Convention to determine the law that should be applied to confirm the validity of the arbitration agreement.[287]

Recognition and enforcement of a foreign arbitral award concerns two issues: where the arbitration is made and what the arbitration is about. The first issue determines whether the New York Convention shall be applied, and the second issue involves application of Chinese law. As to the first issue, given the reservations China made in acceding to the New York Convention, Chinese courts will only recognize and enforce arbitral awards made by arbitration bodies within the territory of another contracting state.[288] Therefore, if an arbitral award is made in a non-contracting state, the New York Convention does not apply, and instead Chinese law will govern.

According to the 1987 Notice, when a people's court is asked to recognize and enforce an arbitral award obtained from an arbitration body of a non-contracting state, the court shall review and examine the request in accordance with the provisions of the CPL.[289] It is now mandated under Article 304 of the CPL that the people's court handle the enforcement petition according to the principle of reciprocity absent treaties.[290] After successful review and examination by a people's

[286] See the SPC, 2017 Rules of Arbitration Review, *supra* note 15, art. 14.

[287] According to Article V(1) of the New York Convention, recognition and enforcement of the award may be refused, at the request of the party against whom it is invoked, only if that party furnishes to the competent authority where the recognition and enforcement is sought, proof that: (a) the parties to the agreement referred to in article II were, under the law applicable to them, under some incapacity, or the said agreement is not valid under the law to which the parties have subjected it or, failing any indication thereon, under the law of the country where the award was made. New York Convention on Recognition and Enforcement of Foreign Arbitral Awards (1958), *supra* note 322.

[288] See the SPC, 1987 Notice, *supra* note 6, art. 1.

[289] See *id.*

[290] See Civil Procedure Law (as amended 2023), *supra* note 12, art. 283.

court, the enforcement shall be granted and made under the procedure provided in the CPL.[291] The enforcement procedure equally applies to arbitral awards that fall within the realm of the New York Convention.

With regard to the second issue, for a foreign arbitral award to be enforced in China under the New York Convention, the dispute must arise from a contractual or non-contractual commercial legal relationship.[292] In other words, for purposes of the New York Convention, only arbitral awards that settle contractual or non-contractual disputes of a commercial legal relationship nature are entitled to recognition and enforcement in China. Also, pursuant to the New York Convention, what would constitute a commercial legal relationship is a matter of domestic law of the enforcing state, and thus is to be determined under Chinese law.[293]

In its 1987 Notice, the SPC defined the "contractual and non-contractual commercial legal relationship" as the economic rights and obligations resulting from contract, torts, or other relevant provisions of law, such as, *inter alia*, the sale of goods, lease of property, project contracting, processing, technology assignment, joint adventure, joint business operation, exploration and development of natural resources, insurance, credit, labor service, surrogate, consultation service, marine/civil aviation/railway/road passenger and cargo transportation, product liability, environment pollution, marine accident, or dispute over ownership.[294] Under the SPC definition, disputes between foreign investors and their host governments are excluded from contractual and non-contractual commercial legal relationships.[295]

c. Review and Examination

Under the SPC's 1997 Notice, the cases that are subject to the court review and examination include those involving (a) confirmation of the validity of arbitration agreements; (b) enforcement of arbitration awards made by arbitration institutions; (c) revocation of arbitration awards made by the Mainland arbitration institutions; (d) recognition and enforcement of arbitration awards made in the Hong Kong and Macao Special Administrative Regions, and Taiwan; (e) recognition and enforcement of foreign arbitration awards; and (f) other arbitration cases requiring judicial reviews.[296]

Once the petition for enforcement is filed, whether the enforcement will be granted under the New York Convention depends on the result of the court's review and examination. It is a bi-faceted process: procedure and substance. Procedurally,

291 See the SPC, Interpretation on the Application of the CPL, *supra* note 13, art. 546.

292 See the New York Convention, *supra* note 322, art. 1.

293 See *id.*

294 See the SPC, 1987 Notice, *supra* note 6, art. 2.

295 See *id.*

296 See *id.*, art. 1.

the arbitral award to be enforced in China shall not violate the two reservations China made to the New York Convention, namely a "commercial nature" and "made within the territory of a contracting state." Substantially, the enforcement sought shall meet the conditions set forth in Article V of the New York Convention as judged by the people's courts.[297]

According to the SPC 1987 Notice, if, upon review and examination, it is found that none of the situations for denial of enforcement as stated in Article V, paragraphs (1) and (2) of the New York Convention exist as to the foreign arbitral award, the People's Court shall recognize its effect and enforce it under the enforcement procedure provided in the law of China.[298]

If, however, any of the Article V situations is found to have occurred, the enforcement petition will be rejected, and as a result, the recognition and enforcement of the arbitral award in question will be denied.[299] It is imperative under the 1987 Notice that the people's courts' review and examination of the foreign arbitral awards covered by the New York Convention be conducted in accordance with the provisions of the Convention.

[297] See New York Convention, *supra* note 322, art. V, providing that:

1. Recognition and enforcement of the award may be refused, at the request of the party against whom it is invoked, only if that party furnishes to the competent authority where the recognition and enforcement is sought, proof that:
   (a) The parties to the agreement referred to in Article II were, under the law applicable to them, under some incapacity, or the said agreement is not valid under the law to which the parties have subjected it or, failing any indication thereon, under the law of the country where the award was made; or
   (b) The party against whom the award is invoked was not given proper notice of the appointment of the arbitrator or of the arbitration proceedings or was otherwise unable to present his case; or
   (c) The award deals with a difference not contemplated by or not falling within the terms of the submission to arbitration, or it contains decisions on matters beyond the scope of the submission to arbitration, provided that, if the decisions on matters submitted to arbitration can be separated from those not so submitted, that part of the award which contains decisions on matters submitted to arbitration may be recognized and enforced; or
   (d) The composition of the arbitral authority or the arbitral procedure was not in accordance with the agreement of the parties, or, failing such agreement, was not in accordance with the law of the country where the arbitration took place; or
   (e) The award has not yet become binding on the parties, or has been set aside or suspended by a competent authority of the country in which, or under the law of which, that award was made.
2. Recognition and enforcement of an arbitral award may also be refused if the competent authority in the country where recognition and enforcement is sought finds that:
   (a) The subject matter of the difference is not capable of settlement by arbitration under the law of that country; or
   (b) The recognition or enforcement of the award would be contrary to the public policy of that country.

[298] See the SPC, 1987 Notice, *supra* note 6, art. 4.

[299] See *id*.

d. Internal Reporting Requirement

Internal reporting refers to a reporting system under which the decision of an Intermediate People's Court to deny the enforcement of a foreign arbitral award is required to be submitted to a High People's Court, as well as to the SPC, for approval before the notice of denial is issued.[300] As discussed, there was no such internal reporting requirement until the SPC 1995 Notice was issued.

Realizing that the standard by which the Intermediate People's Court examines the foreign arbitral award could vary from court to court, and in some instances create cause for abuse of the established process, the SPC, through its 1995 Notice, unified the criterion for review and examination via the reporting requirement. The purpose was to ensure that the New York Convention would be implemented and strictly adhered to.[301]

The 1995 Notice contains only two articles. The first article deals with the invalidation of an arbitration agreement, and the second involves other conditions under which the recognition and enforcement of foreign arbitral awards would be denied. The invalidation provision describes the manner in which the people's court is to determine whether or not to take and hear the enforcement petition. The condition provision describes the qualifications the people's court must consider to determine the eligibility for enforcement. In both situations, the SPC explicitly reserves the power to have the final say through the system of internal reporting, because in either case the enforceability of the foreign arbitral award is at issue.[302]

Under Article 1 of the 1995 Notice, when asked to render an arbitration agreement invalid, ineffective, or unenforceable on the merits, an Intermediate People's Court is required to report to the High People's Court in the same jurisdiction, and if necessary, the SPC for review.[303] Prior to the review, the intermediate court may remove the case from the SPC's docket.

Article 2 of the 1995 Notice is aimed at establishing the process to deny recognition and enforcement of foreign arbitral awards. It provides that if a people's court finds a foreign arbitral award ineligible for enforcement, before it decides to deny recognition and enforcement, the court must report the case to the High People's Court in the same jurisdiction for review. If the High People's Court agrees to the denial, it shall be submitted to the SPC for opinion. Only after obtaining the SPC's approval would formal denial be tendered to the parties.[304]

The 2017 Rules on Reporting amend Article 1 of the 1995 Notice with regard to the invalidation of an arbitration agreement. It simply requires that the Intermediate

[300] See Yves Hu and Clarisse von Wunschheim, *Reforms on the "Prior Reporting System" – A Praiseworthy Effort by the PRC Supreme People's Court, or Not?* KLUWER ARB. BLOG (Jan. 8, 2018).

[301] See the SPC, 1995 Notice, *supra* note 10.

[302] See *id.*

[303] See *id.*, art. 1.

[304] See *id.*, art. 2.

People's Court decision to invalidate an arbitration agreement, like the decision to deny enforcement of a foreign arbitration award, be submitted to the High People's Court in the same jurisdiction for review, and to the Supreme People's Court for approval if the High People's Court agrees with the decision of the lower court. Thus, under the 2017 Notice on Reporting, the decision to invalidate an arbitration agreement may only be made after the SPC's review.[305]

B. *Foreign Arbitral Award*

As discussed, foreign arbitral award in China may refer to an award made by a Chinese foreign arbitration institution or an award made by a foreign arbitration institution. The former is called foreign related arbitral award while the latter is labeled as foreign arbitral award. To trigger application of the New York Convention, there must be a foreign arbitral award. Under the New York Convention, a foreign arbitral award is an award "made in the territory of a State other than the State where the recognition and enforcement of such awards are sought."[306] In addition, the New York Convention also applies to "arbitral awards not considered as domestic awards in the State where their recognition and enforcement are sought." The former generally refers to foreign arbitral awards, while the latter is phrased as "non-domestic awards."[307]

a. Reciprocity Rule

When acceding to the New York Convention in 1986, China, through its reciprocity reservation, limited the award to one "made only in the territory of another Contracting State."[308] An implication of the reciprocity reservation is that the term "foreign" in defining an arbitral award is based on the territory or location where the arbitral award is made. But under Article 283 of the CPL (as amended 2017), foreign arbitral award is described as "an award made by a foreign arbitration institution."[309] To solve this discrepancy, the SPC in its 1987 Notice phrased a foreign arbitral award as "an award made in the territory of another contracting state," conforming to the New York Convention language.[310] At the time the 2015 Notice was issued, the SPC dropped the term "territory of another contracting state," and simply used "foreign country arbitral award" instead.[311] Not until 2023, when the CPL was

[305] See the SPC, 1995 Notice, *supra* note 10, art. 2.
[306] See New York Convention, *supra* note 322, art. 1.
[307] See *id.*
[308] See *id.*
[309] See the CPL (as amended 2017), art. 283, available at https://cicc.court.gov.cn/html/1/219/199/200/644.html.
[310] See the SPC, 1987 Notice, *supra* note 6, art. 1.
[311] See the SPC, Interpretation on the Application of the CPL, *supra* note 13, arts. 546-548.

amended again, was the foreign arbitral award then referred to as the award "made outside the territory of the People's Republic of China."[312]

b. Awards of Foreign Nature

In general, whether an arbitral award is "foreign" depends on the "nationality" of the award. Under the New York Convention, the decisive factor is the place where the arbitration is made. As noted, the New York Convention applies to both foreign arbitral awards and non-domestic awards. The non-domestic arbitral awards are to be determined under the law of the country where the recognition and enforcement of the awards are sought.

In its 2017 Rules of Arbitration Review, the SPC defines foreign arbitration and foreign arbitral award on the basis of a "foreign element." Under Article 12 of the 2017 Rules of Arbitration Review, if an arbitration agreement or arbitral award contains any of the foreign elements as specified in the SPC's interpretation of the application of the Choice of Law Statute (2012),[313] the agreement or the award should be classified as a foreign arbitration agreement or foreign arbitral award.[314] Article 12 appears to be a compromise between "an award made by a foreign arbitration institution" and "an award made in the territory of another contracting state" in identifying "foreign." However, confusion may arise, because "foreign element" as interpreted by the SPC carries no meaning of "another contracting state" for the purpose of the New York Convention.

A separate but relevant issue is *ad hoc* arbitration. As discussed, under Article 27 of the Arbitration Law of China, in order to be valid, an arbitration agreement must include a choice of an arbitration institution.[315] Since the arbitration institution is defined in the Arbitration law to include legally established arbitration commission or arbitration court, it would be difficult, if not impossible, for the parties to designate an "arbitration institution" as such in an *ad hoc* arbitration. On the other hand, pursuant to the Article 82 of the Arbitration Law, an *ad hoc* arbitration may take place in certain cases if the parties choose China as the seat of arbitration, and form an arbitral tribunal composed of persons who meet the conditions stipulated in the Arbitration Law.

[312] See the CPL (as amended 2023), *supra* note 12, art. 304.

[313] See the SPC, Interpretation on Several Issues Concerning the Application of the Choice of Law Statute (I), *supra* note 261. Under Article 1 of the Interpretation, foreign elements include: (a) One or both parties are foreign citizens, foreign legal persons, other organizations, or stateless persons; (b) One or both parties have their habitual residence outside the territory of China; (c) The subject matter is outside the territory of China; (d) The legal facts that give rise to, change, or eliminate the civil relationship occur outside the territory of China; or (e) Other circumstances that can be determined as foreign-related civil relations.

[314] See the SPC 2017 Rules of Arbitration Review, *supra* note 15, art. 12.

[315] See Arbitration Law, *supra* note 31, art. 27.

Because arbitral tribual is not included in the arbitration institution as defined in Article 89 of the Arbitration Law (arbitration commission and arbitration court), the validity rule in Article 27 does not seem to be applicalbe to *ad hoc* arbitration pertaining to the requirement of arbitration institution designation. In other words, an *ad hoc* arbitration agreement can be held valid and enforceable if it contains (a) a location in China as the seat of arbitration, (b) selected arbitrator, and (c) agreed arbitration rules

Nevertheless, the *ad hoc* arbitration is now available under the Arbitration Law in specified geographic areas. Note, however, an *ad hoc* arbitral award made in a foreign country under foreign law will be treated differently. According to the 2015 Interpretation of the SPC, if a party asks a People's Court to recognize and enforce an arbitral award made outside the territory of China by an ad hoc arbitration tribunal, the people's court shall handle it either under the provisions of the treaties, including the New York Convention, or on the basis of the principle of reciprocity.[316]

c. Non-Domestic Awards

Under the New York Convention, non-domestic awards are the awards "not considered as domestic awards in the State where their recognition and enforcement are sought."[317] But China does not seem to clearly separate foreign arbitration awards from non-domestic awards. Instead, it treats both as foreign arbitral awards with a focus on arbitral body.

For example, in the 2003 case of *TH&T International Corp. v. Chengdu Hualong Auto Parts Co., Ltd.*,[318] the petitioner filed a petition with Chengdu Municipality Intermediate People's Court to enforce an arbitral award made by the ICA of the ICC in Los Angeles. When determining the enforceability of the ICA arbitral award, the court opined that for purposes of the New York Convention, the "territory of another contracting state" should be understood as the state where the arbitration body is situated rather than the state in which the arbitration is made. In that case, the court regarded France as the "other contracting state." According to the court, the ICA is located in Paris, and France is a member of the New York Convention. On those grounds, the court granted the petitioner's request for enforcement under the Convention.

As noted, in *Anhui Long Li De Packaging and Printing Co., Ltd. v. BP Agnati S. R. L.*,[319] the parties formed a sales contract. The contract contained an arbitration

[316] See the SPC, Interpretation on the Application of the CPL, *supra* note 13, art. 545.

[317] See New York Convention, *supra* note 282, art. I. See also generally Albert Jan Van Den Berger, *When Is an Arbitral Award Nondomestic Under the New York Convention of 1958?*, 6 Pace L. Rev. 25 (1985).

[318] See generally *THandT Int'l Corp. v. Chengdu Hualong Auto Parts Co., Ltd.*, FShou (Chengdu Interm. People's Ct. of Sichuan Province Dec. 12, 2003).

[319] See *Supreme People's Court on the Applicant Anhui Longlide Packaging and Printing Co., Ltd. and the Respondent BP Agnati S.R.L Reply to the Request for Confirmation of the Validity of*

agreement designating ICA as arbitration body and Shanghai as the "place of jurisdiction." When the parties disputed the contract during its performance, the ICA conducted arbitration in Shanghai. After the arbitral award was entered, *Long Li De* asked Hefei Intermediate People's Court to deny the enforcement of the arbitral award. One of the key arguments *Long Li De* made was that since the arbitral award was made by the ICA within the territory of China, it was therefore a "domestic award" under the Arbitration Law of China, and thus should not be enforced under the New York Convention.

Through the internal reporting process, the case was submitted to Anhui High People's Court for review. A highly divided Anhui High People's Court sent the case to the SPC for guidance. In its reply, the SPC took the position that for the purpose of the determination of the validity of the foreign arbitration agreement in the case, the "place of adjudication" in the agreement should be interpreted to mean "the place of arbitration." The SPC then held that because its contents met the requirements of the Arbitration Law of China, the arbitration agreement should be deemed valid and enforceable.[320]

Although the SPC's reply did not respond directly to *Long Li De*'s argument about the domestic nature of the ICA's arbitration in China, it implicated that since the ICA is a foreign arbitration body, its arbitral award, though made within the territory of China, was a foreign arbitral award to which the New York Convention was applicable. However, under the territory standard, this arbitral award may not be characterized as one made in "the territory of another contracting state." The SPC's holding in this case recognizes the foreign status of an in-country arbitration award by a foreign arbitration institution.

A question then is whether the ICA award made in Shanghai should be deemed as a non-domestic award so that the New York Convention would apply. China does not have a law that defines non-domestic awards. By its reservation to the New York Convention, China has limited the application of the New York Convention only to the arbitral awards of another contracting state. Some then argue that the non-domestic awards are out of the coverage of the New York Convention as applied in China.[321]

Many in China believe that even though the arbitral award was made by the ICA in Shanghai, to hold it as a non-domestic award for enforcement under the New York Convention would step over the line of the reservation China made to the New York Convention.[322] Others disagree, asserting that the reservation operates only in the sense that China does not have any obligation to recognize and enforce non-

the Arbitration Agreement, SHANTOU ARB. COMMISSION (Feb. 22, 2016), available at https://web.archive.org/web/20160325031054/http://stzc.shantou.gov.cn/html/law/460.html.

320 See *id.*

321 See *Lv Binwu, Issues on the Arbitration by Foreign Arbitration Institutions within China*, 10 RES. ON THE RULE OF L. 71 (2010), www.docin.com/p-945660114.html.

322 See *id.* at 73.

domestic awards, but carries no meaning that China could not do it.[323] Between the two is an opinion that since the ICA is a non-Chinese arbitration institution, it meets the standard of "foreign" as prescribed in Chinese law.[324]

C. *Grounds of Denial*

Like a foreign judgment, a foreign arbitral award, in order to be recognized and enforced in China, must meet certain conditions. As noted, foreign arbitral awards in China include awards made by Chinese foreign arbitration insititutions and award made by foreign arbitration insitituion. According to Article 291 of the CPL, an award issued by a Chinese foreign arbitration institution will not be enforced under any of the following circumstances: (a) the parties do not have an arbitration clause in the contract or do not reach a written arbitration agreement afterwards; (b) the respondent did not receive notice of the appointment of an arbitrator or the conduct of arbitration proceedings, or was not given opportunity to be heard due to other reasons beyond the respondent's responsibility; (c) the composition of the arbitral tribunal or the arbitration procedures are inconsistent with the arbitration rules; (d) the matter of the award does not fall within the scope of the arbitration agreement or the arbitration institution has no authority to arbitrate.[325] In addition, if the court determines that the enforcement of the award is against social and public interests, it shall rule to deny its enforcement.[326]

The Arbitration Law now integrates article 291 of the CPL into two articles that apply unformly to both foreign-related arbitral awards and foreign arbitral awards. One is article 83 that deals with annulment revocation of an arbitral award. Under 83 of the Arbitration Law, a foreign-related arbitration award may be annuled and arevoked by a court after a collegial panel review under any of the following proved circumstances: (a) there is no arbitration agreement; (b) the respondent did not receive notice of the appointment of an arbitrator or the conduct of arbitration proceedings, or unable to state its opinion due to other reasons that were not the responsibility of the respondent; (c) the composition of the arbitral tribunal or the arbitration procedures are inconsistent with the arbitration rules; or (d) the matter arbitrated does not fall within the scope of the arbitration agreement or the arbitration institution has no authority to arbitrate. In addition, if an arbitral award is found by the court to be contrary to the public interest, the award will be annulled.[327] Since the power to annul and recoke an arbitral award rests only with the court of the place where the arbitral award is made, article 83 does not apply to foreign arbitral award (award made in foreign country).

[323] See *id.* at 74.
[324] See *id.* at 73.
[325] See the CPL (as amended 2023), *supra* note 12, art. 291.
[326] See *id.*
[327] See the Arbitration law, *supra* note 31, art. 83.

Article 84 of the Arbitration Law provides that the same conditions as provided in article 83 apply to the enforcement of foreign arbitral awards. But, the recognition and enforcement of foreign country arbitral awards in Chinese courts generally are matters of application of treaties, including the New York Convention and bilateral treaties. Again, absent a treaty, recognition and enforecement will be made on a reciprocity basis. In this context, article 83 of the Arbitration Law is a clause that implements the New York Convention.

Under Article V of the New York Convention, a request for recognition and enforcement of a foreign arbitration award may be denied if any of the following is found: (a) incapacity of the parties or invalidity of the arbitration agreement; (b) violation of due process rules; (c) disputes arbitrated not falling within the terms of, or decisions on matters beyond the scope of, the arbitration agreement; (d) improper composition of the arbitral tribunal or non-respect of arbitral procedure; (e) award not binding, has been set aside or suspended; (f) disputes not arbitrable; or (g) violation of public policy of the forum.[328]

In many cases, the enforceability of foreign country awards often depends on the existence and validity of the arbitration agreement. During the years 2000 to 2020, there were a total of 39 cases where enforcement was denied in China (30 out of 94 from 2001-2015, and 8 out of 104 from 2016-2020), of which 12 cases involved defects in the arbitration agreement. The issues ranged from the lack of capacity of a party, to the failure to specify an arbitration body, and from absence of mutual consent to arbitration to non-existence of an arbitration agreement.

In addition to the validity of an arbitration agreement, there are several other grounds or conditions on which the recognition and enforcement of foreign country awards could be rejected by the Chinese courts. A published summary of denied enforcement cases reveals that the other reasons prompting denial include: violations of due process in arbitral proceedings; exceeding arbitral authority; improper composition of the arbitral tribunal; non-compliance with settled arbitration procedure; non-arbitrable subject matters; offense to public policy; and violation of the provisions of enforcement law.[329]

Due process in arbitral proceedings requires proper notice and an opportunity to present a case.[330] In one case where the petitioner sent the respondent emails to notify the respondent to appoint an arbitrator, but failed to prove that the respondent actually received the emails, the request for enforcement of a British arbitral award so obtained was denied by the Chinese court for a lack of due process.[331] In another case, the SPC rejected the enforcement of a Japanese arbitral award because it was found that the arbitral tribunal did not provide the parties with notice of

[328] See the New York Convention, *supra* note 322, art. V.

[329] See Wan E'xiang and Xia Xiaohong, *supra* note 60, at 8.

[330] See the New York Convention, *supra* note 322, art. V(1)(b).

[331] See *Cosmos Marine Management S.A. v. Tianjin Kaiqiang Commerce and Trade Co., Ltd.*, CHINESE CT. DECISION SUMMARIES ON ARB. (Sup. People's Ct. 2007) (China).

postponement of the award decision, which violated both the rules of arbitration and the law of the place of arbitration.[332]

The improper composition of an arbitral tribunal and incompliance with the arbitration procedure agreed to by the parties are the issues that concern an arbitral award entered into in violation of the arbitration agreement. There are two cases in which the enforcement of Swedish arbitral awards was denied.[333] In both of the cases, the arbitration agreement provided a settled procedure, which included a buffer or grace period (45 days and 90 days, respectively) for negotiation before the arbitration. However, in both cases the petitioner initiated arbitration without going through the negotiation period as required in the arbitration agreement.[334] It was held in the two cases that the skipping of the negotiation grace period violated the arbitration procedure agreed upon by the parties.[335]

Exceeding arbitral authority, as discussed, is an issue pertaining to the scope of the arbitration agreement. In certain cases, however, the nature of the dispute may also become relevant to the issue of the authority of the arbitral body. In one case where the parties formed a joint venture, the joint venture contract provided for arbitration by the ICC and its subsidiary, the ICA, if any disputes arose out of the contract.[336] The facts on record involved the performance of a leasing agreement between a foreign investor in the joint venture and the joint venture itself.[337]

In denying recognition and enforcement of the arbitral award, the SPC made a rule that the arbitration clause in a joint venture contract may only bind the parties pertaining to disputes of matters involving the joint venture, and that the arbitration clause shall have no effect to disputes arising between one of the parties and the joint venture entity.[338] Therefore, if an arbitral decision is made on the basis of the arbitration clause in a joint venture contract, and if the parties in disagreement are a joint venture and one of the individual parties in the joint venture, Chinese courts regard the decision as having exceeded arbitral authority.

The issues of arbitrability, public policy, and compliance with Chinese law of enforcement each deserve more discussion. These conditions are either provided explicitly in the law, or serve as the last resort to safeguard national interests. Each of the conditions have been employed in the Chinese courts, though not often, to deny

332 See *Shin-Etsu Chemical Co., Ltd. v. Jiangsu Zhongtian Technology JSCL*, CHINESE CT. DECISION SUMMARIES ON ARB. (Sup. People's Ct. 2008) (China).

333 *PepsiCo Inc. v. Sichuan Pepsi-Cola Beverage Co. Limited* CHINESE CT. DECISION SUMMARIES ON ARB. (Chengdun Interm. People's Ct. 2006) (China); PepsiCo Investment (China) Ltd. v. Sichuan Yunlv Co., Industry Development Co. CHINESE CT. DECISION SUMMARIES ON ARB. (Chengdun Intermediate People's Ct. 2006) (China).

334 See *id*.

335 See *id*.

336 *Hemofarm DD v. Ji'nan Yongning Pharmaceutical Co., Ltd.*, N.Y. CONVENTION GUIDE (Sup. People's Ct. 2008) (China).

337 See *id*.

338 See *id*.

foreign arbitral awards that otherwise would be recognized and enforced. Unlike other conditions that may not be examined by the people's courts without the request of a party, both arbitrability and public policy are reviewable by the People's Court *ex officio* (by virtue of the office).[339]

a. Arbitrability

Although the parties have the freedom to subject their civil commercial disputes to arbitration by agreement, not every matter in a dispute is arbitrable. Under the New York Convention, recognition and enforcement of an arbitral award may be refused if the subject matter over which the two parties disagree is not capable of settlement by arbitration under the law of that country.[340] In China, the Arbitration Law, as noted, defines the scope of arbitration as disputes concerning contractual or other property rights between citizens, legal persons, or other non-legal person organizations.[341]

The matters expressly excluded from arbitration include two categories: (1) disputes arising from marriage, adoption, guardianship, support, and succession; and (2) disputes prescribed by the law to be resolved by administrative agencies.[342] It is unclear in the legal provisions, however, whether the disputes related to such legal areas as antitrust, bankruptcy, and securities may be submitted to arbitration. However, the general holding in China is that those matters are not arbitrable.[343]

As discussed, in the Chinese Contract Law, contracts are described as agreements creating, modifying, or terminating the relationship of civil rights and obligations between natural persons, legal persons, or other organizations of equal footing.[344] Therefore, any dispute concerning such relationship is arbitrable. But the contract provisions in the Civil Code do not cover labor contracts, because they are subject to a different legislation, namely the Labor Contract Law. Article 77 of the Labor Contract Law allows a worker whose legitimate rights and interests are infringed upon to apply for arbitration.[345] Thus, the contractual rights as provided in Article 2 of the Arbitration Law include the rights that arise under a labor contract.

In one case, a request for recognition and enforcement was rejected on the grounds that the subject matter in dispute was non-arbitrable under Chinese law.[346] The facts of the case were quite simple. Two Chinese nationals entered into

339 See the SPC, Interpretation on the Application of the CPL, *supra* note 13, art. 92.

340 New York Convention, *supra* note 322, art. V(2)(a).

341 See the Arbitration Law, *supra* note 31, art. 3.

342 See *id.*, art. 3.

343 See Jiang Wei and Xiao Jianguo, *supra* note 2, at 140-144.

344 See Contract Law of China, *supra* note 225, art. 2.

345 See Labor Contract Law of the People's Republic of China (promulgated by Standing Comm. Nat'l People's Cong., June 29, 2007, effective Jan. 1, 2008), art. 77, P.R.C. LAWS, www.npc.gov.cn/englishnpc/Law/2009-02/20/content_1471106.htm [https://perma.cc/F9NJ-NCSC].

346 *Wu Chunying v. Zhang Guiwen*, CHINESE CT. DECISION SUMMARIES ON ARB. (Sup. People's Ct. Sept. 2, 2009) (China).

an investment contract to establish and register a business corporation in Mongolia.[347] The contract contained an arbitration clause under which the parties agreed to submit their disputes for arbitration to the Mongolian National Arbitration Court (MNAC).[348] During the business operation, one party to the contract died.[349] The widow of the deceased then filed a petition with the MNAC to persuade the commission to confirm, inter alia, her 50 percent ownership in the registered capital of the corporation.[350]

In its arbitral award, the MNAC held that the widow was the successor of the deceased, and thus was legally entitled to 50 percent of the invested capital contributed by the deceased.[351] However, when the widow took the arbitral award to a Chinese people's court in the Shandong Province for enforcement, the court rejected her enforcement request.[352] In its approval of the denial made by the lower courts, the SPC concluded that the subject matter arbitrated, though related to a contract, actually concerned succession – inheriting property rights from the widow's late husband.[353] Thus, ruled the SPC, under Article V, paragraph (2), subparagraph (a) of the New York Convention and Article 3 of the Arbitration Law of China, the MNAC's arbitral award could not be recognized and enforced in China because the subject matter was non-arbitrable.[354]

b. Public Policy

As discussed, public policy is an "escape mechanism" that enables a court to refuse recognition and enforcement of a foreign arbitral award that otherwise would be recognized and enforced.[355] The Arbitration Law makes public policy an affirmative defense to the enforcement of foreign arbitral awards in court.[356] It is considered a judicial function of Chinese courts to review and examine, in light of public policy, foreign arbitral awards submitted for enforcement. Although the phrase "public policy" is not defined in Chinese law, it is generally defined as social and public interests. Under Article 84 of the Arbitration Law, a foreign arbitral award shall not be enforced if the court determines that enforcement of the award would be against

[347] See *id.*
[348] See *id.*
[349] See *id.*
[350] See *id.*
[351] See *id.*
[352] See *id.*
[353] See *id.*
[354] See *id.*
[355] New York Convention, *supra* note 322, art. V(2)(b) (providing that recognition and enforcement of an arbitral award may also be refused if the competent authority in the country where recognition and enforcement is sought finds that the recognition or enforcement of the award would be contrary to the public policy of that country).
[356] See Arbitration law, *supra* note 31, art. 84.

the public interest.[357] In Article 282 of the CPL, public policy is referred to as basic principles of law, national sovereignty and security, or social and public interests.[358]

According to Chinese scholars, in addition to basic principles of law, public policy shall also include the core social values and morals, and basic obligations of treaties to which China is a member.[359] The scholarly understanding in China is that public policy must involve something fundamental to the law and society. As required by Chinese law, the public policy exclusion applies to three areas: (1) application of foreign law; (2) recognition and enforcement of foreign judgment; and (3) recognition and enforcement of foreign arbitral awards.[360] In addition, for the purpose of public policy, the exclusion also applies to international customs,[361] which is deemed a unique feature of Chinese law.[362]

In practice, the SPC seems to have cautiously narrowed down the application of public policy as a defense to the third category, the recognition and enforcement of foreign arbitral awards. There has been one case in which the public policy exclusion was applied in Chinese courts pertaining to the recognition and enforcement of foreign arbitral awards. In *Hemofarm DD, MAG International Trading Co. and Sulamo Media Co. Ltd. v. Jinan Yongning Pharmaceutics Co. Ltd.*, the Supreme People's Court allowed the lower court to deny recognition and enforcement of an ICA arbitral award on the grounds of public policy. The court made this decision because the award as it stood was considered to have encroached on the judicial sovereignty of China, and the adjudicative jurisdiction of Chinese courts.[363]

The case involved unpaid rent that incurred to a joint venture formed between a Chinese company and a Liechtenstein firm in 1995.[364] In addition to the joint venture contract, the parties had signed a rental agreement under which the respondent would lease its property to the joint venture, and the joint venture would pay rent to the respondent. In the joint venture contract, there was an arbitration clause providing for arbitration by the ICA in Paris under the ICC arbitration rules in case disputes arose between the parties pertaining to the joint venture contract. Later, a dispute arose over unpaid rent, and in 2002, the respondent sued the joint venture in Ji Nan Intermediate People's Court for the payment of the rent balance.[365]

[357] See *id.*

[358] See the CPL (as amended 2023), *supra* note 12, art. 282.

[359] See Huang Jin, Private International Law 295 (Law Press, 1999).

[360] See the CPL (as amended 2023), *supra* note 12, arts. 274, 282; see also Choice of Law Statute, *supra* note 205.

[361] See General Principles of the Civil Law of the People's Republic of China (Apr. 12, 1986, effective Jan. 1, 1987), art. 150, available at www.china.org.cn/china/LegislationsForm2001-2010/2011-02/11/content_21898337.htm.

[362] See Huang Jin, *supra* note 416, at 291.

[363] *Hemofarm DD v. Ji'nan Yongning Pharmaceutical Co., Ltd.*, N.Y. CONVENTION GUIDE (Sup. People's Ct. 2008) (China).

[364] See *id.*

[365] See *id.*

The joint venture challenged the court's jurisdiction on the basis of the arbitration clause in the joint venture contract. The court rejected the jurisdictional argument. During trial, the respondent moved to take protective measures of property preservation to ensure the enforcement of the judgment. Upon the receipt of a money guarantee from the respondent, the court granted the respondent's motion and ordered to freeze part of the joint venture's assets, including bank accounts and certain products. In 2003, the court entered a judgment in favor of the respondent. On appeal, Shandong High People's Court affirmed in 2004.[366]

In 2004, the petitioners filed an arbitration request with the ICA pursuant to the arbitration clause in the joint venture contract. The ICA issued an arbitral award in 2007 against the respondent. One of the major reasons that the award was made was that the Chinese court decision on the property preservation issue did not have any legal nor commercial appropriateness, and the freeze of the assets caused damage to, and ultimately the failure of, the business operation of the joint venture. The arbitral award held the respondent liable for breach of the joint venture contract.[367]

In September 2007, the petitioners made a petition to Ji Nan Intermediate People's Court for recognition and enforcement of the ICA arbitral award.[368] The court, upon the SPC's approval, denied the petition. The grounds for the denial were mainly that (a) the rental agreement was not part of the joint venture contract, and thus was not subject to arbitration as agreed in the joint venture contract, and (b) the property preservation made by the lower People's Court was an exercise of judicial function *ex officio* under Chinese law, and therefore the appropriateness of such exercise was not arbitrable.[369] The court then concluded that recognizing and enforcing the ICA arbitral award would violate China's public policy.[370]

Hemofarm DD is the only case where the SPC allowed the public policy defense to stand in recent decades. In all other cases, the SPC rejected the lower courts' holding on the application of public policy. The issues raised in those cases, and the SPC's rulings, have had considerable impact on how the public policy exception should be handled in people's courts. The SPC's actions also suggest that the use of public policy to deny an award, though not well defined, may only be applied in a situation where the national (legal or judicial) interest is at stake.

There are three issues, each encompassing a different type of regulation, that involve the public policy exception. The first issue is the fairness of a foreign arbitral award, and the question is whether the recognition and enforcement of a foreign arbitral award should be denied on the finding that the arbitral award is unfair and unjust. In *GRD Minproc Ltd. v. Shanghai Flyingwheel Industry Co.*, Shanghai No. 1 Intermediate People's Court and the Shanghai High People's Court decided not to

366 See *id.*
367 See *id.*
368 See *id.*
369 See *id.*
370 See *id.*

recognize and enforce an arbitral award made by the Arbitration Court of Stockholm Chamber of Commerce. The denial relied on the argument that the arbitral award did not consider the potential harm to the health of the workers or to the working environment caused by the failure of the equipment purchased under the contract to meet the safety standard of the industry. Therefore, it would violate the fairness principle of the Contract Law of China if the respondent was required to make full payment for the equipment.[371]

The SPC rejected the denial. According to the SPC, there may have been various causes that contribute to the potential harm. The SPC further reasoned that since the arbitration was requested in order to resolve the quality issue disputes under the valid arbitration agreement, it was within the authority of the arbitral body to review that issue, and the parties should be expected to bear the result of the arbitration. The SPC then held that the public policy exception should not be made when considering whether the substantial result of the arbitral award is fair and reasonable. The SPC was also of the opinion that the arbitral award in this case contained no violation of fundamental social interests, basic principles of law, nor good morals of China.[372]

The second issue concerns mandatory provisions of law. The focal point is whether a violation of the mandatory provisions of law should be deemed a violation of public policy for which the recognition and enforcement of a foreign arbitral award would be denied. In *ED&F Man (Hong Kong) Co., Ltd. v. China Nat'l. Sugar Alcohol Group Co.*, the parties agreed to a contract for the purchase of sugar, under which the petitioner was to supply raw sugar to the respondent.[373] The parties in the contract also agreed to subject any disputes arising from the contract to arbitration by the London Sugar Industry Association (LSIA).[374] During contract performance, the petitioner, with the knowledge of the respondent, opened an account with New York Futures Exchange (NYFE) to conduct future trading on part of the contracted sugar.[375]

The performance of the contract did not go as the parties anticipated, so the petitioner requested arbitration, and won an award from the LSIA. While attempting to enforce the arbitral award in Beijing No. 1 Intermediate People's Court, the petitioner was denied enforcement. The Intermediate People's Court and the Beijing High People's Court agreed that future trading (which was unauthorized by the respondent and was conducted for the purpose of illegal profit gains) is prohibited under Chinese law, and as such the arbitral award upholding the underlying contract of the future trading should not be recognized and enforced,

371 See *id.*

372 See *id.*

373 *ED and F Man (Hong Kong) Co., Ltd. v. China National Sugar Alcohol Group Co.*, CHINESE CT. DECISION SUMMARIES ON ARB. (Sup. People's Ct. July 1, 2003) (China).

374 See *id.*

375 See *id.*

because the non-observance of a mandatory provision of law constitutes a violation of public policy.[376]

In rejecting the denial, the SPC acknowledged that because future trading engaged by a Chinese domestic entity is barred under the law unless otherwise authorized, the conduct of such trading in this case should be regarded invalid.[377] The SPC, however, held that a violation of a mandatory provision of law did not necessarily mean a violation of public policy for the purpose of recognition and enforcement of a foreign arbitral award had occurred. The SPC further opined that the dispute between the parties in this case, with regard to the performance of a future trading contract, by its nature fell within the dispute arising out of the contract-based commercial legal relationship, and therefore could be subject to arbitration by the agreement of the parties.[378]

The third issue involves administrative regulations, and to a certain extent it is related to the second issue, because some regulations contain compulsory rules. The question is whether a failure to follow administrative regulations would amount to a violation of public policy. In *Japan Shanjin Property Co. v. Textile Industrial Company of Hainan Province*, the respondent, a state enterprise, entered into a contract with the petitioner, a Japanese company, for which the payment would be made in foreign currency.[379] Under the foreign currency regulations at the time of the contract, a state enterprise was required to obtain an approval from the state foreign exchange administration, and to have the amount of foreign currency needed for international payment registered before the foreign contract could be released for its use.[380]

The respondent, however, failed to obtain approval when the contract was signed. Following a dispute over the contract, the petitioner won an arbitration award from the Arbitration Court of the Stockholm Chamber of Commerce, and sought to enforce it in Hainan. The lower people's courts in Hainan decided to reject the enforcement, because the arbitration award was made on an invalid agreement under Chinese law (because of its violation of foreign currency control). The SPC, however, ruled to enforce the arbitral award. According to the SPC, a violation of administrative rules or regulations should not necessarily trigger the application of public policy to exclude the enforcement of a foreign arbitral award.[381]

[376] See *id.*

[377] See *id.*

[378] See *id.*

[379] *Mitsui and Co., Ltd. v. Hainan Textile Industry Co.*, CHINESE CT. DECISION SUMMARIES ON ARB. (Sup. People's Ct. July 13, 2005) (China).

[380] See *id.*

[381] See *id.*; see also *Noble Resources Pte. Ltd. v. Zhoushan Zhonghai Cereals and Oils Industry Co.*, CHINESE CT. DECISION SUMMARIES ON ARB. (Sup. People's Ct. Mar. 18, 2009) (China) (holding that without evidence to prove that the imported beans at issue could cause serious food safety problems, public policy should not become the reason to block recognition and enforcement of a foreign arbitral award).

In short, all of the cases related to public policy seem to be evidence that when addressing public policy issues in the enforcement of foreign arbitral awards, the SPC has taken a restrictive approach to the application of public policy and has limited it to very narrowly tailored cases. In addition, the SPC has taken the stringent position that if other grounds exist where a foreign arbitral award should not be recognized and enforced, the public policy exception should generally not be applied.[382]

c. Non-Compliance

It is a commonly accepted principle that the recognition and enforcement of foreign arbitral awards are subject to the law of the country where the recognition and enforcement is sought. The language in Article III of the New York Convention also suggests that the enforcement of a foreign arbitral award is subject to the procedures of the place where the enforcement is sought.[383] Under this principle, a violation of, or non-compliance with, the procedure of the enforcing country would result in a denial of the recognition and enforcement of the arbitral award.

To enforce a foreign arbitral award in China, the requesting party is required to follow the procedures set forth in the CPL. There are several issues that are procedurally important to the recognition and enforcement of foreign arbitral awards. One of those issues is the statute of limitations. The SPC has specifically ruled on enforcement denials based on the party's failure to bring up the request for enforcement within the statutory time period.[384] Before 2007, the time limit for the enforcement of an arbitral award was one year for natural persons and 6 months for legal persons.[385] After the CPL amendment in October of 2007, the time limit for submission was extended to two years, irrespective of natural or legal persons.[386] Under the Arbitration Law, if a party applies to revoke an award, the application must be filed within three months from the date of receipt of the award.[387]

[382] *Shin-Etsu Chemical Co. Ltd. v. Jiangsu Zhongtian Technology JSCL*, *supra* note 389.

[383] U.N. Comm'n on Int'l Trade Law, UNCITRAL Secretariat Guide on the Convention on the Recognition and Enforcement of Foreign Arbitral Awards, at 77, U.N. Sales No. E.16.V.7 (amended 2016), http://newyorkconvention1958.org/pdf/guide/2016_Guide_on_the_NY_Convention.pdf#page=89 [https://perma.cc/6999-R2KH] ("Following lengthy discussions between the drafters, the final text of Article III achieved a balanced solution that permits each Contracting State to apply its own national rules of procedure to the recognition and enforcement of arbitral awards, while guaranteeing that such recognition and enforcement will comply with a number of fundamental principles.").

[384] *Peter J. Scheuer v. Edward E. Lehman*, Peking U. L. (Sup. People's Ct. Jan. 22, 2007) (China) (rejecting petitioner's request for recognition and enforcement of an American arbitral award because the petitioner failed to meet the time limit set forth in art. 239 of the CPL).

[385] See the CPL (as amended 2023), *supra* note 12, art. 219.

[386] See *id.*, art. 239.

[387] See the Arbitration Law, *supra* note 31, art. 72.

Normally, the statute of limitations runs from the last day of performance if the arbitral award provides a performance date.[388] If, however, there is no fixed performance date, the time period will be calculated from the date when the arbitral award takes effect.[389] Under certain circumstances, the statutory time period may be suspended or discontinued as required by law.[390] According to the SPC's interpretation of the CPL, the enforcement time period may be discontinued in the case where the parties have settled the dispute through an agreement during the enforcement period.[391] In that case, the statute of limitations will restart and run from the last day of performance.[392]

But if a party is unable to meet the time limit, due to an event of *force majeure* or other legitimate reasons, the party may apply to the court for an extension under Article 86 of the CPL.[393] There are two preconditions for an extension made under Article 86. First, the application for extension must be made within 10 days after the resolution of the obstacle preventing the party from complying with the statute of limitations.[394] Second, the court must approve the application for extension.[395] It follows that an extension is not automatic, but instead is subject to the court's discretion.

Another issue concerns the documents required. To apply for recognition and enforcement of a foreign arbitral award in China under the New York Convention, the applying party shall, at the time of the application, provide such documents as: (a) the duly authenticated original award or a duly certified copy thereof; and (b) the original agreement or a duly certified copy thereof.[396] In addition, all of the documents would need to be translated into the Chinese language.[397] It is also required that the translation be certified.[398]

What appears to be problematic is the certified translation of the documents. Under the New York Convention, the translation certification can be made by an official or sworn translator, or by a diplomatic or consular agent.[399] However, in Chinese courts, the requesting party is required to provide an authenticated translation by the Chinese embassy or consular office in the relevant country,[400] or, as an

[388] See *id.*
[389] See *id.*
[390] See the SPC, Interpretation on the Application of the CPL, *supra* note 13, art. 468.
[391] See *id.*
[392] See *id.*
[393] See the CPL (as amended 2023), *supra* note 12, art. 83.
[394] See *id.*
[395] See *id.*
[396] New York Convention, *supra* note 282, art. IV(1).
[397] See *id.*, art. IV(2).
[398] See *id.*
[399] See *id.*
[400] See the SPC, Provisions on Several Issues Concerning the Judicial Enforcement (Trial Implementation), 1998, art. 21, available at http://gongbao.court.gov.cn/Details/a76a77ab3bdb8ee78e4189146c3444.html.

alternative, a notarized translation by a Chinese notary public agency.[401] Failure to provide the translation as required may result in a rejection of enforcement.[402] In actual practice, however, the People's Court will ask the requesting party to amend the filing by submitting an acceptable translation before the rejection is made.

A final issue is identifying the parties. When making a request to the People's Court for recognition and enforcement of a foreign arbitral award, the requesting party must be a party to the arbitral award.[403] In addition, the person against whom the recognition and enforcement of the foreign arbitral award is sought must exist under Chinese law; otherwise, the request is denied. In *Subway International B.V. v. Beijing Sabowei Food and Beverage Co. Ltd.*, the U.S. petitioner obtained a default arbitral award made by the International Centre for Settlement of Investment Disputes against the Chinese respondent, and attempted to enforce it in China.[404] Its request was rejected because it was found that the respondent did not exist as an entity in China.[405]

The disputes in the case arose from a franchising agreement between the petitioner and respondent.[406] The petitioner claimed that the respondent violated the agreement entered into by the parties in January 2005. In the arbitral award, the respondent was required to stop using the petitioner's name, trademarks, and business symbols. The respondent also had to pay $250 per day from the date of arbitral award to the date of enforcement, plus other costs and fees. When reviewing the petitioner's request, Beijing No. 2 Intermediate People's Court found that the respondent listed in the arbitral award was not registered as a business entity with the Beijing Bureau of Administration of Industries and Commerce. Since the identity of the respondent was unknown, the arbitral award went unrecognized and unenforced.[407]

[401] See *id*.

[402] See *id*., art. 20.

[403] An arbitrator has no standing to request enforcement of a foreign arbitral award to recover the arbitration fee decided in the award because he is not a party to the award. See the SPC, Provisions on Several Matters Concerning Adjudicative Jurisdiction in Foreign Related Civil and Commercial Cases, 2002. A full text of the Provisions is available at http://gongbao.court.gov.cn/Details/8942d8e04099f5e0de897fa83b1c3b.html.

[404] *Subway International, B.V. v. Beijing Sabaiwei Catering Co., Ltd.*, PEKING U. L. (Sup. People's Ct. Feb. 26, 2009) (China).

[405] See *id*.

[406] See *id*.

[407] See *id*.

Index

Printed by Integrated Books International,
United States of America